HAMMOND®

WORLD ATLAS

Gemini Edition

MAPLEWOOD, NEW JERSEY 07040-1396

HAMMOND PUBLICATIONS ADVISORY BOARD

PRINTED IN THE UNITED STATES OF AMERICA

Library of Congress Cataloging in Publication Data

Hammond Incorporated.
Hammond world atlas.

1. Atlases. I. Title. II. Title: World atlas.
G1021.H284 1984 912 84-675204
ISBN 0-8437-1135-3 (pbk.)

CONTENTS

The Hammond World Atlas — Gemini Edition *contains maps and indexes of the major world divisions, namely continents and countries. Maps and indexes of the individual states and of the history of the United States may be found in the companion volume,* Hammond United States Atlas — Gemini Edition.

GAZETTEER-INDEX OF THE WORLD

This alphabetical list of grand divisions, countries, states, colonial possessions, etc., gives area in both square miles and square kilometers, population, capital or chief town, and index references and page numbers on which they are shown on the largest scale. The index reference shows the square on the respective map in which the name of the entry may be located.

Country	Area Square Miles	Area Square Kilometers	Population	Capital or Chief Town	Index Ref.	Page No.
*Afghanistan	250,775	649,507	15,540,000	Kabul	A 2	68
Africa	11,707,000	30,321,130	469,000,000	......	......	102
Alabama, U.S.A.	51,705	133,916	3,893,888	Montgomery	J 4	188
Alaska, U.S.A.	591,004	1,530,700	401,851	Juneau	C 5	188
*Albania	11,100	28,749	2,590,600	Tiranë	E 5	45
Alberta, Canada	255,285	661,185	2,237,724	Edmonton	......	182
*Algeria	919,591	2,381,740	17,422,000	Algiers	D 3	106
American Samoa	77	199	32,297	Pago Pago	J 7	87
Andorra	188	487	31,000	Andorra la Vella	G 1	33
*Angola	481,351	1,246,700	7,078,000	Luanda	C 6	114
Anguilla	35	91	6,519	The Valley	F 3	156
Antarctica	5,500,000	14,245,000	....	......	......	5
*Antigua and Barbuda	171	443	75,000	St. John's	G 3	156
*Argentina	1,072,070	2,776,661	28,438,000	Buenos Aires	......	143
Arizona, U.S.A.	114,000	295,260	2,718,425	Phoenix	D 4	188
Arkansas, U.S.A.	53,187	137,754	2,286,435	Little Rock	H 3	188
Ascension Island, St. Helena	34	88	719	Georgetown	A 5	102
Asia	17,128,500	44,362,815	2,633,000,000	......	......	54
*Australia	2,966,136	7,682,300	14,576,330	Canberra	......	88
*Austria	32,375	83,851	7,507,000	Vienna	B 3	40
*Bahamas	5,382	13,939	209,505	Nassau	C 1	156
*Bahrain	240	622	358,857	Manama	F 4	58
*Bangladesh	55,126	142,776	87,052,024	Dhaka	G 4	68
*Barbados	166	430	248,983	Bridgetown	B 8	161
*Belgium	11,781	30,513	9,855,110	Brussels	E 7	27
*Belize	8,867	22,966	144,857	Belmopan	C 2	154
*Benin	43,483	112,620	3,338,240	Porto-Novo	E 6	106
Bermuda	21	54	67,761	Hamilton	H 3	156
*Bhutan	18,147	47,000	1,298,000	Thimphu	G 3	68
*Bolivia	424,163	1,098,582	5,600,000	La Paz; Sucre	......	136
*Botswana	224,764	582,139	819,000	Gaborone	C 4	119
*Brazil	3,284,426	8,506,663	119,098,992	Brasília	......	132
British Columbia, Canada	366,253	948,596	2,744,467	Victoria	......	184
British Indian Ocean Terr.	29	75	2,000	(London, U.K.)	L10	54
Brunei	2,226	5,765	192,832	Bandar Seri Begawan	E 4	85
*Bulgaria	42,823	110,912	8,862,000	Sofia	F 4	45
*Burma	261,789	678,034	32,913,000	Rangoon	B 2	72
*Burundi	10,747	27,835	4,021,910	Bujumbura	E 4	114
California, U.S.A.	158,706	411,049	23,667,565	Sacramento	B 3	188
*Cambodia (Kampuchea)	69,898	181,036	5,200,000	Phnom Penh	E 4	72
*Cameroon	183,568	475,441	8,503,000	Yaoundé	B 2	114
*Canada	3,851,787	9,976,139	24,343,181	Ottawa	......	162
*Cape Verde	1,557	4,033	324,000	Praia	B 8	106
Cayman Islands	100	259	18,000	Georgetown	B 3	156
*Central African Republic	242,000	626,780	2,284,000	Bangui	C 2	114
Central America	197,480	511,475	21,000,000	......	......	154
Ceylon, see Sri Lanka						
*Chad	495,752	1,283,998	4,309,000	N'Djamena	C 4	111
Channel Islands	75	194	133,000	St. Helier; St. Peter Port	E 8	13
*Chile	292,257	756,946	11,275,440	Santiago	......	138
*China, People's Rep. of	3,691,000	9,559,690	958,090,000	Peking (Beijing)	......	77
China, Republic of (Taiwan)	13,971	36,185	16,609,961	Taipei	K 7	77
*Colombia	439,513	1,138,339	27,520,000	Bogotá	......	126
Colorado, U.S.A.	104,091	269,596	2,889,735	Denver	E 3	188
*Comoros	719	1,862	290,000	Moroni	G 2	119
*Congo	132,046	342,000	1,537,000	Brazzaville	B 4	114
Connecticut, U.S.A.	5,018	12,997	3,107,576	Hartford	M 2	188
Cook Islands	91	236	17,695	Avarua	K 7	87
*Costa Rica	19,575	50,700	2,245,000	San José	E 5	154
*Cuba	44,206	114,494	9,706,369	Havana	......	158
*Cyprus	3,473	8,995	629,000	Nicosia	E 5	62
*Czechoslovakia	49,373	127,876	15,276,799	Prague	C 2	41
Delaware, U.S.A.	2,044	5,294	594,317	Dover	L 3	188
*Denmark	16,629	43,069	5,124,000	Copenhagen	......	21
District of Columbia, U.S.A.	69	179	638,432	Washington	L 3	188
*Djibouti	8,880	23,000	386,000	Djibouti	H 5	111
*Dominica	290	751	74,089	Roseau	E 7	161
*Dominican Republic	18,704	48,443	5,647,977	Santo Domingo	D 6	158
*Ecuador	109,483	283,561	8,644,000	Quito	C 3	128
*Egypt	386,659	1,001,447	41,572,000	Cairo	E 2	110
*El Salvador	8,260	21,393	4,813,000	San Salvador	C 4	154
England, U.K.	50,516	130,836	46,220,955	London	......	13
*Equatorial Guinea	10,831	28,052	244,000	Malabo	A 3	114
*Ethiopia	471,776	1,221,900	31,065,000	Addis Ababa	G 5	110
Europe	4,057,000	10,507,630	676,000,000	......	......	7
Faeroe Islands, Denmark	540	1,399	41,969	Tórshavn	B 2	21
Falkland Islands & Dependencies	6,198	16,053	1,813	Stanley	E 8	120
*Fiji	7,055	18,272	588,068	Suva	H 8	87
*Finland	130,128	337,032	4,788,000	Helsinki	O 6	18
Florida, U.S.A.	58,664	151,940	9,746,342	Tallahassee	K 5	188
*France	210,038	543,998	53,788,000	Paris	......	28
French Guiana	35,135	91,000	73,022	Cayénne	E 3	131
French Polynesia	1,544	4,000	137,382	Papeete	L 8	87
*Gabon	103,346	267,666	551,000	Libreville	B 4	114
*Gambia	4,127	10,689	601,000	Banjul	A 6	106
Georgia, U.S.A.	58,910	152,577	5,463,105	Atlanta	K 4	188
*Germany, East (German Democratic Republic)	41,768	108,179	16,737,000	Berlin (East)	......	22
*Germany, West (Federal Republic)	95,985	248,601	61,658,000	Bonn	......	22
*Ghana	92,099	238,536	11,450,000	Accra	D 7	106
Gibraltar	2.28	5.91	29,760	Gibraltar	D 4	33
*Great Britain & Northern Ireland (United Kingdom)	94,399	244,493	55,672,000	London	......	10
*Greece	50,944	131,945	9,599,000	Athens	F 6	45
Greenland	840,000	2,175,600	49,773	Nuuk (Godthåb)	B12	4
*Grenada	133	344	103,103	St. George's	G 4	156
Guadeloupe & Dependencies	687	1,779	328,400	Basse-Terre	F 4	156
Guam	209	541	105,979	Agaña	E 4	87
*Guatemala	42,042	108,889	7,262,419	Guatemala	B 3	154
*Guinea	94,925	245,856	5,143,284	Conakry	B 6	106
*Guinea-Bissau	13,948	36,125	777,214	Bissau	A 6	106
*Guyana	83,000	214,970	793,000	Georgetown	B 3	131
*Haiti	10,694	27,697	5,053,792	Port-au-Prince	C 5	158
Hawaii, U.S.A.	6,471	16,760	964,691	Honolulu	E 5	188
Holland, see Netherlands						
*Honduras	43,277	112,087	3,691,000	Tegucigalpa	D 3	154
Hong Kong	403	1,044	5,022,000	Victoria	H 7	77
*Hungary	35,919	93,030	10,709,536	Budapest	D 3	41
*Iceland	39,768	103,000	228,785	Reykjavík	B 1	21
Idaho, U.S.A.	83,564	216,431	944,038	Boise	D 2	188
Illinois, U.S.A.	56,345	145,934	11,426,596	Springfield	J 3	188
*India	1,269,339	3,287,588	683,810,051	New Delhi	D 4	68
Indiana, U.S.A.	36,185	93,719	5,490,260	Indianapolis	J 3	188
*Indonesia	788,430	2,042,034	147,490,298	Jakarta	D 7	85
Iowa, U.S.A.	56,275	145,752	2,913,808	Des Moines	H 2	188
*Iran	636,293	1,648,000	37,447,000	Tehran	F 4	66
*Iraq	172,476	446,713	12,767,000	Baghdad	C 4	66
*Ireland	27,136	70,282	3,440,427	Dublin	......	17
Ireland, Northern, U.K.	5,452	14,121	1,543,000	Belfast	F 2	17
Isle of Man	227	588	64,000	Douglas	C 3	13
*Israel	7,847	20,324	3,878,000	Jerusalem	B 4	65
*Italy	116,303	301,225	57,140,000	Rome	......	34
*Ivory Coast	124,504	322,465	7,920,000	Abidjan	C 7	106
*Jamaica	4,411	11,424	2,184,000	Kingston	......	158
*Japan	145,730	377,441	117,057,485	Tokyo	......	81
*Jordan	35,000	90,650	2,152,273	Amman	D 3	65
*Kampuchea (Cambodia)	69,898	181,036	5,200,000	Phnom Penh	E 4	72
Kansas, U.S.A.	82,277	213,097	2,364,236	Topeka	G 3	188
Kentucky, U.S.A.	40,409	104,659	3,660,257	Frankfort	J 3	188
*Kenya	224,960	582,646	15,327,061	Nairobi	G 3	115
Kiribati	291	754	56,213	Bairiki	J 6	87
Korea, North	46,540	120,539	17,914,000	P'yŏngyang	D 3	80
Korea, South	38,175	98,873	37,448,836	Seoul	D 5	80
*Kuwait	6,532	16,918	1,355,827	Al Kuwait	E 4	58
*Laos	91,428	236,800	3,721,000	Vientiane	D 3	72
*Lebanon	4,015	10,399	3,161,000	Beirut	F 6	62
*Lesotho	11,720	30,355	1,339,000	Maseru	D 5	119
*Liberia	43,000	111,370	1,873,000	Monrovia	C 7	106
*Libya	679,358	1,759,537	2,856,000	Tripoli	B 2	110
Liechtenstein	61	158	25,220	Vaduz	J 2	39
Louisiana, U.S.A.	47,752	123,678	4,206,312	Baton Rouge	H 4	188
*Luxembourg	999	2,587	364,000	Luxembourg	J 9	27
Macau	6	16	271,000	Macau	H 7	77
*Madagascar	226,657	587,041	8,742,000	Antananarivo	H 3	119
Maine, U.S.A.	33,265	86,156	1,125,027	Augusta	N 1	188
*Malawi	45,747	118,485	5,968,000	Lilongwe	F 6	114
Malaya, Malaysia	50,806	131,588	11,138,227	Kuala Lumpur	D 6	72
*Malaysia	128,308	332,318	13,435,588	Kuala Lumpur	D 6 E 4	72 85
*Maldives	115	298	143,046	Male	L 9	54
*Mali	464,873	1,204,021	6,906,000	Bamako	C 6	106
*Malta	122	316	343,970	Valletta	E 7	34

*Member of the United Nations

GAZETTEER-INDEX OF THE WORLD

Country	Area		Population	Capital or Chief Town	Index Ref.	Page No.
	Square Miles	Square Kilometers				
Manitoba, Canada	250,999	650,087	1,026,241	Winnipeg	......	179
Martinique	425	1,101	308,000	Fort-de-France	D 5	161
Maryland, U.S.A.	10,460	27,091	4,216,975	Annapolis	L 3	188
Massachusetts, U.S.A.	8,284	21,456	5,737,037	Boston	M 2	188
*Mauritania	419,229	1,085,803	1,634,000	Nouakchott	B 5	106
*Mauritius	790	2,046	959,000	Port Louis	G 5	119
Mayotte	144	373	47,300	Dzaoudzi	G 2	119
*Mexico	761,601	1,972,546	67,395,826	Mexico City	......	150
Michigan, U.S.A.	58,527	151,585	9,262,078	Lansing	J 1	188
Midway Islands	1.9	4.9	453	......	J 3	87
Minnesota, U.S.A.	84,402	218,601	4,075,970	St. Paul	H 1	188
Mississippi, U.S.A.	47,689	123,515	2,520,638	Jackson	J 4	188
Missouri, U.S.A.	69,697	180,515	4,916,759	Jefferson City	H 3	188
Monaco	368 acres	149 hectares	25,029	Monaco	G 6	28
*Mongolia	606,163	1,569,962	1,594,800	Ulaanbaatar	E 2	77
Montana, U.S.A.	147,046	380,849	786,690	Helena	D 1	188
Montserrat	40	104	12,073	Plymouth	G 3	157
*Morocco	172,414	446,550	20,242,000	Rabat	C 2	106
*Mozambique	303,769	786,762	12,130,000	Maputo	E 4	119
Namibia (South-West Africa)	317,827	823,172	1,200,000	Windhoek	B 3	118
Nauru	7.7	20	7,254	Yaren (district)	G 6	87
Nebraska, U.S.A.	77,355	200,349	1,569,825	Lincoln	F 2	188
*Nepal	54,663	141,577	14,179,301	Kathmandu	E 3	68
*Netherlands	15,892	41,160	14,227,000	The Hague; Amsterdam	F 5	27
Netherlands Antilles	390	1,010	246,000	Willemstad	E 4	156
Nevada, U.S.A.	110,561	286,353	800,493	Carson City	C 3	188
New Brunswick, Canada	28,354	73,437	696,403	Fredericton	......	170
New Caledonia & Dependencies	7,335	18,998	133,233	Nouméa	G 8	87
Newfoundland, Canada	156,184	404,517	567,681	St. John's	......	166
New Hampshire, U.S.A.	9,279	24,033	920,610	Concord	M 2	188
New Hebrides, see Vanuatu						
New Jersey, U.S.A.	7,787	20,168	7,364,823	Trenton	M 3	188
New Mexico, U.S.A.	121,593	314,926	1,302,981	Santa Fe	E 4	188
New York, U.S.A.	49,108	127,190	17,558,072	Albany	L 2	188
*New Zealand	103,736	268,676	3,175,737	Wellington	......	100
*Nicaragua	45,698	118,358	2,703,000	Managua	D 4	154
*Niger	489,189	1,267,000	5,098,427	Niamey	F 5	106
*Nigeria	357,000	924,630	82,643,000	Lagos	F 6	106
Niue	100	259	3,578	Alofi	K 7	87
North America	9,363,000	24,250,170	370,000,000	......	......	146
North Carolina, U.S.A.	52,669	136,413	5,881,813	Raleigh	K 3	188
North Dakota, U.S.A.	70,702	183,118	652,717	Bismarck	F 1	188
Northern Ireland, U.K.	5,452	14,121	1,543,000	Belfast	F 2	17
Northwest Territories, Canada	1,304,896	3,379,683	45,741	Yellowknife	G 3	187
*Norway	125,053	323,887	4,092,000	Oslo	F 7	18
Nova Scotia, Canada	21,425	55,491	847,442	Halifax	......	168
Ohio, U.S.A.	41,330	107,045	10,797,624	Columbus	K 2	188
Oklahoma, U.S.A.	69,956	181,186	3,025,290	Oklahoma City	G 3	188
*Oman	120,000	310,800	891,000	Muscat	G 6	58
Ontario, Canada	412,580	1,068,582	8,625,107	Toronto	..	175, 177
Oregon, U.S.A.	97,073	251,419	2,633,149	Salem	B 2	188
Pacific Islands, Territory of the	533	1,380	133,929	Saipan	F 5	87
*Pakistan	310,403	803,944	83,782,000	Islamabad	B 3	68
*Panama	29,761	77,082	1,830,175	Panamá	G 6	154
*Papua New Guinea	183,540	475,369	3,010,727	Port Moresby	E 6	87
*Paraguay	157,047	406,752	2,973,000	Asunción	......	144
Pennsylvania, U.S.A.	45,308	117,348	11,863,895	Harrisburg	L 2	188
Persia, see Iran						
*Peru	496,222	1,285,215	17,031,221	Lima	......	128
*Philippines	115,707	299,681	48,098,460	Manila	......	82
Pitcairn Islands	18	47	54	Adamstown	O 8	87
*Poland	120,725	312,678	35,815,000	Warsaw	......	47
*Portugal	35,549	92,072	9,933,000	Lisbon	B 3	32
Prince Edward Island, Canada	2,184	5,657	122,506	Charlottetown	E 2	168
Puerto Rico	3,515	9,104	3,196,520	San Juan	......	161
*Qatar	4,247	11,000	220,000	Doha	F 4	58
Québec, Canada	594,857	1,540,680	6,438,403	Québec	..	172, 174
Réunion	969	2,510	491,000	St-Denis	F 5	119
Rhode Island, U.S.A.	1,212	3,139	947,154	Providence	M 2	188
Rhodesia, see Zimbabwe						
*Romania	91,699	237,500	22,048,305	Bucharest	F 3	45
*Rwanda	10,169	26,337	4,819,317	Kigali	E 4	114
Sabah, Malaysia	29,300	75,887	1,002,608	Kota Kinabalu	F 4	85
Saint Christopher (St. Kitts)-Nevis	104	269	44,404	Basseterre	F 3	156
Saint Helena & Dependencies	162	420	5,147	Jamestown	B 6	102
*Saint Lucia	238	616	115,783	Castries	G 6	161
Saint Pierre & Miquelon	93.5	242	6,034	Saint-Pierre	C 4	166
*Saint Vincent & the Grenadines	150	388	124,000	Kingstown	G 4	156
San Marino	23.4	60.6	19,149	San Marino	D 3	34
*São Tomé e Príncipe	372	963	85,000	São Tomé	F 8	106
Sarawak, Malaysia	48,202	124,843	1,294,753	Kuching	E 5	85
Saskatchewan, Canada	251,699	651,900	968,313	Regina	......	181
*Saudi Arabia	829,995	2,149,687	8,367,000	Riyadh	D 4	58
Scotland, U.K.	30,414	78,772	5,117,146	Edinburgh	......	15
*Senegal	75,954	196,720	5,508,000	Dakar	A 5	106
*Seychelles	145	375	63,000	Victoria	H 5	119
Siam, see Thailand						
*Sierra Leone	27,925	72,325	3,470,000	Freetown	B 7	106
*Singapore	226	585	2,413,945	Singapore	F 6	72
*Solomon Islands	11,500	29,785	221,000	Honiara	G 6	87
*Somalia	246,200	637,658	3,645,000	Mogadishu	H 3	115
*South Africa	455,318	1,179,274	23,771,970	Cape Town; Pretoria	C 5	118
South America	6,875,000	17,806,250	245,000,000	......	......	120
South Carolina, U.S.A.	31,113	80,583	3,121,833	Columbia	K 4	188
South Dakota, U.S.A.	77,116	199,730	690,768	Pierre	F 2	188
South-West Africa (Namibia)	317,827	823,172	1,200,000	Windhoek	B 3	118
*Spain	194,881	504,742	37,430,000	Madrid	......	33
*Sri Lanka	25,332	65,610	14,850,001	Colombo	E 7	68
*Sudan	967,494	2,505,809	18,691,000	Khartoum	E 4	110
*Suriname	55,144	142,823	354,860	Paramaribo	C 3	131
*Swaziland	6,705	17,366	547,000	Mbabane	E 5	119
*Sweden	173,665	449,792	8,320,000	Stockholm	J 8	18
Switzerland	15,943	41,292	6,365,960	Bern	......	39
*Syria	71,498	185,180	8,979,000	Damascus	G 5	62
Taiwan	13,971	36,185	16,609,961	Taipei	K 7	77
*Tanzania	363,708	942,003	17,527,560	Dar es Salaam	F 5	114
Tennessee, U.S.A.	42,144	109,153	4,591,120	Nashville	J 3	188
Texas, U.S.A.	266,807	691,030	14,229,288	Austin	G 4	188
*Thailand	198,455	513,998	46,455,000	Bangkok	D 3	72
*Togo	21,622	56,000	2,472,000	Lomé	E 7	106
Tokelau	3.9	10	1,575	Fakaofo	J 6	87
Tonga	270	699	90,128	Nuku'alofa	J 8	87
*Trinidad and Tobago	1,980	5,128	1,067,108	Port-of-Spain	G 5	157
Tristan da Cunha, St. Helena	38	98	251	Edinburgh	J 7	2
*Tunisia	63,378	164,149	6,367,000	Tunis	F 1	106
*Turkey	300,946	779,450	45,217,556	Ankara	D 3	62
Turks and Caicos Islands	166	430	7,436	Cockburn Town, Grand Turk	D 2	156
Tuvalu	9.78	25.33	7,349	Fongafale, Funafuti	H 6	87
*Uganda	91,076	235,887	12,630,076	Kampala	F 3	114
*Ukrainian S.S.R., U.S.S.R.	233,089	603,700	49,755,000	Kiev	D 5	52
*Union of Soviet Socialist Republics	8,649,490	22,402,179	262,436,227	Moscow	......	48
*United Arab Emirates	32,278	83,600	1,040,275	Abu Dhabi	F 5	58
*United Kingdom	94,399	244,493	55,672,000	London	......	10
*United States of America	3,623,420	9,384,658	226,504,825	Washington	......	188
*Upper Volta	105,869	274,200	6,908,000	Ouagadougou	D 6	106
*Uruguay	72,172	186,925	2,899,000	Montevideo	......	145
Utah, U.S.A.	84,899	219,888	1,461,037	Salt Lake City	D 3	188
*Vanuatu	5,700	14,763	112,596	Vila	G 7	87
Vatican City	108.7 acres	44 hectares	728	......	B 6	34
*Venezuela	352,143	912,050	14,313,000	Caracas	......	124
Vermont, U.S.A.	9,614	24,900	511,456	Montpelier	M 2	188
*Vietnam	128,405	332,569	52,741,766	Hanoi	E 3	72
Virginia, U.S.A.	40,767	105,587	5,346,818	Richmond	L 3	188
Virgin Islands, British	59	153	11,006	Road Town	H 1	157
Virgin Islands, U.S.A.	132	342	96,569	Charlotte Amalie	A 4	161
Wake Island	2.5	6.5	302	Wake Islet	G 4	87
Wales, U.K.	8,017	20,764	2,790,462	Cardiff	D 5	13
Wallis and Futuna	106	275	9,192	Mata Utu	J 7	87
Washington, U.S.A.	68,139	176,480	4,132,180	Olympia	B 1	188
Western Sahara	102,703	266,000	76,425	......	B 3	106
*Western Samoa	1,133	2,934	158,130	Apia	J 7	87
West Virginia, U.S.A.	24,231	62,758	1,950,279	Charleston	K 3	188
*White Russian S.S.R. (Byelorussian S.S.R.), U.S.S.R.	80,154	207,600	9,560,000	Minsk	C 4	52
Wisconsin, U.S.A.	56,153	145,436	4,705,521	Madison	H 2	188
World (land)	57,970,000	150,142,300	4,415,000,000	......	......	1, 2
Wyoming, U.S.A.	97,809	253,325	469,557	Cheyenne	E 2	188
*Yemen, People's Democratic Rep. of	111,101	287,752	1,969,000	Aden	E 7	58
*Yemen Arab Republic	77,220	200,000	6,456,189	San'a	D 6	58
*Yugoslavia	98,766	255,804	22,471,000	Belgrade	C 3	45
Yukon Territory, Canada	207,075	536,324	23,153	Whitehorse	E 3	186
*Zaire	905,063	2,344,113	28,291,000	Kinshasa	D 4	114
*Zambia	290,586	752,618	5,679,808	Lusaka	E 7	114
*Zimbabwe	150,803	390,580	7,360,000	Harare (Salisbury)	D 3	119

WORLD STATISTICS

Elements of the Solar System

	Mean Distance from Sun: in Miles	Mean Distance from Sun: in Kilometers	Period of Revolution around Sun	Period of Rotation on Axis	Equatorial Diameter: in Miles	Equatorial Diameter: in Kilometers	Surface Gravity (Earth = 1)	Mass (Earth = 1)	Mean Density (Water = 1)	Number of Satellites
MERCURY	35,990,000	57,900,000	87.97 days	59 days	3,032	4,880	0.38	0.055	5.5	0
VENUS	67,240,000	108,200,000	224.70 days	243 days†	7,523	12,106	0.90	0.815	5.25	0
EARTH	93,000,000	149,700,000	365.26 days	23h 56m	7,926	12,755	1.00	1.00	5.5	1
MARS	141,730,000	228,100,000	687.00 days	24h 37m	4,220	6,790	0.38	0.107	4.0	2
JUPITER	483,880,000	778,700,000	11.86 years	9h 50m	88,750	142,800	2.87	317.9	1.3	16
SATURN	887,130,000	1,427,700,000	29.46 years	10h 14m	74,580	120,020	1.32	95.2	0.7	17
URANUS	1,783,700,000	2,870,500,000	84.01 years	10h 49m†	31,600	50,900	0.93	14.6	1.3	5
NEPTUNE	2,795,500,000	4,498,800,000	164.79 years	15h 48m	30,200	48,600	1.23	17.2	1.8	3
PLUTO	3,667,900,000	5,902,800,000	247.70 years	6.39 days(?)	1,500	2,400	0.03 (?)	0.01(?)	0.7(?)	1

†Retrograde motion

Facts About the Sun

Equatorial diameter	865,000 miles	1,392,000 kilometers
Period of rotation on axis	25-35 days*	
Orbit of galaxy	every 225 million years	
Surface gravity (Earth = 1)	27.8	
Mass (Earth = 1)	333,000	
Density (Water = 1)	1.4	
Mean distance from Earth	93,000,000 miles	149,700,000 kilometers

*Rotation of 25 days at Equator, decreasing to about 35 days at the poles.

Facts About the Moon

Equatorial diameter	2,160 miles	3,476 kilometers
Period of rotation on axis	27 days, 7 hours, 43 minutes	
Period of revolution around Earth (sidereal month)	27 days, 7 hours, 43 minutes	
Phase period between new moons (synodic month)	29 days, 12 hours, 44 minutes	
Surface gravity (Earth = 1)	0.16	
Mass (Earth = 1)	0.0123	
Density (Water = 1)	3.34	
Maximum distance from Earth	252,710 miles	406,690 kilometers
Minimum distance from Earth	221,460 miles	356,400 kilometers
Mean distance from Earth	238,860 miles	384,400 kilometers

Dimensions of the Earth

	Area in Sq. Miles	Sq. Kilometers
Superficial area	197,751,000	512,175,090
Land surface	57,970,000	150,142,300
Water surface	139,781,000	362,032,790

	Miles	Kilometers
Equatorial circumference	24,902	40,075
Polar circumference	24,860	40,007
Equatorial diameter	7,926.68	12,756.4
Polar diameter	7,899.99	12,713.4
Equatorial radius	3,963.34	6,378.2
Polar radius	3,949.99	6,356.7

Volume of the Earth	2.6×10^{11} cubic miles	10.84×10^{11} cubic kilometers
Mass or weight	6.6×10^{21} short tons	6.0×10^{21} metric tons
Maximum distance from Sun	94,600,000 miles	152,000,000 kilometers
Minimum distance from Sun	91,300,000 miles	147,000,000 kilometers

The Continents

	Area in: Sq. Miles	Sq. Km.	Percent of World's Land
Asia	17,128,500	44,362,815	29.5
Africa	11,707,000	30,321,130	20.2
North America	9,363,000	24,250,170	16.2
South America	6,875,000	17,806,250	11.8
Antarctica	5,500,000	14,245,000	9.5
Europe	4,057,000	10,507,630	7.0
Australia	2,966,136	7,682,300	5.1

Oceans and Major Seas

	Area in: Sq. Miles	Sq. Km.	Greatest Depth in: Feet	Meters
Pacific Ocean	64,186,000	166,241,700	36,198	11,033
Atlantic Ocean	31,862,000	82,522,600	28,374	8,648
Indian Ocean	28,350,000	73,426,500	25,344	7,725
Arctic Ocean	5,427,000	14,056,000	17,880	5,450
Caribbean Sea	970,000	2,512,300	24,720	7,535
Mediterranean Sea	969,000	2,509,700	16,896	5,150
Bering Sea	875,000	2,266,250	15,800	4,800
Gulf of Mexico	600,000	1,554,000	12,300	3,750
Sea of Okhotsk	590,000	1,528,100	11,070	3,370
East China Sea	482,000	1,248,400	9,500	2,900
Sea of Japan	389,000	1,007,500	12,280	3,740
Hudson Bay	317,500	822,300	846	258
North Sea	222,000	575,000	2,200	670
Black Sea	185,000	479,150	7,365	2,245
Red Sea	169,000	437,700	7,200	2,195
Baltic Sea	163,000	422,170	1,506	459

Major Ship Canals

	Length in: Miles	Kms.	Minimum Feet	Depth in: Meters
Volga-Baltic, U.S.S.R.	225	362	—	—
Baltic-White Sea, U.S.S.R.	140	225	16	5
Suez, Egypt	100.76	162	42	13
Albert, Belgium	80	129	16.5	5
Moscow-Volga, U.S.S.R.	80	129	18	6
Volga-Don, U.S.S.R.	62	100	—	—
Göta, Sweden	54	87	10	3
Kiel (Nord-Ostsee), W. Ger.	53.2	86	38	12
Panama Canal, Panama	50.72	82	41.6	13
Houston Ship, U.S.A.	50	81	36	11

Largest Islands

	Area in: Sq. Mi.	Sq. Km.
Greenland	840,000	2,175,600
New Guinea	305,000	789,950
Borneo	290,000	751,100
Madagascar	226,400	586,376
Baffin, Canada	195,928	507,454
Sumatra, Indonesia	164,000	424,760
Honshu, Japan	88,000	227,920
Great Britain	84,400	218,896
Victoria, Canada	83,896	217,290
Ellesmere, Canada	75,767	196,236
Celebes, Indonesia	72,986	189,034
South I., New Zealand	58,393	151,238
Java, Indonesia	48,842	126,501
North I., New Zealand	44,187	114,444
Newfoundland, Canada	42,031	108,860
Cuba	40,533	104,981
Luzon, Philippines	40,420	104,688
Iceland	39,768	103,000
Mindanao, Philippines	36,537	94,631
Ireland	31,743	82,214
Sakhalin, U.S.S.R.	29,500	76,405
Hispaniola, Haiti & Dom. Rep.	29,399	76,143
Hokkaido, Japan	28,983	75,066
Banks, Canada	27,038	70,028
Ceylon, Sri Lanka	25,332	65,610
Tasmania, Australia	24,600	63,710
Svalbard, Norway	23,957	62,049
Devon, Canada	21,331	55,247
Novaya Zemlya (north isl.), U.S.S.R.	18,600	48,200
Marajó, Brazil	17,991	46,597
Tierra del Fuego, Chile & Argentina	17,900	46,360
Alexander, Antarctica	16,700	43,250

WORLD STATISTICS

Principal Mountains of the World

	Feet	Meters
Everest, Nepal-China	29,028	8,848
Godwin Austen (K2), Pakistan-China	28,250	8,611
Kanchenjunga, Nepal-India	28,208	8,598
Lhotse, Nepal-China	27,923	8,511
Makalu, Nepal-China	27,824	8,481
Dhaulagiri, Nepal	26,810	8,172
Nanga Parbat, Pakistan	26,660	8,126
Annapurna, Nepal	26,504	8,078
Gasherbrum, Pakistan-China	26,740	8,068
Nanda Devi, India	25,645	7,817
Rakaposhi, Pakistan	25,550	7,788
Kamet, India	25,447	7,756
Gurla Mandhada, China	25,355	7,728
Kongur Shan, China	25,325	7,719
Tirich Mir, Pakistan	25,230	7,690
Gongga Shan, China	24,790	7,556
Muztagata, China	24,757	7,546
Communism Peak, U.S.S.R.	24,599	7,498
Pobeda Peak, U.S.S.R.	24,406	7,439
Chomo Lhari, Bhutan-China	23,997	7,314
Muztag, China	23,891	7,282
Cerro Aconcagua, Argentina	22,831	6,959
Ojos del Salado, Chile-Argentina	22,572	6,880
Bonete, Chile-Argentina	22,541	6,870
Tupungato, Chile-Argentina	22,310	6,800

	Feet	Meters
Pissis, Argentina	22,241	6,779
Mercedario, Argentina	22,211	6,770
Huascarán, Peru	22,205	6,768
Llullaillaco, Chile-Argentina	22,057	6,723
Nevada Ancohuma, Bolivia	21,489	6,550
Illampu, Bolivia	21,276	6,485
Chimborazo, Ecuador	20,561	6,267
McKinley, Alaska	20,320	6,194
Logan, Canada (Yukon)	19,524	5,951
Cotopaxi, Ecuador	19,347	5,897
Kilimanjaro, Tanzania	19,340	5,895
El Misti, Peru	19,101	5,822
Pico Cristóbal Colón, Colombia	19,029	5,800
Huila, Colombia	18,865	5,750
Citlaltépetl (Orizaba), Mexico	18,855	5,747
El'brus, U.S.S.R.	18,510	5,642
Damavand, Iran	18,376	5,601
St. Elias, Alaska-Canada (Yukon)	18,008	5,489
Vilcanota, Peru	17,999	5,486
Popocatépetl, Mexico	17,887	5,452
Dykhtau, U.S.S.R.	17,070	5,203
Kenya, Kenya	17,058	5,199
Ararat, Turkey	16,946	5,165
Vinson Massif, Antarctica	16,864	5,140
Margherita (Ruwenzori), Africa	16,795	5,119

	Feet	Meters
Kazbek, U.S.S.R.	16,512	5,033
Puncak Jaya, Indonesia	16,503	5,030
Tyree, Antarctica	16,289	4,965
Blanc, France	15,771	4,807
Klyuchevskaya Sopka, U.S.S.R.	15,584	4,750
Fairweather (Br. Col., Canada)	15,300	4,663
Dufourspitze (Mte. Rosa), Italy-Switzerland	15,203	4,634
Ras Dashan, Ethiopia	15,157	4,620
Matterhorn, Switzerland	14,691	4,478
Whitney, California, U.S.A.	14,494	4,418
Elbert, Colorado, U.S.A.	14,433	4,399
Rainier, Washington, U.S.A.	14,410	4,392
Shasta, California, U.S.A.	14,162	4,350
Pikes Peak, Colorado, U.S.A.	14,110	4,301
Finsteraarhorn, Switzerland	14,022	4,274
Mauna Kea, Hawaii, U.S.A.	13,796	4,205
Mauna Loa, Hawaii, U.S.A.	13,677	4,169
Jungfrau, Switzerland	13,642	4,158
Cameroon, Cameroon	13,350	4,069
Grossglockner, Austria	12,457	3,797
Fuji, Japan	12,389	3,776
Cook, New Zealand	12,349	3,764
Etna, Italy	11,053	3,369
Kosciusko, Australia	7,310	2,228
Mitchell, North Carolina, U.S.A.	6,684	2,037

Longest Rivers of the World

	Length in: Miles	Kms.
Nile, Africa	4,145	6,671
Amazon, S. Amer.	3,915	6,300
Chang Jiang (Yangtze), China	3,900	6,276
Mississippi-Missouri-Red Rock, U.S.A.	3,741	6,019
Ob'Irtysh-Black Irtysh, U.S.S.R.	3,362	5,411
Yenisey-Angara, U.S.S.R.	3,100	4,989
Huang He (Yellow), China	2,877	4,630
Amur-Shilka-Onon, Asia	2,744	4,416
Lena, U.S.S.R.	2,734	4,400
Congo (Zaire), Africa	2,718	4,374
Mackenzie-Peace-Finlay, Canada	2,635	4,241
Mekong, Asia	2,610	4,200
Missouri-Red Rock, U.S.A.	2,564	4,125
Niger, Africa	2,548	4,101
Paraná-La Plata, S. Amer.	2,450	3,943
Mississippi, U.S.A.	2,348	3,778
Murray-Darling, Australia	2,310	3,718
Volga, U.S.S.R.	2,194	3,531
Madeira, S. Amer.	2,013	3,240
Purus, S. Amer.	1,995	3,211
Yukon, Alaska-Canada	1,979	3,185
St. Lawrence, Canada-U.S.A.	1,900	3,058
Rio Grande, Mexico-U.S.A.	1,885	3,034
Syrdar'ya-Naryn, U.S.S.R.	1,859	2,992

	Length in: Miles	Kms.
São Francisco, Brazil	1,811	2,914
Indus, Asia	1,800	2,897
Danube, Europe	1,775	2,857
Salween, Asia	1,770	2,849
Brahmaputra, Asia	1,700	2,736
Euphrates, Asia	1,700	2,736
Tocantins, Brazil	1,677	2,699
Xi (Si), China	1,650	2,655
Amudar'ya, Asia	1,616	2,601
Nelson-Saskatchewan, Canada	1,600	2,575
Orinoco, S. Amer.	1,600	2,575
Zambezi, Africa	1,600	2,575
Paraguay, S. Amer.	1,584	2,549
Kolyma, U.S.S.R.	1,562	2,514
Ganges, Asia	1,550	2,494
Ural, U.S.S.R.	1,509	2,428
Japurá, S. Amer.	1,500	2,414
Arkansas, U.S.A.	1,450	2,334
Colorado, U.S.A.-Mexico	1,450	2,334
Negro, S. Amer.	1,400	2,253
Dnieper, U.S.S.R.	1,368	2,202
Orange, Africa	1,350	2,173
Irrawaddy, Burma	1,325	2,132
Brazos, U.S.A.	1,309	2,107

	Length in: Miles	Kms.
Ohio-Allegheny, U.S.A.	1,306	2,102
Kama, U.S.S.R.	1,262	2,031
Red, U.S.A.	1,222	1,966
Don, U.S.S.R.	1,222	1,967
Columbia, U.S.A.-Canada	1,214	1,953
Saskatchewan, Canada	1,205	1,939
Peace-Finlay, Canada	1,195	1,923
Tigris, Asia	1,181	1,901
Darling, Australia	1,160	1,867
Angara, U.S.S.R.	1,135	1,827
Sungari, Asia	1,130	1,819
Pechora, U.S.S.R.	1,124	1,809
Snake, U.S.A.	1,000	1,609
Churchill, Canada	1,000	1,609
Pilcomayo, S. Amer.	1,000	1,609
Magdalena, Colombia	1,000	1,609
Uruguay, S. Amer.	994	1,600
Platte-N. Platte, U.S.A.	990	1,593
Ohio, U.S.A.	981	1,578
Pecos, U.S.A.	926	1,490
Oka, U.S.S.R.	918	1,477
Canadian, U.S.A.	906	1,458
Colorado, Texas, U.S.A.	894	1,439
Dniester, U.S.S.R.	876	1,410

Principal Natural Lakes

	Area in: Sq. Miles	Sq. Km.	Max. Depth in: Feet	Meters
Caspian Sea, U.S.S.R.-Iran	143,243	370,999	3,264	995
Lake Superior, U.S.A.-Canada	31,820	82,414	1,329	405
Lake Victoria, Africa	26,724	69,215	270	82
Aral Sea, U.S.S.R.	25,676	66,501	256	78
Lake Huron, U.S.A.-Canada	23,010	59,596	748	228
Lake Michigan, U.S.A.	22,400	58,016	923	281
Lake Tanganyika, Africa	12,650	32,764	4,700	1,433
Lake Baykal, U.S.S.R.	12,162	31,500	5,316	1,620
Great Bear Lake, Canada	12,096	31,328	1,356	413
Lake Nyasa (Malawi), Africa	11,555	29,928	2,320	707
Great Slave Lake, Canada	11,031	28,570	2,015	614
Lake Erie, U.S.A.-Canada	9,940	25,745	210	64
Lake Winnipeg, Canada	9,417	24,390	60	18
Lake Ontario, U.S.A.-Canada	7,540	19,529	775	244
Lake Ladoga, U.S.S.R.	7,104	18,399	738	225
Lake Balkhash, U.S.S.R.	7,027	18,200	87	27
Lake Maracaibo, Venezuela	5,120	13,261	100	31
Lake Chad, Africa	4,000-10,000	10,360-25,900	25	8
Lake Onega, U.S.S.R.	3,710	9,609	377	115

	Area in: Sq. Miles	Sq. Km.	Max. Depth in: Feet	Meters
Lake Eyre, Australia	3,500-0	9,000-0	—	—
Lake Titicaca, Peru-Bolivia	3,200	8,288	1,000	305
Lake Nicaragua, Nicaragua	3,100	8,029	230	70
Lake Athabasca, Canada	3,064	7,936	400	122
Reindeer Lake, Canada	2,568	6,651	—	—
Lake Turkana (Rudolf), Africa	2,463	6,379	240	73
Issyk-Kul', U.S.S.R.	2,425	6,281	2,303	702
Lake Torrens, Australia	2,230	5,776	—	—
Vänern, Sweden	2,156	5,584	328	100
Nettilling Lake, Canada	2,140	5,543	—	—
Lake Winnipegosis, Canada	2,075	5,374	38	12
Lake Mobutu Sese Seko (Albert), Africa	2,075	5,374	160	49
Kariba Lake, Zambia-Zimbabwe	2,050	5,310	295	90
Lake Nipigon, Canada	1,872	4,848	540	165
Lake Mweru, Zaire-Zambia	1,800	4,662	60	18
Lake Manitoba, Canada	1,799	4,659	12	4
Lake Taymyr, U.S.S.R.	1,737	4,499	85	26
Lake Khanka, China-U.S.S.R.	1,700	4,403	33	10
Lake Kioga, Uganda	1,700	4,403	25	8

GLOSSARY OF ABBREVIATIONS

A
A. A. F. — Army Air Field
Acad. — Academy
A. C. T. — Australian Capital Territory
adm. — administration; administrative
A. F. B. — Air Force Base
Afgh., Afghan. — Afghanistan
Afr. — Africa
Ala. — Alabama
Alb. — Albania
Alg. — Algeria
Alta. — Alberta
Amer. — American
Amer. Samoa — American Samoa
And. — Andorra
Ant., Antarc. — Antarctica
Ant. & Bar. — Antigua and Barbuda
Ar. — Arabia
arch. — archipelago
Arg. — Argentina
Ariz. — Arizona
Ark. — Arkansas
A. S. S. R. — Autonomous Soviet Socialist Republic
Aust. — Austria
Aust. Cap. Terr. — Australian Capital Territory
Austr., Austral. — Australian, Australia
aut. — autonomous
Aut. Obl. — Autonomous Oblast

B
B. — bay
Bah. — Bahamas
Barb. — Barbados
Battlef. — Battlefield
Bch. — Beach
Belg. — Belgium
Berm. — Bermuda
Bol. — Bolivia
Bots. — Botswana
Br. — Branch
Br. — British
Braz. — Brazil
Br. Col. — British Columbia
Br. Ind. Oc. Terr. — British Indian Ocean Territory
Bulg. — Bulgaria

C
C. — cape
Calif. — California
Can. — Canada
can. — canal
cap. — capital
Cent. Afr. Rep. — Central African Republic
Cent. Amer. — Central America
C. G. Sta. — Coast Guard Station
C. H. — Court House
chan. — channel
Chan. Is. — Channel Islands
Chem. Ctr. — Chemical Center
co. — county
C. of G. H. — Cape of Good Hope
Col. — Colombia
Colo. — Colorado
comm. — commissary
Conn. — Connecticut
cont. — continent
cord. — cordillera (mountain range)
C. Rica — Costa Rica
C. S. — County Seat
C. Verde — Cape Verde
Czech. — Czechoslovakia

D
D. C. — District of Columbia
Del. — Delaware
Dem. — Democratic
Den. — Denmark
depr. — depression
dept. — department
des. — desert
dist., dist's — district, districts
div. — division
Dom. Rep. — Dominican Republic

E
E. — East
Ec., Ecua. — Ecuador
E. Ger. — East Germany
elec. div. — electoral division
El Salv. — El Salvador
Eng. — England
Equat. Guinea, Eq. Guin — Equatorial Guinea
escarp. — escarpment
est. — estuary
Eth. — Ethiopia

F
Falk. Is. — Falkland Islands
Fin. — Finland
Fk., Fks. — Fork, Forks
Fla. — Florida
for. — forest
Fr. — France, French
Fr. Gui. — French Guiana
Fr. Poly. — French Polynesia
Ft. — Fort

G
G. — gulf
Ga. — Georgia
Game Res. — Game Reserve
Ger. — Germany
geys. — geyser
Gibr. — Gibraltar
glac. — glacier
gov. — governorate
Gr. — Group
Greenl. — Greenland
Gren. — Grenada
Gt. Brit. — Great Britain
Guad. — Guadeloupe
Guat. — Guatemala
Guinea-Biss. — Guinea-Bissau
Guy. — Guyana

H
har., harb., hbr. — harbor
hd. — head
highl. — highland, highlands
Hist. — Historic, Historical
Hond. — Honduras
Hts. — Heights
Hung. — Hungary

I
i., isl. — island, isle
I. C. — independent city
Ice., Icel. — Iceland
Ida. — Idaho
Ill. — Illinois
Ind. — Indiana
ind. city — independent city
Indon. — Indonesia
Ind. Res. — Indian Reservation
int. div. — internal division
inten. — intendency
Int'l — International
Ire. — Ireland
is., isls. — islands
Isr. — Israel
isth. — isthmus
Iv. Coast — Ivory Coast

J
Jam. — Jamaica
Jct. — Junction

K
Kans. — Kansas
Ky. — Kentucky

L
L. — Lake, Loch, Lough
La. — Louisiana
Lab. — Laboratory
lag. — lagoon
Ld. — Land
Leb. — Lebanon
Les. — Lesotho
Liecht. — Liechtenstein
Lux. — Luxembourg

M
Mad., Madag. — Madagascar
Man. — Manitoba
Mart. — Martinique
Mass. — Massachusetts
Maur. — Mauritania
Md. — Maryland
met. area — metropolitan area
Mex. — Mexico
Mich. — Michigan
Minn. — Minnesota
Miss. — Mississippi
Mo. — Missouri
Mon. — Monument
Mong. — Mongolia
Mont. — Montana
Mor. — Morocco
Moz., Mozamb. — Mozambique
mt. — mount
mtn. — mountain

N
N., No., North. — North, Northern
N. Amer. — North America
Nam., Namib. — Namibia
N. A. S. — Naval Air Station
Nat'l — National
Nat'l Cem. — National Cemetery
Nat'l Mem. Park — National Memorial Park
Nat'l Mil. Park — National Military Park
Nat'l Pkwy. — National Parkway
Nav. Base — Naval Base
Nav. Sta. — Naval Station
N. B., N. Br. — New Brunswick
N. C. — North Carolina
N. Dak. — North Dakota
Nebr. — Nebraska
Neth. — Netherlands
Neth. Ant. — Netherlands Antilles
Nev. — Nevada
New Bruns. — New Brunswick
New Cal., New Caled. — New Caledonia
Newf. — Newfoundland
New Hebr. — New Hebrides
N. H. — New Hampshire
Nic. — Nicaragua
N. Ire. — Northern Ireland
N. J. — New Jersey
N. Mex. — New Mexico
Nor. — Norway, Norwegian
North. — Northern
North. Terr., No. Terr. — Northern Territory (Australia)
N. S. — Nova Scotia
N. S. W., N.S. Wales — New South Wales
N. W. T., N. W. Terrs. — Northwest Territories (Canada)
N. Y. — New York
N. Z., N. Zealand — New Zealand

O
Obl. — Oblast
O. F. S. — Orange Free State
Okla. — Oklahoma
Okr. — Okrug
Ont. — Ontario
Ord. Depot — Ordnance Depot
Oreg. — Oregon

P
Pa. — Pennsylvania
Pac. Is. — Pacific Islands, Territory of the
Pak. — Pakistan
Pan. — Panama
Papua N. G. — Papua New Guinea
Par. — Paraguay
par. — parish
passg. — passage
P.D.R. Yemen — People's Democratic Republic of Yemen
P. E. I. — Prince Edward Island
pen. — peninsula
Phil., Phil. Is. — Philippines
Pk. — Park
pk. — peak
plat. — plateau
P. N. G. — Papua New Guinea
Pol. — Poland
Port. — Portugal, Portuguese
Pr. Edward I. — Prince Edward Island
pref. — prefecture
P. Rico — Puerto Rico
prom. — promontory
prov. — province, provincial
pt. — point

Q
Que. — Québec
Queens. — Queensland

R
R. — River
ra. — range
Rec., Recr. — Recreation, Recreational
reg. — region
Rep. — Republic
res. — reservoir
Res. — Reservation, Reserve
R. I. — Rhode Island
riv. — river
Rom. — Romania

S
S. — South
Sa. — Sierra, Serra
S. Afr., S. Africa — South Africa
salt dep. — salt deposit
salt des. — salt desert
S. Amer. — South America
São T. & Pr. — São Tomé and Príncipe
Sask. — Saskatchewan
Saudi Ar. — Saudi Arabia
S. Aust., S. Austral. — South Australia
S. C. — South Carolina
Scot. — Scotland
Sd. — Sound
S. Dak. — South Dakota
Sen. — Senegal
sen. dist. — senatorial district
Seych. — Seychelles
S. F. S. R. — Soviet Federated Socialist Republic
Sing. — Singapore
S. Leone — Sierra Leone
S. Marino — San Marino
Sol. Is. — Solomon Islands
Sp. — Spanish
Spr., Sprs. — Spring, Springs
S. S. R. — Soviet Socialist Republic
St., Ste. — Saint, Sainte
Sta. — Station
St. Chris.-Nevis — Saint Christopher-Nevis
St. P. & M. — Saint Pierre and Miquelon
St. Vin. & Grens. — St. Vincent & The Grenadines
str., strs. — strait, straits
Sur. — Suriname
S. W. Afr. — South-West Africa
Swaz. — Swaziland
Switz. — Switzerland

T
Tanz. — Tanzania
Tas. — Tasmania
Tenn. — Tennessee
terr., terrs. — territory, territories
Tex. — Texas
Thai. — Thailand
trad. — traditional
Trin. & Tob. — Trinidad and Tobago
Tun. — Tunisia
twp. — township

U
U.A.E. — United Arab Emirates
U. K. — United Kingdom
Upp. Volta — Upper Volta
urb. area — urban area
Urug. — Uruguay
U. S. — United States
U. S. S. R. — Union of Soviet Socialist Republics

V
Va. — Virginia
Ven., Venez. — Venezuela
V. I. (Br.) — Virgin Islands (British)
V. I. (U. S.) — Virgin Islands (U. S.)
Vic. — Victoria
Viet. — Vietnam
Vill. — Village
vol. — volcano
Vt. — Vermont

W
W. — West, Western
Wash. — Washington
W. Aust., W. Austral. — Western Australia
W. Ger. — West Germany
W. Indies — West Indies
Wis. — Wisconsin
W. Samoa — Western Samoa
W. Va. — West Virginia
Wyo. — Wyoming

Y
Yugo. — Yugoslavia
Yukon — Yukon Territory

Z
Zim. — Zimbabwe

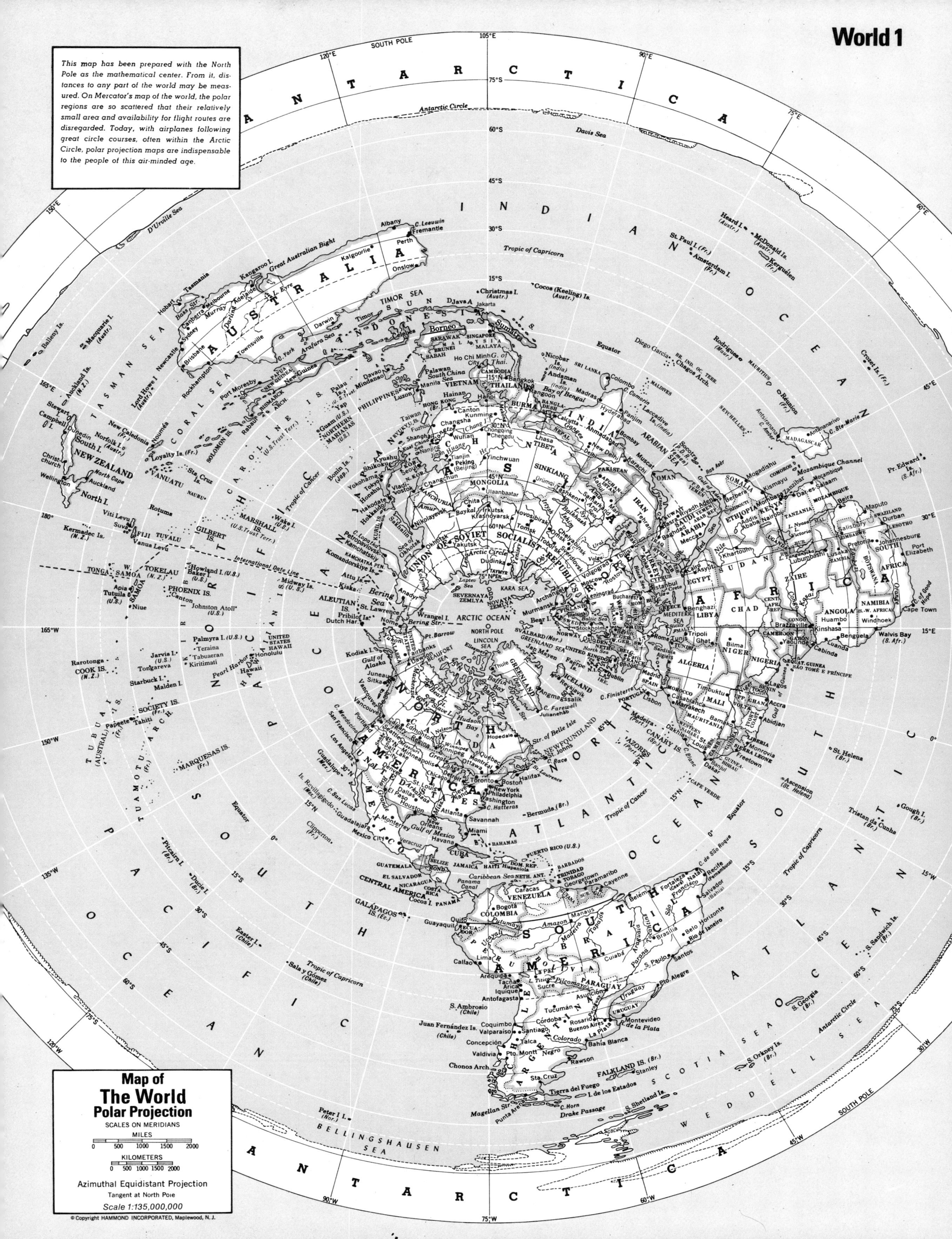
World 1
This map has been prepared with the North Pole as the mathematical center. From it, distances to any part of the world may be measured. On Mercator's map of the world, the polar regions are so scattered that their relatively small area and availability for flight routes are disregarded. Today, with airplanes following great circle courses, often within the Arctic Circle, polar projection maps are indispensable to the people of this air-minded age.
Map of
The World
Polar Projection
SCALES ON MERIDIANS
MILES
0 500 1000 1500 2000
KILOMETERS
0 500 1000 1500 2000
Azimuthal Equidistant Projection
Tangent at North Pole
Scale 1:135,000,000
© Copyright HAMMOND INCORPORATED, Maplewood, N. J.
SOUTH POLE
ANTARCTICA
INDIAN OCEAN
PACIFIC OCEAN
SOUTH PACIFIC OCEAN
NORTH ATLANTIC OCEAN
SOUTH ATLANTIC OCEAN
ARCTIC OCEAN
NORTH POLE
AUSTRALIA
ASIA
UNION OF SOVIET SOCIALIST REPUBLICS
EUROPE
AFRICA
NORTH AMERICA
SOUTH AMERICA
Tropic of Capricorn
Tropic of Cancer
Equator
Antarctic Circle
Arctic Circle
International Date Line

The World

BRIESEMEISTER ELLIPTICAL
EQUAL-AREA PROJECTION

Capitals of Countries ⊛
Other Capitals ◉
International Boundaries – – –

Scale 1:80,000,000

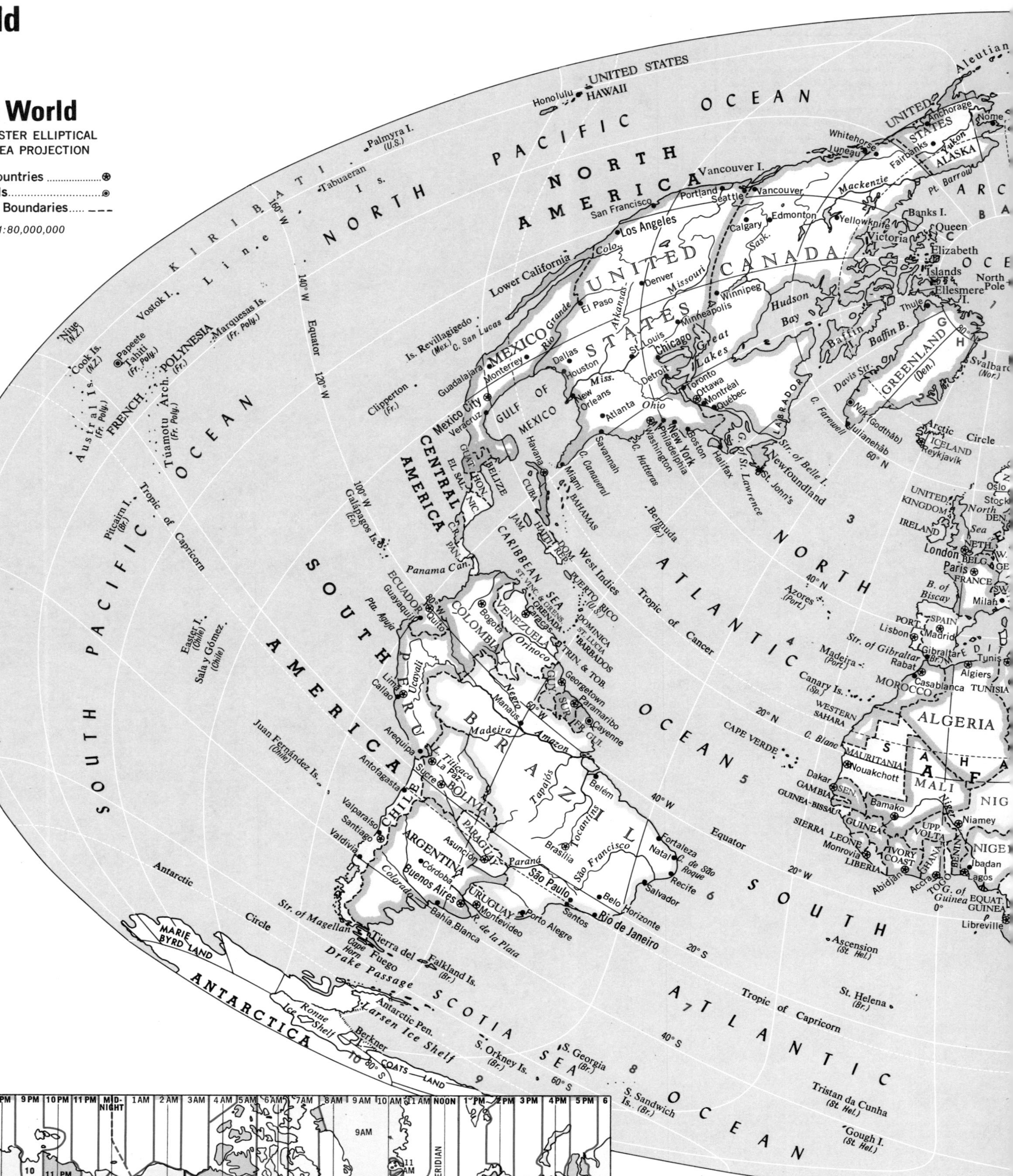

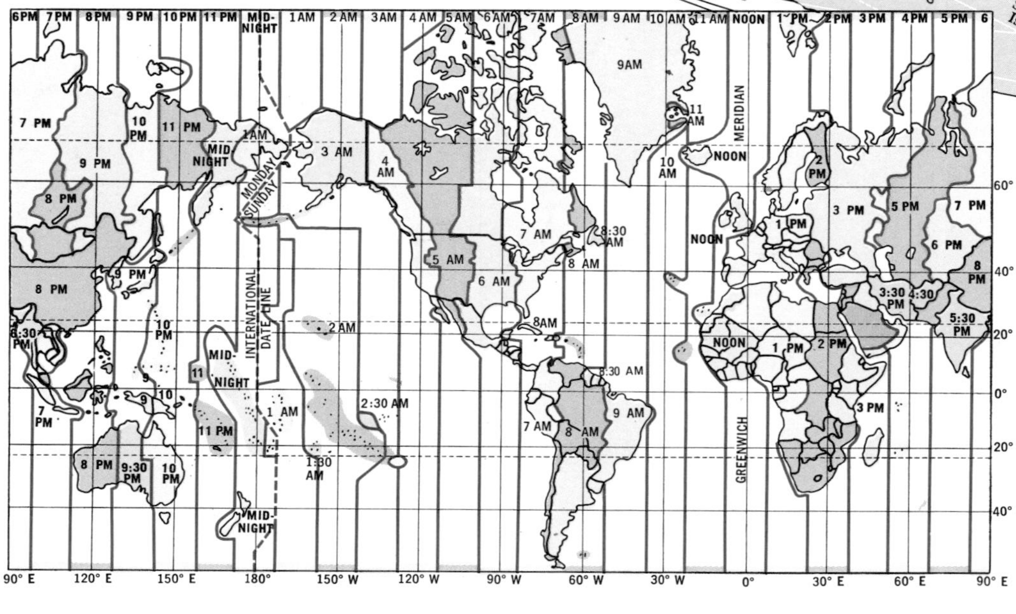

Time Zones

STANDARD TIME ZONES

Areas using half hour deviations.

Areas not using zone system.

NOTE: Standard time zones in the U.S.S.R. are always advanced one hour.

LAND AREA 57,970,000 sq. mi.
(150,142,300 sq. km.)
WATER AREA 139,781,000 sq. mi.
(362,032,790 sq. km.)
TOTAL SURFACE AREA 197,751,000 sq.mi.
(512,175,090 sq. km.)
POPULATION 4,415,000,000

Antarctica

AZIMUTHAL EQUIDISTANT PROJECTION

Scale 1:62,000,000

4 Arctic Ocean

Alaska (gulf), U.S. D17
Alaska (pen.), U.S. D18
Alaska (range), U.S. C17
Alaska (reg.) C17
Aleutian (isls.), U.S. D18
Alexander (arch.), U.S. D16
Alexandra Land (isl.), U.S.S.R. A8
Amundsen (gulf), Canada B16
Anadyr' (gulf), U.S.S.R. C18
Anadyr' (riv.), U.S.S.R. C1
Arctic Ocean A15
Atlantic Ocean D11
Attu (isl.), U.S. D1
Axel Heiberg (isl.), Canada A14
Baffin (bay) B13
Baffin (isl.), Canada C13
Banks (isl)., Canada B16
Barents (sea) B8
Barrow (pt.), U.S. B18
Bathurst (isl.), Canada B14
Bear (isl.), Norway B9
Bear (isls.), U.S.S.R. B1
Beaufort (sea) B16
Belyy (isl.), U.S.S.R. B6
Bering (str.) C18
Bilibino, U.S.S.R. C1
Bol'shevik (isl.), U.S.S.R. A4
Boothia (gulf), Canada B14
Boothia (pen.), Canada B14
Borden (isl.), Canada B15
Bristol (bay), U.S. D18
Brodeur (pen.), Canada B14
Brooks (range), U.S. C17
Canada C13
Chelyuskin (cape), U.S.S.R. B4
Cherskiy, U.S.S.R. C1
Chukchi (pen.), U.S.S.R. C18
Chukchi (sea) C18
Columbia (cape), Canada A13
Cook (inlet), U.S. D17
Cumberland (sound), Canada C13
Davis (str.) C12
Denmark (strait) C11
Devon (isl.), Canada B14
Dezhnev (cape), U.S.S.R. C18
Disko (isl.), Greenl. C12
Dmitriya Lapteva (str.), U.S.S.R. B2
Dvina, Northern (riv.), U.S.S.R. C7
East (Dezhnev) (cape), U.S.S.R. C18
East Siberian (sea), U.S.S.R. B1
Edge (isl.), Norway B8
Ellef Ringnes (isl.), Canada B15
Ellesmere (isl.), Canada B14
Faddeyevskiy (isl.), U.S.S.R. B2
Farewell (cape), Greenl. D12
Finland C8
Foxe (basin), Canada C13
Franz Josef Land (isls.), U.S.S.R. A7
Frederikshåb, Greenl. C12
Garry (lake), Canada C14
George Land (isl.), U.S.S.R. B7
Godhavn, Greenl. C12
Godthåb (Nûk) (cap.), Greenl. C12
Graham Bell (isl.), U.S.S.R. A6
Great Bear (lake), Canada C16
Great Slave (lake), Canada C15
Greenland B12
Greenland (sea) B10
Grise Fiord, Canada B13
Grønnedal, Greenl. C12
Gunnbjørn (mt.), Greenl. C11
Gyda (pen.), U.S.S.R. C6
Hammerfest, Norway B9
Hayes (pen.), Greenl. B13
Hekla (mt.), Ice. C11
Holman Island, Canada B15
Holsteinsborg, Greenl. C12
Hope (isl.), Norway B8
Iceland C10
Igarka, U.S.S.R. C5
Igloolik, Canada B14
Indigirka (riv.), U.S.S.R. C2

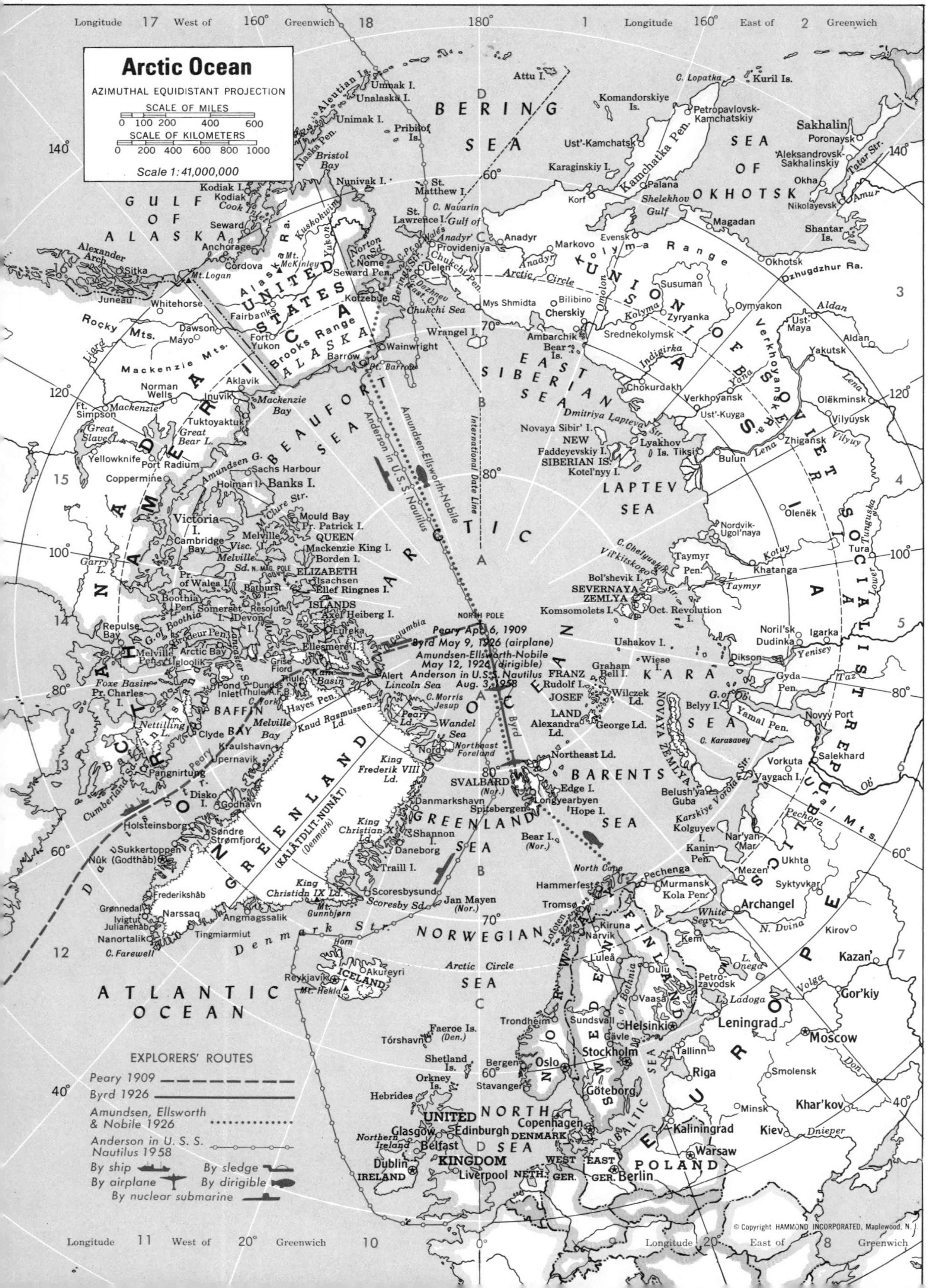

Arctic Ocean

AZIMUTHAL EQUIDISTANT PROJECTION

SCALE OF MILES: 0 100 200 400 600

SCALE OF KILOMETERS: 0 200 400 600 800 1000

Scale 1:41,000,000

EXPLORERS' ROUTES
Peary 1909
Byrd 1926
Amundsen, Ellsworth & Nobile 1926
Anderson in U. S. S. Nautilus 1958
By ship — By sledge
By airplane — By dirigible
By nuclear submarine

Inuvik, Canada C16
Ivigtut, Greenl. D12
Isachsen, Canada B15
Jan Mayen (isl.), Norway B10
Julianehåb, Greenl. D12
Juneau, U.S. D16
Kalâtdlit-Nunât (Greenland) B12
Kane (basin) B13
Kanin (pen.), U.S.S.R. C7
Kara (sea), U.S.S.R. B6
Karasavey (cape), U.S.S.R. B6
Karskiye Vorota (str.), U.S.S.R. B7
Kem', U.S.S.R. C8
Khatanga, U.S.S.R. B4
King Christian IX Land (reg.), Greenl. C11
King Christian X Land (reg.), Greenl. B11
King Frederik VIII Land (reg.), Greenl. B11
Kiruna, Sweden C8
Knud Rasmussen Land (reg.), Greenl. B12
Kodiak, U.S. D17
Kodiak (isl.), U.S. D17
Kola (pen.), U.S.S.R. C8
Kolguyev (isl.), U.S.S.R. B7
Kolyma (range), U.S.S.R. C1
Kolyma (riv.), U.S.S.R. C2
Komsomolets (isl.), U.S.S.R. A5
Korf, U.S.S.R. C1
Kotel'nyy (isl.), U.S.S.R. B2
Kotuy (riv.), U.S.S.R. B4
Kotzebue, U.S. C18
Kraulshavn, Greenl. B13
Kuskokwim (riv.), U.S. C17
Lancaster (sound), Canada B14
Laptev (sea), U.S.S.R. B3
Lena (riv.), U.S.S.R. C3
Lincoln (sea) A12
Lofoten (isls.), Norway C9
Logan (mt.), Canada C17
Longyearbyen, Norway B8
Lyakhov (isls.), U.S.S.R. B3
Mackenzie (bay), Canada B16
Mackenzie (mts.), Canada C16
Mackenzie (riv.), Canada C16
Mackenzie King (isl.), Canada B15
Markovo, U.S.S.R. C1
Mayo, Canada C16
M'Clure (str.), Canada B15
McKinley (mt.), U.S. C17
Melville (bay), Greenl. B13
Melville (isl.), Canada B15
Melville (pen.), Canada C14
Mezen', U.S.S.R. C7
Morris Jesup (cape), Greenl. A11
Mould Bay, Canada B16
Murmansk, U.S.S.R. C8
Mys Shmidta, U.S.S.R. C1
Nanortalik, Greenl. D12
Narssaq, Greenl. C12
Narvik, Norway C9
Nar'yan-Mar, U.S.S.R. C7
Navarin (cape), U.S.S.R. C18
Nettilling (lake), Canada C13
New Siberian (isls.), U.S.S.R. B2
Nikolayevsk, U.S.S.R. D2
Nome, U.S. C18
Nord, GreenL A10
Nordvik-Ugol'naya, U.S.S.R. B4
Noril'sk, U.S.S.R. B5
Norman Wells, Canada C16
North (cape), Ice. C11
North (cape), Norway B8
Northeast Foreland (pen.), Greenl. A10
Northeast Land (isl.), Norway B8
North Magnetic Pole, Canada B15
North Pole A1
Norton (sound), U.S. C18
Norway C9
Norwegian (sea) C10
Novaya Sibir' (isl.), U.S.S.R. B2
Novaya Zemlya (isls.), U.S.S.R. B7
Novyy Port, U.S.S.R. C6
Nûk (cap.), Greenl. C12
Nunivak (isl.), U.S. D18
Ob' (gulf), U.S.S.R. B6
Ob' (riv.), U.S.S.R. C6
October Revolution (isl.), U.S.S.R. B5
Olenek, U.S.S.R. C4
Omolon (riv.), U.S.S.R. C1
Oymyakon, U.S.S.R. C2
Pangnirtung, Canada C13
Peary Land (reg.), Greenl. A11
Pechenga, U.S.S.R. C8
Pechora (riv.), U.S.S.R. C7
Pond Inlet, Canada B13
Port Radium, Canada C15
Pribilof (isls.), U.S. D18
Prince Charles (isl.), Canada C13
Prince of Wales (cape), U.S. C18
Prince of Wales (isl.), Canada B14
Prince Patrick (isl.), Canada B16
Provideniya, U.S.S.R. C18
Queen Elizabeth (isls.), Canada B15
Repulse Bay, Canada C14
Resolute, Canada B14
Reykjavík (cap.), Ice. C11
Rocky (mts.), Canada D16
Rudolf (isl.), U.S.S.R. A7
Sachs Harbour, Canada B16
Saint Lawrence (isl.), U.S. C18
Saint Matthew (isl.), U.S. C18
Salekhard, U.S.S.R. C6
Scoresby (sound), Greenl. B10
Scoresbysund, Greenl. B10
Severnaya Zemlya (isls.), U.S.S.R. A4
Seward, U.S. D17
Seward (pen.), U.S. C18
Shannon (isl.), Greenl. B10
Siberia (reg.), U.S.S.R. C2
Sitka, U.S. D16
Somerset (isl.), Canada B14
Søndre Strømfjord, Greenl. C12
Spitsbergen (isl.), Norway B9
Srednekolymsk, U.S.S.R. C2
Sukkertoppen, Greenl. C12
Susuman, U.S.S.R. C2
Svalbard (isls.), Norway B9
Sweden D9
Taymyr (lake), U.S.S.R. B5
Taymyr (pen.), U.S.S.R. B4
Taz (river), U.S.S.R. C5
Thule, Greenl. B13
Thule A.F.B. (Dundas), Greenl. B13
Tiksi, U.S.S.R. B3
Tingmiarmiut, Greenl. C12
Traill (isl.), Greenl. B10
Tromsø, Norway B9
Tuktoyaktuk, Canada C16
Uelen, U.S.S.R. C18
Umnak (isl.), U.S. D18
Unalaska (isl.), U.S. D18
Unimak (isl.), U.S. D18
Union of Soviet Socialist Republics C2
United States C17
Upernavik, Greenl. B12
Ural (mts.), U.S.S.R. C6
Ushakov (isl.), U.S.S.R. B5
Ust'-Kuyga, U.S.S.R. C3
Vaygach (isl.), U.S.S.R. C6
Verkhoyansk, U.S.S.R. C3
Verkhoyansk (range), U.S.S.R. C3
Victoria (isl.), Canada B15
Vil'kitskogo (str.), U.S.S.R. B4
Viscount Melville (sound), Canada B15
Vorkuta, U.S.S.R. C6
Wainwright, U.S. B18
Wandel (sea), Greenl. A10
White (sea), U.S.S.R. C8
Whitehorse, Canada C16
Wiese (isl.), U.S.S.R. B6
Wilczek Land (isl.), U.S.S.R. B6
Wrangel (isl.), U.S.S.R. B18
Yamal (pen.), U.S.S.R. B6
Yana (riv.), U.S.S.R. C3
Yellowknife, Canada C15
Yenisey (riv.), U.S.S.R. C5
York (cape), Greenl. B13
Yukon (riv.) C17
Zhigansk, U.S.S.R. C3
Zyryanka, U.S.S.R. C2

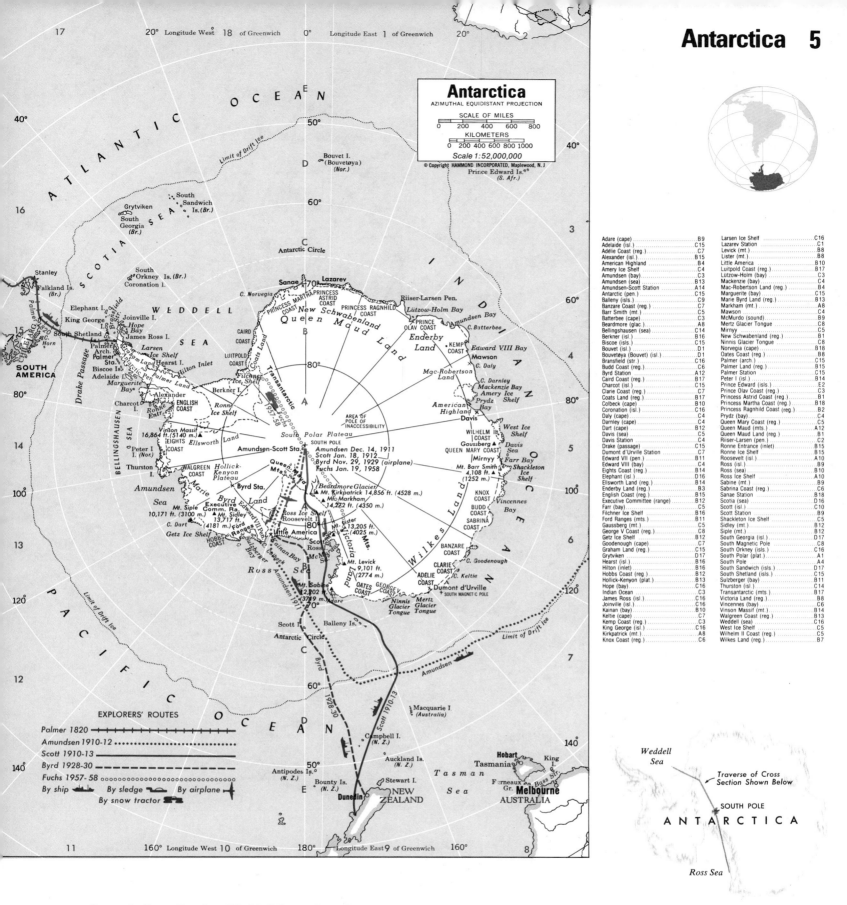

Antarctica

AZIMUTHAL EQUIDISTANT PROJECTION

SCALE OF MILES: 0 200 400 600 800

KILOMETERS: 0 200 400 600 800 1000

Scale 1:52,000,000

EXPLORERS' ROUTES

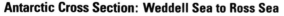

- Palmer 1820
- Amundsen 1910-12
- Scott 1910-13
- Byrd 1928-30
- Fuchs 1957-58
- By ship
- By sledge
- By airplane
- By snow tractor

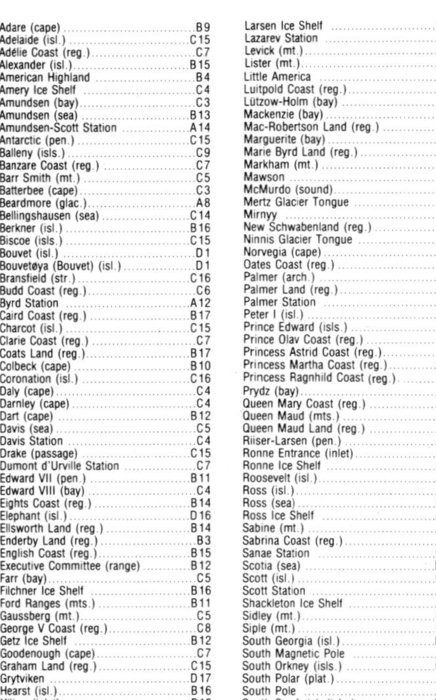

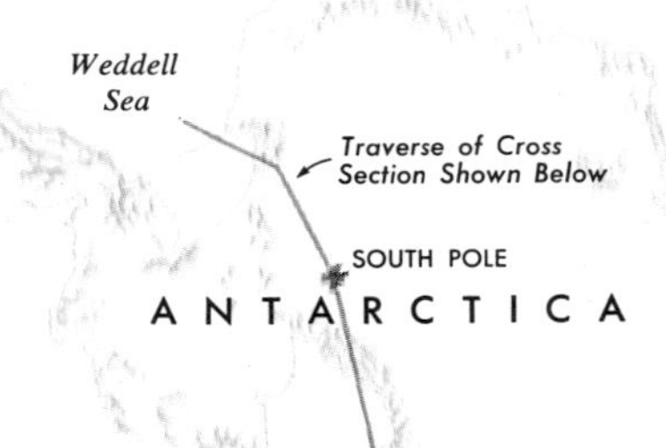

Antarctic Cross Section: Weddell Sea to Ross Sea

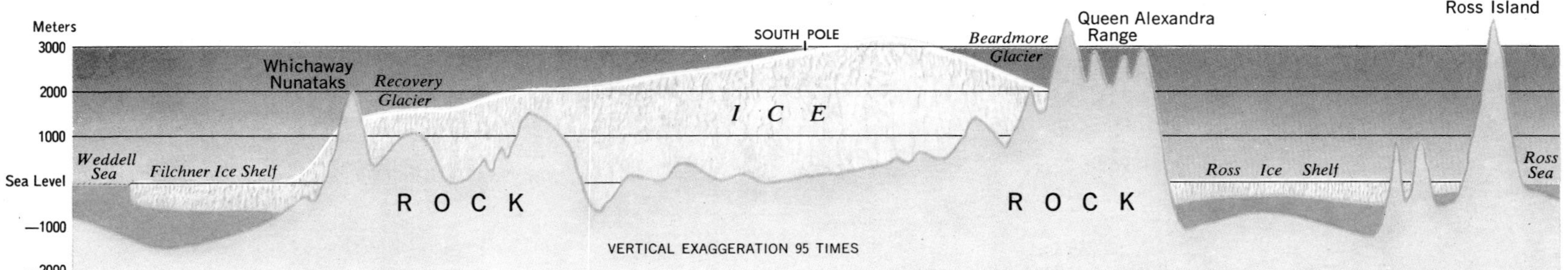

Information Based on American Geographical Society's "Antarctic Map Folio Series"

Europe
POLYCONIC PROJECTION
SCALE OF MILES
0 100 200 300 400
KILOMETERS
0 100 200 300 400
Capitals of Countries
Other Capitals
International Boundaries
Internal Boundaries
Canals
Scale 1:20,800,000
Longitude West of Greenwich 0° Longitude East of Greenwich

AREA 4,057,000 sq. mi.
(10,507,630 sq. km.)
POPULATION 676,000,000
LARGEST CITY Paris
HIGHEST POINT El'brus 18,510 ft.
(5,642 m.)
LOWEST POINT Caspian Sea -92 ft.
(-28 m.)

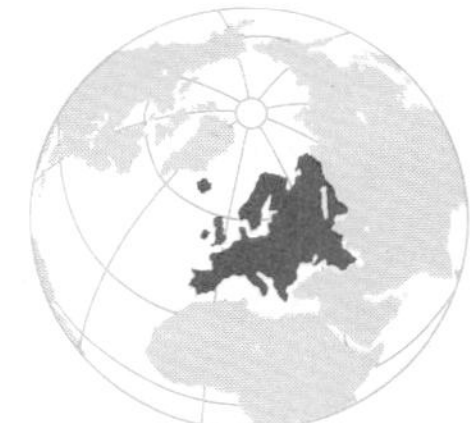

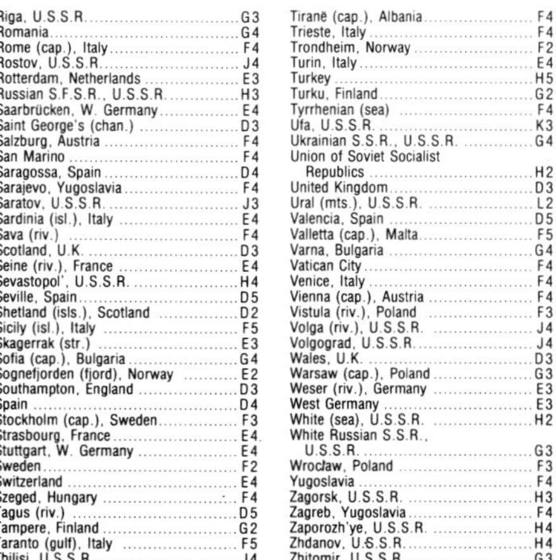

Population Distribution

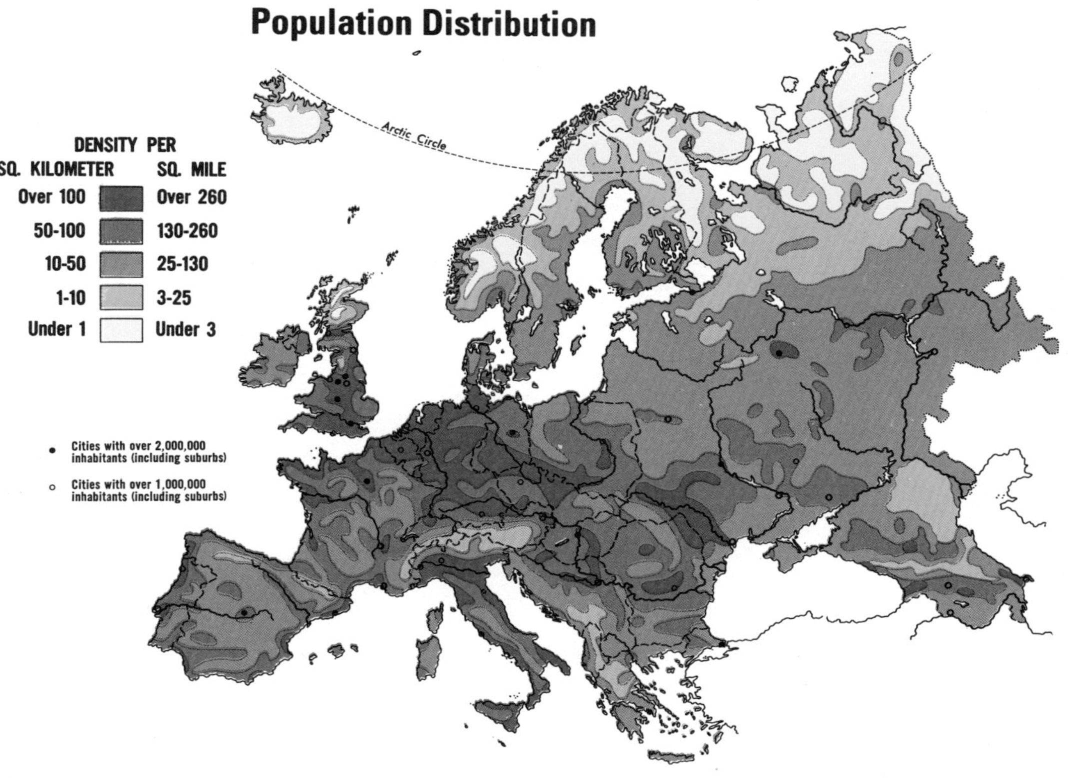

Vegetation

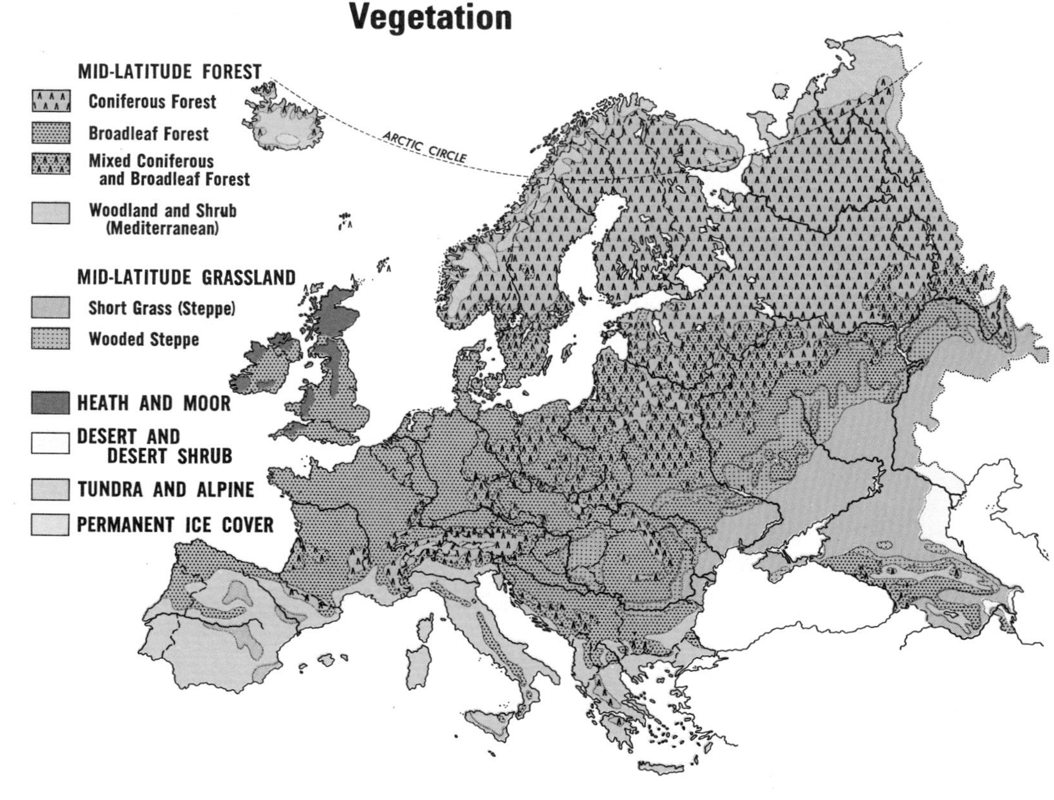

8 Europe

30° 20° 10° 0° 10° 20° 30° 40° 50° 60°

60° 50° 40°

ICELAND
Reykjavík
Horn
Fontur
Arctic Circle
NORWEGIAN SEA
Faeroe Is. (Den.)
Shetland Is.
Orkney Is.
Hebrides
Moray Firth
Hardangerfjord
Aberdeen
Ben Nevis 4,406 ft. (1343 m.)
Glasgow
U.K.
Belfast
Dublin
IRELAND
IRISH SEA
St. Georges Chan.
C. Clear
Liverpool
Birmingham
UNITED KINGDOM
London
Land's End
English Channel
Channel Is. (U.K.)
NORTH SEA
ATLANTIC OCEAN
Bay of Biscay
C. Finisterre
Nordkapp
Sørøy
Hammerfest
Vesterålen
Lofoten
Vestfjord
Kiruna
NORWAY
SWEDEN
Trondheim
Glittertind 8,110 ft. (2472 m.)
Bergen
Oslo
Lindesnes
Skagerrak
Kattegat
Vänern
Göteborg
Västerås
Stockholm
Gotland
Sundsvall
Dal
Gulf of Bothnia
Åland Is.
Oulu
FINLAND
Tampere
Helsinki
Gulf of Finland
Hiiumaa
Saaremaa
Riga
BALTIC SEA
Copenhagen
DENMARK
Bornholm
Rügen
Gdańsk
Frisian Is.
NETHERLANDS
Amsterdam
Hamburg
Elbe
EAST
Berlin
WEST
GERMANY
BELGIUM
Brussels
Cologne
Bonn
Leipzig
LUX.
Le Havre
Seine
Paris
Nantes
Loire
FRANCE
Bordeaux
Dordogne
Garonne
Rhône
Lyon
Stuttgart
Munich
Bern
SWITZ.
LIECH.
Mt. Blanc 15,771 ft. (4807 m.)
Milan
Turin
Genoa
MONACO
Marseille
Gulf of Lions
Corsica
Sardinia
Pyrenees
ANDORRA
Bilbao
Porto
Douro
Ebro
SPAIN
PORTUGAL
Lisbon
Madrid
Saragossa
Barcelona
Tagus
Guadiana
Valencia
C. de São Vicente
Balearic Is.
Minorca
Majorca
Ibiza
Cádiz
Málaga
Str. of Gibraltar
Tangier
GIBRALTAR (U.K.)
Rabat
Casablanca
MOROCCO
Oran
Algiers
ALGERIA
Constantine
Tunis
TUNISIA
C. Bon
AFRICA
C. Teulada
MEDITERRANEAN SEA
TYRRHENIAN SEA
Palermo
Sicily
Etna 11,053 ft. (3369 m.)
C. Passero
MALTA
Valletta
Venice
SAN MARINO
VATICAN CITY
Rome
Naples
ITALY
Apennines
ADRIATIC SEA
IONIAN SEA
POLAND
Vistula
Warsaw
Łódź
Oder
Bug
Prague
Cracow
CZECHOSLOVAKIA
Brno
Danube
Vienna
AUSTRIA
Graz
Budapest
HUNGARY
Cluj-Napoca
Carpathian Mts.
ROMANIA
Zagreb
Sava
Belgrade
YUGOSLAVIA
Bucharest
Balkan Mts.
Sofia
BULGARIA
Skopje
Tirana
ALBANIA
Thessaloniki
GREECE
Évvoia
Athens
Lésvos
AEGEAN SEA
C. Tainaron
Crete
Rhodes
Istanbul
Bosporus
Sea of Marmara
Dardanelles
Izmir
Ankara
TURKEY
CYPRUS
Nicosia
LEBANON
Beirut
Damascus
BLACK SEA
Odessa
Crimea
SEA OF AZOV
Krasnodar
Donetsk
Dnieper
Kiev
Khar'kov
Don
L'vov
Minsk
Western Dvina
Leningrad
Lake Ladoga
Lake Onega
Moscow
Volga
Gor'kiy
UNION OF SOVIET SOCIALIST
Murmansk
Kola Pen.
WHITE SEA
Archangel
Northern Dvina
BARENTS SEA
Kolguyev I.
Kanin Pen.
Cheshskaya Bay
Pechora

Longitude West of Greenwich 0° Longitude East of Greenwich 10° 20° 30°

Vegetation/Relief

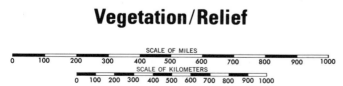

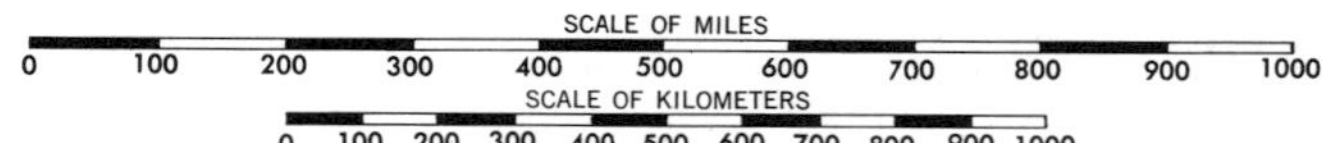

Depths in Fathoms

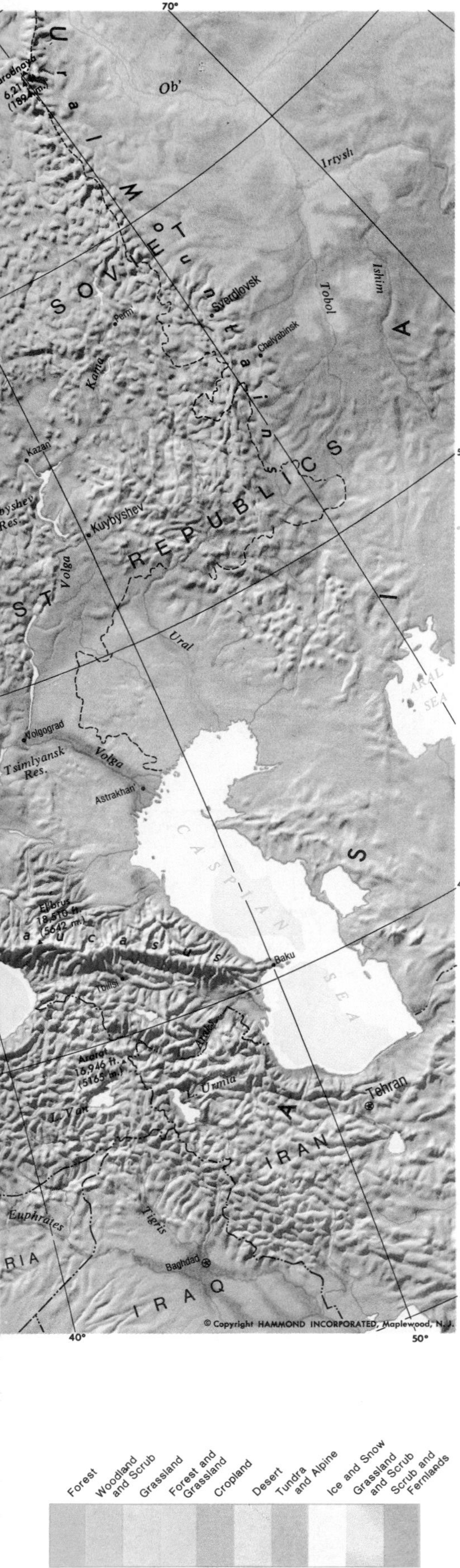

Forest | Woodland and Scrub | Grassland | Forest and Grassland | Cropland | Desert | Tundra and Alpine | Ice and Snow | Grassland and Scrub | Scrub and Fernlands

COLOR KEY

Rainfall

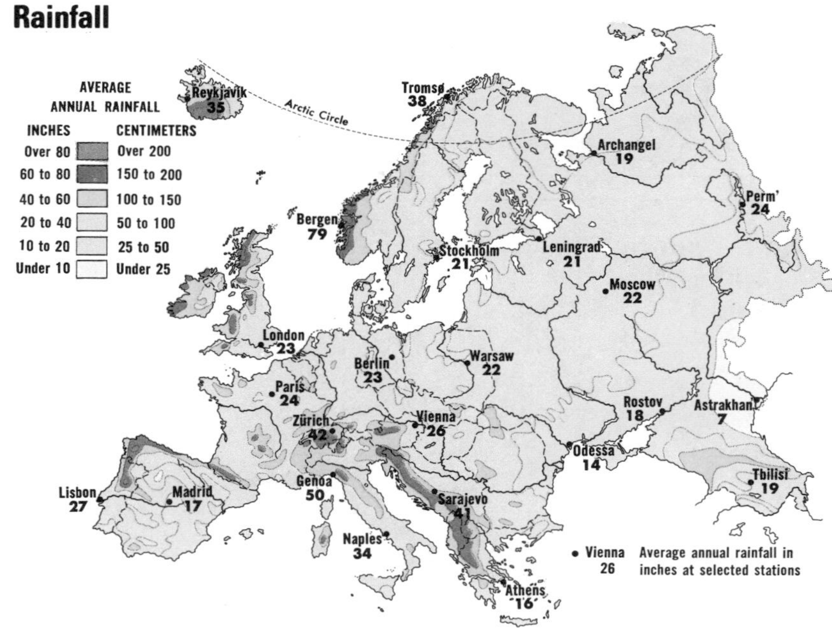

Average January Temperature

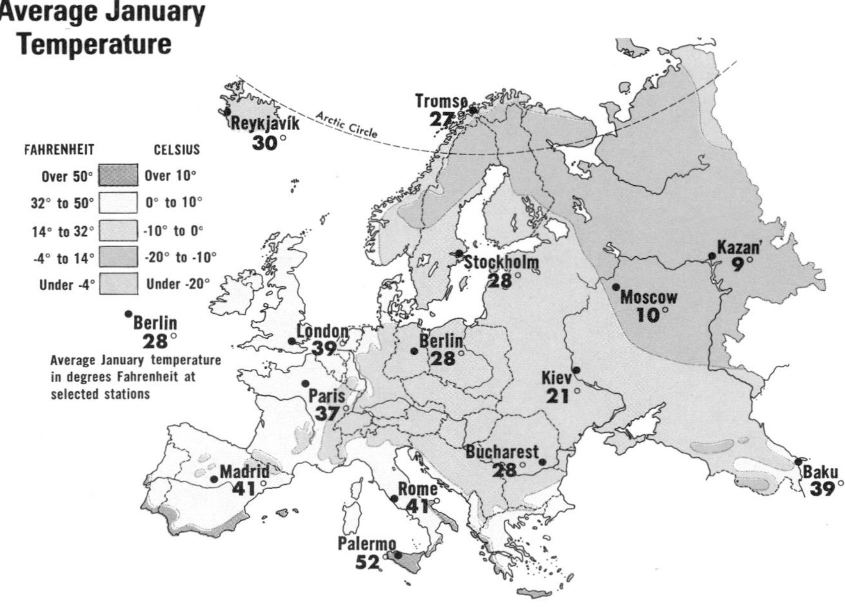

Average July Temperature

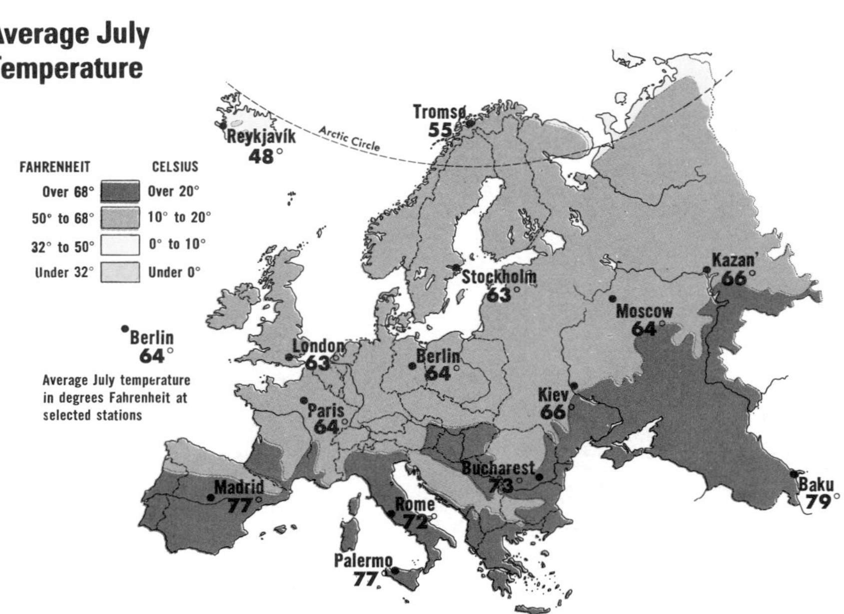

United Kingdom and Ireland
BONNE PROJECTION
SCALE OF MILES
0 10 20 40 60 80
SCALE OF KILOMETERS
0 10 20 40 60 80
Capitals of Countries
International Boundaries
Other Boundaries
Canals
Scale 1:4,200,000
Shetland Islands
Same scale as main map.
GREATER LONDON
ATLANTIC OCEAN
NORTH SEA
IRISH SEA
ENGLISH CHANNEL
SCOTLAND
ENGLAND
WALES
NORTHERN IRELAND
IRELAND
FRANCE
SHETLAND ISLANDS
ORKNEY ISLANDS
OUTER HEBRIDES
INNER HEBRIDES
CHANNEL ISLANDS
North Channel
St. George's Channel
Bristol Channel
Strait of Dover
Isle of Man
Isle of Wight
LONDON
Edinburgh
Belfast
Dublin (Baile Átha Cliath)
Cardiff
Glasgow
Birmingham
Manchester
Liverpool
Ben Nevis 4,406 ft. (1343 m.)
Snowdon 3,560 ft. (1085 m.)
Scafell Pike 3,210 ft. (978 m.)
Snaefell 2,034 ft. (620 m.)
Slieve Donard 2,796 ft. (852 m.)
Carrantuohill 3,415 ft. (1041 m.)
Longitude West of Greenwich

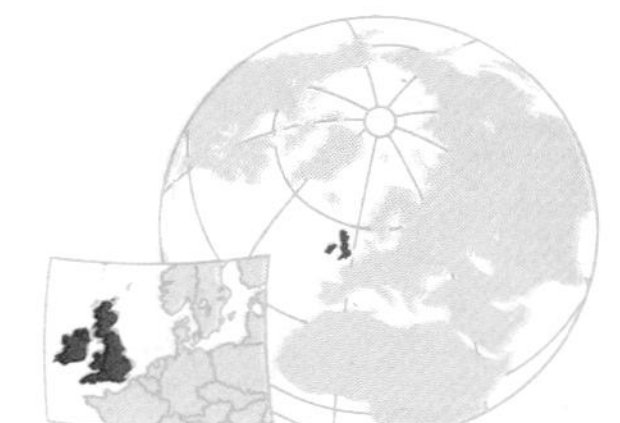

UNITED KINGDOM

AREA 94,399 sq. mi. (244,493 sq. km.)
POPULATION 55,672,000
CAPITAL London
LARGEST CITY London
HIGHEST POINT Ben Nevis 4,406 ft. (1,343 m.)
MONETARY UNIT pound sterling
MAJOR LANGUAGES English, Gaelic, Welsh
MAJOR RELIGIONS Protestantism, Roman Catholicism

IRELAND

AREA 27,136 sq. mi. (70,282 sq. km.)
POPULATION 3,440,427
CAPITAL Dublin
LARGEST CITY Dublin
HIGHEST POINT Carrantuohill 3,415 ft. (1,041 m.)
MONETARY UNIT Irish pound
MAJOR LANGUAGES English, Gaelic (Irish)
MAJOR RELIGION Roman Catholicism

UNITED KINGDOM

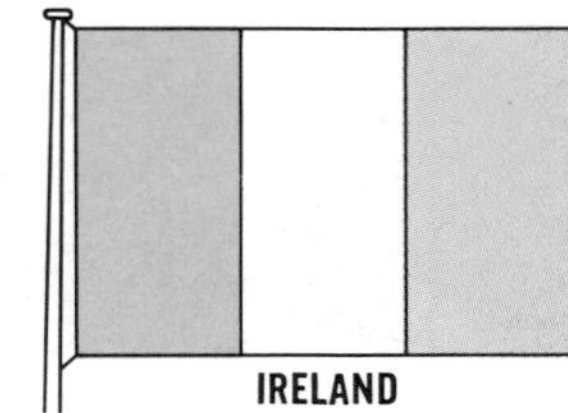
IRELAND

ENGLAND

AREA 50,516 sq. mi. (130,836 sq. km.)
POPULATION 46,220,955
CAPITAL London
LARGEST CITY London
HIGHEST POINT Scafell Pike 3,210 ft. (978 m.)

WALES

AREA 8,017 sq. mi. (20,764 sq. km.)
POPULATION 2,790,462
CAPITAL Cardiff
LARGEST CITY Cardiff
HIGHEST POINT Snowdon 3,560 ft. (1,085 m.)

SCOTLAND

AREA 30,414 sq. mi. (78,772 sq. km.)
POPULATION 5,117,146
CAPITAL Edinburgh
LARGEST CITY Glasgow
HIGHEST POINT Ben Nevis 4,406 ft. (1,343 m.)

NORTHERN IRELAND

AREA 5,452 sq. mi. (14,121 sq. km.)
POPULATION 1,543,000
CAPITAL Belfast
LARGEST CITY Belfast
HIGHEST POINT Slieve Donard 2,796 ft. (852 m.)

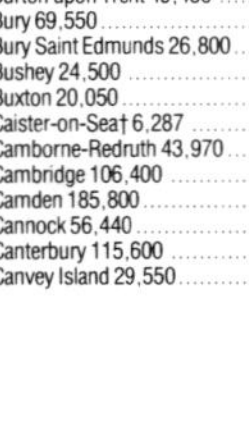

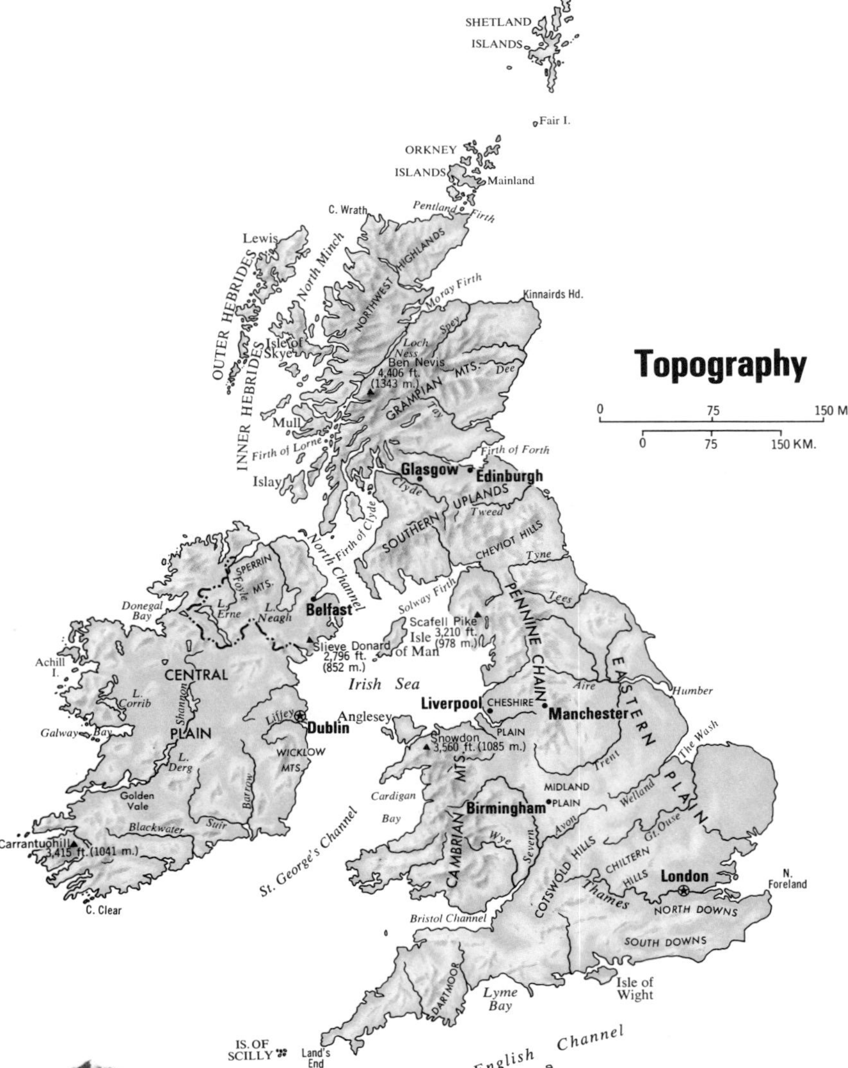

ENGLAND

COUNTIES

Avon, 920,200 . . . E 6
Bedfordshire, 491,700 . . . G 5
Berkshire, 659,000 . . . F 6
Buckinghamshire, 512,000 . . . G 6
Cambridgeshire, 563,000 . . . G 5
Cheshire, 916,400 . . . E 4
Cleveland, 567,900 . . . F 3
Cornwall, 405,200 . . . C 7
Cumbria, 473,600 . . . D 3
Derbyshire, 887,600 . . . F 5
Devon, 942,100 . . . D 7
Dorset, 575,800 . . . E 7
Durham, 610,400 . . . F 3
East Sussex, 655,600 . . . H 7
Essex, 1,426,200 . . . H 6
Gloucestershire, 491,500 . . . E 6
Greater London, 7,028,200 . . . H 8
Greater Manchester, 2,684,100 . . . H 2
Hampshire, 1,456,100 . . . F 6
Hereford and Worcester, 594,200 . . . E 5
Hertfordshire, 937,300 . . . G 6
Humberside, 848,600 . . . G 4
Isle of Wight, 111,300 . . . F 7
Isles of Scilly, 1,900 . . . A 7
Kent, 1,448,100 . . . H 6
Lancashire, 1,375,500 . . . E 4
Leicestershire, 837,900 . . . F 5
Lincolnshire, 524,500 . . . G 4
London, Greater, 7,028,200 . . . H 8
Manchester, Greater, 2,684,100 . . . H 2
Merseyside, 1,578,000 . . . G 2
Norfolk, 662,500 . . . H 5
Northamptonshire, 505,900 . . . G 5
Northumberland, 287,300 . . . E 2
North Yorkshire, 653,000 . . . F 3
Nottinghamshire, 977,500 . . . F 4
Oxfordshire 541,800 . . . F6
Shropshire (Salop) 359,000 . . . E5
Somerset 404,400 . . . E6
South Yorkshire 1,318,300 . . . F4
Staffordshire 997,600 . . . E5
Suffolk 577,600 . . . H5
Surrey 1,002,900 . . . G6
Sussex, East 655,600 . . . H7
Sussex, West 623,400 . . . G7
Tyne and Wear 1,182,900 . . . H3
Warwickshire 471,000 . . . F5
West Midlands 2,743,300 . . . F5
West Sussex 623,400 . . . G7
West Yorkshire 2,072,500 . . . J1
Wiltshire 512,800 . . . E6
Yorkshire, North 653,000 . . . F3
Yorkshire, South 1,318,300 . . . F4
Yorkshire, West 2,072,500 . . . J1

CITIES and TOWNS

Abingdon, 20,130 . . . F 6
Accrington, 36,470 . . . H 1
Adwick le Street, 17,650 . . . K 2
Aldeburgh, 2,750 . . . J 5
Aldershot, 33,750 . . . G 8
Aldridge Brownhills, 89,370 . . . E 5
Alfreton, 21,560 . . . F 4
Alnwick, 7,300 . . . F 2
Altrincham, 40,800 . . . H 2
Amersham, ⊙17,254 . . . G 7
Andover, 27,620 . . . F 6
Appleby, 2,240 . . . E 3
Arnold, 35,090 . . . F 4
Arundel, 2,390 . . . G 7
Ashford, 36,380 . . . H 6
Ashington, 24,720 . . . F 2
Ashton-under-Lyne, 48,500 . . . H 2
Axminster, ⊙4,515 . . . D 7
Aycliffe, ⊙20,203 . . . F 3
Aylesbury, 41,420 . . . G 7
Bacup, 14,990 . . . H 1
Bakewell, 4,100 . . . J 2
Banbury, 31,060 . . . F 5
Banstead, 44,100 . . . H 8
Barking, 153,800 . . . H 8
Barnet, 305,200 . . . H 7
Barnsley, 74,730 . . . J 2
Barnstaple, 17,820 . . . D 6
Barrow-in-Furness, 73,400 . . . D 3
Barton-upon-Humber, 7,750 . . . G 4
Basildon, 135,720 . . . J 8
Basingstoke, 60,910 . . . F 6
Bath, 83,100 . . . E 6
Batley, 41,630 . . . J 1
Battle, ⊙4,987 . . . H 7
Bebington, 62,500 . . . G 2
Bedford, 74,390 . . . G 5
Bedlington, 27,200 . . . F 2
Bedworth, 41,600 . . . F 5
Beeston and Stapleford, 65,360 . . . F 5
Benfleet, 49,180 . . . J 8
Bentley with Arksey, 22,320 . . . F 4
Berkhamsted, 15,920 . . . G 7
Beverley, 16,920 . . . G 4
Bexhill, 34,680 . . . H 7
Bexley, 213,500 . . . H 8
Biddulph, 18,720 . . . H 2
Birkenhead, 135,750 . . . G 2
Birmingham, 1,058,800 . . . F 5
Bishop Auckland, 32,940 . . . E 3
Bishop's Stortford, 21,720 . . . H 6
Blackburn, 101,670 . . . H 1
Blackpool, 149,000 . . . G 1
Blaydon, 31,940 . . . H 3
Blyth, 35,390 . . . F 2
Bodmin, 10,430 . . . C 7
Bognor Regis, 34,620 . . . G 7
Boldon, 24,430 . . . J 3
Bolton, 154,480 . . . H 2
Bootle 71,160 . . . G2
Boston 26,700 . . . G5
Bournemouth 144,100 . . . F7
Bracknell† 34,067 . . . G8
Bradford 458,900 . . . J1
Braintree and Bocking 26,300 . . . H6
Brent 256,500 . . . H8
Brentwood 58,690 . . . J8
Bridgwater 26,700 . . . E6
Bridlington 26,920 . . . G3
Bridport 6,660 . . . E7
Brigg 4,870 . . . G4
Brighouse 35,320 . . . J1
Brightlingsea 7,170 . . . J6
Brighton 156,500 . . . G7
Bristol 416,300 . . . E6
Broadstairs and Saint Peter's 21,670 . . . J6
Bromley 299,100 . . . H8
Bromsgrove 41,430 . . . E5
Buckfastleigh 2,870 . . . C7
Buckingham 5,290 . . . G6
Bude-Stratton 5,750 . . . C7
Bungay 4,120 . . . J5
Burgess Hill 20,030 . . . G7
Burnham-on-Crouch 4,920 . . . H6
Burnley 74,300 . . . H1
Burntwood† 23,088 . . . F5
Burton upon Trent 49,480 . . . F5
Bury 69,550 . . . H2
Bury Saint Edmunds 26,800 . . . H5
Bushey 24,500 . . . H7
Buxton 20,050 . . . J2
Caister-on-Sea† 6,287 . . . J5
Camborne-Redruth 43,970 . . . B7
Cambridge 106,400 . . . G5
Camden 185,800 . . . H8
Cannock 56,440 . . . E5
Canterbury 115,600 . . . H6
Canvey Island 29,550 . . . J8
Carlisle, 99,600 . . . D 3
Carlton, 46,690 . . . F 5
Caterham and Warlingham, 35,840 . H 8
Chatham, 59,550 . . . J 8
Cheadle and Gatley, 62,460 . . . H 2
Chelmsford, 58,320 . . . J 7
Cheltenham, 75,910 . . . E 6
Chertsey, 45,070 . . . G 8
Chesham, 20,830 . . . G 7
Cheshunt, 45,750 . . . H 7
Chester, 117,200 . . . G 2
Chesterfield, 69,480 . . . J 2
Chester-le-Street, 20,720 . . . J 3
Chichester, 20,940 . . . G 7
Chigwell, 54,220 . . . H 8
Chippenham, 18,550 . . . E 6
Chorley, 31,800 . . . G 2
Christchurch, 31,610 . . . F 7
Cirencester, 14,500 . . . E 6
Clacton, 39,380 . . . J 6
Clay Cross, 9,630 . . . J 2
Cleator Moor, ⊙7,686 . . . D 3
Cleethorpes, 37,200 . . . H 4
Clevedon, 15,140 . . . D 6
Clun, ⊙1,261 . . . D 6
Coalville, 28,740 . . . F 5
Cockermouth, 6,480 . . . D 3
Colchester, 79,600 . . . H 6
Colne, 19,030 . . . H 1
Colne Valley, 21,190 . . . J 2
Congleton, 21,500 . . . H 2
Consett, 35,080 . . . H 3
Corby, 48,850 . . . G 5
Coventry, 336,800 . . . F 5
Cowes, 19,190 . . . F 7
Crawley, 72,600 . . . G 6
Crewe and Nantwich, 98,100 . . . E 4
Cromer, 5,720 . . . J 5
Crook and Willington, 21,120 . . . E 3
Crosby, 56,750 . . . G 2
Croydon, 330,600 . . . H 8
Cuckfield, 26,500 . . . G 6
Darlington, 85,120 . . . F 3
Dartford, 44,130 . . . J 8
Darton, 15,710 . . . J 2
Darwen, 29,290 . . . H 1
Deal, 26,840 . . . J 6
Dearne, 24,780 . . . K 2
Denton, 38,110 . . . H 2
Derby, 213,700 . . . F 5
Dewsbury, 50,560 . . . J 1
Didcot, ⊙14,277 . . . F 6
Doncaster, 81,530 . . . F 4
Dorking, 22,410 . . . G 8
Dover, 34,160 . . . J 6
Downham Market, 4,120 . . . H 5
Droitwich, 13,950 . . . E 5
Dronfield, 20,000 . . . J 2
Dudley, 187,110 . . . E 5
Dunstable, 32,090 . . . G 6
Durham, 88,800 . . . J 3
Ealing, 293,800 . . . H 8
Eastbourne, 73,200 . . . H 7
East Grinstead, 19,420 . . . G 6
Eastleigh, 46,340 . . . F 7
East Retford, 18,260 . . . G 4
Egham, 30,320 . . . G 8
Egremont, ⊙7,253 . . . D 3
Eling, ⊙20,006 . . . F 7
Ellesmere, ⊙2,630 . . . E 5
Ellesmere Port, 63,870 . . . G 2
Enfield, 260,900 . . . H 7
Epsom and Ewell, 70,700 . . . G 8
Esher, 63,970 . . . H 8
Eston, ⊙46,219 . . . F 3
Eton, 4,950 . . . G 8
Evesham, 14,090 . . . F 5
Exeter, 93,300 . . . D 7
Exminster, ⊙3,181 . . . D 7
Exmouth, 26,840 . . . D 7
Falmouth, 17,530 . . . B 7
Fareham, 86,300 . . . F 7
Farnborough, 43,520 . . . G 8
Farnham, 33,140 . . . G 8
Farnworth, 26,110 . . . H 2
Faversham, 15,010 . . . H 6
Felixstowe, 19,460 . . . J 6
Felling, 38,990 . . . J 3
Filey, 5,660 . . . G 3
Fleet, 22,930 . . . G 8
Fleetwood, 30,070 . . . D 4
Folkestone, 45,610 . . . J 6
Formby, 24,850 . . . G 2
Framlingham, ⊙2,258 . . . J 5
Frimley and Camberley, 47,390 . . . G 8
Fulwood, 22,910 . . . G 1
Gainsborough, 17,440 . . . G 4
Gateshead, 91,230 . . . J 3
Gillingham, Dorset, ⊙4,050 . . . E 6
Gillingham, Kent, 93,900 . . . J 8
Glastonbury, 6,580 . . . E 6
Glossop, 24,820 . . . J 2
Gloucester, 91,600 . . . E 6
Godalming, 18,840 . . . G 8
Golborne, 28,720 . . . G 2
Goole, 17,920 . . . G 4
Gosport, 82,300 . . . F 7
Grange, 3,520 . . . E 3
Grantham 27,830 . . . G5
Gravesend 53,500 . . . J8
Great Grimsby 93,800 . . . G4
Great Torrington 3,430 . . . C7
Great Yarmouth 49,410 . . . J5
Greenwich 207,200 . . . H8
Guildford 58,470 . . . G8
Guisborough 14,860 . . . F3
Hackney 192,500 . . . H8
Hale 17,080 . . . H2
Halesowen 54,120 . . . E5
Halifax 88,580 . . . J1
Haltemprice 54,850 . . . G4
Haltwhistle† 3,511 . . . E2
Hammersmith 170,000 . . . H8
Haringey 228,200 . . . H8
Harlow 79,160 . . . H7
Harrogate 64,620 . . . F4
Harrow 200,200 . . . B5
Hartlepool 97,100 . . . F3
Harwich 15,280 . . . J6
Haslingden 15,140 . . . H1
Hastings 74,600 . . . H7
Hatfield† 25,359 . . . H7
Havant and Waterloo 112,430 . . . G7
Haverhill 14,550 . . . H5
Havering 239,200 . . . J8
Hayle† 5,378 . . . B7
Hazel Grove and Bramhall 40,400 . . . H2
Heanor 24,590 . . . F4
Hebburn 23,150 . . . J3
Hedon 3,010 . . . G4
Hemel Hempstead 71,150 . . . G7
Hereford 47,800 . . . E5
Hertford 20,760 . . . H7
Hetton 16,810 . . . J3
Hexham 9,820 . . . E3
Heywood 31,720 . . . H2
High Wycombe 61,190 . . . G8
Hillingdon 230,800 . . . G8
Hinckley 49,310 . . . F5
Hinderwell† 2,551 . . . G3
Hitchin 29,190 . . . G6
Hoddesdon 27,510 . . . H7
Holmfirth 19,790 . . . J2
Horley† 18,593 . . . H8
Hornsea 7,280 . . . G4
Horsham 26,770 . . . G6
Horwich 16,670 . . . G2
Houghton-le-Spring 33,150 . . . J3
Hounslow, 199,100 . . . G 8
Hove, 72,000 . . . G 7
Hoylake, 32,000 . . . G 2
Hoyland Nether, 15,500 . . . J 2
Hucknall, 27,110 . . . F 4
Huddersfield, 130,060 . . . J 2
Hugh Town, ⊙1,958 . . . A 8
Hull, 276,600 . . . G 4
Hunstanton, 4,140 . . . H 5
Huntingdon and Godmanchester, 17,200 . . . G 5
Huyton-with-Roby, 65,950 . . . G 2
Hyde, 37,040 . . . H 2
Ilfracombe, 9,350 . . . C 6
Ilkeston, 33,690 . . . F 5
Immingham, ⊙10,259 . . . G 4
Ipswich, 121,500 . . . J 5
Islington, 171,600 . . . H 8
Jarrow, 28,510 . . . J 3
Kendal, 22,440 . . . E 3
Kenilworth, 19,730 . . . F 5
Kensington and Chelsea, 161,400 . . G 8
Keswick, 4,790 . . . D 3
Kettering, 44,480 . . . G 5
Keynsham, 18,970 . . . E 6
Kidderminster, 49,960 . . . E 5
Kidsgrove, 22,690 . . . E 4
King's Lynn, 29,990 . . . H 5
Kingston upon Thames, 135,600 . . H 8
Kingswood, 30,450 . . . E 6
Kirkburton, 20,320 . . . J 2
Kirkby, 59,100 . . . G 2
Kirkby Lonsdale, ⊙1,506 . . . E 3
Kirkby Stephen, ⊙1,539 . . . E 3
Knutsford, 14,840 . . . H 2
Lambeth, 290,300 . . . H 8
Lancaster, 126,300 . . . E 3
Leatherhead, 40,830 . . . G 8
Leeds, 744,500 . . . J 1
Leek, 19,460 . . . H 2
Leicester, 289,400 . . . F 5
Leigh, 46,390 . . . H 2
Leighton-Linslade, 22,590 . . . F 7
Letchworth, 31,520 . . . G 6
Lewes, 14,170 . . . H 7
Lewisham, 237,300 . . . H 8
Leyland, 23,690 . . . G 1
Lichfield, 23,690 . . . F 5
Lincoln, 73,700 . . . G 4
Liskeard, 5,360 . . . C 7
Litherland, 23,530 . . . G 2
Littlehampton, 20,320 . . . G 7

(continued on following page)

12 United Kingdom and Ireland
(continued)

Liverpool, 539,700 G 2
Loftus, 7,850 G 3
London (cap.), 7,028,200 H 8
London, ★12,332,900 H 8
Long Eaton, 33,560 F 5
Longbenton, 50,120 J 3
Looe, 4,060 C 7
Loughborough, 49,010 F 5
Lowestoft, 53,260 J 5
Ludlow, ⊙7,466 E 5
Luton, 164,500 G 6
Lydd, 4,670 H 7
Lyme Regis, 3,460 E 7
Lymington, 36,780 F 7
Lynton, 1,770 D 6
Lytham Saint Anne's, 42,120 G 1
Mablethorpe and Sutton, 6,750 H 4
Macclesfield, 45,420 H 2
Maidenhead, 48,210 G 8
Maidstone, 72,110 J 8
Maldon, 14,350 H 6
Malmesbury, 2,550 E 6
Malton, 4,010 G 3
Malvern, 30,420 E 5
Manchester, 490,000 H 2
Mangotsfield, 23,000 E 6
Mansfield, 58,450 K 2
Mansfield Woodhouse, 25,400 F 4
March, 14,560 H 5
Margate, 50,290 J 6
Market Harborough, 15,230 G 5
Marlborough, 6,370 F 6
Matlock, 20,300 J 2
Melton Mowbray, 20,680 G 5
Merton, 169,400 H 8
Middlesbrough, 153,900 F 3
Middleton, 53,340 H 2
Middlewich, 7,600 H 2
Mildenhall, ⊙9,269 H 5
Millom, ⊙7,101 D 3
Milton Keynes, 89,900 F 5
Minehead, 8,230 D 6
Moretonhampstead, ⊙1,440 C 7
Morpeth, 14,450 F 2
Mundesley, ⊙1,536 J 5
Nelson, 31,220 H 1
Neston, 18,210 G 2
Newark, 24,760 G 4
Newbury, 24,850 F 6
Newcastle upon Tyne, 295,800 H 3
Newcastle-under-Lyme, 75,940 E 4
Newham, 228,900 H 8
Newhaven, 9,970 H 7
Newport, 22,430 F 7
New Romney, 3,830 J 7
Newton Abbot, 19,940 D 7
Newton-le-Willows, 21,780 H 2
New Windsor, 29,660 G 8
Northallerton F 3
Northam, 8,310 C 6
Northampton, 128,290 F 5
Northfleet, 27,150 J 8
North Sunderland, ⊙1,725 F 2
Northwich, 17,710 H 2
Norton, 5,580 G 3
Norton-Radstock, 15,900 E 6
Norwich, 119,200 J 5
Nottingham, 280,300 F 5
Nuneaton, 69,210 F 5
Oadby, 20,700 F 5
Oakham, 7,280 G 5
Okehampton, 4,000 D 7
Oldham, 103,690 H 2
Ormskirk, 28,860 G 2
Oswaldtwistle, 14,270 H 1
Oxford, 117,400 F 6
Padstow, ⊙2,802 B 7
Penryn, 5,660 B 7
Penzance, 19,360 B 7
Peterborough, 118,900 G 5
Peterlee, ⊙21,846 J 3
Plymouth, 259,100 C 7
Polperro, ⊙1,491 C 7
Poole, 110,600 E 7
Porlock, ⊙1,290 D 6
Portishead, 9,680 E 6
Portland, 14,860 E 7
Portslade-by-Sea, 18,040 G 7
Portsmouth, 198,500 F 7
Potters Bar, 24,670 H 7
Poulton-le-Fylde, 16,340 G 1
Preston, 94,760 G 1
Prestwich, 32,850 H 2
Queenborough, 31,550 H 6
Radcliffe, 29,630 H 2
Ramsbottom, 16,710 H 2
Ramsgate, 40,090 J 6
Rawtenstall, 20,950 H 1
Rayleigh, 26,740 J 8
Reading, 131,200 G 8
Redbridge, 231,600 H 8
Redcar, ⊙46,325 F 3
Redditch, 44,750 E 5
Reigate, 55,600 H 8
Richmond upon Thames, 166,800 H 8
Rickmansworth, 29,030 G 8
Ripley, 18,060 F 4
Rochdale, 93,780 H 2
Rochester, 56,030 J 8
Rothbury, ⊙1,818 E 2
Rotherham, 84,770 K 2
Royal Leamington Spa, 44,950 F 5
Royal Tunbridge Wells, 44,800 H 6
Rugby, 60,380 F 5
Rugeley, 24,440 E 5
Runcorn, 42,730 G 2
Rushden, 21,840 G 5
Ryde, 23,170 F 7
Rye, 4,530 H 7
Ryton, 15,170 H 3
Saddleworth, 21,340 J 2
Saint Agnes, ⊙4,747 B 7
Saint Albans, 123,800 H 7
Saint Austell-with-Fowey, 32,710 C 7
Saint Columb Major, ⊙3,953 B 7
Saint Helens, 104,890 G 2
Saint Ives, Cornwall, 9,760 B 7
Saint Neots, 17,940 G 5
Salcombe, 2,370 D 7
Sale, 59,060 H 2
Salford, 261,100 H 2
Salisbury, 35,460 F 6
Saltburn and Marske-by-the-Sea, 21,170 G 3
Sandbach, 14,280 H 2
Sandown-Shanklin, 14,800 F 7
Sandwich, 4,420 J 6
Saxmundham, 1,820 J 5
Scarborough, 43,300 G 3
Scunthorpe, 68,100 G 4
Seaford, 18,020 H 7
Seaham, 22,470 J 3
Seascale, ⊙2,106 D 3
Seaton, 4,500 D 7
Seaton Valley, 35,880 J 3
Sedbergh, ⊙2,741 E 3
Selsey, ⊙6,491 G 7
Sevenoaks, 18,160 J 8
Shaftesbury, 4,180 E 7
Sheffield, 558,000 J 2
Sherborne, 9,230 E 7
Sheringham, 4,940 J 5
Shildon, 15,360 F 3
Shoreham-by-Sea, 19,620 G 7
Shrewsbury, 56,120 E 5
Silloth, ⊙2,662 D 3
Sittingbourne and Milton, 32,830 H 6
Skelmersdale, 35,850 G 2
Skelton and Brotton, 15,930 G 3
Sleaford, 8,050 G 5
Slough, 89,060 G 8
Solihull, 108,230 F 5
Southampton, 213,700 F 7
Southend-on-Sea, 159,300 H 6
Southport, 86,030 G 1
South Shields, 96,900 J 3
Southwark, 224,900 H 8
Southwold, 1,960 J 5
Sowerby Bridge, 15,700 H 1
Spalding, 17,040 G 5
Spenborough, 41,460 J 1
Spennymoor, 19,050 F 3
Stafford, 54,860 E 5
Staines, 56,380 G 8
Stamford, 14,980 G 5
Stanley, 42,280 H 3
Staveley, 17,620 K 2
Stevenage, 72,600 G 6
Stockport, 138,350 H 2
Stockton-on-Tees, 165,400 F 3
Stoke-on-Trent, 256,200 E 4
Stourbridge, 56,530 E 5
Stourport-on-Severn, 19,430 E 5
Stowmarket, 9,020 J 5
Stratford-upon-Avon, 20,080 F 5
Stretford, 52,450 H 2
Stroud, 19,600 E 6
Sudbury, 8,860 H 5
Sunbury-on-Thames, 40,070 G 8
Sunderland, 214,820 J 3
Sutton, 166,700 H 8
Sutton Bridge, ⊙3,113 H 5
Sutton in Ashfield, 40,330 K 2
Swadlincote, 21,060 F 5
Swanage, 8,000 E 7
Swindon, 90,680 F 6
Tamworth, 46,960 F 5
Taunton, 37,570 D 6
Tavistock, ⊙7,620 C 7
Telford, ⊙79,451 E 5
Tenbury, ⊙2,151 E 5
Tewkesbury, 9,210 E 6
Thetford, 15,690 H 5
Thirsk, ⊙2,884 F 3
Thornaby-on-Tees, ⊙42,385 F 3
Thorne, ⊙16,694 F 4
Thornton Cleveleys, 27,090 G 1
Thurrock, 127,700 J 8
Tiverton, 16,190 D 7
Todmorden, 14,540 H 1
Tonbridge, 31,410 H 8
Torbay, 109,900 D 7
Torpoint, 6,840 C 7
Tower Hamlets, 146,100 H 8
Tow Law, 2,460 H 4
Trowbridge, 20,120 E 6
Truro, 15,690 B 7
Turton, 22,800 H 2
Tynemouth, 67,090 J 3
Upton upon Severn, ⊙2,048 E 5
Urmston, 44,130 H 2
Uttoxeter, 9,100 E 5
Ventnor, 6,980 F 7
Wainfleet All Saints, ⊙1,116 H 4
Wakefield, 306,500 J 2
Wallasey, 94,520 G 2
Wallsend, 45,490 J 3
Walsall, 182,430 E 5
Waltham Forest, 223,700 H 8
Waltham Holy Cross, 14,810 H 7
Walton and Weybridge, 51,270 G 8
Walton-le-Dale, 27,660 G 1
Wandsworth, 284,600 H 8
Wantage, 8,490 F 6
Ware, 14,900 H 7
Wareham, 4,630 E 7
Warley, 161,260 E 5
Warminster, 14,440 E 6
Warrington, 65,320 G 2
Warwick, 17,870 F 5
Washington, 27,720 J 3
Watchet, 2,980 D 6
Watford, 77,000 H 7
Wellingborough, 39,570 G 5
Wells, 8,960 E 6
Wells-next-the-Sea, 2,450 H 5
Welwyn, 39,900 H 7
Wem, ⊙3,411 E 5
West Bridgford, 28,340 F 5
West Bromwich, 162,740 F 5
West Mersea, 4,730 H 6
Westminster, 216,100 H 8
Weston-super-Mare, 51,960 D 6
Weymouth and Melcombe Regis, 41,080 E 7
Whickham, 29,710 J 3
Whitchurch, ⊙7,142 E 5
Whitehaven, 26,260 D 3
Whitley Bay, 37,010 J 3
Widnes, 58,330 G 2
Wigan, 80,920 G 2
Wigston, 31,650 F 5
Wilmslow, 31,250 H 2
Wilton, 4,090 F 6
Winchester, 88,900 F 6
Windermere, 7,860 E 3
Winsford, 26,920 G 2
Wirral, 27,510 G 2
Wisbech, 16,990 H 5
Witham, 19,730 H 6
Withernsea, 6,300 H 4
Wivenhoe, 5,630 J 6
Woking, 79,300 G 8
Wokingham, 22,390 G 8
Wolverhampton, 266,400 E 5
Wombwell, 17,850 K 2
Woodhall Spa, 2,420 G 4
Woodley and Sandford, ⊙24,581 G 8
Woodstock, 2,070 F 6
Wooler, ⊙1,833 F 2
Worcester, 73,900 E 5
Workington, 28,260 D 3
Worksop, 36,590 F 4
Worsbrough, 15,180 J 2
Worsley, 49,530 H 2
Worthing, 89,100 G 7
Wymondham, 9,390 J 5
Yateley, ⊙16,505 G 8
Yeovil, 26,180 E 7
York, 101,900 F 4

OTHER FEATURES

Aire (riv.) F 4
Atlantic Ocean A 7
Avon (riv.) F 5
Avon (riv.) F 7
Axe Edge (mt.) H 2
Barnstaple (bay) C 6
Beachy (head) H 7
Bigbury (bay) C 7
Blackwater (riv.) H 6
Bristol (chan.) C 6
Brown Willy (mt.) C 7
Cheviot (hills) E 2
Cheviot, The (mt.) E 2
Chiltern (hills) G 6
Cleveland (hills) F 3
Colne (riv.) G 8
Cornwall (cape) B 7
Cotswold (hills) E 6
Cross Fell (mt.) E 3
Cumbrian (mts.) D 3
Dart (riv.) D 7
Dartmoor National Park C 7
Dee (riv.) D 4
Derwent (riv.) G 3
Derwent (riv.) H 3
Don (riv.) F 4
Dorset Heights (hills) E 7
Dove (riv.) J 2
Dover (str.) J 7
Dungeness (prom.) J 7
Dunkery (hill) D 6
Eddystone (rocks) C 7
Eden (riv.) E 3
English (chan.) D 8
Esk (riv.) D 2
Exe (riv.) D 7
Exmoor National Park D 6
Fens, The (reg.) G 5
Flamborough (head) G 3
Formby (head) G 2
Foulness Island (pen.) J 6
Gibraltar (pt.) H 4
Great Ouse (riv.) H 5
Hartland (pt.) C 6
High Willhays (mt.) C 7
Hodder (riv.) H 1
Holderness (pen.), 43,900 G 4
Holy (isl.), 189 F 2
Humber (riv.) G 4
Irish (sea) B 4
Kennet (riv.) F 6
Lake District National Park D 3
Land's End (prom.) B 7
Lea (riv.) G 6
Lincoln Wolds (hills) G 4
Lindisfarne (Holy) (isl.), 189 F 2
Liverpool (bay) D 4
Lizard, The (pen.), 7,371 B 8
Lundy (isl.), 49 C 6
Lune (riv.) E 3
Lyme (bay) D 7
Manacle (pt.) C 7
Medway (riv.) H 6
Mendip (hills) E 6
Mersea (isl.), 4,423 J 6
Mersey (riv.) G 2
Morecambe (bay) D 3
Mounts (bay) B 7
Naze, The (prom.) J 6
Nene (riv.) H 5
New (for.) F 6
North (sea) J 4
North Downs (hills) G 6
North Foreland (prom.) J 6
Northumberland National Park E 2
North York Moors National Park G 3
Orford Ness (prom.) J 5
Ouse (riv.) G 4
Ouse (riv.) G 6
Parrett (riv.) E 6
Peak District National Park F 4
Peak, The (mt.) J 2
Peel Fell (mt.) E 2
Pennine Chain (range) E 3
Plymouth (sound) C 7
Portland, Bill of (pt.) E 7
Prawle (pt.) D 7
Purbeck, Isle of (pen.), 39,500 F 7
Ribble (riv.) E 4
Saint Alban's (head) F 7
Saint Bees (head) D 3
Saint Martin's (isl.), 106 A 8
Saint Mary's (isl.), 1,958 A 8
Scafell Pike (mt.) D 3
Scilly (isls.), 1,900 A 7
Selsey Bill (prom.) G 7
Severn (riv.) E 6
Sheppey (isl.), 31,550 J 6
Sherwood (for.) F 4
Skiddaw (mt.) D 3
Solent (chan.) F 7
Solway (firth) D 3
South Downs (hills) G 7
Spithead (chan.) F 7
Spurn (head) H 4
Stonehenge (ruins) F 6
Stour (riv.) E 7
Stour (riv.) H 6
Stour (riv.) J 6
Swale (riv.) F 3
Tamar (riv.) C 7
Taw (riv.) D 7
Tees (riv.) F 3
Test (riv.) F 6
Thames (riv.) H 6
Tintagel (head) C 7
Torridge (riv.) C 7
Trent (riv.) G 4
Tresco (isl.), 246 A 8
Tweed (riv.) E 2
Tyne (riv.) F 3
Ure (riv.) F 3
Ver (riv.) H 7
Walney, Isle of (isl.), 11,241 D 3
Wash, The (bay) H 5
Weald, The (reg.) H 6
Wear (riv.) F 3
Weaver (riv.) G 2
Welland (riv.) G 5
Wey (riv.) G 6
Wharfe (riv.) E 3
Wirral (pen.), 432,900 G 2
Witham (riv.) G 4
Wolds, The (hills) G 4
Wye (riv.) D 5
Wyre (riv.) G 1
Yare (riv.) J 5
Yorkshire Dales National Park E 3

CHANNEL ISLANDS

CITIES and TOWNS

Saint Anne E 8
Saint Helier (cap.), Jersey, ⊙28,135 E 8
Saint Peter Port (cap.), Guernsey, ⊙16,303 E 8
Saint Sampson's, ⊙6,534 E 8

OTHER FEATURES

Alderney (isl.), 1,686 E 8
Guernsey (isl.), 51,351 E 8
Herm (isl.), 96 E 8
Jersey (isl.), 72,629 E 8
Sark (isl.), 590 E 8

ISLE of MAN

CITIES and TOWNS

Castletown, 2,620 C 3
Douglas (cap.), 20,389 C 3
Laxey, 1,170 C 3
Michael, 408 C 3
Onchan, 4,807 C 3
Peel, 3,081 C 3
Port Erin, 1,714 C 3
Port Saint Mary, 1,508 C 3
Ramsey, 5,048 C 3

OTHER FEATURES

Ayre (pt.) C 3
Calf of Man (isl.) C 3
Langness (prom.) C 3
Snaefell (mt.) C 3
Spanish (head) C 3

WALES

COUNTIES

Clwyd, 376,000 D 4
Dyfed, 323,100 C 6
Gwent, 439,600 D 6
Gwynedd, 225,100 C 4
Mid Glamorgan, 540,400 D 6
Powys, 101,500 D 5
South Glamorgan, 389,200 A 7
West Glamorgan, 371,900 D 6

CITIES and TOWNS

Aberaeron, 1,340 C 5
Abercarn, 18,370 B 6
Aberdare, 38,030 A 6
Abertillery, 20,550 B 6
Amlwch, 3,630 C 4
Bala, 1,650 D 5
Bangor, 16,030 C 4
Barmouth, 2,070 C 5
Barry, 42,780 B 7
Beaumaris, 2,090 C 4
Bedwellty, 25,460 B 6
Bethesda, 4,180 D 4
Betws-y-Coed, 720 D 4
Brecknock (Brecon), 6,460 D 6
Brecon, 6,460 D 6
Bridgend, 14,690 A 7
Brynmawr, 5,970 B 6
Builth Wells, 1,480 D 5
Burry Port, 5,990 C 6
Caernarfon, 8,840 C 4
Caerphilly, 42,190 B 6
Cardiff, 281,500 B 7
Cardigan, 3,830 C 5
Chepstow, 8,260 E 6
Chirk, ⊙3,564 D 5
Colwyn Bay, 25,370 D 4
Criccieth, 1,590 C 5
Cwmamman, 3,950 D 6
Cwmbran, 32,980 B 6
Denbigh, 8,420 D 4
Dolgellau, 2,430 D 5
Ebbw Vale, 25,670 B 6
Ffestiniog, 5,510 D 5
Fishguard and Goodwick, 5,020 B 5
Flint, 15,070 G 2
Gelligaer, 33,820 A 6
Harlech, ⊙332 C 5
Haverfordwest, 8,930 B 6
Hawarden, ⊙20,389 G 2
Hay, 1,200 D 5
Holywell, 8,570 G 2
Kidwelly, 3,090 C 6
Knighton, 2,190 D 5
Llandeilo, 1,780 C 6
Llandovery, 2,040 D 5
Llandrindod Wells, 3,460 D 5
Llandudno, 17,700 D 4
Llanelli, 25,870 C 6
Llanfairfechan, 3,800 D 4
Llangefni, 4,070 C 4
Llangollen, 3,050 D 5
Llanguicke, ⊙15,029 D 6
Llanidloes, 2,390 D 5
Llantrisant, ⊙27,490 A 7
Llanwrtyd Wells, 460 D 5
Llwchwr, 27,530 D 6
Machynlleth, 1,830 D 5
Maesteg, 21,100 D 6
Menai Bridge, 2,730 C 4
Merthyr Tydfil, 61,500 A 6
Milford Haven, 13,960 B 6
Mold, 8,700 G 2
Montgomery, 1,000 D 5
Mountain Ash, 27,710 A 6
Mynyddislwyn, 15,590 B 6
Narberth, 970 C 6
Neath, 27,280 D 6
Nefyn, ⊙2,086 C 5
Newcastle Emlyn, 690 C 5
Newport, Dyfed, ⊙1,062 C 5
Newport, Gwent, 110,090 B 6
New Quay, 760 C 5
Newtown, 6,400 D 5
Neyland, 2,690 B 6
Ogmore and Garw, 19,680 A 6
Pembroke, 14,570 C 6
Penarth, 24,180 B 7
Penmaenmawr, 4,050 C 4
Pontypool, 36,710 B 6
Pontypridd, 34,180 A 6
Porthcawl, 14,980 D 6
Porthmadog, 3,900 C 5
Port Talbot, 58,200 D 6
Prestatyn, 15,480 D 4
Presteigne, 1,330 D 5
Pwllheli, 4,020 C 5
Rhondda, 85,400 A 6
Rhyl, 22,150 D 4
Risca, 15,780 B 6
Ruthin, 4,780 D 4
Saint David's, ⊙1,638 B 6
Swansea, 190,800 C 6
Tenby, 4,930 C 6
Tredegar, 17,450 B 6
Tywyn, 3,850 C 5
Welshpool, 7,370 D 5
Wrexham, 39,530 E 4

OTHER FEATURES

Anglesey (isl.), 64,500 C 4
Aran Fawddwy (mt.) C 5
Bardsey (isl.), 9 C 5
Berwyn (mts.) D 5
Black (mts.) D 6
Braich-y-Pwll (prom.) C 5
Brecon Beacons (mt.) D 6
Brecon Beacons National Park D 6
Caldy (isl.), 70 C 6
Cambrian (mts.) D 5
Cardigan (bay) C 5
Carmarthen (bay) C 6
Cemmaes (head) C 5
Dee (riv.) D 4
Dovey (riv.) D 5
Ely (riv.) B 7
Gower (pen.), 17,220 C 6
Great Ormes (head) C 4
Holy (isl.), 13,715 C 4
Lleyn (pen.), 25,800 C 5
Menai (str.) C 4
Milford Haven (inlet) B 6
Pembrokeshire Coast National Park C 6
Plynlimon (mt.) D 5
Preseli (mts.) C 6
Radnor (for.) D 5
Rhymney (riv.) B 6
Saint Brides (bay) B 6
Saint David's (head) B 6
Saint George's (chan.) B 5
Saint Gowans (head) C 6
Severn (riv.) E 5
Snowdon (mt.) D 4
Snowdonia National Park D 4
Taff (riv.) B 7
Teifi (riv.) C 5
Towy (riv.) D 6
Tremadoc (bay) C 5
Usk (riv.) B 6
Wye (riv.) D 5
Ynys Môn (Anglesey) (isl.), 64,500 C 4

★Population of met. area.
⊙Population of parish.

SCOTLAND
(map on page 15)

REGIONS

Borders, 99,409 E 5
Central, 269,281 D 4
Dumfries and Galloway, 143,667 E 5
Fife, 336,339 E 4
Grampian, 448,772 F 3
Highland, 182,044 D 3
Lothian, 754,008 E 5
Orkney (islands area), 17,675 E 1
Shetland (islands area), 18,494 F 2
Strathclyde, 2,504,909 C 4
Tayside, 401,987 E 4
Western Isles (islands area), 29,615 A 3

CITIES and TOWNS

Aberchirder, 877 F 3
Aberdeen, 210,362 F 3
Aberdour, 1,576 D 1
Aberfeldy, 1,552 E 4
Aberfoyle, 793 D 4
Aberlady, 737 F 4
Aberlour, 842 E 3
Abernethy, 776 E 4
Aboyne, 1,040 F 3
Acharacle, ⊙764 C 4
Achiltibuie, ⊙1,564 C 3
Achnasheen, ⊙1,078 C 3
Ae, 239 E 5
Airdrie, 38,491 C 2
Alexandria, 9,758 A 1
Alford, 764 F 3
Alloa, 13,558 C 1
Alness, 2,560 D 3
Altnaharra, ⊙1,227 D 2
Alva, 4,593 C 1
Alyth, 1,738 E 4
Ancrum, 266 F 5
Annan, 6,250 E 6
Annat, ⊙550 C 3
Annbank Station, 2,530 D 5
Applecross, ⊙550 C 3
Arbroath, 22,706 F 4
Ardavasar, ⊙449 B 3
Ardersier, 942 E 3
Ardgay, 193 D 3
Ardrishaig, 946 C 4
Ardrossan, 11,072 D 5
Armadale, 7,200 C 2
Arrochar, 543 D 4
Ascog, 230 A 2
Auchenblae, 339 F 4
Auchencairn, 215 E 6
Auchinleck, 4,883 D 5
Auchterarder, 1,738 E 4
Auchtermuchty, 1,426 E 4
Auldearn, 405 E 3
Aviemore, 1,224 E 3
Avoch, 776 D 3
Ayr, 47,990 D 5
Ayton, 410 F 5
Bailivanish, 347 A 3
Baillieston, 7,671 B 2
Balallan, 283 B 2
Balerno, 3,576 D 2
Balfron, 1,149 B 1
Ballantrae, 262 C 5
Ballater, 981 F 3
Ballingry, 4,332 D 1
Ballinluig, 188 E 4
Balloch, Highland, 572 D 3
Balloch, Strathclyde, 1,484 B 1
Baltasound, 246 G 2
Banchory, 2,435 F 3
Banff, 3,832 F 3
Bankfoot, 868 E 4
Bankhead, 1,492 F 3
Bannockburn, 5,889 C 1
Barrhead, 18,736 B 2
Barrhill, 236 D 5
Barvas, 279 B 2
Bathgate, 14,038 C 2
Bayble, 543 B 2
Bearsden, 25,128 B 2
Beattock, 309 E 5
Beauly, 1,141 D 3
Beith, 5,859 D 5
Bellsbank, 3,066 D 5
Bellshill, 18,166 C 2
Berriedale, ⊙1,927 E 2
Bieldside, 1,137 F 3
Biggar, 1,718 E 5
Birnam, 659 E 4
Bishopbriggs, 21,570 B 2
Bishopton, 2,931 B 2
Blackburn, 7,636 C 2
Blackford, 529 E 4
Blair Atholl, 437 E 4
Blairgowrie and Rattray, 5,681 E 4
Blanefield, 835 B 1
Blantyre, 13,992 B 2
Blyth Bridge, ⊙441 E 5
Bo'ness, 12,959 C 1
Boat of Garten, 406 E 3
Boddam, 1,429 G 3
Bonar Bridge, 519 D 3
Bonhill, 4,385 B 1
Bonnybridge, 5,701 C 1
Bonnyrigg and Lasswade, 7,429 D 2
Bowmore, 947 B 5
Braemar, 394 E 3
Breasclete, 234 B 2
Brechin, 6,759 F 4
Bridge of Allan, 4,638 C 1
Bridge of Don, 4,086 F 3
Bridge of Weir, 4,724 A 2
Brightons, 3,106 C 1
Broadford, 310 B 3
Brodick, 630 C 5
Brora, 1,436 E 2
Broxburn, 7,776 D 1
Buchlyvie, 412 B 1
Buckhaven and Methil, 17,930 F 4
Buckie, 8,145 E 3
Bucksburn, 6,567 F 3
Bunessan, ⊙585 B 4
Burghead, 1,321 E 3
Burnmouth, 300 F 5
Burntisland, 5,626 D 1
Cairndow, ⊙874 D 4
Cairnryan, 199 D 6
Callander, 1,805 D 4
Cambuslang, 14,607 B 2
Campbeltown, 6,428 C 5
Cannich, 203 D 3
Canonbie, 234 F 5
Caol, 3,719 C 4
Carbost, ⊙772 B 3
Cardenden, 6,802 D 1
Carloway, 178 B 2
Carluke, 8,864 E 5
Carnoustie, 6,838 F 4
Carnwath, 1,246 E 5
Carradale, 262 C 5
Carrbridge, 416 E 3
Carron, 2,626 C 1
Carsphairn, 186 D 5
Castlebay, 284 A 4
Castle Douglas, 3,384 E 6
Castle Kennedy, 307 D 6
Castletown, 902 E 2
Catrine, 2,681 D 5
Cawdor, 111 E 3
Chirnside, 888 F 5
Chryston, 8,322 C 2
Clackmannan, 3,248 C 1
Clarkston, 8,404 B 2
Closeburn, 225 E 5
Clovulin, ⊙315 C 4
Clydebank, 47,538 B 2
Coalburn, 1,460 E 5
Coatbridge, 50,806 C 2
Cockburnspath, 233 F 5
Cockenzie and Port Seton, 3,539 D 1
Coldingham, 423 F 5
Coldstream, 1,393 F 5
Coll, 305 B 2
Colmonell, 218 D 5
Comrie, 1,119 E 4
Connel, 300 C 4
Cononbridge, 914 D 3
Corpach, 1,296 C 4
Coupar Angus, 2,010 E 4
Cove and Kilcreggan, 1,402 A 1
Cove Bay, 765 F 3
Cowdenbeath, 10,215 D 1
Cowie, 2,751 C 1
Craigellachie, 382 E 3
Craignure, ⊙544 C 4
Crail, 1,033 F 4
Crawford, 384 E 5
Creetown, 769 D 6
Crieff, 5,718 E 4
Crimond, 313 G 3
Crinan, ⊙462 C 4
Cromarty, 492 E 3
Crosshill, 535 D 5
Crossmichael, 317 D 6
Cruden Bay, 528 G 3
Cullen, 1,199 F 3
Culross, 504 C 1
Cults, 3,336 F 3
Cumbernauld, 41,200 C 1
Cumnock and Holmhead, 6,298 D 5
Cupar, 6,607 E 4
Currie, 6,764 D 2
Dailly, 1,258 D 5
Dalbeattie, 3,659 E 6
Daliburgh, 261 A 3
Dalkeith, 9,713 D 2
Dalmally, 283 D 4
Dalmellington, 1,949 D 5
Dalry, 5,833 D 5
Dalrymple, 1,336 D 5
Darvel, 3,177 D 5
Daviot, ⊙513 D 3
Denholm, 581 F 5
Denny and Dunipace, 10,424 C 1
Dervaig, ⊙1,081 B 4
Dingwall, 4,275 D 3
Dollar, 2,573 E 4
Dornoch, 880 D 3
Douglas, 1,843 E 5
Doune, 859 D 4
Drongan, 3,609 D 5
Drumbeg, ⊙833 C 2
Drummore, 336 D 6
Drumnadrochit, 359 D 3
Drymen, 659 B 1
Dufftown, 1,481 E 3
Dumbarton, 25,469 B 1
Dumfries, 29,259 E 5
Dunbar, 4,609 F 4
Dunbeath, 161 E 2
Dunbeg, 939 C 4
Dunblane, 5,222 E 4
Dundee, 194,732 F 4
Dundonald, 2,256 D 5
Dunfermline, 52,098 D 1
Dunkeld, 273 E 4
Dunning, 564 E 4
Dunoon, 8,759 A 2
Dunragit, 323 D 6
Duns, 1,812 F 5
Duntochter, 3,532 B 2
Dunure, 452 D 5
Dunvegan, 301 B 3
Dyce, 2,733 F 3
Eaglesfield, 581 E 5
Eaglesham, 2,788 D 5
Earlston, 1,415 F 5
East Calder, 2,690 D 2
East Kilbride, 71,200 B 2
East Linton, 882 F 5
Eastriggs, 1,455 E 5
Ecclefechan, 844 E 5
Edinburgh (cap.), 470,085 D 1
Edzell, 658 F 4
Elderslie, 5,204 B 2
Elgin, 17,042 E 3
Elie and Earlsferry, 807 F 4
Ellon, 2,855 F 3
Embo, 260 E 3
Errol, 762 E 4
Evanton, 562 D 3
Eyemouth, 2,704 F 5
Fairlie, 1,029 D 5
Falkirk, 36,901 C 1
Falkland, 998 E 4
Fallin, 3,159 C 1
Fauldhouse, 5,247 C 2
Ferness, ⊙287 E 3
Ferryden, 740 F 4
Findhorn, 664 E 3
Findochty, 1,229 E 3
Fintry, 296 B 1
Fochabers, 1,238 E 3
Forfar, 11,179 F 4
Forres, 5,317 E 3
Fort Augustus, 670 D 3
Forth, 2,929 C 2
Fortrose, 1,150 D 3
Fort William, 4,370 C 4
Foyers, 276 D 3
Fraserburgh, 10,930 G 3
Friockheim, 807 F 4
Furnace, 220 C 4
Fyvie, 405 F 3
Gairloch, 125 C 3
Galashiels, 12,808 F 5
Galston, 4,256 D 5
Gardenstown, 892 F 3
Garelochhead, 1,552 A 1
Gargunnock, 457 B 1
Garlieston, 385 D 6
Garmouth, 352 E 3
Garrabost, 307 B 2
Gartmore, 253 B 1
Gatehouse-of-Fleet, 835 D 6
Giffnock, 10,987 B 2
Gifford, 575 F 5
Girvan, 7,597 D 5
Glamis, 190 F 4
Glasgow, 880,617 B 2
Glasgow, ★1,674,789 B 2
Glenbarr, ⊙691 C 5
Glencaple, 275 E 5
Glencoe, 195 C 4
Glenelg, ⊙1,468 C 3
Glenluce, 725 D 6
Glenrothes, 31,400 E 4
Golspie, 1,374 E 3
Gordon, 320 F 5
Gorebridge, 3,426 D 2
Gourock, 11,192 A 1
Grangemouth, 24,430 C 1
Grantown-on-Spey, 1,578 E 3
Greenlaw, 574 F 5
Greenock, 67,275 A 2
Gretna, 1,907 E 5
Gullane, 1,701 F 4
Haddington, 6,767 F 5
Halkirk, 679 E 2
Hamilton, 45,495 C 2
Hamnavoe, 307 G 2
Harthill, 4,712 C 2
Hatton, 315 G 3
Hawick, 16,484 F 5
Heathhall, 1,365 E 5
Helensburgh, 13,327 A 1
Helmsdale, 727 E 2
Hill of Fearn, 233 D 3
Hillside, 692 F 4
Hillswick, ⊙696 G 2
Hopeman, 1,248 E 3
Huntly, 4,078 F 3
Hurlford, 4,294 D 5
Inchnadamph, ⊙833 D 2
Innellan, 922 A 2
Innerleithen, 2,293 E 5
Insch, 881 F 3
Inveraray, 473 C 4
Inverbervie, 853 F 4
Invercassley, ⊙1,067 D 3
Invergordon, 2,385 D 3
Invergowrie, 1,389 E 4
Inverie, ⊙1,468 C 3
Inverkeithing, 6,102 D 1
Inverness, 35,801 D 3
Inverurie, 5,534 F 3
Irvine, 48,500 D 5
Isle of Whithorn, 222 D 6
Jedburgh, 3,953 F 5
John O'Groats, 195 E 2
Johnshaven, 544 F 4
Johnstone, 23,251 B 2
Kames, 230 C 5
Keiss, 344 E 2
Keith, 4,192 F 3
Kelso, 4,934 F 5
Kelty, 6,573 D 1
Kemnay, 1,042 F 3
Kenmore, 211 E 4
Kilbarchan, 2,669 A 2
Kilbirnie, 8,259 A 2
Kilchoan, ⊙764 B 4
Kildonan, ⊙1,105 E 2
Killearn, 1,086 B 1
Killin, 600 D 4
Kilmacolm, 3,348 A 2
Kilmarnock, 50,175 D 5
Kilmaurs, 2,518 D 5
Kilninver, ⊙247 C 4
Kilrenny and Anstruther, 2,951 F 4
Kilsyth, 10,210 B 1
Kilwinning, 8,460 D 5
Kinbrace, ⊙1,105 E 2
Kincardine, 3,278 C 1
Kinghorn, 2,163 D 1
Kingussie, 1,036 D 3
Kinlochewe, ⊙1,794 C 3
Kinlochleven, 1,243 D 4
Kinloch Rannoch, 241 D 4
Kinloss, 2,378 E 3
Kinross, 2,829 E 4
Kintore, 970 F 3
Kippen, 529 B 1
Kirkcaldy, 50,207 D 1
Kirkcolm, 346 C 6
Kirkconnel, 3,318 E 5
Kirkcowan, 354 D 6
Kirkcudbright, 2,690 E 6
Kirkhill, 210 D 3
Kirkintilloch, 26,664 B 2
Kirkmuirhill, 2,575 E 5
Kirkton of Glenisla, ⊙331 E 4
Kirkwall, 4,777 E 2
Kirriemuir, 4,295 E 4
Kyleakin, 268 C 3
Kyle of Lochalsh, 687 C 3
Kylestrome, ⊙745 D 2
Ladybank, 1,216 E 4
Laggan, 393 D 3
Lairg, 572 D 2
Lamlash, 613 C 5
Lanark, 8,842 E 5
Langholm, 2,509 E 5
Larbert, 4,922 C 1
Largs, 9,461 A 2
Larkhall, 15,926 E 5
Lauder, 639 F 5
Laurencekirk, 1,416 F 4

(continued)

England and Wales
CONIC PROJECTION
MILES
KILOMETERS
Capitals of Countries
Administrative Centers
Other Capitals
Canals
International Boundaries
County Boundaries
Other Boundaries
Scale 1:2,886,000
The administrative centers for MID GLAMORGAN, NORTHUMBERLAND and SURREY are Cardiff, Newcastle upon Tyne and Kingston upon Thames, respectively.
© Copyright HAMMOND INCORPORATED, Maplewood, N. J.
SCOTLAND
NORTH SEA
IRISH SEA
NORTHERN IRELAND
IRELAND
WALES
ATLANTIC OCEAN
ENGLISH CHANNEL
Bristol Channel
St. George's Channel
North Channel
CHANNEL ISLANDS
FRANCE
ISLE OF MAN
ISLES OF SCILLY
Longitude West of Greenwich
Longitude East of Greenwich
TYNE AND WEAR
GREATER MANCHESTER
MERSEYSIDE
LANCASHIRE
WEST YORKSHIRE
GREATER LONDON
SURREY
KENT
ESSEX
SOUTH GLAMORGAN
MID GLAMORGAN
GWENT

Lennoxtown, 3,070 B 1
Lerwick, 6,195 G 2
Leslie, 3,303 E 4
Lesmahagow, 3,906 E 5
Leswalt, 237 C 6
Letham, 804 F 4
Leuchars, 2,482 F 4
Leurbost, 461 B 2
Leven, 9,507 F 4
Leverburgh, 223 B 3
Lhanbryde, 1,184 E 3
Lilliesleaf, 212 F 5
Limekilns, 812 D 1
Linlithgow, 6,098 C 1
Linwood, 10,510 B 2
Lionel, 187 B 2
Livingston, 21,900 C 2
Loanhead, 5,971 D 2
Lochailort, ⊙673 C 4
Lochaline, 213 C 4
Lochans, 355 D 6
Locharbriggs, 2,561 E 5
Lochawe, 200 C 4
Lochboisdale, 382 A 3
Lochcarron, 204 C 3
Lochgelly, 7,754 D 1
Lochgilphead, 1,217 C 4
Lochgoilhead, 216 D 4
Lochinver, 283 C 2
Lochmaben, 1,304 E 5
Lochmaddy, 307 A 3
Lochore, 2,994 D 1
Lochwinnoch, 2,064 A 2
Lockerbie, 3,135 E 5
Lossiemouth and Branderburgh, 5,817 E 3
Lumsden, 248 F 3
Luncarty, 584 E 4
Lybster, 554 E 2
Lyness, ⊙454 E 2
Macduff, 3,682 F 3
Machrihanish, 212 C 5
Maidens, 536 D 5
Mallaig, 903 C 4
Markinch, 2,366 E 4
Mauchline, 3,612 D 5
Maud, 634 F 3
Maybole, 4,703 D 5
Mayfield, 8,232 D 2
Meigle, 357 E 4
Melrose, 2,197 F 5
Melvaig, ⊙1,794 C 3
Methlick, 315 F 3
Methven, 806 E 4
Mid Yell, 220 G 2
Millport, 1,161 A 2
Milnathort, 1,099 E 4
Milngavie, 10,846 B 1
Minnigaff, 658 D 6
Mintlaw, 657 F 3
Moffat, 2,041 E 5
Moniaive, 342 E 5
Monifieth, 7,100 F 4
Montrose, 4,704 F 4
Morar, 184 C 4
Motherwell and Wishaw, 72,991 C 2
Muirkirk, 2,607 E 5
Muir of Ord, 1,339 D 3
Musselburgh, 17,045 D 2
Muthill, 672 E 4
Nairn, 5,821 E 3
Neilston, 4,358 B 2
Nethy Bridge, 431 E 3
New Abbey, 339 E 6
Newarthill, 7,003 C 2
Newburgh, Fife, 2,124 E 4
Newburgh, Grampian, 447 G 3
Newcastleton, 903 F 5
New Cumnock, 5,077 D 5
New Deer, 601 F 3
New Galloway, 337 D 5
Newmains, 6,847 C 2
Newmarket, 613 B 2
Newmill, 449 E 3
Newmilns and Greenholm, 3,509 D 5
New Pitsligo, 1,125 F 3
Newport-on-Tay, 3,762 F 4
New Scone, 3,830 E 4
Newtongrange, 4,555 D 2
Newton Mearns, 6,901 B 2
Newtonmore, 894 D 3
Newton Stewart, 1,983 D 6
Newtown Saint Boswells, 1,101 F 5
Newtyle, 664 E 4
North Berwick, 4,317 F 4
North Tolsta, 527 B 2
Oakley, 3,499 C 1
Oban, 6,515 C 4
Old Kilpatrick, 3,256 B 2
Oldmeldrum, 1,103 F 3
Oykel Bridge, ⊙742 D 3
Paisley, 94,833 B 2
Palnackie, 225 E 6
Patna, 2,867 D 5
Peebles, 6,049 E 5
Penicuik, 10,476 D 2
Penpont, 364 E 5
Perth, 43,098 E 4
Peterculter, 3,226 F 3
Peterhead, 14,846 G 3
Pierowall, ⊙735 E 1
Pitlochry, 2,468 E 4
Pitmedden, 313 F 3
Pittenweem, 1,548 F 4
Plockton, 288 C 3
Poolewe, ⊙1,794 C 3
Port Appin, ⊙2,172 C 4
Port Askaig, ⊙1,795 B 5
Port Bannatyne, 730 A 2
Port Charlotte, 240 B 5
Port Ellen, 932 B 5
Port Glasgow, 22,189 A 2
Portgordon, 814 F 3
Portknockie, 1,217 F 3
Portmahomack, 226 E 3
Portpatrick, 643 C 6
Portree, 1,374 B 3
Portsoy, 1,717 F 3
Port William, 517 D 6
Prestonpans, 3,272 D 1
Prestwick, 13,218 D 5
Queensferry, 5,339 D 1
Reay, 283 E 2
Renfrew, 18,880 B 2
Renton, 3,443 A 1
Rhu, 1,540 A 1
Rhynie, 333 F 3
Rigside, 1,195 E 5
Rosehearty, 1,220 F 3
Rosneath, 946 A 1
Rothes, 1,240 E 3
Rothesay, 6,285 A 2
Rutherglen, 24,091 B 2
Saint Abbs, 203 F 5
Saint Andrews, 12,837 F 4
Saint Combs, 738 G 3
Saint Cyrus, 340 F 4
Saint Margaret's Hope, 210 F 2
Saint Monance, 1,205 F 4
Saline, 831 C 1
Saltcoats, 14,861 D 5
Sandbank, 850 A 1
Sandhead, 248 D 6
Sandwick, 603 B 2
Sanquhar, 2,030 D 5
Sauchie, 6,082 C 1
Scalasaig, ⊙137 B 4
Scalloway, 896 G 2
Scarinish, ⊙875 B 4
Scourie, ⊙745 C 2
Scrabster, 273 E 2
Selkirk, 5,635 F 5
Shader, 258 B 2
Shawbost, 458 B 2
Shieldaig, ⊙550 C 3
Shotts, 9,512 C 2
Skateraw, 674 F 3
Skelmorlie, 1,535 A 2
Skipness, ⊙765 C 5
Slamannan, 1,584 C 2
Spean Bridge, 235 D 4
Springholm, 340 E 5
Stanley, 1,385 E 4
Stenhousemuir, 8,203 C 1
Stevenston, 11,786 D 5
Stewarton, 5,165 D 5
Stirling, 29,799 C 1
Stonehaven, 4,837 F 4
Stonehouse, 7,900 D 5
Stornoway, 5,371 B 2
Stow, 485 F 5
Strachan, ⊙390 F 3
Strachur Bay, ⊙678 C 4
Stranraer, 10,174 C 6
Strathaven, 5,464 D 5
Strathpeffer, 874 D 3
Strichen, 962 F 3
Stromeferry, ⊙1,724 C 3
Stromness, 1,680 E 2
Strontian, ⊙764 C 4
Struan, ⊙772 B 3
Swinton, 235 F 5
Tain, 2,057 D 3
Tarbert, Strathclyde, 1,391 C 5
Tarbert, W. Isles, 479 B 3
Tarbolton, 2,224 D 5
Tarland, 452 F 3
Tayport, 2,848 F 4
Thornhill, Central, 443 D 4
Thornhill, Dumf. & Gall., 1,510 E 5
Thurso, 9,113 E 2
Tillicoultry, 4,320 C 1
Tobermory, 652 B 4
Tolob, ⊙2,033 G 2
Tomatin, 214 D 3
Tomintoul, 306 E 3
Torphins, 499 F 3
Tradespark, 425 E 3
Tranent, 7,212 F 5
Troon, 11,656 D 5
Tullibody, 6,082 C 1
Turriff, 3,051 F 3
Tweedsmuir, ⊙105 E 5
Twynholm, 274 D 6
Tyndrum, ⊙1,153 D 4
Uddingston, 5,278 B 2
Uig, Highland, 103 B 3
Uig, W. Isles, ⊙1,948 A 2
Ullapool, 807 C 3
Uphall, 3,035 C 1
Viewpark, 9,812 C 2
Walkerburn, 842 F 5
Watten, 347 E 2
Wemyss Bay, 323 A 2
West Barns, 659 F 5
West Calder, 2,005 C 2
West Kilbride, 3,883 D 5
West Linton, 705 D 2
Whitburn, 11,647 C 2
Whitehills, 875 F 3
Whithorn, 990 D 6
Whiting Bay, 352 C 5
Wick, 7,804 E 2
Wigtown, 1,118 D 6
Winchburgh, 2,409 D 1
Yetholm, 435 F 5

OTHER FEATURES

A'Chralaig (mt.) C 3
Ailsa Craig (isl.), 3 C 5
Almond (riv.) E 4
Annan (riv.) E 5
Appin (dist.), 2,006 C 4
Ardgour (dist.), 315 C 4
Ardle (riv.) E 4
Ardnamurchan (pen.), 764 B 4
Argyll (dist.), 4,940 C 4
Arkaig, Loch (lake) C 4
Arran (isl.), 3,564 C 5
Askival (mt.) B 4
Assynt (dist.), 833 C 2
Athol (dist.), 1,082 D 4
Atlantic Ocean B 2
Avon (riv.) C 1
Avon (riv.) E 3
Awe, Loch (lake) C 4
Ayr (riv.) D 5
Ayr, Heads of (cape) D 5
Badenoch (dist.), 2,717 D 4
Baleshare (isl.), 64 A 3
Balmoral Castle E 3
Barra (sound) A 3
Barra (isl.), 1,005 A 4
Barra (head) A 4
Barra Isles (isls.), 1,092 A 4
Battock (mt.) F 4
Beauly (riv.) D 3
Beinn Dearg (mt.) D 3
Beinn a Ghlo (mt.) E 4
Bell Rock (isl.), 3 F 4
Ben Alder (mt.) D 4
Ben Avon (mt.) E 3
Benbecula (isl.), 1,355 A 3
Ben Cruachan (mt.) C 4
Ben Lawers (mt.) D 4
Ben Lui (mt.) D 4
Ben Macdhui (mt.) E 3
Ben Mhor (mt.) A 3
Ben More (mt.) B 4
Ben More (mt.) D 4
Ben More Assynt (mt.) D 2
Ben Nevis (mt.) D 4
Bernera (isl.), 276 B 2
Berneray (isl.), 131 A 3
Berneray (isl.), 6 A 4
Bidean nam Bian (mt.) D 4
Black Isle (pen.), 7,209 D 3
Blackwater (res.) D 4
Boisdale, Loch (inlet) A 3
Bracadale, Loch (inlet) B 3
Braemar (dist.), 7,624 E 3
Breadalbane (dist.), 3,649 D 4
Bressay (isl.), 248 G 2
Broad (bay) B 2
Broad Law (mt.) E 5
Broom, Loch (inlet) C 3
Brough Ness (prom.) F 2
Buchan (dist.), 40,089 F 3
Buddon Ness (prom.) F 4
Burray (isl.), 209 F 2
Burrow (head) D 6
Bute (isl.), 8,423 C 5
Bute (sound) C 5
Butt of Lewis (prom.) B 2
Cairn Gorm (mt.) E 3
Cairngorm (mts.) E 3
Cairn Toul (mt.) E 3
Caledonian (canal) D 3
Canna (isl.), 22 B 3
Carn Ban (mt.) D 3
Carn Eige (mt.) C 3
Carrick (dist.), 21,425 D 5
Carron (riv.) C 1
Carron (riv.) C 3
Cheviot (hills) F 5
Cheviot, The (mt.) F 5
Clisham (mt.) B 3
Clyde (riv.) D 5
Clyde (firth) D 5
Coll (isl.), 144 B 4
Colonsay (isl.), 137 B 4
Copinsay (isl.), 3 F 2
Cowal (dist.), 15,548 C 4
Creag Meagaidh (mt.) D 4
Cromarty (firth) D 3
Cuillin (hills) B 3
Cuillin (sound) B 3
Dee (riv.) D 5
Dee (riv.) F 3
Dennis (head) F 1
Deveron (riv.) F 3
Don (riv.) F 3
Doon (riv.) D 5
Dornoch (firth) E 3
Duirinish (dist.), 1,085 B 3
Duncansby (head) F 2
Dunnet (head) E 2
Earn (riv.) E 4
Earn, Loch (lake) D 4
Eday (isl.), 179 F 1
Eddrachillis (bay) C 2
Eden (riv.) F 4
Egilsay (isl.), 39 F 1
Eigg (isl.), 69 B 4
Eil, Loch (lake) C 4
Eishort, Loch (inlet) B 3
Enard (bay) C 2
Eriboll, Loch (inlet) D 2
Ericht, Loch (lake) D 4
Eriskay (isl.), 219 A 3
Erisort, Loch (inlet) B 2
Esk (riv.) F 5
Etive, Loch (inlet) C 4
Ewe, Loch (inlet) C 3
Eye (pen.), 850 B 2
Fair Isle (isl.), 65 F 3
Fetlar (isl.), 88 G 2
Fife Ness (prom.) F 4
Findhorn (riv.) E 3
Flannan (isls.), 3 A 2
Formartine (dist.), 10,768 F 3
Forth (riv.) B 1
Forth (firth) F 4
Forth and Clyde (canal) B 2
Foula (isl.), 33 F 2
Fyne, Loch (inlet) C 5
Galloway (dist.), 54,972 D 5
Galloway, Mull of (prom.) D 6
Gare Loch (inlet) A 1
Garioch (dist.), 6,863 F 3
Garry, Loch (lake) D 3
Gigha (isl.), 174 C 5
Girdle Ness (prom.) G 3
Glass (riv.) D 3
Glen More (dist.), 55,035 D 3
Goat Fell (mt.) C 5
Gometra (isl.), 10 B 4
Grampian (mts.) D 4
Great Cumbrae (isl.), 1,296 A 2
Gruinard (bay) C 3
Hallandale (riv.) E 2
Harris (sound) A 3
Harris (dist.), 2,175 B 3
Hebrides (sea) B 3
Hebrides, Inner (isls.), 14,881 B 4
Hebrides, Outer (isls.), 29,615 A 3
Helmsdale (riv.) E 2
Herma Ness (prom.) G 2
Holy (isl.), 10 C 5
Holy Loch (inlet) A 1
Hoy (isl.), 419 E 2
Inchcape (Bell Rock) (isl.), 3 F 4
Inchkeith (isl.), 3 D 1
Indaal, Loch (inlet) B 5
Inner (sound) C 3
Inner Hebrides (isls.), 14,881 B 4
Iona (isl.), 145 B 4
Isla (riv.) E 4
Islay (isl.), 3,816 B 5
Jura (isl.), 210 C 5
Jura (sound) C 5
Katrine, Loch (lake) D 4
Kerrera (isl.), 27 C 4
Kilbrannan (sound) C 5
Kinnairds (head) G 3
Kintyre (pen.), 10,077 C 5
Kintyre, Mull of (prom.) C 5
Knapdale (dist.), 4,082 C 5
Kyle of Tongue (inlet) D 2
Laggan (bay) B 5
Lammermuir (hills) F 5
Lennox (hills) B 1
Leven (lake) E 4
Leven, Loch (inlet) D 4
Lewis (dist.), 20,047 B 2
Liddel Water (riv.) F 5
Linnhe, Loch (inlet) C 4
Lismore (isl.), 166 C 4
Little Minch (sound) B 3
Lochaber (dist.), 13,813 D 4
Lochnagar (mt.) E 4
Lochy, Loch (lake) D 3
Lomond, Loch (lake) D 4
Long, Loch (inlet) D 4
Lorne (dist.), 12,162 C 4
Lorne (firth) C 4
Loyal, Loch (lake) D 2
Luce (bay) D 6
Luing (isl.), 151 C 4
Lyon (riv.) D 4
Machers, The (pen.), 6,192 D 6
Mainland (isl.), 12,747 E 1
Mainland (isl.), 12,944 G 2
Mar (dist.), 23,931 F 3
Maree, Loch (lake) C 3
May, Isle of (isl.), 10 F 4
Merrick (mt.) D 5
Minginish (dist.), 772 B 3
Moidart (dist.), 155 C 4
Monach (sound) A 3
Monadhliath (mts.) D 3
Moorfoot (hills) E 5
Moray (firth) E 3
Moriston (riv.) D 3
Morven (dist.), 398 C 4
Morven (mt.) E 2
Muck (isl.), 24 B 4
Muckle Flugga (isl.), 3 G 2
Mull (isl.), 2,024 C 4
Mull (head) F 1
Mull (sound) C 4
Nairn (riv.) D 3
na Keal, Loch (inlet) B 4
Naver (riv.) D 2
Ness, Loch (lake) D 3
Nevis, Loch (inlet) C 3
Nith (riv.) E 5
North (chan.) C 5
North (sound) F 1
North (sound) G 4
North Esk (riv.) F 4
North Minch (sound) B 3
North Ronaldsay (isl.), 134 F 1
North Uist (isl.), 1,469 A 3
Oa, Mull of (prom.) B 5
Ochil (hills) E 4
Oich (riv.) D 3
Orchy (riv.) D 4
Orkney (isls.), 17,675 F 1
Oronsay (isl.), 2 B 4
Outer Hebrides (isls.), 29,615 A 3
Oykel (riv.) D 3
Pabbay (isl.), 4 A 3
Papa Stour (isl.), 24 F 2
Papa Westray (isl.), 106 F 1
Paps of Jura (mt.) C 5
Park (dist.), 210 B 2
Peel Fell (mt.) F 5
Pentland (hills) D 2
Pentland (firth) E 2
Pladda (isl.), 2 C 5
Quoich, Loch (lake) C 3
Raasay (isl.), 163 C 3
Rannoch (dist.), 1,177 D 4
Rannoch, Loch (lake) D 4
Rhinns, The (pen.), 8,295 C 6
Roag, Loch (inlet) B 2
Rona (isl.), 3 B 3
Ross of Mull (pen.), 585 B 4
Rousay (isl.), 181 E 1
Rudha Hunish (cape) B 3
Rudh Re (cape) C 3
Rum (isl.), 40 B 3
Ryan, Loch (inlet) C 5
Saint Kilda (isl.), 65 A 2
Saint Magnus (bay) F 2
Sanda (isl.), 9 C 5
Sanday (isl.), 11 B 3
Sanday (isl.), 592 F 1
Scalpay (isl.), 483 B 3
Scalpay (isl.), 5 C 3
Scapa Flow (chan.) E 2
Scarp (isl.), 12 A 2
Scridain, Loch (inlet) B 4
Scurdie Ness (prom.) F 4
Seaforth, Loch (inlet) B 3
Seil (isl.), 326 C 4
Sgurr a Choire Ghlais (mt.) D 3
Sgurr Alasdair (mt.) B 3
Sgurr Mor (mt.) C 3
Sgurr na Lapaich (mt.) C 3
Shapinsay (isl.), 346 F 1
Shetland (isls.), 18,494 G 2
Shiant (sound) B 3
Shiel, Loch (lake) C 4
Shin (falls) D 3
Shin, Loch (lake) D 2
Shona (isl.), 17 C 4
Sidlaw (hills) E 4
Sinclair's (bay) E 2
Skye, Isle of (isl.), 7,183 B 3
Sleat (pt.) B 4
Sleat (dist.), 449 C 3
Small Isles (isls.), 171 B 4
Snizort, Loch (inlet) B 3
Soay (isl.), 5 B 3
Solway (firth) E 6
South Esk (riv.) F 4
South Ronaldsay (isl.), 776 F 2
South Uist (isl.), 2,281 A 3
Spean (riv.) D 4
Spey (riv.) E 3
Start (pt.) F 1
Stinchar (riv.) D 5
Strathbogie (dist.), 7,959 F 3
Strathmore (valley) E 4
Strathspey (dist.), 6,668 E 3
Strathy (pt.) E 2
Stroma (isl.), 8 E 2
Stronsay (isl.), 436 F 1
Sumburgh (head) G 2
Sunart, Loch (inlet) C 4
Swona (isl.), 3 E 2
Taransay (isl.), 5 A 3
Tarbat Ness (prom.) E 3
Tarbert, East Loch (inlet) B 3
Tarbert, Loch (inlet) B 5
Tarbert, West Loch (inlet) A 3
Tay (riv.) E 4
Tay (firth) F 4
Tay, Loch (lake) D 4
Teith (riv.) D 4
Teviot (riv.) F 5
Thurso (riv.) E 2
Tiree (isl.), 875 B 4
Tolsta (head) B 2
Tor Ness (prom.) E 2
Torridon, Loch (inlet) C 3
Trossachs, The (valley) D 4
Trotternish (dist.), 1,948 B 3
Tweed (riv.) F 5
Tyne (riv.) F 5
Ulva (isl.), 23 B 4
Unst (isl.), 1,124 G 2
Vaternish (dist.), 162 B 3
Vatersay (isl.), 77 A 4
West Burra (isl.), 501 G 2
Westray (firth) E 1
Westray (isl.), 735 E 1
Whalsay (isl.), 870 G 2
White Coomb (mt.) E 5
Wigtown (bay) D 6
Wrath (cape) C 2
Wyre (isl.), 36 F 1
Yarrow (riv.) E 5
Yell (isl.), 1,143 G 2
Ythan (riv.) F 3

★Population of met. area
⊙Population of parish.

Agriculture, Industry and Resources

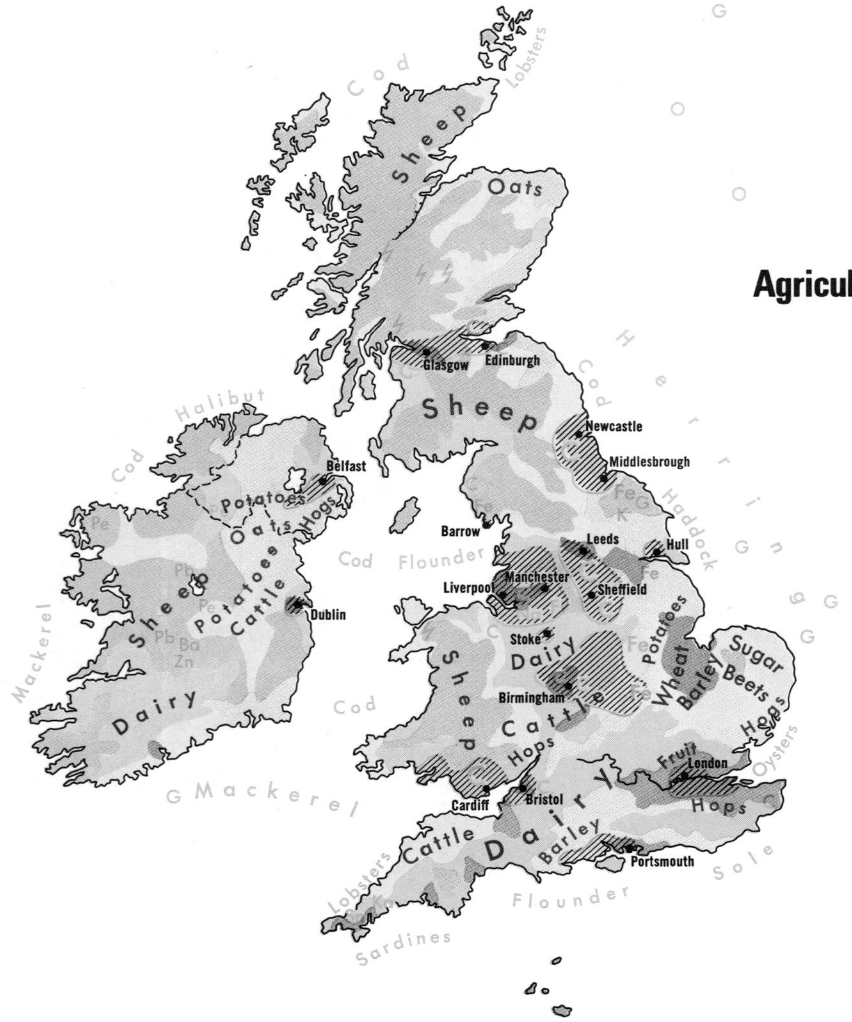

DOMINANT LAND USE

Cereals (chiefly oats, barley)
Truck Farming, Horticulture
Dairy, Mixed Farming
Livestock, Mixed Farming
Pasture Livestock

MAJOR MINERAL OCCURRENCES

Ba Barite
C Coal
F Fluorspar
Fe Iron Ore
G Natural Gas
K Potash
Ka Kaolin (china clay)
Na Salt
O Petroleum
Pb Lead
Pe Peat
Sn Tin
Zn Zinc

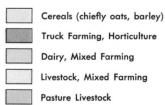

Water Power
Major Industrial Areas

Scotland
CONIC PROJECTION
MILES
KILOMETERS
Capital
Regional Centers
Canals
International Boundaries
Regional Boundaries
Other Boundaries
Scale 1:1,850,000
© Copyright HAMMOND INCORPORATED, Maplewood, N. J.
Former Counties
1 CLACKMANNAN
2 DUNBARTON
3 KINROSS
4 MIDLOTHIAN
5 PEEBLES
6 RENFREW
7 SELKIRK
8 STIRLING
9 W. LOTHIAN
ORKNEY
(OFF MAP) ZETLAND
SUTHERLAND
CAITHNESS
ROSS AND CROMARTY
INVERNESS
ABERDEEN
KINCARDINE
ANGUS
PERTH
FIFE
ARGYLL
E. LOTHIAN
BERWICK
ROXBURGH
LANARK
AYR
BUTE
DUMFRIES
WIGTOWN
KIRKCUDBRIGHT
Shetland Islands
ATLANTIC OCEAN
SHETLAND
Mainland
Yell
Unst
Fetlar
Whalsay
Foula
Fair Isle
Lerwick
Scalloway
Sumburgh Head
Muckle Flugga
ORKNEY ISLANDS
Mainland
Hoy
Kirkwall
Stromness
Westray
Sanday
Stronsay
Shapinsay
S. Ronaldsay
Pentland Firth
Same scale as main map
St. Kilda
Boreray
Soay
Dun
ATLANTIC OCEAN
NORTH SEA
NORTH MINCH
Little Minch
Sea of the Hebrides
INNER HEBRIDES
OUTER HEBRIDES
WESTERN ISLES
North Channel
Solway Firth
Firth of Forth
Moray Firth
Firth of Clyde
Firth of Lorne
Dornoch Firth
Pentland Firth
HIGHLAND
GRAMPIAN
TAYSIDE
CENTRAL
FIFE
LOTHIAN
STRATHCLYDE
BORDERS
DUMFRIES & GALLOWAY
ENGLAND
NORTHERN IRELAND
IRELAND
Lewis
Harris
North Uist
Benbecula
South Uist
Barra
Skye
Rum
Eigg
Mull
Coll
Tiree
Islay
Jura
Arran
Bute
Colonsay
Grampian Mountains
Cairngorm Mts.
Monadhliath Mts.
Ochil Hills
Sidlaw Hills
Pentland Hills
Moorfoot Hills
Lammermuir Hills
Cheviot Hills
Ben Nevis 4,406 ft. (1343 m.)
Ben Macdhui 4,296 ft. (1309 m.)
Cairn Gorm 4,084 ft. (1245 m.)
Ben Lawers 3,984 ft. (1214 m.)
Ben More 3,843 ft. (1171 m.)
Ben Lomond 3,192 ft. (973 m.)
Loch Ness
Loch Lomond
Loch Tay
Loch Rannoch
Loch Shin
Loch Awe
Loch Fyne
Loch Linnhe
Caledonian Canal
Edinburgh
Glasgow
Aberdeen
Dundee
Inverness
Perth
Stirling
Kirkcaldy
Falkirk
Paisley
Ayr
Kilmarnock
Dumfries
Oban
Fort William
Stornoway
Thurso
Wick
Elgin
Peterhead
Montrose
Arbroath
St. Andrews
Dunfermline
Greenock
Hamilton
Motherwell & Wishaw
Coatbridge
Airdrie
Carlisle
Berwick-upon-Tweed
Stranraer
Campbeltown
Longitude 5° West of Greenwich

16 United Kingdom and Ireland
(continued)

IRELAND

Carlow 34,237 H6
Cavan 52,618 G4
Clare 75,008 D6
Cork 352,883 D7
Donegal 108,344 K2
Dublin 852,219 J5
Galway 149,223 D5
Kerry 112,772 B7
Kildare 71,977 H5
Kilkenny 61,473 G6
Laois 45,259 G6
Leitrim 28,360 E3
Leix (Laois) 45,259 G6
Limerick 140,459 D7
Longford 28,250 F4
Louth 74,951 J4
Mayo 109,525 C4
Meath 71,729 H4
Monaghan 46,242 H3
Offaly 51,829 F5
Roscommon 53,519 E4
Sligo 50,275 D3
Tipperary 123,565 F6
Waterford 77,315 F7
Westmeath 53,570 G5
Wexford 86,351 H7
Wicklow 66,295 J5

CITIES and TOWNS

Abbeydorney, 188 B 7
Abbeyfeale, 1,337 C 7
Abbeylara, ‡290 F 4
Abbeyleix, 1,033 G 6
Achill Sound, ‡1,163 B 4
Aclare, ‡336 D 3
Adare, 545 D 6
Aghada-Farsid-Rostellan, 461 E 8
Aghadoe, ‡497 B 7
Aghagower, ‡693 C 4
Ahascragh, 221 E 5
Annagry, 201 E 1
Annascaul, 236 B 7
An Uaimh, 4,605 H 4
An Uaimh, *6,665 H 4
Ardagh, Limerick, 213 C 7
Ardagh, Longford, ‡974 F 4
Ardara, 683 E 2
Ardee, *3,183 H 4
Ardee, 3,096 H 4
Ardfert, 286 B 7
Ardfinnan, 510 F 7
Ardmore, 233 F 8
Ardrahan, ‡239 D 5
Arklow, 6,948 J 6
Arthurstown, 1,188 H 7
Arva, 370 F 4
Ashford, 341 J 5
Askeaton, 844 D 6
Athboy, 705 H 4
Athea, 328 C 7
Athenry, 1,240 D 5
Athleague, ‡955 E 4
Athlone, 9,825 F 5
Athlone, *11,611 F 5
Athy, 4,270 H 6
Athy, *4,654 H 6
Aughrim, 451 J 6
Avoca, ‡620 J 6
Bagenalstown (Muinebeag), 2,321 H 6
Baile Átha Cliath (Dublin) (cap.), 567,866 K 5
Bailieborough, 1,293 G 4
Balbriggan, 3,741 J 4
Balla, 293 C 4
Ballaghaderreen, 1,121 E 4
Ballina, Mayo, 6,063 C 3
Ballina, *6,369 C 3
Ballina, Tipperary, 336 E 6
Ballinagh, 459 G 4
Ballinakill, 300 G 6
Ballineen D 8
Ballinamore, 808 F 3
Ballinasloe, 5,969 E 5
Ballincollig-Carrigrohane, 2,110 D 8
Ballindine, 232 C 4
Ballingarry, Limerick, 422 D 7
Ballingarry, Tipperary, ‡574 F 6
Ballinlough, 242 D 4
Ballinrobe, 1,272 C 4
Ballintober, ‡867 E 4
Ballintra, 197 E 2
Ballisodare, 486 E 3
Ballivor, 287 H 4
Ballybay, 754 G 3
Ballybay, *1,159 G 3
Ballybofey-Stranorlar, 2,214 F 2
Ballybunion, 1,287 B 7
Ballycanew, ‡460 J 6
Ballycarney, ‡294 J 6
Ballycastle, ‡724 C 3
Ballyconnell, 421 F 3
Ballycotton, 389 F 8
Ballydehob, 253 C 8
Ballyduff, 406 B 7
Ballygar, 359 E 4
Ballygeary, 725 J 7
Ballyhaise, 274 G 3
Ballyhaunis, 1,093 D 4
Ballyheigue, 450 B 7
Ballyjamesduff, 673 G 4
Ballylanders, 266 E 7
Ballylongford, 504 B 6
Ballymahon, 707 F 4
Ballymakeery, 272 C 8
Ballymore, ‡447 F 5
Ballymore Eustace, 433 J 5
Ballymote, 952 D 3
Ballyporeen, ‡810 E 7
Ballyragget, 519 G 6
Ballyroan, ‡478 G 6
Ballyshannon, 2,325 E 3
Ballytore, ‡580 H 5
Baltimore, 200 C 9
Baltinglass, 909 H 6
Baltray, 236 J 4
Banagher, 1,052 F 5
Bandon, 2,257 D 8
Bandon, *4,071 D 8
Bannow, ‡798 H 7
Bansha, 184 E 7
Bantry, 2,579 C 8
Barna, ‡1,734 C 5
Belmullet, 744 B 3
Belturbet, 1,092 G 3
Bennettsbridge, 367 G 6
Birr, 3,319 F 5
Birr, *3,881 F 5
Blanchardstown, 3,279 H 5
Blarney, 1,128 D 8
Blessington, 637 J 5
Boherbue, 372 C 7
Borris, 430 H 6
Borris-in-Ossory, 276 F 6
Borrisokane, 769 E 6
Borrisoleigh, 471 E 6
Boyle, 1,727 E 4
Boyle, *1,939 E 4
Bray, 14,467 K 5
Bray, *15,841 K 5
Brí Chualann (Bray), 14,467 K 5
Broadford, 226 C 7
Brosna, 250 C 7
Bruff, 547 D 7
Bruree, 243 D 7
Bunbeg-Derrybeg, 878 E 1
Bunclody-Carrickduff, 929 H 6
Buncrana, 2,955 G 1
Buncrana, *3,334 G 1
Bundoran, 1,337 E 3
Burtonport, ‡1,288 E 2
Buttevant, 1,045 D 7
Cahir, 1,747 F 7
Cahirciveen, 1,547 A 8
Callan, 1,283 G 7
Camolin, 306 J 6
Campile, 231 H 7
Cappamore, 567 E 6
Cappawhite, 305 E 6
Cappoquin, 872 F 7
Carbury, ‡894 H 5
Carlingford, 559 J 3
Carlow, 9,588 H 6
Carlow, *10,399 H 6
Carndonagh, 1,146 G 1
Carnew, 570 H 6
Carrickmacross, 2,100 H 4
Carrickmacross, *2,475 H 4
Carrick-on-Shannon, 1,854 F 4
Carrick-on-Suir, 5,006 F 7
Carrigaholt, ‡493 B 6
Carrigaline, 951 E 8
Carrigallen, 230 F 4
Carrigart, ‡753 F 1
Carrigtwohill, 622 E 8
Carrowkeel, ‡326 G 1
Cashel, 2,692 F 7
Castlebar, 5,979 C 4
Castlebar, *6,476 C 4
Castlebellingham, 407 J 4
Castleblayney, 2,118 H 3
Castleblayney, *2,395 H 3
Castlecomer-Donaguile, 1,244 G 6
Castledermot, 583 H 6
Castlefin, 610 F 2
Castlegregory, 216 A 7
Castleisland, 1,929 B 7
Castlemartyr, 491 E 8
Castlepollard, 693 G 4
Castlerea, 1,752 D 4
Castletown, ‡504 F 6
Castletownbere, 812 B 8
Castletownroche, 399 D 7
Castletownshend, 170 C 9
Causeway, 215 B 7
Cavan, 3,273 G 3
Cavan, *4,312 G 3
Ceanannus Mór, 2,391 G 4
Ceanannus Mór, *2,653 G 4
Celbridge, 1,568 H 5
Charlestown-Bellahy, 677 D 4
Charleville (Rathluirc), 2,232 D 7
Clara, 2,156 F 5
Claregalway, ‡594 D 5
Claremorris, 1,718 C 4
Clashmore, ‡379 F 8
Clifden, 790 B 5
Cloghan, 404 F 5
Clogh-Chatsworth, 324 G 6
Clogheen, 530 F 7
Clogherhead, 649 J 4
Clonakilty, 2,430 D 8
Clonaslee, 285 F 5
Clondalkin, 7,009 J 5
Clonegal, 202 H 6
Clones, 2,164 G 3
Clonfert, ‡430 E 5
Clonmany, ‡936 G 1
Clonmel, 11,622 F 7
Clonmel, *12,291 F 7
Clonmellon, 328 H 4
Clonroche, 222 H 7
Clontuskert, 351 E 4
Cloone, ‡460 F 4
Cloughjordan, 480 E 6
Cloyne, 654 E 8
Coachford, 290 D 8
Cóbh, 6,076 E 8
Cóbh, *7,141 E 8
Coill Dubh, 920 H 5
Collon, 262 J 4
Collooney, 546 E 3
Cong, 233 C 4
Convoy, 654 F 2
Coolaney, ‡352 D 3
Coolgreany, ‡603 J 6
Cootehill, 1,415 G 3
Cootehill, *1,542 G 3
Cork, 128,645 E 8
Cork, *134,430 E 8
Corofin, 342 C 6
Courtmacsherry, 210 D 8
Courtown Harbour, 291 J 6
Creeslough, 269 F 1
Crookhaven, ‡400 B 9
Croom, 756 D 6
Crosshaven, 1,222 E 8
Crossmolina, 1,077 C 3
Crusheen, ‡405 D 6
Culdaff, ‡621 G 1
Daingean, 492 G 5
Delvin, 223 G 4
Dingle, 1,401 A 7
Doaghbeg, ‡701 F 1
Donabate, 426 J 5
Donegal, 1,725 F 2
Doneraile, 799 D 7
Dooagh-Keel, 649 A 4
Doon, 387 E 6
Douglas, ‡4,448 D 8
Drimoleague, 415 C 8
Drishane, ‡1,548 C 7
Drogheda, 19,762 J 4
Drogheda, *20,095 J 4
Droichead Nua, 5,053 H 5
Droichead Nua, *6,444 H 5
Dromahair, 177 E 3
Drumcar, ‡1,215 J 4
Drumconrath, ‡1,044 H 4
Drumkeerin, ‡467 E 3
Drumlish, 205 F 4
Drumshanbo, 576 E 3
Dublin (cap.), 567,866 K 5
Dublin, *679,748 K 5
Duleek, 658 J 4
Duncannon, 228 H 7
Dundalk, 21,672 H 3
Dundalk, *23,816 H 3
Dunfanaghy, 303 F 1
Dungarvan, 5,583 F 7
Dungloe, 940 E 2
Dunkineely, 288 E 2
Dún Laoghaire, 53,171 K 5
Dún Laoghaire, *98,379 K 5
Dunlavin, 423 H 5
Dunleer 855 J4
Dunmanway 1,392 C8
Dunmore 522 D4
Dunmore East 656 G7
Dunshaughlin⊙ 283 H5
Durrow, Laois 596 G6
Durrow, Offaly⊙ 441 F5
Easky 184 D3
Edenderry 2,953 G5
Edenderry* 3,116 G5
Elphin 489 E4
Emyvale 281 G3
Ennis 5,972 D6
Ennis* 10,840 D6
Enniscorthy 5,704 J7
Enniscorthy* 6,642 J7
Enniskerry 772 J5
Ennistymon 1,013 C6
Eyrecourt 314 E5
Fahan⊙ 1,023 G1
Falcarragh 506 E1
Feakle⊙ 398 D6
Fenit 360 B7
Ferbane 1,064 F5
Fermoy 3,237 E7
Fermoy* 4,033 E7
Ferns 712 J6
Fethard, Tipperary 1,064 F7
Fethard, Wexford⊙ 637 H7
Foxford 868 C4
Foynes 624 C6
Frankford (Kilcormac) 1,089 F5
Frenchpark⊙ 693 E4
Freshford 585 G6
Galbally 258 E7
Galway 27,726 C5
Galway* 29,375 C5
Geashill⊙ 751 G5
Glandore⊙ 695 C8
Glanmire-Riverstown 1,113 E8
Glanworth 335 E7
Glenamaddy 315 D4
Glenbeigh 266 B7
Glencolumbkille⊙ 787 D2
Glengarriff 244 C8
Glenties 734 E2
Glenville⊙ 264 D7
Glin 623 C6
Golden⊙ 640 F7
Gorey 2,946 J6
Gorey* 3,024 J6
Gormanston⊙ 1,384 J4
Gort 975 D5
Gowran 402 G6
Graiguenamanagh-Tinnahinch 1,303 H6
Granard 1,054 F4
Greencastle 322 H1
Greenore 882 J4
Greystones-Delgany 4,517 K5
Gurteen 165 D3
Hacketstown 574 H6
Headford 673 C5
Holycross⊙ 902 F6
Hospital 525 E7
Inchigeelagh⊙ 516 C8
Inishannon 190 D8
Inistioge 179 G7
Inniscrone 582 C3
Johnstown 303 G6
Kanturk 2,063 D7
Keel-Dooagh 649 A4
Kells⊙ 423 G6
Kells (Ceanannus Mór) 2,391 G4
Kenmare 903 B8
Kilbaha⊙ 471 B6
Kilbeggan 635 G5
Kilcar 273 D2
Kilcock 827 H5
Kilconnell⊙ 629 E5
Kilcoole 679 K5
Kilcormac 1,089 F5
Kilcullen 880 H5
Kildare 3,137 H5
Kildysart 239 C6
Kilfenora⊙ 441 C6
Kilfinane 561 D7
Kilgarvan 228 B8
Kilkee 1,287 B6
Kilkelly 225 D4
Kilkenny 9,838 G6
Kilkenny* 13,306 G6
Killala 368 C3
Killaloe 871 D6
Killarney 7,184 C7
Killarney* 7,541 C7
Killavullen 221 D7
Killenaule 592 F6
Killeshandra 432 F3
Killimor 221 E5
Killinaboy⊙ 297 C6
Killorglin 1,150 B7
Killucan-Rathwire 290 G4
Killybegs 1,094 E2
Kilmacrennan 274 F1
Kilmacthomas 396 G7
Kilmallock 1,170 D7
Kilmeadan⊙ 262 G7
Kilmihill 284 C6
Kilmoganny 181 G7
Kilmore Quay 273 H7
Kilmurry⊙ 387 C6
Kilnaleck 273 G4
Kilronan 243 B5
Kilrush 2,671 C6
Kilsheelan⊙ 665 F7
Kiltimagh 978 C4
Kilworth 360 E7
Kingscourt 1,016 H4
Kingstown (Dún Laoghaire) 53,171 K5
Kinlough 160 E3
Kinnegad 362 G5
Kinnitty⊙ 420 F5
Kinsale 1,622 D8
Kinsale* 1,989 D8
Kinvara 293 D5
Knightstown 236 A8
Knock⊙ 1,202 D4
Knocklong 248 D7
Knocknagashel 168 C7
Labasheeda⊙ 468 C6
Laghy⊙ 625 E2
Lahinch 455 C6
Lanesborough-Ballyleague 906 E4
Laracor⊙ 404 H4
Laytown-Bettystown-Mornington 1,882 J4
Leenane⊙ 271 B4
Leighlindridge 379 H6
Leitrim⊙ 544 F3
Leixlip 2,402 H5
Letterkenny 4,930 F2
Letterkenny* 5,207 F2
Lifford 1,121 F2
Limerick 57,161 D6
Limerick* 63,002 D6
Liscarroll 231 D7
Lisdoonvarna 459 C5
Lismore 884 F7
Lismore⊙ 1,041 F7
Listowel 3,021 C7
Littleton 322 F6
Longford 3,876 F4
Longford* 4,791 F4
Lorrha⊙ 685 E5
Loughrea 3,075 E5
Louisburgh 310 B4
Louth 208 J4
Lucan-Doddsborough 4,245 J5
Luimneach (Limerick) 57,161 D6
Lusk 553 J4
Macroom 2,256 C8
Malahide 3,834 J5
Malin⊙ 552 G1
Mallow 5,901 D7
Mallow* 6,506 D7
Manorhamilton 858 E3
Manulla⊙ 660 C4
Maryborough (Portlaoise) 3,902 G5
Maynooth 1,296 H5
Meathas Truim 546 G4
Midleton 3,075 E8
Midleton* 4,666 E8
Milford 763 F1
Millstreet 1,319 D7
Milltown 260 A7
Miltown-Malbay 677 C6
Minard⊙ 397 A7
Mitchelstown 2,783 E7
Moate 1,378 F5
Mohill 868 F4
Monaghan 5,256 G3
Monasterevan 1,619 H5
Moneygall 282 F6
Monivea⊙ 405 D5
Mooncoin 413 G7
Mount Bellew 275 D5
Mountcharles 445 E2
Mountmellick 2,595 G5
Mountmellick* 2,864 G5
Mountrath 1,098 F5
Moville 1,089 G1
Moycullen⊙ 498 C5
Moynalty⊙ 583 H4
Muff 240 G1
Muinebeag 2,321 H6
Mullagh 293 H4
Mullaghmore⊙ 629 D3
Mullinahone 262 F7
Mullinavat 343 G7
Mullingar 6,790 G4
Mullingar* 9,245 G4
Naas 5,078 H5
Navan (An Uaimh) 4,605 H4
Nenagh 5,085 E6
Nenagh* 5,174 E6
Newbliss⊙ 547 G3
Newbridge (Droichead Nua) 5,053 H5
Newcastle 2,549 D7
Newcastle* 2,680 D7
Newmarket 886 C7
Newmarket-on-Fergus 1,052 D6
New Pallas⊙ 1,271 E6
Newport, Mayo 420 C4
Newport, Tipperary 582 E6
New Ross 4,775 H7
New Ross* 5,153 H7
Newtown Forbes⊙ 495 F4
Newtownmountkennedy 882 J5
Newtownsandes 268 C6
O'Briensbridge-Montpelier 237 D6
Oldcastle 759 G4
Old Leighlin⊙ 309 G6
Oola 348 E6
Oranmore 440 D5
Oughterard 628 C5
Passage East 408 G7
Passage West 2,709 E8
Patrickswell 415 D6
Pettigo 332 F2
Piltown 456 G7
Portarlington 3,117 G5
Portlaoise 3,902 G5
Portlaoise* 6,470 G5
Portlaw 1,166 G7
Portmarnock 1,726 J5
Portumna 913 E5
Queenstown (Cóbh) 6,076 E8
Rahan⊙ 531 F5
Ramelton 807 F1
Raphoe 945 F2
Rathangan 868 G5
Rathcoole 1,740 J5
Rathcormac 191 E7
Rathdowney 892 F6
Rathdrum 1,141 J6
Rathgormuck⊙ 231 F7
Rathkeale 1,543 D7
Rathluirc 2,232 D7
Rathmore 437 J5
Rathmullen 486 F1
Rathnew-Merrymeeting 954 J6
Rathowen⊙ 294 F4
Rathvilly 230 H6
Ratoath 300 J5
Riverstown 236 E3
Rockcorry 233 H3
Rosapenna⊙ 822 F1
Roscommon 1,556 E4
Roscommon* 2,821 E4
Roscrea 3,855 F6
Rosscarbery 309 C8
Rosses Point 464 D3
Rosslare 588 J7
Rosslare Harbour (Ballygeary) 725 J7
Roundstone 204 A5
Roundwood 260 J5
Rush 2,633 J4
Saint Johnston 463 F2
Scarriff 619 E6
Schull 457 B8
Scotstown 264 H3
Shanagolden 231 C6
Shannon Airport 3,657 D6
Shannon Bridge 188 F5
Shercock 313 G4
Shillelagh 246 J6
Shinrone 365 F5
Shrule 288 C4
Sixmilebridge 567 D6
Skerries 3,044 J4
Skibbereen 2,104 C8
Slane 483 H4
Sligo 14,080 E3
Sligo* 14,456 E3
Sneem 285 B8
Spiddal⊙ 819 C5
Stepaside 748 J5
Stradbally, Laois 891 G5
Stradbally, Waterford 158 F7
Strokestown 563 E4
Swanlinbar 257 F3
Swinford 1,105 C4
Swords 4,133 J5
Taghmon 369 H7
Tallaght 6,174 J5
Tallow, 883 F 7
Tarbert, 485 C 6
Teltown, ‡739 H 4
Templemore, 2,174 F 6
Templetuohy, 197 F 6
Termonfeckin, 328 J 4
Thomastown, 1,270 G 7
Thurles, 6,840 F 6
Thurles, *7,087 F 6
Timoleague, 257 D 8
Tinahely, 450 H 6
Tipperary, 4,631 E 7
Tipperary, *4,717 E 7
Toomevara, 272 E 6
Tralee, 12,287 B 7
Tralee, *13,263 B 7
Tramore, 3,792 G 7
Trim, 1,700 H 4
Trim, *2,255 H 4
Tuam, 3,808 D 4
Tuam, *4,952 D 4
Tubbercurry, 959 D 3
Tulla, 415 D 6
Tullamore, 6,809 G 5
Tullamore, *7,474 G 5
Tullaroan, ‡301 G 6
Tullow, 1,838 H 6
Tullow, *1,945 H 6
Tynagh, ‡452 E 5
Tyrrellspass, 289 G 5
Urlingford, 652 F 6
Virginia, 583 G 4
Waterford, 31,968 G 7
Waterford, *33,676 G 7
Waterville, 547 A 8
Westport, 3,023 C 4
Wexford, 11,849 H 7
Wexford, *13,293 H 7
Whitegate, 370 E 8
Wicklow, 3,786 K 6
Wicklow, *3,915 K 6
Woodenbridge, ‡620 J 6
Woodford, 198 E 5
Youghal, 5,445 F 8
Youghal, *5,626 F 8

OTHER FEATURES

Achill (isl.), 3,129 A 4
Allen (lake) E 3
Allen, Bog of (marsh) H 5
Aran (isl.), 773 D 2
Aran (isls.), 1,499 B 5
Arklow (bank) K 6
Arrow (lake) E 3
Awbeg (riv.) D 7
Ballinskelligs (bay) A 8
Ballycotton (bay) F 8
Ballyheige (bay) B 7
Ballyhoura (hills) E 7
Ballyteige (bay) H 7
Bandon (riv.) D 8
Bann (riv.) J 6
Bantry (bay) B 8
Barrow (riv.) H 7
Baurtregaum (mt.) A 7
Bear (isl.), 288 B 8
Blacksod (bay) A 3
Blackstairs (mt.) H 6
Blackwater (riv.) D 7
Blackwater (riv.) H 4
Blasket (isls.) A 7
Bloody Foreland (prom.) E 1
Blue Stack (mts.) E 2
Boderg (lake) E 4
Boggeragh (mts.) D 7
Boyne (riv.) J 4
Brandon (head) A 7
Bride (riv.) E 7
Broad Haven (harb.) B 3
Brosna (riv.) F 5
Bull, The (isl.), 5 A 8
Caha (mts.) B 8
Carlingford (inlet) J 3
Carnsore (pt.) J 7
Carrantuohill (mt.) B 7
Clare (riv.) D 5
Clare (isls.), 168 A 4
Clear (cape) B 9
Clear (isl.), 192 C 9
Clew (bay) B 4
Comeragh (mts.) F 7
Conn (lake) C 3
Connacht (prov.), 390,902 C 4
Connemara (dist.), 7,599 B 5
Cork (harb.) E 8
Corrib (lake) C 5
Courtmacsherry (bay) D 8
Curragh, The H 5
Dee (riv.) H 4
Deel (riv.) D 7
Deele (riv.) F 2
Derg (lake) E 6
Derravaragh (lake) G 4
Derryveagh (mts.) E 2
Dingle (bay) A 7
Donegal (bay) D 3
Drum (hills) F 7
Dublin (bay) J 5
Dundalk (bay) J 4
Dunmanus (bay) B 8
Dursey (isl.), 38 A 8
Ennell (lake) G 5
Erne (riv.) E 3
Errigal (mt.) E 1
Erris (head) A 3
Fanad (head) F 1
Fastnet Rock (isl.), 3 B 9
Feale (riv.) C 7
Fergus (riv.) D 6
Finn (riv.) F 2
Finn (riv.) G 3
Flesk (riv.) C 7
Foyle (inlet) G 1
Foyle (riv.) G 2
Galley (head) D 9
Galtee (mts.) E 7
Galtymore (mt.) E 7
Galway (bay) C 5
Gara (lake) D 4
Garadice (lake) F 3
Gill (lake) E 3
Glyde (riv.) H 4
Golden Vale (plain) E 7
Gorumna (isl.), 1,108 B 5
Gowna (lake) G 4
Grand (canal) G 5
Greenore (pt.) J 7
Gweebarra (bay) D 2
Hags (head) B 6
Helvick (head) G 7
Hook (head) H 7
Horn (head) E 1
Iar Connacht (dist.), 10,774 C 5
Inishbofin (isl.), 236 A 4
Inishbofin (isl.), 103 E 1
Inisheer (isl.), 313 B 5
Inishmaan (isl.), 319 C 5
Inishmore (isl.), 864 B 5
Inishowen (head) H 1
Inishowen (pen.), 24,109 G 1
Inishtrahull (isl.), 3 G 1
Inishturk (isls.), 83 A 4
Inny (riv.) A 8
Inny (riv.) F 4
Inver (bay) E 2
Ireland's Eye (isl.) K 5
Irish (sea) K 4
Joyce's Country (dist.), 2,021 B 4
Kenmare (riv.) A 8
Kerry (head) A 7
Key (lake) E 3
Kilkieran (bay) B 5
Killala (bay) C 3
Killary (harb.) A 4
Kinsale (harb.) E 8
Kippure (mt.) J 5
Knockboy (mt.) B 8
Knockmealdown (mts.) F 7
Lady's Island Lake (inlet) J 7
Lambay (isl.), 24 K 4
Laune (riv.) B 7
Leane (lake) B 7
Leane (lake) G 4
Lee (riv.) D 8
Leinster (mt.) H 6
Leinster (prov.), 1,498,140 G 5
Lettermullan (isl.), 221 B 5
Liffey (riv.) H 5
Liscannor (bay) B 6
Long Island (bay) B 9
Loop (head) A 6
Lugnaquillia (mt.) J 5
Macgillicuddy's Reeks (mts.) B 7
Macnean (lake) F 3
Maigue (riv.) D 6
Maine (riv.) C 7
Malin (head) F 1
Mask (lake) C 4
Maumturk (mts.) B 5
Melvin (lake) E 3
Mizen (head) B 9
Moher (cliffs) B 6
Monavullagh (mts.) F 7
Moy (riv.) C 3
Mulkear (riv.) E 6
Mullaghareirk (mts.) C 7
Mulroy (bay) F 1
Munster (prov.), 882,002 D 7
Mweelrea (mt.) B 4
Mweenish (isl.), 198 B 5
Nagles (mts.) E 7
Nenagh (riv.) E 6
Nephin (mt.) C 3
Nore (riv.) G 7
North (sound) B 5
Omey (isl.), 34 A 5
Oughter (lake) G 3
Ovoca (riv.) J 6
Owenmore (riv.) D 3
Owey (isl.), 51 D 1
Paps, The (mt.) C 7
Partry (mts.) C 4
Pollaphuca (res.) J 5
Punchestown H 5
Rathlin O'Birne (isl.), 3 C 2
Ree (lake) F 5
Roaringwater (bay) B 9
Rosses (bay) D 1
Rosskeeragh (pt.) D 3
Royal (canal) G 4
Saint Finan's (bay) A 8
Saint George's (chan.) K 7
Saint John's (pt.) D 2
Saltee (isls.) H 7
Seven (heads) D 8
Seven Hogs, The (isls.) A 7
Shannon (riv.) E 6
Sheeffry (hills) B 4
Sheelin (lake) G 4
Sheep Haven (harb.) F 1
Sheeps (head) B 8
Sherkin (isl.), 82 C 9
Silvermine (mts.) E 6
Slaney (riv.) H 7
Slieve Aughty (mts.) D 5
Slieve Bloom (mts.) F 5
Slieve Gamph (mts.) D 3
Slievenaman (mt.) F 7
Sligo (bay) D 3
Slyne (head) A 5
South (sound) C 5
Stacks (mts.) B 7
Suck (riv.) E 5
Suir (riv.) G 7
Swilly (inlet) F 1
Tara (hill) H 4
Tory (isl.), 273 E 1
Tory (sound) E 1
Tralee (bay) B 7
Trawbreaga (bay) F 1
Ulster (part) (prov.), 207,204 G 2
Valencia (Valentia) (isl.), 770 A 8
Valentia (isl.), 770 A 8
Waterford (harb.) G 7
Wexford (bay) J 7
Wicklow (head) K 6
Wicklow (mts.) J 6
Youghal (bay) F 8

NORTHERN IRELAND

DISTRICTS

Antrim, 37,600 J 2
Ards, 52,100 K 2
Armagh, 47,500 H 3
Ballymena, 52,200 J 2
Ballymoney, 22,700 J 1
Bainbridge, 28,800 J 3
Belfast, 368,200 J 2
Carrickfergus, 27,500 K 2
Castlereagh, 63,600 K 2
Coleraine, 44,900 H 1
Cookstown, 27,500 H 2
Craigavon, 71,200 J 3
Down, 48,800 K 3
Dungannon, 43,000 H 3
Fermanagh, 50,900 F 3
Larne, 29,000 K 2
Limavady, 25,000 H 1
Lisburn, 80,800 J 2
Londonderry, 86,600 G 2
Magherafelt, 32,200 H 2
Mourne (Newry and Mourne), 75,300 J 3
Moyle, 13,400 J 1
Newtownabbey, 71,500 J 2
North Down, 59,600 K 2
Omagh, 41,800 G 2
Strabane, 35,500 G 2

CITIES and TOWNS

Ahoghill, ‡1,929 J 2
Annalong, 1,001 K 3
Antrim, 8,351 J 2
Ardglass, 1,052 K 3
Armagh, 13,606 H 3
Armoy, ‡1,051 J 1
Augher, ‡1,986 G 3
Aughnacloy, ‡1,885 H 3
Ballycastle, 2,899 J 1
Ballyclare, 5,155 J 2
Ballygawley, ‡2,165 G 3
Ballykelly, 1,116 G 1
Ballymena, 23,386 J 2
Ballymoney, 5,697 J 1
Ballynahinch, 3,485 J 3
Banbridge, 7,968 J 3
Bangor, 35,260 K 2
Belfast (cap.), 353,700 J 2
Belfast, *551,940 J 2
Bellaghy, ‡2,265 H 2
Belleek, ‡2,487 E 3
Beragh, ‡2,137 G 2
Bessbrook, 2,619 J 3
Brookeborough, ‡2,534 G 3
Broughshane, 1,288 J 2
Bushmills, 1,288 J 1
Caledon, ‡1,828 H 3
Carnlough, 1,416 J 2
Carrickfergus, 16,603 K 2
Carrowdore, 2,548 K 2
Castledawson, 1,162 H 2
Castlederg, 1,766 F 2
Castlewellan, 1,488 K 3
Claudy, ‡2,507 G 2
Clogher, ‡1,888 G 3
Coalisland, 3,614 H 2
Coleraine, 16,354 H 1
Comber, 5,575 K 2
Cookstown, 6,965 H 2
Craigavon, 12,740 J 3
Crossgar, 1,098 K 3
Crossmaglen, 1,085 H 3
Crumlin, 1,450 J 2
Cullybackey, 1,649 J 2
Derrygonnelly, ‡2,539 F 3
Dervock, ‡1,191 J 1
Donaghadee, 4,008 K 2
Downpatrick, 7,918 K 3
Draperstown, ‡2,247 H 2
Dromore, Bainbridge, 2,848 J 3
Dromore, Omagh, ‡2,224 G 3
Drumquin, ‡1,982 F 2
Dundrum, ‡2,245 K 3
Dungannon, 8,190 H 3
Dungiven, 1,536 H 2
Dunnamanagh, ‡2,242 G 2
Ederny and Kesh, ‡2,497 F 2
Enniskillen, 9,679 F 3
Feeny, ‡1,459 H 2
Fintona, 1,190 G 3
Fivemiletown, ‡1,649 G 3
Garvagh, ‡2,363 H 2
Gilford, 1,592 J 3
Glenarm, ‡1,728 J 2
Glenavy, ‡2,360 J 2
Glynn, ‡1,872 K 2
Gortin, ‡2,033 G 2
Greyabbey, ‡2,646 K 2
Hillsborough, 1,021 J 3
Holywood, 9,892 K 2
Irvinestown, 1,457 F 3
Keady, 2,145 H 3
Kells, ‡2,560 J 2
Kesh, ‡2,497 F 3
Kilkeel, 4,090 K 3
Killough, ‡3,295 K 3
Killyleagh, 2,359 K 3
Kilrea, 1,196 H 2
Kircubbin, 1,075 K 3
Larne, 18,482 K 2
Limavady, 6,004 H 1
Lisburn, 31,836 J 2
Lisnaskea, 1,443 G 3
Londonderry, 51,200 G 2
Loughbrickland, ‡2,056 J 3
Maghera, 2,085 H 2
Magherafelt, 4,704 H 2
Markethill, ‡2,352 H 3
Millisle, 1,172 K 2
Moneymore, 1,178 H 2
Moy, ‡2,349 H 3
Moygashel, 1,086 H 3
Newcastle, 4,647 J 3
Newry, 20,279 J 3
Newtownabbey, 58,114 K 2
Newtownards, 15,484 K 2
Newtownbutler, ‡2,663 G 3
Newtownhamilton, ‡1,936 H 3
Newtownstewart, 1,433 G 2
Omagh, 14,594 G 2
Pomeroy, ‡1,786 H 2
Portaferry, 1,730 K 3
Portavogie, 1,310 K 3
Portglenone, ‡2,061 H 2
Portrush, 5,376 H 1
Portstewart, 5,085 H 1
Randalstown, 2,799 J 2
Rathfriland, 1,886 J 3
Rostrevor, 1,617 J 3
Saintfield, ‡2,198 K 3
Sion Mills, 1,588 G 2
Sixmilecross, ‡1,980 G 2
Stewartstown, ‡1,759 H 2
Strabane, 9,413 G 2
Strangford, ‡1,987 K 3
Tandragee, 1,725 J 3
Tempo, ‡2,282 G 3
Trillick, ‡2,167 G 3
Warrenpoint, 4,291 J 3
Whitehead, 2,642 K 2

OTHER FEATURES

Bann (riv.) H 2
Belfast (inlet) K 2
Blackwater (riv.) H 3
Bush (riv.) H 1
Derg (riv.) F 2
Divis (mt.) J 2
Dundrum (bay) K 3
Erne (lake) F 3
Foyle (inlet) G 1
Foyle (riv.) G 2
Giant's Causeway H 1
Lagan (riv.) K 2
Larne (inlet) K 2
Magee, Island (pen.), 1,581 K 2
Magilligan (pt.) H 1
Main (riv.) J 2
Mourne (mts.) J 3
Mourne (riv.) G 2
Neagh (lake) J 2
North (chan.) K 1
Rathlin (isl.), 109 J 1
Red (bay) K 1
Roe (riv.) H 1
Saint John's (pt.) K 3
Slieve Donard (mt.) K 3
Sperrin (mts.) G 2
Strangford (inlet) K 3
Torr (head) K 1
Ulster (part) (prov.), 1,537,200 G 2
Upper Lough Erne (lake) F 3

*City and suburbs.
‡Population of district.

Ireland
CONIC PROJECTION
SCALE OF MILES
0 5 10 20 30 40
SCALE OF KILOMETERS
0 5 10 20 30 40
Capitals
County Towns & District Capitals
Country Boundaries
County & District Boundaries
Canals
Scale 1:1,660,000
NORTHERN IRELAND is divided internally into 26 districts bearing the same names as their respective capitals, except:
DISTRICTS / CAPITALS
ARDS — Newtownards
CASTLEREAGH ①* — Belfast†
DOWN — Downpatrick
FERMANAGH — Enniskillen
MOURNE — Newry
MOYLE — Ballycastle
NEWTOWNABBEY ②* — Belfast†
NORTH DOWN — Bangor
* Indicated by number on map
† Belfast also serves as capital of Belfast District
Traditional Divisions
ULSTER
CONNACHT
LEINSTER
MUNSTER
DONEGAL
LONDONDERRY
ANTRIM
TYRONE
FERMANAGH
ARMAGH
DOWN
SLIGO
LEITRIM
MONAGHAN
CAVAN
LOUTH
MAYO
ROSCOMMON
LONGFORD
W. MEATH
MEATH
GALWAY
OFFALY
KILDARE
DUBLIN
LEIX
WICKLOW
CARLOW
CLARE
TIPPERARY
KILKENNY
WEXFORD
LIMERICK
KERRY
CORK
WATERFORD
ATLANTIC OCEAN
IRISH SEA
North Channel
St. George's Channel
NORTHERN IRELAND
IRELAND (EIRE)
Longitude West of Greenwich
© Copyright HAMMOND INCORPORATED, Maplewood, N. J.

Norway, Sweden, Finland and Denmark
CONIC PROJECTION
SCALE OF MILES
0 50 100 150
SCALE OF KILOMETERS
0 50 100 150 200
Capitals of Countries
Administrative Centers
International Boundaries
Internal Boundaries
Canals
SUBDIVISIONS Indicated by Numbers
Counties in NORWAY
1 Akershus G 6
2 Vestfold G 7
3 Østfold G 7
4 Oslo G 7
Oslo is the administrative center for Akershus and Oslo County.
Counties in SWEDEN
5 Göteborg och Bohus G 7
6 Västmanland K 7
7 Södermanland K 7
8 Östergötland J 7
9 Malmöhus H 9
10 Kristianstad J 8
Svalbard
NORWEGIAN SEA
STOCKHOLM
ARCTIC OCEAN
BARENTS SEA
NORWEGIAN SEA
ATLANTIC OCEAN
NORTH SEA
SKAGERRAK
KATTEGAT
GULF OF BOTHNIA
BALTIC SEA
Gulf of Finland
Gulf of Riga
DENMARK
WEST GERMANY
EAST GERMANY
POLAND
U.S.S.R.
Oslo
Stockholm
Helsinki
Copenhagen
Leningrad
Berlin
Warsaw
Arctic Circle
© Copyright HAMMOND INCORPORATED, Maplewood, N. J.
16° Longitude East of 18° Greenwich

AREA 125,053 sq. mi. (323,887 sq. km.)
POPULATION 4,092,000
CAPITAL Oslo
LARGEST CITY Oslo
HIGHEST POINT Glittertinden 8,110 ft. (2,472 m.)
MONETARY UNIT krone
MAJOR LANGUAGE Norwegian
MAJOR RELIGION Protestantism

AREA 173,665 sq. mi. (449,792 sq. km.)
POPULATION 8,320,000
CAPITAL Stockholm
LARGEST CITY Stockholm
HIGHEST POINT Kebnekaise 6,946 ft. (2,117 m.)
MONETARY UNIT krona
MAJOR LANGUAGE Swedish
MAJOR RELIGION Protestantism

AREA 130,128 sq. mi. (337,032 sq. km.)
POPULATION 4,788,000
CAPITAL Helsinki
LARGEST CITY Helsinki
HIGHEST POINT Haltiatunturi 4,343 ft. (1,324 m.)
MONETARY UNIT markka
MAJOR LANGUAGES Finnish, Swedish
MAJOR RELIGION Protestantism

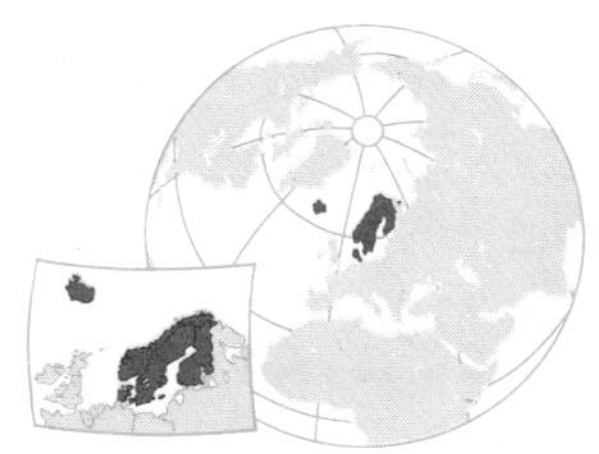

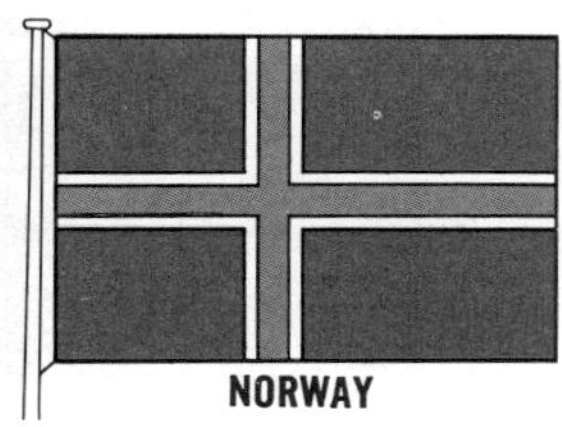

NORWAY

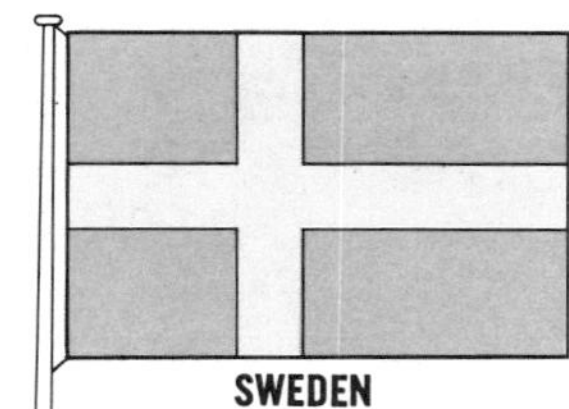

SWEDEN

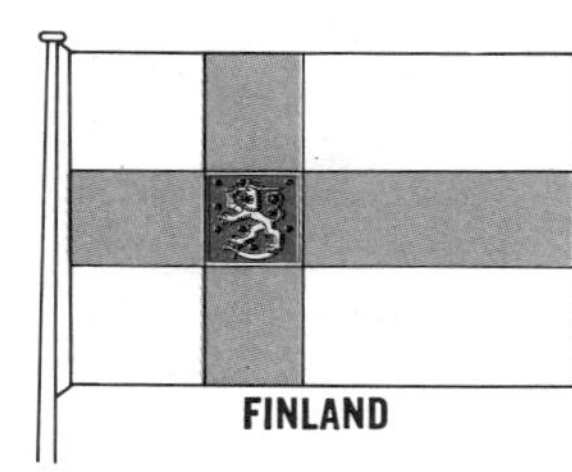

FINLAND

FINLAND

PROVINCES

- Ahvenanmaa 22,380 ... L6
- Åland (Ahvenanmaa) 22,380 ... L6
- Häme 662,500 ... O6
- Keski-Suomi 241,770 ... O5
- Kuopio 252,023 ... P5
- Kymi 346,478 ... Q6
- Lappi 196,792 ... P3
- Mikkeli 211,453 ... P6
- Oulu 406,309 ... P4
- Pohjois-Karjala 179,065 ... Q5
- Turku ja Pori 697,988 ... N6
- Uusimaa 1,085,625 ... O6
- Vaasa 425,283 ... N5

CITIES and TOWNS

- Äänekoski 10,725 ... O5
- Åbo (Turku) 164,857 ... N6
- Alavus 10,285 ... N5
- Borgaå 18,740 ... O6
- Ekenäs 7,391 ... N6
- Espoo 117,090 ... O6
- Forssa 18,442 ... N6
- Haapajärvi 7,791 ... O5
- Hämeenlinna 40,761 ... O6
- Hamina 11,055 ... P6
- Hangö 10,374 ... N7
- Hanko (Hangö) 10,374 ... N7
- Harjavalta 8,445 ... M6
- Heinola 15,350 ... P6
- Helsinki (cap.) 502,961 ... O6
- Helsinki* 794,746 ... O6
- Huutokoski† 6,458 ... P5
- Hyvinkää 35,865 ... O6
- Iisalmi 21,159 ... P5
- Ikaalinen 8,364 ... N6
- Imatra 35,590 ... Q6
- Ivalo 2,661 ... P2
- Jakobstad 20,397 ... N5
- Jämsä 12,526 ... O6
- Järvenpää 16,259 ... O6
- Joensuu 41,429 ... R5
- Jyväskylä 61,209 ... O5
- Jyväskylä* 84,185 ... O5
- Kajaani 20,583 ... P4
- Kalajoki 3,624 ... N4
- Kankaanpää 12,564 ... M6
- Karhula 21,834 ... P6
- Karis 8,152 ... N6
- Karjaa (Karis) 8,152 ... N6
- Karkkila 8,678 ... N6
- Kauniainien 6,219 ... O6
- Kauttua 3,297 ... M6
- Kelloselkä† 8,200 ... Q3
- Kemi 27,893 ... O4
- Kemijärvi 12,951 ... P3
- Kerava 19,966 ... O6
- Kokemäki 10,188 ... N6
- Kokkola 22,096 ... N5
- Kotka 34,026 ... P6
- Kotka* 60,235 ... P6
- Kouvola 29,383 ... P6
- Kouvola* 59,507 ... P6
- Kristiinankaupunki (Kristinestad) 9,331 ... N5
- Kristinestad 9,331 ... N5
- Kuhmo 4,150 ... Q4
- Kuopio 71,684 ... Q5
- Kurikka 11,177 ... M5
- Kuusamo 4,449 ... Q4
- Kuusankoski 22,342 ... P6
- Lahti 94,864 ... O6
- Lahti* 112,129 ... O6
- Lappeenranta 52,682 ... P6
- Lapua 15,189 ... N5
- Lieksa 20,274 ... R5
- Loimaa 6,575 ... N6
- Lovisa 8,674 ... P6
- Maarianhamina (Mariehamn) 9,574 ... M7
- Mänttä 7,910 ... O6
- Mariehamn 9,574 ... M7
- Mikkeli 27,112 ... P6
- Naantali 7,814 ... M6
- Nokia 22,308 ... N6
- Nurmes 11,721 ... Q5
- Nykarleby 7,408 ... N5
- Oulainen 7,322 ... O4
- Oulu 93,707 ... O4
- Oulu* 103,044 ... O4
- Outokumpu 10,736 ... Q5
- Parainen 10,170 ... M6
- Parkano 8,518 ... N6
- Pieksämäki 12,923 ... P5
- Pietarsaari (Jakobstad) 20,397 ... N5
- Pori 80,343 ... M6
- Pori* 86,635 ... M6
- Posio† 6,205 ... Q3
- Pudasjärvi† 12,594 ... P4
- Raahe 15,379 ... O4
- Raisio 14,271 ... M6
- Rauma 29,081 ... M6
- Riihimäki 24,106 ... O6
- Rovaniemi 28,411 ... O3
- Saarijärvi 2,714 ... O5
- Salo 19,176 ... N6
- Savonlinna 28,336 ... Q6
- Seinäjoki 22,123 ... N5
- Sodankylä 3,304 ... P3
- Sotkamo 2,316 ... Q4
- Suolahti 5,936 ... O5
- Suonenjoki 9,286 ... P5
- Tammisaari (Ekenäs) 7,391 ... N6
- Tampere 168,118 ... N6
- Tampere* 220,920 ... N6
- Toijala 8,080 ... N6
- Tornio 19,971 ... O4
- Turku 164,857 ... N6
- Turku* 217,423 ... N6
- Turtola† 5,852 ... O3
- Ulvila† 8,040 ... N6
- Uusikaarlepyy (Nykarleby) 7,408 ... N5
- Uusikaupunki 11,915 ... M6
- Vaasa 54,402 ... M5
- Vaasa* 58,224 ... M5
- Valkeakoski 22,588 ... N6
- Vammala 16,363 ... N6
- Varkaus 24,450 ... Q5
- Vasa (Vaasa) 54,402 ... M5
- Vuotso† 10,186 ... P2
- Ylivieska 10,827 ... O4

OTHER FEATURES

- Åland (isls.) ... L6
- Baltic (sea) ... K9
- Bothnia (gulf) ... M5
- Finland (gulf) ... P7
- Hailuoto (isl.) ... O4
- Haltiatunturi (mt.) ... M2
- Hangöudd (prom.) ... N7
- Haukivesi (lake) ... Q5
- Iijoki (riv.) ... O4
- Inari (lake) ... P2
- Ivalojoki (riv.) ... P2
- Juojärvi (lake) ... Q5
- Kalajoki (riv.) ... O4
- Kallavesi (lake) ... P5
- Karlö (Hailuoto) (isl.) ... O4
- Keitele (lake) ... O5
- Kemijärvi (lake) ... Q3
- Kemijoki (riv.) ... O3
- Kiantajärvi (lake) ... Q4
- Kilpisjärvi (lake) ... M2
- Kitinen (riv.) ... P3
- Kivijärvi (lake) ... O5
- Koitere (lake) ... R5
- Kuusamojärvi (lake) ... Q4
- Längelmävesi (lake) ... O6
- Lapland (reg.) ... O2
- Lappajärvi (lake) ... O5
- Lapuanjoki (riv.) ... N5
- Lestijärvi (lake) ... O5
- Lokka (res.) ... Q3
- Muojärvi (lake) ... R4
- Muonio (riv.) ... M2
- Näsijärvi (lake) ... O6
- Onkivesi (lake) ... P5
- Orihvesi (lake) ... Q5
- Oulujärvi (lake) ... P4
- Oulujoki (riv.) ... O4
- Ounasjoki (riv.) ... O3
- Päijänne (lake) ... O6
- Pielinen (lake) ... Q5
- Puruvesi (lake) ... Q6
- Puulavesi (lake) ... P5
- Pyhäjärvi (lake) ... O5
- Pyhäjärvi (lake) ... M6
- Saimaa (lake) ... Q6
- Siikajoki (riv.) ... O4
- Simojärvi (lake) ... P3
- Simojoki (riv.) ... O4
- Tana (riv.) ... P2
- Tornio (riv.) ... O3
- Vallgrund (isl.) ... M5
- Ylikitka (lake) ... Q3

NORWAY

COUNTIES

- Akershus 355,196 ... G6
- Aust-Agder 86,216 ... E7
- Buskerud 209,684 ... F6
- Finnmark 79,373 ... O2
- Hedmark 183,465 ... G6
- Hordaland 386,492 ... E6
- Møre og Romsdal 231,944 ... E5
- Nordland 243,233 ... J3
- Nord-Trøndelag 122,886 ... H4
- Oppland 178,259 ... F6
- Oslo (city) 462,732 ... D3
- Østfold 228,546 ... G7
- Rogaland 287,653 ... E7
- Sogn og Fjordane 103,135 ... E6
- Sør-Trøndelag 241,361 ... G5
- Telemark 158,853 ... F7
- Troms 144,111 ... L2
- Vest-Agder 131,659 ... E7
- Vestfold 182,433 ... G7

CITIES and TOWNS

- Ålesund 40,868 ... D5
- Ålgård 2,322 ... D7
- Alta 5,582 ... N2
- Åndalsnes 2,574 ... F5
- Årdalstangen 2,360 ... F6
- Arendal 11,701 ... F7
- Arendal* 21,228 ... F7
- Årnes 2,267 ... G6
- Askim 8,413 ... E4
- Bamble† 7,031 ... F7
- Barentsburg ... C2
- Bergen 213,434 ... D6
- Bodø 31,077 ... J3
- Borge† 3,294 ... H2
- Brønnøysund 3,130 ... G4
- Dombås 1,114 ... F5
- Drammen 50,777 ... C4
- Drammen* 56,521 ... C4
- Drøbak 4,538 ... D4
- Eidsvoll 2,906 ... G6
- Eigersund 11,379 ... D7
- Elverum 7,391 ... G6
- Farsund 8,908 ... E7
- Flekkefjord 8,750 ... E7
- Flora 8,822 ... D6
- Fredrikstad 29,024 ... D4
- Fredrikstad* 51,141 ... D4
- Gjøvik 25,963 ... G6
- Grimstad 13,091 ... F7
- Halden 27,087 ... G7
- Hamar 16,418 ... G6
- Hamar* 25,138 ... G6
- Hammerfest 7,610 ... N1
- Hammerfest* 8,005 ... N1
- Harstad 21,125 ... K2
- Haugesund 27,386 ... D7
- Haugesund* 29,277 ... D7
- Hermansverk 706 ... E6
- Holmestrand 8,246 ... C4
- Holmsbu 273 ... D4
- Honningsvag 3,780 ... O1
- Horten 13,746 ... D4
- Horten* 17,246 ... D4
- Kirkenes 4,466 ... Q2
- Kongsberg 19,854 ... F7
- Kongsvinger 16,146 ... H6
- Kopervik 4,221 ... D7
- Kornsjø† 6,079 ... G7
- Kragerø 5,249 ... F7
- Kristiansand 59,488 ... F8
- Kristiansund 18,847 ... E5
- Kvinnherad† 2,898 ... E6
- Larvik 9,097 ... C4
- Larvik* 19,202 ... C4
- Lenvik† 11,098 ... L2
- Levanger 5,066 ... G5
- Lillehammer 21,248 ... F6
- Lillesand 3,028 ... F7
- Lillestrøm† 11,550 ... E3
- Longyearbyen ... D2
- Lysaker† 81,612 ... D3
- Mandal 11,579 ... E7
- Meråker† 2,907 ... G5
- Mo 21,033 ... J3
- Molde 20,334 ... E5
- Mosjøen 9,341 ... H4
- Moss 25,786 ... D4
- Moss* 27,430 ... D4
- Mysen 3,760 ... G7
- Namsos 11,452 ... G4
- Narvik 19,582 ... K2
- Nesttun† 11,519 ... D6
- Nittedal† 8,889 ... D3
- Notodden 12,970 ... F7
- Nøtterøy 11,944 ... D4
- Ny-Ålesund ... C2
- Odda 7,401 ... E6
- Oppdal 2,173 ... F5
- Orkanger 3,685 ... F5
- Oslo (cap.) 462,732 ... D3
- Oslo* 645,413 ... D3
- Porsgrunn 31,709 ... G7
- Rakkestad 2,392 ... G7
- Ringerike 30,156 ... C3
- Risør 6,560 ... F7
- Rjukan 5,334 ... F7
- Røros 3,041 ... G5
- Sandefjord 33,350 ... C4
- Sandnes 33,934 ... D7
- Sandvika† 34,337 ... C3
- Sarpsborg 12,889 ... D4
- Sarpsborg* 36,449 ... D4
- Selje† 3,386 ... D5
- Ski 9,081 ... D4
- Skien 47,105 ... F7
- Stavanger 86,639 ... D7
- Stavern 2,604 ... D4
- Steinkjer 20,553 ... G4
- Stor-Elvdal† 2,993 ... G6
- Sunndalsøra 5,114 ... F5
- Sveagruva ... D2
- Svolvaer 3,942 ... J2
- Tønsberg 9,964 ... D4
- Tønsberg* 36,374 ... D4
- Tromsø 43,830 ... L2
- Trondheim 134,910 ... F5
- Ullensvang† 2,326 ... E6
- Vadsø 6,019 ... Q1
- Vardø 3,875 ... R1
- Vik 1,019 ... E6
- Volda 3,511 ... E5
- Voss 5,944 ... E6

OTHER FEATURES

- Alsten (isl.) ... H4
- Andøya (isl.) ... J2
- Barduelv (riv.) ... L2
- Bellsund ... C2
- Bjørnafjorden (fjord) ... D6
- Bjornøya (isl.) ... D3
- Boknafjord (fjord) ... D7
- Bremanger (isl.) ... D6
- Dønna (isl.) ... H3
- Dovrefjell (hills) ... F5
- Edgeøya (isl.) ... E2
- Femundsjø (lake) ... G5
- Folda (fjord) ... G4
- Folda (fjord) ... J3
- Frohavet (bay) ... F5
- Frøya (isl.) ... F5
- Glittertinden (mt.) ... F6
- Hardangervidda (plat.) ... E6
- Hardangerfjord (fjord) ... D7
- Hinlopenstreten (str.) ... C1
- Hinnøya (isl.) ... K2
- Hitra (isl.) ... F5
- Hopen (isl.) ... E2
- Isfjorden (fjord) ... C2
- Jostedalsbreen (glac.) ... E6
- Kjölen (mts.) ... K3
- Kongsfjorden (fjord) ... B2
- Kvaløya (isl.) ... O1
- Lågen (riv.) ... G6
- Laksefjorden (fjord) ... P1
- Langøy (isl.) ... J2
- Lapland (reg.) ... K2
- Leka (isl.) ... G4
- Lindesnes (cape) ... E8
- Lista (pen.) ... E7
- Lofoten (isls.) ... H2
- Lopphavet (bay) ... M1
- Magerøya (isl.) ... P1
- Moskenesøya (isl.) ... H3
- Namsen (riv.) ... H4
- Nordaustlandet (isl.) ... D1
- Nordfjord (fjord) ... E6
- Nordkapp (pt.) ... C1
- Nordkinn (headland) ... Q1
- Nordkinn (pen.) ... P1
- North Cape (Nordkapp) (pt.) ... P1
- Norwegian (sea) ... F3
- Ofotfjorden (fjord) ... K2
- Oslofjord (fjord) ... D4
- Otra (riv.) ... E7
- Otterøya (isl.) ... E5
- Pasvikelv (riv.) ... Q2
- Platen, Kapp (pt.) ... D1
- Porsangen (fjord) ... O1
- Rana (fjord) ... H3
- Rauma (riv.) ... F5
- Ringvassøy (isl.) ... L2
- Romsdalsfjorden (fjord) ... E5
- Saltfjorden (fjord) ... J3
- Seiland (isl.) ... N1
- Senja (isl.) ... K2
- Skagerrak (str.) ... F8
- Smøla (isl.) ... E5
- Sognafjorden (fjord) ... D6
- Sørkapp (pt.) ... C2
- Sorøya (isl.) ... N1
- Spitsbergen (isl.) ... C2
- Storfjorden (fjord) ... D2
- Sulitjelma (mt.) ... J3
- Svalbard (isls.) ... C3
- Tana (riv.) ... P1
- Tanafjord (fjord) ... Q1
- Tokke (riv.) ... F7
- Trondheimsfjorden (fjord) ... G5
- Tyrifjord (lake) ... C3
- Vaerøy (isl.) ... H3
- Vagåvatn (lake) ... F6
- Vannøy (isl.) ... L1
- Varangerhalvøya (pen.) ... Q1
- Varangerfjord (fjord) ... Q2
- Vega (isl.) ... G4
- Vesterålen (isls.) ... J2
- Vestfjord (fjord) ... H3
- Vestvågøya (isl.) ... H3
- Vikna (isls.) ... G4

SWEDEN

COUNTIES

- Älvsborg 418,150 ... H7
- Blekinge 155,391 ... J8
- Gävleborg 294,595 ... K6
- Göteborg och Bohus 714,660 ... G7
- Gotland 54,447 ... L8
- Halland 219,767 ... H8
- Jämtland 133,559 ... J5
- Jönköping 301,905 ... H8
- Kalmar 240,768 ... K8
- Kopparberg 281,082 ... J6
- Kristianstad 272,090 ... J8

(continued on following page)

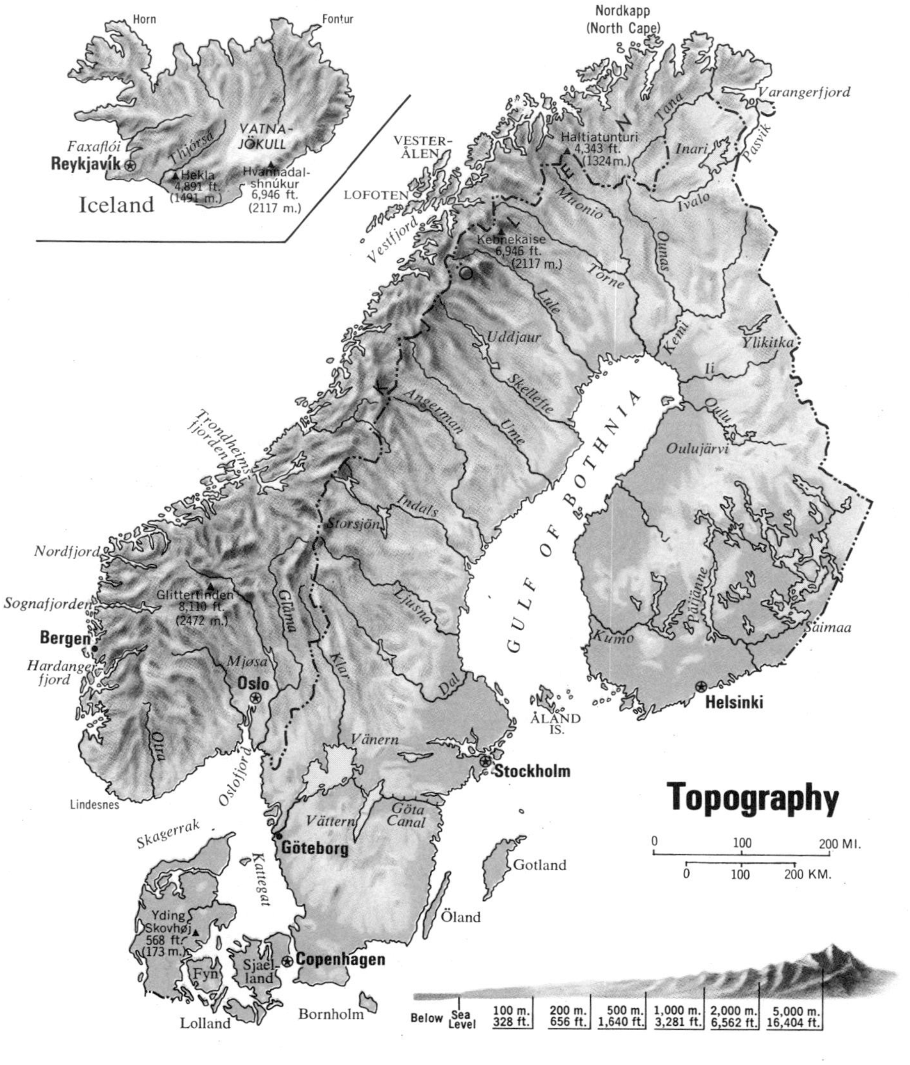

Topography

Norway, Sweden, Finland, Denmark and Iceland

(continued)

Place	Key
Kronoberg 169,454	J8
Malmöhus 740,137	H9
Norrbotten 264,215	L3
Örebro 273,994	J7
Östergötland 387,104	J7
Skaraborg 263,382	H7
Södermanland 252,030	K7
Stockholm 1,493,052	L7
Uppsala 229,879	K7
Värmland 284,442	H7
Västerbotten 236,367	K4
Västernorrland 268,202	K5
Västmanland 259,872	K7

CITIES and TOWNS

Place	Key
Åhus 6,125	J9
Alingsås 18,892	H7
Älmhult 7,390	H8
Alvesta 7,261	J8
Älvsbyn 4,707	M4
Åmål 9,556	H7
Ånge 3,760	J5
Ängelholm 16,016	H8
Arboga 11,819	J7
Arbrå 2,734	K6
Årjäng† 2,596	H7
Arvidsjaur 4,194	L4
Arvika 13,934	H7
Åseda 2,465	J8
Askim 17,609	G8
Åtvidaberg 8,436	K7
Avesta 19,095	J6
Bålsta 8,243	G1
Båstad 2,452	H8
Bengtsfors 3,535	H7
Boden 19,590	M4
Bollnäs 13,305	K6
Bollstabruk 3,548	L5
Borås 67,537	H8
Borås* 187,710	H8
Borgholm 2,789	K8
Borlänge 40,158	J6
Brunflo 3,460	J5
Dalby† 4,013	H6
Danderyd† 36,596	H1
Dannemora 291	K6
Edsbyn 4,388	J6
Eksjö 9,686	J8
Emmaboda 5,652	J8
Enköping 18,541	G1
Eskilstuna 66,409	K7
Eslöv 13,629	H9
Fagersta† 14,778	J6
Falkenberg 14,148	H8
Falköping 15,126	H7
Falun 30,073	J6
Färjestaden 2,995	K8
Filipstad 7,835	H7
Finspång 16,346	J7
Flen 6,770	K7
Forshaga 6,000	H7
Frösö 10,274	J5
Frövi 2,583	J7
Gällivare 8,669	M3
Gamleby 3,666	J8
Gävle 67,454	K6
Gimo 3,154	K6
Gislaved 8,564	H8
Gnesta 3,835	G2
Göteborg 444,540	G8
Göteborg* 690,767	G8
Hagfors 8,060	H6
Hällefors 7,862	J7
Hallsberg 6,799	J7
Hallstahammar 13,583	K7
Hallstavik 5,162	L6
Halmstad 49,558	H8
Haparanda 5,031	N4
Härnösand 18,971	L5
Hässleholm 16,813	H8
Hedemora 7,039	K6
Helsingborg 80,986	H8
Helsingborg* 215,894	H8
Hjo 4,615	J7
Hofors 11,459	K6
Höganäs 10,866	H8
Holmsund 5,467	M5
Hörnefors 2,441	L5
Huddinge 48,339	H1
Hudiksvall 15,004	K6
Hultsfred 5,763	K8
Husum 2,517	L5
Hyltebruk 3,469	H8
Iggesund 4,448	K6
Järna 6,237	G2
Jokkmokk 3,186	L3
Jönköping 78,650	H8
Jönköping* 131,499	H8
Kalix 7,668	N4
Kalmar 32,049	K8
Karlshamn 17,447	J8
Karlskoga† 35,425	J7
Karlskrona 33,414	J8
Karlstad 51,243	H7
Katrineholm 22,884	K7
Kinna 13,676	H8
Kiruna 25,410	L3
Kisa 4,323	J7
Köping 20,059	J7
Kopparberg 3,942	J7
Kramfors 7,719	L5
Kristianstad 30,780	J9
Kristinehamn 21,146	H7
Kumla 11,451	J7
Kungälv† 12,764	G8
Kungsbacka† 11,986	G8
Kvissleby 3,413	K5
Laholm 3,898	H8
Landskrona 29,486	H9
Långshyttan 2,744	K6
Laxå 5,166	J7
Leksand 4,410	J6
Lessebo 2,991	J8
Lidingö 30,098	H1
Lidköping 21,001	H7
Lindesberg 8,247	J7
Linköping 80,274	K7
Linköping* 132,839	K7
Ljungby 12,969	J8
Ljusdal 7,075	J6
Ljusne 3,578	K6
Ludvika 18,217	J6
Luleå 42,139	N4
Lund 55,047	H9
Lycksele 8,586	L4
Lysekil 7,815	G7
Malmberget 10,239	M3
Malmö 241,191	H9
Malmö* 453,339	H9
Malung 6,211	H6
Mariefred 2,553	F1
Mariestad 16,454	H7
Markaryd 4,266	H8
Märsta 17,066	K7
Marstrand 1,168	G8
Mellerud 3,579	H7
Mjölby 12,488	J7
Mölndal† 47,248	H8
Mönsterås 5,005	K8
Mora 8,772	J6
Motala 29,454	J7
Nacka 19,708	H1
Nässjö 18,634	J8
Nora 5,515	J7
Norberg 5,438	K6
Norrköping 85,244	K7
Norrköping* 163,206	K7
Norrtälje 12,784	L7
Nybro 13,010	J8
Nyköping 30,352	K7
Nynäshamn 11,070	L7
Ockelbo 2,810	K6
Olofström 10,096	J8
Örebro 117,877	J7
Örebro* 171,440	J7
Örnsköldsvik 29,514	L5
Orrefors 919	J8
Orsa 5,099	J6
Oskarshamn 19,021	K8
Östersund 40,056	J5
Östhammar 1,783	L6
Oxelösund 13,862	K7
Piteå 16,169	M4
Rättvik 4,087	J6
Rimbo 3,404	L7
Ronneby 12,086	J8
Säffle 11,428	H7
Sala 11,216	K7
Saltsjöbaden 8,113	J1
Sandviken 27,994	K6
Säter 4,297	J6
Sävsjö 4,913	J8
Sigtuna 4,780	H1
Simrishamn 5,834	J9
Skanör med Falsterbo 4,909	H9
Skara 10,138	H7
Skellefteå 29,353	M4
Skövde 29,945	H7
Skutskär 7,174	K6
Smedjebacken 8,418	J6
Söderhamn 14,673	K6
Söderköping 5,310	K7
Södertälje 58,408	G1
Sollefteå 8,923	K5
Sollentuna† 40,905	H1
Solna† 53,992	H1
Sölvesborg 7,292	J9
Stenungsund 8,361	G7
Stockholm (cap.) 665,550	G1
Stockholm* 1,357,183	G1
Storuman 2,587	K4
Storvik 2,748	K6
Strängnäs 10,255	F1
Strömstad 4,735	G7
Strömsund 4,119	K5
Sundbyberg† 27,058	G1
Sundsvall 52,268	K5
Sunne 4,273	H7
Surahammar 6,509	J7
Sveg 2,608	J5
Svenljunga 3,189	H8
Täby† 41,285	H1
Tibro 8,476	J7
Tidaholm 8,039	J7
Tierp 5,005	K6
Timrå 11,416	K5
Tomelilla 5,371	J9
Torsby 3,632	H6
Torshälla 8,231	K7
Tranås 14,854	J7
Trelleborg 22,559	H9
Trollhättan 42,499	H7
Trosa 3,128	K7
Uddevalla 32,700	G7
Ulricehamn 7,827	H8
Umeå 49,715	M5
Uppsala 101,850	K7
Uppsala* 157,202	L7
Vadstena 5,294	J7
Vaggeryd 3,974	J8
Valdemarsvik 3,558	K7
Vallentuna 10,477	H1
Vänersborg 20,510	G7
Vännäs 3,876	L5
Vansbro 2,708	H6
Vara 3,049	H7
Varberg 19,467	G8
Värnamo 15,726	J8
Västerås 98,858	K7
Västerås* 147,508	K7
Västerhaninge 14,125	H1
Västervik 21,239	K8
Vaxholm† 3,744	J1
Växjö 40,328	J8
Vetlanda 12,358	J8
Vilhelmina 4,060	K4
Vimmerby 7,405	J8
Virserum 2,495	J8
Visby 19,886	L8
Ystad 14,286	H9

OTHER FEATURES

Place	Key
Ångermanälven (riv.)	K5
Åsnen (lake)	J8
Baltic (sea)	K9
Bolmen (lake)	H8
Bothnia (gulf)	N4
Dalälven (riv.)	K6
Fårö (isl.)	L8
Göta (canal)	J7
Göta (riv.)	H7
Gotland (isl.)	L8
Gräsö (isl.)	L6
Hanöbukten (bay)	J9
Hjälmaren (lake)	J7
Hoburgen (cliff)	L8
Hornslandet (pen.)	K6
Indalsälven (riv.)	H5
Kalixälv (riv.)	N3
Kalmarsund (sound)	K8
Kattegat (str.)	G8
Kebnekaise (mt.)	L3
Kölen (mts.)	K3
Klarälv (riv.)	H6
Lapland (reg.)	M2
Ljusnan (riv.)	H5
Luleälv (riv.)	M4
Mälaren (lake)	G1
Muonioälv (riv.)	M2
Öland (isl.)	K8
Öresund (sound)	H9
Ornö (isl.)	J2
Österdalälven (riv.)	H6
Piteälv (riv.)	M4
Siljan (lake)	J6
Skagerrak (str.)	F8
Sommen (lake)	J8
Stora Lulevatten (lake)	L3
Storsjön (lake)	J5
Sulitelma (mt.)	K3
Torneälv (riv.)	M3
Uddjaur (lake)	L4
Umeälv (riv.)	L4
Vänern (lake)	H7
Västerdalälven (riv.)	H6
Vättern (lake)	J7

*City and suburbs.
†Population of commune.
‡Population of parish.

DENMARK

COUNTIES

Place	Key
Århus 534,333	D5
Bornholm 47,241	F9
Copenhagen (commune) 622,612	F6
Faerøe Islands 41,969	B2
Frederiksberg (commune) 101,874	F6
Frederiksborg 260,825	E5
Fyn 433,765	D7
København (Copenhagen) (commune) 622,612	F6
Københaven 616,571	F6
Nordjylland 457,165	D4
Ribe 198,153	B7
Ringkøbing 242,006	B5
Roskilde 154,314	E6
Sønderjylland 238,502	C7
Storstrøm 252,780	E7
Vejle 306,809	C6
Vestsjaelland 259,484	E6
Viborg 221,002	C4

CITIES and TOWNS

Place	Key
Åbenrå 15,196	C7
Åbybro 2,897	C3
Åkirkeby 2,001	F9
Ålborg 154,582	D4
Ålestrup 1,926	C4
Århus 245,941	D5
Års 4,266	C4
Årup 1,675	D7
AErøskøbing 1,223	D8
Agerbaek 935	B6
Allingaåbro 1,385	D5
Allinge-Sandvig 1,991	F8
Ansager 1,157	B6
Arden 1,303	C4
Asaå 1,344	D3
Askov 904	C7
Asnaes 1,413	E6
Assens, Århus 1,341	D4
Assens, Fyn 5,139	D7
Augustenborg 2,628	D8
Auning 1,516	D5
Avlum 1,729	B5
Baelum 1,169	D4
Bagenkop 776	D8
Ballerup 50,673	F6
Bandholm 693	E8
Bedsted 965	B4
Birkerød 13,663	F6
Bjerringbro 4,761	C5
Bogense 2,861	D6
Bolderslev 774	C8
Børkop 1,410	C6
Borup 1,591	E7
Braedstrup 2,163	C6
Bramming 3,678	B7
Brande 4,784	B6
Bredebro 1,173	B7
Broager 2,143	C8
Brønderslev 10,247	C3
Brørup 2,584	C7
Brovst 4,200	C3
Bryrup 579	C5
Christiansfeld 1,994	C7
Copenhagen (cap.) 603,368	F6
Copenhagen* 1,327,940	F6
Dronninglund 4,661	D3
Dybvad 805	D3
Ebeltoft 3,017	D5
Egernsund 1,323	C8
Egtved 1,311	C6
Ejby 1,372	C7
Esbjerg 68,097	B7
Faåborg 6,495	D7
Fakse 2,720	F7
Fakse Ladeplads 1,799	F7
Farsø 2,821	C4
Farum 9,936	F6
Fjerritslev 2,134	C3
Fredensborg 4,709	F6
Fredericia 36,157	C6
Frederiksberg 101,874	F6
Frederikshavn 24,846	D3
Frederikssund 11,272	E6
Frederiksvaerk 8,903	E6
Fuglebjerg 1,094	E7
Gedser 1,200	F8
Gedsted 1,006	C4
Gelsted 1,307	C7
Gentofte 77,744	F6
Gilleleje 2,943	F5
Give 2,366	C6
Glamsbjerg 2,226	D7
Glostrup 28,326	F6
Glumsø 1,027	E7
Glyngøre 1,071	C4
Gørding 1,261	B7
Gørlev 1,542	E7
Graested 1,654	F5
Gram 2,061	C7
Graåsten 2,947	C8
Grenaå 12,569	D5
Grindsted 7,558	B6
Haårby 1,506	D7
Haderslev 20,042	C7
Hadsten 3,914	C5
Hadsund 3,652	D4
Hals 1,654	D3
Hammel 3,247	C5
Hammerum 3,227	C5
Hanstholm 1,716	B3
Harboør 1,359	B4
Haårlev 1,228	F7
Hasle 18	
Haslev 6,925	E7
Havdrup 1,833	F6
Hedensted 2,659	C6
Hellebaek 2,911	F5
Helsinge 3,613	F6
Helsingør 42,425	F6
Herning 32,973	B5
Hillerød 23,963	F6
Hinnerup 2,061	D5
Hirtshals 6,861	C2
Hjallerup 1,573	C3
Hjerm 647	B5
Hjørring 19,692	C3
Hobro 8,737	C4
Højer 1,416	B8
Højslev 1,641	C4
Holbaek 19,485	E6
Holeby 1,434	E8
Holstebro 25,006	B5
Holsted 1,390	B6
Høng 2,488	E7
Hornslet 2,561	D5
Horsens 44,120	C6
Hørsholm 19,346	F6
Hørve 1,139	E6
Hov 635	D6
Humlum 546	B4
Hundested 5,443	E6
Hurup 2,287	B4
Hvidbjerg 994	B4
Hvide Sande 2,129	A6
Ikast 9,222	C5
Jelling 1,540	C6
Jerslev 798	D3
Juelsminde 1,991	D6
Jyderup 2,901	E6
Kalundborg 12,248	D6
Karise 1,184	F7
Karup 1,694	C5
Kastrup† 17,391	F6
Kerteminde 5,007	D7
Kibaek 1,279	B5
Kjellerup 3,245	C5
Klitmøller 542	B3
København (Copenhagen) (cap.) 603,368	F6
Køge 18,608	F7
Kolding 41,602	C7
Kolind 1,036	D5
Korsør 15,502	E7
Kvaerndrup 891	D7
Langaå 2,320	C5
Lem 1,026	B5
Lemvig 6,448	B4
Løgstør 3,633	C4
Løgumkloster 2,091	B7
Lohals 580	D7
Løjt Kirkeby 1,203	C7
Løkken 1,345	C3
Løsning 1,967	C6
Lundby 747	E7
Lunderskov 1,494	C7
Lyngby 61,516	F6
Malling 1,584	D5
Mariager 1,692	D4
Maribo 5,287	E8
Marstal 4,124	D8
Middelfart 13,315	C7

Agriculture, Industry and Resources

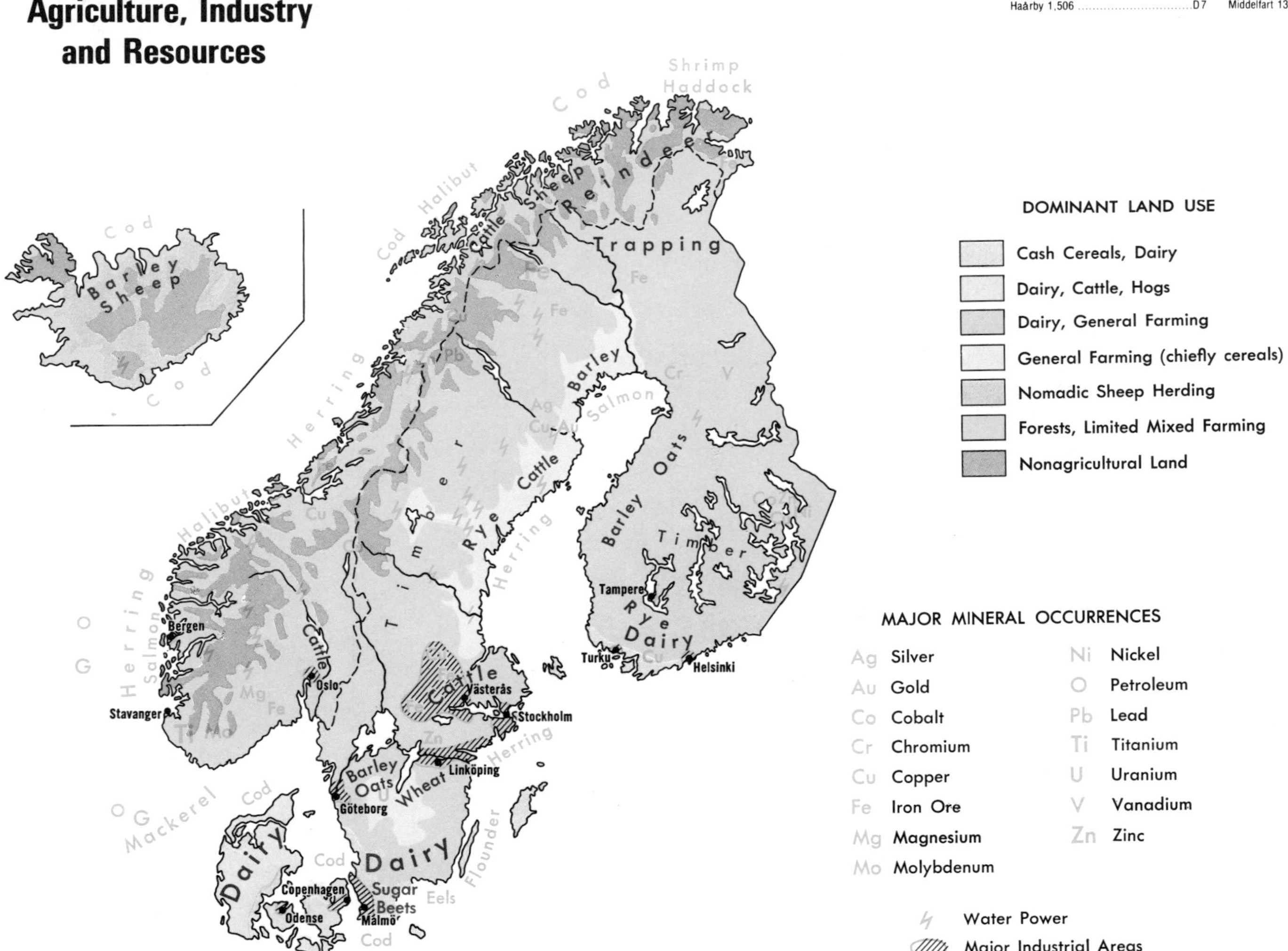

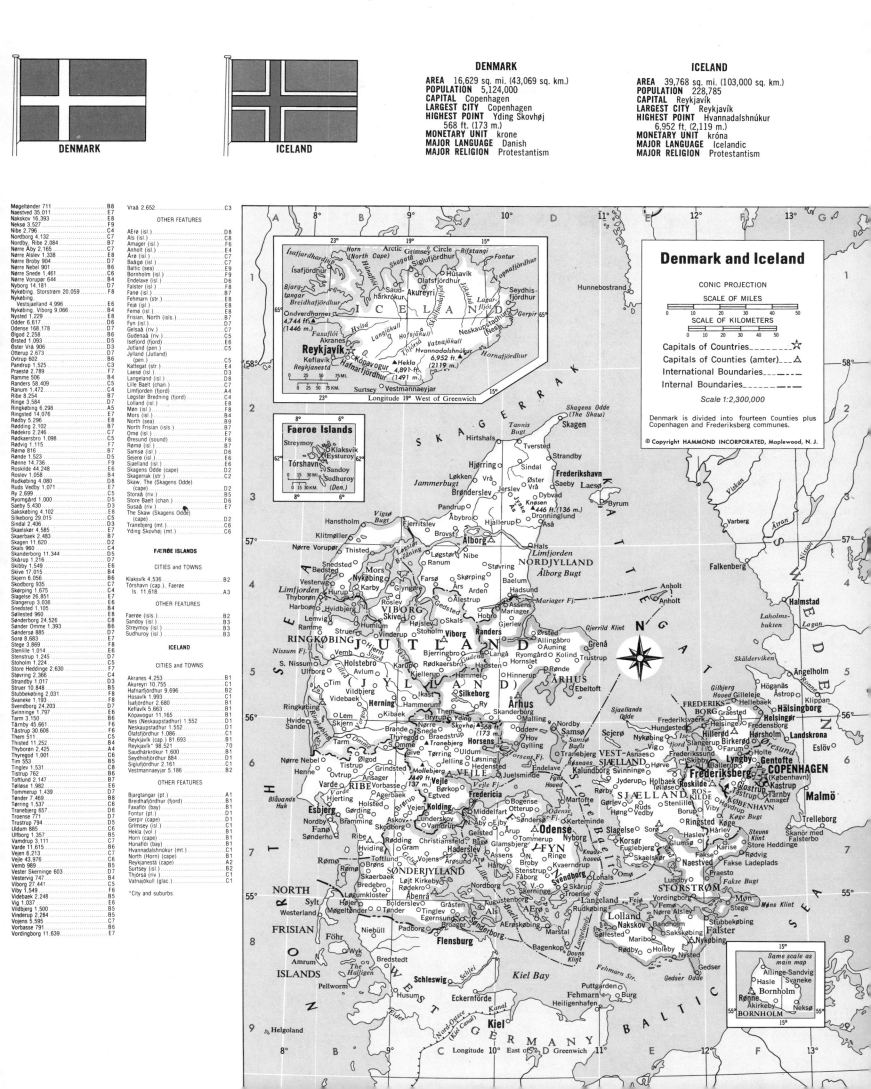

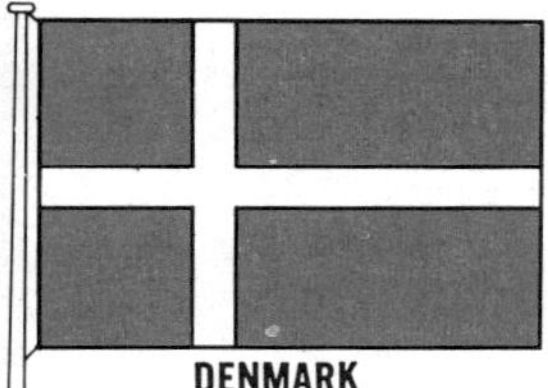

DENMARK

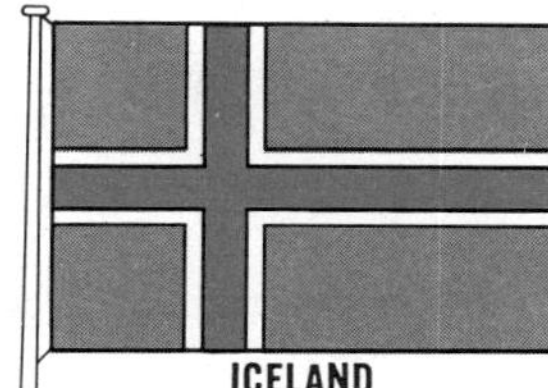

ICELAND

DENMARK

AREA 16,629 sq. mi. (43,069 sq. km.)
POPULATION 5,124,000
CAPITAL Copenhagen
LARGEST CITY Copenhagen
HIGHEST POINT Yding Skovhøj 568 ft. (173 m.)
MONETARY UNIT krone
MAJOR LANGUAGE Danish
MAJOR RELIGION Protestantism

ICELAND

AREA 39,768 sq. mi. (103,000 sq. km.)
POPULATION 228,785
CAPITAL Reykjavík
LARGEST CITY Reykjavík
HIGHEST POINT Hvannadalshnúkur 6,952 ft. (2,119 m.)
MONETARY UNIT króna
MAJOR LANGUAGE Icelandic
MAJOR RELIGION Protestantism

Møgeltønder 711 ... B8
Naestved 35,011 ... E7
Nakskov 16,393 ... E8
Neksø 3,527 ... F9
Nibe 2,796 ... C4
Nordborg 4,132 ... C7
Nordby, Ribe 2,084 ... B7
Nørre Åby 2,165 ... C7
Nørre Alslev 1,338 ... E8
Nørre Broby 904 ... D7
Nørre Nebel 901 ... B6
Nørre Snede 1,461 ... C6
Nørre Vorupør 644 ... B4
Nyborg 14,181 ... D7
Nykøbing, Storstrøm 20,059 ... F8
Nykøbing, Vestsjaelland 4,996 ... E6
Nykøbing, Viborg 9,066 ... B4
Nysted 1,229 ... E8
Odder 6,617 ... D6
Odense 168,178 ... D7
Ølgod 2,258 ... B6
Ørsted 1,093 ... D5
Øster Vrå 906 ... D3
Otterup 2,673 ... D7
Ovtrup 602 ... B6
Pandrup 1,525 ... C3
Praestø 2,789 ... F7
Ramme 506 ... B4
Randers 58,409 ... C5
Ranum 1,472 ... C4
Ribe 8,254 ... B7
Ringe 3,584 ... D7
Ringkøbing 6,298 ... A5
Ringsted 14,076 ... E7
Rødby 5,296 ... E8
Rødding 2,102 ... B7
Rødekro 2,246 ... C7
Rødkaersbro 1,098 ... C5
Rødvig 1,115 ... F7
Rømø 816 ... B7
Rønde 1,523 ... D5
Rønne 14,736 ... F9
Roskilde 44,248 ... E6
Roslev 1,058 ... B4
Rudkøbing 4,080 ... D8
Ruds Vedby 1,071 ... E7
Ry 2,699 ... C5
Ryomgård 1,000 ... D5
Saeby 5,430 ... D3
Sakskøbing 4,102 ... E8
Silkeborg 29,015 ... C5
Sindal 2,406 ... D3
Skaelskør 4,585 ... E7
Skaerbaek 2,483 ... B7
Skagen 11,620 ... D2
Skals 960 ... C4
Skanderborg 11,344 ... D5
Skårup 1,216 ... D7
Skibby 1,549 ... E6
Skive 17,015 ... B4
Skjern 6,056 ... B6
Skodborg 935 ... C7
Skørping 1,675 ... C4
Slagelse 26,851 ... E7
Slangerup 3,036 ... E6
Snedsted 1,105 ... B4
Søllested 960 ... E8
Sønderborg 24,526 ... C8
Sønder Omme 1,393 ... B6
Søndersø 885 ... D7
Sorø 8,683 ... E7
Stege 3,869 ... F8
Stenlille 1,014 ... E6
Stenstrup 1,245 ... D7
Stoholm 1,224 ... C5
Store Heddinge 2,630 ... F7
Støvring 2,366 ... C4
Strandby 1,017 ... D3
Struer 10,848 ... B5
Stubbekøbing 2,031 ... F8
Svaneke 1,193 ... F8
Svendborg 24,203 ... D7
Svinninge 1,797 ... E6
Tarm 3,150 ... B6
Tårnby 45,661 ... F6
Tåstrup 30,608 ... F6
Them 511 ... C5
Thisted 11,252 ... B4
Thyborøn 2,425 ... A4
Thyregod 1,001 ... C6
Tim 553 ... B5
Tinglev 1,531 ... C8
Tistrup 762 ... B6
Toftlund 2,147 ... B7
Tølløse 1,982 ... E6
Tommerup 1,439 ... D7
Tønder 7,469 ... B8
Tørring 1,537 ... C6
Tranebjerg 657 ... D6
Troense 771 ... D7
Trustrup 794 ... D5
Uldum 885 ... C6
Ulfborg 1,357 ... B5
Vamdrup 3,111 ... C7
Varde 11,615 ... B6
Vejen 6,213 ... C7
Vejle 43,976 ... C6
Vemb 989 ... B5
Vester Skerninge 603 ... D7
Vestervig 747 ... B4
Viborg 27,441 ... C5
Viby 1,549 ... F6
Videbaek 2,248 ... B5
Vig 1,037 ... E6
Vildbjerg 1,500 ... B5
Vinderup 2,284 ... B5
Vojens 5,595 ... C7
Vorbasse 791 ... B6
Vordingborg 11,639 ... E7
Vraå 2,652 ... C3

OTHER FEATURES

AErø (isl.) ... D8
Als (isl.) ... C8
Amager (isl.) ... F6
Anholt (isl.) ... E4
Årø (isl.) ... C7
Baågø (isl.) ... C7
Baltic (sea) ... E9
Bornholm (isl.) ... F9
Endelave (isl.) ... D6
Falster (isl.) ... F8
Fanø (isl.) ... B7
Fehmarn (str.) ... E8
Fejø (isl.) ... E8
Femø (isl.) ... E8
Frisian, North (isls.) ... B7
Fyn (isl.) ... D7
Gelsaå (riv.) ... C7
Gudenaå (riv.) ... C5
Isefjord (fjord) ... E6
Jutland (pen.) ... C5
Jylland (Jutland) (pen.) ... C5
Kattegat (str.) ... E4
Laesø (isl.) ... D3
Langeland (isl.) ... D8
Lille Baelt (chan.) ... C7
Limfjorden (fjord) ... A4
Løgstør Bredning (fjord) ... C4
Lolland (isl.) ... E8
Møn (isl.) ... F8
Mors (isl.) ... B4
North (sea) ... B9
North Frisian (isls.) ... B7
Omø (isl.) ... E7
Øresund (sound) ... F6
Rømø (isl.) ... B7
Samsø (isl.) ... D6
Sejerø (isl.) ... E6
Sjaelland (isl.) ... E6
Skagens Odde (cape) ... D2
Skagerrak (str.) ... C2
Skaw, The (Skagens Odde) (cape) ... D2
Storaå (riv.) ... B5
Store Baelt (chan.) ... D6
Susaå (riv.) ... E7
The Skaw (Skagens Odde) (cape) ... D2
Tranebjerg (mt.) ... C6
Yding Skovhøj (mt.) ... C6

FÆRØE ISLANDS

CITIES and TOWNS

Klaksvík 4,536 ... B2
Tórshavn (cap.), Faerøe Is. 11,618 ... A3

OTHER FEATURES

Faerøe (isls.) ... B2
Sandoy (isl.) ... B3
Streymoy (isl.) ... B3
Sudhuroy (isl.) ... B3

ICELAND

CITIES and TOWNS

Akranes 4,253 ... B1
Akureyri 10,755 ... C1
Hafnarfjördhur 9,696 ... B2
Húsavík 1,993 ... C1
Ísafjördhur 2,680 ... B1
Keflavík 5,663 ... B1
Kópavogur 11,165 ... B1
Nes (Neskaupstadhur) 1,552 ... D1
Neskaupstadhur 1,552 ... D1
Ólafsfjördhur 1,086 ... C1
Reykjavík (cap.) 81,693 ... B1
Reykjavík* 98,521 ... 70
Saudhárkrókur 1,600 ... B1
Seydhisfjördhur 884 ... D1
Siglufjördhur 2,161 ... C1
Vestmannaeyjar 5,186 ... B2

OTHER FEATURES

Bjargtangar (pt.) ... A1
Breidhafjördhur (fjord) ... B1
Faxaflói (bay) ... B1
Fontur (pt.) ... D1
Gerpir (cape) ... D1
Grímsey (isl.) ... C1
Hekla (vol.) ... B1
Horn (cape) ... B1
Húnaflói (bay) ... B1
Hvannadalshnúkur (mt.) ... C1
North (Horn) (cape) ... B1
Reykjanestá (cape) ... A2
Surtsey (isl.) ... B2
Thjórsá (riv.) ... C1
Vatnajökull (glac.) ... C1

*City and suburbs.

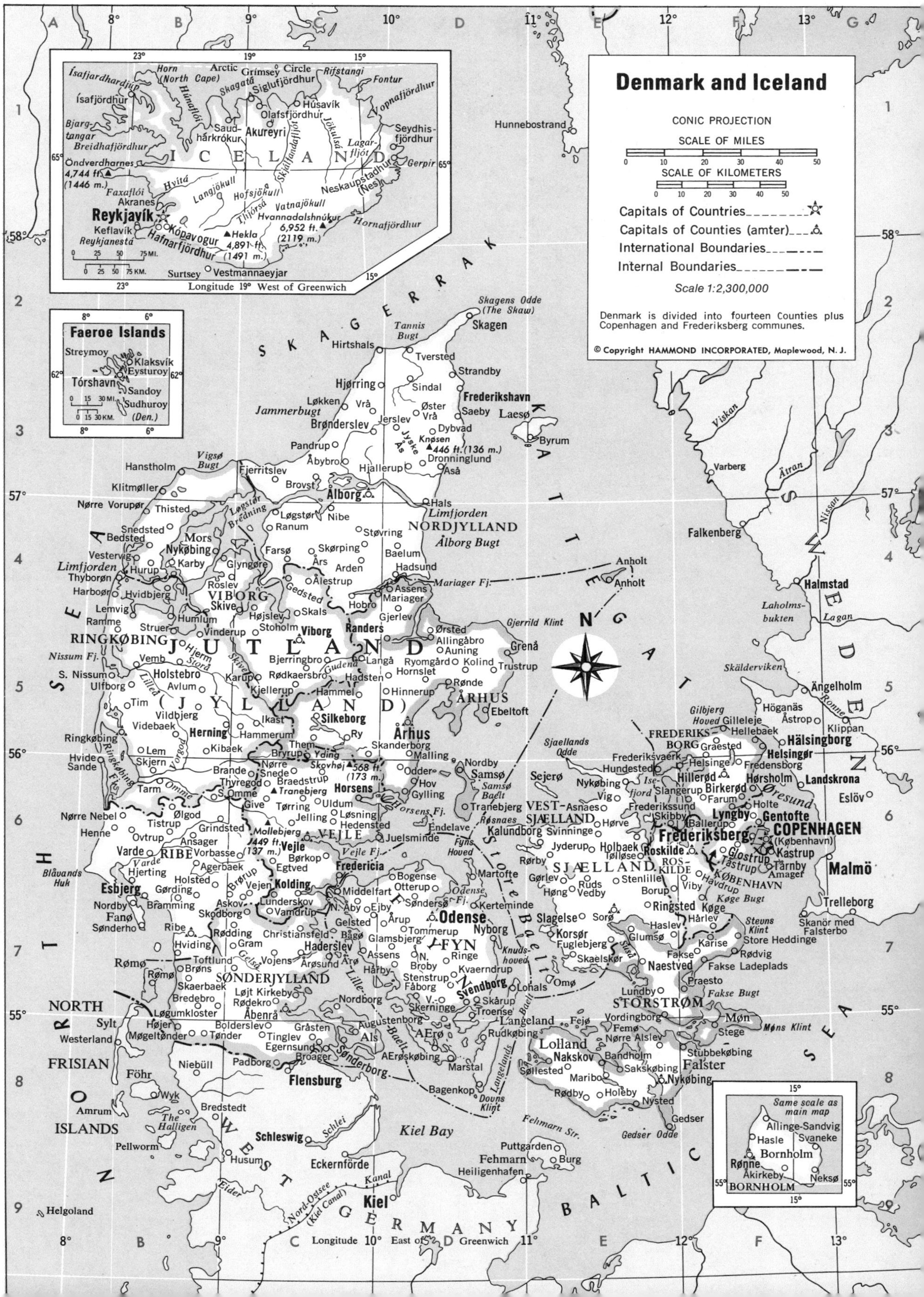

Denmark and Iceland

CONIC PROJECTION

SCALE OF MILES
0 10 20 30 40 50

SCALE OF KILOMETERS
0 10 20 30 40 50

Capitals of Countries
Capitals of Counties (amter)
International Boundaries
Internal Boundaries

Scale 1:2,300,000

Denmark is divided into fourteen Counties plus Copenhagen and Frederiksberg communes.

Longitude 10° East of Greenwich

Germany
CONIC PROJECTION
SCALE OF MILES
0 20 40 60 80
SCALE OF KILOMETERS
0 20 40 60 80
Capitals of Countries
State and District Capitals
International Boundaries
State and District Boundaries
Canals
Scale 1:3,040,000
East Germany is divided into districts bearing the same name as their respective capitals.
DENMARK
NORTH FRISIAN ISLANDS
NORTH SEA
BALTIC SEA
EAST FRISIAN ISLANDS
WEST FRISIAN ISLANDS
SCHLESWIG-HOLSTEIN
MECKLENBURG
Pomerania
BRANDENBURG
EAST GERMANY
LOWER SAXONY
NORTH RHINE-WESTPHALIA
HESSE
THURINGIA
SAXONY
RHINELAND-PALATINATE
SAARLAND
BADEN-WÜRTTEMBERG
BAVARIA
WEST GERMANY
NETHERLANDS
BELGIUM
LUXEMBOURG
FRANCE
SWITZERLAND
AUSTRIA
CZECHOSLOVAKIA
POLAND
Kiel Bay
Mecklenburg Bay
Pomeranian Bay
Helgoland Bay
Lüneburger Heide
Altmark
Teutoburger Wald
Black Forest (Schwarzwald)
Swabian Jura
Franconian Jura
Thüringer Wald
Erzgebirge
Bohemian Forest
Bavarian Forest
Bavarian Alps
Allgäu Alps
Kiel
HAMBURG
Bremen
Hannover
Magdeburg
BERLIN
Potsdam
Schwerin
Rostock
Leipzig
Dresden
Halle
Erfurt
Karl-Marx-Stadt (Chemnitz)
Düsseldorf
Cologne
Bonn
Frankfurt am Main
Wiesbaden
Mainz
Saarbrücken
Stuttgart
Nuremberg (Nürnberg)
MUNICH (München)
Augsburg
Berlin
WEST
EAST
Longitude East 10° of Greenwich
© Copyright HAMMOND INCORPORATED, Maplewood, N.J.

AREA 95,985 sq. mi. (248,601 sq. km.)
POPULATION 61,658,000
CAPITAL Bonn
LARGEST CITY Berlin (West)
HIGHEST POINT Zugspitze 9,718 ft. (2,962 m.)
MONETARY UNIT Deutsche mark
MAJOR LANGUAGE German
MAJOR RELIGIONS Protestantism, Roman Catholicism

AREA 41,768 sq. mi. (108,179 sq. km.)
POPULATION 16,737,000
CAPITAL Berlin (East)
LARGEST CITY Berlin (East)
HIGHEST POINT Fichtelberg 3,983 ft. (1,214 m.)
MONETARY UNIT East German mark
MAJOR LANGUAGE German
MAJOR RELIGIONS Protestantism, Roman Catholicism

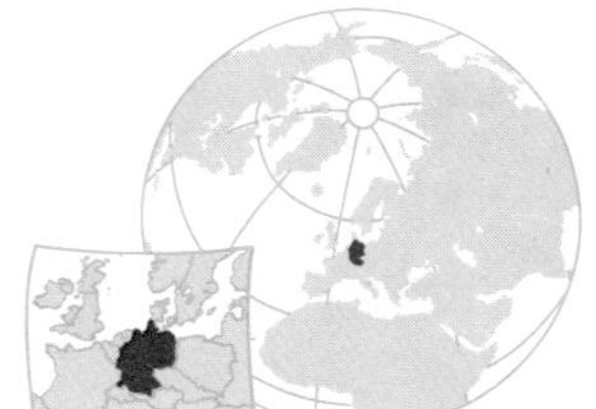

WEST GERMANY

EAST GERMANY

Topography

0 50 100 MI.
0 50 100 KM.

Below Sea Level | 100 m. 328 ft. | 200 m. 656 ft. | 500 m. 1,640 ft. | 1,000 m. 3,281 ft. | 2,000 m. 6,562 ft. | 5,000 m. 16,404 ft.

EAST GERMANY

DISTRICTS

Berlin 1,094,147	F4
Cottbus 872,242	F3
Dresden 1,845,459	E3
Erfurt 1,247,213	D3
Frankfurt 688,637	F2
Gera 738,847	D3
Halle 1,890,187	D3
Karl-Marx-Stadt 1,994,115	E3
Leipzig 1,457,817	E3
Magdeburg 1,297,881	D2
Neubrandenburg 628,686	E2
Potsdam 1,124,892	E2
Rostock 867,806	E1
Schwerin 592,334	D2
Suhl 550,497	D3

CITIES and TOWNS

Aken 11,742	D3
Altenburg 51,193	E3
Angermünde 11,786	E2
Anklam 19,099	E2
Annaberg-Buchholz 26,561	E3
Apolda 28,649	D3
Arnstadt 29,462	D3
Aschersleben 36,674	D3
Aue 32,622	E3
Auerbach 18,168	E3
Bad Doberan 12,541	D1
Bad Dürrenberg 15,192	D3
Bad Langensalza 166,282	D3
Bad Salzungen 17,277	C3
Barth 12,069	E1
Bautzen 45,851	F3
Bergen 13,244	E1
Berlin, East (cap.) 1,094,147	F4
Bernau bei Berlin 15,749	E2
Bernburg 44,428	D3
Bischofswerda 11,540	F3
Bitterfeld 27,062	E3
Blankenburg am Harz 18,784	D3
Boizenburg an der Elbe 12,428	D2
Borna 21,807	E3
Brandenburg 94,071	E2
Burg bei Magdeburg 29,027	D2
Calbe 15,976	D3
Chemnitz (Karl-Marx-Stadt) 303,811	E3
Coswig, Dresden 22,149	E3
Coswig, Halle 12,473	E3
Cottbus 94,293	F3
Crimmitschau 28,845	E3
Delitzsch 24,076	E3
Demmin 17,270	E2
Dessau 100,820	E3
Döbeln 27,624	E3
Dresden 507,692	E3
Ebersbach 12,694	F3
Eberswalde-Finow 47,141	E2
Eilenburg 22,245	E3
Eisenach 49,954	D3
Eisenberg 13,450	D3
Eisenhüttenstadt 46,455	F2
Eisleben 29,297	D3
Erfurt 202,979	D3
Falkensee 25,295	E3
Falkenstein 14,367	E3
Finsterwalde 22,466	E3
Forst 28,084	F3
Frankfurt an der Oder 70,817	F2
Freiberg 50,815	E3
Freital 46,061	E3
Friedland	E2
Fürstenwalde 31,065	F2
Gardelegen 12,987	D2
Genthin 15,916	E2
Gera 113,108	E3
Glauchau 30,927	E3
Görlitz 84,658	F3
Gotha 59,243	D3
Greifswald 53,940	E1
Greiz 37,612	E3
Grevesmühlen 12,005	D2
Grimma 17,100	E3
Grimmen 14,571	E1
Grossenhain 18,712	E3
Grossräschen 12,889	E3
Guben (Wilhelm-Pieck-Stadt) 32,731	F3
Güstrow 36,824	E2
Halberstadt 46,669	D3
Haldensleben 19,194	D2
Halle 241,425	D3
Halle-Neustadt 67,956	D3
Havelberg	D2
Heidenau 21,315	E3
Heiligenstadt 13,931	D3
Hennigsdorf bei Berlin 24,853	E3
Hettstedt 20,291	D3
Hildburghausen 11,372	D3
Hoyerswerda 64,904	F3
Ilmenau 22,021	D3
Jena 99,431	D3
Johanngeorgenstadt 10,328	E3
Jüterbog 13,477	E3
Kamenz 18,221	F3
Karl-Marx-Stadt 303,811	E3
Kleinmachnow 14,059	E4
Klingenthal 13,614	E3
Königs Wusterhausen 11,825	E2
Köpenick 130,987	F4
Köthen 35,451	E3
Kühlungsborn	D1
Lauchhammer 26,939	E3
Leipzig 570,972	E3
Lichtenberg 192,063	F4
Limbach-Oberfrohna 25,706	E3
Löbau 18,077	F3
Lübben 14,224	E3
Lübbenau 22,350	F3
Luckenwalde 28,544	E2
Ludwigslust 13,280	D2
Magdeburg 276,089	D2
Markkleeberg 22,380	E3
Meerane 25,037	E3
Meiningen 26,134	D3
Meissen 43,561	E3
Merseburg 54,269	D3
Meuselwitz 13,585	E3
Mittweida 19,259	E3
Mühlhausen (Thomas-Müntzer-Stadt) 44,106	D3
Nauen 11,940	E2
Naumburg 36,358	D3
Neubrandenburg 59,971	E2
Neuenhagen bei Berlin 12,603	F4
Neuruppin 24,888	E2
Neustrelitz 27,074	E2
Nordhausen 44,442	D3
Oelsnitz 15,084	E3
Oelsnitz im Erzgebirge 16,063	E3
Olbernhau 13,479	E3
Oranienburg 24,452	E2
Oschatz 18,974	E3
Oschersleben 17,377	D2
Pankow 136,527	F3
Parchim 22,927	D2
Pasewalk 15,099	F2
Peenemünde	E1
Perleberg 15,029	D2
Pirna 49,771	E3
Plauen 80,353	E3
Pössneck 18,648	D3
Potsdam 117,236	E2
Prenzlau 22,738	E2
Pritzwalk 11,887	E2
Quedlinburg 29,796	D3
Radeberg 18,528	E3
Radebeul 38,383	E3
Rathenow 32,011	E2
Reichenbach 27,440	E3
Ribnitz-Damgarten 17,254	E1
Riesa 49,989	E3
Rosslau 16,520	E3
Rostock 210,167	E1
Rudolstadt 31,698	D3
Saalfeld 33,648	D3
Salzwedel 21,741	D2
Sangerhausen 32,721	D3
Sassnitz 13,857	E1
Schkeuditz 15,585	E3
Schmalkalden 15,017	D3
Schmölln 13,406	E3
Schneeberg 20,376	E3
Schönebeck 45,197	D2
Schwedt 45,729	F2
Schwerin 104,984	D2
Sebnitz 13,470	F3
Senftenberg 29,953	F3
Sömmerda 20,712	D3
Sondershausen 23,383	D3
Sonneberg 29,193	D3
Spremberg 22,862	F3
Stassfurt 26,225	D3
Stendal 39,647	D2
Stralsund 72,167	E1
Strausberg 21,334	F2
Suhl 36,642	D3
Tangermünde 12,898	D2
Teltow 16,171	E4
Templin 11,718	E2
Thale 17,248	D3
Thomas-Müntzer-Stadt 44,106	D3
Torgau 21,613	E3
Torgelow 14,320	F2
Treptow 127,448	F4
Ueckermünde 11,423	F2
Waldheim 11,925	E3
Waltershausen 13,893	D3
Waren 22,921	E2
Weida 11,816	D3
Weimar 63,144	D3
Weissenfels 43,191	D3
Weissensee 78,451	F3
Weisswasser 25,910	F3
Werdau 22,249	E3
Wernigerode 34,658	D3
Wilhelm-Pieck-Stadt 32,731	F3
Wismar 56,765	D2
Wittenberg 51,364	E3
Wittenberge 32,907	D2
Wolfen 27,570	E3
Wolgast 16,384	E1
Wurzen 20,501	E3
Zehdenick 12,651	E2
Zeitz 44,582	E3
Zella-Mehlis 16,301	D3
Zerbst 19,356	E3
Zeulenroda 13,452	D3
Zittau 42,298	F3
Zwickau 123,069	E3

OTHER FEATURES

Altmark (reg.)	D2
Arkona (cape)	E1
Baltic (sea)	E1
Black Elster (riv.)	E3
Brandenburg (reg.)	E2
Elbe (riv.)	D2
Elde (riv.)	D2
Elster, Black (riv.)	E3
Elster, White (riv.)	E3
Erzgebirge (mts.)	E3
Fichtelberg (mt.)	E3
Harz (mts.)	D3
Havel (riv.)	E2
Lusatia (reg.)	F3
Mecklenburg (bay)	D1
Mecklenburg (reg.)	E2
Mulde (riv.)	E3
Neisse (riv.)	F3
Oder (riv.)	F2
Peene (riv.)	E2
Pomerania (reg.)	E2
Pomeranian (bay)	F1
Rhön (mts.)	D3
Rügen (isl.)	E1
Saale (riv.)	D3
Saxony (reg.)	E3
Spree (riv.)	F3
Spreewald (for.)	F3
Thüringer Wald (for.)	D3
Thuringia (reg.)	D3
Ücker (riv.)	E2
Unstrut (riv.)	D3
Usedom (isl.)	F1
Warnow (riv.)	D2
Werra (riv.)	D3
White Elster (riv.)	E3

WEST GERMANY

STATES

Baden-Württemberg 9,152,700	C4
Bavaria 10,810,400	D4
Berlin (West) (free city) 1,984,800	E4
Bremen 716,800	C2
Hamburg 1,717,400	D2
Hesse 5,549,800	C3
Lower Saxony 7,238,500	C2
North Rhine-Westphalia 17,129,600	B3
Rhineland-Palatinate 3,665,800	B4
Saarland 1,096,300	B4
Schleswig-Holstein 2,582,400	C1

CITIES and TOWNS

Aachen 242,453	B3
Aalen 64,735	D4
Ahaus 27,126	B2
Ahlen 54,214	B3
Ahrensburg 24,964	D2
Alfeld 24,273	C2
Alsdorf 47,473	B3
Alsfeld 18,091	C3
Altena 26,753	B3
Altona	C2
Alzey 15,190	C4
Amberg 46,934	D4
Andernach 27,132	B3
Ansbach 39,117	D4
Arnsberg 80,287	C3
Arolsen 15,619	C3
Aschaffenburg 55,398	C4
Augsburg 249,943	D4
Aurich 34,194	B2
Backnang 29,614	C4
Bad Berleburg 20,415	C3
Bad Driburg 17,478	C3
Bad Dürkheim 16,133	C4
Bad Ems 10,487	B3
Baden-Baden 49,718	C4
Bad Gandersheim 11,614	D3
Bad Harzburg 25,786	D3
Bad Hersfeld 29,248	C3
Bad Homburg vor der Höhe 51,196	C3
Bad Honnef 20,903	B3
Bad Kissingen 22,279	D3
Bad Kreuznach 42,588	B4
Bad Lauterberg im Harz 14,715	D3
Bad Mergentheim 19,895	C4
Bad Münstereifel 14,340	B3
Bad Nauheim 25,916	C3
Bad Neuenahr-Ahrweiler 26,371	B3
Bad Oldesloe 19,640	D2
Bad Pyrmont 21,896	C3
Bad Reichenhall 13,048	E5
Bad Salzuflen 50,924	C2
Bad Schwartau 18,696	D2
Bad Segeberg 13,320	D2
Bad Tölz 12,458	D5
Bad Vilbel 25,012	C3
Bad Waldsee 14,296	C5
Bad Wildungen 15,418	C3
Bad Wimpfen 5,536	C4
Baiersbronn 14,845	C4
Balingen 29,310	C4
Bamberg 74,236	D4
Barsinghausen 32,873	C2
Bassum 14,113	C2
Bayreuth 67,035	D4
Bayrischzell 1,639	E5
Bebra 15,740	C3
Bendorf 15,943	B3
Bensheim 32,653	C4
Bentheim 13,681	B2
Berchtesgaden 8,558	E5
Bergisch Gladbach 99,517	B3
Berleburg (Bad Berleburg) 20,415	C3
Berlin (West) 1,984,837	E4
Biberach an der Riss 28,891	C4
Bielefeld 316,058	C2
Bietigheim-Bissingen 34,042	C4
Bingen 24,541	B4
Birkenfeld 5,883	B4
Blaubeuren 11,652	C4
Böblingen 40,547	C4
Bocholt 65,460	B3
Bochum 414,842	B3
Bonn (cap.) 283,711	B3
Boppard 16,888	B3
Borghorst 17,238	B2
Borken 30,212	B3
Bornheim 32,847	B3
Bottrop 101,495	B3
Brake 18,089	C2
Bramsche 24,119	B2
Braunschweig (Brunswick) 268,519	D2
Breisach am Rhein 9,230	B4
Bremen 572,969	C2
Bremerhaven 143,836	C2
Bremervörde 17,565	C2
Bretten 22,140	C4
Brilon 24,595	C3
Bruchsal 38,929	C4
Brühl 44,305	B3
Brunsbüttel 11,451	C2
Brunswick 268,519	D2
Buchholz in der Nordheide 25,713	C2
Bückeburg 21,393	C2
Büdingen 16,845	C3
Bühl 21,596	C4
Bünde 40,021	C2
Büren 17,352	C3
Burg auf Fehmarn 5,874	D1
Burghausen 16,892	E4
Burgsteinfurt 31,367	B2
Butzbach 20,592	C3
Buxtehude 30,249	C2
Castrop-Rauxel 82,373	B3
Celle 74,347	D2
Cham 12,423	E4
Charlottenburg 201,732	E4
Clausthal-Zellerfeld 16,690	D3
Cloppenburg 19,757	B2
Coburg 46,244	D3
Coesfeld 30,617	B3
Cologne 1,013,771	B3
Crailsheim 24,506	D4
Cuxhaven 60,353	C2
Dachau 33,207	D4
Dahlem	E4
Darmstadt 137,018	C4
Deggendorf 25,188	E4
Delmenhorst 71,488	C2
Detmold 65,629	C3
Diepholz 14,201	C2
Dillenburg 14,068	C3
Dillingen 21,369	B4
Dillingen an der Donau 11,601	D4
Dingolfing 13,325	E4
Dinkelsbühl 10,034	D4
Donaueschingen 17,578	C5
Donauwörth 17,077	D4
Dorsten 65,718	B3
Dortmund 630,609	B3
Duderstadt 23,255	D3
Dudweiler 27,877	B4
Duisburg 591,635	B3
Dülmen 37,013	B3
Düren 87,774	B3
Düsseldorf 664,336	B3
Eberbach 15,834	C4
Ebingen 22,594	C4
Eckernförde 22,938	D1
Ehingen 21,600	C4
Eichstätt 13,080	D4
Einbeck 29,821	C3
Eiserfeld 22,346	C3
Ellwangen 21,994	D4
Elmshorn 41,355	C2
Emden 53,509	B2
Emmendingen 24,722	B4
Emmerich 29,113	B3
Emsdetten 30,195	B2
Erlangen 100,671	D4
Eschwege 24,882	C3
Eschweiler 53,603	B3
Espelkamp 22,670	C2
Essen 677,568	B3
Esslingen am Neckar 95,298	C4
Ettlingen 35,159	C4
Euskirchen 43,558	B3
Eutin 17,701	D1
Fellbach 42,501	C4
Flensburg 93,213	C1
Forchheim 23,430	D4
Frankenberg-Eder 15,337	C3
Frankenthal 43,684	C4
Frankfurt am Main 636,157	C3
Frechen 41,453	B3
Freiburg im Breisgau 175,371	B5
Freising 31,524	D4
Freudenstadt 19,454	C4
Friedberg 24,762	C3
Friedrichshafen 51,544	C5
Fritzlar 15,079	C3
Fulda 58,976	C3
Fürstenfeldbruck 27,194	D4
Fürth 101,639	D4
Füssen 10,506	D5
Gaggenau 28,846	C4
Garbsen 56,337	C2
Garmisch-Partenkirchen 26,831	D5
Gatow	E4
Geesthacht 24,745	D2
Geislingen an der Steige 28,693	C4
Geldern 24,082	B3
Gelnhausen 17,889	C3
Gelsenkirchen 322,584	B3
Georgsmarienhütte 30,259	B2
Geretsried 17,330	D5
Germersheim 12,041	C4
Gerolstein 6,857	B3
Gifhorn 31,635	D2
Glückstadt 12,159	C2
Goch 28,213	B3
Göggingen 15,980	D4
Göppingen 54,365	C4
Goslar 53,957	D3
Göttingen 123,797	D3
Greven 27,479	B2
Grevenbroich 56,392	B3
Griesheim 18,548	C4
Gronau 40,527	B2
Gummersbach 49,316	B3
Günzburg 13,528	D4
Gunzenhausen 13,565	D4
Gütersloh 77,128	C3
Haar 18,824	D4
Hagen 229,224	B3
Haltern 29,750	B3
Hamburg 1,717,383	D2
Hameln 61,066	C2
Hamm 172,210	B3
Hammelburg 12,350	C3
Hanau 86,676	C3
Hannover 552,955	C2
Harburg-Wilhelmsburg	C2
Hassloch 17,752	C4
Haunstetten 21,810	D4
Hechingen 15,926	C4
Heide 21,918	C1
Heidelberg 129,368	C4
Heidenheim an der Brenz 49,943	D4
Heilbronn 113,177	C4
Helmstedt 28,095	D2
Hennef 27,815	B3
Herford 64,385	C2
Herne 190,561	B3
Hildesheim 105,290	D2
Hockenheim 16,890	C4
Hof 54,357	D3
Hofgeismar 13,380	C3
Holzminden 23,650	C3
Homburg 41,861	B4
Horn-Bad Meinberg 16,927	C3
Höxter 32,759	C3
Hückelhoven 34,865	B3
Hünfeld 13,873	C3
Hürth 51,692	B3
Husum 24,984	C1
Hüttental 39,561	C3
Ibbenbüren 42,202	B2
Idar-Oberstein 37,179	B4
Immenstadt im Allgäu 13,720	C5
Ingolstadt 88,500	D4
Iserlohn 96,174	B3
Isny im Allgäu 12,367	D5
Itzehoe 35,077	C2
Jever 12,096	B2
Jülich 31,564	B3
Kaiserslautern 100,886	B4
Karlsruhe 280,448	C4
Kassel 205,534	C3
Kaufbeuren 42,224	D5
Kehl 29,861	B4
Kelheim 11,996	D4
Kempten 56,944	D5
Kevelaer 20,971	B3
Kiel 262,164	D1
Kirchheim unter Teck 31,666	C4
Kitzingen 19,116	C4
Kleve 44,043	B3
Koblenz 118,394	B3
Köln (Cologne) 1,013,771	B3
Königswinter 34,586	B3
Konstanz 70,152	C5
Korbach 22,998	C3
Kornwestheim 27,771	C4
Krefeld 228,463	B3
Kreutztal 30,473	C3
Kronach 11,538	D3
Kulmbach 25,711	D3
Lage 31,724	C3
Lahnstein 19,725	B3
Lahr 35,570	B4
Lampertheim 31,993	C4
Landau in der Pfalz 37,661	C4
Landsberg am Lech 15,862	D4
Landshut 55,858	E4
Langen 30,227	C4
Langenhagen 47,092	C2
Lauenburg an der Elbe 11,077	D2
Lauf an der Pegnitz 19,443	D4
Lauingen 8,778	D4
Lauterbach 15,007	C3
Leer 32,785	B2
Lehrte 38,272	D2
Lemgo 39,664	C2
Lengerich 20,836	B2
Leverkusen 165,947	B3
Lichtenfels 13,719	D3
Limburg an der Lahn 28,606	C3
Lindau 23,930	C5

(continued on following page)

24 Germany
(continued)

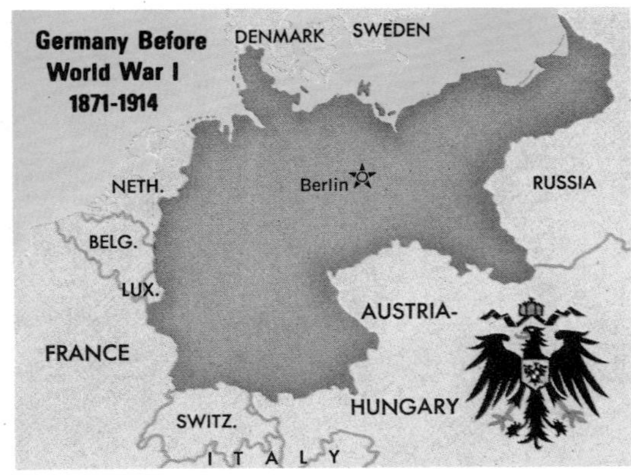

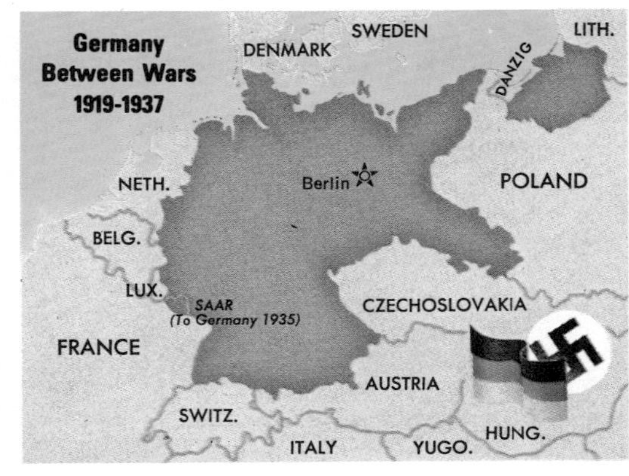

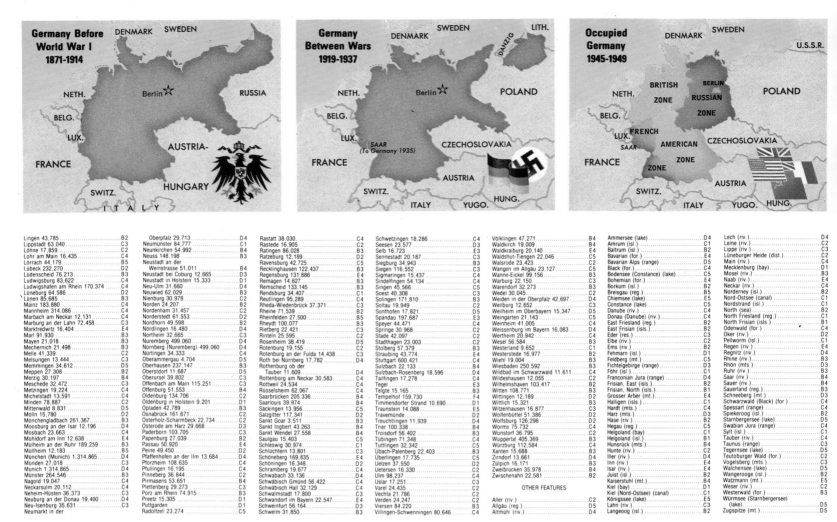

Lingen 43,785 B2
Lippstadt 63,040 C3
Löhne 17,859 C2
Lohr am Main 16,435 C4
Lörrach 44,179 B5
Lübeck 232,270 D2
Lüdenscheid 76,213 B3
Ludwigsburg 83,622 C4
Ludwigshafen am Rhein 170,374 C4
Lüneburg 64,586 D2
Lünen 85,685 B3
Mainz 183,880 C4
Mannheim 314,086 C4
Marbach am Neckar 12,131 C4
Marburg an der Lahn 72,458 C3
Marktredwitz 16,404 E4
Marl 91,930 B3
Mayen 21,018 B3
Mechernich 21,498 B3
Melle 41,339 C2
Melsungen 13,444 C3
Memmingen 34,612 D5
Meppen 27,308 B2
Merzig 30,197 B4
Meschede 32,472 C3
Metzingen 19,224 C4
Michelstadt 13,591 C4
Minden 78,887 C2
Mittenwald 8,831 D5
Mölln 15,780 D2
Mönchengladbach 261,367 B3
Moosburg an der Isar 12,196 D4
Mosbach 23,663 C4
Mühldorf am Inn 12,638 E4
Mülheim an der Ruhr 189,259 B3
Müllheim 12,183 B5
München (Munich) 1,314,865 D4
Münden 27,018 C3
Munich 1,314,865 D4
Münster 264,546 B3
Nagold 19,047 C4
Neckarsulm 20,112 C4
Neheim-Hüsten 36,373 C3
Neuburg an der Donau 19,400 D4
Neu-Isenburg 35,631 C3
Neumarkt in der
Oberpfalz 29,713 D4
Neumünster 84,777 C1
Neunkirchen 54,992 B4
Neuss 148,198 B3
Neustadt an der
Weinstrasse 51,011 B4
Neustadt bei Coburg 12,665 D3
Neustadt in Holstein 15,333 D1
Neu-Ulm 31,660 D4
Neuwied 62,029 B3
Nienburg 30,978 C2
Norden 24,207 B2
Nordenham 31,457 C2
Norderstedt 61,553 D2
Nordhorn 49,598 B2
Nördlingen 16,480 D4
Northeim 32,665 C3
Nuremberg 499,060 D4
Nürnberg (Nuremberg) 499,060 D4
Nürtingen 34,333 C4
Oberammergau 4,704 D5
Oberhausen 237,147 B3
Oberstdorf 11,687 D5
Oberursel 39,802 C3
Offenbach am Main 115,251 C3
Offenburg 51,553 B4
Oldenburg 134,706 C2
Oldenburg in Holstein 9,201 D1
Opladen 42,789 B3
Osnabrück 161,671 C2
Osterholz-Scharmbeck 22,734 C2
Osterode am Harz 29,668 D3
Paderborn 103,705 C3
Papenburg 27,039 B2
Passau 50,920 E4
Peine 49,450 D2
Pfaffenhofen an der Ilm 13,684 D4
Pforzheim 108,635 C4
Pfullingen 16,195 C4
Pinneberg 36,844 C2
Pirmasens 53,651 B4
Plettenberg 29,273 C3
Porz am Rhein 74,915 B3
Preetz 15,305 D1
Puttgarden D1
Radolfzell 23,274 C5
Rastatt 38,030 C4
Rastede 16,905 C2
Ratingen 86,028 B3
Ratzeburg 12,189 D2
Ravensburg 42,725 C5
Recklinghausen 122,437 B3
Regensburg 131,886 E4
Remagen 14,627 B3
Remscheid 133,145 B3
Rendsburg 34,407 C1
Reutlingen 95,289 C4
Rheda-Wiedenbrück 37,371 C3
Rheine 71,539 B2
Rheinfelden 27,500 B5
Rheydt 100,077 B3
Rietberg 22,421 C3
Rinteln 25,595 C2
Rosenheim 38,419 D5
Rotenburg 19,155 C2
Rotenburg an der Fulda 14,438 C3
Roth bei Nürnberg 17,782 D4
Rothenburg ob der
Tauber 11,609 D4
Rottenburg am Neckar 30,583 C4
Rottweil 24,534 C4
Rüsselsheim 62,067 C4
Saarbrücken 205,336 B4
Saarlouis 39,974 B4
Säckingen 13,956 C5
Salzgitter 117,341 D2
Sankt Goar 3,511 B3
Sankt Ingbert 43,263 B4
Sankt Wendel 27,558 B4
Saulgau 15,403 C5
Schleswig 30,974 C1
Schlüchtern 13,801 C3
Schöneberg 169,835 E4
Schöningen 16,348 D2
Schramberg 19,677 C4
Schwabach 33,136 D4
Schwäbisch Gmünd 56,422 C4
Schwäbisch Hall 32,129 C4
Schwalmstadt 17,800 C3
Schwandorf im Bayern 22,547 E4
Schweinfurt 56,164 D3
Schwelm 31,850 B3
Schwetzingen 18,286 C4
Seesen 23,577 D3
Selb 16,723 E3
Sennestadt 20,187 C3
Siegburg 34,943 B3
Siegen 116,552 C3
Sigmaringen 15,437 C4
Sindelfingen 54,134 C4
Singen 45,566 C5
Soest 40,308 C3
Solingen 171,810 B3
Soltau 19,949 C2
Sonthofen 17,821 D5
Spandau 197,687 E3
Speyer 44,471 C4
Springe 30,968 C2
Stade 42,097 C2
Stadthagen 23,003 C2
Stolberg 57,379 B3
Straubing 43,774 E4
Stuttgart 600,421 C4
Sulzbach 22,133 B4
Sulzbach-Rosenberg 18,596 D4
Tailfingen 17,278 C4
Tegel E3
Telgte 15,165 B3
Tempelhof 159,730 F4
Timmendorfer Strand 10,690 D1
Traunstein 14,088 E5
Travemünde D2
Treuchtlingen 11,939 D4
Trier 100,338 B4
Troisdorf 56,402 B3
Tübingen 71,348 C4
Tuttlingen 32,342 C5
Übach-Palenberg 22,403 B3
Überlingen 17,735 C5
Uelzen 37,550 D2
Uetersen 16,330 C2
Ulm 98,237 C4
Uslar 17,251 C3
Varel 24,435 C2
Vechta 21,786 C2
Verden 24,247 C2
Viersen 84,220 B3
Villingen-Schwenningen 80,646 C4
Völklingen 47,271 B4
Waldkirch 19,009 B4
Waldkraiburg 20,140 E4
Waldshut-Tiengen 22,046 C5
Walsrode 23,423 C2
Wangen im Allgäu 23,127 C5
Wanne-Eickel 99,156 B3
Warburg 22,150 C3
Warendorf 32,273 B3
Wedel 30,045 C2
Weiden in der Oberpfalz 42,697 D4
Weilburg 12,652 C3
Weilheim im Oberbayern 15,347 D5
Weingarten 21,143 C5
Weinheim 41,005 C4
Weissenburg im Bayern 16,083 D4
Wertheim 20,942 C4
Wesel 56,584 B3
Westerland 9,652 C1
Westerstede 16,977 B2
Wiehl 19,004 B3
Wiesbaden 250,592 B3
Wildbad im Schwarzwald 11,611 C4
Wildeshausen 12,055 C2
Wilhelmshaven 103,417 B2
Witten 108,771 B3
Wittingen 12,189 D2
Wittlich 15,321 B3
Witzenhausen 16,877 C3
Wolfenbüttel 51,386 D2
Wolfsburg 126,298 D2
Worms 75,732 C4
Wunstorf 36,795 C2
Wuppertal 405,369 B3
Würzburg 112,584 C4
Xanten 15,688 B3
Zirndorf 13,661 D4
Zülpich 16,171 B3
Zweibrücken 35,978 B4
Zwischenahn 22,581 B2

OTHER FEATURES

Aller (riv.) C2
Allgäu (reg.) D5
Altmühl (riv.) D4
Ammersee (lake) D4
Amrum (isl.) C1
Baltrum (isl.) B2
Bavarian (for.) E4
Bavarian Alps (range) D5
Black (for.) C4
Bodensee (Constance) (lake) C5
Bohemian (for.) E4
Borkum (isl.) B2
Breisgau (reg.) B5
Chiemsee (lake) E5
Constance (lake) C5
Danube (riv.) C4
Donau (Danube) (riv.) C4
East Friesland (reg.) B2
East Frisian (isls.) B2
Eder (res.) C3
Elbe (riv.) C2
Ems (riv.) B2
Fehmarn (isl.) D1
Feldberg (mt.) C5
Fichtelgebirge (range) D3
Föhr (isl.) C1
Franconian Jura (range) D4
Frisian, East (isls.) B2
Frisian, North (isls.) B1
Grosser Arber (mt.) E4
Halligen (isls.) C1
Hardt (mts.) C4
Harz (mts.) D3
Hase (riv.) B2
Hegau (reg.) C5
Helgoland (bay) C1
Helgoland (isl.) B1
Hunsrück (mts.) B4
Hunte (riv.) C2
Iller (riv.) D4
Inn (riv.) E4
Isar (riv.) E4
Juist (isl.) B2
Kaiserstuhl (mt.) B4
Kiel (bay) D1
Kiel (Nord-Ostsee) (canal) C1
Königssee (lake) E5
Lahn (riv.) C3
Langeoog (isl.) B2
Lech (riv.) D4
Leine (riv.) C2
Lippe (riv.) C3
Lüneburger Heide (dist.) C2
Main (riv.) C4
Mecklenburg (bay) D1
Mosel (riv.) B3
Naab (riv.) E4
Neckar (riv.) C4
Norderney (isl.) B2
Nord-Ostsee (canal) C1
Nordstrand (isl.) C1
North (sea) B2
North Friesland (reg.) C1
North Frisian (isls.) B1
Odenwald (for.) C4
Oker (riv.) D2
Pellworm (isl.) C1
Regen (riv.) E4
Regnitz (riv.) D4
Rhine (riv.) B3
Rhön (mts.) D3
Ruhr (riv.) B3
Saar (riv.) B4
Sauer (riv.) B4
Sauerland (reg.) B3
Schneeberg (mt.) D3
Schwarzwald (Black) (for.) C4
Spessart (range) C4
Spiekeroog (isl.) B2
Starnbergersee (lake) D5
Swabian Jura (range) C4
Sylt (isl.) C1
Tauber (riv.) C4
Taunus (range) C3
Tegernsee (lake) D5
Teutoburger Wald (for.) C2
Vogelsberg (mts.) C3
Walchensee (lake) D5
Wangerooge (isl.) B2
Watzmann (mt.) E5
Weser (riv.) C2
Westerwald (for.) B3
Würmsee (Starnbergersee)
(lake) D5
Zugspitze (mt.) D5

Agriculture, Industry and Resources

DOMINANT LAND USE

- Wheat, Sugar Beets
- Cereals (chiefly rye, oats, barley)
- Potatoes, Rye
- Dairy, Livestock
- Mixed Cereals, Dairy
- Truck Farming
- Grapes, Fruit
- Forests

MAJOR MINERAL OCCURRENCES

Ag	Silver	K	Potash
Ba	Barite	Lg	Lignite
C	Coal	Na	Salt
Cu	Copper	O	Petroleum
Fe	Iron Ore	Pb	Lead
G	Natural Gas	U	Uranium
Gr	Graphite	Zn	Zinc

Water Power
Major Industrial Areas

AREA 15,892 sq. mi. (41,160 sq. km.)
POPULATION 14,227,000
CAPITALS The Hague, Amsterdam
LARGEST CITY Amsterdam
HIGHEST POINT Vaalserberg 1,056 ft. (322 m.)
MONETARY UNIT guilder (florin)
MAJOR LANGUAGE Dutch
MAJOR RELIGIONS Protestantism, Roman Catholicism

AREA 11,781 sq. mi. (30,513 sq. km.)
POPULATION 9,855,110
CAPITAL Brussels
LARGEST CITY Brussels (greater)
HIGHEST POINT Botrange 2,277 ft. (694 m.)
MONETARY UNIT Belgian franc
MAJOR LANGUAGES French (Walloon), Flemish
MAJOR RELIGION Roman Catholicism

AREA 999 sq. mi. (2,587 sq. km.)
POPULATION 364,000
CAPITAL Luxembourg
LARGEST CITY Luxembourg
HIGHEST POINT Ardennes Plateau 1,825 ft. (556 m.)
MONETARY UNIT Luxembourg franc
MAJOR LANGUAGES Luxembourgeois (Letzeburgisch), French, German
MAJOR RELIGION Roman Catholicism

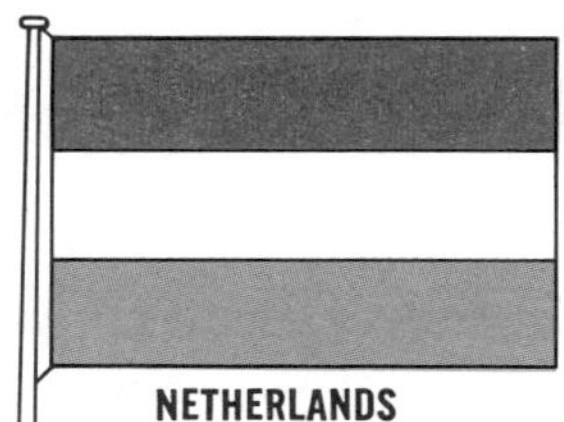
NETHERLANDS

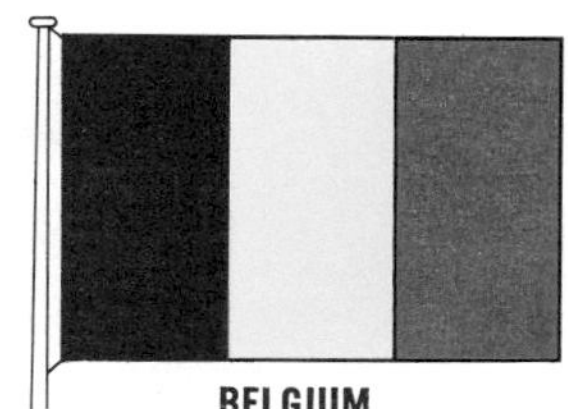
BELGIUM

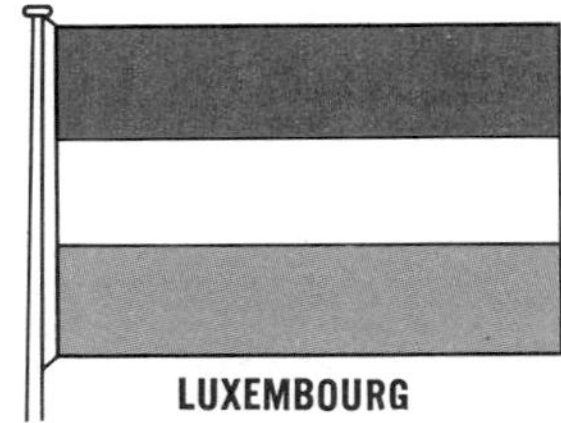
LUXEMBOURG

BELGIUM

PROVINCES

Antwerp 1,533,249 F6
Brabant 2,176,373 F7
East Flanders 1,310,117 D7
Hainaut 1,317,453 D7
Liège 1,008,905 H7
Limburg 652,547 G7
Luxembourg 217,310 G9
Namur 380,561 F8
West Flanders 1,054,429 B7

CITIES and TOWNS†

Aalst 46,659 D7
Aalter 9,173 C6
Aarlen (Arlon) 13,745 H9
Aarschot 12,474 F7
Aat (Ath) 11,842 D7
Alken 8,677 G7
Alost (Aalst) 46,659 D7
Amay 7,617 G7
Andenne 8,091 G8
Anderlecht 103,796 B9
Anderlues 12,176 E8
Ans H7
Antoing 3,426 C7
Antwerp 224,543 E6
Antwerp* 928,000 E6
Antwerpen (Antwerp) 224,543 E6
Ardooie 7,081 C7
Arendonk 9,919 G6
Arlon 13,745 H9
As 5,496 H6
Asse 6,583 E7
Ath 11,842 D7
Attert H9
Aubange 3,761 H9
Audenarde (Oudenaarde) 26,615 D7
Auderghem 34,546 C9
Auvelais 8,287 F8
Aywaille 3,850 H8
Baerle-Hertog F6
Balen 15,110 G6
Basse-Sambre F8
Bastenaken (Bastogne) 6,816 H9
Bastogne 6,816 H9
Beernem C6
Beloeil D7
Berchem 50,241 F6
Berchem-Sainte-Agathe 19,087 B9
Bergen (Mons) 59,362 E8
Beringen G6
Bertogne H8
Bertrix 4,562 G9
Beveren 15,913 E6
Bilzen 7,178 G7
Binche 10,098 E8
Blankenberge 13,969 C6
Bocholt 6,497 H6
Boom 16,584 E6
Borgerhout 49,002 E6
Borgloon 3,412 G7
Borgworm (Waremme) 10,956 G7
Bourg-Léopold (Leopoldsburg) 9,593 G6
Boussu 11,474 D8
Braine-l'Alleud 18,531 E7
Braine-le-Comte 11,957 D7
Brecht F6
Bredene 9,244 B6
Bree 10,389 H6
Bruges 117,220 C6
Brugge (Bruges) 117,220 C6
Brussels (cap.)* 1,054,970 C9
Bruxelles (Brussels) (cap.)* 1,054,970 C9
Cerfontaine E8
Charleroi 23,689 E8
Charleroi* 458,000 E8
Chastre F7
Châtelet 14,752 F8
Chièvres 3,283 D7
Chimay 3,288 E8
Chiny G9
Ciney 7,536 G8
Comblain-au-Pont 3,582 G8
Comines 8,192 B7
Courcelles 17,015 E8
Courtrai (Kortrijk) 44,961 C7
Couvin 4,234 F8
Damme C6
De Haan C6
Deinze 16,711 C7
Denderleeuw 9,925 E7
Dendermonde 22,119 E6
De Panne 6,985 B6
Dessel 7,505 G6
Destelbergen D6
Deurne 80,766 F6
Diest 10,799 F7
Diksmuide 6,669 B6
Dilbeek 15,108 B9
Dilsen H6
Dinant 9,747 G8
Dison 8,466 H7
Dixmude (Diksmuide) 6,669 B6
Doische F8
Doornik (Tournai) 32,794 C7
Dour 10,059 D8
Drogenbos 4,840 B10
Duffel 13,802 F6
Durbuy H8
Ecaussinnes 6,630 E7
Edingen (Enghien) 4,115 D7
Eeklo 19,144 D6
Éghezée F7
Eigenbrakel (Braine-l'Alleud) 18,531 E7
Ekeren 27,648 E6
Ellezelles 3,556 D7
Enghien 4,115 D7
Érezée G8
Erquelinnes 4,471 E8
Esneux 6,183 H7
Essen 10,795 F6
Estampuis C7
Etterbeek 51,030 B9
Eupen 14,879 J7
Evere 26,957 C9
Evergem 12,886 D6
Farciennes E8
Fernelmont F7
Ferrières H8
Flémalle 8,135 G7
Fleurus 8,523 E8
Florennes 4,107 F8
Forest 55,135 B9
Fosses-La-Ville 3,972 F8
Frameries 11,224 D8
Froidchapelle E8
Furnes (Veurne) 9,496 B6
Ganshoren 21,147 B9
Geel 29,346 F6
Geldenaken (Jodoigne) 4,132 F7
Gembloux-sur-Orneau 11,249 F7
Genk 57,913 H7
Gent (Ghent) 148,860 D6
Geraardsbergen 17,533 D7
Gerpinnes F8
Ghent 148,860 D6
Ghent* 477,000 D6
Gistel B6
Gooik E7
Gouvy H8
Grammont (Geraardsbergen) 17,533 D7
Grez-Doiceau F7
Grimbergen E7
Haacht 4,436 F7
Habay H9
Hal (Halle) 20,017 E7
Halen 5,322 G7
Halle 20,017 E7
Hamme 17,559 E6
Hamois G8
Hamont-Achel 6,893 H6
Hannuit (Hannut) 7,232 G7
Hannut 7,232 G7
Harelbeke 18,498 C7
Hasselt 39,663 G7
Hastière F8
Heist-Knokke 27,582 C6
Heist-op-den-Berg 13,472 F6
Hensies D8
Herentals 18,639 F6
Herne E7
Herselt 7,412 F6
Herstal 29,600 H7
Herve 4,118 H7
Heuvelland B7
Hoboken 33,693 E6
Hoei (Huy) 12,736 G8
Hoeselt 6,884 G7
Honnelles D8
Hoogstraten 4,381 F6
Hotton G8
Huy 12,736 G8
Ichtegem B6
Ieper 20,825 B7
Ingelmunster 10,245 C7
Ittre E7
Ixelles 86,450 C9
Izegem 22,928 C7
Jabbeke C6
Jemappes 18,632 D8
Jette 40,013 B9
Jodoigne 4,132 F7
Kalmthout 12,724 F6
Kapellen 13,352 E6
Kasterlee F6
Kinrooi H6
Knokke-Heist 27,582 C6
Koekelare 7,807 B6
Koekelberg 17,570 B9
Koksijde B6
Kontich 14,432 E6
Kortemark 5,904 C6
Kortrijk 44,961 C7
Kraainem 11,390 C9
La Louvière 23,310 E8
La Louvière* 113,259 E8
Lanaken 8,659 H7
Landen 5,740 G7
Langemark-Poelkapelle 5,457 B7
Lasne F7
Lede 10,316 D7
Léglise H9
Leopoldsburg 9,593 G6
Le Roeulx E8
Lessen (Lessines) 8,906 D7
Lessines 8,906 D7
Leuven 30,623 F7
Leuze-en-Hainaut 7,185 D7
Libin G9
Libramont-Chevigny 2,975 G9
Lichtervelde 7,459 C6
Liedekerke 10,482 D7
Liège 145,573 H7
Liège* 622,000 H7
Lier 28,416 F6
Lierre (Lier) 28,416 F6
Limbourg 3,762 J7
Limburg (Limbourg) 3,762 J7
Linkebeek 4,265 C10
Linter G7
Lochristi D6
Lokeren 26,740 D6
Lommel 21,984 G6
Lontzen H9
Looz (Borgloon) 3,412 G7
Lo-Reninge B7
Louvain (Leuven) 30,623 F7
Luik (Liège) 145,573 H7
Lummen G7
Maaseik 8,622 H6
Maasmechelen H7
Machelen 7,057 C9
Maldegem 14,474 C6
Malines (Mechelen) 65,466 F6
Malmédy 6,464 J8
Manage E7
Manhay H8
Marche-en-Famenne 4,567 G8
Marchin 4,206 G8
Mechelen 65,466 F6
Meerhout 8,567 G6
Meise E7
Menen 22,037 C7
Menin (Menen) 22,037 C7
Merchtem 8,998 E7
Merelbeke 13,837 D7
Merksem 39,768 E6
Merksplas 5,065 F6
Messancy 3,150 H9
Mettet 3,372 F8
Meulebeke 10,458 C7
Middelkerke B6
Moeskroen (Mouscron) 37,311 C7
Mol 28,823 G6
Molenbeek-Saint-Jean 68,411 B9
Momignies E8
Mons 59,362 E8
Montigny-le-Tilleul E8
Moorslede B7
Mortsel 28,012 E6
Mouscron 37,311 C7
Namen (Namur) 32,269 F8
Namur 32,269 F8
Nassogne G8
Nazareth D7
Neerpelt 8,771 G6
Neufchâteau 2,670 G9
Nevele D6
Nieuport (Nieuwpoort) 8,273 B6
Nieuwpoort 8,273 B6
Nijvel (Nivelles) 16,126 E7
Ninove 12,428 D7
Nivelles 16,126 E7
Ohey G8
Onhaye F8
Oostende (Ostend) 71,227 B6
Oostkamp 8,999 C6
Opwijk 9,699 E7
Ostend 71,227 B6
Oudenaarde 26,615 D7
Oudenburg B6
Oud-Turnhout 9,245 F6
Oupeye H7
Overijse 16,181 F7
Overpelt 10,470 G6
Paliseul G9
Peer 7,201 G6
Péruwelz 7,878 D8
Philippeville 2,076 E8
Plombières F7
Pont-à-Celles E8
Poperinge 12,671 B7
Profondeville F8
Putte 6,953 F6
Quaregnon 17,688 D8
Quévy D8
Quiévrain 5,510 D8
Raeren 3,655 J7
Ravels G6
Rebecq 3,744 E7
Renaix (Ronse) 25,056 D7
Rendeux H8
Retie 6,619 G6
Rochefort 4,357 G8
Roeselare 40,428 C7
Ronse 25,056 D7
Roulers (Roeselare) 40,428 C7
Rouvroy G9
Ruislede C6
Sainte-Ode H8
Saint-Georges-sur-Meuse 6,003 G7
Saint-Gilles 55,055 B9
Saint-Hubert 3,091 G8
Saint-Josse-ten-Noode 23,633 C9
Saint-Nicolas G7
Saint-Trond (Sint-Truiden) 21,473 G7
Saint-Vith (Sankt Vith) 3,001 J8
Sankt Vith 3,001 J8
Schaerbeek 118,950 C9
Schoten 29,914 F6
Seraing 40,545 G7
's-Gravenbrakel (Braine-le-Comte) 11,957 D7
Sint-Laureins D6
Sint-Niklaas 49,214 E6

(continued on following page)

Agriculture, Industry and Resources

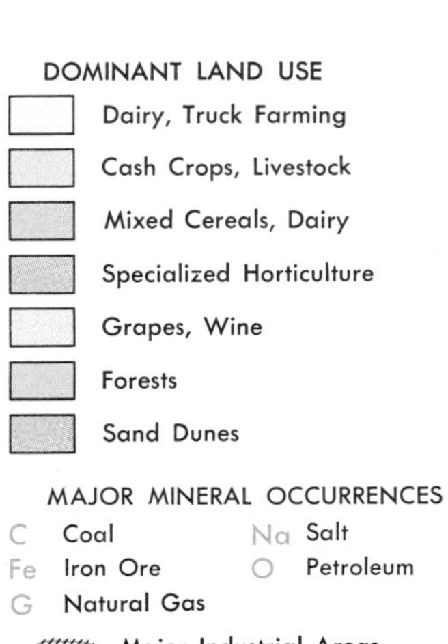

Netherlands, Belgium and Luxembourg

(continued)

Sint-Pieters-Leeuw 16,856 ... B9
Sint-Truiden 21,473 ... G7
Soignies 12,006 ... D7
Somme-Leuze ... G8
Spa 9,504 ... H8
Sprimont ... H8
Staden 5,499 ... B7
Stavelot 4,723 ... H8
Steenokkerzeel 4,037 ... C9
Stekene ... E6
Stoumont ... H8
Tamise (Temse) 14,950 ... E6
Tellin ... G8
Temse 14,950 ... E6
Tenneville ... H8
Termonde (Dendermonde) 22,119 ... E6
Tessenderlo 11,778 ... G6
Theux 5,316 ... H8
Thuin 5,777 ... E8
Tielt 14,077 ... C7
Tielt-Winge 3,743 ... F7
Tienen 24,134 ... F7
Tintigny ... G9
Tirlemont (Tienen) 24,134 ... F7
Tongeren 20,136 ... G7
Tongres (Tongeren) 20,136 ... G7
Torhout 15,156 ... C6
Tournai 32,794 ... C7
Trois-Ponts ... H8
Tubeke (Tubize) 11,507 ... E7
Tubize 11,507 ... E7
Turnhout 38,007 ... F6
Uccle 78,909 ... B9
Ukkel (Uccle) 78,909 ... B9
Vaux-sur-Sûre ... H9
Verviers 33,587 ... H7
Veurne 9,496 ... B6
Vielsalm 3,587 ... H8
Vilvoorde 34,633 ... F7
Vilvorde (Vilvoorde) 34,633 ... F7
Viroinval ... F8
Virton 3,558 ... H9
Visé 6,880 ... H7
Vleteren ... B7
Vorst (Forest) 55,135 ... B9
Vresse-sur-Semois ... F9
Waarschoot 7,905 ... D6
Wachtebeke ... D6
Waregem 17,725 ... C7
Waremme 10,956 ... G7
Waterloo 17,764 ... E7
Watermaal-Bosvoorde
(Watermael-Boitsfort ... C9
Watermael-Boitsfort 25,123 ... C9
Waver (Wavre) 11,767 ... F7
Wavre 11,767 ... F7
Wellin ... G8
Wemmel 12,631 ... B9
Wervik 12,672 ... B7
Westerlo 14,173 ... F6
Westmalle ... F6
Wetteren 20,816 ... D7
Wezembeek-Oppem 10,899 ... D9
Wezet (Visé) 6,880 ... H7
Willebroek 15,726 ... E6
Wilrijk 43,485 ... E6
Wingene 7,140 ... C6
Woluwe-Saint-Lambert 47,360 ... C9
Woluwe-Saint-Pierre 40,884 ... C9
Ypres (Ieper) 20,825 ... B7
Zaventem 10,625 ... C9
Zedelgem ... C6
Zeebrugge ... C6
Zele 18,585 ... E6
Zelzate 12,785 ... D6
Zemst ... E7
Zinnik (Soignies) 12,006 ... D7
Zonhoven 13,484 ... G6
Zottegem 21,461 ... D7
Zuienkerke ... C6

OTHER FEATURES

Albert, (canal) ... F6
Ardennes, (for.) ... F9
Botrange, (mt.) ... J8
Dender, (riv.) ... D7
Deûle, (riv.) ... B7
Dyle, (riv.) ... F7
Hohe Venn, (plat.) ... H8
Lesse, (riv.) ... F8
Lys, (riv.) ... B7
Mark, (riv.) ... F6
Meuse, (riv.) ... F8
Nethe, (riv.) ... F6
North, (sea) ... D4
Ourthe, (riv.) ... G8
Rupel, (riv.) ... F7
Sambre, (riv.) ... D8
Schelde (Scheldt), (riv.) ... C7
Scheldt, (riv.) ... C7
Schnee Eifel, (plat.) ... J8
Semois, (riv.) ... G9
Senne, (riv.) ... E7
Vaalserberg, (mt.) ... J7
Vesdre, (riv.) ... H7
Weisserstein, (mt.) ... J8
Yser, (riv.) ... B7
Zitterwald, (plat.) ... J8

LUXEMBOURG

CITIES and TOWNS

Clervaux 916 ... J8
Diekirch† 5,059 ... J9
Differdange 9,287 ... H9
Dudelange† 14,615 ... J10
Echternach† 3,792 ... J9
Esch-sur-Alzette† 27,574 ... J9
Ettelbruck† 5,990 ... J9
Grevenmacher† 2,918 ... J9
Luxembourg (cap.) 78,272 ... J9
Mamer 3,123 ... H9
Mersch 1,869 ... J9
Pétange 6,234 ... H9
Remich† 12,138 ... J9
Vianden† 1,520 ... J9
Wiltz 1,601 ... H9

OTHER FEATURES

Alzette, (riv.) ... J9
Clerf, (riv.) ... J8
Eisling, (mts.) ... H9
Mosel, (riv.) ... J9
Our, (riv.) ... J9
Sauer, (riv.) ... J9

NETHERLANDS

PROVINCES

Drenthe 405,924 ... K3
Dronten 15,343 ... H4
Friesland 560,614 ... H2
Gelderland 1,639,997 ... H4
Groningen 540,062 ... K2
Lelystad ... H4
Limburg 1,051,620 ... H6
North Brabant 1,967,261 ... F5
North Holland 2,295,875 ... F3
Overijssel 985,569 ... J4
South Holland 3,048,648 ... E5
Utrecht 867,909 ... G4
Zeeland 332,286 ... D6
Zuidelijke
IJsselmeerpolders 14,231 ... H4

CITIES and TOWNS†

Aalsmeer 20,779 ... F4
Aalten 17,486 ... K5
Aardenburg 3,869 ... C6
Akkrum 5,044 ... H2
Alkmaar 65,199 ... F3
Almelo 62,634 ... K4
Alphen aan de Rijn 46,065 ... F4
Amersfoort 87,784 ... G4
Amstelveen 71,803 ... B5
Amsterdam (cap.) 751,156 ... B4
Amsterdam* 987,205 ... B4
Andijk 5,301 ... G3
Apeldoorn 134,055 ... H4
Apeldoorn* 237,231 ... H4
Appingedam 13,295 ... K2
Arnhem 126,051 ... H4
Arnhem* 281,126 ... H4
Assen 43,783 ... K3
Asten 12,295 ... H6
Axel 12,072 ... D6
Baarle-Nassau 5,583 ... F6
Baarn 25,045 ... G4
Barneveld 34,189 ... H4
Bath ... E6
Beilen 12,948 ... K3
Bemmel 14,218 ... H5
Bergeijk 9,009 ... G6
Bergen 14,306 ... F3
Bergen op Zoom 40,770 ... E5
Bergum 28,047 ... H2
Berkel 9,367 ... F5
Berkhout 5,167 ... F3
Beverwijk 37,551 ... F4
Blerick ... J6
Bloemendaal 17,940 ... E4
Blokzijl ... H3
Bodegraven 15,848 ... F4
Bolsward 9,934 ... H2
Borculo 9,859 ... J4
Borger 12,017 ... K3
Borne 18,216 ... K4
Boskoop 12,985 ... F4
Boxmeer 12,662 ... H5
Boxtel 22,465 ... G5
Breda 118,086 ... F5
Breda* 151,182 ... F5
Breezand ... F3
Breskens ... C6
Brielle 10,620 ... E5
Brouwershaven 3,263 ... D5
Brummen 20,460 ... J4
Brunssum 26,116 ... J7
Buiksloot ... C4
Bussum 37,848 ... G4
Capelle 35,696 ... F5
Coevorden 13,089 ... K3
Colijnsplaat ... D5
Culemborg 17,682 ... G5
Cuyk 15,366 ... H5
Dalen 5,084 ... K3
De Bilt 32,588 ... G4
Dedemsvaart 12,975 ... J3
De Koog ... F2
Delft 86,103 ... E4
Delfzijl 23,316 ... K2
Den Burg 12,132 ... F2
Denekamp 11,533 ... L4
Den Helder 60,421 ... F3
Deurne 26,539 ... H6
Deventer 65,557 ... J4
Didam 14,263 ... J5
De Wijk 4,631 ... J3
Diemen 13,704 ... C5
Dieren ... J4
Diever 3,162 ... J3
Dinxperlo 7,296 ... K5
Dirksland 6,495 ... E5
Doesburg 9,759 ... J4
Doetinchem 34,915 ... J5
Dokkum 11,203 ... H2
Domburg 3,874 ... C5
Dongen 19,219 ... F5
Doorn 11,966 ... G4
Dordrecht 101,840 ... F5
Dordrecht* 186,793 ... F5
Drachten 45,390 ... J2
Driebergen 17,022 ... G4
Dronten 16,544 ... H3
Druten 11,113 ... H5
Echt 17,035 ... H6
Edam-Volendam 21,507 ... G4
Ede 79,897 ... H4
Egmond aan Zee 5,734 ... E3
Eindhoven 192,562 ... G6
Eindhoven* 358,234 ... G6
Elburg 18,082 ... H4
Elst 16,686 ... H5
Emmeloord 34,467 ... H3
Emmen 86,700 ... K3
Enkhuizen 13,430 ... G3
Enschede 141,597 ... K4
Enschede* 239,015 ... K4
Epe 32,267 ... H4
Erica ... K3
Ermelo 23,835 ... H4
Etten-Leur 26,167 ... F5
Europoort ... E5
Flushing 43,806 ... C6
Franeker 11,415 ... H2
Geertruidenberg 6,185 ... F5
Geldermalsen 8,952 ... G5
Geldrop 25,879 ... H6
Geleen 35,910 ... H7
Gemert 15,267 ... H5
Gendringen 19,086 ... J5
Genemuiden 6,058 ... H3
Gennep 14,773 ... H5
Giessendam-Hardinxveld 15,523 ... F5
Giethoorn ... J3
Gilze 19,603 ... F5
Goes 28,505 ... D6
Goirle 13,447 ... G5
Goor 11,435 ... K4
Gorinchem 28,337 ... G5
Gorredijk ... J2
Gouda 56,403 ... F4
Graauw ... E6
Gramsbergen 5,866 ... K3
Grave 9,492 ... H5
Groenlo 8,693 ... K4
Groesbeek 18,094 ... H5
Groningen 163,357 ... K2
Groningen* 201,662 ... K2
Grouw 8,567 ... H2
Haamstede 4,575 ... D5
Haarlem 164,672 ... F4
Haarlem* 232,048 ... F4

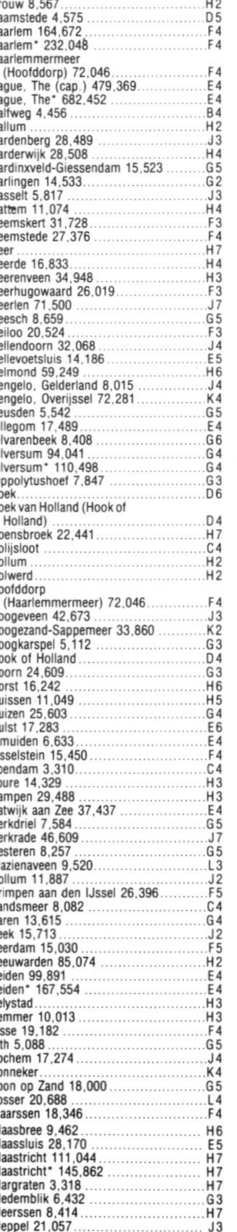

Haarlemmermeer
(Hoofddorp) 72,046 ... F4
Hague, The (cap.) 479,369 ... E4
Hague, The* 682,452 ... E4
Halfweg 4,456 ... B4
Hallum ... H2
Hardenberg 28,489 ... J3
Harderwijk 28,508 ... H4
Hardinxveld-Giessendam 15,523 ... G5
Harlingen 14,533 ... G2
Hasselt 5,817 ... J3
Hattem 11,074 ... H4
Heemskert 31,728 ... F3
Heemstede 27,376 ... F4
Heer ... H7
Heerde 16,833 ... H4
Heerenveen 34,948 ... H3
Heerhugowaard 26,019 ... F3
Heerlen 71,500 ... J7
Heesch 8,659 ... G5
Heiloo 20,524 ... F3
Hellendoorn 32,068 ... J4
Hellevoetsluis 14,186 ... E5
Helmond 59,249 ... H6
Hengelo, Gelderland 8,015 ... J4
Hengelo, Overijssel 72,281 ... K4
Heusden 5,542 ... G5
Hillegom 17,489 ... E4
Hilvarenbeek 8,408 ... G6
Hilversum 94,041 ... G4
Hilversum* 110,498 ... G4
Hippolytushoef 7,847 ... G3
Hoek ... D6
Hoek van Holland (Hook of
Holland) ... D4
Hoensbroek 22,441 ... H7
Holijsloot ... C4
Hollum ... H2
Holwerd ... H2
Hoofddorp
(Haarlemmermeer) 72,046 ... F4
Hoogeveen 42,673 ... J3
Hoogezand-Sappemeer 33,860 ... K2
Hoogkarspel 5,112 ... G3
Hook of Holland ... D4
Hoorn 24,609 ... G3
Horst 16,242 ... H6
Huissen 11,049 ... H5
Huizen 25,603 ... G4
Hulst 17,283 ... E6
IJmuiden 6,633 ... E4
IJsselstein 15,450 ... F4
Ilpendam 3,310 ... C4
Joure 14,329 ... H3
Kampen 29,488 ... H3
Katwijk aan Zee 37,437 ... E4
Kerkdriel 7,584 ... G5
Kerkrade 46,609 ... J7
Kesteren 8,257 ... G5
Klazienaveen 9,520 ... L3
Kollum 11,887 ... J2
Krimpen aan den IJssel 26,396 ... F5
Landsmeer 8,082 ... C4
Laren 13,615 ... G4
Leek 15,713 ... J2
Leerdam 15,030 ... F5
Leeuwarden 85,074 ... H2
Leiden 99,891 ... E4
Leiden* 167,554 ... E4
Lelystad ... H3
Lemmer 10,013 ... H3
Lisse 19,182 ... F4
Lith 5,088 ... G5
Lochem 17,274 ... J4
Lonneker ... K4
Loon op Zand 18,000 ... G5
Losser 20,688 ... L4
Maarssen 18,346 ... F4
Maasbree 9,462 ... H6
Maassluis 28,170 ... E5
Maastricht 111,044 ... H7
Maastricht* 145,862 ... H7
Margraten 3,318 ... H7
Medemblik 6,432 ... G3
Meerssen 8,414 ... H7
Meppel 21,057 ... J3
Middelburg 36,372 ... C6
Middelharnis 14,245 ... E5
Middenmeer ... F3
Millingen aan den Rijn 5,035 ... J5
Moerdijk ... F5
Monnickendam 8,127 ... C4
Montfoort 3,442 ... G4
Muiden 6,567 ... G4
Muntendam 4,147 ... K2
Naaldwijk 24,117 ... E4
Naarden 17,319 ... G4
Nagele ... H3
Neede 10,842 ... K4
Nes 3,012 ... H2
Nieuwegein 22,648 ... G4
Nieuwe-Pekela 5,086 ... L2
Nieuwkoop 8,923 ... F4
Nieuw-Schoonebeek 7,556 ... L3
Nijkerk 21,615 ... H4
Nijmegen 148,493 ... H5
Nijmegen* 213,981 ... H5
Noordwijk 22,386 ... E4
Norg 6,041 ... J2
Numansdorp 7,072 ... E5
Nunspeet 21,340 ... H4
Odoorn 11,973 ... K3
Oisterwijk 16,263 ... G5
Oldenzaal 26,624 ... K4
Olst 8,480 ... J4
Ommen 16,136 ... J3
Onstwedde ... K2
Oostburg 18,461 ... C6
Oosterhout 40,077 ... F5
Ooosterwolde 5,845 ... J2
Oostmahorn ... J2
Oostzaan 6,336 ... C4
Ootmarsum 3,901 ... K4
Oss 45,643 ... H5
Otterlo ... H4
Oud-Beijerland 14,251 ... E5
Ouddorp 9,091 ... D5
Oudenbosch 11,061 ... E5
Oude-Pekela 8,067 ... K2
Oudewater 6,870 ... F4
Purmerend 32,614 ... F4
Putten 18,243 ... H4
Raalte 23,598 ... J4
Renkum 34,547 ... H5
Reusel 6,901 ... G6
Rheden 49,755 ... J4
Rhenen 16,893 ... H5
Ridderkerk 45,069 ... F5
Rijnsburg 10,698 ... F4
Rijssen 20,008 ... J4
Rijswijk 54,123 ... E4
Roden 16,437 ... J2
Roermond 36,695 ... J6
Roosendaal 51,685 ... F5
Rotterdam 614,767 ... E5
Rotterdam* 1,016,505 ... E5
Rutten ... H3
Ruurlo 7,557 ... J4
Sappemeer-Hoogezand 33,860 ... K2
Schagen 13,929 ... F3
Scheveningen ... E4
Schiedam 78,068 ... E5
Schijndel 18,658 ... G5
Schiphol ... B5
Schoonhoven 10,753 ... F5
's Gravendeel 7,242 ... E5
's Gravenhage (The Hague)
(cap.) 479,369 ... E4
's Gravenhage* 682,452 ... E4
's Gravenzande 15,833 ... E4
's Heerenberg 18,326 ... J5
's Hertogenbosch 86,184 ... G5
Simpelveld 6,783 ... H7
Sint Annaland ... E5
Sint Jacobiparochie ... H2
Sittard 34,278 ... H6
Sliedrecht 21,839 ... F5
Slochteren 13,447 ... K2
Sloten, North Holland ... B5
Sloterdijk ... B4
Sluis 3,140 ... C6
Smilde 8,247 ... K3
Sneek 28,123 ... H2
Soest 40,165 ... G4
Soesterberg ... G4
Stadskanaal 13,946 ... L3
Staphorst 11,608 ... J3
Steenbergen 12,930 ... E5
Steenwijk 20,721 ... J3
Stiens 7,711 ... H2
Swifterbant ... H3
Tegelen 18,386 ... J6
Ter Apel ... L3
Termunten 4,803 ... K2
Terneuzen 33,731 ... D6
Tholen 17,213 ... E5
Tiel 24,974 ... G5
Tilburg 151,513 ... G5
Tilburg* 212,510 ... G5
Twello 22,542 ... J4
Uden 28,946 ... H5
Uithoorn 22,812 ... F4
Uithuizen 5,194 ... K2
Ulrum 3,665 ... J2
Urk 9,397 ... H3
Utrecht 250,887 ... G4
Utrecht* 464,357 ... G4
Vaals 11,057 ... H7
Vaassen 7,225 ... H4
Valkenswaard 27,121 ... H6
Veendam 26,168 ... K2
Veenendaal 35,845 ... G4
Veenhuizen ... J2
Veere 4,252 ... D5
Veghel 22,308 ... H5
Veldhoven 30,030 ... G6
Velp ... J5
Velsen 64,035 ... F4
Venlo 61,659 ... J6
Venraij 31,526 ... H6
Vianen 12,821 ... G5
Vlaardingen 78,311 ... E5
Vlagtwedde 16,719 ... L3
Vlijmen 13,515 ... G5
Vlissingen (Flushing) 43,806 ... C6
Volendam-Edam 21,507 ... G4
Voorburg 45,209 ... E4
Voorst 22,542 ... J4
Vorden 7,276 ... J4
Vriezenveen 16,025 ... K4
Vught 23,261 ... G5
Waalre 13,219 ... G6
Waalwijk 25,977 ... F5
Wageningen 28,659 ... H5
Wamel 8,979 ... H5
Warmenhuizen 3,818 ... F3
Weert 36,850 ... H6
Weesp 17,037 ... C5
West-Terschelling 4,542 ... G2
Wierden 20,618 ... K4
Wijhe 6,888 ... J4
Wijk bij Duurstede 7,927 ... G5
Wijk en Aalburg 9,266 ... F5
Winschoten 19,760 ... L2
Winsum 5,007 ... K2
Winterswijk 27,413 ... K5
Woensdrecht 9,101 ... E6
Woerden 22,064 ... F4
Wolvega 22,812 ... J3
Workum 4,135 ... G3
Zaandam (Zaanstad) 124,795 ... B4
Zaandam (Zaanstad)* 137,371 ... B4
Zaltbommel 8,010 ... G5
Zandvoort 16,289 ... E4
Zeist 58,630 ... G4
Zevenaar 26,560 ... J5
Zevenbergen 13,307 ... E5
Zierikzee 8,816 ... D5
Zundert 12,444 ... F6
Zutphen 29,188 ... J4
Zwartsluis 4,391 ... H3
Zwijndrecht 38,271 ... E5
Zwolle 77,826 ... J3

OTHER FEATURES

Alkmaardermeer (lake) ... F3
Ameland (isl.) ... H2
Bergumermeer (lake) ... J2
Beulaker Wijde (lake) ... H3
Borndiep (chan.) ... H2
De Fluessen (lake) ... G3
De Honte (bay) ... D6
De Peel (reg.) ... H6
De Twente (reg.) ... K4
De Zaan (riv.) ... B4
Dollard (bay) ... L2
Dommel (riv.) ... H6
Duiveland (isl.) ... D5
Eastern Scheldt (est.) ... D5
Eems (riv.) ... K2
Eijerlandsche Gat (str.) ... F2
Flevoland Polders 35,618 ... G4
Friesche Gat (chan.) ... J2
Frisian, West (isls.) ... G2
Galgenberg (hill) ... H4
Goeree (isl.) ... D5
Grevelingen (str.) ... E5
Griend (isl.) ... G2
Groninger Wad (sound) ... J2
Groote IJ Polder ... B4
Haarlemmermeer Polder 72,046 ... B5
Haringvliet (str.) ... E5
Het IJ (est.) ... C4
Hoek van Holland (cape) ... D5
Hondsrug (hills) ... K3
Houtrak Polder ... A4
Hunse (riv.) ... K3
IJmeer (bay) ... C4
IJssel (riv.) ... J4
IJsselmeer (lake) ... G3
Lauwers (chan.) ... J1
Lauwers Zee (bay) ... J2
Lek (riv.) ... F5
Lemelerberg (hill) ... J4
Lower Rhine (riv.) ... H5
Maas (riv.) ... G5
Mark (riv.) ... F6
Marken (isl.) ... G4
Markerwaard Polder ... G3
Marsdiep (chan.) ... F3
North (sea) ... E3
North Beveland (isl.) ... D5
North East Polder 34,467 ... H3
North Holland (canal) ... C4
North Sea (canal) ... F4
Old Rhine (riv.) ... E4
Oostzaan Polder 6,336 ... B4
Orange (canal) ... K3
Overflakkee (isl.) ... E5
Pinke Gat (chan.) ... H2
Regge (riv.) ... K4
Rhine (riv.) ... J5
Roer (riv.) ... J6
Rottumeplaat (isl.) ... J1
Rottumeroog (isl.) ... J1
Schiermonnikoog (isl.) ... J1
Schouwen (isl.) ... D5
Slotermeer (lake) ... H3
Sneekermeer (lake) ... H2
South Beveland (isl.) ... D6
Terschelling (isl.) ... G2
Texel (isl.) ... F2
Tjeukemeer (lake) ... H3
Tjonger (riv.) ... J3
Vaalserberg (mt.) ... J7
Vecht (riv.) ... F4
Vechte (riv.) ... J3
Veersche Meer (lake) ... D5
Veluwe (reg.) ... H4
Vlieland (isl.) ... F2
Vliestroom (str.) ... G2
Voorne (isl.) ... D5
Waal (riv.) ... G5
Waddenzee (sound) ... G2
Walcheren (isl.) ... C5
Wester Eems (chan.) ... K1
Western Scheldt (De Honte)
(bay) ... D6
West Frisian (isls.) ... F2
Westgat (chan.) ... F3
Wieringermeer Polder 11,870 ... G3
Wilhelmina (canal) ... G6
Willems (canal) ... G5

*City and suburbs.
†Population of cities in Belgium & Netherlands are communes

Land from the Sea

NORTH SEA
WEST FRISIAN ISLANDS
WADDENZEE
Enclosing Dam 1932
Leeuwarden
Wieringermeer Polder 1930
IJSSELMEER (ZUIDER ZEE)
North East Polder 1942
Markerwaard (planned)
East Flevoland 1957
South Flevoland 1969
Amsterdam
Haarlemmer Lake 1852
Reclaimed Land and Dates of Completion
Future Polders
=10 Square Miles

For centuries the Dutch have been renowned for the drainage of marshes and the construction of polders, i.e., arable land reclaimed from the sea. Future projects will convert much of the present IJsselmeer to agricultural land.

Topography

0 25 50 MI.
0 25 50 KM.

WEST FRISIAN ISLANDS
Waddenzee
IJsselmeer
NORTH EAST POLDER
FLEVOLAND
Amsterdam
North Sea Canal
Amsterdam-Rhine Canal
The Hague
Old Rhine
Rotterdam
Lek
Lower Rhine
Waal
Goeree
Schouwen
Walcheren
Maas
Antwerp
Albert Canal
Demer
Scheldt
Lys
Brussels
Senne
Vaalserberg 1,056 ft. (322 m.)
Botrange 2,277 ft. (694 m.)
Meuse
Sambre
Ourthe
ARDENNES
Semois
Alzette
Luxembourg
Sauer
Our
Mosel

5,000 m. 16,404 ft. | 2,000 m. 6,562 ft. | 1,000 m. 3,281 ft. | 500 m. 1,640 ft. | 200 m. 656 ft. | 100 m. 328 ft. | Sea Level | Below

Netherlands, Belgium and Luxembourg
CONIC PROJECTION
SCALE OF MILES
0 5 10 20 30 40
SCALE OF KILOMETERS
0 5 10 20 30 40 50
Capitals of Countries
Provincial Capitals
International Boundaries
Provincial Boundaries
Canals
Scale 1:1,670,000
© Copyright HAMMOND INCORPORATED, Maplewood, N. J.
NORTH SEA
WEST FRISIAN ISLANDS
WADDEN ZEE
IJSSELMEER
MARKERWAARD
NORTH EAST POLDER
FLEVOLAND
GRONINGEN
FRIESLAND
DRENTHE
OVERIJSSEL
GELDERLAND
UTRECHT
NORTH HOLLAND
SOUTH HOLLAND
ZEELAND
NORTH BRABANT
LIMBURG
ANTWERP
WEST FLANDERS
EAST FLANDERS
BRABANT
HAINAUT
NAMUR
LIÈGE
LUXEMBOURG
GERMANY
FRANCE
SAAR
HUNSRÜCK
EIFEL
AMSTERDAM
The Hague ('s Gravenhage)
Rotterdam
Utrecht
Groningen
Leeuwarden
Haarlem
Arnhem
Zwolle
Assen
Maastricht
's Hertogenbosch
Middelburg
Antwerp (Antwerpen)
BRUSSELS (Bruxelles)
Ghent (Gent)
Bruges (Brugge)
Liège (Luik)
Namur (Namen)
Mons (Bergen)
Hasselt
Arlon (Aarlen)
Luxembourg
Aachen
Cologne (Köln)
Düsseldorf
Bonn
Trier
Lille
Emden
Longitude 5° East of Greenwich
© Copyright HAMMOND INCORPORATED, Maplewood, N.J.

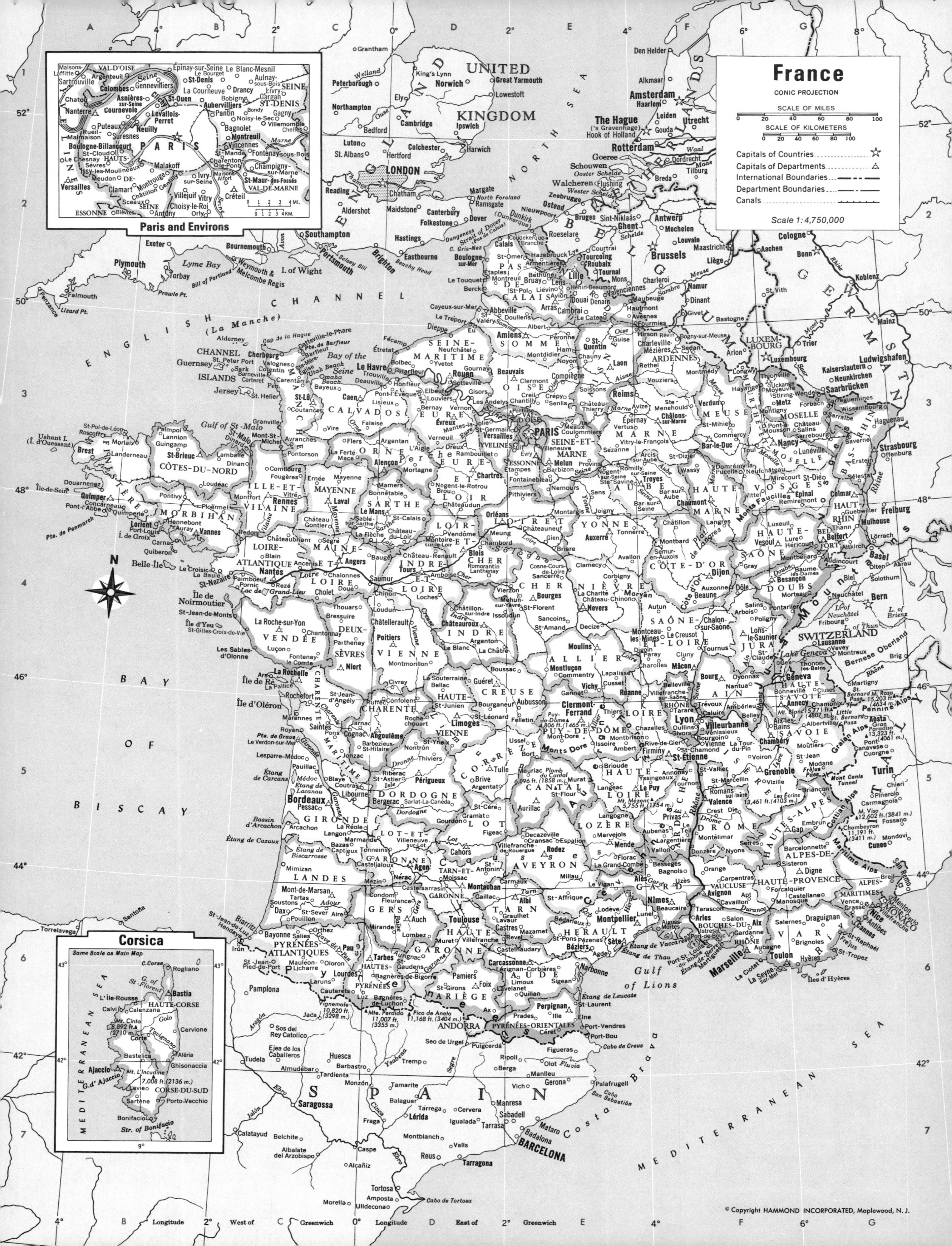
France
CONIC PROJECTION
SCALE OF MILES
0 20 40 60 80 100
SCALE OF KILOMETERS
0 20 40 60 80 100
Capitals of Countries
Capitals of Departments
International Boundaries
Department Boundaries
Canals
Scale 1:4,750,000
Paris and Environs
Corsica
Same Scale as Main Map
UNITED KINGDOM
ENGLAND
LONDON
ENGLISH CHANNEL
(La Manche)
CHANNEL ISLANDS
NORTH SEA
NETHERLANDS
BELGIUM
GERMANY
LUXEMBOURG
SWITZERLAND
ITALY
SPAIN
ANDORRA
MONACO
BAY OF BISCAY
Gulf of Lions
MEDITERRANEAN SEA
MEDITERRANEAN SEA
PARIS
Brussels
Amsterdam
The Hague
Luxembourg
Bern
Turin
BARCELONA
Lyon
Marseille
Bordeaux
Toulouse
Nantes
Lille
Strasbourg
Nice
Ajaccio
Bastia
HAUTE-CORSE
CORSE-DU-SUD
Str. of Bonifacio
© Copyright HAMMOND INCORPORATED, Maplewood, N. J.
Longitude 2° West of 0° Greenwich
Longitude 2° East of Greenwich

DEPARTMENTS

Ain 376,477 F4
Aisne 533,862 E3
Allier 378,406 E4
Alpes-de-Haute-Provence 112,178 G5
Alpes-Maritimes 816,681 G6
Ardèche 257,065 F5
Ardennes 309,306 F3
Ariège 137,857 D6
Aube 284,823 E3
Aude 272,366 E6
Aveyron 278,306 E5
Bas-Rhin 882,121 G3
Belfort (terr.) 128,125 G4
Bouches-du-Rhône 1,632,974 F6
Calvados 560,967 C3
Cantal 166,549 E5
Charente 337,064 D5
Charente-Maritime 497,859 C5
Cher 316,350 E4
Corrèze 240,363 D5
Corse du Sud 128,634 B6
Côte-d'Or 456,070 F4
Côtes-du-Nord 525,556 B3
Creuse 146,214 D4
Deux-Sèvres 335,829 C4
Dordogne 373,179 D5
Doubs 471,082 G4
Drôme 361,847 F5
Essonne 923,063 E3
Eure 422,952 D3
Eure-et-Loir 335,151 D3
Finistère 804,088 A3
Gard 494,575 F6
Gers 175,366 D6
Gironde 1,061,480 C5
Haute-Corse 161,208 B6
Haute-Garonne 777,431 D6
Haute-Loire 205,491 E5
Haute-Marne 212,304 F3
Hautes-Alpes 97,358 G5
Haute-Saône 222,254 G4
Haute-Savoie 447,795 G5
Hautes-Pyrénées 227,222 D6
Haute-Vienne 352,149 D5
Haut-Rhin 635,209 G4
Hauts-de-Seine 1,438,930 A2
Hérault 648,202 E6
Ille-et-Vilaine 702,199 C3
Indre 248,523 D4
Indre-et-Loire 478,601 D4
Isère 860,339 F5
Jura 238,856 F4
Landes 288,323 C5
Loire 742,396 F5
Loire-Atlantique 934,499 C4
Loiret 490,189 E4
Loir-et-Cher 283,686 D4
Lot 150,778 D5
Lot-et-Garonne 292,616 D5
Lozère 74,825 E5
Maine-et-Loire 629,849 C4
Manche 451,662 C3
Marne 530,399 F3
Mayenne 261,789 C3
Meurthe-et-Moselle 722,588 G3
Meuse 203,904 F3
Morbihan 563,588 B4
Moselle 1,006,373 G3
Nièvre 245,212 E4
Nord 2,510,738 E2
Oise 606,320 E3
Orne 293,523 C3
Paris (city) 2,299,830 B2
Pas-de-Calais 1,403,035 E2
Puy-de-Dôme 580,033 E5
Pyrénées-Atlantiques 534,748 C6
Pyrénées-Orientales 299,506 E6
Rhône 1,429,647 F5
Saône-et-Loire 569,810 F4
Sarthe 490,385 D3
Savoie 305,118 G5
Seine-et-Marne 755,762 E3
Seine-Saint-Denis 1,322,127 C1
Somme 538,462 E3
Tarn 338,024 E6
Tarn-et-Garonne 183,314 D5
Val-de-Marne 1,215,713 C1
Val-d'Oise 840,885 E3
Var 626,093 G6
Vaucluse 390,446 F6
Vendée 450,641 C4
Vienne 357,366 D4
Vosges 397,957 G3
Yonne 299,851 E4
Yvelines 1,082,255 D3

CITIES and TOWNS

Abbeville 25,252 D2
Agde 9,856 E6
Agen 33,763 D5
Aix-en-Provence 91,665 F6
Aix-les-Bains 21,884 G5
Ajaccio 47,065 B7
Albert 11,746 E2
Albertville 16,630 G5
Albi 43,942 E6
Alençon 32,917 D3
Alès 33,315 E5
Ambérieu-en-Bugey 9,294 F5
Amboise 10,498 D4
Amiens 129,453 D3
Ancenis 6,689 C4
Angers 136,603 C4
Angoulême 46,293 D5
Annecy 53,058 G5
Annonay 19,234 F5
Antibes 44,226 G6
Antony 57,450 B2
Apt 9,735 F6
Arcachon 13,856 C5
Argentan 16,063 D3
Argenteuil 101,542 A1
Arles 37,337 F6
Armentières 23,850 E2
Arras 45,804 E2
Asnières-sur-Seine 75,328 A1
Aubagne 26,145 F6
Aubenas 11,967 F5
Aubervilliers 72,859 B1
Auch 18,767 D6
Audincourt 18,570 G4
Aulnay-sous-Bois 77,982 B1
Auray 10,006 B4
Aurignac 744 D6
Aurillac 29,458 E5
Autun 19,441 F4
Auxerre 36,039 E4
Auxonne 6,414 F4
Avallon 8,518 E4
Avignon 73,482 F6
Avion 22,860 E2
Avranches 10,128 C3
Ax-les-Thermes 1,456 D6
Bagnères-de-Bigorre 9,080 D6
Bagnolet 35,858 B2
Bagnols-sur-Cèze 13,111 F5
Barbizon 1,189 E3
Barcelonnette 2,523 G5
Barfleur 701 C3
Bar-le-Duc 19,188 F3
Bar-sur-Aube 7,227 F3
Bastia 45,387 B6
Bayeux 13,381 C3
Bayonne 41,281 C6
Beaucaire 10,189 F6
Beaune 16,386 F4
Beauvais 53,493 E3
Belfort 54,469 G4
Belley 6,612 F5
Berck 14,104 D2
Bergerac 25,488 D5
Bernay 9,928 D3
Besançon 119,803 G4
Béthune 26,208 E2
Béziers 79,213 E6
Biarritz 27,453 C6
Blois 49,134 D4
Bobigny 43,041 B1
Bogny-sur-Meuse 6,845 F3
Bolbec 12,347 D3
Bondy 48,285 B1
Bonneville 6,717 G4
Bordeaux 220,830 C5
Boulogne-Billancourt 103,527 A2
Boulogne-sur-Mer 48,309 D2
Bourg-en-Bresse 40,052 F4
Bourges 75,200 E4
Bourgoin-Jallieu 18,504 F5
Bressuire 9,778 C4
Brest 163,940 A3
Briançon 8,523 G5
Brignoles 8,784 G6
Brioude 7,756 E5
Brive-la-Gaillarde 49,276 D5
Bruay-en-Artois 25,544 E2
Caen 116,987 C3
Cahors 19,288 D5
Calais 73,009 D2
Caluire-et-Cuire 43,024 F5
Cambrai 38,706 E2
Cannes 70,226 G6
Carcassonne 38,887 D6
Carmaux 11,970 E5
Carpentras 20,169 F5
Castelnaudary 8,947 E6
Castelsarrasin 6,562 D6
Castres 41,037 E6
Cavaillon 17,383 F6
Châlons-sur-Marne 50,870 F3
Chalon-sur-Saône 55,495 F4
Chambéry 52,286 F5
Chambord 166 D4
Chamonix-Mont-Blanc 6,246 G5
Champigny-sur-Marne 80,189 C2
Chantilly 10,517 E3
Charenton-le-Pont 20,383 B2
Charleville-Mézières 59,513 F3
Chartres 38,574 D3
Châteaubriant 12,417 C4
Château-du-Loir 5,598 D4
Châteaudun 14,634 D3
Château-Gontier 8,301 C4
Châteauroux 53,166 D4
Château-Thierry 13,379 E3
Châtellerault 33,811 D4
Châtillon 26,562 B2
Châtillon-sur-Seine 7,367 F4
Chatou 26,415 A1
Chaumont 26,568 F3
Chauny 14,324 E3
Chelles 24,192 C1
Cherbourg 31,333 C3
Chinon 5,378 D4
Choisy-le-Roi 38,629 B2
Cholet 49,887 C4
Clamart 52,881 A2
Clermont 7,834 E3
Clermont-Ferrand 153,379 E5
Clichy 47,731 B1
Cluny 4,335 F4
Cluses 12,713 G4
Cognac 21,567 C5
Colmar 58,585 G3
Colombes 83,241 A1
Commentry 8,074 E4
Commercy 6,918 F3
Compiègne 37,009 E3
Concarneau 15,096 A4
Cosne-Cours-sur-Loire 9,768 E4
Coudekerque-Branche 24,702 E2
Coulommiers 11,363 E3
Courbevoie 54,391 A1
Coutances 8,286 C3
Creil 31,893 E3
Crépy-en-Valois 10,661 E3
Créteil 58,665 B2
Cusset 13,672 E4
Dax 18,019 C6
Deauville 5,655 C3
Decazeville 9,318 E5
Decize 6,853 E4
Denain 26,096 E2
Dieppe 25,607 D3

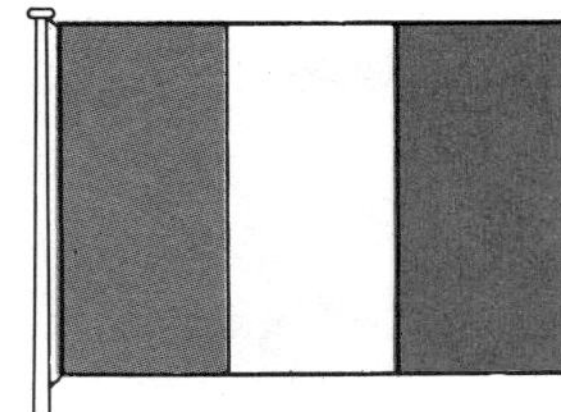

AREA 210,038 sq. mi. (543,998 sq. km.)
POPULATION 53,788,000
CAPITAL Paris
LARGEST CITY Paris
HIGHEST POINT Mont Blanc 15,771 ft. (4,807 m.)
MONETARY UNIT franc
MAJOR LANGUAGE French
MAJOR RELIGION Roman Catholicism

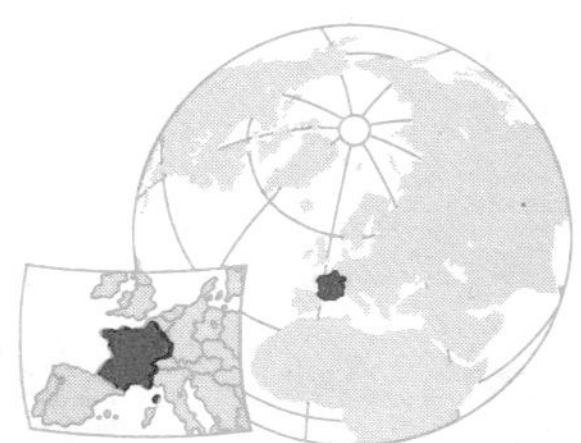

Topography

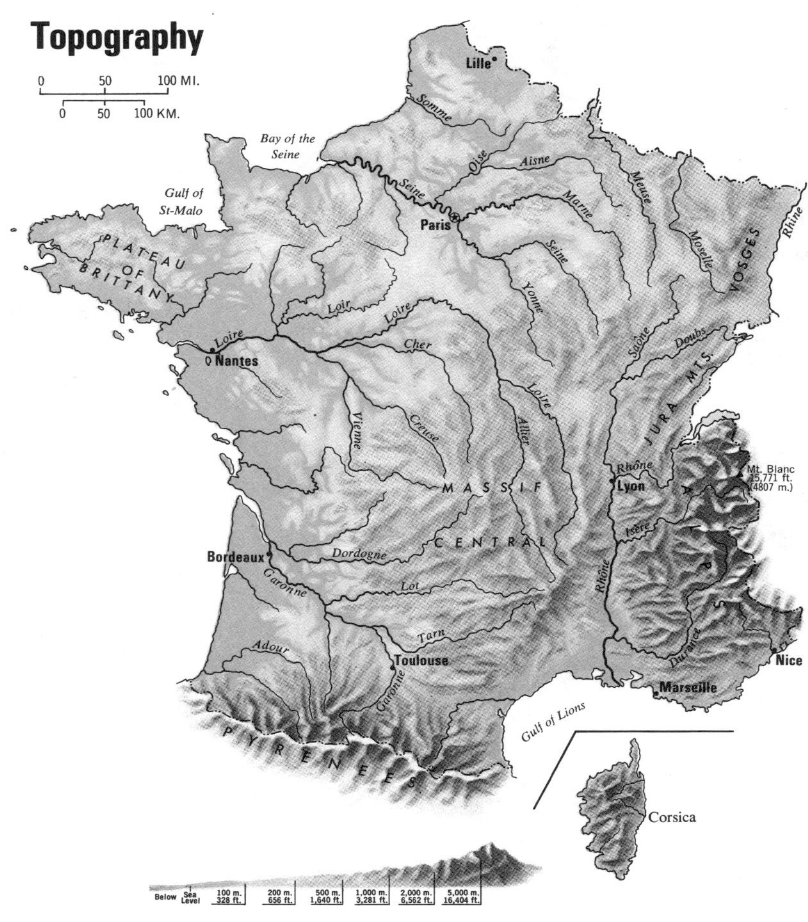

Historic Provinces

A resident of the city of Caen thinks of himself as a Norman rather than as a citizen of the modern department of Calvados. In spite of the passing of nearly two centuries, the historic provinces which existed before 1790 command the local patriotism of most Frenchmen.

Digne 13,140 G5
Digoin 10,449 F4
Dijon 149,899 F4
Dinan 13,303 B3
Dinard 9,211 B3
Dôle 28,109 F4
Domrémy-la-Pucelle 190 F3
Douai 43,954 E2
Douarnenez 17,851 A3
Doullens 6,806 E2
Draguignan 19,653 G6
Drancy 64,258 B1
Dreux 31,503 D3
Dunkirk (Dunkerque) 78,171 E2
Elbeuf 18,642 D3
Épernay 29,286 E3
Épinal 39,000 G3
Épinay-sur-Seine 46,458 B1
Erstein 6,494 G3
Étampes 18,810 E3
Étaples 10,423 D2
Eu 8,349 D3
Évreux 46,181 D3
Évry 15,300 E3
Falaise 8,133 C3
Fécamp 20,835 D3
Figeac 8,675 D5
Firminy 23,776 F5
Flers 18,590 C3
Foix 9,569 D6
Fontainebleau 16,436 E3
Fontenay-le-Comte 12,301 C4
Fontenay-sous-Bois 46,200 C2
Forbach 24,812 G3
Fougères 26,260 C3
Fourmies 15,318 F2
Fréjus 27,805 G6
Gagny 36,714 C1
Gaillac 7,653 D6
Gap 24,962 G5
Gardanne 8,175 F6
Gennevillers 50,154 B1
Gentilly 16,843 B2
Gex 3,959 G4
Gien 13,817 E4
Gif 10,866 E3
Gisors 7,591 D3
Givet 7,787 F2
Givors 19,356 F5
Granville 12,869 C3
Grasse 24,260 G6
Graulhet 11,099 E6
Gray 8,718 F4
Grenoble 165,431 F5
Guebwiller 10,477 G4
Guéret 14,418 D4
Guingamp 9,269 B3
Guise 6,642 E3
Haguenau 23,023 G3
Harfleur 9,857 D3
Hautmont 19,130 F2
Hayange 8,479 F3
Hazebrouck 18,867 E2
Hendaye 9,404 C6
Hénin-Beaumont 26,296 E2
Hennebont 8,978 B4
Héricourt 8,481 G4
Hirson 11,909 F3
Honfleur 8,995 D3
Hyères 29,366 G6
Issoire 13,560 E5
Issoudun 15,065 D4
Issy-les-Moulineaux 47,355 A2
Istres 10,127 F6
Ivry-sur-Seine 62,804 B2
Joigny 10,825 E3
La Baule-Escoublac 13,854 B4
La Ciotat 29,290 F6
La Courneuve 37,917 B1
La Flèche 12,743 C4
La Grand-Combe 9,406 E5
L'Aigle 9,198 D3
Landerneau 13,983 B3
Langres 10,745 F4
Lannion 13,692 B3
Laon 27,420 E3
La Pallice C4
La Rochelle 72,936 C4
La Roche-sur-Yon 40,789 C4
La Seyne-sur-Mer 50,059 F6
Laval 50,734 C3
Lavelanet 9,278 E6
Le Blanc 7,431 D4
Le Blanc-Mesnil 49,062 B1
Le Bourget 10,520 B1
Le Cateau 8,680 E2
Le Chesnay 24,590 A2
Le Creusot 31,643 F4
Le Havre 216,917 C3
Le Mans 150,289 C3
Lens 39,973 E2
Le Puy 24,793 F5
Les Andelys 7,524 D3
Les Sables-d'Olonne 17,157 B4
Le Teil 7,993 F5
Le Tréport 6,463 D2
Levallois-Perret 52,460 A1
Lézignan-Corbières 6,929 E6
Libourne 21,265 C5
Liévin 33,040 E2
Lille 171,010 E2
Limoges 136,059 D5
Limoux 9,595 E6
Lisieux 24,972 D3
Livry-Gargan 32,879 C1
Lodève 7,131 E6
Longwy 20,107 F3
Lons-le-Saunier 20,897 F4
Lorient 68,655 B4
Loudéac 7,173 B3
Loudun 7,060 D4
Lourdes 17,685 C6
Louviers 17,919 D3
Luçon 8,834 C4
Lunel 12,392 E6
Lunéville 22,438 G3
Lure 8,538 G4
Luxeuil-les-Bains 10,061 G4
Lyon 454,265 F5
Mâcon 39,130 F4
Maisons-Alfort 53,963 B2
Maisons-Laffitte 23,465 A1
Malakoff 34,100 A2
Manosque 17,256 G6
Mantes-la-Jolie 42,408 D3
Marmande 13,223 C5
Marseille 901,421 F6
Martigues 26,850 F6
Maubeuge 34,152 F2
Mayenne 11,278 C3
Mazamet 13,148 E6
Meaux 41,831 E3
Mehun-sur-Yèvre 6,533 E4
Melun 36,913 E3
Mende 10,040 E5
Menton 24,736 G6
Metz 110,939 G3
Meudon 31,294 A2
Millau 20,401 E5
Mimizan 6,826 C5
Mirecourt 7,160 G3
Moissac 7,403 D5
Montargis 18,021 E3
Montauban 35,344 D5
Montbard 7,477 F4
Montbéliard 29,968 G4
Montbrison 9,945 E5
Montceau-les-Mines 28,093 F4
Mont-de-Marsan 24,812 C6
Mont-Dore 2,074 E5
Montélimar 25,422 F5
Montfort 2,701 C3
Montigny-les-Metz 24,208 G3
Montluçon 56,337 E4
Montmédy 1,859 F3
Montpellier 178,136 E6
Montreuil,
Seine-Saint-Denis 96,441 B2
Montrouge 40,189 B2
Mont-Saint-Michel 88 C3
Morlaix 15,919 B3
Morteau 6,515 G4
Moulins 25,856 E4
Moyeuvre-Grande 12,448 G3
Mulhouse 116,494 G4
Muret 13,041 D6
Nancy 106,906 G3
Nanterre 94,441 A1
Nantes 252,537 C4
Narbonne 36,525 E6
Nemours 11,159 E3
Neufchâteau 8,582 F3
Neuilly-sur-Seine 65,941 A1
Nevers 45,122 E4
Nice 331,002 G6
Nîmes 123,914 F6
Niort 59,297 C4
Nogent-le-Rotrou 12,284 D3
Noisy-le-Sec 37,674 B1
Noyon 13,784 E3
Oloron-Sainte-Marie 11,616 C6
Orange 19,847 F5
Orléans 88,503 D3
Orly 26,090 B2
Orthez 9,639 C6
Oullins 27,731 F5
Oyonnax 22,548 F4
Pamiers 12,906 D6
Pantin 42,651 B1
Paray-le-Monial 11,523 F4
Paris (cap.) 2,291,554 B2
Parthenay 12,549 C4
Pau 81,560 C6
Périgueux 34,779 D5
Péronne 8,358 E3
Perpignan 101,198 E6
Pessac 50,333 C5
Pézenas 6,768 E6
Pithiviers 9,976 E3
Poitiers 78,739 D4
Pont-à-Mousson 14,461 G3
Pontarlier 17,778 G4
Pontivy 9,478 B3
Pont-l'Abbe 6,618 A4
Pontoise 26,702 E3
Port-de-Bouc 20,448 F6
Port-Saint-Louis-du-Rhône 9,649 F6
Port-Vendres 5,448 E6
Privas 9,385 F5
Provins 12,281 E3
Puteau 35,366 A2
Quimper 50,856 A4
Quimperlé 9,783 B4
Rambouillet 18,446 D3
Redon 9,528 C4
Reims 177,320 E3
Remiremont 10,250 G3
Rennes 194,094 C3

(continued on following page)

30 France

(continued)

Rethel 8,189 ..... F3
Révin 11,459 ..... F3
Rezé 35,512 ..... C4
Rive-de-Gier 17,369 ..... F5
Roanne 54,999 ..... E4
Rochechouart 2,953 ..... D5
Rochefort 27,264 ..... C4
Rodez 24,898 ..... E5
Romans-sur-Isère 30,974 ..... F5
Romilly-sur-Seine 17,276 ..... F3
Romorantin-Lanthenay 15,727 ..... D4
Roubaix 109,473 ..... E2
Rouen 113,536 ..... D3
Royan 17,978 ..... C5
Rueil-Malmaison 62,504 ..... A2
Sablé-sur-Sarthe 9,913 ..... C4
Saint-Affrique 6,842 ..... E6
Saint-Amand-Mont-Rond 11,896 ..... E4
Saint-Brieuc 51,838 ..... B3
Saint-Chamond 39,236 ..... F5
Saint-Claude 12,651 ..... F4
Saint-Cloud 28,052 ..... A2
Saint-Denis 95,808 ..... B1
Saint-Dié 22,834 ..... G3
Saint-Dizier 36,377 ..... F3
Sainte-Mère-Église 1,041 ..... C3
Saintes 24,946 ..... C5
Sainte-Savine 10,526 ..... E3
Saint-Étienne 218,289 ..... F5
Saint-Florent-sur-Cher 6,385 ..... E4
Saint-Flour 6,900 ..... E5
Saint-Gaudens 12,103 ..... D6
Saint-Germain-en-Laye 35,351 ..... D3
Saint-Gilles-Croix-de-Vie 6,569 ..... B4
Saint-Girons 7,259 ..... D6
Saint-Jean-d'Angély 8,801 ..... C4
Saint-Jean-de-Luz 10,921 ..... C6
Saint-Jean-de-Maurienne 9,525 ..... G5
Saint-Jean-Pied-de-Port 1,725 ..... C6
Saint-Junien 9,281 ..... D5
Saint-Lô 21,670 ..... C3
Saint-Malo 43,277 ..... B3
Saint-Mandé 20,714 ..... B2
Saint-Marcellin 6,768 ..... F5
Saint-Maur-des-Fossés 80,797 ..... B2
Saint-Mihiel 5,544 ..... F3
Saint-Nazaire 65,228 ..... B4
Saint-Omer 16,419 ..... E2
Saint-Ouen 43,569 ..... B1
Saint-Pol-de-Léon 6,571 ..... A3
Saint-Quentin 69,956 ..... E3
Saint-Raphaël 19,499 ..... G6
Saint-Tropez 4,484 ..... G6
Saint-Vallier 10,000 ..... F5
Salon-de-Provence 31,783 ..... F6
Sancerre 2,029 ..... E4
Sarlat-La-Canéda 8,191 ..... D5
Sarrebourg 12,442 ..... G3
Sarreguemines 24,570 ..... G3
Sartrouville 42,092 ..... A1
Saumur 30,984 ..... D4
Saverne 10,015 ..... G3
Sceaux 19,651 ..... A2
Sedan 23,867 ..... F3
Sélestat 15,209 ..... G3
Senlis 13,481 ..... E3
Sens 25,621 ..... E3
Sète 39,075 ..... E6
Sèvres 21,100 ..... A2
Sisteron 6,434 ..... G5
Soissons 29,694 ..... E3
Sotteville-les-Rouen 30,393 ..... D3
Stiring-Wendel 12,665 ..... G3
Strasbourg 251,520 ..... H3
Suresnes 37,456 ..... A2
Tarare 11,931 ..... F5
Tarascon 8,522 ..... F6
Tarbes 54,286 ..... D6
Thann 8,508 ..... G4
Thiers 14,534 ..... E5
Thionville 37,943 ..... G3
Thonon-les-Bains 24,673 ..... G4
Thouars 11,835 ..... C4
Tonneins 7,256 ..... D5
Toul 16,141 ..... F3
Toulon 180,508 ..... F6
Toulouse 371,143 ..... D6
Tourcoing 102,092 ..... E2
Tournon 8,568 ..... F5
Tournus 7,284 ..... F4
Tours 139,560 ..... D4
Troyes 71,600 ..... F3
Tulle 18,375 ..... D5
Uckange 11,552 ..... G3
Ussel 9,816 ..... E5
Uzès 6,470 ..... F5
Valence 67,101 ..... F5
Valenciennes 41,976 ..... E2
Vannes 36,722 ..... B4
Vence 7,332 ..... G6
Vendôme 17,828 ..... D4
Vénissieux 74,264 ..... F5
Verdun-sur-Meuse 22,889 ..... F3
Vernon 21,184 ..... D3
Versailles 93,359 ..... A2
Vesoul 17,883 ..... F4
Vichy 32,107 ..... E4
Vienne 25,981 ..... F5
Vierzon 33,057 ..... D4
Villefranche 6,600 ..... G6
Villefranche-de-Rouergue 10,848 ..... E5
Villefranche-sur-Saône 29,996 ..... F4
Villejuif 53,884 ..... B2
Villemomble 28,684 ..... C1
Villeneuve-Saint-Georges 31,378 ..... E3
Villeneuve-sur-Lot 17,818 ..... D5
Villeurbanne 115,913 ..... F5
Vincennes 44,256 ..... B2
Vire 12,832 ..... C3
Vitré 10,989 ..... C3
Vitry-le-François 19,075 ..... F3
Vitry-sur-Seine 87,119 ..... B2
Vittel 6,791 ..... F3
Vizille 6,810 ..... F5
Voiron 17,879 ..... F5
Wissembourg 6,679 ..... G3
Yvetot 10,088 ..... D3

OTHER FEATURES

Adour (riv.) C6
Ain (riv.) F4
Aisne (riv.) E3
Ajaccio (gulf) B7
Allier (riv.) E5
Aube (riv.) F3
Auvergne (mts.) E5
Belle-Île (isl.) B4
Biscay (bay) B5
Blanc (mt.) G5
Bonifacio (str.) B7
Calais (Dover) (str.) D2
Causses (reg.) D5
Cévennes (mts.) E5
Charente (riv.) C5
Cher (riv.) D4
Corse (cape) B6
Corsica (isl.) B6
Côte-d'Or (mts.) F4
Cotentin (pen.) C3
Cottian Alps (range) G5
Creuse (riv.) D4
Dordogne (riv.) D5
Dore Alps (mts.) E5
Doubs (riv.) G4
Drôme (riv.) F5
Dronne (riv.) D5
Durance (riv.) F6
English (chan.) B3
Eure (riv.) D3
Faucilles (mts.) G3
Forez (mts.) E5
Fréjus (pass) G5
Gard (riv.) F5
Garonne (riv.) C5
Gave de Pau (riv.) C6
Geneva (lake) G4
Gers (riv.) D6
Gironde (riv.) C5
Graian Alps (range) G5
Groix (isl.) B4
Hague (cape) C3
Hérault (riv.) E6
Hyères (isls.) G6
Indre (riv.) D4
Isère (riv.) F5
Isle (riv.) D5
Langres (plat.) F4
Limousin (reg.) D5
Lions (gulf) F6
Little Saint Bernard (pass) G5
Loir (riv.) D4
Loire (riv.) C4
Lot (riv.) D5
Manche, La (English) (chan.) B3
Maritime Alps (range) G5
Marne (riv.) C2
Mayenne (riv.) C4
Mediterranean (sea) E7
Médoc (reg.) C5
Meuse (riv.) F3
Mont Cenis (tunnel) G5
Morvan (plat.) F4
Moselle (riv.) G3
Noirmoutier (isl.) B4
North (sea) E1
Oise (riv.) E3
Oléron (isl.) C5
Omaha (beach) C3
Orb (riv.) E6
Orne (riv.) C3
Ouessant (isl.) A3
Penmarch (pt.) A4
Perche (reg.) D3
Puy-de-Dôme (mt.) E5
Pyrenees (range) C6
Ré (isl.) C4
Rhine (riv.) G3
Rhône (riv.) F5
Risle (riv.) D3
Riviera (reg.) G6
Saint-Florent (gulf) B6
Saint-Malo (gulf) B3
Saône (riv.) F4
Sarthe (riv.) D4
Sein (isl.) A3
Seine (bay) C3
Seine (riv.) D3
Sologne (reg.) E4
Somme (riv.) D2
Tarn (riv.) E6
Ushant (Ouessant) (isl.) A3
Utah (beach) C3
Vaccarès (lag.) F6
Vienne (riv.) D4
Vilaine (riv.) C4
Vosges (mts.) G3
Yonne (riv.) E3

MONACO

CITIES and TOWNS

Monte Carlo 11,599 ..... G6

* City and suburbs

MONACO

AREA 368 acres (149 hectares)
POPULATION 25,029

Wine Regions

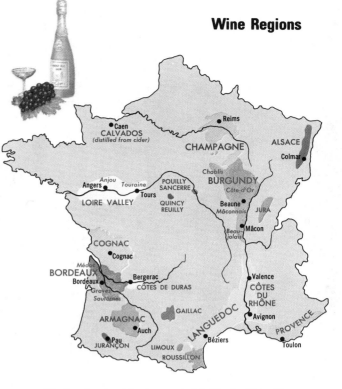

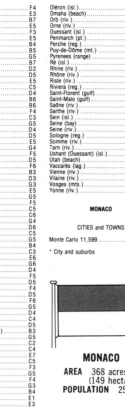

Climate, soil and variety of grape planted determine the quality of wine. Long, hot and fairly dry summers with cool, humid nights constitute an ideal climate. The nature of the soil is such a determining influence that identical grapes planted in Bordeaux, Burgundy and Champagne, will yield wines of widely different types.

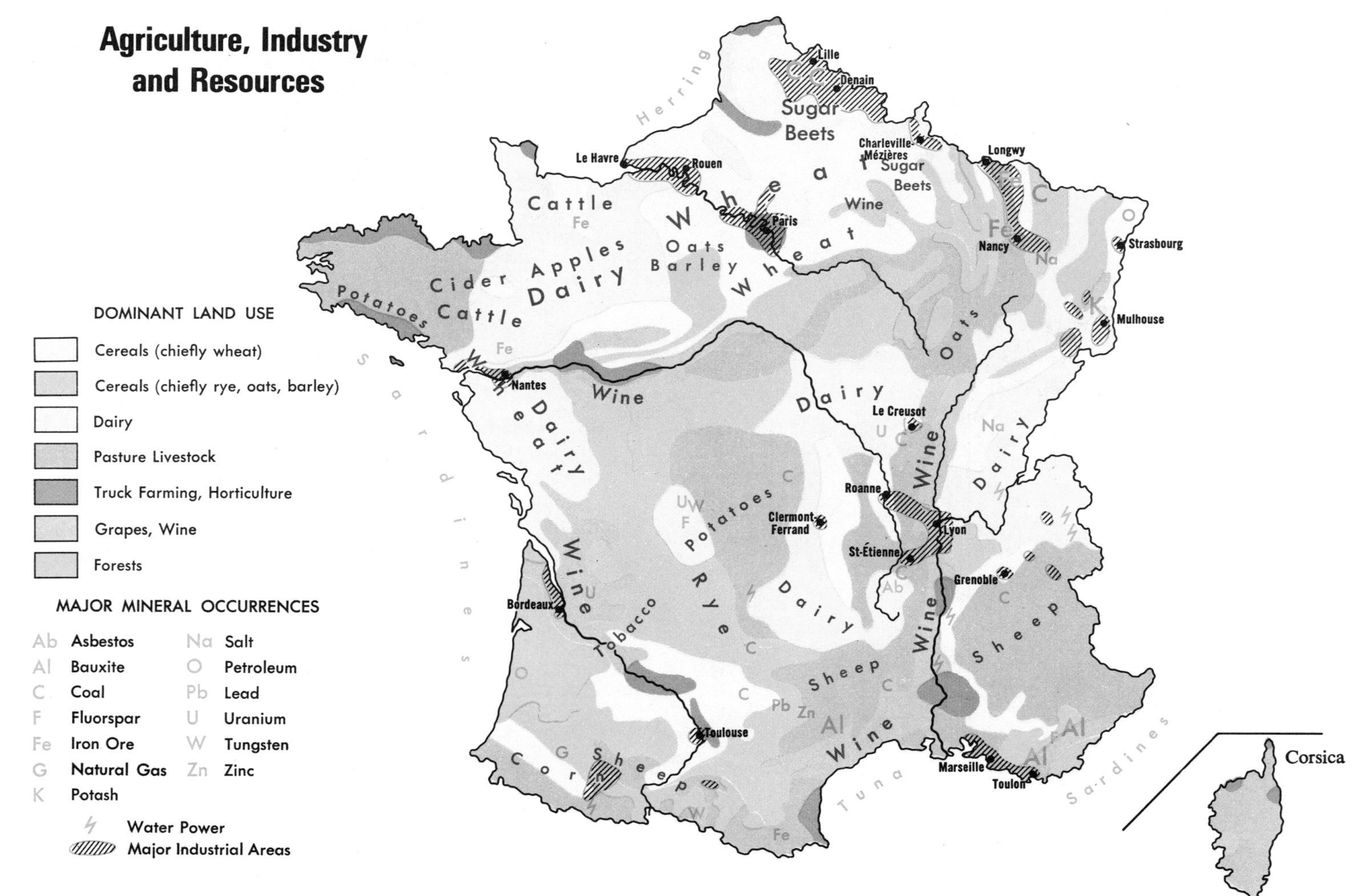

SPAIN

PROVINCES

Álava 204,323 E1
Albacete 335,026 E3
Alicante 920,105 F3
Almería 375,004 E4
Ávila 203,798 D2
Badajoz 687,599 C3
Baleares 558,287 H3
Barcelona 3,929,194 G2
Burgos 358,075 E1
Cáceres 457,777 C3
Cádiz 885,433 D4
Castellón 385,823 G2
Ciudad Real 507,650 D3
Córdoba 724,116 D3
Cuenca 247,158 E2
Gerona 414,397 H1
Granada 733,375 E4
Guadalajara 147,732 E2
Guipúzcoa 631,003 E1
Huelva 397,683 C4
Huesca 222,238 F1
Jaén 661,146 E4
La Coruña 1,004,188 B1
Las Palmas 579,710 C4
León 548,721 C1
Lérida 347,015 G2
Logroño 235,713 E1
Lugo 415,052 C1
Madrid 3,792,561 E2
Málaga 867,330 D4
Murcia 832,313 F4
Navarra 464,867 F1
Orense 413,733 C1
Oviedo 1,045,635 C1
Palencia 198,763 D1
Pontevedra 750,701 B1
Salamanca 371,607 C2
Santa Cruz de Tenerife 590,514 B5
Santander 467,138 D1
Segovia 162,770 D2
Sevilla 1,327,190 D4
Soria 114,956 E2
Tarragona 431,961 G2
Teruel 170,284 F2
Toledo 468,925 D3
Valencia 1,767,327 F3
Valladolid 412,572 D2
Vizcaya 1,043,310 E1
Zamora 251,934 D2
Zaragoza 760,186 F2

CITIES and TOWNS

Adra 10,851 E4
Aguilar 12,893 D4
Aguilas 15,525 F4
Alagón 5,114 F2
Alayor 5,124 J3
Albacete 82,607 F3
Albox 5,072 E4
Alburquerque 7,530 C3
Alcalá de Guadaira 28,781 D4
Alcalá de Henares 59,783 G4
Alcalá de los Gazules 5,262 D4
Alcalá la Real 9,849 E4
Alcanar 5,961 G2
Alcañiz 10,229 F2
Alcantarilla 19,895 F4
Alcaudete 8,557 E4
Alcázar de San Juan 24,620 E3
Alcira 30,493 F3
Alcora 6,711 F2
Alcoy 61,371 F3
Altaro 8,766 F1
Algeciras 74,754 D4
Algemesí 21,158 F3
Alhama de Granada 6,148 E4
Alhama de Murcia 9,274 F4
Alicante 177,918 F3
Almadén 10,713 D3
Almagro 9,066 E3
Almansa 16,965 F3
Almendralejo 21,929 C3
Almería 104,008 E4
Almodóvar del Campo 7,310 D3
Almonte 9,960 C4
Almuñécar 7,812 E4
Álora 8,209 D4
Altea 7,262 G3
Amposta 11,767 G2
Andorra 6,485 F2
Andújar 25,962 D3
Antequera 28,039 D4
Aracena 5,390 C4
Aranda de Duero 18,183 E2
Aranjuez 28,559 E2
Archena 7,118 F3
Archidona 6,084 D4
Arcos de la Frontera 16,217 D4
Arenas de San Pedro 5,225 D2
Arenys de Mar 8,325 H2
Arévalo 5,807 D2
Argamasilla de Alba 6,192 E3
Arganda 11,876 G4
Arnedo 9,809 E1
Arrecife 21,310 C4
Arroyo de la Luz 8,130 C3
Artá 5,284 H3
Arucas 9,095 B5
Aspe 13,229 F3
Astorga 11,794 C1
Ávila de los Caballeros 30,958 D2
Avilés 67,186 C1
Ayamonte 9,897 C4
Ayora 5,249 F3
Azpeitia 7,835 E1
Azuaga 10,719 D3
Badajoz 80,793 C3
Badalona 162,888 H2
Baena 16,496 D4
Baeza 12,607 E4
Bailén 13,207 E3
Balaguer 11,676 G2
Bañolas 9,807 H1
Baracaldo 108,757 E1
Barbastro 13,243 F1
Barcarrota 5,012 C3
Barcelona 1,741,144 H2
Barcelona‡ 2,000,000 H2
Baza 14,290 E4
Beas de Segura 6,592 E3
Béjar 16,804 D2
Bélmez 5,161 D3
Benavente 11,779 D1
Benicarló 12,831 G2
Berga 11,163 G1
Berja 7,081 E4
Bermeo 16,714 E1
Betanzos 7,283 B1
Bilbao 393,179 E1
Bilbao‡ 450,000 E1
Binéfar 6,821 G2
Blanes 15,810 H2
Borjas Blancas 4,991 G2
Bujalance 8,236 D4
Bullas 8,131 F4
Burgos 118,366 E1
Burriana 21,298 G3
Cabeza del Buey 8,704 D3
Cabra 16,177 D4

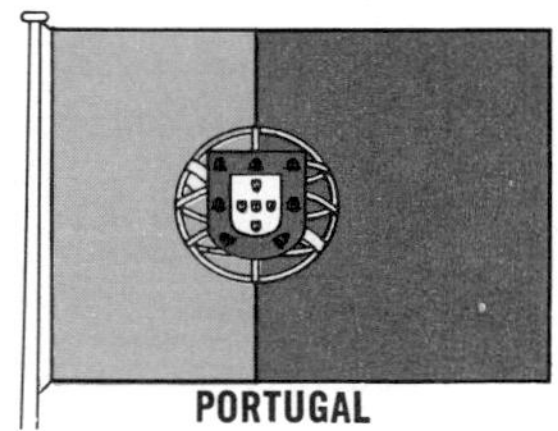

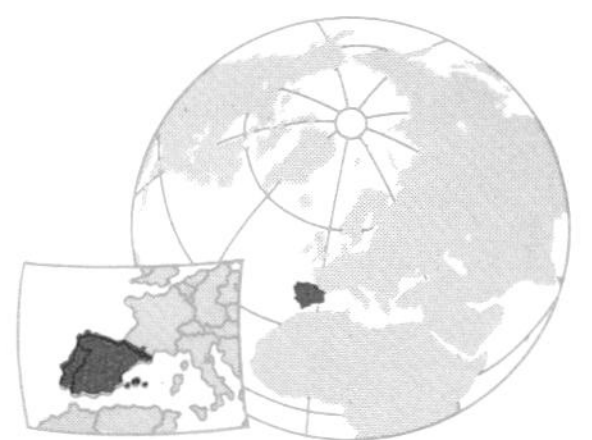

SPAIN

AREA 194,881 sq. mi. (504,742 sq. km.)
POPULATION 37,430,000
CAPITAL Madrid
LARGEST CITY Madrid
HIGHEST POINT Pico de Teide 12,172 ft. (3,710 m.) (Canary Is.); Mulhacén 11,411 ft. (3,478 m.) (mainland)
MONETARY UNIT peseta
MAJOR LANGUAGES Spanish, Catalan, Basque, Galician, Valencian
MAJOR RELIGION Roman Catholicism

ANDORRA

AREA 188 sq. mi. (487 sq. km.)
POPULATION 31,000
CAPITAL Andorra la Vella
MONETARY UNITS French franc, Spanish peseta
MAJOR LANGUAGE Catalan
MAJOR RELIGION Roman Catholicism

PORTUGAL

AREA 35,549 sq. mi. (92,072 sq. km.)
POPULATION 9,933,000
CAPITAL Lisbon
LARGEST CITY Lisbon
HIGHEST POINT Malhão da Estrela 6,532 ft. (1,991 m.)
MONETARY UNIT escudo
MAJOR LANGUAGE Portuguese
MAJOR RELIGION Roman Catholicism

GIBRALTAR

AREA 2.28 sq. mi. (5.91 sq. km.)
POPULATION 29,760
CAPITAL Gibraltar
MONETARY UNIT pound sterling
MAJOR LANGUAGES English, Spanish
MAJOR RELIGION Roman Catholicism

Cáceres 53,108 C3
Cádiz 135,743 C4
Calahorra 16,315 E1
Calasparra 7,238 F3
Calatayud 16,524 F2
Calella 9,696 H2
Callosa de Ensarriá 5,701 G3
Calzada de Calatrava 5,751 E3
Campanario 7,722 D3
Campillos 7,014 D4
Campo de Criptana 12,604 E3
Candás 5,517 D1
Candeleda 5,153 D2
Cangas de Narcea 4,826 C1
Caniles 5,099 E4
Caravaca de le Cruz 10,411 E3
Carballo 5,542 B1
Carcagente 18,223 F3
Carmona 22,832 D4
Cartagena 52,312 F4
Caspe 8,766 G2
Cassá de la Selva 5,248 H2
Castellón de la Plana 79,773 G2
Castro del Río 10,087 D4
Castro-Urdiales 8,369 E1
Castuera 8,060 D3
Caudete 7,332 F3
Cazalla de la Sierra 5,382 D4
Cazorla 6,938 E4
Cehegín 9,661 F3
Cervera 5,693 G2
Ceuta 60,639 D5
Chiclana de la Frontera 22,986 C4
Chiva 5,394 F3
Ciempozuelos 9,185 F5
Cieza 22,929 F3
Ciudadela 13,701 H2
Ciudad Real 39,931 D3
Ciudad-Rodrigo 11,694 C2
Cocentaina 8,375 F3
Coín 14,190 D4
Colmenar de Oreja 4,930 G5
Colmenar Viejo 12,886 F4
Constantina 10,227 D4
Consuegra 10,026 E3
Córdoba 216,049 D4
Corella 5,850 F1
Coria 8,083 C3
Coria del Río 18,085 C4
Corral de Almaguer 8,006 E3
Crevillente 15,749 F3
Cuéllar 6,118 D2
Cuenca 33,980 E2
Cullera 15,128 F3
Daimiel 17,710 E3
Denia 14,514 G3
Dolores 5,420 F3
Don Benito 21,351 C3
Dos Hermanas 36,921 D4
Durango 20,403 E1
Écija 27,295 D4
Eibar 36,729 E1
Ejea de los Caballeros 9,766 F1
El Arahal 14,703 D4
Elche 101,271 F3
Elda 41,404 F3
Elizondo 2,516 F1
El Puerto de Santa María 36,451 C4
Espejo 5,925 D4
Estella 10,371 E1
Estepa 9,376 D4
Estepona 18,560 D4
Felanitx 9,100 H3
Ferrol del Caudillo 75,464 B1
Figueras 22,087 H1
Fraga 9,665 G2
Fregenal de la Sierra 6,826 C3
Fuengirola 20,597 D4
Fuente de Cantos 5,967 C3
Fuenterrabiá 2,350 E1
Fuentes de Andalucía 8,257 D4
Gandía 30,702 F3
Gerona 37,095 H2
Getafe 68,680 F4
Gijón 159,806 D1
Granada 185,799 E4
Granollers 30,066 H2
Guadalajara 30,924 E2
Guadix 15,311 E4
Guareña 7,706 C3
Guernica y Luno 12,046 E1
Haro 8,393 E1
Hellín 15,934 F3
Herencia 8,212 E3
Hinojosa del Duque 9,873 D3
Hortaleza G4
Hospitalet 241,978 H2
Huelma 5,260 E4
Huelva 96,689 C4
Huercal-Overa 5,158 F4
Huesca 33,076 F1
Huéscar 6,384 E4
Ibiza 16,943 G3
Igualada 27,941 G2
Inca 16,930 H3
Irún 38,014 F1
Iscar 5,192 D2
Isla Cristina 11,402 C4
Iznalloz 4,814 E4
Jaca 9,936 F1
Jaén 71,145 E4
Jaraíz de la Vera 6,379 D2
Játiva 20,934 F3
Jávea 6,228 G3
Jerez de la Frontera 112,411 C4
Jerez de los Caballeros 8,607 C3
Jijona 8,117 F3
Jódar 11,973 E4
Jumilla 16,407 F3
La Almunia de Doña Godina 4,835 F2
La Bañeza 8,480 C1
La Bisbal 6,374 H1
La Carolina 13,138 E3
La Coruña 184,372 B1
La Granja (San Ildefonso) 3,198 E2
La Guardia 4,967 B2
La Línea de la Concepción 51,021 D4
La Orotava 8,246 B4
La Palma del Condado 9,256 C4
La Puebla 9,923 H3
La Puebla de Montalbán 6,629 D3
La Rambla 6,525 D4
Laredo 9,114 E1
La Roda 11,460 E3
La Solana 13,894 E3
Las Palmas de Gran Canaria 260,368 B4
Las Pedroñeras 5,846 E3
La Unión 9,998 F4
Lebrija 15,081 D4
Leganés 57,537 F4
León 99,702 D1
Lérida 73,148 G2
Linares 45,330 E3
Liria 11,323 F3
Llerena 5,728 C3
Llivia 801 G1
Llodio 15,587 E1
Lluctmayor 9,630 H3
Logroño 83,117 E1
Loja 11,549 D4
Lora del Río 15,741 D4
Lorca 25,208 F4
Los Santos de Maimona 7,899 C3
Los Yébenes 5,477 E3
Lucena 21,527 D4
Lugo 53,504 C1
Madrid (cap.) 3,146,071 F4
Madrid‡ 3,500,000 F4
Madridejos 9,948 E3
Madroñera 5,397 D3
Mahón 17,802 J3
Málaga 334,988 D4
Málaga‡ 400,000 D4
Malagón 7,732 E3
Malpartida de Cáceres 5,054 C3
Manacor 20,266 H3
Mancha Real 7,547 E4
Manlleu 13,169 H1
Manresa 52,526 G2
Manzanares 15,024 E3
Marbella 19,648 D4
Marchena 16,227 D4
Marín 10,948 B1
Martos 16,395 E4
Mataró 73,129 H2
Medina del Campo 16,345 D2
Medina de Rioseco 4,874 D2
Medina-Sidonia 7,523 D4
Mérida 36,916 C3
Miajadas 8,042 D3
Mieres 22,790 D1
Minas de Ríotinto 3,939 C4
Miranda de Ebro 29,355 E1
Moguer 7,629 C4
Mollerusa 6,685 G2
Monesterio 5,923 C3
Monforte 14,002 C1
Monóvar 9,071 F3
Montehermoso 5,952 C2
Montellano 6,658 D4
Montijo 11,931 C3
Montilla 18,670 D4
Montoro 9,295 D3
Monzón 14,089 G2
Mora 10,523 E3
Moratalla 5,101 E3
Morón de la Frontera 25,662 D4
Mota del Cuervo 5,130 E3
Motril 25,121 E4
Mula 9,168 F3
Munera 5,003 E3
Murcia 102,242 F4
Navalcarnero 6,212 F4
Navalmoral de la Mata 9,650 D3
Nerja 7,413 E4
Nerva 10,830 C4
Novelda 16,867 F3
Nules 9,027 F3
Ocaña 5,603 E3
Oliva 16,717 F3
Oliva de la Frontera 8,560 C3
Olivenza 7,616 C3
Olot 18,062 H1
Olvera 9,825 D4
Onda 13,012 F3
Onteniente 23,685 F3
Orense 63,542 C1
Orihuela 17,610 F3
Osuna 17,384 D4
Oviedo 130,021 C1
Padul 6,377 E4
Palafrugell 10,421 H2
Palamós 7,679 H2
Palencia 58,327 D2
Palma 191,416 H3
Palma del Río 15,075 D4
Pamplona 142,686 F1
Pego 8,861 F3
Peñafiel 4,794 E2
Peñaranda de Bracamonte 6,094 D2
Peñarroya-Pueblonuevo 15,649 D3
Pinos-Puente 7,634 E4
Plasencia 26,897 C2
Pola de Lena 5,760 D1
Pollensa 7,625 H3
Ponferrada 22,838 C1
Pontevedra 27,118 B1
Porcuna 8,169 D4
Port-Bou 2,230 H1
Portugalete 45,589 E1
Posadas 7,245 D4
Pozoblanco 13,280 D3
Pozuelo de Alarcón 14,041 D2
Priego de Córdoba 12,676 D4
Puente-Genil 22,888 D4
Puertollano 50,609 D3
Puerto Real 13,993 D4
Puigcerdá 4,418 G1
Quesada 6,965 E4
Quintana de la Serena 5,171 D3
Quintanar de la Orden 7,764 E3
Reinosa 10,863 D1
Requena 9,836 F3
Reus 47,240 G2
Ripoll 9,283 H1
Ronda 22,094 D4
Roquetas 5,617 G2
Rosas 5,448 H1
Rota 20,021 C4
Rute 8,294 D4
Sabadell 148,223 H2
Sagunto 17,052 F3
Salamanca 125,132 D2
Sallent 7,118 H2
Salobreña 5,961 E4
Salt 5,572 H1
Sama 9,863 D1
San Carlos de la Rápita 8,946 G2
San Clemente 6,016 E3
San Feliu de Guíxols 12,006 H2
San Fernando 59,309 C4
San Ildefonso 3,198 E2

Agriculture, Industry and Resources

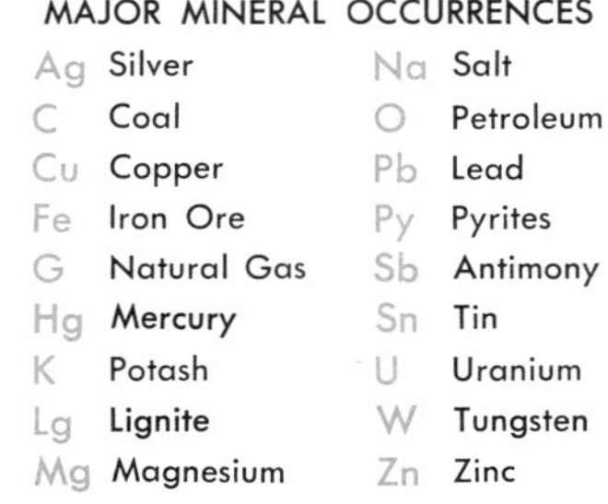

(continued on following page)

(continued)

San Lorenzo de El Escorial 8,098 E2
Sanlúcar de Barrameda 29,483 C4
Sanlúcar la Mayor 6,121 C4
San Roque 8,224 D4
San Sebastián 159,557 E1
Santa Cruz de la Palma 10,393 B4
Santa Cruz de Mudela 6,354 E3
Santa Cruz de Tenerife 74,910 B4
Santa Eugenia 5,946 B1
Santa Fé 8,990 E4
Santander 130,019 D1
Santiago 51,620 B1
Santo Domingo de la Calzada 5,638 E1
Santoña 9,546 E1
San Vicente de Alcántara 7,006 C3
Saragossa 449,319 F2
Saragossa‡ 500,000 F2
Segorbe 6,962 F3
Segovia 41,880 D2
Seo de Urgel 6,604 G1
Seville 511,447 D4
Seville‡ 560,000 D4
Sitges 8,906 G2
Socuéllamos 12,610 E3
Sóller 6,470 H3
Solsona 5,346 G2
Sonseca 6,594 D3
Soria 24,744 E2
Sotrondio 5,914 D1
Sueca 20,019 F3
Tabernes de Valldigna 13,962 G3
Tafalla 8,858 F1
Talavera de la Reina 39,889 D2
Tarancón 8,238 E3
Tarazona 11,067 E2
Tarazona de la Mancha 5,952 F3
Tarifa 9,201 D4
Tarragona 53,548 G2
Tarrasa 134,481 G2
Tárrega 9,036 G2
Tauste 6,832 F2
Telde 13,257 B5
Teruel 20,614 F2
Tobarra 5,887 F3
Toledo 43,905 D3
Tolosa 15,164 F1
Tomelloso 26,041 E3
Tordesillas 5,815 D2
Toro 8,455 D2
Torredonjimeno 12,507 D4
Torrejón de Ardoz 21,081 G4
Torrelavega 19,933 D1
Torremolinos 20,484 D4
Torrente 38,397 F3
Torrevieja 9,431 F4
Torrijos 6,362 D2
Torrox 5,583 E4
Tortosa 20,030 G2
Totana 12,714 F4
Trigueros 6,280 C4
Trujillo 9,024 D3
Tudela 20,942 F1
Úbeda 28,306 E3
Ubrique 13,166 D4
Utiel 9,168 F3
Utrera 28,287 D4
Valdemoro 6,263 F4
Valdepeñas 24,018 E3
Valencia 626,675 F3
Valencia‡ 700,000 F3
Valencia de Alcántara 5,963 C3
Valladolid 227,511 D2
Vall de Uxó 23,976 F3
Vallecas G4
Valls 14,189 G2
Valverde del Camino 10,566 C4
Vejer de la Frontera 6,184 C4
Vélez-Málaga 20,794 E4
Vendrell 7,951 G2
Vera 4,903 F4
Vergara 11,541 E1
Vicálvaro G4
Vich 23,449 H2
Vigo 114,526 B1
Vilafranca del Penedés 16,875 G2
Villacañas 9,883 E3
Villacarrillo 9,452 E3
Villafranca de los Barros 12,610 C3
Villagarcía 6,601 B1
Villajoyosa 12,573 F3
Villanueva de Córdoba 11,270 D3
Villanueva del Arzobispo 8,076 E3
Villanueva de la Serena 16,687 D3
Villanueva de los Infantes 8,154 E3
Villanueva y Geltrú 35,714 G2
Villarreal de los Infantes 29,482 G3
Villarrobledo 19,698 E3
Villarrubia de los Ojos 9,144 E3
Villaverde F4
Villena 23,483 F3
Vinaroz 13,727 G2
Vitoria 124,791 E1
Yecla 19,352 F3
Zafra 11,583 C3
Zalamea de la Serena 6,017 D3
Zamora 48,791 D2
Zaragoza (Saragossa) 449,319 F2

OTHER FEATURES

Alborán (isl.) E5
Alcaraz, Sierra de (range) E3
Alcudia (bay) H3
Almanzor (mt.) D2
Almanzora (riv.) F4
Andalusia (reg.) C4
Aneto (peak) G1
Aragón (reg.) F2
Arosa, Ria de (est.) B1
Asturias (reg.) C1
Balaitous (mt.) F1
Balearic (Baleares) (isls.) H3
Barbate (riv.) D4
Biscay (bay) E1
Cabrera (isl.) H3
Cádiz (gulf) C4
Cala Burras (pt.) D4
Canary (isls.) B4
Cantabrian (range) C1
Catalonia (reg.) G2
Cinca (riv.) G2
Columbretes (isls.) G3
Costa Brava (reg.) H2
Costa de Sola (Costa del Sol) (reg.) D4
Creus (cape) H1
Cuenca, Sierra de (range) F3
Demanda, Sierra de la (range) E1
Douro (riv.) C2
Duero (Douro) (riv.) C2
Ebro (riv.) G2
Eresma (riv.) D2
Esla (riv.) D2
Estats (peak) G1
Estremadura (reg.) C3
Finisterre (cape) B1
Formentera (isl.) G3
Formentor (cape) H2
Fuerteventura (isl.) C4
Galicia (reg.) B1
Gata (cape) F4
Gata (mts.) C2
Genil (riv.) D4
Gibraltar (str.) D5
Gomera (isl.) B5
Gran Canaria (isl.) B5
Gredos, Sierra de (range) D2
Guadalimar (riv.) E3
Guadalquivir (riv.) C4
Guadarrama, Sierra de (range) E2
Guadarrama (riv.) F4
Guadiana (riv.) D3
Gúdar, Sierra de (range) F2
Henares (riv.) G4
Hierro (isl.) A5
Ibiza (isl.) G3
Jalón (riv.) E2
Jarama (riv.) E2
Júcar (riv.) F3
Lanzarote (isl.) C4
La Palma (isl.) A4
León (reg.) C1
Llobregat (riv.) H2
Majorca (isl.) H3
Mallorca (Majorca) (isl.) H3
Mancha, La (reg.) E3
Manzanares (riv.) F4
Marismas, Las (marsh) C4
Mar Menor (lag.) F4
Mayor (cape) E1
Menorca (Minorca) (isl.) J2
Miño (riv.) B1
Minorca (isl.) J2
Moncayo, Sierra de (range) F2
Montserrat (mt.) G2
Morena, Sierra (range) E3
Mulhacén (mt.) E4
Murcia (reg.) F3
Nao (cape) G3
Navia (riv.) C1
Nevada, Sierra (mts.) E4
New Castile (reg.) E3
Odiel (riv.) C4
Old Castile (reg.) D2
Órbigo (riv.) D1
Palos (cape) F4
Peñalara (mt.) E2
Peñas (cape) D1
Peña Vieja (mt.) D1
Penibética, Sistema (range) E4
Perdido (mt.) G1
Pyrenees (range) F1
Rosas (gulf) H1
San Jorge (gulf) G2
Segre (riv.) G2
Segura (riv.) F3
Sil (riv.) C1
Tagus (riv.) D3
Tajo (Tagus) (riv.) D3
Teide, Pico de (peak) B5
Tenerife (isl.) B5
Ter (riv.) H1
Tinto (riv.) C4
Toledo (mts.) E3
Tortosa (cape) G2
Trafalgar (cape) C4
Turia (riv.) F3
Ulla (riv.) B1
Urgel, Llanos de (plain) G2
Valencia (gulf) G3
Valencia (reg.) F3
Valencia, Albufera de (lag.) G3
Vascongadas (reg.) E1

PORTUGAL

DISTRICTS

Aveiro 545,230 B2
Beja 204,440 C3
Braga 609,415 B2
Bragança 180,395 C2
Castelo Branco 254,355 C3
Coimbra 399,380 B2
Évora 178,475 C3
Faro 268,040 B4
Funchal 251,135 A2
Guarda 210,720 C2
Leiria 376,940 B3
Lisbon 1,568,020 A1
Oporto (Porto) 1,309,560 B2
Portalegre 145,545 C3
Porto 1,309,560 B2
Santarém 427,995 B3
Sétubal 469,555 B3
Viano do Castelo 250,510 B2
Vila Real 265,605 C2
Viseu 410,795 C2

CITIES and TOWNS

Abrantes 11,775 B3
Águeda 9,343 B2
Albufeira 7,479 B4
Alcácer do Sal 13,187 B3
Alcântara 23,699 A1

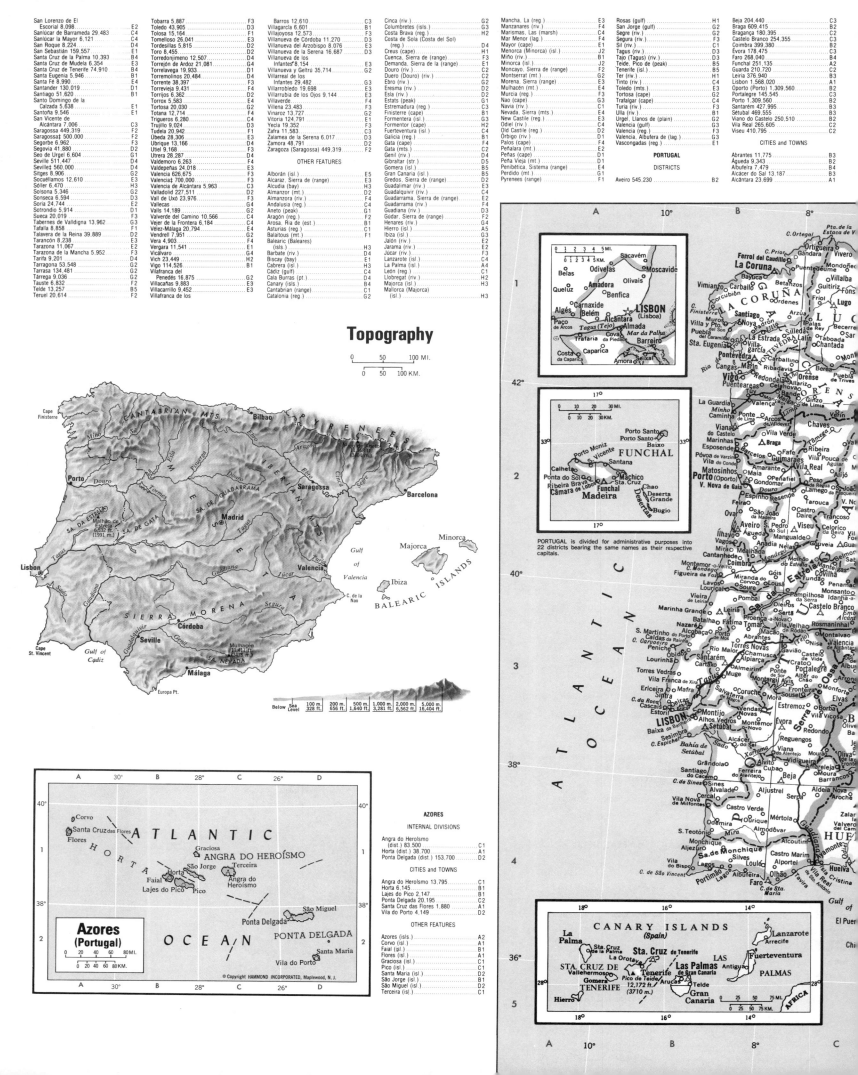

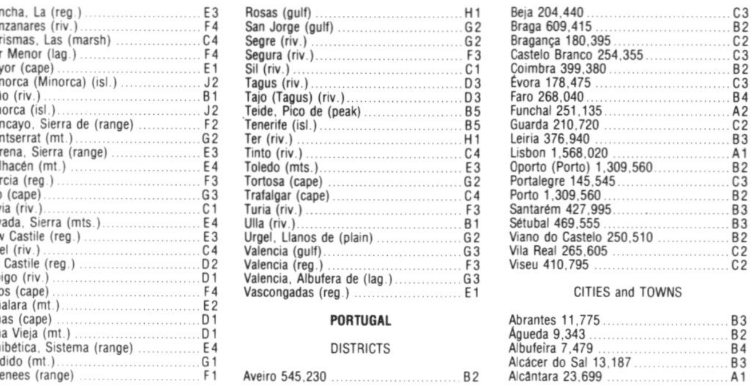

PORTUGAL is divided for administrative purposes into 22 districts bearing the same names as their respective capitals.

Topography

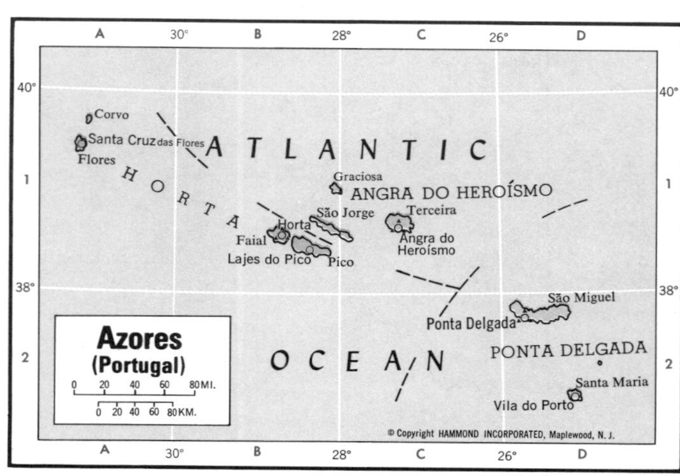

AZORES

INTERNAL DIVISIONS

Angra do Heroísmo (dist.) 83,500 C1
Horta (dist.) 38,700 A1
Ponta Delgada (dist.) 153,700 D2

CITIES and TOWNS

Angra do Heroísmo 13,795 C1
Horta 6,145 B1
Lajes do Pico 2,147 B1
Ponta Delgada 20,195 C2
Santa Cruz das Flores 1,880 A1
Vila do Porto 4,149 D2

OTHER FEATURES

Azores (isls.) A2
Corvo (isl.) A1
Faial (isl.) B1
Flores (isl.) A1
Graciosa (isl.) C1
Pico (isl.) C1
Santa Maria (isl.) D2
São Jorge (isl.) B1
São Miguel (isl.) D2
Terceira (isl.) C1

Alcobaça 4,799 ..... B3
Aldeia Nova de São Bento 5,228 ..... C4
Algés 18,010 ..... A1
Alhos Vedros 7,915 ..... B3
Aljustrel 7,473 ..... B4
Almada 38,990 ..... A1
Almeirim 8,780 ..... B3
Alpiarça 7,623 ..... B3
Alportel 7,632 ..... C4
Amadora 65,870 ..... A1
Amarante 6,067 ..... B2
Amora 10,330 ..... A1
Aveiro 19,905 ..... B2
Avis 1,686 ..... C3
Baixa da Banheira 18,550 ..... B3
Barreiro 53,690 ..... B1
Batalha 6,673 ..... B3
Beja 14,760 ..... C3
Belas 12,001 ..... A1
Belém 19,043 ..... A1
Benfica 39,459 ..... A1
Borba 4,879 ..... C3
Braga 48,735 ..... B2
Bragança 9,310 ..... C2
Caldas da Rainha 13,070 ..... B3
Câmara de Lobos 14,068 ..... A2
Campo Maior 7,405 ..... C3
Cantanhede 6,734 ..... B2
Caparica 13,315 ..... A1
Carnaxide 38,309 ..... A1
Cartaxo 6,628 ..... B3
Cascais 14,925 ..... B3
Castelo Branco 18,740 ..... C3
Cercal 5,021 ..... B4
Chaves 11,465 ..... C2
Coimbra 55,985 ..... B2
Coruche 17,461 ..... B3
Cova da Piedade 21,000 ..... A1
Covilhã 26,530 ..... C2
Elvas 10,305 ..... C3
Espinho 11,745 ..... B2
Estoril 15,740 ..... B3
Estremoz 9,565 ..... C3
Évora 23,665 ..... C3
Fafe 8,142 ..... B2
Faro 20,470 ..... B4
Fátima 6,433 ..... B3
Feira 5,222 ..... B2
Ferreira do Alentejo 6,153 ..... B3
Figueira da Foz 10,485 ..... B2
Funchal 38,340 ..... A2
Fundão 5,081 ..... C2
Gondomar 14,105 ..... B2
Grândola 9,698 ..... B3
Guarda 9,735 ..... C2
Guimarães 24,280 ..... B2
Ílhavo 11,083 ..... B2
Lagoa 5,694 ..... B4
Lagos 10,359 ..... B4
Lamego 10,350 ..... C2
Lavos 5,051 ..... B2
Leiria 7,540 ..... B3
Lisbon (Lisboa) (cap.) 769,410 ..... A1
Lisbon‡ 1,100,000 ..... A1
Loulé 12,777 ..... B4
Louriçal 6,087 ..... B3
Lourinhã 7,340 ..... B3
Lousã 7,341 ..... B2
Machico 10,905 ..... A2
Mafra 7,149 ..... B3
Mangualde 4,839 ..... C2
Marinha Grande 18,548 ..... B3
Matosinhos 22,505 ..... B2
Mira 12,740 ..... B2
Mirandela 5,203 ..... C2
Monchique 8,155 ..... B4
Montargil 5,070 ..... B3
Montemor-o-Novo 9,284 ..... B3
Montijo 26,730 ..... B3
Moscavide 21,765 ..... A1
Moura 9,351 ..... C3
Nazaré 8,553 ..... B3
Odemira 6,793 ..... B4
Odivelas 26,020 ..... A1
Oeiras 14,880 ..... B3
Olhão 11,155 ..... C4
Olivais 55,138 ..... A1
Oporto (Porto) 300,925 ..... B2
Ovar 16,004 ..... B2
Paço de Arcos 11,791 ..... A1
Penafiel 6,463 ..... B2
Peniche 12,555 ..... B3
Peso da Régua 5,376 ..... C2
Pombal 12,508 ..... B3
Ponta do Sol 5,599 ..... A2
Ponte de Sor 9,951 ..... C3
Portalegre 10,970 ..... C3
Portimão 10,300 ..... B4
Porto 300,925 ..... B2
Póvoa de Varzim 17,415 ..... B2
Proença-a-Nova 4,792 ..... B3
Queluz 25,845 ..... A1
Redondo 6,858 ..... C3
Reguengos de Monsaraz 5,806 ..... C3
Ribeira Brava 7,416 ..... A2
Rio Maior 10,206 ..... B3
Sacavém 12,625 ..... A1
Salvaterra de Magos 6,265 ..... B3
Santa Cruz 6,348 ..... A2
Santarém 16,850 ..... B3
Santiago do Cacem 5,887 ..... B3
São Brás de Alportel (Alportel) 7,632 ..... C4
São João da Madeira 14,225 ..... B2
São Teotónio 6,146 ..... B4
São Vicente 5,147 ..... A2
Serpa 7,991 ..... C4
Sertã 6,043 ..... B3
Sesimbra 16,614 ..... B3
Setúbal 49,670 ..... B3
Silves 9,493 ..... B4
Sines 6,996 ..... B4
Sintra 15,994 ..... B3
Soure 7,620 ..... B2
Tavira 10,263 ..... C4
Tomar 10,905 ..... B3
Torres Novas 13,806 ..... B3
Torres Vedras 14,833 ..... B3
Trafaria 6,145 ..... A1
Vagos 5,088 ..... B2
Vendas Novas 8,979 ..... B3
Viana do Castelo 12,510 ..... B2
Vila do Conde 16,485 ..... B2
Vila Franca de Xira 13,070 ..... B3
Vila Nova de Gaia Gaia 50,805 ..... B2
Vila Real Real 10,050 ..... C2
Vila Real de Santo Antonio 10,320 ..... C4
Viseu 16,140 ..... C2

OTHER FEATURES

Atlantic Ocean A3
Carvoeiroeiro (cape) B3
Desertasrtas (isls.) A2
Douro (riv.) B2
Espichel (cape) B3
Estrela, Serra da (mts.) C2
Guadiana (riv.) C4
Lima (riv.) B2
Madeira (isl.) .....
Madeira (isls.) A2
Minho (riv.) B2
Mira (riv.) B4
Monchique, Serra de (mts.) B4
Mondego (riv.) B2
Monsanto (mt.) A1
Ossa, Serra da (mts.) C3
Palha, Mar da (bay) A1
Porto Santo (isl.) B2
Roca (cape) B3
Sadu (riv.) B3
São Vincent (cape) B4
Santa María (cape) C4
Setúbal (bay) B3
Tagus (riv.) B3
Tâmega (riv.) C2
Tejo (Tagus) (riv.) B3
Xarrama (riv.) B3

ANDORRA

CITIES and TOWNS

Andorra la Vella (cap.) 12,000 ..... G1

GIBRALTAR

Gibraltar 29,760 ..... D4

PHYSICAL FEATURES

Europa (pt.) D4

‡Population of metropolitan area.

Spain and Portugal

CONIC PROJECTION

SCALE OF MILES
0 20 40 60 80 100

KILOMETERS
0 20 40 60 80 100

Capitals of Countries ..... ☆
Provincial and District Capitals ..... △
International Boundaries ..... —·—
Provincial & District Boundaries ..... - - -

Scale 1:4,240,000

In SPAIN, following the referenda of October 29, 1979, autonomous status was granted to CATALONIA and the BASQUE COUNTRY *(País Vasco)*. Catalonia consists of the provinces of Barcelona, Gerona, Lerida and Tarragona; the Basque Country consists of Alava, Guipuzcoa and Vizcaya.

Italy
CONIC PROJECTION
SCALE OF MILES
0 20 40 60 80 100
SCALE OF KILOMETERS
0 20 40 60 80 100
Capitals of Countries
Regional Capitals
Provincial Capitals
International Boundaries
Regional Boundaries
Scale 1:4,710,000
The regions are subdivided into provinces bearing the same names as their respective capitals, except:
PROVINCE
CAPITAL
MASSA-CARRARA
Massa
PESARO-URBINO
Pesaro
WEST GERMANY
AUSTRIA
SWITZERLAND
LIECHTENSTEIN
FRANCE
MONACO
YUGOSLAVIA
TUNISIA
CORSICA
SARDINIA
SICILY
MALTA
VATICAN CITY
SAN MARINO
ROME
MILAN
NAPLES
Turin
Genoa
Venice
Florence
Bologna
Palermo
Bari
Trieste
Cagliari
Catania
Messina
Reggio di Calabria
Taranto
Ancona
Pescara
Perugia
Verona
Padua
Trento
Bolzano
Aosta
Potenza
Catanzaro
Campobasso
L'Aquila
ABRUZZI
MOLISE
BASILICATA
CAMPANIA
CALABRIA
APULIA
UMBRIA
MARCHE
TUSCANY
LAZIO
LIGURIA
PIEDMONT
LOMBARDY
VENETO
EMILIA-ROMAGNA
TRENTINO-ALTO ADIGE
FRIULI-VENEZIA GIULIA
ADRIATIC SEA
LIGURIAN SEA
TYRRHENIAN SEA
IONIAN SEA
MEDITERRANEAN SEA
Gulf of Venice
Gulf of Taranto
Gulf of Genoa
Gulf of Naples
Gulf of Salerno
Gulf of Gaeta
Strait of Messina
Strait of Sicily
Strait of Otranto
Malta Channel
Str. of Bonifacio
LIPARI ISLANDS
EGADI ISLANDS
PONTINE ISLANDS
PELAGIE ISLANDS
TUSCAN ARCH.
Elba
Capri
Ischia
Pantelleria
Lampedusa
Alps
Apennines
Dolomite Alps
Carnic Alps
Julian Alps
Mt. Blanc 15,771 ft. (4807 m.)
Etna 11,053 ft. (3369 m.)
Vesuvius 4,190 ft. (1277 m.)
Mt. Corno 9,560 ft. (2914 m.)
Lake Maggiore
Lake Como
Lake Garda
Lake Constance
Po
Tiber
Arno
Vatican City
SCALE
St. Peters
Piazza S. Pietro
Vatican Gar.
Papal Pal.
Rome and Environs
L. Bracciano
TYRRHENIAN SEA
Ostia Antica
Lido di Ostia
Fiumicino
Frascati
Tivoli
Castel Gandolfo
L. Albano
Velletri
Pomezia
© Copyright HAMMOND INCORPORATED, Maplewood, N. J.
Longitude East of Greenwich

VATICAN CITY

AREA 108.7 acres (44 hectares)
POPULATION 728

SAN MARINO

AREA 23.4 sq. mi. (60.6 sq. km.)
POPULATION 19,149

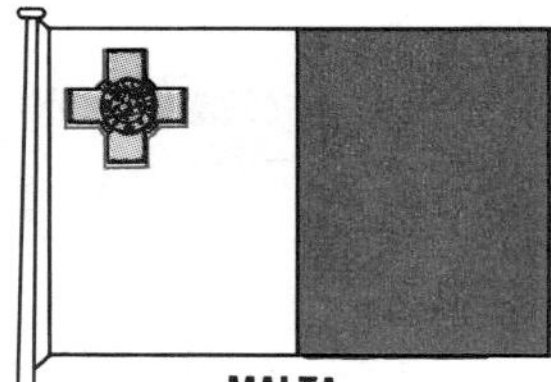

MALTA

AREA 122 sq. mi. (316 sq. km.)
POPULATION 343,970
CAPITAL Valletta
LARGEST CITY Sliema
HIGHEST POINT 787 ft. (240 m.)
MONETARY UNIT Maltese pound
MAJOR LANGUAGES Maltese, English
MAJOR RELIGION Roman Catholicism

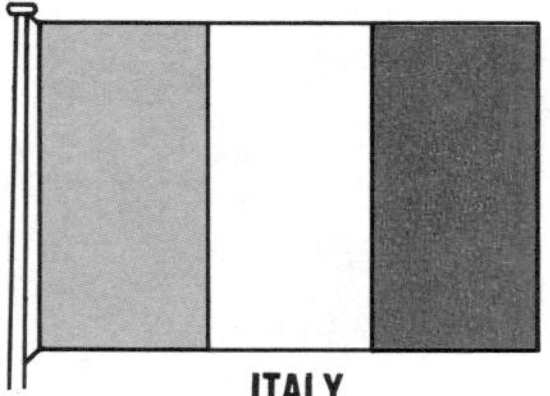

ITALY

AREA 116,303 sq. mi. (301,225 sq. km.)
POPULATION 57,140,000
CAPITAL Rome
LARGEST CITY Rome
HIGHEST POINT Dufourspitze (Mte. Rosa) 15,203 ft. (4,634 m.)
MONETARY UNIT lira
MAJOR LANGUAGE Italian
MAJOR RELIGION Roman Catholicism

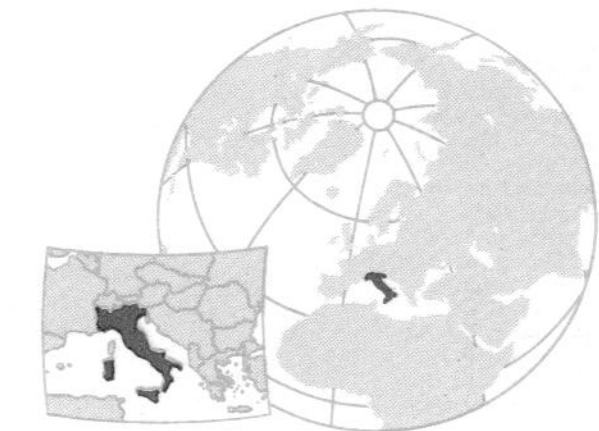

ITALY

REGIONS

Abruzzi 1,166,664 D3
Aosta 109,150 A2
Apulia (Puglia) 3,582,787 F4
Basilicata 603,064 F4
Calabria 1,988,051 F5
Campania 5,059,348 E4
Emilia-Romagna 3,846,755 C2
Friuli-Venezia Giulia 1,213,532 D1
Latium (Lazio) 4,689,482 D3
Liguria 1,853,578 B2
Lombardy 8,543,657 B2
Marche 1,359,907 D3
Molise 319,807 E4
Piedmont 4,432,313 A2
Sardinia 1,473,800 B4
Sicily 4,680,715 D6
Trentino-Alto Adige 841,886 C1
Tuscany 3,473,097 C3
Umbria 775,783 D3
Veneto 2,109,502 D3

PROVINCES

Agrigento 454,045 D6
Alessandria 483,183 B2
Ancona 416,611 D3
Aosta 109,150 A2
Arezzo 306,340 C3
Ascoli Piceno 340,758 D3
Asti 218,547 B2
Avellino 427,509 E4
Bari 1,351,288 F4
Belluno 221,155 D1
Benevento 286,499 E4
Bergamo 829,019 B2
Bologna 918,844 C2
Bolzano-Bozen 414,041 C1
Brescia 957,686 C2
Brindisi 366,027 G4
Cagliari 802,888 B5
Caltanissetta 282,069 D6
Campobasso 227,641 E4
Caserta 677,959 E4
Catania 938,273 E6
Catanzaro 718,069 F5
Chieti 351,567 E3
Como 720,463 B2
Cosenza 691,659 F5
Cremona 334,281 B2
Cuneo 540,504 A2
Enna 202,131 E6
Ferrara 383,639 C2
Florence 1,146,367 C3
Foggia 657,292 E4
Forlì 565,470 D2
Frosinone 422,630 D4
Genoa 1,087,973 B2
Gorizia 142,412 D2
Grosseto 216,315 C3
Imperia 225,127 B3
Isernia 92,166 E4
L'Aquila 293,066 D3
La Spezia 244,435 B2
Latina 376,238 D4
Lecce 696,503 G4
Leghorn 335,265 C3
Lucca 380,356 C3
Macerata 286,155 D3
Mantua 376,892 C2
Massa-Carrara 200,955 C2
Matera 194,629 F4
Messina 654,703 E5
Milan 3,903,685 B2
Modena 553,852 C2
Naples 2,709,929 E4
Novara 496,811 B2
Nuoro 273,021 B4
Padua 762,998 C2
Palermo 1,124,015 D5
Parma 395,497 C2
Pavia 526,389 B2
Perugia 552,936 D3
Pesaro e Urbino 316,383 D3
Pescara 264,981 E3
Piacenza 284,881 B2
Pisa 375,933 C3
Pistoia 254,335 C2
Pordenone 253,906 D2
Potenza 408,435 E4
Ragusa 255,047 E6
Ravenna 351,876 D2
Reggio di Calabria 578,323 E5
Reggio nell'Emilia 392,696 C2
Rieti 143,162 D3
Rome 3,490,377 F6
Rovigo 251,908 C2
Salerno 957,452 E4
Sassari 397,891 B4
Savona 296,043 B2
Siena 257,221 C3
Sondrio 169,149 B1
Syracuse 365,039 E6
Taranto 511,677 F4
Teramo 257,080 D3
Terni 222,847 D3
Trapani 405,393 D5
Trento 427,845 C1
Treviso 668,620 D2
Trieste 300,304 E2
Turin 2,287,016 A2
Udine 516,910 D1
Varese 725,823 B2
Venice 807,251 D2
Vercelli 406,252 B2
Verona 733,595 C2
Vicenza 677,884 C2
Viterbo 257,075 C3

CITIES and TOWNS

Acireale 34,081 E6
Acqui Terme 20,099 B2
Acri 8,150 F5
Adrano 31,988 E6
Adria 11,951 D2
Agira 11,262 E6
Agnone 3,965 E4
Agrigento 40,513 D6
Agropoli 9,413 E4
Alassio 13,512 A2
Alatri 5,710 D4
Alba 23,522 B2
Albano Laziale 15,561 F7
Albenga 13,397 B3
Albino 8,837 B2
Alcamo 41,448 D6
Alessandria 78,644 B2
Alghero 28,454 B4
Altamura 44,879 F4
Amalfi 4,205 E4
Amantea 6,132 E5
Amelia 4,331 D3
Ancona 88,427 D3
Andria 76,405 F4
Anguillara Sabazia 3,241 F6
Anzio 14,966 D4
Aosta 35,053 A2
Aprilia 18,412 D4
Aragona 11,213 D6
Arezzo 56,693 C3
Argenta 6,682 D2
Ariano Irpino 9,796 E4
Ariccia 7,287 F7
Artena 5,034 F7
Ascoli Piceno 43,041 D3
Assisi 4,630 D3
Asti 62,277 B2
Atessa 3,079 E3
Atri 4,686 D3
Augusta 32,501 E6
Avellino 44,750 E4
Aversa 46,536 E4
Avezzano 26,456 D3
Avigliano 5,400 E4
Avola 29,089 E6
Bagheria 32,465 D5
Barcellona Pozzo di Gotto 25,280 E5
Bari 339,110 F4
Barletta 75,116 F4
Bassano del Grappa 33,002 C2
Bellagio 3,258 B2
Belluno 22,180 D1
Benevento 48,523 E4
Bergamo 127,553 B2
Biancavilla 18,743 E6
Biella 46,453 B2
Bisceglie 45,014 F4
Bitonto 39,714 F4
Bitti 4,606 B4
Bologna 493,282 C2
Bolzano (Bolzen) 102,806 C1
Bondeno 7,451 C2
Bonorva 5,232 B4
Bordighera 8,994 A3
Borgo 4,013 C1
Borgomanero 16,655 B2
Bórgo San Lorenzo 7,699 C2
Bosa 8,045 B4
Boves 3,896 A2
Bra 18,399 A2
Bracciano 7,681 C3
Brescia 189,092 C2
Bressanone 12,261 C1
Brindisi 76,612 G4
Bronte 17,823 E6
Brunico 5,175 D1
Budrio 5,635 C2
Busto Arsizio 72,400 B2
Cagli 4,356 D3
Cagliari 211,015 B5
Caltagirone 34,444 E6
Caltanissetta 52,838 D6
Camaiore 8,578 C3
Camerino 4,644 D3
Campobasso 35,551 E4
Campo Tures 1,325 C1
Canicatti 28,761 E6
Canosa di Puglia 30,263 E4
Cantù 28,617 B2
Capua 13,938 E4
Caravaggio 11,298 B2
Carbonia 23,031 B5
Carini 14,255 D5
Carloforte 6,671 B5
Carmagnola 16,469 A2
Carpi 41,789 C2
Carrara 56,236 C2
Casale Monferrato 35,156 B2
Casalmaggiore 6,374 C2
Cascina-Navacchio 28,263 C3
Caserta 51,621 E4
Cassano allo Ionio 9,661 F5
Cassino 14,747 D4
Castelfranco Veneto 16,042 D2
Castel Gandolfo 2,965 F7
Castellammare del Golfo 13,144 D5
Castellammare di Stabia 64,341 E4
Castel San Pietro Terme 6,985 C2
Castelvetrano 29,167 D6
Castiglion Fiorentino 3,797 C3
Castrovillari 15,207 F5
Catania 403,390 E6
Catanzaro 52,054 F5
Caulonia 3,402 F5
Cava de'Tirreni 33,868 E4
Cavarzere 7,917 D2
Cecina 19,415 C3
Cefalù 11,043 E5
Ceglie Messapico 17,512 F4
Celano 9,531 D3
Cerignola 44,648 E4
Cernobbio 8,026 B2
Cerveteri 5,239 E6
Cesano 2,883 F6
Cesena 49,915 D2
Cesenatico 12,805 D2
Chiari 12,017 C2
Chiavari 29,950 B2
Chieri 27,548 A2
Chieti 31,895 E3
Chioggia 24,044 D2
Chivasso 21,369 A2
Ciampino 36,728 F7
Cittadella 9,321 C2
Città di Castello 18,880 C3
Cittanova 11,045 F5
Cividale del Friuli 8,345 D1
Civitavecchia 41,305 C3
Clusone-Fiorine 6,428 C2
Codroipo 6,117 D2
Colle di Val d'Elsa 8,657 C3
Comacchio 10,437 D2
Comiso 24,508 E6
Como 73,257 B2
Conegliano 28,635 D2
Conversano 16,805 F4
Corato 38,163 F4
Cori 6,829 F7
Corigliano Calabro 14,518 F5
Corleone 11,057 D6
Correggio 11,415 C2
Cortina d'Ampezzo 7,285 D1
Cortona 3,482 C3
Cosenza 94,565 F5
Courmayeur 1,401 A2
Crema 26,061 B2
Cremona 75,988 B2
Crotone 44,081 F5
Cuneo 41,633 A2
Cuorgnè 6,752 A2
Desenzano del Garda 14,624 C2
Diano Marina 6,001 B3
Domodossola 18,562 A1
Dorgali 6,714 B4
Eboli 19,787 E4
Edolo 3,707 C1
Empoli 30,526 C3
Enna 27,351 E6
Este 12,992 C2
Fabriano 18,355 D3
Faenza 36,241 D2
Fano 31,238 D3
Fasano 21,247 F4
Favara 27,940 D6
Feltre 11,806 C1
Fermo 17,521 D3
Ferrandina 8,372 F4
Ferrara 97,507 C2
Fidenza 18,064 B2
Fiesole 3,772 C3
Finale Emilia 7,474 C2
Finale Ligure 11,461 B2
Firenze (Florence) 441,654 C3
Fiumicino 13,180 F7
Florence 441,654 C3
Floridia 16,562 E6
Foggia 136,436 E4
Foligno 26,887 D3
Fondi 16,472 D4
Forlì 83,303 D2
Formia 18,978 D4
Fossano 15,857 A2
Fossombrone 5,882 D3
Francavilla Fontana 30,347 F4
Frascati 14,217 F7
Frosinone 34,066 D4
Gaeta 21,973 D4
Galatina 22,137 G4
Galatone 13,880 F4
Gallarate 43,773 B2
Gallipoli 16,878 F4
Garessio 3,359 A2
Gela 66,845 E6
Gemona 6,863 D1
Genoa 787,011 B2
Genova (Genoa) 787,011 B2
Genzano di Roma 14,147 F7
Giarre 18,233 E6
Gioia del Colle 23,299 F4
Gioiosa Ionica 3,811 F5
Giovinazzo 17,768 F4
Giulianova 17,926 E3
Gorizia 35,912 D2
Gravina in Puglia 32,006 F4
Grosseto 48,309 C3
Grottaferrata 10,639 F7
Grottaglie 23,556 F4
Guardiagrele 4,122 E3
Guastalla 7,639 C2
Gubbio 12,371 D3
Guidonia 8,413 F6
Iglesias 24,472 B5
Imola 42,111 C2
Imperia 37,585 B3
Isernia 12,290 E4
Ivrea 26,530 B2
Jesi 33,011 D3
Ladispoli 6,625 E6
Lagonegro 5,613 E4
La Maddalena 10,405 B4
Lanciano 19,652 E3
Lanusei 5,508 B5
Lanuvio 2,970 F7
L'Aquila 36,233 D3
Larino 5,166 E4
La Spezia 121,254 B2
Latina 53,003 D4
Lauria 4,927 E4
Lavello 11,486 E4
Lecce 80,114 G4
Lecco 53,165 B2
Leghorn 170,369 C3
Legnago 15,534 C2
Lendinara 7,079 C2
Lentini 31,429 E6
Leonforte 16,317 E6
Lerici 5,407 B2
Licata 40,997 D6
Lido di Ostia 61,492 F7
Lido di Venezia 18,794 D2
Lipari 3,886 E5
Livigno 2,135 C1
Livorno (Leghorn) 170,369 C3
Lodi 42,489 B2
Lonigo 6,368 C2
Lucca 54,280 C3
Lucera 29,355 E4
Lugo 19,497 D2
Macerata 33,470 D3
Macomer 9,433 B4
Maglie 13,326 G4
Manduria 25,194 F4
Manfredonia 44,463 F4
Mantua 59,529 C2
Marino 12,135 F7
Marsala 34,150 D6
Marsciano 5,372 D3
Martina Franca 31,811 F4
Massa 56,591 C2
Massafra 22,610 F4
Massa Marittima 6,438 C3
Matera 43,026 F4
Mazara del Vallo 37,441 D6
Mazzarino 14,981 E6
Melfi 13,355 E4
Menfi 12,386 D6
Merano 30,951 C1
Mesagne 26,955 G4
Messina 203,937 E5
Mestre 184,818 D2
Milan 1,724,557 B2
Milazzo 18,576 E5
Minturno 2,428 D4
Mirandola 11,551 C2
Mira Taglio 10,194 D2
Mistretta 6,631 E6
Modena 149,029 C2
Modica 31,074 E6
Mola di Bari 23,778 F4
Molfetta 63,250 F4
Moncalieri 49,953 A2
Mondovì Breo 12,524 A2
Monfalcone 29,589 D2
Monopoli 29,776 F4
Monreale 19,348 D5
Monselice 9,047 C2
Montalto Uffugo 3,173 E5
Montebelluna 9,573 D2
Montefiascone 6,885 D3
Montepulciano 4,069 C3
Monterotondo 15,869 F6
Monte Sant'Angelo 17,756 F4
Montevarchi 16,849 C3
Monza 110,735 B2
Mortara 13,929 B2
Naples 1,214,775 E4
Nardò 24,142 F4
Narni 6,213 D3
Naro 13,171 D6
Nettuno 20,927 D4
Nicastro 27,206 F5
Nicosia 13,982 E6
Niscemi 23,925 E6
Nizza Monferrato 7,532 B2
Nocera Inferiore 44,415 E4
Noto 21,606 E6
Novara 92,634 B2
Novi Ligure 29,944 B2
Nuoro 30,551 B4
Olbia 20,998 B4
Oliena 7,030 B4
Orbetello 6,884 C3
Oristano 20,966 B5
Ortona 11,966 E3
Orvieto 8,813 D3
Osimo 12,034 D3
Ostia Antica 2,583 F7
Ostuni 27,241 F4
Otranto 3,707 G4
Ozieri 9,149 B4
Pachino 20,427 E6
Padua 210,950 C2
Palazzolo Acreide 8,981 E6
Palermo 556,374 D5
Palestrina 9,239 F7
Palma di Montechiaro 22,381 D6
Palmi 14,405 E5
Palombara Sabina 5,292 F6
Pantelleria 3,116 C6
Paola 11,330 E5
Parma 151,967 C2
Partanna 10,303 D6
Partinico 25,447 D6
Paterno 41,504 E6
Patti 7,500 E5
Pavia 80,639 B2
Pavullo nel Frignano 5,026 C2
Penne 5,889 D3
Pergine Valsugana 6,248 C1
Pergola 3,866 D3
Perugia 65,975 D3
Pesaro 72,104 D3
Pescara 125,391 E3
Pescia 9,918 C3
Piacenza 100,001 B2
Piazza Armerina 21,754 E6
Pietrasanta 6,620 B3
Pinerolo 33,935 A2
Piombino 35,641 C3
Piove di Sacco 7,035 C2
Pisa 91,156 C3
Pisticci 11,239 F4
Pistoia 55,403 C2
Poggibonsi 21,271 C3
Pomezia 11,915 F7
Pont Canavese 4,075 A2
Pontecorvo 5,986 D4
Pontinia 3,166 D4
Pontremoli 5,222 B2
Popoli 5,372 E3
Pordenone 43,230 D2
Portocivitanova 25,773 D3
Porto Empedocle 15,986 D6
Portoferraio 7,579 C3
Portofino 720 B2
Portogruaro 12,258 D2
Portomaggiore 6,343 C2
Porto Recanati 5,389 D3
Porto Torres 15,422 B4
Potenza 46,869 E4
Pozzallo 12,199 E6
Pozzuoli 53,546 D4
Prato 108,385 C3
Prima Porta 11,393 F6
Priverno 9,950 D4
Putignano 19,290 F4
Quartu Sant'Elena 29,715 B5
Ragusa 55,751 E6
Rapallo 22,272 B2
Ravenna 75,153 D2
Recanati 10,176 D3
Reggio di Calabria 110,291 E5
Reggio nell'Emilia 102,337 C2
Rho 39,206 B2
Riesi 15,855 E6
Rieti 26,775 D3
Rimini 101,579 D2
Rionero in Vulture 11,230 E4
Riva del Garda 8,513 C2
Roccastrada 2,629 C3
Rome (cap.) 2,535,018 F6
Ronciglione 5,900 C3
Rossano 12,119 F5
Rovereto 26,827 C2
Rovigo 31,124 C2
Ruvo di Puglia 23,133 F4

(continued on following page)

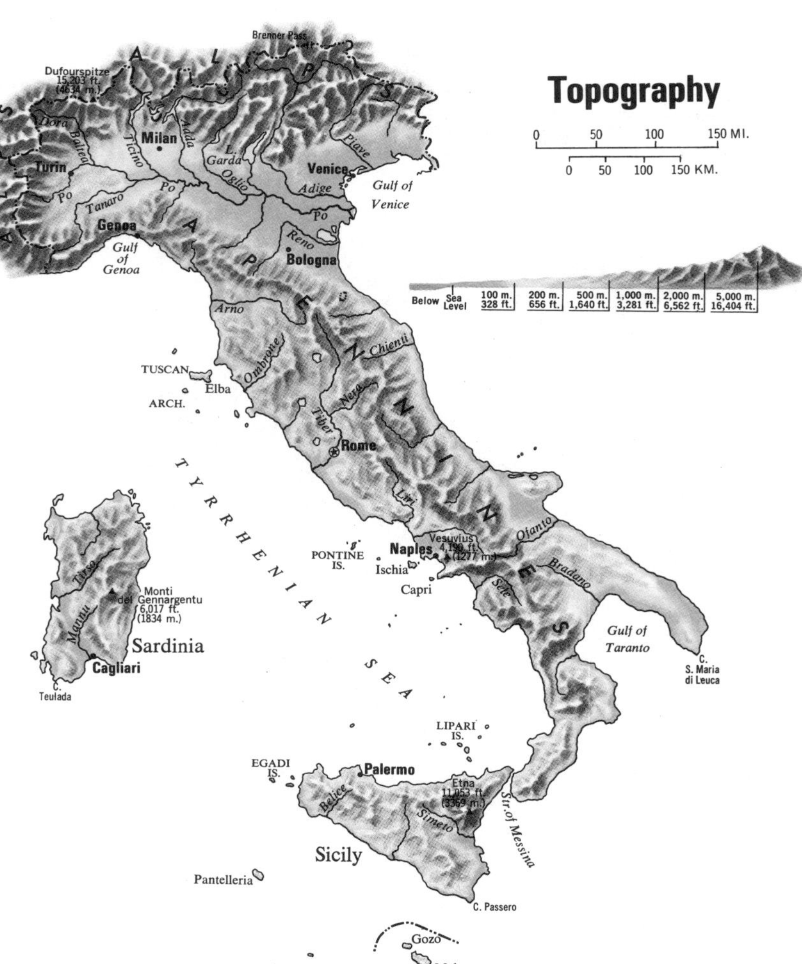

Sabaudia 4,501 .... D4
Saint Vincent 3,737 .... A2
Sala Consilina 8,177 .... E4
Salemi 10,180 .... D6
Salerno 146,534 .... E4
Salsomaggiore Terme 13,677 .... B2
Saluzzo 13,929 .... A2
Sambiase 10,567 .... F5
San Bartolomeo in Galdo 6,943 .... E4
San Benedetto del Tronto 40,108 .... E3
San Cataldo 19,609 .... D6
San Giovanni in Fiore 16,116 .... F5
San Giovanni in Persiceto 12,151 .... C2
San Marco in Lamis 15,817 .... E4
San Miniato 3,245 .... C3
Sannicandro Garganico 17,939 .... E4
San Remo 47,684 .... A3
Sansepolcro 11,443 .... C3
San Severino Marche 6,447 .... D3
San Severo 49,622 .... E4
Santa Maria Capua Vetere 31,077 .... E4
Sant'Elpidio a Mare 4,446 .... E3
Santeramo in Colle 19,758 .... F4
San Vito 3,901 .... B5
San Vito al Tagliamento 6,328 .... D2
San Vito dei Normanni 18,447 .... F4
San Vito Romano 3,256 .... F6
Saronno 32,477 .... B2
Sarroch 3,560 .... B5
Sassari 94,312 .... B4
Sassuolo 33,451 .... C2
Savigliano 14,036 .... A2
Savona 76,274 .... B2
Schio 27,890 .... C2
Sciacca 29,803 .... D6
Scicli 18,405 .... E6
Segni 7,193 .... F7
Senigallia 25,413 .... D3
Sesto Fiorentino 41,636 .... C3
Sestri Levante 18,331 .... B2
Settebagni 5,022 .... F6
Sezze 7,043 .... D4
Siderno 8,023 .... F5
Siena 56,539 .... C3
Siniscola 6,149 .... B4
Sinnai 8,499 .... B5
Siracusa (Syracuse) 93,006 .... E6
Sondrio 19,724 .... B1
Sora 14,031 .... D4
Soresina 9,300 .... C2
Sorrento 13,078 .... E4
Sorso 10,741 .... B4
Spoleto 18,013 .... D3
Squinzano 14,053 .... G4
Stresa 3,758 .... B2
Sulmona 18,221 .... D3
Susa 5,773 .... A2
Suzzara 12,013 .... C2
Syracuse 93,006 .... E6
Taormina 6,696 .... E6
Taranto 205,158 .... F4
Tarquinia 10,300 .... C3
Taurianova 12,198 .... E5
Tempio Pausania 10,382 .... B4
Teramo 31,163 .... D3
Termini Imerese 24,085 .... D6
Termoli 13,986 .... E3
Terni 75,873 .... D3
Terracina 24,092 .... D4
Terralba 8,551 .... B5
Tirano 7,413 .... C1
Tivoli 28,393 .... F6
Todi 5,705 .... D3
Tolentino 11,642 .... D3
Torino (Turin) 1,181,698 .... A2
Torre Annunziata 71,068 .... E4
Torre del Greco 74,752 .... E4
Torremaggiore 16;171 .... E4
Tortona 24,165 .... B2
Trani 40,508 .... F4
Trapani 90,305 .... D5
Trento 64,272 .... C1
Treviglio 21,920 .... B2
Treviso 87,447 .... D2
Tricase 10,481 .... G5
Trieste 257,259 .... E2
Trino 8,722 .... B2
Turin 1,181,698 .... A2
Udine 97,544 .... D2
Umbertide 6,640 .... D3
Urbino 7,735 .... D3
Valdagno 20,342 .... C2
Valenza 20,533 .... B2
Valmontone 6,543 .... F7
Varallo Pombia 3,118 .... B2
Varazze 11,676 .... B2
Varese 65,978 .... B2
Vasto 17,295 .... E3
Velletri 22,020 .... F7
Venafro 5,156 .... E4
Venezia (Venice) 108,082 .... D2
Venice 108,082 .... D2
Venosa 10,993 .... E4
Ventimiglia 20,343 .... A3
Verbania 29,894 .... B2
Vercelli 54,934 .... B2
Veroli 2,793 .... D4
Verona 227,032 .... C2
Viadana 6,667 .... C2
Viareggio 49,965 .... C3
Vibo Valentia 18,005 .... F5
Vicenza 99,451 .... C2
Vicovaro 3,005 .... F6
Vigevano 62,855 .... B2
Villacidro 12,651 .... B5
Villafranca di Verona 11,762 .... C2
Viterbo 39,291 .... C3
Vittoria 43,673 .... E6
Vittorio Veneto 25,476 .... D1
Vizzini 8,583 .... E6
Voghera 37,316 .... B2
Volterra 10,732 .... C3
Zagarolo 4,232 .... F7

OTHER FEATURES

Adda (riv.) B2
Adige (riv.) C2
Adriatic (sea) E3
Alicudi (isl.) E5
Apennines, Central (range) D3
Apennines, Northern (range) B2
Apennines, Southern (range) E4
Arno (riv.) C3
Asinara (isl.) B4
Bernina, Piz (peak) B1
Blanc (mt.) A2
Bolsena (lake) C3
Bonifacio (str.) B4
Bracciano (lake) D3
Brenner (pass) C1
Capraia (isl.) B3
Capri (isl.) E4
Carbonara (cape) B5
Carnic Alps (range) D1
Castellammare (gulf) D5
Circeo (cape) D4
Como (lake) B1
Cottian Alps (range) A2
Dolomite Alps (range) C1
Dora Baltea (riv.) A2
Dora Riparia (riv.) A2
Egadi (isls.) C6
Elba (isl.) C3
Etna (vol.) E6
Favignana (isl.) D6
Filicudi (isl.) E5
Gaeta (gulf) D4
Garda (lake) C2
Gennargentu, Monti del (mt.) B5
Genoa (gulf) B2
Giannutri (isl.) C3
Giglio (isl.) C3
Gorgona (isl.) B3
Graian Alps (range) A2
Gran Paradiso (mt.) A2
Great Saint Bernard (pass) A2
Ionian (sea) F6
Ischia (isl.) D4
Julian Alps (range) D1
Lampedusa (isl.) D7
Lepontine Alps (range) B1
Levanzo (isl.) D5
Ligurian (sea) B3
Linosa (isl.) D7
Lipari (isl.) E5
Lipari (isls.) E5
Maggiore (lake) B1
Manfredonia (gulf) F4
Marettimo (isl.) C6
Maritime Alps (range) A2
Marmolada (mt.) C1
Mediterranean (sea) B6
Messina (str.) E6
Metauro (riv.) D3
Mincio (riv.) C2
Montecristo (isl.) C3
Nera (riv.) D3
Oglio (riv.) C2
Ombrone (riv.) C3
Oristano (gulf) B5
Orosei (gulf) B4
Ortles (range) C1
Otranto (str.) G5
Ötztal Alps (range) C1
Panarea (isl.) E5
Panaro (riv.) C2
Pantelleria (isl.) D6
Pelagie (isls.) D7
Pennine Alps (range) A2
Pianosa (isl.) C3
Piave (riv.) D2
Po (riv.) C2
Pompeii (ruins) E4
Pontine (isls.) D4
Ponza (isl.) D4
Rosa (mt.) A1
Salina (isl.) E5
Salso (riv.) D6
San Pietro (isl.) B5
Santa Maria di Leuca (cape) G5
Sant'Antioco (pen.) B5
Sant'Eufemia (gulf) F5
Sardinia (isl.) B4
Sicily (isl.) E6
Sicily (str.) D6
Simplon (tunnel) A1
Spartivento (cape) B5
Spartivento (cape) F6
Squillace (gulf) F5
Stromboli (isl.) E5
Tagliamento (riv.) D1
Tanaro (riv.) B2
Taranto (gulf) F5
Testa del Gargano (cape) F4
Tiber (riv.) D3
Trasimeno (lake) D3
Tremiti (isls.) E3
Trieste (gulf) D2
Tuscan (arch.) B3
Tyrrhenian (sea) C4
Ustica (isl.) D5
Vaticano (cape) E5
Venice (gulf) D2
Ventotene (isl.) D4
Vesuvius (vol.) E4
Viso (mt.) A2
Volturno (riv.) E4
Vulcano (isl.) E5

MALTA

CITIES and TOWNS

Sliema 20,095 .... E7
Valletta (cap.) 14,042 .... E7
Victoria 5,249 .... E6

SAN MARINO

CITIES and TOWNS

San Marino (cap.) 4,628 .... D3
San Marino* 5,410 .... D3

VATICAN CITY

Vatican City 728 .... B6

*City and suburbs.

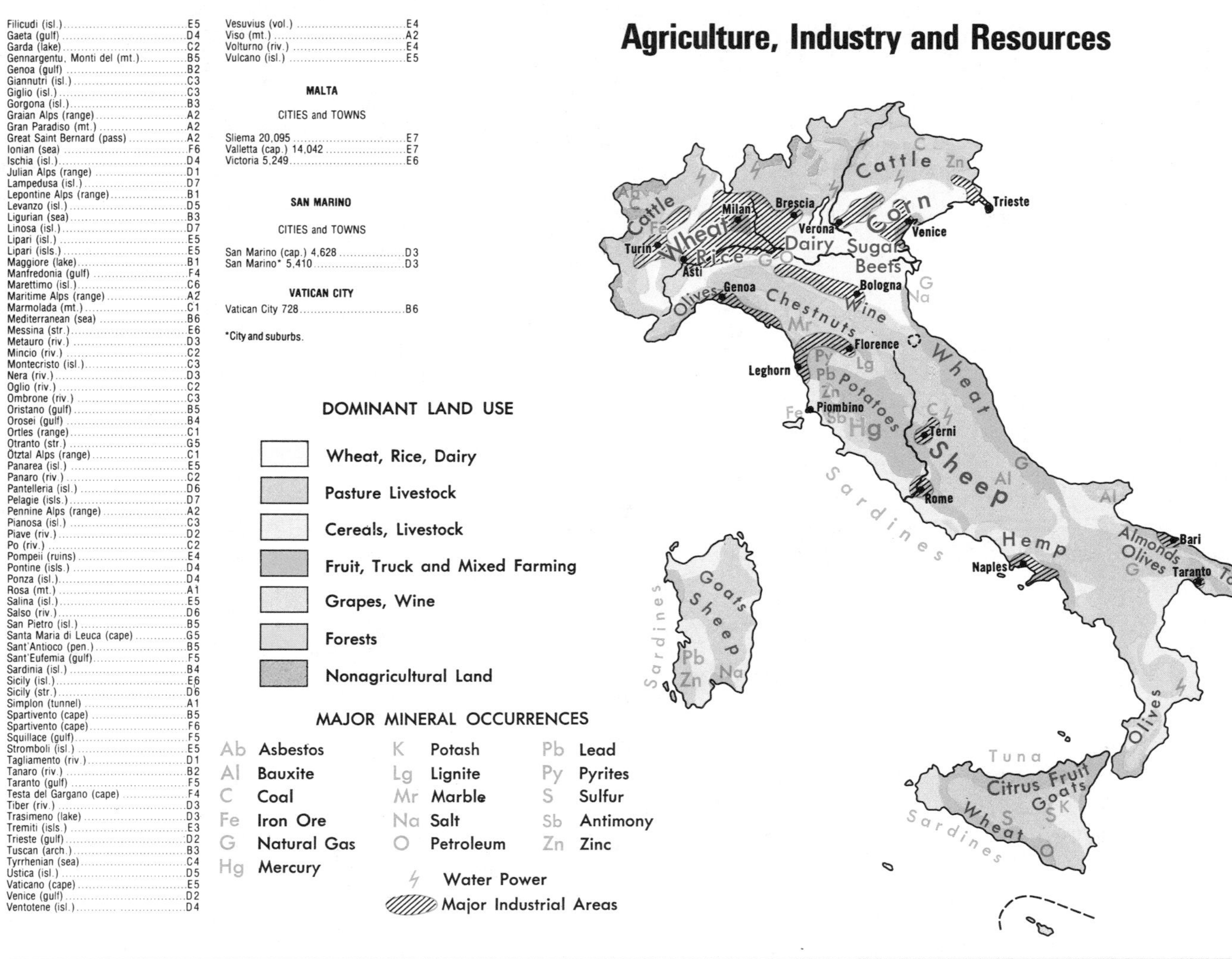

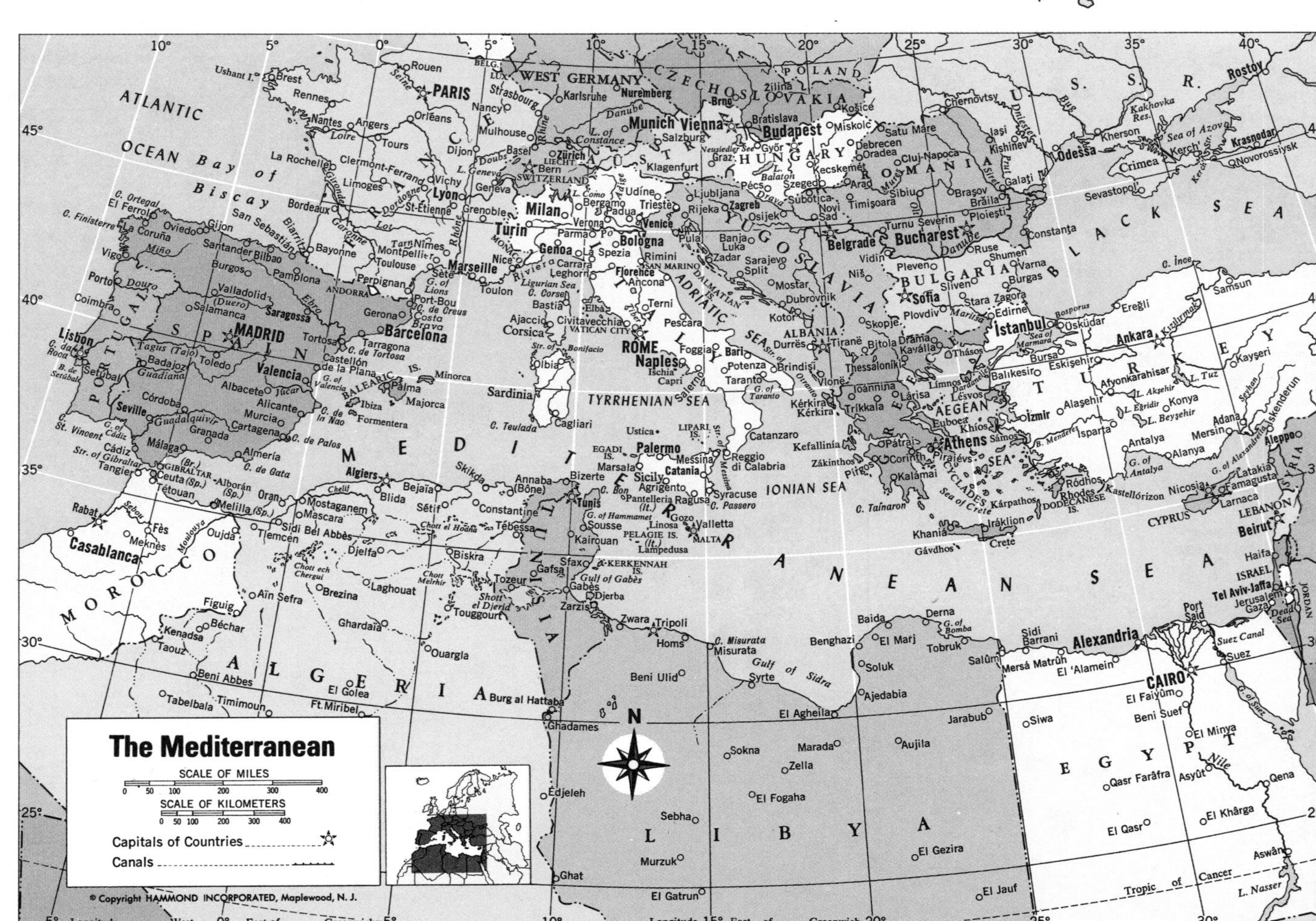

SWITZERLAND

AREA 15,943 sq. mi. (41,292 sq. km.)
POPULATION 6,365,960
CAPITAL Bern
LARGEST CITY Zürich
HIGHEST POINT Dufourspitze (Mte. Rosa) 15,203 ft. (4,634 m.)
MONETARY UNIT Swiss franc
MAJOR LANGUAGES German, French, Italian, Romansch
MAJOR RELIGIONS Protestantism, Roman Catholicism

LIECHTENSTEIN

AREA 61 sq. mi. (158 sq. km.)
POPULATION 25,220
CAPITAL Vaduz
LARGEST CITY Vaduz
HIGHEST POINT Grauspitze 8,527 ft. (2,599 m.)
MONETARY UNIT Swiss franc
MAJOR LANGUAGE German
MAJOR RELIGION Roman Catholicism

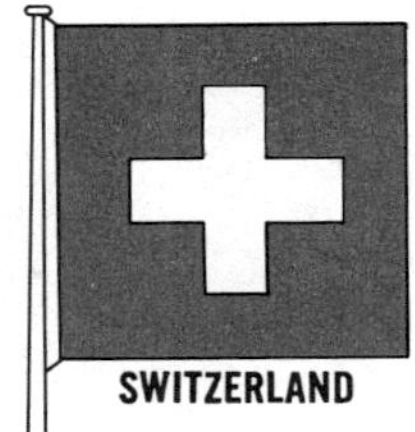
SWITZERLAND

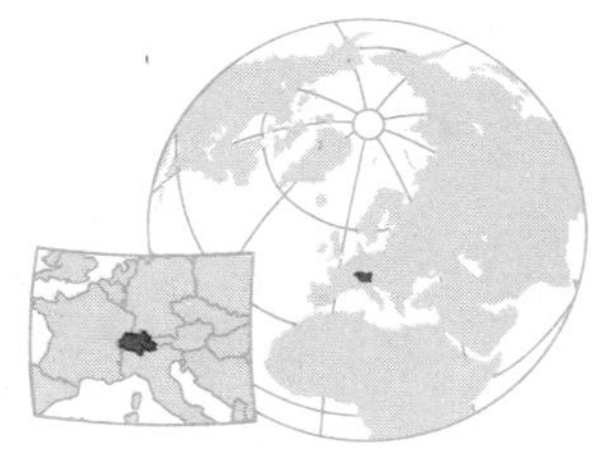

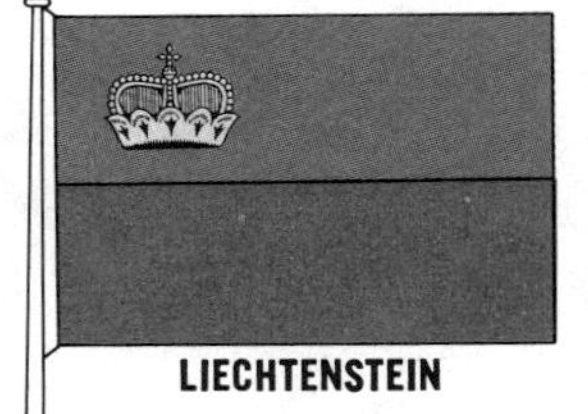
LIECHTENSTEIN

Languages

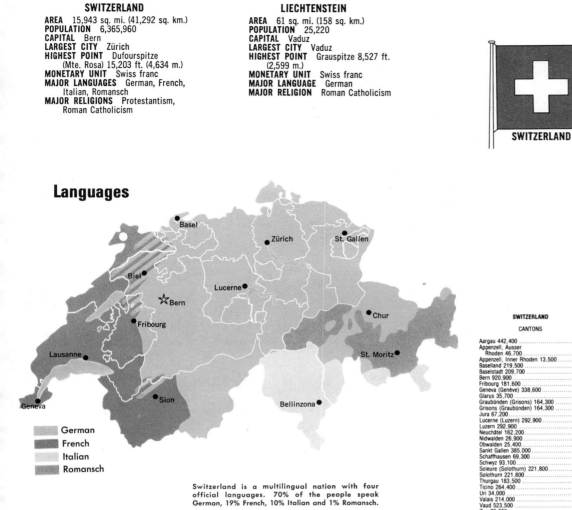

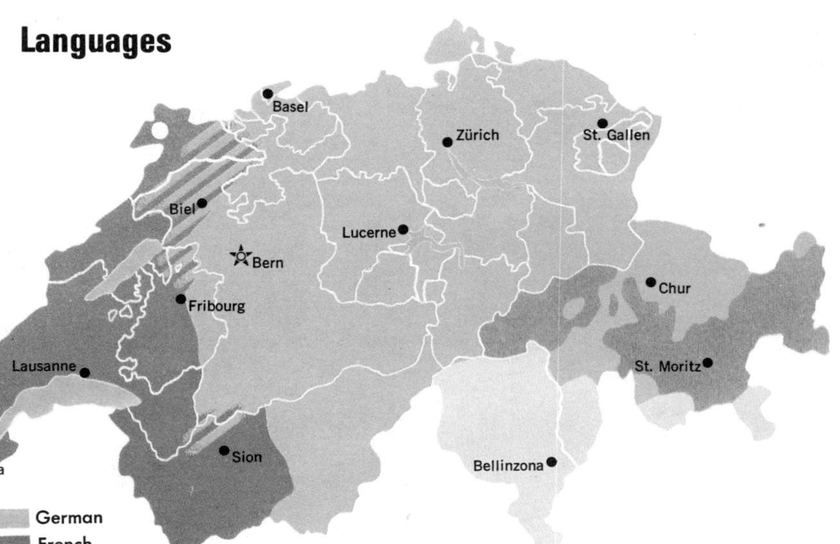

Switzerland is a multilingual nation with four official languages. 70% of the people speak German, 19% French, 10% Italian and 1% Romansch.

SWITZERLAND

CANTONS

Aargau 442,400 F2
Appenzell, Ausser Rhoden 46,700 H2
Appenzell, Inner Rhoden 13,500 H2
Baselland 219,500 E2
Baselstadt 209,700 E1
Bern 920,900 D2
Fribourg 181,600 D3
Geneva (Genève) 338,600 B4
Glarus 35,700 H3
Graubünden (Grisons) 164,300 H3
Grisons (Graubünden) 164,300 H3
Jura 67,200 D2
Lucerne (Luzern) 292,900 F2
Luzern 292,900 F2
Neuchâtel 162,200 C3
Nidwalden 26,900 F3
Obwalden 25,400 F3
Sankt Gallen 385,000 H2
Schaffhausen 69,300 G1
Schwyz 93,100 G2
Soleure (Solothurn) 221,800 E2
Solothurn 221,800 E2
Thurgau 183,500 H1
Ticino 264,400 G4
Uri 34,000 G3
Valais 214,000 D4
Vaud 523,500 B3
Zug 73,600 G2
Zürich 1,117,300 G2

CITIES and TOWNS

Aadorf 3,022 G2
Aarau 16,881 F2
Aarau* 51,800 F2
Aarberg 3,122 D2
Aarburg 5,943 E2
Adelboden 3,326 E3
Adliswil 15,920 F2
Aeschi bei Spiez 1,402 E3
Affoltern am Albis 7,363 F2
Affoltern im Emmental 1,223 E2
Aigle 6,532 C4
Airolo 2,140 G3
Alle 1,615 D2
Allschwil 17,638 D1
Alpnach 3,277 F3
Altdorf 8,647 G3
Altstätten 9,084 J2
Amriswil 7,601 H1
Andelfingen 1,453 G1
Andermatt 1,589 G3
Appenzell 5,217 H2
Arbedo-Castione 2,456 G4
Arbon 12,227 H1
Arbon* 15,400 H1
Ardon 1,498 D4
Arosa 2,717 J3
Arth 7,580 F2
Ascona 4,086 G4
Attalens 1,116 C3
Au 4,944 J2
Aubonne 1,983 B4
Avenches 2,235 D3
Baar 14,074 F2
Baden 14,115 F2
Baden* 66,800 F2
Bad Ragaz 3,713 H2
Balerna 3,885 G5
Balsthal 5,607 E2
Bäretswil 2,733 G2
Basel 199,600 E1
Basel* 379,700 E1
Bassecourt 2,985 D2
Bätterkinden 1,757 E2
Bauma 3,159 G2
Beatenberg 1,263 E3
Beinwil am See 2,520 F2
Belfaux 1,075 D3
Bellinzona 16,979 H4
Bellinzona* 31,000 H4
Belp 6,981 D3
Berg 1,039 H1
Bern (cap.) 154,700 D3
Bern* 285,300 D3
Beromünster 1,552 F2
Bettlach 4,046 D2
Bex 5,069 D4
Biasca 4,696 H4
Biberist 7,769 D2
Biel 63,400 D2
Biel** 89,900 D2
Bière 1,252 B3
Binningen 15,344 D1
Bischofszell 4,233 H1
Blumenstein 1,049 E3
Bodio 1,425 G4
Bolligen 26,121 E3
Boltigen 1,519 D3
Bonaduz 1,289 H3
Boncourt 1,528 C2
Bönigen 1,738 E3
Boswil 1,904 F2
Boudry 4,372 C3
Bourg Saint-Pierre 236 D5
Breil-Brigels 1,215 H3
Breitenbach 2,455 E2
Bremgarten 4,873 F2
Brienz 2,796 F3
Brig 5,191 F4
Brissago 2,120 G4
Brittnau 2,888 E2
Broc 1,842 D3
Brugg 8,635 F2
Brusio 1,344 K4
Bubendorf 2,070 E2
Bubikon 3,244 G2
Buchs 8,454 H2
Bülach 11,043 G1
Bulle 7,556 D3
Buochs 3,232 F3
Büren an der Aare 3,085 D2
Burgdorf 15,888 E2
Burgdorf* 18,400 E2
Bürglen, Thurgau 1,920 H1
Bürglen, Uri 3,401 G3
Bussigny-près-Lausanne 4,509 B3
Bütschwil 3,270 H2
Carouge 14,055 B4
Castagnola 4,430 G4
Cazis 1,687 H3
Cernier 1,717 C2
Chalais 1,651 E4
Cham 8,209 F2
Chamoson 2,049 D4
Charmey 1,155 D3
Château-d'Oex 3,203 D4
Châtel-Saint-Denis 2,842 C3
Chêne-Bougeries 8,670 B4
Chavornay 1,521 C3
Chexbres 1,607 C3
Chiasso 8,868 G5
Chippis 1,561 E4
Chur 32,400 J3
Churwalden 1,052 J3
Claro 1,143 G4
Collombey-Muraz 2,279 C4
Collonge-Bellerive 3,541 B4
Conthey 4,259 D4
Coppet 1,097 B4
Corcelles-près-Payerne 1,256 C3
Corgémont 1,645 D2
Cossonay 1,529 B3
Courgenay 1,954 D2
Courrendlin 2,656 D2
Courroux 1,788 D2
Courtelary 1,462 C2
Courtételle 1,864 D2
Couvet 3,481 C3
Cully 1,535 C4
Davos 10,238 J3
Degersheim 3,400 H2
Delémont 11,797 D2
Derendingen 4,917 E2
Dielsdorf 2,691 F1
Diemtigen 1,913 D3
Diepoldsau 3,311 J2
Diessenhofen 2,532 G1
Dietikon 22,705 F2
Disentis-Mustér 2,319 G3
Domat-Ems 5,701 H3
Dombresson 1,109 C2
Dornach 5,258 E2
Döttingen 3,380 F1
Dübendorf 19,639 G2
Düdingen 4,932 D3
Dürnten 4,820 G2
Dürrenroth 1,084 E2
Ebnat-Kappel 5,131 H2
Echallens 1,643 C3
Ecublens 6,379 B3
Egg 5,250 G2
Eggiwil 2,391 E3
Eglisau 2,160 G1
Egnach 3,466 H1

(continued on following page)

Agriculture, Industry and Resources

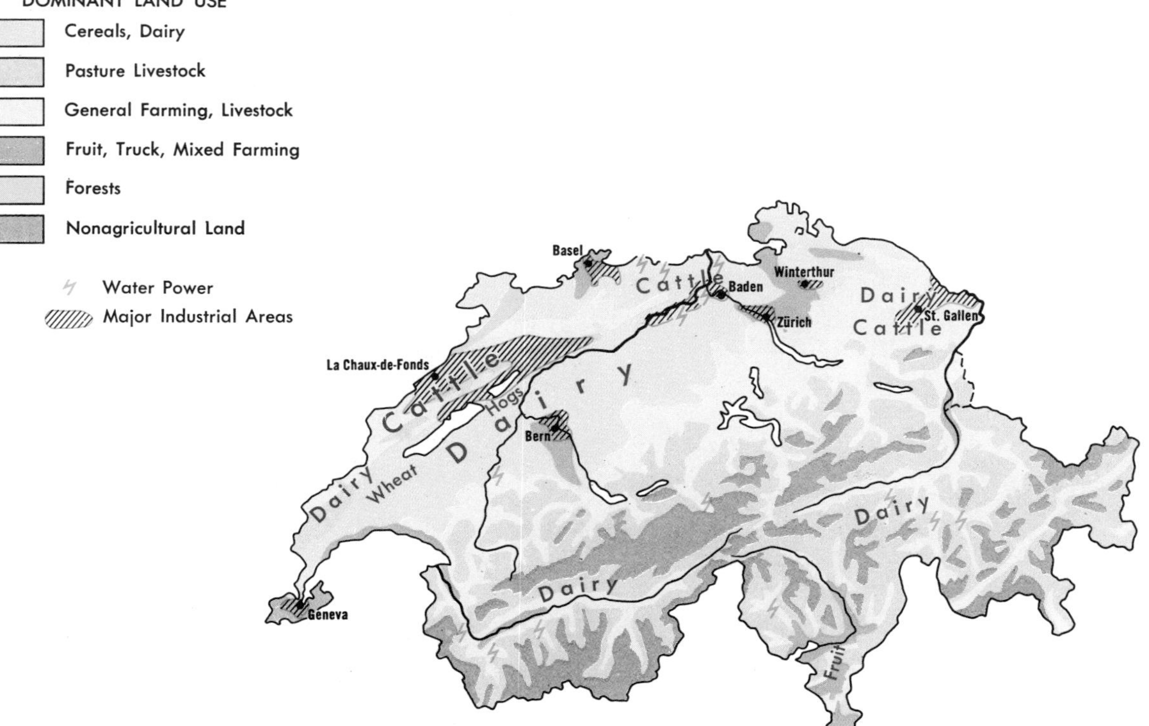

38 Switzerland and Liechtenstein

(continued)

Topography

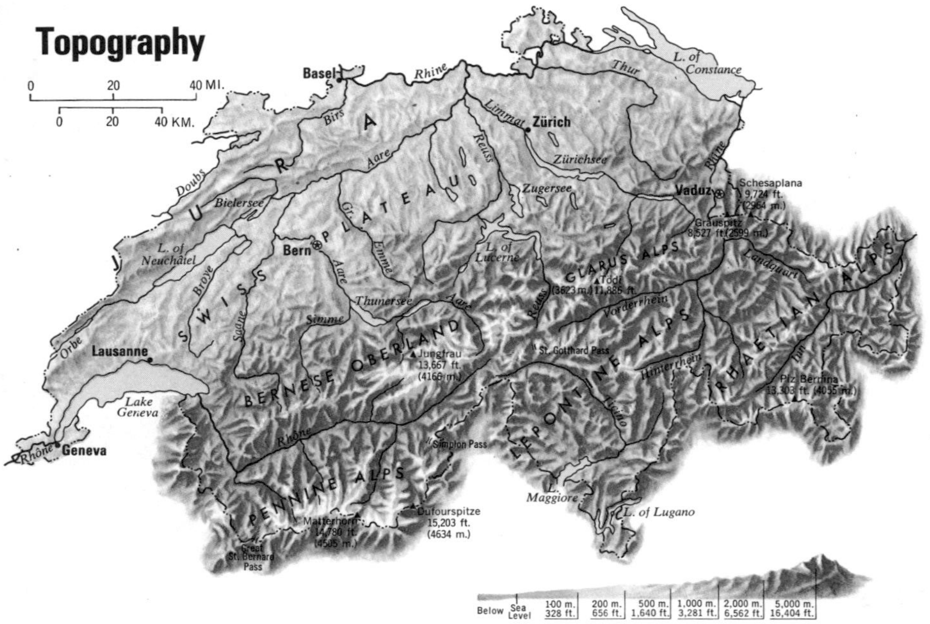

Einsiedeln 10,020 G2
Elgg 2,970 G2
Emmen 22,040 F2
Engelberg 2,841 F3
Ennenda 2,762 H2
Entlebuch 3,310 F3
Erlach 1,052 D2
Erlenbach im Simmental 1,436 E3
Ermatingen 1,787 H1
Erstfeld 4,516 G3
Eschenbach 3,387 G2
Escholzmatt 3,161 E3
Estavayer-le-Lac 3,439 C3
Evolène 1,403 D4
Faido 1,866 G4
Felsberg 1,321 H3
Feuerthalen 3,118 G1
Flawil 8,474 H2
Fleurier 4,124 C3
Flims 1,936 H3
Flüelen 1,731 G3
Flums 4,474 H2
Frauenfeld 17,576 G1
Freienbach 8,429 G2
Fribourg 41,600 D3
Fribourg* 53,500 D3
Frick 3,112 E1
Frutigen 5,796 E3
Fully 3,643 D4
Gais 2,344 H2
Gelterkinden 5,157 E2
Geneva (Genève) 163,100 B4
Geneva (Genève)* 320,200 B4
Gersau 1,753 G2
Gimel 1,205 B3
Giornico 1,389 G4
Giswil 2,760 F3
Giubiasco 5,796 H4
Gland 2,404 B4
Glarus 6,189 H2
Glattfelden 2,857 F1
Glis 3,389 E4
Gordola 2,586 G4
Gossau 12,793 H2
Grabs 4,245 H2
Grächen 1,063 E4
Grandson 2,135 C3
Grenchen 20,051 D2
Grenchen* 28,300 D2
Grindelwald 3,511 E3
Grosswangen 2,213 F2
Gruyères 1,234 D3
Gstaad D4
Gsteig 865 D4
Guggisberg 1,739 D3
Gurtnellen 1,048 G3
Guttingen 1,060 H1
Hallau 1,836 F1
Heiden 3,716 H2
Heimberg 3,046 E3
Hérémence 1,484 D4
Hergiswil 4,364 F3
Herisau 14,597 H2
Herzogenbuchsee 5,140 E2
Hilterfingen 3,647 E3
Hinwil 6,547 G2
Hitzkirch 1,468 F2
Hochdorf 5,222 F2
Horgen 15,691 G2
Huttwil 4,800 E2
Igis 5,283 J3
Ilanz 1,783 H3
Illnau 13,693 G2
Ingenbohl 5,111 G2
Innertkirchen 1,064 F3
Ins 2,435 D2
Interlaken 4,735 E3
Jegenstorf 2,858 D2
Jenaz 1,124 J3
Jona 9,286 G2
Jungfraujoch E3
Kaltbrunn 2,751 H2
Kandersteg 957 E4
Kerns 3,807 F3
Kerzers 2,688 D3
Kirchberg, Bern 3,595 E2
Kirchberg, St. Gallen 6,309 G2
Kleinlützel 1,271 D2
Klingnau 2,545 F1
Klosters Dorf 3,534 J3
Kloten 16,388 G2
Koblenz 1,439 F1
Kölliken 3,219 F2
Köniz 33,800 D3
Konolfingen 4,137 E3
Kreuzlingen 15,760 H1
Kriens 20,409 F2
Krummenau 1,904 H2
Küsnacht 12,193 G2
Küssnacht am Rigi 7,956 F2
Küttigen 4,181 F2
L'Abbaye 1,319 B3
La Chaux-de-Fonds 42,500 C2
Lachen 4,914 G2
Lancy 20,523 B4
La Neuveville 3,917 D2
Langenthal 13,077 E2
Langenthal* 22,100 E2
Langnau am Albis 4,879 G2
Langnau in Emmental 8,950 E3
La Roche 1,069 D3
La Sarraz 1,190 C3
La Tour-de-Peilz 8,864 C4
Läufelfingen 1,243 E2
Laufen 4,723 D2
Laufenburg 2,128 F1
Laupen 2,139 D3
Lauperswil 2,542 E3
Lausanne 136,100 C3
Lausanne* 228,700 C3
Lauterbrunnen 3,431 E3
Le Brassus 5,465 B3
Le Châble 4,541 D4
Le Chenit (Le Brassus) 5,465 B3
Le Landeron 2,768 C2
Le Locle 14,452 C2
Le Mont-sur-Lausanne 2,692 C3
Lengau 4,736 D2
Lenk 1,876 D4
Le Noirmont 1,516 C2
Lens 2,052 D4
Lenzburg 7,594 F2
Les Bois 1,110 C2
Les Ponts-de-Martel 1,327 C2
Leuk 2,796 E4
Leukerbad 1,056 E4
Leysin 2,752 C4
Liechtensteig 2,131 H2
Liestal 12,500 E2
Liestal-Sissach* 40,800 E2
Linthal 1,458 H3
Littau 13,495 F2
Locarno 14,143 G4
Locarno* 39,200 G4
Lodrino 1,075 G4
Lotzwil 2,323 E2
Lucens 2,144 C3
Lucerne 70,200 F2
Lucerne* 158,600 F2
Lugano 22,280 G4
Lugano* 64,200 G4
Lungern 1,813 F3
Luthern 1,706 E2
Lutry 4,994 C3
Lützelflüh 3,842 E3
Luzern (Lucerne) 70,200 F2
Lyss 8,131 D2
Maienfeld 1,542 J2
Malans 1,294 J3
Malleray 1,969 D2
Malters 5,100 F2
Malvaglia 1,099 H4
Männedorf 7,419 G2
Marbach 1,265 E3
Martigny 10,478 C4
Meilen 9,881 G2
Meiringen 3,759 F3
Melide 1,315 G5
Mellingen 3,211 F2
Mels 5,969 H2
Mendrisio 6,223 G5
Menzingen 3,483 G2
Menznau 2,185 E2
Mesocco 1,376 H4
Meyrin 14,255 B4
Minusio 5,027 G4
Möhlin 6,003 E1
Mollis 2,628 H2
Montana 1,725 D4
Monthey 10,114 C4
Montreux 20,421 C4
Morges 11,931 B3
Morges* 17,200 B3
Moudon 3,773 C3
Moutier 8,794 D2
Müllheim 1,620 G1
Mümliswil-Ramiswil 2,702 E2
Münchenbuchsee 6,459 E2
Münsingen 8,350 E3
Muotathal 2,763 G3
Muri 4,853 F2
Muri bei Bern 3,057 E3
Mürren E3
Murten 4,256 D3
Muttenz 15,518 E1
Näfels 3,739 H2
Naters 5,517 E4
Nebikon 1,378 F2
Nendaz 4,051 D4
Nesslau 1,934 H2
Netstal 2,771 H2
Neuchâtel 38,400 C3
Neuchâtel* 61,700 C3
Neuenegg 3,452 D3
Neuhausen am Rheinfall 12,103 G1
Neunkirch 1,239 F1
Nidau 7,962 D2
Niederbipp 3,293 E2
Niederurnen 3,354 G2
Nunningen 1,450 E2
Nyon 11,424 B4
Oberägeri 2,992 G2
Oberburg 3,015 E2
Oberdiessbach 2,145 E3
Oberdorf 1,953 E2
Oberriet 6,123 J2
Obersiggenthal 6,623 F1
Oberzwil 4,659 H2
Oensingen 3,387 E2
Oftringen 9,189 E2
Ollon 4,470 D4
Olten 21,209 E2
Olten* 49,000 E2
Opfikon 11,115 G2
Orbe 4,522 C3
Orsières 2,470 D4
Ouchy C4
Paradiso 3,101 G5
Payerne 6,899 C3
Penthalaz 1,701 C3
Péry 1,486 D2
Peseux 5,578 C3
Pfaffnau 2,584 E2
Pieterlen 3,485 D2
Plaffeien 1,448 D3
Pontresina 1,646 J3
Porrentruy 7,827 C2
Port-Valais 1,363 C4
Poschiavo 3,563 J4
Prangins 1,466 B4
Pratteln 15,127 E1
Pully 15,917 C4
Quinto 1,490 G3
Rafz 2,215 G1
Ramsen 1,217 G1
Rapperswil 8,713 G2
Raron 1,257 E4
Regensdorf 8,566 F2
Reichenbach im Kandertal 2,900 E3
Reiden 3,275 F2
Reinach in Aargau 5,862 F2
Reinach in Baselland 13,419 E2
Renan 1,094 C2
Renens 17,391 C3
Rheinau 2,075 G1
Rheineck 3,275 J2
Rheinfelden 6,866 E1
Richterswil 7,380 G2
Riehen 21,026 E1
Riggisberg 2,193 E3
Riva San Vitale 1,607 G5
Rivera 1,146 G4
Roggwil 3,403 E2
Rolle 3,658 B4
Romanshorn 8,329 H1
Romont 3,276 C3
Rorschach 11,963 H2
Rorschach* 24,200 H2
Rosenlaui F3
Rothrist 5,883 E2
Roveredo 2,037 H4
Rüeggisberg 1,857 E3
Rumlang 5,677 G2
Rüschegg 1,346 D3
Ruswil 4,756 F2
Rüthi 1,493 J2
Rüti, Zürich 9,546 G2
Saanen 5,840 D4
Sachseln 3,059 F3
Saignelégier 1,745 D2
Saint-Aubin-Sauges 2,058 C3
Saint-Blaise 2,586 D2
Sainte-Croix 6,240 B3
Saint-Imier 6,740 D2
Saint-Légier-La Chiésaz 2,230 C4
Saint-Martin 1,120 E4
Saint-Maurice 3,808 C4
Saint Moritz 5,699 J3
Saint Niklaus 2,043 E4
Saint-Prex 2,306 B4
Saint Stephan 1,213 D3
Saint-Ursanne 1,073 D2
Samedan 2,574 J3
Sankt Gallen 81,900 H2
Sankt Gallen* 90,400 H2
Sankt Margrethen 5,101 J2
Sargans 4,058 H2
Sarnen 6,952 F3
Satigny 1,877 A4
Savièse 3,585 D4
Saxon 2,409 D4
Schaffhausen 36,800 G1
Schaffhausen* 55,800 G1
Schänis 2,355 H2
Schattdorf 3,292 G3
Scherzingen 1,420 H1
Schiers 2,342 J3
Schinznach-Dorf 1,154 F2
Schleitheim 1,544 G1
Schlieren 11,869 F2
Schönenwerd 4,793 E2
Schübelbach 4,395 G2
Schüpfheim 3,773 F3
Schwanden 2,823 H2
Schwyz 12,194 G2
Scuol 1,686 K3
Sempach 1,619 F2
Seon 3,628 F2
Seuzach 3,258 G1
Sevelen 2,742 H2
Sierre 11,017 D4
Signau 2,642 E3
Sigriswil 3,540 E3
Silenen 2,338 G3
Sils im Domleschg 762 H3
Silvaplana 714 J4
Sins 2,435 F2
Sion 21,925 D4
Sirnach 3,706 G2
Sissach 4,938 E2
Solothurn (Soleure) 17,708 E2
Solothurn* 35,600 E2
Somvix 1,555 G3
Sonvico 1,129 G4
Spiez 9,911 E3
Stäfa 9,937 G2
Stalden 1,121 E4
Stans 5,180 F3
Steckborn 3,752 G1
Steffisburg 12,621 E3
Stein 1,763 E1
Stein am Rhein 2,751 G1
Suhr 7,223 F2
Sulgen 1,834 H1
Sumiswald 5,334 E2
Sursee 7,052 F2
Tafers 2,021 D3
Täuffelen 1,761 D2
Tavannes 3,869 D2
Tavetsch 1,273 G3
Teufen 5,300 H2
Thal 4,919 J2
Thalwil 13,591 G2
Thayngen 3,640 G1
Therwil 5,412 E1
Thun 37,000 E3
Thun* 63,600 E3
Thunstetten 2,483 E2
Thusis 2,381 H3
Trachselwald 1,199 E2
Tramelan 5,549 D2
Trimmis 1,109 J3
Troistorrents 2,208 C4
Trub 1,833 E3
Trun 1,607 G3
Turbenthal 2,939 G2
Uetendorf 3,132 E3
Unterägeri 4,671 G2
Unteriberg 1,344 G2
Unterkulm 2,596 F2
Unterseen 4,192 E3
Untervaz 1,230 H3
Urnäsch 2,313 H2
Uster 21,819 G2
Utzenstorf 3,193 E2
Uznach 3,984 H2
Uzwil 9,133 H2
Vallorbe 4,028 B3
Vaz-Obervaz 2,003 J3
Vechigen 3,595 E3
Vernayaz 1,356 D4
Versoix 5,627 B4
Vevey 17,957 C4
Vevey-Montreux* 62,300 C4
Villeneuve 3,705 C4
Visp 5,252 E4
Vouvry 1,851 C4
Vuadens 1,278 C3
Wädenswil 15,695 G2
Wahlern 4,832 D3
Wald 8,185 G2
Waldenburg 1,449 E2
Waldkirch 2,669 H2
Walenstadt 3,446 H2
Wallisellen 10,415 G2
Walzenhausen 2,082 J2
Wangen an der Aare 2,013 E2
Wängi 2,730 H1
Wartau 3,604 H2
Wattwil 8,566 H2
Weesen 1,308 H2
Weggis 2,517 F2
Weinfelden 8,621 H1
Wettingen 19,900 F2
Wetzikon 13,469 G2
Wil 14,646 H2
Wil* 20,500 H2
Wilchingen 1,066 F1
Wilderswil 1,666 E3
Wildhaus 1,104 H2
Willisau 2,728 F2
Wimmis 1,833 E3
Windisch 7,444 F1
Winterthur 93,500 G1
Winterthur* 110,100 G1
Wohlen 12,024 F2
Wohlen* 16,000 F2
Wohlen bei Bern 4,190 D3
Wolfenschiessen 1,470 F3
Wolhusen 3,556 F2
Worb 9,526 E3
Wünnewil 3,652 D3
Wynigen 1,986 E2
Yverdon 20,538 C3
Yvonand 1,321 C3
Zell, Luzern 1,590 E2
Zell, Zürich 4,008 G2
Zermatt 3,101 E4
Zizers 1,913 J3
Zofingen 9,292 F2
Zollikofen 9,069 E3
Zollikon 12,117 G2
Zug 22,972 G2
Zug* 51,300 G2
Zuoz 1,165 J3
Zürich 401,600 F2
Zürich* 718,100 F2
Zurzach 3,098 F1
Zweisimmen 2,738 D3

OTHER FEATURES

Aa (riv.) F3
Aare (riv.) E3
Ägerisee (lake) G2
Aiguille d'Argentière (mt.) C5
Aletschhorn (mt.) F4
Aroser Rothorn (mt.) J3
Ault (peak) H3
Balmhorn (mt.) E4
Bernese Oberland (reg.) E3
Bernina (peak) J4
Bernina (pass) K4
Bielersee (lake) D2
Bietschhorn (mt.) E4
Birs (riv.) D2
Blinnenhorn (mt.) F4
Blümlisalp (mt.) E3
Bodensee (Constance) (lake) H1
Borgne (riv.) D4
Breithorn (mt.) E5
Breithorn (mt.) E4
Brienzer Rothorn (mt.) F3
Brienzersee (lake) F3
Broye (riv.) C3
Buchegg (mts.) D2
Buin (peak) K3
Campo Tencia (peak) G4
Chasseron (mt.) C3
Churfirsten (mt.) H2
Clariden (mt.) G3
Constance (lake) H1
Cornettes de Bise (mts.) C4
Dammastock (mt.) F3
Davos (valley) J3
Dent Blanche (mt.) E4
Dent de Lys (mt.) D4

Dent de Ruth (mt.) D3
Dent d'Hérens (mt.) E5
Dents du Midi (mt.) C4
Diablerets (mt.) D4
Doldenhorn (mt.) E4
Dolent (mt.) C5
Dom (mt.) E4
Doubs (riv.) C2
Drance (riv.) D4
Dufourspitze (mt.) E5
Emmental (riv.) E3
Engadine (valley) K3
Err (peak) J3
Finsteraarhorn (mt.) F3
Finstermünz (pass) K3
Fletschhorn (mt.) F4
Fluchthorn (mt.) K3
Flüela (pass) J3
Furka (pass) F3
Generoso (mt.) H5
Geneva (lake) C4
Glärnisch (mt.) H2
Glarus Alps (mts.) H3
Grand Combin (mt.) D5
Grande Dixence (dam) D4
Grand Muveran (mt.) D4
Grauehörner (mts.) H3
Great Saint Bernard (mt.) D5
Great Saint Bernard (pass) D5
Greifensee (lake) G2
Greina (pass) G3
Grimsel (pass) F3
Gross Emme (riv.) E2
Gross Litzner (mt.) K3
Hinterrhein (riv.) H3
Hochwang (mt.) J3
Hohenstollen (mt.) F3
Hörnli (mt.) G2
Inn (riv.) K3
Jorat (mt.) C3
Jungfrau (mt.) E3
Jura (mts.) B3
Kaiseregg (mt.) D3
Kesch (peak) J3
La Dôle (mt.) B4
Landquart (riv.) J3
Le Chasseral (mt.) D2
Le Gros Crêt (mt.) B3
Léman (Geneva) (lake) C4
Leone (mt.) F4
Lepontine Alps (range) G4
Limmat (riv.) F2
Linard (peak) K3
Linden (mts.) F2
Linth (riv.) G3
Lötschberg (tunnel) E4
Lower Engadine (valley) K3
Lucerne (lake) F3
Lugano (lake) H5
Madrisahorn (mt.) J3
Maggia (riv.) G4
Maggiore (lake) G5
Männlifluh (mt.) E3
Marmontana (mt.) H4
Matterhorn (mt.) E4
Mauvoisin (dam) D4
Moësa (riv.) H4
Morat (lake) D3
Muota (riv.) G3
Murg (riv.) G1
Murtaröl (peak) K3
Muttler (mt.) K3
Naafkopf (mt.) J2
Napf (mt.) E3
National Park K3
Neuchâtel (lake) C3
Noirmont (mt.) B4
Oberalp (pass) G3
Oberalpstock (mt.) G3
Ochsen (mt.) D3
Ofen (pass) K3
Ofenhorn (mt.) F4
Orbe (riv.) C3
Pennine Alps (range) D5
Pilatus (mt.) F2
Plessur (riv.) J3
Poschiavo (valley) K4
Pragel (pass) G2
Quatervals (peak) K3
Reuss (riv.) F2
Rhaetian Alps (range) J3
Rhätikon (mts.) J2
Rheinwaldhorn (mt.) G4
Rhine (riv.) J2
Rhône (riv.) D4
Rigi (mt.) F2
Rimpfischhorn (mt.) E4
Ringelspitz (mt.) H3
Risoux (mt.) B3
Rosa (mt.) E5
Rosstock (mt.) G3
Rothorn (mt.) D4
Saane (Sarine) (riv.) D3
Saint Gotthard (pass) G3
Saint Gotthard (tunnel) G3
San Bernardino (pass) H3
Säntis (mt.) H2
Sarine (Saane) (riv.) D3
Sarnen (lake) F3
Schesaplana (mt.) J2
Scherhorn (mt.) G3
Schreckhorn (mt.) F3
Schwarzhorn (mt.) E4
Schwarzhorn (mt.) F3
Seez (riv.) H2
Sempach (lake) F2
Septimer (pass) J4
Sesvenna (peak) K3
Sihlsee (lake) G2
Silvretta (mts.) K3
Simme (riv.) D3
Simplon (pass) F4
Simplon (tunnel) F4
Sonnenhorn (mt.) F4
Splügen (pass) H3
Stockhorn (mt.) E3
Sulzflüh (mt.) J2
Susten (pass) G3
Sustenhorn (mt.) G3
Tamaro (mt.) G4
Tamina (riv.) H3
Tendre (peak) B3
Terri (peak) H3
Thunersee (lake) E3
Thur (riv.) G1
Ticino (riv.) G4
Titlis (mt.) F3
Tödi (mt.) G3
Toggenburg (dist.) H2
Töss (riv.) G1
Tour d'Ai (mt.) C4
Umbrail (peak) K3
Untersee (lake) H1
Unterwalden (reg.) F3
Upper Engadine (valley) J4
Urirotstock (mt.) G3
Vadret (peak) J3
Valserrhein (riv.) H3
Vanil Noir (mt.) D3
Vélan (mt.) D5
Visp (riv.) E4
Vorab (mt.) H3
Vorderrhein (riv.) G3
Wandfluhhorn (mt.) G4
Weissenstein (mts.) D2
Weisshorn (mt.) E4
Weisshorn (mt.) J3
Weissmies (mt.) F4
Wetterhorn (mt.) F3
Wildhorn (mt.) D4
Wildstrubel (mt.) E4
Zellersee (lake) G1
Zugersee (lake) F2
Zürichsee (lake) G2

LIECHTENSTEIN

CITIES and TOWNS

Schaan 4,552 ..... H2
Triesen 2,971 ..... H2
Vaduz (cap.) 4,614 ..... H2

OTHER FEATURES

Grauspitz (mt.) J2
Ochsenkopf (mt.) J2
Rhätikon (mts.) J2
Rhine (riv.) J2

*City and suburbs.

Austria, Czechoslovakia and Hungary

Topography

0 50 100 MI.
0 50 100 KM.

5,000 m. 16,404 ft. | 2,000 m. 6,562 ft. | 1,000 m. 3,281 ft. | 500 m. 1,640 ft. | 200 m. 656 ft. | 100 m. 328 ft. | Sea Level | Below

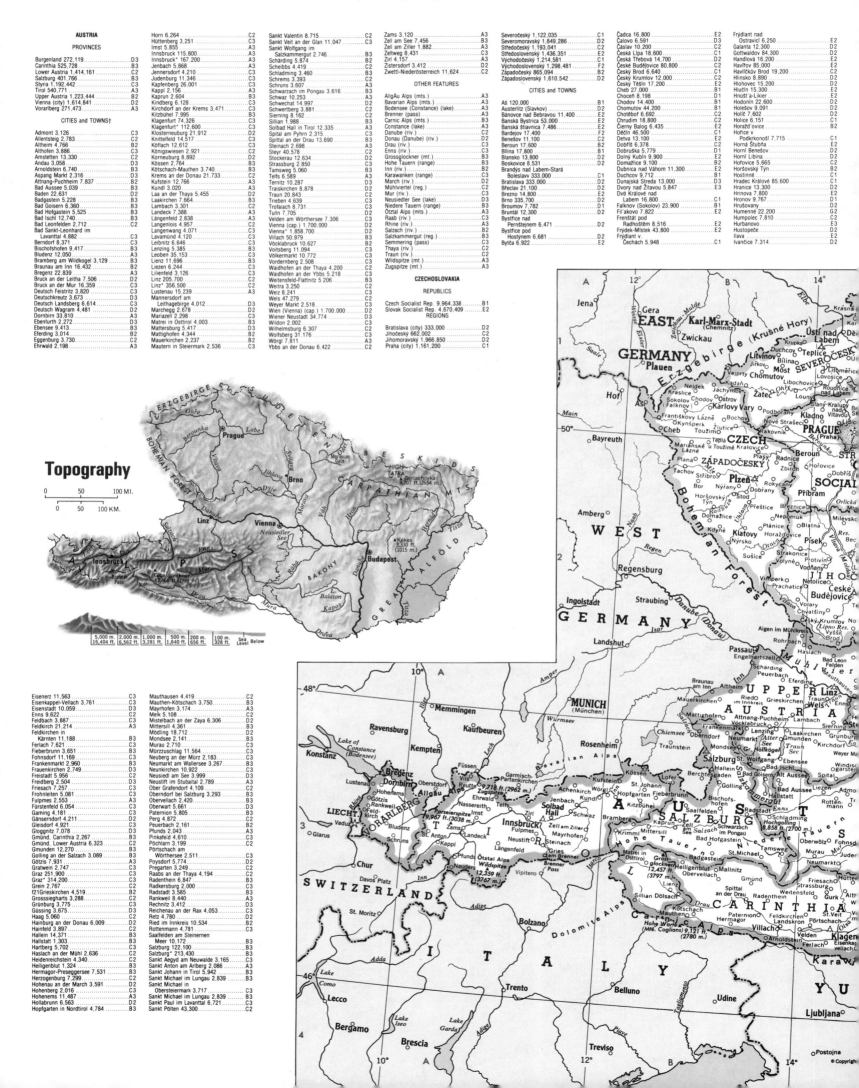

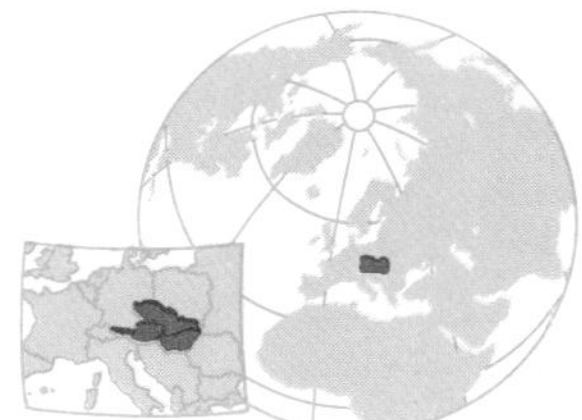

AREA 32,375 sq. mi. (83,851 sq. km.)
POPULATION 7,507,000
CAPITAL Vienna
LARGEST CITY Vienna
HIGHEST POINT Grossglockner 12,457 ft. (3,797 m.)
MONETARY UNIT schilling
MAJOR LANGUAGE German
MAJOR RELIGION Roman Catholicism

AREA 49,373 sq. mi. (127,876 sq. km.)
POPULATION 15,276,799
CAPITAL Prague
LARGEST CITY Prague
HIGHEST POINT Gerlachovka 8,707 ft. (2,654 m.)
MONETARY UNIT koruna
MAJOR LANGUAGES Czech, Slovak
MAJOR RELIGIONS Roman Catholicism, Protestantism

AREA 35,919 sq. mi. (93,030 sq. km.)
POPULATION 10,709,536
CAPITAL Budapest
LARGEST CITY Budapest
HIGHEST POINT Kékes 3,330 ft. (1,015 m.)
MONETARY UNIT forint
MAJOR LANGUAGE Hungarian
MAJOR RELIGIONS Roman Catholicism, Protestantism

AUSTRIA

CZECHOSLOVAKIA

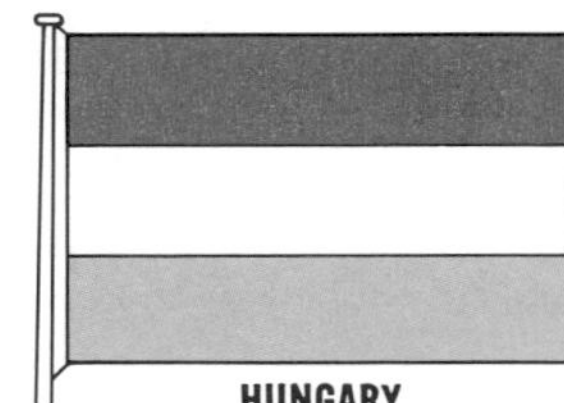

HUNGARY

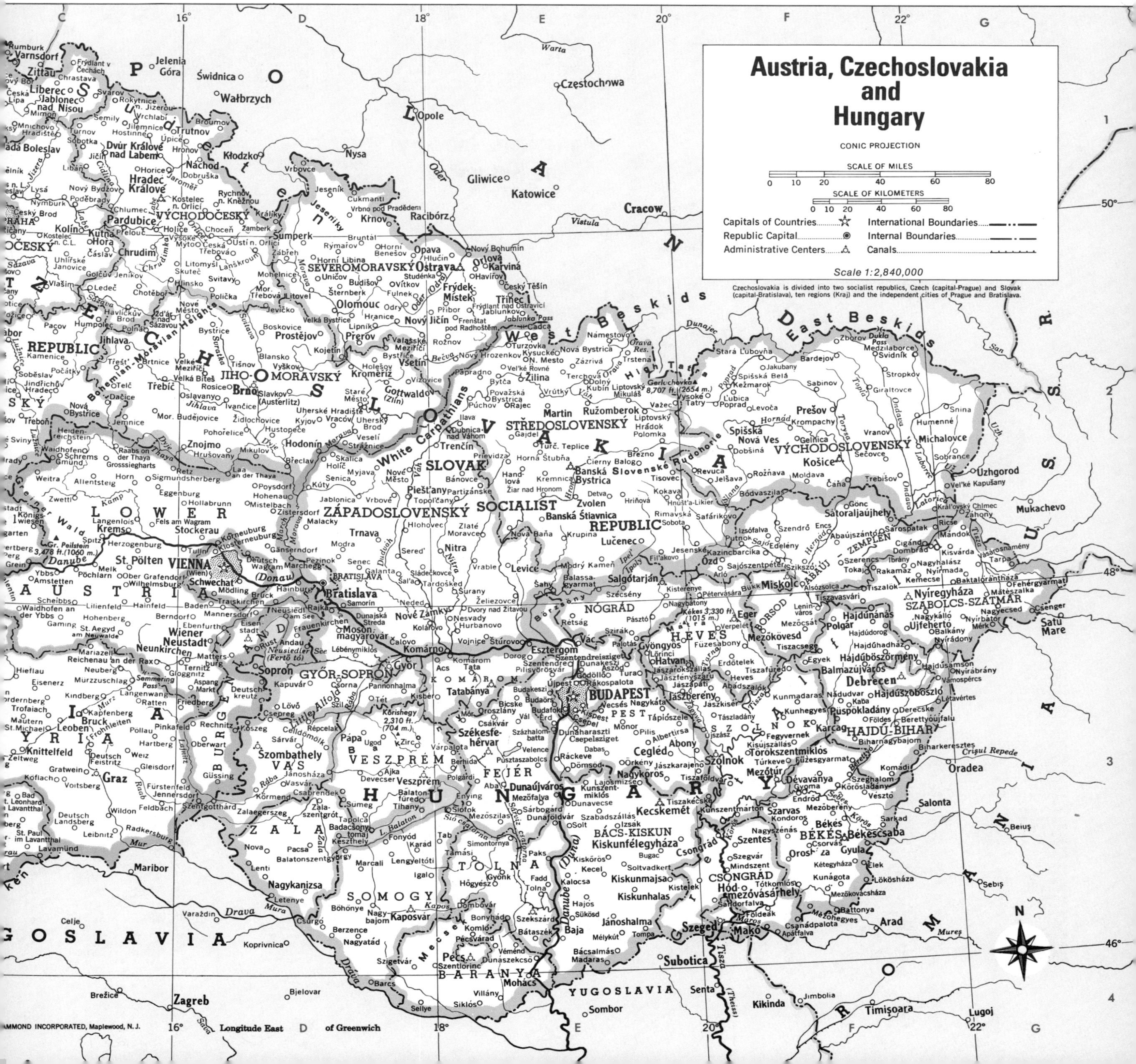

Austria, Czechoslovakia and Hungary

CONIC PROJECTION

SCALE OF MILES: 0 10 20 40 60 80

SCALE OF KILOMETERS: 0 10 20 40 60 80

Capitals of Countries ☆ · International Boundaries
Republic Capital ◉ · Internal Boundaries
Administrative Centers △ · Canals

Scale 1:2,840,000

Czechoslovakia is divided into two socialist republics, Czech (capital-Prague) and Slovak (capital-Bratislava), ten regions (Kraj) and the independent cities of Prague and Bratislava.

HAMMOND INCORPORATED, Maplewood, N.J. 16° Longitude East D of Greenwich 18° E 20° F 22° G

Austria, Czechoslovakia and Hungary

(continued)

Jablonec nad Nisou 36,300 ....C1
Jablonica D2
Jablunkov 9,405 ....E2
Jáchymov B1
Jakubany F2
Jaroměř 11,600 ....C1
Jelšava F2
Jemnice C2
Jeseník 10,900 ....D1
Jesenské F2
Jevíčko D2
Jičín 13,200 ....C1
Jihlava 44,500 ....C2
Jilemnice C1
Jindřichův Hradec 15,700 ....C2
Jiřkov 11,400 ....B1
Kadaň 18,100 ....B1
Kamenice C2
Kaplice C2
Karlovy Vary 43,300 ....B1
Karviná 79,100 ....E2
Kdyně B2
Kežmarok 11,000 ....F2
Kladno 61,200 ....B1
Klatovy 18,500 ....B2
Kojetín 5,852 ....D2
Kokava nad Rimavicou 5,391 ....E2
Kolárovo 10,500 ....D3
Kolín 29,100 ....C1
Komárno 28,200 ....D3
Košice 169,100 ....F2
Kostelec nad Orlicí 5,575 ....D1
Král'ovský Chlmec 5,329 ....G2
Kralupy nad Vltavou 16,900 ....C1
Kraslice 6,733 ....B1
Kremnica 5,941 ....E2
Krnov 25,000 ....D1
Kroměříž 23,200 ....D2
Krompachy 6,332 ....F2
Krupina 6,627 ....E2
Krupka 8,301 ....B1
Kutná Hora 19,200 ....C2
Kyjov 10,700 ....D2
Kynšperk 5,524 ....B1
Kysucké Nové Mesto 11,700 ....E2
Lanškroun 8,683 ....D2
Levice 19,000 ....E2
Levoča 10,100 ....F2
Libáň C1
Liberec 75,600 ....C1
Lidice C1
Lipník nad Bečvou 7,358 ....D2
Liptovský Mikuláš 19,400 ....E2
Litoměřice 19,700 ....C1
Litomyšl 8,112 ....D2
Litovel 5,805 ....D2
Litvínov 23,300 ....B1
Lomnice C2
Louny 15,200 ....B1
Lovosice 9,323 ....C1
L'ubica F2
Lučenec 23,300 ....E2
Lysá nad Labem 9,920 ....C1
Malacky 13,200 ....D2
Mariánské Lázně 14,600 ....B2
Martin 47,800 ....E2
Medzilaborce F2
Mělník 17,800 ....C1
Michalovce 23,600 ....G2
Mikulov 6,267 ....D2
Milevsko 7,091 ....C2
Mimoň 6,773 ....C1
Mladá Boleslav 36,900 ....C1
Mladá Vožice C2
Mnichovo Hradiště 5,239 ....C1
Modra 7,219 ....D2
Modrý Kameň 6,200 ....E2
Mohelnice 6,050 ....D2
Moldava nad Bodvou 5,397 ....F2
Moravská Třebová 9,052 ....D2
Moravské Budějovice 5,576 ....D2
Most 59,400 ....B1
Myjava 6,657 ....D2
Náchod 19,300 ....D1
Námestovo E2
Neded D2
Nejdek 8,187 ....B1
Nepomuk B2
Nesvady 5,453 ....E3
Netolice C2
Nitra 50,000 ....E2
Nová Baňa 6,218 ....E2
Nová Bystrica E2
Nová Bystřice C2
Nové Hrady C2
Nové Město na Moravě 6,581 ....D2
Nové Město nad Váhom 15,900 ....D2
Nové Strašecí B1
Nové Zámky 27,300 ....D3
Nový Bohumín 16,700 ....E2
Nový Bor 7,621 ....C1
Nový Bydžov 6,824 ....C1
Nový Hrozenkov E2
Nový Jičín 21,400 ....E2
Nymburk 13,600 ....C1
Nýřany 6,204 ....B2
Nýrsko B2
Odry D2
Olomouc 82,800 ....D2
Opava 53,800 ....E2
Orlová 25,500 ....E2
Ostrava 293,500 ....E2
Ostrov 18,200 ....B1
Pardubice 78,500 ....C1
Partizánske 15,100 ....E2
Pelhřimov 11,900 ....C2
Pezinok 13,100 ....D2
Piešt'any 25,400 ....D2
Písek 25,100 ....C2
Plzeň 155,000 ....B2
Počátky C2
Podbořany B1
Poděbrady 13,400 ....C1
Pohořelice D2
Polička 6,529 ....D2
Polná C2
Polomka E2
Poprad 25,800 ....F2
Považská Bystrica 19,300 ....E2
Prachatice 7,900 ....B2
Prague (Praha) (cap.) 1,161,200 ....C1
Přelouč 6,251 ....C1
Přerov 43,500 ....D2
Prešov 61,000 ....F2
Přeštice B2
Příbor 7,726 ....E2
Příbram 31,300 ....B2
Prievidza 30,900 ....E2
Prostějov 44,200 ....D2
Protivín C2
Púchov 9,306 ....E2
Radnice B2
Rajec E2
Rakovník 14,200 ....B1
Revúca 5,901 ....F2
Říčany u Prahy 8,407 ....C2
Rimavská Sobota 5,800 ....E2
Rokycany 12,800 ....B2
Rokytnice nad Jizerou C1
Rosice D2
Roudnice nad Labem 11,800 ....C1
Rožňava 12,400 ....F2
Rožnov pod Radhoštěm 11,600 ....E2
Rumburk C1
Ružomberok 22,600 ....E2
Rychnov nad Kněžnou 7,500 ....D1
Rýmařov 7,522 ....D2
Sabinov 5,473 ....F2
Šafárikovo F2
Šahy 5,049 ....E2
Šal'a 15,200 ....D2
Samorín 8,287 ....D2
Sečovce 5,744 ....F2
Sedlčany C2
Semily 8,200 ....C1
Senec 8,544 ....D2
Senica 12,300 ....D2
Sered' 12,500 ....D2
Skalica 11,100 ....D2
Skuteč D2
Sládečkovce 5,598 ....D2
Slaný 13,200 ....C1
Slavkov D2
Snina 10,900 ....G2
Soběslav 6,140 ....C2
Sobotka C1
Sobrance G2
Sokolov 23,900 ....B1
Spišská Belá F2
Spišská Nová Ves 26,100 ....F2
Stará L'ubovňa 5,800 ....F2
Staré Město 6,293 ....D2
Šternberk 13,700 ....D2
Stod B2
Strakonice 19,000 ....B2
Strážnice 5,482 ....D2
Stříbro B2
Stropkov 5,645 ....F2
Studénka 9,744 ....D2
Štúrovo 8,287 ....E3
Šumperk 25,900 ....D1
Šurany 6,693 ....E2
Sušice 10,300 ....B2
Svárov C1
Svidník 4,600 ....F2
Svitavy 15,000 ....D2
Tábor 28,100 ....C2
Tachov 11,400 ....B2
Telč 5,285 ....C2
Teplice 52,300 ....B1
Tišnov 8,263 ....D2
Topol'čany 17,500 ....D2
Třebíč 23,900 ....C2
Trebišov 13,700 ....F2
Třeboň 6,068 ....C2
Trenčín 38,800 ....E2
Třešt' 5,053 ....C2
Třinec 32,000 ....E2
Trnava 48,600 ....D2
Trutnov 24,500 ....D1
Turnov 13,600 ....C1
Turzovka 6,107 ....E2
Uherské Hradiště 32,100 ....D2
Uherský Brod 12,800 ....D2
Uničov 10,800 ....D2
Úpice 6,323 ....C1
Ústí nad Labem 74,900 ....C1
Ústí nad Orlicí 13,700 ....D2
Valašské Meziříčí 19,400 ....D2
Varnsdorf 14,700 ....C1
Važec E2
Vejprty B1
Velká Bíteš D2
Velká Bystřice D2
Vel'ké Kapušany G2
Velké Meziříčí 7,590 ....D2
Vel'ké Rovné E2
Veselí nad Lužnicí C2
Veselí nad Moravou 11,500 ....D2
Vimperk 5,749 ....B2
Vítkov 5,138 ....D2
Vizovice D2
Vlašim 8,873 ....C2
Vodňany 5,620 ....C2
Vojnice E3
Volary B2
Volyně B2
Votice C2
Vráble E2
Vracov D2
Vranov nad Teplou 14,700 ....F2
Vrbno pod Pradědem 5,594 ....D1
Vrbovce D1
Vrbové D2
Vrchlabí 11,700 ....C1
Vrútky 5,756 ....E2
Vsetín 24,100 ....D2
Vyškov 15,100 ....D2
Vysoké Mýto 8,830 ....D2
Vysoké Tatry F2
Vyšší Brod C2
Zábřeh 11,300 ....D2
Žamberk 5,040 ....D1
Žatec 17,400 ....B1
Zázrivá E2
Zbiroh B2
Zborov F2
Žd'ár nad Sázavou 17,800 ....C2
Želiezovce 5,478 ....E2
Žiar nad Hronom 14,800 ....E2
Židlochovice D2
Žilina 56,000 ....E2
Zlaté Moravce 10,300 ....E2
Zlín (Gottwaldov) 84,300 ....D2
Žlutice B1
Znojmo 28,500 ....D2
Zvolen 29,000 ....E2

OTHER FEATURES

Berounka (riv.) C2
Beskids, East (mts.) F1
Beskids, West (mts.) E2
Bohemian (for.) B2
Bohemian-Moravian Heights (hills) C2
Danube (riv.) C2
Dunajec (riv.) F2
Dyje (riv.) D2
Erzgebirge (mts.) B1
Gerlachovka (mt.) E2
Hornád (riv.) F2
Hron (riv.) E2
Ipel' (riv.) E2
Jablunka (pass) E2
Jeseníky (mts.) D1
Jihlava (riv.) D2
Krušné Hory (Erzgebirge) (mts.) B1
Labe (riv.) C1
Lipno (res.) C2
Lužnice (riv.) C2
Moldau (Vltava) (riv.) C2
Morava (riv.) D2
Nitra (riv.) E2
Oder (Odra) (riv.) D2
Ohře (riv.) B1
Ondava (riv.) F2
Orava (riv.) E2
Orlická (res.) C2
Sázava (riv.) C2
Slovenské Rudohorie (mts.) E2
Sudeten (mts.) C1
Svitava (riv.) D2
Svratka (riv.) D2
Tatra, High (mts.) E2
Torysa (riv.) F2
Úhlava (riv.) B2
Váh (riv.) D2
Vltava (riv.) C2
White Carpathians (mts.) E2

HUNGARY

COUNTIES

Bács-Kiskun 568,532 ....E3
Baranya 434,030 ....E4
Békés 436,987 ....F3
Borsod-Abaúj-Zemplén 808,924 ....F2
Budapest (city) 2,060,170 ....E3
Csongrád 456,862 ....F3
Fejér 421,568 ....E3
Győr-Sopron 428,476 ....D3
Hajdú-Bihar 552,417 ....F3
Heves 350,874 ....F3
Komárom 321,579 ....E3
Nógrád 239,907 ....E3
Pest 973,486 ....E3
Somogy 360,308 ....D3
Szabolcs-Szatmár 593,746 ....G3
Szolnok 446,379 ....F3
Tolna 266,414 ....E3
Vas 285,527 ....D3
Veszprém 386,740 ....D3
Zala 316,610 ....D3

CITIES and TOWNS

Aba 4,271 ....E3
Abádszalók 6,386 ....F3
Abaújszántó 4,209 ....F2
Abony 15,624 ....E3
Ács 8,423 ....E3
Ajka 29,601 ....D3
Albertirsa 11,252 ....E3
Alsózsolca 5,045 ....F2
Arló 4,203 ....F2
Aszód 6,218 ....E3
Bácsalmás 9,025 ....E3
Badacsonytomaj 2,933 ....D3
Baja 38,456 ....E3
Baktalórántháza 3,736 ....G2
Balassagyarmat 18,534 ....E2
Balatonfüred 12,599 ....D3
Balkány 7,667 ....G3
Balmazújváros 17,371 ....F3
Barcs 11,448 ....D4
Bátaszék 7,274 ....E3
Battonya 9,324 ....F3
Békés 22,287 ....F3
Békéscsaba 67,266 ....F3
Berettyóújfalu 16,406 ....F3
Berzence 3,406 ....D3
Bicske 10,720 ....E3
Biharkeresztes 4,788 ....F3
Biharnagybajom 4,093 ....F3
Böhönye 3,215 ....D3
Bonyhád 14,841 ....E3
Budafok 40,623 ....E3
Budaörs 13,958 ....E3
Budakeszi 10,429 ....E3
Budapest (cap.) 2,060,170 ....E3
Bugak 4,989 ....E3
Cegléd 40,567 ....E3
Celldömölk 12,533 ....D3
Cigánd 4,767 ....F2
Csabrendek 3,045 ....D3
Csákvár 5,238 ....E3
Csanádpalota 4,642 ....F3
Csenger 4,792 ....G3
Csepel 71,693 ....E3
Csepreg 4,079 ....D3
Csongrád 22,202 ....E3
Csorna 12,131 ....D3
Csorvás 6,826 ....F3
Csurgó 5,463 ....D3
Dabas 13,075 ....E3
Debrecen 192,484 ....F3
Derecske 9,579 ....F3
Dévaványa 11,208 ....F3
Devecser 5,482 ....D3
Dombóvár 19,917 ....E3
Dombrád 6,328 ....F2
Dömsöd 6,545 ....E3
Dorog 10,754 ....E3
Dunaföldvár 10,318 ....E3
Dunaharaszti 15,788 ....E3
Dunakeszi 25,187 ....E3
Dunaszekcső 2,999 ....E3
Dunaújváros 60,694 ....E3
Dunavecse 4,521 ....E3
Edelény 9,559 ....F2
Eger 61,283 ....F3
Egyek 7,956 ....F3
Elek 6,032 ....F3
Enes 2,565 ....F2
Endrőd 8,136 ....F3
Enying 7,518 ....E3
Érd 41,210 ....E3
Erdőtelek 4,250 ....F3
Esztergom 30,476 ....E3
Fadd 4,805 ....E3
Fegyvernek 8,421 ....F3
Fehérgyarmat 6,729 ....G3
Földeák 3,855 ....F3
Földes 5,293 ....F2
Fonyód 3,957 ....D3
Füzesabony 6,965 ....F3
Füzesgyarmat 7,097 ....F3
Gödöllő 28,057 ....E3
Gönc 2,875 ....F2
Gyoma 10,392 ....F3
Gyöngyös 36,927 ....E3
Győnk 2,507 ....E3
Győr 123,618 ....D3
Gyula 34,514 ....F3
Hajdúböszörmény 32,145 ....F3
Hajdúdorog 10,118 ....F3
Hajdúhadház 13,626 ....F3
Hajdúnánás 18,146 ....F3
Hajdúsámson 7,492 ....F3
Hajdúszoboszló 23,374 ....F3
Hajós 5,113 ....E3
Hatvan 24,790 ....E3
Heves 10,943 ....F3
Hódmezővásárhely 54,481 ....F3
Hőgyész 3,534 ....E3
Ibrány 7,037 ....F2
Izsák 7,686 ....E3
Izsófalva 6,816 ....F2
Jánoshalma 12,534 ....E3
Jánosháza 3,274 ....D3
Jászapáti 10,424 ....E3
Jászárokszállás 10,139 ....E3
Jászberény 31,347 ....E3
Jászfényszaru 6,869 ....E3
Jászkarajenő 4,101 ....E3
Jászkisér 6,816 ....F3
Jászladány 7,823 ....F3
Kaba 6,654 ....F2
Kalocsa 18,613 ....E3
Kaposvár 72,330 ....D3
Kapuvár 11,243 ....D3
Karád 2,754 ....D3
Karcag 25,264 ....F3
Kazincbarcika 37,481 ....F2
Kecel 10,493 ....E3
Kecskemét 91,929 ....E3
Kemecse 4,583 ....F2
Keszthely 21,671 ....D3
Kétegyháza 4,728 ....F3
Kisbér 4,562 ....D3
Kiskőrös 15,499 ....E3
Kiskunfélegyháza 35,339 ....E3
Kiskunhalas 30,552 ....E3
Kiskunmajsa 14,439 ....E3
Kispest 65,106 ....E3
Kistelek 8,544 ....E3
Kisterenye 6,844 ....E2
Kisújszállás 13,699 ....F3
Kisvárda 17,828 ....G2
Komádi 8,765 ....F3
Komárom 19,955 ....E3
Komló 30,301 ....E3
Kondoros 7,319 ....F3
Körmend 11,787 ....D3
Körösladány 6,565 ....F3
Kőszeg 12,705 ....D3
Kunágota 4,622 ....F3
Kunhegyes 10,116 ....F3
Kunmadaras 7,343 ....F3
Kunszentmárton 11,103 ....F3
Kunszentmiklós 7,952 ....E3
Lajosmizse 12,872 ....E3
Lébénymiklós 6,190 ....D3
Lengyeltóti 3,389 ....D3
Leninváros 18,667 ....F3
Lenti 8,106 ....D3
Létavértes 9,106 ....G3
Letenye 4,395 ....D3
Lökösháza 2,514 ....F3
Lőrinci 10,679 ....E3
Madaras 4,519 ....E3
Makó 29,943 ....F3
Mándok 5,093 ....G2
Marcali 12,485 ....D3
Mátészalka 17,709 ....G3
Mélykút 7,640 ....E3
Mérk 3,211 ....G3
Mezőberény 12,702 ....F3
Mezőcsát 6,729 ....F3
Mezőfalva 5,008 ....E3
Mezőhegyes 8,631 ....F3
Mezőkovácsháza 7,473 ....F3
Mezőkövesd 18,435 ....F3
Mezőszilas 2,792 ....E3
Mezőtúr 22,018 ....F3
Mindszent 8,730 ....F3
Miskolc 206,727 ....F2
Mohács 21,385 ....E4
Monor 16,838 ....E3
Mór 12,066 ....E3
Mosonmagyaróvár 29,732 ....D3
Nádudvar 9,447 ....F3
Nagyatád 12,946 ....D3
Nagybajom 4,402 ....D3
Nagyecsed 8,225 ....G3
Nagyhalász 6,437 ....F2
Nagykálló 11,282 ....F3
Nagykanizsa 48,494 ....D3
Nagykáta 11,922 ....E3
Nagykőrös 27,900 ....E3
Nagyszénás 7,124 ....F3
Nyírábrány 4,509 ....G3
Nyíradony 7,146 ....G3
Nyírbátor 13,388 ....G3
Nyíregyháza 108,156 ....F3
Nyírmada 4,744 ....F2
Örkény 5,013 ....E3
Orosháza 36,243 ....F3
Oroszlány 20,604 ....E3
Ózd 48,521 ....F2
Pacsa 1,984 ....D3
Paks 19,514 ....E3
Pannonhalma 3,731 ....D3
Pápa 32,202 ....D3
Pásztó 7,962 ....E3
Pécs 168,788 ....E3
Pécsvárad 3,672 ....E3
Pétervására 2,753 ....F3
Pilis 9,055 ....E3
Pilisvörösvár 10,217 ....E3
Polgár 9,429 ....F3
Polgárdi 5,767 ....E3
Püspökladány 15,730 ....F3
Pusztaszabolcs 5,794 ....E3
Putnok 7,103 ....F2
Ráckeve 7,534 ....E3
Rajka 2,448 ....D3
Rakamaz 5,407 ....F2
Rákospalota 60,983 ....E3
Répcelak 1,997 ....D3
Ricse 2,992 ....G2
Sajószentpéter 13,992 ....F2
Salgótarján 49,320 ....E2
Sándorfalva 5,949 ....F3
Sárbogárd 11,178 ....E3
Sarkad 11,937 ....F3
Sárospatak 15,316 ....F2
Sárvár 15,126 ....D3
Sátoraljaújhely 19,252 ....F2
Sellye 2,804 ....D4
Siklós 10,567 ....E4
Simontornya 4,892 ....E3
Siófok 20,084 ....E3
Solt 6,911 ....E3
Soltvadkert 7,934 ....E3
Sopron 53,930 ....D3
Sükösd 4,430 ....E3
Sümeg 6,229 ....D3
Szabadszállás 8,223 ....E3
Szarvas 20,598 ....F3
Szécsény 5,690 ....E2
Százhalombatta 13,963 ....E3
Szeged 171,342 ....E3
Szeghalom 9,736 ....F3
Szegvár 6,395 ....F3
Székesfehérvár 103,197 ....E3
Szekszárd 34,592 ....E3
Szendrő 4,098 ....F2
Szentendre 16,844 ....E3
Szentes 35,326 ....F3
Szentgotthárd 5,837 ....D3
Szentlőrinc 3,926 ....E3
Szerencs 8,612 ....F2
Szigetvár 12,114 ....D3
Szikszó 6,419 ....F2
Szil 2,073 ....D3
Szolnok 75,203 ....F3
Szombathely 82,830 ....D3
Tab 3,922 ....E3
Tamási 7,602 ....E3
Tápiószele 5,575 ....E3
Tapolca 17,161 ....D3
Tarpa 3,436 ....G2
Tata 24,114 ....E3
Tatabánya 75,942 ....E3
Tét 4,441 ....D3
Tiszacsege 6,263 ....F3
Tiszaföldvár 12,560 ....F3
Tiszafüred 12,259 ....F3
Tiszakécske 12,378 ....E3
Tiszalök 6,230 ....F2
Tiszavasvári 13,292 ....F3
Tokaj 4,845 ....F2
Tolna 8,997 ....E3
Tompa 5,365 ....E3
Törökszentmiklós 25,551 ....F3
Tótkomlós 8,803 ....F3
Tura 8,235 ....E3
Túrkeve 11,393 ....F3
Újfehértó 14,412 ....F3
Újpest 80,384 ....E3
Újszász 7,098 ....F2
Vác 34,837 ....E3
Vál 2,488 ....E3
Vámospércs 5,213 ....F3
Várpalota 28,293 ....E3
Vásárosnamény 8,637 ....G2
Vasvár 4,275 ....D3
Vecsés 19,193 ....E3
Velence 3,463 ....E3
Véménd 2,293 ....E3
Verpelét 4,622 ....F2
Veszprém 54,898 ....D3
Vésztő 9,815 ....F3
Villány 2,764 ....E4
Záhony 3,049 ....G2
Zalaegerszeg 39,671 ....D3
Zalaszentgrót 5,346 ....D3
Zirc 5,980 ....D3

OTHER FEATURES

Bakony (mts.) D3
Balaton (lake) D3
Berettyó (riv.) F3
Bükk (mts.) F2
Csepelsziget (isl.) E3
Danube (riv.) E3
Dráva (riv.) D3
Duna (Danube) (riv.) E3
Fertő tó (Neusiedler See) (lake) D3
Great Alföld (plain) F3
Hernád (riv.) F2
Kapos (riv.) D3
Kékes (mt.) E3
Körös (riv.) F3
Maros (riv.) F3
Mátra (mts.) E3
Mecsek (mts.) D3
Mura (riv.) D3
Rába (riv.) D3
Sajó (riv.) F2
Sárviz csatorna (canal) E3
Sió csatorna (canal) E3
Szentendreisziget (isl.) E3
Tisza (riv.) F3
Zala (riv.) D3

*City and suburbs.
†Population of Austrian cities are communes.

Agriculture, Industry and Resources

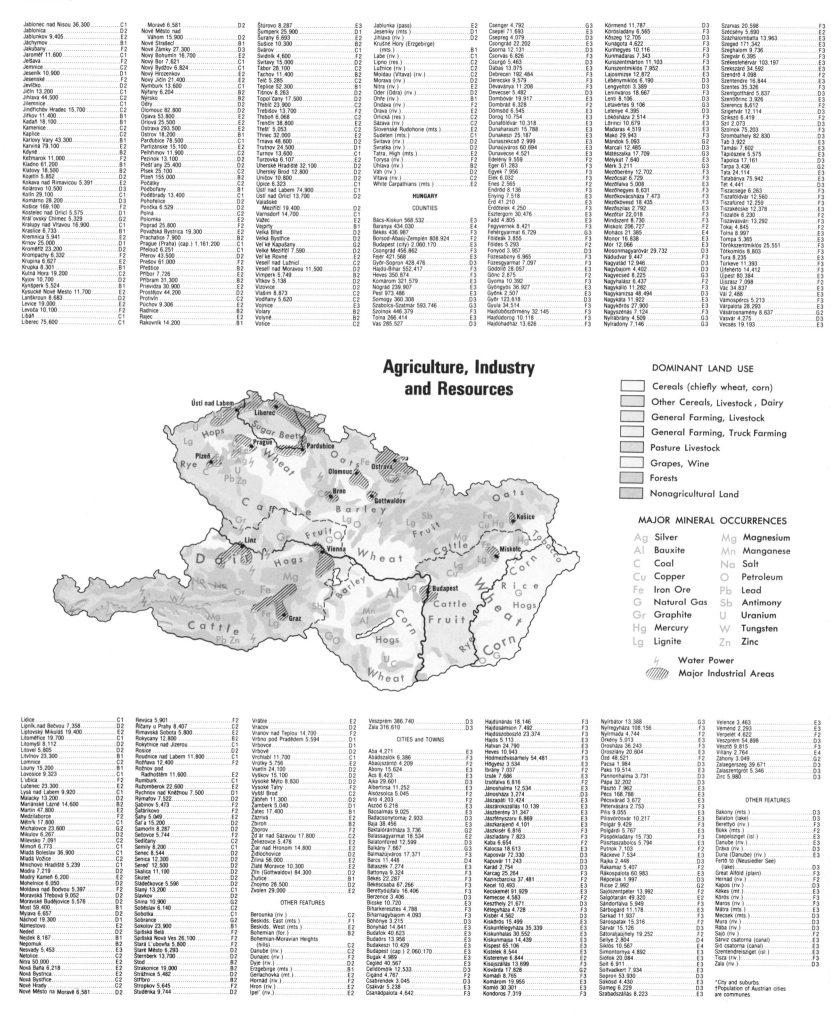

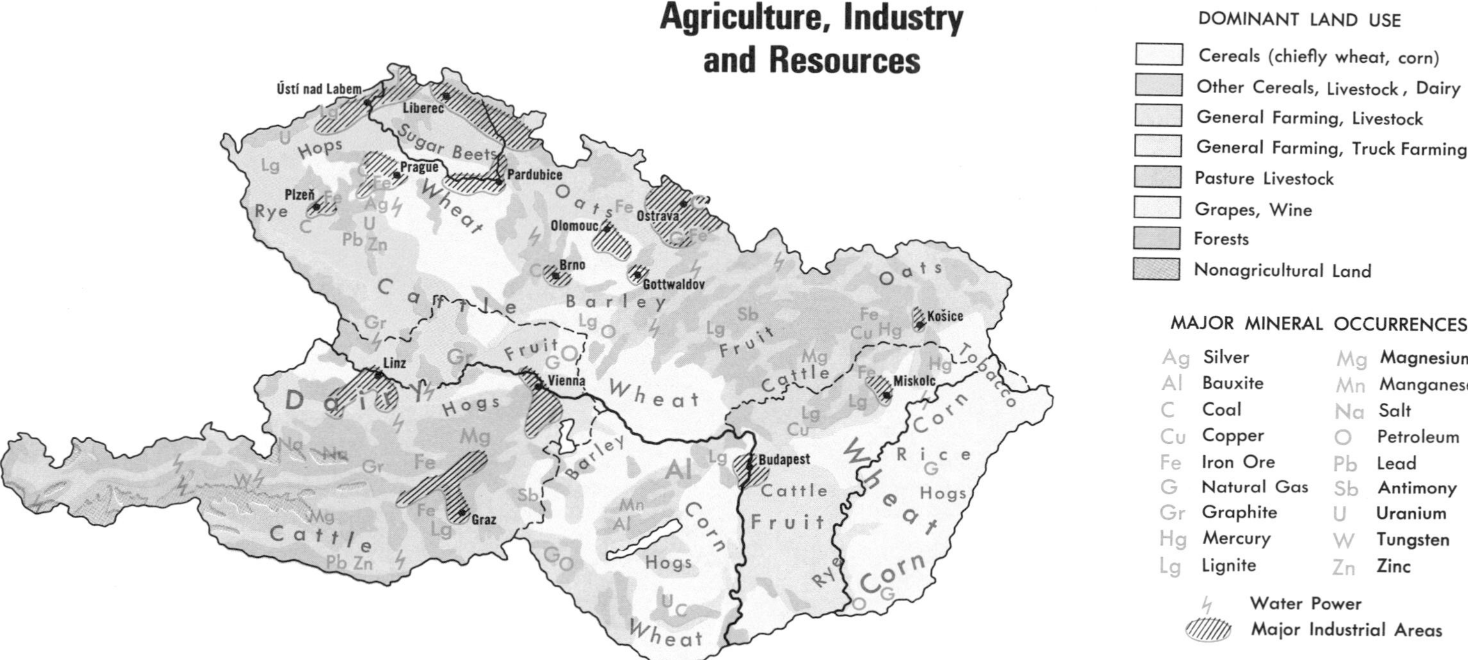

YUGOSLAVIA

AREA 98,766 sq. mi. (255,804 sq. km.)
POPULATION 22,471,000
CAPITAL Belgrade
LARGEST CITY Belgrade
HIGHEST POINT Triglav 9,393 ft. (2,863 m.)
MONETARY UNIT Yugoslav dinar
MAJOR LANGUAGES Serbo-Croation, Slovenian, Macedonian, Montenegrin, Albanian
MAJOR RELIGIONS Eastern Orthodoxy, Roman Catholicism, Islam

ALBANIA

AREA 11,100 sq. mi. (28,749 sq. km.)
POPULATION 2,590,600
CAPITAL Tiranë
LARGEST CITY Tiranë
HIGHEST POINT Korab 9,026 ft. (2,751 m.)
MONETARY UNIT lek
MAJOR LANGUAGE Albanian
MAJOR RELIGIONS Islam, Eastern Orthodoxy, Roman Catholicism

ROMANIA

AREA 91,699 sq. mi. (237,500 sq. km.)
POPULATION 22,048,305
CAPITAL Bucharest
LARGEST CITY Bucharest
HIGHEST POINT Moldoveanul 8,343 ft. (2,543 m.)
MONETARY UNIT leu
MAJOR LANGUAGES Romanian, Hungarian
MAJOR RELIGION Eastern Orthodoxy

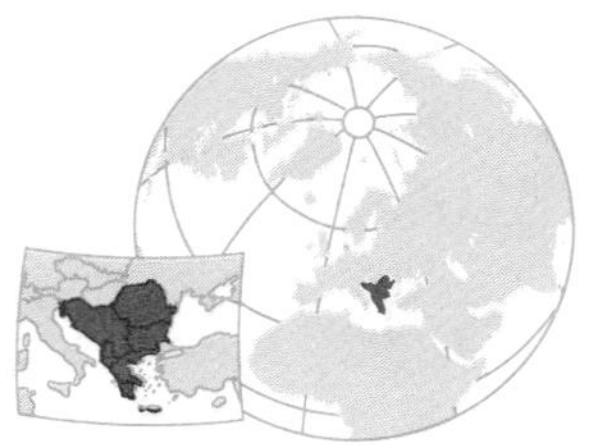

BULGARIA

AREA 42,823 sq. mi. (110,912 sq. km.)
POPULATION 8,862,000
CAPITAL Sofia
LARGEST CITY Sofia
HIGHEST POINT Musala 9,597 ft. (2,925 m.)
MONETARY UNIT lev
MAJOR LANGUAGE Bulgarian
MAJOR RELIGION Eastern Orthodoxy

GREECE

AREA 50,944 sq. mi. (131,945 sq. km.)
POPULATION 9,599,000
CAPITAL Athens
LARGEST CITY Athens
HIGHEST POINT Olympus 9,570 ft. (2,917 m.)
MONETARY UNIT drachma
MAJOR LANGUAGE Greek
MAJOR RELIGION Eastern (Greek) Orthodoxy

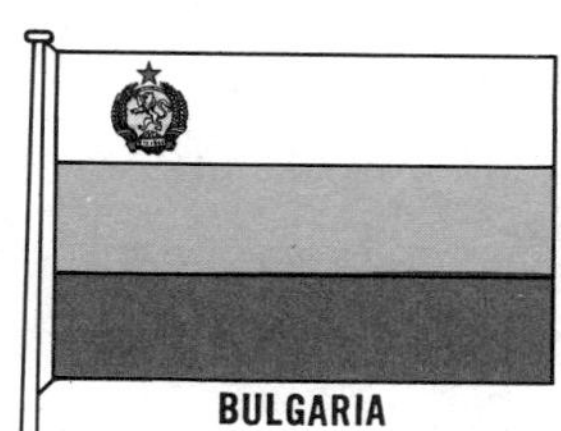
BULGARIA

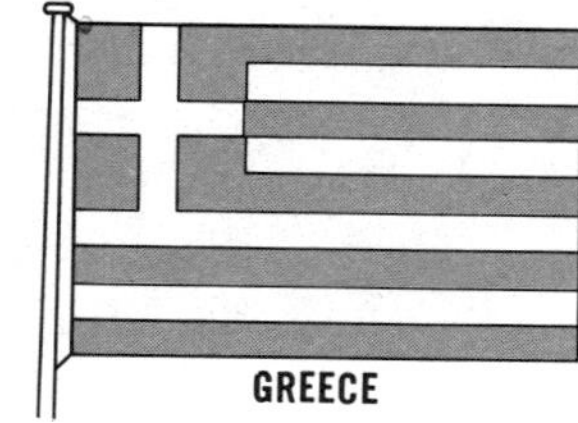
GREECE

YUGOSLAVIA

ALBANIA

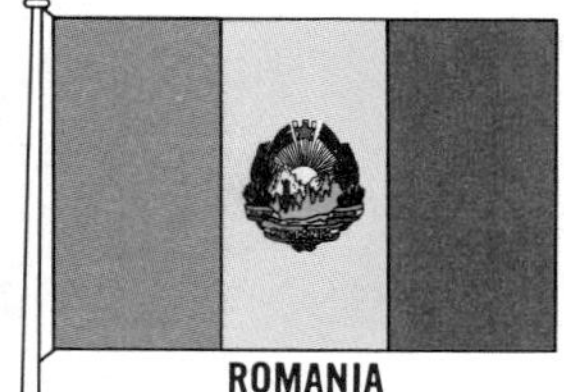
ROMANIA

Agriculture, Industry and Resources

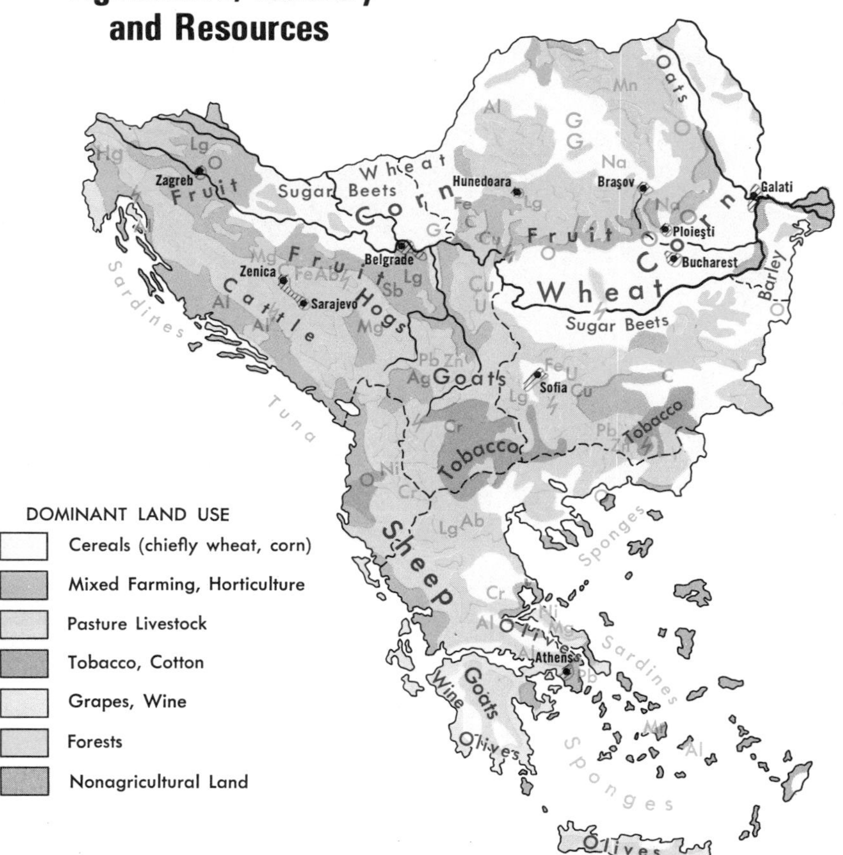

MAJOR MINERAL OCCURRENCES

Ab Asbestos
Ag Silver
Al Bauxite
C Coal
Cr Chromium
Cu Copper
Fe Iron Ore
G Natural Gas
Hg Mercury
Lg Lignite
Mg Magnesium
Mn Manganese
Mr Marble
Na Salt
Ni Nickel
O Petroleum
Pb Lead
Sb Antimony
U Uranium
Zn Zinc

Water Power
Major Industrial Areas

ALBANIA

CITIES and TOWNS

- Berat 25,700 ... D5
- Çorovodë ... E5
- Burrel ... D5
- Delvinë 6,000 ... D6
- Durrës (Durazzo) 53,800 ... D5
- Elbasan 41,700 ... E5
- Ersekë ... E5
- Fier 23,000 ... D5
- Gjirokastër 17,100 ... D5
- Kavajë 18,700 ... D5
- Korçë 47,300 ... E5
- Krujë 7,900 ... D5
- Kuçovë (Stalin) 14,000 ... D5
- Kukës 6,100 ... E4
- Leskovik ... E5
- Lezhë ... D5
- Lushnje 18,900 ... D5
- Memaliaj ... D5
- Peqin ... D5
- Përmet ... E5
- Peshkopi 6,600 ... E5
- Pogradec 10,100 ... E5
- Pukë ... E4
- Sarandë 8,700 ... E6
- Shëngjin ... D5
- Shijak 6,200 ... D5
- Shkodër 55,300 ... D5
- Stalin 14,000 ... D5
- Tepelenë ... D5
- Tiranë (Tirana) (cap.) 171,300 ... E5
- Vlorë 50,000 ... D5

OTHER FEATURES

- Adriatic (sea) ... B4
- Drin (riv.) ... E4
- Korab (mt.) ... E5
- Ohrid (lake) ... E5
- Otranto (str.) ... D5
- Prespa (lake) ... E5
- Sazan (isl.) ... D5
- Scutari (lake) ... D4
- Vijosë (riv.) ... D5

BULGARIA

CITIES and TOWNS

- Akhtopol 938 ... H4
- Alfatar 3,249 ... H4
- Ardino 5,080 ... G5
- Asenovgrad 43,049 ... G5
- Aytos 20,967 ... H4
- Balchik 11,070 ... H4
- Bansko 10,011 ... F5
- Belogradchik 6,892 ... F4
- Berkovitsa 16,253 ... F4
- Blagoevgrad 50,043 ... F5
- Botevgrad 17,789 ... F4
- Bregovo 5,567 ... F3
- Breznik 4,699 ... F4
- Burgas 144,449 ... H4
- Byala 10,564 ... G4
- Byala Slatina 15,788 ... F4
- Chirpan 20,595 ... G4
- Devin 7,120 ... G5
- Dimitrovgrad 45,596 ... G4
- Dobrich (Tolbukhin) 86,184 ... H4
- Dryanovo 9,804 ... G4
- Elena 7,008 ... G4
- Elin Pelin 5,499 ... F4
- Elkhovo 12,397 ... H4
- Gabrovo 75,034 ... G4
- General-Toshevo 8,928 ... H4
- Godech 5,225 ... F4
- Gorna Oryakhovitsa 34,157 ... G4
- Gotse Delchev 17,015 ... F5
- Grudovo 9,871 ... H4
- Ikhtiman 11,482 ... F4
- Isperikh 10,500 ... H4
- Ivaylovgrad 3,900 ... H5
- Karapelit ... H4
- Karlovo 25,472 ... G4
- Karnobat 21,480 ... H4
- Kavarna 10,872 ... J4
- Kazanlŭk 53,607 ... G4
- Kharmanli 19,240 ... H5
- Khaskovo 75,031 ... G5
- Kotel 8,229 ... H4
- Krumovgrad 5,211 ... G5
- Kubrat 9,826 ... H4
- Kula 5,667 ... F4
- Kŭrdzhali 47,757 ... G5
- Kyustendil 48,239 ... F4
- Lom 30,538 ... F4
- Lovech 43,858 ... G4
- Lukovit 10,400 ... G4
- Malko Tŭrnovo 4,233 ... H4
- Maritsa 8,664 ... H4
- Michurin 4,434 ... H4
- Mikhaylovgrad 40,064 ... F4
- Momchilgrad 8,185 ... G5
- Nesebŭr 6,768 ... H4
- Nikopol 5,563 ... G4
- Nova Zagora 21,872 ... H4
- Novi Pazar 15,751 ... H4
- Omurtag 9,067 ... H4
- Oryakhovo 14,012 ... F4
- Panagyurishte 20,649 ... F4
- Pazardzhik 65,577 ... G4
- Pernik 87,432 ... F4
- Peshtera 16,882 ... G4
- Petrich 24,381 ... F5
- Pirdop 8,248 ... G4
- Pleven 107,567 ... G4
- Plovdiv 300,242 ... G4
- Pomorie 11,960 ... H4
- Popina ... H3
- Popovo 19,428 ... H4
- Provadiya 15,143 ... H4
- Radomir 10,436 ... F4
- Razgrad 42,486 ... H4
- Razlog 13,690 ... F5
- Rositsa ... H4
- Ruse 160,351 ... H4
- Samokov 25,763 ... F4
- Sandanski 19,003 ... F5
- Sevlievo 24,421 ... G4
- Shabla 4,471 ... J4
- Shumen 83,525 ... H4
- Silistra 58,270 ... H3
- Simeonovgrad (Maritsa) 8,664 ... H4
- Sliven 90,137 ... H4
- Smolyan 29,032 ... G5
- Smyadovo 5,020 ... H4
- Sofia (cap.) 965,728 ... F4
- Sozopol 3,877 ... H4
- Stanke Dimitrov 42,034 ... F4
- Stara Zagora 122,200 ... G4
- Svilengrad 15,150 ... G5
- Svishtov 29,412 ... G4
- Teteven 12,555 ... G4
- Tolbukhin 86,184 ... H4
- Topolovgrad 7,230 ... H4
- Troyan 23,692 ... G4
- Trŭn 3,435 ... F4
- Tŭrgovishte 38,796 ... H4
- Tutrakan 11,447 ... H4
- Varna 251,654 ... J4
- Veliko Tŭrnovo 56,497 ... G4
- Vidin 53,030 ... F4
- Vratsa 61,265 ... F4
- Yambol 75,861 ... H4
- Zimnitsa ... H4
- Zlatograd 7,732 ... G5

OTHER FEATURES

- Balkan (mts.) ... G4
- Black (sea) ... J4
- Danube (riv.) ... H4
- Dunav (Danube) (riv.) ... H4
- Emine (cape) ... J4
- Iskŭr (riv.) ... G4
- Kaliakra (cape) ... J4
- Maritsa (riv.) ... G4
- Mesta (riv.) ... F5
- Midzhur (mt.) ... F4
- Musala (mt.) ... F4
- Osŭm (riv.) ... G4
- Rhodope (mts.) ... G5
- Rujen (mt.) ... F4
- Struma (riv.) ... F5
- Timok (riv.) ... F3
- Tundzha (riv.) ... G4
- Vit (riv.) ... G4

GREECE

REGIONS

- Aegean Islands 417,813 ... G6
- Athens, Greater 2,566,775 ... F7
- Áyion Óros (aut. dist.) 1,732 ... G5
- Central Greece and Euboea 966,543 ... F6
- Crete 456,642 ... G8
- Epirus 310,334 ... E6
- Ionian Islands 184,443 ... D6
- Macedonia 1,888,952 ... E5
- Pelopónnisos 986,912 ... F7
- Thessaly 659,913 ... F6
- Thrace 329,582 ... G5

CITIES and TOWNS

- Agrínion 30,973 ... E6
- Aíyina 5,704 ... F7
- Aíyion 18,829 ... F6
- Alexandroúpolis 22,995 ... H5
- Alivérion 4,414 ... G6
- Almirós 5,680 ... F6
- Amaliás 14,177 ... E7
- Amfilokhía 4,668 ... E6
- Ámfissa 6,605 ... F6
- Ándissa 1,762 ... H6
- Andravídha 3,046 ... E6
- Ándros 1,827 ... G7
- Áno Viánnos 1,431 ... G8
- Anóyia 2,750 ... G8
- Ardhéa 3,555 ... F5
- Areópolis 674 ... F7
- Argalastí 1,621 ... F6
- Árgos 18,890 ... F7
- Argostólion 7,060 ... E6
- Arkhángelos 3,016 ... J7
- Arnaía 2,424 ... F5
- Árta 19,498 ... E6
- Astipálaia 787 ... H7
- Atalándi 4,581 ... F6
- Athens (cap.) 867,023 ... F7
- Athens* 2,566,775 ... F7
- Ayiá 3,241 ... F6
- Áyios Kírikos 1,083 ... H7
- Áyios Matthaíos 1,596 ... D6
- Áyios Nikólaos 5,002 ... G8
- Candia (Iráklion) 77,506 ... G8
- Canea (Khaniá) 40,564 ... G8
- Corinth 20,773 ... F7
- Delfí 1,185 ... F6
- Delvinákion 1,067 ... E6
- Dhidhimótikhon 8,388 ... H5
- Dhíkaia 1,222 ... H5
- Dhimitsána 996 ... F7
- Dhomokós 1,991 ... F6
- Dráma 29,692 ... F5
- Édhessa 13,967 ... F5
- Elassón 7,200 ... F6
- Elevtheroúpolis 4,888 ... G5
- Ermoúpolis 13,502 ... G7
- Fársala 6,967 ... F6
- Filiátes 2,579 ... E6
- Filiatrá 5,919 ... E7
- Filippiás 3,248 ... E6
- Flórina 11,164 ... E5
- Gargaliánoi 5,888 ... E7
- Grevená 8,106 ... E5
- Ídhra 2,381 ... F7
- Ierápetra 7,055 ... G8
- Igoumenítsa 4,109 ... E6
- Ioánnina 40,130 ... E6
- Íos 1,270 ... G7
- Iráklion 77,506 ... G8
- Istiaía 4,059 ... F6
- Itháki 2,293 ... E6
- Kalámai 39,133 ... F7
- Kalampáka 5,453 ... E6
- Kalávrita 1,948 ... F6
- Kálimnos 6,492 ... H7
- Kándanos 403 ... F8
- Kardhítsa 25,685 ... E6
- Kariá 1,350 ... E6
- Kariaí 301 ... G5
- Káristos 3,550 ... G6
- Kárpathos 1,363 ... H8
- Karpenísion 4,414 ... E6
- Kastéllion (Kíssamos) 2,996 ... F8
- Kastéllion 1,152 ... G8
- Kastoría 15,407 ... E5
- Katákolon 690 ... E7
- Kateríni 28,808 ... F5
- Kaválla 46,234 ... G5
- Kéa 693 ... G7
- Kérkira 28,630 ... D6
- Khalkís 36,300 ... F6
- Khaniá 40,564 ... G8
- Khíos 24,084 ... G6
- Khóra Sfakíon 246 ... G8
- Kiáton 7,392 ... F6
- Kilkís 10,538 ... F5
- Kími 2,772 ... F6
- Kiparissía 3,882 ... E7
- Kíssamos 2,996 ... G8
- Kíthira 349 ... F7
- Komotiní 28,896 ... G5
- Kónitsa 3,150 ... E5
- Koropí 9,367 ... G7
- Kos 7,828 ... H7
- Kozáni 23,240 ... F5
- Kranídhion 3,657 ... F7
- Lagkadia 1,350 ... E7
- Lamía 37,872 ... F6
- Langadhás 6,707 ... F5
- Langádhia ... F7
- Lárisa 72,336 ... F6
- Lávrion 8,283 ... G7
- Leonídhion 3,181 ... F7
- Levádhia 15,445 ... F6
- Levkás 6,818 ... E6
- Limenária 1,507 ... G5

(continued on following page)

(continued)

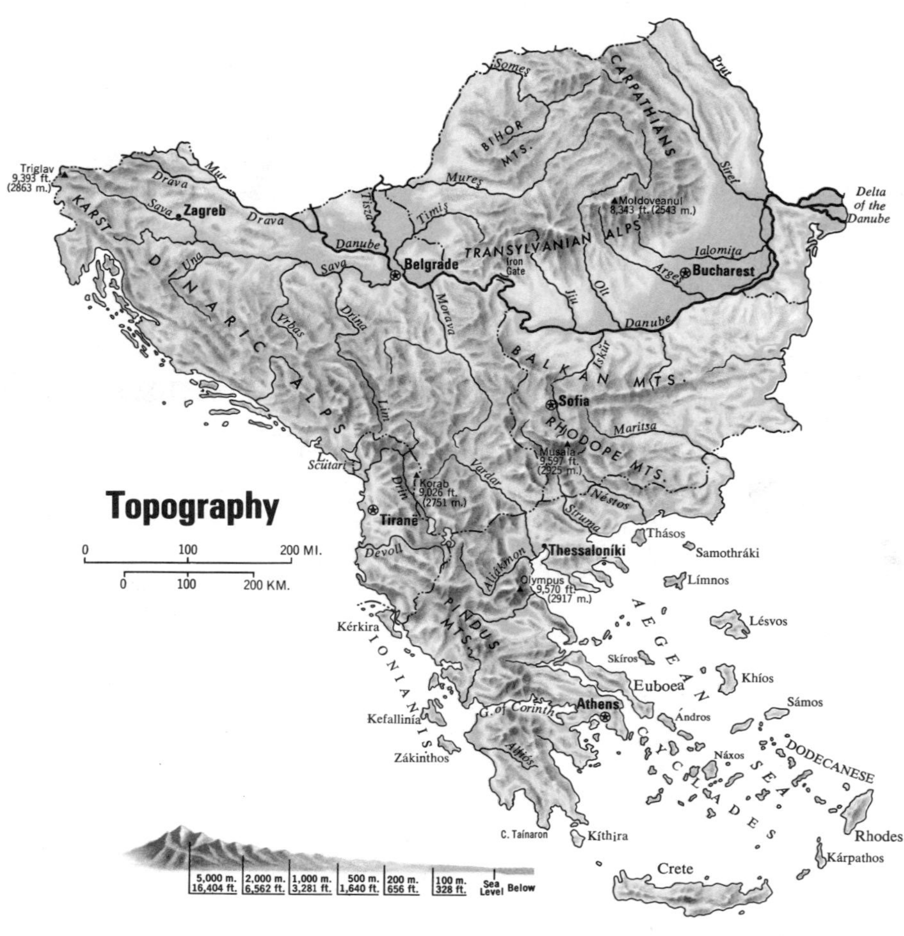

Límni 2,394 F6
Líndos 700 J7
Litókhoron 5,561 F5
Lixoúrion 3,364 E6
Loutrá Aidhipsoú 2,195 F6
Marathón 1,976 G6
Megalópolis 3,357 E7
Mégara 17,294 F6
Meligalá 1,724 F7
Mesolóngion 11,614 E6
Messíni 6,625 E7
Métsovon 2,823 E6
Mikínai 390 F7
Mílos 850 G7
Mírina 3,982 G6
Míthimna 1,414 G6
Mitilíni 23,426 H6
Moírai 2,948 G8
Moláoi 2,484 F7
Monólithos 247 H7
Moúdhros 1,024 G6
Náousa 17,375 F5
Návpaktos 8,170 F6
Návplion 9,281 F7
Náxos 2,892 G7
Neápolis 3,070 F7
Neméa 4,356 F7
Néon Karlóvasi 4,401 H7
Nestórion 1,143 E5
Nigríta 7,301 F5
Oinói 188 F6
Orestías 10,727 H5
Paramithía 2,747 E6
Pátrai 111,607 E6
Pérdika 1,198 E6
Péta 2,116 E6
Pílos 2,258 E7
Piraiévs (Piraeus) 187,362 F7
Pírgos 20,599 E7
Pirgí 1,455 G6
Píthion 1,047 H5
Plomárion 4,353 H6
Políkastron 5,279 F5
Políkhnitos 4,152 G6
Políyiros 3,707 F5
Póros 4,051 F7
Préveza 11,439 E6
Psakhná 4,650 F6
Psári 622 E7
Ptolemaís 16,588 E5
Réthimnon 14,969 G8
Rhodes (Ródhos) 32,092 J7
Salamís 18,256 F6
Salonika
(Thessaloníki) 345,799 F5
Sámi 957 E6
Sámos 5,146 H7
Samothráki 508 G5
Sápai 2,456 G5
Sérrai 39,897 F5
Sérvia 3,834 F5
Siátista 4,852 E5
Sidhirókastron 6,363 F5
Sími 2,344 H7
Sitía 6,167 H8
Skíathos 3,707 F6
Skíros 1,925 G6
Skópelos 2,545 F6
Souflíon 5,637 H5
Sparta 10,549 F7
Spétsai 3,427 F7
Spíli 789 G8
Stavrós 1,700 F5
Stílis 4,427 F6
Thásos 2,052 G5
Thessaloníki 345,799 F5
Thessaloníki* 482,361 F5
Thíra 1,322 G7
Thívai 15,971 F6
Timbákion 3,229 G8
Tínos 3,423 G7
Tírnavos 10,451 F6
Tríkkala 34,794 E6
Trípolis 20,209 F7
Vámos 652 F8
Vartholomión 3,015 E7
Vathí 2,491 H7
Velvendós 4,063 F5
Vérroia 29,528 F5
Vólos 51,290 F6
Vónitsa 3,324 E6
Vrondádhes 4,253 G6
Xánthi 24,867 G5
Yerolimín 73 F7
Yiannitsá 18,151 F5
Yíthion 4,915 F7
Zákinthos 9,339 E7
Zante (Zákinthos) 9,339 E7

OTHER FEATURES

Aegean (sea) G6
Akrítas (cape) E7
Aktí (pen.) G5
Amorgós (isl.) G7
Anáfi (isl.) G7
Andikíthira (isl.) F8
Ándros (isl.) G7
Arda (riv.) G5
Argolís (gulf) F7
Astipálaia (isl.) H7
Áthos (mt.) G5
Áyios Evstrátios
(isl.) G6
Áyios Yeóryios (cape) G5
Cephalonia (Kefallinía)
(isl.) E6
Corfu (Kérkira) (isl.) D6
Corinth (gulf) F6
Crete (isl.) G8
Crete (sea) G7
Cyclades (isls.) G7
Día (isl.) G8
Dodecanese (isls.) H8
Euboea (Évvoia)
(isl.) G6
Évros (riv.) H5
Évvoia (isl.) G6
Gávdhos (isl.) F8
Ídhi (mt.) G8
Ikaría (isl.) G7
Ionian (sea) D7
Íos (isl.) G7
Itháki (Ithaca) (isl.) E6
Kafirévs (cape) G6
Kálimnos (isl.) H7
Kárpathos (isl.) H8
Kásos (isl.) H8
Kassándra (pen.) F6
Kéa (isl.) G7
Kefallinía (isl.) E6
Kérkira (isl.) D6
Khálki (isl.) H7
Khaniá (gulf) G8
Khíos (isl.) G6
Kímolos (isl.) G7
Kiparissía (gulf) E7
Kíthira (isl.) F7
Kíthnos (isl.) G7
Kos (isl.) H7
Kriós (cape) F8
Kríti (Crete) (isl.) G8
Lakonía (gulf) F7
Léros (isl.) H7
Lésvos (isl.) G6
Levítha (isl.) H7
Levkás (isl.) E6
Límnos (isl.) G6
Maléa (cape) F7
Matapan (Taínaron) (cape) F7
Merabéllou (gulf) H8
Mesará (gulf) G8
Messíni (gulf) E7
Míkonos (isl.) G7
Mílos (isl.) G7
Mirtóön (sea) F7
Náxos (isl.) G7
Néstos (riv.) G5
Nísiros (isl.) H7
Northern Sporades (isls.) F6
Olympia (isls.) E7
Olympus (mt.) F5
Parnassus (mt.) F6
Páros (isl.) G7
Pátmos (isl.) H7
Paxoí (isl.) D6
Pindus (mts.) E6
Piniós (riv.) E6
Prespa (lake) E5
Psará (isl.) G6
Psevdhókavos (cape) G6
Rhodes (isl.) H7
Rhodope (mts.) G5
Salonika (Thermaic) (gulf) F6
Sámos (isl.) H7
Samothráki (isl.) G5
Saría (isl.) H8
Saronic (gulf) F7
Sérifos (isl.) G7
Sídheros (cape) H8
Sífnos (isl.) G7
Sími (isl.) H7
Síros (isl.) G7
Sithoniá (pen.) F5
Skíros (isl.) G6
Spátha (cape) F8
Strimón (gulf) G5
Strofádhes (isls.) E7
Taínaron (cape) F7
Thásos (isl.) G5
Thermaic (gulf) F6
Thíra (isl.) G7
Tílos (isl.) H7
Tínos (isl.) G7
Toronaic (gulf) F5
Vardar (riv.) E5
Voívis (lake) F6
Vólvi (lake) F5
Voúxa (cape) F8
Zákinthos (Zante)
(isl.) E7

ROMANIA

CITIES and TOWNS

Aiud 25,173 F2
Alba Iulia 44,552 F2
Alexandria 38,296 G3
Anina 11,594 E3
Arad 161,568 E2
Babadag 8,423 J3
Bacău 131,413 H2
Baia de Aramă 5,065 F3
Baia Mare 112,893 F2
Băile Herculane 4,606 F3
Băileşti 21,246 F3
Balş 16,091 G3
Beiuş 9,992 F2
Bereşti Tîrg H2
Bicaz 9,490 G2
Bîrlad 59,059 H2
Bistrița 47,562 G2
Bivolari H2
Blaj 21,678 F2
Borşa 25,287 G2
Botoşani 69,881 H2
Brad 18,391 F2
Brăila 203,983 H3
Braşov 259,108 G3
Bucharest (Bucureşti)
(cap.) 1,832,015 G3
Bucharest* 1,960,097 G3
Buhuşi 20,204 H2
Buzău 106,738 H3
Buziaş 8,310 E3
Calafat 16,421 F3
Călăraşi 58,960 H3
Caracal 31,159 G3
Caransebeş 27,429 F3
Carei 24,496 F2
Cernavodă 14,686 J3
Chişineu Criş 9,344 E2
Cîmpeni 7,722 F2
Cîmpia Turzii 23,745 F2
Cîmpina 33,259 H3
Cîmpulung 33,448 G3
Cîmpulung Moldovenesc 19,270 G2
Cisnădie 21,114 G3
Cluj-Napoca 274,095 F2
Cogealac J3
Comaneşti 18,177 H2
Constanța 279,308 J3
Corabia 20,454 G4
Costeşti 10,446 G3
Craiova 220,893 F3
Cujmir F3
Curtea de Argeş 23,555 G3
Dăbuleni F4
Dăeni J3
Darabani 12,207 H1
Dej 35,396 F2
Deta 6,956 E3
Deva 68,290 F3
Dorohoi 23,121 H2
Drăgăneşti Olt 11,606 G3
Drăgăşani 16,290 F3
Drobeta-Turnu Severin 80,114 F3
Făgăraş 34,762 G3
Fălciu J2
Fălticeni 22,463 H2
Făurei 3,620 H3
Feteşti 28,730 H3
Focşani 62,275 H3
Folteşti H3
Găeşti 13,384 G3
Galați 252,884 H3
Gheorghe Gheorghiu-Dej 41,297 H2
Gheorghieni 20,592 G2
Gherla 19,303 G2
Giurgiu 53,241 G3
Hațeg 9,706 F3
Hîrlău 8,135 H2
Hîrşova 8,434 J3
Huedin 8,557 F2
Hunedoara 83,159 F3
Huşi 24,329 J2
Iaşi 262,493 H2
Ineu 10,414 E2
Isaccea 5,283 J3
Jibou F2
Jimbolia 15,325 E3
Lipova 12,427 E2
Luduş 15,771 G2
Lugoj 48,558 F3
Lupeni 28,251 F3
Mangalia 27,263 J4
Medgidia 43,691 J3
Mediaş 68,442 G2
Miercurea Ciuc 38,097 G2
Mizil 14,294 H3
Mociu G2
Moineşti 21,015 H2
Moldova Nouă 18,498 E3
Moreni 17,743 G3
Nădlac 8,407 E2
Năsăud 8,646 G2
Negreşti 7,435 H2
Ocna Mureş 16,381 G2
Odobeşti 8,440 H3
Odorheiu Secuiesc 33,392 G2
Oltenița 25,536 H3
Oradea 175,400 E2
Orăştie 18,769 F3
Oravița 13,628 E3
Orşova 14,873 F3
Panciu 7,772 H3
Paşcani 26,937 H2
Pătulele F3
Pechea H3
Pecica E2
Periam E2
Petrila 25,087 F3
Petroşeni 42,316 F3
Piatra Neamț 84,192 G2
Pincota 7,494 E2
Piteşti 125,029 G3
Plenița F3
Ploieşti 207,009 H3
Poenari Burchi G3
Poiana Mare F4
Pucioasa 14,056 G3
Rădăuți 24,222 G2
Reghin 31,948 G2
Reşița 90,698 E3
Rîmnicu Sărat 29,815 H3
Rîmnicu Vîlcea 75,070 G3
Roman 56,466 H2
Roşiori de Vede 28,832 G3
Săcele 29,391 G3
Salonta 19,698 E2
Satu Mare 108,152 F2
Săveni 7,913 H1
Sebeş 27,448 F3
Sebiş 6,401 F2
Segarcea 8,783 F3
Sfîntu Gheorghe 51,210 G3
Sfîntu Gheorghe J3
Sibiu 156,854 G3
Sighetu Marmației 38,879 F2
Sighişoara 32,296 G2
Şimleul Silvaniei 14,780 F2
Sinaia 14,215 G3
Sînnicolaul Mare 13,565 E2
Siret 6,677 G1
Slănic 8,017 G3
Slatina 54,954 G3
Slobozia 35,207 H3
Solca 4,835 G2
Sovata 10,745 G2
Ştefăneşti H2
Strehaia 11,431 F3
Suceava 66,857 G2
Sulina 5,240 J3
Tăşnad 10,441 F2
Techirghiol 11,228 J3
Tecuci 37,928 H3
Timişoara 281,320 E3
Tinca F2
Tîrgovişte 71,533 G3
Tîrgu Cărbuneşti 7,536 F3
Tîrgu Frumos 6,428 H2
Tîrgu Jiu 70,629 F3
Tîrgu Mureş 129,284 G2
Tîrgu Neamț 15,756 G2
Tîrgu Ocna 12,960 H2
Tîrgu Secuiesc 18,265 H2
Tîrnăveni 27,799 F2
Toplița 14,347 G2
Tulcea 67,091 J3
Turda 57,972 F2
Turnu Măgurele 30,003 G4
Urlața 10,900 H3
Urziceni 13,500 H3
Vasile Roaită J3
Vaslui 44,134 H2
Vatra Dornei 16,748 G2
Videle 11,323 G3
Vişeul de Sus 20,697 F2
Viziru H3
Zalău 36,158 F2
Zărneşti 23,378 G3
Zimnicea 15,111 G4

OTHER FEATURES

Argeş (riv.) G3
Bîrlad (riv.) H2
Black (sea) J4
Brăila (marshes) H3
Buzău (riv.) H3
Carpathian (mts.) G2
Crişul Alb (riv.) F2
Crişul Repede (riv.) F2
Danube (delta) J3
Danube (riv.) H4
Ialomița (marshes) J3
Ialomița (riv.) H3
Jijia (riv.) H2
Jiu (riv.) F3
Moldoveanul (mt.) G3
Mureş (riv.) E2
Olt (riv.) G3
Peleaga (mt.) F3
Pietrosul (mt.) G2
Prut (riv.) J2
Siret (riv.) H2
Someş (riv.) F2
Timiş (riv.) E3
Tîrnava Mare (riv.) G2
Transylvanian Alps (mts.) G3

YUGOSLAVIA

INTERNAL DIVISIONS

Bosnia and Hercegovina
(rep.) 3,710,965 C3
Croatia (rep.) 4,396,397 C3
Kosovo (aut. reg.) 1,240,919 E4
Macedonia (rep.) 1,623,598 E5
Montenegro (rep.) 527,207 D4
Serbia (rep.) 8,401,673 E3
Slovenia (rep.) 1,697,068 B2
Vojvodina (aut.
prov.) 1,953,980 D3

CITIES and TOWNS

Aleksinac 11,943 E4
Apatin 17,501 D3
Arendjelovac 15,659 E3
Bačka Topola 16,028 D3
Bakar B3
Banja Luka 85,786 C3
Bar 3,594 D4
Bečej 26,616 E3
Bela Crkva 11,137 E3
Belgrade (cap.) 727,945 E3
Beli Manastir 7,325 D3
Beograd (Belgrade)
(cap.) 727,945 E3
Berovo 5,053 F5
Bihać 24,155 B3
Bijeljina 24,888 D3
Bijelo Polje 9,298 D4
Bileća 4,083 D4
Biograd 3,595 B4
Bitola 64,467 E5
Bjelovar 21,019 C3
Blato 5,591 C4
Bled 4,710 A2
Bor 27,520 E3
Bosanska Dubica 9,191 C3
Bosanska Gradiška 9,742 C3
Bosanska Kostajnica 2,535 B3
Bosanska Krupa 8,947 C3
Bosanski Brod 10,113 D3
Bosanski Novi 9,861 C3
Bosanski Petrovac 4,113 C3
Bosanski Šamac 4,949 D3
Brčko 25,575 D3
Brežice 3,271 B3
Budva 2,483 D4
Bugojno 9,079 C3
Čačak 38,890 E4
Čakovec 11,766 C2
Čapljina 4,677 C4
Caribrod (Dimitrovgrad) 5,449 F4
Cazin 1,213 B3
Celje 30,827 B2
Cetinje 12,089 D4
Ćuprija 17,691 E4
Daruvar 8,478 C3
Debar 8,597 E5
Derventa 11,887 C3
Dimitrovgrad 5,449 F4
Djakovica 29,499 E4
Djakovo 15,833 D3
Doboj 18,073 C3
Donji Vakuf 4,928 C3
Drvar 6,237 C3
Dubrovnik 31,213 C4
Fiume (Rijeka) 128,883 B3
Foča 9,370 D4
Gacko 1,641 D4
Gevgelija 9,319 F5
Glamoč 2,627 C3
Gnjilane 21,359 E4
Gornji Milanovac 11,114 D3
Gornji Vakuf 2,429 C4
Gospić 8,238 B3
Gostivar 18,805 E5
Gračac 3,228 B3
Gračanica 9,302 D3
Gradačac 7,571 D3
Grubišno Polje 2,771 C3
Gusinje 2,616 D4
Herceg Novi 6,645 D4
Ivangrad 11,373 E4
Ivanjica 5,719 E4
Jajce 9,221 C3
Jesenice 16,163 A2
Kanjiža 11,348 D2
Karlovac 47,046 B3
Kavadarci 17,974 E5
Kičevo 14,189 E5
Kikinda 37,392 E3
Kladanj 3,255 D3
Ključ 3,466 C3
Knin 7,279 C3
Knjaževac 11,734 F4
Kočani 16,611 F5
Kočevje 7,277 B3
Kolašin 2,111 D4
Konjic 9,161 D4
Koper 16,683 A3
Koprivnica 16,398 C2
Kosovska Mitrovica 42,526 E4
Kostajnica 9,161 C3
Kotor 5,728 D4
Kragujevac 72,080 E3
Kraljevo 28,065 E4
Kranj 26,341 B2
Križevci 8,501 C2
Krk 1,500 B3
Krško 4,451 B3
Kruševac 29,902 E4
Kulen Vakuf 1,078 B3
Kumanovo 44,791 E4
Kutina 10,892 C3
Leskovac 46,050 E4
Livno 7,223 C4
Ljubinje 785 D4
Ljubljana 169,064 B3
Ljubuški 2,891 C4
Loznica 13,513 D3
Maglaj 5,869 D3
Makarska 6,589 C4
Maribor 94,976 B2
Modriča 7,406 D3
Mostar 47,821 D4
Murska Sobota 9,665 C2
Našice 5,836 C3
Negotin 11,325 F3
Nevesinje 3,077 D4
Nikšić 28,940 D4
Nin 1,782 B3
Niš 128,231 F4
Nova Gorizia A2
Nova Gradiška 11,765 C3
Novi 2,682 B3
Novi Pazar 28,696 E4
Novi Sad 143,591 D3
Novo Mesto 9,553 B3
Novska 5,168 C3
Ogulin 9,975 B3
Ohrid 26,352 E5
Omiš 3,515 C4
Opatija 9,238 A3
Osijek 94,989 D3
Pag 2,318 B3
Pančevo 53,979 E3
Paraćin 21,555 E4
Peć 41,783 E4
Petrinja 12,296 B3
Piran 5,485 A3
Pirot 29,658 F4
Plav 3,072 D4
Pljevlja 14,459 D4
Pločce 4,257 C4
Pola (Pula) 47,117 A3
Poreč 4,512 A3
Postojna 6,085 B3
Požarevac 33,336 E3
Preševo 7,634 E4
Priboj 12,556 D4
Prijedor 22,379 C3
Prijepolje 7,960 D4
Prilep 48,045 E5
Priština 71,264 E4
Prizren 41,875 E4
Prokuplje 20,617 E4
Prozor 1,420 C4
Ptuj 9,245 C2
Pula 47,117 A3
Rab 1,675 B3
Radoviš 9,373 F5
Ragusa (Dubrovnik) 31,213 C4
Raška 3,935 E4
Ravne na Koroškem 6,529 B2
Rijeka 128,883 B3
Rogatica 4,801 D4
Rovinj 8,998 A3
Rožaj E4
Ruma 24,180 D3
Šabac 43,539 D3
Samobor 7,821 B3
Sanski Most 8,718 C3
Sarajevo 245,058 D4
Senj 4,927 B3
Senta 24,694 D3
Šibenik 29,619 C4
Šid 11,867 D3
Sinj 4,705 C4
Sisak 37,215 C3
Sjenica 9,118 E4
Škofja Loka 4,971 A2
Skopje 308,117 E5
Skradin 893 B4
Slavonska Požega 18,160 C3
Slavonski Brod 38,829 D3
Smederevo 39,200 E3
Smederevska Palanka 18,837 E3
Sombor 44,210 D3
Split 150,739 C4
Srebrenica 3,101 D3
Sremska Mitrovica 32,569 D3
Štip 27,218 F5
Stolac 3,862 D4
Ston 407 C4
Struga 11,369 E5
Strumica 22,770 F5
Subotica 89,476 D2
Surdulica 7,048 F4
Svetozarevo 27,812 E4
Svilajnac 7,848 E3
Teslić 4,940 C3
Tetovo 35,293 E5
Titograd 54,639 D4
Titovo Užice 35,465 D4
Titov Veles 35,583 E5
Travnik 12,745 C3
Trbovlje 16,393 B2
Trebinje 3,553 D4
Trogir 6,162 C4
Trstenik 7,167 E4
Tržič 4,435 B2
Tuzla 53,836 D3
Ub 3,785 E3
Ulcinj 7,472 D5
Umag 3,228 A3
Uroševac E4
Valjevo 26,655 D3
Varaždin 34,662 B2
Vareš 7,632 D3
Velenje 11,225 B2
Velika Plana E3
Veliki Bečkerek
(Zrenjanin) 60,201 E3
Vinkovci 29,257 D3
Virovitica 16,389 C3
Višegrad 4,753 D4
Visoko 9,365 D4
Vlasenica 4,033 D3
Vranje 25,909 F4
Vrbas 22,502 D3
Vršac 33,573 E3
Vučitrn 11,701 E4
Vukovar 29,500 D3
Žabljak 1,023 D4
Zadar 43,588 B3
Zagreb 561,773 C3
Zaječar 27,724 E4
Zara (Zadar) 43,588 B3
Zenica 49,522 C3
Žepče 3,177 D3
Zrenjanin 60,201 E3
Zvornik 8,498 D3

OTHER FEATURES

Adriatic (sea) B4
Bobotov Kuk (mt.) D4
Bosna (riv.) D3
Brač (isl.) C4
Cazma (riv.) C3
Cres (isl.) B3
Čvrsnica (mt.) C4
Dalmatia (reg.) C4
Danube (riv.) E3
Dinaric Alps (mts.) B3
Drava (riv.) C3
Drina (riv.) D3
Dugi Otok (isl.) B3
Hvar (isl.) C4
Ibar (riv.) E4
Istria (pen.) A3
Kamenjak (cape) A3
Kladovo F3
Korab (mt.) E5
Korčula (isl.) C4
Kornat (isl.) B4
Krk (isl.) B3
Kupa (riv.) B3
Kvarner (gulf) B3
Lastovo (Lagosta) (isl.) C4
Lim (riv.) D4
Lošinj (isl.) B3
Midzhur (mt.) F4
Mljet (isl.) C4
Morava (riv.) E3
Mur (riv.) B2
Neretva (riv.) D4
Ohrid (lake) E5
Pag (isl.) B3
Palagruža (Pelagosa) (isl.) C4
Prespa (lake) E5
Rab (isl.) B3
Rujen (mt.) F4
Sava (riv.) D3
Scutari (lake) D4
Slavonia (reg.) C3
Šolta (isl.) C4
Tara (riv.) D4
Timok (riv.) F3
Tisa (riv.) E3
Triglav (mt.) A2
Una (riv.) C3
Vardar (riv.) E5
Vis (isl.) C4
Vrbas (riv.) C3
Žirje (isl.) B4

*City and suburbs.

The Balkan States
CONIC PROJECTION
SCALE OF MILES
0 25 50 75 100 125 150 175
SCALE OF KILOMETERS
0 25 50 75 100 125 150 175
Capitals of Countries
Administrative Centers
International Boundaries
Major Internal Boundaries
Minor Internal Boundaries
Canals
Scale 1:6,150,000
BULGARIA and GREECE are divided into counties and departments, respectively. Because of the scale no attempt has been made to delimit and name these subdivisions; their administrative centers have, however, been designated.
The larger divisions named in Greece are well-known geographical regions, without administrative function.
ROMANIA consists of thirty-nine counties and three cities of regional status, Bucharest, Constanţa and Petroşeni. Scale does not permit delimiting these counties.
ALBANIA is divided into twenty-seven districts. Scale does not permit the delimitation of these divisions.
YUGOSLAVIA is a federation of six republics. The Serbian republic includes an autonomous province (Vojvodina), and an autonomous region (Kosovo).
WEST GERMANY
CZECHOSLOVAKIA
AUSTRIA
HUNGARY
U. S. S. R.
ROMANIA
YUGOSLAVIA
BOSNIA AND HERCEGOVINA
MONTENEGRO
MACEDONIA
ALBANIA
BULGARIA
GREECE
TURKEY
ITALY
ADRIATIC SEA
TYRRHENIAN SEA
IONIAN SEA
AEGEAN SEA
SEA OF MARMARA
SEA OF CRETE
BLACK SEA
MEDITERRANEAN SEA
VIENNA
BUDAPEST
BELGRADE
BUCHAREST
Sofia
Tiranë
Athens
ISTANBUL
Longitude East of 22° Greenwich
© Copyright HAMMOND INCORPORATED, Maplewood, N. J.

Topography

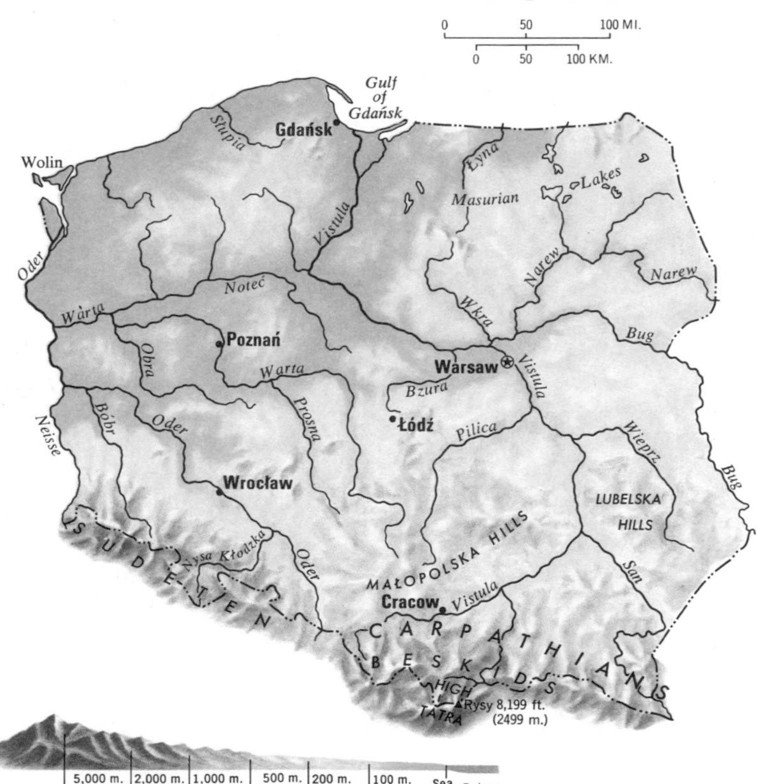

PROVINCES	
Biata Podlaska 283,200	F3
Białystok 613,800	F2
Bielsko 765,500	D4
Bydgoszcz 982,100	C2
Chełm 221,000	F3
Ciechanów 398,500	E2
Cracow (Kraków) 1,097,600	E4
Cracow (city) 651,300	E4
Częstochowa 723,200	D3
Elbląg 419,800	D1
Gdańsk 1,312,300	D1
Gorzów 428,700	B2
Jelenia Góra 483,400	B3
Kalisz 640,300	D3
Katowice 3,439,700	D3
Kielce 1,030,400	E3
Konin 423,700	D2
Koszalin 428,500	C1
Krosno 418,000	E4
Legnica 405,600	C4
Leszno 340,600	C3
Łódź 1,063,700	D3
Łódź (city) 777,800	D3
Łomza 320,600	F2
Lublin 875,300	F3
Nowy Sącz 600,300	E4
Olsztyn 654,400	E2
Opole 961,600	C3
Ostrołęka 360,700	E2
Piła 414,000	C2
Piotrków 581,900	D3
Płock 479,700	D2
Poznań 1,156,500	C2
Przemyśl 373,100	F4
Radom 674,400	E3
Rzeszów 602,200	F4
Siedlce 602,100	F2
Sieradz 388,000	D3
Skierniewice 388,300	E3
Słupsk 352,900	C1
Suwałki 412,700	F1
Szczecin 841,400	B2
Tarnobrzeg 532,200	E3
Tarnów 573,900	E4
Torún 580,500	D2
Wałbrzych 709,600	C3
Warsaw 2,117,700	E2
Warsaw (city) 1,377,100	E2
Włocławek 402,000	D2
Wrocław 1,014,600	C3
Zamość 472,300	F3
Zielona Góra 575,000	B3

CITIES and TOWNS	
Aleksandrów Kujawski 9,600	D2
Aleksandrów Łódzki 14,400	D3
Allenstein (Olsztyn) 94,119	E2
Andrespol 12,400	D3
Andrychów 14,300	D4
Augustów 19,784	F2
Auschwitz (Oświęcim) 39,600	D3
Bartoszyce 15,500	E1
Będzin 42,787	B3
Beuthen (Bytom) 186,993	A3
Biała Podlaska 26,100	F3
Białogard 20,500	C1
Białystok 166,619	F2
Bielawa 30,900	C3
Bielsk Podlaski 14,000	F2
Bielsko-Biała 105,601	D4
Biłgoraj 12,888	F3
Błonie 12,500	E2
Bochnia 14,500	E4
Bogatynia 11,800	B3
Boguszów-Gorce 11,900	B3
Bolesławiec 30,500	B3

Poland 1938
0 50 100 MILES

Agriculture, Industry and Resources

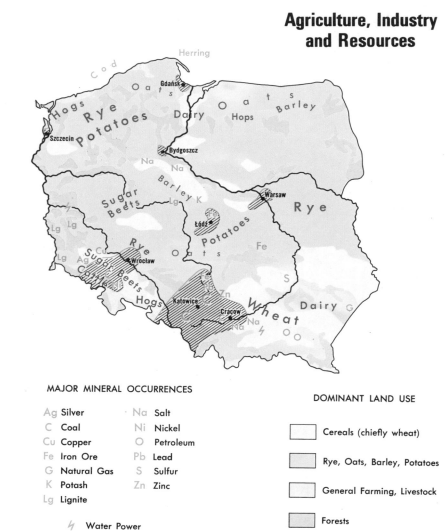

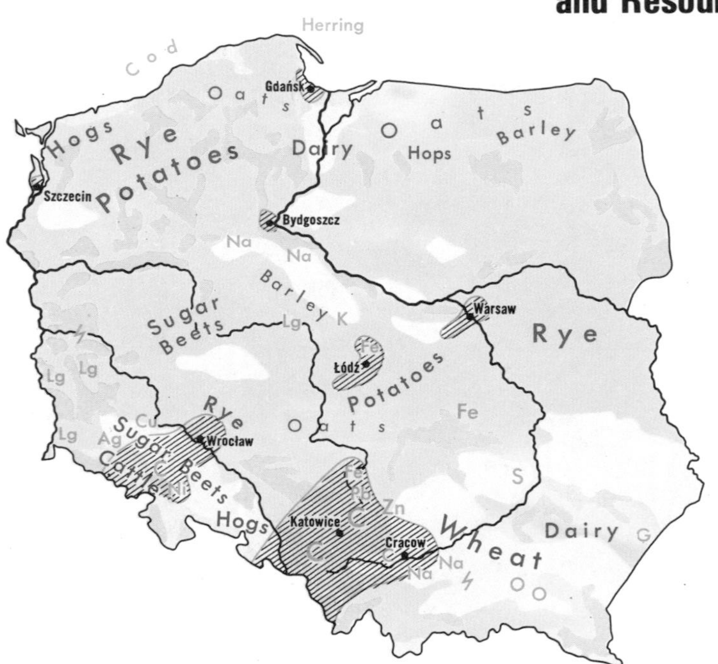

Poland 1945
0 50 100 MILES

MAJOR MINERAL OCCURRENCES

- Ag Silver
- C Coal
- Cu Copper
- Fe Iron Ore
- G Natural Gas
- K Potash
- Lg Lignite
- Na Salt
- Ni Nickel
- O Petroleum
- Pb Lead
- S Sulfur
- Zn Zinc

Water Power
Major Industrial Areas

DOMINANT LAND USE

- Cereals (chiefly wheat)
- Rye, Oats, Barley, Potatoes
- General Farming, Livestock
- Forests

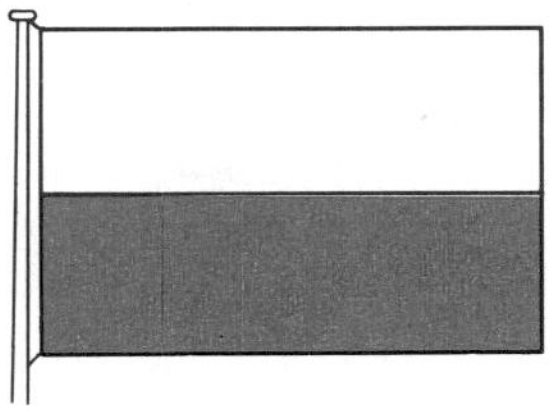

Braniewo 12,100 D1
Breslau (Wrocław) 461,900 C3
Brieg (Brzeg) 30,780 C3
Brodnica 17,300 D2
Brzeg 30,780 C3
Brzeg Dolny 10,800 C3
Brzesko 9,701 E3
Busko Zdrój 11,100 E3
Bydgoszcz 280,460 C2
Bytom 186,993 A3
Bytów 10,642 C1
Chełm 38,789 F3
Chełmno 17,906 D2
Chełmza 14,200 D2
Chodziez 14,100 C2
Chojnice 23,500 C2
Chojnów 11,000 B3
Chorzów 151,338 B4
Choszczno 9,800 B2
Chrzanów 29,300 B4
Ciechanów 28,500 E2
Ciep ice
  Śląskie-Zdrój 15,400 B3
Cieszyn 25,234 D4
Cracow 651,300 E4
Czechowice-Dziedzice 25,400 D4
Czeladź 31,843 B4
Częstochowa 187,613 D3
Dąbrowa Górnicza 61,660 B3
Danzig (Gdańsk) 364,285 D1
Darłowo 11,200 C1
Dębica 22,900 E3
Dęblin 14,600 E3
Dębno 10,700 B2
Działdowo 10,100 E2
Dzierzoniów 32,800 C3
Elbing (Elblag) 89,835 D1
Ełk 27,188 F2
Gdansk 364,285 D1
Gdynia 190,125 D1
Gizycko 18,200 E1
Gleiwitz (Gliwice) 170,912 A4
Głogów (Glogau) 20,226 C3
Głowno 12,800 D2
Głubczyce 11,300 C3
Głuchołazy 13,200 C3
Gniezno 50,643 C2
Goleniów 14,600 B2
Gorlice 15,200 E4
Gorzów Wielkopolski 74,267 B2
Gostyń 13,000 C3
Gostynin 12,000 D2
Grajewo 11,200 F2
Grodzisk Mazowiecki 20,400 E2
Grójec 10,300 E3
Grudziądz 75,511 D2
Grünberg (Zielona
  Góra) 59,700 B3
Gryfice 13,200 B2
Guben (Gubin) 14,600 B3
Hajnowka m4,345 F2
Hindenburg (Zabrze) 199,400 A4
Hirschberg (Jelenia
  Góra) 55,720 B3
Hrubieszów 14,999 F3
Iława 16,400 D2
Inowrocław 54,817 D2
Jarocin 18,100 C3
Jarosław 29,000 F4
Jasło 17,025 E4
Jastrzębie Zdroj 34,400 D3
Jaworzno 63,271 B4
Jędrzejów 13,264 E3
Jelenia Góra 55,720 B3
Kalisz 81,227 D3
Kamienna Góra 21,000 B3
Kartuzy 10,558 C1
Katowice 303,264 B4
Kedzierzyn-Koźle 45,600 C3
Kępno 10,151 C3
Kętrzyn 19,300 E1
Kielce 125,952 E3
Kłobuck 12,600 D3
Kłodzko 26,000 C3
Kluczbork 18,000 D3
Knurów 28,400 A4
Kolberg (Kołobrzeg) 25,419 B1
Koło 13,100 D2
Kołobrzeg 25,419 B1
Konin 40,600 D2
Końskie 13,100 E3
Konstantynów
  Łódzki 12,800 D3
Kościan 18,700 C2
Kościerzyna 18,914 C1
Köslin (Koszalin) 64,414 C1
Kostrzyń 11,200 B2
Koszalin 64,414 C1
Kraków (Cracow) 651,300 E4
Krapkowice 13,800 D3
Kraśnik Fabryczny 14,600 F3
Krasnystaw 12,495 F3
Krosno 26,500 E4
Krotoszyn 21,900 C3
Krynica 10,200 E4
Küstrin 11,200 B2
Kutno 30,000 D2
Kwidzin 23,104 D2
Łancut 12,049 F3
Landsberg (Gorzów
  Wielkepolski) 74,267 B2
Łaziska Górne 10,800 A4
Lębork 25,000 C1
Łęczyca 13,900 D2
Legionowo 20,800 E2
Legnica 75,843 C3
Leszcyny 12,200 A4
Leszno 33,890 C3
Libiaz 10,600 D3
Lidzbark Warmiński 12,900 E1
Liegnitz (Legnica) 75,843 C3
Lipno 10,900 D2
Łódź 777,800 D3
Łomza 25,500 F2
Łowicz 20,400 D2
Lubań 17,200 B3
Lubartów 10,000 F3
Lubin 28,400 C3
Lublin 235,937 F3
Lubliniec 19,800 D3
Luboń 16,400 C2
Lubsko 12,600 B3
Łuków 15,500 F3
Malbork (Marienburg) 30,900 D1

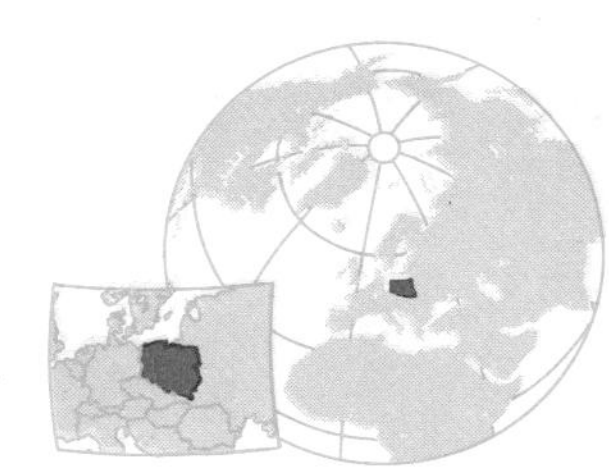

AREA 120,725 sq. mi. (312,678 sq. km.)
POPULATION 35,815,000
CAPITAL Warsaw
LARGEST CITY Warsaw
HIGHEST POINT Rysy 8,199 ft. (2,499 m.)
MONETARY UNIT zloty
MAJOR LANGUAGE Polish
MAJOR RELIGION Roman Catholicism

Międzyrzec Podlaski 13,500 F3
Międzyrzecz 14,900 B2
Mielec 26,800 E3
Mikłów 21,300 B4
Mińsk Mazowiecki 24,200 E2
Mława 20,007 E2
Mońki 9,560 F2
Morąg 9,681 E2
Mrągowo 13,400 E2
Myślenice 12,100 E4
Mysłowice 44,737 C4
Myszków 18,000 D3
Nakło nad Notecia 16,800 C2
Namysłów 11,076 C3
Neisse (Nysa) 31,837 C3
Nidzica 9,642 E2
Nisko 10,000 E3
Nowa Ruda 18,100 C3
Nowa Sól 33,300 B3
Nowy Dwór Mazowiecki 16,900 E2
Nowy Sącz 41,103 E4
Nowy Targ 21,900 E4
Nysa 31,837 C3
Oborniki 10,200 C2
Oława 17,746 C3
Oleśnica 27,500 C3
Olkusz 15,800 D3
Olsztyn 94,119 E2
Opoczno 12,168 E3
Opole 86,510 C3
Oppeln 86,510 C3
Orzesze 9,600 A4
Ostróda 21,300 D2
Ostrołęka 21,981 E2
Ostrów Mazowiecka 15,000 E2
Ostrów Wielkopolski 49,530 C3
Ostrowiec
  Świętokrzyski 49,958 E3
Oświęcim 39,600 D3
Otwock 39,863 E2
Ozorków 18,200 D3
Pabianice 62,275 D3
Piekary Śląskie 36,300 B4
Piła 43,778 C2
Pionki 13,600 E3
Piotrków Trybunalski 59,683 D3
Pisz 11,100 E2
Pleszew 13,348 C3
Płock 71,727 D2
Płońsk 11,619 E2
Police 12,700 B2
Poznań 469,085 C2
Prudnik 20,300 C3
Pruszcz Gdanski 13,000 D1
Pruszków 42,961 E2
Przasnysz 11,100 E2
Przemyśl 53,228 F4
Puck 9,500 D1
Puławy 34,800 F3
Pułtusk 12,600 E2
Rabka 10,700 D4
Racibórz 40,418 C3
Radom 158,640 E3
Radomsko 31,179 D3
Ratibor (Racibórz) 40,418 C3
Rawa Mazowiecka 9,800 E3
Rawicz 14,100 C3
Ruda Śląska 142,407 B4
Rumia 23,300 D1
Rybnik 43,415 D3
Rypin 10,029 D2
Rzeszów 82,192 F4
Sandomierz 16,800 E3
Sanok 21,600 F4
Schneidemühl (Piła) 36,600 C2
Schweidnitz
  (Świdnica) 47,542 C3
Siedlce 38,983 F2
Siemianowice
  Śląskie 67,278 B4
Sieradz 18,500 D3
Sierpc 12,700 D2
Skarzysko-Kamienna 39,194 E3
Skawina 15,900 D4
Skierniewice 25,590 E2
Sławno 10,700 C1
Słubice 12,000 B2
Słupsk 68,311 C1
Sochaczew 20,500 E2
Sokółka 10,023 F2
Sokołów Podlaski 9,569 F2
Sopot 47,573 D1
Sosnowiec 144,652 B4
Śrem 15,600 C2
Środa Śląska 10,259 C3
Środa Wielkopolska 14,800 C2
Stalowa Wola 29,768 F3
Starachowice 42,807 E3
Stargard Szeciński 44,400 B2
Starogard Gdański 33,400 D2
Stary Sacz 57,400 E4
Stettin (Szczecin) 337,294 B2
Stolp (Słupsk) 68,311 C1
Strzegom 14,000 C3
Strzelce Opolskie 14,700 D3
Strzelin 9,800 C3
Sulechów 10,200 B2
Suwałki 25,360 F1
Swarzędz 12,100 C2
Świdnica 47,542 C3
Świdnik 21,900 F3
Świdwin 12,500 B2
Świebodzice 18,500 C3
Świebodzin 14,900 B2
Świecie 17,900 D2
Świętochłowice 57,633 A4
Świnoujście
  (Swinemünde) 27,900 B1
Szamotuły 14,600 C2
Szczecin 337,204 B2
Szczecinek 28,600 C2
Szczytno 17,371 E2
Szprotawa 11,200 B3
Tarnobrzeg 18,800 E3
Tarnów 85,514 E4
Tarnowskie Góry 34,200 A3
Tczew 40,794 D1
Tomaszów Lubelski 12,329 F3
Tomaszów Mazowiecki 54,911 E3
Toruń 129,152 D2
Trzcianka 10,900 C2
Trzebinia-Siersza C4
Turek 18,500 D2
Tychy 71,384 B4
Ustka 9,900 C1
Wąbrzeźno 11,800 D2
Wadowice 11,700 D4
Wągrowiec 15,600 C2
Wałbrzych 125,048 C3
Wałcz 18,900 C2
Waldenburg
  (Wałbrzych) 125,048 C3
Warsaw (Warszawa)
  (cap.) 1,377,100 E2
Wejherowo 33,600 D1
Wieliczka 13,600 E3
Wieluń 14,300 D3
Wisła 9,800 D4
Włocławek 77,169 D2
Wodzisław Śłaski 25,600 D4
Wolin 35,458 B2
Wołomin 24,000 E2
Wołów 10,500 C3
Wrocław 523,318 C3
Września 17,800 C2
Wschowa 10,000 C3
Wyszków E2
Ząbki 16,000 E2
Ząbkowice Śląskie 13,800 C3
Zabrze 197,214 A4
Zagań 21,400 B3
Zakopane 27,039 D4
Zambrów 14,082 E2
Zamość 34,734 F3
Zary 28,300 B3
Zawiercie 39,410 D3
Zduńska Wola 29,066 D3
Zgierz 42,838 D3
Zgorzelec 28,400 B3
Ziębice 9,700 C3
Zielona Góra 73,156 B3
Złocieniec 10,100 C2
Złotoryja 12,200 C3
Złotów 11,600 C2
Znin 9,600 C2
Zyrardów 33,196 E2
Zywiec 22,400 D4

OTHER FEATURES

Baltic (sea) B1
Beskids (range) D4
Brda (riv.) C2
Brynica (riv.) B4
Bug (riv.) F2
Danzig (Gdańsk) (gulf) D1
Dukla (pass) E4
Dunajec (riv.) E4
Gwda (riv.) C2
Hel (pen.) D1
High Tatra (range) D4
Kłodnica (riv.) A4
Łyna (riv.) E1
Mamry, Jezioro (lake) E1
Masurian (lkes) E2
Narew (riv.) E2
Neisse (riv.) B3
Noteć (riv.) B2
Nysa Kłodzka (riv.) C3
Nysa Łuzycka (Neisse)
  (riv.) B3
Oder (riv.) B2
Orava (res.) D4
Pilica (riv.) D3
Pomeranian (bay) B1
Prosna (riv.) C3
Przemsza (riv.) B4
Rysy (mt.) D4
San (riv.) F3
Słupia (riv.) C1
Śniardwy, Jezioro (lake) E2
Sudeten (range) B3
Uznam (Usedom) (isl.) B1
Vistula (riv.) D2
Warmia (reg.) D1
Warta (riv.) B2
Wieprz (riv.) F3
Wisła (Vistula) (riv.) D2
Wkra (riv.) E2
Wolin (Wollin) (isl.) B2

Poland
CONIC PROJECTION
SCALE OF MILES 0 10 20 40 60 80
SCALE OF KILOMETERS 0 10 20 40 60 80
Capitals of Countries
Other Capitals
International Boundaries
Internal Boundaries
Canals
Scale 1:4,500,000

Poland is divided into 49 provinces (bearing the same name as their capitals) and the autonomous cities of Warsaw, Łódź and Cracow.

48 Union of Soviet Socialist Republics

UNION REPUBLICS

Armenian S.S.R. 3,031,000 .... E6
Azerbaidzhan S.S.R. 6,028,000 .... E5
Estonian S.S.R. 1,466,000 .... C4
Georgian S.S.R. 5,015,000 .... D5
Kazakh S.S.R. 14,684,000 .... G5
Kirgiz S.S.R. 3,529,000 .... H5
Latvian S.S.R. 2,521,000 .... C4
Lithuanian S.S.R. 3,398,000 .... C4
Moldavian S.S.R. 3,947,000 .... C5
Russian S.F.S.R. 137,551,000 .... D4
Tadzhik S.S.R. 3,801,000 .... H6
Turkmen S.S.R. 2,759,000 .... F6
Ukrainian S.S.R. 49,755,000 .... C5
Uzbek S.S.R. 15,391,000 .... G5
White Russian S.S.R. 9,560,000 .... C4

INTERNAL DIVISIONS

Abkhaz A.S.S.R. 505,000 .... E5
Adygey Aut. Obl. 405,000 .... D5
Adzhar A.S.S.R. 354,000 .... E5
Aginsk Buryat Aut. Okr. 69,000 .... M4
Bashkir A.S.S.R. 3,849,000 .... F4
Buryat A.S.S.R. 900,000 .... M4
Chechen-Ingush A.S.S.R. 1,154,000 .... E5
Chukchi Aut. Okr. 133,000 .... R3
Chuvash A.S.S.R. 1,292,000 .... E4
Dagestan A.S.S.R. 1,628,000 .... E5
Evenki Aut. Okr. 16,000 .... K3
Gorno-Altay Aut. Obl. 172,000 .... J4
Gorno-Badakhshan Aut. Obl. 127,000 .... H6
Jewish Aut. Obl. 190,000 .... O5
Kabardin-Balkar A.S.S.R. 674,000 .... E5
Kalmuck A.S.S.R. 294,000 .... E5
Karachay-Cherkess Aut. Obl. 368,000 .... E5
Karakalpak A.S.S.R. 904,000 .... G5
Karelian A.S.S.R. 736,000 .... D3
Khakass Aut. Obl. 500,000 .... J4
Khanty-Mansi Aut. Okr. 569,000 .... H3
Komi A.S.S.R. 1,119,000 .... F3
Komi-Permyak Aut. Okr. 173,000 .... F4
Koryak Aut. Okr. 34,000 .... R3
Mari A.S.S.R. 703,000 .... E4
Mordvinian A.S.S.R. 991,000 .... E4
Nagorno-Karabakh Aut. Obl. 161,000 .... E5
Nakhichevan' A.S.S.R. 239,000 .... E6
Nenets Aut. Okr. 47,000 .... F3
North Ossetian A.S.S.R. 597,000 .... E5
South Ossetian Aut. Obl. 98,000 .... E5
Tatar A.S.S.R. 3,436,000 .... F4
Taymyr Aut. Okr. 44,000 .... K2
Tuvinian A.S.S.R. 267,000 .... K4
Udmurt A.S.S.R. 1,494,000 .... F4
Ust'-Ordynskiy Buryat Aut. Okr. 133,000 .... L4
Yakut A.S.S.R. 839,000 .... N3
Yamal-Nenets Aut. Okr. 158,000 .... H3

CITIES and TOWNS

Abakan 128,000 .... K4
Abay 34,245 .... H5
Abaza 15,202 .... J4
Achinsk 117,000 .... K4
Agata K3
Aginskoye 7,922 .... M4
Akmolinsk (Tselinograd) 234,000 .... H4
Aksay 10,010 .... F4
Aktas G5
Aktash J4
Aktyubinsk 191,000 .... F4
Aldan 17,689 .... N4
Aleksandrovsk-Sakhalinskiy 20,342 .... P5
Alekseyevka 18,041 .... H4
Aleysk 32,487 .... J4
Alga 12,000 .... F5
Aliskerovo R3
Allakh-Yun' O3
Alma-Ata 910,000 .... H5
Almaznyy M3
Ambarchik R3
Amderma F3
Amursk 24,010 .... O4
Anadyr' 7,703 .... S3
Andizhan 230,000 .... H5
Angarsk 239,000 .... L4
Angren H5
Anzhero-Sudzhensk 105,000 .... J4
Aral'sk 37,722 .... G5
Archangel (Arkhangel'sk) 385,000 .... E3
Arkalyk 15,108 .... G4
Armavir 162,000 .... E5
Arsen'yev 60,000 .... O5
Artem 69,000 .... O5
Artemovskiy M4
Arys' 26,414 .... G5
Arzamas 93,000 .... E4
Asbest 79,000 .... G4
Ashkhabad 312,000 .... F6
Asino 29,395 .... J4
Astrakhan' 461,000 .... E5
Atbasar 37,228 .... G4
Atka Q3
Ayaguz 35,827 .... J5
Ayan O4
Aykhal M3
Bagdarin M4
Baku 1,022,000 .... F5
Baku* 1,550,000 .... F5
Balakovo 152,000 .... E4
Balashov 93,000 .... E4
Baley 27,215 .... M4
Balkhash 78,000 .... H5
Balykshi 22,397 .... F5
Bam N4
Barabinsk 37,274 .... H4
Baranovichi 131,000 .... C4
Barnaul 533,000 .... J4
Batagay 10,000 .... O3
Batumi 123,000 .... E5
Baykit K3
Baykonyr G5
Bayram-Ali 31,987 .... G6
Belgorod 240,000 .... D4
Belogorsk 63,000 .... N4
Belomorsk 16,595 .... D3
Beloretsk 71,000 .... F4
Belovo 112,000 .... J4
Berdichev 80,000 .... C5
Berdsk 67,000 .... J4
Berezniki 185,000 .... F4
Berezovo 6,000 .... G3
Beringovskiy T3
Bikin 17,473 .... O5
Bira O5
Birobidzhan 69,000 .... O5
Biruni G5
Biysk 212,000 .... J4
Blagoveshchensk 172,000 .... N4
Bobruysk 192,000 .... C4
Bodaybo 19,000 .... M4
Borisoglebsk 68,000 .... E4
Borzya 27,815 .... M4
Bratsk 214,000 .... L4
Brest 177,000 .... C4
Brindakit O4
Bryansk 394,000 .... D4
Bugul'ma 80,000 .... F4
Bukachacha 10,000 .... M4
Bukhara 185,000 .... G5
Bulun N2
Buzuluk 76,000 .... F4
Chadan K4
Chapayevsk 85,000 .... F4
Chara M4
Chardzhou 140,000 .... G6
Charsk 10,100 .... J5
Cheboksary 308,000 .... E4
Chegdomyn 16,499 .... O4
Chelkar 19,377 .... F5
Chelyabinsk 1,030,000 .... G4
Cheremkhovo 77,000 .... L4
Cherepovets 266,000 .... D4
Cherkessk 91,000 .... E5
Chernigov 238,000 .... D4
Chernogorsk 71,000 .... K4
Chernovtsy 219,000 .... C5
Chernyshevsk 10,000 .... M4
Cherskiy Q3
Chimbay 18,899 .... F5
Chimkent 322,000 .... H5
Chirchik 132,000 .... H5
Chita 303,000 .... M4
Chokurdakh P2
Chumikan O4
Dal'negorsk 33,506 .... O5
Dal'nerechensk 28,224 .... O5
Daugavpils 116,000 .... C4
Denau G6
Dikson J2
Dimitrovgrad 106,000 .... F4
Dnepropetrovsk 1,066,000 .... D5
Donetsk 1,021,000 .... D5
Drogobych 66,000 .... C5
Druzhba J5
Druzhina P3
Dudinka 19,701 .... J3
Dushanbe 494,000 .... G6
Dzerzhinsk 257,000 .... E4
Dzhalal-Abad 55,000 .... H5
Dzhalinda N4
Dzhambul 264,000 .... H5
Dzhelinda M2
Dzhetygara 32,169 .... G4
Dzhezkazgan 89,000 .... G5
Dzhusaly 20,658 .... G5
Egvekinot S3
Ekibastuz 66,000 .... H4
Ekimchan O4
El'dikan O3
Elista 70,000 .... E5
Emba 17,820 .... F5
Engel's 161,000 .... E4
Erivan 1,019,000 .... E6
Evensk Q3
Fergana 176,000 .... H5
Fort-Shevchenko 12,000 .... F5
Frolovo 33,398 .... E5
Frunze 533,000 .... H5
Gasan-Kuli F6
Gol'chikha J2
Gomel' 383,000 .... D4
Gor'kiy 1,344,000 .... E4
Gorno-Altaysk 34,413 .... J4
Gornyak 16,643 .... J4
Grodno 195,000 .... C4
Groznyy 375,000 .... E5
Gubakha 33,243 .... F4
Gulistan 30,879 .... G5
Gur'yev 131,000 .... F5
Gusinoozersk 10,000 .... L4
Gyda H2
Igarka 15,624 .... J3
Igrim G3
Ilanskiy 22,852 .... K4
Indiga E3
Inta 51,000 .... G3
Iolotan' 10,000 .... G6
Irkutsk 550,000 .... L4
Ishim 63,000 .... H4
Isil'kul' 25,958 .... H4
Iul'tin T3
Ivano-Frankovsk 150,000 .... C5
Ivanovo 465,000 .... E4
Ivdel 15,308 .... G3
Izhevsk 549,000 .... F4
Izmail 83,000 .... C5
Kachug L4
Kagan 34,117 .... G6
Kalachinsk 20,809 .... H4
Kalakan M4
Kalinin 412,000 .... D4
Kaliningrad 355,000 .... B4
Kalmykovo F5
Kaluga 265,000 .... D4
Kamen'-na-Obi 35,604 .... H4

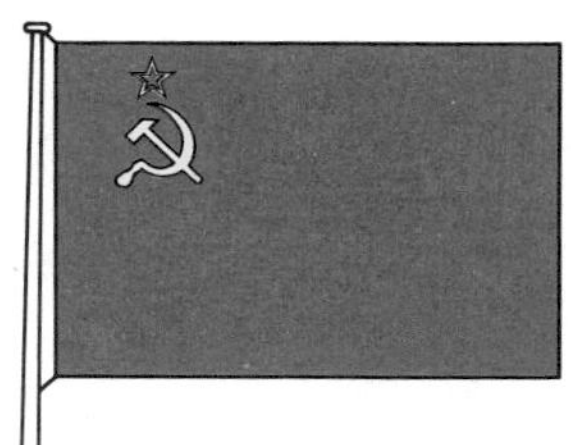

AREA 8,649,490 sq. mi. (22,402,179 sq. km.)
POPULATION 262,436,227
CAPITAL Moscow
LARGEST CITY Moscow
HIGHEST POINT Communism Peak 24,599 ft. (7,498 m.)
MONETARY UNIT ruble
MAJOR LANGUAGES Russian, Ukrainian, White Russian, Uzbek, Azerbaidzhani, Tatar, Georgian, Lithuanian, Armenian, Yiddish, Latvian, Mordvinian, Kirgiz, Tadzhik, Estonian, Kazakh, Moldavian (Romanian), German, Chuvash, Turkmenian, Bashkir
MAJOR RELIGIONS Eastern (Russian) Orthodoxy, Islam, Judaism, Protestantism (Baltic States)

Kamenskoye R3
Kamensk-Ural'skiy 187,000 ..... G4
Kamyshin 112,000 ..... E4
Kandalaksha 42,656 ..... C3
Kansk 101,000 ..... K4
Kapchagay H5
Kara G3
Karaganda 572,000 ..... H5
Karasuk 22,637 ..... H4
Karatau 26,962 ..... H5
Karazhal 17,702 ..... H5
Kargasok J4
Karpinsk F4
Karshi 108,000 ..... G6
Kartaly 42,801 ..... G4
Katangli P4
Kattakurgan 53,000 ..... G5
Kaunas 370,000 ..... C4
Kavalerovo 16,415 ..... O5
Kazan' 993,000 ..... F4
Kem' 21,025 ..... D3
Kemerovo 471,000 ..... J4
Kentau 52,000 ..... G5
Kerki 10,000 ..... G6
Khabarovsk 528,000 ..... O5
Khandyga O3
Khanty-Mansiysk 24,754 ..... H3
Khar'kov 1,444,000 ..... D4
Khatanga L2
Kherson 319,000 ..... D5
Khilok 17,000 ..... M4
Khiva 24,139 ..... F5
Khodzheyli 36,435 ..... F5
Kholmsk 37,412 ..... P5
Khorog 12,295 ..... H6
Kiev 2,144,000 ..... D4

UNION REPUBLICS

	AREA (sq. mi.)	AREA (sq. km.)	POPULATION	CAPITAL and LARGEST CITY
RUSSIAN S.F.S.R.	6,592,812	17,075,400	137,551,000	Moscow 7,831,000
KAZAKH S.S.R.	1,048,300	2,715,100	14,684,000	Alma-Ata 910,000
UKRAINIAN S.S.R.	233,089	603,700	49,755,000	Kiev 2,144,000
TURKMEN S.S.R.	188,455	488,100	2,759,000	Ashkhabad 312,000
UZBEK S.S.R.	173,591	449,600	15,391,000	Tashkent 1,780,000
WHITE RUSSIAN S.S.R.	80,154	207,600	9,560,000	Minsk 1,262,000
KIRGIZ S.S.R.	76,641	198,500	3,529,000	Frunze 533,000
TADZHIK S.S.R.	55,251	143,100	3,801,000	Dushanbe 494,000
AZERBAIDZHAN S.S.R.	33,436	86,600	6,028,000	Baku 1,022,000
GEORGIAN S.S.R.	26,911	69,700	5,015,000	Tbilisi 1,066,000
LITHUANIAN S.S.R.	25,174	65,200	3,398,000	Vilna 481,000
LATVIAN S.S.R.	24,595	63,700	2,521,000	Riga 835,000
ESTONIAN S.S.R.	17,413	45,100	1,466,000	Tallinn 430,000
MOLDAVIAN S.S.R.	13,012	33,700	3,947,000	Kishinev 503,000
ARMENIAN S.S.R.	11,506	29,800	3,031,000	Erivan 1,019,000

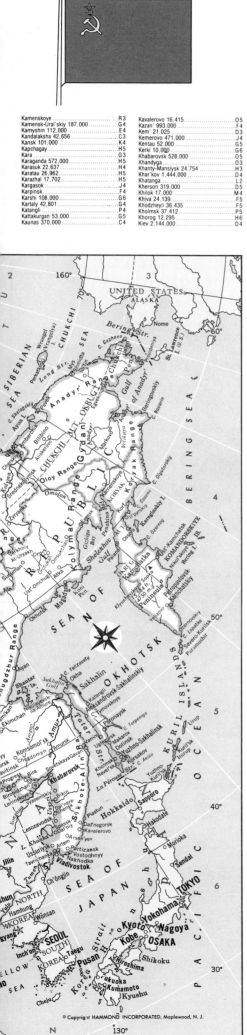

Kirensk 10,000 ..... L4
Kirov 390,000 ..... E4
Kirovabad 232,000 ..... E5
Kirovograd 237,000 ..... D5
Kirovskiy H5
Kiselevsk 122,000 ..... J4
Kishinev 503,000 ..... C5
Kizel 46,264 ..... F4
Kizyl-Arvat 21,671 ..... F6
Klaipeda 176,000 ..... B4
Kokand 153,000 ..... H5
Kokchetav 103,000 ..... H4
Kolomna 147,000 ..... D4
Kolpashevo 24,911 ..... J4
Komsomol'sk 15,385 ..... G4
Komsomol'sk-na-Amure 264,000 ..... O4
Kondopoga 27,908 ..... D3
Kopeysk 146,000 ..... G4
Korf R3
Korsakov 38,210 ..... P5
Koslan E3
Kostroma 255,000 ..... E4
Kotlas 61,000 ..... E3
Kovel' 33,351 ..... C4
Kovrov 143,000 ..... E4
Kozhevnikovo L2
Krasino F2
Krasnodar 560,000 ..... E5
Krasnokamensk 51,000 ..... M4
Krasnokamsk 56,000 ..... F4
Krasnotur'insk 61,000 ..... G3
Krasnoural'sk 39,743 ..... G4
Krasnovodsk 53,000 ..... F5
Krasnoyarsk 796,000 ..... K4
Kremenchug 210,000 ..... D5
Krivoy Rog 650,000 ..... D5
Kudymkar 26,350 ..... F4
Kul'sary 16,427 ..... F5
Kulunda 15,264 ..... H4
Kulyab 55,000 ..... H6
Kum-Dag 10,000 ..... F6
Kungur 80,000 ..... F4
Kupino 20,799 ..... H4
Kurgan 310,000 ..... G4
Kurgan-Tyube 34,620 ..... G6
Kursk 375,000 ..... D4
Kushka G6
Kustanay 165,000 ..... G4
Kutaisi 194,000 ..... E5
Kuybyshev 1,216,000 ..... F4
Kuybyshev 40,166 ..... H4
Kyakhta 15,316 ..... L4
Kyusyur N2
Kyzyl 66,000 ..... K4
Kzyl-Orda 156,000 ..... G5
Labytnangi G3
Lebedinyy N4
Leninabad 130,000 ..... G5
Leninakan 207,000 ..... E5
Leningrad 4,073,000 ..... D4
Leningrad* 4,588,000 ..... D4
Leninogorsk 54,000 ..... J5
Leninsk G5
Leninsk-Kuznetskiy 132,000 ..... J4
Leninskoye O5
Lenkoran' 35,505 ..... E6
Lensk 16,758 ..... M3
Lesosibirsk K4
Lesozavodsk 34,957 ..... O5
Liepāja 108,000 ..... B4
Lipetsk 396,000 ..... E4
Luga 31,905 ..... D4
Lutsk 137,000 ..... C4
L'vov 667,000 ..... C4
Lys'va 75,000 ..... F4
Magadan 121,000 ..... P4
Magdagachi 15,059 ..... N4
Magnitogorsk 406,000 ..... G4
Makhachkala 251,000 ..... E5
Makinsk 22,850 ..... H4
Mama M4
Markovo S3
Mary (Merv) 74,000 ..... G6
Maykop 128,000 ..... D5
Mednogorsk 38,024 ..... F4
Medvezh'yegorsk 17,465 ..... D3
Mezen' E3
Miass 150,000 ..... G4
Michurinsk 101,000 ..... E4
Millerovo 34,627 ..... E5
Minsk 1,262,000 ..... C4
Minsk* 1,276,000 ..... C4
Minusinsk 56,000 ..... K4
Mirnyy 23,826 ..... M3
Mogilev 290,000 ..... D4
Mogocha 17,884 ..... N4
Molodechno 73,000 ..... C4
Monchegorsk 51,000 ..... C3
Moscow (cap.) 7,831,000 ..... D4
Moscow* 8,011,000 ..... D4
Motygino 10,000 ..... K4
Mozyr' 73,000 ..... C4
Murgab H6
Murmansk 381,000 ..... D3
Muynak 12,000 ..... F5
Mys Shmidta T3
Nadym H3
Nagornyy N4
Nakhichevan' 33,279 ..... E6
Nakhodka 133,000 ..... O5
Nal'chik 207,000 ..... E5
Namangan 227,000 ..... H5
Naminga M4
Nar'yan-Mar 16,864 ..... F3
Naryn 21,098 ..... H5
Navoi 84,000 ..... G6
Nazarovo 54,000 ..... K4
Nazyvayevsk 15,792 ..... H4
Nebit-Dag 71,000 ..... F6
Nefteyugansk 52,000 ..... H3
Nel'kan O4
Nepa L4
Neryungri N4
Nevel'sk 20,726 ..... P5
Nikolayev 440,000 ..... D5
Nikolayevsk-na-Amure 30,082 ..... P4
Nikol'skoye R4
Nizhneudinsk 39,743 ..... K4
Nizhnevartovsk 109,000 ..... H3
Nizhneyansk O3
Nizhniy Tagil 398,000 ..... G4
Nordvik-Ugol'naya M2
Noril'sk 180,000 ..... J3
Novaya Kazanka F5
Novgorod 186,000 ..... D4
Novokazalinsk 34,815 ..... G5
Novokuznetsk 541,000 ..... J4
Novomoskovsk 147,000 ..... E4
Novorossiysk 159,000 ..... D5
Novosibirsk 1,312,000 ..... J4
Novozybkov 34,433 ..... D4
Novyy Port G3
Novyy Uzen' 18,073 ..... F5
Novyy Urengoy H3
Nukus 109,000 ..... G5

Topography

50 Union of Soviet Socialist Republics

(continued)

Nyandoma 23,366 E3
Nyurba M3
Obluch'ye 17,000 N5
Odessa 1,046,000 D5
Okha 30,890 P4
Okhotsk P4
Olëkminsk N3
Olënek M3
Omsk 1,014,000 H4
Omsukchan Q3
Omutninsk 28,777 F4
Onega 25,047 D3
Ordzhonikidze 279,000 E5
Orel 305,000 D4
Orenburg 459,000 F4
Orotukan Q3
Orsk 247,000 F4
Osh 169,000 H5
Ostrogozhsk 29,921 D4
Oymyakon O3
Ozernovskiy Q4
Palana 2,735 R4
Panfilov 19,173 H5
Pärnu 51,000 C4
Partizansk 48,345 O5
Pavlodar 273,000 H4
Pechenga D2
Pechora 56,000 F3
Peleduy M4
Penza 483,000 E4
Perkatkin T2
Perm' 999,000 F4
Pervoural'sk 129,000 F4
Petropavlovsk 207,000 G4
Petropavlovsk-Kamchatskiy 215,000 R4
Petrovsk-Zabaykal'skiy 28,313 L4
Petrozavodsk 234,000 D3
Pevek S3
Pikol'skiy 32,862 G5
Pinsk 90,000 C4
Plastun O5
Podol'sk 202,000 D4
Pokrovsk N3
Poligus K3
Poltava 279,000 D5
Polyarnyy 15,321 D3
Ponoy E3
Poronaysk 23,610 P5
Prikumsk 35,768 E5
Progress 10,000 O5
Prokop'yevsk 266,000 J4
Provideniya T3
Przheval'sk 51,000 H5
Pskov 176,000 C4
Pushkin 90,000 C4
Raychikhinsk 25,157 N5
Riga 835,000 C4
Rostov-na-Donu 934,000 E5
Rovno 179,000 C4
Rubtsovsk 157,000 J4
Ruch'i E3
Rudnyy 110,000 G4
Ryazan' 453,000 E4
Rybach'ye H5
Rybinsk 239,000 D4
Rzhev 69,000 D4
Saksaul'skiy F5
Salekhard 21,929 G3
Sal'sk 57,000 E5
Samagaltay K4
Samarkand 477,000 G6
Sangar N3
Saran' 55,000 H5
Saransk 263,000 E4
Sarapul 107,000 F4
Saratov 856,000 E4
Sarkand 18,296 J5
Segezha 28,810 D3
Semipalatinsk 283,000 H4
Serakhs G6
Serov 101,000 G4
Serpukhov 140,000 D4
Sevastopol' 301,000 D5
Severobaykal'sk M4
Severodvinsk 197,000 E3
Severo-Kuril'sk 8,000 Q4
Severoural'sk 29,880 G3
Severo-Yeniseysk K3
Shadrinsk 82,000 G4
Shakhtinsk 50,000 H5
Shakhty 209,000 E5
Shar'ya 25,788 E4
Shchuchinsk 40,432 H4
Shenkursk E3
Shevchenko 111,000 F5
Shilka 16,065 M4
Shimanovsk 16,880 N4
Shushenskoye 10,000 K4
Šiauliai 118,000 C4
Siktyakh N3
Simferopol' 302,000 D5
Skovorodino 10,000 N4
Slavgorod 32,908 H4
Slobodskoy 34,374 E4
Slyudyanka 20,639 L4
Smolensk 276,000 D4
Snezhnogorsk J3
Sochi 287,000 D5
Sokol 48,253 E4
Solikamsk 101,000 F3
Sortavala 22,188 C3
Sosnogorsk 24,688 F3
Sosnovo-Ozerskoye M4
Sovetskaya Gavan' 28,455 P5
Spassk-Dal'niy 53,000 O5
Srednekolymsk Q3
Sretensk 16,000 M4
Stalingrad (Volgograd) 929,000 E5
Stavropol' 258,000 E5
Stepanakert 30,293 E6
Sterlitamak 220,000 F4
Strezhevoy H3
Sukhana M3
Sukhumi 114,000 D5
Sumy 228,000 D4
Suntar M3
Surgut 107,000 H3
Susuman 12,000 P3
Sverdlovsk 1,211,000 F4
Svobodnyy 75,000 N4
Syktyvkar 171,000 F3
Syzran' 178,000 E4
Taganrog 276,000 D5
Takhiatash F5
Takhta-Bazar G6
Taksimo M4
Taldy-Kurgan 88,000 H5
Talgar 31,273 H5
Tallinn 430,000 C4
Tambey G2
Tambov 270,000 E4
Tara 22,358 H4
Tarko-Sale H3
Tartu 105,000 C4
Tashauz 84,000 F5
Tashkent 1,780,000 G5
Tatarsk 29,589 H4
Tavda G4
Tayshet 34,232 K4
Tazovskiy J3
Tbilisi 1,066,000 E5
Tedzhen 25,708 F6
Tekeli 29,846 H5
Temirtau 213,000 H4
Termez 57,000 G6
Ternopol' 144,000 C5
Tiksi N2
Tobol'sk 62,000 G4
Togliatti (Tol'yatti) 502,000 F4
Tokmak 59,000 H5
Tommot 8,000 N4
Tomsk 421,000 J4
Tot'ma E4
Troitsk 88,000 G4
Tselinograd 234,000 H4
Tskhinvali 30,311 E5
Tula 514,000 D4
Tulun 52,000 L4
Tura 3,528 L3
Turan K4
Turgay G5
Turkestan 67,000 G5
Tynda N4
Tyumen' 359,000 G4
Uelen T3
Ufa 969,000 F4
Uglegorsk 17,921 P5
Ukhta 87,000 F3
Ulan-Ude 300,000 L4
Ul'yanovsk 464,000 E4
Ural'sk 167,000 F4
Uray 17,385 G3
Urgench 100,000 G5
Ushtobe 24,484 H5
Usol'ye-Sibirskoye 103,000 L4
Ussuriysk 147,000 O5
Ust'-Ilimsk 69,000 L4
Ust'-Kamchatsk 10,000 R4
Ust'-Kamenogorsk 274,000 J5
Ust'-Kut 50,000 L4
Ust'-Kuyga O3
Ust'-Maya O3
Ust'-Nera P3
Ust'-Omchug P3
Ust'-Olenëk M2
Ust'-Ordynskiy 10,693 L4
Ust'-Port J2
Vanavara L3
Vanino 15,401 P5
Velikiye Luki 102,000 D4
Velikiy Ustyug 36,737 E3
Vel'sk 21,899 E3
Ventspils 40,467 B4
Verkhnevilyuysk N3
Verkniy At-Uryakh Q3
Verkhoyansk 2,000 N3
Vilna (Vilnius) 481,000 C4
Vilyuysk N3
Vinnitsa 314,000 C5
Vitebsk 297,000 D4
Vitimskiy M4
Vladimir 296,000 D4
Vladivostok 550,000 O5
Volgograd 929,000 E5
Volochanka K2
Vologda 237,000 E4
Vorkuta 100,000 G3
Voronezh 783,000 E4
Voroshilovgrad 463,000 E5
Vostochnyy O5
Votkinsk 90,000 F4
Voy-Vozh 10,000 F3
Vyazemskiy 18,365 O5
Vyborg 76,000 C3
Vyshniy Volochek 72,000 D4
Yakutsk 152,000 N3
Yalutorsk 25,426 G4
Yamsk Q4
Yaroslavl' 597,000 D4
Yartsevo J4
Yelets 112,000 D4
Yelizovo 10,000 Q4
Yeniseysk 19,880 K4
Yermak 28,133 H4
Yermentau 15,276 H4
Yesil' 15,000 G4
Yessey L3
Yoshkar-Ola 201,000 E4
Yurga 78,000 J4
Yuzhno-Sakhalinsk 140,000 P5
Zabaykal'sk M5
Zakamensk 10,000 L4
Zaozernyy 27,216 K4
Zaporozh'ye 781,000 D5
Zarafshan G5
Zavitinsk 19,009 O4
Zaysan 10,000 J5
Zeya 16,684 N4
Zhatay O3
Zhdanov 503,000 D5
Zheleznogorsk-Ilimskiy 22,179 L4
Zhigalovo L4
Zhigansk N3
Zhitomir 244,000 C4
Zima 41,567 L4
Zlatoust 198,000 F4
Zyryanka Q3

OTHER FEATURES

Alakol' (lake) J5
Alazeya (riv.) Q3
Aldan (plat.) N4
Aldan (riv.) O3
Alexandra Land (isl.) E1
Altay (mts.) J5
Amga (riv.) O3
Amgun' (riv.) O4
Amudar'ya (riv.) G5
Amur (riv.) O4
Anabar (riv.) M2
Anadyr' (gulf) T3
Anadyr' (range) S3
Anadyr' (riv.) S3
Angara (riv.) K4
Aniva (cape) P5
Aral (sea) F5
Arctic Ocean K1
Argun (riv.) M4
Arkticheskiy Institut (isls.) H2
Atrek (riv.) F6
Ayon (isl.) R2
Azov (sea) D5
Balkhash (lake) H5
Baltic (sea) B4
Barents (sea) D2
Baykal (lake) L4
Baykal (mts.) L4
Beloye (lake) D3
Belyy (isl.) G2
Bering (isl.) R4
Bering (sea) S4
Bering (str.) U3
Bet-Pak-Dala (des.) H5
Black (sea) D5
Bol'shevik (isl.) K2
Bol'shoy Lyakhovskiy (isl.) P2
Bolvanskiy Nos (cape) G2
Bratsk (res.) L4
Caspian (sea) F6
Caucasus (mts.) E5
Chelyuskin (cape) M2
Cherskiy (range) P3
Chu (riv.) H5
Chukchi (pen.) T3
Chukchi (sea) T2
Chulym (riv.) J4
Chuna (riv.) K4
Chunya (riv.) K3
Communism (peak) H6
Crimea (pen.) D5
Dezhnev (cape) T3
Dmitriya Lapteva (str.) O2
Dnieper (riv.) D5
Dniester (riv.) C5
Don (riv.) E5
Donets (riv.) D5
Dulgalakh (riv.) O3
Dvina, Northern (riv.) E3
Dvina, Western (riv.) C4
Dzhugdzhur (range) O4
East Siberian (sea) S2
Emba (riv.) F5
Faddeyevskiy (isl.) P2
Finland (gulf) C4
Franz Josef Land (isls.) F1
George Land (isl.) E1
Gizhiga (bay) Q3
Govena (cape) R4
Graham Bell (isl.) G1
Gyda (pen.) H2
Gydan (Kolyma) (range) Q3
Hiiumaa (isl.) C4
Ili (riv.) H5
Imandra (lake) D3
Indigirka (riv.) P3
Irtysh (riv.) H4
Ishim (riv.) G4
Issyk-Kul' (lake) H5
Iturup (isl.) P5
Japan (sea) O6
Kakhovka (res.) D5
Kamchatka (pen.) Q4
Kanin (pen.) E3
Kanin Nos (cape) E3
Kara (sea) G2
Kara-Bogaz-Gol (gulf) F5
Karaginskiy (isl.) R4
Kara-Kum (canal) F6
Kara-Kum (des.) F5
Karskiye Vorota (str.) F2
Khanka (lake) O5
Kharasavey (cape) G2
Kheta (riv.) K2
Klyuchevskaya Sopka (vol.) Q4
Kola (pen.) D3
Kolguyev (isl.) E3
Kolyma (range) Q3
Kolyma (riv.) Q3
Komandorskiye (isls.) R4
Komsomolets (isl.) L1
Koni (pen.) Q4
Koryak (range) S3
Kotel'nyy (isl.) O2
Kotuy (riv.) L3
Kuma (riv.) E5
Kura (riv.) E6
Kuril (isls.) P5
Kuybyshev (res.) F4
Kyzyl-Kum (des.) G5
Ladoga (lake) D3
La Pérouse (str.) P5
Laptev (sea) N2
Lena (riv.) N3
Little Yenisey (riv.) K4
Long (str.) S2
Lopatka (cape) Q4
Lower Tunguska (riv.) K3
Lyatkhovskiye (isls.) O2
Mangyshlak (pen.) F5
Markha (riv.) M3
Matochkin Shar (str.) F2
Maya (riv.) O4
Mezen' (riv.) E3
Murgab (riv.) G6
Nadym (riv.) H3
Narodnaya (mt.) G3
Navarin (cape) T3
New Siberian (isls.) P2
Northern Dvina (riv.) E3
Novaya Sibir' (isl.) Q2
Novaya Zemlya (isls.) F2
Ob' (gulf) H3
Ob' (riv.) G3
October Revolution (isl.) L2
Oka (riv.) L4
Okhotsk (sea) P4
Olëkma (riv.) N4
Olënek (bay) N2
Olënek (riv.) M3
Oloy (range) R3
Olyutorskiy (cape) S4
Omolon (riv.) Q3
Omoloy (riv.) O3
Onega (lake) D3
Onega (riv.) D3
Ozernoy (cape) R4
Paramushir (isl.) Q4
Pechora (riv.) F3
Peipus (lake) C4
Penzhina (bay) R3
Pioner (isl.) J2
Pobeda (peak) J5
Pur (riv.) H3
Pyasina (riv.) J2
Riga (gulf) C4
Rybachiy (pen.) D2
Rybinsk (res.) D4
Saaremaa (isl.) B4
Sakhalin (gulf) P4
Sakhalin (isl.) P4
Sannikova (str.) O2
Sary Su (riv.) H5
Sayan (mts.) K4
Selemdzha (riv.) O4
Sergeya Kirova (isls.) J2
Severnaya Zemlya (isls.) L1
Shantar (isls.) O4
Shelagskiy (cape) R2
Shelekhov (gulf) Q4
Siberia (reg.) 38,524,000 M3
Sikhote-Alin' (range) O5
Stanovoy (range) N4
Stony Tunguska (riv.) K3
Syrdar'ya (riv.) G5
Tannu-Ola (range) K5
Tatar (str.) P4
Taymyr (lake) K2
Taymyr (pen.) L2
Taymyr (riv.) K2
Taz (riv.) J3
Tengiz (lake) G4
Terpeniye (cape) P5
Tobol (riv.) G4
Tsimlyansk (res.) E5
Tym (riv.) J3
Tyung (riv.) M3
Uda (riv.) O4
Ulutau (mts.) G5
Ural (mts.) F4
Ural (riv.) F5
Urup (isl.) Q5
Ussuri (riv.) O5
Ust'-Urt (plat.) F5
Vakh (riv.) J3
Velikaya (riv.) S3
Verkhoyansk (range) N3
Vil'kitskogo (str.) L2
Vilyuy (range) M3
Vilyuy (res.) M3
Vilyuy (riv.) L3
Vitim (riv.) M4
Volga (riv.) E5
Western Dvina (riv.) C4
White (sea) D3
Wiese (isl.) H2
Wilczek Land (isl.) G1
Wrangel (isl.) T2
Yablonovyy (range) M4
Yamal (pen.) G2
Yana (riv.) O3
Yelizavety (cape) P4
Yenisey (riv.) J3
Zaysan (lake) J5
Zeya (riv.) N4
Zhelaniye (cape) H2

*City and suburbs.

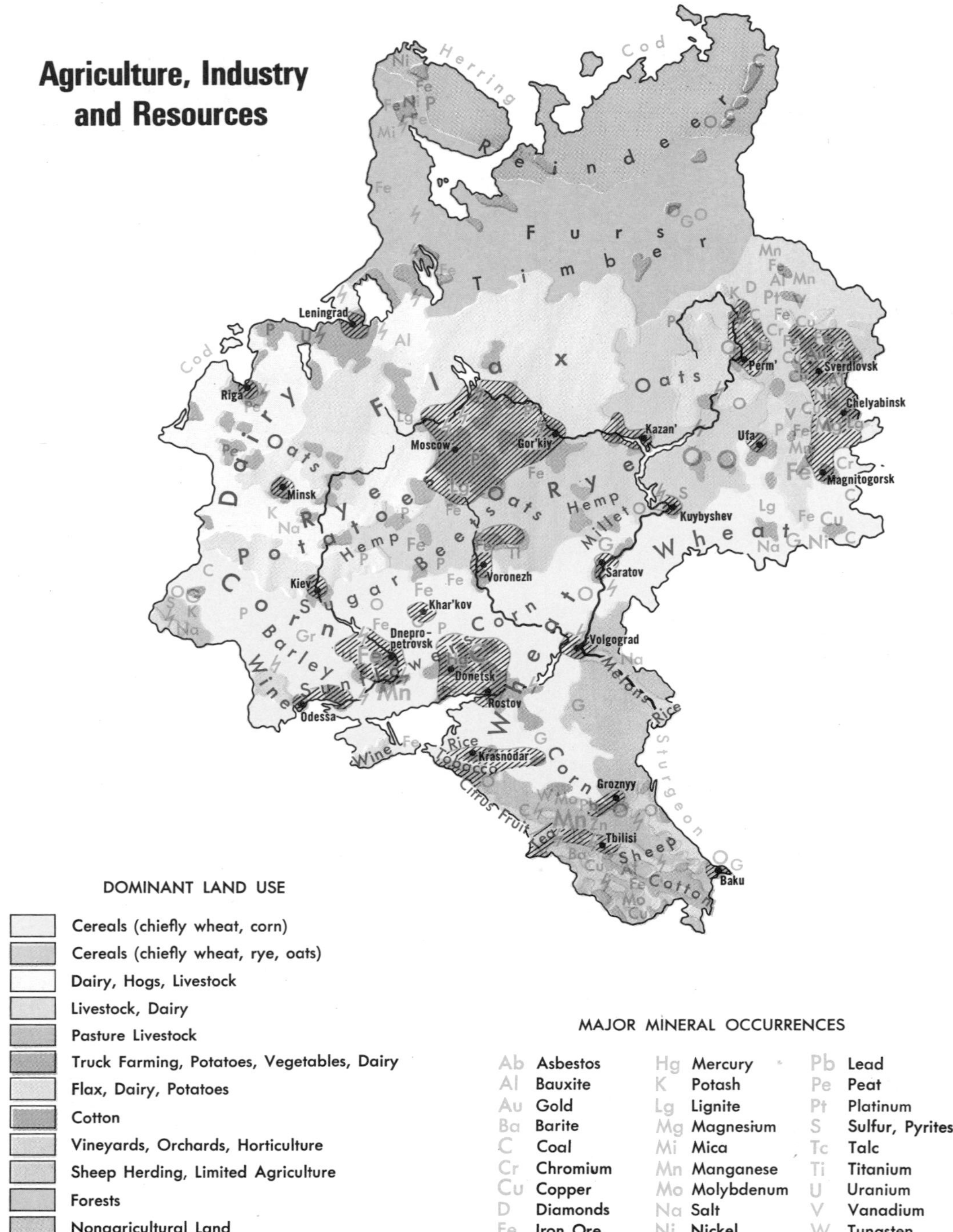

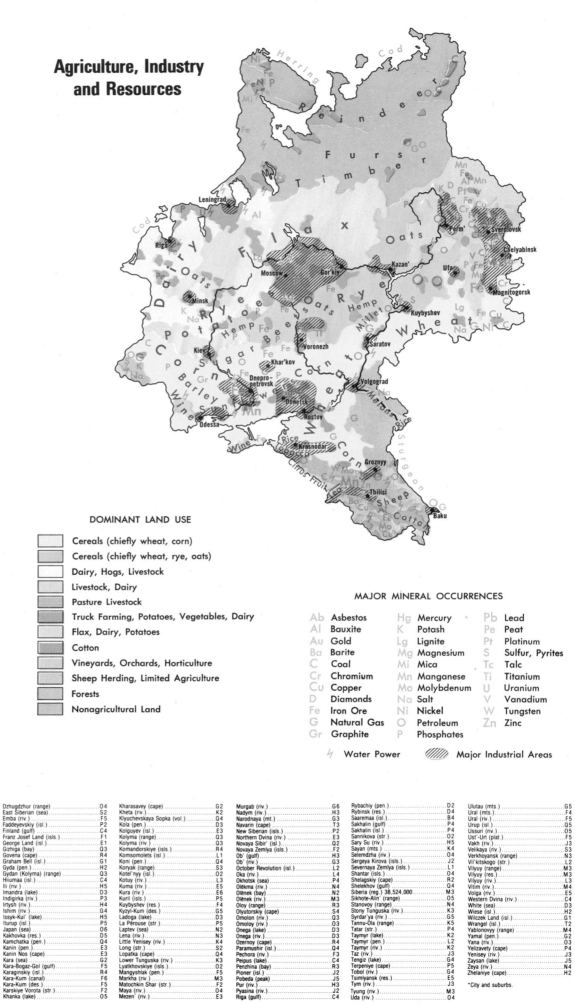

Agriculture, Industry and Resources

DOMINANT LAND USE

- Cereals (chiefly wheat, corn)
- Livestock, Dairy
- Truck Farming, Potatoes, Vegetables, Dairy
- Cotton
- Sheep Herding, Limited Agriculture
- Forests
- Nonagricultural Land

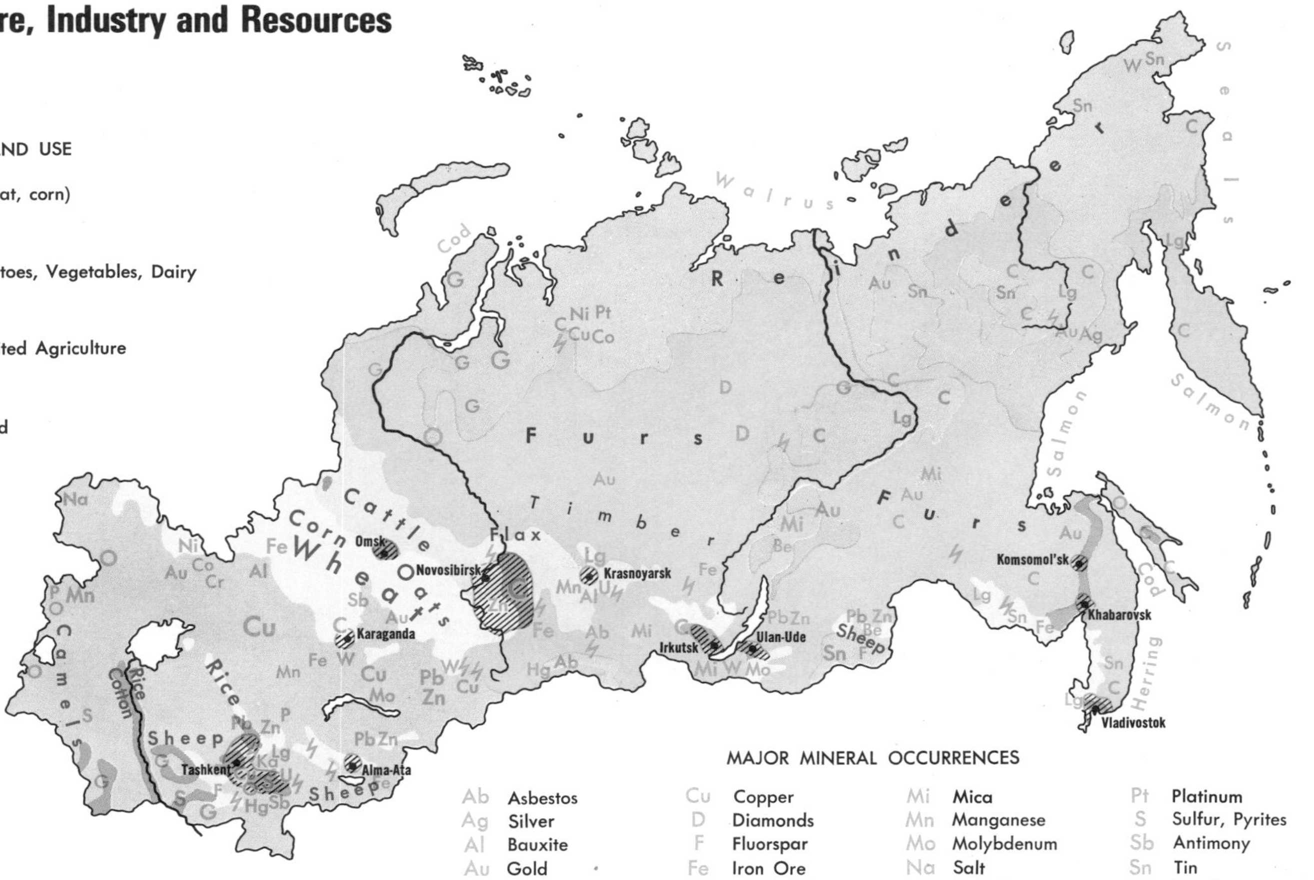

MAJOR MINERAL OCCURRENCES

Ab	Asbestos	Cu	Copper	Mi	Mica	Pt	Platinum
Ag	Silver	D	Diamonds	Mn	Manganese	S	Sulfur, Pyrites
Al	Bauxite	F	Fluorspar	Mo	Molybdenum	Sb	Antimony
Au	Gold	Fe	Iron Ore	Na	Salt	Sn	Tin
Be	Beryl	G	Natural Gas	Ni	Nickel	U	Uranium
C	Coal	Hg	Mercury	O	Petroleum	W	Tungsten
Co	Cobalt	Ka	Kaolin	P	Phosphates	Zn	Zinc
Cr	Chromium	Lg	Lignite	Pb	Lead		

Water Power

Major Industrial Areas

U.S.S.R.–Railroads and Navigation

Principal Railroads
Navigable Rivers
Canals
Main Sea Routes
Major Russian Ports

SCALE OF MILES 0 500 1000

SCALE OF KILOMETERS 0 500 1000

(continued on following page)

Division	Capital	Key
Abkhaz A.S.S.R.	Sukhumi	F6
Adygey Aut. Oblast	Maykop	F6
Adzhar A.S.S.R.	Batumi	F6
Bashkir A.S.S.R.	Ufa	J4
Chechen-Ingush A.S.S.R.	Groznyy	G6
Chuvash A.S.S.R.	Cheboksary	G3
Crimean Oblast	Simferopol'	D6
Dagestan A.S.S.R.	Makhachkala	G6
Kabardin-Balkar A.S.S.R.	Nal'chik	F6
Kalmuck A.S.S.R.	Elista	F5
Karachay-Cherkess Aut. Obl.	Cherkessk	F6
Karelian A.S.S.R.	Petrozavodsk	D2
Komi A.S.S.R.	Syktyvkar	H2
Komi-Permyak Aut. Okrug	Kudymkar	H3
Mari A.S.S.R.	Yoshkar-Ola	G3
Mordvinian A.S.S.R.	Saransk	G4
Nagorno-Karabakh Aut. Obl.	Stepanakert	G7
Nenets Aut. Okrug	Nar'yan-Mar	H1
North Ossetian A.S.S.R.	Ordzhonikidze	F6
South Ossetian Aut. Obl.	Tskhinvali	F6
Tatar A.S.S.R.	Kazan'	G3
Trans-Carpathian Oblast	Uzhgorod	B5
Udmurt A.S.S.R.	Izhevsk	H3
Volyn Oblast	Lutsk	C4

U.S.S.R. — EUROPEAN

UNION REPUBLICS

Armenian S.S.R. 3,031,000 F6
Azerbaidzhan S.S.R. 6,028,000 G6
Estonian S.S.R 1,466,000 C3
Georgian S.S.R. 5,015,000 F6
Latvian S.S.R 2,521,000 B3
Lithuanian S.S.R. 3,398,000 B3
Moldavian S.S.R. 3,947,000 C5
Russian S.F.S.R. 137,551,000 F3
Ukrainian S.S.R. 49,755,000 D5
White Russian S.S.R. 9,560,000 C4

INTERNAL DIVISIONS

Abkhaz A.S.S.R. 505,000 F6
Adygey Aut. Obl. 405,000 F6
Adzhar A.S.S.R. 354,000 F6
Bashkir A.S.S.R. 3,849,000 J4
Chechen-Ingush A.S.S.R. 1,154,000 G6
Chuvash A.S.S.R. 1,292,000 G3
Crimean Oblast 2,183,000 D6
Dagestan A.S.S.R. 1,628,000 G6
Kabardin-Balkar A.S.S.R. 674,000 F6
Kalmuck A.S.S.R. 294,000 F5
Karachay-Cherkess Aut. Obl. 368,000 F6
Karelian A.S.S.R. 736,000 D2
Komi A.S.S.R. 1,119,000 H2
Komi-Permyak Aut. Okr. 173,000 H3
Mari A.S.S.R. 703,000 G3
Mordvinian A.S.S.R. 991,000 G4
Nagorno-Karabakh Aut. Obl. 161,000 G7
Nakhichevan' A.S.S.R. 239,000 F7
Nenets Aut. Okr. 47,000 H1
North Ossetian A.S.S.R. 597,000 F6
South Ossetian Aut. Obl. 98,000 F6
Tatar A.S.S.R. 3,436,000 G3
Trans-Carpathian Oblast 1,155,000 B5
Udmurt A.S.S.R. 1,494,000 H3
Volyn Oblast 1,015,000 C4

CITIES and TOWNS

Abdulino 26,010 H4
Agdam 21,277 G6
Agryz 19,267 H3
Akhaltsikhe 18,972 F6
Akhtubinsk 43,466 G5
Akhty G6
Akhtyrka 41,354 E4
Akkerman (Belgorod-Dnestrovskiy) 32,928 D5
Alagir 18,161 F6
Alatyr' 43,499 G4
Alaverdi 21,311 F6
Aleksandriya 82,000 D5
Aleksandrovsk 18,286 J3
Alekseyevka 25,562 E4
Aleksin 67,000 E4
Ali-Bayramly 33,828 G7
Al'met'yevsk 110,000 H3
Alushta 22,016 D6
Amderma K1
Anapa 29,900 E6
Apatity 62,000 D1
Apsheronsk 32,867 F6
Archangel (Arkhangel'sk) 385,000 F2
Armavir 162,000 F5
Arzamas 93,000 F3
Astara G7
Astrakhan' 461,000 G5
Atkarsk 28,881 G4
Azov 75,000 E5
Bakhchisaray 15,912 D6
Baku 1,022,000 H6
Baku* 1,550,000 H6
Balakhna 36,542 F3
Balaklava D6
Balakovo 152,000 G4
Balashov 93,000 F4
Baltiysk 20,300 A4
Baranovichi 131,000 C4
Barysh 20,792 G4
Bataysk 90,000 E5
Batumi 123,000 F6
Belaya Tserkov' 151,000 C5
Belebey 32,460 H4
Belev 17,733 E4
Belgorod 240,000 E4
Belgorod-Dnestrovskiy 32,928 D5
Belomorsk 16,595 D2
Belorechensk 35,970 E6
Beloretsk 71,000 J4
Belozersk E3
Bel'tsy 125,000 C5
Belush'ya Guba H1
Bendery 101,000 C5
Berdichev 80,000 C5
Berdyansk 122,000 E5
Beregovo 27,308 B5
Berezniki 185,000 J3
Beslan 26,893 F6
Bezhetsk 30,030 E3
Birsk 29,607 J3
Bobrov 17,977 F4
Bobruysk 192,000 C4
Bologoye 33,949 D3
Bor 63,000 F3
Borislav 33,800 B5
Borisoglebsk 68,000 F4
Borisov 112,000 C4
Borovichi 60,000 D3
Brest 177,000 B4
Brezhnev 301,000 H3
Bryansk 394,000 D4
Bugul'ma 80,000 H4
Buguruslan 54,000 H4
Buturlinovka 21,643 F4
Buy 29,946 F3
Buynaksk 37,946 G6
Buzuluk 76,000 H4
Bykhov 17,371 C4
Cēsis 17,696 C3
Chadyr-Lunga 20,474 C5
Chapayevsk 85,000 G4
Chaykovskiy 48,034 H3
Cheboksary 308,000 G3
Cherepovets 266,000 E3
Cherkassy 228,000 D5
Cherkessk 91,000 F6
Chernigov 238,000 D4
Chernovtsy 219,000 C5
Chernushka 21,106 J3
Chervonograd 55,000 B4
Chiatura 25,474 F6
Chistopol' 64,000 H3
Chortkov 19,183 B5
Chudovo D3
Chusovoy 56,000 J3
Danilov 17,500 E3
Dankov 20,030 E4
Daugavpils 116,000 C3
Davlekanovo 20,123 H4
Derbent 70,000 G6
Dimitrovgrad 106,000 G4
Dneprodzerzhinsk 250,000 D5
Dnepropetrovsk 1,066,000 D5
Dobrush 16,809 D4
Dobryanka 18,349 J3
Donetsk 1,021,000 E5
Drogobych 66,000 B5
Dubna 55,000 E3
Dubna E4
Dubno 25,442 C4
Dvinsk (Daugavpils) 116,000 C3
Dyat'kovo 26,825 D4
Dzerzhinsk 257,000 F3
Dzhankoy 43,459 D5
Dzhul'fa G7
Echmiadzin 31,819 F6
Elektrostal' 139,000 E3
Elista 70,000 F5
El'ton G5
Engel's 161,000 G4
Erivan 1,019,000 F6
Fastov 51,000 C4
Feodosiya 76,000 D5
Frolovo 33,398 F5
Furmanov 40,155 F3
Gagra 23,025 E6
Galich 19,374 F3
Gandzha (Kirovabad) 232,000 G6
Gatchina 75,000 C3
Gay 28,250 J4
Gaysin 23,741 C5
Gdov C3
Gelendzhik 29,086 E6
Genichesk 20,031 E5
Georgiu-Dezh 52,000 E4
Glazov 81,000 H3
Glubokoye C3
Glukhov 27,096 D4
Gomel' 383,000 D4
Gori 56,000 F6
Gorki 22,117 D4
Gor'kiy 1,344,000 F3
Gorlovka 336,000 E5
Gorodets 34,229 F3
Gremikha E1
Gremyachinsk 29,975 J3
Grodno 195,000 B4
Groznyy 375,000 G6
Gryazi 41,292 F4
Gubakha 33,243 J3
Gubkin 65,000 E4
Gudauta F6
Gudermes 32,445 G6
Gukovo 68,000 F5
Gus'-Khrustal'nyy 72,000 F3
Imishli 17,839 G7
Inta 51,000 K1
Inza 19,060 G4
Ishimbay 57,000 J4
Ivano-Frankovsk 150,000 B5
Ivanovo 465,000 E3
Izberbash 17,299 G6
Izhevsk 549,000 H3
Izmail 83,000 C5
Izyum 61,000 E5
Jēkabpils 22,440 C3
Jelgava 68,000 B3
Jurmala 61,000 B3
Kadiyevka (Stakhanov) 108,000 E5
Kafan 29,916 G7
Kagul 26,249 C5
Kakhovka 28,472 D5
Kalach 18,475 F4
Kalach-na-Donu 20,795 F5
Kalinin 412,000 E3
Kaliningrad, Kaliningrad 355,000 B4
Kaliningrad, Moscow Oblast 133,000 E3
Kalinkovichi 23,918 C4
Kaluga 265,000 E4
Kalush 60,000 B5
Kamenets-Podol'skiy 81,000 C5
Kamenka, Penza 30,067 F4
Kamensk-Shakhtinskiy 72,000 F5
Kamyshin 112,000 F4
Kanash 40,682 G3
Kandalaksha 42,656 D1
Kapsukas 28,763 B4
Karachayevsk F6
Karachev 15,972 E4
Kashin 17,678 E3
Kasimov 33,066 F4
Kaspiysk 38,990 G6
Kaunas 370,000 B4
Kazan' 993,000 G3
Kazatin 26,649 C5
Kem' 21,025 D2
Kerch' 157,000 E5
Keret' D1
Khachmas 22,313 G6
Khadyzhensk 17,856 E6
Khar'kov 1,444,000 E5
Khasavyurt 65,000 G6
Khashuri 24,469 F6
Kherson 319,000 D5
Khmel'nitskiy 172,000 C5
Khotin C5
Khust 23,810 B5
Khvalynsk 16,249 G4
Kiev 2,144,000 D4
Kiliya 24,276 C5
Kimovsk 44,490 E4
Kimry 58,000 E3
Kinel' 39,373 H4
Kineshma 101,000 F3
Kirishi 27,252 D3
Kirov, Kaluga 29,355 D4
Kirov, Kirov 390,000 G3
Kirovabad 232,000 G6
Kirovakan 146,000 G6
Kirovo-Chepetsk 71,000 H3
Kirovograd 237,000 D5
Kirovsk 38,484 D1
Kirsanov 21,795 F4
Kishinev 503,000 C5
Kislovodsk 101,000 F6
Kizel 46,264 J3
Kizlyar 29,745 G6
Klaipeda 176,000 B3
Klintsy 67,000 D4
Kobrin 24,935 B4
Kobuleti 18,051 F6
Kohtla-Järve 73,000 C3
Kolomiya 52,000 B5
Kolomna 147,000 E4
Kolpino 114,000 D3
Kommunarsk 120,000 E5
Komrat 21,369 C5
Komsomol'skiy 17,078 K1
Kondopoga 27,908 D2
Königsberg (Kaliningrad) 355,000 B4
Konotop 82,000 D4
Konstantinovka 112,000 E5
Korenovsk 26,323 E5
Korosten' 65,000 C4
Korostyshev 21,153 C4
Koryazhma 33,230 G2
Kostopol' 17,548 C4
Kostroma 255,000 F3
Kotel'nich 29,196 G3
Kotel'nikovo 19,063 F5
Kotlas 61,000 G2
Kotovo 20,553 G4
Kotovsk, Odessa 36,463 C5
Kotovsk, Tambov 33,347 F4
Kovel' 33,351 C4
Kovrov 143,000 F3
Kovylkino 17,300 F4
Kramatorsk 178,000 E5
Krasnoarmeysk 60,000 G4
Krasnodar 560,000 E6
Krasnograd 18,386 E5
Krasnokamsk 56,000 H3
Krasnoslobodsk 17,749 G5
Krasnovishersk J2
Krasnyy Kut 17,087 G4
Krasnyy Luch 106,000 E5
Krasnyy Sulin 41,684 F5
Kremenchug 210,000 D5
Krichev 25,682 D4
Krivoy Rog 650,000 D5
Krolevets 18,307 D4
Kronshtadt 39,477 C3
Kropotkin 70,000 F5
Krymsk 41,430 E5
Kuba 18,871 G6
Kudymkar 26,350 H3
Kulebaki 46,252 F3
Kumertau 52,000 J4
Kunda C3
Kungur 80,000 J3
Kupyansk 30,055 E5
Kuressaare 12,140 B3
Kursk 375,000 E4
Kutaisi 194,000 F6
Kuvandyk 22,914 J4
Kuybyshev 1,216,000 H4
Kuznetsk 94,000 G4
Kuzomen' E1
Labinsk 54,000 F6
Lakhdenpokh'ya C2
Lebedin 29,240 D4
Leninakan 207,000 F6
Leningrad 4,073,000 C3
Leningrad* 4,588,000 C3
Leninogorsk 54,000 H4
Lenkoran' 35,505 G7
L'gov 25,110 E4
Lida 66,000 C4
Liepāja 108,000 B3
Likhoslavl' E3
Lipetsk 396,000 E4
Lisichansk 119,000 E5
Livny 37,290 E4
Lodeynoye Pole 19,632 D2
Lozovaya 53,000 E5
Lubny 54,000 D4
Luga 31,905 C3
Lutsk 137,000 B4
L'vov (Lwów) 667,000 B5
Lys'va 75,000 J3
Lyubertsy 160,000 E3
Lyubotin 33,324 E4
Lyudinovo 33,871 D4
Makeyevka 436,000 E5
Makhachkala 251,000 G6
Makharadze 21,679 F6
Malaya Vishera 15,381 D3
Malgobek 20,548 F6
Manturovo 21,510 F3
Marganets 50,000 E5
Mariupol' (Zhdanov) 503,000 E5
Marks 17,132 G4
Maykop 128,000 F6
Mednogorsk 38,024 J4
Medvezh'yegorsk 17,465 D2
Melenki 18,545 F3
Meleuz 24,851 J4
Melitopol' 161,000 D5
Memel (Klaipeda) 176,000 B3
Merefa 29,985 E5
Mezen' F1
Michurinsk 101,000 F4
Mikhaylovka 58,000 F4
Millerovo 34,627 F5
Mineral'nye Vody 67,000 F6
Mingechaur 60,000 G6
Minsk 1,262,000 C4
Minsk* 1,276,000 C4
Mirgorod 28,407 D5
Mogilev 290,000 C4
Mogilev-Podol'skiy 26,051 C5
Molodechno 73,000 C4
Molotov (Perm') 999,000 J3
Monchegorsk 51,000 D1
Morshansk 44,245 F4
Moscow (Moskva) (cap.) 7,831,000 E3
Moscow* 8,011,000 E3
Mozhaysk 20,321 E3
Mozhga 38,930 H3
Mozyr' 73,000 C4
Mtsensk 27,833 E4
Mukachevo 72,000 B5
Murmansk 381,000 D1
Murom 114,000 F3
Mytishchi 141,000 E3
Nakhichevan' 33,279 F7
Nal'chik 207,000 F6
Narva 73,000 C3
Nar'yan-Mar 16,864 H1
Neftekamsk 70,000 J3
Nelidovo 29,813 D3
Nerekhta 25,722 F3
Nevel' 17,804 D3
Nevinnomyssk 104,000 F6
Nezhin 70,000 D4
Nikel' 21,299 C1
Nikolayev 440,000 D5
Nikol'sk 20,740 G4
Nikopol' 146,000 D5
Nizhnekamsk 134,000 H3
Nizhniy Lomov 17,460 F4
Nizhniy Novgorod (Gor'kiy) 1,344,000 F3
Nosovka 19,430 D4
Novaya Kakhovka 52,000 D5
Novgorod 186,000 D3
Novgorod-Severskiy D4
Novoanninskiy 20,461 F4
Novocherkassk 183,000 F5
Novograd-Volynskiy 41,194 C4
Novogrudok 19,374 C4
Novokuybyshevsk 109,000 G4
Novomoskovsk 147,000 E4
Novopolotsk 67,000 C3
Novorossiysk 159,000 E6
Novoshakhtinsk 104,000 E5
Novotroitsk 95,000 J4
Novoukrainka 19,554 D5
Novouzensk G4
Novovolynsk 41,187 B4
Novovyatsk 26,408 G3
Novozybkov 34,433 D4
Nurlat 17,533 H4
Nyandoma 23,366 F2
Nytva 17,491 H3
Nyuvchim H2
Obninsk 73,000 E3
Ochamchira 18,718 F6
Odessa 1,046,000 D5
Oktyabr'sk 33,981 G4
Oktyabr'skiy 88,000 H4
Okulovka 19,194 D3
Olenegorsk 21,485 D1
Olonets D2
Omutninsk 28,777 H3
Onega 25,047 E2
Ordzhonikidze 279,000 F6
Orel 305,000 E4
Orenburg 459,000 J4
Orgeyev 25,798 C5
Orsha 112,000 C4
Orsk 247,000 J4
Osa 15,038 J3
Osipenko (Berdyansk) 122,000 E5
Osipovichi 19,705 C4
Ostashkov 23,419 D3
Ostrogozhsk 29,921 E4
Ostrov 22,369 C3
Otradnyy 44,426 H4
Panevežys 102,000 B3
Pärnu 51,000 C3
Pavlograd 107,000 E5
Pavlovo 68,000 F3
Pechenga D1
Pechora 56,000 J1
Penza 483,000 G4
Perm' 999,000 J3
Pervomaysk 72,000 D5
Petrokrepost' D3
Petrovsk 30,953 G4
Petrozavodsk 234,000 D2
Petsamo (Pechenga) D1
Pinsk 90,000 C4
Podol'sk 202,000 E3
Podporozh'ye 21,545 D2
Pokhvistnevo 26,125 H4
Polonnoye 22,484 C4
Polotsk 71,000 C3
Poltava 279,000 D5
Polyarnyy 15,321 D1
Ponoy F1
Poti 45,979 F6
Povenets E2
Povorino 20,591 F4
Prikumsk 35,768 F6
Priluki 65,000 D4
Primorsk C2
Primorsko-Akhtarsk 25,981 E5
Priozersk 16,652 D2
Privolzhskiy 23,041 G4
Priyutovo 21,051 H4
Prokhladnyy 40,074 F6
Pskov 176,000 C3
Pugachev 33,963 G4
Pushkin 90,000 C3
Pyatigorsk 110,000 F6
Rabocheostrovsk D1
Rakhov B5
Rakvere 17,891 C3
Rasskazovo 40,038 F4
Razdan 26,833 G6
Rechitsa 60,000 C4
Reni 19,625 C5
Revel (Tallinn) 430,000 B3
Rēzekne 30,803 C3
Riga 835,000 B3
Romny 53,000 D4
Roslavl' 56,000 D4
Rossosh' 36,438 E4
Rostov 30,815 E3
Rostov-na-Donu 934,000 F5
Rovno 179,000 C4
Rtishchevo 37,146 F4
Rubezhnoye 66,000 E5
Rustavi 129,000 G6
Ruzayevka 41,084 F4
Ryazan' 453,000 E4
Ryazhsk 25,425 F4
Rybinsk 239,000 E3
Rybnitsa 32,266 C5
Rzhev 69,000 D3
Safonovo 53,000 D3
Saki 24,208 D5
Salavat 137,000 H4
Sal'sk 57,000 F5
Sal'yany 24,228 G7
Samara (Kuybyshev) 1,216,000 H4
Sambor 29,253 B5
Saransk 263,000 G4
Sarapul 107,000 H3
Saratov 856,000 G4
Sasovo 27,228 F4
Segezha 28,810 D2
Semenov 23,633 F3
Semiluki 18,221 E4
Sengiley G4
Serdobol (Sortavala) 22,188 D2
Serdobsk 33,783 F4
Sergach 22,509 F3
Serpukhov 140,000 E4
Sevastopol' 301,000 D6
Severodonetsk 113,000 E5
Severodvinsk 197,000 E2
Severomorsk 50,000 D1
Shakhty 209,000 F5
Shakhun'ya 20,009 G3
Shar'ya 25,788 G3
Shchekino 70,000 E4
Shchigry 17,133 E4
Sheki 43,158 G6
Shemakha 17,986 G6
Shepetovka 38,707 C4
Shostka 82,000 D4
Shpola 19,806 D5
Shumerlya 33,816 G3
Shuya 72,000 F3
Šiauliai 118,000 B3
Sibay 37,656 J4
Simferopol' 302,000 D6
Skadovsk D5
Skopin 24,429 F4
Slantsy 41,146 C3
Slavuta 25,573 C4
Slavyansk 140,000 E5
Slavyansk-na-Kubani 54,000 E5
Slobodskoy 34,374 H3
Slonim 30,279 B4
Slutsk 35,609 C4
Smela 62,000 D5
Smolensk 276,000 D4
Sochi 287,000 E6
Sokol 48,243 F3
Soligorsk 65,000 C4
Solikamsk 101,000 J3
Sol'-Iletsk 22,227 J4
Sorochinsk 23,235 H4
Soroki 21,924 C5
Sortavala 22,188 D2
Sosnogorsk 24,688 H2
Sovetsk (Tilsit) 38,456 B4
Sovetsk 17,027 G3
Stakhanov 108,000 E5
Stalingrad (Volgograd) 929,000 F5
Staraya Russa 34,577 D3
Staryy Oskol 115,000 E4
Stavropol' 258,000 F5
Stepanakert 30,293 G7
Sterlitamak 220,000 J4
Stupino 70,000 E4
Sudak E6
Sukhumi 114,000 F6
Sumgait 190,000 G6
Sumy 228,000 E4
Svetlogorsk 55,000 C4
Svetlograd 40,265 F5
Syktyvkar 171,000 H2
Syzran' 178,000 G4
Taganrog 276,000 E5
Tallinn 430,000 B3
Tambov 270,000 F4
Tartu 105,000 C3
Taurage 19,461 B3
Tbilisi 1,066,000 F6
Telavi 21,179 G6
Telšiai 20,220 B3
Temryuk 23,172 E5
Ternopol' 144,000 C5
Teykovo 41,607 E3
Tiflis (Tbilisi) 1,066,000 F6
Tighina (Bendery) 101,000 C5
Tikhoretsk 64,000 F5
Tikhvin 59,000 D3
Tilsit (Sovetsk) 38,456 B4
Timashevsk 29,055 E5
Tiraspol' 139,000 D5
Togliatti (Tol'yatti) 502,000 G4
Tokmak 59,000 E5
Toropets 16,863 D3
Torzhok 45,443 D3
Troitsko-Pechorsk J2
Tskhinvali 30,311 F6
Tuapse 60,000 E6
Tukums 14,800 B3
Tula 514,000 E4
Tutayev 16,839 E3
Tuymazy 37,021 H4
Tver (Kalinin) 412,000 E3
Tyrnyauz 18,253 F6
Uchaly 21,808 J4
Ufa 969,000 J4
Uglich 35,463 E3
Ukmerge 21,663 C3
Ul'yanovsk 464,000 G4
Uman' 79,000 D5
Unecha 21,749 D4
Ungeny 17,228 C5
Uryupinsk 38,192 F4
Usinsk J1
Usman' 20,150 E4
Uvarovo 24,946 F4
Uzhgorod 91,000 B5
Uzlovaya 65,000 E4
Valga 16,795 C3
Valmiera 20,331 C3
Valuyki 29,093 E4
Vasil'kov 26,741 D4
Velikiye Luki 102,000 D3
Velikiy Ustyug 36,737 F2
Vel'sk 21,899 F2
Ventspils 40,467 B3
Vereshchagino 23,585 H3
Vichuga 52,000 F3
Viipuri (Vyborg) 76,000 C2
Vileyka C4
Vilna (Vilnius) 481,000 C4
Vinnitsa 314,000 C5
Vinogradov 20,580 B5
Vitebsk 297,000 C3
Vladimir 296,000 F3
Vladimir-Volynskiy 28,412 B4
Volgodonsk 91,000 F5
Volgograd 929,000 F5
Volkhov 47,025 D3
Volkovysk 28,266 B4
Vologda 237,000 F3
Vol'sk 66,000 G4
Volzhsk 52,000 G3
Volzhskiy 209,000 G5
Vorkuta 100,000 K1
Voronezh 783,000 E4
Voroshilovgrad 463,000 E5
Voskresensk 76,000 E3
Votkinsk 90,000 H3
Voznesensk 36,457 D5
Vyatskiye Polyany 32,729 H3
Vyaz'ma 52,000 D3
Vyborg 76,000 C2
Vyksa 54,000 F3
Vyshniy Volochek 72,000 D3
Yalta 80,000 D6
Yanaul 20,115 J3
Yaroslavl' 597,000 E3
Yartsevo 36,662 D3
Yefremov 53,000 E4
Yelabuga 31,728 H3
Yelets 112,000 E4
Yenakiyevo 114,000 E5
Yershov 21,731 G4
Yessentuki 78,000 F6
Yevlakh 29,462 G6
Yevpatoria 93,000 D5
Yeysk 71,000 E5
Yoshkar-Ola 201,000 G3
Yur'yevets 20,144 F3
Zagorsk 107,000 E3
Zapolyarnyy 22,084 D1
Zaporozh'ye 781,000 E5
Zelenodol'sk 85,000 G3
Zelenokumsk 29,691 F6
Zernograd 20,324 F5
Zhdanov 503,000 E5
Zheleznodorozhnyy 76,000 H2
Zheleznogorsk 65,000 E4
Zhigulevsk 52,130 G4
Zhitomir 244,000 C4
Zhlobin 25,359 D4
Zhmerinka 36,195 C5
Zhodino 22,083 C4
Zhovtnevoye 31,102 D5
Znamenka 27,393 D5
Zolotonosha 27,639 D5
Zugdidi 39,896 F6
Zuyevka 17,001 H3

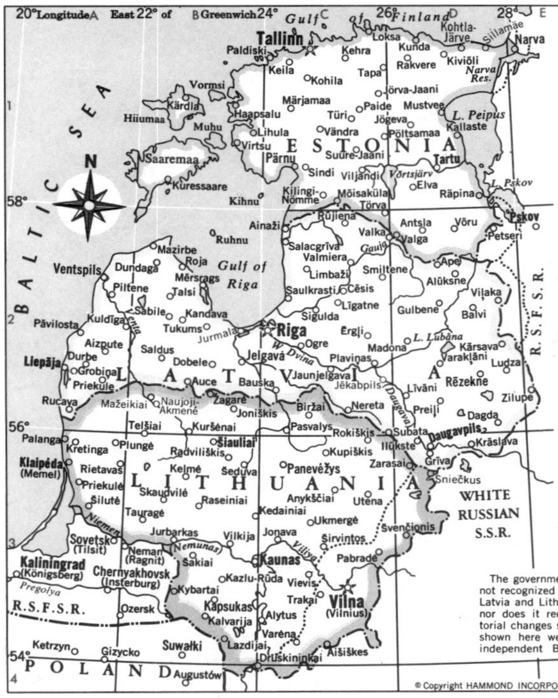

OTHER FEATURES

Apsheron (pen.) H6
Araks (riv.) G7
Azov (sea) E5
Baltic (sea) B3
Barents (sea) E1
Belaya (riv.) H3
Beloye (lake) E2
Black (sea) D6
Bug (riv.) B4
Bug (riv.) D5
Caspian (sea) G6
Caucasus (mts.) F6
Crimea (pen.) D5
Desna (riv.) D4
Dnieper (riv.) D5
Dniester (riv.) C5
Don (riv.) F5
Donets (riv.) E5
Dvina (bay) E2
Dvina, Northern (riv.) F2
Dvina, Western (riv.) C3
Dykh-Tau (mt.) F6
El'brus (mt.) F6
Finland (gulf) C3
Hiiumaa (isl.) B3
Il'men' (lake) D3
Imandra (lake) D1
Kakhovka (res.) D5
Kama (riv.) H2
Kandalaksha (gulf) D1
Kanin (pen.) G1
Kara (sea) K1
Karskiye Vorota (str.) J1
Kazbek (mt.) F6
Khoper (riv.) F4
Kola (pen.) E1
Kolguyev (isl.) G1
Kuban' (riv.) E5
Kura (riv.) G6
Kuybyshev (res.) G4
Ladoga (lake) D2
Lapland (reg.) D1
Mezen' (riv.) G1
Moksha (riv.) F4
Narodnaya (mt.) J1
Niemen (riv.) B4
Novaya Zemlya (isls.) H1
Oka (riv.) F4
Onega (bay) E2
Onega (lake) E2
Onega (riv.) E2
Pechora (riv.) H1
Peipus (lake) C3
Pripet (marshes) C4
Pripyat' (riv.) C4
Prut (riv.) C5
Riga (gulf) B3
Rybachiy (pen.) D1
Rybinsk (res.) E3
Saaremaa (isl.) B3
Samara (riv.) H4
Sevan (lake) G6
Seym (riv.) D4
Sura (riv.) G4
Svir' (riv.) D2
Timan (ridge) G1
Tsil'ma (riv.) H1
Tsimlyansk (res.) F5
Tuloma (riv.) D1
Ural (mts.) J2
Ural (riv.) J4
Usa (riv.) K1
Valday (hills) D3
Vaygach (isl.) K1
Velikaya (riv.) C3
Volga (riv.) G5
Volga-Don (canal) F5
Volgograd (res.) G5
Volkhov (riv.) D3
Vorskla (riv.) E4
Vyatka (riv.) H3
Vychegda (riv.) G2
Vyg (lake) E2
White (sea) E1
Yamantau (mt.) J4
Yugorskiy (pen.) K1

*City and suburbs.

The Baltic States

SCALE OF MILES
SCALE OF KILOMETERS

Capitals ☆
International Boundaries
Union Republic Boundaries
Prewar boundaries of the Baltic States where divergent from present boundaries

ESTONIA

LATVIA

LITHUANIA

The government of the United States has not recognized the incorporation of Estonia, Latvia and Lithuania into the Soviet Union, nor does it recognize other post-war territorial changes shown on this map. The flags shown here were the official flags of the independent Baltic States prior to 1939.

BALTIC STATES

Alytus 55,000 C3
Biržai 11,400 C2
Cēsis 17,696 C2
Daugava (Western Dvina) (riv.) D2
Daugavpils 116,000 D3
Dobele 10,100 B2
Druskininkai 11,200 C3
Dvina, Western (riv.) C2
Finland (gulf) D1
Gauja (riv.) C2
Haapsalu 11,483 B1
Hiiumaa (isl.) B1
Jēkabpils 22,400 C2
Jelgava 68,000 B2
Jonava 14,400 C3
Jurmala 61,000 B2
Kapsukas 28,763 B3
Kaunas 370,000 C3
Kedainiai 19,677 C3
Kihnu (isl.) B1
Kingisepp (Kuressaare) 12,140 B1
Kiviõli 11,153 D1
Klaipeda 176,000 A3
Kohtla-Järve 73,000 D1
Kretinga 13,000 A3
Kuldīga 12,300 A2
Kuressaare 12,140 B1
Kuršenai 11,500 B2
Liepāja 108,000 A2
Lubāna (lake) D2
Mažeikiai 13,400 A2
Memel (Klaipeda) 176,000 A3
Muhu (isl.) B1
Narva 73,000 E1
Naujoji-Akmene 10,200 B2
Niemen (riv.) A3
Ogre 15,708 C2
Panevežys 102,000 C3
Pärnu 51,000 C1
Peipus (lake) D1
Plunge 13,600 B3
Radviliškis 16,841 B3
Rakvere 17,891 D1
Rēzekne 30,803 D2
Riga (cap.), Latvia 835,000 C2
Riga (gulf) B2
Saaremaa (isl.) B1
Saldus 10,000 B2
Šiauliai 118,000 B3
Sillamäe 13,505 D1
Šilute 12,400 A3
Tallinn (cap.), Estonia 430,000 C1
Tapa 10,037 C1
Tartu 105,000 D1
Taurage 19,461 B3
Telšiai 20,220 B2
Tukums 14,800 B2
Ukmerge 21,663 C3
Utena 13,300 C3
Valga 16,795 D2
Valmiera 20,331 C2
Venta (riv.) B2
Ventspils 40,467 A2
Viliya (riv.) C3
Viljandi 20,814 C1
Vilna (Vilnius) (cap.), Lithuania 481,000 C3
Vormosi (isl.) B1
Võrtsjärv (lake) D1
Võru 15,398 D2
Western Dvina (riv.) C2

Asia
LAMBERT AZIMUTHAL EQUAL-AREA PROJECTION
SCALE OF MILES
0 100 200 400 600 800 1000 1200
SCALE OF KILOMETERS
0 200 400 600 800 1000 1200
Capitals of Countries
Other Capitals
International Boundaries
Other Boundaries
Canals
Scale 1: 46,500,000
© Copyright HAMMOND INCORPORATED, Maplewood, N.J.
ATLANTIC OCEAN
ARCTIC OCEAN
North Pole
Longitude East of Greenwich
NORWEGIAN SEA
BARENTS SEA
KARA SEA
LAPTEV SEA
EAST SIBERIAN SEA
CHUKCHI SEA
BERING SEA
SEA OF OKHOTSK
PACIFIC OCEAN
SEA OF JAPAN
EAST CHINA SEA
SOUTH CHINA SEA
PHILIPPINE SEA
MEDITERRANEAN SEA
BLACK SEA
CASPIAN SEA
RED SEA
ARABIAN SEA
BAY OF BENGAL
INDIAN OCEAN
UNION OF SOVIET SOCIALIST REPUBLICS
RUSSIAN SOVIET FEDERATED SOCIALIST REPUBLIC
Siberia
KAZAKH S.S.R.
MONGOLIA
CHINA
Tibet
Sinkiang
Inner Mongolia
INDIA
PAKISTAN
AFGHANISTAN
IRAN
IRAQ
TURKEY
SAUDI ARABIA
JAPAN
KOREA
BURMA
THAILAND
VIETNAM
MALAYSIA
INDONESIA
PHILIPPINES
AUSTRALIA
NORTH AMERICA
UNITED STATES
ALASKA
Tropic of Cancer
Tropic of Capricorn
Arctic Circle
Equator

Population Distribution

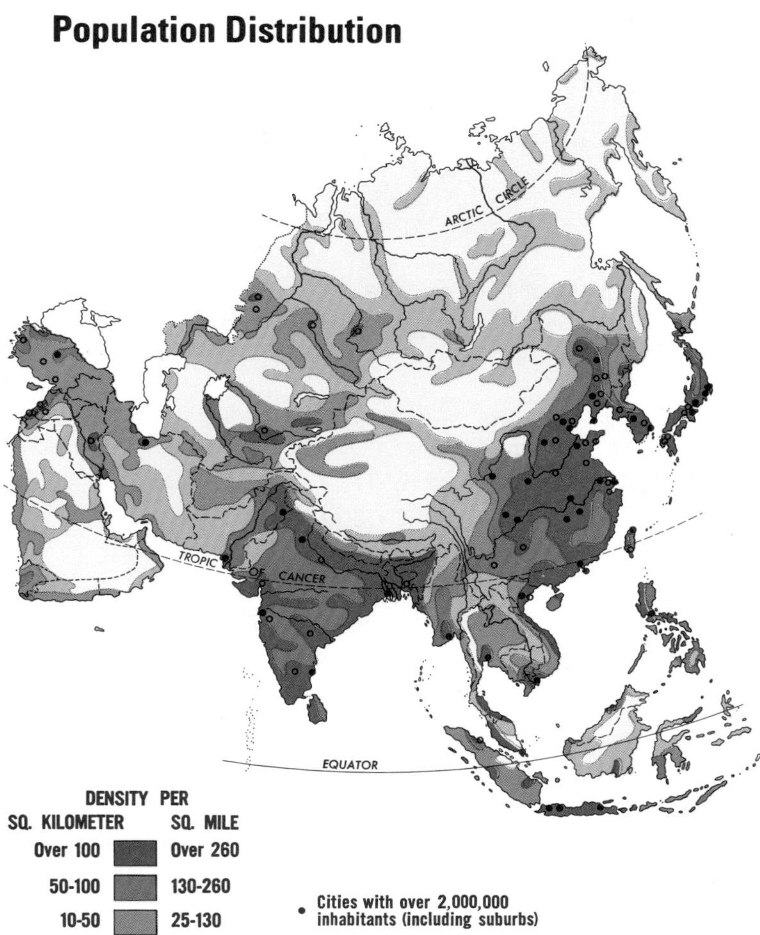

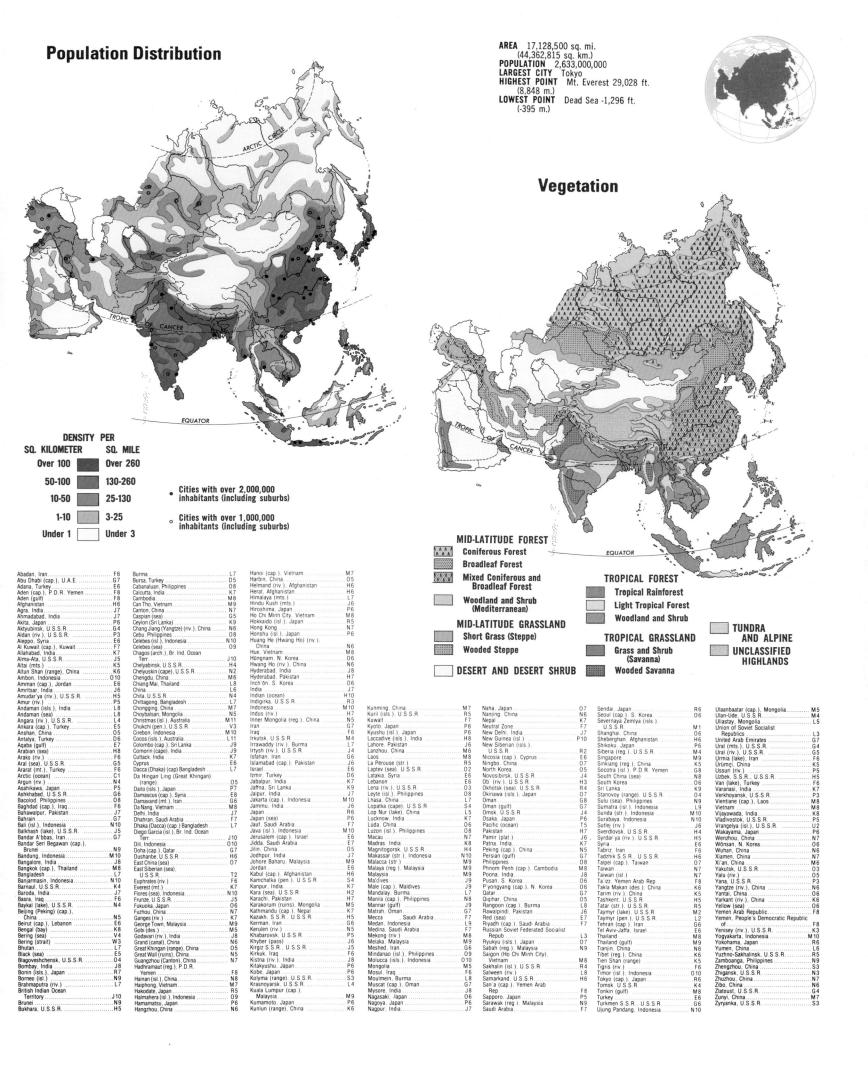

DENSITY PER

SQ. KILOMETER	SQ. MILE
Over 100	Over 260
50-100	130-260
10-50	25-130
1-10	3-25
Under 1	Under 3

• Cities with over 2,000,000 inhabitants (including suburbs)

∘ Cities with over 1,000,000 inhabitants (including suburbs)

AREA 17,128,500 sq. mi. (44,362,815 sq. km.)
POPULATION 2,633,000,000
LARGEST CITY Tokyo
HIGHEST POINT Mt. Everest 29,028 ft. (8,848 m.)
LOWEST POINT Dead Sea -1,296 ft. (-395 m.)

Vegetation

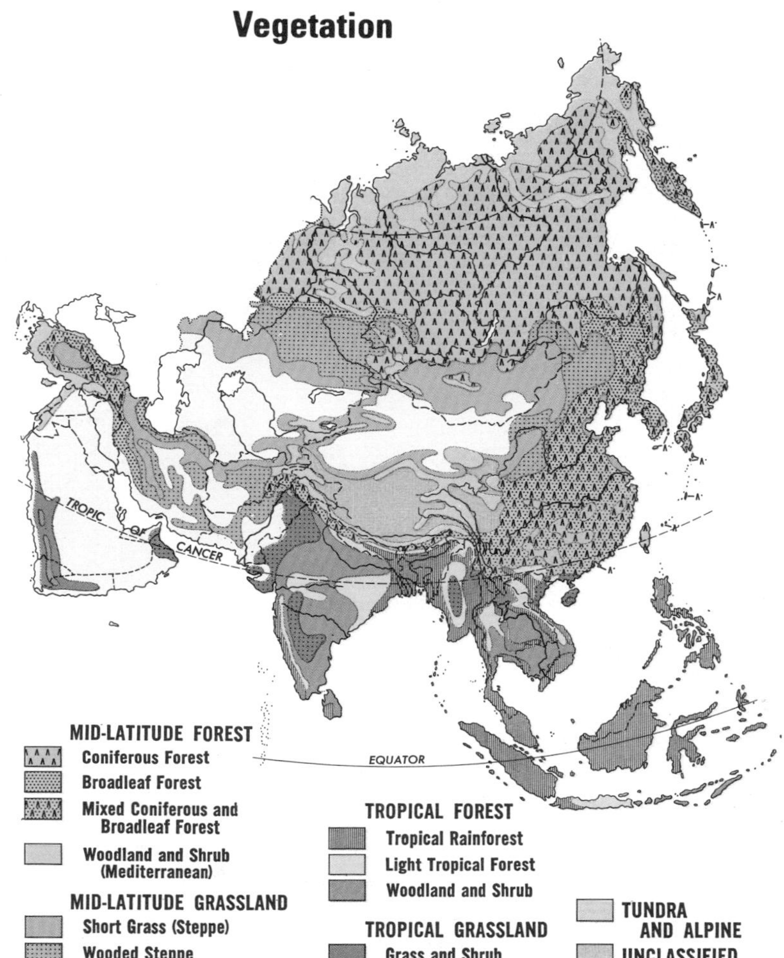

MID-LATITUDE FOREST
- Coniferous Forest
- Broadleaf Forest
- Mixed Coniferous and Broadleaf Forest
- Woodland and Shrub (Mediterranean)

MID-LATITUDE GRASSLAND
- Short Grass (Steppe)
- Wooded Steppe

DESERT AND DESERT SHRUB

TROPICAL FOREST
- Tropical Rainforest
- Light Tropical Forest
- Woodland and Shrub

TROPICAL GRASSLAND
- Grass and Shrub (Savanna)
- Wooded Savanna

TUNDRA AND ALPINE

UNCLASSIFIED HIGHLANDS

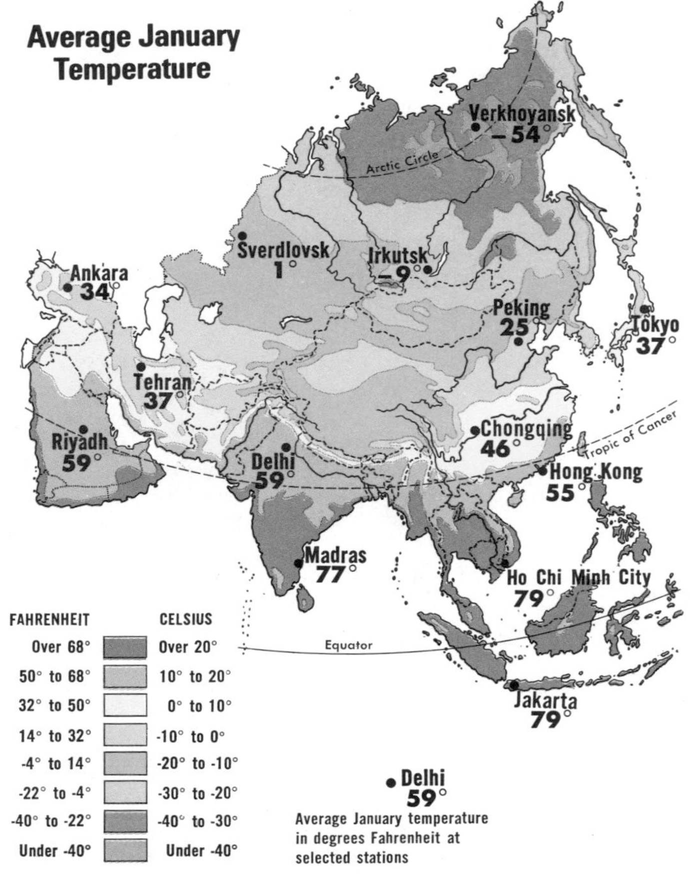
Average January Temperature
Verkhoyansk −54°
Arctic Circle
Sverdlovsk 1°
Irkutsk −9°
Ankara 34°
Peking 25°
Tokyo 37°
Tehran 37°
Riyadh 59°
Chongqing 46°
Tropic of Cancer
Delhi 59°
Hong Kong 55°
Madras 77°
Ho Chi Minh City 79°
Equator
Jakarta 79°
FAHRENHEIT
CELSIUS
Over 68° Over 20°
50° to 68° 10° to 20°
32° to 50° 0° to 10°
14° to 32° -10° to 0°
-4° to 14° -20° to -10°
-22° to -4° -30° to -20°
-40° to -22° -40° to -30°
Under -40° Under -40°
Delhi 59°
Average January temperature in degrees Fahrenheit at selected stations

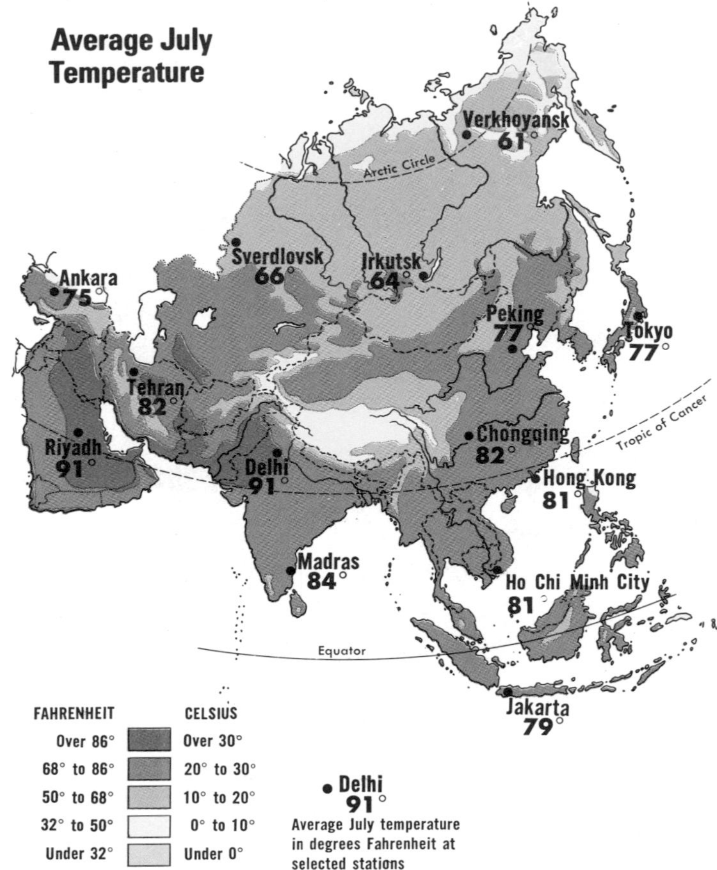
Average July Temperature
Verkhoyansk 61°
Arctic Circle
Sverdlovsk 66°
Irkutsk 64°
Ankara 75°
Peking 77°
Tokyo 77°
Tehran 82°
Riyadh 91°
Chongqing 82°
Tropic of Cancer
Delhi 91°
Hong Kong 81°
Madras 84°
Ho Chi Minh City 81°
Equator
Jakarta 79°
FAHRENHEIT
CELSIUS
Over 86° Over 30°
68° to 86° 20° to 30°
50° to 68° 10° to 20°
32° to 50° 0° to 10°
Under 32° Under 0°
Delhi 91°
Average July temperature in degrees Fahrenheit at selected stations

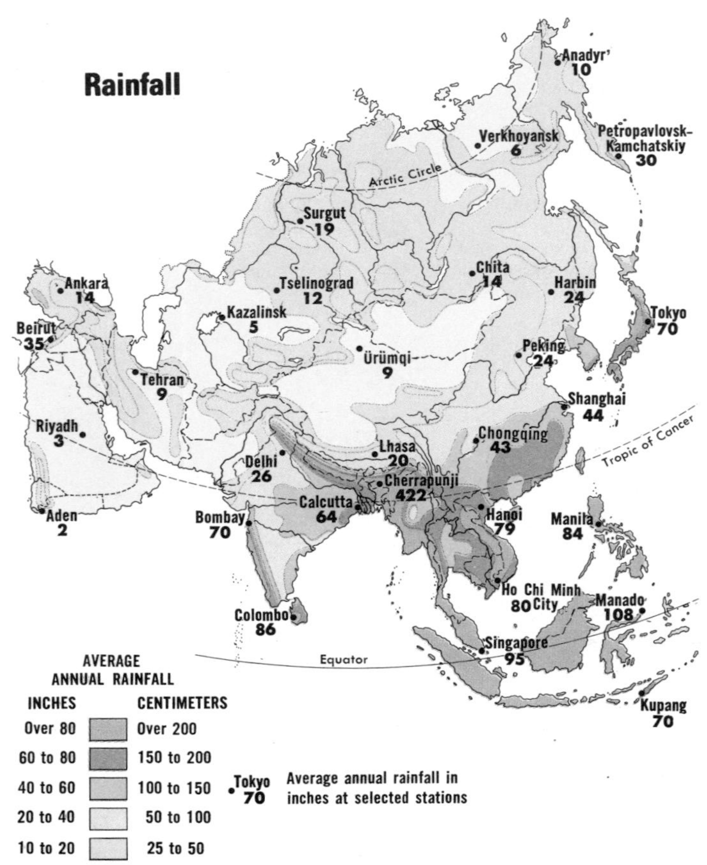
Rainfall
Anadyr' 10
Verkhoyansk 6
Petropavlovsk-Kamchatskiy 30
Arctic Circle
Surgut 19
Chita 14
Ankara 14
Tselinograd 12
Harbin 24
Kazalinsk 5
Tokyo 70
Beirut 35
Ürümqi 9
Peking 24
Tehran 9
Shanghai 44
Riyadh 3
Chongqing 43
Lhasa 20
Tropic of Cancer
Delhi 26
Cherrapunji 422
Aden 2
Calcutta 64
Bombay 70
Hanoi 79
Manila 84
Ho Chi Minh City 80
Colombo 86
Manado 108
Singapore 95
Equator
Kupang 70
AVERAGE ANNUAL RAINFALL
INCHES
CENTIMETERS
Over 80 Over 200
60 to 80 150 to 200
40 to 60 100 to 150
20 to 40 50 to 100
10 to 20 25 to 50
Under 10 Under 25
Tokyo 70
Average annual rainfall in inches at selected stations

Vegetation/Relief

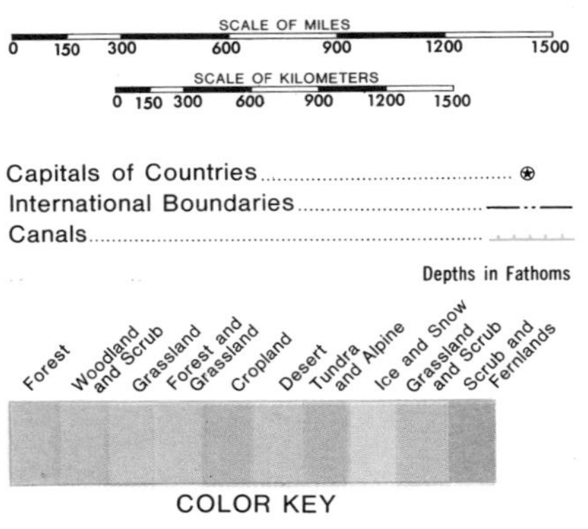
SCALE OF MILES
0 150 300 600 900 1200 1500
SCALE OF KILOMETERS
0 150 300 600 900 1200 1500
Capitals of Countries
International Boundaries
Canals
Depths in Fathoms
Forest
Woodland and Scrub
Grassland
Forest and Grassland
Cropland
Desert
Tundra and Alpine
Ice and Snow
Grassland and Scrub
Scrub and Fernlands
COLOR KEY

ATLANTIC OCEAN
ICELAND
GREENLAND
Arctic Circle
NORWEGIAN SEA
North Pole
IRELAND
UNITED KINGDOM
London
NORTH SEA
PORTUGAL
SPAIN
Bay of Biscay
FRANCE
Paris
BELG.
NETH.
GERMANY
Berlin
DEN.
POLAND
BALTIC SEA
NORWAY
SWEDEN
FINLAND
Nordkapp
Svalbard (Nor.)
Franz Josef Ld.
ARCTIC OCEAN
BARENTS SEA
Novaya Zemlya
KARA SEA
Severnaya Zemlya
C. Chelyuskin
LAPTEV SEA
New Siberian Is.
EAST SIBERIAN SEA
C. Dezhnev
Bering Str.
Alaska
UNITED STATES
BERING SEA
Aleutian Islands
Kolyma
Kamchatka Peninsula
C. Lopatka
SEA OF OKHOTSK
Sakhalin
Kuril Is.
PACIFIC OCEAN
EUROPE
Rome
YUGOSLAVIA
ROMANIA
Danube
BULG.
ALB.
GREECE
MEDITERRANEAN SEA
Moscow
Volga
UNION OF SOVIET SOCIALIST REPUBLICS
Ural Mountains
Ob'
Siberia
Yenisey
Noril'sk
Lena
Vilyuy
Yakutsk
Aldan
Sverdlovsk
Chelyabinsk
Tobol
Omsk
Irtysh
Novosibirsk
Krasnoyarsk
Angara
Lake Baykal
Irkutsk
Yablonovyy Ra.
Amur
Khabarovsk
BLACK SEA
Caucasus
CASPIAN SEA
TURKEY
CYPRUS
LEBANON
SYRIA
ISRAEL
Damascus
Cairo
EGYPT
Suez Canal
JORDAN
IRAQ
Baghdad
Euphrates
Zagros Mts.
Tehran
IRAN
ARAL SEA
Syrdar'ya
Amudar'ya
Karaganda
L. Balkhash
Tashkent
Alma-Ata
Urümqi
Altai Mts.
Ulaanbaatar
MONGOLIA
Gobi
Great Khingan Ra.
Harbin
Vladivostok
Shenyang
N. KOREA
S. KOREA
Seoul
SEA OF JAPAN
Hokkaido
Honshu
Tokyo
Nagoya
Osaka
Shikoku
Kyushu
JAPAN
Tien Shan
Tarim
Takla Makan
Peking (Beijing)
Luda
Tianjin
YELLOW SEA
Hwang Ho
Taiyuan
(Huang He)
Lanzhou
Xi'an
Nanjing
Shanghai
CHINA
EAST CHINA SEA
Chengdu
Wuhan
(Chang Jiang)
Chongqing
Yangtze
Tibet
Kunlun
Hindu Kush
K2 (Godwin Austen) 28,250 ft. (8611 m.)
Kabul
AFGHANISTAN
Islamabad
Helmand
Lahore
PAKISTAN
Indus
Delhi
New Delhi
Himalaya
NEPAL
Mt. Everest 29,028 ft. (8848 m.)
BHUTAN
Brahmaputra
Kanpur
Ganges
Jumna
Karachi
INDIA
Ahmadabad
Narbada
BANGLADESH
Dhaka
Calcutta
Bombay
Godavari
Hyderabad
Kistna
Western Ghats
Madras
Bangalore
C. Comorin
SRI LANKA (CEYLON)
Colombo
Dondra Head
MALDIVES
ARABIAN SEA
BAY OF BENGAL
SAUDI ARABIA
Riyadh
Mecca
KUWAIT
Persian Gulf
BAHRAIN
QATAR
U.A.E.
Gulf of Oman
Muscat
OMAN
Rub' al Khali
YEMEN ARAB REP.
PEOP. DEM. REP. YEMEN
Aden
Gulf of Aden
Socotra
Ras Asèr
SOMALIA
ETHIOPIA
SUDAN
AFRICA
Nile
RED SEA
Taipei
Taiwan
Ryukyu Is.
Tropic of Cancer
Canton (Guangzhou)
HONG KONG (U.K.)
Xi
Red
Mekong
Salween
Irrawaddy
Hanoi
Hainan
BURMA
Rangoon
THAILAND
Bangkok
CAMBODIA
VIETNAM
Ho Chi Minh City
Gulf of Siam
SOUTH CHINA SEA
ANDAMAN SEA
Andaman Is.
Nicobar Is.
C. Engaño
Luzon
Manila
PHILIPPINES
Palawan
SULU SEA
Mindanao
MALAYSIA
BRUNEI
Kuala Lumpur
SINGAPORE
CELEBES SEA
Celebes
New Guinea
Sumatra
Borneo
INDONESIA
BANDA SEA
Jakarta
Java
Surabaya
JAVA SEA
FLORES SEA
Timor
TIMOR SEA
Sunda Islands
Equator
INDIAN OCEAN
SEYCHELLES
COMOROS
BRITISH INDIAN OCEAN TERR.
MADAGASCAR
Réunion (Fr.)
MAURITIUS
Tropic of Capricorn
AUSTRALIA
Longitude 70° East of Greenwich

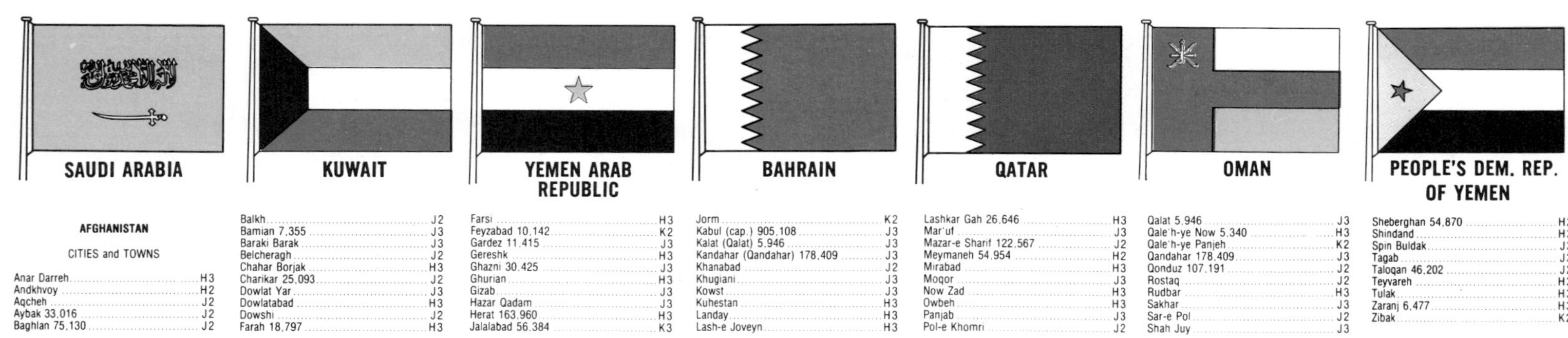

AFGHANISTAN

CITIES and TOWNS

Place	Key
Anar Darreh	H3
Andkhvoy	H2
Aqcheh	J2
Aybak 33,016	J2
Baghlan 75,130	J2
Balkh	J2
Bamian 7,355	J3
Baraki Barak	J3
Belcheragh	J2
Chahar Borjak	H3
Charikar 25,093	J2
Dowlat Yar	J3
Dowlatabad	H3
Dowshi	J2
Farah 18,797	H3
Farsi	H3
Feyzabad 10,142	K2
Gardez 11,415	J3
Gereshk	H3
Ghazni 30,425	J3
Ghurian	H3
Gizab	J3
Hazar Qadam	J3
Herat 163,960	H3
Jalalabad 56,384	K3
Jorm	K2
Kabul (cap.) 905,108	J3
Kalat (Qalat) 5,946	J3
Kandahar (Qandahar) 178,409	J3
Khanabad	J2
Khugiani	J3
Kowst	J3
Kuhestan	H3
Landay	H3
Lash-e Joveyn	H3
Lashkar Gah 26,646	H3
Mar'uf	J3
Mazar-e Sharif 122,567	J2
Meymaneh 54,954	H2
Mirabad	H3
Moqor	J3
Now Zad	H3
Owbeh	H3
Panjab	J3
Pol-e Khomri	J2
Qalat 5,946	J3
Qale'h-ye Now 5,340	H3
Qale'h-ye Panjeh	K2
Qandahar 178,409	J3
Qonduz 107,191	J2
Rostaq	J2
Rudbar	H3
Sakhar	J3
Sar-e Pol	J2
Shah Juy	J3
Sheberghan 54,870	H2
Shindand	H3
Spin Buldak	J3
Tagab	J3
Taloqan 46,202	J2
Teyvareh	H3
Tulak	H3
Zaranj 6,477	H3
Zibak	K2

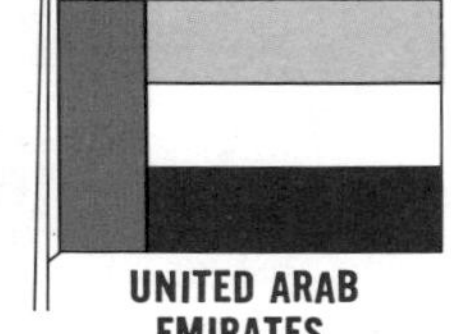

UNITED ARAB EMIRATES

OTHER FEATURES

Farah Rud (riv.) H3
Gowd-e Zerreh (depr.) H4
Harirud (riv.) H3
Helmand (riv.) J3
Hindu Kush (mts.) J2
Kabul (riv.) K3
Konar (riv.) K2
Lurah (riv.) J3
Margow, Dasht-e (des.) H3
Murghab (riv.) H2
Namaksar (salt lake) H3
Paropamisus (mts.) H3
Rigestan (reg.) H3

BAHRAIN

CITIES and TOWNS

Manama (cap.) 88,785 .... F4
Muharraq 37,732 .... F4

GAZA STRIP

CITIES and TOWNS

Gaza* 118,272 .... B3

IRAN

CITIES and TOWNS

Abadan 296,081 .... E3
Abadeh 16,000 .... F3
Abarqu 8,000 .... F3
Ahvaz 329,006 .... E3
Amol 68,782 .... F2
Anar 463 .... G3
Anarak 2,038 .... F3
Arak 114,507 .... E3
Ardabil 147,404 .... E2
Ardestan 5,868 .... F3
Asterabad (Gorgan) 88,348 .... F2
Babol 67,790 .... F2
Bafq 5,000 .... G3
Baft 6,000 .... G4

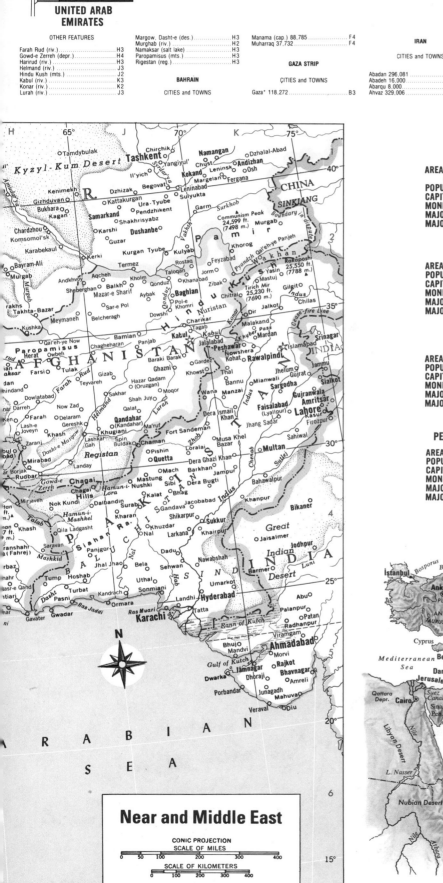

(continued on following page)

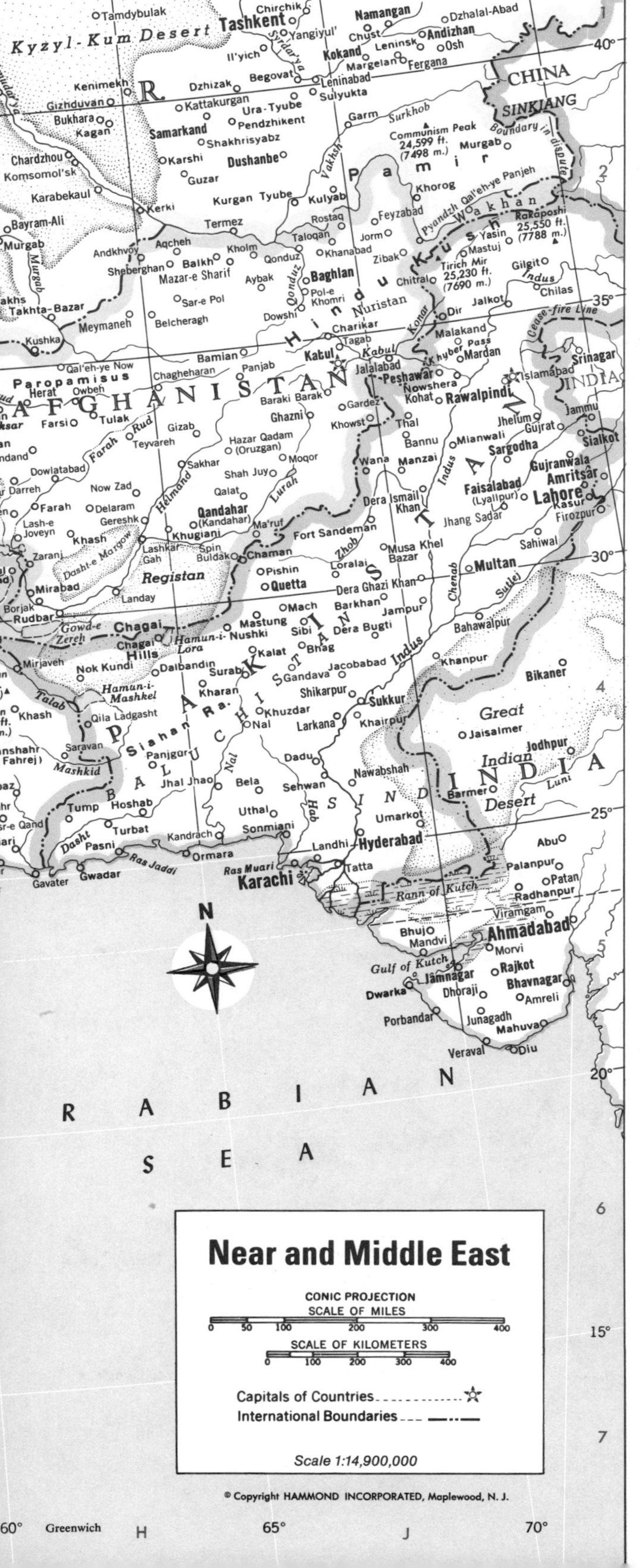

SAUDI ARABIA

AREA 829,995 sq. mi. (2,149,687 sq. km.)
POPULATION 8,367,000
CAPITAL Riyadh
MONETARY UNIT Saudi riyal
MAJOR LANGUAGE Arabic
MAJOR RELIGION Islam

YEMEN ARAB REPUBLIC

AREA 77,220 sq. mi. (200,000 sq. km.)
POPULATION 6,456,189
CAPITAL San'a
MONETARY UNIT Yemeni rial
MAJOR LANGUAGE Arabic
MAJOR RELIGION Islam

QATAR

AREA 4,247 sq. mi. (11,000 sq. km.)
POPULATION 220,000
CAPITAL Doha
MONETARY UNIT Qatari riyal
MAJOR LANGUAGE Arabic
MAJOR RELIGION Islam

PEOPLE'S DEM. REP. OF YEMEN

AREA 111,101 sq. mi. (287,752 sq. km.)
POPULATION 1,969,000
CAPITAL Aden
MONETARY UNIT Yemeni dinar
MAJOR LANGUAGE Arabic
MAJOR RELIGION Islam

KUWAIT

AREA 6,532 sq mi. (16,918 sq. km.)
POPULATION 1,355,827
CAPITAL Al Kuwait
MONETARY UNIT Kuwaiti dinar
MAJOR LANGUAGE Arabic
MAJOR RELIGION Islam

BAHRAIN

AREA 240 sq. mi. (622 sq. km.)
POPULATION 358,857
CAPITAL Manama
MONETARY UNIT Bahraini dinar
MAJOR LANGUAGE Arabic
MAJOR RELIGION Islam

OMAN

AREA 120,000 sq. mi. (310,800 sq. km.)
POPULATION 891,000
CAPITAL Muscat
MONETARY UNIT Omani rial
MAJOR LANGUAGE Arabic
MAJOR RELIGION Islam

UNITED ARAB EMIRATES

AREA 32,278 sq. mi. (83,600 sq. km.)
POPULATION 1,040,275
CAPITAL Abu Dhabi
MONETARY UNIT dirham
MAJOR LANGUAGE Arabic
MAJOR RELIGION Islam

Topography

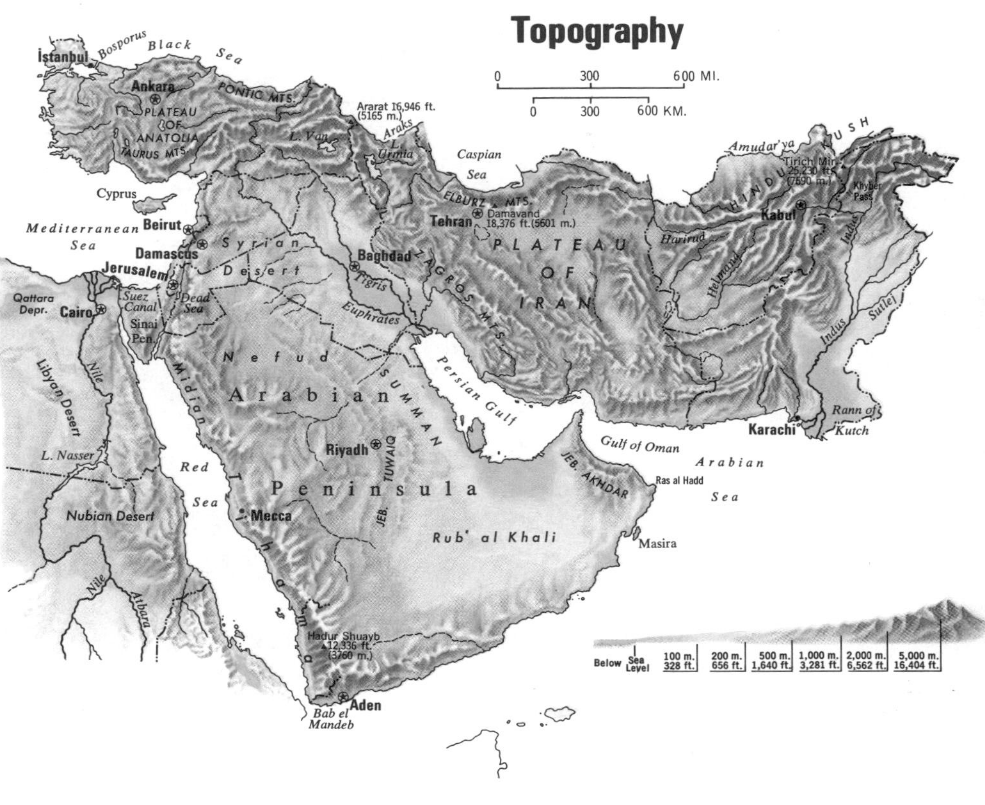

(continued)

Bam 22,000 G4
Bampur 1,585 H4
Bandar A'bbas 89,103 G4
Bandar-e Anzali (Enzeli) 55,978 E2
Bandar-e Khomeyni 6,000 E3
Bandar-e Lengeh 4,920 F4
Bandar-e Rig 1,889 F4
Bandar-e Torkeman 13,000 F2
Bejestan 3,823 G3
Bir Bala 103 G4
Birjand 25,854 G3
Bojnurd 31,248 G2
Borazjan 20,000 F4
Borujerd 100,103 E3
Bushehr 57,681 F4
Chah Bahar 1,800 H4
Chalus 15,000 F2
Damghan 13,000 F2
Darab 13,000 G4
Dasht-e Azadegan 21,000 E3
Dashtiari H4
Dezful 110,287 E3
Dezh Shahpur 1,384 E2
Emamshahr 30,767 G2
Enzeli 55,978 E2
Estahbanat 18,187 F4
Fahrej (Iranshahr) 5,000 H4
Fasa 19,000 F4
Ferdows 11,000 G3
Gach Saran F3
Garmsar 4,723 F2
Golpayegan 20,515 F3
Gonabad 8,000 G3
Gorgan 88,348 F2
Hamadan 155,846 E3
Iranshahr 5,000 H4
Isfahan 617,825 F3
Jahrom 38,236 F4
Jask 1,078 G4
Kangan 2,682 F4
Kangavar 9,414 E3
Kashan 84,545 F3
Kashmar 17,000 G2
Kazerun 51,309 F4
Kerman 140,309 G3
Kermanshah 290,861 E3
Khash 7,439 H4
Khorramabad 104,928 E3
Khorramshahr 146,709 E3
Khvor 2,912 G3
Khvoy 70,040 E2
Lar 22,000 F4
Mahabad 28,610 E2
Maragheh 60,820 E2
Marand 24,000 E2
Meshed 670,180 H2
Mianeh 28,447 E2
Minab 4,228 G2
Mirjaveh 11,000 H4
Nahavand 24,000 E3
Na'in 5,925 F3
Najafabad 76,236 F3
Nasratabad (Zabol) 20,000 H3
Natanz 4,370 F3
Nehbandan 2,130 G3
Neyshabur 59,101 G2
Nikshahr H4
Pahlevi (Enzeli) 55,978 E2
Qasr-e Qand 1,879 H4
Qayen 6,000 G3
Qazvin 138,527 E2
Qom 246,831 F3
Quchan 29,133 G2
Qum (Qom) 246,831 F3
Rafsanjan 21,000 G3
Rasht 187,203 E2
Ravar 5,074 G3
Rey 102,825 F2
Reza'iyeh (Urmia) 163,991 D2
Sabzevar 69,174 G2
Sabzvaran 7,000 G4
Sai'dabad 20,000 G4
Sanandaj 95,834 E2
Saqqez 17,000 E2
Saravan H4
Sari 70,936 F2
Saveh 17,565 F2
Semnan 31,058 F2
Shahdad 2,777 G3
Shahreza 34,220 F3
Shiraz 416,408 F4
Shirvan 11,000 G2
Shustar 24,000 E3
Sirjan (Sai'dabad) 20,000 G4
Tabas 10,000 G3
Tabas-Masina (Tabas) 466 H3
Tabriz 598,576 E2
Tarom 394 G4
Tehran (cap.) 4,496,159 F2
Tonekabon 12,000 F2
Torbat-e Heydariyeh 30,106 G2
Torbat-e Jam 13,000 H2
Torud 721 F2
Turan G2
Turbat-i-Shaikh Jam 13,000 H2
Urmia 163,991 D2
Yazd 135,978 F3
Yazdan H3
Zabol 20,000 H3
Zahedan 92,628 H4
Zanjan 99,967 E2
Zarand 5,000 G3

OTHER FEATURES

Araks (riv.) E2
Atrek (riv.) G2
Bazman, Kuh-e (mt.) H4
Damavand (mt.) F2
Dez (riv.) E3
Elburz (mts.) F2
Gavkhuni (lake) F3
Gorgan (riv.) F2
Halil (riv.) G4
Jaz Murian, Hamun-e (marsh) G4
Karun (riv.) E3
Kavir, Dasht-e (salt des.) G3
Kavir-e Namak (salt des.) G3
Lut, Dasht-e (des.) G3
Maidani, Ras (cape) G4
Mand Rud (riv.) F4
Mashkid (riv.) H4
Mehran (riv.) F4
Namak, Daryacheh-ye (salt lake) F3
Namaksar (salt lake) H3
Namakzar-e Shahdad (salt lake) G3
Oman (gulf) G5
Persian (gulf) F4
Qeys (isl.) F4
Qezel Owzan (riv.) E2
Qeshm (isl.) G4
Safidar, Kuh-e (mt.) F4
Shaikh Shua'ib (isl.) F4
Shir Kuh (mt.) F3
Taftan, Kuh-e (mt.) H4
Talab (riv.) H4
Tashk (lake) F4
Urmia (lake) E2
Zagros (mts.) E3

IRAQ

CITIES and TOWNS

Al'Aziziya 7,450 E3
Al Falluja 38,072 D3
Al Fatha† 15,329 D2
Al Musaiyib 15,955 D3
Al Qurna 5,638 E3
'Amadiya 2,578 D2
'Amara 64,847 E3
'Ana 15,729 D3
An Najaf 128,096 D3
An Nasiriya 60,405 E3
Arbela (Erbil) 90,320 D2
Ar Rahhaliya 1,579 D3
As Salman 3,584 E3
Baghdad (cap.) 502,503 E3
Baghdad* 1,745,328 E3
Baq'uba 34,575 D3
Basra 313,327 E3
Erbil 90,320 D2
Habbaniya 14,405 D3
Haditha 6,870 D3
Hai 16,988 E3
Hilla 84,717 D3
Hit 9,131 D3
Karbal'a 83,301 D3
Khanaqin 23,522 D3
Kirkuk 167,413 D2
Kirkuk* 176,794 D2
Kut 42,116 E3
Maidan 354 E3
Mosul 315,157 D2
Qala' Sharqat 2,434 D2
Ramadi 28,723 D3
Rutba 5,091 D3
Samarra 24,746 D3
Samawa 33,473 D3
Shithatha 2,326 D3
Sulaimaniya 86,822 E2
Tikrit 9,921 D3

OTHER FEATURES

'Aneiza, Jebel (mt.) C3
'Ara'r, Wadi (dry riv.) D3
Batin, Wadi al (dry riv.) E4
Euphrates (riv.) E3
Hauran, Wadi (dry riv.) D3
Mesopotamia (reg.) D3
Syrian (El Hamad) (des.) D3
Tigris (riv.) E3

KUWAIT

CITIES and TOWNS

Al Kuwait (cap.) 181,774 E4
Mina al Ahmadi E4
Mina Saud E4

OTHER FEATURES

Bubiyan (isl.) E4
Persian (gulf) F4

OMAN

CITIES and TOWNS

Adam G5
Buraimi G5
Dhank G5
Ibra G5
I'bri G5
Juwara G6
Kamil G5
Khaluf G5
Khasab G4
Manah G5
Masqat (Muscat) (cap.) 7,500 G5
Matrah 15,000 G5
Mina al Fahal G5
Murbat G6
Muscat (cap.) 7,500 G5
Nizwa G5
Quryat G5
Raysut (Risut) F6
Salala 4,000 F6
Sarur G5
Shinas G5
Sohar G5
Sur G5
Suwaiq G5

OTHER FEATURES

Akhdar, Jebel (range) G5
Batina (reg.) G5
Dhofar (reg.) F6
Hadd, Ras al (cape) G5
Jibsh, Ras (cape) G5
Kuria Muria (isls.) G6
Madraka, Ras (cape) G6
Masira (gulf) G6
Masira (isl.) G5
Musandam, Ras (cape) G4
Nus, Ras (cape) G6
Oman (gulf) G5
Oman (reg.) G5
Ruus al Jibal (dist.) G4
Sauqira (bay) G6
Sauqira, Ras (cape) G6
Sham, Jebel (mt.) G5
Sharbatat, Ras (cape) G6

QATAR

CITIES and TOWNS

Doha (cap.) 150,000 F4
Dukhan F4
Umm Sai'd F5

OTHER FEATURES

Persian (gulf) F4
Rakan, Ras (cape) F4

SAUDI ARABIA

CITIES and TOWNS

Aba as Sau'd 47,501 D6
'Abaila F5
Abha 30,150 D6
Abqaiq E4
Abu 'Arish D6
Abu Hadriya E4
'Ain al Mubarrak C5
Al 'Ain C4
Al 'Ala C4
Al 'Auda E4
Al Birk D6
Al Hilla E5
Al Lidam D5
Al Lith C5
Al Muadhdam C4
'Anaiza D4
Artawiya E4
'Ashaira D5
Ayun D4
Badr C5
Buraida 69,940 D4
Dam D5
Dammam 127,844 F4
Dar al Hamra C4
Dhaba C4
Dhahran E4
Dharma E5
Dilam E5
Doqa D6
Duwadami D5
Er Ras D4
Faid D4
Gail E5
Haddar E5
Hadiya C4
Hafar al Batin E4
Hail 40,502 D4
Hamar E5
Hamda D6
Hanakiya D5
Haql C4
Harad E5
Haraja D6
Hariq E5
Hofuf 101,271 E4
Jabrin E5
Jauf C4
Jidda 561,104 C5
Jizan (Qizan) 32,812 D6
Jubail F4
Jubba D4
Junaina D5
Kaf C3
Khaibar, 'Asir D5
Khaibar, Hejaz C4
Khamis Mushait 49,581 D6
Khay D6
Khurma D5
Laila E5
Majmaa' D4
Maqna C4
Marib E6
Mastaba C5
Mastura C5
Mecca (cap.) 366,801 C5
Medain Salih C4
Medina 198,186 D5
Mendak D5
Mina Sau'd E4
Mubarraz 54,325 E4
Mudhnib D4
Muwailih C4
Najran (Aba as Sau'd) 47,501 D6
Nisab D4
O'qair E4
Qadhima C5
Qafar D4
Qasr al Haiyanya D4
Qatif E4
Qizan 32,812 D6
Qunfidha D6
Qusaiba D4
Rabigh C5
Ra's al Khafji E4
Ras Tanura F4
Riyadh (cap.) 666,840 E5
Rumah E4
Sabya D6
Sakaka D4
Salwa F5
Shaqra D4
Shuqaiq D6
Sufeina D5
Sulaiyil E5
Taif 204,857 D5
Taima C4
Tamra E5
Tathlith D6
Tebuk (Tabuk) 74,825 C4
Truba D4
Turaba D5
Umm Lajj C4
Wejh C4
Yamama E5
Yenbo C5
Zahran D6
Zalim D5
Zilfi E4

OTHER FEATURES

Abu-Mad, Ras (cape) C5
'Aneiza, Jebel (mt.) C3
'Aqaba (gulf) C4
Arafat, Jebel (mt.) D5
'Ara'r, Wadi (dry riv.) D3
Arma (plat.) E4
Aswad, Ras al (cape) C5
Bahr es Safi (des.) E6
Barida, Ras (cape) C5
Bisha, Wadi (dry riv.) D5
Dahana (des.) E4
Dawasir, Wadi (dry riv.) E5
Dawasir, Hadhb (range) D5
Farasan (isls.) D6
Hatiba, Ras (cape) C5
Jafura (des.) F5
Mashabi (isl.) C4
Midian (dist.) C4
Mishaa'b, Ras (cape) E4
Nefud (des.) D4
Nefud Dahi (des.) D5
Persian (gulf) F4
Ranya, Wadi (dry riv.) D5
Red (sea) C5
Rima, Wadi (dry riv.) D4
Rimal, Ar (des.) F5
Rub al Khali (des.) F5
Safaniya, Ras (cape) E4
Salma, Jebel (mts.) D4
Shaibara (isl.) C4
Shammar, Jebel (plat.) D4
Sirhan, Wadi (dry riv.) C3
Subh, Jebel (mt.) C5
Summan (plat.) E4
Tihama (reg.) C5
Tiran (isl.) C4
Tiran (str.) C4
Tuwaiq, Jebel (range) E5

UNITED ARAB EMIRATES

CITIES and TOWNS

Abu Dhabi (cap.) 347,000 F5
'AJman G4
'Aradah F5
Buraimi G5
Dubai F4
Fujairah G4
Jebel Dhanna F5
Ras al Khaimah G4
Ruwais F5
Sharjah F4
Umm al Qaiwain G4

OTHER FEATURES

Das (isl.) F4
Oman (gulf) G5
Yas (isl.) F5
Zirko (isl.) F5

WEST BANK

CITIES and TOWNS

Hebron 38,309 C3

OTHER FEATURES

Dead (sea) C3

YEMEN ARAB REP.

CITIES and TOWNS

'Amran D6
Bait al Faqih D7
Dhamar 19,467 D7
El Beida 5,975 E7
Hajja 5,814 D6
Harib E7
Hodeida 80,314 D7
Huth D6
Ibb 19,066 D7
Luhaiya D6
Marib 292 D6
Mocha D7
Saa'da 4,252 D6
Sana' (cap.) 134,588 D6
Sheikh Sai'd D7
Tai'zz 78,642 D7
Yarim D7
Zabid D7

OTHER FEATURES

Hanish (isls.) D7
Manar, Jebel (mt.) D7
Mandeb, Bab el (str.) D7
Red (sea) C5
Sabir, Jebel (mt.) D7
Tihama (reg.) C5
Zuqar (isl.) D7

YEMEN, PEOPLE'S DEM. REPUBLIC OF

CITIES and TOWNS

Aden (cap.) 240,370 E7
Ahwar E7
Balhaf E7
Bir 'Ali E7
Damqut F6
Ghaida F6
Habban E7
Hadibu F7
Hajarain E6
Haura E7
Hureidha E6
I'rqa E7
Lahej E7
Leijun E6
Lodar E7
Madinat ash Shab' E7
Meifa E7
Mukalla 45,000 E7
Nisab E7
Nuqub E6
Qishn F6
Riyan E7
Saihut F6
Seiyun 20,000 E6
Shabwa E6
Shibam E6
Shihr E7
Shuqra E7
Tarim E6
Yeshbum E7
Zinjibar E7

OTHER FEATURES

Fartak, Ras (cape) F6
Hadhramaut (dist.) E7
Hadhramaut, Wadi (dry riv.) F7
Kamaran (isl.) D6
Perim (isl.) D7
Socotra (isl.) F7

*City and suburbs.

Agriculture, Industry and Resources

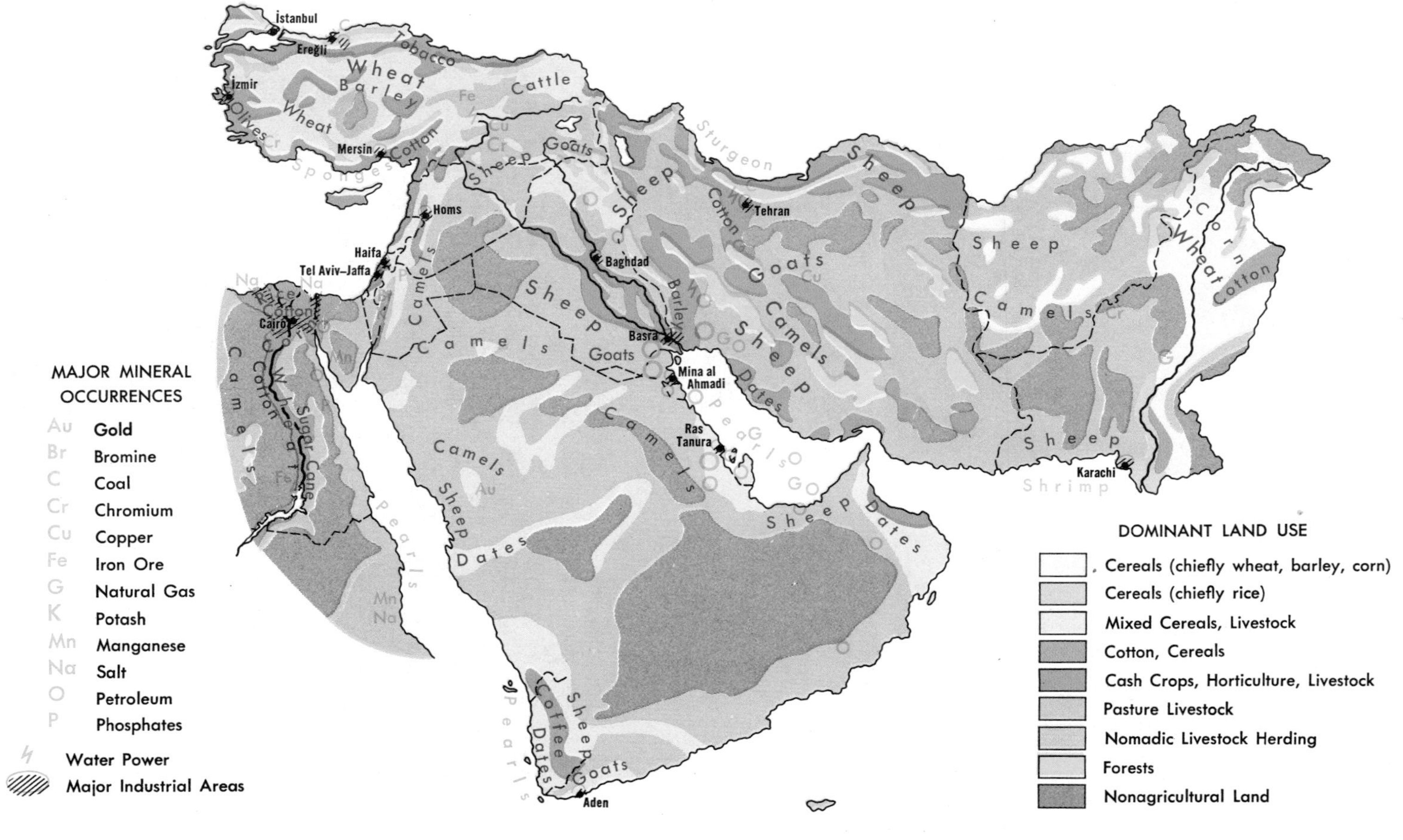

TURKEY

SYRIA

LEBANON

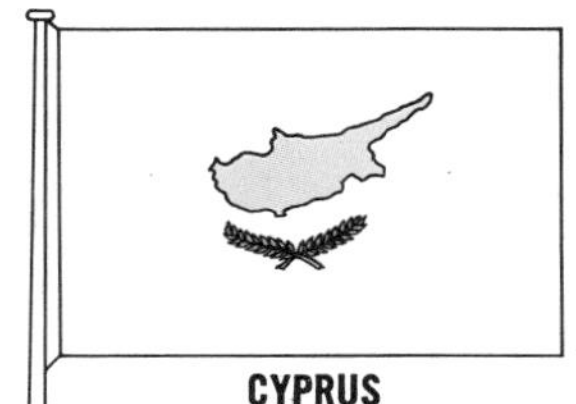

CYPRUS

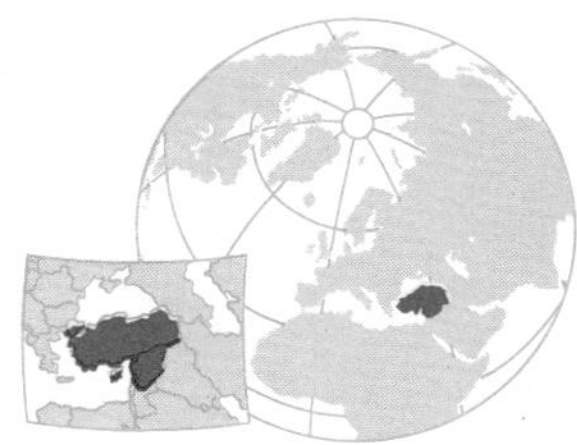

AREA 300,946 sq. mi. (779,450 sq. km.)
POPULATION 45,217,556
CAPITAL Ankara
LARGEST CITY Istanbul
HIGHEST POINT Ararat 16,946 ft. (5,165 m.)
MONETARY UNIT Turkish lira
MAJOR LANGUAGE Turkish
MAJOR RELIGION Islam

AREA 71,498 sq. mi. (185,180 sq. km.)
POPULATION 8,979,000
CAPITAL Damascus
LARGEST CITY Damascus
HIGHEST POINT Hermon 9,232 ft. (2,814 m.)
MONETARY UNIT Syrian pound
MAJOR LANGUAGES Arabic, French, Kurdish, Armenian
MAJOR RELIGIONS Islam, Christianity

AREA 4,015 sq. mi. (10,399 sq. km.)
POPULATION 3,161,000
CAPITAL Beirut
LARGEST CITY Beirut
HIGHEST POINT Qurnet es Sauda 10,131 ft. (3,088 m.)
MONETARY UNIT Lebanese pound
MAJOR LANGUAGES Arabic, French
MAJOR RELIGIONS Christianity, Islam

AREA 3,473 sq. mi. (8,995 sq. km.)
POPULATION 629,000
CAPITAL Nicosia
LARGEST CITY Nicosia
HIGHEST POINT Troödos 6,406 ft. (1,953 m.)
MONETARY UNIT Cypriot pound
MAJOR LANGUAGES Greek, Turkish, English
MAJOR RELIGIONS Eastern (Greek) Orthodoxy, Islam

CYPRUS

CITIES and TOWNS

Dhali 2,970 E5
Episkopi 2,150 E5
Famagusta 38,960 F5
Ktima E5
Kyrenia 3,892 E5
Kythrea 3,400 E5
Lapithos 3,600 E5
Larnaca 19,608 E5
Lefka 3,650 E5
Limassol 79,641 E5
Morphou 9,040 E5
Nicosia (cap.) 115,718 E5
Paphos 8,984 E5
Polis 2,200 E5
Rizokarpasso 3,600 F5
Yialousa 2,750 E5

OTHER FEATURES

Andreas (cape) F5
Arnauti (cape) E5
Gata (cape) E5
Greco (cape) F5
Kormakiti (cape) E5
Troodos (mt.) E5

LEBANON

CITIES and TOWNS

A'leih 18,630 F6
Amyun 7,926 F5
Baa'lbek 15,560 G5
Batrun 5,976 F5
Beirut (cap.) 474,870 F6
Beirut* 938,940 F6
Hermil 2,652 G5
Merj U'yun 9,318 F6
Rasheiya 6,731 F6
Rayak 1,480 G6
Saida 32,200 F6
Sidon (Saida) 32,200 F6
Sur 16,483 F6
Tripoli (Tarabulus) 127,611 F5
Tyre (Sur) 16,483 F6
Zahle 53,121 F6
Zegharta 18,210 G5

OTHER FEATURES

Lebanon (mts.) F6
Leontes (Litani) (riv.) F6
Litani (riv.) F6
Sauda, Qurnet es (mt.) G5

SYRIA

PROVINCES

Aleppo 1,316,872 G4
Damascus 1,457,934 G6
Deir ez Zor 292,780 H5
Dera' 230,481 G6
El Quneitra 16,490 F6
Es Suweida 139,650 G6
Hama 514,748 G5
Haseke 468,506 J4
Homs 546,176 G5
Idlib 383,695 G5
Latakia 389,552 G5
Rashid 243,736 H5
Tartus 302,065 G5

CITIES and TOWNS

Abu Kemal 6,907 J5
A'in el A'rab 4,529 H4
Aleppo 639,428 G4
Azaz 13,923 G4
Baniyas 8,537 F5
Busra G6
Damascus (cap.) 836,668 G6
Damascus* 923,253 G6
Deir ez Zor 66,164 H5
Dera' 27,651 G6
Dimashq (Damascus) (cap.) 836,668 G6
Duma 30,050 G6
El Bab 27,366 G4
El Haseke 32,746 J4
El Ladhiqiya (Latakia) 125,716 F5
El Quryatein G5
El Quneitra 17,752 F6
El Rashid 37,151 H5
En Nebk 16,334 G5
Es Suweide 29,524 G6
Et Tell el Abyad H4
Haffe 4,656 G5
Haleb (Aleppo) 639,428 G4
Hama 137,421 G5
Harim 6,837 G4
Homs 215,423 G5
Idlib 34,515 G5
Izra 3,226 G6
Jeble 15,715 F5
Jerablus 8,610 G4
Jisr esh Shughur 13,131 G5
Khan Sheikhun G5
Latakia 125,716 F5
Masyaf 7,058 G5
Membij 13,796 G4
Meskene H5
Meyadin 12,515 J5
Qala't es Salihiye J5
Qamishliye 31,448 J4
Quteife 4,993 G6
Raqqa (El Rashid) 37,151 H5
Sabkha 3,375 H5
Safita 9,650 G5
Selemiya 21,677 G5
Tadmur 10,670 H5
Tartus 29,842 F5
Telkalakh 6,242 F5
Zebdani 10,010 G6

OTHER FEATURES

A'mrit (ruins) F5
Arwad (Ruad) (isl.) F5
A'si (Orontes) (riv.) G5
Druz, Jebel ed (mts.) G6
El Furat (riv.) H4
Euphrates (El Furat) (riv.) H4
Hermon (mt.) F6
Khabur (riv.) J5
Orontes (riv.) G5
Palmyra (Tadmor) (ruins) H5
Ruwaq, Jebel er (mts.) G5

TURKEY

PROVINCES

Adana 1,240,475 F4
Adiyaman 346,892 H4
Afyonkarahisar 579,171 D3
Ağri 330,201 K3
Amasya 322,806 F2
Ankara 2,585,293 E3
Antalya 669,357 D4
Artvin 228,026 J2
Aydin 609,869 B4
Balikesir 789,255 B3
Bilecik 137,120 D2
Bingöl 210,804 J3
Bitlis 218,305 J3
Bolu 428,704 D2
Burdur 222,896 D4
Bursa 961,639 C2
Çanakkale 369,385 B2
Çankiri 265,468 E2
Çorum 547,580 F2
Denizli 560,916 C4
Diyarbakir 651,233 H4
Edirne 340,732 B2
Elâziğ 417,924 H3
Erzincan 283,683 H3
Erzurum 746,666 J3
Eskişehir 495,097 D3
Gaziantep 715,939 G4
Giresun 463,587 H2
Gümüşhane 293,673 H2
Hakkâri 126,036 K4
Hatay 744,113 G4
Içel 714,817 F4
Isparta 322,685 D4
Istanbul 3,904,588 C2
Izmir 1,673,966 B3
Kahramanmaraş 641,480 G4
Kars 707,398 K2
Kastamonu 438,243 E2
Kayseri 676,809 F3
Kirklareli 268,399 B2
Kirşehir 232,853 F3
Kocaeli 477,736 C2
Konya 1,422,461 E4
Kütahya 470,423 C3
Malatya 574,558 H3
Manisa 872,375 B3
Mardin 519,687 J4
Muğla 400,796 C4
Muş 267,203 J3
Nevşehir 249,308 F3
Niğde 463,121 F4
Ordu 664,290 G2
Rize 336,278 J2
Sakarya 495,649 D2
Samsun 906,381 F2
Siirt 381,503 J4
Sinop 267,605 F2
Sivas 741,713 G3
Tekirdağ 319,987 B2
Tokat 599,166 G2
Trabzon 719,008 H2
Tunceli 164,591 H3
Urfa 597,277 H4
Uşak 229,679 C3
Van 386,314 K3
Yozgat 500,371 F3
Zonguldak 836,156 D2

CITIES and TOWNS

Acigöl 3,934 F3
Acipayam 5,046 C4
Adalia (Antalya) 130,774 D4
Adana 475,384 F4
Adapazari 114,130 D2
Adilcevaz 9,022 K3
Adiyaman 43,782 H4
Afşin 18,231 G3
Afyonkarahisar 60,150 D3
Ağlasun 4,288 D4
Ağli 3,399 E2
Ağri (Karaköse) 35,284 K3
Ahlat 7,995 K3
Akçaabat 10,756 H2
Akçadağ 7,366 G3
Akçakoca 9,066 D2
Akdağmadeni 7,909 F3
Akhisar 53,357 B3
Aksaray 45,564 F3
Akşehir 35,544 D3
Akseki 5,141 D4
Akviran 3,799 E4
Akyazi 12,438 D2
Alaca 12,552 F2
Alacahan 2,321 G3
Alaçam 10,013 F2
Alanya 18,520 D4
Alaşehir 23,243 C3
Alexandretta (Iskenderun) 107,437 G4
Aliağa 5,727 B3
Alibeyköyü 33,387 D6
Almus 4,225 G2
Alpu 3,718 D3
Altindağ 512,392 E2
Altinova 6,980 B3
Altintaş 3,386 C3
Altinözü 5,158 G4
Alucra 7,070 H2
Amasra 4,369 E2
Amasya 41,496 G2
Anamur 21,475 E4
Andirin 5,018 G4
Ankara (cap.) 1,701,004 E3
Antakya 77,518 G4
Antalya 130,774 D4
Antioch (Antakya) 77,518 G4
Araç 3,594 E2
Aralik 4,155 L3
Arapkir 8,436 H3
Ardahan 16,285 K2
Ardeşen 7,980 J2
Ardanuç 2,942 K2
Arguvan 2,461 H3
Arhavi 6,311 J2
Arpaçay 2,651 K2
Arsin 6,557 H2
Artova 2,813 G2
Artvin 13,390 J2
Aşkale 10,817 J3
Avanos 8,635 F3
Ayancik 7,202 F1
Ayaş 4,575 E2
Aybasti 13,180 G2
Aydin 59,579 B4
Aydincik 6,739 E4
Ayranci 2,664 E4
Ayvacik 3,120 B3
Ayvalik 18,041 B3
Babadağ 5,890 C4
Babaeski 17,090 B2
Bafra 34,288 F2
Bahçe 10,212 G4
Bakirköy 200,942 D6
Baklan 3,327 C4
Balâ 4,107 E3
Balikesir 99,443 B3
Balya 2,362 B3
Banaz 6,264 C3
Bandirma 45,752 B2
Bartin 18,409 E2
Başkale 8,558 K3
Başmakçi 5,925 C4
Batman 64,384 J4
Bayat 4,671 F2
Bayburt 20,156 J2
Bayindir 14,078 B3
Baykan 2,690 J3
Bayramiç 6,385 B3
Bergama 29,749 B3
Beşiktaş 174,931 D6
Beşiri 4,165 J4
Besni 16,313 G4
Beykoz 76,804 D5
Beyoğlu 230,532 D6
Beypazari 14,963 D2
Beyşehir 15,060 D4
Beytüşşebap 2,766 K4
Biga 15,188 B2
Bigadiç 7,535 C3
Bilecik 11,269 D2
Bingöl (Çapakçur) 22,047 J3
Birecik 20,104 H4
Bismil 12,775 J4
Bitlis 25,054 J3
Bodrum 7,858 B4
Boğazliyan 10,329 F3
Bolu 32,812 D2
Bolvadin 29,218 D3
Bor 16,560 F4
Borçka 4,636 J2
Bornova 45,096 B3
Boyabat 13,139 F2
Bozdoğan 7,218 C4
Bozkir 5,294 E4
Bozkurt 2,948 F2
Bozova 5,462 H4
Bozüyük 15,197 C3
Bucak 15,090 D4
Bulancak 14,153 H2
Bulanik 8,296 K3
Buldan 11,115 C3
Bünyan 12,277 G3
Burdur 36,633 D4
Burhaniye 12,800 B3
Bursa 346,103 C2
Büyükada D6
Büyükdere D5
Çal 3,274 C3
Çala 2,450 K2
Caldiran 3,366 K3

(continued on following page)

Agriculture, Industry and Resources

DOMINANT LAND USE

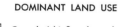

- Cereals (chiefly wheat, barley), Livestock
- Cash Crops, Horticulture, Livestock
- Pasture Livestock
- Nomadic Livestock Herding
- Forests
- Nonagricultural Land

MAJOR MINERAL OCCURRENCES

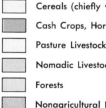

- Ab Asbestos
- Al Bauxite
- C Coal
- Cr Chromium
- Cu Copper
- Fe Iron Ore
- Hg Mercury
- Mg Magnesium
- Na Salt
- O Petroleum
- P Phosphates
- Pb Lead
- Py Pyrites
- Sb Antimony
- Zn Zinc

Water Power
Major Industrial Areas

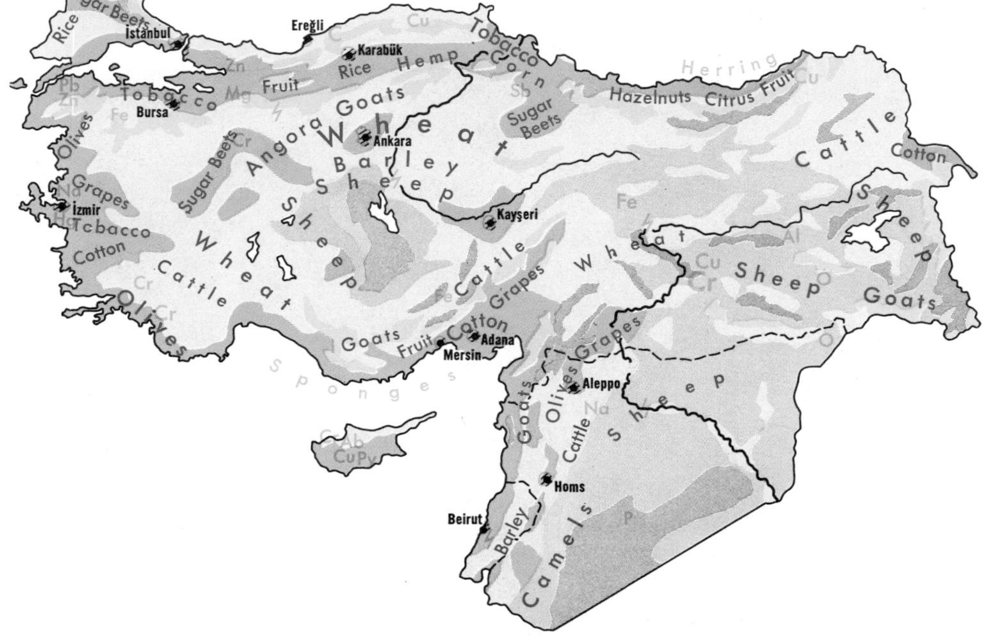

Turkey, Syria, Lebanon and Cyprus

(continued)

Çalköy 3,002 .... C3
Çamardi 2,419 .... F4
Çameli 2,502 .... C4
Çamlidere 4,386 .... E2
Çan 11,797 .... B2
Çanakkale 30,788 .... B6
Çandir 6,986 .... F3
Çankaya 895,005 .... E3
Çankiri 28,512 .... E2
Çapakçur 22,047 .... J3
Çardak 4,232 .... C6
Çarşamba 23,973 .... G2
Çatak 2,366 .... K4
Çatalca 7,693 .... C2
Çatalzeytin 2,271 .... F1
Çay 12,200 .... D3
Çaycuma 8,118 .... E2
Çayeli 13,480 .... J2
Çayiralan 8,071 .... F3
Çayirli 4,580 .... J3
Çekerek 3,796 .... F2
Çelikhan 5,066 .... H3
Çemişkezek 3,048 .... H3
Çerkeş 3,780 .... E2
Çerkezköy 8,428 .... C2
Çermik 9,749 .... H3
Çeşme 5,284 .... B3
Çetinkaya 3,616 .... G3
Ceyhan 62,909 .... F4
Ceylânpinar 20,171 .... H4
Çiçekdagi 3,203 .... F3
Cide 3,520 .... E2
Çifteler 8,163 .... D3
Cihanbeyli 10,079 .... E3
Çildir 2,260 .... K2
Cimin 5,341 .... H3
Çine 11,308 .... B4
Çivril 7,721 .... C3
Cizre 15,557 .... K4
Çölemerik 11,735 .... K4
Çorlu 40,134 .... B2
Çorum 64,852 .... F2
Çubuk 13,793 .... E2
Çukur 5,479 .... F3
Çukurca 3,019 .... K4
Çumra 19,225 .... E4
Çüngüş 2,616 .... H3
Daday 2,528 .... E2
Darende 8,055 .... G3
Dazkiri 3,912 .... D4
Delice 3,462 .... E3
Demirci 15,016 .... C3
Demirkent 4,204 .... E4
Demirköy 4,257 .... B2
Denizli 106,902 .... C4
Dereli 4,188 .... H2
Derik 13,292 .... J4
Derinkuyu 5,618 .... F3
Develi 17,323 .... F3
Devrek 9,164 .... D2
Devrekâni 4,014 .... E2
Dicle 5,247 .... J3
Dikili 6,916 .... B3
Dinar 19,873 .... D3
Dirmil 3,476 .... C4
Divriği 12,302 .... H3
Diyadin 5,094 .... K3
Diyarbakir 169,535 .... H4
Doğanbey 3,077 .... D4
Doğanhisar 9,487 .... D3
Doğanşehir 10,280 .... G3
Döger 3,478 .... D3
Doğubeyazit 17,612 .... K3
Domaniç 2,729 .... C3
Dörtyol 19,390 .... F4
Dumlu 4,206 .... J2
Durağan 3,259 .... F2
Dursunbey 8,615 .... C3
Düzce 32,129 .... D2
Eceabat 3,642 .... B6
Edirne 63,001 .... B2
Edremit 26,110 .... B3
Eflâni 3,793 .... E2
Eğridir 9,799 .... D4
Elâziğ 131,415 .... H3
Elbistan 26,048 .... G3
Eldivan 3,302 .... E2
Eleşkirt 8,202 .... K3
Elmali 10,184 .... C4
Emet 6,239 .... C3
Emirdağ 13,184 .... D3
Emirgazi 5,244 .... E4
Enez 2,486 .... B2
Erbaa 20,315 .... G2
Erciş 22,351 .... K3
Erdek 8,685 .... B2
Erdemli 19,936 .... F4
Ereğli 45,992 .... D2
Ereğli 50,354 .... F4
Ergani 21,936 .... H3
Erkilet 3,924 .... F3
Ermenak 13,464 .... E4
Eruh 5,340 .... K4
Erzin 15,314 .... G4
Erzincan 60,351 .... H3
Erzurum 162,973 .... J3
Eskimalatya 10,182 .... H3
Eskipazar 2,865 .... E2
Eskişehir 259,952 .... D3
Eşme 7,828 .... C3
Espiye 8,168 .... H2
Eynesil 6,081 .... H2
Eyüp 95,486 .... D6
Ezibider 3,631 .... H2
Ezine 9,359 .... B3
Fakili 4,173 .... F3
Fatih 504,127 .... D6
Fatsa 19,758 .... G2
Feke 5,576 .... G4
Fethiye 12,700 .... C4
Fevzipaşa 5,495 .... G4
Findikli 5,008 .... J2
Finike 4,200 .... D4
Foça 4,829 .... B3
Gallipoli 13,466 .... C5
Gaziantep 300,882 .... G4
Gazipaşa 6,696 .... E4
Gebze 33,110 .... C2
Gediz 10,649 .... C3
Gelibolu (Gallipoli) 13,466 .... C5
Gemerek 5,769 .... G3
Gemlik 20,704 .... C2
Genç 7,671 .... J3
Genezin 4,925 .... F3
Gercüş 4,393 .... J4
Gerede 8,259 .... E2
Gerger 2,773 .... H3
Germencik 10,558 .... B4
Gerze 7,313 .... F2
Gevaş 6,333 .... K3
Geyve 7,806 .... D2
Giresun 38,236 .... H2
Gökçe 4,470 .... B2
Göksun 10,481 .... G3
Gölbaşi 15,103 .... G4
Gölcük 33,279 .... C2
Göle 7,680 .... K2
Gölhisar 7,095 .... C4
Gölköy 10,022 .... G2
Gölmarmara 11,982 .... C3
Gölpazari 5,002 .... D2
Gönen 16,091 .... B2
Gördes 7,909 .... C3
Görele 8,079 .... H2
Göynücek 2,600 .... F2
Göynük 2,519 .... D2
Güdül 4,746 .... E2
Gülnar 6,344 .... E4
Gülşehir 6,188 .... F3
Gümüş 3,066 .... F2
Gümüşhaciköy 12,789 .... F2
Gümüşhane 11,166 .... H2
Güney 7,154 .... C3
Gürün 9,138 .... G3
Hacibektaş 5,032 .... F3
Hacilar 15,622 .... F3
Hadim 10,467 .... E4
Hafik 5,398 .... G3
Hakkâri
(Çöelemerik) 11,735 .... K4
Halfeti 3,689 .... H4
Hamur 2,267 .... K3
Hanac 2,581 .... K2
Hani 7,559 .... J3
Harput 3,231 .... H3
Haruniye 12,837 .... G4
Hassa 10,926 .... G4
Hatay (Antakya) 77,518 .... G4
Havran 7,552 .... B3
Havsa 4,298 .... B2
Havza 15,341 .... F2
Haymana 6,123 .... E3

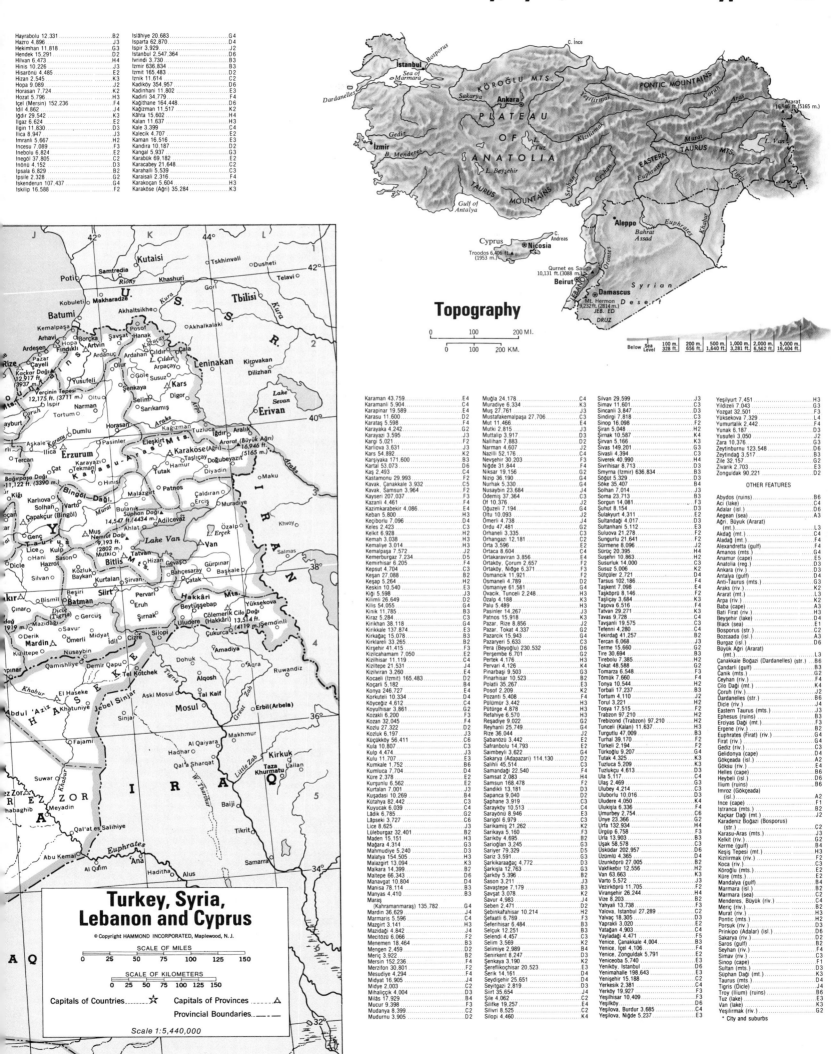

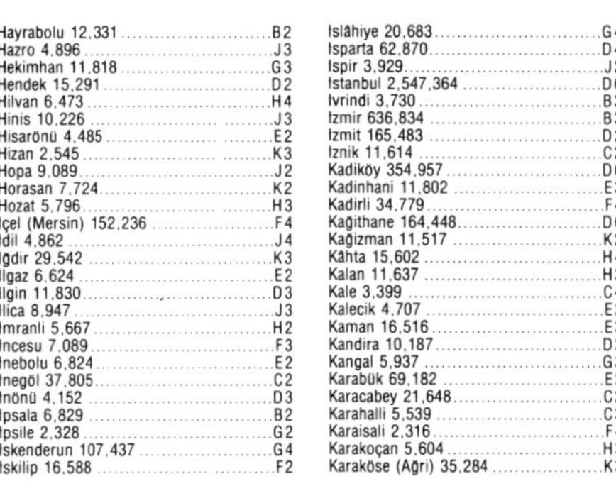
Hayrabolu 12,331 B2
Hazro 4,896 J3
Hekimhan 11,818 G3
Hendek 15,291 D2
Hilvan 6,473 H4
Hinis 10,226 J3
Hisarönü 4,485 E2
Hizan 2,545 K3
Hopa 9,089 J2
Horasan 7,724 K2
Hozat 5,796 H3
Içel (Mersin) 152,236 F4
Idil 4,862 J4
Iğdir 29,542 K3
Ilgaz 6,624 E2
Ilgin 11,830 D3
Ilica 8,947 J3
Imranli 5,667 H2
Incesu 7,089 F3
Inebolu 6,824 E2
Inegöl 37,805 C2
Inönü 4,152 D3
Ipsala 6,829 B2
Ipsile 2,328 G2
Iskenderun 107,437 G4
Iskilip 16,588 F2
Islâhiye 20,683 G4
Isparta 62,870 D4
Ispir 3,929 J2
Istanbul 2,547,364 D6
Ivrindi 3,730 B3
Izmir 636,834 B3
Izmit 165,483 D2
Iznik 11,614 C2
Kadiköy 354,957 D6
Kadinhani 11,802 E3
Kadirli 34,779 F4
Kağithane 164,448 D6
Kağizman 11,517 K2
Kâhta 15,602 H4
Kalan 11,637 H3
Kale 3,399 C4
Kalecik 4,707 E2
Kaman 16,516 E3
Kandira 10,187 D2
Kangal 5,937 G3
Karabük 69,182 E2
Karacabey 21,648 C2
Karahalli 5,539 C3
Karaisali 2,316 F4
Karakoçan 5,604 H3
Karaköse (Ağri) 35,284 K3

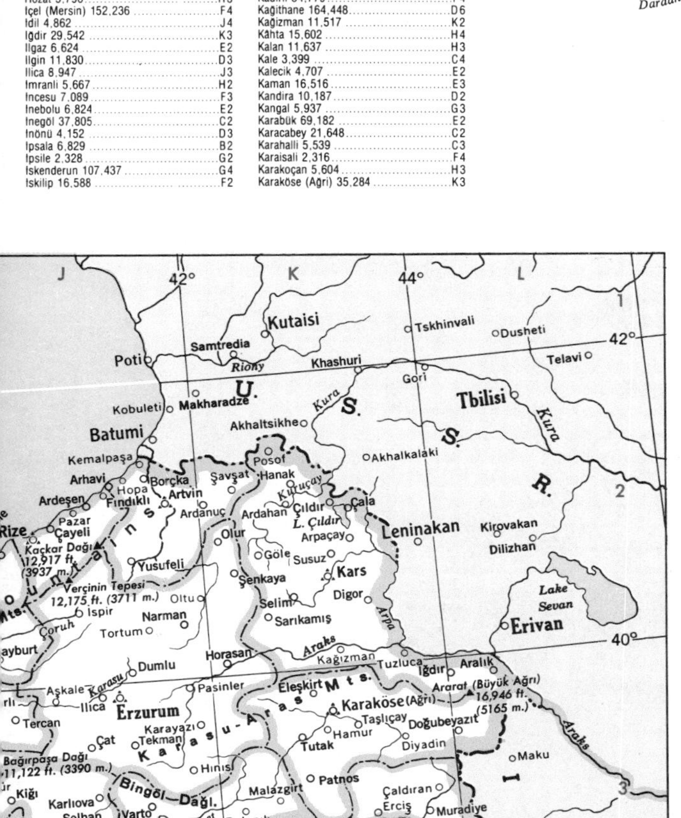

Karaman 43,759 E4
Karamanli 5,904 C4
Karapinar 19,589 E4
Karasu 11,600 D2
Karataş 5,598 F4
Karayaka 4,242 G2
Karayazi 3,595 J3
Kargi 5,021 F2
Karliova 3,631 J3
Kars 54,892 K2
Karşiyaka 171,600 B3
Kartal 53,073 D6
Kaş 2,493 C4
Kastamonu 29,993 F2
Kavak, Çanakkale 3,932 C5
Kavak, Samsun 3,964 F2
Kayseri 207,037 F3
Kazanli 4,461 F4
Kazimkarabekir 4,086 E4
Keban 5,800 H3
Keçiborlu 7,096 D4
Keles 2,423 C3
Kelkit 6,928 H2
Kemah 3,038 H3
Kemaliye 3,014 H3
Kemalpaşa 7,572 J2
Kemerburgaz 7,234 D5
Kemirhisar 6,205 F4
Kepsut 4,704 C3
Keşan 27,088 B2
Keşap 5,264 H2
Keskin 10,540 E3
Kiği 5,598 J3
Kilimli 26,649 D2
Kilis 54,055 G4
Kinik 11,785 B3
Kiraz 5,284 C3
Kirikhan 38,118 G4
Kirikkale 137,874 E3
Kirkağaç 15,078 B3
Kirklareli 33,265 B2
Kirşehir 41,415 F3
Kizilcahamam 7,050 E2
Kizilhisar 11,119 C4
Kiziltepe 21,531 J4
Kizilviran 3,260 E4
Kocaeli (Izmit) 165,483 D2
Koçarli 5,182 B4
Konya 246,727 E4
Korkuteli 10,334 D4
Köyceğiz 4,612 C4
Koyulhisar 3,861 G2
Kozakli 6,200 F3
Kozan 32,045 F4
Kozlu 27,322 D2
Kozluk 6,197 J3
Küçükköy 56,411 C6
Kula 10,807 C3
Kulp 4,474 J3
Kulu 11,707 E3
Kumkale 1,752 B6
Kumluca 7,704 D4
Küre 2,378 E2
Kurşunlu 6,562 E2
Kurtalan 7,001 J3
Kuşadasi 10,269 B4
Kütahya 82,442 C3
Kuyucak 6,039 C4
Lâdik 6,785 G2
Lâpseki 3,727 C6
Lice 8,625 J3
Lüleburgaz 32,401 B2
Maden 15,151 H3
Mağara 4,314 G3
Mahmudiye 5,240 D3
Malatya 154,505 H3
Malazgirt 13,094 K3
Malkara 14,399 B2
Maltepe 66,343 D6
Manavgat 10,804 D4
Manisa 78,114 B3
Manyas 4,410 B3
Maraş
(Kahramanmaraş) 135,782 G4
Mardin 36,629 J4
Marmaris 5,596 C4
Mazgirt 3,141 H3
Mazidaği 4,842 J4
Mecitözü 6,066 F2
Menemen 18,464 B3
Mengen 2,459 D2
Meriç 3,922 B2
Mersin 152,236 F4
Merzifon 30,801 F2
Mesudiye 4,294 F4
Midyat 16,905 J4
Midye 2,003 C2
Mihaliççik 4,004 D3
Milâs 17,929 B4
Mucur 9,398 F3
Mudanya 8,399 C2
Mudurnu 3,905 D2
Muğla 24,178 C4
Muradiye 6,334 K3
Muş 27,761 J3
Mustafakemalpaşa 27,706 C3
Mut 11,466 E4
Mutki 2,815 J3
Muttalip 3,917 D3
Nallihan 7,883 D2
Narman 4,607 J2
Nazilli 52,176 C4
Nevşehir 30,203 F3
Niğde 31,844 F4
Niksar 19,156 G2
Nizip 36,190 G4
Nurhak 5,330 G4
Nusaybin 23,684 J4
Ödemiş 37,364 C3
Of 10,376 J2
Oğuzeli 7,194 G4
Oltu 10,093 J2
Ömerli 4,738 J4
Ordu 47,481 G2
Orhaneli 3,335 C3
Orhangazi 12,181 C2
Orta 3,596 E2
Ortaca 8,604 C4
Ortakaraviran 3,856 E4
Ortaköy, Çorum 2,657 F2
Ortaköy, Niğde 6,371 F3
Osmancik 11,921 F2
Osmaneli 4,789 D2
Osmaniye 61,581 G4
Ovacik, Tunceli 2,248 H3
Özalp 4,188 K3
Palu 5,489 H3
Pasinler 14,267 J3
Patnos 15,918 K3
Pazar, Rize 8,856 J2
Pazar, Tokat 4,337 G2
Pazarcik 15,943 G4
Pazaryeri 5,633 C3
Pera (Beyoğlu) 230,532 D6
Perşembe 6,701 G2
Pertek 4,176 H3
Pervari 4,126 K4
Pinarbaşi 9,503 G3
Pinarhisar 10,523 B2
Polatli 35,267 E3
Posof 2,209 K2
Pozanti 5,408 F4
Pülümür 3,442 H3
Pütürge 4,878 H3
Refahiye 6,570 H3
Reşadiye 9,022 G2
Reyhanli 25,749 G4
Rize 36,044 J2
Şabanözü 3,442 E2
Safranbolu 14,793 E2
Saimbeyli 3,622 G4
Sakarya (Adapazari) 114,130 D2
Salihli 45,514 C3
Samandaği 22,540 F4
Samsat 2,083 H4
Samsun 168,478 F2
Sandikli 13,181 D3
Sapanca 9,040 D2
Şaphane 3,919 C3
Sarayköy 10,513 C4
Sarayönü 8,946 E3
Sarigöl 6,979 C3
Sarikamiş 21,262 K2
Sarikaya 5,160 F3
Sariköy 4,695 B2
Sarioğlan 3,245 G3
Sariyer 79,329 D5
Sariz 3,591 G3
Şarkikaraağaç 4,772 D3
Şarkişla 12,763 G3
Şarköy 5,396 B2
Sason 3,211 J3
Savaştepe 7,179 B3
Şavşat 3,078 K2
Savur 4,983 J4
Seben 2,471 D2
Şebinkarahisar 10,214 H2
Şefaatli 6,769 F3
Seferihisar 6,484 B3
Selçuk 12,251 B3
Selendi 4,457 C3
Selim 3,569 K2
Selimiye 2,989 B4
Senirkent 8,247 D3
Şenkaya 3,190 K2
Şereflikoçhisar 20,523 E3
Serik 14,161 D4
Seydişehir 25,651 D4
Seyitgazi 2,819 D3
Siirt 35,654 J4
Şile 4,062 C2
Silifke 19,257 E4
Silivri 8,525 C2
Silopi 4,460 K4
Silvan 29,599 J3
Simav 11,601 C3
Sincanli 3,847 D3
Sindirgi 7,818 C3
Sinop 16,098 F2
Şiran 5,048 H2
Şirnak 10,587 K4
Şirvan 5,166 K3
Sivas 149,201 G3
Sivasli 4,394 C3
Siverek 40,990 H4
Sivrihisar 8,713 D3
Smyrna (Izmir) 636,834 B3
Söğüt 5,329 D3
Söke 35,407 B4
Solhan 7,014 J3
Soma 23,713 B3
Sorgun 14,081 F3
Şuhut 8,154 D3
Sulakyurt 4,311 E2
Sultandaği 4,017 D3
Sultanhani 5,112 E3
Suluova 21,278 F2
Sungurlu 21,641 F2
Sürmene 8,096 J2
Sürüç 20,395 H4
Suşehri 10,863 H2
Susurluk 14,000 C3
Susuz 5,006 K2
Sütçüler 2,721 D4
Tarsus 102,186 F4
Taşkent 7,098 E4
Taşköprü 8,146 F2
Taşliçay 3,684 K3
Taşova 6,516 F4
Tatvan 29,271 K3
Tavas 9,728 C4
Tavşanli 19,575 C3
Tefenni 4,280 C4
Tekirdağ 41,257 B2
Tercan 6,068 J3
Terme 15,660 G2
Tire 30,694 B3
Tirebolu 7,385 H2
Tokat 48,588 G2
Tomarza 6,548 F3
Tömük 7,660 F4
Tonya 10,544 H2
Torbali 17,237 B3
Tortum 4,110 J2
Torul 3,221 H2
Tosya 17,515 F2
Trabzon 97,210 H2
Trebizond (Trabzon) 97,210 H2
Tunceli (Kalan) 11,637 H3
Turgutlu 47,009 B3
Turhal 39,170 F2
Türkeli 2,194 F2
Türkoğlu 9,207 G4
Tutak 4,325 K3
Tuzluca 5,209 K3
Tuzlukçu 4,613 D3
Ula 5,117 C4
Ulaş 2,469 G3
Ulubey 4,214 C3
Uluborlu 10,016 D3
Uludere 4,050 K4
Ulukişla 6,336 F4
Umurbey 2,754 C6
Ünye 23,366 G2
Urfa 132,934 H4
Ürgüp 6,758 F3
Urla 13,903 B3
Uşak 58,578 C3
Üsküdar 202,957 D6
Üzümlü 4,365 D4
Uzunköprü 27,005 B2
Vakfikebir 12,556 H2
Van 63,663 K3
Varto 5,572 J3
Vezirköprü 11,705 F2
Viranşehir 26,244 H4
Vize 8,203 B2
Yahyali 13,738 F3
Yalova, Istanbul 27,289 C2
Yalvaç 18,305 D3
Yaprakli 3,020 E2
Yatağan 4,903 C4
Yayladaği 4,471 F5
Yenice, Çanakkale 4,004 B3
Yenice, Içel 4,106 F4
Yenice, Zonguldak 5,791 E2
Yeniceoba 5,740 E3
Yeniköy, Istanbul D6
Yenimahalle 198,643 E3
Yenişehir 15,188 C2
Yerkesik 2,381 C4
Yerköy 19,927 F3
Yeşilhisar 10,409 F3
Yeşilköy D6
Yeşilova, Burdur 3,685 C4
Yeşilova, Niğde 5,237 E3
Yeşilyurt 7,451 H3
Yildizeli 7,043 G3
Yozgat 32,501 F3
Yüksekova 7,329 L4
Yumurtalik 2,442 F4
Yunak 6,187 D3
Yusufeli 3,050 J2
Zara 10,376 G3
Zeytinburnu 123,548 D6
Zeytindağ 3,517 B3
Zile 32,157 G2
Zivarik 2,703 E3
Zonguldak 90,221 D2

OTHER FEATURES

Abydos (ruins) B6
Aci (lake) C4
Adalar (isl.) D6
Aegean (sea) A3
Ağri, Büyuk (Ararat)
(mt.) L3
Akdağ (mt.) C4
Aladağ (mt.) F4
Alexandretta (gulf) F4
Amanos (mts.) G4
Anamur (cape) E5
Anatolia (reg.) D3
Ankara (riv.) D3
Antalya (gulf) D4
Anti-Taurus (mts.) G3
Araks (riv.) K2
Ararat (mt.) L3
Arpa (riv.) K2
Baba (cape) A3
Bati Firat (riv.) H3
Beyşehir (lake) D4
Black (sea) E1
Bosporus (str.) C2
Bozcaada (isl.) A3
Burgaz (isl.) D6
Büyük Ağri (Ararat)
(mt.) L3
Çanakkale Boğazi (Dardanelles) (str.) B6
Çandarli (gulf) B3
Canik (mts.) G2
Ceyhan (riv.) F4
Cilo Daği (mt.) K4
Çoruh (riv.) J2
Dardanelles (str.) B6
Dicle (riv.) J4
Eastern Taurus (mts.) J3
Ephesus (ruins) B3
Erciyas Daği (mt.) F3
Ergene (riv.) B2
Euphrates (Firat) (riv.) G4
Firat (riv.) G4
Gediz (riv.) C3
Gelidonya (cape) D4
Gökçeada (isl.) A2
Göksu (riv.) E4
Helles (cape) B6
Heybeli (isl.) D6
Ilium (ruins) B6
Imroz (Gökçeada)
(isl.) A2
Ince (cape) F1
Istranca (mts.) B2
Kaçkar Daği (mt.) J2
Karadeniz Boğazi (Bosporus)
(str.) C2
Karasu-Aras (mts.) J3
Kelkit (riv.) G2
Kerme (gulf) B4
Keşiş Tepesi (mt.) H3
Kizilirmak (riv.) F2
Koca (riv.) C3
Köroğlu (mts.) E2
Küre (mts.) E2
Mandalya (gulf) B4
Marmara (isl.) B2
Marmara (sea) C2
Menderes, Büyük (riv.) C4
Meriç (riv.) B2
Murat (riv.) H3
Pontic (mts.) H2
Porsuk (riv.) D3
Prinkipo (Adalar) (isl.) D6
Sakarya (riv.) D2
Saros (gulf) B2
Seyhan (riv.) F4
Simav (riv.) C3
Sinop (cape) F1
Sultan (mts.) D3
Süphan Daği (mt.) K3
Taurus (mts.) D4
Tigris (Dicle) J4
Troy (Ilium) (ruins) B6
Tuz (lake) E3
Van (lake) K3
Yeşilirmak (riv.) G2

* City and suburbs

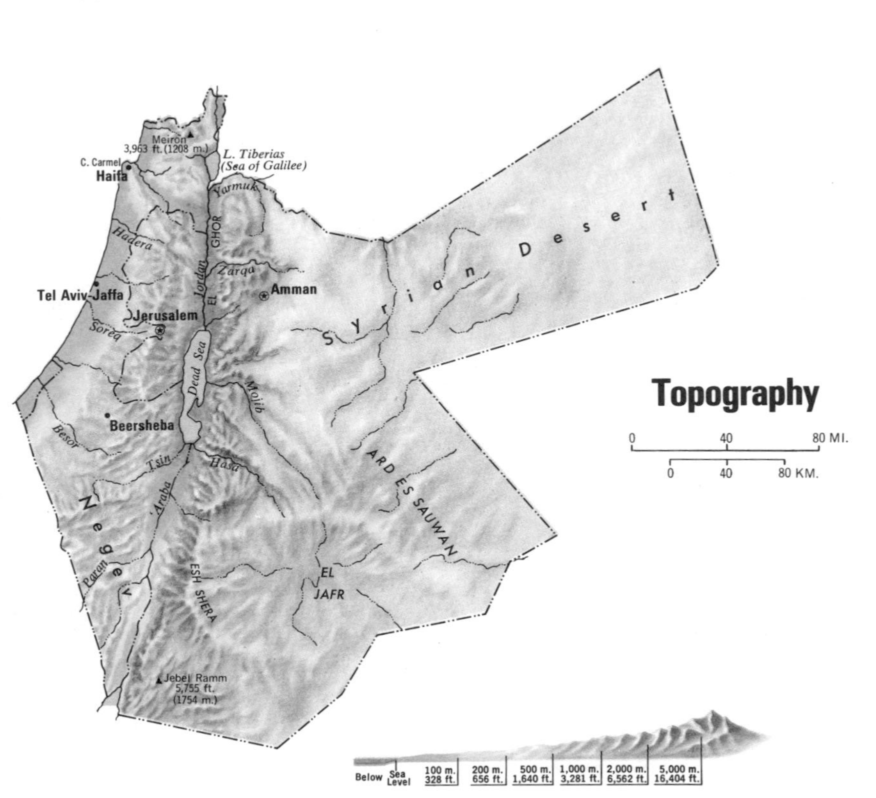

ISRAEL

DISTRICTS

Central 572,300 ..... B3
Haifa 480,800 ..... C2
Jerusalem 338,600 ..... B4
Northern 473,700 ..... C2
Southern 351,300 ..... B5
Tel Aviv 905,100 ..... B3

CITIES and TOWNS

Acre 34,400 ..... C2
Afiqim 1,243 ..... D2
'Afula 17,400 ..... C2
Ahuzzam 407 ..... B4
Akko (Acre) 34,400 ..... C2
Arad 5,400 ..... C5
'Arrabe 6,000 ..... C2
Ashdod 40,500 ..... B4
Ashdot Yaa'qov 1,197 ..... D2
Ashqelon 43,100 ..... A4
Atlit 1,516 ..... B2
Avihayil 579 ..... B3
Bat Shelomo 218 ..... B2
Bat Yam 124,100 ..... B3
Be'eri 390 ..... A5
Be'er Menuha D5
Beersheba (Be'er Sheva) 101,000 ..... B5
Be'er Tuveya 602 ..... B4
Beit Guvrin B4
Bene Beraq 74,100 ..... B3
Bet Qama 228 ..... B5
Bet She'an 11,300 ..... D3
Bet Shemesh 10,100 ..... B4
Binyamina 2,701 ..... B2
Carmiel C2
Dafna 577 ..... D1
Dalyat al-Karmel 6,200 ..... B2
Dan 498 ..... D1
Dimona 23,700 ..... D4
Dor 195 ..... B2
E'in Gedi C5
E'in Harod 1,372 ..... C2
Elat D6
Elath (Elat) 12,800 ..... D6
El 'Auja D5
Elyakim 568 ..... C2
Elyashiv 435 ..... B3
Even Yehuda 3,464 ..... B3
Gal'on 356 ..... B4
Gat 430 ..... B4
Gedera 5,400 ..... B4
Gerofit D5
Gesher 360 ..... C2
Gesher Haziv 238 ..... C1
Gevara'm 283 ..... B4
Gilat 561 ..... B5
Ginnosar 473 ..... D2
Giv'atayim 48,500 ..... B3
Giva't Brenner 1,505 ..... B4
Giv'at Hayyim 1,360 ..... B3
Habonim 189 ..... B2
Hadera 31,900 ..... B3
Haifa 227,800 ..... B2
Haifa* 367,400 ..... B2
Hatseva D5
Hazerim 127 ..... B5
Hazor Hagelilit D2
Helez 466 ..... B4
Herzeliyya 41,200 ..... B3
Hod Hasharon 13,500 ..... B3
Hodiyya 400 ..... B4
Holon 121,200 ..... B3
Iksal 2,156 ..... C2
Jerusalem (cap.) 376,000 ..... C4
Jish 1,498 ..... C1
Kafar Kanna 5,200 ..... C2
Kafr Yasif 2,975 ..... C2
Karkur-Pardes Hanna 13,600 ..... C3
Kefar Blum 565 ..... D1
Kefar Gila'di 701 ..... C1
Kefar Ruppin 306 ..... D3
Kefar Sava 26,500 ..... B3
Kefar Vitkin 808 ..... B3
Kefar Zekhariya 420 ..... B4
Kinneret 909 ..... D2
Lod (Lydda) 30,500 ..... B4
Lydda 30,500 ..... B4
Magen 149 ..... A5
Maa'lot-Tarshiha C1
Malkiya D1
Mash 'Abbe Sade 238 ..... B6
Mavqii'm 177 ..... B4
Megiddo C2
Metula 261 ..... D1
Migdal 688 ..... C2
Migdal Ha E'meq C2
Mikhmoret 608 ..... B3
Mishmar Hanegev 336 ..... B5
Mishmar Hayarden D1
Mivtahim 398 ..... A5
Mizpe Ramon 331 ..... D5
Moza Illit 219 ..... C4
Mughar 4,010 ..... C2
Muqeible 459 ..... C2
Nahariyya 24,000 ..... C1
Nazareth 33,300 ..... C2
Nazerat I'llit C2
Negba 453 ..... B4
Nes Ziyyona 11,700 ..... B4
Netanya 70,700 ..... B3
Netivot B5
Nevatim 436 ..... B5
Newe Yam 211 ..... B2
Newe Zohar C5
Nir Yitzhaq 209 ..... A5
Nizzanim 479 ..... B4
Ofaqim B5
O'mer B5
Oron C6
Or Yehuda B4
Pardes Hanna-Karkur 13,600 ..... B2
Peduyim 361 ..... B5
Petah Tiqwa 112,000 ..... B3
Qadima 2,937 ..... B3
Qalansuwa B3
Qedma 157 ..... B4
Qiryat Atta C2
Qiryat Bialik 18,000 ..... C2
Qiryat Gat 19,200 ..... B4
Qiryat Mal'akhi B4
Qiryat Motzkin 17,600 ..... C2
Qiryat Shemona 15,200 ..... C1
Qiryat Tivo'n 9,800 ..... C2
Qiryat Yam 19,800 ..... C2
Raa'nana 14,900 ..... B3
Ramat Gan 120,900 ..... B3
Ramat Hasharon 20,100 ..... B3
Rame 2,986 ..... C2
Ramla 34,100 ..... B4
Rehovot 39,200 ..... B4
Rei'm 155 ..... A5
Revadim 175 ..... B4
Revivim 258 ..... D5
Rishon Le Ziyyon 51,900 ..... B4
Rosh Ha 'Ayin B3
Rosh Pinna 700 ..... D2
Ruhama 497 ..... B4
Saa'd 418 ..... B5
Safad (Zefat) 13,600 ..... C2
Sakhnin 8,400 ..... C2
Sede Boqer D5
Sederot B4
Sedom D5
Sedot Yam 511 ..... B3
Shave Ziyyon 269 ..... B2
Shefara'm 11,800 ..... C2
Shefayim 614 ..... B3
Shoval 393 ..... B5
Tayibe 11,700 ..... C3
Tel Aviv-Jaffa 343,300 ..... B3
Tel Aviv-Jaffa* 1,219,900 ..... B3
Tiberias 23,800 ..... C2
Tirat Hakarmel 14,400 ..... B2
Tirat Zevi 353 ..... D3
Tur'an 2,304 ..... C2
Umm el Fahm 13,300 ..... C2
Urim 203 ..... B5
Uzza 487 ..... B4
Yad Mordekhai 416 ..... A4
Yagur 1,266 ..... C2
Yahav D5
Yavne 10,100 ..... B4
Yavne'el 1,580 ..... D2
Yehud 8,900 ..... B3
Yeroham 5,800 ..... B6
Yesodot 293 ..... B4
Yesud Hamaa'la 428 ..... D1
Yiftah D1
Yirka 2,715 ..... C2
Yotvata D5
Zavdi'el 396 ..... B4
Ze'elim 148 ..... A5
Zefat 13,600 ..... C2
Zikhron Yaa'qov 6,500 ..... B2
Zippori 241 ..... C2

OTHER FEATURES

Aqaba (gulf) D6
'Araba, Wadi (valley) D5
Beer Sheva' (dry riv.) B5
Besor (riv.) B5
Carmel (cape) B2
Carmel (mt.) C2
Dead (sea) C4
Galilee, Sea of (Tiberias) (lake) D2
Galilee (reg.) C2
Gerar (dry riv.) B5
Hadera (dry riv.) B3
Haniqra, Rosh (cape) C1
Jordan (riv.) D3
Judaea (reg.) B5
Lakhish (dry riv.) B4
Meiron (mt.) C1
Negev (reg.) D5

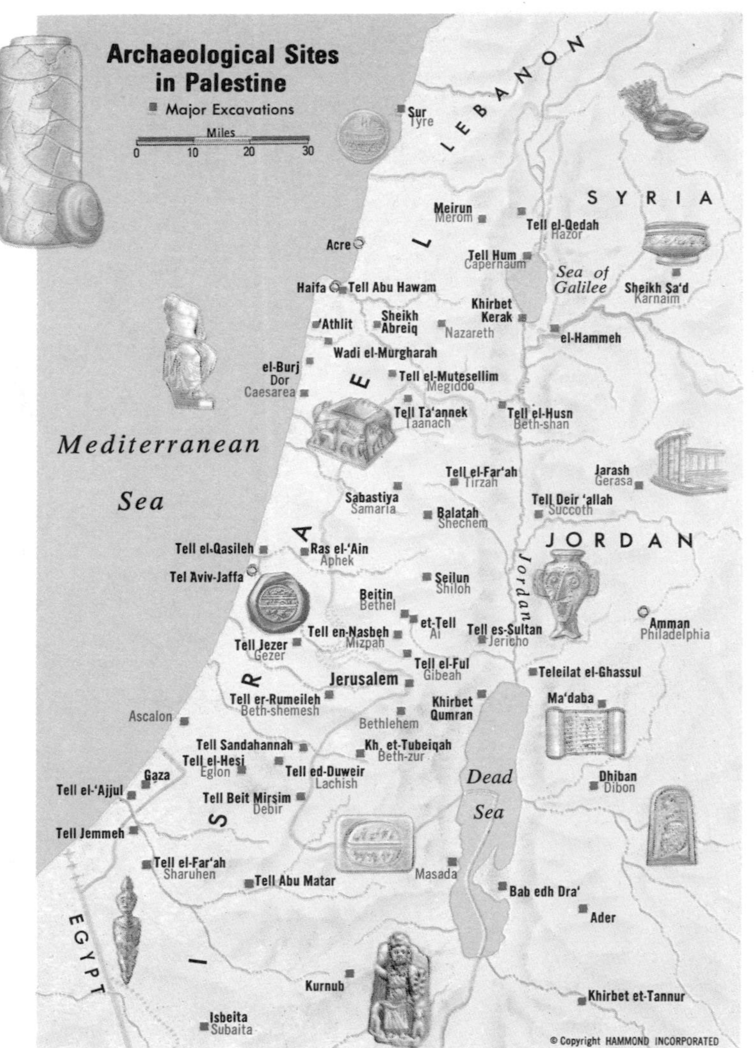

Agriculture, Industry and Resources

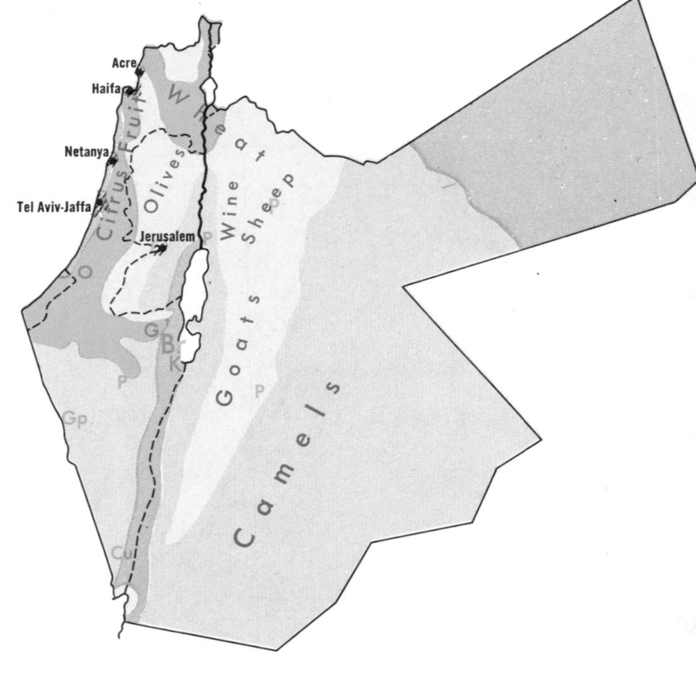

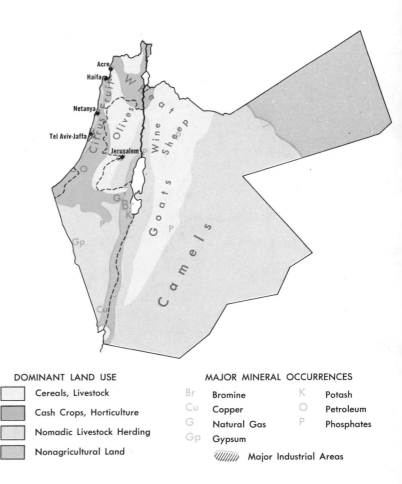

DOMINANT LAND USE

- Cereals, Livestock
- Cash Crops, Horticulture
- Nomadic Livestock Herding
- Nonagricultural Land

MAJOR MINERAL OCCURRENCES

- Br Bromine
- Cu Copper
- G Natural Gas
- Gp Gypsum
- K Potash
- O Petroleum
- P Phosphates

Major Industrial Areas

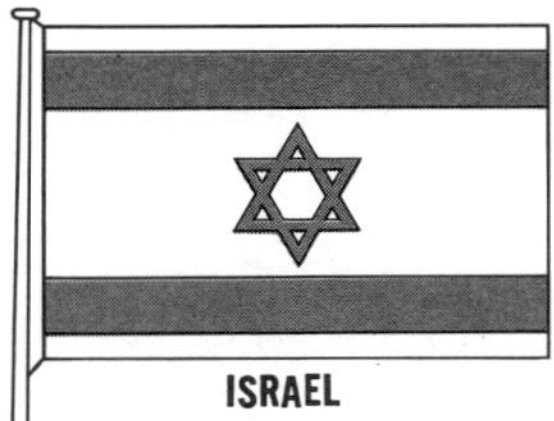

ISRAEL

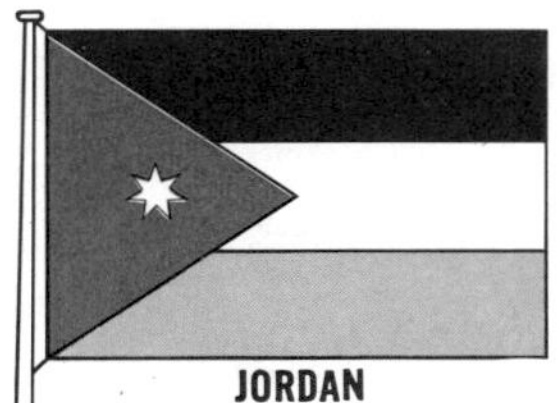

JORDAN

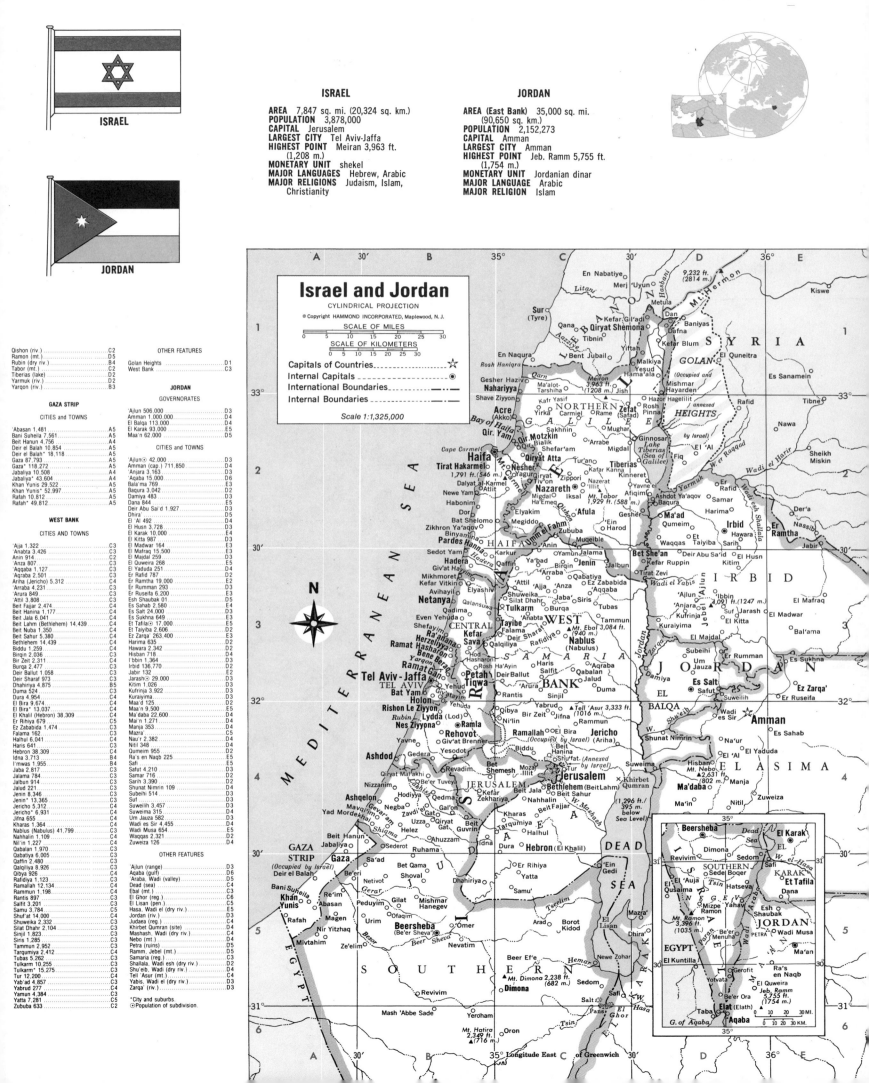

ISRAEL

AREA 7,847 sq. mi. (20,324 sq. km.)
POPULATION 3,878,000
CAPITAL Jerusalem
LARGEST CITY Tel Aviv-Jaffa
HIGHEST POINT Meiran 3,963 ft. (1,208 m.)
MONETARY UNIT shekel
MAJOR LANGUAGES Hebrew, Arabic
MAJOR RELIGIONS Judaism, Islam, Christianity

JORDAN

AREA (East Bank) 35,000 sq. mi. (90,650 sq. km.)
POPULATION 2,152,273
CAPITAL Amman
LARGEST CITY Amman
HIGHEST POINT Jeb. Ramm 5,755 ft. (1,754 m.)
MONETARY UNIT Jordanian dinar
MAJOR LANGUAGE Arabic
MAJOR RELIGION Islam

Qishon (riv.) C2
Ramon (mt.) D5
Rubin (dry riv.) B4
Tabor (mt.) C2
Tiberias (lake) D2
Yarmuk (riv.) D2
Yarqon (riv.) B3

GAZA STRIP

CITIES and TOWNS

'Abasan 1,481 ..... A5
Bani Suheila 7,561 ..... A5
Beit Hanun 4,756 ..... A4
Deir el Balah 10,854 ..... A5
Deir el Balah* 18,118 ..... A5
Gaza 87,793 ..... A5
Gaza* 118,272 ..... A5
Jabaliya 10,508 ..... A4
Jabaliya* 43,604 ..... A4
Khan Yunis 29,522 ..... A5
Khan Yunis* 52,997 ..... A5
Rafah 10,812 ..... A5
Rafah* 49,812 ..... A5

WEST BANK

CITIES AND TOWNS

'Ajja 1,322 ..... C3
'Anabta 3,426 ..... C3
Anin 914 ..... C2
'Anza 807 ..... C3
'Aqqaba 1,127 ..... C3
'Aqraba 2,501 ..... C3
Ariha (Jericho) 5,312 ..... C4
'Arraba 4,231 ..... C3
'Arura 849 ..... C3
'Attil 3,808 ..... C3
Beit Fajjar 2,474 ..... C4
Beit Hanina 1,177 ..... C4
Beit Jala 6,041 ..... C4
Beit Lahm (Bethlehem) 14,439 ..... C4
Beit Nuba 1,350 ..... C4
Beit Sahur 5,380 ..... C4
Bethlehem 14,439 ..... C4
Biddu 1,259 ..... C4
Birqin 2,036 ..... C3
Bir Zeit 2,311 ..... C4
Burqa 2,477 ..... C3
Deir Ballut 1,058 ..... C3
Deir Sharaf 973 ..... C3
Dhahiriya 4,875 ..... B5
Duma 524 ..... C3
Dura 4,954 ..... C4
El Bira 9,674 ..... C4
El Bira* 13,037 ..... C4
El Khalil (Hebron) 38,309 ..... C4
Er Rihiya 679 ..... C5
Ez Zababida 1,474 ..... C3
Falama 162 ..... C3
Halhul 6,041 ..... C4
Haris 641 ..... C3
Hebron 38,309 ..... C4
Idna 3,713 ..... B4
I'mwas 1,955 ..... B4
Jaba 2,817 ..... C3
Jalama 784 ..... C3
Jalbun 914 ..... C3
Jalud 221 ..... C3
Jenin 8,346 ..... C3
Jenin* 13,365 ..... C3
Jericho 5,312 ..... C4
Jericho* 6,931 ..... C4
Jifna 655 ..... C4
Kharas 1,364 ..... C4
Nablus (Nabulus) 41,799 ..... C3
Nahhalin 1,109 ..... C4
Nil'in 1,227 ..... C4
Qabalan 1,970 ..... C3
Qabatiya 6,005 ..... C3
Qaffin 2,480 ..... C3
Qalqiliya 8,926 ..... C3
Qibya 926 ..... C4
Rafidiya 1,123 ..... C3
Ramallah 12,134 ..... C4
Rammun 1,198 ..... C4
Rantis 897 ..... C3
Salfit 3,201 ..... C3
Samu 3,784 ..... C5
Shuf'at 14,000 ..... C4
Shuweika 2,332 ..... C3
Silat Dhahr 2,104 ..... C3
Sinjil 1,823 ..... C3
Siris 1,285 ..... C3
Tammun 2,952 ..... C3
Tarqumiya 2,412 ..... C4
Tubas 5,262 ..... C3
Tulkarm 10,255 ..... C3
Tulkarm* 15,275 ..... C3
Tur 12,200 ..... C4
Yab'ad 4,857 ..... C3
Yabrud 277 ..... C4
Yamun 4,384 ..... C3
Yatta 7,281 ..... C5
Zububa 633 ..... C2

OTHER FEATURES

Golan Heights D1
West Bank C3

JORDAN

GOVERNORATES

'Ajlun 506,000 ..... D3
Amman 1,000,000 ..... D4
El Balqa 113,000 ..... D4
El Karak 93,000 ..... E5
Maa'n 62,000 ..... D5

CITIES and TOWNS

'Ajlun⊙ 42,000 ..... D3
Amman (cap.) 711,850 ..... D4
'Anjara 3,163 ..... D3
'Aqaba 15,000 ..... D6
Bala'ma 769 ..... E3
Baqura 3,042 ..... D2
Damiya 483 ..... D3
Dana 844 ..... E5
Deir Abu Sai'd 1,927 ..... D3
Dhira' D5
El 'Al 492 ..... D4
El Husn 3,728 ..... D3
El Karak 10,000 ..... E4
El Kitta 987 ..... D3
El Madwar 164 ..... E3
El Mafraq 15,500 ..... E3
El Majdal 259 ..... D3
El Quweira 268 ..... E5
El Yaduda 251 ..... D4
Er Rafid 787 ..... D2
Er Ramtha 19,000 ..... E2
Er Rumman 293 ..... D3
Er Ruseifa 6,200 ..... E3
Esh Shaubak 01 ..... D5
Es Sahab 2,580 ..... E4
Es Salt 24,000 ..... D3
Es Sukhna 649 ..... E3
Et Tafila⊙ 17,000 ..... E5
Et Taiyiba 2,606 ..... D2
Ez Zarqa' 263,400 ..... E3
Harima 635 ..... D2
Hawara 2,342 ..... D2
Hisban 718 ..... D4
I'bbin 1,364 ..... D3
Irbid 136,770 ..... D2
Jabir 132 ..... E2
Jarash⊙ 29,000 ..... D3
Kitim 1,026 ..... D3
Kufrinja 3,922 ..... D3
Kuraiyima D3
Maa'd 125 ..... D2
Maa'n 9,500 ..... E5
Ma'daba 22,600 ..... D4
Mai'n 1,271 ..... D4
Manja 353 ..... D4
Mazra' C5
Nau'r 2,382 ..... D4
Nitil 348 ..... D4
Qumeim 955 ..... D2
Ra's en Naqb 225 ..... E5
Safi E5
Safut 4,210 ..... D3
Samar 716 ..... D2
Sarih 3,390 ..... D2
Shunat Nimrin 109 ..... D4
Subeihi 514 ..... D3
Suf D3
Suweilih 3,457 ..... D3
Suweima 315 ..... D4
Um Jauza 582 ..... D3
Wadi es Sir 4,455 ..... D4
Wadi Musa 654 ..... E5
Waqqas 2,321 ..... D2
Zuweiza 126 ..... D4

OTHER FEATURES

'Ajlun (range) D3
Aqaba (gulf) D6
'Araba, Wadi (valley) D5
Dead (sea) C4
Ebal (mt.) C3
El Ghor (reg.) C6
El Lisan (pen.) C5
Hasa, Wadi el (dry riv.) E5
Jordan (riv.) D3
Judaea (reg.) C4
Khirbet Qumran (site) D4
Mashash, Wadi (dry riv.) C4
Nebo (mt.) D4
Petra (ruins) D5
Ramm, Jebel (mt.) D5
Samaria (reg.) C3
Shallala, Wadi esh (dry riv.) D2
Shu'eib, Wadi (dry riv.) D4
Tell 'Asur (mt.) C4
Yabis, Wadi el (dry riv.) D3
Zarqa' (riv.) D3

*City and suburbs.
⊙Population of subdivision.

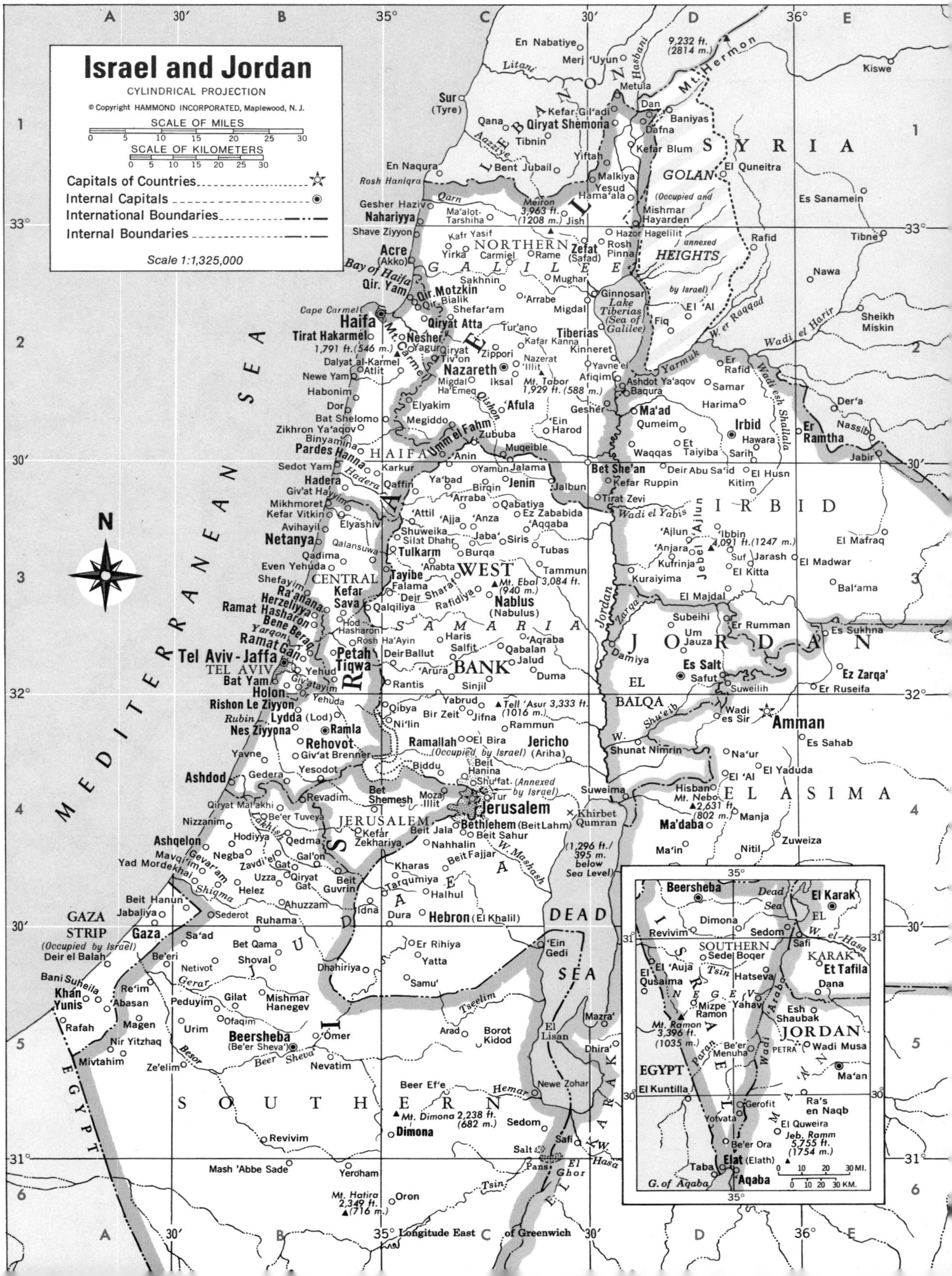

Israel and Jordan

CYLINDRICAL PROJECTION

SCALE OF MILES
SCALE OF KILOMETERS

Capitals of Countries
Internal Capitals
International Boundaries
Internal Boundaries

Scale 1:1,325,000

IRAN

INTERNAL DIVISIONS

Azerbaijan, East (prov.) 3,194,543 ..... E1
Azerbaijan, West (prov.) 1,404,875 ..... D1
Bakhtiari (governorate) 394,300 ..... F4
Boyer Ahmediyeh and Kohkiluyeh (governor 244,750 ..... G5
Bushehr (prov.) 345,427 ..... G6
Central (Markazi) (prov.) 6,921,283 ..... G3
Esfahan (Isfahan) (prov.) 1,974,938 ..... H4
Fars (prov.) 2,020,947 ..... H6
Gilan (prov.) 1,577,800 ..... F2
Hamadan (governorate) 1,086,512 ..... F3
Hormozgan (prov.) 463,419 ..... J7
Ilam (governorate) 244,222 ..... E4
Isfahan (prov.) 1,974,938 ..... H4
Kerman (prov.) 1,088,045 ..... K6
Kermanshahan (prov.) 1,016,199 ..... E3
Khorasan (prov.) 3,266,650 ..... K3
Khuzestan (prov.) 2,176,612 ..... F5
Kordestan (Kurdistan) (prov.) 781,889 ..... E3
Lorestan (Luristan) (governorate) 924,848 ..... F4
Mazandaran (prov.) 2,384,226 ..... H2
Semnan (governorate) 485,875 ..... J3
Sistan and Baluchestan (prov.) 659,297 ..... M6
Yazd (governorate) 356,218 ..... J5
Zanjan (governorate) 579,000 ..... F2

CITIES and TOWNS

Abadan 296,081 ..... F5
Abadeh 16,000 ..... H5
Abarqu 8,000 ..... H5
Abhar 24,000 ..... F2
Agha Jari 24,195 ..... F5
Ahar 24,000 ..... E1
Ahvaz (Ahwaz) 329,006 ..... F5
Amol 68,782 ..... H2
Anarak 2,038 ..... H4
Andimeshk 16,000 ..... F4
Aradan 8,978 ..... H3
Arak 114,507 ..... F3
Ardabil 147,404 ..... F1
Ardestan 5,868 ..... H4
Asadabad 7,000 ..... F3
Asterabad (Gorgan) 88,348 ..... J2
Azaran 3,153 ..... E2
Babol 67,790 ..... H2
Babol Sar 7,237 ..... H2
Bafq 5,000 ..... J5
Baft 6,000 ..... K6
Bajgiran 1,151 ..... L2
Bam 22,000 ..... L6
Bampur 1,585 ..... M7
Bandar A'bbas 89,103 ..... J7
Bandar-e Anzali (Enzeli) 55,978 ..... F2
Bandar-e Deylam 3,691 ..... G5
Bandar Khomeyni 6,000 ..... F5
Bandar-e Lengeh 4,920 ..... J7
Bandar-e Mas'hur 17,000 ..... F5
Bandar-e Rig 1,889 ..... G6
Bandar-e Torkeman 13,000 ..... H2
Bandar Shahpur 6,000 ..... F5
Bastak 2,473 ..... J7
Bastam 3,296 ..... J2
Behbehan 39,874 ..... G5
Behshahr 26,032 ..... H2
Bejestan 3,823 ..... K3
Bijar 12,000 ..... E3
Birjand 25,854 ..... L4
Bojnurd 31,248 ..... K2
Borazjan 20,000 ..... G6
Borujerd 100,103 ..... F4
Bostan 4,619 ..... F5
Bowkan 9,000 ..... E2
Bushehr (Bushire) 57,681 ..... G6
Chah Bahar 1,800 ..... M8
Chalus 15,000 ..... G2
Damavand 5,319 ..... H3
Damghan 13,000 ..... J2
Darab 13,000 ..... J6
Daran 4,609 ..... G4
Darreh Gaz 11,000 ..... L2
Dasht-e-Azadegan 21,000 ..... F5
Dehkhvareqan 6,000 ..... D2
Delijan 6,000 ..... G4
Dezful 110,287 ..... F4
Dizful (Dezful) 110,287 ..... F4
Duzdab (Zahedan) 92,628 ..... M6
Emamshahr 30,767 ..... J2
Enzeli 55,978 ..... F2
Esfahan (Isfahan) 671,820 ..... G4
Elamabad 12,000 ..... E3
Estahbanat 18,187 ..... J6
Evaz 6,064 ..... J7
Ezna 5,000 ..... F4
Fahrej (Iranshahr) 5,000 ..... M7
Fariman 8,000 ..... L3
Farrashband 3,532 ..... G6
Fasa 19,000 ..... H6
Ferdows 11,000 ..... K3
Firuzabad 8,718 ..... H6
Firuzkuh 4,684 ..... H3
Fowman 9,000 ..... F2
Gach Saran G5
Ganaveh 9,000 ..... G6
Garmsar 4,723 ..... H3
Gavater M8
Ghaemshahr 63,289 ..... H2
Golpayegan 20,515 ..... G4
Golshan (Tabas) 10,000 ..... K4
Gomishan 6,000 ..... J2
Gonabad 8,000 ..... L3
Gonbad-e Kavus 59,868 ..... J2
Gonbadli 531 ..... M2
Gorgan (Gurgan) 88,348 ..... J2
Haft Gel 10,000 ..... F5
Hamadan 155,846 ..... F3
Hashtpar 5,000 ..... F2
Hormoz 2,569 ..... J7
Huzgan 4,722 ..... F5
Ilam 15,000 ..... E4
Iranshahr 5,000 ..... M7
Isfahan 671,825 ..... G4
Izeh 1,983 ..... F5
Jahrom 38,236 ..... H6
Jajarm 3,641 ..... K2
Jask 1,078 ..... K8
Kakhk 4,043 ..... L3
Kangan 2,682 ..... G7
Kangavar 9,414 ..... F3
Karaj 138,774 ..... G3
Kashan 84,545 ..... G3
Kashmar 17,000 ..... L3
Kazerun 51,309 ..... G6
Kazvin (Qazvin) 138,527 ..... F2
Kerman 140,309 ..... K5
Kermanshah 290,861 ..... E3
Khaf 5,000 ..... L3
Khalkhal 5,422 ..... F2
Khash 7,439 ..... M6
Khiyav 9,000 ..... E1
Khoman 3,054 ..... F2
Khomeinishar 46,836 ..... G4
Khorramabad 104,928 ..... F4
Khorramshahr 146,709 ..... F5
Khvaf 5,000 ..... L3
Khvonsar 10,947 ..... F4
Khvor 2,912 ..... J4
Khvoy (Khoi) 70,040 ..... D1
Kord Kuy 9,855 ..... J2
Lahijan 25,725 ..... G2
Lar 22,000 ..... J7
Mahabad 28,610 ..... D2
Mahallat 12,000 ..... G4
Mahan 8,000 ..... K5
Maku 7,000 ..... D1
Malamir (Izeh) 1,983 ..... F5
Malayer 28,434 ..... F3
Maragheh 60,820 ..... E2
Marand 24,000 ..... D1
Marv Dasht 25,498 ..... H6
Mashhad (Meshed) 670,180 ..... L2
Masjed Soleyman 77,161 ..... F5
Medishahr 9,000 ..... H3
Mehran 664 ..... E4
Meshed 670,180 ..... L2
Meshed-i-Sar (Babol Sar) 12,000 ..... H2
Meybod 15,000 ..... J4
Miandowab 19,000 ..... E2
Mianeh 28,447 ..... E2
Minab 4,228 ..... K7
Mirjaveh 11,000 ..... M6
Naft-e Shah 3,043 ..... D4
Nahavand 24,000 ..... F3
Na'in 5,925 ..... H4
Najafabad 76,236 ..... G4
Naraq 2,725 ..... G3
Nasratabad (Zabol) 20,000 ..... M5
Natanz 4,370 ..... H4
Neyriz 16,114 ..... J6
Neyshabur 59,101 ..... L2
Nishapur (Neyshabur) 59,101 ..... L2
Nosratabad 20,000 ..... L6
Now Shahr 8,000 ..... G2
Orumiyeh (Urmia) 163,991 ..... D2
Oshnoviyeh 5,000 ..... D2
Pahlevi (Enzeli) 55,978 ..... F2
Pazanan 81 ..... F5
Qasr-e-Shirin 15,094 ..... E3
Qayen 6,000 ..... L4
Qazvin 138,527 ..... F2
Qom 246,831 ..... G3
Qorveh 2,929 ..... E3
Quchan 29,133 ..... L2
Qum (Qom) 246,831 ..... G3
Rafsanjan 21,000 ..... K5
Ramhormoz 9,000 ..... F5
Rasht 187,203 ..... F2
Ravar 5,074 ..... K5
Resht (Rasht) 187,203 ..... F2
Rey 102,825 ..... G3
Reza'iyeh (Urmia) 163,991 ..... D2
Rigan 8,255 ..... L6
Rud Sar 7,460 ..... G2
Sabzevar 69,174 ..... K2
Sabzvaran 7,000 ..... K6
Saeendey 4,195 ..... E2
Sai'dabad 20,000 ..... J6
Sakht-Sar 12,000 ..... G2
Salmas 13,161 ..... D1
Sanandaj 95,834 ..... E3
Saqqez 17,000 ..... E2
Sarab 16,000 ..... E2
Sarakhs 3,461 ..... M2
Saravan 4,012 ..... N7
Sar Dasht 6,000 ..... D2
Sari 70,936 ..... H2
Savanat (Estahbanat) 18,187 ..... J6
Saveh 17,565 ..... G3
Semnan 31,058 ..... H3
Shadegan 6,000 ..... F5
Shahdad 2,777 ..... K5
Shahistan (Saravan) 4,012 ..... N7
Shahreza 34,220 ..... H4
Shahr Kord 24,000 ..... G4
Shahrud (Emamshahr) 30,767 ..... J2
Sharafkhaneh 1,260 ..... D1
Shiraz 416,408 ..... H6
Shirvan 11,000 ..... K2
Shush 1,433 ..... F4
Shushtar 24,000 ..... F4
Sinneh (Sanandaj) 95,834 ..... E3
Sirjan (Sai'dabad) 20,000 ..... J6
Sivand 1,811 ..... H5
Sonqor 10,433 ..... E3
Sufian 2,914 ..... E1
Sultanabad (Kashmar) 17,000 ..... L3
Tabas 10,000 ..... K4
Tabriz 598,576 ..... D2
Taft 7,000 ..... J5
Tajrish 157,486 ..... G3
Takestan 13,485 ..... F2
Tehran (cap.) 4,496,159 ..... G3
Tonekabon 12,000 ..... G2
Torbat-e-Heydariyeh 30,106 ..... L3
Torbat-e Jam 13,000 ..... M3
Tun (Ferdows) 11,000 ..... K3
Turbat-i-Shaikh Jam 13,000 ..... M3
Tuysarkan 12,000 ..... F3
Urmia 163,991 ..... D2
Varamin 11,183 ..... G3
Yazd (Yezd) 135,978 ..... J5
Yazd-e Khvasat 3,544 ..... H5
Zabol 20,000 ..... M5
Zahedan 92,628 ..... M6
Zanjan 99,967 ..... K5
Zarand 5,000 ..... H6
Zarqam 7,000 ..... H6
Zenjan (Zanjan) 99,967 ..... F2

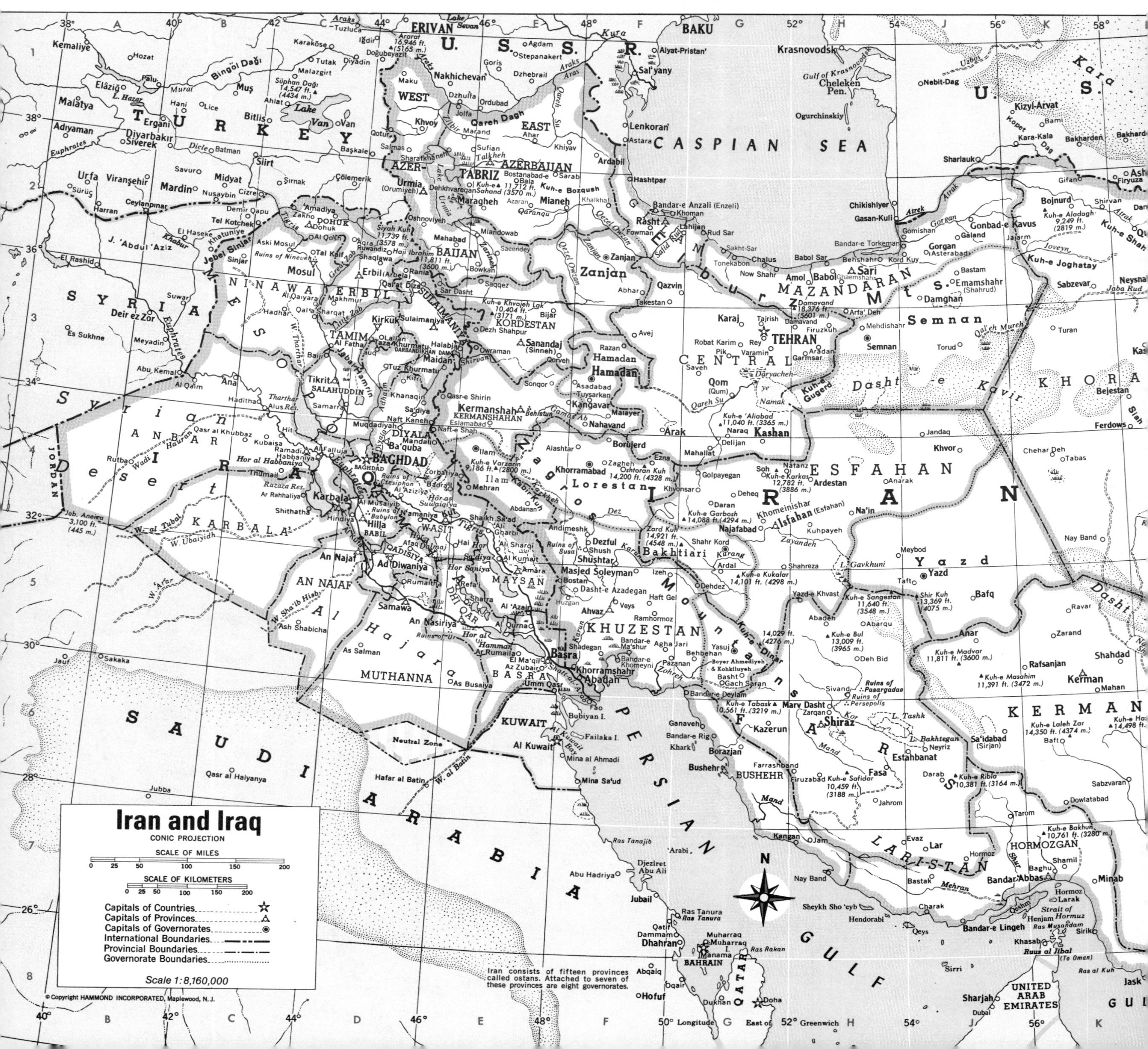

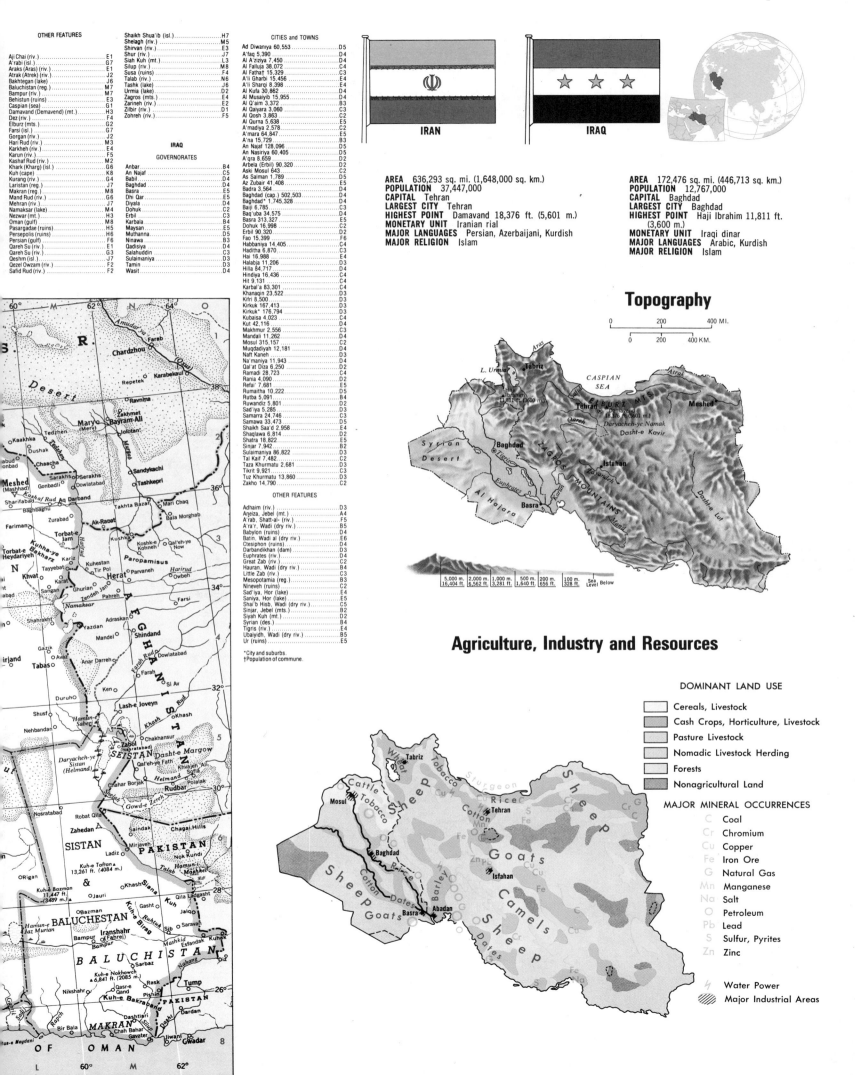

OTHER FEATURES

Aji Chai (riv.) E1
A'rabi (isl.) G7
Araks (Aras) (riv.) E1
Atrak (Atrek) (riv.) J2
Bakhtegan (lake) J6
Baluchistan (reg.) M7
Bampur (riv.) M7
Behistun (ruins) E3
Caspian (sea) G1
Damavand (Demavend) (mt.) H3
Dez (riv.) F4
Elburz (mts.) G2
Farsi (isl.) G7
Gorgan (riv.) J2
Hari Rud (riv.) M3
Karkheh (riv.) E4
Karun (riv.) F5
Kashaf Rud (riv.) M2
Khark (Kharg) (isl.) G6
Kuh (cape) K8
Kurang (riv.) G4
Laristan (reg.) J7
Makran (reg.) M8
Mand Rud (riv.) G6
Mehran (riv.) J7
Namaksar (lake) M4
Nezwar (mt.) H3
Oman (gulf) M8
Pasargadae (ruins) H5
Persepolis (ruins) H6
Persian (gulf) F6
Qareh Su (riv.) E1
Qareh Su (riv.) G3
Qeshm (isl.) J7
Qezel Owzam (riv.) F2
Safid Rud (riv.) F2
Shaikh Shua'ib (isl.) H7
Shelagh (riv.) M5
Shirvan (riv.) E3
Shur (riv.) J7
Siah Kuh (mt.) L3
Silup (riv.) M8
Susa (ruins) F4
Talab (riv.) N6
Tashk (lake) J6
Urmia (lake) D2
Zagros (mts.) E4
Zarineh (riv.) E2
Zilbir (riv.) D1
Zohreh (riv.) F5

IRAQ

GOVERNORATES

Anbar B4
An Najaf C5
Babil D4
Baghdad D4
Basra E5
Dhi Qar E5
Diyala D4
Dohuk C2
Erbil C3
Karbala B4
Maysan E5
Muthanna D5
Ninawa B3
Qadisiya D4
Salahuddin C3
Sulaimaniya D3
Tamin D3
Wasit D4

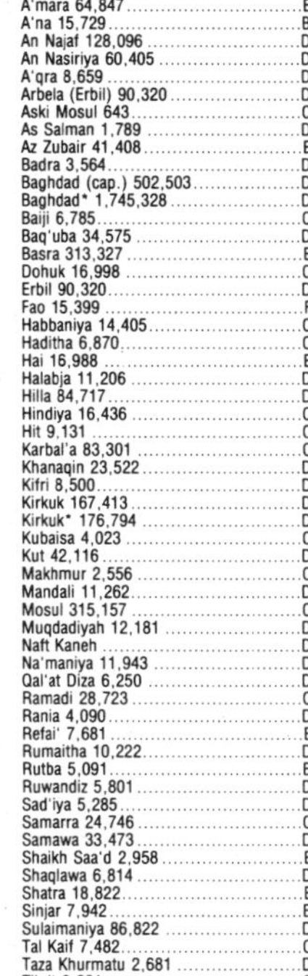

CITIES and TOWNS

Ad Diwaniya 60,553 .... D5
A'faq 5,390 .... D4
Al A'ziziya 7,450 .... D4
Al Falluja 38,072 .... C4
Al Fatha† 15,329 .... C3
A'li Gharbi 15,456 .... E4
A'li Sharqi 8,398 .... E4
Al Kufa 30,862 .... D4
Al Musaiyib 15,955 .... D4
Al Q'aim 3,372 .... B3
Al Qaiyara 3,060 .... C3
Al Qosh 3,863 .... C2
Al Qurna 5,638 .... E5
A'madiya 2,578 .... C2
A'mara 64,847 .... E5
A'na 15,729 .... B3
An Najaf 128,096 .... D5
An Nasiriya 60,405 .... D5
A'qra 8,659 .... D2
Arbela (Erbil) 90,320 .... D2
Aski Mosul 643 .... C2
As Salman 1,789 .... D5
Az Zubair 41,408 .... E5
Badra 3,564 .... D4
Baghdad (cap.) 502,503 .... D4
Baghdad* 1,745,328 .... D4
Baiji 6,785 .... C3
Baq'uba 34,575 .... D4
Basra 313,327 .... E5
Dohuk 16,998 .... C2
Erbil 90,320 .... D2
Fao 15,399 .... F6
Habbaniya 14,405 .... C4
Haditha 6,870 .... C3
Hai 16,988 .... E4
Halabja 11,206 .... D3
Hilla 84,717 .... D4
Hindiya 16,436 .... C4
Hit 9,131 .... C4
Karbal'a 83,301 .... C4
Khanaqin 23,522 .... D3
Kifri 8,500 .... D3
Kirkuk 167,413 .... D3
Kirkuk* 176,794 .... D3
Kubaisa 4,023 .... C4
Kut 42,116 .... D4
Makhmur 2,556 .... C3
Mandali 11,262 .... D4
Mosul 315,157 .... C2
Muqdadiyah 12,181 .... D4
Naft Kaneh D3
Na'maniya 11,943 .... D4
Qal'at Diza 6,250 .... D2
Ramadi 28,723 .... C4
Rania 4,090 .... D2
Refai' 7,681 .... E5
Rumaitha 10,222 .... D5
Rutba 5,091 .... B4
Ruwandiz 5,801 .... D2
Sad'iya 5,285 .... D3
Samarra 24,746 .... C3
Samawa 33,473 .... D5
Shaikh Saa'd 2,958 .... E4
Shaqlawa 6,814 .... D2
Shatra 18,822 .... E5
Sinjar 7,942 .... B2
Sulaimaniya 86,822 .... D3
Tal Kaif 7,482 .... C2
Taza Khurmatu 2,681 .... D3
Tikrit 9,921 .... C3
Tuz Khurmatu 13,860 .... D3
Zakho 14,790 .... C2

OTHER FEATURES

Adhaim (riv.) D3
Aneiza, Jebel (mt.) A4
A'rab, Shatt-al- (riv.) F5
A'ra'r, Wadi (dry riv.) B5
Babylon (ruins) D4
Batin, Wadi al (dry riv.) E6
Ctesiphon (ruins) D4
Darbandikhan (dam) D3
Euphrates (riv.) D4
Great Zab (riv.) C2
Hauran, Wadi (dry riv.) B4
Little Zab (riv.) C3
Mesopotamia (reg.) B3
Nineveh (ruins) C2
Sad'iya, Hor (lake) E4
Saniya, Hor (lake) E5
Shai'b Hisb, Wadi (dry riv.) C5
Sinjar, Jebel (mts.) B2
Siyah Kuh (mt.) D2
Syrian (des.) B4
Tigris (riv.) E4
Ubaiyidh, Wadi (dry riv.) B5
Ur (ruins) E5

*City and suburbs.
†Population of commune.

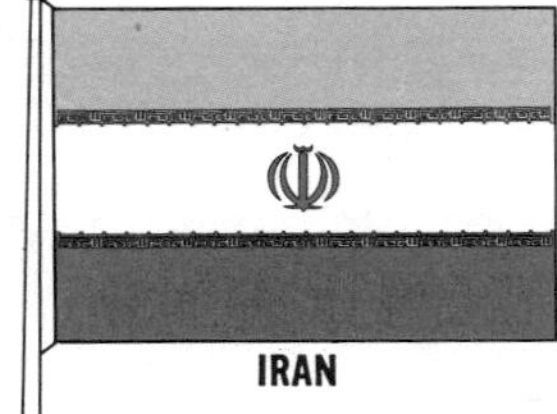

IRAN

IRAQ

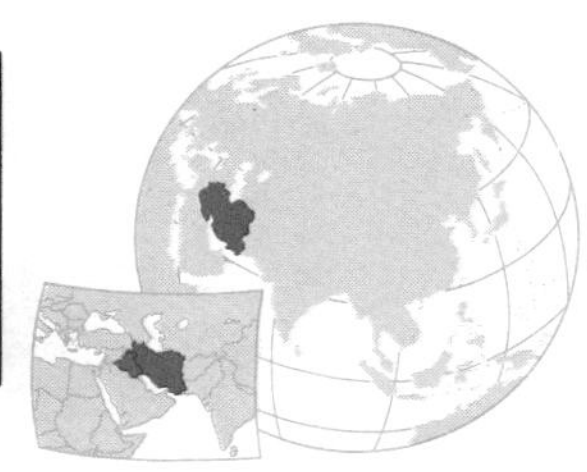

AREA 636,293 sq. mi. (1,648,000 sq. km.)
POPULATION 37,447,000
CAPITAL Tehran
LARGEST CITY Tehran
HIGHEST POINT Damavand 18,376 ft. (5,601 m.)
MONETARY UNIT Iranian rial
MAJOR LANGUAGES Persian, Azerbaijani, Kurdish
MAJOR RELIGION Islam

AREA 172,476 sq. mi. (446,713 sq. km.)
POPULATION 12,767,000
CAPITAL Baghdad
LARGEST CITY Baghdad
HIGHEST POINT Haji Ibrahim 11,811 ft. (3,600 m.)
MONETARY UNIT Iraqi dinar
MAJOR LANGUAGES Arabic, Kurdish
MAJOR RELIGION Islam

Topography

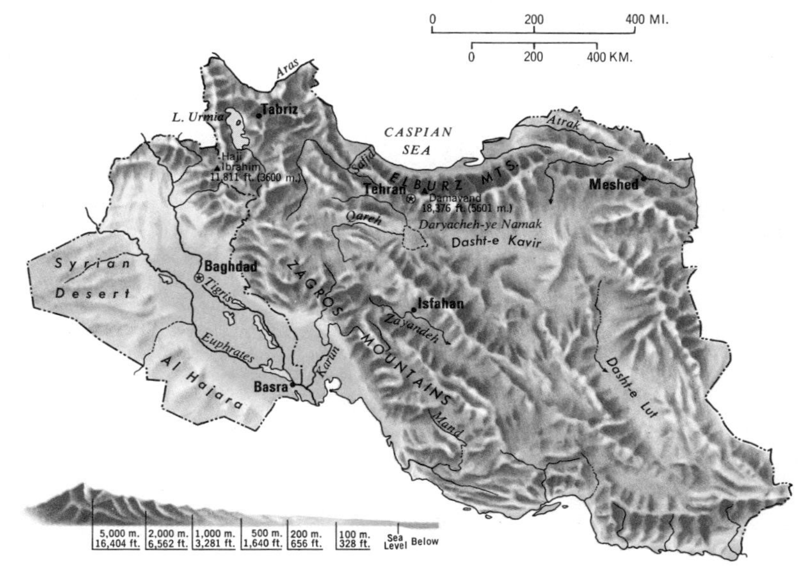

Agriculture, Industry and Resources

DOMINANT LAND USE

- Cereals, Livestock
- Cash Crops, Horticulture, Livestock
- Pasture Livestock
- Nomadic Livestock Herding
- Forests
- Nonagricultural Land

MAJOR MINERAL OCCURRENCES

- C Coal
- Cr Chromium
- Cu Copper
- Fe Iron Ore
- G Natural Gas
- Mn Manganese
- Na Salt
- O Petroleum
- Pb Lead
- S Sulfur, Pyrites
- Zn Zinc

- Water Power
- Major Industrial Areas

Tabriz, Mosul, Tehran, Baghdad, Isfahan, Basra, Abadan, Wheat, Tobacco, Sturgeon, Rice, Cotton, Cattle, Sheep, Goats, Camels, Barley, Dates

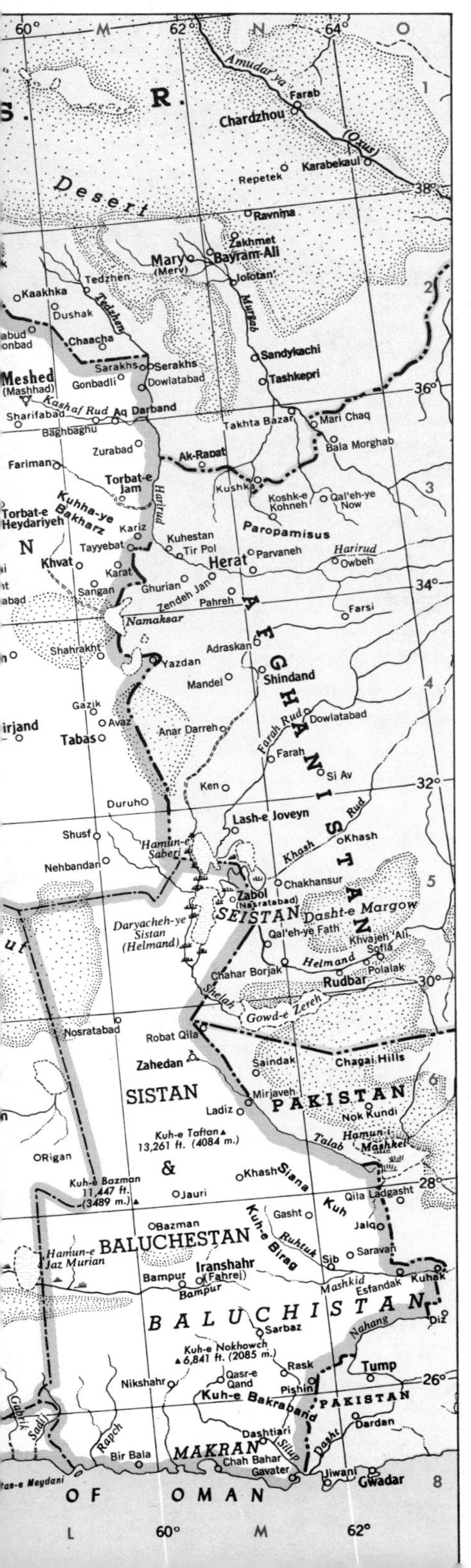

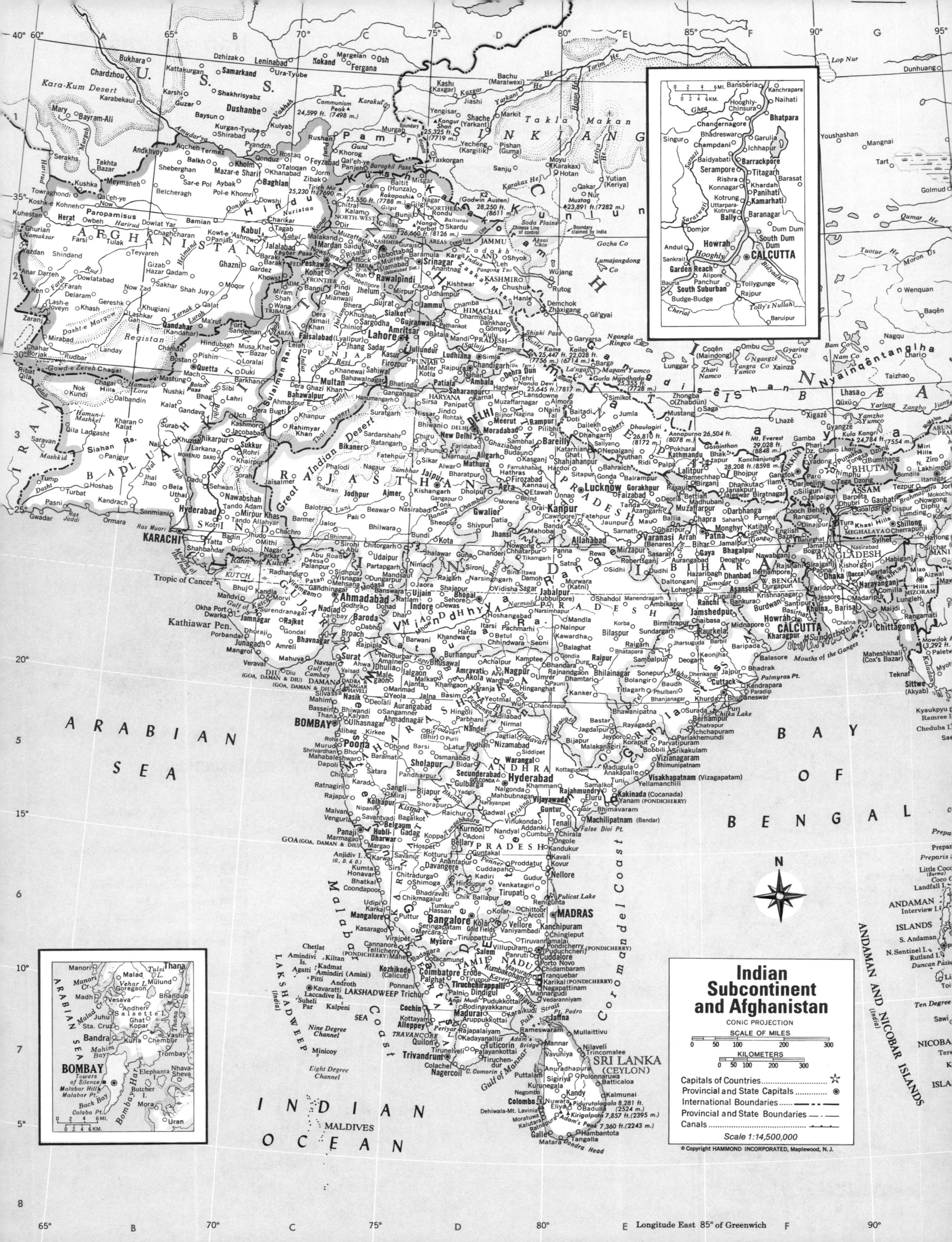

Indian Subcontinent and Afghanistan
CONIC PROJECTION
SCALE OF MILES
0 50 100 200 300
KILOMETERS
0 100 200 300
Capitals of Countries
Provincial and State Capitals
International Boundaries
Provincial and State Boundaries
Canals
Scale 1:14,500,000
© Copyright HAMMOND INCORPORATED, Maplewood, N. J.
U. S. S. R.
AFGHANISTAN
PAKISTAN
INDIA
SINKIANG
NEPAL
BHUTAN
BANGLADESH
SRI LANKA (CEYLON)
MALDIVES
ARABIAN SEA
BAY OF BENGAL
INDIAN OCEAN
LAKSHADWEEP (India)
ANDAMAN AND NICOBAR ISLANDS (India)
Tropic of Cancer
Kathiawar Pen.
BOMBAY
CALCUTTA
MADRAS
DELHI
KARACHI
Longitude East 85° of Greenwich
N

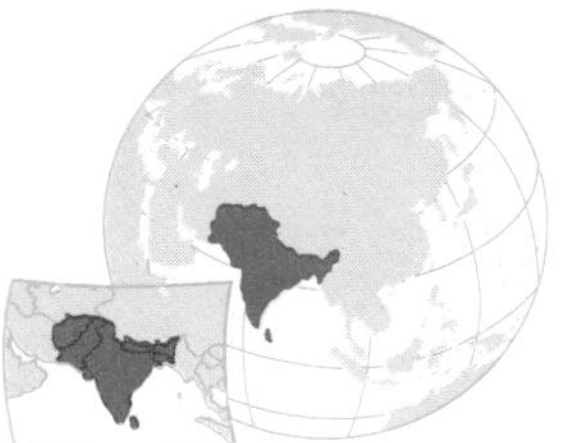

INDIA

AREA 1,269,339 sq. mi. (3,287,588 sq. km.)
POPULATION 683,810,051
CAPITAL New Delhi
LARGEST CITY Calcutta (greater)
HIGHEST POINT Nanda Devi 25,645 ft. (7,817 m.)
MONETARY UNIT Indian rupee
MAJOR LANGUAGES Hindi, English, Bihari, Telugu, Marathi, Bengali, Tamil, Gujarati, Rajasthani, Kanarese, Malayalam, Oriya, Punjabi, Assamese, Kashmiri, Urdu
MAJOR RELIGIONS Hinduism, Islam, Christianity, Sikhism, Buddhism, Jainism, Zoroastrianism, Animism

PAKISTAN

AREA 310,403 sq. mi. (803,944 sq. km.)
POPULATION 83,782,000
CAPITAL Islamabad
LARGEST CITY Karachi
HIGHEST POINT K2 (Godwin Austen) 28,250 ft. (8,611 m.)
MONETARY UNIT Pakistani rupee
MAJOR LANGUAGES Urdu, English, Punjabi, Pushtu, Sindhi, Baluchi, Brahui
MAJOR RELIGIONS Islam, Hinduism, Sikhism, Christianity, Buddhism

SRI LANKA (CEYLON)

AREA 25,332 sq. mi. (65,610 sq. km.)
POPULATION 14,850,001
CAPITAL Colombo
LARGEST CITY Colombo
HIGHEST POINT Pidurutalagala 8,281 ft. (2,524 m.)
MONETARY UNIT Sri Lanka rupee
MAJOR LANGUAGES Sinhala, Tamil, English
MAJOR RELIGIONS Buddhism, Hinduism, Christianity, Islam

AFGHANISTAN

AREA 250,775 sq. mi. (649,507 sq. km.)
POPULATION 15,540,000
CAPITAL Kabul
LARGEST CITY Kabul
HIGHEST POINT Nowshak 24,557 ft. (7,485 m.)
MONETARY UNIT afghani
MAJOR LANGUAGES Pushtu, Dari, Uzbek
MAJOR RELIGION Islam

NEPAL

AREA 54,663 sq. mi. (141,577 sq. km.)
POPULATION 14,179,301
CAPITAL Kathmandu
LARGEST CITY Kathmandu
HIGHEST POINT Mt. Everest 29,028 ft. (8,848 m.)
MONETARY UNIT Nepalese rupee
MAJOR LANGUAGES Nepali, Maithili, Tamang, Newari, Tharu
MAJOR RELIGIONS Hinduism, Buddhism

MALDIVES

AREA 115 sq. mi. (298 sq. km.)
POPULATION 143,046
CAPITAL Male
LARGEST CITY Male
HIGHEST POINT 20 ft. (6 m.)
MONETARY UNIT Maldivian rupee
MAJOR LANGUAGE Divehi
MAJOR RELIGION Islam

BHUTAN

AREA 18,147 sq. mi. (47,000 sq. km.)
POPULATION 1,298,000
CAPITAL Thimphu
LARGEST CITY Thimphu
HIGHEST POINT Kula Kangri 24,784 ft. (7,554 m.)
MONETARY UNIT ngultrum
MAJOR LANGUAGES Dzongka, Nepali
MAJOR RELIGIONS Buddhism, Hinduism

BANGLADESH

AREA 55,126 sq. mi. (142,776 sq. km.)
POPULATION 87,052,024
CAPITAL Dhaka
LARGEST CITY Dhaka
HIGHEST POINT Keokradong 4,034 ft. (1,230 m.)
MONETARY UNIT taka
MAJOR LANGUAGES Bengali, English
MAJOR RELIGIONS Islam, Hinduism Christianity

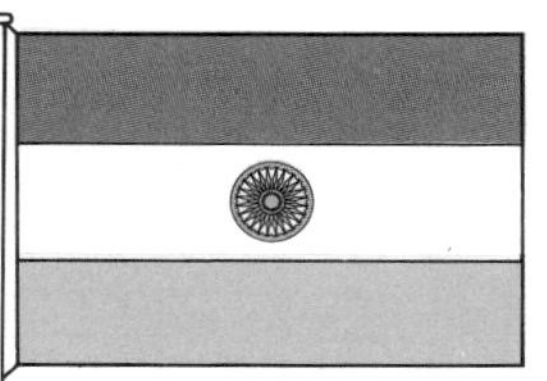

INDIA

PAKISTAN

SRI LANKA (CEYLON)

BHUTAN

AFGHANISTAN

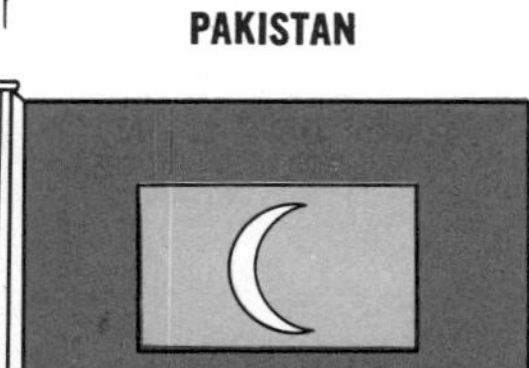

MALDIVES

BANGLADESH

NEPAL

AFGHANISTAN

CITIES and TOWNS

Name	Key
Andkhvoy	A1
Aqcheh	B1
Aybak 33,016	B1
Baghlan 75,130	B1
Balkh	B1
Bamian 7,355	B2
Belcheragh	B1
Chaghcharan 2,974	B2
Chahar Borjak	A2
Charikar 25,093	B1
Delaram	A2
Dowlatabad	A2
Dowlat Yar	B2
Dowshi	B1
Farah 18,797	A2
Farsi	A2
Feyzabad 10,142	C1
Gardez 11,415	B2
Gereshk	A2
Ghazni 30,425	B2
Ghurian	A2
Gizab	B2
Hazar Qadam	B2
Herat 163,960	A2
Jalalabad 56,384	B2
Jorm	C1
Kabul (cap.) 905,108	B2
Kalat (Qalat) 5,946	B2
Kandahar (Qandahar) 178,409	B2
Ken	A2
Khanabad	B1
Khash	A2
Kholm	B1
Khowst	B2
Khugiani	B2
Koshke-e Kohneh	A2
Kowt-e 'Ashrow	B2
Kuhestan	A2
Landay	A2
Lash-e Joveyn	A2
Lashkar Gah 26,646	A2
Mar'uf	B2
Mazar-e Sharif 122,567	B1
Meymaneh 54,954	A1
Mirabad	A2
Moqor	B2
Now Zad	A2
Oruzgan (Hazar Qadam)	B2
Owbeh	A2
Panjab	B2
Pol-e Khomri	B1
Qalat 5,946	B2
Qale'h-ye Now 5,340	A1
Qale'h-ye Panjeh	C1
Qandahar 178,409	B2
Qonduz 107,191	B1
Rostaq	B1
Rudbar	A2
Sakhar	B2
Sar-e Pol	B1
Shay Juy	B2
Sheberghan 54,870	B1
Shindand	A2
Spin Buldak	B2
Tagab	B2
Taloqan 46,202	B1
Teyvareh	A2
Towraghondi	A1
Tulak	A2
Zaranj 6,477	A2
Zibak	C1

OTHER FEATURES

Name	Key
Farah Rud (riv.)	A2
Harirud (riv.)	A1
Helmand (riv.)	B2
Hindu Kush (mts.)	B1
Kabul (riv.)	C2
Konar (riv.)	C1
Lurah (riv.)	B2
Margow, Dasht-e (des.)	A2
Namaksar (salt lake)	A2
Paropamisus (range)	A2
Tarnak (riv.)	B2

BANGLADESH

CITIES and TOWNS

Name	Key
Barisal 98,127	G4
Bogra 47,154	F4
Chalna Port 14,590	F4
Chittagong 889,760	G4
Comilla 86,446	G4
Cox's Bazar (Maheshkhali) 15,720	G4
Dhaka (Dacca) (cap.) 1,679,572	G4
Dinajpur 61,866	F3
Faridpur 46,232	F4
Habiganj 16,281	G4
Jamalpur 60,261	F4
Jessore 76,168	F4
Khulna 437,304	F4
Kishorganj 35,605	G4
Madaripur 32,488	G4
Maheshkhali 15,720	G4
Mymensingh (Nasirabad) 182,153	G4
Narayanganj 270,680	G4
Nasirabad 182,153	G4
Nawabganj 46,059	F4
Noakhali 32,490	G4
Pabna 62,254	F4
Rajshahi 132,909	F4
Rangamati 20,473	G4
Rangpur 72,829	F3
Sirajganj 74,457	F4
Sylhet 59,546	G4
Teknaf	G4

OTHER FEATURES

Name	Key
Bengal, Bay of (sea)	F5
Brahmaputra (riv.)	G3
Ganges (riv.)	F3
Sundarbans (reg.)	F4

BHUTAN

CITIES and TOWNS

Name	Key
Bumthang 10,000	G3
Paro 35,000	F3
Punakha 12,000	G3
Taga Dzong 18,000	G3
Thimphu (cap.) 50,000	G3
Tongsa Dzong 2,500	G3

OTHER FEATURES

Name	Key
Chomo Lhari (mt.)	F3
Himalaya (mts.)	E2
Kula Kangri (mt.)	G3

INDIA

INTERNAL DIVISIONS

Name	Key
Andaman and Nicobar Isls. (terr.) 188,254	G6
Andhra Pradesh (state) 53,403,619	D5
Arunachal Pradesh (terr.) 628,050	G3

(continued on following page)

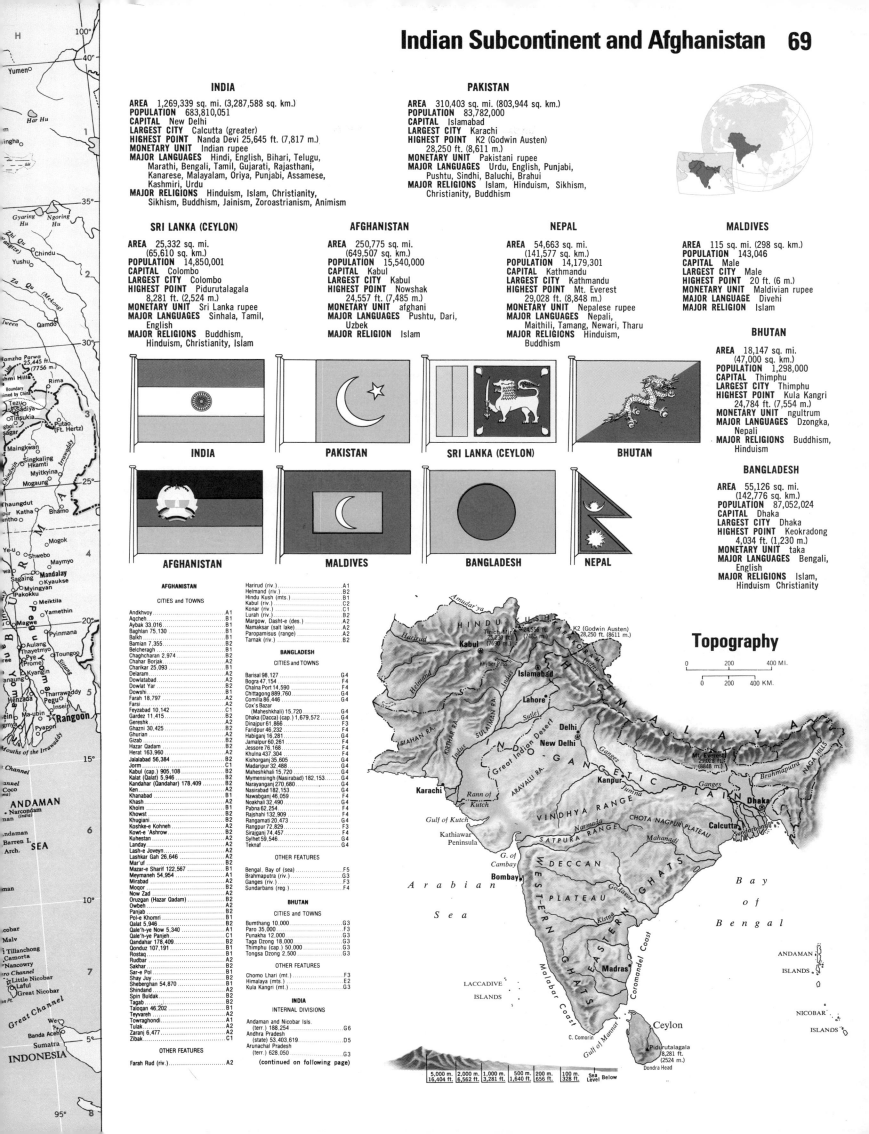

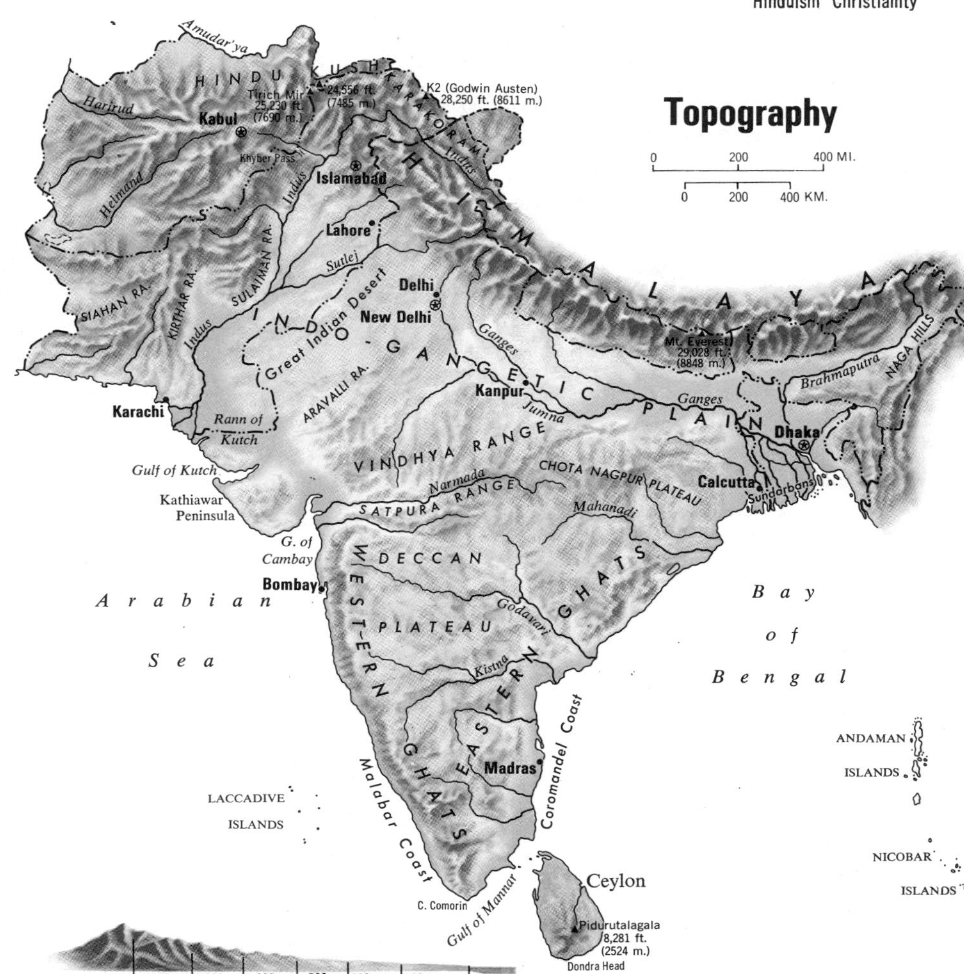

Indian Subcontinent and Afghanistan

(continued)

Assam (state) 19,902,826 ... G3
Bihar (state) 69,823,154 ... F4
Chandigarh (terr.) 450,061 ... D2
Dadra and Nagar Haveli (terr.) 103,677 ... C4
Delhi (terr.) 6,196,414 ... D3
Goa, Daman and Diu (terr.) 1,082,117 ... C4
Gujarat (state) 33,960,905 ... C4
Haryana (state) 12,850,902 ... D3
Himachal Pradesh (state) 4,237,569 ... D2
Jammu and Kashmir (state) 5,981,600 ... D2
Karnataka (state) 37,043,451 ... D6
Kerala (state) 25,403,217 ... D6
Lakshadweep (terr.) 40,237 ... C6
Madhya Pradesh (state) 52,131,717 ... D4
Maharashtra (state) 62,693,898 ... C5
Manipur (state) 1,433,691 ... G4
Meghalaya (state) 1,327,874 ... G3
Mizoram (terr.) 487,774 ... G4
Nagaland (state) 773,281 ... G3
Orissa (state) 26,272,054 ... E5
Pondicherry (terr.) 604,136 ... E6
Punjab (state) 16,669,755 ... D2
Rajasthan (state) 34,102,912 ... C3
Sikkim (state) 315,682 ... F3
Tamil Nadu (state) 48,297,456 ... D6
Tripura (state) 2,060,189 ... G4
Uttar Pradesh (state) 110,858,019 ... D3
West Bengal (state) 54,485,560 ... F4

CITIES and TOWNS

Abu 9,840 ... C4
Abu Road 25,331 ... C4
Achalpur 42,326 ... D4
Addanki 10,223 ... D5
Adilabad 30,368 ... D5
Adoni 85,311 ... D5
Agartala 59,625 ... G4
Agartala□ 100,264 ... G4
Agra 591,917 ... D3
Agra□ 634,622 ... D3
Ahmadabad 1,591,832 ... C4
Ahmadabad□ 1,741,522 ... C4
Ahmadnagar 118,236 ... C5
Ahmadnagar□ 148,405 ... C5
Aizwal 31,740 ... G4
Ajanta ... D4
Ajmer 262,851 ... C3
Akola 168,438 ... D4
Alibag 11,913 ... C5
Aligarh 252,314 ... D3
Alipore ... F2
Allahabad 490,622 ... E3
Allahabad□ 513,036 ... E3
Alleppey-Cochin 160,166 ... D7
Almora 19,671 ... D3
Along 3,524 ... G3
Alwar 100,378 ... D3
Amalner 55,544 ... C4
Ambala 83,633 ... D2
Ambala□ 186,168 ... D2
Ambikapur 23,087 ... E4
Amravati 193,800 ... D4
Amreli 39,520 ... C4
Amritsar 407,628 ... C2
Amritsar□ 458,029 ... C2
Anakapalle 57,273 ... E5
Anantapur 80,069 ... D6
Anantnag 27,643 ... D2
Andheri ... B7
Andul 3,602 ... F2
Arcot 30,230 ... D6
Arrah 92,919 ... E3
Aruppukkottai 62,223 ... D7
Arvi 26,494 ... D4
Asansol 155,968 ... F4
Asansol□ 241,792 ... F4
Aurangabad, Bihar 18,714 ... E4
Aurangabad, Maharashtra 150,483 ... D5
Aurangabad□ 165,253 ... D5
Azamgarh 40,963 ... E3
Badagara 53,938 ... D6
Bagalkot 51,746 ... D5
Bahraich 73,931 ... E3
Baidyabati 54,130 ... F1
Balaghat 27,872 ... E4
Balasore 46,239 ... F4
Ballia 47,101 ... E3
Bally 38,892 ... F1
Balotra 17,595 ... C3
Balrampur 36,191 ... E3
Balurghat 67,088 ... F3
Banda 50,575 ... D3
Bandar (Machilipatnam) 112,612 ... E5
Bandra ... B7
Bangalore 1,540,741 ... D6
Bangalore□ 1,653,779 ... D6
Bankura 79,129 ... F4
Bansberia 61,748 ... F1
Banswara 27,363 ... C4
Baramati 27,912 ... C5
Baramula 26,334 ... C2
Baranagar 136,842 ... F1
Barasat 42,642 ... F1
Barbil 24,342 ... F4
Bareilly 296,248 ... D3
Bareilly□ 326,106 ... D3
Baripada 28,725 ... F4
Barmer 38,630 ... C3
Baroda (Vadodara) 466,696 ... C4
Barpeta 26,479 ... G3
Barrackpore 96,889 ... F1
Barrackpore□ 198,255 ... F1
Barsi 62,374 ... D5
Baruipur 20,501 ... F2
Barwani 22,099 ... D4
Basim 32,496 ... D4
Basirhat 63,816 ... F4
Bassein 30,594 ... C5
Bastar ... E5
Batala 58,200 ... D2
Baudh 8,891 ... E4
Bauria 10,610 ... E2
Beawar 66,114 ... C3
Belgaum 192,427 ... C5
Belgaum□ 213,872 ... C5
Bellary 125,183 ... D5
Benares (Varanasi) 583,856 ... E3
Berhampore 72,605 ... F4
Berhampur 117,662 ... F5
Bettiah 51,018 ... E3
Betul 30,862 ... D4
Bhadrak 40,487 ... F4
Bhadravati 40,203 ... D6
Bhadravati□ 101,358 ... D6
Bhadreswar 45,586 ... F1
Bhagalpur 172,202 ... F4
Bhandara 39,423 ... E4
Bhandup ... B7
Bhanjanagar 12,353 ... E4
Bharatpur 68,036 ... D3
Bharuch 91,589 ... C4
Bhatapara 20,980 ... E4
Bhatinda 53,684 ... C2
Bhatkal 18,732 ... C6
Bhatpara 204,750 ... F1
Bhavnagar 225,358 ... C4
Bhavnagar□ 225,974 ... C4
Bhawanipatna 22,808 ... E5
Bhilai 157,173 ... E4
Bhilwara 82,155 ... C3
Bhimavaram 63,762 ... E5
Bhimunipatnam 14,291 ... E5
Bhind 42,371 ... D3
Bhinmal 14,050 ... C3
Bhir (Bir) 49,965 ... D5
Bhiwandi 79,576 ... C5
Bhiwani 73,086 ... D3
Bhopal 298,022 ... D4
Bhor 10,708 ... C5
Bhubaneswar 105,491 ... F4
Bhuj 52,177 ... B4
Bhusawal 96,800 ... D4
Bhusawal□ 104,708 ... D4
Bidar 50,670 ... D5
Bihar 100,046 ... F3
Bijapur, Karnataka 103,931 ... D5
Bijapur, Madhya Pradesh 5,289 ... E5
Bijnor 43,290 ... D3
Bikaner 188,518 ... C3
Bikaner□ 208,894 ... C3
Bilaspur 98,410 ... E4
Bina-Itawa 33,106 ... D4
Bir 49,965 ... D5
Birmitrapur 28,063 ... E4
Bobbili 30,649 ... E5
Bodhan 37,589 ... D5
Bodinayakkanur 54,176 ... D6
Bolangir 35,748 ... E4
Bombay (Greater)* 5,970,575 ... B7
Bomdila 2,264 ... G3
Broach (Bharuch) 91,589 ... C4
Budaun 72,204 ... D3
Budge-Budge 51,039 ... F2
Bundi 34,279 ... D3
Burdwan 143,318 ... F4
Burhanpur 105,246 ... D4
Calcutta 3,148,746 ... F2
Calcutta□ 7,031,382 ... F2
Calicut (Kozhikode) 333,979 ... D6
Cambay 62,097 ... C4
Cannanore 55,162 ... C6
Cawnpore (Kanpur) 1,154,388 ... E3
Chaibasa 35,386 ... F4
Chamba 11,814 ... D2
Champdani 58,596 ... F1
Chanderi 10,294 ... D4
Chandernagore 75,238 ... F1
Chandigarh 218,743 ... D2
Chandigarh□ 232,940 ... D2
Chandrapur 75,134 ... D5
Chapra 83,101 ... F3
Chatrapur 10,835 ... F5
Chembur ... B7
Cherrapunji⊙ 83,987 ... G3
Chhatarpur 32,271 ... D4
Chhindwara 53,492 ... D4
Chidambaram 48,811 ... E6
Chik Ballapur 29,227 ... D6
Chikmagalur 41,639 ... D6
Chingleput 38,419 ... E6
Chiplun 20,942 ... C5
Chirala 54,487 ... E5
Chitorgarh 25,917 ... C4
Chitradurga 50,254 ... D6
Chittoor 63,035 ... D6
Churachandpur 8,706 ... G4
Churu 52,502 ... D3
Chushul ... D2
Cocanada (Kakinada) 164,200 ... E5
Cochin-Alleppey 439,066 ... D6
Coimbatore 356,368 ... D6
Coimbatore□ 736,203 ... D6
Colachel 18,819 ... D7
Cooch Behar 53,684 ... F3
Coondapoor 23,831 ... C6
Cuddalore 101,335 ... E6
Cuddapah 66,195 ... D6
Cumbum 9,745 ... D5
Cuttack 194,068 ... F4
Cuttack□ 205,759 ... F4
Dabhoi 37,892 ... C4
Daltonganj 32,367 ... E4
Damoh 59,489 ... D4
Dapoli 6,296 ... C5
Darbhanga 132,059 ... F3
Darjeeling 42,873 ... F3
Datia 36,439 ... D3
Davangere 121,110 ... D6
Deesa 28,324 ... C4
Dehra Dun 166,073 ... D2
Dehra Dun□ 203,464 ... D2
Delhi 3,287,883 ... D3
Delhi□ 3,647,023 ... D3
Demchok ... D2
Deogarh, Orissa 8,906 ... E4
Deoghar, Bihar 40,356 ... F4
Deolali 55,436 ... C5
Deoria 38,161 ... E3
Dewas 51,545 ... D4
Dhamtari 34,546 ... E4
Dhanbad 79,838 ... F4
Dhanbad□ 434,031 ... F4
Dhar 36,172 ... C4
Dharmsala 10,939 ... D2
Dharwar-Hubli 379,166 ... C5
Dhenkanal 19,615 ... E4
Dholpur 31,865 ... D3
Dhond 16,583 ... C5
Dhoraji 59,773 ... C4
Dhubri 36,503 ... G3
Dhulia 137,129 ... C4
Dibrugarh 80,348 ... G3
Digboi 16,538 ... H3
Dindigul 128,429 ... D6
Diphu 10,200 ... G3
Dispur 1,725 ... G3
Diu 6,214 ... C4
Dohad 44,506 ... C4
Domjor 10,896 ... F1
Dudhi 5,084 ... E4
Dum Dum 31,363 ... F1
Dum Dum□ 273,812 ... F1
Dungarpur 19,773 ... C4
Durg 67,892 ... E4
Durgapur 206,638 ... F4
Dwarka 17,801 ... B4
Eluru 127,023 ... E5
English Bazar 61,335 ... F3
Erode 105,111 ... D6
Etawah 85,894 ... D3
Faizabad-cum-Ayodhya 102,835 ... E3
Faridabad 85,762 ... D3
Farrukhabad-cum-Fatehgarh 102,768 ... D3
Farrukhabad-cum-Fatehgarh□ 110,835 D3
Fatehpur, Rajasthan 34,929 ... C3
Fatehpur, Uttar Pradesh 54,665 ... E3
Firozabad 133,863 ... D3
Firozpur 49,545 ... C2
Gadag-Betgeri 95,426 ... D5
Gadwal 21,828 ... D5
Gandhinagar 24,055 ... C4
Ganganagar 90,042 ... C3
Gangapur 27,453 ... D3
Gangtok 12,000 ... F3
Garden Reach 154,913 ... F2
Garulia 44,271 ... F1
Gauhati 123,783 ... G3
Gauhati□ 200,377 ... G3
Gaya 179,884 ... F4
Ghat Kopar 34,256 ... B7
Ghaziabad 118,836 ... D3
Ghaziabad□ 127,700 ... D3
Ghazipur 45,635 ... E3
Goalpara 16,703 ... G3
Godhra 66,403 ... C4
Gonda 52,662 ... E3

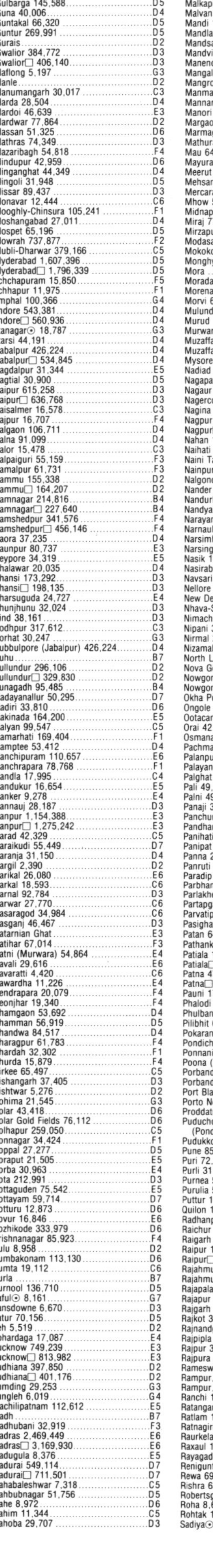

Gondal 54,928 ... C4
Gondia 77,992 ... E4
Gorakhpur 230,911 ... E3
Goregaon ... B7
Gudur 33,778 ... D6
Gulbarga 145,588 ... D5
Guna 40,006 ... D4
Guntakal 66,320 ... D5
Guntur 269,991 ... D5
Gurais ... D2
Gwalior 384,772 ... D3
Gwalior□ 406,140 ... D3
Haflong 5,197 ... G3
Hanle ... D2
Hanumangarh 30,017 ... C3
Harda 28,504 ... D4
Hardoi 46,639 ... E3
Hardwar 77,864 ... D2
Hassan 51,325 ... D6
Hathras 74,349 ... D3
Hazaribagh 54,818 ... F4
Hindupur 42,959 ... D6
Hinganghat 44,349 ... D4
Hingoli 31,948 ... D5
Hissar 89,437 ... D3
Honavar 12,444 ... C6
Hooghly-Chinsura 105,241 ... F1
Hoshangabad 27,011 ... D4
Hospet 65,196 ... D5
Howrah 737,877 ... F2
Hubli-Dharwar 379,166 ... C5
Hyderabad 1,607,396 ... D5
Hyderabad□ 1,796,339 ... D5
Ichchapuram 15,850 ... F5
Ichhapur 11,975 ... F1
Imphal 100,366 ... G4
Indore 543,381 ... D4
Indore□ 560,936 ... D4
Itanagar⊙ 18,787 ... G3
Itarsi 44,191 ... D4
Jabalpur 426,224 ... D4
Jabalpur□ 534,845 ... D4
Jagdalpur 31,344 ... E5
Jagtial 30,900 ... D5
Jaipur 615,258 ... D3
Jaipur□ 636,768 ... D3
Jaisalmer 16,578 ... C3
Jajpur 16,707 ... F4
Jalgaon 106,711 ... D4
Jalna 91,099 ... D4
Jalor 15,478 ... C3
Jalpaiguri 55,159 ... F3
Jamalpur 61,731 ... F3
Jammu 155,338 ... D2
Jammu□ 164,207 ... D2
Jamnagar 214,816 ... B4
Jamnagar□ 227,640 ... B4
Jamshedpur 341,576 ... F4
Jamshedpur□ 456,146 ... F4
Jaora 37,235 ... D4
Jaunpur 80,737 ... E3
Jeypore 34,319 ... E5
Jhalawar 20,035 ... D4
Jhansi 173,292 ... D3
Jhansi□ 198,135 ... D3
Jharsuguda 24,727 ... E4
Jhunjhunu 32,024 ... D3
Jind 38,161 ... D3
Jodhpur 317,612 ... C3
Jorhat 30,247 ... G3
Jubbulpore (Jabalpur) 426,224 ... D4
Juhu ... B7
Jullundur 296,106 ... D2
Jullundur□ 329,830 ... D2
Junagadh 95,485 ... B4
Kadayanallur 50,295 ... D7
Kadiri 33,810 ... D6
Kakinada 164,200 ... E5
Kalyan 99,547 ... C5
Kamarhati 169,404 ... F1
Kamptee 53,412 ... D4
Kanchipuram 110,657 ... E6
Kanchrapara 78,768 ... F1
Kandla 17,995 ... C4
Kandukur 16,654 ... E5
Kanker 9,278 ... E4
Kannauj 28,187 ... D3
Kanpur 1,154,388 ... E3
Kanpur□ 1,275,242 ... E3
Karad 42,329 ... C5
Karaikudi 55,449 ... D7
Karanja 31,150 ... D4
Kargil 2,390 ... D2
Karikal 26,080 ... E6
Karkal 18,593 ... C6
Karnal 92,784 ... D3
Karwar 27,770 ... C6
Kasaragod 34,984 ... C6
Kasganj 46,467 ... D3
Katarnian Ghat ... E3
Katihar 67,014 ... F3
Katni (Murwara) 54,864 ... E4
Kavali 29,616 ... E6
Kavaratti 4,420 ... C6
Kawardha 11,226 ... E4
Kendrapara 20,079 ... F4
Keonjhar 19,340 ... F4
Khamgaon 53,692 ... D4
Khamman 56,919 ... D5
Khandwa 84,517 ... D4
Kharagpur 61,783 ... F4
Khardah 32,302 ... F1
Khurda 15,879 ... F4
Kirkee 65,497 ... C5
Kishangarh 37,405 ... D3
Kishtwar 5,276 ... D2
Kohima 21,545 ... G3
Kolar 43,418 ... D6
Kolar Gold Fields 76,112 ... D6
Kolhapur 259,050 ... C5
Konnagar 34,424 ... F1
Koppal 27,277 ... D5
Koraput 21,505 ... E5
Korba 30,963 ... E4
Kota 212,991 ... D3
Kottaguden 75,542 ... E5
Kottayam 59,714 ... D7
Kotturu 12,873 ... D6
Kovur 16,846 ... E6
Kozhikode 333,979 ... D6
Krishnanagar 85,923 ... F4
Kulu 8,958 ... D2
Kumbakonam 113,130 ... D6
Kumta 19,112 ... C6
Kurla ... B7
Kurnool 136,710 ... D5
Laful⊙ 8,161 ... G7
Lansdowne 6,670 ... D3
Latur 70,156 ... D5
Leh 5,519 ... D2
Lohardaga 17,087 ... E4
Lucknow 749,239 ... E3
Lucknow□ 813,982 ... E3
Ludhiana 397,850 ... D2
Ludhiana□ 401,176 ... D2
Lumding 29,253 ... G3
Lungleh 6,019 ... G4
Machilipatnam 112,612 ... E5
Madh ... B7
Madhubani 32,919 ... F3
Madras 2,469,449 ... E6
Madras□ 3,169,930 ... E6
Madugula 8,376 ... E5
Madurai 549,114 ... D7
Madurai□ 711,501 ... D7
Mahabaleshwar 7,318 ... C5
Mahbubnagar 51,756 ... D5
Mahe 8,972 ... D6
Mahim 11,344 ... C5
Mahoba 29,707 ... D3
Mahuva 39,497 ... C4
Malad ... B6
Malakanagiri 7,494 ... E5
Malegaon 191,847 ... C4
Maler Kotla 48,536 ... D2
Malkapur 35,476 ... D4
Malvan 17,579 ... C5
Mandi 16,849 ... D2
Mandla 24,406 ... E4
Mandsaur 52,347 ... C4
Mandvi 27,849 ... B4
Manendragarh 11,936 ... E4
Mangalore 165,174 ... C6
Mangrol 27,183 ... B4
Manmad 29,571 ... C4
Mannargudi 42,783 ... E6
Manori ... B6
Margao 41,655 ... C5
Marmagao 44,065 ... C5
Mathura 132,028 ... D3
Mau 64,058 ... E3
Mayuram 60,195 ... D6
Meerut 270,993 ... D3
Mehsana 51,598 ... C4
Mercara 19,357 ... D6
Mhow 59,037 ... D4
Midnapore 71,326 ... F4
Miraj 77,606 ... D5
Mirzapur-cum-Vindhyachal 105,939 ... E4
Modasa 22,483 ... C4
Mokokchung 17,423 ... G3
Monghyr 102,474 ... F3
Mora ... B7
Moradabad 258,590 ... D3
Morena 44,901 ... D3
Morvi 60,976 ... C4
Mulund ... B6
Murud 11,210 ... C5
Murwara 54,864 ... E4
Muzaffarnagar 114,783 ... D3
Muzaffarpur 126,379 ... E3
Mysore 355,685 ... D6
Nadiad 108,269 ... C4
Nagapattinam 68,026 ... E6
Nagaur 36,448 ... C3
Nagercoil 141,288 ... D7
Nagina 37,066 ... D3
Nagpur 866,076 ... D4
Nagpur□ 930,459 ... D4
Nahan 16,017 ... D2
Naihati 82,080 ... F1
Naini Tal 23,986 ... D3
Nainpur 14,683 ... E4
Nalgonda 33,126 ... D5
Nander 126,538 ... D5
Nandurbar 54,070 ... C4
Nandyal 63,193 ... D5
Narayanpet 21,744 ... D5
Narnaul 31,875 ... D3
Narsimhapur 25,552 ... D4
Narsinghgarh 13,814 ... D4
Nasik 176,091 ... C5
Nasirabad 25,732 ... C3
Navsari 72,979 ... C4
Nellore 133,590 ... E6
New Delhi (cap.) 301,801 ... D3
Nhava-Sheva ... B7
Nimach 47,113 ... D4
Nipani 35,116 ... C5
Nirmal 28,529 ... D5
Nizamabad 115,640 ... D5
North Lakhimpur 20,094 ... G3
Nova Goa (Panaji) 34,953 ... C5
Nowgong, Assam 56,537 ... G3
Nowgong, Madhya Pradesh 10,248 ... D3
Okha Port 10,687 ... B4
Ongole 53,330 ... E5
Ootacamund 63,310 ... D6
Orai 42,513 ... D3
Osmanabad 27,279 ... D5
Pachmarhi 1,212 ... D4
Palanpur 42,114 ... C4
Palayankottai 70,070 ... D7
Palghat 95,788 ... D6
Pali 49,834 ... C3
Palni 49,575 ... D6
Panaji 34,953 ... C5
Panchur 59,021 ... F2
Pandharpur 53,638 ... D5
Panihati 148,046 ... F1
Panipat 87,981 ... D3
Panna 22,316 ... E4
Panruti 34,065 ... D6
Paradip ... F4
Parbhani 61,570 ... D5
Parlakhemundi 26,917 ... E5
Partapgarh 17,402 ... C4
Parvatipuram 30,025 ... E5
Pasighat 5,116 ... G3
Patan 64,519 ... C4
Pathankot 76,355 ... D2
Patiala 148,686 ... D2
Patiala□ ... D2
Patna 473,001 ... F3
Patna□ ... F3
Pauni 17,781 ... E4
Phalodi 17,379 ... C3
Phulbani 10,677 ... E4
Pilibhit 68,273 ... D3
Pokaran 7,769 ... C3
Pondicherry 90,537 ... E6
Ponnani 35,723 ... D6
Poona (Pune)□ ... C5
Porbandar 96,881 ... B4
Porbandar□ ... B4
Port Blair 26,218 ... G6
Porto Novo 17,412 ... E6
Proddatur 70,822 ... D6
Puduchcheri (Pondicherry) 90,537 ... E6
Pudukkottai 66,384 ... D6
Pune 856,105 ... C5
Puri 72,674 ... F5
Purli 31,078 ... D5
Purnea 56,484 ... F3
Purulia 57,708 ... F4
Puttur 17,483 ... D6
Quilon 124,208 ... D7
Radhanpur 18,360 ... C4
Raichur 79,831 ... D5
Raigarh 46,745 ... E4
Raipur 174,518 ... E4
Raipur□ ... E4
Rajahmundry 165,912 ... E5
Rajahmundry□ ... E5
Rajapalaiyam 86,952 ... D7
Rajapur 9,017 ... C5
Rajgarh 11,475 ... D4
Rajkot 300,612 ... C4
Rajnandgaon 41,183 ... E4
Rajpipla 25,769 ... C4
Rajpur 34,393 ... F2
Rajpura 14,840 ... D2
Rameswarem 16,755 ... D7
Rampur, Him. Pradesh 2,623 ... D2
Rampur, Uttar Pradesh 161,417 ... D3
Ranchi 175,934 ... F4
Ratangarh 31,506 ... C3
Ratlam 106,666 ... C4
Ratnagiri 37,551 ... C5
Raurkela 47,076 ... F4
Raxaul 12,064 ... E3
Rayagada 25,064 ... E5
Renigunta 8,567 ... E6
Rewa 69,182 ... E4
Rishra 63,486 ... F1
Robertsganj 7,093 ... E4
Roha 8,631 ... C5
Rohtak 124,783 ... C5
Sadiya⊙ 64,252 ... H3

Sagar 118,574 .... D4
Saharanpur 225,396 .... D3
Saharsa 23,217 .... F3
Salem 308,716 .... D6
Salem□ 416,440 .... D6
Samalkot 34,607 .... E5
Sambalpur 64,675 .... E4
Sambhal 86,323 .... D3
Sangamner 28,594 .... C5
Sangli 115,138 .... C5
Sankrail 11,300 .... E2
Santa·Cruz B7
Santipur 61,166 .... F4
Sardarshahr 37,703 .... C3
Sarnath E3
Sasaram 48,282 .... E4
Satara 66,433 .... C5
Satna 57,531 .... E4
Savantvadi 16,873 .... C5
Savanur 18,302 .... D6
Sawi⊙ 13,504 .... G7
Secunderabad 250,636 .... D5
Secunderabad□ 345,052 .... D5
Sehore 35,657 .... D4
Seoni 38,396 .... D4
Serampore 102,023 .... F1
Seringapatam 14,100 .... D6
Shahdol 28,490 .... E4
Shahjahanpur 135,604 .... E3
Shajapur 25,189 .... D4
Sheopur 16,418 .... D3
Shillong 87,659 .... G3
Shimoga 102,709 .... D6
Shivpuri 42,120 .... D3
Sholapur 398,361 .... D5
Shorapur 21,056 .... D5
Shyok D2
Sibsagar 27,426 .... H3
Siddipet 26,296 .... D5
Sidhi 8,341 .... E4
Sidhpur 40,521 .... C4
Sikar 70,987 .... D3
Silchar 52,596 .... G4
Siliguri 97,484 .... F3
Silvassa C4
Simla 55,368 .... D2
Singur 10,957 .... F1
Sirohi 18,774 .... C4
Sironj 22,413 .... D4
Sirsa 48,808 .... D3
Sirsi 28,576 .... D6
Sitapur 66,715 .... E3
Sonepur 8,084 .... E4
South Dum Dum 174,538 .... F2
South Suburban 272,600 .... F2
Srikakulam 45,179 .... E5
Srinagar 403,413 .... D2
Srinagar□ 423,253 .... D2
Srivardhan 12,342 .... C5
Sundargarh 17,244 .... E4
Surada 9,833 .... E5
Surat 471,656 .... C4
Surat□ 493,001 .... C4
Suratgarh 14,491 .... C3
Surendranagar 66,667 .... C4
Tanda 41,611 .... E3
Tehri 5,480 .... D2
Tellicherry 68,759 .... C6
Tenali 102,937 .... E5
Tezpur 39,870 .... G3
Tezu 3,055 .... H3
Thana 170,675 .... B6
Thanjavur 140,547 .... D6
Tikamgarh 27,007 .... D4
Tinsukia 54,911 .... H3
Tiruchchirappalli 307,400 .... D6
Tiruchchirappalli□ 464,624 .... D6
Tiruchendur 18,126 .... D7
Tirunelveli 108,498 .... D7
Tirupati 65,843 .... D6
Tiruppattur 40,357 .... D6
Tiruppur 113,302 .... D6
Tiruvannamalai 61,370 .... D6
Titagarh 88,218 .... F1
Titlagarh 14,504 .... E4
Toibalawe G6
Tollygunge F2
Tonk 55,866 .... D3
Tranquebar 17,318 .... E6
Trichur 76,241 .... D6
Trivandrum 409,627 .... D7
Trombay B7
Tumkur 70,476 .... D6
Tuni 28,344 .... E5
Tura 15,489 .... G3
Tuticorin 155,310 .... D7
Udaipur 161,278 .... C4
Udhampur 16,392 .... D2
Udipi 29,753 .... C6
Ujjain 203,278 .... D4
Ulhasnagar 168,462 .... C5
Umrer 27,092 .... D4
Unnao 38,195 .... E3
Uran 12,616 .... B7
Uttarpara-Kotrung 67,568 .... F1
Vadodara 466,696 .... C4
Vadodara□ 467,487 .... C4
Valsad 43,254 .... C4
Vaniyambadi 51,810 .... D6
Varanasi 583,856 .... E3
Varanasi□ 606,721 .... E3
Vashi B7
Vedaranniyam 21,471 .... E6
Vellore 139,082 .... D6
Vellore□ 178,554 .... D6
Vengurla 11,805 .... C5
Venkatagiri 17,546 .... D6
Veraval 58,771 .... C4
Vesava B7
Vidisha 43,212 .... D4
Vijayawada 317,258 .... D5
Villupuram 60,242 .... D6
Vinukonda 16,259 .... D5
Virajpet 9,782 .... D6
Viramgam 43,790 .... C4
Visakhapatnam 352,504 .... E5
Visnagar 34,863 .... C4
Vizagapatam (Visakhapatnam) 352,504 .... E5
Vizianagaram 86,608 .... E5
Warangal 207,520 .... D5
Wardha 69,037 .... D4
Wun 24,455 .... D5
Yadgir 32,756 .... D5
Yanam 8,291 .... E5
Yellamanchili 15,318 .... E5
Yeola 24,533 .... C4
Yeotmal 64,836 .... D4

OTHER FEATURES

Abor (hills) G3
Adam's Bridge (sound) D7
Agatti (isl.) C6
Amindiri (isl.) C6
Amindivi (isls.) C6
Amini (Amindiri) (isl.) C6
Andaman (isls.) G6
Andaman (sea) G6
Androth (isl.) C6
Anjidiv (Angedeva) (isl.) C6
Arabian (sea) B5
Back (bay) B7
Bengal, Bay of (sea) F5
Berar (reg.) D4
Brahmaputra (riv.) G3
Butcher (isl.) B7
Cambay (gulf) C4
Car Nicobar⊙ (isl.) G7
Chambal (riv.) D3
Chenab (riv.) C2
Chetlat (isl.) C6
Chilka (lake) F5
Coco (chan.) G6
Colaba (pt.) B7
Colair (lake) E5
Comorin (cape) D7
Coromandel Coast (reg.) E6
Daman (dist.) C4
Damodar (riv.) F4
Deccan (plat.) D6
Diu (dist.) C4
Eastern Ghats (mts.) D6
Elephanta (isl.) B7
Ganga (Ganges) (riv.) F3
Ganges, Mouths of the (delta) F4
Ganges (riv.) F3
Ghaghra (riv.) E3
Goa (dist.) C5
Godavari (riv.) D5
Golconda (ruins) D5
Great (chan.) G7
Great Indian (des.) C3
Great Nicobar (isl.) G7
Himalaya (mts.) D2
Hindu Kush (mts.) C1
Hooghly (riv.) F2
Indus (riv.) B3
Jhelum (riv.) C2
Jumna (riv.) E3
Kadmat (isl.) C6
Kalpeni (isl.) C7
Kamet (mt.) D2
Kanchenjunga (mt.) F3
Karakoram (mts.) D1
Kaveri (riv.) D6
Khasi (hills) G3
Kiltan (isl.) C6
Kistna (Krishna) (riv.) D5
Krishna (Kistna) (riv.) D5
Kunlun (range) D1
Kutch (gulf) B4
Kutch, Rann of (salt marsh) B4
Laccadive (isls.) C6
Ladakh (reg.) D2
Little Andaman (isl.) G6
Little Nicobar (isl.) G7
Mahanadi (riv.) E4
Malabar (hill) B7
Malabar Coast (reg.) C6
Mannar (gulf) D7
Middle Andaman (isl.) G6
Minicoy (isl.) C7
Miri (hills) G3
Mishmi (hills) H3
Nancowry⊙ (isl.) G7
Nanda Devi (mt.) D2
Narmada (riv.) D4
North Andaman⊙ (isl.) G6
Palk (str.) D7
Penganga (riv.) D5
Periyar (lake) D7
Pitti (isl.) C6
Pulicat (lake) E6
Salsette (isl.) B7
Sambhar (lake) C3
Satpura (range) D4
Shipki (pass) D2
South Andaman (isl.) G6
Sundarbans (reg.) F4
Sutlej (riv.) C3
Ten Degree (chan.) G7
Towers of Silence B7
Travancore (reg.) D7
Tungabhadra (riv.) D5
Vindhya (range) D4
Western Ghats (mts.) C5
Zaskar (mts.) D2

MALDIVES

Maldives 143,046 .... C7

NEPAL

CITIES and TOWNS

Bhaktapur 40,112 .... F3
Bhaktapur⊙ 110,157 .... F3
Biratnagar 45,100 .... F3
Birganj 12,999 .... F3
Dhangarhi E3
Ilam 7,299 .... F3
Jaleswar F3
Janakpur 14,294 .... F3
Jumla⊙ 122,753 .... E3
Kathmandu (cap.) 150,402 .... E3
Kathmandu⊙ 353,752 .... E3
Lalitpur 59,049 .... E3
Lalitpur⊙ 154,998 .... E3
Mustang⊙ 26,944 .... E3
Nepalganj 23,523 .... E3
Pokhara 20,611 .... E3
Pyuthan⊙ 137,338 .... E3
Ridi E3
Sallyan⊙ 141,457 .... E3
Simikot E3

OTHER FEATURES

Annapurna (mt.) E3
Bheri (riv.) E3
Dhaulagiri (mt.) E3
Everest (mt.) F3
Himalaya (mts.) D2
Kanchenjunga (mt.) F3

PAKISTAN

PROVINCES

Azad Kashmir C2
Baluchistan 2,409,000 .... B3
Federal Administrated Tribal Areas C2
Islamabad District 235,000 .... C2
Northern Areas D1
North-West Frontier 10,909,000 .... C2
Punjab 37,374,000 .... C2
Sind 13,965,000 .... B3

CITIES and TOWNS

Abbottabad 47,011 .... C2
Ahmadpur East 32,423 .... C3
Attock C2
Badin 6,387 .... B4
Bahawalnagar 36,290 .... C2
Bahawalpur 133,956 .... C3
Baltit C1
Bannu 43,795 .... C2
Barkhan 930 .... B3
Bhag 4,316 .... B3
Bhera 17,992 .... C2
Bostan B2
Bunji C1
Campbellpore 19,041 .... C2
Chachro C3
Chagai⊙ 41,263 .... A3
Chaman 12,208 .... B2
Chilas C1
Chiniot 69,124 .... C2
Chitral C1
Dadu 19,142 .... B3
Dalbandin 1,724 .... A3
Dera Ghazi Khan 71,429 .... C3
Dera Ismail Khan 59,892 .... C2
Diplo B4
Dir C1
Duki 464 .... B2
Faisalabad 822,263 .... C2
Fort Sandeman 8,058 .... B2
Ghizar C1
Gilgit C1
Gujranwala 360,419 .... C2
Gujrat 100,581 .... C2
Gwadar 8,146 .... A4
Hindubagh 2,217 .... B2
Hoshab A3
Hunza (Baltit) C1
Hyderabad 628,310 .... B3
Islamabad (cap.) 77,318 .... C2
Jacobabad 57,292 .... B3
Jhal Jhao B3
Jhang Sadar 135,722 .... C2
Jhelum 63,653 .... C2
Jhudo 6,950 .... B3
Kalam C1
Kalat 5,321 .... B3
Kandrach A3
Karachi 3,498,634 .... B4
Karachi* 3,650,000 .... B4
Kashmor C3
Kasur 102,531 .... C2
Khairpur 34,144 .... B3
Khanewal 67,617 .... C2
Khanpur 31,465 .... C3
Kharan Kalat 2,692 .... A3
Khushab 24,851 .... C2
Kohat 64,634 .... C2
Kotri 20,262 .... B3
Ladgasht (Qila Ladgasht) A3
Lahore 2,165,372 .... C2
Lahri B3
Larkana 71,943 .... B3
Leiah 19,608 .... C2
Loralai 5,519 .... B2
Lyallpur (Faisalabad) 822,263 .... C2
Mach 4,921 .... B3
Malakand C2
Mardan 115,218 .... C2
Mastung 5,962 .... B3
Mianwali 31,398 .... C2
Miram Shah C2
Mirpur C2
Mirpur Khas 81,617 .... B3
Misgar C1
Mithi C4
Multan 542,195 .... C2
Multan* 723,000 .... C2
Murree 13,486 .... C2
Musa Khel Bazar 429 .... B2
Muzaffarabad C2
Nagar D1
Nagar Parkar C4
Nal B3
Nawabshah 80,779 .... B3
Nok Kundi 861 .... A3
Nowshera 56,117 .... C2
Nushki 3,153 .... B3
Ormara A3
Panjgur 2,032 .... A3
Pasni 7,483 .... A3
Peshawar 268,366 .... C2
Pindi Gheb 12,416 .... C2
Pishin 2,906 .... B2
Qila Ladgasht A3
Quetta 156,000 .... B2
Rahimyar Khan 74,407 .... C3
Rawalpindi 615,392 .... C2
Ribat Qila A3
Risalpur Cantonment 11,291 .... C2
Rohri 19,072 .... B3
Rondu D1
Sahiwal 106,213 .... C2
Saidu 15,920 .... C2
Sargodha 201,407 .... C2
Sehwan 4,169 .... B3
Shahbandar B4
Shikarpur 70,301 .... B3
Sialkot 203,779 .... C2
Sibi 13,327 .... B3
Skardu D1
Sonmiani B3
Sorah B3
Sui 1,082 .... B3
Sukkur 158,876 .... B3
Surab B3
Tando Adam 31,246 .... B3
Tando Allahyar B3
Tatta 12,786 .... B4
Tump A3
Turbat 4,578 .... A3
Uch 5,483 .... B3
Uthal B3
Wah 107,671 .... C2
Wana C2
Yasin C1

OTHER FEATURES

Arabian (sea) B5
Bolan (pass) B3
Chagai (hills) A3
Chenab (riv.) C2
Hindu Kush (mts.) B1
Indus (riv.) B3
Jhelum (riv.) C2
K2 (mt.) D1
Konar (riv.) C1
Kutch, Rann of (salt marsh) B4
Mohenjo Daro (ruins) B3
Muari, Ras (cape) B4
Ravi (riv.) C2
Siahan (range) A3
Sulaiman (range) C3
Sutlej (riv.) C3
Talab (riv.) A3
Taxila (ruins) C2
Tirich Mir (mt.) C1
Zhob (riv.) B2

SRI LANKA (CEYLON)

CITIES and TOWNS

Anuradhapura 34,836 .... E7
Badulla 34,658 .... E7
Batticaloa 36,761 .... E7
Colombo (cap.) 618,000 .... D7
Colombo* 852,098 .... D7
Dehiwala-Mt. Lavinia 154,785 .... D7
Galle 72,720 .... D7
Hambantota 6,908 .... E7
Jaffna 112,000 .... E7
Kalmunai 19,176 .... E7
Kalutara 28,748 .... D7
Kandy 93,602 .... E7
Kurunegala 25,189 .... E7
Mannar 11,157 .... E7
Matara 36,641 .... E7
Moratuwa 96,489 .... D7
Mullaittivu 4,930 .... E7
Negombo 57,115 .... D7
Nilaveli 4,556 .... E7
Nuwara Eliya 16,347 .... E7
Polonnaruwa 9,551 .... E7
Puttalam 17,982 .... D7
Ratnapura 29,1[illegible]6 .... D7
Sigiriya 1,446 .... E7
Tangalla 8,748 .... E7
Trincomalee 41,780 .... E7
Vavuniya 15,639 .... E7

OTHER FEATURES

Adam's (peak) E7
Adam's Bridge (shoals) D7
Dondra (head) E7
Kirigalpota (mt.) E7
Mannar (gulf) D7
Palk (str.) D7
Pedro (pt.) E6
Pidurutalagala (mt.) E7

*City and suburbs.
⊙Population of district.
□Population of urban areas.

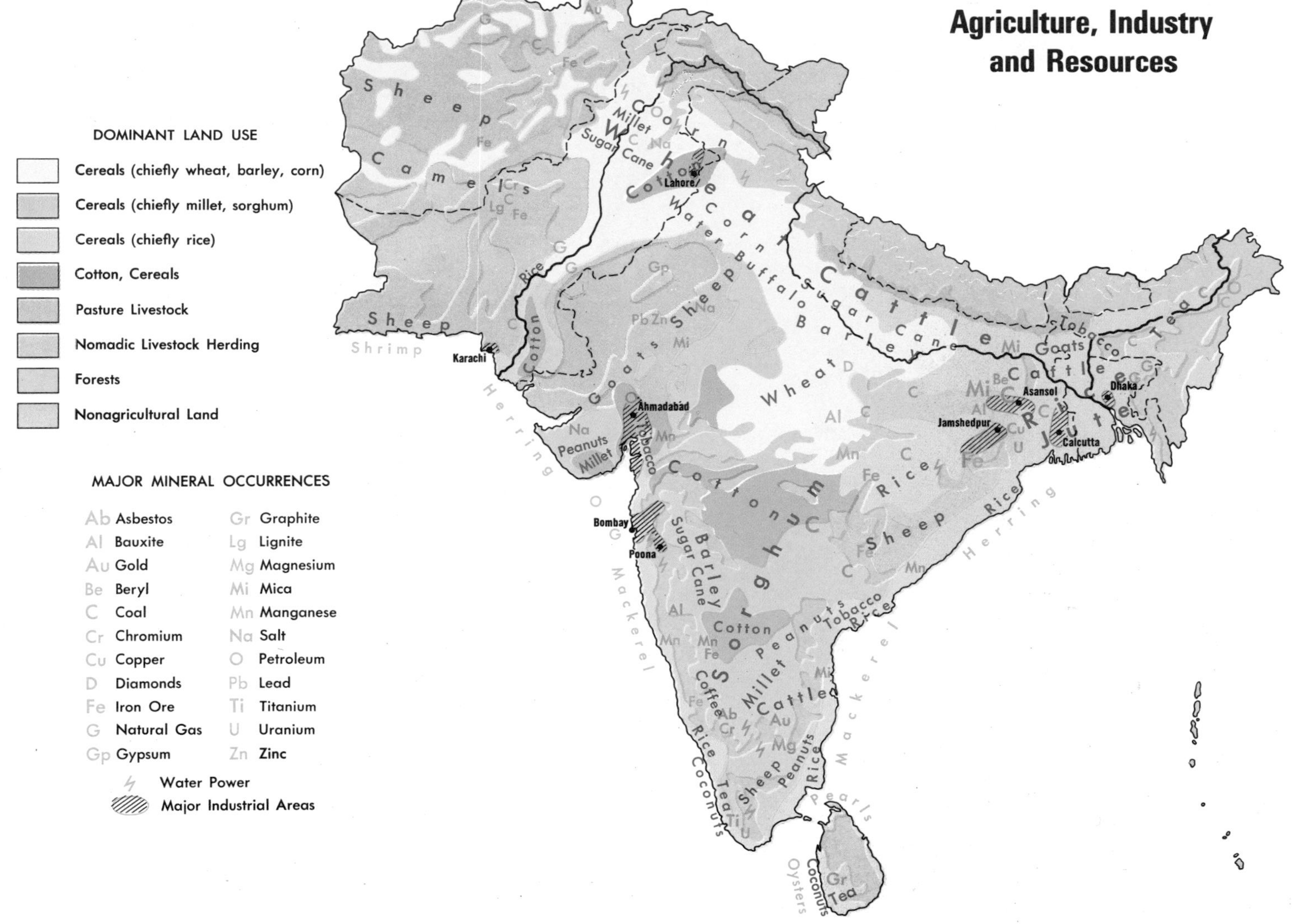

Burma, Thailand, Indochina and Malaya
CONIC PROJECTION
SCALE OF MILES
0 50 100 150 200
SCALE OF KILOMETERS
0 50 100 200 300
International Boundaries
Division and State Boundaries
Capitals of Countries
Division and State Capitals
Scale 1:10,000,000
© Copyright HAMMOND INCORPORATED, Maplewood, N. J.
Longitude East 96° of Greenwich
BHUTAN
INDIA
BANGLADESH
CHINA
BURMA
KACHIN STATE
SHAN STATE
KAYAH STATE
KAREN STATE
CHIN STATE
SAGAING
MANDALAY
MAGWE
ARAKAN
IRRAWADDY
RANGOON
TENASSERIM
THAILAND
LAOS
CAMBODIA
VIETNAM
MALAYA
MALAYSIA
INDONESIA
SUMATRA
HAINAN
JOHOR
SINGAPORE
BAY OF BENGAL
ANDAMAN SEA
GULF OF THAILAND
GULF OF TONKIN
SOUTH CHINA SEA
ANDAMAN IS. (India)
NICOBAR IS. (India)
Strait of Malacca
Tropic of Cancer
Rangoon
Mandalay
Bangkok (Krung Thep)
Vientiane (Viangchan)
Phnom Penh
Hanoi
Haiphong
Ho Chi Minh City (Saigon)
Kuala Lumpur
Kunming
Nanning
Moulmein
Chiang Mai
Luang Prabang
Hue
Da Nang
George Town
Paracel Is.
Anambas Is. (Indon.)

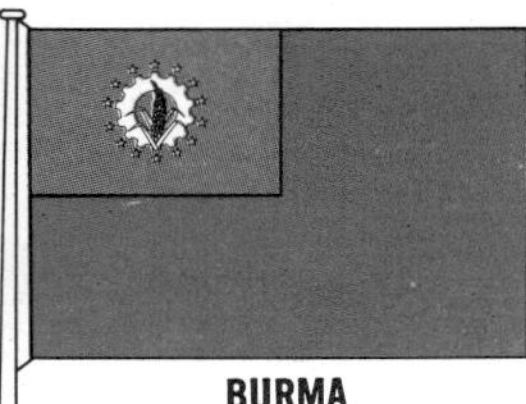

BURMA

THAILAND

LAOS

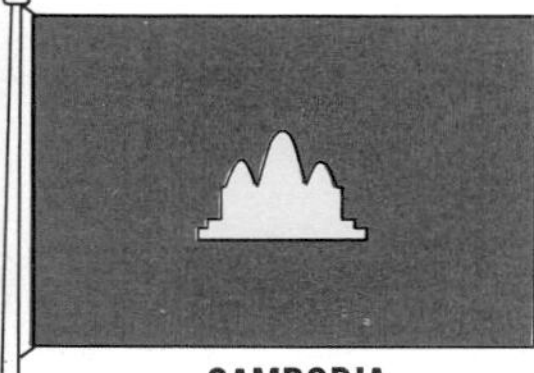

CAMBODIA

VIETNAM

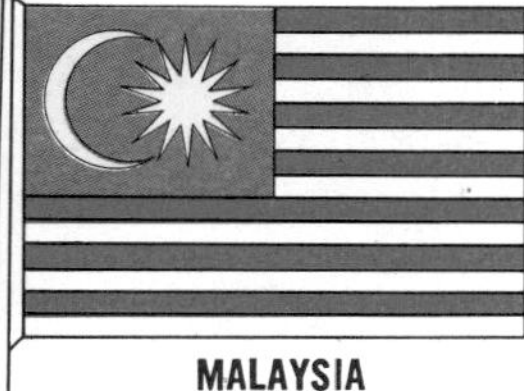

MALAYSIA

SINGAPORE

BURMA

AREA 261,789 sq. mi. (678,034 sq. km.)
POPULATION 32,913,000
CAPITAL Rangoon
LARGEST CITY Rangoon
HIGHEST POINT Hkakabo Razi 19,296 ft. (5,881 m.)
MONETARY UNIT kyat
MAJOR LANGUAGES Burmese, Karen, Shan, Kachin, Chin, Kayah, English
MAJOR RELIGIONS Buddhism, tribal religions

THAILAND

AREA 198,455 sq. mi. (513,998 sq. km.)
POPULATION 46,455,000
CAPITAL Bangkok
LARGEST CITY Bangkok
HIGHEST POINT Doi Inthanon 8,452 ft. (2,576 m.)
MONETARY UNIT baht
MAJOR LANGUAGES Thai, Lao, Chinese, Khmer, Malay
MAJOR RELIGIONS Buddhism, tribal religions

LAOS

AREA 91,428 sq. mi. (236,800 sq. km.)
POPULATION 3,721,000
CAPITAL Vientiane
LARGEST CITY Vientiane
HIGHEST POINT Phou Bia 9,252 ft. (2,820 m.)
MONETARY UNIT kip
MAJOR LANGUAGE Lao
MAJOR RELIGIONS Buddhism, tribal religions

CAMBODIA

AREA 69,898 sq. mi. (181,036 sq. km.)
POPULATION 5,200,000
CAPITAL Phnom Penh
LARGEST CITY Phnom Penh
HIGHEST POINT 5,948 ft. (1,813 m.)
MONETARY UNIT riel
MAJOR LANGUAGE Khmer (Cambodian)
MAJOR RELIGION Buddhism

VIETNAM

AREA 128,405 sq. mi. (332,569 sq. km.)
POPULATION 52,741,766
CAPITAL Hanoi
LARGEST CITY Ho Chi Minh City (Saigon)
HIGHEST POINT Fan Si Pan 10,308 ft. (3,142 m.)
MONETARY UNIT dong
MAJOR LANGUAGES Vietnamese, Thai, Muong, Meo, Yao, Khmer, French, Chinese, Cham
MAJOR RELIGIONS Buddhism, Taoism, Confucianism, Roman Catholicism, Cao-Dai

MALAYSIA

AREA 128,308 sq. mi. (332,318 sq. km.)
POPULATION 13,435,588
CAPITAL Kuala Lumpur
LARGEST CITY Kuala Lumpur
HIGHEST POINT Mt. Kinabalu 13,455 ft. (4,101 m.)
MONETARY UNIT ringgit
MAJOR LANGUAGES Malay, Chinese, English, Tamil, Dayak, Kadazan
MAJOR RELIGIONS Islam, Confucianism, Buddhism, tribal religions, Hinduism, Taoism, Christianity, Sikhism

SINGAPORE

AREA 226 sq. mi. (585 sq. km.)
POPULATION 2,413,945
CAPITAL Singapore
LARGEST CITY Singapore
HIGHEST POINT Bukit Timah 581 ft. (177 m.)
MONETARY UNIT Singapore dollar
MAJOR LANGUAGES Chinese, Malay, Tamil, English, Hindi
MAJOR RELIGIONS Confucianism, Buddhism, Taoism, Hinduism, Islam, Christianity

Topography

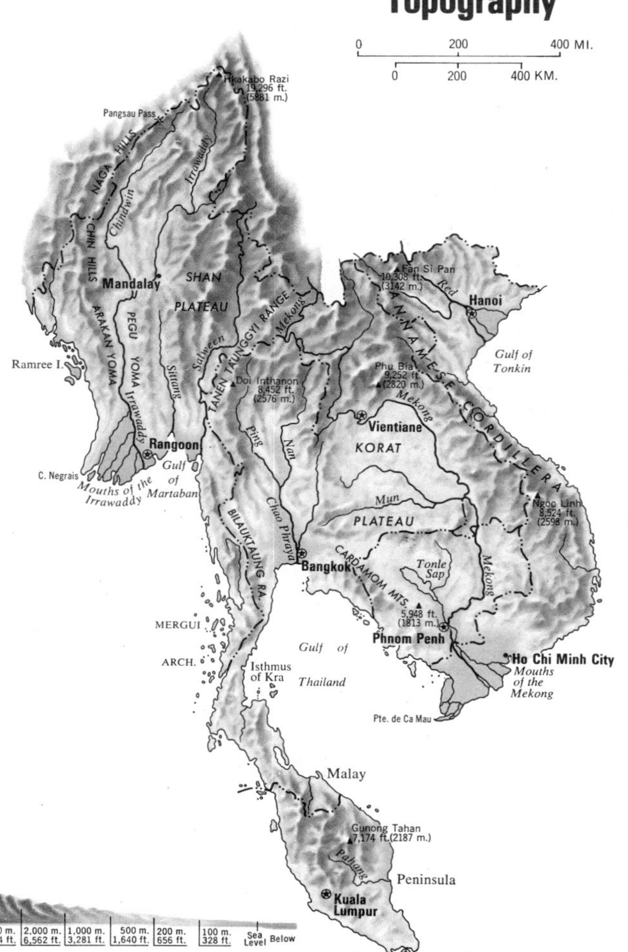

BURMA

INTERNAL DIVISIONS

Arakan (state) 1,710,913 .... B3
Chin (state) 323,094 .... B2
Irrawaddy (div.) 4,152,521 .... B3
Kachin (state) 735,144 .... C1
Karen (state) 865,218 .... C3
Kayah (state) 126,492 .... C3
Magwe (div.) 2,632,144 .... B2
Mandalay (div.) 3,662,312 .... B2
Mon (state) 1,313,111 .... C3
Pegu (div.) 3,174,109 .... C3
Rangoon (div.) 3,186,886 .... C3
Sagaing (div.) 3,115,502 .... B1
Shan (state) 3,178,214 .... C2
Tenasserim (div.) 717,607 .... C4

CITIES and TOWNS

Akyab (Sittwe) 42,329 .... B2
Allanmyo 15,580 .... B3
Amarapura 11,268 .... B2
Amherst 6,000 .... C3
An B3
Anin C4
Bassein 126,045 .... B3
Bhamo 9,821 .... C1
Chauk 24,466 .... B2
Danubyu B3
Falam B2
Fort Hertz (Putao) C1
Gawai C1
Gokteik C2
Gwa B3
Gyobingauk 9,922 .... C3
Haka B2
Henzada 61,972 .... B3
Hmawbi 23,032 .... C3
Homalin B1
Hsenwi C2
Hsipaw C2
Htawgaw C1
Insein 143,625 .... C3
Kamaing C1
Karathuri C5
Katha 7,648 .... C1
Kawludo C3
Kawthaung 1,520 .... C5
Keng Hkam C2
Keng Tung C2
Koma C4
Kunlong C2
Kyaikto 13,154 .... C3
Kya-in Seikkyi C3
Kyangin 6,073 .... B3
Kyaukme C2
Kyaukpadaung 5,480 .... B2
Kyaukpyu 7,335 .... B3
Kyaukse 8,659 .... C2
Labutta 12,982 .... B3
Lai-hka C2
Lamu B3
Lashio C2
Lenya C5
Letpadan 15,896 .... C3
Lewe B3
Loi-kaw C3
Lonton B1
Magwe 13,270 .... B2
Maingkwan C1
Maliwun C5
Mandalay 418,008 .... C2
Man Hpang C2
Martaban 5,661 .... C3
Ma-ubin 23,362 .... B3
Maungdaw 3,772 .... B2
Mawkmai C2
Mawlaik 2,993 .... B2
Mawlu C1
Maymyo 22,287 .... C2
Meiktila 19,474 .... B2
Mergui 33,697 .... C4
Minbu 9,096 .... B2
Minhla 6,470 .... B3
Mogaung 2,920 .... C1
Mogok 8,334 .... C2
Mohnyin C1
Möng Hsat C2
Möng Maü C3
Möng Mit C2
Möng Pan C2
Möng Si C2
Möng Tön C2
Möng Tung C2
Monywa 26,279 .... B2
Moulmein 171,977 .... C3
Mudon 20,136 .... C3
Myanaung 11,155 .... B3
Myaungmya 24,532 .... B3
Myingyan 36,439 .... B2
Myitkyina 12,382 .... C1
Myohaung 6,534 .... B2
Naba B1
Namhkam C2
Namlan C2
Namtu C2
Natmauk B2
Okkan 14,443 .... B3
Okpo 12,155 .... C3
Pakokku 30,943 .... B2
Palaw 5,596 .... C4
Paletwa B2
Pantha B2
Papun C3
Pasawng C3
Paungde 17,286 .... B3
Pegu 47,378 .... C3
Prome (Pye) 36,997 .... B3
Putao C1
Pyapon 19,174 .... B3
Pye 36,997 .... B3
Pyinmana 22,025 .... C3
Pyu 10,443 .... C3
Rangoon (cap.) 1,586,422 .... C3
Rangoon* 2,055,365 .... C3
Rathedaung 2,969 .... B2
Sadon C1
Sagaing 15,382 .... B2
Samka C2
Sandoway 5,172 .... B3
Shingbwiyang B1
Shwebo 17,827 .... B2
Shwenyaung C2
Singkaling Hkamti B1
Singu 4,027 .... C2
Sinlumkaba C1
Sittwe 42,329 .... B2
Sumprabum C1
Syriam 15,296 .... C3
Taungdwingyi 16,233 .... C2
Taunggyi C2
Tavoy 40,312 .... C4
Tharrawaddy 8,977 .... C3
Thaton 38,047 .... C3
Thaungdut B1
Thayetmyo 11,649 .... B3
Thazi 7,531 .... C2
Thongwa 10,829 .... C3
Toungoo 31,589 .... C3
Wakema 20,716 .... B3
Yamethin 11,167 .... C2
Yandoon 15,245 .... B3
Ye 12,852 .... C4
Yenangyaung 24,416 .... B2
Yesagyo 7,880 .... B2
Ye-u 5,307 .... B2
Ywathit C3
Zadi C4
Zalun 899 .... B3

OTHER FEATURES

Amya (pass) C4
Andaman (sea) B4
Arakan Yoma (mts.) B3
Ataran (riv.) C4
Bengal, Bay of (sea) B3
Bentinck (isl.) C5

(continued on following page)

Bilauktaung (range) C4
Chaukan (pass) C1
Cheduba (isl.) B3
Chin (hills) B2
Chindwin (riv.) B2
Coco (chan.) B4
Combermere (bay) B3
Daung Kyun (isl.) C4
Dawna (range) C3
Great Coco (isl.) B4
Great Tenasserim (riv.) C4
Heinze Chaung (bay) C4
Heywood (chan.) B3
Hka, Nam (riv.) C2
Hkakabo Razi (mt.) C1
Indawgyi (lake) C1
Inle (lake) C2
Irrawaddy (riv.) B3
Irrawaddy, Mouths of the (delta) B4
Kadan Kyun (isl.) C4
Kaladan (riv.) B2
Kalegauk (isl.) C4
Khao Luang (mt.) C5
Lanbi Kyun (isl.) C5
Launglon Bok (isls.) C4
Loi Leng (mt.) C2
Manipur (riv.) B2
Martaban (gulf) C4
Mekong (riv.) D2
Mergui (arch.) C5
Mon (riv.) B2
Mu (riv.) B2
Negrais (cape) B3
Pakchan (riv.) C5
Pangsau (pass) C1
Pawn, Nam (riv.) C2
Pegu Yoma (mts.) B3
Preparis (isl.) B4
Ramree (isl.) B3
Salween (riv.) C3
Shan (plat.) C2
Sittang (riv.) C3
Taungthonton (mt.) B1
Tavoy (pt.) C4
Tenasserim (isl.) C4
Teng, Nam (riv.) C2
Three Pagodas (pass) C4
Victoria (mt.) B2

CAMBODIA (KAMPUCHEA)

CITIES and TOWNS

Batdambang (Battambang) D4
Choam Khsant E4
Kampong Cham E4
Kampong Chhnang D4
Kampong Khleang E4
Kampong Saom D5
Kampong Spoe E5
Kampong Thum E4
Kampong Trabek E5
Kampot E5
Kaoh Nhek E4
Kracheh E4
Krong Kaoh Kong D4
Krong Keb E5
Kulen E4
Lumphat E4
Moung Roessei D4
Pailin D4
Paoy Pet D4
Phnom Penh (cap.) c. 300,000 E5
Phnum Tbeng Meanchey E4
Phsar Ream D5
Phumi Banam E5
Phumi Phsar E4
Phumi Prek Kak E4
Phumi Samraong D4
Pouthisat D4
Prek Pouthi E5
Prey Veng E5
Pursat (Pouthisat) D4
Rovieng Tbong E4
Sambor E4
Senmonoron E4
Siempang E4
Siemreab D4
Sisophon D4
Sre Ambel D5
Sre Khtum E4
Stoeng Treng E4
Suong E5
Svay Rieng E5
Takev E5
Virochey E4

OTHER FEATURES

Angkor Wat (ruins) E4
Dangrek (mts.) D4
Drang, Ia (riv.) E4
Joncs (plain) E5
Khong, Se (riv.) E4
Kong, Kaoh (isl.) D5
Mekong (riv.) E4
Rung, Kaoh (isl.) D5
San, Se (riv.) E4
Sen, Stoeng (riv.) E4
Srepok (riv.) E4
Tang, Kaoh (isl.) D5
Thailand (gulf) D5
Tonle Sap (lake) D4
Wai, Poulo (isls.) D5

LAOS

CITIES and TOWNS

Attapu 2,750 E4
Ban Khon E4
Ban Lahanam E3
Borikan D3
Champasak 3,500 E4
Dônghén E3
Khamkeut⊙ 31,206 E3
Louang Namtha 1,459 D2
Louangphrabang 7,596 D3
Muang Hinboun 1,750 E3
Muang Kènthao D3
Muang Khammoun 5,500 E3
Muang Không 1,750 E4
Muang Khôngxédôn 2,000 E4
Muang Khoua D2
Muang May E4
Muang Ou Tai D2
Muang Paktha D2
Muang Phin E3
Muang Tahoi F3
Muang Vapi E4
Muang Xaignabouri (Sayaboury) 2,500 D3
Mounlapamôk E4
Napè E3
Nong Het E3
Pakxé 8,000 E4
Phiafai⊙ 17,216 E4
Phôngsali 2,500 D2
San Nua (Sam Neua) 3,000 E2
Saravan 2,350 E4
Savannakhét 8,500 E3
Sayaboury (Muang Xaignabouri) 2,500 D3
Thakhek (Muang Khammouan) 5,500 E3
Tourakom D3
Viangchan (Vientiane) 132,253 D3
Vientiane (cap.) 132,253 D3
Xiangkhoang 3,500 D3

OTHER FEATURES

Bolovens (plat.) E4
Hou, Nam (riv.) D2
Jars (plain) D3
Mekong (riv.) D3
Ou, Nam (riv.) D2
Phou Bia (mt.) D3
Phou Cô Pi (mt.) E3
Phou Loi (mt.) D2
Rao Co (mt.) E3
Se Khong (riv.) E4
Tha, Nam (riv.) D2
Xianghoang (plat.) D3

MALAYA, MALAYSIA*

STATES

Federal Territory 937,875 D7
Johor (Johore) 1,601,504 D7
Kedah 1,102,200 D6
Kelantan 877,575 D6
Melaka 453,153 D7
Negeri Sembilan 563,955 D7
Pahang 770,644 D7
Perak 1,762,288 D6
Perlis 147,726 D6
Pinang (Penang) 911,586 D6
Selangor 1,467,441 D7
Terengganu 542,280 D6

CITIES and TOWNS

Alor Gajah 2,222 D7
Alor Setar 66,260 D6
Bandar Maharani (Muar) 61,218 D7
Bandar Penggaram (Batu Pahat) 53,291 D7
Batu Gajah 10,692 D6
Batu Pahat 53,291 D7
Bentong 22,683 D7
Butterworth 61,187 D6
Chukai 12,514 D6
Gemas 5,214 D7
George Town (Pinang) 269,603 C6
Ipoh 247,953 D6
Johor Baharu (Johore Bharu) 136,234 F5
Kampar 26,591 D6
Kangar 8,758 D6
Kelang 113,611 D7
Keluang 43,272 D7
Kota Baharu 55,124 D6
Kota Tinggi 8,725 F5
Kuala Dungun 17,560 D6
Kuala Lipis 9,270 D6
Kuala Lumpur (cap.) 451,977 D7
Kuala Lumpur* 937,875 D7
Kuala Pilah 12,508 D7
Kuala Rompin 1,384 D7
Kuala Selangor 3,132 D7
Kuala Terengganu 53,320 D6
Kuantan 43,358 D7
Kulai 11,841 F5
Lumut 3,255 D6
Malacca (Melaka) 87,160 D7
Mawai F5
Melaka 87,160 D7
Mersing 18,246 E7
Muar 61,218 D7
Pekan 4,682 D7
Pekan Nanas 9,003 E5
Pinang (George Town) 269,603 C6
Pontian Kechil 8,349 E5
Port Dickson 10,300 D7
Port Kelang D7
Port Weld 3,233 D6
Raub 18,433 D7
Segamat 17,796 D7
Seremban 80,921 D7
Sungai Petani 35,959 C6
Taiping 54,645 D6
Tanah Merah 7,012 D6
Telok Anson 44,524 D6
Tumpat 10,673 D6

OTHER FEATURES

Aur, Pulau (isl.) E7
Belumut, Gunong (mt.) D7
Gelang, Tanjong (pt.) D6
Johor, Sungai (riv.) F5
Johore (str.) E6
Kelantan, Sungai (riv.) D6
Langkawi, Pulau (isl.) C6
Ledang, Gunong (mt.) D7
Lima, Pulau (isl.) F6
Malacca (str.) D7
Malay (pen.) D6
Pahang, Sungai (riv.) D7
Pangkor, Pulau (isl.) D6
Perak, Gunong (mt.) D6
Perhentian, Kepulauan (isls.) D6
Pulai, Sungai (riv.) E5
Ramunia, Tanjong (pt.) F6
Redang, Pulau (isl.) D6
Sedili Kechil, Tanjong (pt.) F5
Tahan, Gunong (mt.) D6
Temiang, Bukit (mt.) D6
Tenggol, Pulau (isl.) D6
Tinggi, Pulau (isl.) E7

SINGAPORE

CITIES and TOWNS

Jurong 50,974 E6
Nee Soon 37,641 F6
Serangoon 89,558 F6
Singapore (cap.) 2,413,945 F6

OTHER FEATURES

Keppel (harb.) F6
Main (str.) F6
Singapore (str.) F6
Tekong Besar, Pulau (isl.) F6

THAILAND (SIAM)

CITIES and TOWNS

Ang Thong 7,267 C4
Ayutthaya (Phra Nakhon Si Ayutthaya) 37,213 D4
Ban Aranyaprathet 12,276 D4
Bangkok (cap.) 1,867,297 D4
Bangkok* 2,495,312 D4
Bang Lamung D4
Bang Saphan C5
Ban Kantang 9,247 C6
Ban Kapong C5
Ban Khlong Yai D5
Ban Kui Nua D4
Ban Ngon D3
Ban Pak Phanang 13,590 D5
Banphot Phisai C3
Ban Pua D3
Ban Sattahip D4
Ban Tha Uthen D3
Bua Chum D4
Buriram 16,431 D4
Chachoengsao 22,106 D4
Chai Badan D4
Chai Buri D3
Chainat 9,944 D4
Chaiya C5
Chaiyaphum 12,540 D4
Chang Khoeng C3
Chanthaburi 15,479 D4
Chiang Dao C3
Chiang Khan D3
Chiang Mai 83,729 C3
Chiang Rai 13,927 C3
Chiang Saen C2
Chon Buri 39,367 D4
Chumphon 11,643 C5
Den Chai C3
Hat Yai 47,953 C6
Hot C3
Hua Hin 21,426 D4
Kalasin 14,960 D3
Kamphaeng Phet 12,378 C3
Kanchanaburi 16,397 C4
Khanu C3
Khemmarat E4
Khon Kaen 29,431 D3
Khorat (Nakhon Ratchasima) 66,071 D4
Krabi 8,764 C5
Krung Thep (Bangkok) (cap.) 1,867,297 D4
Kumphawapi D3
Lae D3
Lampang 40,100 C3
Lamphun 11,309 C3
Lang Suan 4,020 C5
Loei 10,137 D3
Lom Sak 10,597 D3
Lop Buri 23,112 D4
Mae Hong Son 3,981 C3
Maha Sarakham 19,707 D3
Mukdahan E3
Nakhon Nayok 8,185 D4
Nakhon Pathom 34,300 C4
Nakhon Phanom 20,385 D3
Nakhon Ratchasima 66,071 D4
Nakhon Sawan 46,853 D4
Nakhon Si Thammarat 40,671 D5
Nan 17,738 D3
Nang Rong D4
Narathiwat 21,256 D6
Ngao D3
Nong Khai 21,150 D3
Pattani 21,938 D6
Phanat Nikhom 10,514 D4
Phangnga 5,738 C5
Phatthalung 13,336 D6
Phayao 20,346 C3
Phet Buri 27,755 C4
Phetchabun 6,240 D3
Phichai D3
Phichit 10,814 D3
Phitsanulok 33,883 D3
Phon Phisai D3
Phrae 17,555 D3
Phra Nakhon Si Ayutthaya 37,213 D4
Phuket 34,362 C6
Phutthaisong D4
Prachin Buri 14,167 D4
Prachuap Khiri Khan 9,075 D5
Pran Buri D4
Rahaeng (Tak) 16,317 C3
Ranong 10,301 C5
Rat Buri 32,271 C4
Rayong 14,846 D4
Roi Et 20,242 D4
Rong Kwang D3
Sakon Nakhon 18,943 E3
Samut Prakan 46,632 D4
Samut Sakhon 33,619 D4
Samut Songkhram 23,574 C4
Sara Buri 25,025 D4
Satun 7,315 C6
Sawankhalok 8,387 C3
Selaphum E3
Sing Buri 9,050 D4
Singora (Songkhla) 41,193 D6
Sisaket 13,662 E4
Songkhla 41,193 D6
Sukhothai 15,488 D3
Suphan Buri 18,768 C4
Surat Thani 24,923 C5
Surin 16,342 D4
Suwannaphum D4
Tak 16,317 C3
Takua Pa 7,825 C5
Thoen C3
Thon Buri 628,015 D4
To Mo D6
Trang 32,985 C6
Trat 7,917 D4
Ubon 40,650 E4
Udon Thani 56,218 D3
Uthai Thani 10,525 C4
Uttaradit 12,022 D3
Warin Chamrap 21,520 E4
Yala 30,051 D6
Yasothon 12,079 D4

OTHER FEATURES

Amya (pass) C4
Bilauktaung (range) C4
Chang, Ko (isl.) D4
Chao Phraya, Mae Nam (riv.) D4
Chi, Mae Nam (riv.) D3
Dangrek (Dong Rak) (mts.) D4
Doi Inthanon (mt.) C3
Doi Pha Hom Pok (mt.) C2
Doi Pia Fai (mt.) D4
Kao Prawa (mt.) C3
Khao Luang (mt.) C5
Khwae Noi, Mae Nam (riv.) C4
Kra (isth.) C5
Kut, Ko (isl.) D5
Laem Pho (cape) D6
Laem Talumphuk (cape) D5
Lanta, Ko (isl.) C6
Luang (mt.) C5
Mae Klong, Mae Nam (riv.) C4
Mekong (riv.) E3
Mun, Mae Nam (riv.) D4
Nan, Mae Nam (riv.) D3
Nong Lahan (lake) D3
Pakchan (riv.) C5
Pa Sak, Mae Nam (riv.) D4
Phangan, Ko (isl.) D5
Phuket, Ko (isl.) C5

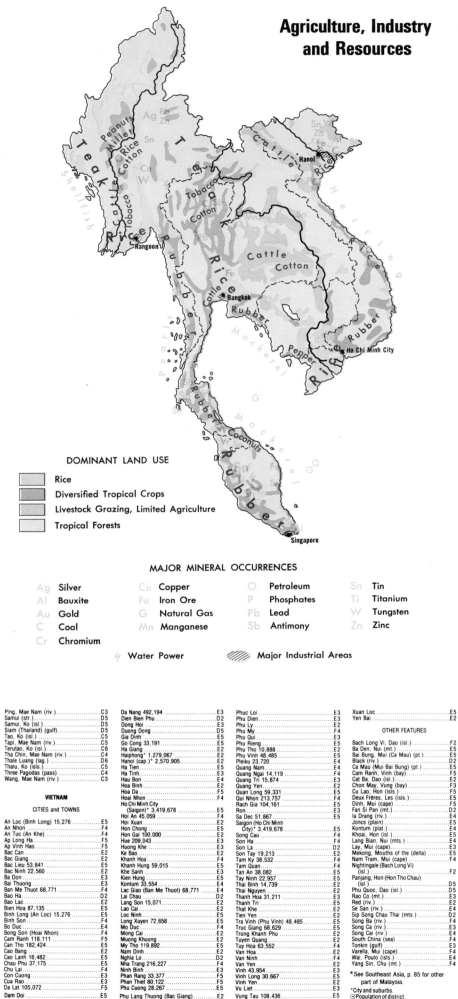

Agriculture, Industry and Resources

DOMINANT LAND USE

Rice
Diversified Tropical Crops
Livestock Grazing, Limited Agriculture
Tropical Forests

MAJOR MINERAL OCCURRENCES

Ag Silver
Al Bauxite
Au Gold
C Coal
Cr Chromium
Cu Copper
Fe Iron Ore
G Natural Gas
Mn Manganese
O Petroleum
P Phosphates
Pb Lead
Sb Antimony
Sn Tin
Ti Titanium
W Tungsten
Zn Zinc

Water Power
Major Industrial Areas

Ping, Mae Nam (riv.) C3
Samui (str.) D5
Samui, Ko (isl.) D5
Siam (Thailand) (gulf) D5
Tao, Ko (isl.) C5
Tapi, Mae Nam (riv.) C5
Terutao, Ko (isl.) C6
Tha Chin, Mae Nam (riv.) C4
Thale Luang (lag.) D6
Thalu, Ko (isls.) C5
Three Pagodas (pass) C4
Wang, Mae Nam (riv.) C3

VIETNAM

CITIES and TOWNS

An Loc (Binh Long) 15,276 E5
An Nhon F4
An Tuc (An Khe) F4
Ap Long Ha F5
Ap Vinh Hao F5
Bac Can E2
Bac Giang E2
Bac Lieu 53,841 E5
Bac Ninh 22,560 E2
Ba Don E3
Bai Thuong E3
Ban Me Thuot 68,771 F4
Bao Ha D2
Bao Lac E2
Bien Hoa 87,135 E5
Binh Long (An Loc) 15,276 E5
Binh Son F4
Bo Duc E4
Bong Son (Hoai Nhon) F4
Cam Ranh 118,111 F5
Can Tho 182,424 E5
Cao Bang E2
Cao Lanh 16,482 E5
Chau Phu 37,175 E5
Chu Lai F4
Con Cuong E3
Cua Rao E3
Da Lat 105,072 F5
Dam Doi E5
Da Nang 492,194 E3
Dien Bien Phu D2
Dong Hoi E3
Duong Dong D5
Gia Dinh E5
Go Cong 33,191 E5
Ha Giang E2
Haiphong* 1,279,067 E2
Hanoi (cap.)* 2,570,905 E2
Ha Tien E5
Ha Tinh E3
Hau Bon E4
Hoa Binh E2
Hoa Da F5
Hoai Nhon F4
Ho Chi Minh City (Saigon)* 3,419,678 E5
Hoi An 45,059 F4
Hoi Xuan E2
Hon Chong E5
Hon Gai 100,000 E2
Hue 209,043 E3
Huong Khe E3
Ke Bao E2
Khanh Hoa F4
Khanh Hung 59,015 E5
Khe Sanh E3
Kien Hung E5
Kontum 33,554 E4
Lac Giao (Ban Me Thuot) 68,771 E4
Lai Chau D2
Lang Son 15,071 E2
Lao Cai E2
Loc Ninh E5
Long Xuyen 72,658 E5
Mo Duc F4
Mong Cai E2
Muong Khuong E2
My Tho 119,892 E5
Nam Dinh E2
Nghia Lo D2
Nha Trang 216,227 F4
Ninh Binh E3
Phan Rang 33,377 F5
Phan Thiet 80,122 F5
Phu Cuong 28,267 E5
Phu Lang Thuong (Bac Giang) E2
Phuc Loi E3
Phu Dien E3
Phu Ly E2
Phu My F4
Phu Qui E3
Phu Rieng E5
Phu Tho 10,888 E2
Phu Vinh 48,485 E5
Pleiku 23,720 E4
Quang Nam E4
Quang Ngai 14,119 F4
Quang Tri 15,874 E3
Quang Yen E2
Quan Long 59,331 E5
Qui Nhon 213,757 F4
Rach Gia 104,161 E5
Ron E3
Sa Dec 51,867 E5
Saigon (Ho Chi Minh City)* 3,419,678 E5
Song Cau F4
Son Ha F4
Son La D2
Son Tay 19,213 E2
Tam Ky 38,532 F4
Tam Quan F4
Tan An 38,082 E5
Tay Ninh 22,957 E5
Thai Binh 14,739 E2
Thai Nguyen E2
Thanh Hoa 31,211 E3
Thanh Tri E5
That Khe E2
Tien Yen E2
Tra Vinh (Phu Vinh) 48,485 E5
Truc Giang 68,629 E5
Trung Khanh Phu E2
Tuyen Quang E2
Tuy Hoa 63,552 F4
Van Hoa E2
Van Ninh F4
Van Yen E2
Vinh 43,954 E3
Vinh Long 30,667 E5
Vinh Yen E2
Vu Liet E3
Vung Tau 108,436 E5
Xuan Loc E5
Yen Bai E2

OTHER FEATURES

Bach Long Vi, Dao (isl.) F2
Ba Den, Nui (mt.) E5
Bai Bung, Mui (Ca Mau) (pt.) E5
Black (riv.) D2
Ca Mau (Mui Bai Bung) (pt.) E5
Cam Ranh, Vinh (bay) F5
Cat Ba, Dao (isl.) E2
Chon May, Vung (bay) F3
Cu Lao, Hon (isls.) F5
Deux Frères, Les (isls.) E5
Dinh, Mui (cape) F5
Fan Si Pan (mt.) D2
Ia Drang (riv.) E4
Joncs (plain) E5
Kontum (plat.) E4
Khoai, Hon (isl.) E5
Lang Bian, Nui (mts.) E4
Lay, Mui (cape) E3
Mekong, Mouths of the (delta) E5
Nam Tram, Mui (cape) F4
Nightingale (Bach Long Vi) (isl.) F2
Panjang, Hon (Hon Tho Chau) (isl.) D5
Phu Quoc, Dao (isl.) D5
Rao Co (mt.) E3
Red (riv.) E2
Se San (riv.) E4
Sip Song Chau Thai (mts.) D2
Song Ba (riv.) F4
Song Ca (riv.) E3
Song Cai (riv.) E4
South China (sea) F4
Tonkin (gulf) E3
Varella, Mui (cape) F4
Wai, Poulo (isls.) E4
Yang Sin, Chu (mt.) F4

*See Southeast Asia, p. 85 for other part of Malaysia.

*City and suburbs.
⊙Population of district.

CHINA (MAINLAND)

AREA 3,691,000 sq. mi. (9,559,690 sq. km.)
POPULATION 958,090,000
CAPITAL Peking (Beijing)
LARGEST CITY Shanghai
HIGHEST POINT Mt. Everest 29,028 ft. (8,848 m.)
MONETARY UNIT yuan
MAJOR LANGUAGES Chinese, Chuang, Uigur, Yi, Tibetan, Miao, Mongol, Kazakh
MAJOR RELIGIONS Confucianism, Buddhism, Taoism, Islam

CHINA (TAIWAN)

AREA 13,971 sq. mi. (36,185 sq. km.)
POPULATION 16,609,961
CAPITAL Taipei
LARGEST CITY Taipei
HIGHEST POINT Yü Shan 13,113 ft. (3,997 m.)
MONETARY UNIT new Taiwan yüan (dollar)
MAJOR LANGUAGES Chinese, Formosan
MAJOR RELIGIONS Confucianism, Buddhism, Taoism, Christianity, tribal religions

MONGOLIA

AREA 606,163 sq. mi. (1,569,962 sq. km.)
POPULATION 1,594,800
CAPITAL Ulaanbaatar
LARGEST CITY Ulaanbaatar
HIGHEST POINT Tabun Bogdo 14,288 ft. (4,355 m.)
MONETARY UNIT tughrik
MAJOR LANGUAGES Khalkha Mongolian, Kazakh (Turkic)
MAJOR RELIGION Buddhism

HONG KONG

AREA 403 sq. mi. (1,044 sq. km.)
POPULATION 5,022,000
CAPITAL Victoria
MONETARY UNIT Hong Kong dollar
MAJOR LANGUAGES Chinese, English
MAJOR RELIGIONS Confucianism, Buddhism, Christianity

MACAU

AREA 6 sq. mi. (16 sq. km.)
POPULATION 271,000
CAPITAL Macau
MONETARY UNIT pataca
MAJOR LANGUAGES Chinese, Portuguese
MAJOR RELIGIONS Confucianism, Buddhism, Taoism, Christianity

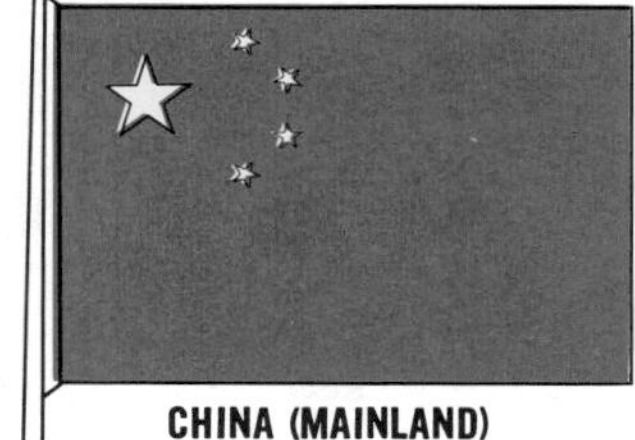

CHINA (MAINLAND)

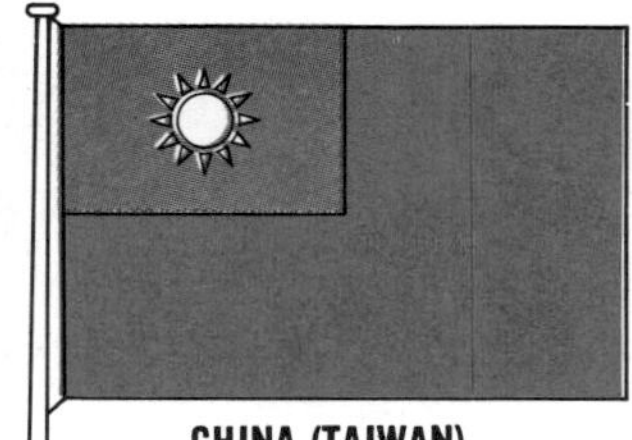

CHINA (TAIWAN)

MONGOLIA

China and Mongolia Transportation

Scale of Miles 0 500 1000
Scale of Kilometers 0 500 1000

Railroads
Under Construction
Connecting Roads
Navigable Rivers
Canals
Major Seaports

CHINA

PROVINCES

Anhui (Anhwei) 47,130,000 ..... J5
Chekiang (Zhejiang) 37,510,000 ..... K6
Fujian (Fukien) 24,500,000 ..... J6
Gansu (Kansu) 18,730,000 ..... E3
Guangdong (Kwangtung) 55,930,000 ..... H7
Guangxi Zhuangzu (Kwangsi Chuang Aut. Reg. 34,020,000 ..... G7
Guizhou (Kweichow) 26,860,000 ..... G6
Heilongjiang (Heilungkiang) 33,760,000 ..... K2
Hebei (Hopei) 50,570,000 ..... J4
Henan (Honan) 70,660,000 ..... H5
Hubei (Hupei) 45,750,000 ..... H5
Hunan 51,660,000 ..... H6
Inner Mongolian Aut. Reg. (Nei Monggol) 8,900,000 ..... H3
Jiangxi (Kiangsi) 31,830,000 ..... J6
Jiangsu (Kiangsu) 58,340,000 ..... K5
Jilin (Kirin) 24,740,000 ..... L3
Kansu (Gansu) 18,730,000 ..... E3
Kiangsi (Jiangxi) 31,830,000 ..... J6
Kiangsu (Jiangsu) 58,340,000 ..... K5
Kirin (Jilin) 24,740,000 ..... L3
Kwangsi Chuang Aut. Reg. (Guangxi Zhuang 34,020,000 ..... G7
Kwangtung (Guangdong) 55,930,000 ..... H7
Kweichow (Guizhou) 26,860,000 ..... G6
Liaoning 37,430,000 ..... K3
Nei Monggol (Inner Mongolian Aut. Reg.) 8,900,000 ..... H3
Ningxia Huizu (Ningsia Hui Aut. Reg.) 3,660,000 ..... F3
Qinghai (Tsinghai) 3,650,000 ..... E4
Shaanxi (Shensi) 27,790,000 ..... G5
Shanxi (Shansi) 24,340,000 ..... H4
Shandong (Shantung) 71,600,000 ..... J4
Sichuan (Szechwan) 97,070,000 ..... F5
Sinkiang-Uigur Aut. Reg. (Xinjiang Uygur 12,330,000 ..... B3
Taiwan 16,609,961 ..... K7
Tibet Aut. Reg. (Xizang) 1,790,000 ..... B5

Tsinghai (Qinghai) 3,650,000 ..... E4
Xinjiang Uygur (Sinkiang-Uigur Aut. Reg. 12,330,000 ..... B3
Xizang (Tibet Aut. Reg.) 1,790,000 ..... B5
Yunnan 30,920,000 ..... F7
Zhejiang (Chekiang) 37,510,000 ..... K6

CITIES AND TOWNS†

Aba F5
Abagnar (Silinhot) J3
Aihui (Aigun) (Heihe) L1
Aksu (Aqsu) B3
Altay C2
Alxa Youqi F4
Alxa Zuoqi F4
Amoy (Xiamen) 400,000 ..... J7
Anda (Anta) L2
Ankang G5
Anqing (Anking) 160,000 ..... J5
Anshan 1,500,000 ..... K3
Anshun G6
Antu L3
Anxi E3
Anyang 225,000 ..... H4
Aqsu (Aksu) B3
Aratürük (Yiwu) D3
Ar Horqin K3
Arixang (Wenquan) B3
Artux (Atushi) A4
Bachu (Maralwexi) A4
Baicheng, Jilin K2
Baicheng (Bay), Xinjiang Uygur B3
Bairin Zuoqi J3
Baoding (Paoting) 350,000 ..... J4
Baoji (Paoki) 275,000 ..... G5
Baoshan E7
Baoting G8
Baotou (Paotow) 800,000 ..... G3
Bargrax (Bohu) C3
Batang E5
Bay (Baicheng) B3
Bayan Obo G3
Ba Xian J4
Bei'an (Pehan) 130,000 ..... L2
Beihai (Pakhoi) 175,000 ..... G7
Beijing (Peking) (cap.)• 8,500,000 ..... J3
Bengbu (Pengpu) 400,000 ..... J5
Benxi (Penki) 750,000 ..... K3
Bohu (Bagrax) C3
Bole B3
Bortala (Bole) B3
Boshan J4
Bo Xian (Pohsien) J5
Butha K2
Cangzhou (Tsangchow) J4
Canton (Guangzhou) 2,300,000 ..... H7
Chamdo (Qamdo) E5
Changchih (Changzhi) H4
Changchow (Changzhou) 400,000 ..... J5
Changchow (Zhangzhou) J7
Changchun 1,500,000 ..... K3
Changde (Changteh) 225,000 ..... H6
Changhua 137,236 ..... K7
Changji C3
Changjiang G8
Changsha 850,000 ..... H6
Changteh (Changde) 225,000 ..... H6
Changyeh (Zhangye) F4
Changzhi (Changchih) H4
Changzhou (Changchow) 400,000 ..... K5
Chankiang (Zhanjiang) 220,000 ..... H7
Chao'an (Chaochow) J7
Chaotung (Zhaotung) F6
Chaoyang, Liaoning J3
Chaoyang, Guangdong J7
Charkhlia (Ruoqiang) C4
Chefoo (Yantai) 180,000 ..... K4
Chengchow (Zhengzhou) 1,500,000 ..... H5
Chengde (Chengteh) 200,000 ..... J3
Chengdu (Chengtu) 2,000,000 ..... F5
Chen Xian H6
Cherchen (Qiemo) C4
Chiai 238,713 ..... K7
Chifeng J3
Chinchow (Jinzhou) 750,000 ..... K3
Chindu E5
Chinkiang (Zhenjiang) 250,000 ..... J5
Chinsi (Jinxi) K3
Chinwangtao (Qinhuangdao) 400,000 ..... K4
Chishui G6
Chongqing (Chungking) 3,500,000 ..... G6
Chüanchow (Quanzhou) 130,000 ..... J7
Chuchow (Zhuzhou) 350,000 ..... H6
Chuguchak (Tacheng) B2
Chumatien (Zhumadian) H5
Chungking (Chongqing) 3,500,000 ..... G6
Chungshan (Zhongshan) 135,000 ..... H7
Da'an (Talai) K2
Danba F5
Dandong (Tantung) 450,000 ..... K3
Dali E6
Dan Xian G8
Da Qaidam E4
Datong (Tatung), Shanxi 300,000 ..... H3
Datong, Qinghai F4
Da Xian G5
Dazhai H4
Dengkou G3
Deyang F5
Dezhou (Tehchow) J4
Dingxing H4
Dongchuan F6
Dongfang G8
Dongsheng H4
Dongtai K5
Dorbiljin (Emin) B2
Dukou F6
Dulan E4
Dunhua (Tunhwa) L3
Dunhuang E3
Duolun J3
Dushan G6
Duyun (Tuyün) G6
Ejin F3
Emin (Dorbiljin) B2
Erenhot H3
Ergun Youqi K1
Ergun Zuoqi K1
Ertai C2
Fatshan (Foshan) H7

(continued on following page)

China and Mongolia

(continued)

Foochow (Fuzhou) 900,000 J6
Foshan (Fatshan) H7
Fowyang (Fuyang) J5
Fushun 1,700,000 K3
Fusingchen (Simao) F7
Fu Xian, Liaoning K4
Fu Xian, Shaanxi G4
Fuxin (Fusin) 350,000 K3
Fuyang (Fowyang) J5
Fuyu, Heilongjiang K2
Fuyu, Jilin L2
Fuyuan, Heilongjiang M2
Fuyuan, Yunnan F6
Fuyun C2
Fuzhou (Foochow) Fujian 900,000 J6
Fuzhou, Jiangxi J6
Ganzhou (Kanchow) 135,000 H6
Garyarsa (Gartok) B5
Gejiu (Kokiu) 250,000 F7
Golmud (Golmo) D4
Gonghe F4
Guangyuan G5
Guan Xian F5
Guangzhou (Canton) 2,300,000 H7
Guilin (Kweilin) 225,000 G6
Guiyang (Kweiyang), Guizhou 1,500,000 G6
Guiyang, Hunan H6
Gulja (Yining) 160,000 B3
Guma (Pishan) A4
Guyang G3
Guyuan G4
Gyaca D6
Gyangzê C6
Habahe C2
Haikou (Hoihow) 500,000 H7
Hailar J2
Hami (Kumul) D3
Hancheng H4
Hanchung (Hanzhong) 120,000 G5
Handan (Hantan) 500,000 H4
Hangzhou (Hangchow) 1,100,000 J5
Hantan (Handan) 500,000 H4
Hanzhong (Hanchung) 120,000 G5
Harbin 2,750,000 L2
Hebi H4
Hechuan (Hochwan) G5
Hefei (Hofei) 400,000 J5
Hegang (Hokang) 350,000 L2
Heihe (Aihui) (Aigun) L1
Hekou F7
Hengchun K7
Hengshan G4
Hengyang 310,000 H6
Hepu (Hoppo) G7
Hexigten J3
Hezuo F5
Hochwan (Hechuan) G5
Hofei (Hefei) 400,000 J5
Hohhot (Huhehot) 700,000 H3
Hoihow (Haikou) 500,000 H7
Hokang (Hegang) 350,000 L2
Hoppo (Hepu) G7
Horqin Youyi Qianqi (Ulanhot) 100,000 K2
Hotan B4
Houma H4
Hsüchang (Xuchang) H5
Huadian L3
Huaibei J5
Huaide (Hwaiteh) K3
Huainan 350,000 J5
Hualien K7
Huangling G4
Huangshi 200,000 J5
Huangzhong F4
Huhehot (Hohhot) 700,000 H3
Huizhou H7
Hulin M2
Hunchun M3
Hunjiang L3
Hwainan (Huainan) 350,000 J5
Hwaiteh (Huaide) K3
Hwangshih (Huangshi) 200,000 J5
Ichang (Yichang) 150,000 H5
Ichun (Yichun) 200,000 L2
Ilan K7
Ipin (Yibin) 275,000 F6
Jeminay C2
Jiamusi (Kiamusze) 275,000 M2
Ji'an (Kian) 100,000 J6
Jiangmen (Kongmoon) 150,000 H7
Jian'ou J6
Jiaozuo (Tsiaotso) 300,000 H4
Jiaxing (Kashing) K5
Jiayuguan E4
Jieyang J7
Jilin (Kirin) 1,200,000 L3
Jinan (Tsinan) 1,500,000 J4
Jingdezhen (Kingtehchen) 300,000 J6
Jinghong F7
Jingxi G7
Jing Xian, Anhui J5
Jing Xian, Hunan H6
Jingyuan F4
Jinhua (Kinhwa) J6
Jining (Tsining), Nei Monggol 160,000 H3
Jining (Tsining), Shandong J4
Jinshi (Tsingshih) 100,000 H6
Jinxi (Chinsi) K3
Jinzhou (Chinchow) 750,000 K3
Jiujiang (Kiukiang) 120,000 J6
Jiuquan (Kiuchüan) E4
Jixi (Kisi) 350,000 M2
Juichin (Ruijin) J6
Jun Xian H5
Kaba (Habahe) C2
Kaifeng 330,000 H5
Kailu K3
Kaiyuan, Liaoning K3
Kaiyuan, Yunnan F7
Kalgan (Zhangjiakou) 1,000,000 J3
Kanchow (Ganzhou) 135,000 H6
Kangding F5
Kaohsiung 1,028,334 J7
Karakax (Kara Kash) (Moyu) A4
Karamay B2
Karghalik (Yecheng) A4
Kashi (Kashgar) 175,000 A4
Kashing (Jiaxing) K5
Kaxgar (Kashi) 175,000 A4
Keelung 342,604 K6
Kenli J4
Keriya (Yutian) B4
Khotan (Hotan) B4
Kiamusze (Jiamusi) 275,000 M2
Kian (Ji'an) 100,000 J6
Kienyang (Qianyang) H6
Kingtehchen (Jingdezhen) 300,000 J6
Kinhwa (Jinhua) J6
Kirin (Jilin) 1,200,000 L3
Kisi (Jixi) 350,000 M2
Kiuchüan (Jiuquan) E4
Kiukiang (Jiujiang) 120,000 J6
Kokiu (Gejiu) 250,000 F7
Kongmoon (Jiangmen) 150,000 H7
Korla C3
Kuldja (Yining) 160,000 B3
Kumul (Hami) D3
Künes (Xinyuan) B3
Kunming 1,700,000 F6
Kuqa B3
Kuytun C3
Kwangchow (Canton) 2,300,000 H7
Kweilin (Guilin) 225,000 G6
Kweisui (Hohhot) 700,000 H3
Kweiyang (Guiyang) 1,500,000 G6
Lanzhou (Lanchow) 1,500,000 F4
Lenghu D4
Lengshuijiang H6
Leshan (Loshan) 250,000 F6
Lhasa 175,000 D6
Lhazê (Lhatse) C6
Lianyungang (Lienyünkang) 300,000 J5
Liaoyang 250,000 K3
Liaoyuan 300,000 K3
Lijiang F6
Linfen H4
Lingling H6
Linhe G3
Linqing (Lintsing) J4
Linxi J3
Linxia (Linsia) F4
Liuzhou (Liuchow) 250,000 G7
Loho (Luohe) H5
Longjiang K2
Lopnur (Yuli) C3
Loshan (Leshan) 250,000 F6
Loyang (Luoyang) 750,000 H5
Lu'an J5
Luchow (Luzhou) 225,000 G6
Lüda (Lüta) 4,000,000 K4
Luohe H5
Luoyang (Loyang) 750,000 H5
Lüshun K4
Lüta (Lüda) 4,000,000 K4
Luxi F7
Luzhou (Luchow) 225,000 G6
Ma'anshan J5
Manas C3
Manchouli (Manzhouli) J2
Manzhouli (Manchouli) J2
Maoming (Mowming) H7
Maralwexi (Bachu) A4
Mengcheng J5
Mengzi F7
Mianyang, Hubei H5
Mianyang, Sichuan G5
Minfeng (Niya) B4
Minle F4
Mowming (Maoming) H7
Moyu (Karakax) A4
Mudanjiang (Mutankiang) 400,000 M3
Mukden (Shenyang) 3,750,000 K3
Muli F6
Nagqu D5
Nanchang 900,000 J6
Nanchong (Nanchung) 275,000 G5
Nanjing (Nanking) 2,000,000 J5
Nanning 375,000 G7
Nanping J6
Nantong 300,000 K5
Nanyang H5
Napo G7
Neijiang (Neikiang) 240,000 G6
Nenjiang L2
Ningbo (Ningpo) 350,000 K6
Ningpo (Ningbo) 350,000 K6
Ningsia (Yinchuan, Yinchwan) 175,000 G4
Niya (Minfeng) B4
Ongniud J3
Oroqen K1
Paicheng (Baicheng) K2
Pakhoi (Beihai) 175,000 G7
Paoki (Baoji) 275,000 G5
Paoting (Baoding) 350,000 J4
Paotow (Baotou) 800,000 G3
Pehan (Bei'an) 130,000 L2
Peking (Beijing) (cap.)● 8,500,000 J3
Pengpu (Bengbu) 400,000 J5
Penki (Benxi) 750,000 K3
Pingdingshan H5
Pingliang G4
Pingtung 165,360 K7
Pingxiang, Guangxi Zhuangzu G7
Pingxiang, Jiangxi H6
Piqan (Shanshan) D3
Pishan (Guma) A4
Pohsien (Bo Xian) J5
Qamdo E5
Qarkilik (Ruoqiang) C4
Qarqan (Qiemo) C4
Qianyang (Kienyang) H6
Qiemo (Qarqan) C4
Qingdao (Tsingtao) 1,900,000 K4
Qingjiang, Jiangxi J6
Qingjiang 110,000 J5
Qinhuangdao (Chinwangtao) 400,000 K4
Qionghai H8
Qiqihar (Tsitsihar) 1,500,000 K2
Qitai C3
Qog G3
Qoqek (Tacheng) B2
Quanzhou (Chüanchow) 130,000 J7
Qu Xian, Sichuan G5
Qu Xian, Zhejiang J6
Qüxü D6
Ruijin (Juichin) J6
Ruoqiang (Qarkilik) C4
Rutog A5
Sanmenxia H5
Sanming J6
Sêrxü E5
Shache (Yarkand) A4
Shandan F4
Shangdu H3
Shanghai● 10,980,000 K5
Shangqiu (Shangkiu) 250,000 J5
Shangrao (Shangjao) 100,000 J6
Shangshui 100,000 J5
Shanshan (Piqan) D3
Shantou (Swatow) 400,000 J7
Shaoguan (Shiukwan) 125,000 H7
Shaoxing (Shaohing) 225,000 K5
Shaoyang 275,000 H6
Shashi 125,000 H5
Shenyang (Mukden) 3,750,000 K3
Shigatse (Xigaze) C6
Shihezi (Shihhotzu) C3
Shijiazhuang (Shihkiachwang) 1,500,000 J4
Shiquanhe A5
Shiukwan (Shaoyuan) 125,000 H7
Shiyan H5
Shizuishan (Shihsuishan) G4
Shuangcheng L2
Shuangyashan 150,000 M2
Shuo Xian H4
Siakwan (Xiaguan) E6
Sian (Xi'an) 1,900,000 G5
Siangfan (Xiangfan) 150,000 H5
Siangtan (Xiangtan) 300,000 H6
Sienyang (Xianyang) 125,000 G5
Silinhot (Abnagar) J3
Simao (Fusingchen) F7
Sinchu 208,038 K7
Singtai (Xingtai) H4
Sining (Xining) 250,000 F4
Sinsiang (Xinxiang) 300,000 H4
Sinyang (Xinyang) 125,000 H5
Siping (Szeping) 180,000 K3
Soche (Shache) A4
Soochow (Suzhou) 1,300,000 K5
Suao K7
Süchow (Xuzhou) 1,500,000 J5
Suifenhe M3
Suihua L2
Suining G5
Suzhou (Soochow) 1,300,000 K5
Swatow (Shantou) 400,000 J7
Szeping (Siping) 180,000 K3
Tacheng (Qoqek) B2
Tai'an J4
Taibus J3
Taichow (Taizhou) 275,000 K5
Taichung 565,255 K7
Taigu H4
Tainan 541,390 J7
Taipei 2,108,193 K7
Taitung K7
Taiyuan 2,725,000 H4
Taizhou (Taichow) 275,000 K5
Talai (Da'an, Dalai) K2
Tali (Dali) E6
Tangshan 1,200,000 J4
Tantung (Dandong) 450,000 K3
Tao'an K2
Taoyuan 105,841 K6
Tart D4
Tatung (Datong) 300,000 H3
Taxkorgan A4
Tehchow (Dezhou) J4
Tengchong E6
Tianjin (Tientsin)● 7,210,000 J4
Tianjun E4
Tianshui 100,000 F5
Tieling K3
Tienshui (Tianshui) 100,000 F5
Tientsin (Tianjin)● 7,210,000 J4
Tingri C6
Togtoh H3
Toksu (Xinhe) B3
Toksun C3
Tongchuan (Tungchwan) G5
Tonghua (Tunghwa) 275,000 L3
Tongjiang (Tungkiang) M2
Tongliao K3
Tongling J5
Tongxin G4
Tongyu K3
Tsangchow (Cangzhou) J4
Tsiaotso (Jiaozuo) 300,000 H4
Tsinan (Jinan) 1,500,000 J4
Tsingkiang (Qingjiang) 110,000 J5
Tsingshih (Jinshi) 100,000 H6
Tsingtao (Qingdao) 1,900,000 K4
Tsining (Jining), Nei Monggol 160,000 H3

Topography

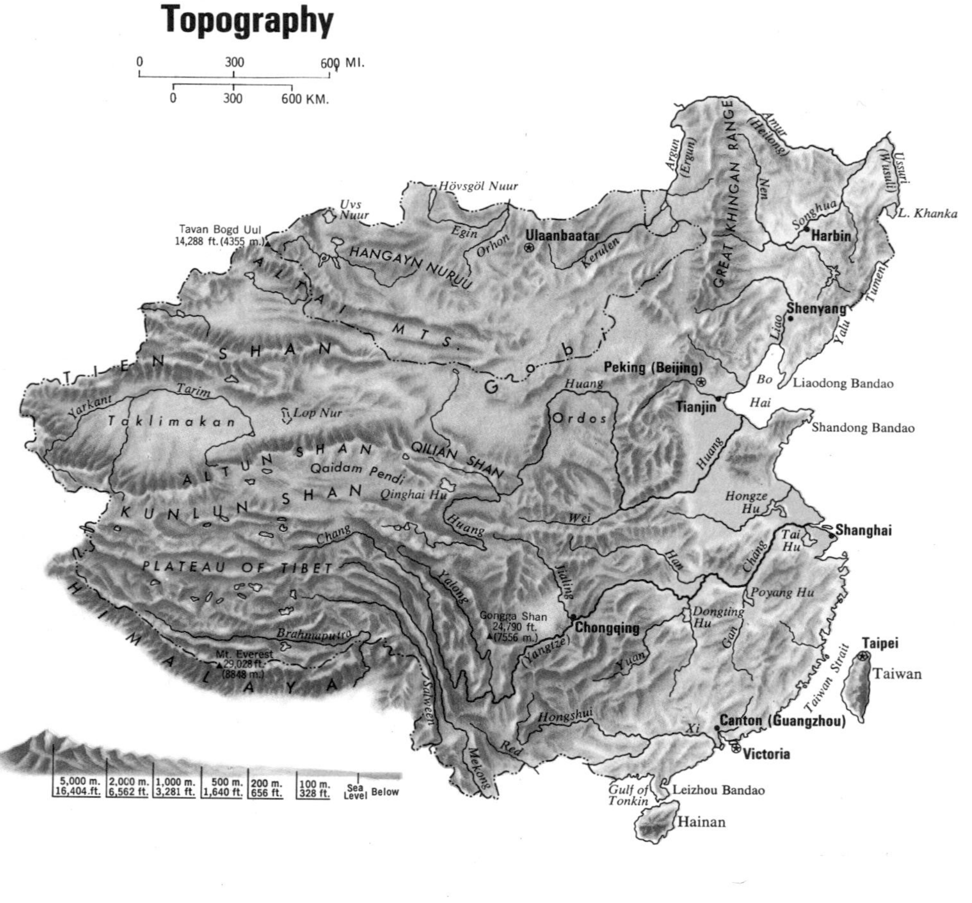

Tsining (Jining), Shandong J4
Tsitsihar (Qiqihar) 1,500,000 .... K2
Tsunyi (Zunyi) 275,000 .... G6
Tumen M3
Tungchwan (Tongchuan) G5
Tunghwa (Tonghua) 275,000 .... L3
Tungkiang (Tongjiang) M2
Tungliao (Tongliao) K3
Tunhwa (Dunhua) L3
Tunxi (Tunki) J6
Turpan (Turfan) C3
Tuyün (Duyun) G6
Tzekung (Zigong) 350,000 .... F6
Tzepo (Zibo) 1,750,000 .... J4
Uch Turfan (Wushi) A3
Ulanhot (Horquin Youyi Qianqi) 100,000 .... K2
Ulughchat (Wuqia) A4
Ürümqi (Urumchi) 500,000 .... C3
Usu B3
Wanning H8
Wanxian (Wanhsien) 175,000 .... G5
Weichang J3
Weifang 260,000 .... J4
Weihai (Weihaiwei) K4
Weixi E6
Weixin F6
Wenchow (Wenzhou) 250,000 .... J6
Wenquan, Qinghai D5
Wenquan, Xinjiang Uygur B3
Wenzhou 250,000 .... J6
Wuchang L3
Wuchow (Wuzhou) 150,000 .... H7
Wuchuan, Guizhou G6
Wuchuan, Nei Monggol H3
Wuchung (Wuzhong) G4
Wuda G4
Wuhai G4
Wuhan 4,250,000 .... H5
Wuhing (Wuxing) 160,000 .... K5
Wuhu 300,000 .... J5
Wuqi G4
Wuqia A4
Wushi A3
Wusih (Wuxi) 900,000 .... J5
Wutai H4
Wuwei F4
Wuxi (Wusih) 900,000 .... K5
Wuxing (Wuhing) 160,000 .... K5
Wuyuan G3
Wuzhong (Wuchung) G4
Wuzhou (Wuchow) 150,000 .... H7
Xiaguan (Siakwan) E6
Xiamen (Amoy) 400,000 .... J7
Xi'an (Sian) 1,900,000 .... G5
Xiangfan (Siangfan) 150,000 .... H5
Xiangtan (Siangtan) 300,000 .... H6
Xianyang (Sienyang) 125,000 .... G5
Xiapu (Siapu) K6
Xichang (Sichang) F6
Xigazê (Shigatse) C6
Ximiao F3
Xin Barag Zuoqi J2
Xingtai (Singtai) H4
Xinhe (Toksu) B3
Xining (Sining) 250,000 .... F4
Xinxiang (Sinsiang) 300,000 .... H4
Xinyang (Sinyang) 125,000 .... H5
Xinyuan (Künes) B3
Xuchang (Hsüchang) H5
Xuguit K2
Xuzhou (Süchow) 1,500,000 .... J5
Ya'an 100,000 .... F6
Yadong C6
Yan'an (Yenan) G4
Yancheng K5
Yangchow (Yangzhou) 210,000 .... J5
Yangchüan (Yangquan) 350,000 .... H4
Yangjiang H7
Yanji (Yenki) 130,000 .... L3
Yangquan (Yangchüan) 350,000 .... H4
Yangzhou (Yangchow) 210,000 .... J5
Yanqi C3
Yantai (Chefoo) 180,000 .... K4
Yarkant (Shache) A4
Ya Xian G8
Yecheng A4
Yenan (Yan'an) G4
Yenki (Yanji) 130,000 .... L3
Yibin (Ipin) 275,000 .... F6
Yichang (Ichang) 150,000 .... H5
Yichun, Jiangxi H6
Yichun, Heilongjiang 200,000 .... L2
Yidu, Hubei H5
Yidu, Shandong J4
Yinchuan (Ningsia) 175,000 .... G4
Yingkou 215,000 .... K3
Yining 160,000 .... B3
Yiwu (Aratürük) D3
Yiyang H6
Yongxin H6
Yuci (Yütze) H4
Yueyang H6
Yuli (Lopnur) C3
Yulin, Guangxi Zhuangzu G7
Yulin, Shanxi G4
Yumen 325,000 .... E4
Yuncheng H4
Yungkia (Wenzhou) 250,000 .... J6
Yushu, Jilin L3
Yushu, Qinghai E5
Yutian, Hebei J4
Yutian, Xinjiang Uygur B4
Yütze (Yuci) H4
Zaozhuang J5
Zayü E6
Zêtang D6
Zhanghei J3
Zhangjiakou (Kalgan) 1,000,000 .... J3
Zhangye (Changyeh) F4
Zhangzhou (Changchow) J7
Zhanjiang (Chankiang) 220,000 .... H7
Zhaodong K2
Zhaojue F6
Zhaoqing H7
Zhaosu B3
Zhaotong (Chaotung) F6
Zhengzhou (Chengchow) 1,500,000 .... H5
Zhenjiang (Chinkiang) 250,000 .... J5
Zhenyuan G6
Zhongba B6
Zhongshan (Chungshan) 135,000 .... H7
Zhongwei F4
Zhumadian (Chumatien) H5
Zhushan G5
Zhuzhou (Chuchow) 350,000 .... H6
Zibo (Tzepo) 1,750,000 .... J4
Zigong (Tzekung) 350,000 .... F6
Zinhui H7
Zunhua J3
Zunyi (Tsunyi) 275,000 .... G6

OTHER FEATURES

Altun Shan (range) C4
Alxa Shamo (des.) F4
Amur (Heilong Jiang) (riv.) L2
A'nyêmaqên Shan (mts.) E5
Aqqikkol Hu (lake) C4
Argun' (Ergun He) (riv.) K1
Bagrax (Bosten Hu) (lake) C3
Bangong Co (lake) A5
Bashi (chan.) K7
Bayan Har Shan (range) E5
Bo Hai (gulf) J4
Bosten (Bagrax) Hu (lake) C3
Chang Jiang (Yangtze) (riv.) K5
Da Hingan Ling (range) J3
Dian Chi (lake) F7
Dongsha (isl.) J7
Dongting Hu (riv.) H6
East China (sea) L6
Ebinur Hu (lake) B2
Ergun He (Argun') (riv.) K1
Er Hai (lake) F6
Everest (mt.) C6
Fen He (riv.) H4
Formosa (Taiwan) (str.) J7
Formosa (Taiwan) (isl.) K7
Gangdisê Shan (range) B5
Gaoyou Hu (lake) J5
Ghenghis Khan Wall (ruin) H2
Gobi (des.) G3
Gongga Shan (mt.) F6
Grand (canal) J4
Great Wall (ruins) G4,J
Gurla Mandhada (mt.) B5
Hailar He (riv.) K2
Hainan (isl.) H8
Hangzhou Wan (bay) K5
Han Shui (riv.) H5
Heilong Jiang (Amur) (riv.) L2
Himalaya (mts.) C6
Hongshui He (riv.) G7
Hongze Hu (lake) J5
Hotan He (riv.) B4
Huang He (Yellow) (riv.) J4
Hulun Nur (lake) J2
Hungtow (isl.) K7
Inner Mongolia (reg.) H3
Jinmen (Quemoy) (isl.) J7
Jinsha Jiang (Yangtze) (riv.) E5
Junggar Pendi (desert basin) C2
Kangrinboqê Feng (mt.) B5
Karakhoto (ruins) F3
Karamiran Shankou (pass) C4
Keriya Shankou (pass) B4
Khanka (lake) M3
Kongur Shan (mt.) A4
Künes He (riv.) B3
Kunlun Shan (range) B4
Kuruktag Shan (range) C3
Lancang Jiang (riv.) F7
Leizhou Bandao (pen.) G7
Liaodong Bandao (pen.) K3
Liao He (riv.) K3
Lop Nor (Lop Nur) (lake) D3
Manas He (riv.) C3
Manas Hu (lake) C2

(continued on following page)

78 China and Mongolia

(continued)

Mazu (Matsu) (isl.) K6
Mekong (Lancang Jiang) (riv.) F7
Min Jiang (riv.) J6
Mudan Jiang (riv.) L3
Muztag (mt.) B4
Muztagata (mt.) A4
Nam Co (lake) D5
Namzha Parwa (mt.) E6
Nan Ling (mts.) H6
Nen Jiang (riv.) K2
Ngangzê Co (lake) C5
Ngoring Hu (lake) E5
Nu Jiang (riv.) E6
Nyainqêntanglha Shan (range) D5
Olwampi (cape) K7
Ordos (reg.) G4
Penghu (Pescadores) (isls.) 113,397 J7
Pingtan (isl.) K6
Pobeda (peak) A3
Poyang Hu (lake) J6
Pratas (Dongsha) (isl.) J7
Qaidam Pendi (basin) (swamp) D4
Qarqan He (riv.) C4
Qilian Shan (range) E4
Qinghai Hu (lake) E4
Qiongzhou Haixia (str.) G7
Quemoy (Jinmen) (isl.) J7
Qumar He (riv.) D4
Salween (Nu Jiang) (riv.) E6
Siling Co (lake) C5
Songhua Hu (lake) L3
Songhua Jiang (Sungari) (riv.) M2
South China (sea) J7
Tachen (Taizhou) (isls.) K6
Tai Hu (lake) J5
Taiwan (Formosa) (isl.) 16,609,961 K7
Taiwan (Formosa) (str.) J7
Taizhou (Tachen) (isls.) K6
Takla Makan (Taklimakan Shamo) (des.) B.
Tanggula Shan (range) D5
Tangra Yumco (lake) C5
Tarim He (riv.) B3
Tarim Pendi (basin) B4
Tian Shan (range) C3
Tibet (reg.) B5
Tongtian He (Zhi Qu) (riv.) E5
Tonkin (gulf) G7
Tumen (riv.) L3
Ulu Muztag (mt.) C4
Ulungur He (riv.) C2
Ulungur Hu (lake) C2
Ussuri (Wusuli Jiang) (riv.) M2
Wei He (riv.) G5
Wu Jiang (riv.) G6
Wusuli Jiang (Ussuri) (riv.) M2
Wuyi Shan (range) J6
Xiang Jiang (riv.) H6
Xi Jiang (riv.) H7
Yagradagzê Shan (mt.) D4
Yalong Jiang (riv.) F6
Yalu (riv.) L3
Yangtze (Chang Jiang) (riv.) K5
Yarkant He (riv.) A4
Yellow (Huang He) (riv.) J4
Yellow (sea) K4
Yin Shan (mts.) G3
Yuhuan (isl.) K6
Yü Shan (mt.) K7
Yushan (isls.) K6
Zhoushan (arch.) K5

HONG KONG

CITIES and TOWNS

Kowloon* 2,378,480 H7
Victoria (cap.)* 1,026,870 H7

MACAU (MACAO)

CITIES and TOWNS

Macau (Macao) (cap.) 226,880 H7

MONGOLIA

PROVINCES

Arhangay 90,500 F2
Bayamhongor 64,900 E2
Bayan-Ölgiy 73,300 C2
Bulgan 45,700 F2
Dornod 51,100 H2
Dornogovĭ 36,400 G3
Dundgovĭ 37,800 G2
Dzavhan 87,600 E2
Govĭ-Altay 59,200 E3
Hentiy 49,900 H2
Hovd 68,300 D2
Hövsgöl 89,600 E1
Ömnögovĭ 32,200 F3
Övörhangay 84,100 F2
Selenge 53,700 G2
Sühbaatar 44,100 H2
Töv 74,900 G2
Uvs 76,300 D2

CITIES AND TOWNS

Altay 10,000 E2
Arvayheer 9,100 F2
Baatsagaan 800 E2
Baruun-Urt 8,200 H2
Bayanbaraat 400 G2
Bayandalay 500 F3
Bayangovĭ 400 F3
Bayanhongor 11,300 E2
Bayan-Öndör 300 E3
Bayan-Uul 1,200 E2
Beger 800 E2
Bulgan, Bulgan 9,800 F2
Bulgan, Hovd 3,100 D2
Bulgan, Ömnögovĭ 700 F3
Bürentsogt 3,000 H2
Chandmanĭ 700 E2
Choybalsan 20,500 J2
Dalandzadgad 6,600 G3
Darhan (Darkhan) 32,900 G2
Dashbalbar 1,100 H2
Dashinchilen 600 F2
Delgertsogt 500 G2
Dzamîn Üüd 1,500 H3
Dzüünharaa 8,100 G2
Dzuunmod 7,200 G2
Erdentsagaan 1,500 J2
Ereen 700 H2
Hanbogd 300 G3
Hanh 500 F1
Hatgal 5,000 E1
Hongor H2
Hovd (Kobdo, Jirgalanta) 12,400 D2
Hyargas 1,600 D2
Jargalant J2
Jibhalanta (Uliastay) 13,000 E2
Jirgalanta (Hovd) 12,400 D2
Kobdo (Hovd) 12,400 D2
Mandah 200 G3
Mandalgovĭ 7,000 G2
Mandal-Ovoo 300 F3
Mönhhaan 400 H2
Mörön (Muren) 10,700 F2
Nalayh (Nalaikha) 14,000 G2
Nomgon 500 G3
Noyon 300 F3
Ölgiy (Ulegei) 11,700 C2
Öndörhaan (Undur Khan) 7,900 G2
Onon 2,600 H2
Sayhan-Ovoo 400 F2
Saynshand 10,000 H3
Selenge 1,300 F2
Sühbaatar (Sukhe Bator) 10,000 G1
Sulanheer 300 G3
Tamsagbulag J2
Tsagaannuur 2,000 C2
Tsagaan-Ovoo 900 H2
Tsagaan-Uul 1,700 E2
Tsetseg 700 D2
Tsetserleg 12,400 F2
Ulaanbaatar (Ulan Bator) (cap.) 345,000 G2
Ulaangom (Ulangom) 14,000 D2
Ulegei (Ölgiy) 11,700 C2
Uliastay (Jibhalanta) 13,000 E2
Urga (Ulaanbaatar) (cap.) 345,000 G2
Yaruu 700 E2

OTHER FEATURES

Altai (mts.) C2
Dörgön Nuur (lake) D2
Dzavhan Gol (riv.) D2
Ghenghis Khan Wall (ruins) H2
Gobi (des.) G3
Hangayn Nuruu (mts.) E2
Har Us Nuur (lake) D2
Herlen Gol (Kerulen) (riv.) H2
Hovd Gol (riv.) D2
Hövsgöl Nuur (lake) F1
Hyargas Nuur (lake) D2
Ider Gol (riv.) E2
Karakorum (ruins) F2
Kerulen (riv.) H2
Munku-Sardyk (mt.) F1
Orhon Gol (riv.) F2
Selenge Mörön (riv.) G2
Tannu-Ola (range) D1
Tavan Bogd Uul (mt.) C2
Uvs Nuur (lake) D1

● Population of municipality
*City and suburbs.

† Populations of mainland cities, excluding Peking (Beijing), Shanghai and Tianjin (Tientsin), courtesy of Kingsley Davis, Office of Int'l Pop. and Research, Inst. of Int'l Studies Univ. of California.

Agriculture, Industry and Resources

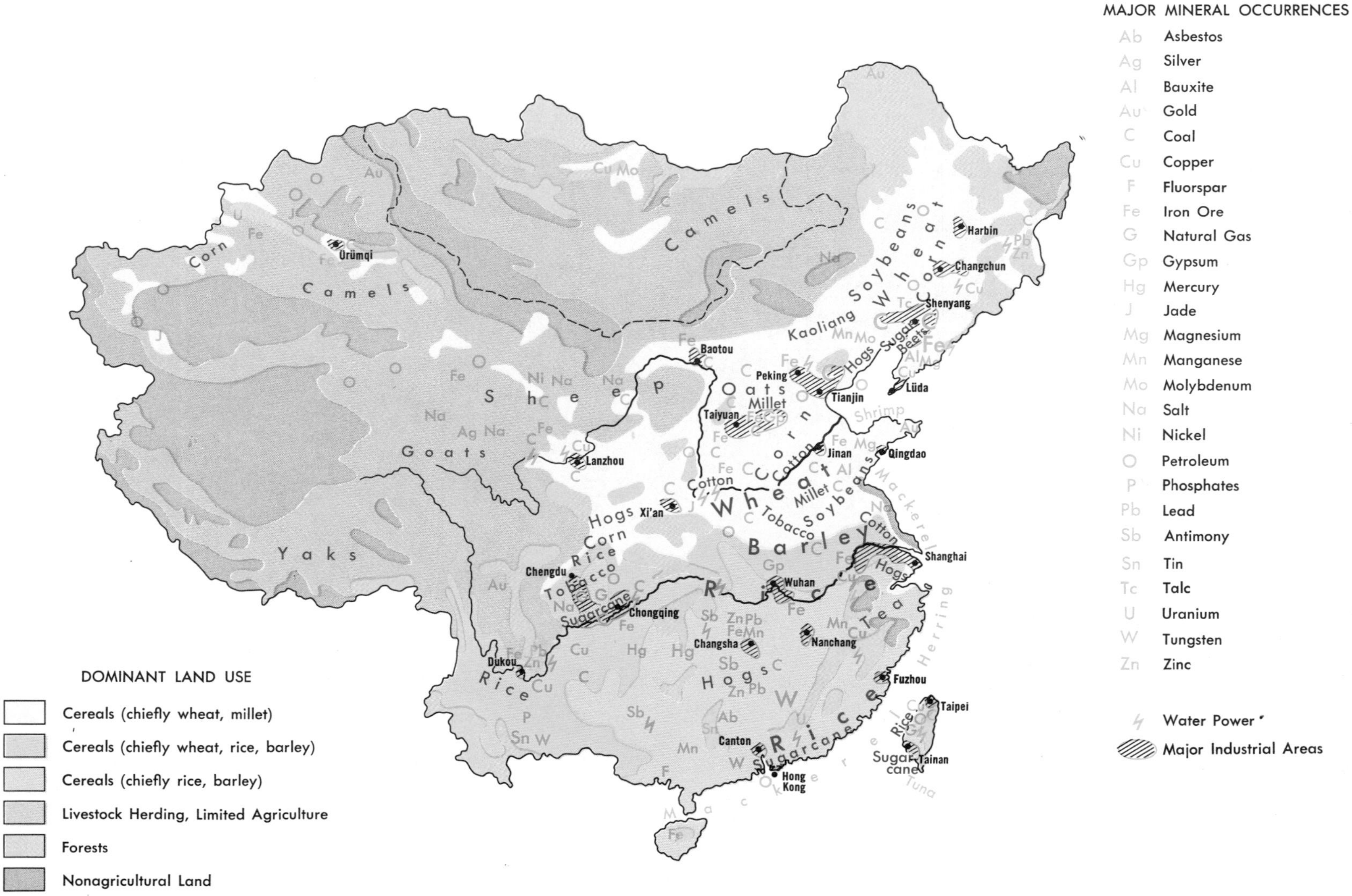

MAJOR MINERAL OCCURRENCES

Ab Asbestos
Ag Silver
Al Bauxite
Au Gold
C Coal
Cu Copper
F Fluorspar
Fe Iron Ore
G Natural Gas
Gp Gypsum
Hg Mercury
J Jade
Mg Magnesium
Mn Manganese
Mo Molybdenum
Na Salt
Ni Nickel
O Petroleum
P Phosphates
Pb Lead
Sb Antimony
Sn Tin
Tc Talc
U Uranium
W Tungsten
Zn Zinc

Water Power
Major Industrial Areas

DOMINANT LAND USE

Cereals (chiefly wheat, millet)
Cereals (chiefly wheat, rice, barley)
Cereals (chiefly rice, barley)
Livestock Herding, Limited Agriculture
Forests
Nonagricultural Land

AREA 145,730 sq. mi. (377,441 sq. km.)
POPULATION 117,057,485
CAPITAL Tokyo
LARGEST CITY Tokyo
HIGHEST POINT Fuji 12,389 ft. (3,776 m.)
MONETARY UNIT yen
MAJOR LANGUAGE Japanese
MAJOR RELIGIONS Buddhism, Shintoism

AREA 46,540 sq. mi. (120,539 sq. km.)
POPULATION 17,914,000
CAPITAL P'yŏngyang
LARGEST CITY P'yŏngyang
HIGHEST POINT Paektu 9,003 ft. (2,744 m.)
MONETARY UNIT won
MAJOR LANGUAGE Korean
MAJOR RELIGIONS Confucianism, Buddhism, Ch'ondogyo

AREA 38,175 sq. mi. (98,873 sq. km.)
POPULATION 37,448,836
CAPITAL Seoul
LARGEST CITY Seoul
HIGHEST POINT Halla 6,398 ft. (1,950 m.)
MONETARY UNIT won
MAJOR LANGUAGE Korean
MAJOR RELIGIONS Confucianism, Buddhism, Ch'ondogyo, Christianity

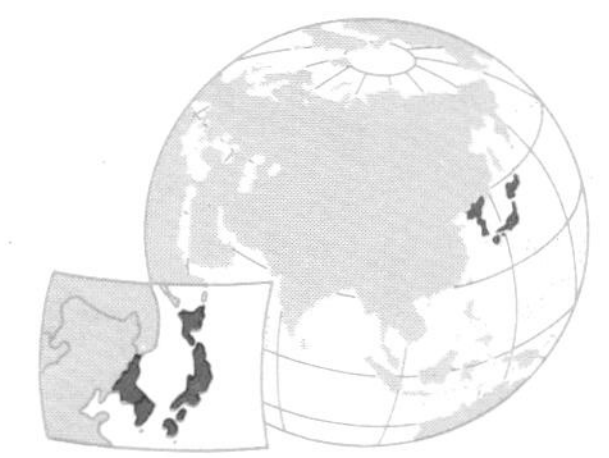

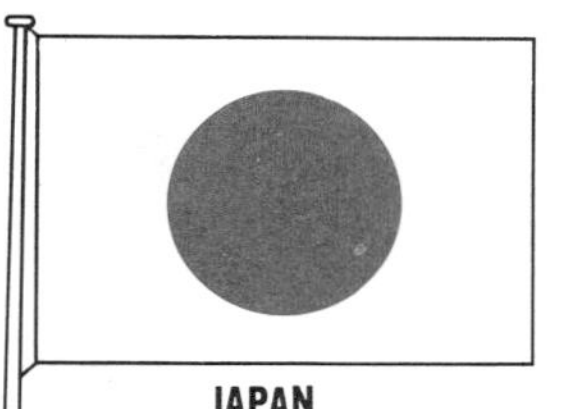

JAPAN

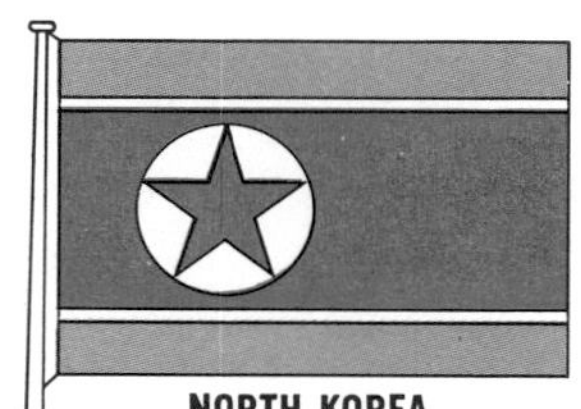

NORTH KOREA

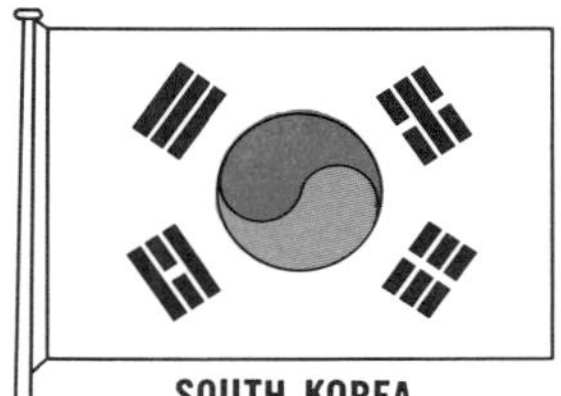

SOUTH KOREA

JAPAN

PREFECTURES

Aichi 5,923,569 ..... H6
Akita 1,232,481 ..... J4
Aomori 1,468,646 ..... K3
Chiba 4,149,147 ..... P2
Ehime 1,465,215 ..... F7
Fukui 773,599 ..... G5
Fukuoka 4,292,963 ..... D7
Fukushima 1,970,616 ..... K5
Gifu 1,867,978 ..... H6
Gumma 1,756,480 ..... J5
Hiroshima 2,646,324 ..... E6
Hokkaido 5,338,206 ..... K2
Hyogo 4,992,140 ..... H7
Ibaraki 2,342,198 ..... K5
Ishikawa 1,069,872 ..... H5
Iwate 1,385,563 ..... K4
Kagawa 961,292 ..... G6
Kagoshima 1,723,902 ..... E8
Kanagawa 6,397,748 ..... O2
Kochi 808,397 ..... F7
Kumamoto 1,715,273 ..... E7
Kyoto 2,424,856 ..... J7
Miė 1,626,002 ..... H6
Miyagi 1,955,267 ..... K4
Miyazaki 1,085,055 ..... E8
Nagano 2,017,564 ..... J5
Nagasaki 1,571,912 ..... D7
Nara 1,077,491 ..... J8
Niigata 2,391,938 ..... J5
Oita 1,190,314 ..... E7
Okayama 1,814,305 ..... F6
Okinawa 1,042,572 ..... N6
Osaka 8,278,925 ..... J8
Saga 837,674 ..... E7
Saitama 4,821,340 ..... O2
Shiga 985,621 ..... J7
Shimane 768,886 ..... F6
Shizuoka 3,308,799 ..... H6
Tochigi 1,698,003 ..... K5
Tokushima 805,166 ..... G7
Tokyo 11,673,554 ..... O2
Tottori 581,311 ..... G6
Toyama 1,070,791 ..... H5
Wakayama 1,072,118 ..... G6
Yamagata 1,220,302 ..... K4
Yamaguchi 1,555,218 ..... E6
Yamanashi 783,050 ..... J6

CITIES and TOWNS

Abashiri 43,825 ..... M1
Ageo 146,358 ..... O2
Aikawa 13,546 ..... H4
Aizuwakamatsu 108,650 ..... J5
Ajigasawa 18,086 ..... J3
Akashi 234,905 ..... H8
Aki 24,480 ..... F7
Akita 261,246 ..... J4
Akkeshi 16,778 ..... M2
Akune 30,295 ..... E7
Amagasaki 545,783 ..... H8
Amagi 42,725 ..... E7
Anan 60,439 ..... G7
Aomori 264,222 ..... K3
Asahi 34,028 ..... K6
Asahikawa 320,526 ..... L2
Ashibetsu 36,520 ..... L2
Ashikaga 162,359 ..... J5
Ashiya 76,211 ..... H8
Atami 51,437 ..... J6
Atsugi 108,955 ..... O2
Awaji 9,623 ..... H8
Ayabe 43,490 ..... G6
Beppu 133,894 ..... E7
Bibai 38,416 ..... L2
Biratori 9,331 ..... L2
Chiba 659,356 ..... P2
Chichibu 61,798 ..... J5
Chigasaki 152,023 ..... O3
Chitose 61,031 ..... K2
Chofu 175,924 ..... O2
Choshi 90,374 ..... K6
Daito 110,829 ..... J8
Ebetsu 77,624 ..... K2
Eniwa 39,884 ..... K2
Esashi, Hokkaido 10,172 ..... L1
Esashi, Hokkaido 14,409 ..... J3
Esashi, Iwate 36,336 ..... K4
Fuchu, Hiroshima 50,217 ..... F6
Fuchu, Tokyo 182,474 ..... O2
Fuji 199,195 ..... J6
Fujieda 90,358 ..... J6
Fujisawa 265,975 ..... O3
Fukagawa 36,000 ..... L2
Fukuchiyama 60,003 ..... G6
Fukue 32,018 ..... D7
Fukui 231,364 ..... G5
Fukuoka 1,002,201 ..... D7
Fukushima 246,531 ..... K5
Fukuyama 329,714 ..... F6
Funabashi 423,101 ..... P2
Furukawa 54,356 ..... K4
Gifu 408,707 ..... H6
Gobo 30,272 ..... G7
Gose 37,554 ..... J8
Gosen 39,376 ..... J5
Goshogawara 49,040 ..... K3
Gotsu 27,992 ..... F6
Habikino 94,160 ..... J8
Haboro 13,624 ..... K1
Hachinohe 224,366 ..... K3
Hachioji 322,580 ..... O2
Hadano 103,663 ..... O3
Hagi 52,724 ..... E6
Hakodate 307,453 ..... K3
Hakui 28,726 ..... H5
Hamada 50,316 ..... E6
Hamamatsu 468,884 ..... H6
Hanamaki 65,826 ..... K4
Hanno 55,926 ..... O2
Haramachi 43,483 ..... K5
Hayama 24,026 ..... O3
Higashiosaka 524,750 ..... J8
Hikone 85,066 ..... H6
Himeji 436,086 ..... G6
Himi 61,789 ..... H5
Hino 126,847 ..... O2
Hirakata 297,618 ..... J7
Hirara 29,301 ..... L7
Hirata 30,942 ..... F6
Hiratsuka 195,635 ..... O3
Hiroo 11,399 ..... L2
Hirosaki 164,911 ..... K3
Hiroshima 852,611 ..... E6
Hitachi 202,383 ..... K5
Hitachiota 35,322 ..... K5
Hitoyoshi 41,118 ..... E7
Hofu 105,540 ..... E6
Hondo 40,432 ..... E7
Honjo 40,488 ..... J4
Hyuga 53,448 ..... E7
Ibaraki 210,286 ..... J7
Ibusuki 32,339 ..... E8
Ichihara 194,068 ..... P3
Ichikawa 319,291 ..... P2
Ichinohe 21,433 ..... K3
Ichinomiya 238,463 ..... H6
Ichinoseki 59,122 ..... K4
Ide 9,112 ..... J7
Iida 77,112 ..... H6
Iizuka 75,417 ..... E7
Ikeda, Hokkaido 12,306 ..... L2
Ikeda, Osaka 100,268 ..... H7
Ikoma 48,848 ..... J8
Ikuno 6,658 ..... G6
Imabari 119,726 ..... F6
Imari 60,913 ..... D7
Imazu 11,519 ..... G6
Ina 54,468 ..... H6
Isahaya 73,341 ..... D7
Ise 104,957 ..... H6
Ishigaki 34,657 ..... L7
Ishige 19,220 ..... P2
Ishinomaki 115,085 ..... K4
Ishioka 43,679 ..... K5
Itami 171,978 ..... H7
Ito 68,072 ..... J6
Itoigawa 36,646 ..... H5
Itoman 39,363 ..... N6
Iwaizumi 20,219 ..... K4
Iwaki 330,213 ..... K5
Iwakuni 111,069 ..... E6
Iwami 16,063 ..... G6
Iwamizawa 72,305 ..... L2
Iwanai 25,823 ..... K2
Iwasaki 4,437 ..... J3
Iwata 67,665 ..... H6
Iwatsuki 83,825 ..... O2
Iyo 27,805 ..... F7
Izuhara 18,460 ..... D6
Izumi 118,237 ..... J8
Izumiotsu 66,250 ..... J8
Izumisano 86,139 ..... G6
Izumo 71,568 ..... F6
Joetsu 123,418 ..... H5
Joyo 58,923 ..... J7
Kadoma 143,238 ..... J7
Kaga 61,599 ..... H5
Kagoshima 456,827 ..... E8
Kaizuka 79,506 ..... H8
Kakogawa 169,293 ..... G6
Kamaishi 68,981 ..... L4
Kamakura 165,552 ..... O3
Kameoka 58,184 ..... J7
Kamiisco 27,229 ..... K3
Kaminoyama 37,858 ..... J4
Kamiyaku 8,668 ..... E8
Kamo 8,953 ..... J7
Kanazawa 395,263 ..... H5
Kanonji 44,131 ..... F6
Kanoya 67,951 ..... E8
Kanuma 81,799 ..... J5
Karatsu 75,224 ..... D7
Kaseda 24,969 ..... D8
Kashihara 95,701 ..... J8
Kashiwa 203,065 ..... P2
Kashiwara 63,586 ..... J8
Kashiwazaki 80,351 ..... J5
Kasugai 213,857 ..... H6
Kasukabe 121,639 ..... O2
Katsuta 79,996 ..... K5
Katsuura 26,755 ..... K6
Kawachinagano 66,936 ..... J8
Kawagoe 225,465 ..... O2
Kawaguchi 345,538 ..... J6
Kawanishi 115,773 ..... H7
Kawasaki 1,014,951 ..... O2
Kesennuma 66,616 ..... K4
Kikonai 10,034 ..... K3
Kimitsu 76,016 ..... O3
Kiryu 134,239 ..... J5
Kisarazu 96,840 ..... P3
Kishiwada 174,952 ..... J8
Kitaibaraki 44,332 ..... K5
Kitakami 48,759 ..... K4
Kitakata 37,471 ..... J5
Kitakyushu 1,058,058 ..... E6
Kitami 91,519 ..... L2
Kizu 11,890 ..... J7
Kobayashi 38,325 ..... E8
Kobe 1,360,605 ..... H7
Kochi 280,962 ..... F7
Kodaira 156,181 ..... O2
Kofu 193,879 ..... J6
Koga 55,973 ..... J5
Koganei 102,714 ..... O2
Kokubu 31,660 ..... E8
Komagane 30,318 ..... H6
Komatsu 100,273 ..... H5
Koriyama 264,628 ..... K5
Koshigaya 195,917 ..... P2
Koyama 16,394 ..... E8
Kubohama 17,817 ..... F7
Kuji 38,122 ..... K3
Kuki 45,797 ..... O2
Kumagaya 131,485 ..... J5
Kumamoto 488,166 ..... E7
Kumano 27,026 ..... G7
Kumiyama 11,540 ..... J7
Kurashiki 392,755 ..... F6
Kurayoshi 50,785 ..... F6
Kure 242,655 ..... F6
Kuroiso 42,349 ..... K5
Kurume 204,474 ..... E7
Kushikino 30,456 ..... E8
Kushima 30,038 ..... E8
Kushimoto 18,997 ..... G7
Kushiro 206,840 ..... M2
Kyonan 13,067 ..... O3
Kyoto 1,461,059 ..... J7
Machida 255,305 ..... O2
Maebashi 250,241 ..... J5
Maihara 12,845 ..... G6
Maizuru 97,780 ..... G6
Makubetsu 18,444 ..... L2
Makurazaki 29,685 ..... O3
Mashike 9,312 ..... K2
Masuda 50,734 ..... E6
Matsubara 132,662 ..... H8
Matsue 127,440 ..... F6
Matsumae 18,307 ..... J3
Matsumoto 185,595 ..... H5
Matsusaka 108,893 ..... H6
Matsuto 36,170 ..... H5
Matsuyama 367,323 ..... F7
Mihara 83,679 ..... F6
Miki 53,731 ..... H7
Mikuni 21,602 ..... G5
Minamata 36,782 ..... E7
Minobu 10,345 ..... J6
Minoo 79,621 ..... J7
Misawa 37,437 ..... K3
Mitaka 164,950 ..... O2
Mito 197,953 ..... K5
Mitsukaido 38,820 ..... P2
Miura 47,888 ..... O3
Miyako 61,912 ..... L4
Miyakonojo 118,289 ..... E8
Miyazaki 234,347 ..... E8
Miyazu 30,194 ..... G6
Miyoshi 37,193 ..... F6
Mizusawa 52,266 ..... K4
Mobara 64,942 ..... K6
Mombetsu 32,825 ..... L1
Monbetsu 15,029 ..... L2
Mooka 47,345 ..... K5
Mori 17,030 ..... K2
Moriguchi 178,383 ..... J7
Morioka 216,223 ..... K4
Motobu 17,823 ..... N6
Muko 45,886 ..... J7
Murakami 32,939 ..... J4
Muroran 158,715 ..... K2
Muroto 26,660 ..... G7
Musashino 139,508 ..... O2
Mutsu 44,646 ..... K3
Nachikatsuura 23,596 ..... H7
Nagahama, Ehime 13,144 ..... F7
Nagahama, Shiga 54,064 ..... H6
Nagano 306,637 ..... J5
Nagaoka, Kyoto 65,557 ..... J7
Nagaoka, Niigata 171,742 ..... J5
Nagaokakyo 65,557 ..... J7
Nagasaki 450,194 ..... D7
Nagato 27,327 ..... E6
Nago 45,210 ..... N6
Nagoya 2,079,740 ..... H6
Naha 295,006 ..... N6
Nakaminato 33,147 ..... K5
Nakamura 34,437 ..... F7
Nakasato 14,248 ..... K3
Nakatsu 59,111 ..... E7
Nanao 49,493 ..... H5
Nankoku 42,832 ..... F7
Nara 257,538 ..... J8
Narashino 117,852 ..... P2
Nayoro 35,145 ..... L1
Naze 46,359 ..... O5
Nemuro 45,817 ..... M2
Neyagawa 254,311 ..... J7
Nichinan 52,171 ..... E8
Niigata 423,188 ..... J5
Niihama 131,712 ..... F6
Niimi 30,014 ..... F6
Niitsu 58,970 ..... J5
Nishinomiya 400,622 ..... H8

(continued on following page)

Agriculture, Industry and Resources

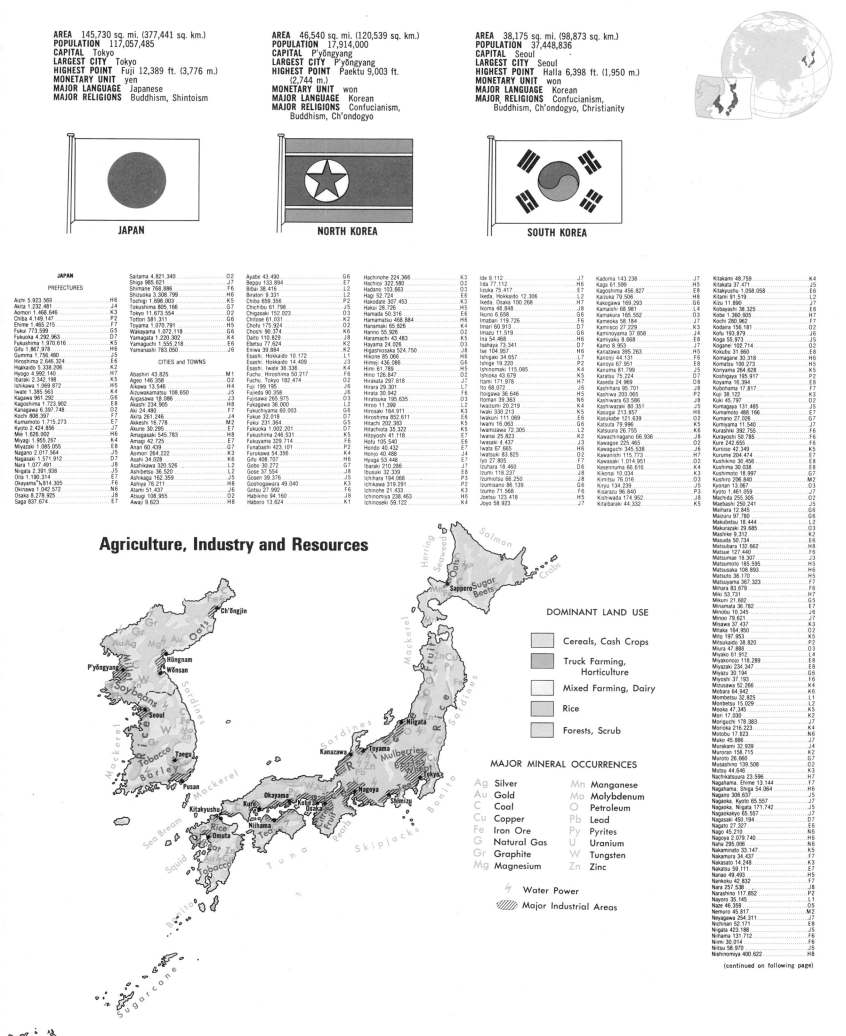

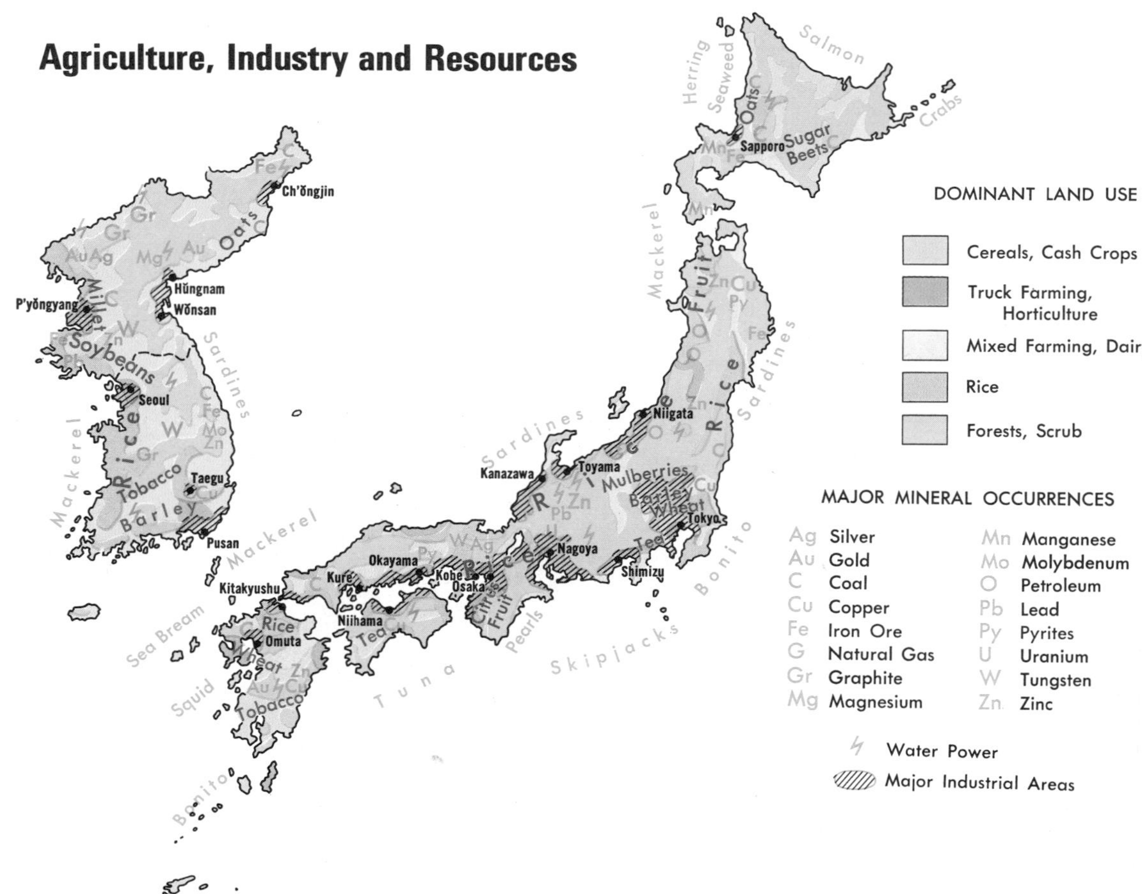

(continued)

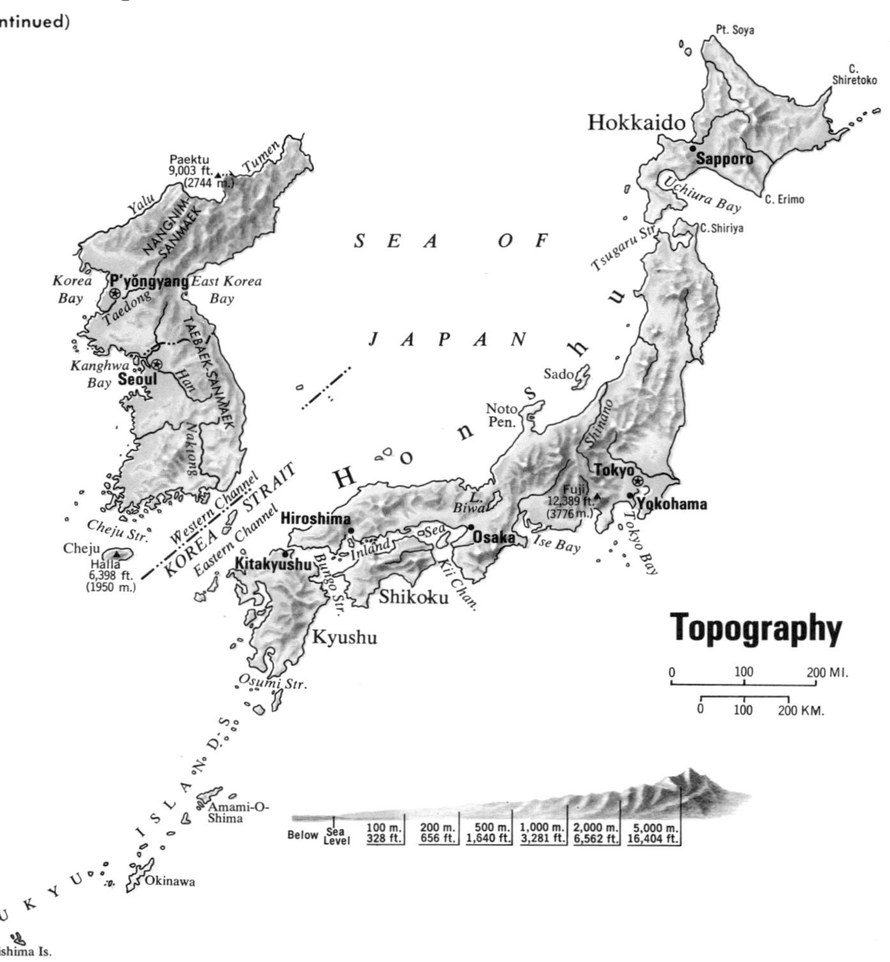

Nishinoomote 24,266 E8
Nobeoka 134,521 E7
Noboribetsu 50,885 K2
Noda 78,193 P2
Nogata 58,551 E7
Nose 9,749 J7
Noshiro 59,215 J3
Noto 15,815 H5
Numata 45,255 J5
Numazu 199,325 J6
Obama 33,890 G6
Obihiro 141,774 L2
Oda 37,449 F6
Odate 71,828 K3
Odawara 173,519 J6
Ofunato 39,632 K4
Oga 39,619 J4
Ogaki 140,424 H6
Ogi 4,717 J5
Ohata 12,632 K3
Oita 320,237 E7
Ojiya 44,375 J5
Okawa 50,395 E7
Okaya 61,776 H5
Okayama 513,471 F6
Okazaki 234,510 H6
Omagari 40,581 K4
Omiya 327,698 O2
Omu 7,407 L1
Omura, Bonin Is. 1,507 M3
Omura, Nagasaki 60,919 E7
Omuta 165,969 E7
Onagawa 16,945 K4
Ono 41,918 H6
Onoda 43,804 E6
Onomichi 102,951 F6
Osaka 2,778,987 J8
Ota 110,723 J5
Otaru 184,406 K2
Otawara 42,332 K5
Otofuke 26,933 L2
Otsu 191,481 J7
Owase 31,797 H6
Oyabe 35,791 H5
Oyama 120,264 J5
Ozu 37,294 F7
Rausu 8,249 M1
Rikuzentakata 29,439 K4
Rumoi 36,882 K2
Ryotsu 22,110 J4
Ryugasaki 40,565 P2
Sabae 57,252 H5
Saga 152,258 E7
Sagamihara 377,398 O2
Saigo 14,409 F5
Saiki 52,863 E7
Saito 37,054 E7
Sakado 51,232 O2
Sakai, Ibaraki 24,347 P1
Sakai, Osaka 750,688 J8
Sakaide 67,624 G6
Sakaiminato 35,821 F6
Sakata 97,723 J4
Saku 56,143 J5
Sakurai 54,314 J8
Sanda 35,261 H7
Sanjo 81,806 J5
Sapporo 1,240,613 K2
Sarufutsu 3,552 L1
Sasebo 250,729 D7
Satte 43,083 O1
Sawara 48,670 K6
Sayama 98,548 O2
Sendai, Kagoshima 61,788 E8
Sendai, Miyagi 615,473 K4
Setouchi 15,290 O5
Settsu 76,704 J8
Shari 15,996 M2
Shibata 74,025 J5
Shibetsu 30,028 M2
Shimabara 45,179 E7
Shimamoto 22,404 J7
Shimizu 243,049 J6
Shimoda 31,700 J6
Shimonoseki 266,593 E6
Shingu 39,023 H7
Shinjo 42,227 K4
Shiogama 59,235 K4
Shirakawa 42,685 K5
Shiranuka 14,897 M2
Shiroishi 40,862 K4
Shizunai 24,833 L2
Shizuoka 446,952 H6
Shobara 23,867 F6
Soka 167,177 O2
Soma 37,551 K5
Sonobe 14,827 J7
Suita 300,956 J7
Sukagawa 54,922 K5
Sukumo 25,340 F7
Sumoto 44,137 G6
Sunagawa 26,023 K2
Susaki 31,019 F7
Suttsu 6,511 J2
Suwa 49,594 H6
Suzu 28,238 H5
Suzuka 141,829 H6
Tachikawa 138,129 O2
Tagawa 61,464 E7
Tajimi 68,901 H6
Takaishi 66,824 H8
Takamatsu 298,999 F6
Takaoka 169,621 H5
Takarazuka 162,624 H7
Takasaki 211,348 J5
Takatsuki 330,570 J7
Takayama 60,504 H5
Takefu 65,012 G6
Takikawa 50,090 K2
Tanabe, Kyoto 30,022 J7
Tanabe, Wakayama 66,999 G7
Tateyama 56,139 K6
Tendo 48,082 K4
Tenri 62,909 J8
Teshio 6,509 K1
Toba 29,346 H6
Tobetsu 17,351 K2
Togane 33,406 K6
Toi 6,983 J6
Tojo 13,796 F6
Tokamachi 50,211 J5
Tokorozawa 196,870 O2
Tokunoshima 35,391 O5
Tokushima 239,281 G7
Tokuyama 106,967 F6
Tokyo (cap.) 8,646,520 O2
Tokyo* 11,673,554 O2
Tomakomai 132,477 K2
Tomiyama 7,389 O3
Tondabayashi 91,393 J8
Tosa 30,679 F7
Tosashimizu 24,856 F7
Tosu 50,733 E7
Tottori 122,312 G6
Towada 54,365 K3
Toyama 290,143 H5
Toyohashi 284,585 H6
Toyonaka 398,384 J7
Toyooka 46,210 G6
Toyota 248,774 H6
Tsu 139,538 H6
Tsubame 43,265 J5
Tsuchiura 104,028 J5
Tsuruga 60,205 G6
Tsuruoka 95,932 J4
Tsuyama 79,907 F6
Ube 161,969 E6
Ueda 105,151 J5
Ugo 21,956 K4
Uji 133,405 J7
Uozu 48,419 H5
Urakawa 20,213 L2
Urawa 331,145 O2
Ushibuka 24,250 D7
Usuki 39,163 F7
Utsunomiya 344,420 K5
Uwajima 70,428 F7
Wajima 33,234 H5
Wakasa 6,989 G6
Wakayama 389,717 G6
Wakkanai 55,464 K1
Warabi 76,311 O2
Yaizu 94,102 J6
Yakumo 19,260 J2
Yamagata 219,773 K4
Yamaguchi 106,099 E6
Yamato 145,881 O2
Yamatokoriyama 71,001 J8
Yamatotakada 58,637 J8
Yao 261,639 J8
Yatabe 22,225 P2
Yatsushiro 103,691 E7
Yawata 50,132 J7
Yawatahama 45,259 F7
Yoichi 25,816 K2
Yokawa 8,015 H7
Yokkaichi 247,001 H6
Yokohama 2,621,771 O3
Yokosuka 389,557 O3
Yokote 43,030 K4
Yonago 118,332 F6
Yonezawa 91,974 K5
Yono 71,044 O2
Yubari 50,131 L2
Yubetsu 6,693 L1
Yukuhashi 53,750 E7
Yuzawa 38,005 K4
Zushi 56,298 O3

OTHER FEATURES

Abashiri (riv.) M1
Abukuma (riv.) K4
Agano (riv.) J4
Akan National Park M2
Amakusa (isls.) D7
Amami (isls.) N5
Amami-O-Shima (isl.) N5
Ara (riv.) O2
Asahi (mt.) J4
Asama (mt.) J5
Ashizuri (cape) F7
Aso (mt.) E7
Aso National Park E7
Atsumi (bay) H6
Awa (isl.) J4
Awaji (isl.) H8
Bandai (mt.) K5
Bandai-Asahi National Park J4
Biwa (lake) H6
Bonin (isls.) M3
Boso (pen.) K6
Bungo (str.) F7
Chichi (isl.) M3
Chichibu-Tama National Park J6
Chokai (mt.) J4
Chubu-Sangaku National Park H5
Dai (mt.) F6
Daimanji (mt.) F5
Daio (cape) H6
Daisen-Oki National Park F6
Daisetsu (mt.) L2
Daisetsu-Zan National Park L2
Dogo (isl.) F5
Dozen (isls.) F5
East China (sea) C8
Edo (riv.) P2
Erimo (cape) L3
Esan (pt.) K3
Fuji (mt.) J6
Fuji (riv.) J6
Fuji-Hakone-Izu National Park H6
Gassan (mt.) J4
Goto (isls.) D7
Habomai (isls.) N2
Hachiro (lag.) J3
Haha (isl.) M3
Hakken (mt.) H6
Haku (mt.) H5
Hakusan National Park H5
Harima (sea) G6
Hida (riv.) H6
Hodaka (mt.) H5
Hokkaido (isl.) L2
Honshu (isl.) J5
Ie (isl.) N6
Iheya (isl.) N6
Iki (isl.) D7
Ina (riv.) H7
Inawashiro (lake) K5
Inubo (cape) K6
Iriomote (isl.) K7
Iro (cape) J6
Ise (bay) H6
Ise-Shima National Park H6
Ishigaki (isl.) L7
Ishikari (bay) K2
Ishikari (riv.) L2
Ishizuchi (mt.) F7
Iwaki (mt.) K3
Iwate (mt.) K4
Iwo (isl.) M4
Iyo (sea) E7
Izu (isls.) J6
Izu (pen.) J6
Japan (sea) G4
Joshinetsu-Kogen National Park J5
Kagoshima (bay) E8
Kamui (cape) K2
Kariba (mt.) K2
Kasumiga (lag.) K5
Kazan-retto (Volcano) (isls.) M4
Kerama (isls.) M6
Kii (chan.) G7
Kikai (isl.) O5
Kino (riv.) G6
Kirishima-Yaku National Park E7
Kita Iwo (isl.) M4
Kitakami (riv.) K4
Komaga (mt.) K2
Koshiki (isls.) D8
Kuchino (isl.) O4
Kuju (mt.) E7
Kume (isl.) M6
Kutcharo (lake) M2
Kyushu (isl.) E7
Meakan (mt.) L2
Minami Iwo (isl.) M5
Miura (pen.) O3
Miyako (isl.) L7
Miyako (isls.) L7
Mogami (riv.) K4
Motsuta (cape) J2
Muko (isl.) M3
Muko (riv.) H7
Muroto (pt.) G7
Mutsu (bay) K3
Naka (riv.) K5
Nampo-Shoto (isls.) M3
Nansei Shoto (Ryukyu) (isls.) M6
Nantai (mt.) J5
Nasu (mt.) J5
Nemuro (str.) M1
Nii (isl.) J6
Nikko National Park J5
Nishino (isl.) M3
Nojima (cape) K6
Nosappu (pt.) N2
Noto (pen.) H5
Nyudo (cape) J4
Oani (riv.) K3
Obitsu (riv.) P3
Oga (pen.) J4
Ogasawara-gunto (Bonin) (isls.) M3
Okhotsk (sea) M1
Oki (isls.) F5
Okinawa (isl.) N6
Okinawa (isls.) N6
Okinoerabu (isl.) N5
Okushiri (isl.) J2
Oma (cape) K3
Omono (riv.) J4
Ono (riv.) E7
Ontake (mt.) H6
Osaka (bay) H8
O-Shima (isl.) J6
Osumi (isls.) E8
Osumi (pen.) E8
Osumi (str.) E8
Otakine (mt.) K5
Rikuchu-Kaigan National Park L4
Rishiri (isl.) K1
Ryukyu (isls.) L7
Sado (isl.) J4
Sagami (bay) O3
Sagami (riv.) O2
Sagami (sea) J6
Saikai National Park D7
Sakishima (isls.) K7
San'in Kaigan National Park G6
Sata (cape) E8
Setonaikai National Park H7
Shikoku (isl.) F7
Shikotan (isl.) N2
Shikotsu (lake) K2
Shikotsu-Toya National Park K2
Shimane (pen.) F6
Shimokita (pen.) K3
Shinano (riv.) J5
Shiono (cape) H7
Shiragami (cape) J3
Shirane (mt.) J5
Shirane (mt.) H6
Shiretoko (cape) M1
Shiriya (cape) K3
Soya (pt.) L1
Suo (sea) E7
Suruga (bay) J6
Suwanose (isl.) O4
Suzu (pt.) H5
Takeshima (isls.) F5
Tama (riv.) O2
Tanega (isl.) E8
Tappi (cape) K3

JAPAN is divided into prefectures bearing the same names as their capitals except:

Prefecture	Capital	Ref.
AICHI	NAGOYA	H 6
EHIME	MATSUYAMA	F 7
GUMMA	MAEBASHI	J 5
HOKKAIDO	SAPPORO	K 2
HYOGO	KOBE	H 7
IBARAKI	MITO	K 5
ISHIKAWA	KANAZAWA	H 5
IWATE	MORIOKA	K 4
KAGAWA	TAKAMATSU	G 6
KANAGAWA	YOKOHAMA	O 3
MIE	TSU	H 6
MIYAGI	SENDAI	K 4
OKINAWA	NAHA	N 6
SAITAMA	URAWA	O 2
SHIGA	OTSU	J 7
SHIMANE	MATSUE	F 6
TOCHIGI	UTSUNOMIYA	K 5
YAMANASHI	KOFU	J 6

KOREA (NORTH)

CITIES and TOWNS

OTHER FEATURES

KOREA (SOUTH)

CITIES and TOWNS

OTHER FEATURES

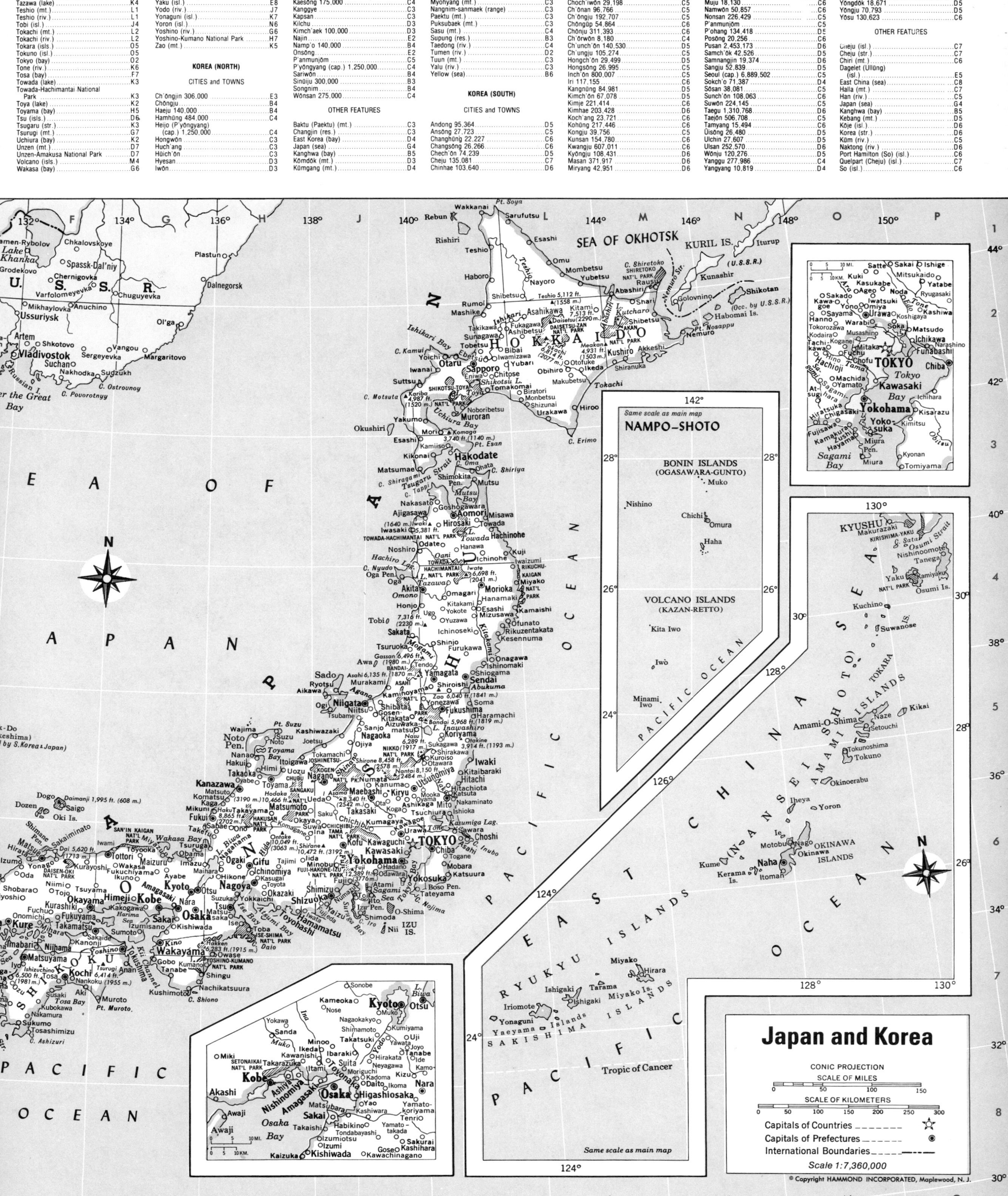

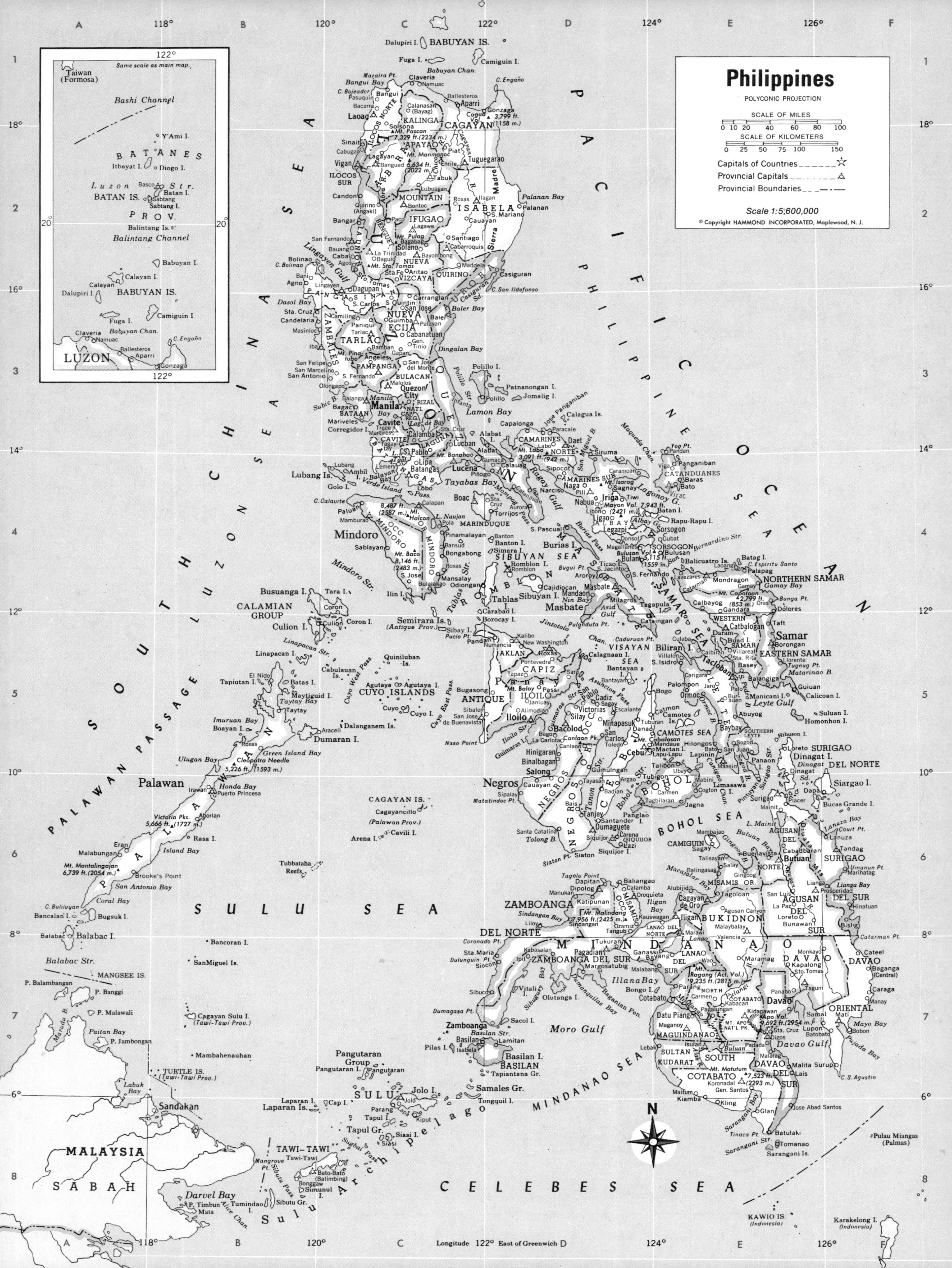

Philippines
POLYCONIC PROJECTION
SCALE OF MILES
0 10 20 40 60 80 100
SCALE OF KILOMETERS
0 25 50 75 100 150
Capitals of Countries
Provincial Capitals
Provincial Boundaries
Scale 1:5,600,000
© Copyright HAMMOND INCORPORATED, Maplewood, N. J.
Same scale as main map.
Taiwan (Formosa)
Bashi Channel
Y'Ami I.
BATANES
Itbayat I.
Diogo I.
Luzon Str.
BATAN IS.
Basco
Batan I.
Sabtang
Sabtang I.
PROV.
Balintang Is.
Balintang Channel
Babuyan I.
Calayan I.
Calayan
Dalupiri I.
BABUYAN IS.
Camiguin I.
Fuga I.
Babuyan Chan.
Claveria
Namuac
C. Engaño
Ballesteros
Aparri
Gonzaga
LUZON
122°
20°
A
B
C
D
E
F
118°
120°
122°
124°
126°
1
2
3
4
5
6
7
8
18°
16°
14°
12°
10°
8°
6°
Dalupiri I.
BABUYAN IS.
Fuga I.
Camiguin I.
Babuyan Chan.
C. Engaño
Maraira Pt.
Bangui Bay
C. Bojeador
Bangui
Pasuquin
Bacarra
Laoag
Claveria
Namuac
Ballesteros
Aparri
Calanasan (Bayag)
Solsona
KALINGA
CAGAYAN
Gonzaga
3,799 ft. (1158 m.)
Mt. Pascan 7,329 ft. (2234 m.)
APAYAO
ILOCOS NORTE
Sinait
Cabugao
Vigan
ILOCOS SUR
Lagayan
Bangued
Mt. Manmanoc 6,634 ft. (2022 m.)
ABRA
Piat
Enrile
Tuguegarao
Tabuk
Lubuagan
Candon
Quirino (Angaki)
MOUNTAIN
Bontoc
Roxas
Ilagan
ISABELA
S. Mariano
Palanan Bay
Palanan
Cauayan
Sierra Madre
Bangar
Paco
IFUGAO
Lagawe
San Fernando
Bauang
Caba
Agoo
Mt. Pulog
Bagabag
Solano
Santiago
Cabarroquis
La Trinidad
Baguio
Bayombong
NUEVA VIZCAYA
Mt. Sto. Tomas
Bolinao
C. Bolinao
Lingayen Gulf
Bani
Agno
Lingayen
Dagupan
PANGASINAN
Sta. Fe
Aritao
QUIRINO
Maddela
Casiguran
C. San Ildefonso
Dasol Bay
Sta. Cruz
Candelaria
Masinloc
ZAMBALES
Camiling
Paniqui
Tarlac
TARLAC
S. Carlos
Quintin
San Jose
Carranglan
Guimba
NUEVA ECIJA
Cabanatuan
Gen. Tinio
Baler
Baler Bay
Palayan
Casiguran Sd.
AURORA
Iba
Mt. Pinatubo
Bamban
Angeles
Gapan
PAMPANGA
San Jose del Monte
Dingalan Bay
San Felipe
San Marcelino
San Antonio
Olongapo
S. Fernando
BULACAN
Malolos
Quezon City
Polillo I.
Polillo Str.
Polillo
Patnanongan I.
Jomalig I.
Subic B.
Balanga
Manila
RIZAL
BATAAN
Bagac
Manila Bay
NAT'L CAP. REG.
Mariveles
Corregidor I.
Cavite
CAVITE
Laguna de Bay
Lamon Bay
Trece Martires
Tagaytay
Calamba
LAGUNA
Sta. Cruz
QUEZON
Infanta
Lucban
Alabat I.
Alabat
Capalonga
Jose Panganiban
Calagua Is.
Paracale
CAMARINES NORTE
Labo
Daet
Mt. Labo 3,091 ft. (942 m.)
San Miguel B.
Maqueda Chan.
Siruma
Yog Pt.
Pandan
Lubang
Ambil I.
Lubang Is.
Golo I.
Taal
Pablo
Lipa
Batangas
BATANGAS
Balayan
Verde Island Pass.
Mt. Banahao
Lucena
Gumaca
Calauag
Pitogo
Tayabas Bay
Ragay Gulf
Sipocot
CAMARINES SUR
Mt. Isarog
Naga
Pili
Caramoan
Sagnay
Lagonoy G.
Iriga
Tiwi
Panganiban
CATANDUANES
Baras
Bato
Virac
C. Calavite
Paluan
Mamburao
OCC. MINDORO
8,487 ft. (2587 m.)
Mt. Halcon
Calapan
Boac
Sta. Cruz
Torrijos
MARINDUQUE
Mompog Pass.
Mayon Vol. 7,943 ft. (2421 m.)
Nabua
Libon
Ligao
ALBAY
Albay G.
Legazpi
Batan I.
Rapu-Rapu I.
Sorsogon
Mindoro
Sablayan
L. Naujan
Pola
Pinamalayan
Bansud
Bongabong
Mt. Baco 8,146 ft. (2483 m.)
S. Jose
OR. MINDORO
Roxas
Mansalay
Bulalacao
Mindoro Str.
Banton
Banton I.
Simara I.
SIBUYAN SEA
Burias I.
Burias Pass
S. Pascual
Donsol
Magallanes
Gubat
SORSOGON
Bulusan
Bulan
5,115 ft. (1559 m.)
S. Bernardino Str.
Balicuatro Is.
Batag I.
C. Espiritu Santo
Palapag
NORTHERN SAMAR
Gamay Bay
Laoang
Lavezares
Mondragon
Catarman
Mt. Capotoan 2,799 ft. (853 m.)
Bunga Pt.
Dolores
Oras
Calbayog
Gandara
Busuanga I.
Tara I.
Coron
CALAMIAN GROUP
Culion I.
Culion
Coron I.
Ilin I.
Romblon I.
Romblon
ROMBLON
Tablas
Odiongan
Tablas Str.
Cajidiocan
Sibuyan I.
Mandaon
Masbate
MASBATE
Nin Bay
Asid Gulf
Aroroy
Ticao I.
S. Jacinto
Bugui Pt.
S. Fernando
Tagapula I.
Cataingan
Carabao I.
Borocay I.
Semirara Is.
(Antique Prov.)
Sibay I.
Pucio Pt.
Jintotolo
Pulgaduta Pt.
Chan.
Caduruan Pt.
WESTERN SAMAR
Catbalogan
Taft
Samar
Borongan
EASTERN SAMAR
Linapacan I.
Linapacan Str.
El Nido
Tapiutan I.
Batas I.
Cabulauan Is.
Quiniluban Is.
Agutaya
CUYO ISLANDS
Cuyo
Cuyo I.
Cuyo West Pass.
Cuyo East Pass.
Maytiguid I.
Taytay Bay
Taytay
Imuruan Bay
Boayan I.
Araceli
Dalanganem Is.
Dumaran I.
Pandan
Kalibo
New Washington
AKLAN
Numancia
Roxas
CAPIZ
Pontevedra
Tapaz
Mt. Baloy
Passi
ILOILO
Januiay
Alimodian
Iloilo
ANTIQUE
Bugasong
Sibalom
San Jose de Buenavista
Naso Point
Iloilo Str.
Guimaras Str.
Guimaras I.
VISAYAN SEA
Calagnaan I.
Bantayan I.
Bantayan
Asuncion Pass.
Sagay
Cadiz
San Carlos
Victorias
Silay
Bacolod
Escalante
Biliran I.
Culaba
Villalon
S. Isidro
Naval
Carigara
Palompon
LEYTE
Ormoc
Jaro
Tacloban
Daram
Basey
Marabut
Manicani I.
Guiuan
Calicoan I.
Leyte Gulf
Suluan I.
Homonhon I.
Bogo
Tuburan
Camotes Is.
CAMOTES SEA
Abuyog
Baybay
SOUTHERN LEYTE
Maasin
Sogod
Hibuson I.
Dinagat I.
Dinagat
SURIGAO DEL NORTE
Siargao I.
Cebu
CEBU
Toledo
Mandaue
Lapu-Lapu
Mactan I.
Danao
Mt. Cabalasan
Hilongos
Bato
Lapinin I.
Ubay
Talibon
BOHOL
Tubigon
Carmen
Tagbilaran
Jagna
Limasawa I.
Mabini
Cogton
Surigao
Panaon I.
Placer
Dapa
Bucas Grande I.
Hinigaran
Binalbagan
Salong
La Carlota
Canlaon Pk.
Canlaon
NEGROS OCC.
Guihulngan
Tayasan
Negros
Cauayan
Sipalay
Matatindoc Pt.
NEGROS OR.
Bais
Tanjay
Dumaguete
Santander I.
Panglao I.
Bohol Str.
Badian
Argao
Santa Catalina
Tolong B.
Siquijor
SIQUIJOR
Larena
Lazi
Siquijor I.
Siaton
Siaton Pt.
BOHOL SEA
Palawan
Irawan
Honda Bay
Puerto Princesa
Ulugan Bay
Roxas
Cleopatra Needle 5,226 ft. (1593 m.)
Green Island Bay
PALAWAN
PALAWAN PASSAGE
Victoria Pks. 5,666 ft. (1727 m.)
Aborlan
Rasa I.
Island Bay
Eran
Malabungan
Mt. Mantalingajan 6,739 ft. (2054 m.)
Brooke's Point
San Antonio Bay
Coral Bay
C. Buliluyan
Bancalan I.
Bugsuk I.
Balabac
Balabac I.
CAGAYAN IS.
Cagayancillo
(Palawan Prov.)
Arena I.
Cavili I.
Tubbataha Reefs
SULU SEA
Bancoran I.
SanMiguel Is.
Balabac Str.
MANGSEE IS.
P. Balambangan
P. Banggi
P. Malawali
Paitan Bay
P. Jambongan
Cagayan Sulu I.
(Tawi-Tawi Prov.)
Mambahenauhan
TURTLE IS.
(Tawi-Tawi Prov.)
Labuk Bay
Sandakan
MALAYSIA
SABAH
Darvel Bay
P. Timbun Mata
Tumindao I.
Sibutu Gr.
Alice Chan.
Sibutu Pass
Mangrove Pt.
Bongao
Bato-Bato (Balimbing)
Simunul I.
TAWI-TAWI
Tawi-Tawi
Sulu Archipelago
Sugbai Pass
Siasi
Siasi I.
Tapul Gr.
Tapul I.
Parang
Kiput I.
Jolo
Jolo I.
SULU
Laparan I.
Laparan Is.
Cap I.
Pangutaran Group
Pangutaran I.
Pangutaran
Samales Gr.
Tongquil I.
Basilan I.
BASILAN
Tapiantana Gr.
Lamitan
Isabela
Basilan
Pilas I.
Basilan Str.
Zamboanga
Sacol I.
Dumagasa Pt.
Sibuco
Vitali I.
Olutanga I.
Sibuguey Bay
Dumanquilas Bay
Baganian Pen.
Moro Gulf
Illana Bay
Bongo I.
Cotabato
MINDANAO SEA
CELEBES SEA
Tagolo Point
Dapitan
Dipolog
Manukan
Katipunan
ZAMBOANGA DEL NORTE
Sindangan Bay
Mt. Malindang 7,956 ft. (2425 m.)
Liloy
Baliangao
Calamba
Oroquieta
MISAMIS OCC.
Iligan Bay
Kauswagan
Ozamiz
Tangub
LANAO DEL NORTE
Iligan
Coronado Pt.
Sta. Maria
Dulunguin Pt.
Siocon
Kabasalan
Ipil
Tukuran
Pagadian
ZAMBOANGA DEL SUR
Margosatubig
Ganassi
Marawi
LANAO DEL SUR
Malabang
MINDANAO
Mt. Ragang (Act. Vol.) 9,235 ft. (2815 m.)
Parang
CAMIGUIN
Mambajao
Sagay
Gingoog Bay
Macajalar Bay
Talisayan
Balingasag
Gingoog
Salay
MISAMIS OR.
Alubijid
Cagayan de Oro
Tagoloan
BUKIDNON
Malaybalay
Valencia
Agusan Canyon
Butuan Bay
Buenavista
Butuan
Cabadbaran
AGUSAN DEL NORTE
L. Mainit
Mainit
Lanuza Bay
Cauit Pt.
Lanuza
Tandag
SURIGAO DEL SUR
Umanun Pt.
Marihatag
Lianga
Lianga Bay
Prosperidad
San Luis
AGUSAN DEL SUR
La Paz
Loreto
Bunawan
Hinatuan
Bislig
Catarman Pt.
Monkayo
DAVAO
Kapalong
Sto. Tomas
Tagum
Cateel
DAVAO ORIENTAL
Baganga (Central)
Caraga
Manay
Maramag
Carmen
NORTH COTABATO
Kabacan
Kidapawan
Mt. Apo Vol. 9,692 ft. (2954 m.)
MT. APO NAT'L PK.
Sta. Cruz
Digos
Davao
Panabo
Samal I.
Lupon
Batobato
Mati
Mayo Bay
Bobon
Pujada Bay
Davao Gulf
Datu Piang
Maganoy
MAGUINDANAO
Lebak
Isulan
SULTAN KUDARAT
SOUTH COTABATO
Koronadal
Mt. Matutum 7,523 ft. (2293 m.)
Gen. Santos
Maitum
Kiamba
Kling
DAVAO DEL SUR
Malita
Surup
Lais
C. S. Agustin
Glan
Jose Abad Santos
Sarangani Bay
Tinaca Pt.
Batulaki
Tomanao
Sarangani Is.
Sarangani Str.
Pulau Miangas (Palmas)
KAWIO IS. (Indonesia)
Karakelong I. (Indonesia)
N
SOUTH CHINA SEA
LUZON SEA
PACIFIC OCEAN
PHILIPPINE SEA
Longitude 122° East of Greenwich

PROVINCES

Abra 160,198 . . . . C2
Agusan del Norte 365,421 . . E6
Agusan del Sur 631,634 . . . . E6
Aklan 324,563 . . . . D5
Albay 809,177 . . . . D4
Antique 344,879 . . . . D5
Aurora 107,145 . . . . C3
Basilan 201,407 . . . . D7
Bataan 323,254 . . . . C3
Batanes 12,091 . . . . A2
Batangas 1,174,201 . . . . C4
Benguet 354,751 . . . . C2
Bohol 806,031 . . . . E6
Bukidnon 631,634 . . . . E6
Bulacan 1,098,046 . . . . C3
Cagayan 711,476 . . . . C1
Camarines Norte 368,007 . . . D3
Camarines Sur 1,099,346 . . D4
Camiguin 57,126 . . . . E6
Capiz 492,231 . . . . D5
Catanduanes 175,247 . . . . . . E4
Cavite 771,320 . . . . C3
Cebu 2,091,602 . . . . D5
Davao 725,153 . . . . E7
Davao del Sur 1,133,599 . . . E7
Davao Oriental 339,931 . . . . . F7
Eastern Samar 320,637 . . . . E5
Ifugao 111,368 . . . . C2
Ilocos Norte 390,666 . . . . . . C1
Ilocos Sur 443,591 . . . . C2
Iloilo 1,433,641 . . . . D5
Isabela 870,604 . . . . C2
Kalinga-Apayao 185,063 . . . . C1
Laguna 973,104 . . . . C3
Lanao del Norte 461,049 . . . E6
Lanao del Sur 404,971 . . . . . E7
La Union 452,578 . . . . C2
Leyte 1,302,648 . . . . E5
Maguindanao 536,546 . . . . . E7
Manila 5,925,884 . . . . C3
Marinduque 173,715 . . . . . . C4
Masbate 584,526 . . . . D4
Misamis Occidental 386,328 D6
Misamis Oriental 690,032 . . . E6
Mountain 103,052 . . . . C2
National Capital Region (Manila) 5,925,884 . . . . . . C3
Negros Occidental 1,930,301 . . . . D6
Negros Oriental 819,399 . . . D6
North Cotabato 564,599 . . . . E7
Northern Samar 378,516 . . . E4
Nueva Ecija 1,069,409 . . . . . C3
Nueva Vizcaya 241,690 . . . . . C2
Occidental Mindoro 222,431 C4
Oriental Mindoro 448,938 . . . C4
Palawan 371,782 . . . . B6
Pampanga 1,181,590 . . . . . . C3
Pangasinan 1,636,057 . . . . . C3
Quezon 1,129,277 . . . . C3
Quirino 83,230 . . . . C2
Rizal 555,533 . . . . C3
Romblon 193,174 . . . . D4
Siquijor 70,300 . . . . D6
Sorsogon 500,685 . . . . E4
South Cotabato 770,473 . . . . E7
Southern Leyte 298,294 . . . . E5
Sultan Kudarat 303,784 . . . . E7
Sulu 360,588 . . . . C7
Surigao del Norte 363,414 . . F5
Surigao del Sur 377,647 . . . . F6
Tarlac 638,457 . . . . C3
Tawi-Tawi 194,651 . . . . B8
Western Samar 501,439 . . . . E5
Zambales 444,037 . . . . C3
Zamboanga del Norte 588,015 . . . . D6
Zamboanga del Sur 1,183,845 . . . . D7

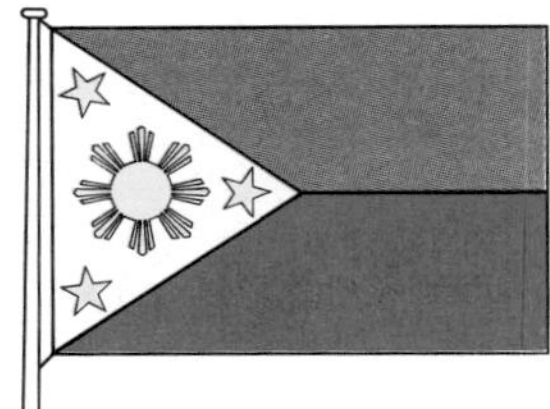

AREA 115,707 sq. mi. (299,681 sq. km.)
POPULATION 48,098,460
CAPITAL Manila
LARGEST CITY Manila
HIGHEST POINT Apo 9,692 ft. (2,954 m.)
MONETARY UNIT piso
MAJOR LANGUAGES Pilipino (Tagalog), English, Spanish, Bisayan, Ilocano, Bikol
MAJOR RELIGIONS Roman Catholicism, Islam, Protestantism, tribal religions

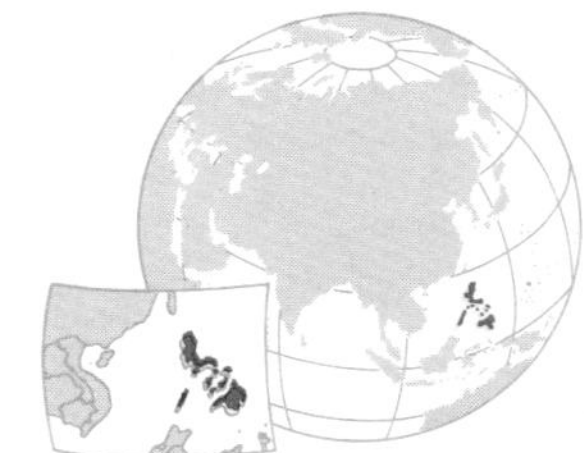

CITIES and TOWNS

Angeles 188,834 . . . . C3
Aparri 45,070 . . . . C1
Bacolod 262,415 . . . . D5
Bagac 13,109 . . . . C3
Bago 99,631 . . . . D5
Baguio 119,009 . . . . C2
Balanga 39,132 . . . . C3
Baler 18,349 . . . . C3
Balimbing (Bato-Bato) 22,189 . . . . C8
Bamban 26,072 . . . . C3
Basco 4,341 . . . . A2
Batangas 143,570 . . . . C4
Bato-Bato 22,189 . . . . C8
Baybay 74,640 . . . . E5
Bislig 81,615 . . . . F6
Boac 37,005 . . . . C4
Bontoc 17,091 . . . . C2
Burauen 48,058 . . . . E5
Butuan 172,489 . . . . E6
Cabanatuan 138,298 . . . . C3
Cabarroquis 17,450 . . . . C2
Cadiz 129,632 . . . . D5
Cagayan de Oro 227,312 . . . E6
Calamba 121,175 . . . . C3
Calbayog 106,719 . . . . E4
Carigara 34,377 . . . . E5
Cauayan 70,017 . . . . D6
Cavite 87,666 . . . . C3
Cebu 490,281 . . . . D5
Cotabato 83,871 . . . . D7
Dagupan 98,344 . . . . C2
Davao 610,375 . . . . E7
Digos 70,065 . . . . E7
Escalante 71,293 . . . . D5
General Santos 149,396 . . . . E7
Gingoog 79,937 . . . . E6
Guihulngan 84,156 . . . . D5
Guimba 58,847 . . . . C3
Iba 22,791 . . . . B3
Ilagan 79,336 . . . . C2
Iligan 167,358 . . . . E6
Iloilo 244,827 . . . . D5
Infanta 27,914 . . . . C3
Jaro 29,739 . . . . E5
Jolo 52,429 . . . . C8
Koronadal 80,566 . . . . E7
Lagawe 15,075 . . . . C2
Lapu-Lapu 98,723 . . . . E5
Legazpi 99,766 . . . . D4
Ligao 69,860 . . . . D4
Lingayen 65,187 . . . . C2
Lipa 121,166 . . . . C4
Lucena 107,880 . . . . C4
Maganoy 45,845 . . . . E7
Mainit 18,078 . . . . E6
Malabang 18,955 . . . . D7
Malolos 95,699 . . . . C3
Mandaue 110,590 . . . . E5
Manila (cap.) 1,630,485 . . . . C3
Mariveles 48,594 . . . . C3
Mati 78,178 . . . . F7
Naga 90,712 . . . . D4
Olongapo 156,430 . . . . C3
Ormoc 104,978 . . . . E5
Ozamiz 77,832 . . . . D6
Pagadian 80,861 . . . . D7
Palo 31,124 . . . . E5
Palompon 40,242 . . . . E5
Panabo 71,098 . . . . E7
Prosperidad 33,824 . . . . F6
Puerto Princesa 60,234 . . . . B6
Quezon City 1,165,865 . . . . . C3
Romblon 24,251 . . . . D4
Roxas 81,183 . . . . D5
Sagay 99,118 . . . . D5
San Antonio 42,969 . . . . B3
San Carlos, Negros Occ. 91,627 . . . . D5
San Carlos, Pangasinan 101,243 . . . . C3
San Fernando, La Union 68,410 . . . . C2
San Fernando, Pampanga 110,891 . . . . C3
San Jose 64,254 . . . . C3
San Jose del Monte 90,732 . C3
San Pablo 131,655 . . . . C3
Santa Fe 6,338 . . . . C2
Santiago 69,877 . . . . C2
Silay 111,131 . . . . D5
Siquijor 17,533 . . . . D6
Surigao 79,745 . . . . E6
Tacloban 102,523 . . . . E5
Tagaytay 16,322 . . . . C3
Tagum 86,201 . . . . E7
Tarlac 175,691 . . . . C3
Toledo 91,668 . . . . D5
Tuguegarao 73,507 . . . . C2
Zamboanga 343,722 . . . . C7

OTHER FEATURES

Agusan (riv.) E6
Alabat (isl.) D3
Apo (vol.) E7
Babuyan (isl.) B2
Balabac (isl.) A7
Balayan (bay) C4
Balintang (chan.) A2
Baloy (mt.) D5
Bantayan (isl.) D5
Banton (isl.) D4
Bashi (chan.) A1
Basilan (isl.) D7
Batan, Albay (isl.) E4
Batan, Batanes (isl.) B2
Batan (isls.) A2
Bay, Laguna de (lake) C3
Biliran (isl.) E5
Bohol (isl.) E6
Bojeador (cape) C1
Borocay (isl.) D5
Bucas Grande (isl.) F6
Bugsuk (isl.) A6
Buliluyan (cape) A6
Bunga (pt.) E4
Burias (isl.) D4
Busuanga (isl.) B4
Cabalasan (mt.) E5
Cabulauan (isls.) C5
Cagayan (isls.) C6
Cagayan (riv.) C2
Cagayan Sulu (isl.) B7
Cagua (vol.) D1
Calagua (isls.) D3
Calamian Group (isls.) B4
Calayan (isl.) A2
Calicoan (isl.) E5
Camiguin, Cagayan (isl.) . . . B3
Camiguin, Camiguin (isl.) . . . E6
Camotes (isls.) E5
Camotes (sea) E5
Canigao (chan.) E5
Canlaon (peak) D5
Capotoan (mt.) E4
Carabao (isl.) D4
Catanduanes (isl.) E4
Cebu (isl.) D5
Celebes (sea) D8
Cleopatra Needle (mt.) B5
Coron (isl.) C5
Corregidor (isl.) C3
Culion (isl.) B5
Cuyo (isl.) C5
Cuyo (isls.) C5
Daram (isl.) E5
Davao (gulf) E7
Dinagat (isl.) E5
Diuata (mts.) E6
Dumanquilas (bay) D7
Dumaran (isl.) C5
Engaño (cape) D1
Espiritu Santo (cape) E4
Fuga (isl.) A3
Guimaras (isl.) D5
Halcon (mt.) C4
Hibuson (isl.) E5
Homonhon (isl.) E5
Honda (bay) B6
Iligan (bay) E6
Ilin (isl.) C4
Illana (bay) D7
Imuruan (bay) B5
Island (bay) B6
Itbayat (isl.) A2
Jintotolo (chan.) D5
Jolo (isl.) C7
Jomalig (isl.) D3
Lagonoy (gulf) E4
Lamon (bay) C3
Lanao (lake) E7
Laparan (isls.) B8
Lapinin (isl.) E5
Leyte (gulf) E5
Leyte (isl.) E5
Limasawa (isl.) E6
Linapacan (isl.) B5
Lingayen (gulf) C2
Lubang (isls.) B4
Luzon (isl.) C3
Luzon (str.) A2
Macajalar (bay) E6
Malindang (mt.) D6
Mangsee (isls.) A7
Manila (bay) C3
Mantalingajan (mt.) A6
Maqueda (chan.) D3
Maraira (pt.) C1
Marinduque (isl.) C4
Masbate (isl.) D4
Mayon (vol.) D4
Maytiguid (isl.) B5
Mindanao (isl.) D7
Mindanao (riv.) E7
Mindoro (isl.) C4
Mindoro (str.) C4
Mompog (passg.) D4
Moro (gulf) D7
Mount Apo National Park . . . E7
Naso (pt.) C5
Negros (isl.) D6
Olutanga (isl.) D7
Pacsan (mt.) C2
Palawan (isl.) B6
Palawan (passg.) A6
Panaon (isl.) E5
Panay (isl.) D5
Panglao (isl.) D6
Pangutaran (isl.) C7
Pangutaran Group (isls.) . . . C7
Patnanongan (isl.) D3
Philippine (sea) D3
Pilas (isl.) C7
Pinatubo (mt.) C3
Polillo (isl.) C3
Pujada (bay) F7
Pulangi (riv.) E7
Ragang (vol.) E7
Ragay (gulf) D4
Rapu-Rapu (isl.) E4
Romblon (isl.) D4
Sabtang (isl.) B2
Sacol (isl.) D7
Samal (isl.) E7
Samales Group (isls.) D7
Samar (isl.) E5
Samar (sea) E4
San Agustin (cape) F7
San Bernardino (str.) E4
San Miguel (bay) D3
San Pedro (bay) E5
Santo Tomas (mt.) C2
Semirara (isls.) C5
Siargao (isl.) F6
Sibay (isl.) C5
Sibuguey (bay) D7
Sibutu Group (isls.) B8
Sibuyan (isl.) D4
Sibuyan (sea) D4
Sierra Madre (mt.) D2
Simunul (isl.) B8
Siquijor (isl.) D6
South China (sea) B3
Subic (bay) C3
Sulu (arch.) B8
Sulu (sea) B6
Suluan (isl.) F5
Surigao (str.) E6
Taal (lake) C4
Tablas (isl.) D4
Tablas (str.) C4
Tagapula (isl.) E4
Tagolo (pt.) D6
Tanon (str.) D6
Tapul (isl.) C8
Tapul Group (isls.) C8
Tara (isl.) C4
Tawi-Tawi (isl.) B8
Tayabas (bay) C4
Ticao (isl.) D4
Tinaca (pt.) E8
Tongquil (isl.) D8
Tumindao (isl.) B8
Turtle (isls.) B7
Verde Island (passg.) C4
Victoria (peaks) B6
Visayan (sea) D5

Topography

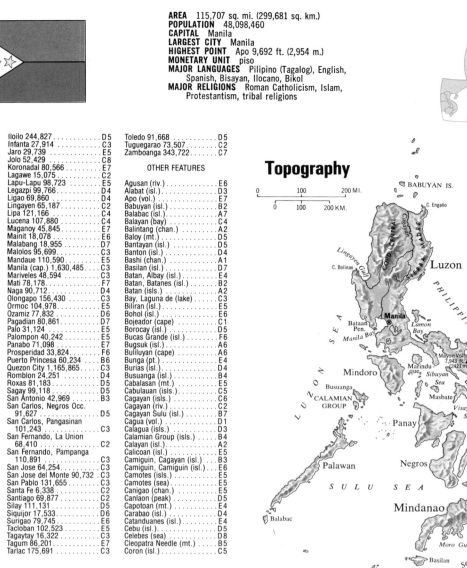

Agriculture, Industry and Resources

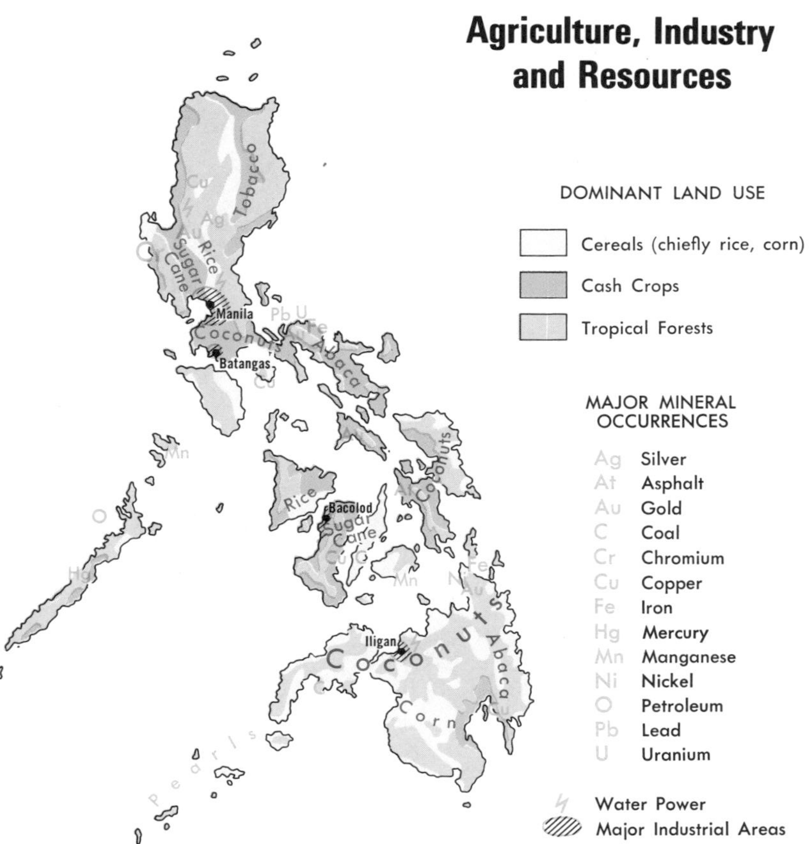

84 Southeast Asia

BRUNEI

CITIES and TOWNS

Bandar Seri Begawan 63,868 E4
Seria 23,511 .... E5

INDONESIA

CITIES and TOWNS

Adaut J7
Agats K7
Ambon (Amboina) 208,898 . H6
Amuntai F6
Amurang G5
Atambua G7
Baa G8
Bagansiapiapi C5
Balikpapan 280,675 .... F6
Banda Aceh 72,090 .... A4
Bandanaira H6
Bandung 1,462,637 .... H2
Banggai G6
Banjarmasin 381,286 .... E6
Banyumas J2
Batang J2
Batavia (Jakarta) (cap.) 6,503,449 .... H1
Bekasi H2
Belawan B5
Bengkulu 64,783 .... C6
Beo H5
Biak K6
Binjai 76,464 .... B5
Bintuhan C6
Blitar 78,503 .... K2
Bogor 247,409 .... H2
Bojonegoro J2
Bukittinggi 70,771 .... B6
Bula J6
Bulukumba G7
Buntok F6
Cianjur H2
Cimahi H2
Cirebon 223,776 .... H2
Demta L6
Denpasar E7
Dili H7
Djambi (Jambi) 230,373 .... C6
Djokjakarta (Yogyakarta) 398,727 .... J2
Dobo J7
Donggala F6
Enaratoli K6
Ende G7
Fakfak J6
Garut H2
Gorontalo 97,628 .... G5
Hollandia (Jayapura) K6
Indramayu H2
Jailolo H5
Jakarta (cap.) 6,503,449 ... H1
Jambi 230,373 .... C6
Jayapura (Hollandia) K6
Jogjakarta (Yogyakarta) 398,727 .... J2
Jombang K2
Kaimana J6
Kampung Baru (Tolitoli) G5
Kediri 221,830 .... K2
Kendari G6
Kepi K7
Ketapang E6
Kokonau K6
Kolonodale G6
Kotabaharu E6
Kotabaru F6
Kotawaringin E6
Kragen K2
Kupang G8
Kutaraja (Banda Aceh) 72,090 .... A4
Labuha H6
Labuhan G2
Laiwui H6
Larantuka G7
Lekitobi G6
Longiram F5
Madiun 150,562 .... K2
Magelang 123,484 .... J2
Majalengka H2
Makassar (Ujung Pandang) 709,038 .... F7
Malang 511,780 .... K2
Malili G6
Manado 217,159 .... G5
Manokwari J6
Maumere G7
Medan 1,378,955 .... B5
Menggala D6
Merauke K7
Mindiptana L7
Mojokerto 68,849 .... K2
Muarasiberut B6
Nangatayap E6
Pacitan J2
Padang 480,922 .... B6
Padangpanjang 34,517 ..... B6
Padangsidempuan B5
Pakanbaru 186,262 .... C5
Palangkaraya 60,447 .... E6
Palembang 787,187 .... D6
Pangkalanbuun E6
Pangkalpinang 90,096 .... D6
Parepare 86,450 .... F6
Pasangkayu F6
Pasuruan 95,864 .... K2
Payakumbuh 78,836 .... C6
Pekalongan 132,558 .... J2
Pemalang J2
Pematangsiantar 150,376 ... B5
Pinrang F6
Plaju D6
Pontianak 304,778 .... D6
Probolinggo 100,296 .... K2
Purbolinggo J2
Raha G6
Rantauprapat C5
Rembang K2
Sabang, Celebes F5
Sabang, Weh 23,821 .... B4
Salatiga 85,849 .... J2
Samarinda 264,718 .... F6
Sampit E6
Sarmi K6
Sawahlunto 13,561 .... C6
Seba G8
Semarang 1,026,671 .... J2
Semitau E5
Serui K6
Sibolga 59,897 .... B5
Sigli B4
Sinabang B5
Singaraja F7
Solo (Surakarta) 469,888 ... J2
Solok 31,724 .... C6
Sorong J6
Sragen J2
Subang H2
Sukabumi 109,994 .... H2
Sumbawa Besar F7
Sumedang H2
Surabaya 2,027,913 .... K2
Surakarta 469,888 .... J2
Tanahmerah K7
Tanjungbalai 41,894 .... C5
Tanjungkarang 284,275 ..... D7
Tanjungpinang C5
Tanjungselor F5
Tarakan F5
Tebingtinggi 92,087 .... B5
Tegal 131,728 .... J2
Telukbayur C6
Tepa H7
Terempa D5
Tjilatjap (Cilicap) H2
Tjirebon (Cirebon) 223,776 . H2
Tolitoli G5
Tuban K2
Ujung Pandang 709,038 ..... F7
Vila Arminda Monteiro H7
Vila Salazar H7
Viquique H7
Wahai H6
Waigama H6
Wajabula H5
Waren K6
Weda H5
Wonreli H7
Yogyakarta 398,727 .... J2

OTHER FEATURES

Anambas (isls.) 29,572 ..... D5
Arafura (sea) J8
Aru (isls.) 34,195 .... K7
Babar (isl.) H7
Bali (isl.) 2,074,438 .... F7
Banda (sea) H7
Banggai (arch.) 169,025 ... G6
Bangka (isl.) 298,017 .... D6
Banyak (isls.) 1,980 .... B5
Barisan (mts.) C6
Barito (riv.) E6
Batu (isls.) 16,390 .... B6
Bawean (isl.) 64,551 .... K1
Belitung (Billiton) (isl.) 128,694 .... D6
Berau (bay) J6
Biak (isl.) K6
Billiton (isl.) 128,694 .... D6
Binongko (isl.) 11,549 .... G7
Bone (gulf) G7
Borneo (isl.) E5
Bosch, van den (cape) J6
Bunguran (Great Natuna) (isl.) D5
Buru (isl.) 23,034 .... H6
Butung (isl.) 188,173 .... G6
Celebes (Sulawesi) (isl.) 7,732,383 .... G5
Celebes (sea) G5
Cenderawasih (bay) K6
Dampier (str.) J6
Digul (riv.) K7
Doberai (pen.) J6
Enggano (isl.) 1,082 .... C7
Ewab (Kai) (isls.) 108,328 ... J7
Flores (isl.) 860,328 .... G7
Flores (sea) F7
Frederik Hendrik (Kolepom) (isl.) K7
Geelvink (Cenderawasih) (bay) K6
Great Kai (isl.) 38,748 .... J7
Halmahera (isl.) 122,521 ... H5
Irian Jaya (reg.) 923,440 ... J6
Jambuair (cape) B4
Jamursba (cape) J5
Java (head) C7
Java (isl.) 73,712,411 .... J2
Java (sea) D6
Jaya, Puncak (mt.) K6
Jayawijaya (range) K6
Jemaja (isl.) 5,628 .... D5
Kabaena (isl.) G7
Kai (isls.) 108,328 .... J7
Kalao (isl.) G7
Kalaotoa (isl.) G5
Kalimantan (reg.) 4,956,865. E5
Kangean (isl.) F7
Kapuas (riv.) D6
Karakelong (isl.) H5
Karimata (arch.) 9,398 .... D6
Karimunjawa (isls.) 5,025 ... J1
Kerinci (mt.) C6
Kisar (isl.) H7
Komodo (isl.) 30,407 .... F7
Krakatau (Rakata) (isl.) C7
Laut (isl.) 55,711 .... F6
Leuser (mt.) B5
Lingga (arch.) 46,658 .... D5
Lingga (isl.) 18,027 .... D6
Lombok (isl.) 1,581,193 .... F7
Madura (isl.) 1,509,774 .... K2
Mahakam (riv.) F6
Makassar (str.) F6
Malacca (str.) C5
Mamberamo (riv.) K6
Maoke (mts.) K6
Mapia (isls.) J5
Mentawai (isls.) 30,107 .... B6
Misool (isl.) J6
Molucca (sea) H6
Moluccas (isls.) 944,240 ... H6
Morotai (isl.) 27,333 .... H5
Muli (str.) K7
Müller (mts.) E5
Muna (isl.) 156,186 .... G7
Musi (riv.) C6
Natuna (isls.) 23,893 .... D5
Ngunju (cape) F8
Nias (isl.) 356,093 .... B5
Numfoor (isl.) J6
Obi (isls.) 12,437 .... H6
Ombai (str.) H7
Pantar (isl.) 28,259 .... G7
Perkam (cape) K6
Puting, Borneo (cape) E6
Puting, Sumatra (cape) C7
Raja Ampat Group (isls.) ... H6
Rakata (isl.) C7
Rantekombola (mt.) F6
Raya (mt.) E6
Riau (arch.) 483,230 .... C5
Rokan (riv.) C5
Roti (isl.) 76,270 .... G8
Salawati (isl.) J6
Sangihe (isl.) H5
Sangihe (isls.) 183,000 .... G5
Sawu (isls.) 51,002 .... G8
Sawu (sea) G7
Schouten (isls.) 110,148 ... K6
Schwaner (mts.) E6
Sebuku (bay) F5
Selatan (cape) E6
Selayar (isl.) 92,342 .... G7
Semeru (mt.) K2
Siau (isl.) 46,801 .... H5
Siberut (str.) B6
Simeulue (isl.) 29,147 ..... A5
Singkep (isl.) 28,631 .... D6
Sipura (isl.) 6,051 .... B6
Slamet (mt.) J2
Sorikmerapi (mt.) B5
South Natuna (isls.) D5
Sudirman (range) K6
Sula (isls.) 36,922 .... H6
Sulawesi (isl.) 7,732,383 ... G6
Sumatra (isl.) 19,360,400 .. B5
Sumba (isl.) 291,190 .... F7
Sumba (str.) F7
Sumbawa (isl.) 621,140 .... F7
Sunda (str.) C7
Tahulandang (isl.) 21,493 .. H5
Talaud (isls.) 46,395 .... H5
Taliabu (isl.) 18,303 .... G6
Tambelan (isls.) 4,032 ..... D5
Tanimbar (isls.) 55,405 ..... J7
Tariku (riv.) K6
Tidore (isl.) 28,655 .... H5
Timor (reg.) 1,435,527 .... H7
Timor (sea) H7
Toba (lake) B5
Tolo (gulf) G6
Tomini (gulf) G6
Tukangbesi (isls.) 73,106 ... G7
Vals (cape) K7
Vogelkop (Doberai) (pen.) ... J6
Waigeo (isl.) J5
Wakde (isl.) K6
Wangiwangi (isl.) 28,469 ... G7
We (isl.) B4
Wetar (isl.) H7
Yapen (isl.) 50,888 .... K6

MALAYSIA

STATES

North Borneo (Sabah) 1,002,608 .... F3
Sarawak 1,294,753 .... E5

CITIES and TOWNS

Beaufort 2,709 .... F4
Bintulu 4,424 .... E5
Kabong E5
Kampong Sibuti E5
Kapit 1,929 .... E5
Keningau 2,037 .... F4
Kota Kinabalu 40,939 .... F4
Kuching 63,535 .... E5
Kudat 5,089 .... F4
Labuan 7,216 .... E4
Lahad Datu 5,169 .... F5
Lamag F4
Marudi 4,700 .... E5
Miri 35,702 .... E5
Mukah 1,717 .... E5

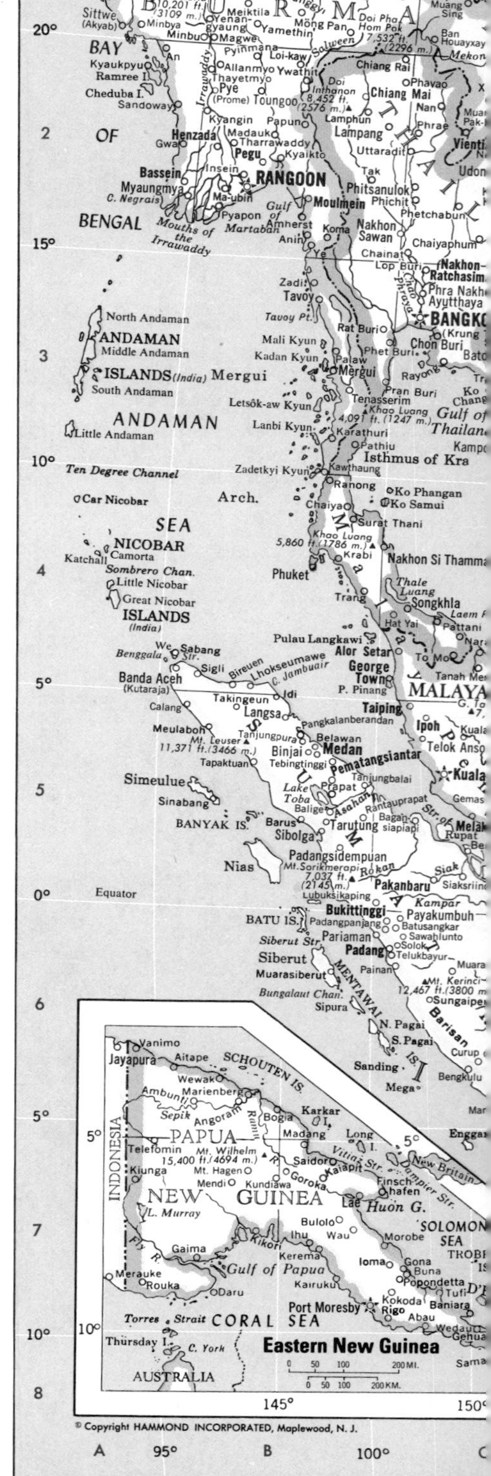

Topography

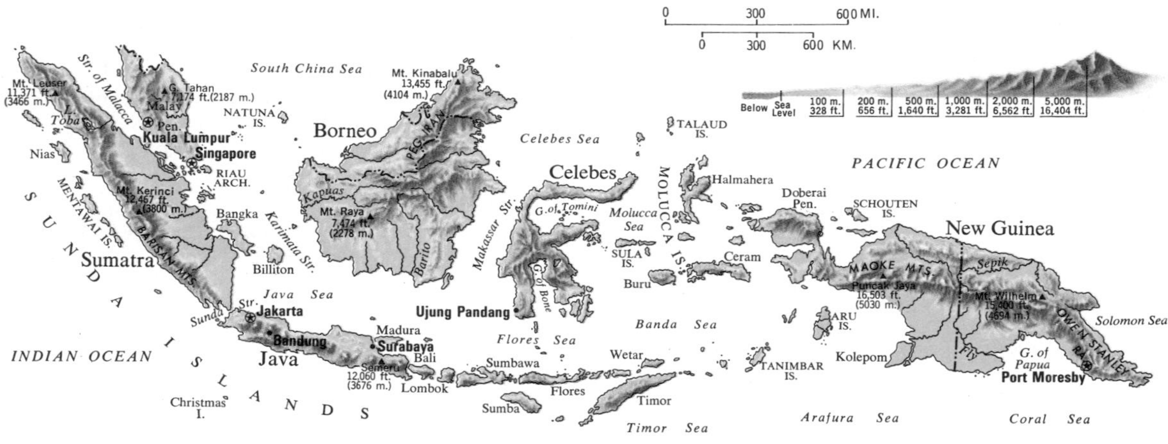

Agriculture, Industry and Resources

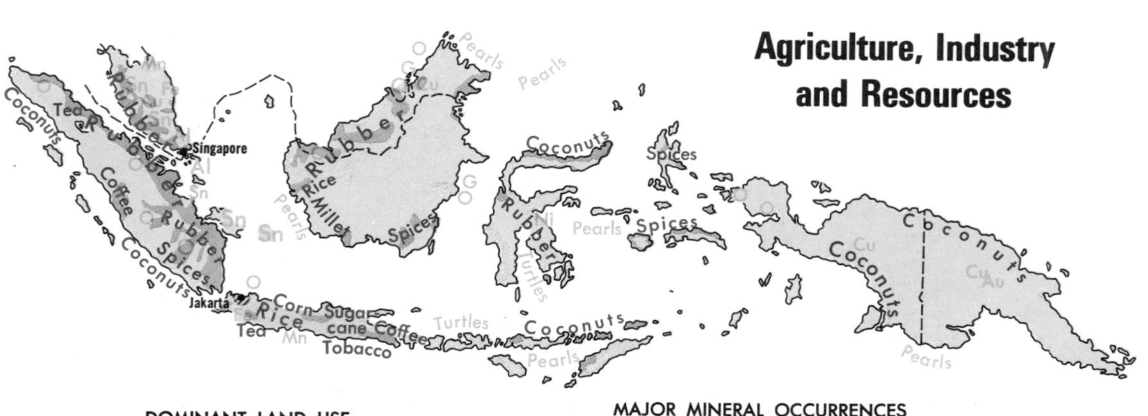

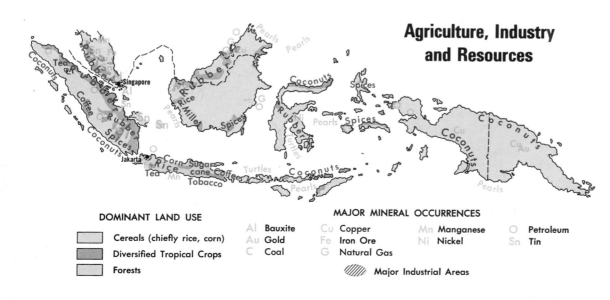

DOMINANT LAND USE

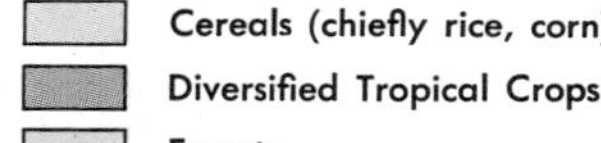

Cereals (chiefly rice, corn)
Diversified Tropical Crops
Forests

MAJOR MINERAL OCCURRENCES

Al Bauxite
Au Gold
C Coal
Cu Copper
Fe Iron Ore
G Natural Gas
Mn Manganese
Ni Nickel
O Petroleum
Sn Tin

Major Industrial Areas

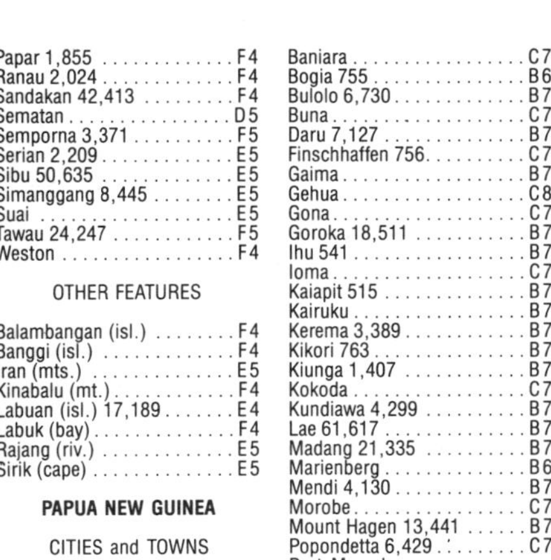

Papar 1,855 . . . . F4
Ranau 2,024 . . . . F4
Sandakan 42,413 . . . . F4
Sematan D5
Semporna 3,371 . . . . F5
Serian 2,209 . . . . E5
Sibu 50,635 . . . . E5
Simanggang 8,445 . . . . E5
Suai E5
Tawau 24,247 . . . . F5
Weston F4

OTHER FEATURES

Balambangan (isl.) F4
Banggi (isl.) F4
Iran (mts.) E5
Kinabalu (mt.) F4
Labuan (isl.) 17,189 . . . . E4
Labuk (bay) F4
Rajang (riv.) E5
Sirik (cape) E5

PAPUA NEW GUINEA

CITIES and TOWNS

Abau C7
Aitape 3,368 . . . . B6
Ambunti 1,035 . . . . B6
Angoram 1,846 . . . . B6
Baniara C7
Bogia 755 . . . . B6
Bulolo 6,730 . . . . B7
Buna C7
Daru 7,127 . . . . B7
Finschhaffen 756 . . . . C7
Gaima B7
Gehua C8
Gona C7
Goroka 18,511 . . . . B7
Ihu 541 . . . . B7
Ioma C7
Kaiapit 515 . . . . B7
Kairuku B7
Kerema 3,389 . . . . B7
Kikori 763 . . . . B7
Kiunga 1,407 . . . . B7
Kokoda C7
Kundiawa 4,299 . . . . B7
Lae 61,617 . . . . B7
Madang 21,335 . . . . B7
Marienberg B6
Mendi 4,130 . . . . B7
Morobe C7
Mount Hagen 13,441 . . . . B7
Popondetta 6,429 . . . . C7
Port Moresby (cap.) 123,624 . . . . B7
Rouka B7
Saidor 500 . . . . B7
Samarai 864 . . . . C8
Telefomin B7
Vanimo 3,071 . . . . B6
Wau 2,349 . . . . B7
Wedau C7
Wewak 19,890 . . . . B6

OTHER FEATURES

Dampier (str.) C7
D'Entrecasteaux (isls.) C7
Fly (riv.) A7
Huon (gulf) C7
Karkar (isl.) B6
Kiriwina (isl.) C7
Long (isl.) B7
Louisiade (arch.) D8
Milne (bay) C8
Misima (isl.) C8
New Britain (isl.) 148,773 . . . . C7
Ramu (riv.) B7
Rossel (isl.) D8
Schouten (isls.) B6
Sepik (riv.) B6
Solomon (sea) C7
Tagula (isl.) C8
Torres (str.) A7
Trobriand (isls.) C7
Vitiaz (str.) B7
Woodlark (isl.) C7

★See page 74 for other Malaysian entries.

INDONESIA

AREA 788,430 sq. mi. (2,042,034 sq. km.)
POPULATION 147,490,298
CAPITAL Jakarta
LARGEST CITY Jakarta
HIGHEST POINT Puncak Jaya 16,503 ft. (5,030 m.)
MONETARY UNIT rupiah
MAJOR LANGUAGES Bahasa Indonesia, Indonesian and Papuan languages, English
MAJOR RELIGIONS Islam, tribal religions, Christianity, Hinduism

PAPUA NEW GUINEA

AREA 183,540 sq. mi. (475,369 sq. km.)
POPULATION 3,010,727
CAPITAL Port Moresby
LARGEST CITY Port Moresby
HIGHEST POINT Mt. Wilhelm 15,400 ft. (4,694 m.)
MONETARY UNIT kina
MAJOR LANGUAGES pidgin English, Hiri Motu, English
MAJOR RELIGIONS Tribal religions, Christianity

BRUNEI

AREA 2,226 sq. mi. (5,765 sq. km.)
POPULATION 192,832
CAPITAL Bandar Seri Begawan
LARGEST CITY Bandar Seri Begawan
HIGHEST POINT Pagon 6,070 ft. (1,850 m.)
MONETARY UNIT Brunei Dollar
MAJOR LANGUAGES Malay, English, Chinese
MAJOR RELIGIONS Islam, Buddhism, Christianity, tribal religions

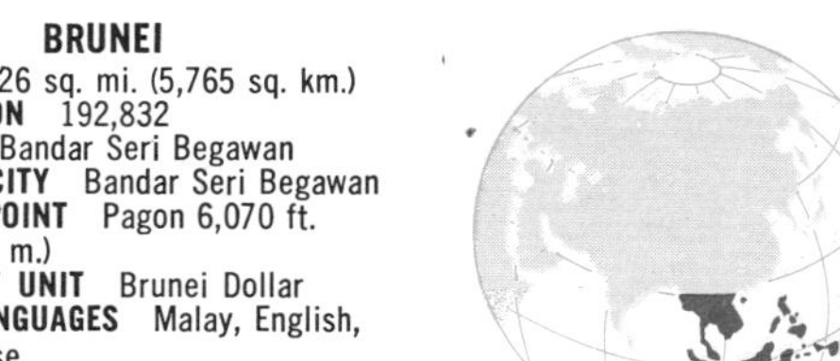

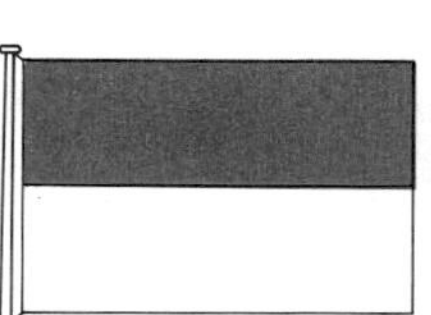

INDONESIA

PAPUA NEW GUINEA

BRUNEI

Southeast Asia

LAMBERT AZIMUTHAL EQUAL-AREA PROJECTION

SCALE OF MILES: 0 100 200 400 600
SCALE OF KILOMETERS: 0 100 200 400 600

Capitals of Countries ☆
Administrative Center ◉
International Boundaries
Other Boundaries

Scale 1:19,000,000

Java

INDIAN OCEAN

PACIFIC OCEAN

SOUTH CHINA SEA

Longitude East of Greenwich

FIJI

AREA 7,055 sq. mi. (18,272 sq. km.)
POPULATION 588,068
CAPITAL Suva
LARGEST CITY Suva
HIGHEST POINT Tomaniivi 4,341 ft. (1,323 m.)
MONETARY UNIT Fijian dollar
MAJOR LANGUAGES Fijian, Hindi, English
MAJOR RELIGIONS Protestantism, Hinduism

KIRIBATI

AREA 291 sq. mi. (754 sq. km.)
POPULATION 56,213
CAPITAL Bairiki (Tarawa)
HIGHEST POINT (on Banaba I.) 285 ft. (87 m.)
MONETARY UNIT Australian dollar
MAJOR LANGUAGES I-Kiribati, English
MAJOR RELIGIONS Protestantism, Roman Catholicism

NAURU

AREA 7.7 sq. mi. (20 sq. km.)
POPULATION 7,254
CAPITAL Yaren (district)
MONETARY UNIT Australian dollar
MAJOR LANGUAGES Nauruan, English
MAJOR RELIGION Protestantism

SOLOMON ISLANDS

AREA 11,500 sq. mi. (29,785 sq. km.)
POPULATION 221,000
CAPITAL Honiara
HIGHEST POINT Mount Popomanatseu 7,647 ft. (2,331 m.)
MONETARY UNIT Solomon Islands dollar
MAJOR LANGUAGES English, pidgin English, Melanesian dialects
MAJOR RELIGIONS Tribal religions, Protestantism, Roman Catholicism

TONGA

AREA 270 sq. mi. (699 sq. km.)
POPULATION 90,128
CAPITAL Nuku'alofa
LARGEST CITY Nuku'alofa
HIGHEST POINT 3,389 ft. (1,033 m.)
MONETARY UNIT pa'anga
MAJOR LANGUAGES Tongan, English
MAJOR RELIGION Protestantism

TUVALU

AREA 9.78 sq. mi. (25.33 sq. km.)
POPULATION 7,349
CAPITAL Fongafale (Funafuti)
HIGHEST POINT 15 ft. (4.6 m.)
MONETARY UNIT Australian dollar
MAJOR LANGUAGES English, Tuvaluan
MAJOR RELIGION Protestantism

Abaiang (atoll) 3,296 . . . . H 5
Abemama (atoll) 2,300. . . . . . . H 5
Adamstown (cap.), Pitcairn Is. 54 . . . . N 8
Admiralty (isls.) . . . . E 6
Agaña (cap.), Guam 896 . . . . . E 4
Agrihan (isl.) . . . . E 4
Ailinglapalap (atoll) 1,385 . . . . G 5
Ailuk (atoll) 413. . . . . H 4
Aitutaki (atoll) 2,348 . . . . K 7
Alofi (cap.), Niue 960 . . . . K 7
Alotau 4,310. . . . . E 7
Ambrym (isl.) 6,324 . . . . G 7
American Samoa 32,297 . . . . . J 7
Anaa (atoll) 444. . . . . M 7
Angaur (isl.) 243 . . . . D 5
Apataki (atoll) . . . . M 7
Apia (cap.), W. Samoa 33,100. J 7
Arno (atoll) 1,487 . . . . H 5
Arorae (atoll) 1,626. . . . . H 6
Atafu (atoll) 577. . . . . J 6
Atiu (isl.) 1,225 . . . . L 8
Austral (isls.) 5,208. . . . . L 8
Avarua (cap.), Cook Is. . . . . L 8
Babelthuap (isl.) 10,391. . . . . . D 5
Bairiki (cap.), Kiribati 1,777 . . . H 5
Baker (isl.) . . . . J 5
Banaba (isl.) 2,314 . . . . G 6
Banks (isls.) 3,158 . . . . G 7
Belau (Palau) 12,116 . . . . D 5
Belep (isls.) 624 . . . . G 7
Bellona (reefs). . . . . G 8
Beru (atoll) 2,318 . . . . H 6
Bikini (atoll) . . . . G 4
Bismarck (arch.) 218,339 . . . . E 6
Bonin (isls.) 1,879. . . . . E 3
Bora-Bora (isl.) 2,572. . . . . L 7
Bougainville (isl.) 71,761 . . . . . F 6
Bounty (isls.) . . . . H 10
Bourail 3,149. . . . . G 8
Butaritari (atoll) 2,971. . . . . H 5
Canton (isl.). . . . . J 6
Capitol Hill (cap.), No. Marianas 592 . . . . E 4
Caroline (isl.). . . . . M 7
Caroline (isls.). . . . . E 5
Chichi (isl.) 1,879 . . . . E 3
Choiseul (isl.) 10,349. . . . . F 6
Christmas (Kirimati) (isl.) 674 . L 5
Cook (isls.) 17,695 . . . . K 7
Coral (sea). . . . . F 7
Danger (Pukapuka) (atoll) 797 . . . . K 7
Daru 7,127. . . . . E 6
Disappointment (isls.) 373. . . . N 7
Ducie (isl.) . . . . O 8
Easter (isl.) 1,598 . . . . Q 8
Ebon (atoll) 887. . . . . G 5
Efate (isl.) 18,038 . . . . G 7
Enderbury (isl.) . . . . J 6
Enewetak (Eniwetok) (atoll) 542 . . . . G 4
Erromanga (isl.) 945. . . . . H 7
Espiritu Santo (isl.) 16,220 . . . G 7
Fais (isl.) 207. . . . . E 5
Fakaofo (atoll) 654 . . . . J 6
Fanning (Tabuaeron) (isl.) 340 L 5
Faraulep (atoll) 132 . . . . E 5
Fatuhiva (isl.) 386. . . . . N 7
Fiji 588,068 . . . . H 8
Flint (isl.) . . . . L 7
Fly (riv.). . . . . E 6
Fongafale (cap.), Tuvalu. . . . . . H 6
French Polynesia 137,382. . . . L 8
Funafuti (atoll) 2,120 . . . . H 6
Futuna (Hoorn) (isls.) 3,173 . . J 7
Gambier (isls.) 556. . . . . N 8
Gardner (isl.) . . . . J 6
Gilbert (isls.) 47,711. . . . . H 6
Greenwich (Kapingamarangi) (atoll) 508 . . . . F 5
Guadalcanal (isl.) 46,619 . . . . F 7
Guam (isl.) 105,979 . . . . E 4
Hall (isls.) 647. . . . . F 5
Hawaiian (isls.) 964,691. . . . . . J 3
Henderson (isl.). . . . . O 8
Hivaoa (isl.) 1,159. . . . . N 6
Honiara (cap.), Solomon Is. 14,942 . . . . F 6
Hoorn (isls.) 3,173 . . . . J 7
Howland (isl.). . . . . J 5
Huahine (isl.) 3,140 . . . . L 7
Hull (isl.). . . . . J 6
Huon (gulf). . . . . E 6
Ifalik (atoll) 389 . . . . E 5
Iwo (isl.) . . . . E 3
Jaluit (atoll) 1,450. . . . . G 5
Jarvis (isl.) . . . . K 6
Johnston (atoll) 327 . . . . K 4
Kadavu (Kandavu) (isl.) 8,699 H 7
Kapingamarangi (atoll) 508. . . F 5
Kavieng 4,633 . . . . E 6
Kermadec (isls.) 5. . . . . J 9
Kieta 3,491. . . . . F 6
Kimbe 4,662. . . . . F 6
Kingman (reef). . . . . K 5
Kiribati 57,500 . . . . J 6
Kirimati (isl.) 674. . . . . L 5
Kolonia (cap.), Micronesia 5,549 . . . . F 5
Koror (cap.), Belau 6,222. . . . . D 5
Kosrae (isl.) 5,491 . . . . G 5
Kwajalein (atoll) 6,624 . . . . G 5
Lae 61,617. . . . . E 6
Lau Group (isls.) 14,452 . . . . . J 7
Lavongai (isl.) . . . . F 6
Lifu (isl.) 7,585. . . . . G 8
Line (isls.). . . . . K 5
Little Makin (atoll) 1,445 . . . . . H 5
Lord Howe (Ontong Java) (isl.) 1,082 . . . . G 6
Lord Howe (isl.) 287 . . . . G 9
Lorengau 3,986. . . . . E 6
Louisiade (arch.). . . . . F 7
Loyalty (isls.) 14,518 . . . . G 8
Luganville 4,935 . . . . G 7
Madang 21,335. . . . . E 6
Majuro (atoll) (cap.), Marshall Is. 8,583. . . . . H 5
Makin (Butaritari) (atoll) 2,971 H 5
Malaita (isl.) 50,912 . . . . G 6
Malden (isl.). . . . . L 6
Malekula (isl.) 15,931. . . . . G 7
Maloelap (atoll) 763 . . . . H 5
Mangaia (isl.) 1,364 . . . . L 8
Mangareva (isl.) 556. . . . . N 8
Manihiki (atoll) 405 . . . . K 7
Manua (isls.), 1,459 . . . . K 7
Manus (isl.) 25,844. . . . . E 6
Marcus (isl.). . . . . F 3
Maré (isl.) 4,156 . . . . G 8
Marianas, Northern 16,780 . . . E 4
Mariana Trench . . . . E 4
Marquesas (isls.) 5,419 . . . . . . N 6
Marshall Islands 30,873. . . . . . G 4
Marutea (atoll). . . . . N 8
Mata Utu (cap.), Wallis and Futuna 558 . . . . J 7
Mauke (isl.) 684 . . . . L 8
Melanesia (reg.) . . . . E 5
Micronesia (reg.). . . . . E 4
Micronesia, Federated States of 73,160 . . . . F 5
Midway (isls.) 453. . . . . J 3
Mili (atoll) 763 . . . . H 5
Moen (isl.) 10,351. . . . . F 5
Moorea (isl.) 5,788 . . . . L 7
Mururoa (isl.). . . . . M 8
Nadi 6,938 . . . . H 7
Namonuito (atoll) 783. . . . . E 5
Namorik (atoll) 617. . . . . G 5
Nanumea (atoll) 844. . . . . H 6
Nauru 7,254. . . . . G 6
Ndeni (isl.) 4,854. . . . . G 7
New Britain (isl.) 148,773 . . . . F 6
New Caledonia 133,233 . . . . . G 8
New Caledonia (isl.) 118,715 . G 8
New Georgia (isl.) 16,472 . . . . F 6
New Guinea (isl.) . . . . E 6
New Ireland (isl.) 65,657 . . . . . F 6
Ngatik (atoll) 560. . . . . F 5
Ngulu (atoll) 21 . . . . D 5
Niuatoputapu (isl.) 1,650 . . . . . J 7
Niue (isl.) 3,578. . . . . K 7
Niutao (atoll) 866 . . . . H 6
Nomoi (isls.) 1,879 . . . . F 5
Nonouti (atoll) 2,223. . . . . H 6
Norfolk Island (terr.) 2,175. . . . G 8
Northern Marianas 16,780 . . . E 4
Nouméa (cap.), New Caled. 56,078 . . . . G 8
Nouméa *74,335. . . . . G 8
Nui (atoll) 603 . . . . H 6
Nuku'alofa (cap.), Tonga 18,356 . . . . J 8
Nukuhiva (isl.) 1,484. . . . . M 6
Ocean (Banaba) (isl.) 2,314 . . G 6

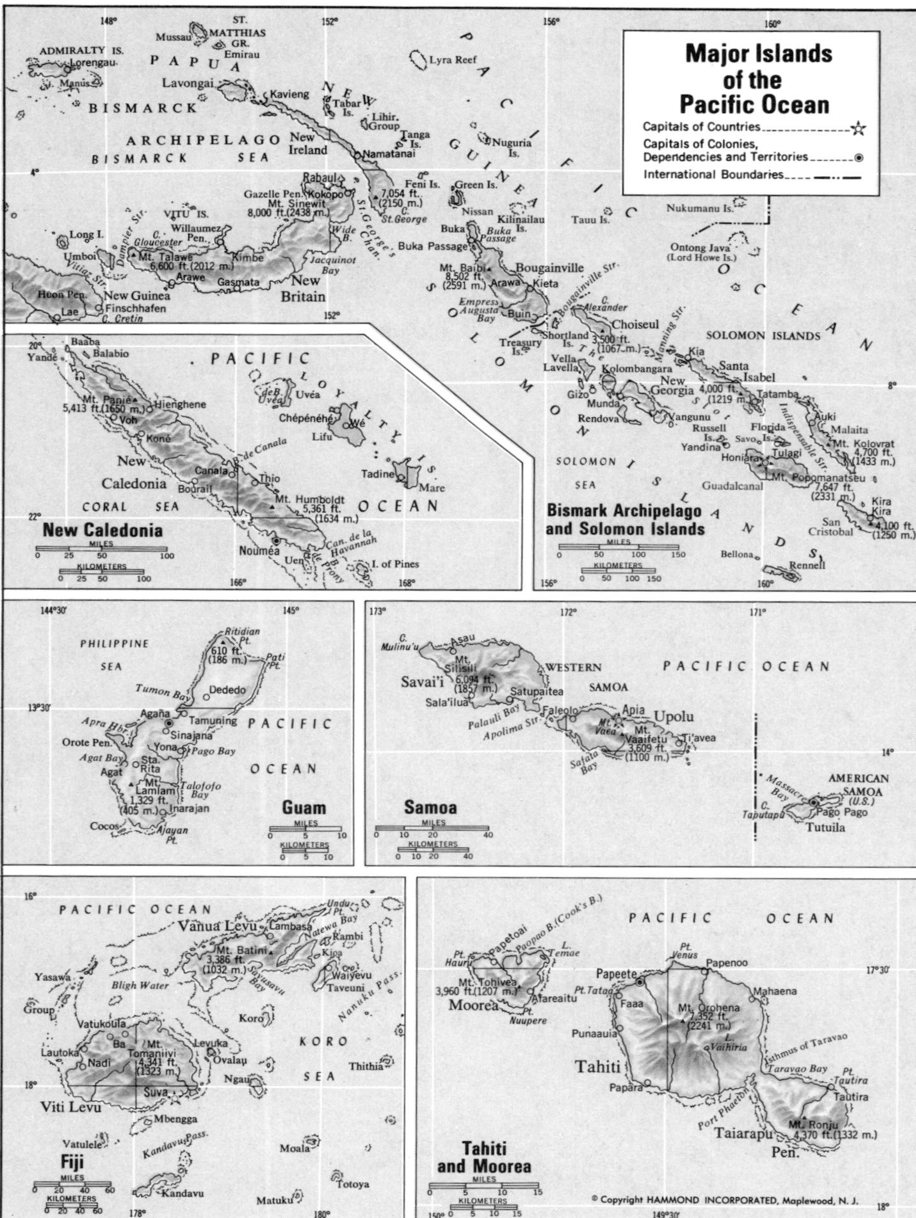

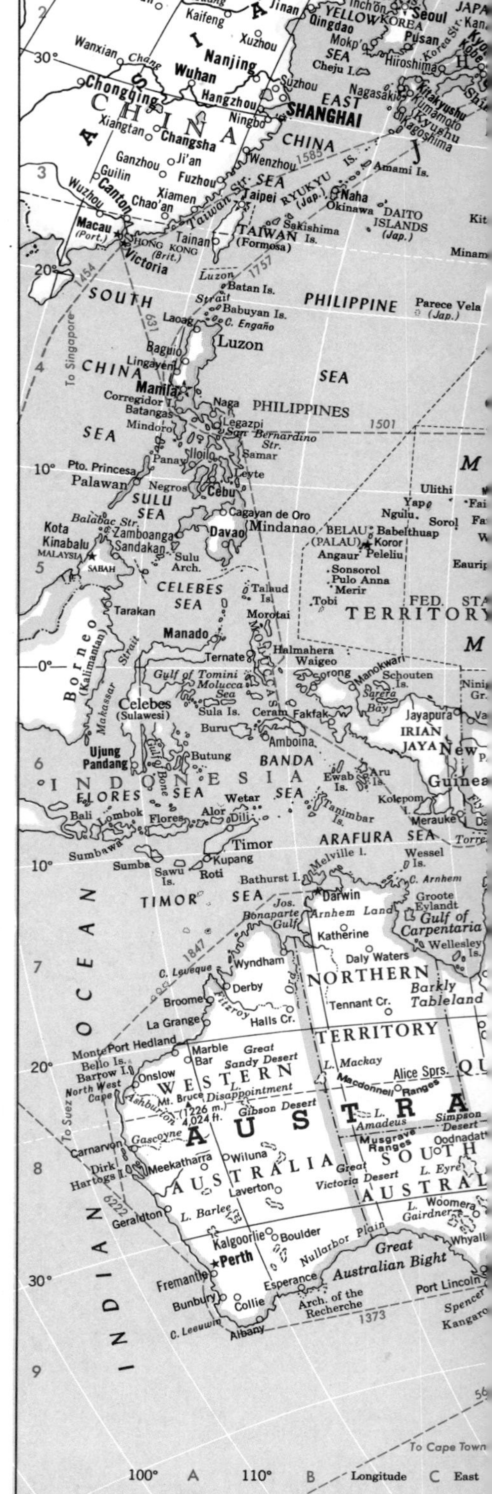

Oeno (isl.) .... O 8
Onotoa (atoll) 1,997 .... H 6
Ontong Java (isl.) 1,082 .... G 6
Pacific Islands, Terr. of the 132,929 .... F 5
Pagan (isl.) .... E 4
Pago Pago (cap.), Amer. Samoa 3,075 .... J 7
Palau (Belau) 12,116 .... D 5
Palmyra (atoll) .... K 5
Papeete (cap.), Fr. Poly. 22,967 .... M 7
Papeete •51,987 .... M 7
Papua (gulf) .... E 6
Papua New Guinea 3,010,727 E 6
Peleliu (isl.) 609 .... D 5
Penrhyn (Tongareva) (atoll) 608 .... L 6
Phoenix (isls.) .... J 6
Pines (isl.) 1,095 .... G 8
Pitcairn (isl.) 54 .... O 8
Polynesia (reg.) .... K 7
Ponape (isl.) 19,935 .... F 5
Popondetta 6,429 .... E 6
Port Moresby (cap.), Papua N.G. 123,624 .... E 6
Pukapuka (atoll) 797 .... K 7
Pulap (atoll) 427 .... E 5
Puluwat (atoll) 441 .... E 5
Rabaul 14,954 .... F 6
Raiatea (isl.) 2,517 .... L 7
Raivavae (isl.) 1,023 .... M 8
Rakahanga (atoll) 269 .... K 7
Ralik Chain (isls.) .... G 5
Rangiroa (atoll) .... M 7
Rapa (isl.) 398 .... M 8
Rarotonga (isl.) 9,477 .... K 8
Ratak Chain (isls.) .... G 5
Reao (atoll) 424 .... N 7
Rennell (isl.) 1,132 .... F 7
Rikitea .... N 8
Rimatara (isl.) 813 .... L 8
Rongelap (atoll) 235 .... G 4
Rota (isl.) 1,261 .... E 4
Rotuma (isl.) 2,805 .... H 7
Rurutu (isl.) 1,555 .... L 8
Saipan (isl.) 14,549 .... E 4
Sala y Gómez (isl.) .... P 8
Samarai 869 .... E 7
Samoa (isls.) .... J 7
San Cristobal (isl.) 11,212 .... G 7
Santa Cruz (isls.) 5,421 .... G 6
Santa Isabel (isl.) 10,420 .... G 6
Savai'i (isl.) 43,150 .... J 7
Senyavin (isls.) 20,035 .... F 5
Society (isls.) 117,703 .... L 7
Solomon (isls.) .... F 6
Solomon (sea) .... F 6
Solomon Islands 221,000 .... G 6
Starbuck (isl.) .... L 6
Suva (cap.), Fiji 63,628 .... H 7
Suva *117,827 .... H 7
Swains (isl.) 27 .... K 7
Sydney (isl.) .... K 6
Tabiteuea (atoll) 3,942 .... H 6
Tabuaeran (isl.) 340 .... L 5
Tahaa (isl.) 3,513 .... L 7
Tahiti (isl.) 95,604 .... L 7
Takaroa (atoll) 337 .... M 7
Tanna (isl.) 15,715 .... H 7
Tarawa (atoll) 17,129 .... H 5
Tasman (sea) .... G 9
Teraina (isl.) 458 .... L 5
Tinian (isl.) 866 .... E 4
Tokelau (isls.) 1,575 .... J 6
Tonga 90,128 .... J 8
Tongareva (atoll) 608 .... L 6
Tongatapu (isls.) 57,130 .... J 8
Torres (isls.) 325 .... G 7
Torres (strait) .... E 7
Trobriand (isls.) .... F 6
Truk (isls.) 37,488 .... F 5
Tuamotu (arch.) 9,052 .... M 7
Tubuai (Austral) (isls.) 5,208 .... M 8
Tubuai (isl.) 1,419 .... M 8
Tutuila (isl.) 30,538 .... J 7
Tuvalu 7,349 .... H 6
Uapou (isl.) 1,563 .... M 6
Ujelang (atoll) 309 .... F 5
Ulithi (atoll) 710 .... D 4

VANUATU

AREA 5,700 sq. mi. (14,763 sq. km.)
POPULATION 112,596
CAPITAL Vila
HIGHEST POINT Mt. Tabwemasana 6,165 ft. (1,879 m.)
MONETARY UNIT vatu
MAJOR LANGUAGES Bislama, English, French
MAJOR RELIGIONS Christian, animist

WESTERN SAMOA

AREA 1,133 sq. mi. (2,934 sq. km.)
POPULATION 158,130
CAPITAL Apia
LARGEST CITY Apia
HIGHEST POINT Mt. Silisili 6,094 ft. (1,857 m.)
MONETARY UNIT tala
MAJOR LANGUAGES Samoan, English
MAJOR RELIGIONS Protestantism, Roman Catholicism

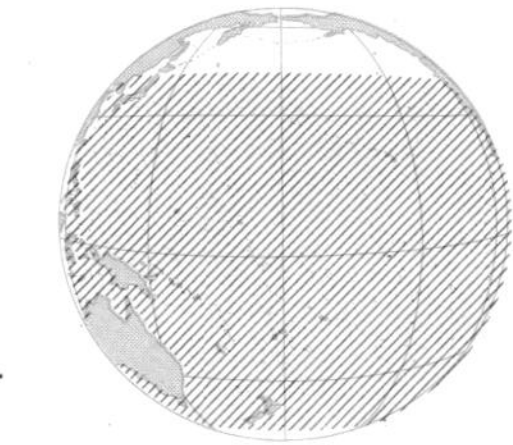

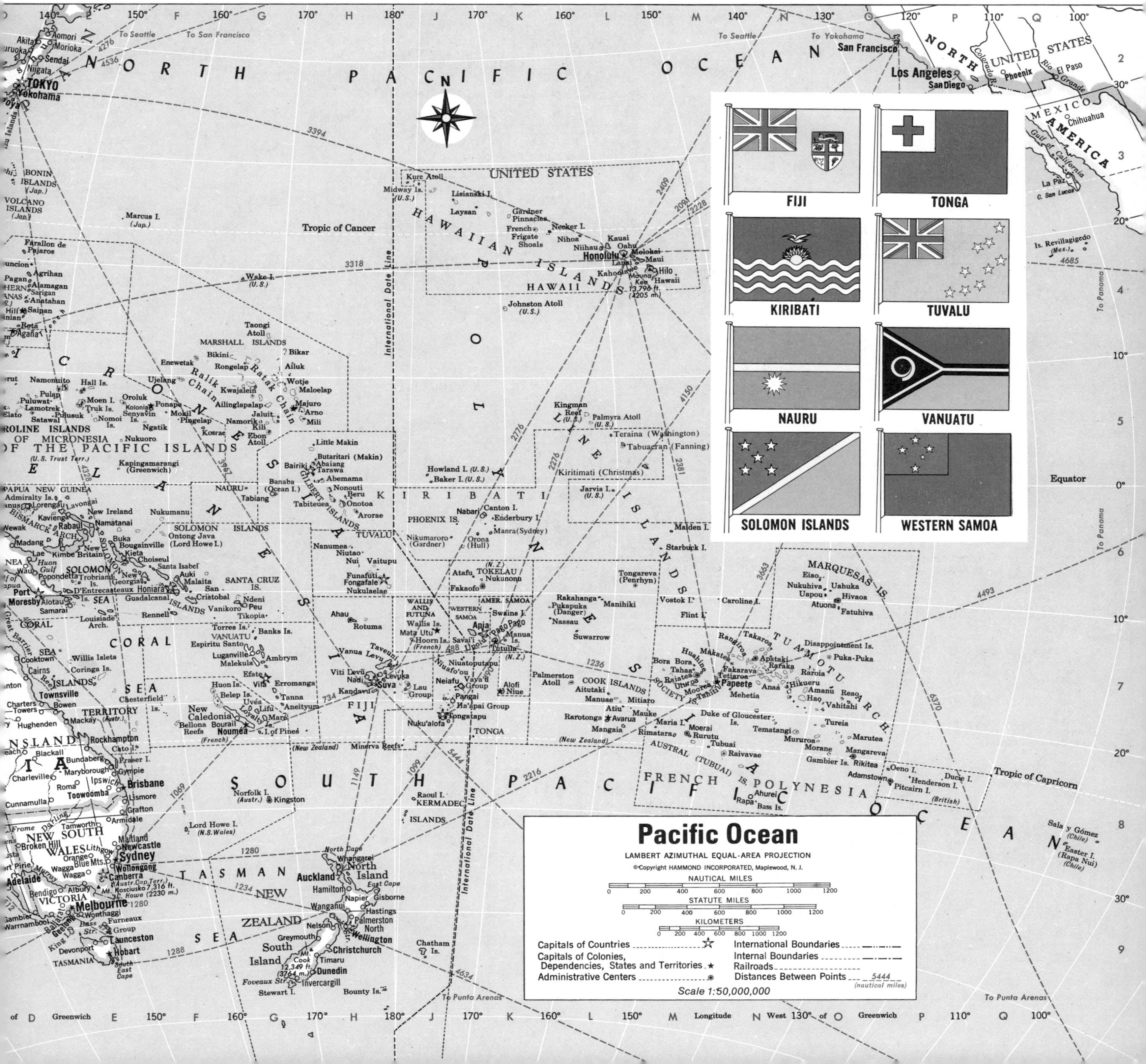

Upolu (isl.) 114,620 .... J 7
Uturoa 2,517 .... L 7
Uvéa (isl.) 2,777 .... G 7
Vaitupu (atoll) 1,273 .... H 6
Vanikoro (isl.) 267 .... G 7
Vanimo 3,071 .... E 6
Vanua Levu (isl.) 103,122 .... H 7
Vanuatu 112,596 .... G 7
Vila (cap.), Vanuatu 4,729 .... G 7
Vila *14,797 .... G 7
Viti Levu (isl.) 445,422 .... H 7
Volcano (isls.) .... E 3
Vostok (isl.) .... L 7
Wake (isl.) 302 .... G 4
Wallis (isls.) 6,019 .... J 7
Wallis and Futuna 9,192 .... J 7
Washington (Teraina) (isl.) 458 .... L 5
Wau 2,349 .... E 6
Western Samoa 158,130 .... J 7
Wewak 19,890 .... E 6
Woleai (isl.) 638 .... E 5
Wotje (atoll) 535 .... H 5
Yap (isl.) 6,670 .... D 5

*City and suburbs.
•Population of urban area.

FIJI
TONGA
KIRIBATI
TUVALU
NAURU
VANUATU
SOLOMON ISLANDS
WESTERN SAMOA

Pacific Ocean

LAMBERT AZIMUTHAL EQUAL-AREA PROJECTION

NAUTICAL MILES 0 200 400 600 800 1000 1200
STATUTE MILES 0 200 400 600 800 1000 1200
KILOMETERS 0 200 400 600 800 1000 1200

Capitals of Countries ★
Capitals of Colonies, Dependencies, States and Territories ★
Administrative Centers ◉
International Boundaries
Internal Boundaries
Railroads
Distances Between Points 5444 (nautical miles)

Scale 1:50,000,000

Adelaide (cap.), S. Austr. D8
Albany B6
Albury H7
Alice Springs E4
Altona K7
Ararat G7
Armidale J6
Ashfield K4
Ashgrove K2
Ashmore and Cartier Is., Terr. of C2
Aspley K2
Auburn K4
Australian Capital Territory H7
Ayr H3
Bairnsdale H7
Ballarat G7
Bankstown K4
Banyo K2
Bathurst H6
Baulkham Hills K4
Beenleigh J5
Bendigo G7
Blacktown K4
Blue Mountains J6
Botany L4
Boulder-Kalgoorlie C6
Bowen H3
Box Hill L7
Brighton D8
Brighton L7
Brisbane (cap.), Queens. K3
Brisbane Water J6
Broadmeadows L6
Broken Hill G6
Brunswick K7
Bunbury B6
Bundaberg J4
Burnie H8
Burnside E8
Burwood K4
Busselton A6
Cairns H3
Caloundra J5
Camberwell L7
Campbelltown E8
Camp Hill K3
Canberra (cap.), Australia H7
Canterbury K4
Carina K3
Casino J5
Caulfield L7
Cessnock-Bellbird J6
Charters Towers H4
Chelsea L8
Chermside K2
Coburg K7
Coffs Harbour J6
Colac G7
Collingwood L7
Concord K4
Cooma H7
Cootamundra H6
Coral Sea Is. Terr. J3
Corinda K3
Cowra H6
Crafters-Bridgewater E8
Cranbourne M8
Croydon M7
Dalby J5
Dandenong M7
Darwin (cap.), North. Terr. E2
Deniliquin G7
Devonport H8
Doncaster and Templestowe L7
Drummoyne K4
Dubbo H6
Echuca G7
Elizabeth E7
Eltham L6
Enfield D7
Enoggera K2
Esperance C6
Essendon K7
Fairfield K4
Fitzroy L7
Footscray K7
Forbes H6
Fremantle B6
Gawler F6
Geelong L7
Geelong West G7
Geraldton A5
Gladstone J4
Glenelg D8
Glen Innes J5
Glenorchy H8
Gold Coast J5
Goulburn J6
Graceville K3
Grafton J5
Greenslopes K3
Griffith H6
Gunnedah H6
Gympie J5
Hamilton G7
Hawthorn L7
Heidelberg L7
Hervey Bay J5
Hindmarsh D8
Hobart (cap.), Tasmania H8
Holyroyd K4
Hornsby K3
Horsham G7
Hunters Hill K4
Hurstville K4
Inala K3
Indooroopilly K3
Innisfail H3
Inverell J5
Ipswich J3
Kalgoorlie C6
Kalgoorlie-Boulder C6
Karratha B4
Keilor K7
Kempsey J6
Kenmore J3
Kensington and Norwood E8
Kew L7
Knox M7
Kogarah K4
Ku-ring-gai K4
Kwinana-New Town B2
Lane Cove L4
Launceston H8
Leeton H6
Leichhardt L4
Lismore J5
Lithgow J6
Liverpool K4
Mackay H4
Maitland J6
Malvern L7
Mandurah B3
Manly L4
Mareeba G3
Marion D8
Maroochydore-Mooloolaba J5
Marrickville L4
Maryborough J5
Maryborough G7
Melbourne (cap.), Victoria H7
Mildura G6
Mitcham D8
Mitchelton J2
Moe H7
Moorabbin L7
Moorooka K3
Mordialloc L7
Moree H5
Morningside K2
Morwell H7
Mosman L4
Mount Gambier G7
Mount Isa F4
Mudgee J6
Murray Bridge F7
Murwillumbah J5
Muswellbrook J6
Narrabri J6
Narrandera H6
Nedlands B2
Newcastle J6
Newman C4
New Norfolk H8
New South Wales H6
Norfolk Island 2,180 L5
Northam B6
Northcote L7
Northern Territory E3
North Sydney L4
Nowra-Bomaderry J6
Nunawading L7
Nundah K2
Oakleigh L7
Orange H6
Parkes H6
Parramatta K4
Payneham E8
Penrith J6
Perth (cap.), W. Austr. B2
Port Adelaide D7
Port Augusta F6
Port Hedland B3
Portland G7
Port Lincoln E6
Port Macquarie J6
Port Melbourne K7
Port Pirie F6
Prahan L7
Preston L7
Prospect D8
Queanbeyan H7
Queensland G4
Randwick L4
Red Cliffe J5
Richmond L7
Ringwood M7
Rockdale K4
Rockhampton H4
Rockingham B2
Roma H5
Ryde K4
Saint Kilda L7
Saint Lucia K3
Sale H7

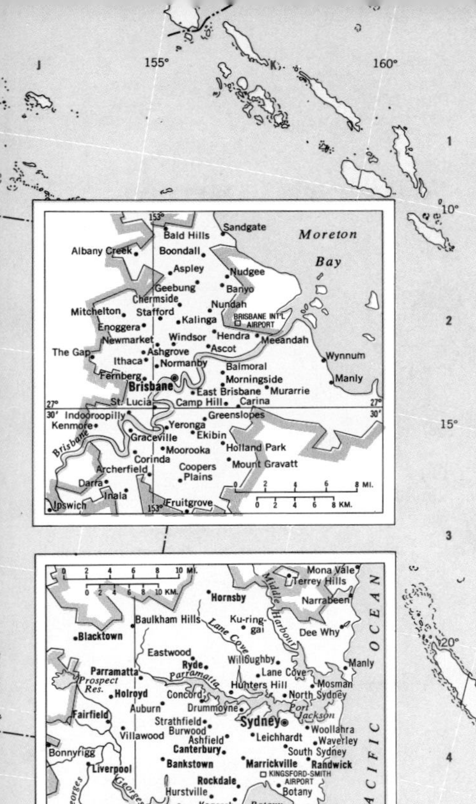

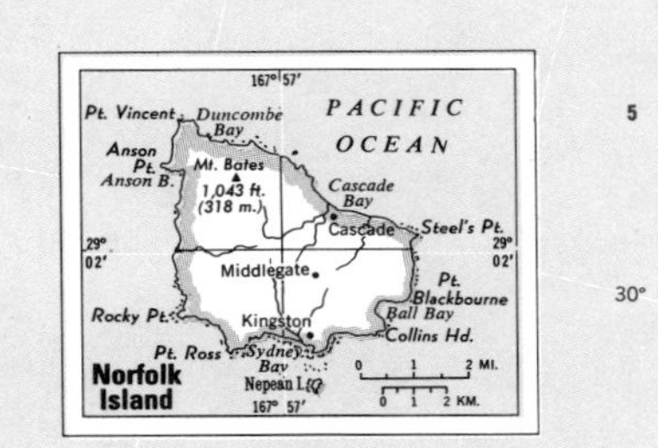

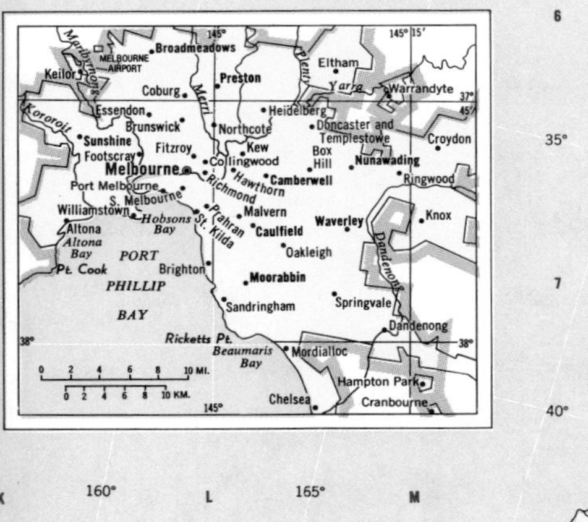

*City and suburbs.
†Population of met. area.
‡Population of urban area.

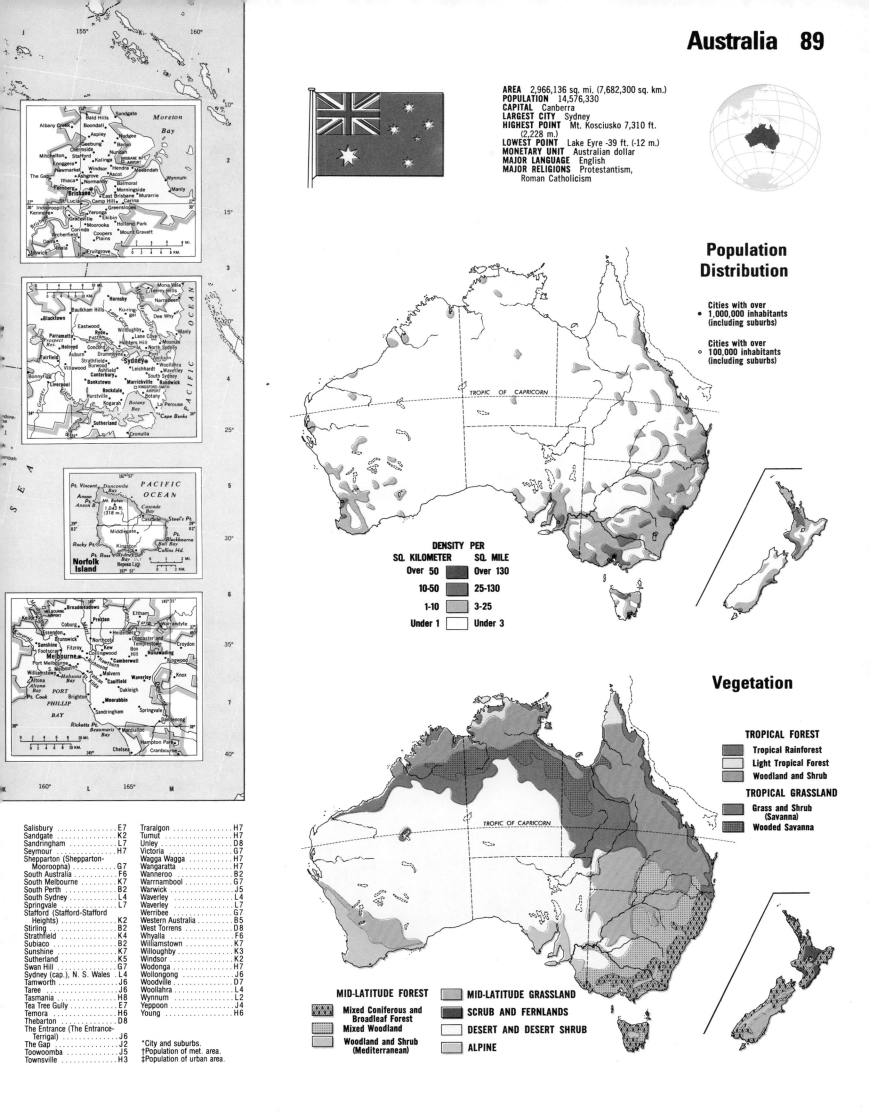

AREA 2,966,136 sq. mi. (7,682,300 sq. km.)
POPULATION 14,576,330
CAPITAL Canberra
LARGEST CITY Sydney
HIGHEST POINT Mt. Kosciusko 7,310 ft. (2,228 m.)
LOWEST POINT Lake Eyre -39 ft. (-12 m.)
MONETARY UNIT Australian dollar
MAJOR LANGUAGE English
MAJOR RELIGIONS Protestantism, Roman Catholicism

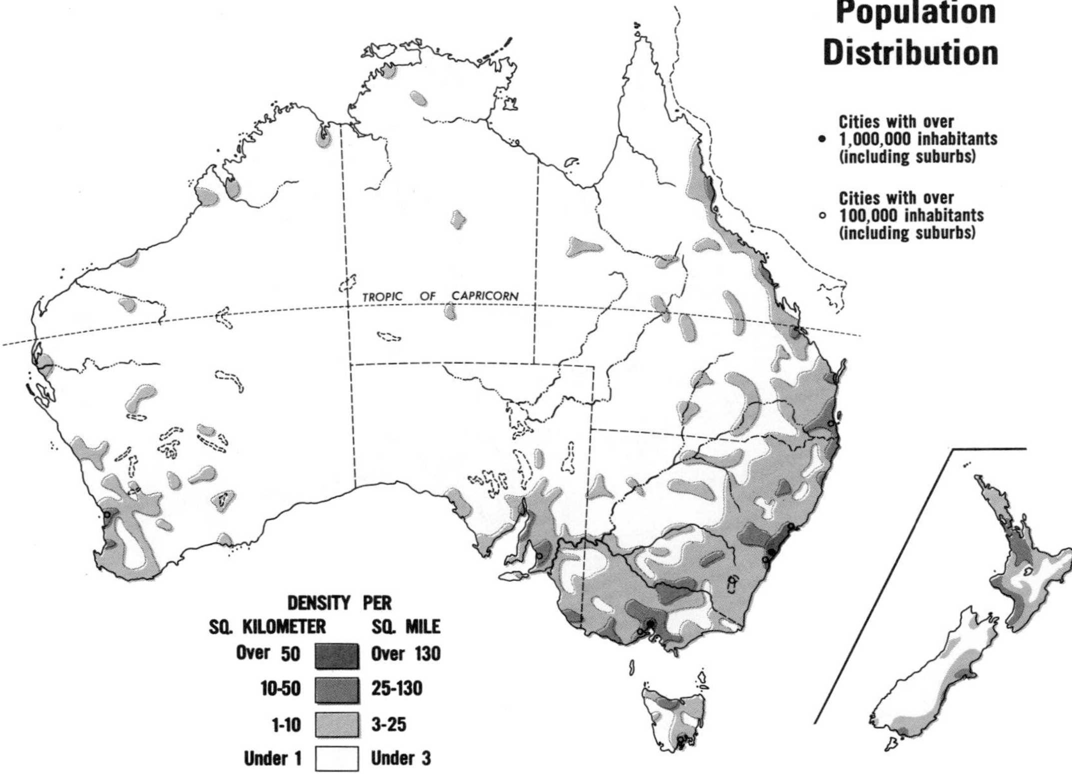

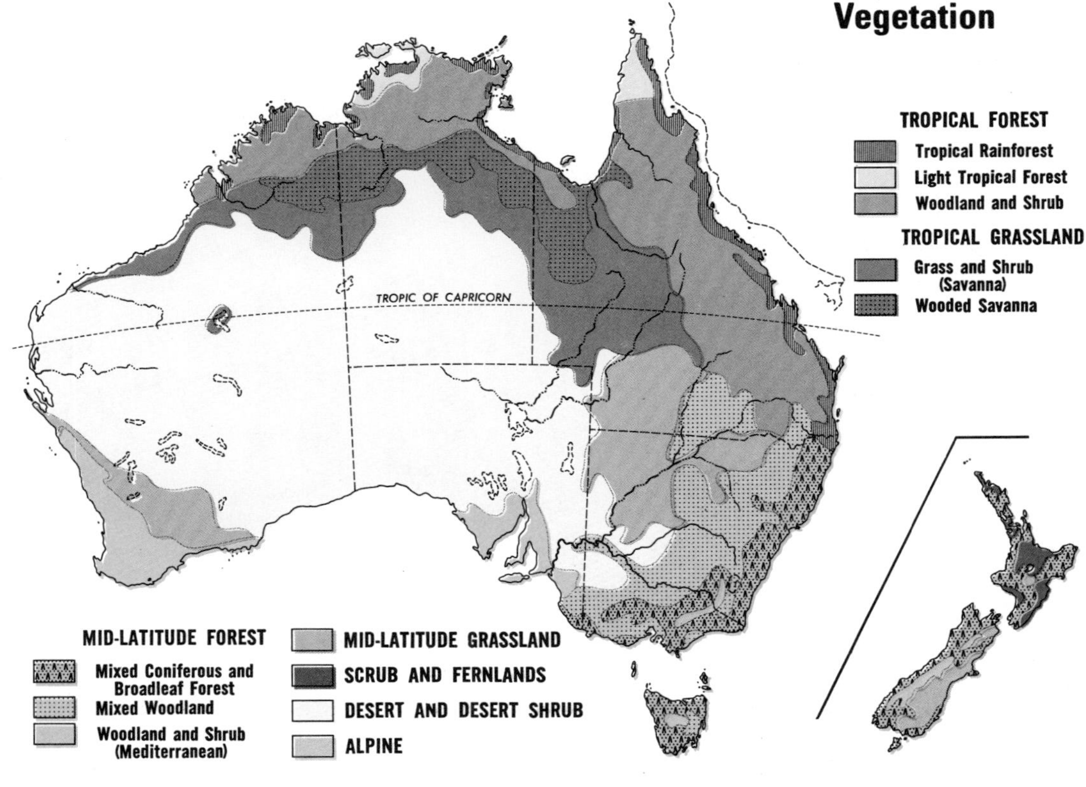

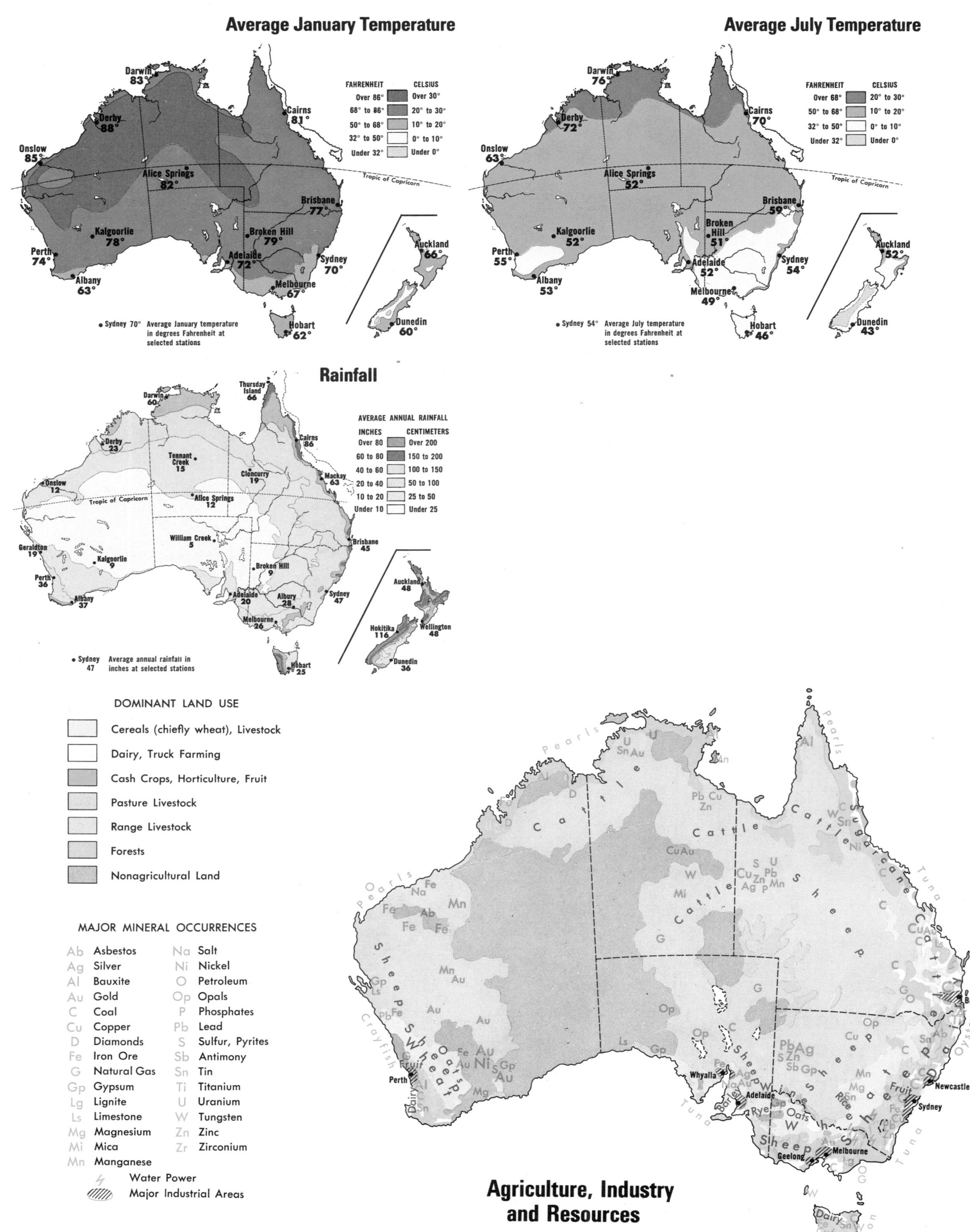
Average January Temperature
FAHRENHEIT
CELSIUS
Over 86°
Over 30°
68° to 86°
20° to 30°
50° to 68°
10° to 20°
32° to 50°
0° to 10°
Under 32°
Under 0°
Darwin 83°
Derby 88°
Onslow 85°
Cairns 81°
Alice Springs 82°
Tropic of Capricorn
Brisbane 77°
Kalgoorlie 78°
Broken Hill 79°
Perth 74°
Adelaide 72°
Sydney 70°
Albany 63°
Melbourne 67°
Auckland 66°
Hobart 62°
Dunedin 60°
• Sydney 70° Average January temperature in degrees Fahrenheit at selected stations
Average July Temperature
FAHRENHEIT
CELSIUS
Over 68°
20° to 30°
50° to 68°
10° to 20°
32° to 50°
0° to 10°
Under 32°
Under 0°
Darwin 76°
Derby 72°
Onslow 63°
Cairns 70°
Alice Springs 52°
Tropic of Capricorn
Brisbane 59°
Kalgoorlie 52°
Broken Hill 51°
Perth 55°
Adelaide 52°
Sydney 54°
Albany 53°
Melbourne 49°
Auckland 52°
Hobart 46°
Dunedin 43°
• Sydney 54° Average July temperature in degrees Fahrenheit at selected stations
Rainfall
AVERAGE ANNUAL RAINFALL
INCHES
CENTIMETERS
Over 80
Over 200
60 to 80
150 to 200
40 to 60
100 to 150
20 to 40
50 to 100
10 to 20
25 to 50
Under 10
Under 25
Thursday Island 66
Darwin 60
Cairns 86
Derby 23
Tennant Creek 15
Cloncurry 19
Mackay 63
Onslow 12
Tropic of Capricorn
Alice Springs 12
William Creek 5
Brisbane 45
Geraldton 19
Kalgoorlie 9
Broken Hill 9
Perth 36
Adelaide 20
Albury 28
Sydney 47
Albany 37
Melbourne 26
Auckland 48
Hokitika 116
Wellington 48
Dunedin 36
Hobart 25
• Sydney 47 Average annual rainfall in inches at selected stations
DOMINANT LAND USE
Cereals (chiefly wheat), Livestock
Dairy, Truck Farming
Cash Crops, Horticulture, Fruit
Pasture Livestock
Range Livestock
Forests
Nonagricultural Land
MAJOR MINERAL OCCURRENCES
Ab Asbestos
Ag Silver
Al Bauxite
Au Gold
C Coal
Cu Copper
D Diamonds
Fe Iron Ore
G Natural Gas
Gp Gypsum
Lg Lignite
Ls Limestone
Mg Magnesium
Mi Mica
Mn Manganese
Na Salt
Ni Nickel
O Petroleum
Op Opals
P Phosphates
Pb Lead
S Sulfur, Pyrites
Sb Antimony
Sn Tin
Ti Titanium
U Uranium
W Tungsten
Zn Zinc
Zr Zirconium
Water Power
Major Industrial Areas
Agriculture, Industry and Resources
Pearls
Cattle
Sheep
Sugarcane
Tuna
Oysters
Crayfish
Oats
Wheat
Barley
Rye
Rice
Fruit
Dairy
Salmon
Perth
Whyalla
Adelaide
Geelong
Melbourne
Sydney
Newcastle
Brisbane

120° 125° 130° 135° 140° 145° 150°

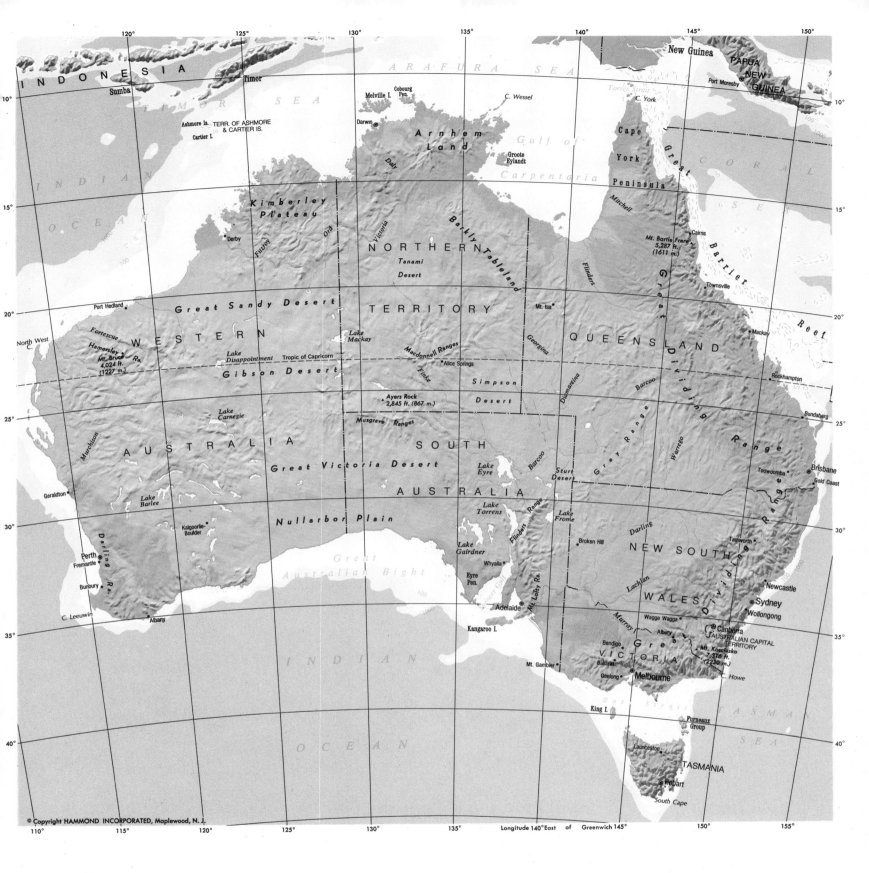

INDONESIA
Timor
Sumba
ARAFURA SEA
TIMOR SEA
New Guinea
PAPUA NEW GUINEA
Port Moresby
Torres Strait
C. York
Melville I.
Cobourg Pen.
C. Wessel
Darwin
Ashmore Is.
TERR. OF ASHMORE & CARTIER IS.
Cartier I.
Arnhem Land
Gulf of Carpentaria
Groote Eylandt
Daly
Cape York Peninsula
Great Barrier Reef
CORAL SEA
INDIAN OCEAN
Kimberley Plateau
Derby
Fitzroy
Ord
Victoria
Mitchell
Barkly Tableland
Mt. Bartle Frere 5,287 ft. (1611 m.)
Cairns
NORTHERN TERRITORY
Tanami Desert
Flinders
Townsville
Port Hedland
Great Sandy Desert
Mt. Isa
Fortescue
North West C.
Hamersley Ra.
Mt. Bruce 4,024 ft. (1227 m.)
WESTERN AUSTRALIA
Lake Mackay
Lake Disappointment
Tropic of Capricorn
Macdonnell Ranges
Alice Springs
Georgina
QUEENSLAND
Mackay
Great Dividing Range
Gibson Desert
Finke
Simpson Desert
Diamantina
Rockhampton
Barcoo
Ayers Rock 2,845 ft. (867 m.)
Lake Carnegie
Musgrave Ranges
Bundaberg
Murchison
SOUTH AUSTRALIA
Grey Range
Warrego
Great Victoria Desert
Lake Eyre
Sturt Desert
Toowoomba
Brisbane
Gold Coast
Geraldton
Lake Barlee
Lake Torrens
Lake Frome
Nullarbor Plain
Kalgoorlie-Boulder
Flinders Range
Broken Hill
Darling
Tamworth
Darling Ra.
Perth
Fremantle
Lake Gairdner
NEW SOUTH WALES
Whyalla
Great Australian Bight
Eyre Pen.
Lachlan
Newcastle
Bunbury
Spencer Gulf
Mt. Lofty Ra.
Sydney
Wollongong
C. Leeuwin
Albany
Adelaide
Murray
Wagga Wagga
Canberra
AUSTRALIAN CAPITAL TERRITORY
Kangaroo I.
Albury
Bendigo
Mt. Kosciusko 7,316 ft. (2230 m.)
VICTORIA
Ballarat
Mt. Gambier
Geelong
Melbourne
C. Howe
Bass Strait
King I.
TASMAN SEA
Furneaux Group
Launceston
TASMANIA
Hobart
South Cape

10° 15° 20° 25° 30° 35° 40°

110° 115° 120° 125° 130° 135° Longitude 140° East of Greenwich 145° 150° 155°

Vegetation/Relief

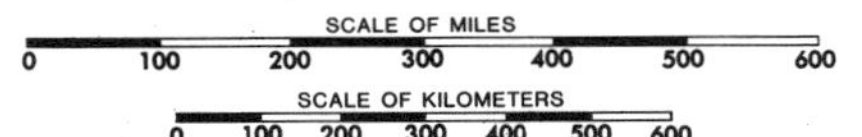

Capital of Country .... ⊛
State and Territorial Capitals .... ◉
International Boundaries .... —·—
State and Territorial Boundaries .... —··—

Depths in Fathoms

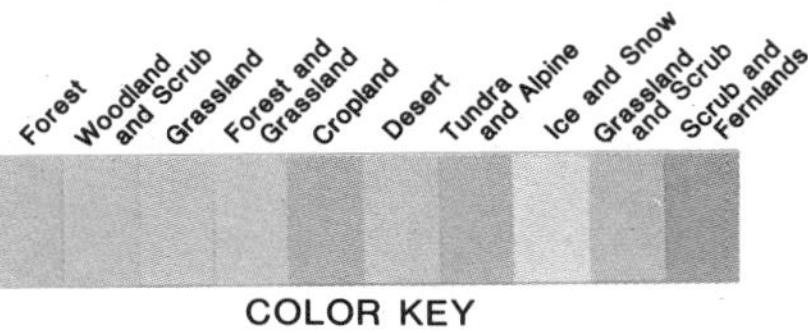

Western Australia

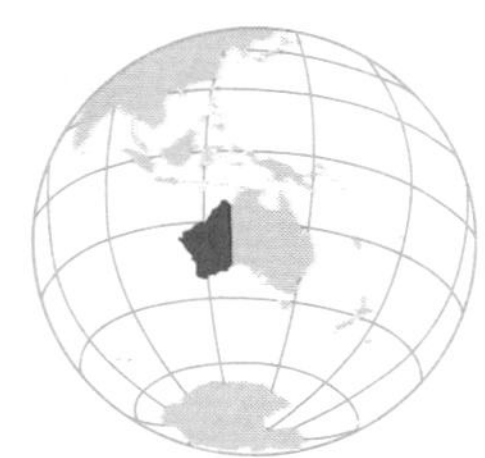

AREA 975,096 sq. mi. (2,525,500 sq. km.)
POPULATION 1,273,624
CAPITAL Perth
LARGEST CITY Perth
HIGHEST POINT Mt. Bruce 4,024 ft. (1,227 m.)

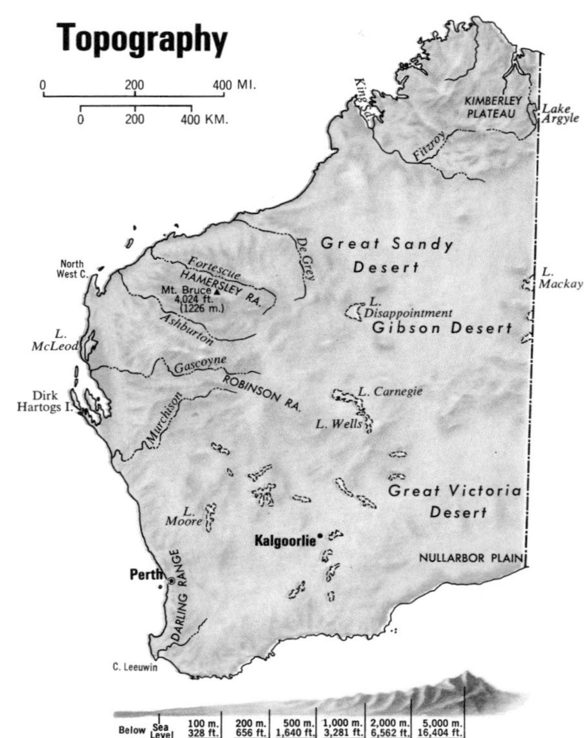

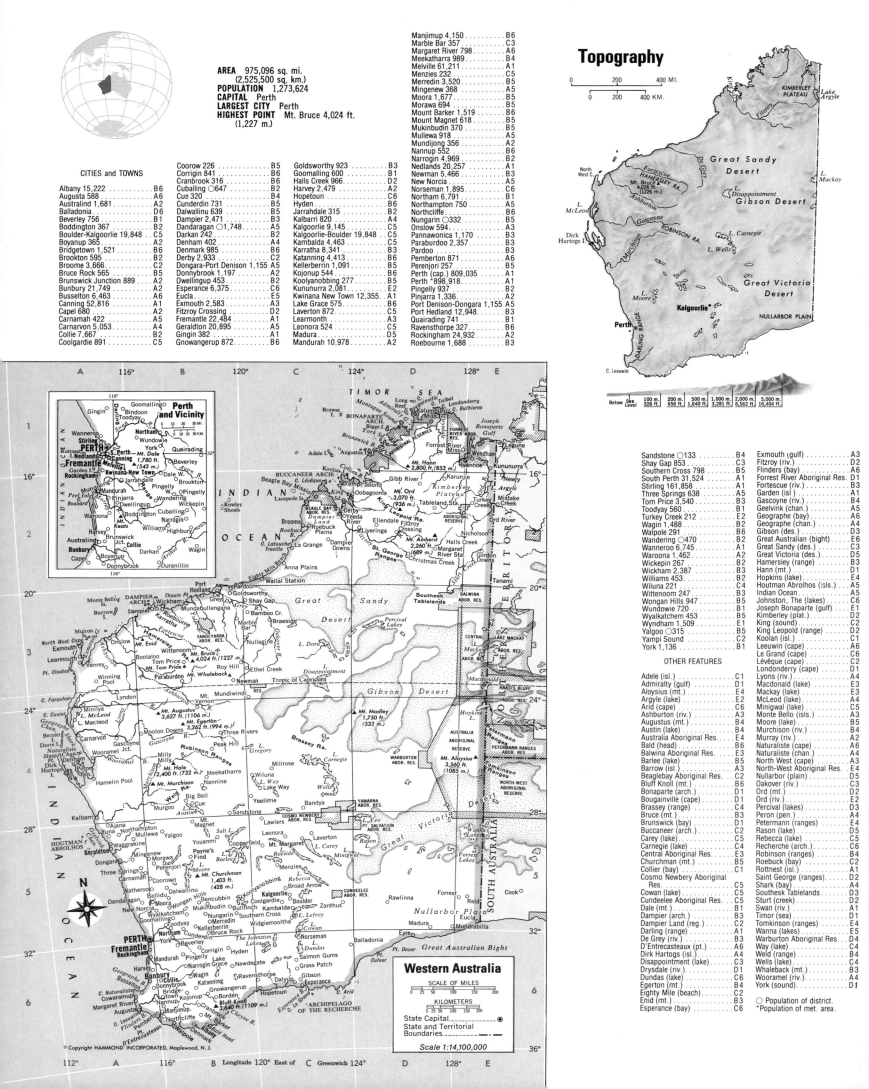

CITIES and TOWNS

Albany 15,222 . . . B6
Augusta 588 . . . A6
Australind 1,681 . . . A2
Balladonia . . . D6
Beverley 756 . . . B1
Boddington 367 . . . B2
Boulder-Kalgoorlie 19,848 . . C5
Boyanup 365 . . . A2
Bridgetown 1,521 . . . B6
Brookton 595 . . . B2
Broome 3,666 . . . C2
Bruce Rock 565 . . . B5
Brunswick Junction 889 . . . A2
Bunbury 21,749 . . . A2
Busselton 6,463 . . . A6
Canning 52,816 . . . A1
Capel 680 . . . A2
Carnamah 422 . . . A5
Carnarvon 5,053 . . . A4
Collie 7,667 . . . B2
Coolgardie 891 . . . C5
Coorow 226 . . . B5
Corrigin 841 . . . B6
Cranbrook 316 . . . B6
Cuballing ○647 . . . B2
Cue 320 . . . B4
Cunderdin 731 . . . B5
Dalwallinu 639 . . . B5
Dampier 2,471 . . . B3
Dandaragan ○1,748 . . . A5
Darkan 242 . . . B2
Denham 402 . . . A4
Denmark 985 . . . B6
Derby 2,933 . . . C2
Dongara-Port Denison 1,155 A5
Donnybrook 1,197 . . . A2
Dwellingup 453 . . . B2
Esperance 6,375 . . . C6
Eucla . . . E5
Exmouth 2,583 . . . A3
Fitzroy Crossing . . . D2
Fremantle 22,484 . . . A1
Geraldton 20,895 . . . A5
Gingin 382 . . . A1
Gnowangerup 872 . . . B6
Goldsworthy 923 . . . B3
Goomalling 600 . . . B1
Halls Creek 966 . . . D2
Harvey 2,479 . . . A2
Hopetoun . . . C6
Hyden . . . B6
Jarrahdale 315 . . . B2
Kalbarri 820 . . . A4
Kalgoorlie 9,145 . . . C5
Kalgoorlie-Boulder 19,848 . . C5
Kambalda 4,463 . . . C5
Karratha 8,341 . . . B3
Katanning 4,413 . . . B6
Kellerberrin 1,091 . . . B5
Kojonup 544 . . . B6
Koolyanobbing 277 . . . B5
Kununurra 2,081 . . . E2
Kwinana New Town 12,355 . . A1
Lake Grace 575 . . . B6
Laverton 872 . . . C5
Learmonth . . . A3
Leonora 524 . . . C5
Madura . . . D5
Mandurah 10,978 . . . A2
Manjimup 4,150 . . . B6
Marble Bar 357 . . . C3
Margaret River 798 . . . A6
Meekatharra 989 . . . B4
Melville 61,211 . . . A1
Menzies 232 . . . C5
Merredin 3,520 . . . B5
Mingenew 368 . . . A5
Moora 1,677 . . . B5
Morawa 694 . . . B5
Mount Barker 1,519 . . . B6
Mount Magnet 618 . . . B5
Mukinbudin 370 . . . B5
Mullewa 918 . . . A5
Mundijong 356 . . . A2
Nannup 552 . . . B6
Narrogin 4,969 . . . B2
Nedlands 20,257 . . . A1
Newman 5,466 . . . B3
New Norcia . . . A5
Norseman 1,895 . . . C6
Northam 6,791 . . . B1
Northampton 750 . . . A5
Northcliffe . . . B6
Nungarin ○332 . . . B5
Onslow 594 . . . A3
Pannawonica 1,170 . . . B3
Paraburdoo 2,357 . . . B3
Pardoo . . . B3
Pemberton 871 . . . A6
Perenjori 257 . . . B5
Perth (cap.) 809,035 . . . A1
Perth *898,918 . . . A1
Pingelly 937 . . . B2
Pinjarra 1,336 . . . A2
Port Denison-Dongara 1,155 A5
Port Hedland 12,948 . . . B3
Quairading 741 . . . B1
Ravensthorpe 327 . . . B6
Rockingham 24,932 . . . A2
Roebourne 1,688 . . . B3
Sandstone ○133 . . . B4
Shay Gap 853 . . . C3
Southern Cross 798 . . . B5
South Perth 31,524 . . . A1
Stirling 161,858 . . . A1
Three Springs 638 . . . A5
Tom Price 3,540 . . . B3
Toodyay 560 . . . B1
Turkey Creek 212 . . . E2
Wagin 1,488 . . . B2
Walpole 291 . . . B6
Wandering ○470 . . . B2
Wanneroo 6,745 . . . A1
Waroona 1,462 . . . A2
Wickepin 267 . . . B2
Wickham 2,387 . . . B3
Williams 453 . . . B2
Wiluna 221 . . . C4
Wittenoom 247 . . . B3
Wongan Hills 947 . . . B5
Wundowie 720 . . . B1
Wyalkatchem 453 . . . B5
Wyndham 1,509 . . . E1
Yalgoo ○315 . . . B5
Yampi Sound . . . C2
York 1,136 . . . B1

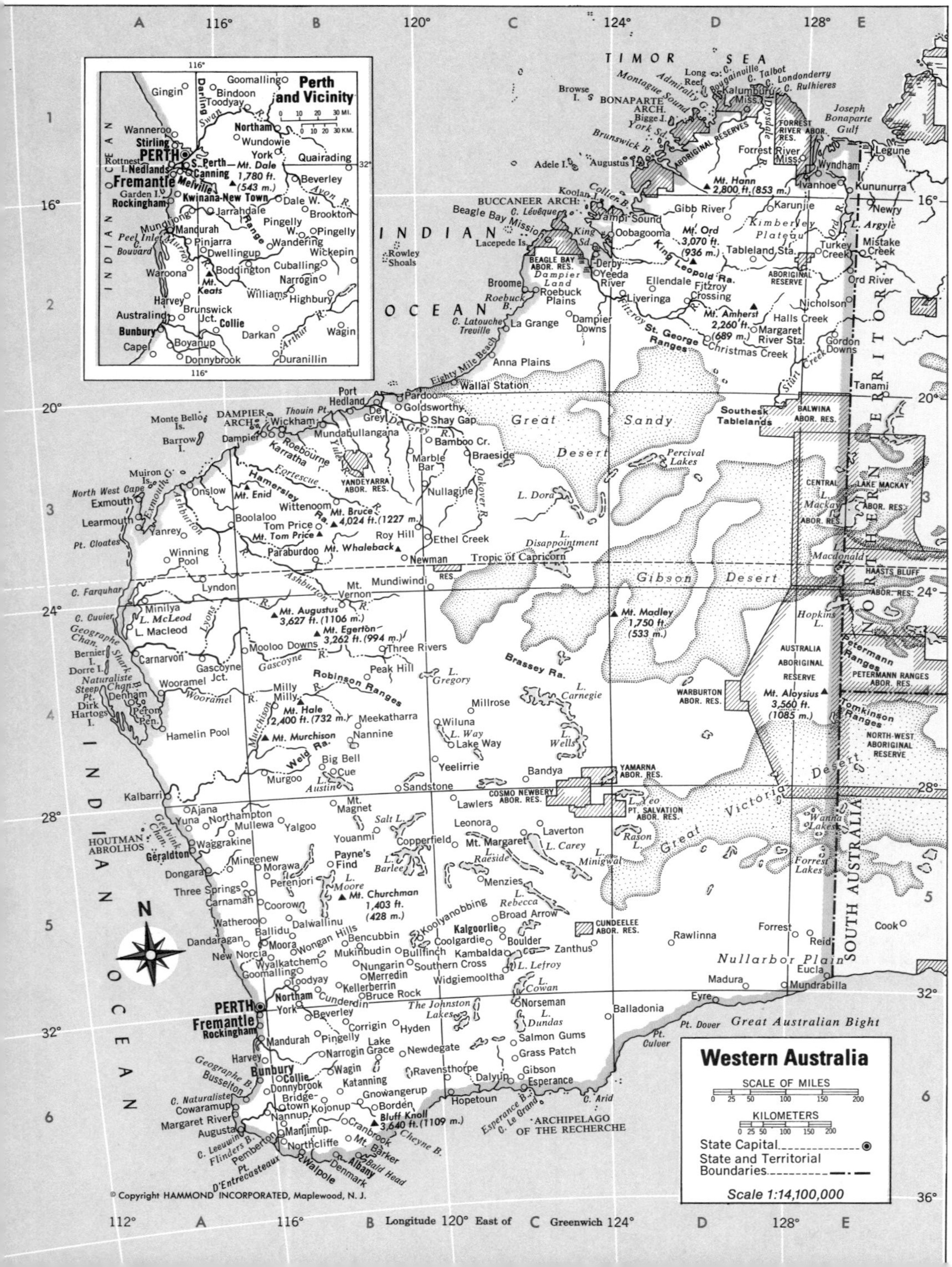

OTHER FEATURES

Adele (isl.) . . . C1
Admiralty (gulf) . . . D1
Aloysius (mt.) . . . E4
Argyle (lake) . . . E2
Arid (cape) . . . C6
Ashburton (riv.) . . . A3
Augustus (mt.) . . . B4
Austin (lake) . . . B4
Australia Aboriginal Res. . . . E4
Bald (head) . . . B6
Balwina Aboriginal Res. . . . E3
Barlee (lake) . . . B5
Barrow (isl.) . . . A3
Beaglebay Aboriginal Res. . . C2
Bluff Knoll (mt.) . . . B6
Bonaparte (arch.) . . . D1
Bougainville (cape) . . . D1
Brassey (range) . . . C4
Bruce (mt.) . . . B3
Brunswick (bay) . . . D1
Buccaneer (arch.) . . . C2
Carey (lake) . . . C5
Carnegie (lake) . . . C4
Central Aboriginal Res. . . . E3
Churchman (mt.) . . . B5
Collier (bay) . . . C1
Cosmo Newbery Aboriginal Res. . . . C5
Cowan (lake) . . . C5
Cundeelee Aboriginal Res. . . C5
Dale (mt.) . . . B1
Dampier (arch.) . . . B3
Dampier Land (reg.) . . . C2
Darling (range) . . . A1
De Grey (riv.) . . . B3
D'Entrecasteaux (pt.) . . . A6
Dirk Hartogs (isl.) . . . A4
Disappointment (lake) . . . C3
Drysdale (riv.) . . . D1
Dundas (lake) . . . C6
Egerton (mt.) . . . B4
Eighty Mile (beach) . . . C2
Enid (mt.) . . . B3
Esperance (bay) . . . C6
Exmouth (gulf) . . . A3
Fitzroy (riv.) . . . D2
Flinders (bay) . . . A6
Forrest River Aboriginal Res. D1
Fortescue (riv.) . . . B3
Garden (isl.) . . . A1
Gascoyne (riv.) . . . B4
Geelvink (chan.) . . . A5
Geographe (bay) . . . A6
Geographe (chan.) . . . A4
Gibson (des.) . . . D3
Great Australian (bight) . . . E6
Great Sandy (des.) . . . C3
Great Victoria (des.) . . . D5
Hamersley (range) . . . B3
Hann (mt.) . . . D1
Hopkins (lake) . . . E4
Houtman Abrolhos (isls.) . . . A5
Indian Ocean . . . A5
Johnston, The (lakes) . . . C6
Joseph Bonaparte (gulf) . . . E1
Kimberley (plat.) . . . D2
King (sound) . . . C2
King Leopold (range) . . . D2
Koolan (isl.) . . . C1
Leeuwin (cape) . . . A6
Le Grand (cape) . . . C6
Lévêque (cape) . . . C2
Londonderry (cape) . . . D1
Lyons (riv.) . . . A4
Macdonald (lake) . . . E3
Mackay (lake) . . . E3
McLeod (lake) . . . A4
Minigwal (lake) . . . C5
Monte Bello (isls.) . . . A3
Moore (lake) . . . B5
Murchison (riv.) . . . B4
Murray (riv.) . . . A2
Naturaliste (cape) . . . A6
Naturaliste (chan.) . . . A4
North West (cape) . . . A3
North-West Aboriginal Res. . E4
Nullarbor (plain) . . . D5
Oakover (riv.) . . . C3
Ord (mt.) . . . D2
Ord (riv.) . . . E2
Percival (lakes) . . . D3
Peron (pen.) . . . A4
Petermann (ranges) . . . E4
Rason (lake) . . . D5
Rebecca (lake) . . . C5
Recherche (arch.) . . . C6
Robinson (ranges) . . . B4
Roebuck (bay) . . . C2
Rottnest (isl.) . . . A1
Saint George (ranges) . . . D2
Shark (bay) . . . A4
Southesk Tablelands . . . D3
Sturt (creek) . . . D2
Swan (riv.) . . . A1
Timor (sea) . . . D1
Tomkinson (ranges) . . . E4
Wanna (lakes) . . . E5
Warburton Aboriginal Res. . . D4
Way (lake) . . . C4
Weld (range) . . . B4
Wells (lake) . . . C4
Whaleback (mt.) . . . B3
Wooramel (riv.) . . . A4
York (sound) . . . D1

○ Population of district.
*Population of met. area.

Western Australia
SCALE OF MILES 0 25 50 100 150 200
KILOMETERS 0 25 50 100 150 200
State Capital
State and Territorial Boundaries
Scale 1:14,100,000

A 116° B 120° C 124° D 128° E
112° A 116° B Longitude 120° East of C Greenwich 124° D 128° E

CITIES and TOWNS

- Adelaide River B2
- Aileron C7
- Alice Springs 18,395 D7
- Alyangula 1,181 E2
- Angurugu 597 E3
- Anthony Lagoon D4
- Areyonga C8
- Arltunga D7
- Avon Downs E5
- Bamyili-Beswick 685 C3
- Banka Banka C5
- Barrow Creek D6
- Batchelor B2
- Bathurst Island 1,032 B1
- Birdum C3
- Birrimbah C3
- Birrindudu A5
- Borroloola 420 E4
- Bundooma D8
- Burramurra E6
- Charlotte Waters D8
- Claravale B3
- Coniston C7
- Coolibah B3
- Creswell Downs E4
- Croker Island Mission C1
- Daly River B2
- Daly Waters C4
- Darwin (cap.) 56,482 B2
- Docker River 217 A8
- Elliott C4
- Epenarra D6
- Erldunda C8
- Eva Downs D5
- Ewaninga D7
- Goulburn Island 277 C1
- Gove (Nhulunbuy) 3,879 E2
- Harts Range D7
- Hatches Creek D6
- Helen Springs C5
- Henbury C8
- Hermannsburg 541 C7
- Hooker Creek 671 B5
- Humpty Doo B2
- Katherine 3,737 B3
- Kildurk A4
- Koolpinyah B2
- Kulgera C8
- Kurundi D6
- Lake Nash E6
- Larrimah C3
- Legune A3
- Limbunya B4
- Lucy Creek E7
- Mainoru C3
- Maningrida 702 C2
- Mataranka C3
- Milingimbi 564 D2
- Mistake Creek A4
- Montejinnie C4
- Mount Cavenagh C8
- Mount Doreen B7
- Murray Downs D6
- Napperby C7
- Newcastle Waters C4
- Nhulunbuy 3,879 E2
- Numbulwar 422 D3
- Oenpelli 452 C2
- O. T. Downs D4
- Papunya 635 B7
- Pine Creek 214 C2
- Plenty River Mine D7
- Port Keats 819 A3
- Powell Creek C5
- Rankine Store E5
- Robinson River E4
- Rockhampton Downs D5
- Rodinga D8
- Rum Jungle B2
- Santa Teresa 479 D8
- Soudan E6
- Stirling Station C6
- Tanami A5
- Tarlton Downs E7
- Tea Tree Well C7
- Tempe Downs C8
- Tennant Creek 3,118 C5
- The Granites B6
- Top Springs C4
- Ucharonidge D4
- Umbakumba 247 E3
- Umbeara C8
- Urapunga D3
- Utopia D7
- Victoria River Downs B4
- Warrabri 459 D6
- Warrego 991 C5
- Wave Hill B4
- White Quartz Hill D7
- Willeroo B3
- Willowra C6
- Wollogorang F4
- Yambah C7
- Yirrkala 543 E2
- Yuendumu 687 B7

OTHER FEATURES

- Amadeus (lake) B8
- Arafura (sea) D1
- Arnhem (cape) E2
- Arnhem Land (reg.) D2
- Arnhem Land Aboriginal Res. C2
- Arnold (riv.) D3
- Ayers Rock Nat'l Park B8
- Barkly Tableland D4
- Bathurst (isl.) A1
- Beagle (gulf) A2
- Beatrice (cape) E3
- Bennett (lake) B7
- Beswick Aboriginal Res. C3
- Bickerton (isl.) E2
- Blaze (pt.) A2
- Carpentaria (gulf) E3
- Central Wedge (mt.) C7
- Clarence (str.) B2
- Cobourg (pen.) C1
- Conner (mt.) B8
- Croker (cape) C1
- Daly (riv.) B2
- Daly River Aboriginal Res. A2
- Davenport (mt.) B7
- Dundas (str.) B1
- East Alligator (riv.) C2
- Ehrenberg (range) B7
- Elcho (isl.) D1
- Finke (riv.) C8
- Fitzmaurice (riv.) B3
- Ford (cape) A2
- Georgina (riv.) E6
- Goulburn (isls.) C1
- Goyder (riv.) D2
- Groote Eylandt (isl.) 2,230 E3
- Haasts Bluff Aboriginal Res. B7
- Hale (riv.) D8
- Hanson (riv.) C6
- Hay (dry riv.) E7
- Hogarth (mt.) E6
- Hopkins (lake) A8
- Joseph Bonaparte (gulf) A3
- Katherine (riv.) C3
- Lake MacKay Aboriginal Res. A6
- Lander (riv.) C6
- Leisler (mt.) A7
- Limmen (bight) D3
- Limmen Bight (riv.) D4
- Macdonald (lake) B7
- Macdonnell (ranges) C7
- MacKay (lake) A7
- Mann (riv.) D2
- Marshall (riv.) D7
- Melville (bay) E2
- Melville (isl.) B1
- Mount Olga Nat'l Park B8
- Murchison (range) D6
- Napier (mt.) A4
- Neale (lake) A8
- Newcastle (creek) C4
- Nicholson (riv.) E5
- Olga (mt.) B8
- Peron (isls.) A2
- Petermann (ranges) A8
- Petermann Ranges Aboriginal Res. A8
- Port Darwin (inlet) B2
- Ranken (riv.) E6
- Robinson (riv.) E4
- Roper (riv.) C3
- Sandover (riv.) D6
- Simpson (des.) E8
- Singleton (mt.) B6
- Sir Edward Pellew Group (isls.) E3
- South Alligator (riv.) C2
- Stanley (mt.) B7
- Stewart (cape) D1
- Stirling (creek) A4
- Sturt (plain) C4
- Tanami (des.) C5
- Timor (sea) A2
- Todd (riv.) D8
- Vanderlin (isl.) E3
- Van Diemen (cape) A1
- Van Diemen (gulf) B1
- Victoria (riv.) B3
- Wagait Aboriginal Res. B2
- Warwick (chan.) E3
- Wessel (cape) E1
- Wessel (isls.) E1
- West Baines (riv.) A4
- White (lake) A6
- Woods (lake) C4
- Young (mt.) D3
- Ziel (mt.) C7

AREA 519,768 sq. mi. (1,346,200 sq. km.)
POPULATION 123,324
CAPITAL Darwin
LARGEST CITY Darwin
HIGHEST POINT Mt. Ziel 4,955 ft. (1,510 m.)

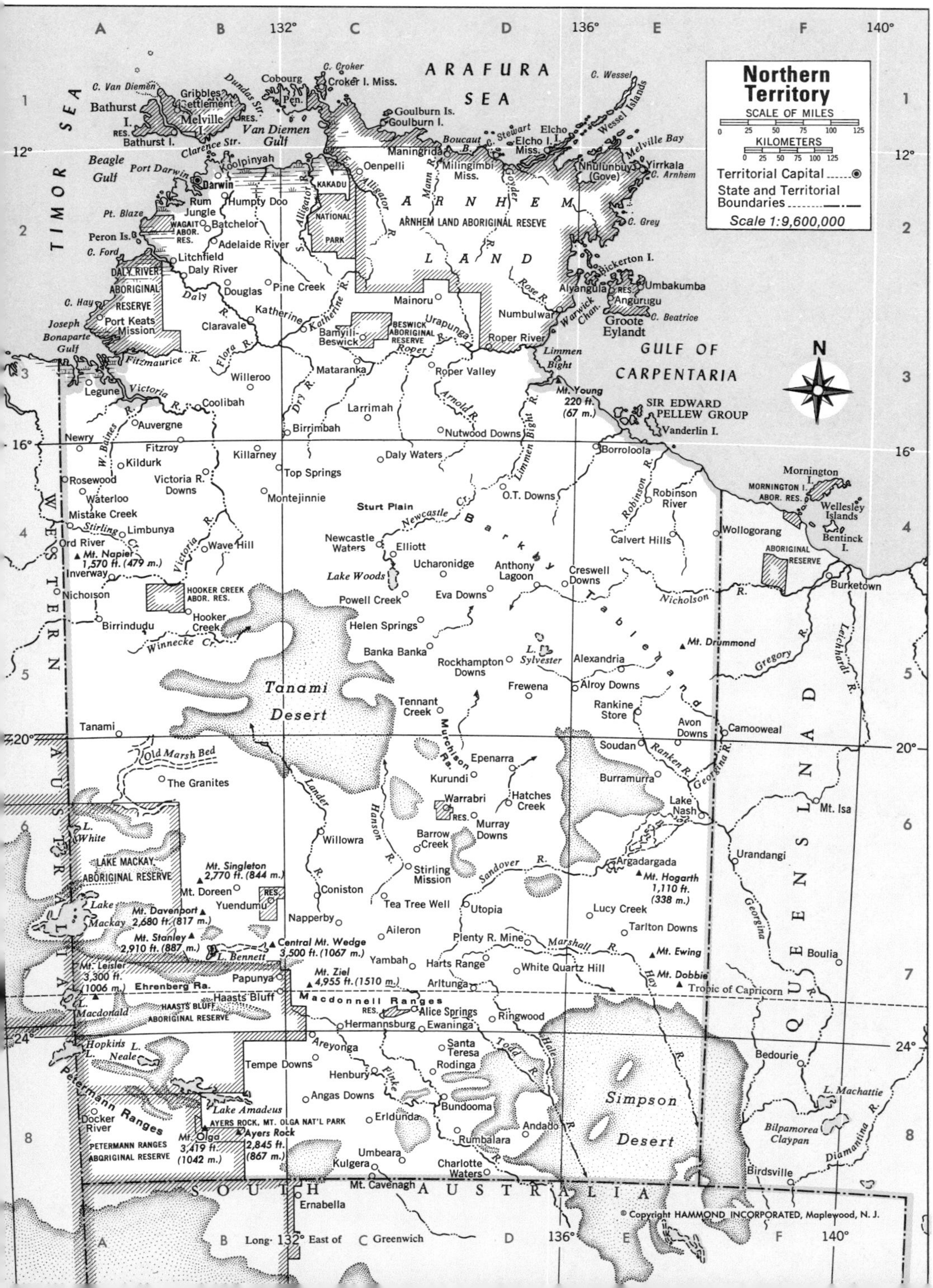

Northern Territory

SCALE OF MILES 0 25 50 75 100 125
KILOMETERS 0 25 50 75 100 125
Territorial Capital
State and Territorial Boundaries
Scale 1:9,600,000

Topography

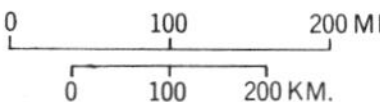

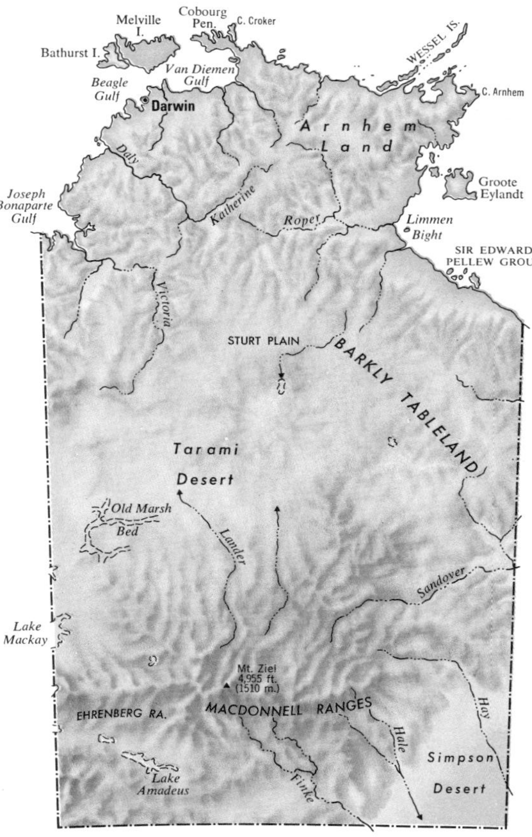

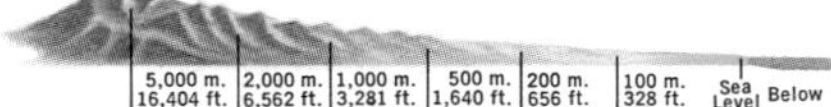

South Australia

AREA 379,922 sq. mi. (984,000 sq. km.)
POPULATION 1,285,033
CAPITAL Adelaide
LARGEST CITY Adelaide
HIGHEST POINT Mt. Woodroffe 4,970 ft. (1,515 m.)

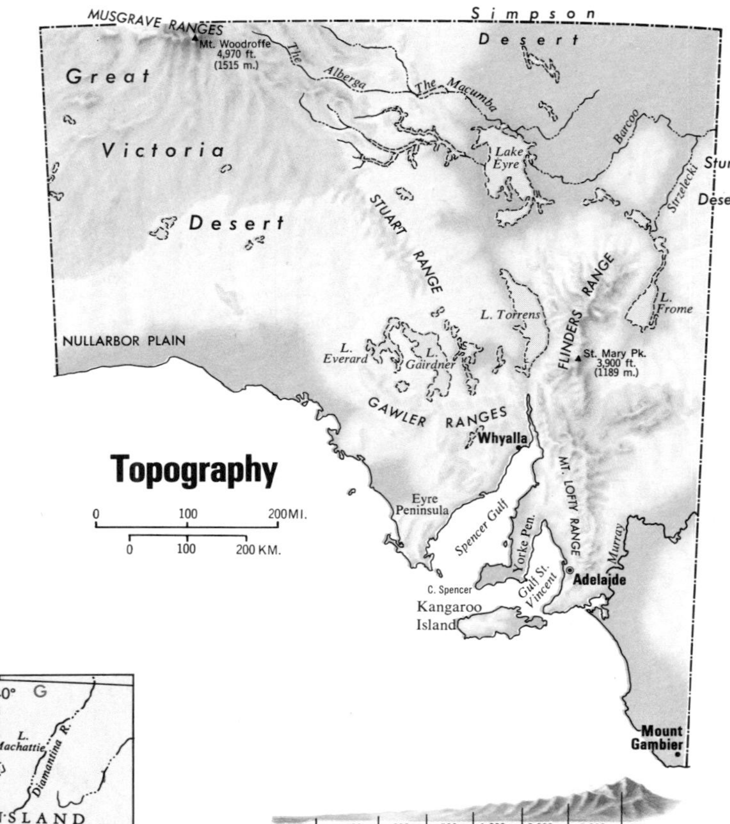

Below Sea Level | 100 m. 328 ft. | 200 m. 656 ft. | 500 m. 1,640 ft. | 1,000 m. 3,281 ft. | 2,000 m. 6,562 ft. | 5,000 m. 16,404 ft.

CITIES and TOWNS

Place	Key
Adelaide (cap.) 882,520	B6
Adelaide *931,886	B6
Andamooka 402	E4
Angaston 1,753	F6
Balaklava 1,306	F6
Barmera 2,014	G6
Beachport 357	F7
Berri 3,419	G6
Birdwood 397	C7
Blinman	F4
Bordertown 2,138	G7
Brighton 19,441	A8
Burnside 37,593	B8
Burra 1,222	F5
Campbelltown 43,084	B7
Ceduna 2,794	D5
Clare 2,381	F5
Cleve 827	E5
Coober Pedy 2,078	D3
Cowell 626	E5
Crafters-Bridgewater 9,764	B8
Crystal Brook 1,240	E5
Cummins 767	D6
Edithburgh 359	E6
Elizabeth 32,608	B7
Elliston ○1,345	D5
Enfield 66,797	B7
Gawler 9,433	B6
Gladstone 680	F5
Glenelg 13,306	A8
Gumeracha 387	C7
Hahndorf 1,274	C8
Hawker 351	F4
Hindmarsh 7,593	A7
Iron Knob 398	E5
Jamestown 1,384	F5
Kadina 2,943	F5
Kapunda 1,340	F6
Keith 1,147	G7
Kensington and Norwood 8,950	B8
Kimba 862	E5
Kingscote 1,236	E6
Kingston 1,325	G7
Lameroo 599	G6
Laura 504	F5
Leigh Creek 1,635	F4
Lobethal 1,522	C7
Lock 213	D5
Loxton 3,100	G6
Lyndoch 539	C6
Maitland 1,085	E6
Mannum 1,984	F6
Marion 66,580	A8
Marree	E3
Meadows 388	B8
Meningie 807	F6
Millicent 5,255	F7
Minlaton 865	E6
Mitcham 60,309	B8
Moonta 1,751	E5
Mount Barker 4,190	C8
Mount Gambier 18,193	G7
Murray Bridge 8,664	F6
Nairne 706	C8
Nangwarry 758	G7
Naracoorte 4,758	G7
Noarlunga 60,928	A8
Nuriootpa 2,851	F6
Oodnadatta	D2
Orroroo 604	F5
Payneham 16,502	B7
Penola 1,205	G7
Peterborough 2,575	F5
Pinnaroo 731	G6
Port Adelaide 35,407	A7
Port Augusta 15,566	E5
Port Broughton 587	F5
Port Lincoln 9,846	E6
Port Pirie 14,695	E5
Prospect 18,591	B7
Quorn 1,049	F5
Renmark 3,475	G5
Robe 590	F7
Salisbury 86,451	B7
Snowtown 492	E5
Strathalbyn 1,756	F6
Streaky Bay 985	D5
Tailem Bend 1,677	F6
Tanunda 2,621	C6
Tea Tree Gully 67,237	B7
Thebarton 9,208	A7
Tumby Bay 933	E6
Unley 35,844	B8
Uraidla 303	B8
Victor Harbor 4,522	F6
Virginia 353	B7
Waikerie 1,629	F6
Wallaroo 2,043	E5
West Torrens 45,099	A8
Whyalla 30,518	E5
Williamstown 495	C7
Willunga 667	F6
Wilmington 227	F6
Woodside 724	C8
Woodville 77,634	A7
Woomera 1,658	E4
Wudinna 572	D5
Yorketown 713	E6

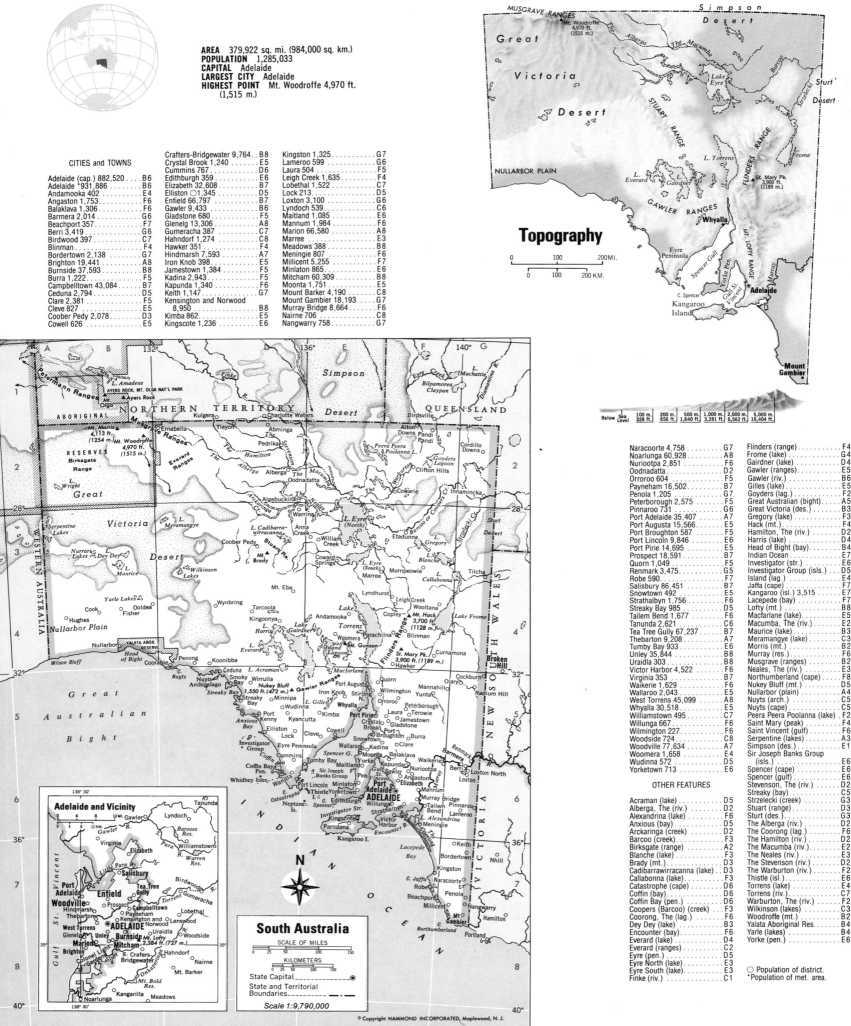

OTHER FEATURES

Feature	Key
Acraman (lake)	D5
Alberga, The (riv.)	D2
Alexandrina (lake)	F6
Anxious (bay)	D5
Arckaringa (creek)	D2
Barcoo (creek)	F3
Birksgate (range)	A2
Blanche (lake)	F3
Brady (mt.)	D3
Cadibarrawirracanna (lake)	D3
Callabonna (lake)	F3
Catastrophe (cape)	D6
Coffin (bay)	D6
Coffin Bay (pen.)	D6
Coopers (Barcoo) (creek)	F3
Coorong, The (lag.)	F6
Dey Dey (lake)	B3
Encounter (bay)	F6
Everard (lake)	D4
Everard (ranges)	C2
Eyre (pen.)	D5
Eyre North (lake)	E3
Eyre South (lake)	E3
Finke (riv.)	C1
Flinders (range)	F4
Frome (lake)	G4
Gairdner (lake)	D4
Gawler (ranges)	E5
Gawler (riv.)	B6
Gilles (lake)	E5
Goyders (lag.)	F2
Great Australian (bight)	A5
Great Victoria (des.)	B3
Gregory (lake)	F3
Hack (mt.)	F4
Hamilton, The (riv.)	D2
Harris (lake)	D4
Head of Bight (bay)	B4
Indian Ocean	E7
Investigator (str.)	E6
Investigator Group (isls.)	D5
Island (lag.)	E4
Jaffa (cape)	F7
Kangaroo (isl.) 3,515	E7
Lacepede (bay)	F7
Lofty (mt.)	B8
Macfarlane (lake)	E5
Macumba, The (riv.)	E2
Maurice (lake)	B3
Meramangye (lake)	C3
Morris (mt.)	B2
Murray (res.)	F6
Musgrave (ranges)	B2
Neales, The (riv.)	E3
Northumberland (cape)	F8
Nukey Bluff (mt.)	D5
Nullarbor (plain)	A4
Nuyts (arch.)	C5
Nuyts (cape)	C5
Peera Peera Poolanna (lake)	F2
Saint Mary (peak)	F4
Saint Vincent (gulf)	F6
Serpentine (lakes)	A3
Simpson (des.)	E1
Sir Joseph Banks Group (isls.)	E6
Spencer (cape)	E6
Spencer (gulf)	E6
Stevenson, The (riv.)	D2
Streaky (bay)	C5
Strzelecki (creek)	G3
Stuart (range)	D3
Sturt (des.)	G3
The Alberga (riv.)	D2
The Coorong (lag.)	F6
The Hamilton (riv.)	D2
The Macumba (riv.)	E2
The Neales (riv.)	E3
The Stevenson (riv.)	D2
The Warburton (riv.)	F2
Thistle (isl.)	E6
Torrens (lake)	E4
Torrens (riv.)	C7
Warburton, The (riv.)	F2
Wilkinson (lakes)	C3
Woodroffe (mt.)	B2
Yalata Aboriginal Res.	B4
Yarle (lakes)	B4
Yorke (pen.)	E6

○ Population of district.
*Population of met. area.

Adelaide and Vicinity

South Australia

SCALE OF MILES: 0 25 50 100 150
KILOMETERS: 0 25 50 100 150
State Capital
State and Territorial Boundaries
Scale 1:9,790,000

Longitude D East 136° of E Greenwich

CITIES and TOWNS

Aramac 428 . . . C4
Archerfield 785 . . . D3
Ascot 4,298 . . . E2
Atherton 4,196 . . . C3
Ayr 8,787 . . . C3
Balmoral 2,915 . . . E2
Barcaldine 1,432 . . . C4
Beaudesert 3,780 . . . E6
Biloela 4,643 . . . D5
Birdsville . . . A5
Blackall 1,609 . . . C5
Blackwater 5,434 . . . D4
Boulia 292 . . . A4
Bowen 7,663 . . . D3
Brisbane (cap.) 689,378 . . . D2
Brisbane *1,028,527 . . . D2
Bucasia 1,356 . . . D4
Bundaberg 32,560 . . . D5
Burketown 210 . . . A3
Cairns 48,557 . . . C3
Caloundra 16,758 . . . E5
Camooweal 251 . . . A3
Camp Hill 8,999 . . . E3
Capella 660 . . . D4
Cardwell 1,249 . . . C3
Charleville 3,523 . . . C5
Charters Towers 6,823 . . . C4
Cherbourg 963 . . . D5
Chermside 6,892 . . . D2
Clermont 1,659 . . . C4
Cloncurry 1,961 . . . B4
Collinsville 2,756 . . . C4
Cooktown 913 . . . C2
Coopers Plains 4,492 . . . D3
Corinda 4,894 . . . D3
Croydon ○255 . . . B3
Cunnamulla 1,627 . . . C5
Dalby 8,784 . . . D5
Dirranbandi 480 . . . D6
East Brisbane 4,853 . . . E3
Eidsvold 613 . . . D5
Emerald 4,628 . . . C4
Esk 676 . . . E5
Gatton 4,190 . . . E5
Gayndah 1,708 . . . D5
Geebung 4,850 . . . E2
Georgetown 319 . . . B3
Gladstone 22,083 . . . D4
Gold Coast 135,437 . . . E6
Goondiwindi 3,576 . . . D6
Gordonvale 2,375 . . . C3
Greenslopes 7,219 . . . E3
Gympie 10,768 . . . E5
Hervey Bay 13,569 . . . E5
Holland Park 7,363 . . . E3
Home Hill 3,138 . . . C3
Hughenden 1,657 . . . B4
Inala 17,383 . . . D3
Indooroopilly 7,959 . . . D3
Ingham 5,598 . . . C3
Injune 407 . . . D5
Innisfail 7,933 . . . C3
Ipswich 68,297 . . . E5
Isisford ○605 . . . C5
Jandowae 781 . . . D5
Jericho ○1,177 . . . C4
Julia Creek 602 . . . B4
Karumba 670 . . . B3
Kilcoy 1,257 . . . E5
Kingaroy 5,134 . . . D5
Longreach 2,971 . . . B4
Mackay 35,361 . . . D4
Mareeba 6,309 . . . C3
Marian 796 . . . D4
Maroochydore-Mooloolaba 17,460 . . . E5
Maryborough 20,111 . . . E5
Mary Kathleen 830 . . . A4
McKinlay ○1,477 . . . B4
Millmerran 1,107 . . . D5
Mitchell 1,171 . . . C5
Mitchelton 5,810 . . . D2
Monto 1,397 . . . D5
Moorooka 8,740 . . . D3
Moranbah 4,362 . . . C9
Mossman 1,614 . . . C3
Mount Isa 23,679 . . . A4
Moura 2,871 . . . D5
Murgon 2,327 . . . D5
Nambour 7,965 . . . E5
Newmarket 3,520 . . . D2
Normanton 926 . . . B3
Nundah 7,358 . . . E2
Proserpine 3,058 . . . D4
Quilpie 694 . . . C5
Ravenshoe 915 . . . C3
Redcliffe 42,223 . . . E5
Richmond 784 . . . B4
Rockhampton 50,146 . . . D4
Roma 5,706 . . . D5
Saint George 2,204 . . . D5
Saint Lucia 6,075 . . . D3
Sandgate 6,776 . . . D2
Sarina 2,815 . . . D4
Springsure 774 . . . D5
Stafford (Stafford Heights) 13,731 . . . D2
Stanthorpe 3,966 . . . D6
Tara 864 . . . D5
Taroom 688 . . . D5
Tewantin-Noosa 9,965 . . . E5
Theodore 643 . . . D5
Thursday Island 2,283 . . . B1
Toowoomba 63,401 . . . D5
Townsville 86,112 . . . C3
Tully 2,728 . . . C3
Walkerston 1,277 . . . D4
Warwick 8,853 . . . D6
Weipa 2,433 . . . B2
Windsor 6,119 . . . D2
Winton 1,259 . . . B4
Wynnum 10,794 . . . E5
Yeppoon 6,447 . . . D4
Yeronga 4,579 . . . D3

OTHER FEATURES

Albatross (bay) . . . B2
Archer (riv.) . . . B2
Balonne (riv.) . . . D6
Banks (isl.) . . . B1
Barcoo (creek) . . . B5
Barkly Tableland . . . A4
Bartle Frere (mt.) . . . C3
Beal (range) . . . B5

AREA 666,872 sq. mi. (1,727,200 sq. km.)
POPULATION 2,295,123
CAPITAL Brisbane
LARGEST CITY Brisbane
HIGHEST POINT Mt. Bartle Frere 5,287 ft. (1,611 m.)

Topography

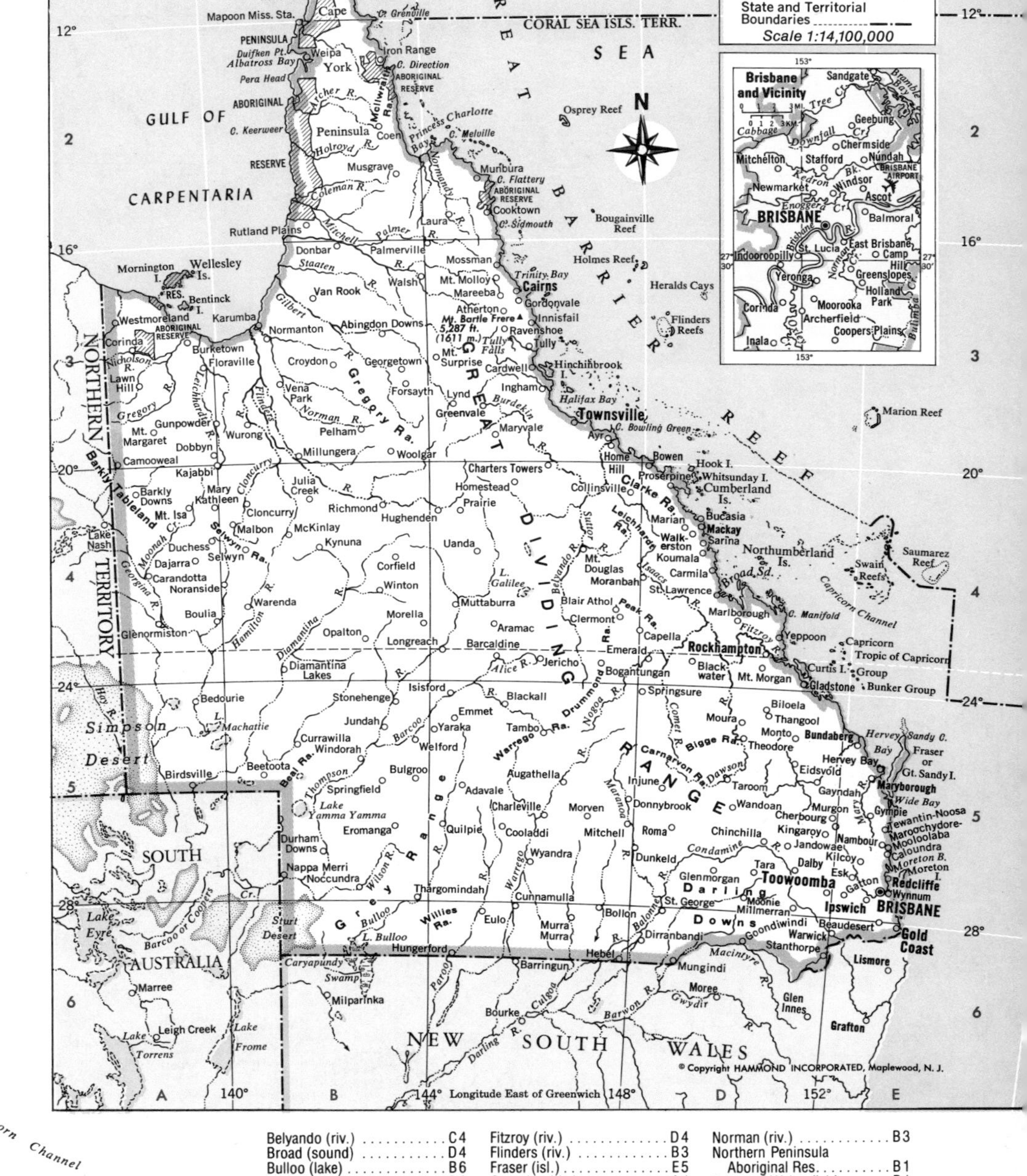

Belyando (riv.) . . . C4
Broad (sound) . . . D4
Bulloo (lake) . . . B6
Bulloo (riv.) . . . B6
Bunker Group (isls.) . . . E4
Burdekin (riv.) . . . C3
Cape York (pen.) . . . B2
Capricorn (chan.) . . . D4
Capricorn Group (isls.) . . . E4
Carnarvon (range) . . . D5
Carpentaria (gulf) . . . A2
Cloncurry (riv.) . . . B4
Coopers (Barcoo) (creek) . . . B5
Coral (sea) . . . C1
Culgoa (riv.) . . . C6
Cumberland (isls.) . . . D4
Curtis (isl.) . . . D4
Darling Downs . . . D5
Dawson (riv.) . . . D5
Diamantina (riv.) . . . B4
Drummond (range) . . . C5
Duifken (pt.) . . . B2
Endeavour (str.) . . . B1
Fitzroy (riv.) . . . D4
Flinders (riv.) . . . B3
Fraser (isl.) . . . E5
Georgina (riv.) . . . A4
Gilbert (riv.) . . . B3
Great Dividing (range) . . . C4
Gregory (range) . . . B3
Gregory (riv.) . . . A3
Grey (range) . . . B5
Hamilton (riv.) . . . B4
Hervey (bay) . . . E5
Hinchinbrook (isl.) . . . C3
Hook (isl.) . . . D4
Leichhardt (riv.) . . . A3
Machattie (lake) . . . B5
Macintyre (riv.) . . . D6
Maranoa (riv.) . . . C5
Mary (riv.) . . . E5
Melville (cape) . . . C2
Mitchell (riv.) . . . B2
Moreton (bay) . . . E5
Moreton (isl.) . . . E5
Mornington (isl.) . . . A3
Norman (riv.) . . . B3
Northern Peninsula Aboriginal Res. . . . B1
Prince of Wales (isl.) . . . B1
Princess Charlotte (bay) . . . C2
Sandy (cape) . . . E5
Selwyn (range) . . . B4
Simpson (des.) . . . A5
Sturt (des.) . . . B3
Suttor (riv.) . . . C4
Swain (reefs) . . . E4
Thompson (riv.) . . . B5
Torres (str.) . . . B1
Warrego (range) . . . C5
Warrego (riv.) . . . C5
Wellesley (isls.) . . . A3
Whitsunday (isl.) . . . D4
Willies (range) . . . C6
Yamma Yamma (lake) . . . B5
York (cape) . . . B1

○ Population of district.
*Population of met. area.

New South Wales and Victoria

AUSTRALIAN CAPITAL TERRITORY

CITIES and TOWNS

NEW SOUTH WALES

CITIES and TOWNS

Cobbadah F2
Coffs Harbour 16,020 . . . . . . G2
Collarenebri 602 . . . . E1
Collie E2
Comboyne G2
Concord 23,926 . . . . J3
Condobolin 3,355 . . . . D3
Conoble C3
Coogee K3
Coolah 878 . . . . E2
Coolamon 1,088 . . . . D4
Cooma 7,978 . . . . E5
Coonabarabran 3,001 . . . . . . E2
Coonamble 3,090 . . . . E2
Cootamundra 6,540 . . . . D4
Copmanhurst ◯2,857 . . . . . G1
Coraki 895 . . . . G1
Coramba 202 . . . . G2
Corowa-Wahgunyah 3,390 . . D4
Cowra 7,900 . . . . E3
Crescent Head 944 . . . . G2
Cronulla J4
Crookwell 2,063 . . . . E4
Cudal 400 . . . . E3
Cullburra-Orient Point 2,068 . F4
Culcairn 1,027 . . . . D4
Cullen Bullen 231 . . . . F3
Cumnock 252 . . . . E3
Curlewis 487 . . . . F2
Dareton 612 . . . . B4
Darlington Point 599 . . . . . . C4
Deepwater 260 . . . . F1
Dee Why K3
Delegate 347 . . . . E5
Delungra 332 . . . . F1
Deniliquin 7,354 . . . . C4
Denman 1,122 . . . . F3
Dorrigo 1,192 . . . . G2
Drummoyne 30,961 . . . . J3
Dubbo 23,986 . . . . E3
Dunedoo 836 . . . . E3
Dungalear Station D1
Dungog 2,126 . . . . F3
Eden 3,107 . . . . E5
Emmaville 503 . . . . F1
Ermeran Station D3
Eugowra 577 . . . . E3
Evans Head 1,802 . . . . G1

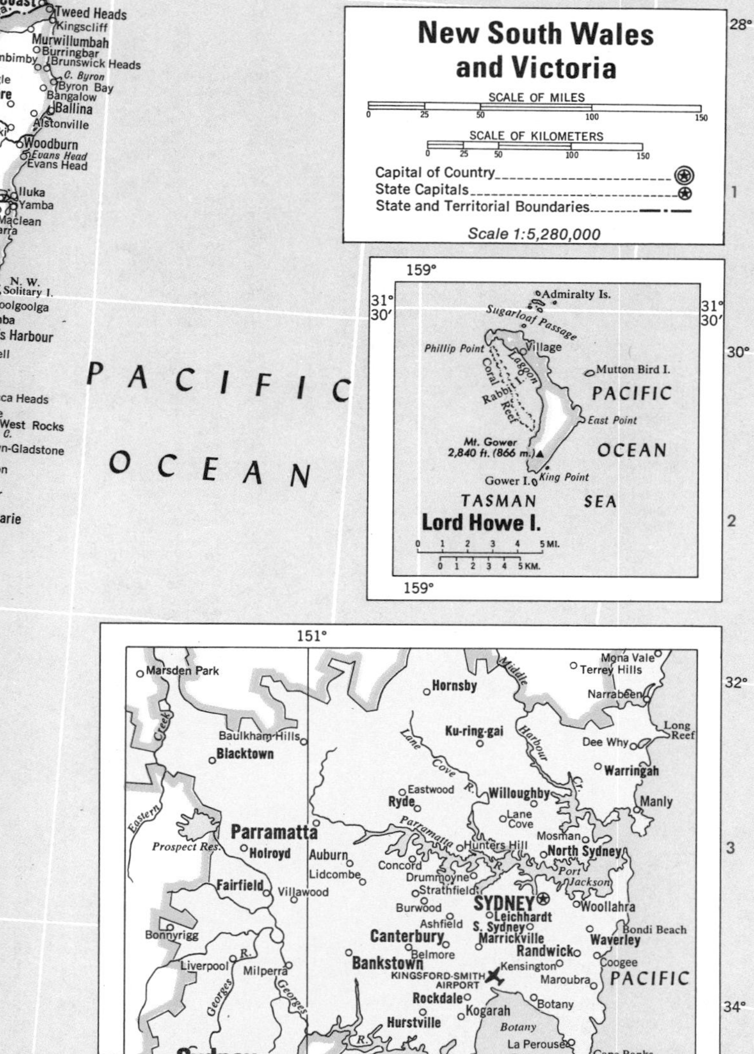

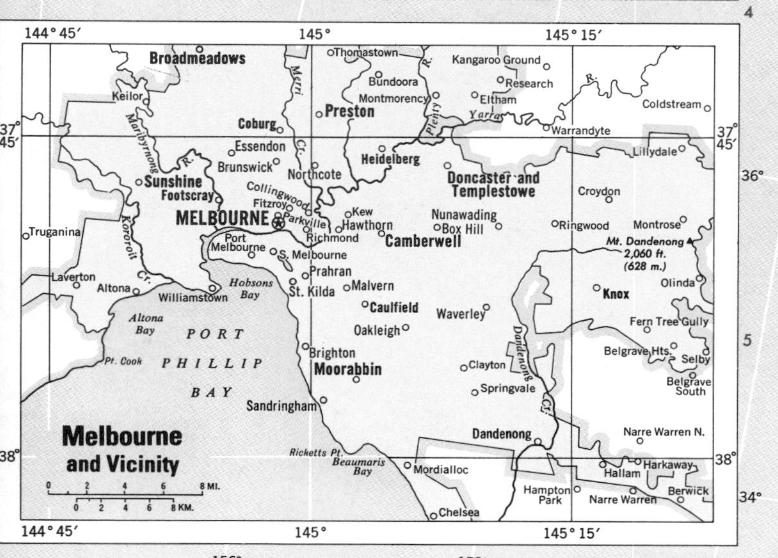

NEW SOUTH WALES

AREA 309,498 sq. mi. (801,600 sq. km.)
POPULATION 5,126,217
CAPITAL Sydney
LARGEST CITY Sydney
HIGHEST POINT Mt. Kosciusko 7,310 ft. (2,228 m.)

VICTORIA

AREA 87,876 sq. mi. (227,600 sq. km.)
POPULATION 3,832,443
CAPITAL Melbourne
LARGEST CITY Melbourne
HIGHEST POINT Mt. Bogong 6,508 ft. (1,984 m.)

Topography

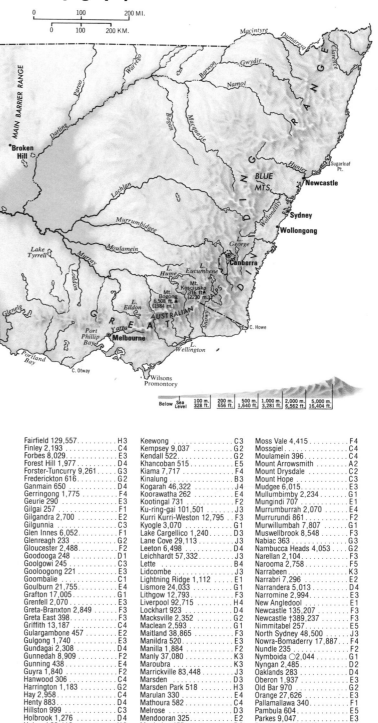

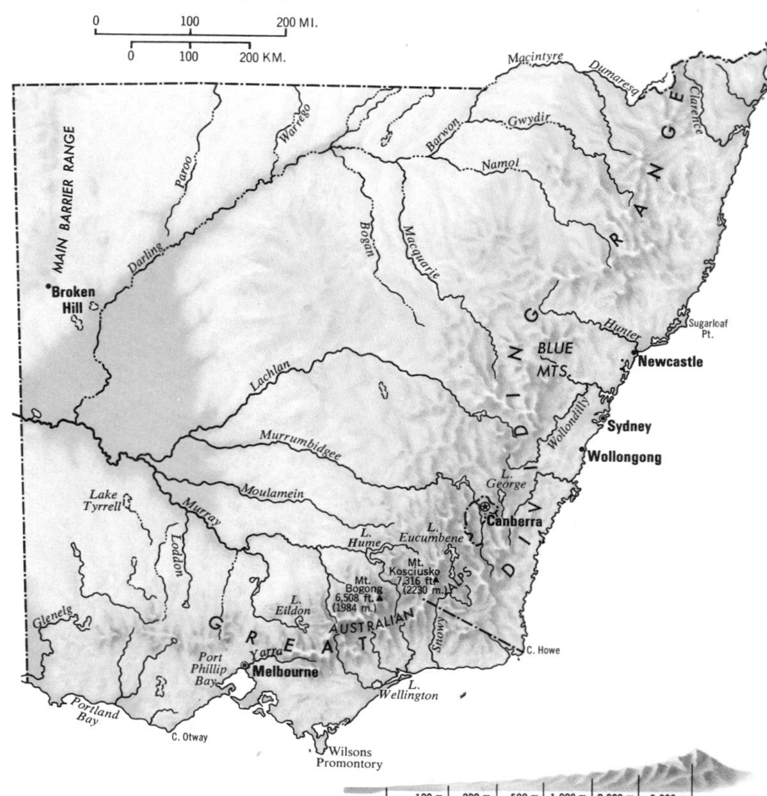

Fairfield 129,557 . . . . H3
Finley 2,193 . . . . C4
Forbes 8,029 . . . . E3
Forest Hill 1,977 . . . . D4
Forster-Tuncurry 9,261 . . . . . G3
Frederickton 616 . . . . G2
Ganmain 650 . . . . D4
Gerringong 1,775 . . . . F4
Geurie 290 . . . . E3
Gilgai 257 . . . . F1
Gilgandra 2,700 . . . . E2
Gilgunnia C3
Glen Innes 6,052 . . . . F1
Glenreagh 233 . . . . G2
Gloucester 2,488 . . . . F2
Goodooga 248 . . . . D1
Goolgowi 245 . . . . C3
Gooloogong 221 . . . . E3
Goombalie C1
Goulburn 21,755 . . . . E4
Grafton 17,005 . . . . G1
Grenfell 2,070 . . . . E3
Greta-Branxton 2,849 . . . . . . F3
Greta East 398 . . . . F3
Griffith 13,187 . . . . C4
Gulargambone 457 . . . . E2
Gulgong 1,740 . . . . E3
Gundagai 2,308 . . . . D4
Gunnedah 8,909 . . . . F2
Gunning 438 . . . . E4
Guyra 1,840 . . . . F2
Hanwood 306 . . . . C4
Harrington 1,183 . . . . G2
Hay 2,958 . . . . C4
Henty 883 . . . . D4
Hillston 999 . . . . C3
Holbrook 1,276 . . . . D4
Holroyd 80,116 . . . . H3
Hornsby 111,081 . . . . J3
Howlong 1,072 . . . . D4
Hunters Hill 12,537 . . . . J3
Hurstville 64,910 . . . . J4
Huskisson 2,296 . . . . F4
Iluka 1,362 . . . . G1
Inverell 9,734 . . . . F1
Ivanhoe 517 . . . . C3
Jerilderie 1,075 . . . . C4
Jindabyne 1,602 . . . . E5
Junee 3,993 . . . . D4
Kandos 1,626 . . . . F3
Karpakora B3
Katoomba-Wentworth Falls 13,942 . . . . F3
Keewong C3
Kempsey 9,037 . . . . G2
Kendall 522 . . . . G2
Khancoban 515 . . . . E5
Kiama 7,717 . . . . F4
Kinalung B3
Kogarah 46,322 . . . . J4
Koorawatha 262 . . . . E4
Kootingal 731 . . . . F2
Ku-ring-gai 101,501 . . . . J3
Kurri Kurri-Weston 12,795 . . F3
Kyogle 3,070 . . . . G1
Lake Cargellico 1,240 . . . . . . D3
Lane Cove 29,113 . . . . J3
Leeton 6,498 . . . . D4
Leichhardt 57,332 . . . . J3
Lette B4
Lidcombe J3
Lightning Ridge 1,112 . . . . . E1
Lismore 24,033 . . . . G1
Lithgow 12,793 . . . . F3
Liverpool 92,715 . . . . H4
Lockhart 923 . . . . D4
Macksville 2,352 . . . . G2
Maclean 2,593 . . . . G1
Maitland 38,865 . . . . F3
Manildra 520 . . . . E3
Manilla 1,884 . . . . F2
Manly 37,080 . . . . K3
Maroubra K3
Marrickville 83,448 . . . . J3
Marsden D3
Marsden Park 518 . . . . H3
Marulan 330 . . . . E4
Mathoura 582 . . . . C4
Melrose D3
Mendooran 325 . . . . E2
Menindee 455 . . . . B3
Merimbula 2,899 . . . . F5
Merriwa 943 . . . . F3
Millthorpe 607 . . . . E5
Milpa B2
Milperra H4
Milton 740 . . . . F4
Mittagong 4,266 . . . . F4
Moama C5
Mogil Mogil E1
Molong 1,374 . . . . E3
Mona Vale K2
Moree 10,459 . . . . E1
Morisset 1,593 . . . . F3
Moruya 2,003 . . . . F4
Mosman 26,200 . . . . J3
Moss Vale 4,415 . . . . F4
Mossgiel C4
Moulamein 396 . . . . C4
Mount Arrowsmith A2
Mount Drysdale C2
Mount Hope C3
Mudgee 6,015 . . . . E3
Mullumbimby 2,234 . . . . G1
Mungindi 707 . . . . E1
Murrumburrah 2,070 . . . . . . E4
Murrurundi 861 . . . . F2
Murwillumbah 7,807 . . . . . . G1
Muswellbrook 8,548 . . . . . . F3
Nabiac 363 . . . . G3
Nambucca Heads 4,053 . . . . G2
Narellan 2,104 . . . . F3
Narooma 2,758 . . . . F5
Narrabeen K3
Narrabri 7,296 . . . . E2
Narrandera 5,013 . . . . D4
Narromine 2,994 . . . . E3
New Angledool E1
Newcastle 135,207 . . . . F3
Newcastle †389,237 . . . . F3
Nimmitabel 257 . . . . E5
North Sydney 48,500 . . . . . . J3
Nowra-Bomaderry 17,887 . . . F4
Nundle 235 . . . . F2
Nymboida ◯2,044 . . . . G1
Nyngan 2,485 . . . . D2
Oaklands 283 . . . . D4
Oberon 1,937 . . . . E3
Old Bar 970 . . . . G2
Orange 27,626 . . . . E3
Pallamallawa 340 . . . . F1
Pambula 604 . . . . E5
Parkes 9,047 . . . . E3
Parramatta 130,943 . . . . . . H3
Peak Hill 1,037 . . . . E3
Penrith 108,720 . . . . F3
Perthville 639 . . . . E3
Picton 1,817 . . . . F4
Pilliga 206 . . . . E2
Popiltah A3
Portland 1,980 . . . . E3
Port Kembla F4
Port Macquarie 19,581 . . . . . G2
Queanbeyan 19,383 . . . . E4
Quirindi 2,851 . . . . F2
Randwick 116,202 . . . . J3
Raymond Terrace 7,548 . . . . F3
Richmond-Windsor 15,491 . . F3
Rockdale 83,719 . . . . J4

(continued on following page)

(continued)

Ryde 88,948 J3
Rylstone 651 E3
Salisbury Downs B1
Sawtell 5,970 G2
Scone 3,949 F3
Shellharbour 41,790 F4
Singleton 9,572 F3
Smithtown-Gladstone 953 G2
South Sydney 30,776 J3
South West Rocks 1,314 G2
Stephen's Creek A2
Strathfield 25,882 J3
Stroud 522 G3
Sussex Inlet 1,293 F4
Sutherland 165,336 J4
Sydney (cap.) 2,876,508 J3
Sydney †3,204,696 J3
Talbingo 481 E4
Tamworth 29,657 F2
Taralga 272 E4
Tarcutta 263 D4
Taree 14,697 G2
Tathra 1,077 F5
Temora 4,350 D4
Tenterfield 3,402 G1
Terrigal-The Entrance 37,891 F3
The Rock 693 D4
Thurloo Downs B1
Tibbita C4
Tibooburra B1
Tiltagara C2
Tingha 886 F1
Tocumwal 1,174 C4
Tongo B2
Torrowangee A2
Tottenham 366 D3
Trangie 977 D3
Trundle 515 D3
Tullamore 324 D3
Tumbarumba 1,536 D4
Tumut 5,816 E4
Tweed Heads G1
Ulladulla 6,018 F4
Ulmarra 395 G1
Ungarie 428 D3
Uralla 2,090 F2
Urana 419 D4
Urbenville 282 G1
Urunga 2,045 G2
Villawood H3
Wagga Wagga 36,837 D4
Wakool 278 C4
Walcha 1,674 F2
Walgett 2,157 E2
Walla Walla 593 D4
Wallerawang 1,855 F3
Wangi-Rathmines 5,106 F3
Warialda 1,340 F1
Warragamba 1,406 F3
Warren 2,153 D2
Warringah ○172,653 K3
Wauchope 3,645 G2
Waverley 61,575 K3
Waverley Downs B1
Wee Waa 1,904 E2
Wellington 5,280 E3
Wentworth 1,180 B4
Werris Creek 1,924 F2
West Wyalong 3,778 D3
Wetuppa B4
White Cliffs B2
Whitton 344 D4
Whyjonta B1
Wilcannia 982 B2
Willoughby 52,120 J3
Willow Tree 258 F2
Wingham 3,937 G2
Wollongong 169,381 F4
Wollongong †222,539 F4
Woodburn 647 G1
Woodenbong 409 G1
Woodstock 266 E3
Woolgoolga 2,081 G2
Wooli 457 G1
Woollahra 51,659 K3
Wyong 3,902 F3
Yallock C3
Yalpunga A1
Yamba 2,528 G1
Yancannia B2
Yanco 415 D4
Yantara B1
Yass 4,283 E4
Yenda 697 D4
Yeoval 288 E3
Young 6,906 E4

OTHER FEATURES

Ana Branch, Darling (riv.) A3
Australian Alps (mts.) D5
Barrington Tops (mt.) F2
Barwon (riv.) D2
Blue (mts.) F3
Bogan (riv.) D2
Bondi (beach) K3
Botany (bay) J4
Broken (bay) F3
Burrinjuck (res.) E4
Byron (cape) G1
Caryapundy (swamp) B1
Castlereagh (riv.) E2
Cawndilla (lake) A3
Clarence (riv.) G1
Colo (riv.) F3
Cowal (lake) D3
Culgoa (riv.) D1
Cuttaburra (creek) C1
Darling (riv.) B3
Dumaresq (riv.) F1
Eucumbene (lake) E5
George (lake) E4
Georges (riv.) H4
Gower (mt.) J2
Great Dividing (range) E3
Green (cape) F5
Gunderbooka (ranges) C2
Gwydir (riv.) E1
Howe (cape) F5
Hume (res.) D4
Hunter (riv.) F3
Kosciusko (mt.) E5
Kurnell (pen.) J4
Lachlan (range) C3
Lachlan (riv.) C3
Liverpool (range) F2
Lord Howe (isl.) 287 J2
Macintyre (riv.) E1
Macquarie (lake) F3
Macquarie (riv.) D2
Main Barrier (range) A2
Manning (riv.) F2
Marthaguy (creek) D2
McPherson (range) G1
Menindee (lake) B3
Monaro (range) E5
Moonie (riv.) E1
Moulamein (creek) C4
Mount Royal (range) F2
Murray (riv.) A4
Murrumbidgee (riv.) C4
Myall (lake) G3
Namoi (riv.) E2
Narran (lake) D1
New England (range) F1
Paroo (riv.) C1
Parramatta (riv.) J3
Poopeloe (lake) C2
Port Jackson (inlet) J3
Port Stephens (inlet) G3
Richmond (range) G1
Richmond (riv.) G1
Riverina (reg.) C4
Robe (mt.) A2
Round, The (mt.) G2
Salt, The (lake) B2
Shoalhaven (riv.) E4
Smoky (cape) G2
Snowy (mts.) E5
Snowy (riv.) E5
Stony (ranges) B2
Sturt (mt.) A1
Sugarloaf (pt.) G3
Talyawalka (creek) B2
Tandou (lake) A3
Tasman (sea) F5
The Round (mts.) G2
The Salt (lake) B2
Timbarra (riv.) G1
Tuggerah (lake) F3
Victoria (lake) A3
Warrego (riv.) C1
Willandra Billabong (creek) C3
Wollondilly (riv.) F4

VICTORIA

CITIES and TOWNS

Alexandra 1,756 C5
Altona 30,909 H5
Apollo Bay 921 B6
Ararat 8,336 B5
Avoca 1,032 B5
Bacchus Marsh 6,224 C5
Bairnsdale 9,459 D5
Ballarat 35,681 C5
Ballarat †71,930 C5
Balmoral 257 A5
Beaufort 1,214 B5
Beechworth 3,154 D5
Belgrave Heights J5
Belgrave South K5
Benalla 8,151 D5
Bendigo 31,841 C5
Bendigo †58,818 C5
Berwick 36,181 K6
Beulah 290 B4
Birchip 895 B4
Birregurra 416 B6
Boort 863 B5
Box Hill 47,579 J5
Bright 1,545 D5
Brighton 33,697 J5
Broadford 1,580 C5
Broadmeadows 103,540 H4
Brunswick 44,464 H5
Bruthen 449 D5
Bundoora J4
Camberwell 85,883 J5
Camperdown 3,545 C6
Cann River 345 E5
Casterton 1,945 A5
Castlemaine 7,583 C5
Caulfield 69,922 J5
Charlton 1,377 B5
Chelsea 26,034 J6
Churchill 4,796 D6
Clunes 761 B5
Cobden 1,453 B6
Cobram 3,817 C4
Coburg 55,035 H5
Cohuna 2,178 C4
Colac 10,587 B6
Coldstream 1,395 K4
Coleraine 1,232 A5
Collingwood 15,089 J5
Corryong 1,320 D5
Craigieburn 4,296 C5
Cranbourne 9,400 C6
Creswick 2,036 B5
Croydon 36,210 K5
Dandenong 54,962 K5
Darby D6
Dartmoor 349 A5
Daylesford 2,883 C5
Derrinallum 287 B5
Dimboola 1,675 B5
Donald 1,609 B5
Doncaster and Templestowe 90,660 J5
Drouin 3,492 C6
Dunkeld 402 B5
Dunolly 621 B5
Eaglehawk 7,355 C5
Echuca 7,943 C5
Edenhope 827 A5
Eildon 737 C5
Eltham 34,648 J4
Erica 236 D5
Essendon 56,380 H5
Euroa 2,640 C5
Fitzroy 19,112 H5
Footscray 49,756 H5
Geelong 14,471 C6
Geelong †137,173 C6
Geelong West 14,823 C6
Goroke 370 A5
Gunbower 259 C4
Hamilton 9,751 B5
Hawthorn 30,689 J5
Healesville 4,526 C5
Heathcote 1,213 C5
Heidelberg 64,757 J5
Heyfield 1,635 D6
Heywood 1,266 A6
Hopetoun 1,832 B4
Horsham 12,034 B5
Inglewood 674 B5
Inverloch 1,523 C6
Kaniva 956 A5
Keilor 81,762 H5
Kerang 4,049 B4
Kew 28,870 J5
Kilmore 1,728 C5
Knox 88,902 K5
Koroit 1,988 B6
Korumburra 2,798 D6
Kyabram 5,414 C5
Kyneton 3,185 C5
Lake Boga 502 B4
Lake Bolac 211 B5
Lakes Entrance 3,414 E5
Lara 4,231 C6
Leongatha 3,736 C6
Lillydale 62,077 J4
Macarthur 322 A6
Maffra 3,822 D5
Maldon 1,009 C5
Mallacoota 726 E5
Malvern 43,211 J5
Mansfield 1,920 D5
Maryborough 7,858 B5
Melbourne (cap.) 2,578,759 H5
Melbourne †2,722,817 H5
Melton 20,599 C5
Merbein 1,735 A4
Merino 298 A5
Mildura 15,763 A4
Minyip 567 B5
Moe 16,649 D6
Montmorency J4
Montrose K5
Moorabbin 97,810 J5
Mooroopna C5
Mordialloc 27,869 J6
Morea A5
Mornington 23,512 C6
Mortlake 1,056 B6
Morwell 16,491 D5
Mount Beauty 1,509 D5
Murrayville 313 A4
Murtoa 946 B5
Myrtleford 2,815 D5
Nagambie 1,102 C5
Narre Warren North 761 K5
Nathalia 1,222 C5
Natimuk 482 A5
Newtown 10,210 C6
Nhill 1,567 A5
Northcote 51,235 J5
Numurkah 2,713 C5
Nunawading 97,052 J5
Nyah 351 B4
Nyah West 535 B4
Oakleigh 55,612 J5
Omeo 272 D5
Orbost 2,586 E5
Ouyen 1,527 B4
Penshurst 558 B5
Porepunkah 268 D5
Port Albert 267 D6
Port Fairy 2,276 B6
Portland 9,353 A6
Port Melbourne 8,585 H5
Prahran 45,018 J5
Preston 84,519 J4
Quambatook 359 B4
Queenscliff 3,420 C6
Rainbow 700 A4
Red Cliffs 2,409 B4
Richmond 24,506 J5
Ringwood 38,665 K5
Robinvale 1,751 B4
Rochester 2,399 C5
Rushworth 994 C5
Rutherglen 1,454 D5
Saint Arnaud 2,721 B5
Saint Kilda 49,366 J5
Sale 12,968 D6
Sandringham 31,175 J5
Sea Lake 943 B4
Sebastopol 6,462 B5
Seymour 6,494 C5
Shepparton-Mooroopna ‡28,373 C5
South Barwon 35,307 C6
South Melbourne 19,955 J5
Springvale 80,186 J5
Stawell 6,160 B5
Sunbury 11,085 C5
Sunshine 94,419 H5
Swan Hill 8,398 B4
Swifts Creek 288 D5
Tallangatta 950 D5
Tatura 2,697 C5
Templestowe and Doncaster 90,660 J5
Terang 2,111 B6
Tongala 994 C5
Traralgon 18,057 D6
Underbool 274 A4
Wangaratta 16,202 D5
Warburton 2,009 C5
Warracknabeal 2,735 B5
Warragul 7,712 D6
Warrnambool 21,414 B6
Waverley 122,471 J5
Wedderburn 868 B5
Werrimull A4
Whittlesea 65,657 C5
Willaura 377 B5
Williamstown 25,554 H5
Winchelsea 825 B6
Wodonga 19,208 D5
Wonthaggi 4,797 C6
Woodend 1,785 C5
Wycheproof 938 B5
Yallourn 26 D6
Yarram 2,085 D6
Yarrawonga 3,442 C5
Yea 996 C5

OTHER FEATURES

Australian Alps (mts.) D5
Avoca (riv.) B5
Barry (mts.) D5
Bogong (mt.) D5
Bridgewater (cape) A6
Buller (mt.) D5
Campaspe (riv.) C5
Corangamite (lake) B6
Corner (inlet) D6
Dandenong (mt.) K5
Difficult (mt.) B5
Discovery (bay) A6
Eildon (lake) C5
French (isl.) 123 C6
Gippsland (reg.) D6
Glenelg (riv.) A5
Goulburn (riv.) C5
Hindmarsh (lake) A5
Hobsons (bay) H5
Hopkins (riv.) B5
Hume (lake) D4
Indian Ocean B6
Loddon (riv.) B5
Mitchell (riv.) D5
Mitta Mitta (riv.) D5
Mornington (pen.) C6
Mount Emu (creek) B5
Murray (riv.) A4
Nelson (cape) A6
Ninety Mile (beach) D6
Otway (cape) B6
Ovens (riv.) D5
Phillip (isl.) 2,832 C6
Portland (bay) A6
Port Phillip (bay) C6
Rocklands (res.) B5
Snowy (riv.) E5
South East (pt.) D6
Tasman (sea) F5
Tyrrell (lake) B4
Waratah (bay) C6
Wellington (lake) D6
Western Port (inlet) C6
Wilsons (prom.) D6
Wimmera (riv.) A5
Yarra (riv.) C5

*City and suburbs.
○ Population of district.
†Population of met. area.
‡Population of urban area.

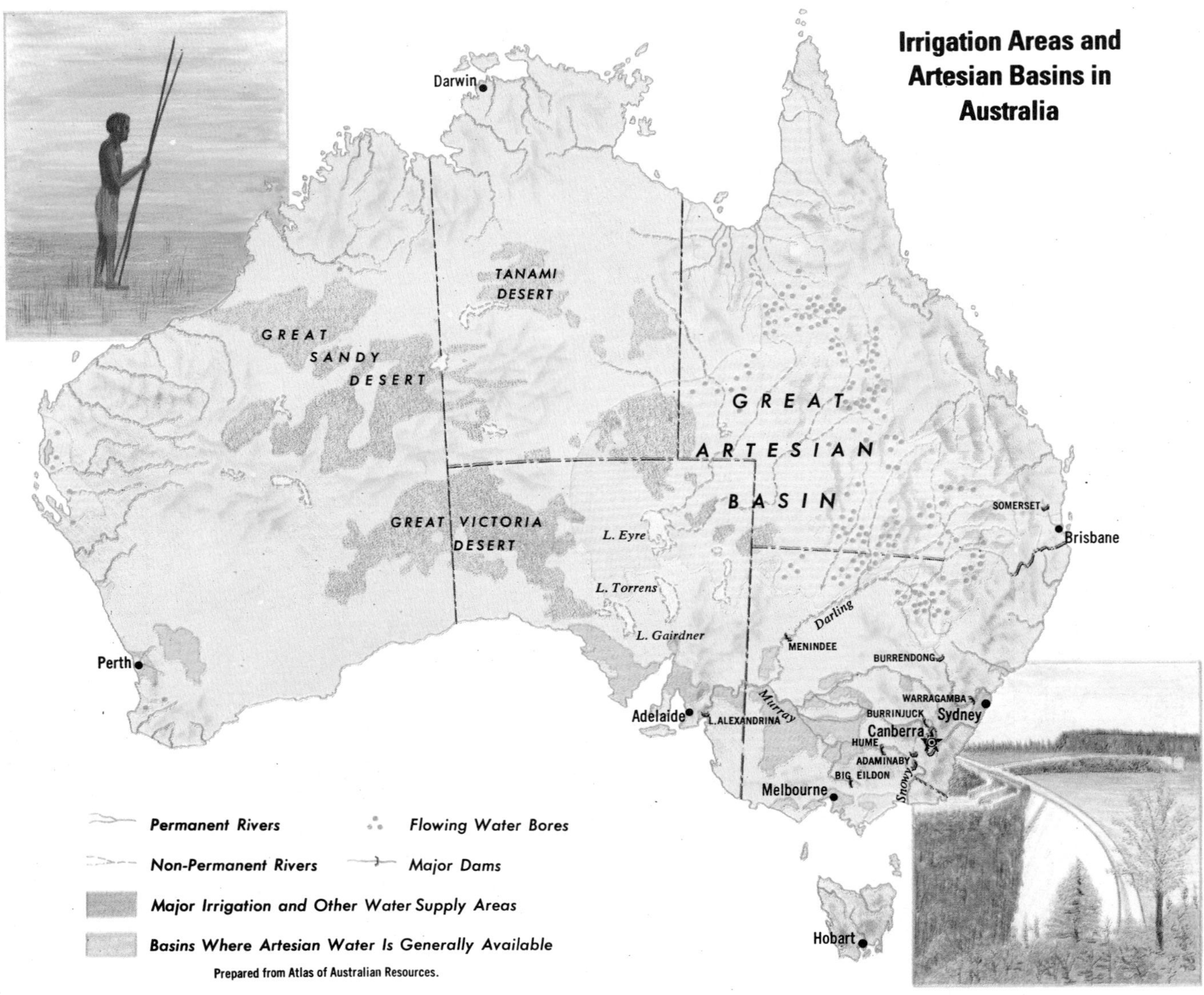

Prepared from Atlas of Australian Resources.

Topography

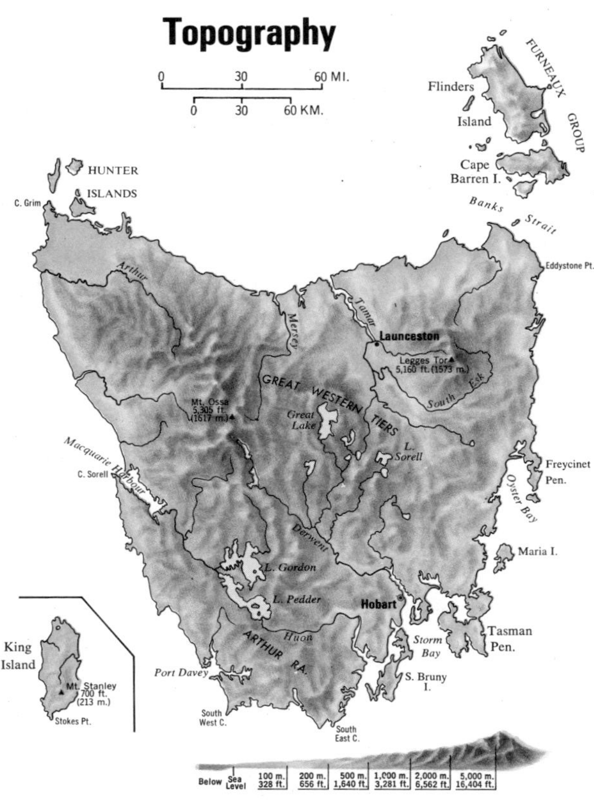

TASMANIA

AREA 26,178 sq. mi. (67,800 sq. km.)
POPULATION 418,957
CAPITAL Hobart
LARGEST CITY Hobart
HIGHEST POINT Mt. Ossa 5,305 ft. (1,617 m.)

CITIES and TOWNS

Adventure Bay ... D5
Avoca ... D3
Bagdad ... D4
Beaconsfield 898 ... C3
Beauty Point 998 ... C3
Bell Bay ... C3
Bicheno 674 ... E3
Boat Harbour ... B2
Bothwell 356 ... C4
Bracknell 347 ... C3
Branxholm 273 ... D3
Bridgewater 6,880 ... D4
Bridport 885 ... D3
Brighton 9,441 ... D4
Burnie 19,994 ... B3
Campbell Town 879 ... D3
Chudleigh ... C3
Colebrook ... D4
Cressy 640 ... C3
Currie 859 ... A1
Cygnet 715 ... C5
Deloraine 1,923 ... C3
Derwent Bridge ... C4
Devonport 21,424 ... C3
Dover 570 ... C5
Dunalley 203 ... D4
Evandale 614 ... D3
Exeter 353 ... C3
Fingal 424 ... E3
Forth 273 ... C3
Franklin 479 ... C5
Geeveston 860 ... C5
George Town 5,592 ... C3
Glenorchy 41,019 ... D4
Gormanston 126 ... B4
Gowrie Park ... C3
Grassy 780 ... B1
Gravelly Beach 535 ... C3
Hadspen 908 ... D3
Hagley 232 ... C3
Hamilton 2,488 ... C4
Heybridge 395 ... C3
Hobart (cap.) 128,603 ... D4
Hobart *168,359 ... D4
Huonville-Ranelagh 1,347 ... C5
Kettering 288 ... D5
Kingston 8,556 ... D4
Latrobe 2,401 ... C3
Lauderdale 2,117 ... D4
Launceston 31,273 ... C3
Launceston *64,555 ... C3
Legana 964 ... C3
Lilydale 308 ... D3
Longford 2,027 ... C3
Luina 522 ... B3
Margate 476 ... D4
Maydena 461 ... C4
Meander ... C3
Mole Creek 303 ... C3
New Norfolk 6,243 ... C4
Nubeena 225 ... D5
Oatlands 545 ... D4
Orford 378 ... D4
Penguin 2,616 ... C3
Perth 1,229 ... D3
Poatina ... C3
Port Sorell 859 ... C3
Queenstown 3,714 ... B4
Railton 857 ... C3
Richmond 587 ... D4
Ridgley 452 ... B3
Ringarooma 223 ... D3
Rosebery 2,675 ... B3
Ross 289 ... D4
Rossarden 365 ... D3
Saint Helens 1,005 ... E3
Saint Marys 653 ... E3
Sassafras ... C3
Savage River 1,141 ... B3
Scottsdale 2,002 ... D3
Sheffield 945 ... C3
Smithton 3,378 ... A2
Snug 684 ... D5
Sorell-Midway Point 2,544 ... D4
Stanley 603 ... B2
Storeys Creek ... D3
Strahan 402 ... B4
Strathgordon ... C4
Sulphur Creek 367 ... C3
Swansea 428 ... D4
Tarraleah 498 ... C4
Temma ... A3
Triabunna 924 ... D4
Tullah 1,894 ... B3
Ulverstone 9,413 ... C3
Waratah 342 ... B3
Wesley Vale ... C3
Westbury 1,161 ... C3
Whitemark ... D2
Woodbridge 259 ... D5
Wynyard 4,582 ... B3
Zeehan 1,750 ... B3

OTHER FEATURES

Anderson (bay) ... D2
Anne (mt.) ... C4
Anser Group (isls.) ... C1
Arthur (lake) ... D4
Arthur (range) ... C5
Arthur (riv.) ... B3
Babel (isl.) ... E1
Banks (str.) ... D2
Barn Bluff (mt.) ... B3
Barren (cape) ... E2
Bass (str.) ... C1
Bathurst (gulf) ... C5
Cape Barren (isl.) ... E2
Chappell (isls.) ... D2
Circular (gulf) ... B2
Clarke (isl.) ... E2
Clyde (riv.) ... D4
Cox (bight) ... C5
Cradle (mt.) ... B3
Cradle Mt. Lake St. Clair Nat'l Park ... B3
Crescent (lake) ... D4
Curtis Group (isls.) ... C1
D'Aguilar (range) ... B4
Davey (riv.) ... B4
Deal (isl.) ... D1
Dee (riv.) ... C4
Denison (range) ... C4
D'Entrecasteaux (chan.) ... D5
Derwent (riv.) ... C4
East Sister (isl.) ... E1
Echo (lake) ... C4
Eddystone (pt.) ... E2
Elliott (bay) ... B5
Fires (bay) ... E3
Flinders (isl.) 2,150 ... D1
Florence (riv.) ... C4
Forestier (chan.) ... E4
Forestier (pen.) ... E4
Forth (riv.) ... C3
Frankland (cape) ... D1
Frankland (range) ... B4
Franklin (riv.) ... B4
Frenchmans Cap (mt.) ... B4
Freycinet (pen.) ... E4
Furneaux Group (isls.) 1,039 ... E1
Gordon (lake) ... C4
Gordon (riv.) ... B4
Great (lake) ... C3
Great Western Tiers (mts.) ... C3
Grim (cape) ... A2
Hartz (mt.) ... C5
Hibbs (pt.) ... B4
Hogan Group (isl.) ... D1
Hummock (isl.) ... D2
Hunter (isl.) ... A2
Hunter (isls.) ... B2
Huon (riv.) ... C5
Indian Ocean ... A4
Kent Group (isls.) ... D1
King (isl.) 2,592 ... A1
King (riv.) ... B4
King William (lake) ... C4
Lake (riv.) ... D3
Legges Tor (mt.) ... D3
Leven (riv.) ... B3
Lofty (range) ... B3
Low Rocky (pt.) ... B4
Lyell (mt.) ... B4
Maatsuyker (isls.) ... C5
Macquarie (harb.) ... B4
Macquarie (riv.) ... D3
Maria (isl.) ... E4
Marion (bay) ... E4
Mersey (riv.) ... C3
Munro (mt.) ... E2
Naturaliste (cape) ... E2
Nive (riv.) ... C4
Norfolk (bay) ... D4
North (pt.) ... E1
North Bruny (isl.) ... D5
North Esk (riv.) ... D3
Ossa (mt.) ... C3
Ouse (riv.) ... C4
Oyster (bay) ... E4
Pedder (riv.) ... B4
Phoques (bay) ... A1
Picton (mt.) ... C5
Pieman (riv.) ... B3
Pillar (cape) ... E5
Port Davey (inlet) ... B5
Portland (cape) ... D2
Ramsey (mt.) ... B3
Raoul (cape) ... D5
Reid (rapid) ... B1
Ringarooma (bay) ... D2
Robbins (isl.) ... B2
Saint Clair (lake) ... C4
Saint Helens (pt.) ... E3
Saint Vincent (cape) ... B5
Savage (riv.) ... B3
Schouten (isl.) ... E4
Sorell (cape) ... B4
Sorell (lake) ... D4
South (cape) ... C5
South Bruny (isl.) ... D5
South East (cape) ... C5
South Esk (riv.) ... D3
South West (cape) ... B5
Stanley (mt.) ... A1
Stokes (pt.) ... A1
Storm (bay) ... D5
Strzelecki (mt.) ... D2
Tamar (riv.) ... D3
Tasman (head) ... D5
Tasman (pen.) ... E5
Tasman (sea) ... E4
Three Hummock (isl.) ... B2
Vansittart (isl.) ... E2
West (pt.) ... A2
West Sister (isl.) ... D1
Wickham (cape) ... A1

○ Population of district.
*Population of met. area.

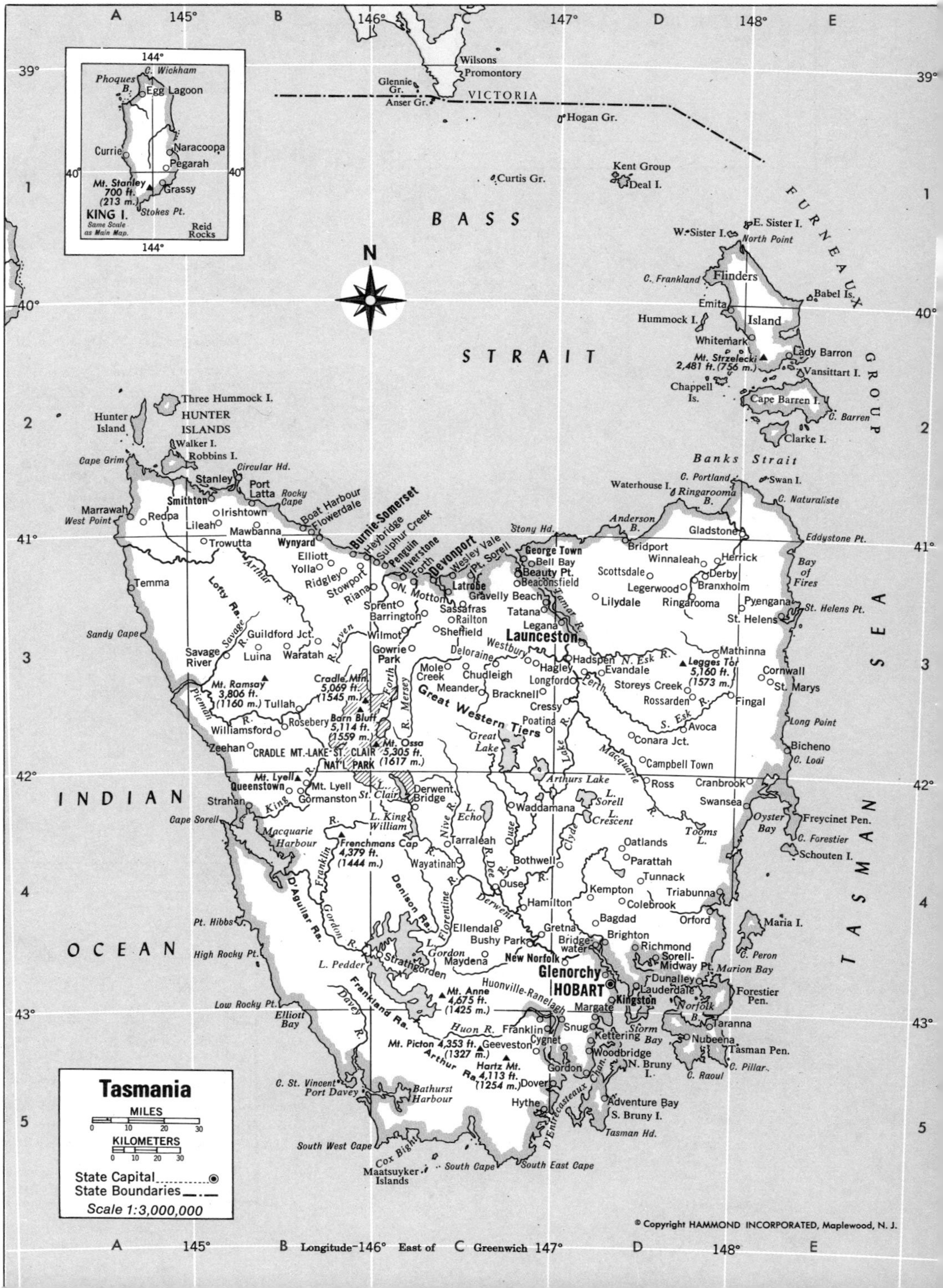

Tasmania

MILES 0 10 20 30
KILOMETERS 0 10 20 30
State Capital ◉
State Boundaries
Scale 1:3,000,000

Longitude 146° East of Greenwich 147°

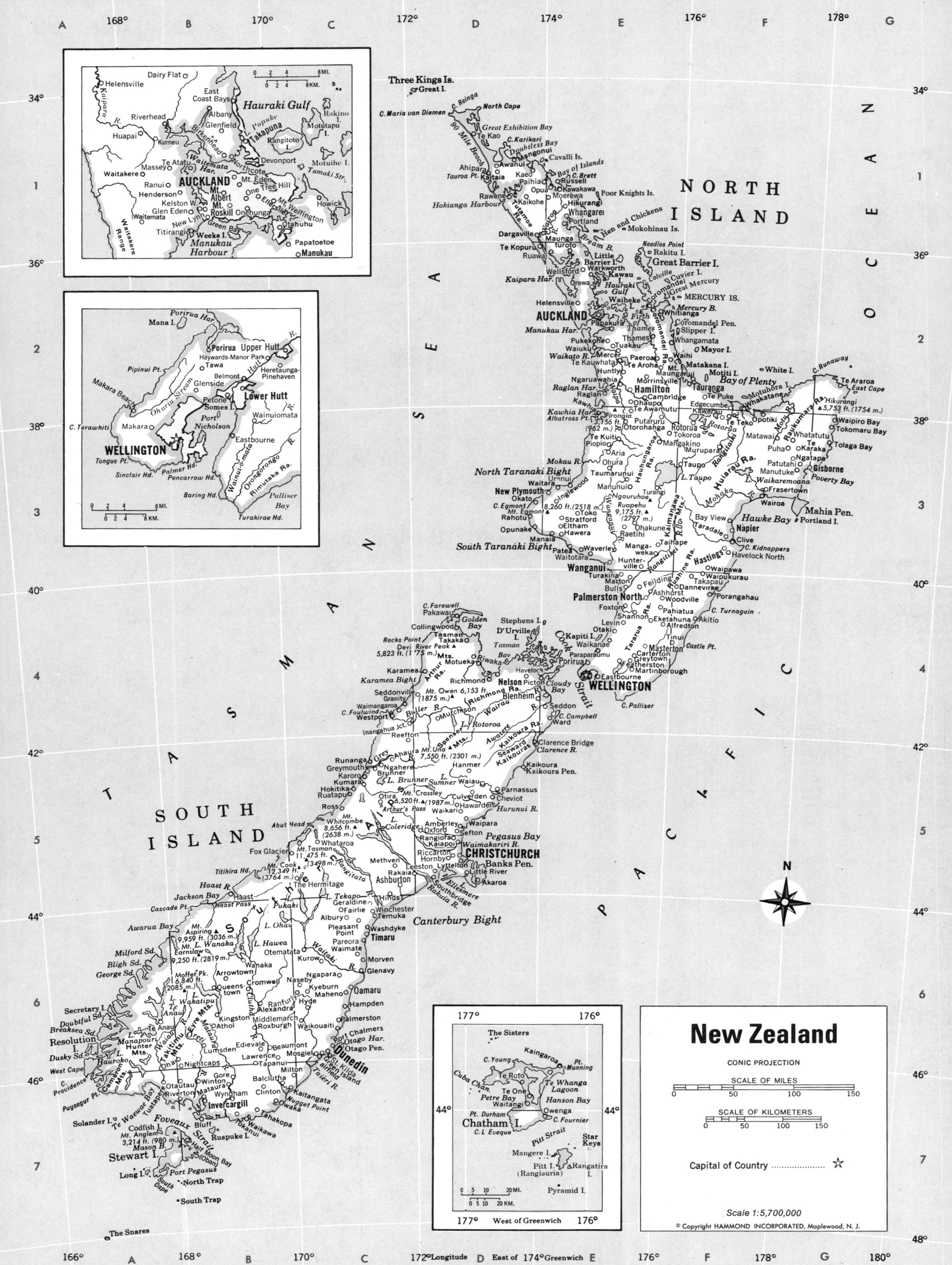

New Zealand
CONIC PROJECTION
SCALE OF MILES
0 50 100 150
SCALE OF KILOMETERS
0 50 100 150
Capital of Country
Scale 1:5,700,000
© Copyright HAMMOND INCORPORATED, Maplewood, N. J.
NORTH ISLAND
SOUTH ISLAND
TASMAN SEA
PACIFIC OCEAN
Longitude East of Greenwich
Three Kings Is.
Great I.
C. Reinga
North Cape
C. Maria van Diemen
90 Mile Beach
Great Exhibition Bay
Te Kao
C. Karikari
Doubtless Bay
Mangonui
Cavalli Is.
Ahipara
Awanui
Tauroa Pt.
Kaitaia
Kaeo
Bay of Islands
C. Brett
Paihia
Russell
Opua
Kawakawa
Poor Knights Is.
Rawene
Kaikohe
Moerewa
Hokianga Harbour
Hikurangi
Whangarei
Portland
Hen and Chickens
Mokohinau Is.
Dargaville
Maunga turoto
Bream B.
Te Kopuru
Ruawai
Needles Point
Rakitu I.
Little Barrier I.
Great Barrier I.
Warkworth
Kawau I.
Wellsford
Kaipara Har.
Orewa
Hauraki Gulf
Colville
Cuvier I.
Great Mercury
MERCURY IS.
Waiheke I.
Helensville
AUCKLAND
Papakura
Firth of Thames
Mercury B.
Whitianga
Coromandel Pen.
Slipper I.
Manukau Har.
Pukekohe
Thames
Whangamata
Waiuku
Tuakau
Mayor I.
Waikato R.
Mercer
Paeroa
Waihi
Te Kauwhata
Te Aroha
Matakana I.
Huntly
Mt. Maunganui
Motiti I.
White I.
C. Runaway
Ngaruawahia
Morrinsville
Bay of Plenty
Te Araroa
Raglan Har.
Hamilton
Tauranga
East Cape
Raglan
Cambridge
Te Puke
Motuhora I.
Hikurangi 5,753 ft. (1754 m.)
Ohaupo
Edgecumbe
Whakatane
Kawhia Har.
Te Awamutu
Kawerau
Albatross Pt.
Pirongia 3,156 ft. (962 m.)
Putaruru
Rotorua
Te Teko
Opotiki
Waipiro Bay
Tokomaru Bay
Otorohanga
Tokoroa
Te Kuiti
Mangakino
Whatatutu
Tolaga Bay
Piopio
Murupara
Matawai
Puha
Te Karaka
Ngatapa
Aria
Patutahi
Gisborne
Mokau R.
Ohura
Taupo
Manutuke
Poverty Bay
North Taranaki Bight
Taumarunui
L. Taupo
Huiarau Ra.
L. Waikaremoana
Urenui
Manunui
Turangi
Frasertown
New Plymouth
Waitara
Ngauruhoe
Okato
Ruapehu 9,175 ft. (2797 m.)
Wairoa
Mahia Pen.
C. Egmont
Mt. Egmont 8,260 ft. (2518 m.)
Toko
Rahotu
Stratford
Hawke Bay
Portland I.
Eltham
Bay View
Opunake
Hawera
Ohakune
Raetihi
Napier
Manaia
Taihape
Clive
South Taranaki Bight
Patea
Waverley
Manga-weka
C. Kidnappers
Waitotara
Hastings
Havelock North
Wanganui
Hunter-ville
Waipawa
Turakina
Waipukurau
Marton
Feilding
Takapau
Bulls
Ashhurst
Dannevirke
Palmerston North
Porangahau
Foxton
Woodville
Pahiatua
C. Turnagain
Levin
Shannon
Eketahuna
Akitio
Otaki
Alfredton
Kapiti I.
Waikanae
Tinui
Paraparaumu
Masterton
Castle Pt.
Porirua
Carterton
Greytown
Featherston
Martinborough
Eastbourne
WELLINGTON
C. Palliser
Cook Strait
Stephens I.
D'Urville I.
C. Farewell
Pakawau
Golden Bay
Collingwood
Tasman Bay
Takaka
Rocks Point
Devil River Peak 5,823 ft. (1775 m.)
Tasman Mts.
Motueka
Riwaka
Havelock
Karamea
Karamea Bight
Richmond
Nelson
Picton
Cloudy Bay
Seddonville
Mt. Owen 6,153 ft. (1875 m.)
Blenheim
Granity
Richmond Ra.
Waimangaroa
Seddon
C. Foulwind
Westport
Buller R.
Murchison
Wairau R.
C. Campbell
Ward
L. Rotoroa
Inangahua Jct.
Reefton
Spenser Mts.
Awatere R.
Kaikoura Ra.
Clarence Bridge
Clarence R.
Ahaura
Mt. Una 7,550 ft. (2301 m.)
Seaward Kaikouras
Runanga
Greymouth
Ngahere
Brunner
Hanmer
Kaikoura
Kaikoura Pen.
Kumara
L. Brunner
L. Sumner
Waiau
Hokitika
Ruatapu
Parnassus
Mt. Crossley 6,520 ft. (1987 m.)
Culverden
Cheviot
Otira
Hawarden
Waikari
Hurunui R.
Ross
Arthur's Pass
Abut Head
Mt. Whitcombe 8,656 ft. (2638 m.)
L. Coleridge
Amberley
Waipara
Oxford
Sefton
Pegasus Bay
Rangiora
Whataroa
Kaiapoi
Waimakariri R.
Fox Glacier
Mt. Tasman 11,475 ft. (3498 m.)
Riccarton
CHRISTCHURCH
Mt. Cook 12,349 ft. (3764 m.)
Methven
Hornby
Lyttelton
Banks Pen.
Titihira Hd.
Rakaia
Leeston
Little River
Rangitata R.
Ashburton
Akaroa
Haast R.
The Hermitage
Lake Ellesmere
Southbridge
Rakaia R.
Jackson Bay
Haast
Haast Pass
L. Tekapo
Geraldine
Hinds
Cascade Pt.
Pukaki
Fairlie
Winchester
Temuka
Canterbury Bight
Awarua Bay
L. Ohau
Albury
Mt. Aspiring 9,959 ft. (3036 m.)
Pleasant Point
Washdyke
Timaru
Mt. Earnslaw 9,250 ft. (2819 m.)
L. Wanaka
L. Hawea
Pareora
Waimate
Otematata
Milford Sd.
Bligh Sd.
Waitaki R.
Morven
Kurow
George Sd.
Wanaka
Glenavy
Moffet Pk. 6,840 ft. (2085 m.)
Arrowtown
Ngapara
Queenstown
Cromwell
Naseby
Oamaru
Kyeburn
Maheno
Secretary I.
L. Wakatipu
Ranfurly
Doubtful Sd.
L. Te Anau
Alexandra
Hyde
Hampden
Breaksea Sd.
Te Anau
Kingston
Middlemarch
Palmerston
Resolution I.
Athol
Roxburgh
Waikouaiti
L. Manapouri
Port Chalmers
Dusky Sd.
Hunter Mts.
Edievale
Beaumont
Otago Har.
Otago Pen.
Lumsden
Mosgiel
Dunedin
West Cape
L. Hauroko
Lawrence
Nightcaps
Tapanui
St. Kilda
Island
Taieri R.
C. Providence
Ohai
Gore
Milton
Winton
Balclutha
Puysegur Pt.
Otautau
Mataura
Kaitangata
Riverton
Wyndham
Clinton
Nugget Point
Owaka
Te Waewae Bay
Invercargill
Solander I.
Bluff
Tahakopa
Foveaux Strait
Waikawa
Tokanui
Codfish I.
Ruapuke I.
Mt. Anglem 3,214 ft. (980 m.)
Half Moon Bay (Oban)
Mason B.
Stewart I.
Long I.
Port Pegasus
South Cape
North Trap
South Trap
The Snares
Helensville
Dairy Flat
Kaipara R.
East Coast Bays
Hauraki Gulf
Riverhead
Albany
Rakino I.
Glenfield
L. Pupuke
Motutapu I.
Huapai
Kumeu
Takapuna
Rangitoto I.
Birkenhead
Te Atatu
Devonport
Motuihe I.
Waitakere
Massey
Waitemata Har.
Northcote
Tamaki Str.
Ranui
AUCKLAND
Mt. Eden
One Tree Hill
Henderson
Mt. Albert
Howick
Kelston W.
Glen Eden
Mt. Roskill
Ellerslie
Mt. Wellington
Waitemata
New Lynn
Onehunga
Otahuhu
Titirangi
Green Bay
Weeks I.
Waitakere Range
Manukau Harbour
Papatoetoe
Manukau
Porirua Har.
Mana I.
Porirua
Upper Hutt
Hutt R.
Haywards-Manor Park
Tawa
Pipinui Pt.
Heretaunga-Pinehaven
Belmont
Makara Beach
Glenside
Ohariu Stream
Petone
Lower Hutt
Somes I.
Port Nicholson
Wainuiomata
C. Terawhiti
Makara
WELLINGTON
Eastbourne
Tongue Pt.
Wainui-o-mata R.
Orongorongo R.
Sinclair Hd.
Palmer Hd.
Pencarrow Hd.
Rimutaka Ra.
Baring Hd.
Palliser Bay
Turakirae Hd.
The Sisters
Kaingaroa
Pt. Munning
C. Young
Cuba Chan.
Te Roto
Te One
Te Whanga Lagoon
Petre Bay
Waitangi
Hanson Bay
Pt. Durham
Chatham I.
Owenga
C. Fournier
C. L. Eveque
Pitt Strait
Star Keys
Mangere I.
Pitt I. (Rangiauria)
Rangatira I.
Pyramid I.
West of Greenwich

Topography

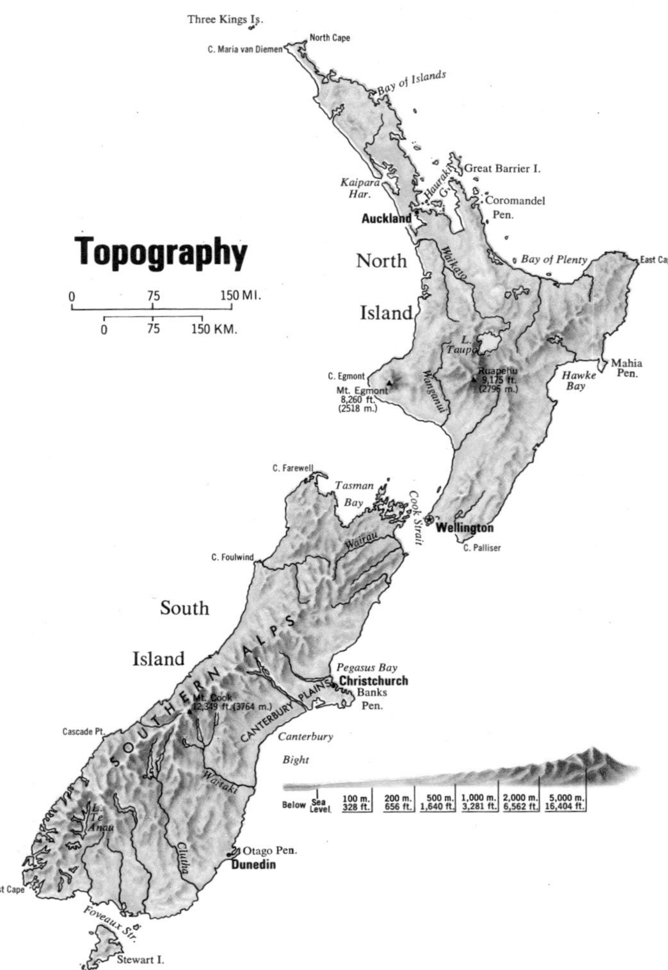

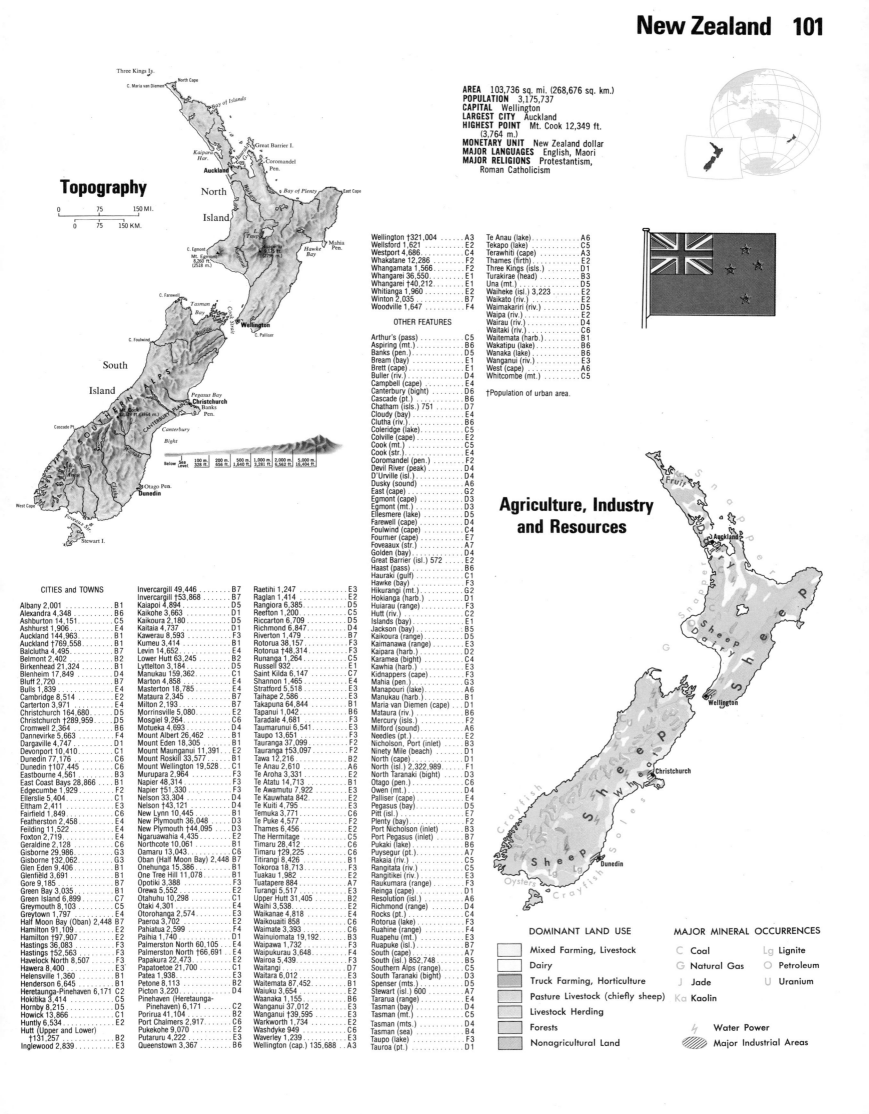

AREA 103,736 sq. mi. (268,676 sq. km.)
POPULATION 3,175,737
CAPITAL Wellington
LARGEST CITY Auckland
HIGHEST POINT Mt. Cook 12,349 ft. (3,764 m.)
MONETARY UNIT New Zealand dollar
MAJOR LANGUAGES English, Maori
MAJOR RELIGIONS Protestantism, Roman Catholicism

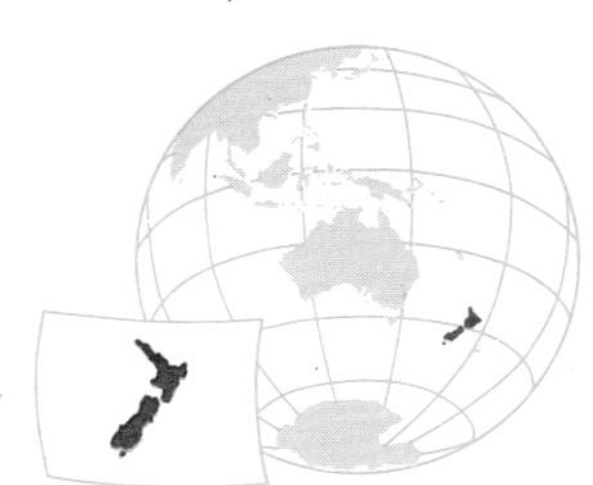

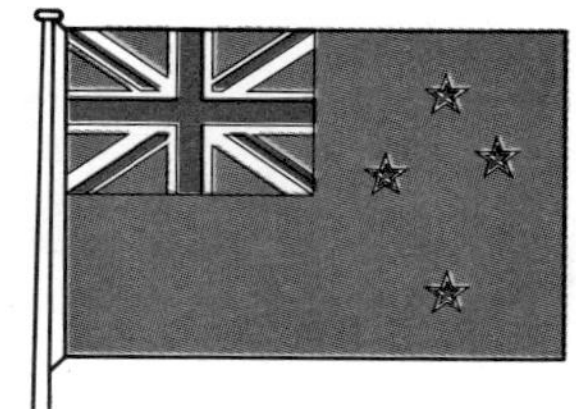

CITIES and TOWNS

Albany 2,001 .... B1
Alexandra 4,348 .... B6
Ashburton 14,151 .... C5
Ashhurst 1,906 .... E4
Auckland 144,963 .... B1
Auckland †769,558 .... B1
Balclutha 4,495 .... B7
Belmont 2,402 .... B2
Birkenhead 21,324 .... B1
Blenheim 17,849 .... D4
Bluff 2,720 .... B7
Bulls 1,839 .... E4
Cambridge 8,514 .... E2
Carterton 3,971 .... E4
Christchurch 164,680 .... D5
Christchurch †289,959 .... D5
Cromwell 2,364 .... B6
Dannevirke 5,663 .... F4
Dargaville 4,747 .... D1
Devonport 10,410 .... C1
Dunedin 77,176 .... C6
Dunedin †107,445 .... C6
Eastbourne 4,561 .... B3
East Coast Bays 28,866 .... B1
Edgecumbe 1,929 .... F2
Ellerslie 5,404 .... C1
Eltham 2,411 .... E3
Fairfield 1,849 .... C6
Featherston 2,458 .... E4
Feilding 11,522 .... E4
Foxton 2,719 .... E4
Geraldine 2,128 .... C6
Gisborne 29,986 .... G3
Gisborne †32,062 .... G3
Glen Eden 9,406 .... B1
Glenfield 3,691 .... B1
Gore 9,185 .... B7
Green Bay 3,035 .... B1
Green Island 6,899 .... C7
Greymouth 8,103 .... C5
Greytown 1,797 .... E4
Half Moon Bay (Oban) 2,448 B7
Hamilton 91,109 .... E2
Hamilton †97,907 .... E2
Hastings 36,083 .... F3
Hastings †52,563 .... F3
Havelock North 8,507 .... F3
Hawera 8,400 .... E3
Helensville 1,360 .... B1
Henderson 6,645 .... B1
Heretaunga-Pinehaven 6,171 C2
Hokitika 3,414 .... C5
Hornby 8,215 .... D5
Howick 13,866 .... C1
Huntly 6,534 .... E2
Hutt (Upper and Lower) †131,257 .... B2
Inglewood 2,839 .... E3
Invercargill 49,446 .... B7
Invercargill †53,868 .... B7
Kaiapoi 4,894 .... D5
Kaikohe 3,663 .... D1
Kaikoura 2,180 .... D5
Kaitaia 4,737 .... D1
Kawerau 8,593 .... F3
Kumeu 3,414 .... B1
Levin 14,652 .... E4
Lower Hutt 63,245 .... B2
Lyttelton 3,184 .... D5
Manukau 159,362 .... C1
Marton 4,858 .... E4
Masterton 18,785 .... E4
Mataura 2,345 .... B7
Milton 2,193 .... B7
Morrinsville 5,080 .... E2
Mosgiel 9,264 .... C6
Motueka 4,693 .... D4
Mount Albert 26,462 .... B1
Mount Eden 18,305 .... B1
Mount Maunganui 11,391 .... E2
Mount Roskill 33,577 .... B1
Mount Wellington 19,528 .... C1
Murupara 2,964 .... F3
Napier 48,314 .... F3
Napier †51,330 .... F3
Nelson 33,304 .... D4
Nelson †43,121 .... D4
New Lynn 10,445 .... B1
New Plymouth 36,048 .... D3
New Plymouth †44,095 .... D3
Ngaruawahia 4,435 .... E2
Northcote 10,061 .... B1
Oamaru 13,043 .... C6
Oban (Half Moon Bay) 2,448 B7
Onehunga 15,386 .... B1
One Tree Hill 11,078 .... B1
Opotiki 3,388 .... F3
Orewa 5,552 .... E2
Otahuhu 10,298 .... C1
Otaki 4,301 .... E4
Otorohanga 2,574 .... E3
Paeroa 3,702 .... E2
Pahiatua 2,599 .... F4
Paihia 1,740 .... D1
Palmerston North 60,105 .... E4
Palmerston North †66,691 .... E4
Papakura 22,473 .... E2
Papatoetoe 21,700 .... C1
Patea 1,938 .... E3
Petone 8,113 .... B2
Picton 3,220 .... D4
Pinehaven (Heretaunga-Pinehaven) 6,171 .... C2
Porirua 41,104 .... B2
Port Chalmers 2,917 .... C6
Pukekohe 9,070 .... E2
Putaruru 4,222 .... E3
Queenstown 3,367 .... B6
Raetihi 1,247 .... E3
Raglan 1,414 .... E2
Rangiora 6,385 .... D5
Reefton 1,200 .... C5
Riccarton 6,709 .... D5
Richmond 6,847 .... D4
Riverton 1,479 .... B7
Rotorua 38,157 .... F3
Rotorua †48,314 .... F3
Runanga 1,264 .... C5
Russell 932 .... E1
Saint Kilda 6,147 .... C7
Shannon 1,465 .... E4
Stratford 5,518 .... E3
Taihape 2,586 .... E3
Takapuna 64,844 .... B1
Tapanui 1,042 .... B6
Taradale 4,681 .... F3
Taumarunui 6,541 .... E3
Taupo 13,651 .... F3
Tauranga 37,099 .... F2
Tauranga †53,097 .... F2
Tawa 12,216 .... B2
Te Anau 2,610 .... A6
Te Aroha 3,331 .... E2
Te Atatu 14,713 .... B1
Te Awamutu 7,922 .... E3
Te Kauwhata 842 .... E2
Te Kuiti 4,795 .... E3
Temuka 3,771 .... C6
Te Puke 4,577 .... F2
Thames 6,456 .... E2
The Hermitage C5
Timaru 28,412 .... C6
Timaru †29,225 .... C6
Titirangi 8,426 .... B1
Tokoroa 18,713 .... F3
Tuakau 1,982 .... E2
Tuatapere 884 .... A7
Turangi 5,517 .... E3
Upper Hutt 31,405 .... B2
Waihi 3,538 .... E2
Waikanae 4,818 .... E4
Waikouaiti 858 .... C6
Waimate 3,393 .... C6
Wainuiomata 19,192 .... B3
Waipawa 1,732 .... F3
Waipukurau 3,648 .... F4
Wairoa 5,439 .... F3
Waitangi D7
Waitara 6,012 .... E3
Waitemata 87,452 .... B1
Waiuku 3,654 .... E2
Waanaka 1,155 .... B6
Wanganui 37,012 .... E3
Wanganui †39,595 .... E3
Warkworth 1,734 .... E2
Washdyke 949 .... C6
Waverley 1,239 .... E3
Wellington (cap.) 135,688 .... A3
Wellington †321,004 .... A3
Wellsford 1,621 .... E2
Westport 4,686 .... C4
Whakatane 12,286 .... F2
Whangamata 1,566 .... F2
Whangarei 36,550 .... E1
Whangarei †40,212 .... E1
Whitianga 1,960 .... E2
Winton 2,035 .... B7
Woodville 1,647 .... F4

OTHER FEATURES

Arthur's (pass) C5
Aspiring (mt.) B6
Banks (pen.) D5
Bream (bay) E1
Brett (cape) E1
Buller (riv.) D4
Campbell (cape) E4
Canterbury (bight) D6
Cascade (pt.) B6
Chatham (isls.) 751 .... D7
Cloudy (bay) E4
Clutha (riv.) B6
Coleridge (lake) C5
Colville (cape) E2
Cook (mt.) C5
Cook (str.) E4
Coromandel (pen.) F2
Devil River (peak) D4
D'Urville (isl.) D4
Dusky (sound) A6
East (cape) G2
Egmont (cape) D3
Egmont (mt.) D3
Ellesmere (lake) D5
Farewell (cape) D4
Foulwind (cape) C4
Fournier (cape) E7
Foveaux (str.) A7
Golden (bay) D4
Great Barrier (isl.) 572 .... E2
Haast (pass) B6
Hauraki (gulf) C1
Hawke (bay) F3
Hikurangi (mt.) G2
Hokianga (harb.) D1
Huiarau (range) F3
Hutt (riv.) C2
Islands (bay) E1
Jackson (bay) B5
Kaikoura (range) D5
Kaimanawa (range) E3
Kaipara (harb.) D2
Karamea (bight) C4
Kawhia (harb.) E3
Kidnappers (cape) F3
Mahia (pen.) G3
Manapouri (lake) A6
Manukau (harb.) B1
Maria van Diemen (cape) D1
Mataura (riv.) B6
Mercury (isls.) F2
Milford (sound) A6
Needles (pt.) E2
Nicholson, Port (inlet) B3
Ninety Mile (beach) D1
North (cape) D1
North (isl.) 2,322,989 .... F1
North Taranaki (bight) D3
Otago (pen.) C6
Owen (mt.) D4
Palliser (cape) E4
Pegasus (bay) D5
Pitt (isl.) E7
Plenty (bay) F2
Port Nicholson (inlet) B3
Port Pegasus (inlet) B7
Pukaki (lake) B6
Puysegur (pt.) A7
Rakaia (riv.) C5
Rangitata (riv.) C5
Rangitikei (riv.) E3
Raukumara (range) F3
Reinga (cape) D1
Resolution (isl.) A6
Richmond (range) D4
Rocks (pt.) C4
Rotorua (lake) F3
Ruahine (range) F4
Ruapehu (mt.) E3
Ruapuke (isl.) B7
South (cape) A7
South (isl.) 852,748 .... B5
Southern Alps (range) C5
South Taranaki (bight) D3
Spenser (mts.) D5
Stewart (isl.) 600 .... A7
Tararua (range) E4
Tasman (bay) D4
Tasman (mt.) C5
Tasman (mts.) D4
Tasman (sea) B4
Taupo (lake) F3
Tauroa (pt.) D1
Te Anau (lake) A6
Tekapo (lake) C5
Terawhiti (cape) A3
Thames (firth) E2
Three Kings (isls.) D1
Turakirae (head) B3
Una (mt.) D5
Waiheke (isl.) 3,223 .... E2
Waikato (riv.) E2
Waimakariri (riv.) D5
Waipa (riv.) E2
Wairau (riv.) D4
Waitaki (riv.) C6
Waitemata (harb.) B1
Wakatipu (lake) B6
Wanaka (lake) B6
Wanganui (riv.) E3
West (cape) A6
Whitcombe (mt.) C5

†Population of urban area.

Agriculture, Industry and Resources

Auckland
Wellington
Christchurch
Dunedin
Fruit
Snapper
Sheep
Dairy
Wheat
Crayfish
Soles
Oysters

DOMINANT LAND USE

- Mixed Farming, Livestock
- Dairy
- Truck Farming, Horticulture
- Pasture Livestock (chiefly sheep)
- Livestock Herding
- Forests
- Nonagricultural Land

MAJOR MINERAL OCCURRENCES

- C Coal
- G Natural Gas
- J Jade
- Ka Kaolin
- Lg Lignite
- O Petroleum
- U Uranium
- Water Power
- Major Industrial Areas

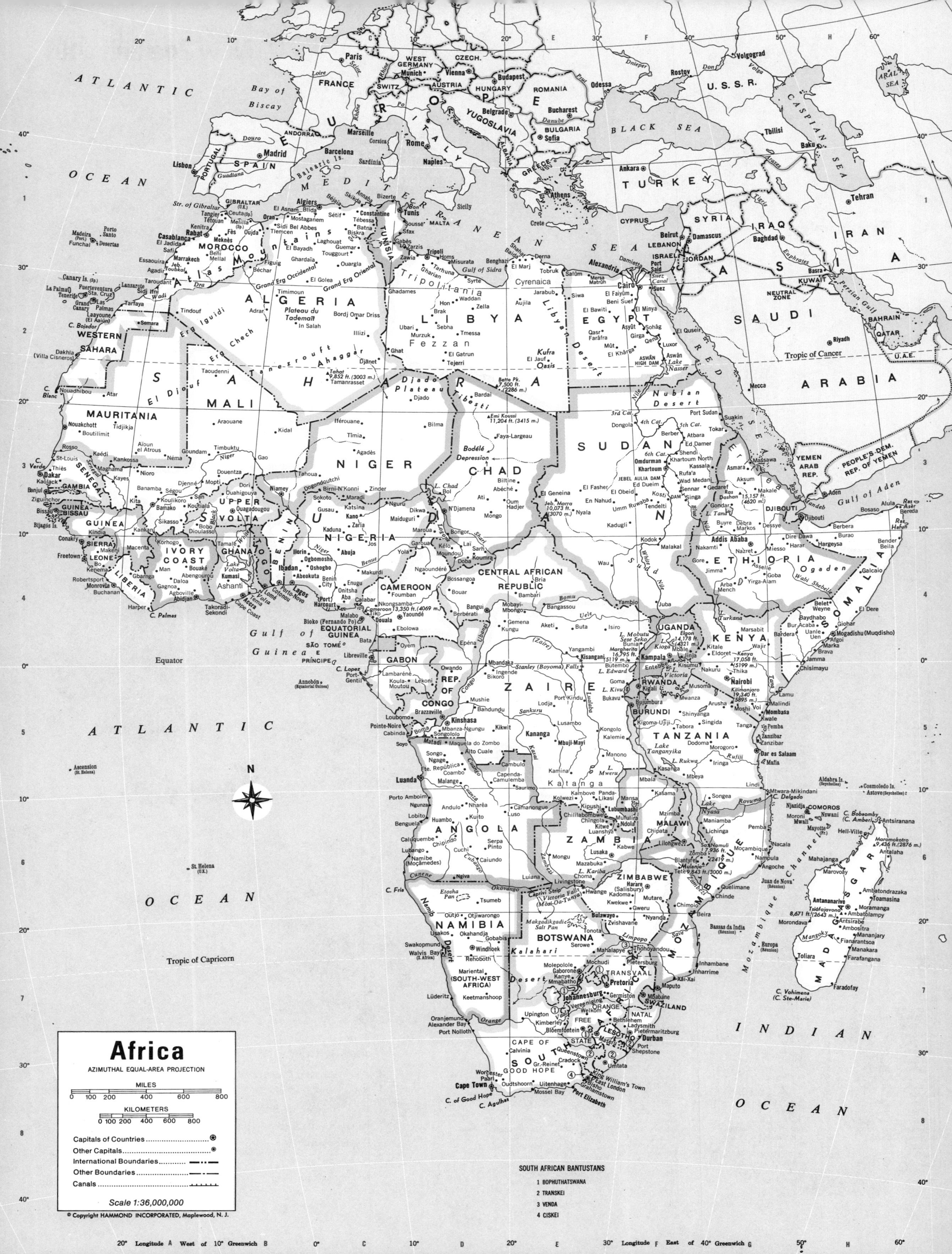

Africa
AZIMUTHAL EQUAL-AREA PROJECTION
MILES
0 100 200 400 600 800
KILOMETERS
0 100 200 400 600 800
Capitals of Countries
Other Capitals
International Boundaries
Other Boundaries
Canals
Scale 1:36,000,000
© Copyright HAMMOND INCORPORATED, Maplewood, N. J.
SOUTH AFRICAN BANTUSTANS
1 BOPHUTHATSWANA
2 TRANSKEI
3 VENDA
4 CISKEI
20° Longitude A West of 10° Greenwich B
0° C 10° D 20° E
30° Longitude F East of 40° Greenwich G
50° H 60°
ATLANTIC OCEAN
INDIAN OCEAN
MEDITERRANEAN SEA
BLACK SEA
CASPIAN SEA
ARAL SEA
RED SEA
Bay of Biscay
Gulf of Guinea
Gulf of Aden
Persian Gulf
Mozambique Channel
Equator
Tropic of Cancer
Tropic of Capricorn
EUROPE
ASIA
SAHARA
FRANCE
SPAIN
PORTUGAL
ITALY
WEST GERMANY
SWITZ.
AUSTRIA
CZECH.
HUNGARY
ROMANIA
BULGARIA
YUGOSLAVIA
ALBANIA
GREECE
TURKEY
U.S.S.R.
SYRIA
LEBANON
ISRAEL
JORDAN
IRAQ
IRAN
KUWAIT
NEUTRAL ZONE
BAHRAIN
QATAR
U.A.E.
SAUDI ARABIA
YEMEN ARAB REP.
PEOPLE'S DEM. REP. OF YEMEN
MOROCCO
ALGERIA
TUNISIA
LIBYA
EGYPT
WESTERN SAHARA
MAURITANIA
MALI
NIGER
CHAD
SUDAN
SENEGAL
GAMBIA
GUINEA-BISSAU
GUINEA
SIERRA LEONE
LIBERIA
IVORY COAST
UPPER VOLTA
GHANA
TOGO
BENIN
NIGERIA
CAMEROON
CENTRAL AFRICAN REPUBLIC
ETHIOPIA
DJIBOUTI
SOMALIA
EQUATORIAL GUINEA
GABON
REP. OF CONGO
ZAIRE
UGANDA
KENYA
RWANDA
BURUNDI
TANZANIA
ANGOLA
ZAMBIA
MALAWI
MOZAMBIQUE
ZIMBABWE
NAMIBIA (SOUTH-WEST AFRICA)
BOTSWANA
SWAZILAND
LESOTHO
SOUTH AFRICA
TRANSVAAL
ORANGE FREE STATE
NATAL
CAPE OF GOOD HOPE
MADAGASCAR
COMOROS
Paris
Madrid
Lisbon
Rome
Vienna
Budapest
Belgrade
Bucharest
Sofia
Athens
Ankara
Tehran
Baghdad
Damascus
Beirut
Riyadh
Cairo
Alexandria
Tripoli
Tunis
Algiers
Rabat
Casablanca
Nouakchott
Dakar
Banjul
Bissau
Conakry
Freetown
Monrovia
Abidjan
Accra
Lomé
Porto-Novo
Lagos
Niamey
Ouagadougou
N'Djamena
Khartoum
Addis Ababa
Djibouti
Mogadishu (Muqdisho)
Nairobi
Kampala
Kigali
Bujumbura
Dar es Salaam
Kinshasa
Brazzaville
Libreville
Malabo
Yaoundé
Bangui
Luanda
Lusaka
Lilongwe
Harare (Salisbury)
Maputo
Gaborone
Windhoek
Pretoria
Johannesburg
Maseru
Mbabane
Cape Town
Durban
Port Elizabeth
East London
Antananarivo
Moroni
Atlas Mountains
Ahaggar
Tibesti
Lake Chad
Lake Victoria
Lake Tanganyika
Lake Nyasa
Nile
Congo
Zambezi
Niger
Kilimanjaro 19,340 ft. (5895 m.)
Kenya 17,058 ft. (5199 m.)
Emi Koussi 11,204 ft. (3415 m.)
Kalahari Desert
Namib Desert
Libyan Desert
Nubian Desert
Canary Is. (Sp.)
Madeira (Port.)
Ascension (St. Helena)
St. Helena (U.K.)
C. of Good Hope
C. Agulhas

AREA 11,707,000 sq. mi. (30,321,130 sq. km.)
POPULATION 469,000,000
LARGEST CITY Cairo
HIGHEST POINT Kilimanjaro 19,340 ft. (5,895 m.)
LOWEST POINT Lake Assal, Djibouti -512 ft. (-156 m.)

Population Distribution

TROPIC OF CANCER
EQUATOR
TROPIC OF CAPRICORN

DENSITY PER SQ. KILOMETER	SQ. MILE
Over 100	Over 260
50-100	130-260
10-50	25-130
1-10	3-25
Under 1	Under 3

• Cities with over 1,000,000 inhabitants (including suburbs)

○ Cities with over 350,000 inhabitants (including suburbs)

Vegetation

EQUATOR
TROPIC OF CAPRICORN

TROPICAL FOREST
- Tropical Rainforest
- Light Tropical Forest
- Woodland and Shrub

TROPICAL GRASSLAND
- Grass and Shrub (Savanna)
- Wooded Savanna

MID-LATITUDE FOREST
- Mixed Coniferous and Broadleaf Forest
- Woodland and Shrub (Mediterranean)

MID-LATITUDE GRASSLAND
- Short Grass (Steppe)

RIVER VALLEY AND OASIS

DESERT AND DESERT SHRUB

UNCLASSIFIED HIGHLANDS

Abéché, Chad . . . D3
Abidjan (cap.), Ivory Coast . . B4
Accra (cap.), Ghana . . . B4
Addis Ababa (cap.), Ethiopia . F4
Aden (gulf) . . . G3
Agulhas (cape), S. Africa . . . D8
Ahaggar (range), Algeria . . . C2
Alexandria, Egypt . . . E1
Algeria . . . C2
Algiers (cap.), Algeria . . . C1
Amber (Bobaomby) (cape), Madagascar . . . G6
Angola . . . D6
Annaba, Algeria . . . C1
Annobon (isl.), Equat. Guinea . . . C5
Antananarivo (cap.), Madagascar . . . G6
Arusha, Tanzania . . . F5
Ascension (isl.), St. Helena . A5
Asmara, Ethiopia . . . F3
Aswân, Egypt . . . F2
Asyût, Egypt . . . F2
Atbara, Sudan . . . F3
Atlas (mts.) . . . B1
Bab el Mandeb (str.) . . . G3
Bamako (cap.), Mali . . . B3
Bangui (cap.), Cent. Afr. Rep. . . . D4
Banjul (cap.), Gambia . . . A3
Béchar, Algeria . . . B1
Beira, Mozambique . . . F7
Benghazi, Libya . . . D1
Benguela, Angola . . . D6
Benin . . . C4
Bioko (isl.), Equat. Guinea . . C4
Biskra, Algeria . . . C1
Bissau (cap.), Guinea-Biss. . A3
Bizerte, Tunisia . . . C1
Blanc (cape), Mauritania . . . A2
Blantyre, Malawi . . . F6
Bloemfontein, S. Africa . . . E7
Blue Nile (riv.) . . . F3
Bobaomby (cape), Madagascar . . . G6
Bobo Dioulasso, Upper Volta . . . B3
Bon (cape), Tunisia . . . D1
Bophuthatswana, S. Africa . . E7
Botswana . . . E7
Bouaké, Ivory Coast . . . B4
Boyoma (Stanley) (falls), Zaire . . . E5
Brazzaville (cap.), Congo . . . D5
Buchanan, Liberia . . . A4
Bujumbura (cap.), Burundi . . F5
Bukavu, Zaire . . . E5
Bulawayo, Zimbabwe . . . E7
Burundi . . . F5
Cabinda, Angola . . . D5
Cairo (cap.), Egypt . . . F2
Cameroon . . . D4
Canary (isls.), Spain . . . A2
Cape of Good Hope (prov.), S. Africa . . . E8
Cape Town (cap.), S. Africa . D8
Casablanca, Morocco . . . B1
Central African Republic . . . D4
Ceuta, Spain . . . B1
Chad . . . D3
Chad (lake) . . . D3
Comoros . . . G6
Conakry (cap.), Guinea . . . A4
Congo . . . D5
Congo (riv.) . . . D5
Constantine, Algeria . . . C1
Cotonou, Benin . . . C4
Cyrenaica (reg.), Libya . . . E1
Dakar (cap.), Senegal . . . A3
Damietta, Egypt . . . F1
Dar es Salaam (cap.), Tanzania . . . F5
Dire Dawa, Ethiopia . . . G4
Djibouti . . . G3
Djibouti (cap.), Djibouti . . . G3
Dodoma, Tanzania . . . F5
Douala, Cameroon . . . D4
Durban, S. Africa . . . F7
East London, S. Africa . . . E8
Edward (lake) . . . E5
Egypt . . . E2
El Bayadh, Algeria . . . C1
El Faiyûm, Egypt . . . E2
El Fasher, Sudan . . . E3
Elgon (mt.) . . . F4
El Minya, Egypt . . . F2
El Obeid, Sudan . . . E3
Emi Koussi (mt.), Chad . . . D3
Entebbe, Uganda . . . F5
Equatorial Guinea . . . C4
Eritrea (reg.), Ethiopia . . . F3
Ethiopia . . . F4
Etosha Salt Pan, Namibia . . . D6
Fernando Po (Bioko) (isl.), Equat. Guinea . . . C4
Fès, Morocco . . . B1
Fezzan (reg.), Libya . . . D2
Fianarantsoa, Madagascar . . G7
Freetown (cap.), S. Leone . . . A4
Funchal (cap.), Madeira, Port. . . . A1
Gabon . . . D4
Gaborone (cap.), Botswana . . E7
Gambia . . . A3
Garoua, Cameroon . . . D4
Germiston, S. Africa . . . E7
Ghana . . . B4
Gharîan, Libya . . . D1
Gibraltar (str.) . . . B1
Good Hope (cape), S. Africa . D8
Grand Erg Occidental (des.), Algeria . . . C1
Grand Erg Oriental (des.), Algeria . . . C1
Guinea . . . A3
Guinea (gulf) . . . C4
Guinea-Bissau . . . A3
Gweru, Zimbabwe . . . F6
Harar, Ethiopia . . . G4
Harare (Salisbury) (cap.), Zimb. . . . E6
Hargeysa, Somalia . . . G4
Huambo, Angola . . . D6
Ibadan, Nigeria . . . C4
Iguidi Erg (des.) . . . B2
Ilorin, Nigeria . . . C4
Ivory Coast . . . B4
Jinja, Uganda . . . F4
Johannesburg, S. Africa . . . E7
Kalahari (des.) . . . E7
Kampala (cap.), Uganda . . . F4
Kananga, Zaire . . . E5
Kankan, Guinea . . . B3
Kano, Nigeria . . . C3
Kaolack, Senegal . . . A3
Kariba (lake) . . . E6
Kasai (riv.) . . . E5
Kassala, Sudan . . . F3
Katanga (reg.), Zaire . . . E5
Kayes, Mali . . . A3
Kenitra, Morocco . . . B1
Kenya . . . F4
Kenya (mt.), Kenya . . . F4
Khartoum (cap.), Sudan . . . F3
Kigali (cap.), Rwanda . . . F5
Kilimanjaro (mt.), Tanzania . . F5
Kimberley, S. Africa . . . E7
Kinshasa (cap.), Zaire . . . D5
Kisangani, Zaire . . . E4
Kisumu, Kenya . . . F5
Kitwe, Zambia . . . E6
Kufra (oasis), Libya . . . E2
Kumasi, Ghana . . . B4
Laayoune, W. Sahara . . . A2
Lagos (cap.), Nigeria . . . C4
Las Palmas (cap.), Canary Is., Spain . . . A2
Lesotho . . . E7
Liberia . . . B4
Libreville (cap.), Gabon . . . C4
Libya . . . D2
Libyan (des.) . . . E2
Lilongwe (cap.), Malawi . . . F6
Limpopo (riv.) . . . E7
Lobito, Angola . . . D6
Lomé (cap.), Togo . . . C4
Luanda (cap.), Angola . . . D5
Luanshya, Zambia . . . E6
Lubumbashi, Zaire . . . E6
Lusaka (cap.), Zambia . . . E6
Luxor, Egypt . . . F2
Madagascar . . . G7
Madeira (isls.), Portugal . . . A1
Malabo (cap.), Equat. Guinea . . . C4
Malawi . . . F6
Mali . . . B2
Maputo (cap.), Mozambique . F7
Marrakech, Morocco . . . B1
Maseru (cap.), Lesotho . . . E8
Massawa, Ethiopia . . . F3
Matadi, Zaire . . . D5
Mauritania . . . A3
Mayotte (isl.), France . . . G6
Mbabane (cap.), Swaziland . . F7
Mbuji-Mayi, Zaire . . . E5
Meknès, Morocco . . . B1
Melilla, Spain . . . B1
Misurata, Libya . . . D1
Mmabatho (cap.), Bophuthatswana, S. Africa . . . E7
Mobuto Sese Seko (lake) . . . F4
Moçambique, Mozambique . . F6
Mogadishu (cap.), Somalia . . G4
Mombasa, Kenya . . . G5
Monrovia (cap.), Liberia . . . A4
Morocco . . . B1
Moroni (cap.), Comoros . . . G6
Mosi-Oa-Tunya (falls) . . . E6
Mostaganem, Algeria . . . C1
Mozambique . . . F6
Mozambique (chan.) . . . G6
Muqdisho (Mogadishu) (cap.), Somalia . . . G4
Nairobi (cap.), Kenya . . . F5
Nakuru, Kenya . . . F5
Namibia . . . D7
Nasser (lake), Egypt . . . F2
Natal (prov.), S. Africa . . . F7
N'Djamena (cap.), Chad . . . D3
Ndola, Zambia . . . E6
Niamey (cap.), Niger . . . C3
Niger . . . C3
Niger (riv.) . . . C4
Nigeria . . . C4
Nile (riv.) . . . F2
Nouadhibou, Mauritania . . . A2
Nouakchott (cap.), Mauritania . . . A3
Nubian (des.), Sudan . . . F2
Nyasa (lake) . . . F6
Ogaden (reg.), Ethiopia . . . G4
Ogbomosho, Nigeria . . . C4
Okovango (riv.) . . . D6
Omdurman, Sudan . . . F3
Oran, Algeria . . . B1
Orange (riv.) . . . D7
Orange Free State (prov.), S. Africa . . . E7
Oshogbo, Nigeria . . . C4
Ouagadougou (cap.), Upper Volta . . . B3
Oujda, Morocco . . . B1
Palmas (cape) . . . B4
Pemba (isl.), Tanzania . . . G5
Pietermaritzburg (cap.), Natal, S. Africa . . . F7
Pointe-Noire, Congo . . . D5
Port Elizabeth, S. Africa . . . E8
Port Harcourt, Nigeria . . . C4
Porto-Novo (cap.), Benin . . . C4
Port Said, Egypt . . . F1
Port Sudan, Sudan . . . F3
Pretoria (cap.), S. Africa . . . E7
Rabat (cap.), Morocco . . . B1
Ras Asèr (cape), Somalia . . . H3
Red (sea) . . . F2
Rufiji (riv.), Tanzania . . . F5
Rwanda . . . F5
Sahara (des.) . . . C2
Saint Helena (isl.), U.K. . . . B6
Saint-Louis, Senegal . . . A3
Sainte-Marie (Vohimena) (cape), Madagascar . . . G7
Salisbury (Harare) (cap.), Zimb. . . . E6
Santa Cruz (cap.), Canary Is., Spain . . . A2
São Tomé e Príncipe . . . C4
Ségou, Mali . . . B3
Senegal . . . A3
Sétif, Algeria . . . C1
Sfax, Tunisia . . . D1
Sidi Bel Abbes, Algeria . . . C1
Sidi Ifni, Morocco . . . B2
Sierra Leone . . . A4
Skikda, Algeria . . . C1
Sohâg, Egypt . . . F2
Somalia . . . G4
Sousse, Tunisia . . . D1
South Africa . . . E7
South-West Africa (Namibia) D7
Stanley (falls), Zaire . . . E5
Sudan . . . E3
Sudan (reg.) . . . D3
Suez, Egypt . . . F2
Suez (canal), Egypt . . . F1
Swaziland . . . F7
Takoradi-Sekondi, Ghana . . . B4
Tamale, Ghana . . . B4
Tana (lake), Ethiopia . . . F3
Tanezrouft (des.), Algeria . . . C2
Tanga, Tanzania . . . F5
Tanganyika (lake) . . . F5
Tangier, Morocco . . . B1
Tanzania . . . F5
Tenerife (isl.), Spain . . . A2
Thiès, Senegal . . . A3
Thohoyandou (cap.), Venda, S. Africa . . . F7
Tibesti (mts.) . . . D2
Tidjikja, Mauritania . . . A3
Timbuktu, Mali . . . B3
Tlemcen, Algeria . . . B1
Toamasina, Madagascar . . . G6
Tobruk, Libya . . . E1
Togo . . . C4
Toubkal, Jebel (mt.), Morocco . . . B1
Touggourt, Algeria . . . C1
Transkei, S. Africa . . . E8
Transvaal (prov.), S. Africa . . E7
Tripoli (cap.), Libya . . . D1
Tripolitania (reg.), Libya . . . D1
Tunis (cap.), Tunisia . . . D1
Tunisia . . . C1
Turkana (lake), Kenya . . . F4
Ubangi (riv.) . . . D4
Uganda . . . F4
Uitenhage, S. Africa . . . E8
Umtata (cap.), Transkei, S. Africa . . . E8
Upper Volta . . . B3
Vaal (riv.), S. Africa . . . E7
Venda, S. Africa . . . F7
Verde (cape), Senegal . . . A3
Victoria (lake) . . . F5
Victoria (Mosi-Oa-Tunya) (falls) . . . E6
Vohimena (cape), Madagascar . . . G7
Volta (lake), Ghana . . . B4
Volta (riv.), Ghana . . . C4
Wabi Shebelle (riv.) . . . G4
Wad Medani, Sudan . . . F3
Walvis Bay, S. Africa . . . D7
Western Sahara . . . A2
White Nile (riv.) . . . F4
Windhoek (cap.), Namibia . . D7
Yaoundé (cap.), Cameroon . . D4
Zaire . . . E5
Zaire (Congo) (riv.) . . . E4
Zambezi (riv.) . . . E6
Zambia . . . E6
Zanzibar, Tanzania . . . F5
Zanzibar (isl.), Tanzania . . . F5
Zimbabwe . . . E6
Zomba, Malawi . . . F6

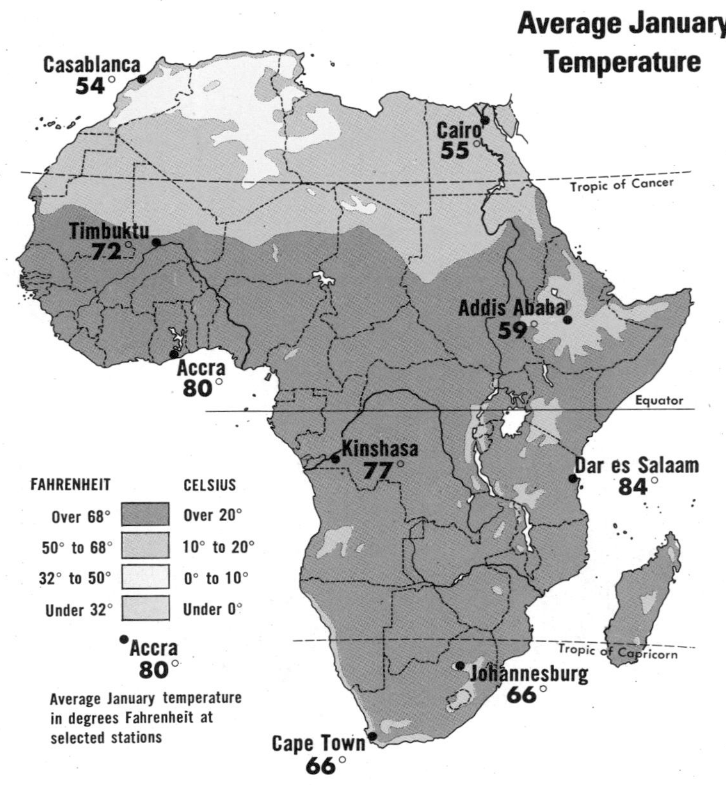
Average January Temperature
Casablanca 54°
Cairo 55°
Tropic of Cancer
Timbuktu 72°
Addis Ababa 59°
Accra 80°
Equator
Kinshasa 77°
Dar es Salaam 84°
FAHRENHEIT
CELSIUS
Over 68°
Over 20°
50° to 68°
10° to 20°
32° to 50°
0° to 10°
Under 32°
Under 0°
Accra 80°
Average January temperature in degrees Fahrenheit at selected stations
Tropic of Capricorn
Johannesburg 66°
Cape Town 66°

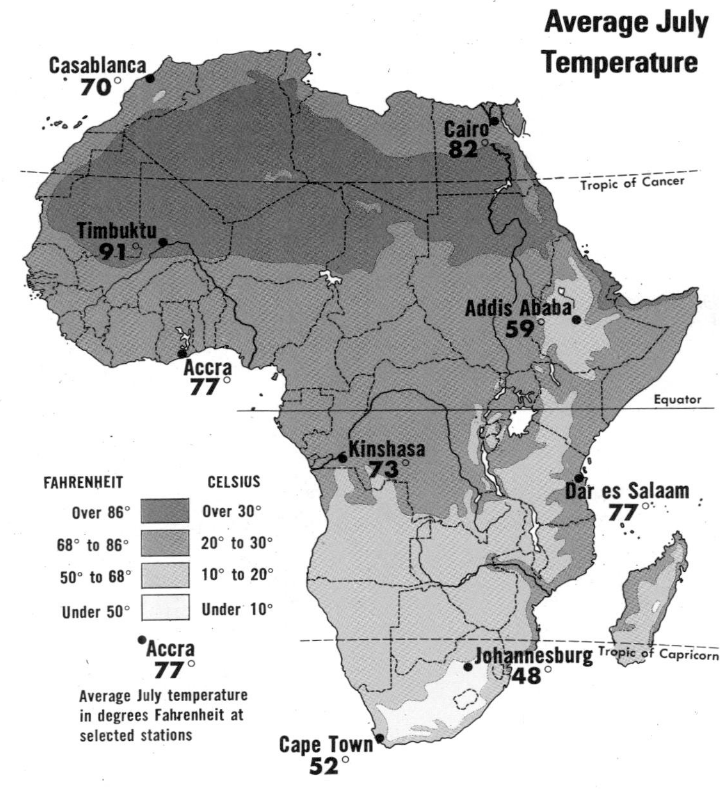
Average July Temperature
Casablanca 70°
Cairo 82°
Tropic of Cancer
Timbuktu 91°
Addis Ababa 59°
Accra 77°
Equator
Kinshasa 73°
Dar es Salaam 77°
FAHRENHEIT
CELSIUS
Over 86°
Over 30°
68° to 86°
20° to 30°
50° to 68°
10° to 20°
Under 50°
Under 10°
Accra 77°
Average July temperature in degrees Fahrenheit at selected stations
Johannesburg 48°
Tropic of Capricorn
Cape Town 52°

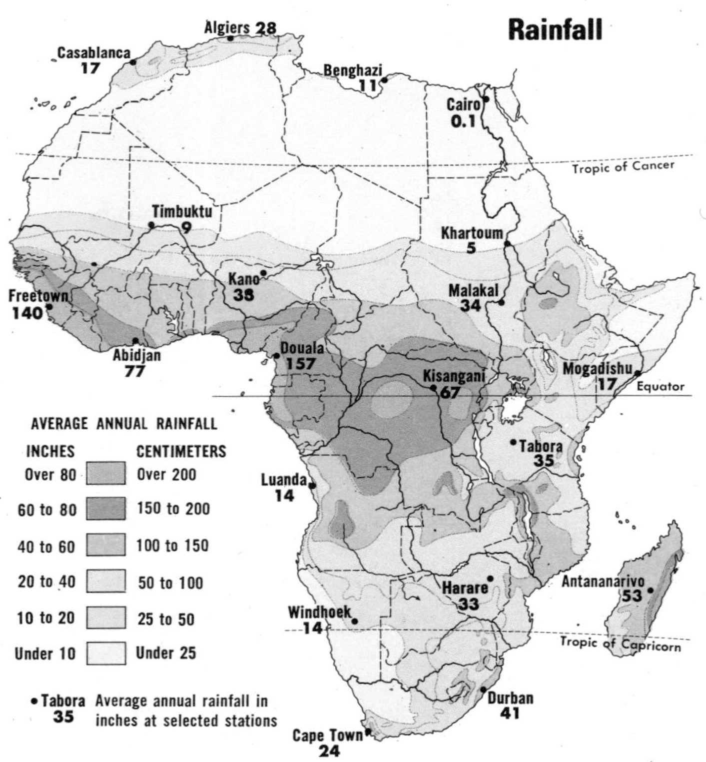
Rainfall
Algiers 28
Casablanca 17
Benghazi 11
Cairo 0.1
Tropic of Cancer
Timbuktu 9
Khartoum 5
Kano 35
Freetown 140
Malakal 34
Abidjan 77
Douala 157
Kisangani 67
Mogadishu 17
Equator
AVERAGE ANNUAL RAINFALL
INCHES
CENTIMETERS
Over 80
Over 200
60 to 80
150 to 200
40 to 60
100 to 150
20 to 40
50 to 100
10 to 20
25 to 50
Under 10
Under 25
Tabora 35
Luanda 14
Harare 33
Antananarivo 53
Windhoek 14
Tropic of Capricorn
Tabora 35 Average annual rainfall in inches at selected stations
Durban 41
Cape Town 24

Vegetation/Relief

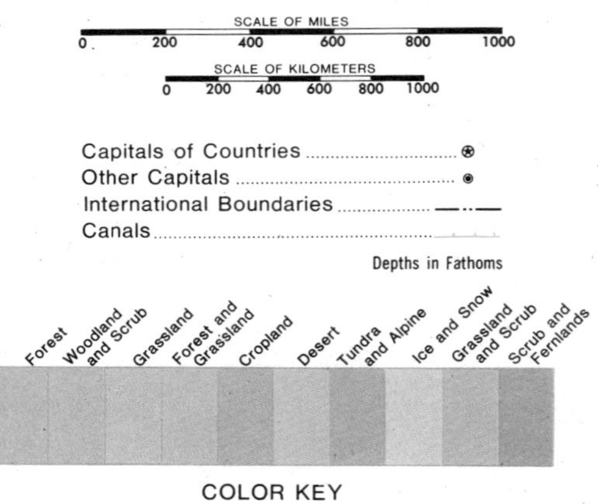
SCALE OF MILES
0 200 400 600 800 1000
SCALE OF KILOMETERS
0 200 400 600 800 1000
Capitals of Countries
Other Capitals
International Boundaries
Canals
Depths in Fathoms
Forest
Woodland and Scrub
Grassland
Forest and Grassland
Cropland
Desert
Tundra and Alpine
Ice and Snow
Grassland and Scrub
Scrub and Fernlands
COLOR KEY

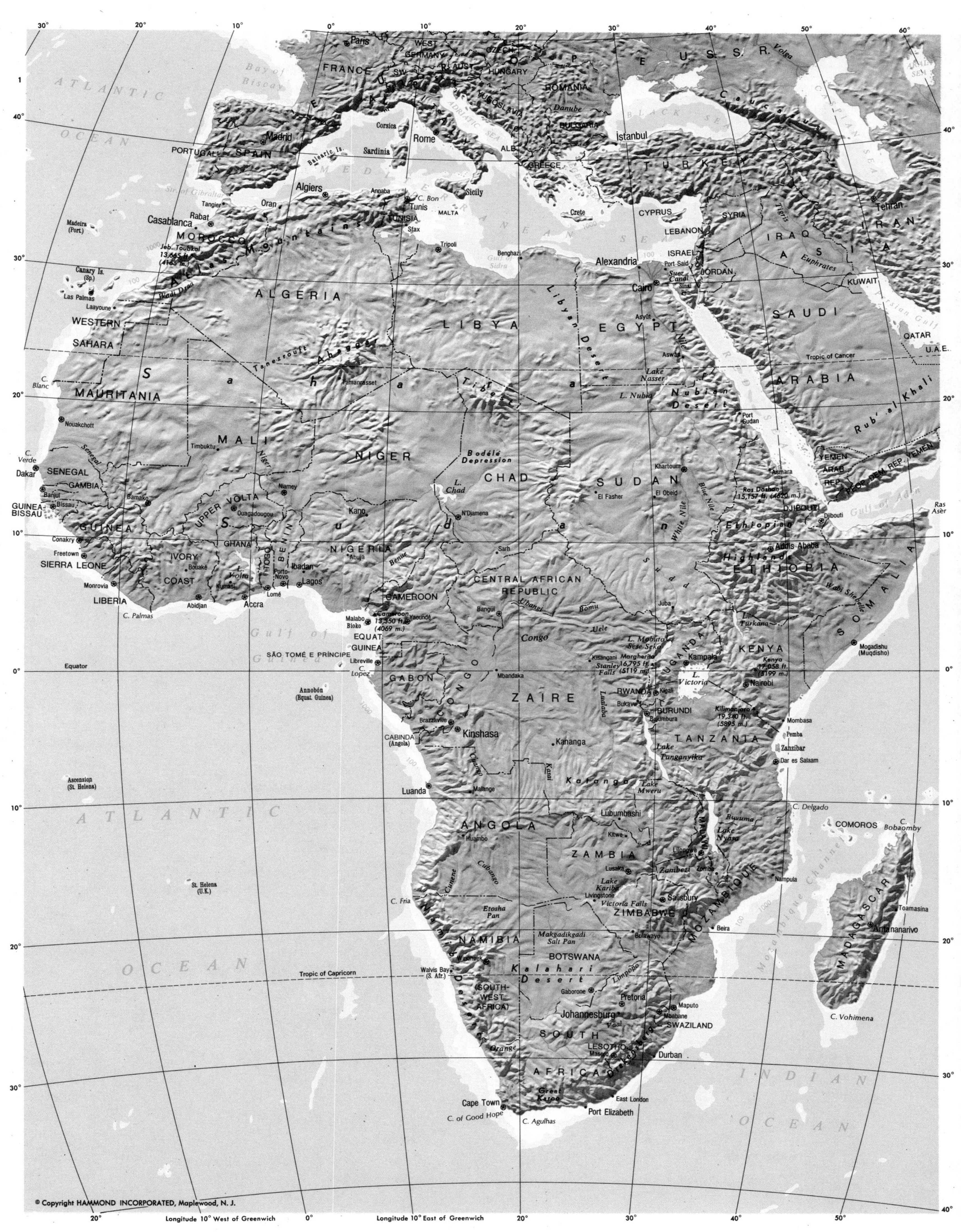

ATLANTIC
OCEAN
Bay of Biscay
Paris
FRANCE
WEST GERMANY
CZECH.
AUST.
SW.
HUNGARY
ROMANIA
YUGOSLAVIA
Danube
BULGARIA
ALB.
GREECE
U.S.S.R.
Volga
Caucasus
BLACK SEA
CASPIAN SEA
ARAL SEA
Istanbul
TURKEY
Madrid
SPAIN
PORTUGAL
Balearic Is.
Corsica
Sardinia
Rome
ADRIATIC SEA
Sicily
MALTA
Str. of Gibraltar
Tangier
Algiers
Oran
Annaba
C. Bon
Tunis
TUNISIA
Sfax
MEDITERRANEAN SEA
Crete
CYPRUS
LEBANON
SYRIA
ISRAEL
JORDAN
IRAQ
IRAN
Tehran
Tigris
Euphrates
ASIA
KUWAIT
Persian Gulf
QATAR
U.A.E.
SAUDI
ARABIA
Rub' al Khali
Tropic of Cancer
Madeira (Port.)
Rabat
Casablanca
MOROCCO
Atlas Mountains
Jeb. Toubkal 13,665 ft. (4165 m.)
Canary Is. (Sp.)
Las Palmas
Laayoune
Wadi Draa
WESTERN SAHARA
Tripoli
Benghazi
Gulf of Sidra
Alexandria
Port Said
Suez Canal
Cairo
Sinai Pen.
ALGERIA
LIBYA
EGYPT
Libyan Desert
Asyût
Nile
Aswân
Lake Nasser
L. Nubia
Nubian Desert
RED SEA
Port Sudan
Tanezrouft
Ahaggar
Tamanrasset
Tibesti
Sahara
C. Blanc
MAURITANIA
Nouakchott
Timbuktu
MALI
Niger
NIGER
Bodélé Depression
L. Chad
CHAD
SUDAN
Khartoum
El Fasher
El Obeid
White Nile
Blue Nile
Asmara
Ras Dashan 15,157 ft. (4620 m.)
YEMEN ARAB REP.
PEOP. DEM. REP. YEMEN
Gulf of Aden
DJIBOUTI
Djibouti
Ras Asir
C. Verde
Senegal
Dakar
SENEGAL
GAMBIA
Banjul
GUINEA-BISSAU
Bissau
Bamako
UPPER VOLTA
Ouagadougou
Niamey
Kano
N'Djamena
GUINEA
Conakry
Freetown
SIERRA LEONE
GHANA
IVORY COAST
Bouaké
L. Volta
TOGO
BENIN
Porto-Novo
NIGERIA
Abuja
Benue
Ibadan
Lagos
Kumasi
Monrovia
LIBERIA
Abidjan
Accra
Lomé
C. Palmas
Sudan
Sarh
Ethiopian Highlands
Addis Ababa
ETHIOPIA
Sudd
CENTRAL AFRICAN REPUBLIC
CAMEROON
Cameroon 13,350 ft. (4069 m.)
Yaoundé
Malabo
Bioko
Bangui
Ubangi
Bomu
Uele
Juba
L. Turkana
Wabi Shebelle
SOMALIA
Mogadishu (Muqdisho)
Gulf of Guinea
EQUAT. GUINEA
SÃO TOMÉ E PRÍNCIPE
Libreville
C. Lopez
Congo
L. Mobutu Sese Seko
Kisangani
Margherita 16,795 ft. (5119 m.)
Stanley Falls
UGANDA
Kampala
KENYA
Kenya 17,058 ft. (5199 m.)
Nairobi
Equator
GABON
CONGO
Mbandaka
ZAIRE
L. Victoria
RWANDA
Kigali
Bukavu
BURUNDI
Bujumbura
Lualaba
Annobón (Equat. Guinea)
Brazzaville
Kinshasa
CABINDA (Angola)
Kananga
Kilimanjaro 19,340 ft. (5895 m.)
Mombasa
Pemba
TANZANIA
Zanzibar
Dar es Salaam
Lake Tanganyika
Kasai
Cuango
Katanga
Lake Mweru
Luanda
Malange
Ascension (St. Helens)
ATLANTIC
Lubumbashi
C. Delgado
COMOROS
C. Bobaomby
ANGOLA
Huambo
Kitwe
Ruvuma
Lake Nyasa
MALAWI
Lilongwe
ZAMBIA
Lusaka
Zambezi
Zomba
MOZAMBIQUE
Nampula
Mozambique Channel
Cunene
Cubango
St. Helena (U.K.)
Lake Kariba
Livingstone
Victoria Falls
Salisbury
ZIMBABWE
C. Fria
Etosha Pan
MADAGASCAR
Toamasina
Antananarivo
Beira
Makgadikgadi Salt Pan
Bulawayo
NAMIBIA
Windhoek
BOTSWANA
Kalahari Desert
OCEAN
Walvis Bay (S. Afr.)
Tropic of Capricorn
Limpopo
Namib Desert
(SOUTH-WEST AFRICA)
Gaborone
Pretoria
Maputo
Mbabane
SWAZILAND
Johannesburg
Vaal
C. Vohimena
SOUTH AFRICA
Orange
LESOTHO
Maseru
Drakensberg
Durban
INDIAN OCEAN
Great Karoo
East London
Cape Town
C. of Good Hope
C. Agulhas
Port Elizabeth
Longitude 10° West of Greenwich
Longitude 10° East of Greenwich

Western Africa
CONIC EQUAL-AREA PROJECTION
SCALE OF MILES
0 100 200 400
SCALE OF KILOMETERS
0 100 200 400
Capitals of Countries
Other Capitals
International Boundaries
Internal Boundaries
Scale 1:15,200,000
© Copyright HAMMOND INCORPORATED, Maplewood, N. J.
NORTH ATLANTIC OCEAN
CANARY ISLANDS (Spanish)
MEDITERRANEAN SEA
SPAIN
PORTUGAL
MOROCCO
ALGERIA
TUNISIA
LIBYA
WESTERN SAHARA
(Occupied by Morocco)
MAURITANIA
MALI
NIGER
SENEGAL
GAMBIA
GUINEA-BISSAU
GUINEA
SIERRA LEONE
LIBERIA
IVORY COAST
UPPER VOLTA
GHANA
TOGO
BENIN
NIGERIA
CAMEROON
EQUATORIAL GUINEA
GABON
SÃO TOME E PRÍNCIPE
S A H A R A
GULF OF GUINEA
Bight of Benin
Bight of Biafra
Ivory Coast
Gold Coast
Slave Coast
Grain Coast
Niger Delta
Equator
ALGIERS
TUNIS
Tripoli
CASABLANCA
Rabat
Marrakech
Dakar
Nouakchott
Bamako
Niamey
Ouagadougou
Accra
Lomé
Porto-Novo
Lagos
Ibadan
Freetown
Conakry
Monrovia
Abidjan
Banjul (Bathurst)
Bissau
Douala
Timbuktu
Kano
Longitude West 5° of Greenwich
Longitude East 5° of Greenwich
Cape Verde
Santo Antão
São Vicente
Santa Luzia
São Nicolau
Sal
Boa Vista
Maio
São Tiago
Fogo
Brava
Praia
NORTH ATLANTIC OCEAN

ALGERIA

AREA 919,591 sq. mi. (2,381,740 sq. km.)
POPULATION 17,422,000
CAPITAL Algiers
LARGEST CITY Algiers
HIGHEST POINT Tahat 9,852 ft. (3,003 m.)
MONETARY UNIT Algerian dinar
MAJOR LANGUAGES Arabic, Berber, French
MAJOR RELIGION Islam

BENIN

AREA 43,483 sq. mi. (112,620 sq. km.)
POPULATION 3,338,240
CAPITAL Porto-Novo
LARGEST CITY Cotonou
HIGHEST POINT Atakora Mts. 2,083 ft. (635 m.)
MONETARY UNIT CFA franc
MAJOR LANGUAGES Fon, Somba, Yoruba, Bariba, French, Mina, Dendi
MAJOR RELIGIONS Tribal religions, Islam, Roman Catholicism

CAPE VERDE

AREA 1,557 sq. mi. (4,033 sq. km.)
POPULATION 324,000
CAPITAL Praia
LARGEST CITY Praia
HIGHEST POINT 9,281 ft. (2,829 m.)
MONETARY UNIT Cape Verde escudo
MAJOR LANGUAGE Portuguese
MAJOR RELIGION Roman Catholicism

GAMBIA

AREA 4,127 sq. mi. (10,689 sq. km.)
POPULATION 601,000
CAPITAL Banjul
LARGEST CITY Banjul
HIGHEST POINT 100 ft. (30 m.)
MONETARY UNIT dalasi
MAJOR LANGUAGES Mandingo, Fulani, Wolof, English, Malinke
MAJOR RELIGIONS Islam, tribal religions, Christianity

GHANA

AREA 92,099 sq. mi. (238,536 sq. km.)
POPULATION 11,450,000
CAPITAL Accra
LARGEST CITY Accra
HIGHEST POINT Togo Hills 2,900 ft. (884 m.)
MONETARY UNIT cedi
MAJOR LANGUAGES Twi, Fante, Dagbani, Ewe, Ga, English, Hausa, Akan
MAJOR RELIGIONS Tribal religions, Christianity, Islam

GUINEA

AREA 94,925 sq. mi. (245,856 sq. km.)
POPULATION 5,143,284
CAPITAL Conakry
LARGEST CITY Conakry
HIGHEST POINT Nimba Mts. 6,070 ft. (1,850 m.)
MONETARY UNIT syli
MAJOR LANGUAGES Fulani, Mandingo, Susu, French
MAJOR RELIGIONS Islam, tribal religions

GUINEA-BISSAU

AREA 13,948 sq. mi. (36,125 sq. km.)
POPULATION 777,214
CAPITAL Bissau
LARGEST CITY Bissau
HIGHEST POINT 689 ft. (210 m.)
MONETARY UNIT Guinea-Bissau escudo
MAJOR LANGUAGES Balante, Fulani, Crioulo, Mandingo, Portuguese
MAJOR RELIGIONS Islam, tribal religions, Roman Catholicism

IVORY COAST

AREA 124,504 sq. mi. (322,465 sq. km.)
POPULATION 7,920,000
CAPITAL Abidjan
LARGEST CITY Abidjan
HIGHEST POINT 5,745 ft. (1,751 m.)
MONETARY UNIT CFA franc
MAJOR LANGUAGES Bale, Bete, Senufu, French, Dioula
MAJOR RELIGIONS Tribal religions, Islam

LIBERIA

AREA 43,000 sq. mi. (111,370 sq. km.)
POPULATION 1,873,000
CAPITAL Monrovia
LARGEST CITY Monrovia
HIGHEST POINT Wutivi 5,584 ft. (1,702 m.)
MONETARY UNIT Liberian dollar
MAJOR LANGUAGES Kru, Kpelle, Bassa, Vai, English
MAJOR RELIGIONS Christianity, tribal religions, Islam

MALI

AREA 464,873 sq. mi. (1,204,021 sq. km.)
POPULATION 6,906,000
CAPITAL Bamako
LARGEST CITY Bamako
HIGHEST POINT Hombori Mts. 3,789 ft. (1,155 m.)
MONETARY UNIT Mali franc
MAJOR LANGUAGES Bambara, Senufu, Fulani, Soninke, French
MAJOR RELIGIONS Islam, tribal religions

MAURITANIA

AREA 419,229 sq. mi. (1,085,803 sq. km.)
POPULATION 1,634,000
CAPITAL Nouakchott
LARGEST CITY Nouakchott
HIGHEST POINT 2,972 ft. (906 m.)
MONETARY UNIT ouguiya
MAJOR LANGUAGES Arabic, Wolof, Tukolor, French
MAJOR RELIGION Islam

MOROCCO

AREA 172,414 sq. mi. (446,550 sq. km.)
POPULATION 20,242,000
CAPITAL Rabat
LARGEST CITY Casablanca
HIGHEST POINT Jeb. Toubkal 13,665 ft. (4,165 m.)
MONETARY UNIT dirham
MAJOR LANGUAGES Arabic, Berber, French
MAJOR RELIGIONS Islam, Judaism, Christianity

NIGER

AREA 489,189 sq. mi. (1,267,000 sq. km.)
POPULATION 5,098,427
CAPITAL Niamey
LARGEST CITY Niamey
HIGHEST POINT Banguezane 6,234 ft. (1,900 m.)
MONETARY UNIT CFA franc
MAJOR LANGUAGES Hausa, Songhai, Fulani, French, Tamashek, Djerma
MAJOR RELIGIONS Islam, tribal religions

NIGERIA

AREA 357,000 sq. mi. (924,630 sq. km.)
POPULATION 82,643,000
CAPITAL Lagos
LARGEST CITY Lagos
HIGHEST POINT Dimlang 6,700 ft. (2,042 m.)
MONETARY UNIT naira
MAJOR LANGUAGES Hausa, Yoruba, Ibo, Ijaw, Fulani, Tiv, Kanuri, Ibibio, English, Edo
MAJOR RELIGIONS Islam, Christianity, tribal religions

SÃO TOMÉ E PRÍNCIPE

AREA 372 sq. mi. (963 sq. km.)
POPULATION 85,000
CAPITAL São Tomé
LARGEST CITY São Tomé
HIGHEST POINT Pico 6,640 ft. (2,024 m.)
MONETARY UNIT dobra
MAJOR LANGUAGES Bantu languages, Portuguese
MAJOR RELIGIONS Tribal religions, Roman Catholicism

SENEGAL

AREA 75,954 sq. mi. (196,720 sq. km.)
POPULATION 5,508,000
CAPITAL Dakar
LARGEST CITY Dakar
HIGHEST POINT Futa Jallon 1,640 ft. (500 m.)
MONETARY UNIT CFA franc
MAJOR LANGUAGES Wolof, Peul (Fulani), French, Mende, Mandingo, Dida
MAJOR RELIGIONS Islam, tribal religions, Roman Catholicism

SIERRA LEONE

AREA 27,925 sq. mi. (72,325 sq. km.)
POPULATION 3,470,000
CAPITAL Freetown
LARGEST CITY Freetown
HIGHEST POINT Loma Mts. 6,390 ft. (1,947 m.)
MONETARY UNIT leone
MAJOR LANGUAGES Mende, Temne, Vai, English, Krio (pidgin)
MAJOR RELIGIONS Tribal religions, Islam, Christianity

TOGO

AREA 21,622 sq. mi. (56,000 sq. km.)
POPULATION 2,472,000
CAPITAL Lomé
LARGEST CITY Lomé
HIGHEST POINT Agou 3,445 ft. (1,050 m.)
MONETARY UNIT CFA franc
MAJOR LANGUAGES Ewe, French, Twi, Hausa
MAJOR RELIGIONS Tribal religions, Roman Catholicism, Islam

TUNISIA

AREA 63,378 sq. mi. (164,149 sq. km.)
POPULATION 6,367,000
CAPITAL Tunis
LARGEST CITY Tunis
HIGHEST POINT Jeb. Chambi 5,066 ft. (1,544 m.)
MONETARY UNIT Tunisian dinar
MAJOR LANGUAGES Arabic, French
MAJOR RELIGION Islam

UPPER VOLTA

AREA 105,869 sq. mi. (274,200 sq. km.)
POPULATION 6,908,000
CAPITAL Ouagadougou
LARGEST CITY Ouagadougou
HIGHEST POINT 2,352 ft. (717 m.)
MONETARY UNIT CFA franc
MAJOR LANGUAGES Mossi, Lobi, French, Samo, Gourounsi
MAJOR RELIGIONS Islam, tribal religions, Roman Catholicism

WESTERN SAHARA

AREA 102,703 sq. mi. (266,000 sq. km.)
POPULATION 76,425
HIGHEST POINT 2,700 ft. (823 m.)
MAJOR LANGUAGE Arabic
MAJOR RELIGION Islam

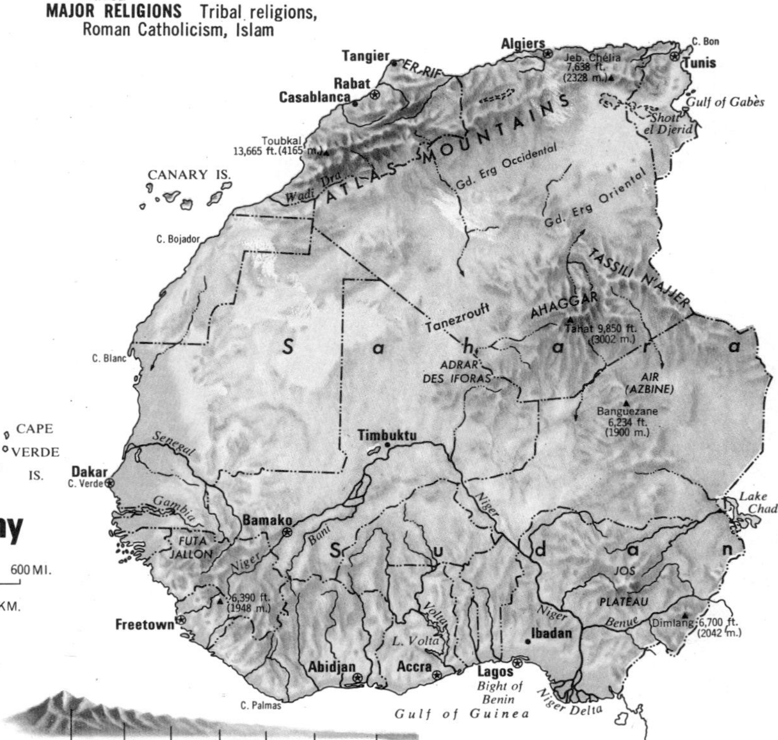

Topography

0 200 400 600 MI.
0 200 400 600 KM.

(continued)

ALGERIA

CITIES and TOWNS

Abadla 12,200 D2
Adrar 22,800 D3
Aîn Beîda 26,976 F1
Aîn Sefra 22,400 D2
Aîn Temouchent 42,000 D1
Algiers (cap.) 1,365,400 E1
Amguid F3
Annaba 255,900 F1
Aoulef 17,200 E3
Arak E3
Batna 112,100 F1
Béchar 72,800 D2
Bejaîa 89,500 F1
Beni Abbès 5,000 D2
Beni Ounif 7,500 D2
Beni Saf 30,700 D1
Berga E3
Bidon 5 (Poste Maurice Cordier) E4
Biskra 90,500 F2
Blida 160,900 E1
Bône (Annaba) 255,900 F1
Bordj Bou Arreridj 65,000 E1
Bordj Fly Sainte Marie D3
Bordj Omar Driss 1,900 F3
Boufarik 50,000 E1
Bougie (Béjaîa) 89,500 F1
Bou Saâda 50,000 E1
Brezina 10,000 E2
Charouine D3
Chenachane D3
Cherchell 36,800 E1
Constantine 335,100 F1
Deldoul E3
Dellys 29,700 E1
Djanet 5,300 F4
Djelfa 51,000 E2
Djemaa 34,600 F2
Edjeleh F3
El Abiod Sidi Cheikh 15,300 E2
El Asnam 106,100 E1
El Bayadh 38,500 E2
El Djezair (Algiers) (cap.) 1,365,400 E1
El Goléa 24,400 E2
El Oued 72,100 F2
Fort Lallemand F2
Fort MacMahon E3
Fort Miribel E3
Fort Tarat F3
Ghardaîa 70,500 E2
Ghazaouet 25,900 D2
Guelma 60,100 F1
Guemar F2
Guerara 22,300 E2
Guerzim D3
Hassi Messaoud F2
Hassi R'Mel E2
Idelès F4
Igli 3,400 D2
Illizi 4,600 F3
In Amenas 4,200 F3
In Amguel E4
In Eker F4
In Guezzam F5
In Rhar E3
In Salah 18,800 E3
Jijel 49,800 F1
Kenadsa 7,600 D2
Kerzaz 2,900 D3
Khemis Miliana 57,800 E1
Ksar el Boukhari 41,200 E1
Laghouat 59,200 E2
Mascara 62,300 D1
Mecheria 22,600 D2
Médéa 72,300 E1
Metlili Chaamba 21,300 E2
Miliana 36,400 E1
Mohammadia 53,700 D1
Mostaganem 101,600 D1
M'Sila 49,100 E1
Oran 491,900 D1
Orléansville (El Asnam) 106,100 E1
Ouallene E4
Ouargla 77,400 F2
Ouled Djellal 22,700 F2
Philippeville (Skikda) 107,700 F1
Poste Maurice Cortier E4
Poste Weygand D4
Reggane 11,300 D3
Relizane 60,000 E1
Saîda 62,100 E2
Sbaa D3
Sétif 144,200 F1
Sidi Bel-Abbes 116,000 D1
Silet E4
Skikda 107,700 F1
Souk Ahras 60,200 F1
Tabelbala 3,100 D3
Taghit 3,500 D2
Tamanrasset 23,200 F4
Tamentit D3
Taourirt E3
Tébessa 67,200 F1
Temacine F2
Ténès 30,100 E1
Tiaret 62,900 E1
Tiguentourine F3
Timgad 9,800 F1
Timimoun 20,500 E3
Tindouf 6,500 C3
Tinjoub C3
Tin-Zaouatene E5
Tizi Ouzou 73,100 E1
Tlemcen 109,400 D2
Touggourt 75,600 F2
Zaouiet Kounta 13,800 D3

OTHER FEATURES

Adrar des Iforas (plat.) E5
Ahaggar (range) F4
Anaî (well) G4
Aouinet Bel Egrâ (well) C3
Atlas (mts.) E2
Aurès (lag.) F1
Azzel Mati, Sebkha (lake) E3
Bougaroun (cape) F1
Chech, Erg (des.) D3
Chelia (mt.) F1
Chelif (riv.) E1
Chergui, Chott Ech (salt lake) E2
Gourara (oasis) E3
Grand Erg Occidental (des.) E2
Grand Erg Oriental (des.) F2
Guir Hamada (des.) D2
High Plateaus (ranges) D2
Iguidi, Erg (des.) C3
In Ezzane (well) G4
Irharhar, Wadi (dry riv.) F3
Issaouane Erg (des.) F3
Kabylia (reg.) E1
Mediterranean (sea) E1
Medjerda (riv.) F1
Melrhir, Chott (salt lake) F2
Mouydir (mts.) E3
Mya, Wadi (dry riv.) E2
M'zab (oasis) E2
Raoui, Erg er (des.) D3
Rhir, Wadi (dry riv.) F2
Sahara (des.) E4
Saharan Atlas (ranges) E2
Saoura, Wadi (dry riv.) D3
Souf (oasis) F2
Tademaît, Plateau du (plat.) E3
Tafassasset, Wadi (dry riv.) F4
Tahat (mt.) F4
Tamanrasset, Wadi (dry riv.) E4
Tanezrouft (des.) E4
Tassili N'Ahagger (plat.) E4
Tassili N'Ajjer (plat.) F3
Tidikelt (oasis) E3
Timmissao (well) E4
Tindouf, Sebkha de (salt lake) C3
Tinrhert, Hamada de (des.) F3
Tni Haîa (well) D4
Touat (oasis) E3
Touila (well) C3

BENIN

CITIES and TOWNS

Abomey 38,000 E7
Cotonou 178,000 E7
Djougou E7
Grand-Popo E7
Kandi E6
Lokossa 6,000 E7
Malanville E6
Natitingou 49,000 E6
Nikki E7
Ouidah E7
Parakou 21,000 E7
Porto-Novo (cap.) 104,000 E7
Savalou E7
Savé E7

OTHER FEATURES

Atakora (mts.) E6
Benin (bight) E8
Guinea (gulf) E8
Mono (riv.) E7
Niger (riv.) E6
Ouémé (riv.) E7
Slave Coast (reg.) E7
Sudan (reg.) E6

CAPE VERDE

CITIES and TOWNS

Mindelo 28,797 A7
Praia (cap.) 21,494 B8
Ribeira Grande 1,892 B7
Sal Rei 1,296 B8
Santa Maria 956 B8

OTHER FEATURES

Boa Vista (isl.) B8
Brava (isl.) B8
Fogo (isl.) B8
Maio (isl.) B8
Sal (isl.) B7
Santa Luzia (isl.) B8
Santo Antão (isl.) A7
São Nicolau (isl.) B8
São Tiago (isl.) B8
São Vicente (isl.) B7

GAMBIA

CITIES and TOWNS

Banjul (cap.) 39,476 A6
Basse Santa Su 2,899 B6
Brikama 9,483 A6
Georgetown 2,510 A6

GHANA

CITIES and TOWNS

Accra (cap.) 564,194 D7
Accra* 738,498 D7
Ada 4,285 E7
Akuse 3,791 E7
Attebubu 6,630 D7
Awaso 5,449 D7
Axim 8,107 D8
Bawku 20,567 D6
Bekwai 11,287 D7
Berekum 14,296 D7
Bole 4,772 D7
Bolgatanga 18,896 D6
Cape Coast 51,653 D7
Daboya 1,872 D7
Damongo 7,760 D7
Dunkwa 15,437 D7
Elmina 11,401 D8
Enchi 4,382 D7
Gambaga 3,730 D6
Gyasikan 6,403 D7
Half Assini 5,429 D8
Ho 24,199 E7
Keta 14,446 E7
Kete Krachi 5,097 E7
Kintampo 7,149 D7
Koforidua 46,235 D7
Kpandu 12,842 D7
Kumasi 260,286 D7
Kumasi* 345,117 D7
Lawra 2,709 D6
Mampong 13,895 D7
Mpraeso 5,908 D7
Navrongo D6
Nsawam 25,518 D7
Nsuta 3,854 D7
Obuasi 31,005 D7
Oda 20,957 D7
Prestea 15,143 D7
Salaga 6,413 D7
Sekondi 33,713 D8
Sekondi-Takoradi* 160,868 D8
Sunyani 23,780 D7
Takoradi 58,161 D8
Tamale 83,653 D7
Tarkwa 14,702 D7
Tema 60,767 E7
Tumu 4,366 D6
Wa 21,374 D6
Wenchi 13,836 D7
Wiawso 5,558 D7
Winneba 30,778 D7
Yapei 1,203 D7
Yendi 22,072 D7

OTHER FEATURES

Ashanti (reg.) D7
Benin (bight) E8
Black Volta (riv.) D6
Gold Coast (reg.) D8
Guinea (gulf) E8
Oti (riv.) E7
Red Volta (riv.) D6
Saint Paul (cape) E7
Three Points (cape) D8
Volta (lake) D7
Volta (riv.) E7
White Volta (riv.) D6

ALGERIA
BENIN
CAPE VERDE
GAMBIA
GHANA
GUINEA
GUINEA-BISSAU
IVORY COAST
LIBERIA
MALI
MAURITANIA
MOROCCO
NIGER
NIGERIA
SÃO TOMÉ E PRÍNCIPE
SENEGAL
SIERRA LEONE
TOGO
TUNISIA
UPPER VOLTA

GUINEA

CITIES and TOWNS

Beyla C7
Boffa B6
Boké B6
Conakry (cap.)* 525,671 B7
Dabola B6
Dalaba B6
Dinguiraye B6
Dubréka B7
Faranah B6
Forécariah B7
Fria B6
Gaoual B6
Guéckédou B7
Kamsar B6
Kankan 85,310 C6
Kérouané C7
Kindia 79,861 B6
Kissidougou B7
Koundara 6,000 B6
Kouroussa C6
Labé 79,670 B6
Macenta C7
Mali B6
Mamou B6
N'Zérékoré 23,000 C7
Sangaredyi B6
Siguiri C6
Télimélé 12,000 B6
Tougué B6
Victoria B6

OTHER FEATURES

Bafing (riv.) B6
Bakoy (riv.) B6
Futa Jallon (lag.) B6
Los (isls.) B7
Milo (riv.) C7
Moa (riv.) B7
Niger (riv.) C6
Nimba (lag.) C7
Verga (cape) B6

GUINEA-BISSAU

CITIES and TOWNS

Bissau (cap.) 109,486 A6
Bolama○ 9,133 A6
Buba○ 6,706 B6
Bubaque○ 8,441 A6
Cacheu○ 15,194 A6

OTHER FEATURES

Bijagós (isls.) A6

IVORY COAST

CITIES and TOWNS

Abengourou 31,239 D7
Abidjan (cap.) 685,828 D7
Aboisso 14,272 D7
Agboville 27,192 D7
Bingerville 18,218 D7
Bondoukou 19,111 D7
Bouaflé 15,917 C7
Bouaké 173,248 D7
Bouna 5,787 D7
Boundiali 9,869 C7
Dabakala 3,272 D7
Dabou 23,870 D7
Daloa 60,958 C7
Danané 19,872 C7
Dimbokro 30,986 D7
Divo 37,896 C7
Ferkessédougou 25,307 D7
Fresco 1,865 C7
Gagnoa 42,362 C7
Grand-Bassam 25,808 D7
Grand-Lahou 4,070 C8
Guiglo 10,441 C7
Issia 11,143 C7
Katiola 21,559 C7
Kong 2,551 D7
Korhogo 47,657 C7
Man 50,315 C7
Mankono 6,570 C7
Odienné 13,864 C7
Port-Bouet 72,616 D7
San Pedro 27,616 C8
Sassandra 9,404 C8
Séguéla 12,587 C7
Sinfra 16,399 C7
Tabou 7,255 C8
Touba 5,256 C7
Toumodi 12,983 D7

OTHER FEATURES

Aby (lag.) D8
Bagoé (riv.) C6
Bandama (riv.) C7
Baoulé (riv.) C6
Black Volta (riv.) D6
Cavally (riv.) C7
Comoé (riv.) D7
Ebrié (lag.) D8
Guinea (gulf) E8
Ivory Coast (reg.) C8
Kossou, Lac de (lake) C7
Nimba (lag.) C7
Sassandra (riv.) C7

LIBERIA

CITIES and TOWNS

Buchanan 23,999 B7
Gbarnga 6,896 C7
Grand Cess C8
Greenville 8,462 C8
Harbel 11,445 B7
Harper 10,627 C8
Kolahun C7
Marshall B7
Monrovia (cap.) 166,507 B7
Plahn C7
River Cess 2,041 C7
Robertsport 2,562 B7
Sasstown C8
Tapeta 3,927 C7
Tchien 6,094 C7
Tubmanburg 14,089 B7

OTHER FEATURES

Bong (range) B7
Cavalla (riv.) C7
Cestos (riv.) C7
Grain Coast (reg.) B8
Kru Coast (reg.) C8
Mano (riv.) B7
Mount (cape) B7
Nimba (lag.) C7
Palmas (cape) C8
Roberts Field Int'l Airport C7

MALI

CITIES and TOWNS

Anéfis E5
Ansongo 3,485 E5
Araouane D5
Bafoulabé 2,163 B6
Bamako (cap.) 404,022 C6
Bamba D5
Banamba 6,776 C6
Bandiagara 8,920 D6
Bankass 3,229 D6
Bou Djebeha D5
Bougouni 17,246 C6
Bourem 4,538 E5
Dioila 4,953 C6
Dire 8,941 D5
Djenné 10,251 D6
Douentza 6,746 D6
Gao 30,714 E5
Goundam 10,262 D5
Gourma-Rharous 4,671 D5
Hombori D5
Kadiolo 3,991 C6
Kangaba 3,184 C6
Kati 24,991 C6
Kayes 44,736 B6
Ké-Macina 5,426 C6
Kéniéba 4,510 B6
Kerchoual E5
Kidal 3,308 E5
Kita 17,538 C6
Kolokani 8,923 C6
Kolondiéba 5,882 C6
Koulikoro 16,376 C6
Kourouba B6
Koutiala 27,497 C6
Mabrouk D5
Ménaka 3,693 E5
Mopti 53,885 D6
Nampala C5
Nara 6,091 C5
Niafunké 6,399 D5
Niono 12,290 C6
Nioro 11,617 C5
San 22,962 D6
Satadougou B6
Ségou 64,890 C6
Sikasso 47,030 C6
Sokolo C6
Taoudenni D4
Ténenkou 4,708 C6
Tessalit E4
Timbuktu (Tombouctou) 20,483 D5
Toukoto C6
Yanfolila 3,809 C6
Yelimané 1,481 B5
Yorosso 2,390 C6

OTHER FEATURES

Achourat (well) D4
Adrar des Iforas (plat.) E5
Asselar (well) D5
Azaouad (reg.) D5
Azaouak (dry riv.) E5
Bafing (riv.) B6
Bagoé (riv.) C6
Bakoy (riv.) B6
Bani (riv.) C6
Baoulé (dry riv.) C6
Baoulé (riv.) C6
Bir Ounane (well) D4
Chech, Erg (des.) D4
Debo (lake) D5
El Mraiti (well) D5
Faguibine (lake) D5
Falémé (riv.) B6
Haricha Hamada (des.) D4
Hombori (mts.) D5
In Dagouber (well) D4
Macina (depr.) D6
Niger (riv.) D5
Oum el Asel (well) D4
Sahara (des.) D4
Sekkane, Erg (des.) D4
Senegal (riv.) B5
Sudan (reg.) D6
Tadjnout Hagguerete (well) D4
Terhazza (ruins) C4
Tilemsi (valley) E5
Toufourine (well) C4

MAURITANIA

CITIES and TOWNS

Aîoun el Atrous C5
Akjoujt 8,044 B5
Akreîjit C5
Aleg 6,415 B5
Atar 16,326 B4
Bassikounou C5
Bir Mogreîn B3
Boutilimit 7,261 B5
Bogué 8,056 B5
Chinguetti B4
Fderik (Fort-Gouraud) 2,160 B4
Kaédi 20,848 B5
Kankossa B5
Kiffa 10,629 B5
Maghama B5
M'Bout B5
Méderdra A5
Néma 8,232 C5
Nouakchott (cap.) 134,986 A5
Nouadhibou 21,961 A4
Ouadane B4
Oualata C5
Oujaf C5
Oujeft B4
Rosso 16,466 A5
Sélibaby 5,994 B5
Tamchakett B5
Tamsagout C4
Tazadit B4
Tichitt C5
Tidjikja 7,870 B5
Timbédra 5,317 C5
Zouîrât 17,474 B4

OTHER FEATURES

Adafer (reg.) B5
Adrar (reg.) B4
Affolé (reg.) B5
Agueraktem (well) C4
Aîn ben Tili (well) C3
Arguin (bay) A4
Assaba (reg.) B5
Atoui, Wadi (dry riv.) B4
Ben Guerdane (well) B3
Bir el Khzaim (well) C4
Blanc (cape) A4
Brakna (reg.) B5
Chegga (well) C3
Djouf, El (des.) C4
El Mrayer (well) C4
El Mreîti (well) C4
Gorgol (reg.) B5
Hodh (reg.) C5
Iguidi, Erg (des.) C3
Inchiri (reg.) A5
Koumbi Saleh (ruins) C5
Lévrier (bay) A4
Makteîr (des.) B4
Meraia (reg.) C5
Mirik (Timiris) (cape) A5
Ouarane (reg.) B4
Sahara (des.) C4
Senegal (riv.) B5
Tagant (reg.) B5
Tidra (isl.) A5
Timiris (cape) A5
Touila (well) C3
Trarza (reg.) A5

MOROCCO

CITIES and TOWNS

Agadir 61,192 C2
Al Hoceima 18,686 D1
Asilah 14,074 C1
Azemmour 17,182 C2
Azrou 20,756 C2
Beni Mellal 53,826 C2
Berguent 3,356 D2
Bou Arfa D2
Bou Izakarn 2,342 C3
Boujad 18,838 C2
Casablanca 1,506,373 C2
Chechaouene 15,362 D1
Dar-el-Beida (Casablanca) 1,506,373 C2
El Jadida 55,501 C2
El Kelaa des Srarhna 17,163 C2
Erfoud 5,400 D2
Er Rachidia 16,775 D2
Essaouira 30,061 B2
Fédala (Mohammedia) 70,392 C2
Fès (Fez) 325,327 D2
Figuig 13,660 D2
Goulmima 4,056 C2
Inezgane 11,495 C2

Jerada 30,633 D2
Kenitra 139,206 C2
Khenifra 25,526 C2
Khouribga 73,667 C2
Ksar el Kebir 48,262 C2
Larache 45,710 C1
Marrakech 332,741 C2
Mazagan (El Jadida) 55,501 C2
Meknès 248,369 C2
Mogador (Essaouira) 30,061 B2
Mohammedia 70,392 C2
Nador 32,490 D1
Ouarzazate 11,142 C2
Oued Zem 33,323 C2
Ouezzane 33,267 C2
Oujda 175,532 D2
Petitjean (Sidi Kacem) 26,831 C2
Port-Lyautey
(Kénitra) 139,206 C2
Rabat (cap.) 367,620 C2
Safi 129,113 C2
Saîdia D2
Salé 155,557 C2
Sefrou 28,607 D2
Settat 42,325 C2
Sidi Ifni 13,650 B3
Sidi Kacem 26,831 C2
Tagounite C3
Tangier (Tanger) 187,894 C1
Tan-Tan 10,772 B3
Taourirt 15,580 D2
Taouz D2
Tarfaya 1,104 B3
Taroudant 22,272 C2
Taza 55,157 D2
Tendrara D2
Tétouan 139,105 C1
Tiznit 11,391 B3
Youssoufia 22,435 C2
Zagora 5,306 C2

OTHER FEATURES

Anti-Atlas (ranges) C3
Atlas (mts.) C2
Bani, Jebel (mts.) C3
Beddouza, Ras (cape) C2
Dra, Wadi (dry riv.) C3
Er Rif (range) D2
Gibraltar (str.) C1
High Atlas (ranges) C2
Juby (cape) B3
Mediterranean (sea) D1
Middle Atlas (ranges) C2
Moulouya (riv.) D2
Rhéris, Wadi (dry riv.) D2
Rhir (cape) B2
Rif, Er (range) D2
Sarhro, Jebel (mts.) C2
Sebou (riv.) C2
Sim (cape) B2
Toubkal, Jebel (mt.) C2
Ziz, Wadi (dry riv.) D2

NIGER

CITIES and TOWNS

Agadès 11,000 F5
Arhli (Arlit) F4
Bilma G5
Birni-N'Konni 10,000 E6
Bosso G6
Chirfa G4
Dakoro F6
Dessa E6
Diffa G6
Djado G4
Dogondoutchi 9,000 E6
Dosso E6
Fachi G5
Filingué 10,000 E6
Gangara F6
Gaya 5,000 E6
Gouré G6
Iférouane F5
Illéla 9,000 F6
In-Gall F5
Madama G4
Madaoua F6
Magaria F6
Mainé-Soroa G6
Maradi 45,852 F6
N'Guigmi G6
Niamey (cap.) 225,314 E6
Quallam E6
Say E6
Tahoua 31,265 F6
Tanout F6
Téra 8,000 E6
Tessaoua 5,000 F6
Tillabéry E6
Tîmia F4
Zinder 58,436 F6

OTHER FEATURES

Achégour (well) G5
Agadem (well) G5
Air (mts.) F5
Anaye (well) G5
Assakarai (dry riv.) F5
Azaoua (reg.) E5
Azbine (Air) (mts.) F5
Bagam (well) F5
Banguezane (mt.) F5
Bedouaram (well) G5
Chad (lake) G6
Dallol Bosso (dry riv.) E6
Dillia (dry riv.) G5
Djado (plat.) G4
El War (well) G4
In Azaoua (well) F4
Komadugu Yobe (riv.) G6
Mantas (well) E5
Niger (riv.) E6
Sahara (des.) F4
Sudan (reg.) F6
Tafassasset, Wadi (dry riv.) F4
Talak (reg.) E5
Ténéré (des.) G5
Timboulaga (well) F5
Tummo (El War) (well) G4
Zoo Baba (well) G5

NIGERIA

STATES

Anambra 2,300,000 F7
Bauchi 2,496,329 F6
Bendel 2,336,000 F7
Benue 2,641,496 F7
Borno 2,853,553 G6
Cross River 3,633,582 F7
Gongola 1,585,200 G7
Imo 5,000,000 F7
Kaduna 4,098,303 F6
Kano 5,775,000 F6
Kwara 1,600,600 E7
Lagos 1,100,000 E7
Niger 2,900,000 F7
Ogun 1,448,966 E7
Ondo 2,727,676 F7
Oyo 5,208,884 E7
Plateau 1,367,450 F7
Rivers 1,544,314 F8
Sokoto 1,367,450 F6

CITIES and TOWNS

Aba 177,000 F7
Abeokuta 253,000 E7
Abuja F7
Ado 213,000 E7
Afikpo F7
Aku F7
Akure F7
Argungu E6
Asaba F7
Azare G6
Baga G6
Bama G6
Baro F7
Bauchi F6
Benin City 136,000 F7
Bida F7
Birnin Kebbi E6
Biu G6
Bonny F8
Brass F8
Burutu F7
Calabar 103,000 F7
Deba Habe G6
Degema F8
Dikwa G6
Donga G7
Ede 182,000 E7
Eha Amufu F7
Enugu 187,000 F7
Forcados E7
Funtua F6
Gashaka G7
Gbogo F7
Geidam G6
Gombe G6
Gumel F6
Gummi F6
Gusau F6
Gwadabawa F6
Hadejia G6
Ibadan 847,000 E7
Ibi F7
Ife 176,000 E7
Ijebu-Ode E7
Ikeja E7
Ikom F7
Ilesha 224,000 F7
Ilorin 282,000 E7
Isa F6
Iseyin 115,083 E7
Iwo 214,000 E7
Jalingo G7
Jebba E7
Jega E6
Jos F7
Kabba F7
Kaduna 202,000 F6
Kaiama E7
Kalmalo F6
Kano 399,000 F6
Katsina 109,424 F6
Katsina Ala F7
Kaura Namoda F6
Keffi F7
Koko F7
Kontagora F6
Kukawa G6
Kumo G7
Kuta F7
Lafia F7
Lafiagi F7
Lagos (cap.) 1,060,848 E7
Laro E7
Lere F7
Lokoja F7
Maiduguri 189,000 G6
Maigatari F6
Makurdi F7
Minna F7
Mubi G6
Nasarawa F7
New Bussa E6
Nguru G6
Nnewi F7
Nsukka F7
Offa E7
Ogbomosho 432,000 E7
Ogoja F7
Okene F7
Ondo F7
Onitsha 220,000 F7
Oron F8
Oshogbo 282,000 F7
Owerri F7
Owo F7
Oyo 152,000 E7
Pankshin F7
Panyam F7
Port Harcourt 242,000 F8
Ringim F6
Sapele F7
Shaki E7
Shendam F7
Sokoto F6
Toungo G7
Uromi F7
Vom F7
Wamba F7
Warri F7
Wukari F7
Yan G7
Yelwa F6
Yola G7
Zaria 224,000 F6
Zungeru F7

OTHER FEATURES

Adamawa (reg.) G7
Benin (bight) E8
Benue (riv.) F7
Biafra (bight) F8
Biu (plat.) G6
Bonny (bight) F8
Chad (lake) G6
Cross (riv.) F7
Dimlang (mt.) G7
Donga (riv.) G7
Foge (isl.) E6
Gongola (riv.) G6
Guinea (gulf) E8
Hadejia (riv.) F6
Jos (plat.) F7
Kaduna (riv.) F7
Kainji (res.) E6
Kebbi (riv.) E6
Komadugu Yobe (riv.) G6
Niger (delta) F8
Niger (riv.) F7
Osse (riv.) F7
Slave Coast (reg.) E7
Sokoto (riv.) F6
Sudan (reg.) F6

PORTUGAL-Madeira

CITIES and TOWNS

Funchal (cap.) 38,340 A2

OTHER FEATURES

Desertas (isls.) A2
Madeira (isl.) A2
Pôrto Santo (isl.) A2
Salvage (isls.) A2

SÃO TOMÉ E PRINCIPE

CITIES and TOWNS

Santo António 1,618 F8
São Tomé (cap.) 7,681 F8

OTHER FEATURES

Guinea (gulf) E8
Príncipe (isl.) F8
São Tomé (isl.) F8

SENEGAL

CITIES and TOWNS

Bakel 6,339 B6
Bignona 14,537 A6
Dagana 10,506 A5
Dakar (cap.) 798,792 A6
Diourbel 50,618 A6
Kaolack 106,899 A6
Kédougou 7,575 B6
Kaffrine 11,211 A6
Kolda 19,302 B6
Linguère 7,890 B5
Louga 35,063 A5
Matam 10,002 B5
M'Bour 37,663 A6
Nioro-du-Rip 7,824 A6
Podor 6,914 B5
Richard Toll A5
Rufisque A6
Saint-Louis 88,404 A5
Sedhiou 9,421 A6
Tambacounda 25,147 B6
Thiès 117,333 A5
Tivaouane 17,351 A5
Touba A6
Yarboutenda B6
Ziguinchor 72,726 A6

OTHER FEATURES

Casamance (riv.) A6
Falémé (riv.) B6
Ferlo (reg.) B6
Gambia (riv.) B6
Senegal (riv.) B5
Verde (cape) A6

SIERRA LEONE

CITIES and TOWNS

Bo 42,216 B7
Bonthe 6,230 B7
Freetown (cap.) 274,000 B7
Kabala 4,610 B7
Kambia 3,700 B7
Kenema 33,880 B7
Lungi 2,170 B7
Marampa B7
Makeni 28,684 B7
Moyamba 4,564 B7
Pendembu 2,696 B7
Pepel 3,793 B7
Port Loko 5,809 B7
Pujehun 1 B7

OTHER FEATURES

Loma, Mansa (lag.) B7
Mano (riv.) B7
Moa (riv.) B7
Sherbro (isl.) B7
Yawri (bay) B7

SPAIN-Canary Islands, Ceuta and Melilla

CITIES and TOWNS

Arrecife 21,310 B3
Ceuta 60,639 C1
La Laguna A3
Las Palmas de Gran
Canaria 260,368 B3
Melilla 64,942 D1
Santa Cruz de la Palma 10,393 A3
Santa Cruz de Tenerife 74,910 A3

OTHER FEATURES

Canary (isls.) A3
Fuerteventura (isl.) B3
Gomera (isl.) A3
Grand Canary (isl.) A3
Hierro (isl.) A3
Lanzarote (isl.) B3
La Palma (isl.) A3
Tenerife (isl.) A3

TOGO

CITIES and TOWNS

Aného (Anécho) 10,889 E7
Atakpamé 17,440 E7
Dapaong 10,100 E6
Kpalimé 19,801 E7
Kpémé 3,600 E7
Lama-Kara 9,400 E7
Lomé (cap.) 148,443 E7
Mango 9,600 E6
Sokodé 29,623 E7

OTHER FEATURES

Benin (bight) E8
Guinea (gulf) E8
Mono (riv.) E7
Oti (riv.) E7
Slave Coast (reg.) E7

TUNISIA

CITIES and TOWNS

Béja 39,226 F1
Ben Gardane 6,593 G2
Bizerte 62,856 F1
Burj al Hattaba F2
El Borma F2
El Djem 10,666 G1
El Kef 27,939 F1
Gabès 40,585 F2
Gafsa 42,225 F2
Halq el Oued 41,912 G1
Jendouba 18,127 F1
Kairouan 54,546 F1
Kalaa-Kebira 23,508 F1
Kasserine 22,594 F1
La Goulette (Halq el
Oued) 41,912 G1
La Skhirra 4,565 G2
Le Kef (El Kef) 27,939 F1
Mahdia 25,711 G1
Mareth 2,185 F2
Mateur 19,645 F1
Médenine 15,826 F2
Menzel Bourguiba 42,111 F1
Menzel Temime 18,857 G1
Moknine 26,035 G1
Monastir 26,759 G1
Msaken 33,559 G1
Nabeul 30,476 G1
Nefta 12,476 F2
Remada 6,100 F2
Sbeitla 8,039 F1
Sfax 171,297 G2
Sousse 69,530 G1
Tabarka 3,140 F1
Tatahouine 10,399 G2
Tozeur 16,772 F2
Tunis (cap.) 550,404 G1
Tunis* 873,515 G1
Zarzis 14,420 G2

OTHER FEATURES

Abiad, Ras el (Blanc) (cape) G1
Blanc (cape) G1
Bon (cape) G1
Chambi, Jebel (mt.) F2
Djerba (isl.) G2
Djerid, Shott el (salt lake) F2
Gabès (gulf) G2
Grand Erg Oriental (des.) F2
Hammamet (gulf) G1
Jefara (reg.) G2
Kerkennah (isls.) G2
Mediterranean (sea) F1
Medjerda (riv.) F1
Tib, Ras el (Bon) (cape) G1
Tunis (gulf) G1

UPPER VOLTA

CITIES and TOWNS

Aribinda D6
Banfora 12,358 D6
Batié D7
Bobo Dioulasso 115,063 D6
Bogandé E6
Dédougou D6
Diapaga E6
Diébougou D6
Djibo D6
Dori D6
Fada-N'Gourma 12,000 E6
Gaoua D6
Houndé D6
Kaya 18,000 D6
Koudougou 36,838 D6
Koupela D6
Léo D6
Ouagadougou (cap.) 172,661 D6
Ouahigouya 25,690 D6
Pama E6
Po D6
Tenkodogo E6
Tougan D6
Yako D6
Zabré D6

OTHER FEATURES

Black Volta (riv.) D6
Comoé (riv.) D7
Oti (riv.) E7
Red Volta (riv.) D6
Sudan (reg.) D6
White Volta (riv.) D6

WESTERN SAHARA

CITIES and TOWNS

Dakhla 6,554 A4
El Aaiún (Laayoune) 24,519 B3
Semara 2,655 B3
Villa Cisneros (Dakhla) 6,554 A4

OTHER FEATURES

Atoui, Wadi (dry riv.) B4
Ausert (well) B4
Barbas (cape) A4
Bir Ganduz (well) A4
Bir Nzaran (well) B4
Blanc (cape) A4
Bojador (cape) B3
Durnford (pt.) A4
Guelta de Zemmur (well) B3
Saguia el Hamra (dry riv.) B3
Tichlá (well) B4

*City and suburbs.
○Population of sub-district or division.

Agriculture, Industry and Resources

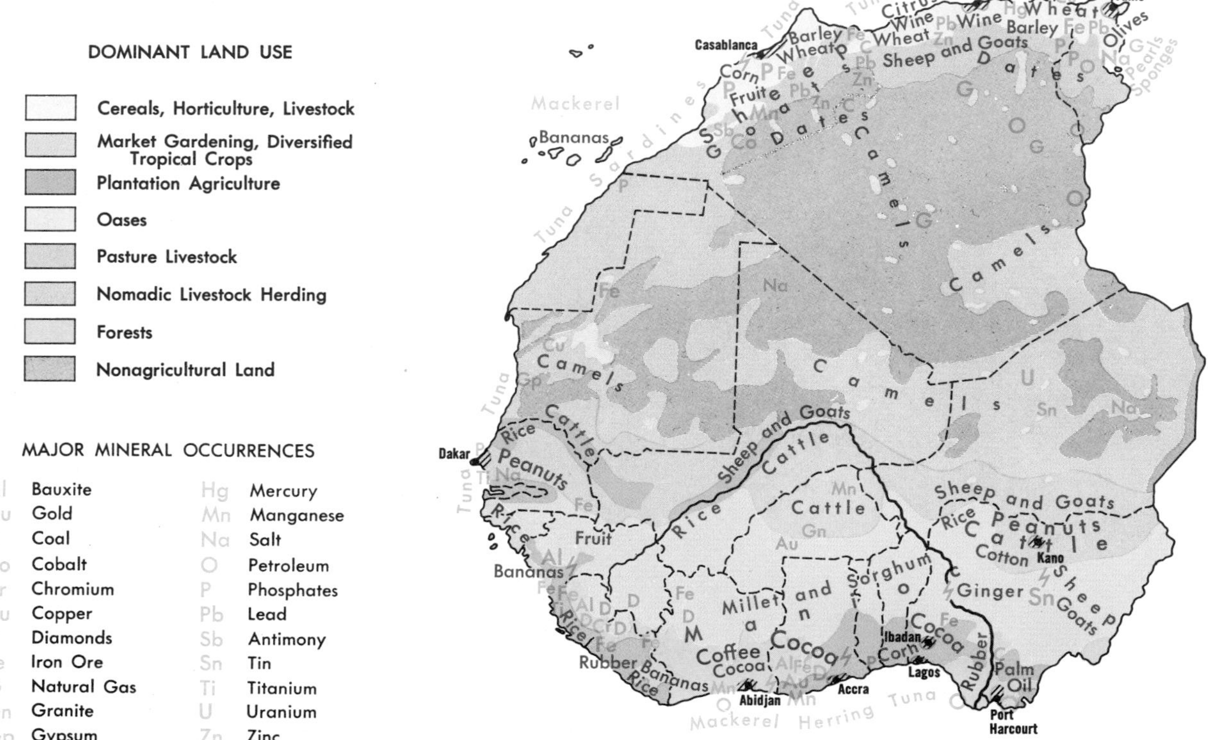

Northeastern Africa

LIBYA EGYPT CHAD SUDAN ETHIOPIA

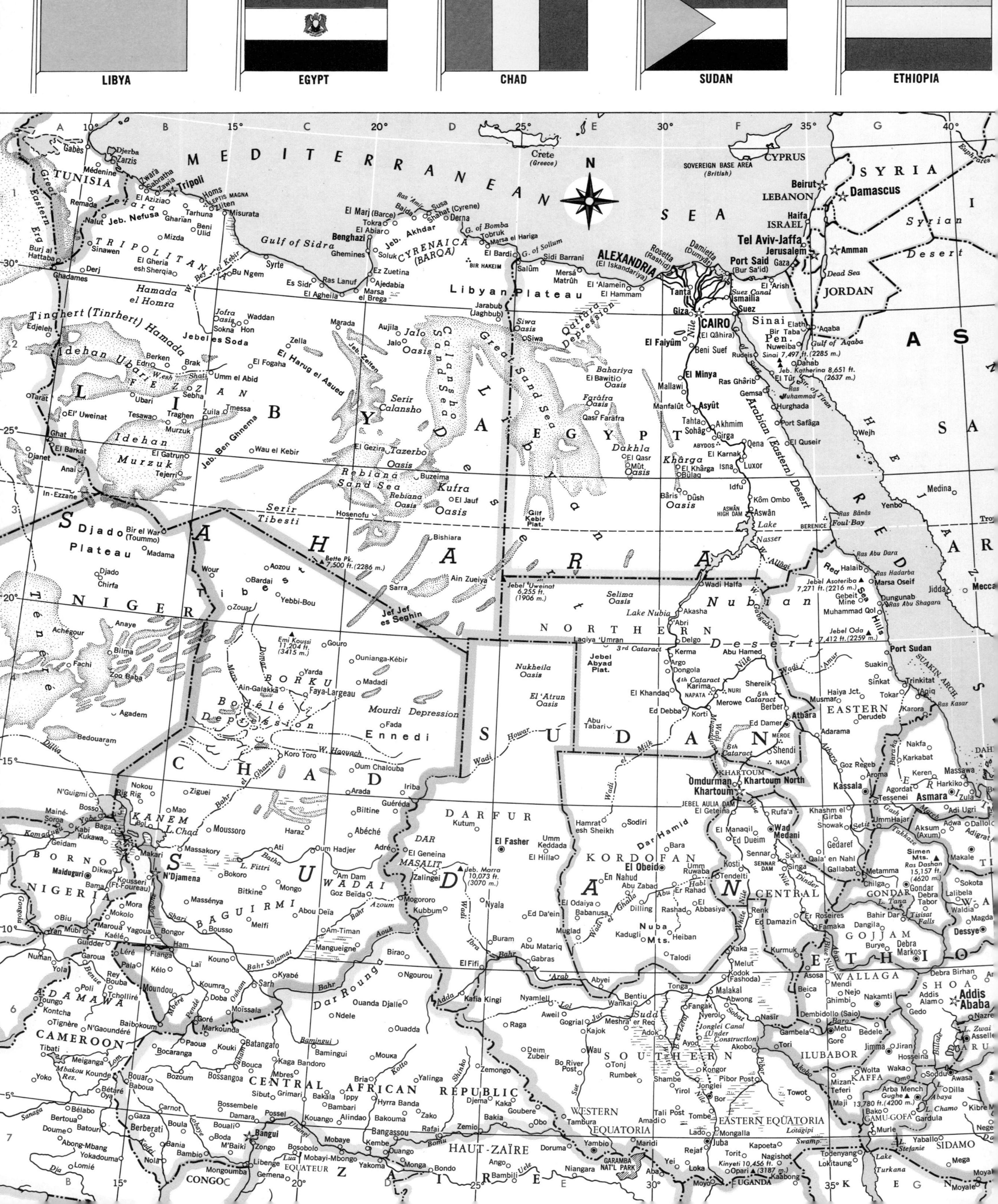

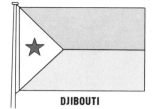

DJIBOUTI

LIBYA

AREA 679,358 sq. mi. (1,759,537 sq. km.)
POPULATION 2,856,000
CAPITAL Tripoli
LARGEST CITY Tripoli
HIGHEST POINT Bette Pk. 7,500 ft. (2,286 m.)
MONETARY UNIT Libyan dinar
MAJOR LANGUAGES Arabic, Berber
MAJOR RELIGION Islam

EGYPT

AREA 386,659 sq. mi. (1,001,447 sq. km.)
POPULATION 41,572,000
CAPITAL Cairo
LARGEST CITY Cairo
HIGHEST POINT Jeb. Katherina 8,651 ft. (2,637 m.)
MONETARY UNIT Egyptian pound
MAJOR LANGUAGE Arabic
MAJOR RELIGIONS Islam, Coptic Christianity

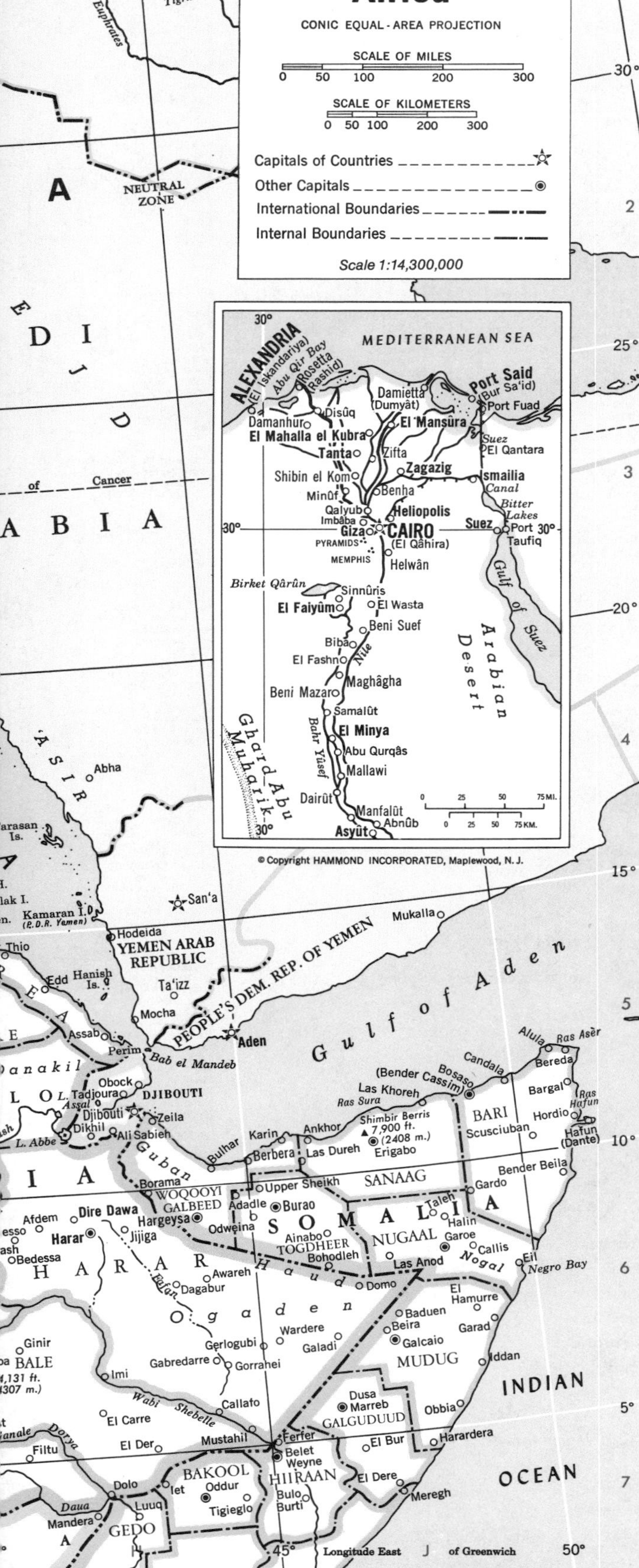

CHAD

AREA 495,752 sq. mi. (1,283,998 sq. km.)
POPULATION 4,309,000
CAPITAL N'Djamena
LARGEST CITY N'Djamena
HIGHEST POINT Emi Koussi 11,204 ft. (3,415 m.)
MONETARY UNIT CFA franc
MAJOR LANGUAGES Arabic, Bagirmi, French, Sara, Massa, Moudang
MAJOR RELIGIONS Islam, tribal religions

SUDAN

AREA 967,494 sq. mi. (2,505,809 sq. km.)
POPULATION 18,691,000
CAPITAL Khartoum
LARGEST CITY Khartoum
HIGHEST POINT Jeb. Marra 10,073 ft. (3,070 m.)
MONETARY UNIT Sudanese pound
MAJOR LANGUAGES Arabic, Dinka, Nubian, Beja, Nuer
MAJOR RELIGIONS Islam, tribal religions

ETHIOPIA

AREA 471,776 sq. mi. (1,221,900 sq. km.)
POPULATION 31,065,000
CAPITAL Addis Ababa
LARGEST CITY Addis Ababa
HIGHEST POINT Ras Dashan 15,157 ft. (4,620 m.)
MONETARY UNIT birr
MAJOR LANGUAGES Amharic, Gallinya, Tigrinya, Somali, Sidamo, Arabic, Ge'ez
MAJOR RELIGIONS Coptic Christianity, Islam

DJIBOUTI

AREA 8,880 sq. mi. (23,000 sq. km.)
POPULATION 386,000
CAPITAL Djibouti
LARGEST CITY Djibouti
HIGHEST POINT Moussa Ali 6,768 ft. (2,063 m.)
MONETARY UNIT Djibouti franc
MAJOR LANGUAGES Arabic, Somali, Afar, French
MAJOR RELIGIONS Islam, Roman Catholicism

(continued on following page)

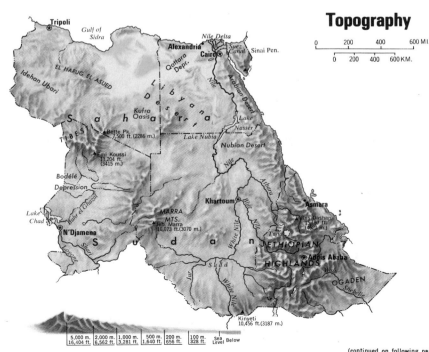

Topography

0 200 400 600 MI.
0 200 400 600 KM.

5,000 m. 16,404 ft. | 2,000 m. 6,562 ft. | 1,000 m. 3,281 ft. | 500 m. 1,640 ft. | 200 m. 656 ft. | 100 m. 328 ft. | Sea Level | Below

(continued on following page)

112 Northeastern Africa

(continued)

Aswan 144,377 F3
Asyût 213,983 J4
Bâris F3
Benha 88,992 J3
Beni Mazar 39,373 J4
Beni Suef 118,148 J3
Biba 33,074 J4
Bûlaq F2
Bur Sai'd (Port Said) 262,620 K2
Cairo (cap.) 5,084,463 J3
Dahab F2
Dairût 31,624 J4
Damanhur 188,927 J3
Damietta 93,546 J3
Disûq 58,650 J3
Dumyât (Damietta) 93,546 J3
Dûsh F3
El A'lamein E1
El A'rish F1
El Bawiti E2
El Faiyûm 167,081 J3
El Fashn 33,506 J4
El Hammam 6,588 E1
El Iskandariya (Alexandria) 2,318,655 J2
El Karnak F2
El Khârga 26,375 F2
El Mahalla el Kubra 292,853 J3
El Mansûra 257,866 K3
El Minya 146,423 J4
El Qâhira (Cairo) (cap.) 5,084,463 J3
El Qantara 919 K3
El Qasr E2
El Quseir 12,297 F2
El Tûr F2
El Wasta 17,659 J3
Gemsa F2
Girga 51,110 F2
Giza 1,246,713 J3
Heliopolis J3
Helwân J3
Hurghada F2
Idfu 34,858 F3
Imbâba J3
Ismailia 145,978 K3
Isna 34,186 F2
Karnak (El Karnak) F2
Kôm Ombo 44,531 F3
Luxor 92,748 F2
Maghâgha 40,802 J4
Mallawi 74,256 J4
Manfalût 41,126 J4
Mersá Matrûh 27,857 E1
Minûf 55,131 J3
Mût 8,032 E2
Nuweiba F2
Port Fuad K3
Port Safâga F2
Port Said 262,620 K2
Port Taufiq K3
Qalyub 62,739 J3
Qasr Farâfra E2
Qena 94,013 F2
Ras Ghârib F2
Rashid (Rosetta) 42,962 J2
Rudeis F2
Salûm 4,161 E1
Samalût 48,146 J4
Shibin el Kom 102,844 J3
Sidi Barrani 1,574 E1
Sinnûris 42,022 J3
Siwa 4,999 E2
Sohâg 101,758 F2
Suez 194,001 K3
Tahta 45,242 F2
Tanta 284,636 J3
Zagazig 202,637 K3
Zifta 50.410 J3

OTHER FEATURES

Abu Qir (bay) J2
Abydos (ruins) F2
A'llaqi, Wadi (dry riv.) F3
A'qaba (gulf) G2
Arabian (des.) F2
Aswân (dam) F3
Aswân High (dam) F3
Bahariya (oasis) E2
Bahr Yusef (stream) J4
Bânâs, Ras (cape) G3
Berenice (ruins) F3
Birket Qârûn (lake) J3
Bir Taba (well) F2
Bitter (lkes) K3
Dakhla (oasis) E2
Eastern (Arabian) (des.) F2
El Sollum (gulf) E1
Farâfra (oasis) E2
Foul (bay) G3
Ghard Abu Muharik (des.) J4
Gilf Kebir (plat.) E3
Great Sand Sea (des.) D2
Katherina, Jebel (mt.) F2
Khârga (oasis) F2
Libyan (des.) E2
Libyan (plat.) E1
Mediterranean (sea) E1
Memphis (ruins) J3
Muhammad, Ras (cape) F2
Nasser (lake) F3
Nile (riv.) F2
Pyramids (ruins) J3
Qattara (depr.) E2
Red (sea) G3
Sahara (des.) E3
Sinai (mt.) F2
Sinai (pen.) F2
Siwa (oasis) E2
Suez (canal) K3
Suez (gulf) F2
Tiran (str.) F2
U'weinat, Jebel (mt.) E3

ETHIOPIA

PROVINCES

Arusi 852,900 G6
Bale 707,800 H6
Begemdir 1,355,800 G5
Eritrea 1,947,600 G4
Gamu-Gofa 698,800 G6
Gojjam 1,750,100 G5
Harar 3,359,200 H6
Ilubabor 688,800 F6
Kaffa 1,693,000 G6
Shoa 5,369,500 G6
Sidamo 2,479,800 G7
Tigre 1,828,900 H5
Wallaga 1,269,100 G6
Wallo 2,459,900 H5

CITIES and TOWNS

Addis Ababa (cap.) 1,196,300 G6
Addis Alam 5,500 G6
Adigrat 9,400 G5
Adi Ugri 12,800 G5
Adwa 16,400 G5
Afdem H6
Agordat G4
Aksum 12,800 G5
Ankober H6
Arba Mench 7,660 G6
Asmara 393,800 G4
Asosa F5
Assab 16,000 H5
Asselle 19,390 G6
Awareh H6
Awasa 16,790 G6
Awash H6
Axum (Aksum) 12,800 G5
Bahir Dar 25,100 G5
Burye G5
Callafo H6
Chilga G5
Dagabur H6
Dallol G5
Dangila G5
Debra Birhan 16,700 G6
Debra Markos 30,260 G5
Debra Tabor 8,700 G5
Dembidollo 7,600 F6
Dessye 49,750 G5
Dilla 13,800 G6
Dire Dawa 63,700 H6
Dolo H7
Domo J6
Edd H5
El Carre H6
El Der H6
Filtu H6
Gabredarre H6
Galadi J6
Gambela F6
Gardula 5,800 G6
Gedo G6
Gerlogubi H6
Ghimbi 8,300 G6
Ginir H6
Goba 13,500 H6
Gondar 38,600 G5
Gore 8,500 G6
Gorrahei H6
Harar 48,440 H6
Harkiko G4
Hosseina 8,500 G6
Imi H6
Jijiga 8,000 H6
Jimma 47,360 G6
Jiran G6
Karkabat G4
Keren G4
Kibre Mengist 8,300 G6
Lalibela G5
Magdala G5
Maji G6
Makale 30,780 G5
Massawa 19,800 G4
Mega G7
Mendi G6
Mersa Fatma H5
Metamma G5
Metu G6
Miesso H6
Mizan Teferi G6
Moyale G7
Murle G6
Mustahil H6
Nakamti 18,310 G6
Nakfa G4
Nazret 42,900 G6
Negelli 8,800 G6
Nejo G6
Saio (Dembidollo) 7,600 F6
Soddu 11,900 G6
Sokota G5
Tessenei G4
Thio H5
Tori F6
Umm Hajar G5
Waka G6
Waldia 9,600 G5
Wardere J6
Wolta G6
Yaballo G6
Zula G4

OTHER FEATURES

Abay (riv.) G5
Abaya (lake) G6
Akobo (riv.) F6
Assale (lake) H5
Atbara (riv.) G4
Awash (riv.) H5
Bale (mt.) G6
Baraka (riv.) G4
Baro (riv.) G6
Billate (riv.) G6
Blue Nile (Abay) (riv.) G5
Buri (pen.) H4
Chamo (lake) G6
Dahlak (arch.) H4
Dahlak (isl.) H4
Danakil (reg.) H5
Dawa (riv.) G7
Fafan (riv.) H6
Ganale Dorya (riv.) H6
Gash Mareb (riv.) G5
Gughe (mt.) G6
Haud (reg.) J6
Kasar, Ras (cape) G4
Ogaden (reg.) H6
Omo (riv.) G6
Ras Dashan (mt.) G5
Red (sea) H4
Rudolf (Turkana) (lake) G7
Simen (mts.) G5
Stefanie (lake) G7
Takkaze (riv.) G5
Tana (lake) G5
Tisisat (fall) G5
Turkana (lake) G7
Wabi (riv.) H6
Wabi Shebelle (riv.) H6
Zwai (lake) G6

LIBYA

CITIES and TOWNS

Ajedabia○ 53,170 D1
Aujila○ 6,695 D2
Baida○ 59,765 D1
Barce (El Marj)○ 55,444 D1
Benghazi (cap.)○ 286,943 C1
Beni Ulid○ 19,113 B1
Berken B2
Brak○ 12,507 B2
Bu Ngem C1
Cyrene (Shahat)○ 17,157 D1
Derj○ 2,152 B1
Derna○ 44,145 D1
Edri B2
El Abiar○ 17,685 D1
El Agheila C1
El Azizia○ 34,077 B1
El Bardi○ 4,330 D1
El Barkat○ 2,139 B3
El Fogaha C2
El Gatrun B3
El Gezira D2
El Jauf○ 6,481 D3
El Marj○ 55,444 D1
El' Uweinat B2
Es Sidr○ 706 C1
Ez Zuetina○ 7,256 D1
Ghadames○ 6,172 A2
Gharfan○ 65,224 B1
Ghat○ 6,924 B3
Ghemines○ 4,313 C1
Homs○ 66,890 B1
Hon○ 2,766 C2
Jaghbub (Jarabub)○ 1,436 D2
Jalo D2
Jarabub○ 1,436 D2
Marada○ 3,201 C2
Marsa el Brega○ 2,618 D1
Marsa el Hariga○ 5,043 D1
Mekili D1
Misurata○ 102,439 C1
Mizda○ 11,472 B1
Murzuk○ 22,185 B2
Nalut○ 23,535 B1
Ras Lanuf○ 1,990 C1
Sabrathaa○ 30,836 B1
Sebha○ 35,879 B2
Shahat○ 17,157 D1
Sinawen○ 1,549 B1
Sokna○ 3,757 C2
Soluk○ 6,501 D1
Susa D1
Syrte○ 22,797 C1
Tarhuna○ 52,657 B1
Tejerri B3
Tesawa B2
Tmessa C2
Tobruk○ 58,384 D1
Tokra○ 10,714 D1
Traghen B2
Tripoli (cap.)○ 550,438 B1
Ubari○ 19,132 B2
Umm el Abid C2
Waddan○ 5,347 C2
Wau el Kebir C2
Zawia○ 72,092 B1
Zella○ 4,835 C2
Zliten○ 58,981 C1
Zuila C2
Zwara○ 15,078 B1

OTHER FEATURES

Ain Zueiya (well) D3
Akhdar, Jebel (mts.) D1
A'mir, Ras (cape) D1
Barqa (Cyrenaica) (reg.) D1
Ben Ghnema, Jebel (mts.) C2
Bette (peak) C3
Bey el Kebir, Wadi (dry riv.) B1
Bir Hakeim (ruins) D1
Bishiara (well) D3
Bomba (gulf) D1
Buzeima (well) D3
Calansho Sand Sea (des.) D2
Calansho, Serir (des.) D2
Cyrenaica (reg.) D1
Fezzan (reg.) B2
Great Sand Sea (des.) D2
Harug el Asued, El (mts.) C2
Homra, Hamada el (des.) B2
Hosenofu (well) D3
Idehan Ubari (des.) B2
Idehan Murzuk (des.) B2
Jalo (oasis) D2
Jefara (reg.) B1
Jef Jef es Seghin (plat.) D3
Jofra (oasis) C2
Kufra (oasis) D3
Leptis Magna (ruins) B1
Libyan (des.) D2
Libyan (plat.) D1
Mediterranean (sea) C1
Nefusa, Jebel (mts.) B1
Rebiana○ (oasis) D3
Rebiana Sand Sea (des.) D3
Sahara (des.) C3
Sarra (well) D3
Shati, Wadi esh (dry riv.) B2
Sidra (gulf) C1
Soda, Jebel es (mts.) C2
Tazerbo○ (oasis) D2
Tibesti, Serir (des.) C3
Tinghert Hamada (Tinrhert) (des.) B2
Tripolitania (reg.) B1
U'weinat, Jebel (mt.) E3
Zelten, Jebel (mts.) D2

SUDAN

PROVINCES

Central F5
Darfur D5
Eastern G4
Khartoum F4
Kordofan E5
Northern E3
Southern E6

CITIES and TOWNS

A'bri F3
Abu Hamed F4
Abu Matariq E5
Abu Zabad E5
Abwong F6
Abyei E6
Adarama G4
Adok F6
Akasha F3
Akobo F6
Amadi F6
A'qiq G4
Argo F4
Aroma G4
Atbara 66,000 F4
Aweil E6
Ayod F6
Babanusa E5
Bara F5
Bentiu E6
Berber F4
Bor F6
Bo River Post E6
Buram E5
Damazin (Ed Damazin) 12,000 F5
Deim Zubeir E6
Delgo F3
Derudeb G4
Dilling E5
Dongola 6,000 F4
Dungunab G3
Ed Dae'in E5
Ed Damer 17,000 F4
Ed Damazin 12,000 F5
Ed Debba F4
Ed Dueim 27,000 F5
El Abbasiya F5
El Fasher 52,000 E5
El Fifi D5
El Geneina 33,000 D5
El Geteina F5
El Hilla E5
El Khandaq E4
El Manaqil F5
El Obeid 90,000 E5
El Odaiya E5
En Nahud 23,000 E5
Er Rahad F5
Er Roseires F5
Famaka F5
Fangak F6
Fashoda (Kodok) F6
Gabras E5
Gallabat G5
Gebeit Mine G3
Gedaref 92,000 G5
Gogrial E6
Goz Regeb G4
Haiya Junction G4
Halaib G3
Heiban F5
Jonglei F6
Juba 57,000 F7
Kadugli 18,000 E5
Kafia Kingi D6
Kajok E6
Kaka F5
Kapoeta F7
Karima F4
Karora G4
Kassala 99,000 G4
Kerma F4
Khartoum (cap.) 334,000 F4
Khartoum North 151,000 F4
Khashm el Girba G5
Kodok F6
Kongor F6
Korti F4
Kosti 57,000 F5
Kubbum D5
Kurmuk F5
Kutum D5
Lado F6
Loka F7
Malakal 35,000 F6
Maridi E7
Marsa Oseif G3
Melut F5
Merowe F4
Meshra er Req E6
Mongalla F6
Muglad E5
Muhammad Qol G3
Musmar G4
Nagishot F7
Nasir F6
Nimule F7
Nyala 60,000 E5
Nyamlell E6
Nyerol F6
Omdurman 299,000 F4
Opari F7
Pibor Post F6
Port Sudan 133,000 G4
Qalae'n Nahl F5
Raga E6
Rashad F5
Rejaf F7
Renk F5
Rufaa' F5
Rumbek 17,000 E6
Sennar F5
Shambe F6
Shendi F4
Shereik F4
Showak G5
Singa F5
Sinkat G4
Sodiri E5
Suakin G4
Suki F5
Tali Post F6
Talodi F5
Tambura E6
Tendelti F5
Tokar G4
Tombe F6
Tonga F6
Tonj E6
Torit F7
Towot F6
Trinkitat G4
Umm Keddada E5
Umm Ruwaba F5
Wadi Halfa F3
Wad Medani 107,000 F5
Wankai E6
Wau 53,000 E6
Yambio 7,000 E7
Yei F7
Yirol F6
Zalingei D5

OTHER FEATURES

Abu Dara, Ras (cape) G3
Abu Habl, Wadi (dry riv.) F5
Abu Shagara, Ras (cape) G3
Abu Tabari (well) E4
Adda (riv.) D6
Akobo (riv.) F6
A'mur, Wadi (dry riv.) G4
Asoteriba, Jebel (mt.) G3
Atbara (riv.) G4
Bahr Azoum (riv.) D5
Bahr el A'rab (riv.) E6
Bahr ez Zeraf (riv.) F6
Baraka (riv.) G4
Blue Nile (riv.) F5
Dar Hamid (reg.) F5
Dar Masalit (reg.) D5
Dinder (riv.) F5
El A'trun (oasis) E4
Fifth Cataract F4
Fourth Cataract F4
Gabgaba, Wadi (dry riv.) F3
Gezira, El (reg.) F5
Ghalla, Wadi el (dry riv.) E5
Hadarba, Ras (cape) G3
Howar, Wadi (dry riv.) E4
Ibra, Wadi (dry riv.) D5
Jebel Abyad (plat.) E4
Jebel Aulia (dam) F4
Jur (riv.) E6
Kasar, Ras (cape) G4
Kinyeti (mt.) F7
Laqiya U'mran (well) E3
Libyan (des.) E3
Lol (dry riv.) E6
Lotagipi Swamp (plain) F6
Marra, Jebel (mt.) D5
Meroe (ruins) F4
Milk, Wadi el (dry riv.) E4
Muqaddam, Wadi (dry riv.) F4
Napata (ruins) F4
Naqa (ruins) F4
Nile (riv.) F4
Nuba (mts.) E5
Nubia (lake) F3
Nubian (des.) F3
Nukheila (oasis) E4
Nuri (ruins) F4
Oda, Jebel (mt.) G3
Pibor (riv.) F6
Red (sea) G3
Sahara (des.) E3
Second Cataract F3
Selima (oasis) E3
Sennar (dam) F5
Setit (riv.) G5
Sixth Cataract F4
Sobat (riv.) F6
Suakin (arch.) G4
Sudan (reg.) E5
Sudd (swamp) F6
Sue (riv.) E6
Third Cataract E4
U'weinat, Jebel (mt.) E3
White Nile (riv.) F5

○Population of sub-district or division.

Agriculture, Industry and Resources

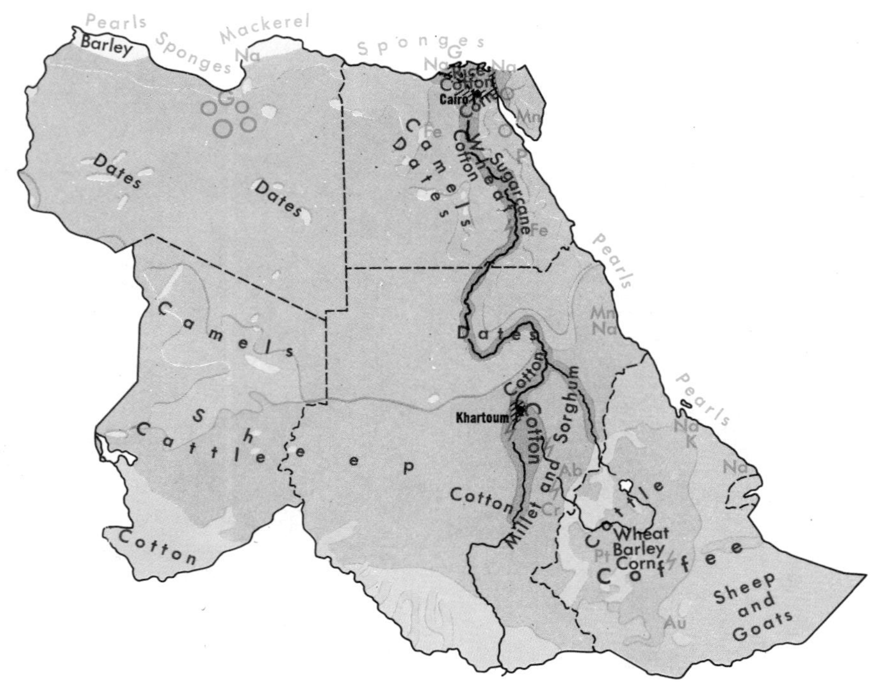

DOMINANT LAND USE

- Cereals, Horticulture, Livestock
- Cash Crops, Mixed Cereals
- Cotton, Cereals
- Market Gardening, Diversified Tropical Crops
- Plantation Agriculture
- Oases
- Pasture Livestock
- Nomadic Livestock Herding
- Forests
- Nonagricultural Land

MAJOR MINERAL OCCURRENCES

Ab	Asbestos	Mn	Manganese
Au	Gold	Na	Salt
Cr	Chromium	O	Petroleum
Fe	Iron Ore	P	Phosphates
G	Natural Gas	Pt	Platinum
K	Potash		

Water Power

Major Industrial Areas

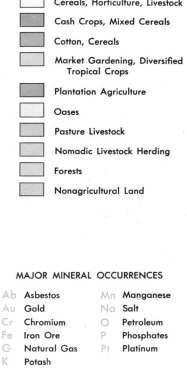

ANGOLA

AREA 481,351 sq. mi. (1,246,700 sq. km.)
POPULATION 7,078,000
CAPITAL Luanda
LARGEST CITY Luanda
HIGHEST POINT Mt. Moco 8,593 ft. (2,620 m.)
MONETARY UNIT kwanza
MAJOR LANGUAGES Mbundu, Kongo, Lunda, Portuguese
MAJOR RELIGIONS Tribal religions, Roman Catholicism

BURUNDI

AREA 10,747 sq. mi. (27,835 sq. km.)
POPULATION 4,021,910
CAPITAL Bujumbura
LARGEST CITY Bujumbura
HIGHEST POINT 8,858 ft. (2,700 m.)
MONETARY UNIT Burundi franc
MAJOR LANGUAGES Kirundi, French, Swahili
MAJOR RELIGIONS Tribal religions, Roman Catholicism, Islam

CAMEROON

AREA 183,568 sq. mi. (475,441 sq. km.)
POPULATION 8,503,000
CAPITAL Yaoundé
LARGEST CITY Douala
HIGHEST POINT Cameroon 13,350 ft. (4,069 m.)
MONETARY UNIT CFA franc
MAJOR LANGUAGES Fang, Bamileke, Fulani, Duala, French, English
MAJOR RELIGIONS Tribal religions, Christianity, Islam

CENTRAL AFRICAN REP.

AREA 242,000 sq. mi. (626,780 sq. km.)
POPULATION 2,284,000
CAPITAL Bangui
LARGEST CITY Bangui
HIGHEST POINT Gao 4,659 ft. (1,420 m.)
MONETARY UNIT CFA franc
MAJOR LANGUAGES Banda, Gbaya, Sangho, French
MAJOR RELIGIONS Tribal religions, Christianity, Islam

CONGO

AREA 132,046 sq. mi. (342,000 sq. km.)
POPULATION 1,537,000
CAPITAL Brazzaville
LARGEST CITY Brazzaville
HIGHEST POINT Leketi Mts. 3,412 ft. (1,040 m.)
MONETARY UNIT CFA franc
MAJOR LANGUAGES Kikongo, Bateke, Lingala, French
MAJOR RELIGIONS Christianity, tribal religions, Islam

EQUATORIAL GUINEA

AREA 10,831 sq. mi. (28,052 sq. km.)
POPULATION 244,000
CAPITAL Malabo
LARGEST CITY Malabo
HIGHEST POINT 9,868 ft. (3,008 m.)
MONETARY UNIT ekuele
MAJOR LANGUAGES Fang, Bubi, Spanish
MAJOR RELIGIONS Tribal religions, Christianity

GABON

AREA 103,346 sq. mi. (267,666 sq. km.)
POPULATION 551,000
CAPITAL Libreville
LARGEST CITY Libreville
HIGHEST POINT Ibounzi 5,165 ft. (1,574 m.)
MONETARY UNIT CFA franc
MAJOR LANGUAGES Fang and other Bantu languages, French
MAJOR RELIGIONS Tribal religions, Christianity, Islam

KENYA

AREA 224,960 sq. mi. (582,646 sq. km.)
POPULATION 15,327,061
CAPITAL Nairobi
LARGEST CITY Nairobi
HIGHEST POINT Kenya 17,058 ft. (5,199 m.)
MONETARY UNIT Kenya shilling
MAJOR LANGUAGES Kikuyu, Luo, Kavirondo, Kamba, Swahili, English
MAJOR RELIGIONS Tribal religions, Christianity, Hinduism, Islam

MALAWI

AREA 45,747 sq. mi. (118,485 sq. km.)
POPULATION 5,968,000
CAPITAL Lilongwe
LARGEST CITY Blantyre
HIGHEST POINT Mulanje 9,843 ft. (3,000 m.)
MONETARY UNIT Malawi kwacha
MAJOR LANGUAGES Chichewa, Yao, English, Nyanja, Tumbuka, Tonga, Ngoni
MAJOR RELIGIONS Tribal religions, Islam, Christianity

RWANDA

AREA 10,169 sq. mi. (26,337 sq. km.)
POPULATION 4,819,317
CAPITAL Kigali
LARGEST CITY Kigali
HIGHEST POINT Karisimbi 14,780 ft. (4,505 m.)
MONETARY UNIT Rwanda franc
MAJOR LANGUAGES Kinyarwanda, French, Swahili
MAJOR RELIGIONS Tribal religions, Roman Catholicism, Islam

SOMALIA

AREA 246,200 sq. mi. (637,658 sq. km.)
POPULATION 3,645,000
CAPITAL Mogadishu
LARGEST CITY Mogadishu
HIGHEST POINT Surud Ad 7,900 ft. (2,408 m.)
MONETARY UNIT Somali shilling
MAJOR LANGUAGES Somali, Arabic, Italian, English
MAJOR RELIGION Islam

TANZANIA

AREA 363,708 sq. mi. (942,003 sq. km.)
POPULATION 17,527,560
CAPITAL Dar es Salaam
LARGEST CITY Dar es Salaam
HIGHEST POINT Kilimanjaro 19,340 ft. (5,895 m.)
MONETARY UNIT Tanzanian shilling
MAJOR LANGUAGES Nyamwezi-Sukuma, Swahili, English
MAJOR RELIGIONS Tribal religions, Christianity, Islam

UGANDA

AREA 91,076 sq. mi. (235,887 sq. km.)
POPULATION 12,630,076
CAPITAL Kampala
LARGEST CITY Kampala
HIGHEST POINT Margherita 16,795 ft. (5,119 m.)
MONETARY UNIT Ugandan shilling
MAJOR LANGUAGES Luganda, Acholi, Teso, Nyoro, Soga, Nkole, English, Swahili
MAJOR RELIGIONS Tribal religions, Christianity, Islam

ZAIRE

AREA 905,063 sq. mi. (2,344,113 sq. km.)
POPULATION 28,291,000
CAPITAL Kinshasa
LARGEST CITY Kinshasa
HIGHEST POINT Margherita 16,795 ft. (5,119 m.)
MONETARY UNIT zaire
MAJOR LANGUAGES Tshiluba, Mongo, Kikongo, Kingwana, Zande, Lingala, Swahili, French
MAJOR RELIGIONS Tribal religions, Christianity

ZAMBIA

AREA 290,586 sq. mi. (752,618 sq. km.)
POPULATION 5,679,808
CAPITAL Lusaka
LARGEST CITY Lusaka
HIGHEST POINT Sunzu 6,782 ft. (2,067 m.)
MONETARY UNIT Zambian kwacha
MAJOR LANGUAGES Bemba, Tonga, Lozi, Luvale, Nyanja, English
MAJOR RELIGIONS Tribal religions

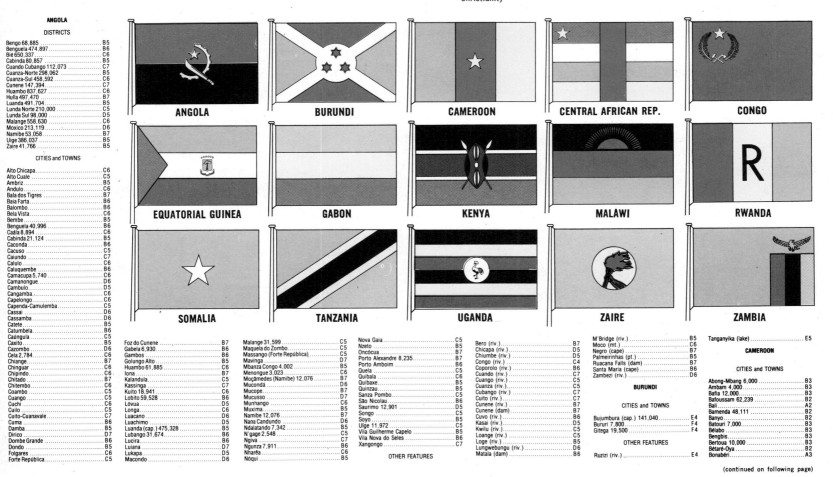

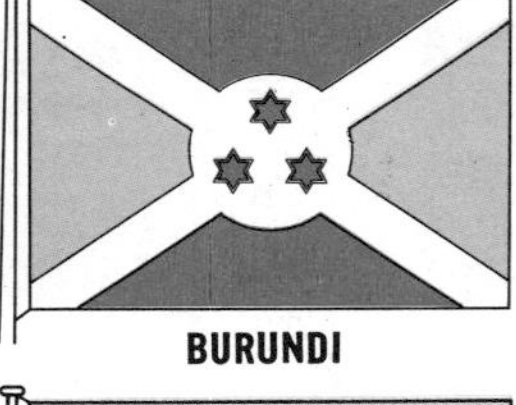

ANGOLA | BURUNDI | CAMEROON | CENTRAL AFRICAN REP. | CONGO

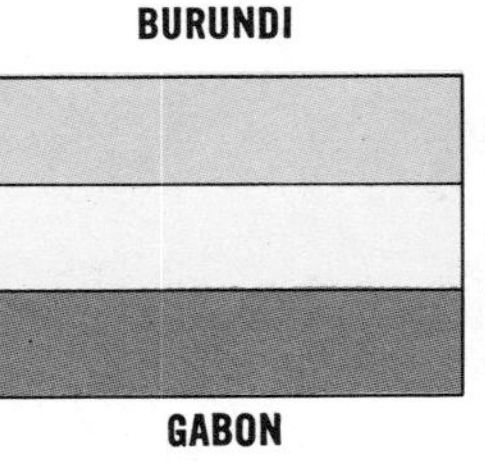

EQUATORIAL GUINEA | GABON | KENYA | MALAWI | RWANDA

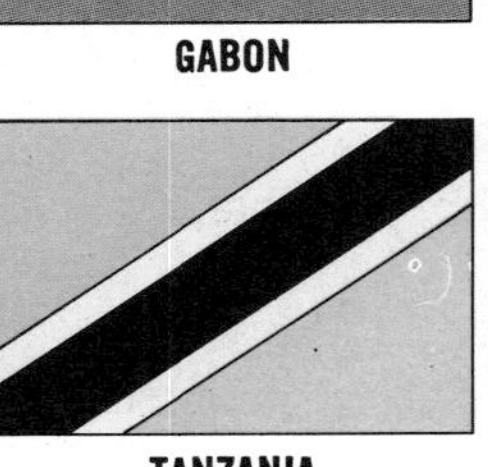
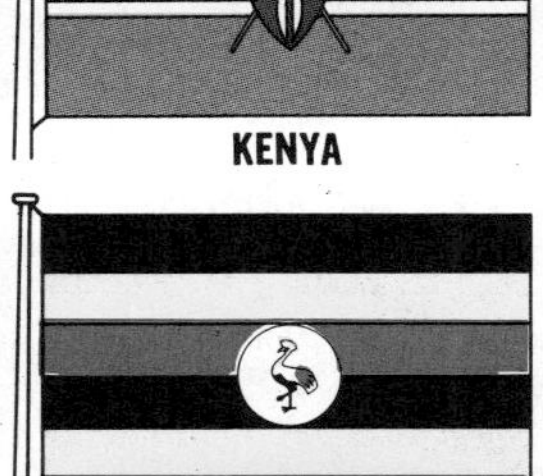
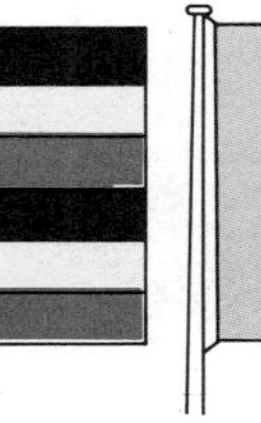

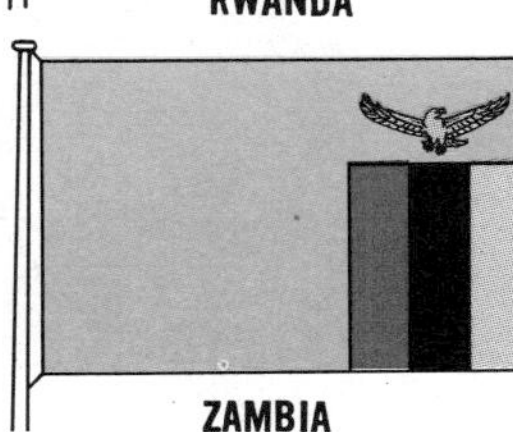

SOMALIA | TANZANIA | UGANDA | ZAIRE | ZAMBIA

ANGOLA

DISTRICTS

Bengo 68,885 B5
Benguela 474,897 B6
Bié 650,337 C6
Cabinda 80,857 B5
Cuando Cubango 112,073 C7
Cuanza-Norte 298,062 B5
Cuanza-Sul 458,592 C6
Cunene 147,394 C7
Huambo 837,627 C6
Hulla 497,470 B7
Luanda 491,704 B5
Lunda Norte 210,000 C5
Lunda Sul 98,000 D5
Malange 558,630 C6
Moxico 213,119 D6
Namibe 53,058 B7
Uige 386,037 B5
Zaire 41,766 B5

CITIES and TOWNS

Alto Chicapa C6
Alto Cuale C5
Ambriz B5
Andulo C6
Bala dos Tigres B7
Baia Farta B6
Balombo B6
Bela Vista C6
Bembe B5
Benguela 40,996 B6
Caála 8,894 C6
Cabinda 21,124 B5
Caconda B6
Cacuso C5
Caiundo C7
Calulo C6
Caluquembe B6
Camacupa 5,740 C6
Camanongue D6
Cambulo D5
Cangamba C6
Capelongo C6
Capenda-Camulemba C5
Cassai D6
Cassamba D6
Catete B5
Catumbela B6
Caúngula C5
Caxito B5
Cazombo D6
Cela 2,784 C6
Chiange B7
Chinguar C6
Chipindo C6
Chitado B7
Chitembo C6
Coambo C5
Cuango C5
Cuchi C6
Cuilo C5
Cuito-Cuanavale C7
Cuma B6
Damba B5
Dirico D7
Dombe Grande B6
Dondo B5
Folgares C6
Forte República C5
Foz do Cunene B7
Gabela 6,930 B6
Gambos B6
Golungo Alto B5
Huambo 61,885 C6
Iona B7
Kalandula C5
Kassinga C7
Kuito 18,941 C6
Lobito 59,528 B6
Lóvua D5
Longa C6
Luacano D6
Luachimo D5
Luanda (cap.) 475,328 B5
Lubango 31,674 B6
Lucira B6
Luiana D7
Lukapa D5
Macondo D6
Malange 31,599 C5
Maquela do Zombo C5
Massango (Forte República) C5
Mavinga D7
Mbanza Congo 4,002 B5
Menongue 3,023 C6
Moçâmedes (Namibe) 12,076 B7
Mucondá D6
Mucope B7
Mucusso D7
Munhango C6
Muxima B5
Namibe 12,076 B7
Nana Candundo D6
Ndalatando 7,342 B5
N'gage 2,548 C5
Ngiva C7
Ngunza 7,911 B6
Nharêa C6
Nóqui B5
Nova Gaia C5
Nzeto B5
Oncócua B7
Porto Alexandre 8,235 B7
Porto Amboim B6
Quela C5
Quibala C6
Quibaxe B5
Quinzau B5
Sanza Pombo C5
São Nicolau B6
Saurimo 12,901 D5
Songo C5
Soyo B5
Uíge 11,972 C5
Vila Guilherme Capelo B5
Vila Nova do Seles B6
Xangongo C7

OTHER FEATURES

Bero (riv.) B7
Chicapa (riv.) D5
Chiumbe (riv.) D5
Congo (riv.) C4
Coporolo (riv.) B6
Cuando (riv.) C7
Cuango (riv.) C5
Cuanza (riv.) C5
Cubango (riv.) C7
Cuito (riv.) C7
Cunene (riv.) B7
Cunene (dam) B7
Cuvo (riv.) B6
Kasai (riv.) D5
Kwilu (riv.) C5
Loange (riv.) C5
Loge (riv.) B5
Lungwebungu (riv.) D6
Matala (dam) B6
M'Bridge (riv.) B5
Moco (mt.) C6
Negro (cape) B7
Palmeirinhas (pt.) B5
Ruacana Falls (dam) B7
Santa Maria (cape) B6
Zambezi (riv.) D6

BURUNDI

CITIES and TOWNS

Bujumbura (cap.) 141,040 E4
Bururi 7,800 F4
Gitega 19,500 F4

OTHER FEATURES

Ruzizi (riv.) E4
Tanganyika (lake) E5

CAMEROON

CITIES and TOWNS

Abong-Mbang 6,000 B3
Ambam 4,000 B3
Bafia 12,000 B3
Bafoussam 62,239 B2
Bali A2
Bamenda 48,111 B2
Banyo B2
Batouri 7,000 B3
Bélabo B3
Bengbis B3
Bertoua 10,000 B3
Bétaré-Oya B2
Bonabéri A3

(continued on following page)

Central Africa

(continued)

Buea 24,584 .... A3
Campo B3
Djoum B3
Douala 458,426 .... B3
Doumé B3
Dschang 20,000 .... A2
Ebolowa 24,000 .... B3
Edéa 25,493 .... B3
Eséka 10,000 .... B3
Essé B3
Fort-Foureau (Kousseri) 7,000 .... B1
Foumban 33,944 .... B2
Garoua 63,900 .... B2
Guidder 10,000 .... B2
Kaélé 17,000 .... B1
Kontcha B2
Kousseri 11,627 .... B1
Kribi 10,512 .... B3
Kumba 44,175 .... A3
Kumbo 11,699 .... B2
Limbe 27,016 .... A3
Lomié B3
Makari B1
Mamfé 10,000 .... A2
Maroua 67,187 .... B1
Mbalmayo 22,106 .... B3
Meiganga 15,906 .... B2
Mokolo 7,000 .... B1
Moloundou C3
Monatélé B3
Mora 6,000 .... B1
Nanga-Eboko B3
Ngaoundéré 38,992 .... B2
Nkambe 5,000 .... B2
Nkongsamba 71,298 .... B3
Poli B2
Rey Bouba B2
Sangmélima 13,776 .... B3
Tcholliré B2
Tibati B2
Tignéré B2
Tiko 13,824 .... A3
Wum 15,149 .... A2
Yabassi 10,000 .... B3
Yagoua 13,541 .... B1
Yaoundé (cap.) 313,706 .... B3
Yokadouma 6,000 .... B3
Yoko B2

OTHER FEATURES

Adamawa (reg.) B2
Benué (riv.) A2
Biafra (bight) A3
Cameroon (mt.) A3
Cross (riv.) A2
Dja (riv.) B3
Donga (riv.) B2
Ivindo (riv.) B3
Kadei (riv.) C3
Logone (riv.) C2
Lom (riv.) B2
Mbéré (riv.) B2
Mbakou (res.) B2
Sanaga (riv.) B3
Sanga (riv.) C3

CENTRAL AFRICAN REPUBLIC

CITIES and TOWNS

Alindao 12,295 .... D2
Baboua 3,999 .... C2
Bakia E2
Bambari 31,285 .... D2
Bangassou 21,773 .... D3
Bangui (cap.) 279,792 .... C3
Bania C3
Batangafo 12,543 .... C2
Berberati 27,285 .... C3
Birao 3,317 .... D1
Bocaranga 6,202 .... C2
Boda 8,771 .... C3
Bossangoa 25,150 .... C2
Bossembele 5,091 .... C2
Bouali C3
Bouar 29,528 .... C2
Bouca 8,874 .... C2
Boula C3
Bozoum 13,573 .... C2
Bria 14,786 .... D2
Carnot 17,863 .... C3
Damara 2,556 .... C2
Dekoa 7,663 .... C2
Gaza C3
Goubere E2
Grimari 7,308 .... C2
Hyrra Banda D2
Ippy 10,816 .... D2
Kaga Bandoro 11,876 .... C2
Kaka E2
Kembe 5,051 .... D3
Kouango 2,602 .... D2
Kouki C2

- Kounde B2
- Mbaïki 12,346 C3
- Mbres 2,622 D2
- Mobaye 4,220 D3
- Mouka D2
- Ndele 5,858 D2
- Ngourou D2
- Nola 6,703 C3
- Obo 3,978 E2
- Ouadda 3,009 D2
- Paoua 7,052 C2
- Possel C2
- Sibut 13,341 C2
- Zako D2
- Zemio 3,259 D2
- Zemongo E2

OTHER FEATURES

- Bamingui (riv.) C2
- Bomu (riv.) D3
- Dar Rounga (reg.) D2
- Gao (mt.) C2
- Kadei (riv.) C3
- Kotto (riv.) D2
- Lobaye (riv.) C2
- Mbéré (riv.) B2
- Ouham (riv.) C2
- Pendé (riv.) C2
- Sanga (riv.) C3
- Sara (riv.) C2
- Shari (riv.) C2
- Shinko (riv.) D2
- Ubangi (riv.) C3

CONGO

CITIES and TOWNS

- Abala C4
- Boko B4
- Brazzaville (cap.) 298,967 C4
- Boundji C4
- Djambala B4
- Dongou C3
- Enyellé C3
- Epéna C3
- Etoumbi B3
- Ewo B4
- Gamboma C4
- Ikelemba C3
- Impfondo C3
- Kellé B4
- Kibangou B4
- Kindama C4
- Kinkala B4
- Komono B4
- Loubomo 29,600 B4
- Loudima B4
- Madingo-Kayes B4
- Madingou B4
- Makoua C3
- Mbinda B4
- Mindouli B4
- Mossaka C4
- Mossendjo B4
- M'Pouya C4
- M'Vouti B4
- Nkayi 30,600 B4
- Okoyo C4
- Ouesso C3
- Owando C4
- Oyo C4
- Pangala B4
- Pointe-Noire 141,700 B4
- Sembé B3
- Sibiti B4
- Souanké B3
- Zanaga B4

OTHER FEATURES

- Alima (riv.) B4
- Congo (riv.) C4
- Crystal (mts.) B4
- Dja (riv.) B3
- Ivindo (riv.) B3
- Kadei (riv.) C3
- Kouilou (riv.) B4
- Likouala (riv.) C3
- N'Gounié (riv.) B4
- Niari (riv.) B4
- Ogooué (riv.) A4
- Sangha (riv.) C3
- Ubangi (riv.) C3

EQUATORIAL GUINEA

TERRITORIES

- Bioko 78,000 A3
- Río Muni 203,000 B3

CITIES and TOWNS

- Bata 27,024 B3
- Luba 19,933 A3
- Malabo (cap.) 37,237 A3
- Mbini 14,503 A3

OTHER FEATURES

- Biafra (bight) A3
- Bioko (isl.) A3
- Corisco (isl.) A3
- Elobey (isls.) A3
- Fernando Po (Bioko) (isl.) A3

GABON

CITIES and TOWNS

- Banda B4
- Bitam 5,936 B3
- Booué B3
- Chinchoua A4
- Cocobeach B3
- Fougamou A4
- Franceville 9,345 B4
- Iguéla A4
- Kango B3
- Kemboma B3
- Koula-Moutou 8,032 B4
- Lalara B3
- Lambaréné 17,770 B4
- Lastoursville B4
- Lekoni B4
- Libreville (cap.) 105,080 A3
- Makokou 5,005 B3
- Mayumba A4
- M'Bigou B4
- Médouneu B3
- Mekambo B3
- Mimongo B4
- Minvoul B3
- Mitzic B3
- Moanda 10,709 B4
- Mouila 15,016 B4
- Mounana 4,000 B4
- N'Dendé B4
- N'Djolé B4
- Nyangá A4
- Okondja B4
- Omboué A4
- Owendo A3
- Oyem 12,455 B3
- Port-Gentil 48,190 A4
- Setté-Cama A4
- Tchibanga 14,001 B4

OTHER FEATURES

- Crystal (mts.) B4
- Ibounzi (mt.) B4
- Ivindo (riv.) B3
- Lopez (cape) A4
- N'Dogo (lag.) B4
- N'Gounié (riv.) B4
- N'Komi (lag.) A4
- Ogooué (riv.) A4
- Onangué (lake) A4
- Pongara (pt.) A3

KENYA

PROVINCES

- Central 1,675,647 G4
- Coast 944,082 G4
- Eastern 1,907,301 G4
- Nairobi 509,286 G4
- North-Eastern 245,757 G3
- Nyanza 2,122,045 F4
- Rift Valley 2,210,289 G3
- Western 1,328,298 G3

CITIES and TOWNS

- Buna G3
- Bunyala F3
- Bura H4
- Eldoret 18,196 G3
- El Wak H3
- Embu 3,928 G4
- Fort Hall 4,750 G4
- Galole 3,609 G4
- Garba Tula G3
- Garissa G4
- Garsen G4
- Gilgil 4,178 G4
- Isiolo 8,201 G3
- Kakamega 6,244 F3
- Kaningo G4
- Kericho 10,144 F4
- Kiambu 2,776 G4
- Kilifi 2,662 G4
- Kipini H4
- Kisii 6,080 F4
- Kisumu 32,431 F3
- Kitale 11,573 G3
- Kitui 3,071 G4
- Kolbio H4
- Konza G4
- Laisamis G3
- Lamu 7,403 H4
- Lodwar G3
- Lokitaung 4,090 G3
- Lolgorien G4
- Machakos 6,312 G4
- Magadi G4
- Malindi 10,757 H4
- Mambrui H4
- Maralal 3,878 G3
- Marsabit 6,635 G3
- Meru 4,475 G3
- Mombasa 247,073 G4
- Moyale G3
- Nairobi (cap.) 509,286 G4
- Naivasha 6,920 G4
- Nakuru 47,151 G4
- Namanga G4
- Nanyuki 11,624 G3
- Narok 2,608 G4
- North Horr G3
- South Horr G3
- Taveta G4
- Thika 18,387 G4
- Thomson's Falls 7,602 G3
- Todenyang G3
- Tsavo G4
- Vanga G4
- Voi 5,313 G4
- Wajir H3
- Wamba 2,650 G3

OTHER FEATURES

- Daua (riv.) H3
- Elgon (mt.) F3
- Formosa (bay) H4
- Galana (riv.) G4
- Gedi (ruins) G4
- Kavirondo (gulf) F4
- Kenya (mt.) G4
- Lak Dera (dry riv.) H3
- Lorian (swamp) G3
- Natron (lake) G4
- Nyiru (mt.) G3
- Patta (isl.) H4
- Rudolf (Turkana) (lake) G3
- Tana (riv.) G4
- Tsavo Nat'l Park G4
- Turkana (lake) G3
- Victoria (lake) F4
- Winam (bay) F4

MALAWI

CITIES and TOWNS

- Bandawe F6
- Blantyre 222,153 F7
- Chilumba F6
- Chipoka F6
- Chiromo F7
- Chitipa 3,079 F5
- Dedza 5,448 F6
- Karonga 11,873 F5
- Kasungu F6
- Lilongwe (cap.) 102,924 F6
- Livingstonia F6
- Mangochi 3,341 G6
- Mzimba 4,962 F6
- Nkhata Bay 4,024 F6
- Nkhotakota 10,312 F6
- Nsanje 6,091 G7
- Rumphi 3,998 F6
- Salima 4,646 F6
- Thyolo 4,186 F7
- Zomba 21,000 G7

OTHER FEATURES

- Chilwa (lake) G7
- Malawi (Nyasa) (lake) F6
- Mulanje (mts.) G7
- Nyasa (lake) F6
- Shire (riv.) G7

RWANDA

CITIES and TOWNS

- Butare 21,691 E4
- Cyangugu 7,042 E4
- Gisenyi 12,436 E4
- Kigali (cap.) 117,749 F4
- Nyabisindu 8,587 F4

OTHER FEATURES

- Kagera Nat'l Park F4
- Karisimbi (mt.) E4
- Kivu (lake) E4
- Ruzizi (riv.) E4
- Virunga (range) E4

SOMALIA

PROVINCES

- Bakool 100,000 H3
- Bari 155,000 J1
- Bay 302,000 H3
- Galguduud 182,000 J2
- Gedo 212,000 H3
- Hiiraan 147,000 J3
- Jubbada Hoose 246,000 H3
- Mogadiscio 371,000 J3
- Mudug 215,000 J2
- Nugaal 85,000 J2
- Sanaag 146,000 J1
- Shabeellaha Dhexe 237,000 J3
- Shabeellaha Hoose 398,000 H3
- Togdheer 258,000 J2
- Woqooyi Galbeed 440,000 H1

CITIES and TOWNS

- Adadle H2
- Afgoi J3
- Afmadu 2,580 H3
- Alula K1
- Ankhor J1
- Audegle J3
- Baduen J2
- Barawa (Brava) H3
- Bardera H3
- Bargal K1
- Baydhabo 14,962 H3
- Belet Weyne 11,426 J3
- Bender Beila K2
- Bender Cassim (Bosaso) J1
- Berbera 12,219 J1
- Bereda K1
- Bircao H4
- Bohodleh J2
- Borama 3,244 H1

(continued on following page)

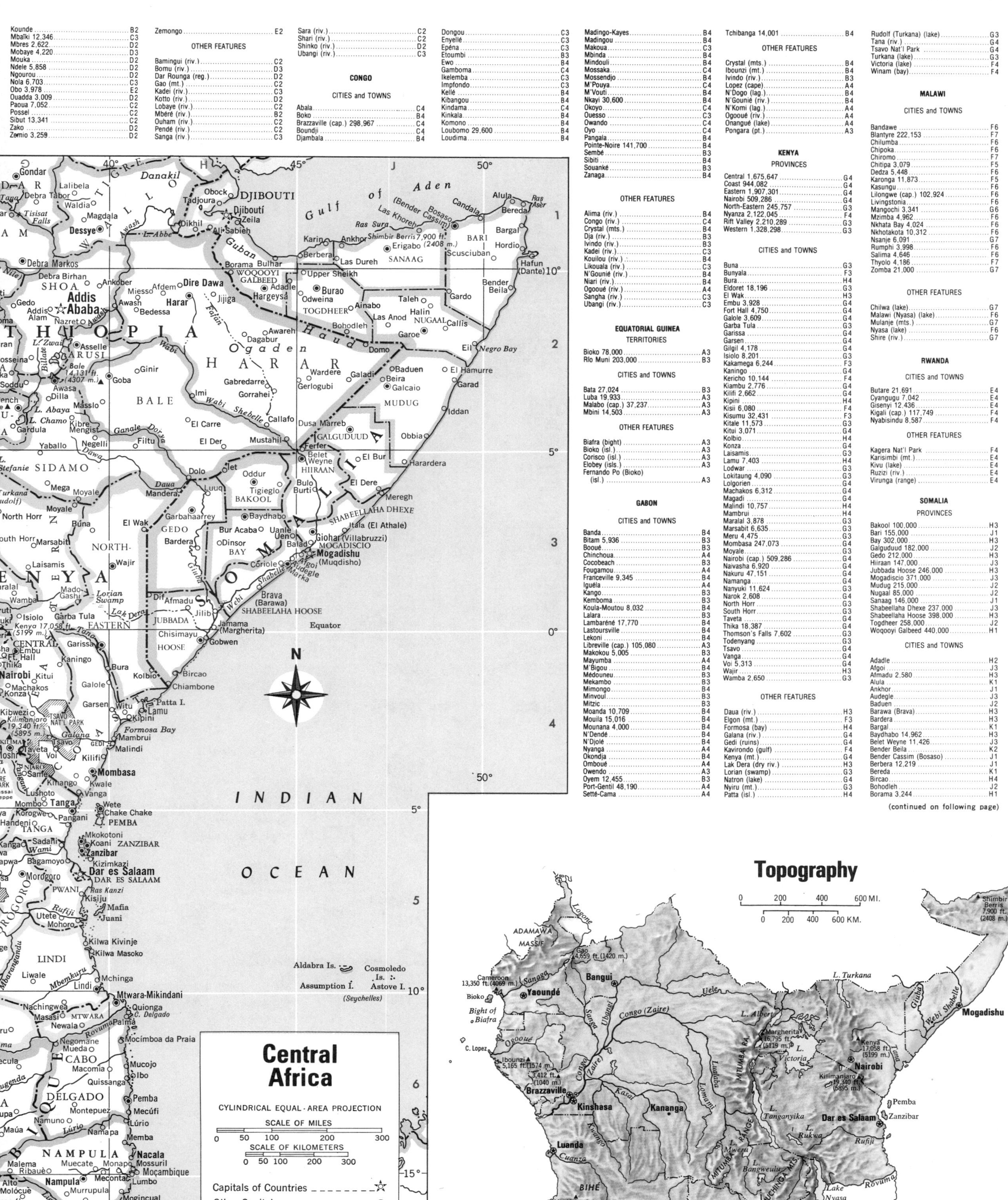

(continued)

Bosaso J1
Brava 6,167 H3
Bulhar H1
Bulo Burti 5,247 J3
Bur Acaba H3
Burao 12,617 J2
Callis J2
Candala J1
Chisimayu 17,872 H4
Chiambone H4
Coriole 4,341 H3
Dante (Hafun) K1
Dif H3
Dinsor H3
Dusa Marreb J2
Eil J2
El Athale (Itala) J3
El Bur J3
El Dere J3
El Hamurre J2
Erigabo 4,279 J1
Ferfer J2
Galcaio J2
Garad J2
Garbahaarrey H3
Gardo J2
Garoe J2
Giohar 13,156 J3
Gobwen H4
Hafun K1
Halin J2
Harardera J3
Hargeysa 40,254 H2
Hordio K1
Iddan J2
Iet H3
Itala J3
Jamama 5,408 H3
Jilib 3,232 H3
Karin J1
Kismayu (Chisimayu) 17,872 H4
Las Dureh J1
Luuq H3
Margherita (Jamama) H3
Marka (Merka) 17,708 H3
Mogadishu (cap.) 371,000 J3
Muqdisho (Mogadishu) (cap.) 371,000 J3
Obbia J2
Oddur H3
Taleh J2
Uanle Uen H3
Upper Sheikh J2
Villabruzzi (Johar) J3
Zeila 1,226 H1

OTHER FEATURES

Aden (gulf) J1
Asèr, Ras (cape) K1
Giuba (riv.) H3
Guban (reg.) H1
Hafun, Ras (cape) K1
Haud (plat.) J2
Lak Dera (dry riv.) H3
Negro (bay) J2
Nogal (reg.) J2
Shimbir Berris (mt.) J1
Sura, Ras (cape) J1
Surud Ad (mt.) J1
Webi Shabelle (riv.) H3

TANZANIA

REGIONS

Arusha 928,478 G4
Dodoma 971,921 G5
Iringa 922,801 G5
Kigoma 648,950 F4
Kilimanjaro 902,394 G4
Lindi 527,902 G5
Mara 723,295 F4
Mbeya 1,080,241 F5
Morogoro 939,190 G5
Mtwara 771,726 G5
Mwanza 1,443,418 F4
Pemba 205,870 H5
Pwani (Coast) 516,949 G5
Rukwa 451,897 F5
Ruvuma 564,113 G6
Shinyanga 1,323,482 F4
Singida 614,030 F5
Tabora 818,049 F5
Tanga 1,088,592 G5
Zanzibar Mjini 143,616 G5
Zanzibar Shambani North 77,424 G5
Zanzibar Shambani South 52,325 G5
Ziwa Magharibi (West Lake) 1,009,379 F4

CITIES and TOWNS

Arusha 55,281 G4
Babati G4
Bagamoyo 5,112 G5
Bukoba 20,430 F4
Chake Chake 4,862 H5
Dar es Salaam (cap.) 757,346 G5
Dodoma 45,703 G5
Geita 3,066 F4
Handeni G5
Ifakara G5
Iringa 57,182 G5
Itigi F5
Kahama 3,211 F4
Kaliua F5
Kanga G5
Karema F5
Kasanga F5
Kasulu F4
Kibara F4
Kibaya G5
Kibondo F4
Kigoma-Ujiji 50,044 E4
Kilosa 4,458 G5
Kilwa Kivinje 2,790 G5
Kilwa Masoko G5
Kinyangiri G4
Kipili F5
Kisiju G5
Kitunda F5
Kizimkazi G5
Kondoa 4,514 G4
Kongwa G5
Korogwe 6,675 G5
Lindi 27,308 G5
Liuli F6
Liwale G5
Longido G4
Mahenge G5
Makumbako G5
Manda F6
Manyoni G5
Masasi G6
Mbamba Bay G6
Mbeya 76,606 F5
Mbulu G4
Mchinga H5
Mohoro G5
Mombo G4
Morogoro 61,890 G5
Moshi 52,223 G4
Mpanda F5
Mtakuja F5
Mtwara-Mikindani 48,510 H6
Murongo F4
Musoma 32,658 F4
Muwale F5
Mwadui 7,383 F4
Mwanza 110,611 F4
Mwaya F5
Mwesi F5
Nachingwea 3,751 G6
Newala G6
Ngara F4
Njombe F5
Pangani 2,955 G5
Rungwa F5
Sadani G5
Same G4
Sekenke F4
Shinyanga 21,703 F4
Singida 29,252 F4
Songea 17,954 G6
Sumbawanga 28,586 F5
Tabora 67,392 F5
Tanga 103,409 G4
Tukuyu 4,089 F5
Tunduru G6
Urambo F4
Utete G5
Uvinza F5
Wete 8,469 G4
Zanzibar 110,669 G5

OTHER FEATURES

Eyasi (lake) F4
Great Ruaha (riv.) G5
Juani (isl.) G5
Kalambo (falls) F5
Kanzi (cape) G5
Kilimanjaro (mt.) G4
Kilombero (riv.) G5
Mafia (isl.) H5
Manyara (lake) G4
Masai (steppe) G4
Mbarangandu (riv.) G5
Mbemkuru (riv.) G5
Meru (mt.) G4
Mikumi Nat'l Park G5
Natron (lake) G4
Ngorongoro (crater) F4
Njombe (riv.) F5
Nyasa (lake) F6
Olduvai Gorge (canyon) G4
Pangani (riv.) G4
Pemba (isl.) H5
Rovuma (riv.) G6
Rufiji (riv.) G5
Ruaha Nat'l Park F5
Rukwa (lake) F5
Rungwa (riv.) F5
Rungwe (mt.) F5
Serengeti Nat'l Park F4
Tanganyika (lake) E5
Tarangire Nat'l Park G4
Victoria (lake) F4
Wami (riv.) G5
Wembere (riv.) F4
Zanzibar (isl.) G5

UGANDA

CITIES and TOWNS

Arua 10,837 F3
Atura F3
Butiaba 261 F3
Entebbe 21,096 F4
Fort Portal 7,947 F3
Gulu 18,170 F3
Hoima 2,339 F3
Jinja 52,509 F3
Kabale 8,234 E4
Kampala (cap.) 478,895 F3
Kasese 7,213 F3
Kilembe F3
Kitgum 3,242 F3
Lira 7,340 F3
Masaka 12,987 F4
Masindi 2,100 F3
Mbale 23,544 F3
Mbarara 16,078 F4
Moroto 5,488 F3
Moyo 2,656 F3
Mubende 6,004 F3
Rhino Camp 198 F3
Soroti 8,130 F3
Tororo 15,977 F3

OTHER FEATURES

Albert (Mobuto Sese Seko) (lake) F3
Edward (lake) E4
Elgon (mt.) F3
George (lake) F4
Kabalega (falls) F3
Kagalega Nat'l Park F3
Kidepo Nat'l Park F3
Kioga (lake) F3
Margherita (mt.) E3
Mobuto Sese Seko (lake) F3
Owen Falls (dam) F3
Ruwenzori (range) E3
Sese (isls.) F4
Victoria (lake) F4
Virunga (range) E4
Virunga Nat'l Park F4

ZAIRE

PRUVINCES

Bandundu 2,600,556 C4
Bas-Zaïre 1,504,361 B4
Equateur 2,431,812 D3
Haut-Zaïre 3,356,419 E3
Kasai-Occidental 2,433,861 D4
Kasai-Oriental 1,872,231 D5
Kinshasa 1,323,039 C4
Kivu 3,361,883 E4
Shaba 2,753,714 E5

CITIES and TOWNS

Aba 7,600 F3
Abumombazi D3
Aketi 17,200 D3
Andoma E3
Ango E3
Ankoro E5
Bagata C4
Balangala D3
Bambesa E3
Bambili E3
Banalia E3
Banana B5
Bandundu 74,467 C4
Baraka E4
Basankusu C3
Basoko 9,100 D3
Basongo D4
Befale D3
Bena-Dibele D4
Beni 22,800 E3
Bikoro C4
Boende 12,800 D4
Bokote D4
Bokungu D4
Bolobo 10,300 C4
Bolomba 7,200 C3
Boma 61,100 B5
Bomboma C3
Bomongo C3
Bondo 10,000 D3
Bongandanga 12,900 D3
Bosobolo 11,100 D3
Budjala C3
Bukama E5
Bukavu 134,861 E4
Bulungu 16,300 C4
Bumba 34,700 D3
Bunia 28,800 E3
Bunkeya 5,100 E6
Businga 11,000 D3
Busu-Djanoa D3
Buta 19,800 D3
Butembo 27,800 E3
Dekese D4
Demba 22,000 D5
Dibaya 11,400 D5
Dibaya-Lubue 7,900 C4
Dilolo 14,000 D6
Dimbelenge D5
Djolu D3
Djugu F3
Dongo C3
Doruma E3
Dungu 9,100 E3
Etoile E6
Faradje 10,400 E3
Feshi C5
Fizi E4
Gandajika 60,100 D5
Gemena 37,300 D3
Goma 48,600 E4
Gungu C5
Idiofa C4
Ikela D4
Ilebo 32,200 D4
Imese C3
Ingende C4
Inongo 14,800 C4
Irumu 9,300 E3
Isangi D3
Isiro 49,300 E3
Kabalo 22,600 E5
Kabambare E4
Kabare 12,600 E4
Kabinda 60,500 D5
Kabongo 6,500 E5
Kahemba C5
Kalehe E4
Kalemie 62,300 E5
Kalima 27,500 E4
Kama 17,700 E4
Kambove 18,900 E6
Kamina 56,300 D5
Kampene 14,600 E4
Kananga 428,960 D5
Kanda-Kanda D5
Kaniama D5
Kapanga D5
Kasaji D6
Kasangulu 11,900 C4
Kasenga E6
Kasenyi E3
Kasese E4
Kasongo 37,800 E4
Kasongo-Lunda C5
Katako-Kombe D4
Katenga E5
Kazumba D5
Kenge 17,500 C4
Kiambi E5
Kibombo E4
Kikwit 111,960 C5
Kilembe C5
Kilwa E5
Kilo E3
Kinda D5
Kiniama E6
Kinshasa (cap.) 1,323,039 C4
Kipushi 32,900 E6
Kiri C4
Kirundu E4
Kisangani 229,596 E3
Kole, Kasai-Oriental D4
Kole, Haut-Zaïre E3
Kolwezi 81,600 E6
Komba D3
Kongolo 14,800 E5
Kungu C3
Kutu 10,000 C4
Kwamouth C4
Libenge 12,500 C3
Likasi, Panda- 146,394 E6
Likati D3
Lisala D3
Lodja 20,300 D4
Lokolama D4
Lomela D4
Loto D4
Luashi D6
Lubefu D4
Lubero E4
Lubudi 6,000 E5
Lubumbashi 318,000 E6
Lubutu E4
Luebo 21,800 D5
Luishia E6
Luiza D5
Lukolela, Equateur C4
Lukolela, Kasai-Oriental D5
Lukula 9,400 B5
Luozi 7,000 B5
Lusambo 13,100 D4
Makanza C3
Malemba-Nkulu E5
Mambasa 7,400 E3
Mangai 15,200 C4
Manono 44,500 E5
Masi-Manimba 6,300 C4
Masisi E4
Matadi 110,436 B5
Mbandaka 107,910 C3
Mbanza-Ngungu 55,800 C5
Mbuji-Mayi 256,154 D5
Mitwaba E5
Moanda 6,400 B5
Mobayi-Mbongo D3
Moliro E5
Monga D3
Monkoto D4
Mulongo E5
Mungbere E3
Mushie 13,700 C4
Mutshatsha D6
Muyumba E5
Mwadingusha E6
Mwanza E5
Mweka 24,900 D4
Mwene-Ditu 71,200 D5
Mwenga E4
Niangara 9,200 E3
Niemba E5
Nyunzu 11,300 E5
Opala D4
Oshwe C4
Panda-Likasi 146,394 E6
Pangi E4
Penge D5
Poko E3
Popokabaka C5
Port Kindu 42,800 E4
Punia E4
Pweto E5
Rutshuru E4
Sakania E6
Sampwe E5
Sandoa D5
Seke-Banza B5
Sentery 24,300 E5
Shabunda 6,900 E4
Songololo 4,600 B5
Tenke E6
Titule E3
Tshela 10,700 B4
Tshikapa 38,900 D5
Tshofa D5
Ubundu 6,300 E4
Uvira 15,900 E4
Virunga 21,900 E5
Waka D3
Walikale E4
Wamba 11,500 E3
Watsa 21,300 E3
Yahuma D3
Yakoma D3
Yangambi 22,600 D3
Zongo C3

OTHER FEATURES

Albert (Mobuto Sese Seko) (lake) F3
Aruwimi (riv.) E3
Bomu (riv.) D3
Boyoma (Stanley) (falls) D3
Chicapa (riv.) D5
Congo (riv.) C4
Edward (lake) E4
Elila (riv.) E4
Fimi (riv.) C4
Garamba Nat'l Park E3
Giri (riv.) C3
Itimbiri (riv.) D3
Ituri (for.) E3
Karisimbi (mt.) E4
Kasai (riv.) C4
Kivu (lake) E4
Kwa (riv.) C4
Kwango (riv.) C5
Kwilu (riv.) C5
Lindi (riv.) E3
Livingstone (falls) B5
Loange (riv.) C5
Lokoro (riv.) C4
Lomami (riv.) D4
Lomela (riv.) D4
Lowa (riv.) E4
Lua (riv.) C3
Lualaba (riv.) E4
Luapula (riv.) E6
Lubilash (riv.) D5
Lufira (riv.) E5
Luilaka (riv.) C4
Lukenie (riv.) D4
Lukuga (riv.) E5
Lulua (riv.) D5
Luvua (riv.) E5
Mai-Ndombe (lake) C4
Malebo (Stanley Pool) (lake) C4
Margherita (mt.) E3
Marungu (mts.) E5
Mobuto Sese Seko (lake) F3
Mweru (lake) E5
Ruwenzori (range) E3
Ruzizi (riv.) E4
Salonga Nat'l Park D4
Sankuru (riv.) D4
Stanley (falls) D3
Stanley Pool (lake) C4
Tanganyika (lake) E5
Tshuapa (riv.) D4
Tumba (lake) C4
Ubangi (riv.) C3
Uele (riv.) E3
Ulindi (riv.) E4
Upemba (lake) E5
Upemba Nat'l Park E5
Virunga (range) E4
Virunga Nat'l Park E4
Zaire (Congo) (riv.) C4

ZAMBIA

CITIES and TOWNS

Abercorn (Mbala) 11,179 F5
Bancroft (Chililabombwe) 61,928 E6
Broken Hill (Kabwe) 143,635 E6
Chibwe E6
Chilanga 12,503 E7
Chililabombwe 61,928 E6
Chingola 145,869 E6
Chinsali 4,211 F6
Chipata 32,291 F6
Choma 17,943 E7
Fort Rosebery (Mansa) 34,801 E6
Isoka 6,832 F6
Kabompo 5,357 D6
Kabwe 143,635 E6
Kafue 29,794 E7
Kalabo 7,398 D6
Kalomo 5,878 E7
Kaoma 6,731 D6
Kapiri Mposhi 13,677 E6
Kasama 38,093 F6
Kasempa 3,063 E6
Kataba D7
Kawambwa 7,235 E5
Kitwe 314,794 E6
Lealui D6
Livingstone 71,987 E7
Luanshya 132,164 E6
Lundazi 4,083 F6
Lusaka (cap.) 538,469 E7
Luwingu 3,763 E6
Mansa 34,801 E6
Mazabuka 29,602 E7
Mbala 11,179 F5
Mkushi 4,104 E6
Mongu 24,919 D7
Monze 13,141 E7
Mpika 25,880 F6
Mporokoso 6,008 F5
Mpulungu 6,354 F5
Mufulira 149,778 E6
Mulobezi 2,589 E7
Mumbwa 7,570 E6
Mwinilunga 3,169 D6
Nakonde 4,599 F5
Namwala 3,008 E7
Ndola 282,439 E6
Petauke 7,531 F6
Senanga 7,204 D7
Serenje 6,008 F6
Sesheke 3,500 D7
Solwezi 15,032 E6
Zambezi 8,166 D6

OTHER FEATURES

Bangweulu (lake) F6
Barotseland (reg.) D7
Chambeshi (riv.) F6
Cuando (riv.) D7
Dongwe (riv.) D6
Kabompo (riv.) D6
Kafue (riv.) E7
Kafue Nat'l Park E6
Kalambo (falls) F5
Kariba (dam) E7
Kariba (lake) E7
Luangwa (riv.) F6
Luapula (riv.) E6
Lungwebungu (riv.) D6
Mosi-Oa-Tunya (Victoria) (falls) E7
Mulungushi (dam) E6
Mweru (lake) E5
Sunzu (mt.) F5
Tanganyika (lake) E5
Victoria (falls) E7
Zambezi (riv.) D7

Agriculture, Industry and Resources

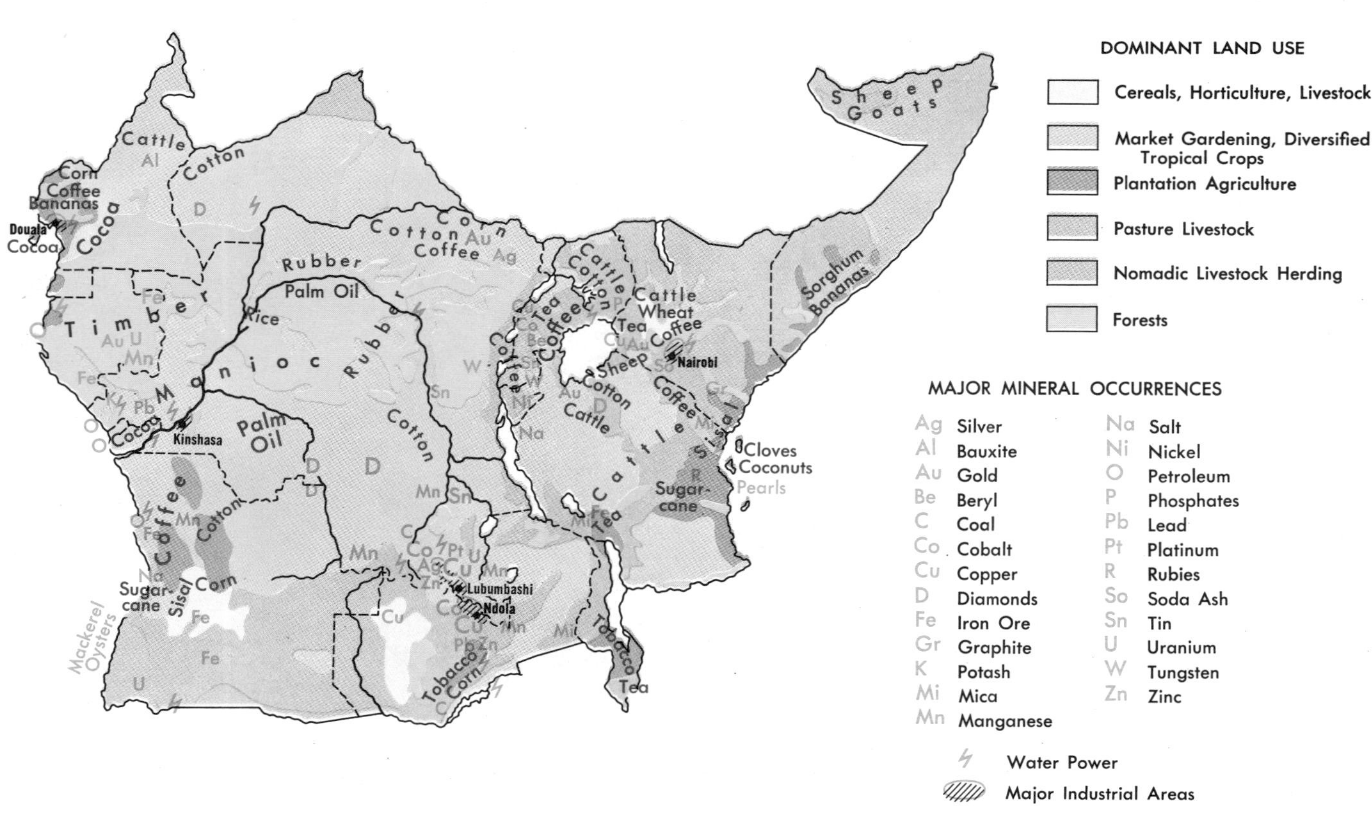

NAMIBIA (SOUTH-WEST AFRICA)

AREA 317,827 sq. mi. (823,172 sq. km.)
POPULATION 1,200,000
CAPITAL Windhoek
LARGEST CITY Windhoek
HIGHEST POINT Brandberg 8,550 ft. (2,606 m.)
MONETARY UNIT rand
MAJOR LANGUAGES Ovambo, Hottentot, Herero, Afrikaans, English
MAJOR RELIGIONS Tribal religions, Protestantism

BOTSWANA

AREA 224,764 sq. mi. (582,139 sq. km.)
POPULATION 819,000
CAPITAL Gaborone
LARGEST CITY Francistown
HIGHEST POINT Tsodilo Hill 5,922 ft. (1,805 m.)
MONETARY UNIT pula
MAJOR LANGUAGES Setswana, Shona, Bushman, English, Afrikaans
MAJOR RELIGIONS Tribal religions, Protestantism

ZIMBABWE

AREA 150,803 sq. mi. (390,580 sq. km.)
POPULATION 7,360,000
CAPITAL Harare
LARGEST CITY Harare
HIGHEST POINT Mt. Inyangani 8,517 ft. (2,596 m.)
MONETARY UNIT Zimbabwe dollar
MAJOR LANGUAGES English, Shona, Ndebele
MAJOR RELIGIONS Tribal religions, Protestantism

SOUTH AFRICA

AREA 455,318 sq. mi. (1,179,274 sq. km.)
POPULATION 23,771,970
CAPITALS Cape Town, Pretoria
LARGEST CITY Johannesburg
HIGHEST POINT Injasuti 11,182 ft. (3,408 m.)
MONETARY UNIT rand
MAJOR LANGUAGES Afrikaans, English, Xhosa, Zulu, Sesotho
MAJOR RELIGIONS Protestantism, Roman Catholicism, Islam, Hinduism, tribal religions

MOZAMBIQUE

AREA 303,769 sq. mi. (786,762 sq. km.)
POPULATION 12,130,000
CAPITAL Maputo
LARGEST CITY Maputo
HIGHEST POINT Mt. Binga 7,992 ft. (2,436 m.)
MONETARY UNIT metical
MAJOR LANGUAGES Makua, Thonga, Shona, Portuguese
MAJOR RELIGIONS Tribal religions, Roman Catholicism, Islam

MADAGASCAR

AREA 226,657 sq. mi. (587,041 sq. km.)
POPULATION 8,742,000
CAPITAL Antananarivo
LARGEST CITY Antananarivo
HIGHEST POINT Maromokotro 9,436 ft. (2,876 m.)
MONETARY UNIT Madagascar franc
MAJOR LANGUAGES Malagasy, French
MAJOR RELIGIONS Tribal religions, Roman Catholicism, Protestantism

MAURITIUS

AREA 790 sq. mi. (2,046 sq. km.)
POPULATION 959,000
CAPITAL Port Louis
LARGEST CITY Port Louis
HIGHEST POINT 2,711 ft. (826 m.)
MONETARY UNIT Mauritian rupee
MAJOR LANGUAGES English, French, French Creole, Hindi, Urdu
MAJOR RELIGIONS Hinduism, Christianity, Islam

LESOTHO

AREA 11,720 sq. mi. (30,355 sq. km.)
POPULATION 1,339,000
CAPITAL Maseru
LARGEST CITY Maseru
HIGHEST POINT 11,425 ft. (3,482 m.)
MONETARY UNIT loti
MAJOR LANGUAGES Sesotho, English
MAJOR RELIGIONS Tribal religions, Christianity

SWAZILAND

AREA 6,705 sq. mi. (17,366 sq. km.)
POPULATION 547,000
CAPITAL Mbabane
LARGEST CITY Manzini
HIGHEST POINT Emlembe 6,109 ft. (1,862 m.)
MONETARY UNIT lilangeni
MAJOR LANGUAGES siSwati, English
MAJOR RELIGIONS Tribal religions, Christianity

COMOROS

AREA 719 sq. mi. (1,862 sq. km.)
POPULATION 290,000
CAPITAL Moroni
LARGEST CITY Moroni
HIGHEST POINT Karthala 7,746 ft. (2,361 m.)
MONETARY UNIT CFA franc
MAJOR LANGUAGES Arabic, French, Swahili
MAJOR RELIGION Islam

SEYCHELLES

AREA 145 sq. mi. (375 sq. km.)
POPULATION 63,000
CAPITAL Victoria
LARGEST CITY Victoria
HIGHEST POINT Morne Seychellois 2,993 ft. (912 m.)
MONETARY UNIT Seychellois rupee
MAJOR LANGUAGES English, French, Creole
MAJOR RELIGION Roman Catholicism

RÉUNION

AREA 969 sq. mi. (2,510 sq. km.)
POPULATION 491,000
CAPITAL St-Denis

MAYOTTE

AREA 144 sq. mi. (373 sq. km.)
POPULATION 47,300
CAPITAL Dzaoudzi

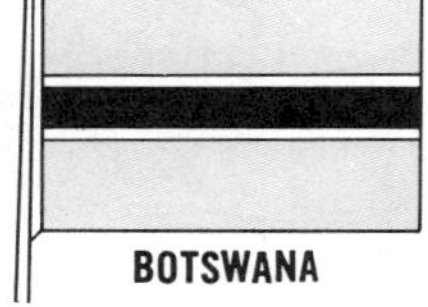

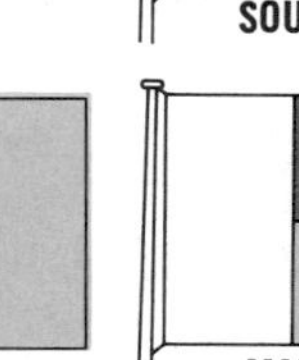
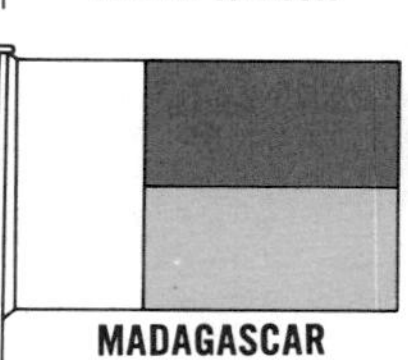
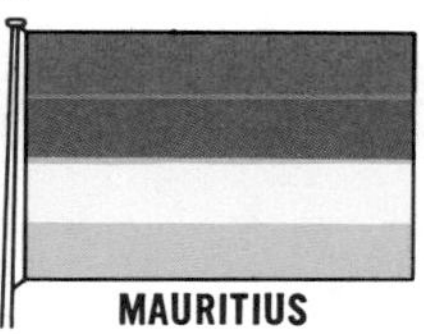
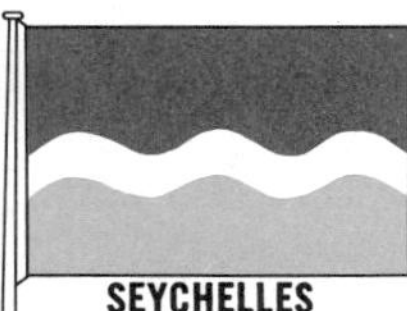

ZIMBABWE | BOTSWANA | SOUTH AFRICA | LESOTHO | SWAZILAND

MOZAMBIQUE | COMOROS | MADAGASCAR | MAURITIUS | SEYCHELLES

Agriculture, Industry and Resources

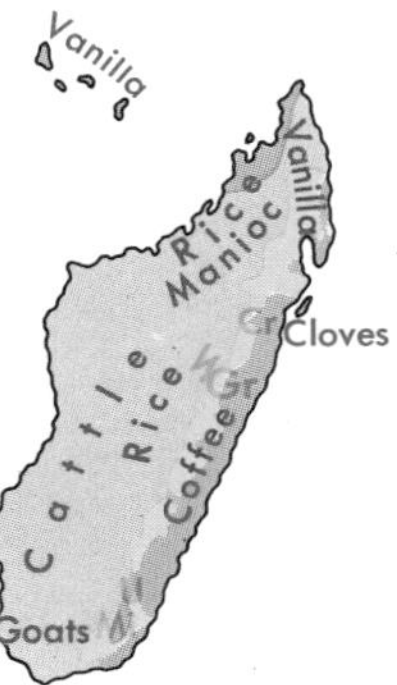

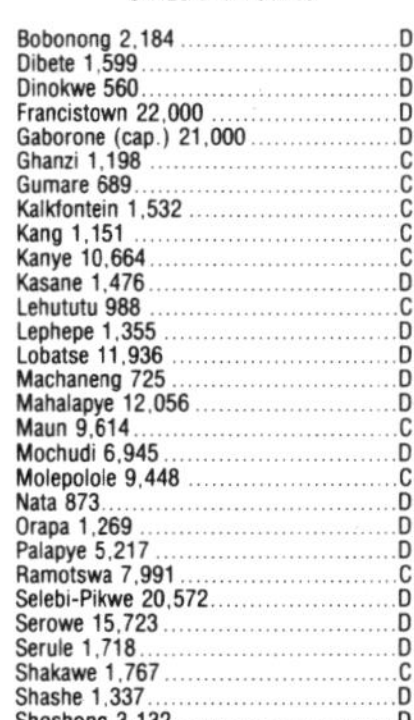

MAJOR MINERAL OCCURRENCES

Ab	Asbestos	Cu	Copper	Pb	Manganese	Sb	Antimony
Ag	Silver	D	Diamonds	Pt	Salt	Sn	Tin
Al	Bauxite	Fe	Iron Ore	Mn	Nickel	U	Uranium
Au	Gold	Gr	Graphite	Na	Phosphates	V	Vanadium
Be	Beryl	Li	Lithium	Ni	Lead	W	Tungsten
C	Coal	Mg	Magnesium	P	Platinum	Zn	Zinc
Cr	Chromium	Mi	Mica				

DOMINANT LAND USE

- Cereals, Horticulture, Livestock
- Market Gardening, Diversified Tropical Crops
- Plantation Agriculture
- Pasture Livestock
- Nomadic Livestock Herding
- Forests
- Nonagricultural Land

- Water Power
- Major Industrial Areas

BOTSWANA

CITIES and TOWNS

Bobonong 2,184 ..... D4
Dibete 1,599 ..... D4
Dinokwe 560 ..... D4
Francistown 22,000 ..... D4
Gaborone (cap.) 21,000 ..... D4
Ghanzi 1,198 ..... C4
Gumare 689 ..... C3
Kalkfontein 1,532 ..... C4
Kang 1,151 ..... C4
Kanye 10,664 ..... C5
Kasane 1,476 ..... D3
Lehututu 988 ..... C4
Lephepe 1,355 ..... D4
Lobatse 11,936 ..... D5
Machaneng 725 ..... D4
Mahalapye 12,056 ..... D4
Maun 9,614 ..... C4
Mochudi 6,945 ..... D4
Molepolole 9,448 ..... C4
Nata 873 ..... D4
Orapa 1,269 ..... D4
Palapye 5,217 ..... D4
Ramotswa 7,991 ..... C4
Selebi-Pikwe 20,572 ..... D4
Serowe 15,723 ..... D4
Serule 1,718 ..... D4
Shakawe 1,767 ..... C3
Shashe 1,337 ..... D4
Shoshong 3,132 ..... D4
Tonota 4,494 ..... D4
Tsau 427 ..... C4
Tshabong 983 ..... C5
Tshane 604 ..... C4

OTHER FEATURES

Chobe (riv.) C3
Kalahari (des.) C4
Limpopo (riv.) D4
Makgadikgadi (salt pan) D3
Molopo (riv.) C5
Ngami (lake) C4
Ngamiland (reg.) C3
Nossob (riv.) B4
Okovango (swamps) C3
Orange (riv.) B5
Shashe (riv.) D4
Tati (riv.) D4

COMOROS

CITIES and TOWNS

Fomboni 3,229 ..... G2
Mitsamiouli 3,196 ..... G2
Moroni (cap.) 12,000 ..... G2
Mutsamudu 7,652 ..... G2

OTHER FEATURES

Anjouan (Nzwani) (isl.) 83,486 ..... G2
Grand Comoro (Njazidja) (isl.) 118,443 ..... G2
Mohéli (Mwali) (isl.) 9,525 ..... G2

LESOTHO

CITIES and TOWNS

Leribe 5,200 ..... D5
Mafeteng 4,600 ..... D5
Maseru (cap.) 71,500 ..... D5
Mohaleshoek 3,600 ..... D6

MADAGASCAR

PROVINCES

Antananarivo 2,167,973 ..... H3
Antsiranana 597,982 ..... H2
Fianarantsoa 1,804,365 ..... H4
Mahajanga 819,750 ..... H3
Toamasina 1,179,660 ..... H3
Toliara 1,034,114 ..... G4

CITIES and TOWNS

Ambalavao 6,988 ..... H4
Ambanja 12,258 ..... H2
Ambato Boeny 3,317 ..... H3
Ambatofinandrahana 2,161 ..... H4
Ambatolampy 11,539 ..... H3
Ambatomainty 1,276 ..... H3
Ambatondrazaka 18,044 ..... H3
Ambilobe 9,415 ..... H2
Amboasary 2,420 ..... H4
Ambodifototra 1,112 ..... J3
Ambohimahasoa 5,851 ..... H4
Ambositra 16,780 ..... H4
Ambovombe 1,375 ..... H5
Ampanihy 2,262 ..... G4
Analalava 5,184 ..... H2
Andapa 6,275 ..... H2
Andilamena 3,512 ..... H3
Androka 1,068 ..... G5
Ankazoabo 1,677 ..... G4
Antalaha 17,541 ..... J2
Antananarivo (cap.) 451,808 ..... H3
Antsalova 2,202 ..... G3
Antsirabe 32,979 ..... H3
Antsiranana 40,443 ..... H2
Antsohihy 8,721 ..... H2
Arivonimamo 8,497 ..... H3
Bealanana 2,299 ..... H2
Befandriana 3,004 ..... H3
Bekily 1,933 ..... G4
Belo-Tsiribihina 4,403 ..... G3
Beroroha 1,742 ..... G4
Besalampy 2,874 ..... G3
Betioky 3,964 ..... G4
Betroka 3,943 ..... H4
Brickaville (Vohibinany) 1,741 ..... H3
Diégo-Suarez (Antsiranana) 40,443 ..... H2
Fandriana 4,139 ..... H4
Faradofay 13,805 ..... H5
Farafangana 10,817 ..... H4
Fenoarivo, Toamasina 7,696 ..... H3
Fianarantsoa 68,054 ..... H4
Fort-Dauphin (Faradofay) 13,805 ..... H5
Foulpointe H3
Hell-Ville 6,183 ..... H2
Ifanadiana 1,111 ..... H4
Ihosy 4,521 ..... H4
Ivohibe 1,254 ..... H4
Madirovalo 3,991 ..... H3
Maevatanana 7,197 ..... H3
Mahabo 4,941 ..... G4
Mahanoro 5,041 ..... H3
Maintirano 6,375 ..... G3
Majunga 65,864 ..... H3
Manakara 19,768 ..... H4
Mananara 3,253 ..... J3
Mananjary 14,638 ..... H4
Mandabe 1,757 ..... G4
Mandritsara 6,826 ..... H3
Manja 4,151 ..... G4
Manombo 2,908 ..... G4
Maroantsetra 6,645 ..... J3
Marovoay 20,253 ..... H3

(continued on following page)

Topography

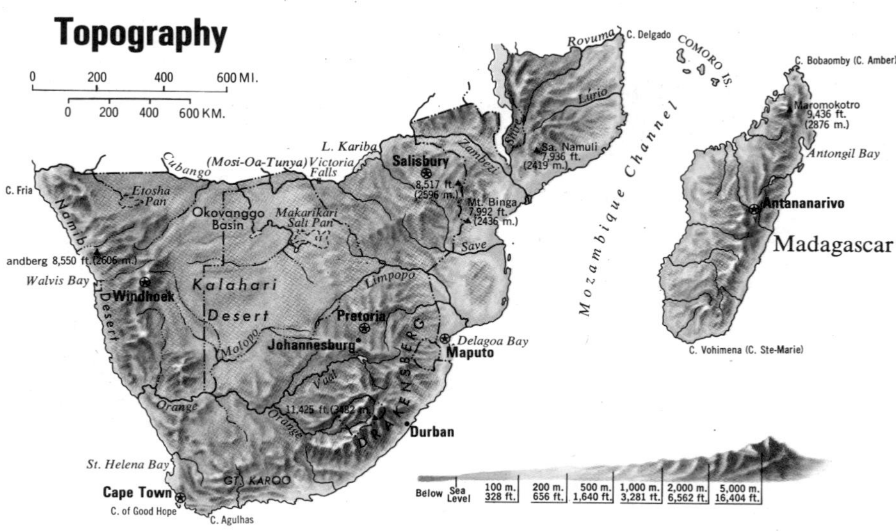

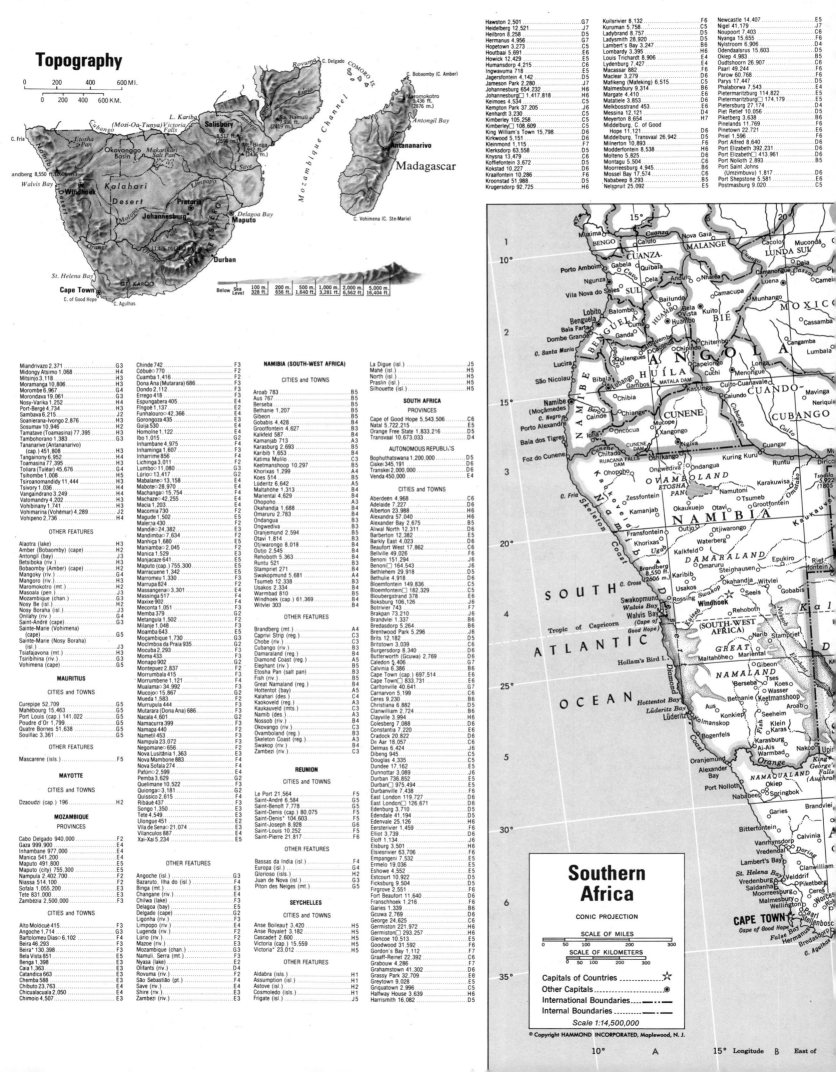

Miandrivazo 2,371 .... G3
Midongy Atsimo 1,068 .... H4
Mitsinjo 3,118 .... H3
Moramanga 10,806 .... H3
Morombe 6,967 .... G4
Morondava 19,061 .... G3
Nosy-Varika 1,252 .... H4
Port-Bergé 4,734 .... H3
Sambava 6,215 .... J2
Soanierana-Ivongo 2,876 .... H3
Sosumav 10,946 .... H2
Tamatave (Toamasina) 77,395 .... H3
Tambohorano 1,383 .... G3
Tananarive (Antananarivo)
(cap.) 451,808 .... H3
Tangainony 6,952 .... H4
Toamasina 77,395 .... H3
Toliara (Tuléar) 45,676 .... G4
Tsihombe 1,008 .... H5
Tsiroanomandidy 11,444 .... H3
Tsivory 1,036 .... H4
Vangaindrano 3,249 .... H4
Vatomandry 4,202 .... H3
Vohibinany 1,741 .... H3
Vohimarina (Vohémar) 4,289 .... J2
Vohipeno 2,736 .... H4

OTHER FEATURES

Alaotra (lake) H3
Amber (Bobaomby) (cape) H2
Antongil (bay) J3
Betsiboka (riv.) H3
Bobaomby (Amber) (cape) H2
Mangoky (riv.) G4
Mangoro (riv.) H3
Maromokotro (mt.) H2
Masoala (pen.) J3
Mozambique (chan.) G3
Nosy Be (isl.) H2
Nosy Boraha (isl.) J3
Onilahy (riv.) G4
Saint-André (cape) G3
Sainte-Marie (Vohimena)
(cape) G5
Sainte-Marie (Nosy Boraha)
(isl.) J3
Tsiafajavona (mt.) H3
Tsiribihina (riv.) G3
Vohimena (cape) G5

MAURITIUS

CITIES and TOWNS

Curepipe 52,709 .... G5
Mahébourg 15,463 .... G5
Port Louis (cap.) 141,022 .... G5
Poudre d'Or 1,799 .... G5
Quatre Bornes 51,638 .... G5
Souillac 3,361 .... G5

OTHER FEATURES

Mascarene (isls.) F5

MAYOTTE

CITIES and TOWNS

Dzaoudzi (cap.) 196 .... H2

MOZAMBIQUE

PROVINCES

Cabo Delgado 940,000 .... F2
Gaza 999,900 .... E4
Inhambane 977,000 .... E4
Manica 541,200 .... E4
Maputo 491,800 .... E5
Maputo (city) 755,300 .... E5
Nampula 2,402,700 .... F2
Niassa 514,100 .... F2
Sofala 1,055,200 .... E3
Tete 831,000 .... E3
Zambézia 2,500,000 .... F3

CITIES and TOWNS

Alto Molócuè 415 .... F3
Angoche 1,714 .... G3
Bartolomeu Dias○ 6,102 .... F4
Beira 46,293 .... F3
Beira* 130,398 .... F3
Bela Vista 851 .... E5
Benga 1,398 .... E3
Caia 1,363 .... E3
Catandica 663 .... E3
Chemba 588 .... E3
Chibuto 23,763 .... E4
Chicualacuala 2,050 .... E4
Chimoio 4,507 .... E3
Chinde 742 .... F3
Cóbuè○ 770 .... F2
Cuamba 1,416 .... F2
Dona Ana (Mutarara) 686 .... F3
Dondo 2,112 .... F3
Errego 418 .... F3
Espungabera 405 .... E4
Fingoè 1,137 .... E2
Funhalouro○ 42,366 .... E4
Gorongoza 435 .... E3
Guija 530 .... E4
Homoíne 1,122 .... E4
Ibo 1,015 .... G2
Inhambane 4,975 .... F4
Inhaminga 1,607 .... F3
Inharrime 856 .... F4
Lichinga 3,011 .... F2
Lumbo○ 11,080 .... G3
Lúrio○ 13,417 .... G2
Mabalane○ 13,158 .... E4
Mabote○ 28,970 .... E4
Machanga○ 15,754 .... F4
Machaze○ 42,255 .... E4
Macia 1,203 .... E4
Macomia 730 .... F2
Magude 1,502 .... E5
Malema 430 .... F2
Mandié○ 24,382 .... E3
Mandimba○ 7,634 .... F2
Manhiça 1,680 .... E5
Maniamba○ 2,045 .... F2
Manica 1,529 .... E3
Manjacaze 641 .... E5
Maputo (cap.) 755,300 .... E5
Marracuene 1,342 .... E5
Marromeu 1,330 .... F3
Marrupa 824 .... F2
Massangena○ 3,301 .... E4
Massinga 517 .... F4
Maxixe 902 .... F4
Meconta 1,051 .... F3
Memba 379 .... G2
Metangula 1,502 .... F2
Milanje 1,048 .... F3
Moamba 643 .... E5
Moçambique 1,730 .... G3
Mocímboa da Praia 935 .... G2
Mocuba 2,293 .... F3
Moma 433 .... F3
Monapo 902 .... G2
Montepuez 2,837 .... F2
Morrumbala 415 .... F3
Morrumbene 1,121 .... F4
Mualama○ 34,992 .... F3
Mucojo○ 15,867 .... G2
Mueda 1,583 .... F2
Murrupula 444 .... F3
Mutarara (Dona Ana) 686 .... F3
Nacala 4,601 .... G2
Namacurra 399 .... F3
Namapa 440 .... F2
Nametil 453 .... F3
Nampula 23,072 .... F3
Negomane○ 656 .... F2
Nova Lusitânia 1,363 .... E3
Nova Mambone 883 .... F4
Nova Sofala 274 .... F4
Pafúrio○ 2,599 .... E4
Pemba 3,629 .... G2
Quelimane 10,522 .... F3
Quionga○ 3,181 .... G2
Quissico 2,615 .... F4
Ribáuè 437 .... F3
Songo 1,350 .... E3
Tete 4,549 .... E3
Ulongue 451 .... E2
Vila de Sena○ 21,074 .... E3
Vilanculos 887 .... E4
Xai-Xai 5,234 .... E5

OTHER FEATURES

Angoche (isl.) G3
Bazaruto, Ilha do (isl.) F4
Binga (mt.) E3
Changane (riv.) E4
Chilwa (lake) F3
Delagoa (bay) E5
Delgado (cape) G2
Ligonha (riv.) F3
Limpopo (riv.) E4
Lugenda (riv.) F2
Lúrio (riv.) F2
Mazoe (riv.) E3
Mozambique (chan.) G3
Namuli, Serra (mt.) F3
Nyasa (lake) E2
Olifants (riv.) D4
Rovuma (riv.) F2
São Sebastião (pt.) F4
Save (riv.) E4
Shire (riv.) E3
Zambezi (riv.) E3

NAMIBIA (SOUTH-WEST AFRICA)

CITIES and TOWNS

Aroab 783 .... B5
Aus 767 .... B5
Berseba B5
Bethanie 1,207 .... B5
Gibeon B5
Gobabis 4,428 .... B4
Grootfontein 4,627 .... B3
Kalkfeld 587 .... B4
Kamanjab 713 .... A3
Karasburg 2,693 .... B5
Karibib 1,653 .... B4
Katima Mulilo C3
Keetmanshoop 10,297 .... B5
Khorixas 1,299 .... A4
Koes 514 .... B5
Lüderitz 6,642 .... A5
Maltahöhe 1,313 .... B4
Mariental 4,629 .... B4
Ohopoho A3
Okahandja 1,688 .... B4
Omaruru 2,783 .... B4
Ondangua B3
Ongwediva B3
Oranjemund 2,594 .... B5
Otavi 1,814 .... B3
Otjiwarongo 8,018 .... B4
Outjo 2,545 .... B4
Rehoboth 5,363 .... B4
Runtu 521 .... B3
Stampriet 271 .... B4
Swakopmund 5,681 .... A4
Tsumeb 12,338 .... B3
Usakos 2,334 .... B4
Warmbad 810 .... B5
Windhoek (cap.) 61,369 .... B4
Witvlei 303 .... B4

OTHER FEATURES

Brandberg (mt.) A4
Caprivi Strip (reg.) C3
Chobe (riv.) C3
Cubango (riv.) B3
Damaraland (reg.) B4
Diamond Coast (reg.) A5
Elephant (riv.) B5
Etosha Pan (salt pan) B3
Fish (riv.) B5
Great Namaland (reg.) B4
Hottentot (bay) A5
Kalahari (des.) C4
Kaokoveld (reg.) A3
Kaukauveld (mts.) C3
Namib (des.) A3
Nossob (riv.) B4
Okovango (riv.) C3
Ovamboland (reg.) B3
Skeleton Coast (reg.) A3
Swakop (riv.) B4
Zambezi (riv.) C3

REUNION

CITIES and TOWNS

Le Port 21,564 .... F5
Saint-André 6,584 .... G5
Saint-Benoît 7,778 .... G5
Saint-Denis (cap.) 80,075 .... F5
Saint-Denis* 104,603 .... F5
Saint-Joseph 8,928 .... G6
Saint-Louis 10,252 .... F5
Saint-Pierre 21,817 .... F6

OTHER FEATURES

Bassas da India (isl.) F4
Europa (isl.) G4
Glorioso (isls.) H2
Juan de Nova (isl.) G3
Piton des Neiges (mt.) G5

SEYCHELLES

CITIES and TOWNS

Anse Boileau† 3,420 .... H5
Anse Royale† 3,182 .... H5
Cascade† 2,600 .... H5
Victoria (cap.) 15,559 .... H5
Victoria* 23,012 .... H5

OTHER FEATURES

Aldabra (isls.) H1
Assumption (isl.) H1
Astove (isl.) H2
Cosmoledo (isls.) H1
Frigate (isl.) J5
La Digue (isl.) J5
Mahé (isl.) H5
North (isl.) H5
Praslin (isl.) H5
Silhouette (isl.) H5

SOUTH AFRICA

PROVINCES

Cape of Good Hope 5,543,506 .... C6
Natal 5,722,215 .... E5
Orange Free State 1,833,216 .... D5
Transvaal 10,673,033 .... D4

AUTONOMOUS REPUBLICS

Bophuthatswana 1,200,000 .... D5
Ciskei 345,191 .... D6
Transkei 2,000,000 .... D6
Venda 450,000 .... E4

CITIES and TOWNS

Aberdeen 4,968 .... C6
Adelaide 7,227 .... D6
Alberton 23,988 .... H6
Alexandra 57,040 .... H6
Alexander Bay 2,675 .... B5
Aliwal North 12,311 .... D6
Barberton 12,382 .... E5
Barkly East 4,023 .... D6
Beaufort West 17,862 .... C6
Bellville 49,026 .... F6
Benoni 151,294 .... J6
Benoni□ 164,543 .... J6
Bethlehem 29,918 .... D5
Bethulie 4,918 .... D6
Bloemfontein 149,836 .... C5
Bloemfontein□ 182,329 .... C5
Bloubergstrand 378 .... E6
Boksburg 106,126 .... J6
Botrivier 743 .... F7
Brakpan 73,210 .... J6
Brandvlei 1,337 .... B6
Bredasdorp 5,264 .... B6
Brentwood Park 5,296 .... J6
Brits 12,182 .... D5
Britstown 3,039 .... C6
Burgersdorp 8,340 .... D6
Butterworth (Gcuwa) 2,769 .... D6
Caledon 5,406 .... G7
Calvinia 6,386 .... B6
Cape Town (cap.) 697,514 .... E6
Cape Town□ 833,731 .... E6
Carltonville 40,641 .... G7
Carnarvon 5,199 .... C6
Ceres 9,230 .... B6
Christiana 6,882 .... D5
Clanwilliam 2,724 .... B6
Clayville 3,994 .... H6
Colesberg 7,088 .... D6
Constantia 7,220 .... E6
Cradock 20,822 .... D6
De Aar 18,057 .... C6
Delmas 6,424 .... J6
Dibeng 945 .... C5
Douglas 4,335 .... C5
Dundee 17,162 .... E5
Dunnottar 3,089 .... J6
Durban 736,852 .... E5
Durban□ 975,494 .... E5
Durbanville 7,438 .... F6
East London 119,727 .... D6
East London□ 126,671 .... D6
Edenburg 3,710 .... D5
Edendale 41,194 .... D5
Edenvale 25,126 .... H6
Eersterivier 1,459 .... F6
Elliot 3,739 .... D6
Eloff 1,134 .... J6
Elsburg 3,501 .... H6
Elsiesrivier 63,706 .... F6
Empangeni 7,532 .... E5
Ermelo 19,036 .... E5
Eshowe 4,552 .... E5
Estcourt 10,922 .... D5
Ficksburg 9,504 .... D5
Firgrove 2,551 .... F6
Fort Beaufort 11,640 .... D6
Franschhoek 1,216 .... F6
Garies 1,339 .... B6
Gcuwa 2,769 .... D6
George 24,625 .... C6
Germiston 221,972 .... H6
Germiston□ 293,257 .... H6
Glencoe 10,513 .... E5
Goodwood 31,592 .... F6
Gordon's Bay 1,112 .... F7
Graaff-Reinet 22,392 .... C6
Grabouw 4,286 .... F7
Grahamstown 41,302 .... D6
Grassy Park 32,709 .... E6
Greytown 9,028 .... E5
Griquatown 2,996 .... C5
Halfway House 3,639 .... H6
Harrismith 16,082 .... D5
Hawston 2,501 .... G7
Heidelberg 12,521 .... J7
Heilbron 8,258 .... D5
Hermanus 4,956 .... G7
Hopetown 3,273 .... C5
Houtbaai 5,691 .... E6
Howick 12,429 .... E5
Humansdorp 4,215 .... C6
Ingwavuma 718 .... E5
Jagersfontein 4,142 .... D5
Jameson Park 2,280 .... J7
Johannesburg 654,232 .... H6
Johannesburg□ 1,417,818 .... H6
Keimoes 4,534 .... C5
Kempton Park 37,205 .... J6
Kenhardt 3,230 .... C5
Kimberley 105,258 .... C5
Kimberley□ 108,609 .... C5
King William's Town 15,798 .... D6
Kirkwood 5,151 .... D6
Kleinmond 1,115 .... F7
Klerksdorp 63,558 .... D5
Knysna 13,479 .... C6
Koffiefontein 3,672 .... D5
Kokstad 10,227 .... D6
Kraaifontein 10,286 .... F6
Kroonstad 51,988 .... D5
Krugersdorp 92,725 .... H6
Kuilsrivier 8,132 .... F6
Kuruman 5,758 .... C5
Ladybrand 8,757 .... D5
Ladysmith 28,920 .... D5
Lambert's Bay 3,247 .... B6
Lombardy 3,395 .... H6
Louis Trichardt 8,906 .... E4
Lydenburg 7,427 .... E4
Macassar 882 .... F6
Maclear 3,279 .... D6
Mafikeng (Mafeking) 6,515 .... C5
Malmesbury 9,314 .... B6
Margate 4,410 .... E6
Matatiele 3,853 .... D6
Melkbosstrand 453 .... E6
Messina 12,121 .... D4
Meyerton 8,654 .... H7
Middelburg, C. of Good
Hope 11,121 .... D6
Middelburg, Transvaal 26,942 .... D5
Milnerton 10,893 .... F6
Modderfontein 8,538 .... H6
Molteno 5,825 .... D6
Montagu 5,504 .... C6
Moorreesburg 4,945 .... B6
Mossel Bay 17,574 .... C6
Nababeep 8,293 .... B5
Nelspruit 25,092 .... E5
Newcastle 14,407 .... E5
Nigel 41,179 .... J7
Noupoort 7,403 .... C6
Nyanga 15,655 .... F6
Nylstroom 6,906 .... D4
Odendaalsrus 15,603 .... D5
Okiep 4,983 .... B5
Oudtshoorn 26,907 .... C6
Paarl 49,244 .... F6
Parow 60,768 .... F6
Parys 17,447 .... D5
Phalaborwa 7,543 .... E4
Pietermaritzburg 114,822 .... E5
Pietermaritzburg□ 174,179 .... E5
Pietersburg 27,174 .... D4
Piet Retief 10,056 .... D5
Piketberg 3,638 .... B6
Pinelands 11,769 .... F6
Pinetown 22,721 .... E6
Pniel 1,596 .... F6
Port Alfred 8,640 .... D6
Port Elizabeth 392,231 .... D6
Port Elizabeth□ 413,961 .... D6
Port Nolloth 2,893 .... B5
Port Saint Johns
(Umzimbuvu) 1,817 .... D6
Port Shepstone 5,581 .... E6
Postmasburg 9,020 .... C5

OTHER FEATURES

SWAZILAND

CITIES and TOWNS

ZIMBABWE

CITIES and TOWNS

OTHER FEATURES

*City and suburbs.
†Population of parish.
○Population of subdivision.
□Population of urban area.

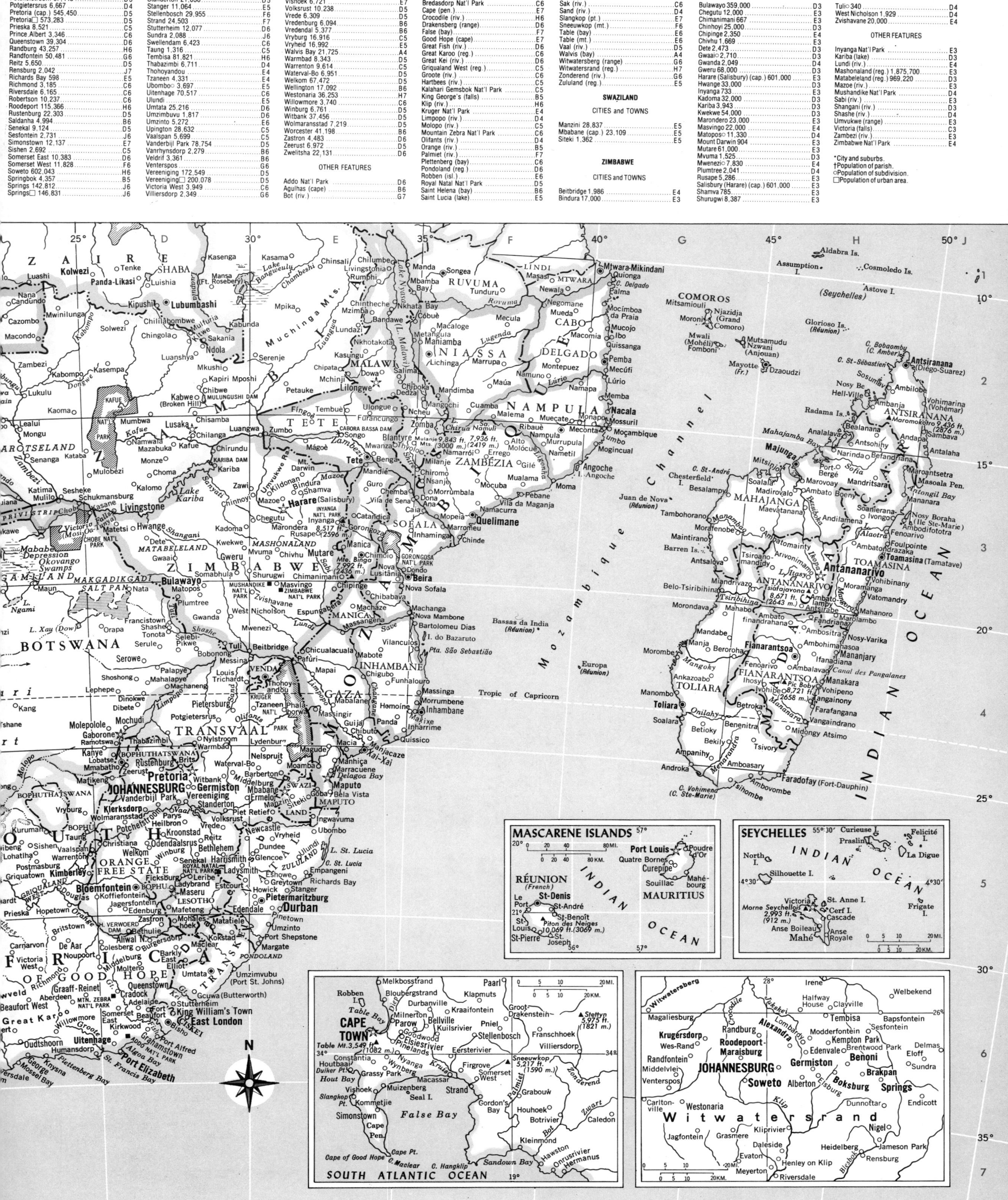

South America
AZIMUTHAL EQUAL-AREA PROJECTION
MILES
0 100 200 400 600
KILOMETERS
0 100 200 400 600
Capitals of Countries
Other Capitals
International Boundaries
Canals
Scale 1:27,000,000
© Copyright HAMMOND INCORPORATED, Maplewood, N. J.
Longitude West 50° of Greenwich
CARIBBEAN SEA
ATLANTIC OCEAN
ATLANTIC OCEAN
PACIFIC OCEAN
NETHERLANDS ANTILLES
ST. VINCENT AND THE GRENADINES
BARBADOS
GRENADA
WEST INDIES
TRINIDAD & TOBAGO
Port of Spain
PANAMA
G. of Panamá
Panama Canal
COLOMBIA
Bogotá
Medellín
Cali
Barranquilla
Cartagena
VENEZUELA
Caracas
Maracaibo
Lake Maracaibo
Ciudad Bolívar
Ciudad Guayana
Angel Fall
GUYANA
Georgetown
SURINAME
Paramaribo
FRENCH GUIANA
Cayenne
ECUADOR
Quito
Guayaquil
Gulf of Guayaquil
Chimborazo 20,561 ft. (6267 m.)
Equator
PERU
Lima
Callao
Cusco
Arequipa
Iquitos
Huascarán 22,205 ft. (6768 m.)
Lake Titicaca
BOLIVIA
La Paz
Sucre
Cochabamba
Santa Cruz
Lake Poopó
Potosí
Nev. Ancohuma 21,489 ft. (6550 m.)
BRAZIL
Brasília
Rio de Janeiro
São Paulo
Belo Horizonte
Salvador
Recife
Fortaleza
Belém
Manaus
Santarém
Porto Alegre
Curitiba
Amazon
Planalto de Mato Grosso
Brazilian Highlands
Guiana Highlands
Selvas
Caatinga
I. de Marajó
Tropic of Capricorn
PARAGUAY
Asunción
ITAIPU DAM
Gran Chaco
CHILE
Santiago
Valparaíso
Antofagasta
Concepción
Punta Arenas
Atacama Desert
ARGENTINA
Buenos Aires
Córdoba
Rosario
Mendoza
Mar del Plata
Bahía Blanca
Cerro Aconcagua 22,831 ft. (6959 m.)
Pampas
Patagonia
URUGUAY
Montevideo
Río de la Plata
Lagoa dos Patos
FALKLAND ISLANDS (U.K.)
Stanley
West Falkland
East Falkland
Tierra del Fuego
Strait of Magellan
Cape Horn
Ushuaia
I. de los Estados
ARCHIPIÉLAGO DE LOS CHONOS
Isla de Chiloé
JUAN FERNÁNDEZ IS. (Chile)
I. Robinson Crusoe
I. Alejandro Selkirk
I. de San Félix (Chile)
I. San Ambrosio (Chile)
Malpelo I. (Col.)
Golfo San Matías
Golfo San Jorge
Rocas
10° 0° 10° 20° 30° 40° 50°
80° 70° 60° 50° 40° 90° 30° 20°
A B C D E F G
1 2 3 4 5 6 7 8

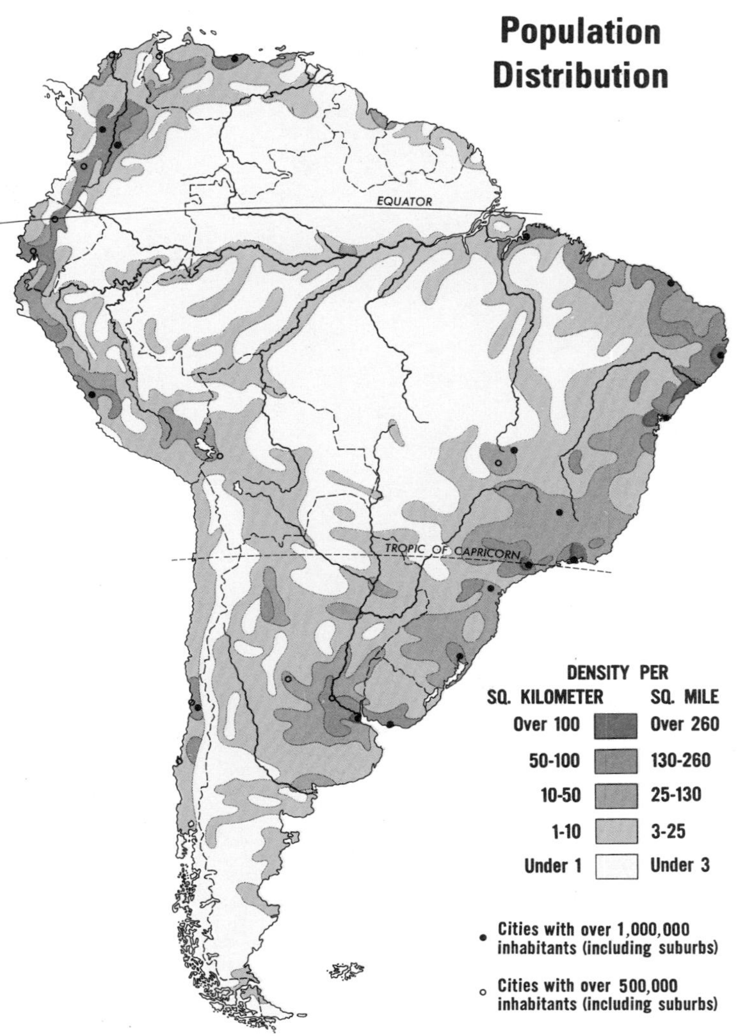

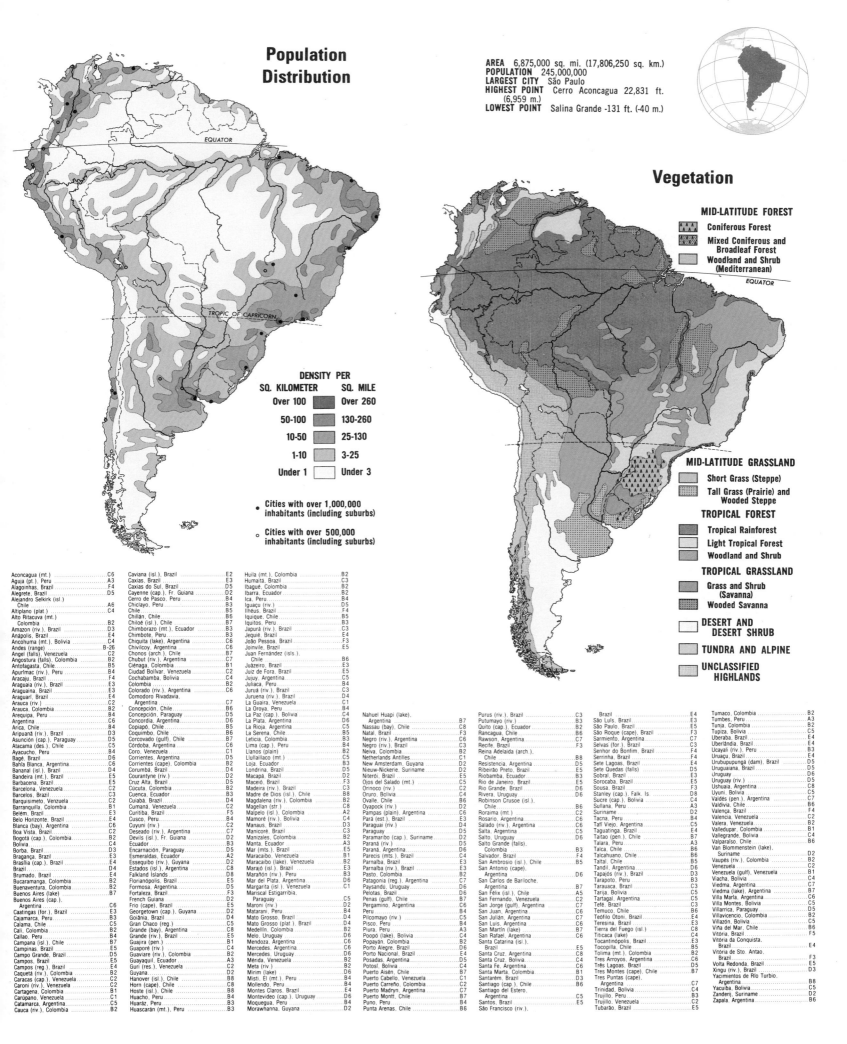

AREA 6,875,000 sq. mi. (17,806,250 sq. km.)
POPULATION 245,000,000
LARGEST CITY São Paulo
HIGHEST POINT Cerro Aconcagua 22,831 ft. (6,959 m.)
LOWEST POINT Salina Grande -131 ft. (-40 m.)

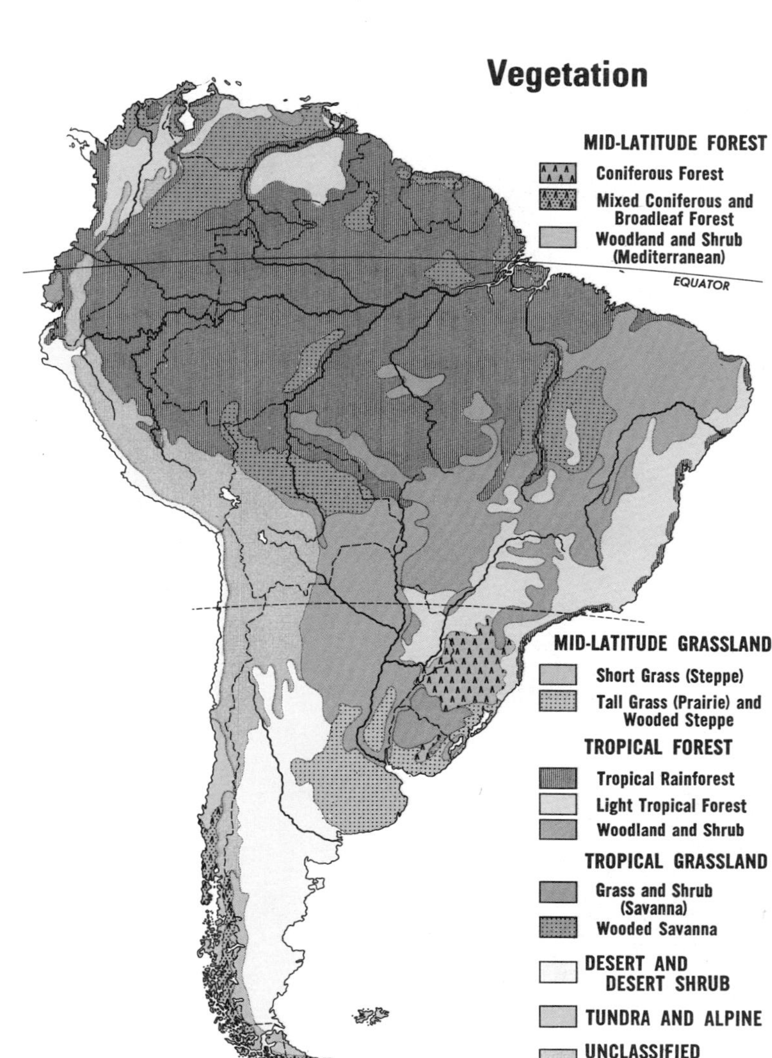

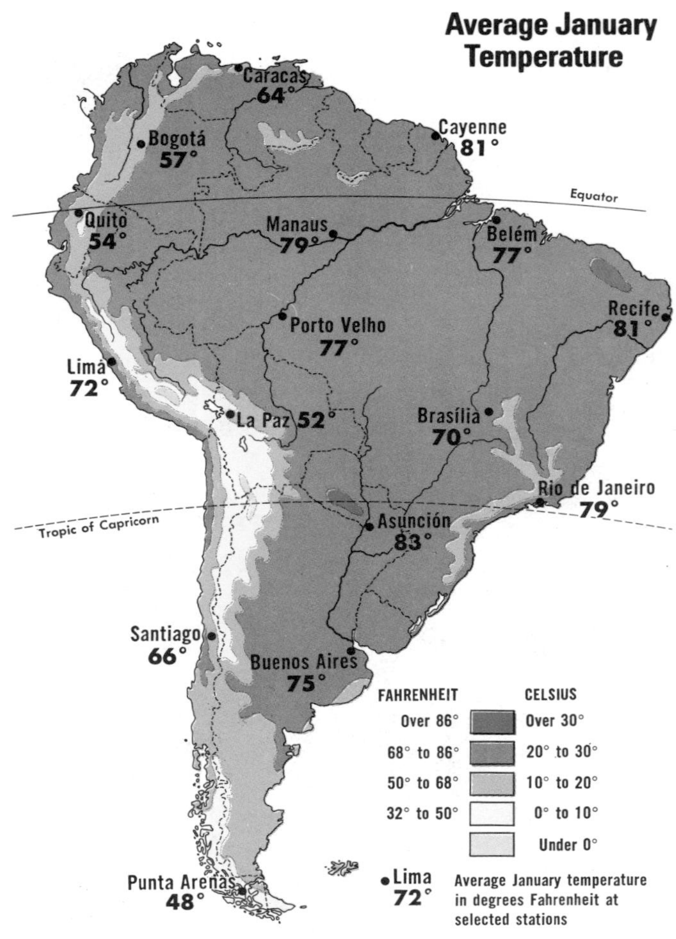
Average January Temperature
Caracas 64°
Cayenne 81°
Bogotá 57°
Equator
Quito 54°
Manaus 79°
Belém 77°
Recife 81°
Porto Velho 77°
Lima 72°
La Paz 52°
Brasília 70°
Rio de Janeiro 79°
Tropic of Capricorn
Asunción 83°
Santiago 66°
Buenos Aires 75°
Punta Arenas 48°
FAHRENHEIT
CELSIUS
Over 86° Over 30°
68° to 86° 20° to 30°
50° to 68° 10° to 20°
32° to 50° 0° to 10°
Under 0°
Lima 72° Average January temperature in degrees Fahrenheit at selected stations

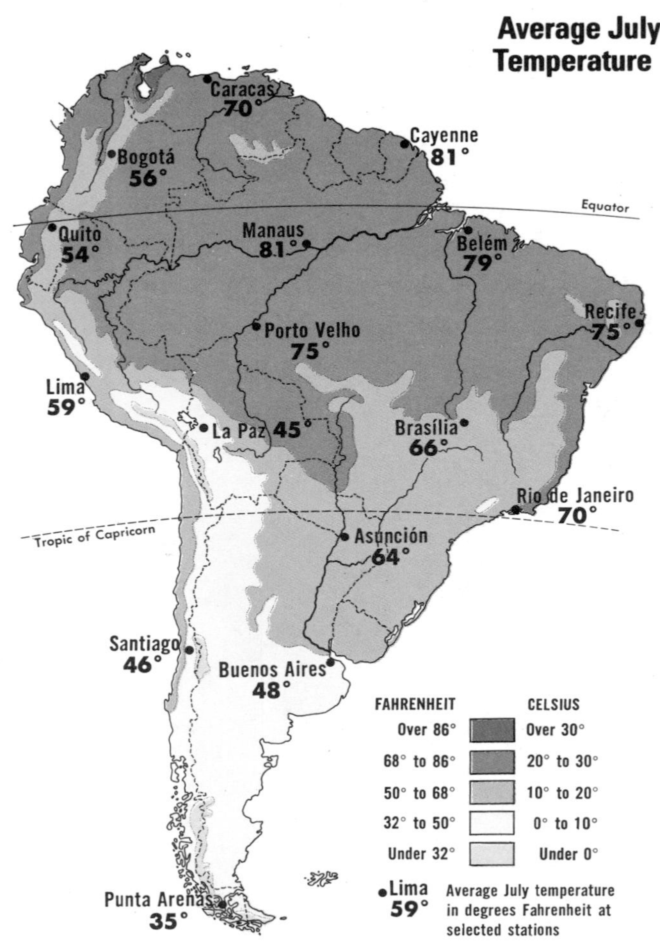
Average July Temperature
Caracas 70°
Cayenne 81°
Bogotá 56°
Equator
Quito 54°
Manaus 81°
Belém 79°
Recife 75°
Porto Velho 75°
Lima 59°
La Paz 45°
Brasília 66°
Rio de Janeiro 70°
Tropic of Capricorn
Asunción 64°
Santiago 46°
Buenos Aires 48°
Punta Arenas 35°
FAHRENHEIT
CELSIUS
Over 86° Over 30°
68° to 86° 20° to 30°
50° to 68° 10° to 20°
32° to 50° 0° to 10°
Under 32° Under 0°
Lima 59° Average July temperature in degrees Fahrenheit at selected stations

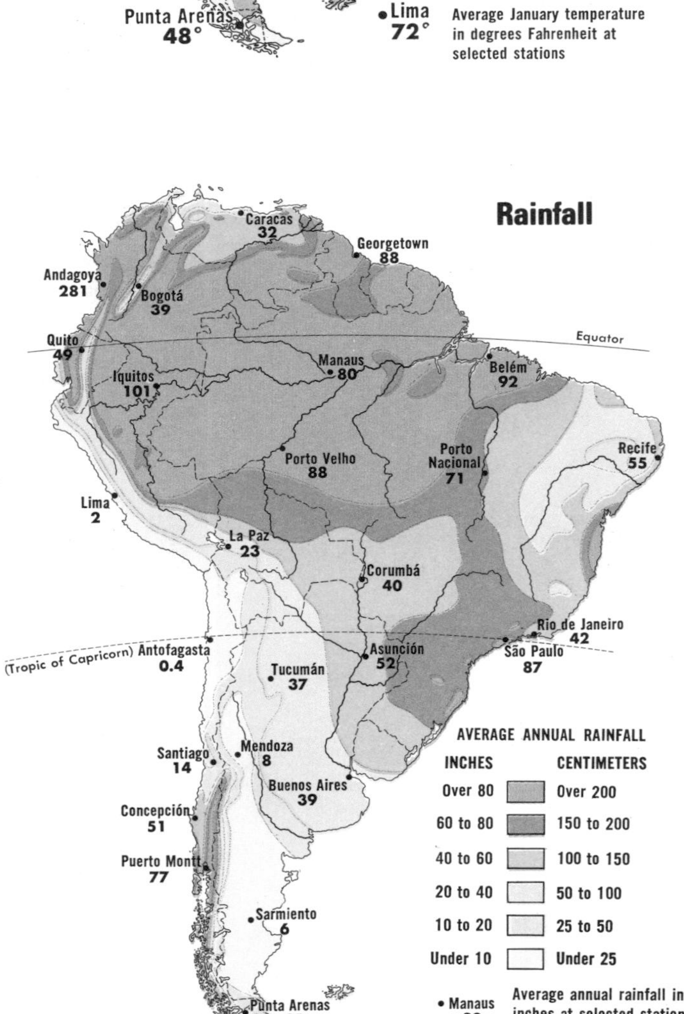
Rainfall
Caracas 32
Georgetown 88
Andagoya 281
Bogotá 39
Equator
Quito 49
Manaus 80
Iquitos 101
Belém 92
Porto Velho 88
Porto Nacional 71
Recife 55
Lima 2
La Paz 23
Corumbá 40
Rio de Janeiro 42
(Tropic of Capricorn) Antofagasta 0.4
Asunción 52
São Paulo 87
Tucumán 37
Santiago 14
Mendoza 8
Buenos Aires 39
Concepción 51
Puerto Montt 77
Sarmiento 6
Punta Arenas 21
AVERAGE ANNUAL RAINFALL
INCHES
CENTIMETERS
Over 80 Over 200
60 to 80 150 to 200
40 to 60 100 to 150
20 to 40 50 to 100
10 to 20 25 to 50
Under 10 Under 25
Manaus 80 Average annual rainfall in inches at selected stations

Vegetation/Relief

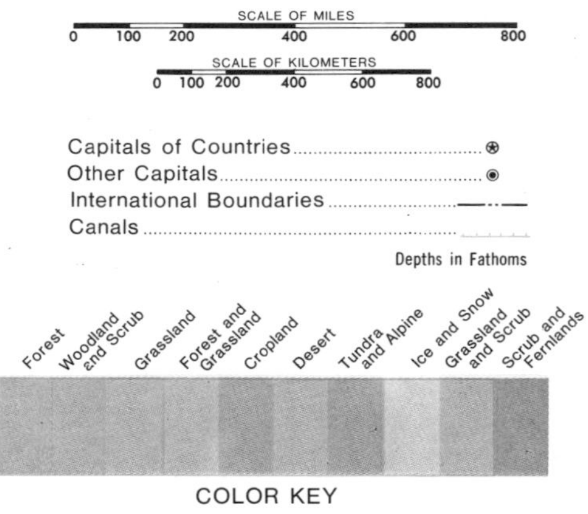
SCALE OF MILES
0 100 200 400 600 800
SCALE OF KILOMETERS
0 100 200 400 600 800
Capitals of Countries
Other Capitals
International Boundaries
Canals
Depths in Fathoms
Forest
Woodland and Scrub
Grassland
Forest and Grassland
Cropland
Desert
Tundra and Alpine
Ice and Snow
Grassland and Scrub
Scrub and Fernlands
COLOR KEY

CARIBBEAN SEA
G. of Venezuela
NETH. ANTILLES
Aruba
Curaçao
Bonaire
Willemstad
Pta. Gallinas
GRENADA
BARBADOS
West Indies
Tobago
TRINIDAD & TOBAGO
Port of Spain
Trinidad
Barranquilla
Maracaibo
Caracas
L. Maracaibo
Pico Bolívar 16,427 ft. (5007 m.)
Ciudad Guayana
Orinoco
Panamá
PANAMÁ
VENEZUELA
Guri Res.
Bucaramanga
Arauca
Medellín
Magdalena
Bogotá
Meta
Angel Fall
GUYANA
Georgetown
Paramaribo
Cayenne
Mt. Roraima 9,094 ft. (2772 m.)
SURINAME
FRENCH GUIANA
Caroní
Essequibo
Courantyne
Maroni
Cali
Cauca
COLOMBIA
Llanos
Guiana Highlands
Orinoco
Branco
Jari
ATLANTIC OCEAN
Pico Phelps (Pico da Neblina) 9,889 ft. (3014 m.)
Vaupés
Caquetá
Quito
Chimborazo 20,561 ft. (6267 m.)
ECUADOR
Putumayo
Negro
Japurá
Equator
I. de Marajó
Amazon
Belém
São Luís
Guayaquil
Gulf of Guayaquil
Içá
Manaus
Amazon
Iquitos
Amazon
Selvas
Tapajós
Xingu
Tocantins
Fortaleza
Teresina
Yavari
Juruá
Madeira
Purus
Pta. Aguja
Ucayali
Marañón
Aripuanã
Teles Pires
Araguaia
Parnaíba
Caatingas
Cabo de São Roque
Natal
Trujillo
Huascarán 22,205 ft. (6768 m.)
Recife
BRAZIL
Maceió
Callao
Lima
Mamoré
Guaporé
Juruena
Planalto de Mato Grosso
Brazilian Plateau
Paraguaçu
Salvador
Beni
BOLIVIA
Cusco
Lake Titicaca
Nev. Ancohuma 21,489 ft. (6550 m.)
La Paz
Arequipa
Cochabamba
Grande
Brasília
Goiânia
São Francisco
Jequitinhonha
Highlands
Arica
Lake Poopó
Sucre
Chaco
Paraguai
Campo Grande
Belo Horizonte
Grande
Pico da Bandeira 9,482 ft. (2890 m.)
Paraná
Tietê
PARAGUAY
Paraíba
C. de São Tomé
C. Frio
Tropic of Capricorn
Antofagasta
Volcán Llullaillaco 22,057 ft. (6723 m.)
Pilcomayo
Bermejo
Asunción
ITAIPU DAM
São Paulo
Santos
Rio de Janeiro
Curitiba
Iguaçu
Iguazú Falls
San Miguel de Tucumán
Salado del Norte
Nev. Ojos del Salado 22,572 ft. (6880 m.)
I. de San Félix (Chile)
I. San Ambrosio (Chile)
I. de Santa Catarina
Serra do Mar
CHILE
Uruguay
Paraná
Gran Chaco
Atacama Desert
Porto Alegre
Córdoba
Santa Fé
Lagoa dos Patos
Cerro Aconcagua 22,831 ft. (6959 m.)
Rosario
Negro
Lagoa Mirim
Valparaíso
Santiago
Mendoza
URUGUAY
I. Robinson Crusoe
I. Alejandro Selkirk
Juan Fernandez Is. (Chile)
Buenos Aires
Salado
Montevideo
La Plata
Río de la Plata
C. San Antonio
Pampas
ARGENTINA
Concepción
Colorado
Bahía Blanca
Limay
Negro
PACIFIC OCEAN
Andes
Golfo San Matías
Puerto Montt
Pen. Valdés
Isla de Chiloé
Chubut
Archipiélago de los Chonos
Golfo San Jorge
C. Tres Puntas
Pen. Taitao
Deseado
G. de Penas
Patagonia
Bahía Grande
Falkland Islands (U.K.)
Stanley
Archipiélago Reina Adelaida
Str. of Magellan
Tierra del Fuego
Punta Arenas
Cape Horn
Longitude West of Greenwich

STATES

Amazonas (terr.) 21,696 ..... E5
Anzoátegui 506,297 ..... F3
Apure 164,705 ..... D4
Aragua 543,170 ..... E3
Barinas 231,046 ..... D3
Bolívar 391,665 ..... F7
Carabobo 659,339 ..... D2
Cojedes 94,351 ..... D3
Delta Amacuro (terr.) 48,139 ..... H3
Dependencias Federales (terr.) 463 ..... E2
Distrito Federal 1,860,637 ..... E2
Falcón 407,957 ..... D2
Guárico 318,905 ..... E3
Lara 671,410 ..... C2
Mérida 347,095 ..... C3
Miranda 856,272 ..... E2
Monagas 298,239 ..... G3
Nueva Esparta 118,830 ..... G2
Portuguesa 297,047 ..... D3
Sucre 469,004 ..... G2
Táchira 511,346 ..... C4
Trujillo 381,334 ..... C3
Yaracuy 223,545 ..... D2
Zulia 1,299,030 ..... B2

CITIES and TOWNS

Acarigua 56,743 ..... D3
Achaguas 4,633 ..... D4
Adícora 707 ..... D2
Aguada Grande 2,901 ..... D2
Agua Fría D2
Agua Linda E5
Aguasay 1,752 ..... G3
Altagracia 11,116 ..... C2
Altagracia de Orituco 18,717 ..... E3
Amuay C2
Anaco 29,487 ..... F3
Aparurén G5
Apurito 740 ..... D4
Arabopó H5
Aragua de Barcelona 9,107 ..... F3
Aragua de Maturín 4,051 ..... G3
Araure 22,466 ..... D3
Aricagua 231 ..... C3
Arichuna 1,204 ..... E4
Aripao 296 ..... F4
Arismendi 1,257 ..... D3
Aroa 5,418 ..... D2
Atapirire 337 ..... F3
Bachaquero C3
Baragua 659 ..... D2
Barbacoas 2,513 ..... E3
Barcelona 78,201 ..... F2
Barinas 56,329 ..... C3
Barinitas 9,644 ..... C3
Barquisimeto 330,815 ..... D2
Barrancas, Barinas 4,489 ..... C3
Barrancas, Monagas 5,738 ..... G3
Betijoque 5,851 ..... C3
Biruaca 2,266 ..... E4
Biscucuy 6,114 ..... D3
Bobare 1,204 ..... D2
Bobures 2,468 ..... C3
Boca de Aroa 2,756 ..... D2
Boca del Mangle D2
Boca del Pao 403 ..... F3
Boconó 15,915 ..... C3
Borbón F4
Borojó 423 ..... C2
Bruzual 941 ..... D3
Buena Vista, Anzoátegui F3
Buena Vista, Apure D4
Buena Vista, Falcón 944 ..... D2
Cabimas 118,037 ..... C2
Cabruta 1,927 ..... E4
Cabudare 14,593 ..... D3
Cabure 1,673 ..... D2
Cachipo G3
Cacuri F5
Cagua 29,601 ..... E2
Caicara 6,092 ..... G3
Caicara de Orinoco 6,867 ..... E4
Calabozo 37,282 ..... E3
Calderas 1,195 ..... C3
Camaguán 4,143 ..... E3
Camatagua 3,335 ..... E3
Campo Claro 1,832 ..... G2
Candelaria F4
Cantaura 15,839 ..... F3
Capatárida 1,375 ..... C2
Capibara E6
Carabobo, Bolívar H4
Carabobo, Carabobo D3
Caracas (cap.) 1,035,499 ..... E2
Caracas* 2,183,935 ..... E2
Carache 3,966 ..... C3
Carapa 119 ..... G3
Cariaco 6,549 ..... G2
Caribén E4
Caripe 4,729 ..... G2
Caripito 19,053 ..... G2
Carirubana 15,701 ..... C2
Carmelo 2,556 ..... C2
Carora 36,115 ..... C2
Carrasquero 2,193 ..... B2
Carúpano 50,935 ..... G2
Casanay 4,985 ..... G2
Casigua, Falcón 460 ..... C2
Casigua, Zulia 3,665 ..... B3
Caucagua 6,218 ..... E2
Cazorla 700 ..... E3
Chaguaramas 2,748 ..... E3
Chichiriviche 3,236 ..... D2
Chivacoa 19,210 ..... D2
Choroní 534 ..... E2
Churuguara 6,636 ..... D2
Ciudad Bolívar 103,728 ..... G3
Ciudad Bolivia 4,864 ..... C3
Ciudad de Nutrias 769 ..... D3
Ciudad Guayana 143,540 ..... G3
Ciudad Ojeda 83,083 ..... C2
Ciudad Piar 3,965 ..... G4
Clarines 2,099 ..... F3
Cojoro C2
Colón E6
Comunidad E6
Coporito H3
Coro 68,701 ..... D2
Corozo Pando E3
Cúa 9,953 ..... E2
Cubiro 1,988 ..... D3
Cuchivero F4
Cumaná 119,751 ..... F2
Cumanacoa 9,179 ..... F2
Cunaviche 795 ..... E4
Curiapo H3
Dabajuro 4,516 ..... C2
Delicias 1,616 ..... B4
Democracia E6
Dolores 1,454 ..... D3
Duaca 7,519 ..... D2
Ejido 11,170 ..... C3
El Almacén G4
El Amparo de Apure 2,015 ..... C4
El Baúl 1,715 ..... D3
El Callao 4,270 ..... G4
El Calvario 384 ..... E3
El Chaparro 3,768 ..... F3
El Cristo G4
El Dorado 1,888 ..... H4
El Empedrado 1,788 ..... C3
El Guapo 1,231 ..... F2
El Manteco 1,962 ..... G4
El Miamo 335 ..... H4
Elorza 3,184 ..... D4
El Oso H5
El Palmar 2,758 ..... G4
El Pao, Anzoátegui 761 ..... F3
El Pao, Bolívar 1,259 ..... G3
El Pao, Cojedes 1,715 ..... D3
El Perú H4
El Pilar 3,278 ..... G2
El Rastro 903 ..... E3
El Roque E2
El Samán de Apure 1,399 ..... D4
El Socorro F3
El Sombrero 8,373 ..... E3
El Tigre 49,801 ..... F3
El Tocuyo 19,351 ..... C3
El Toro H3
El Vigía 20,970 ..... C3
El Vínculo D1
El Yagual 699 ..... D4
Encontrados 5,607 ..... B3
Esperanza E6
Espino 559 ..... F3
Garcitas C3
Guacara 35,111 ..... D2
Guachara 577 ..... D4
Guadarrama 334 ..... D3
Guaina G5
Guana G5
Guanare 34,148 ..... D3
Guanarito 3,150 ..... D3
Guanoco G2
Guanta 9,017 ..... F2
Guardatinajas 1,206 ..... E3
Guarero B2
Guarico 3,259 ..... D3
Guariquén 619 ..... G2
Guasdualito 7,793 ..... C4
Guasimal 582 ..... D4
Guasipati 4,807 ..... H4
Guayabal, Amazonas E6
Guayabal, Guárico 1,403 ..... E3
Güiria 13,905 ..... G2
Guri G4
Guzmán Blanco E6
Higuerote 5,008 ..... F2
Icabarú H5
Independencia 4,897 ..... B4
Irapa 4,470 ..... G2
Juangriego 6,062 ..... G2
Judibana C2
Jusepín G3
Kavanayen H5
La Aduana D3
La Asunción 6,381 ..... G2
La Canoa G3
La Ceiba, Apure C4
La Ceiba, Trujillo 212 ..... C3
La Concepción B2
La Concepción 13,885 ..... C2
La Esmeralda F6
La Esperanza H3
La Fría 8,134 ..... B3
La Grita 9,954 ..... C3
La Guaira 20,344 ..... E2
Lagunetas C3
Lagunillas C2

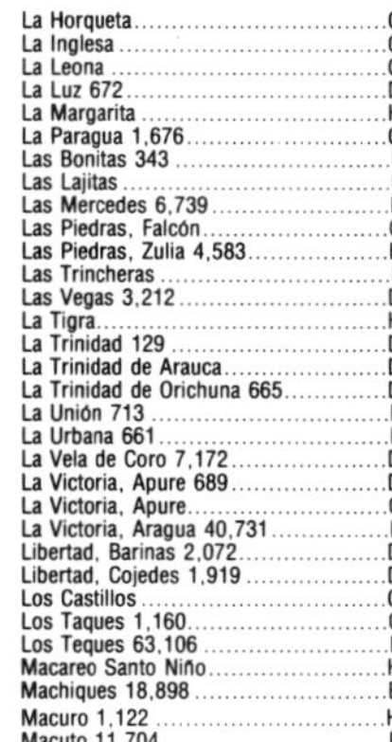

La Horqueta G3
La Inglesa G3
La Leona G3
La Luz 672 D3
La Margarita H3
La Paragua 1,676 G4
Las Bonitas 343 F4
Las Lajitas F4
Las Mercedes 6,739 E3
Las Piedras, Falcón C2
Las Piedras, Zulia 4,583 B2
Las Trincheras F4
Las Vegas 3,212 D3
La Tigra H4
La Trinidad 129 D3
La Trinidad de Arauca D4
La Trinidad de Orichuna 665 D4
La Unión 713 E3
La Urbana 661 E4
La Vela de Coro 7,172 D2
La Victoria, Apure 689 D4
La Victoria, Apure C4
La Victoria, Aragua 40,731 E2
Libertad, Barinas 2,072 D3
Libertad, Cojedes 1,919 D3
Los Castillos G3
Los Taques 1,160 C2
Los Teques 63,106 E2
Macareo Santo Niño H3
Machiques 18,898 B3
Macuro 1,122 H2
Macuto 11,704 E2

Maiquetía 59,238 E2
Mantecal, Apure 1,136 D4
Mantecal, Bolívar F4
Maparari 1,376 D2
Mapire 1,195 F4
Maporal 249 C4
Maracaibo 651,574 C2
Maracay 255,134 E2
Marigüitar 5,645 G2
Maripa 913 F4
Maroa 408 E6
Matu F4
Maturín 98,188 G3
Mene de Mauroa 4,336 C2
Mene Grande 11,498 C3
Mérida 74,214 C3
Mesa Bolívar 956 C3
Mirimire 3,424 D2
Moitaco 458 F4
Morganito E5
Morón 19,451 D2
Mucuchachí 472 C3
Mucuchíes 1,625 C3
Naricual 1,047 F2
Nirgua 11,918 D2
Nuevo Mamo G3
Obispos 1,140 D3
Ocumare de la Costa 2,840 E2
Ocumare del Tuy 24,229 E2
Onoto 1,991 F3
Ortiz 1,793 E3
Ospino 3,544 D3
Palmarejo C2
Palmarito, Apure 926 D4
Palmarito, Guárico F3
Palmarito, Mérida 988 C3
Papelón 774 D3
Paraguaipoa 3,850 C2
Paraíso de
  Chabasquén 2,094 D3
Pariaguán 8,173 F3
Parmana F4
Pedernales G3
Pedregal 1,317 C2
Peraitepuí H5
Piacoa H3
Pimichín E6
Píritu, Anzoátegui 2,479 F2
Píritu, Falcón 1,186 D2
Píritu, Portuguesa 8,128 D3
Platanal F6
Porlamar 31,985 G2
Pozuelos 45,391 F2
Pregonero 3,598 C3
Pueblo Hondo B3
Pueblo Nuevo 3,426 D1
Puerto Ayacucho 10,417 E5
Puerto Cabello 72,103 E2
Puerto Cumarebo 10,064 D2
Puerto de Nutrias 675 D3
Puerto Hierro H2
Puerto La Cruz 63,276 F2
Puerto Miranda E4
Puerto Páez 954 E4
Puerto Píritu 3,495 F2
Punta Cardón 18,182 C2
Punta de Mata 7,777 G3
Punta de Piedras 2,826 F2
Punto Fijo 5,548 D2
Puruey F4
Puruname E6
Quibor 12,216 D3
Quiriquire 7,304 G3
Quisiro 1,383 C2
Río Caribe 8,963 G2
Río Chico 4,491 F2
Río Claro 2,460 D3
Río Tocuyo 916 C2
Rosario B2
Rubio 19,156 B4
Sabaneta, Barinas 4,680 D3
Sabaneta, Falcón 650 D2
Samariapo E5
San Antonio, Amazonas E6
San Antonio, Monagas 4,235 G2
San Antonio, Zulia C3
San Antonio de Caparo 289 C4
San Antonio del
  Táchira 20,342 B4
San Antonio de Tabasca G3
Sanare 6,717 D3
San Carlos, Cojedes 21,029 D3
San Carlos, Zulia 749 C2

San Carlos del Zulia 26,762 C3
San Carlos de Río Negro 515 E7
San Casimiro 4,843 E3
San Cristóbal 151,717 B4
San Diego de Cabrutica 432 F3
San Felipe, Yaracuy 43,801 D2
San Felipe, Zulia B3
San Félix 379 C2
San Fernando de Apure 38,960 E4
San Fernando de Atabapo 1,537 E5
San Francisco, Lara 861 C2
San Ignacio B2
San José, Amazonas E5
San José, Zulia 4,498 B3
San José de Amacuro H3
San José de Areocuar 985 G2
San José de Guanipa 22,530 G3
San José de la Costa D2
San José de Río
  Chico 3,600 F2
San José de Tiznados 666 E3
San Juan de Colón B3
San Juan de las Galdonas 1,196 G2
San Juan de los Cayos 1,692 D2
San Juan de los Morros 38,265 E3
San Juan de Manapiare E5
San Juan de Payara 1,018 E4
San Lorenzo, Falcón 716 D2
San Lorenzo, Zulia C3
San Luis 1,405 D2
San Mateo 2,424 F3
San Mauricio E3
San Pedro de las Bocas G4
San Rafael 10,910 C2
San Rafael de Atamaica 635 E4
San Rafael de Orituco 1,378 E3
San Sebastián 5,582 E2
San Simón del Cocuy E3
Santa Ana, Anzoátegui 3,558 F3
Santa Ana, Táchira 5,116 B4
Santa Bárbara, Amazonas E6
Santa Bárbara, Barinas 6,155 C4
Santa Bárbara, Monagas 2,034 G3
Santa Bárbara, Zulia C3
Santa Catalina, Barinas 1,077 D4
Santa Catalina, Delta
  Amacuro H3
Santa Cruz C3
Santa Cruz de Bucaral 2,904 D2
Santa Cruz del Zulia 4,221 B3
Santa Cruz de Mara 5,773 C2
Santa Cruz de Orinoco 513 F3
Santa Elena 608 H5
Santa Inés,
  Anzoátegui 1,049 F3
Santa Inés, Barinas 391 C3
Santa Isabel F7
Santa Lucía 619 D3
Santa María, Bolívar G3
Santa María de Erebató F5
Santa María de Ipire 3,307 F3
Santa María del Orinoco E4
Santa Rita, Guárico E3
Santa Rita, Zulia 15,668 C2
Santa Rosa, Anzoátegui 954 F3

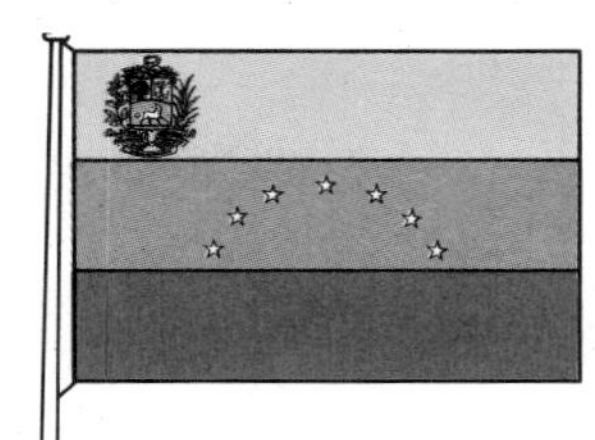

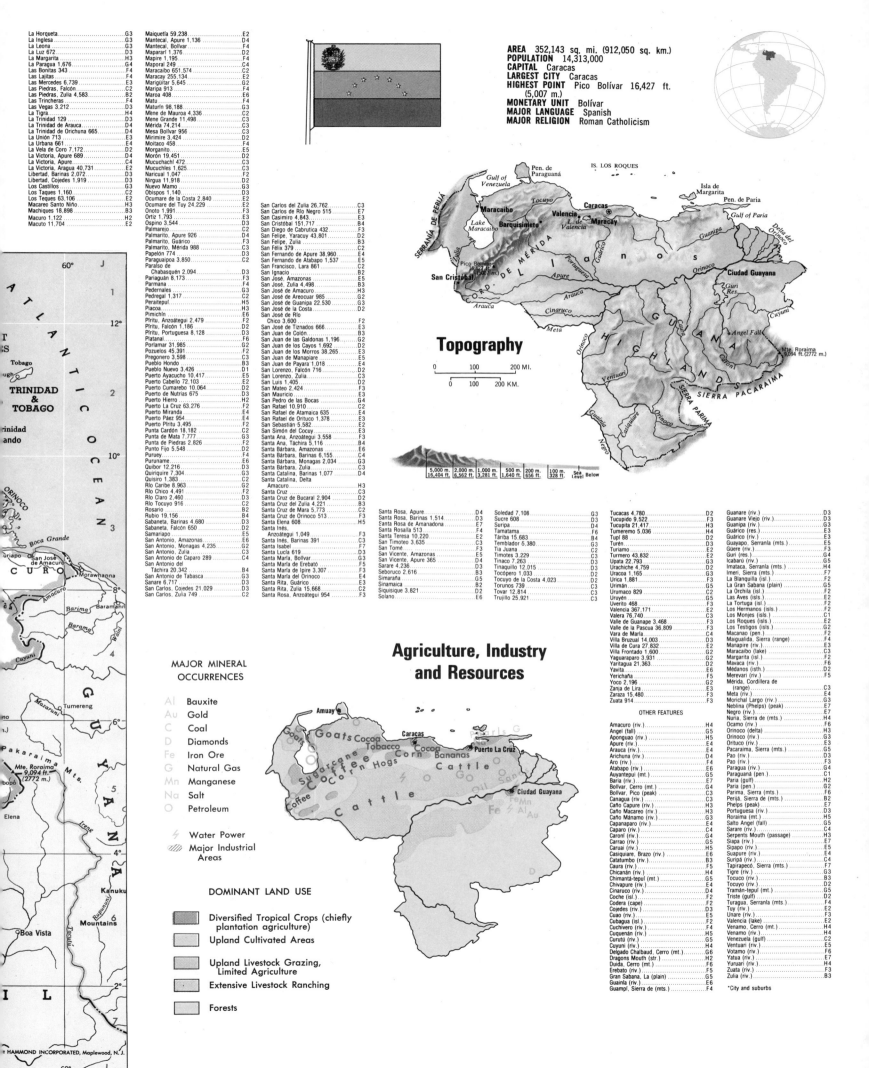

AREA 352,143 sq. mi. (912,050 sq. km.)
POPULATION 14,313,000
CAPITAL Caracas
LARGEST CITY Caracas
HIGHEST POINT Pico Bolívar 16,427 ft. (5,007 m.)
MONETARY UNIT Bolívar
MAJOR LANGUAGE Spanish
MAJOR RELIGION Roman Catholicism

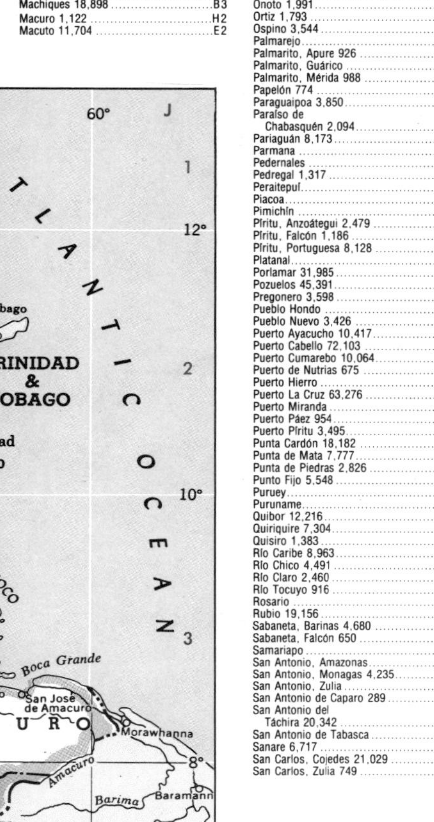

Topography

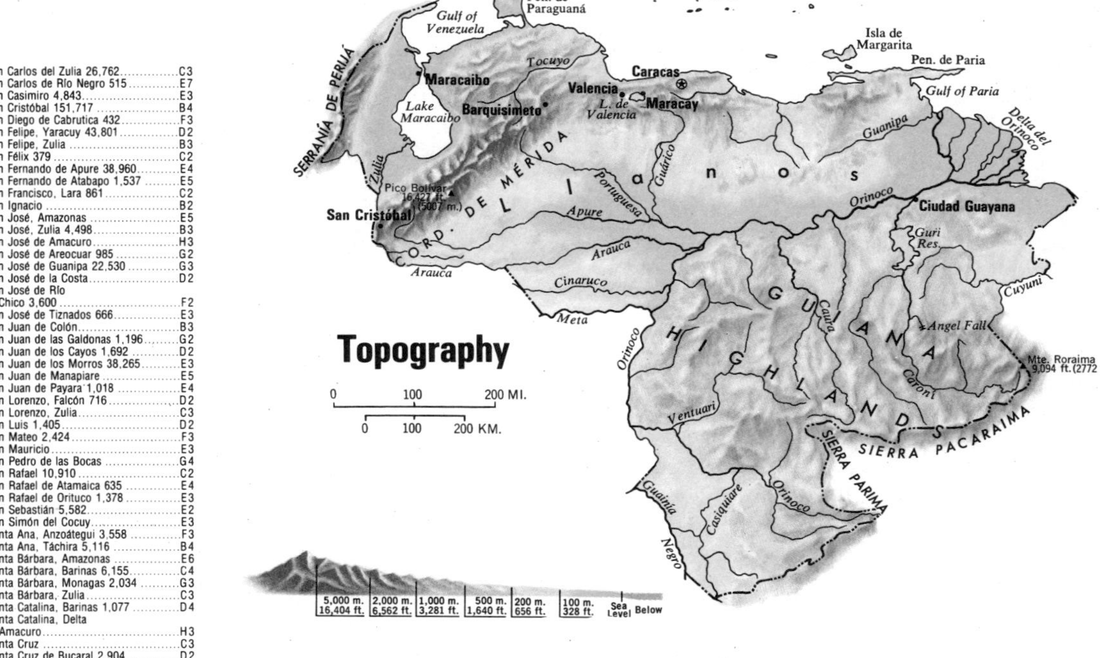

Santa Rosa, Apure D4
Santa Rosa, Barinas 1,514 D3
Santa Rosa de Amanadona E7
Santa Rosalía 513 F4
Santa Teresa 10,220 E2
San Timoteo 3,635 C3
San Tomé F3
San Vicente, Amazonas E5
San Vicente, Apure 365 D4
Sarare 4,236 D3
Seboruco 2,616 B3
Simaraña G5
Sinamaica B2
Siquisique 3,821 D2
Solano E6

Soledad 7,108 G3
Sucre 608 D3
Suripa D4
Tamatama F6
Táriba 15,683 B4
Temblador 5,380 G3
Tia Juana C2
Timotes 3,229 C3
Tinaco 7,263 D3
Tinaquillo 12,015 D3
Tocópero 1,033 D2
Tocuyo de la Costa 4,023 D2
Torunos 739 C3
Tovar 12,814 C3
Trujillo 25,921 C3

Tucacas 4,780 D2
Tucupido 9,522 F3
Tucupita 21,417 H3
Tumeremo 5,036 H4
Tupí 88 D2
Turén D3
Turiamo E2
Turmero 43,832 E2
Upata 22,793 G3
Urachiche 4,759 D2
Uracoa 1,165 G3
Urica 1,881 F3
Urimán G5
Urumaco 829 C2
Uruyén G5
Uverito 468 F3
Valencia 367,171 E2
Valera 76,740 C3
Valle de Guanape 3,468 F3
Valle de la Pascua 36,809 F3
Vara de María C4
Villa Bruzual 14,003 D3
Villa de Cura 27,832 E2
Villa Frontado 1,600 G2
Yaguaraparo 3,931 G2
Yaritagua 21,363 D2
Yavita E6
Yerichaña F5
Yoco 2,196 G2
Zanja de Lira E3
Zaraza 15,480 F3
Zuata 914 F3

OTHER FEATURES

Amacuro (riv.) H4
Angel (fall) G5
Aponguao (riv.) H5
Apure (riv.) E4
Arauca (riv.) E4
Arichuna (riv.) D4
Aro (riv.) F4
Atabapo (riv.) E6
Auyantepui (mt.) G5
Baria (riv.) E7
Bolívar, Cerro (mt.) G4
Bolívar, Pico (peak) C3
Canagua (riv.) C3
Caño Capure (riv.) H3
Caño Macareo (riv.) H3
Caño Mánamo (riv.) G3
Capanaparo (riv.) E4
Caparo (riv.) C4
Caroní (riv.) G4
Carrao (riv.) G5
Caruai (riv.) H5
Casiquiare, Brazo (riv.) E6
Catatumbo (riv.) B3
Caura (riv.) F5
Chicanán (riv.) H4
Chimantá-tepuí (mt.) G5
Chivapure (riv.) E4
Cinaruco (riv.) D4
Coche (isl.) F2
Codera (cape) F2
Cojedes (riv.) D3
Cuao (riv.) E5
Cubagua (isl.) F2
Cuchivero (riv.) F4
Cuquenán (riv.) H5
Curutú (riv.) G5
Cuyuni (riv.) H4
Delgado Chalbaud, Cerro (mt.) G6
Dragons Mouth (str.) H2
Duida, Cerro (mt.) F6
Erebato (riv.) F5
Gran Sabana, La (plain) G5
Guainía (riv.) E6
Guampí, Sierra de (mts.) F4

Guanare (riv.) D3
Guanare Viejo (riv.) D3
Guanipa (riv.) G3
Guárico (res.) E3
Guárico (riv.) E3
Guayapo, Serranía (mts.) E5
Güere (riv.) F3
Guri (res.) G4
Icabarú (riv.) G5
Imataca, Serranía (mts.) H4
Imeri, Sierra (mts.) F7
La Blanquilla (isl.) F2
La Gran Sabana (plain) G5
La Orchila (isl.) F2
Las Aves (isls.) E2
La Tortuga (isl.) F2
Los Hermanos (isls.) F2
Los Monjes (isls.) C1
Los Roques (isls.) E2
Los Testigos (isls.) G2
Macanao (pen.) F2
Maigualida, Sierra (range) F4
Manapire (riv.) E3
Maracaibo (lake) C3
Margarita (isl.) F2
Mavaca (riv.) F6
Médanos (isth.) D2
Merevari (riv.) F5
Mérida, Cordillera de
  (range) C3
Meta (riv.) E4
Morichal Largo (riv.) G3
Neblina (Phelps) (peak) E7
Negro (riv.) E7
Nuria, Sierra de (mts.) H4
Ocamo (riv.) F6
Orinoco (delta) H3
Orinoco (riv.) G3
Orituco (riv.) E3
Pacaraima, Sierra (mts.) G5
Pao (riv.) D3
Pao (riv.) F3
Paragua (riv.) G4
Paraguaná (pen.) C1
Paria (gulf) H2
Paria (pen.) G2
Parima, Sierra (mts.) F6
Perijá, Sierra de (mts.) B2
Phelps (peak) E7
Portuguesa (riv.) D3
Roraima (mt.) H5
Salto Angel (fall) G5
Sarare (riv.) C4
Serpents Mouth (passage) H3
Siapa (riv.) E7
Sipapo (riv.) E5
Suapure (riv.) E4
Suripá (riv.) C4
Tapirapecó, Sierra (mts.) F7
Tigre (riv.) G3
Tocuco (riv.) B3
Tocuyo (riv.) D2
Tramán-tepuí (mt.) G5
Triste (gulf) D2
Turagua, Serranía (mts.) F4
Tuy (riv.) E2
Unare (riv.) F3
Valencia (lake) E2
Venamo, Cerro (mt.) H4
Venamo (riv.) H4
Venezuela (gulf) C2
Ventuari (riv.) E5
Votamo (riv.) F6
Yatua (riv.) E7
Yuruari (riv.) H4
Zuata (riv.) F3
Zulia (riv.) B3

*City and suburbs

Agriculture, Industry and Resources

MAJOR MINERAL OCCURRENCES

Al Bauxite
Au Gold
C Coal
D Diamonds
Fe Iron Ore
G Natural Gas
Mn Manganese
Na Salt
O Petroleum

Water Power
Major Industrial Areas

DOMINANT LAND USE

Diversified Tropical Crops (chiefly plantation agriculture)
Upland Cultivated Areas
Upland Livestock Grazing, Limited Agriculture
Extensive Livestock Ranching
Forests

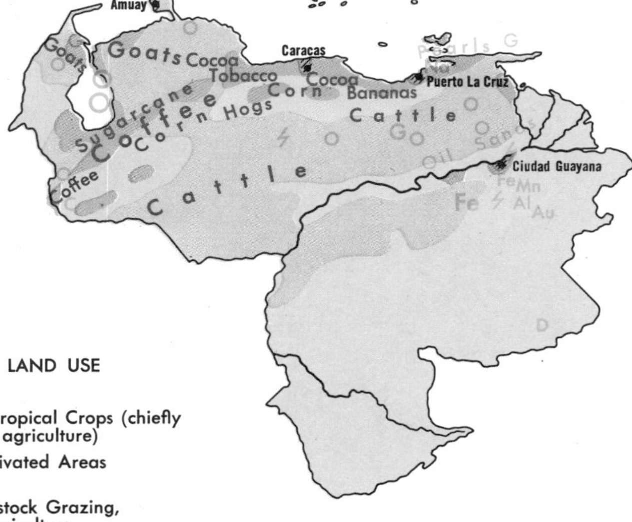

Colombia
MERCATOR PROJECTION
SCALE OF MILES
0 25 50 75 100 125 150
SCALE OF KILOMETERS
0 25 50 75 100 125 150
Capitals of Countries
Other Capitals
International Boundaries
Other Boundaries
Canals
Scale 1:6,800,000
CARIBBEAN SEA
PACIFIC OCEAN
PANAMA
VENEZUELA
ECUADOR
PERU
BRAZIL
NETH. ANTILLES
Aruba
Curaçao
Bonaire
Willemstad
Guajira Peninsula
Paraguana Peninsula
Gulf of Venezuela
Lake Maracaibo
Maracaibo
Cabimas
Barquisimeto
Coro
Puerto Cabello
CARACAS
Maracay
Valencia
Lago de Valencia
Trujillo
Mérida
San Cristóbal
San Fernando de Apure
Puerto Ayacucho
Gulf of Panamá
ARCH. DE LAS PERLAS
Panamá
Quito
Tulcán
Ibarra
Iquitos
Leticia
Benjamin Constant
Pebas
Tabatinga
LA GUAJIRA
MAGDALENA
ATLÁNTICO
CÉSAR
BOLÍVAR
SUCRE
CÓRDOBA
ANTIOQUIA
CHOCÓ
SANTANDER
NORTE DE SANTANDER
BOYACÁ
CALDAS
RISARALDA
QUINDÍO
CUNDINAMARCA
TOLIMA
HUILA
VALLE DEL CAUCA
CAUCA
NARIÑO
PUTUMAYO
CAQUETÁ
META
ARAUCA
CASANARE
VICHADA
GUAINÍA
GUAVIARE
VAUPÉS
AMAZONAS
BOGOTÁ
DISTRITO ESPECIAL
Barranquilla
Santa Marta
Cartagena
Riohacha
Valledupar
Sincelejo
Montería
Medellín
Quibdó
Manizales
Pereira
Armenia
Ibagué
Bucaramanga
Cúcuta
Pamplona
Tunja
Yopal
Villavicencio
Neiva
Popayán
Pasto
Ipiales
Tumaco
Buenaventura
Cali
Palmira
Florencia
Mocoa
Mitú
Puerto Carreño
Inírida
Barrancabermeja
Sierra Nevada de Santa Marta
Serranía de Perijá
Cordillera Oriental
Cordillera Central
Cordillera Occidental
Serranía de la Macarena
Serranía de Baudó
Nevado del Huila
Alto Ritacuva
Magdalena
Cauca
Atrato
Orinoco
Meta
Guaviare
Vichada
Caquetá
Putumayo
Apaporis
Amazon
Negro
Japurá
Napo
Equator
Isla Gorgona
Bahía de Tumaco
INTENDENCIA DE SAN ANDRÉS Y PROVIDENCIA
Same scale as main map
Banco de Serranilla
Banco Alicia
Bajo Nuevo
Roca que Vela
Banco de Quitasueño
Banco de Serrana
Cayos de Roncador
I. Sta. Catalina
Sta. Isabel
Isla de Providencia
San Andrés
Isla de San Andrés
Vigía
Cayos del E.S.E. (Courtown Cays)
Cayos de Albuquerque
Longitude West of Greenwich
© Copyright HAMMOND INCORPORATED, Maplewood, N.J.

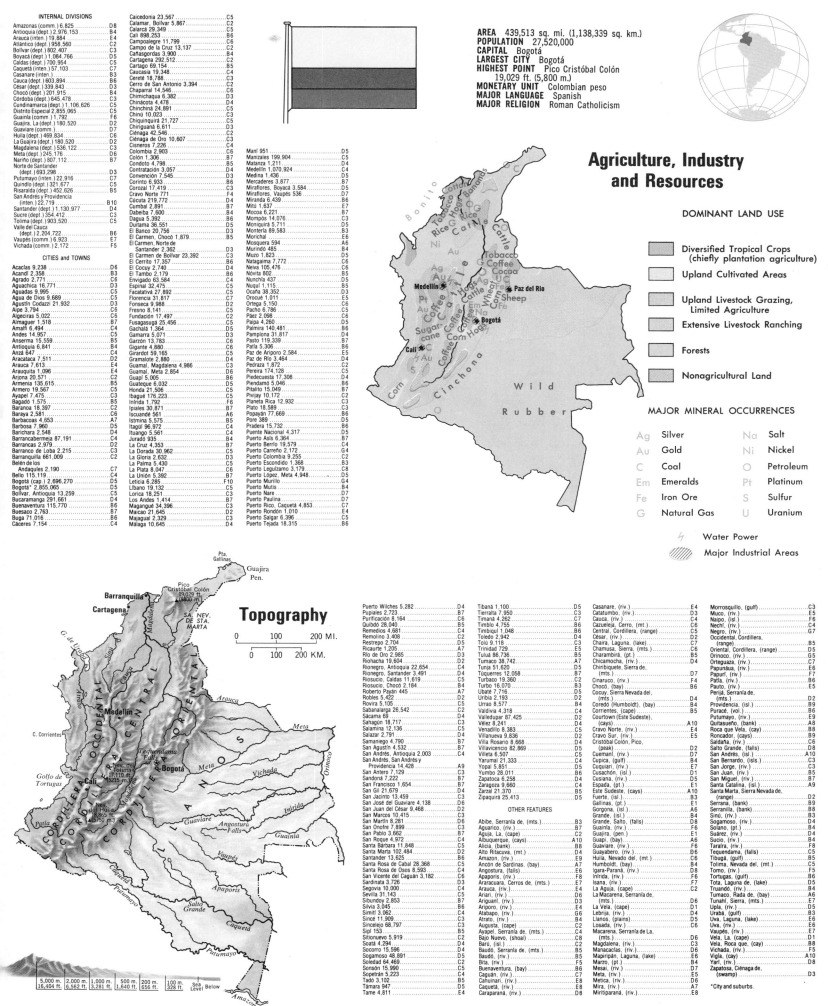

INTERNAL DIVISIONS

Amazonas (comm.) 6,825 ... D8
Antioquia (dept.) 2,976,153 ... B4
Arauca (inten.) 19,884 ... E4
Atlántico (dept.) 958,560 ... C2
Bolívar (dept.) 802,407 ... C3
Boyacá (dept.) 1,084,766 ... D5
Caldas (dept.) 700,954 ... C5
Caquetá (inten.) 57,103 ... C7
Casanare (inten.) ... B3
Cauca (dept.) 603,894 ... B6
César (dept.) 339,843 ... D3
Chocó (dept.) 201,915 ... B4
Córdoba (dept.) 645,478 ... C3
Cundinamarca (dept.) 1,106,626 ... C5
Distrito Especial 2,855,065 ... C5
Guainía (comm.) 1,792 ... F6
Guajira, La (dept.) 180,520 ... D2
Guaviare (comm.) ... D7
Huila (dept.) 469,834 ... C6
La Guajira (dept.) 180,520 ... D2
Magdalena (dept.) 536,122 ... C3
Meta (dept.) 245,176 ... D6
Nariño (dept.) 807,112 ... B7
Norte de Santander (dept.) 693,298 ... D3
Putumayo (inten.) 22,916 ... C7
Quindío (dept.) 321,677 ... C5
Risaralda (dept.) 452,626 ... B5
San Andrés y Providencia (inten.) 22,719 ... B10
Santander (dept.) 1,130,977 ... D4
Sucre (dept.) 354,412 ... C3
Tolima (dept.) 903,520 ... C5
Valle del Cauca (dept.) 2,204,722 ... B6
Vaupés (comm.) 6,923 ... E7
Vichada (comm.) 2,172 ... F5

CITIES and TOWNS

Acacías 9,238 ... D6
Acandí 2,358 ... B3
Agrado 2,771 ... C6
Aguachica 16,771 ... D3
Aguadas 9,995 ... C5
Agua de Dios 9,689 ... C5
Agustín Codazzi 21,932 ... D3
Aipe 3,794 ... C6
Algeciras 5,022 ... C6
Almaguer 1,518 ... B7
Amalfi 6,494 ... C4
Andes 14,957 ... C5
Anserma 15,559 ... B5
Antioquia 6,841 ... B4
Anzá 647 ... C4
Aracataca 7,511 ... D2
Arauca 7,613 ... E4
Arauquita 1,096 ... E4
Arjona 20,571 ... C2
Armenia 135,615 ... B5
Armero 19,567 ... C5
Ayapel 7,475 ... C3
Bagadó 1,575 ... B5
Baranoa 18,397 ... C2
Baraya 2,581 ... C6
Barbacoas 4,653 ... A7
Barbosa 7,960 ... D5
Barichara 2,548 ... D4
Barrancabermeja 87,191 ... C4
Barrancas 2,979 ... D2
Barranco de Loba 2,215 ... C3
Barranquilla 661,009 ... C2
Belén de los Andaquíes 2,190 ... C7
Bello 115,119 ... C4
Bogotá (cap.) 2,696,270 ... D5
Bogotá* 2,855,065 ... D5
Bolívar, Antioquia 13,259 ... C5
Bucaramanga 291,661 ... D4
Buenaventura 115,770 ... B6
Buesaco 2,763 ... B7
Buga 71,016 ... B6
Cáceres 7,154 ... C4
Caicedonia 23,567 ... C5
Calamar, Bolívar 5,867 ... C2
Calarcá 29,349 ... C5
Cali 898,253 ... B6
Campoalegre 11,799 ... C6
Campo de la Cruz 13,137 ... C2
Cañasgordas 3,900 ... B4
Cartagena 292,512 ... C2
Cartago 69,154 ... B5
Caucasia 19,348 ... C4
Cereté 18,788 ... C3
Cerro de San Antonio 3,394 ... C2
Chaparral 14,546 ... C6
Chimichaqua 6,382 ... D3
Chinácota 4,478 ... D4
Chinchiná 24,891 ... C5
Chinú 10,023 ... C3
Chiquinquirá 21,727 ... C5
Chiriguaná 6,611 ... D3
Ciénaga 42,546 ... C2
Ciénaga de Oro 10,607 ... C3
Cisneros 7,226 ... C4
Colombia 2,903 ... C6
Colón 1,306 ... B7
Condoto 4,798 ... B5
Contratación 3,057 ... D4
Convención 7,545 ... D3
Corinto 6,933 ... B6
Corozal 17,419 ... C3
Cravo Norte 771 ... F4
Cúcuta 219,772 ... D4
Cumbal 2,891 ... B7
Dabeiba 7,600 ... B4
Dagua 5,392 ... B6
Duitama 36,551 ... D5
El Banco 20,756 ... D3
El Carmen, Chocó 1,879 ... B5
El Carmen, Norte de Santander 2,362 ... D3
El Carmen de Bolívar 23,392 ... C3
El Cerrito 17,357 ... B6
El Cocuy 2,740 ... D4
El Tambo 2,179 ... B6
Envigado 63,584 ... C4
Espinal 32,475 ... C5
Facatativá 27,892 ... C5
Florencia 31,817 ... C7
Fonseca 9,988 ... D2
Fresno 8,141 ... C5
Fundación 17,497 ... C2
Fusagasugá 25,456 ... C5
Gachalá 1,364 ... D5
Gamarra 5,071 ... D3
Garzón 13,783 ... C6
Gigante 4,880 ... C6
Girardot 59,165 ... C5
Gramalote 2,880 ... D4
Guamal, Magdalena 4,986 ... C3
Guamal, Meta 2,854 ... D6
Guapí 5,005 ... B6
Guateque 6,032 ... D5
Honda 21,506 ... C5
Ibagué 176,223 ... C5
Inírida 1,792 ... F6
Ipiales 30,871 ... B7
Iscuandé 561 ... A6
Istmina 5,575 ... B5
Itagüí 96,972 ... C4
Ituango 5,561 ... C4
Juradó 935 ... B4
La Cruz 4,353 ... B7
La Dorada 30,962 ... C5
La Gloria 2,632 ... D3
La Palma 5,430 ... C5
La Plata 8,047 ... C6
La Unión 5,392 ... B7
Leticia 6,285 ... F10
Líbano 19,132 ... C5
Lorica 18,251 ... C3
Los Andes 1,414 ... B7
Magangué 34,396 ... C3
Maicao 21,645 ... D2
Majagual 2,329 ... C3
Málaga 10,645 ... D4

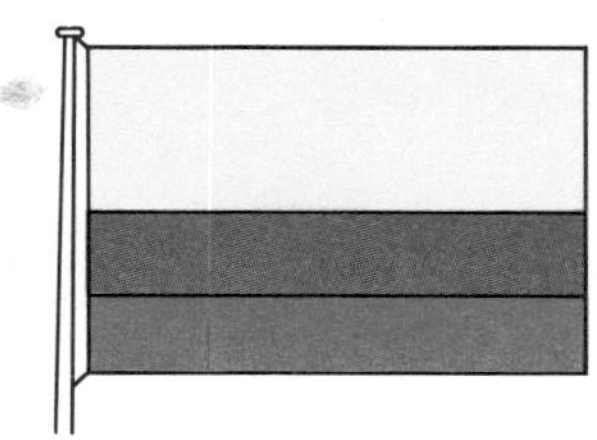

AREA 439,513 sq. mi. (1,138,339 sq. km.)
POPULATION 27,520,000
CAPITAL Bogotá
LARGEST CITY Bogotá
HIGHEST POINT Pico Cristóbal Colón 19,029 ft. (5,800 m.)
MONETARY UNIT Colombian peso
MAJOR LANGUAGE Spanish
MAJOR RELIGION Roman Catholicism

Maní 951 ... D5
Manizales 199,904 ... C5
Matanza 1,211 ... D4
Medellín 1,070,924 ... C4
Medina 1,436 ... D5
Mercaderes 3,877 ... B7
Miraflores, Boyacá 3,584 ... D5
Miraflores, Vaupés 536 ... D7
Miranda 6,439 ... B6
Mitú 1,637 ... E7
Mocoa 6,221 ... B7
Mompós 14,076 ... C3
Moniquirá 5,711 ... D5
Montería 89,583 ... B3
Morichal ... E6
Mosquera 594 ... A6
Murindó 485 ... B4
Muzo 1,823 ... D5
Natagaima 7,772 ... C6
Neiva 105,476 ... C6
Nóvita 802 ... B5
Nunchía 437 ... D5
Nuquí 1,115 ... B5
Ocaña 38,352 ... D3
Orocué 1,011 ... E5
Ortega 5,150 ... C6
Pacho 6,786 ... C5
Páez 2,098 ... C6
Paipa 4,260 ... D5
Palmira 140,481 ... B6
Pamplona 31,817 ... D4
Pasto 119,339 ... B7
Patía 5,306 ... B6
Paz de Ariporo 2,584 ... E5
Paz de Río 3,464 ... D4
Pedraza 1,872 ... C2
Pereira 174,128 ... C5
Piedecuesta 17,308 ... D4
Piendamó 5,046 ... B6
Pitalito 15,049 ... B7
Pivijay 10,172 ... C2
Planeta Rica 12,932 ... C3
Plato 18,589 ... C3
Popayán 77,669 ... B6
Pore 389 ... D5
Pradera 15,732 ... B6
Puente Nacional 4,317 ... D5
Puerto Asís 6,364 ... B7
Puerto Berrío 19,579 ... C4
Puerto Carreño 2,172 ... G4
Puerto Colombia 9,255 ... C2
Puerto Escondido 1,368 ... B3
Puerto Leguízamo 3,179 ... C8
Puerto López, Meta 4,948 ... D5
Puerto Murillo ... G4
Puerto Mutis ... B4
Puerto Nare ... D7
Puerto Paulina ... D7
Puerto Rico, Caquetá 4,853 ... C7
Puerto Rondón 1,010 ... E4
Puerto Salgar 6,396 ... C5
Puerto Tejada 18,315 ... B6

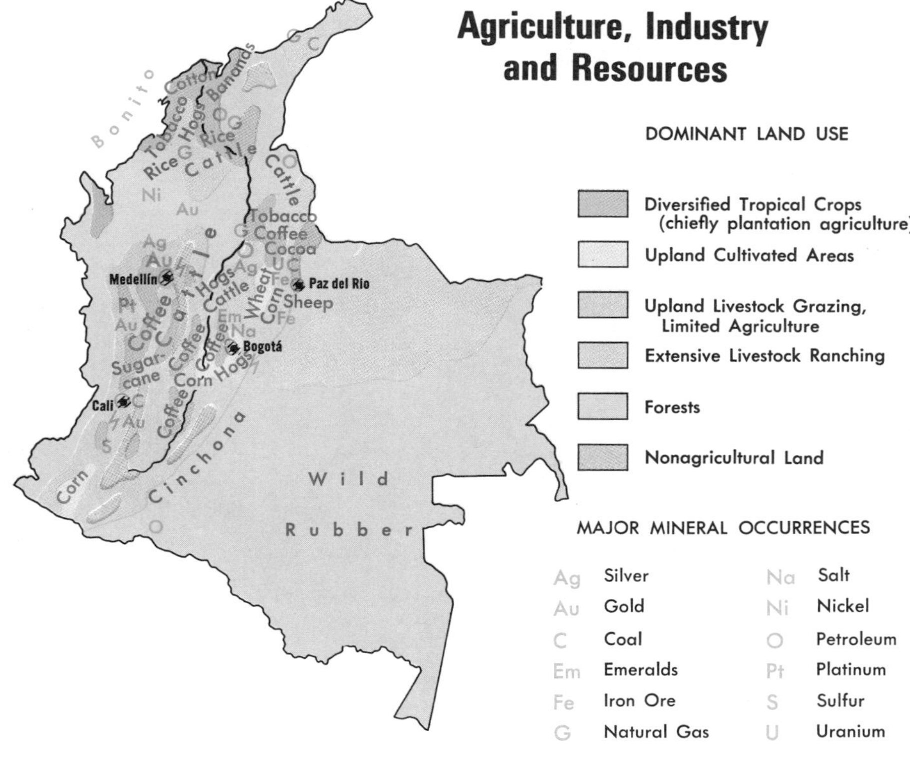

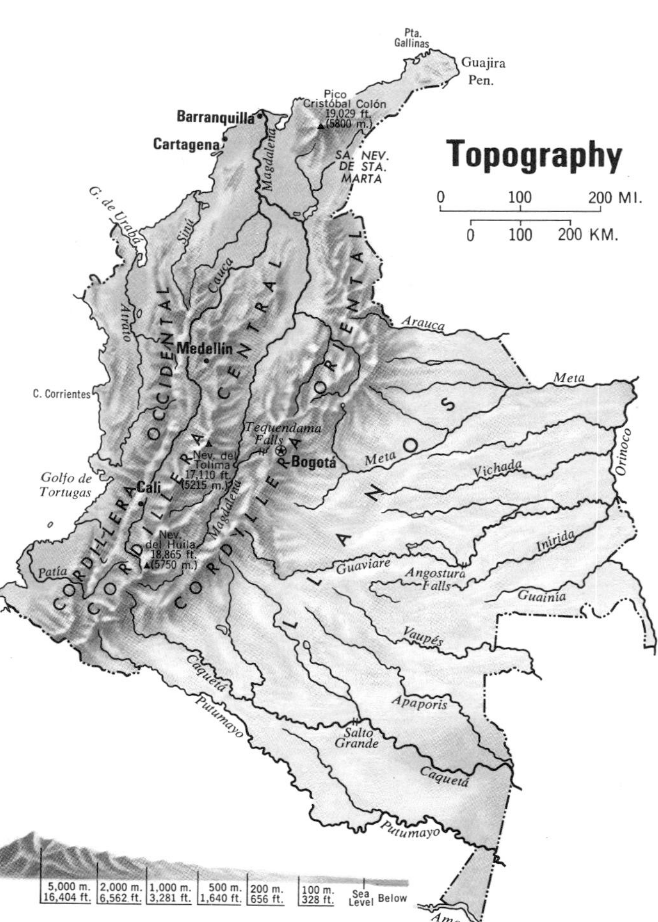

Puerto Wilches 5,282 ... D4
Pupiales 2,723 ... B7
Purificación 8,164 ... C6
Quibdó 28,040 ... B5
Remedios 4,681 ... C4
Remolino 3,408 ... C2
Restrepo 2,704 ... D5
Ricaurte 1,205 ... A7
Río de Oro 2,985 ... D3
Riohacha 19,604 ... D2
Rionegro, Antioquia 22,654 ... C4
Rionegro, Santander 3,491 ... D4
Riosucio, Caldas 11,619 ... C5
Riosucio, Chocó 2,184 ... B4
Roberto Payán 445 ... A7
Robles 5,422 ... D2
Rovira 5,105 ... C5
Sabanalarga 26,542 ... C2
Sácama 69 ... D4
Sahagún 18,717 ... C3
Salamina 12,136 ... C5
Salazar 2,791 ... D4
Samaniego 4,790 ... B7
San Agustín 4,532 ... B7
San Andrés, Antioquia 2,003 ... C4
San Andrés, San Andrés y Providencia 14,428 ... A9
San Antero 7,129 ... C3
Sandoná 7,222 ... B7
San Francisco 1,654 ... B7
San Gil 21,679 ... D4
San Jacinto 13,459 ... C3
San José del Guaviare 4,138 ... D6
San Juan del César 9,468 ... D2
San Marcos 10,415 ... C3
San Martín 8,281 ... D6
San Onofre 7,899 ... C3
San Pablo 3,662 ... B7
San Roque 4,972 ... C4
Santa Bárbara 11,848 ... C5
Santa Marta 102,484 ... D2
Santander 13,625 ... B6
Santa Rosa de Cabal 28,368 ... C5
Santa Rosa de Osos 8,593 ... C4
San Vicente del Caguán 3,182 ... C6
Sardinata 3,726 ... D3
Segovia 10,000 ... C4
Sevilla 31,143 ... C5
Sibundoy 2,853 ... B7
Silvia 3,045 ... B6
Simití 3,062 ... C4
Sincé 11,909 ... C3
Sincelejo 68,797 ... C3
Sipí 153 ... B5
Sitionuevo 5,919 ... C2
Soatá 4,294 ... D4
Socorro 15,596 ... D4
Sogamoso 48,891 ... D5
Soledad 64,469 ... C2
Sonsón 15,990 ... C5
Sopetrán 5,223 ... C4
Tadó 3,102 ... B5
Támara 947 ... D5
Tame 4,811 ... E4
Tibaná 1,100 ... D5
Tierralta 7,950 ... C3
Timaná 4,262 ... C7
Timbío 4,755 ... B6
Timbiquí 1,048 ... B6
Toledo 2,942 ... D4
Tolú 9,118 ... C3
Trinidad 729 ... E5
Tuluá 86,736 ... B5
Tumaco 38,742 ... A7
Tunja 51,620 ... D5
Túquerres 12,058 ... B7
Turbaco 19,360 ... C2
Turbo 16,070 ... B3
Ubaté 7,716 ... D5
Uribia 2,193 ... D2
Urrao 8,577 ... B4
Valdivia 4,318 ... C4
Valledupar 87,425 ... D2
Vélez 8,241 ... D4
Venadillo 8,383 ... C5
Villanueva 9,836 ... D2
Villa Rosario 8,668 ... D4
Villavicencio 82,869 ... D5
Villeta 6,507 ... C5
Yarumal 21,333 ... C4
Yopal 5,851 ... D5
Yumbo 28,011 ... B6
Zapatoca 6,258 ... D4
Zaragoza 9,660 ... C4
Zarzal 21,370 ... B5
Zipaquirá 25,413 ... D5

OTHER FEATURES

Abibe, Serranía de, (mts.) ... B3
Aguarico, (riv.) ... B7
Aguja, La, (cape) ... C2
Albuquerque, (cays) ... A10
Alicia, (bank) ... B8
Alto Ritacuva, (mt.) ... D4
Amazon, (riv.) ... E9
Ancón de Sardinas, (bay) ... A7
Angostura, (falls) ... E6
Apaporis, (riv.) ... F8
Araracuara, Cerros de, (mts.) ... E7
Arauca, (riv.) ... E4
Ariari, (riv.) ... D6
Ariguaní, (riv.) ... D3
Ariporo, (riv.) ... E4
Atabapo, (riv.) ... G6
Atrato, (riv.) ... B4
Augusta, (cape) ... C2
Ayapel, Serranía de, (mts.) ... C4
Bajo Nuevo, (shoal) ... C8
Barú, (isl.) ... C2
Baudó, Serranía de, (mts.) ... B5
Baudó, (riv.) ... B5
Bita, (riv.) ... F5
Buenaventura, (bay) ... B6
Caguán, (riv.) ... C7
Cahuinari, (riv.) ... E8
Caquetá, (riv.) ... E8
Caraparaná, (riv.) ... D8
Casanare, (riv.) ... E4
Catatumbo, (riv.) ... D3
Cauca, (riv.) ... C4
Cazueleja, Cerro, (mt.) ... C6
Central, Cordillera, (range) ... C5
César, (riv.) ... D2
Chaira, Laguna, (lake) ... C7
Chamusa, Sierra, (mts.) ... C6
Charambirá, (pt.) ... B5
Chicamocha, (riv.) ... D4
Chiribiquete, Sierra de, (mts.) ... D7
Cinaruco, (riv.) ... F4
Chocó, (bay) ... B6
Cocuy, Sierra Nevada del, (mts.) ... D4
Coredó (Humboldt), (bay) ... B4
Corrientes, (cape) ... B5
Courtown (Este Sudeste), (cays) ... A10
Cravo Norte, (riv.) ... E4
Cravo Sur, (riv.) ... E5
Cristóbal Colón, Pico, (peak) ... D2
Cuemaní, (riv.) ... D7
Cupica, (gulf) ... B4
Cuquiari, (riv.) ... E7
Cusachón, (isl.) ... D1
Cusiana, (riv.) ... D5
Espada, (pt.) ... E1
Este Sudeste, (cays) ... A10
Fuerte, (isl.) ... B3
Gallinas, (pt.) ... E1
Gorgona, (isl.) ... A6
Grande, (isl.) ... B4
Grande, Salto, (falls) ... D8
Guainía, (riv.) ... F6
Guajira, (pen.) ... E1
Guapi, (bay) ... A6
Guaviare, (riv.) ... F6
Guayabero, (riv.) ... D6
Huila, Nevado del, (mt.) ... C6
Humboldt, (bay) ... B4
Igara-Paraná, (riv.) ... D8
Inírida, (riv.) ... F6
Isana, (riv.) ... F7
La Aguja, (cape) ... C2
La Macarena, Serranía de, (mts.) ... D6
La Vela, (cape) ... D1
Lebrija, (riv.) ... D4
Llanos, (plains) ... D5
Losada, (riv.) ... C6
Macarena, Serranía de La, (mts.) ... D6
Magdalena, (riv.) ... C3
Manacacías, (riv.) ... D6
Mapiripán, Laguna, (lake) ... E6
Marzo, (pt.) ... B4
Mesai, (riv.) ... D7
Meta, (riv.) ... E5
Metica, (riv.) ... D6
Mira, (riv.) ... A7
Miritiparaná, (riv.) ... E8
Morrosquillo, (gulf) ... C3
Muco, (riv.) ... E5
Naipo, (isl.) ... F6
Nechí, (riv.) ... C4
Negro, (riv.) ... G7
Occidental, Cordillera, (range) ... B5
Oriental, Cordillera, (range) ... D5
Orinoco, (riv.) ... G5
Orteguaza, (riv.) ... C7
Papunáua, (riv.) ... E6
Papurí, (riv.) ... F7
Patía, (riv.) ... B6
Pauto, (riv.) ... E5
Perijá, Serranía de, (mts.) ... D2
Providencia, (isl.) ... B9
Puracé, (vol.) ... B6
Putumayo, (riv.) ... E9
Quitasueño, (bank) ... A8
Roca que Vela, (cay) ... B8
Roncador, (cays) ... B9
Saldaña, (riv.) ... C6
Salto Grande, (falls) ... D8
San Andrés, (isl.) ... A10
San Bernardo, (isls.) ... C3
San Jorge, (riv.) ... C3
San Juan, (riv.) ... B5
San Miguel, (riv.) ... B7
Santa Catalina, (isl.) ... A9
Santa Marta, Sierra Nevada de, (range) ... D2
Serrana, (bank) ... B9
Serranilla, (bank) ... B8
Sinú, (riv.) ... B3
Sogamoso, (riv.) ... D4
Solano, (pt.) ... B4
Suárez, (riv.) ... D4
Sucio, (riv.) ... B4
Taraíra, (riv.) ... F8
Tequendama, (falls) ... C5
Tibugá, (gulf) ... B5
Tolima, Nevada del, (mt.) ... C5
Tomo, (riv.) ... F5
Tortugas, (gulf) ... B6
Tota, Laguna de, (lake) ... D5
Truandó, (riv.) ... B4
Tumaco, Rada de, (bay) ... A6
Tunahí, Sierra, (mts.) ... E7
Upía, (riv.) ... D5
Urabá, (gulf) ... B3
Uva, Laguna, (lake) ... E6
Uva, (riv.) ... E6
Vaupés, (riv.) ... E7
Vela, La, (cape) ... D1
Vela, Roca que, (cay) ... B8
Vichada, (riv.) ... F5
Vigía, (cay) ... A10
Yarí, (riv.) ... D8
Zapatosa, Ciénaga de, (swamp) ... D3

*City and suburbs.

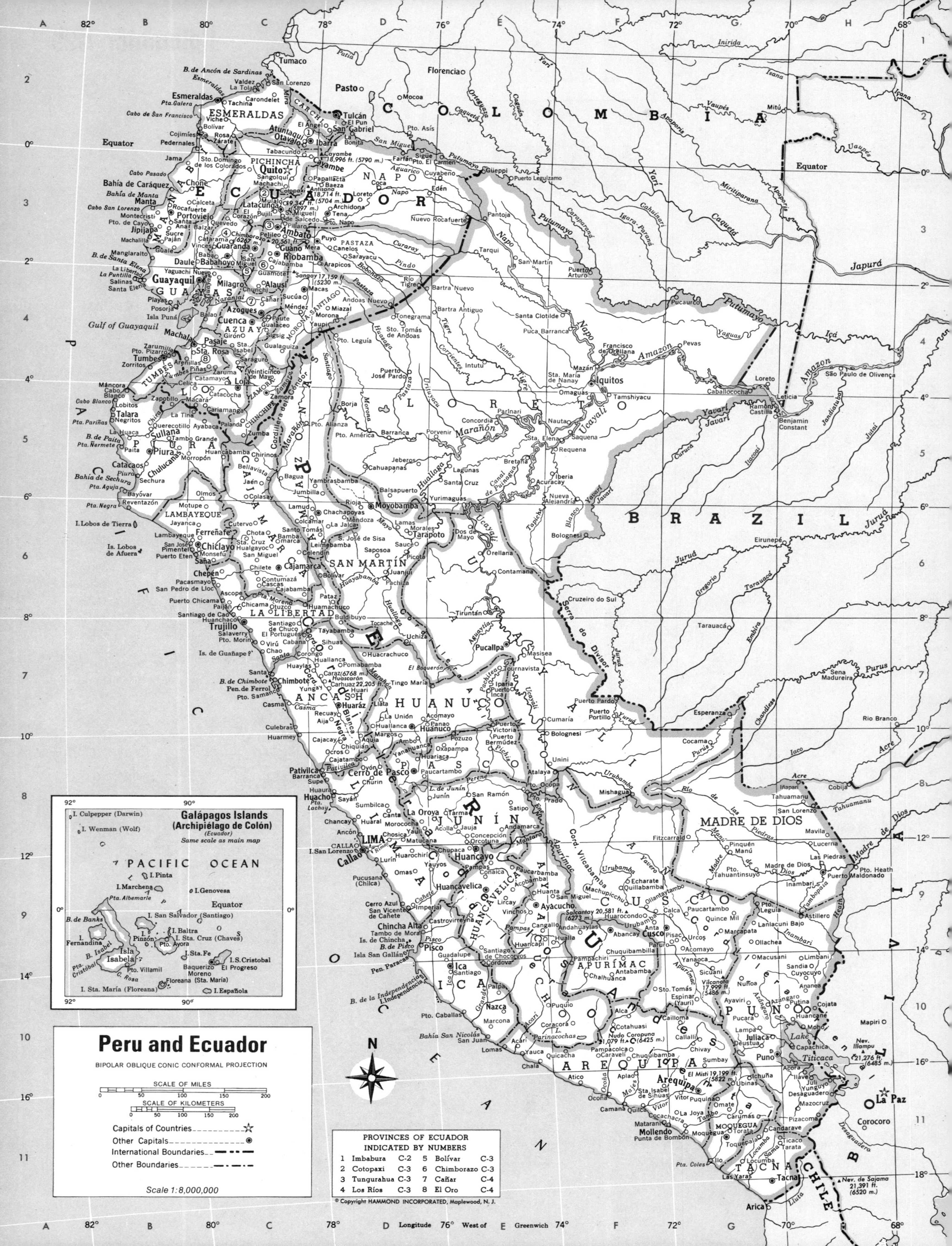

Peru and Ecuador
BIPOLAR OBLIQUE CONIC CONFORMAL PROJECTION
SCALE OF MILES
0 50 100 150 200
SCALE OF KILOMETERS
0 50 100 150 200
Capitals of Countries
Other Capitals
International Boundaries
Other Boundaries
Scale 1:8,000,000
PROVINCES OF ECUADOR INDICATED BY NUMBERS
1 Imbabura C-2
2 Cotopaxi C-3
3 Tungurahua C-3
4 Los Ríos C-3
5 Bolívar C-3
6 Chimborazo C-3
7 Cañar C-4
8 El Oro C-4
Galápagos Islands (Archipiélago de Colón)
(Ecuador)
Same scale as main map
PACIFIC OCEAN
C O L O M B I A
E C U A D O R
P E R U
B R A Z I L
B O L I V I A
CHILE
PACIFIC OCEAN
Longitude 76° West of Greenwich
© Copyright HAMMOND INCORPORATED, Maplewood, N. J.

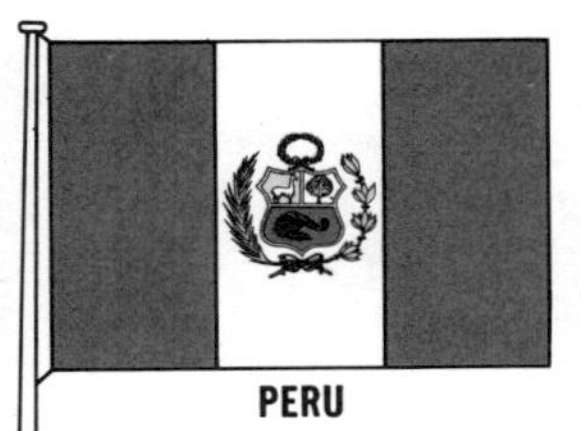

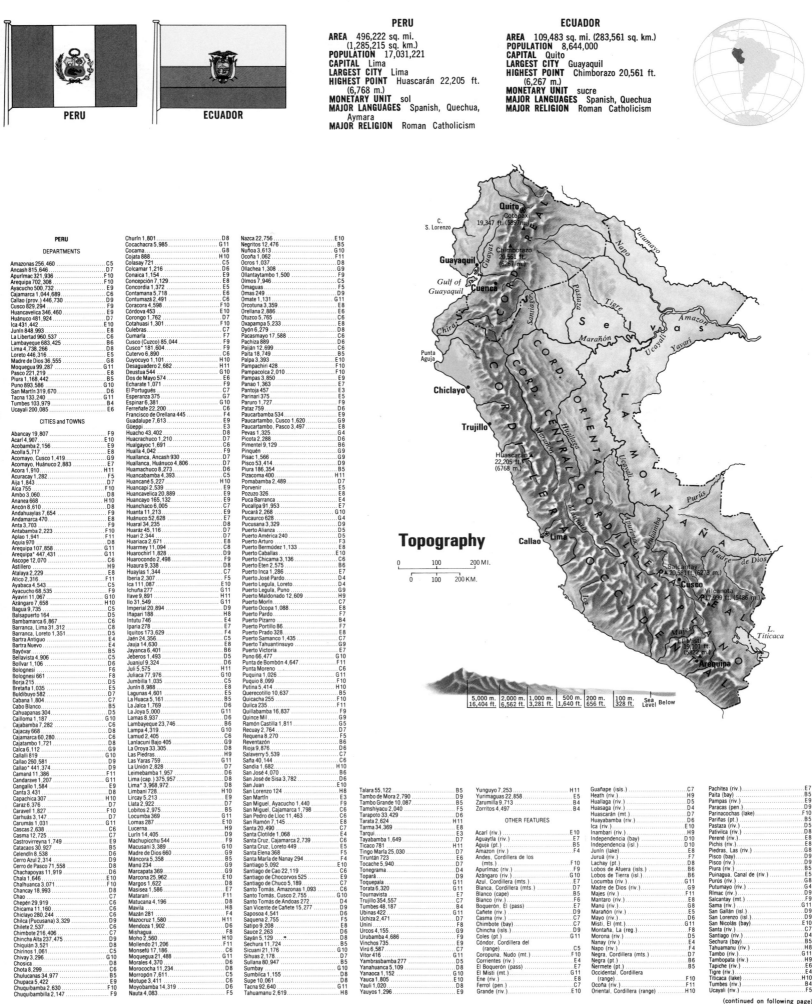

PERU

AREA 496,222 sq. mi. (1,285,215 sq. km.)
POPULATION 17,031,221
CAPITAL Lima
LARGEST CITY Lima
HIGHEST POINT Huascarán 22,205 ft. (6,768 m.)
MONETARY UNIT sol
MAJOR LANGUAGES Spanish, Quechua, Aymara
MAJOR RELIGION Roman Catholicism

ECUADOR

AREA 109,483 sq. mi. (283,561 sq. km.)
POPULATION 8,644,000
CAPITAL Quito
LARGEST CITY Guayaquil
HIGHEST POINT Chimborazo 20,561 ft. (6,267 m.)
MONETARY UNIT sucre
MAJOR LANGUAGES Spanish, Quechua
MAJOR RELIGION Roman Catholicism

Topography

0 100 200 MI.
0 100 200 KM.

5,000 m. 16,404 ft. | 2,000 m. 6,562 ft. | 1,000 m. 3,281 ft. | 500 m. 1,640 ft. | 200 m. 656 ft. | 100 m. 328 ft. | Sea Level | Below

PERU

DEPARTMENTS

Amazonas 256,460 C5
Ancash 815,646 D7
Apurímac 321,936 F10
Arequipa 702,308 F10
Ayacucho 500,732 E9
Cajamarca 1,044,689 C6
Callao (prov.) 446,730 D9
Cusco 829,294 F9
Huancavelica 346,460 E9
Huánuco 481,924 D7
Ica 431,442 E10
Junín 848,993 E8
La Libertad 960,537 C6
Lambayeque 683,425 B6
Lima 4,738,266 D8
Loreto 446,316 E5
Madre de Dios 36,555 G8
Moquegua 99,287 G11
Pasco 221,219 E8
Piura 1,168,442 B5
Puno 893,586 G10
San Martín 319,670 D6
Tacna 133,240 G11
Tumbes 103,979 B4
Ucayali 200,085 E6

CITIES and TOWNS

Abancay 19,807 F9
Acarí 4,907 E10
Acobamba 2,156 E9
Acolla 5,717 E8
Acomayo, Cusco 1,419 G9
Acomayo, Huánuco 2,883 E7
Acora 1,910 H11
Acuracay 1,282 F5
Aija 1,843 D7
Alca 755 F10
Ambo 3,060 D8
Ananea 668 H10
Ancón 8,610 D8
Andahuaylas 7,654 F9
Andamarca 470 E8
Anta 3,703 F9
Antabamba 2,223 F10
Aplao 1,941 F11
Aquia 970 D8
Arequipa 107,858 G11
Arequipa* 447,431 G11
Ascope 12,070 C6
Astillero H9
Atalaya 2,229 E8
Atico 2,316 F11
Ayabaca 4,543 C5
Ayacucho 68,535 F9
Ayaviri 11,067 G10
Azángaro 7,658 H10
Bagua 9,735 C5
Balsapuerto 164 D5
Bambamarca 6,867 C6
Barranca, Lima 31,312 C8
Barranca, Loreto 1,351 D5
Bartra Antiguo E4
Bartra Nuevo E4
Bayóvar B5
Bellavista 4,906 C5
Bolívar 1,106 D6
Bolognesi F6
Bolognesi 661 E8
Borja 215 D5
Bretaña 1,035 E5
Buldibuyo 582 D7
Cabana 1,804 C7
Cabo Blanco B5
Cahuapanas 304 D5
Cailloma 1,187 G10
Cajabamba 7,282 C6
Cajacay 668 D8
Cajamarca 60,280 C6
Cajatambo 1,721 D8
Calca 6,112 G9
Callalli 619 G10
Callao 260,581 D9
Callao* 441,374 D9
Camaná 11,386 F11
Candarave 1,207 G11
Cangallo 1,584 E9
Canta 3,431 D8
Capachica 307 H10
Caraz 6,376 D7
Caravelí 1,827 F10
Carhuás 3,147 D7
Carumás 1,031 G11
Cascas 2,638 C6
Casma 12,725 C7
Castrovirreyna 1,749 E9
Catacaos 30,927 B5
Celendín 8,538 D6
Cerro Azul 2,314 D9
Cerro de Pasco 71,558 D8
Chachapoyas 11,919 D6
Chala 1,646 E10
Chalhuanca 3,071 F10
Chancay 18,993 D8
Chao C7
Chepén 29,919 C6
Chicama 11,160 C6
Chiclayo 280,244 C6
Chilca (Pucusana) 3,329 D9
Chilete 2,537 C7
Chimbote 216,406 C7
Chincha Alta 237,475 D9
Chiquián 3,521 D8
Chirinos 1,061 C5
Chivay 3,296 G10
Chosica D8
Chota 8,299 C6
Chulucanas 34,977 B5
Chupaca 5,422 E9
Chuquibamba 2,630 F10
Chuquibambilla 2,147 F9
Churín 1,801 D8
Cocachacra 5,985 G11
Cocama G8
Cojata 888 H10
Colasay 721 C5
Colcamar 1,216 D6
Conaica 1,154 E9
Concepción 7,129 E8
Concordia 1,372 E5
Contamana 5,718 E6
Contumazá 2,491 C6
Coracora 4,598 F10
Córdova 453 E10
Corongo 1,762 D7
Cotahuasi 1,301 F10
Culebras C7
Cumaría F7
Cusco (Cuzco) 85,044 F9
Cusco* 181,604 F9
Cutervo 6,890 C6
Cuyocuyo 1,101 H10
Desaguadero 2,682 H11
Deustua 544 G10
Dos de Mayo 574 E6
Echarate 1,071 F9
El Portugués C7
Esperanza 375 G7
Espinar 6,381 G10
Ferreñafe 22,200 C6
Francisco de Orellana 445 F4
Guadalupe 7,613 E9
Güeppí E3
Huacho 43,402 D8
Huacrachuco 1,210 D7
Hualgayoc 1,691 C6
Hualla 4,042 F9
Huallanca, Ancash 930 D7
Huallanca, Huánuco 4,806 D7
Huamachuco 8,273 D6
Huancabamba 4,393 C5
Huancané 5,227 H10
Huancapi 2,539 E9
Huancavelica 20,889 E9
Huancayo 165,132 E9
Huanchaco 6,005 C7
Huanta 11,213 E9
Huánuco 52,628 E7
Huaral 34,235 D8
Huaraz 45,116 D7
Huari 2,344 D7
Huariaca 2,671 E8
Huarmey 11,094 C8
Huarochirí 1,828 D9
Huarocondo 2,498 F9
Huaura 9,338 D8
Huaylas 1,344 C7
Iberia 2,307 F5
Ica 111,087 E10
Ichuña 277 G11
Ilave 9,891 H11
Ilo 31,549 G11
Imperial 20,894 D9
Iñapari 188 H8
Intutu 746 E4
Iparia 278 E7
Iquitos 173,629 F4
Jaén 24,356 C5
Jauja 14,630 E8
Jayanca 6,401 B6
Jeberos 1,493 D5
Juanjuí 9,324 D6
Juli 5,575 H11
Juliaca 77,976 G10
Jumbilla 1,035 C5
Junín 8,988 E8
Lagunas 4,601 E5
La Huaca 5,161 B5
La Jalca 1,769 D6
La Joya 5,000 G11
Lamas 8,937 D6
Lambayeque 23,746 B6
Lampa 4,319 G10
Lamud 2,405 C6
Lanlacuni Bajo 405 G9
La Oroya 33,305 D8
Las Piedras H9
Las Yaras 759 G11
La Unión 2,828 D7
Leimebamba 1,957 D6
Lima (cap.) 375,957 D8
Lima* 3,968,972 D8
Limbani 728 H10
Lircay 5,213 E9
Llata 2,922 D7
Lobitos 2,975 B5
Locumba 369 G11
Lomas 287 E10
Lucerna H9
Lurín 14,405 D9
Machupicchu 544 F9
Macusani 3,389 G10
Madre de Dios 660 G9
Máncora 5,358 B5
Manú 234 G9
Marcapata 369 G9
Marcona 25,962 E10
Margos 1,622 D8
Masisea 1,586 E7
Matarani F11
Matucana 4,196 D8
Mavila H8
Mazán 281 F4
Mazocruz 1,580 H11
Mendoza 1,902 D6
Mishagua F8
Moho 2,560 H10
Mollendo 21,206 F11
Monsefú 17,186 C6
Moquegua 21,488 G11
Morales 4,370 D6
Morococha 11,234 D8
Morropón 7,611 C5
Motupe 3,411 C6
Moyobamba 14,319 D6
Nauta 4,083 F5
Nazca 22,756 E10
Negritos 12,476 B5
Nuñoa 3,613 G10
Ocoña 1,062 F11
Ocros 1,037 D8
Ollachea 1,308 G9
Ollantaytambo 1,500 F9
Olmos 7,946 C5
Omaguas F5
Omas 249 D9
Omate 1,131 G11
Orcotuna 3,359 E8
Orellana 2,886 E6
Otuzco 5,765 C6
Oxapampa 5,233 E8
Oyón 6,279 D8
Pacasmayo 17,588 C6
Pachiza 889 D6
Paiján 12,699 C6
Paita 18,749 B5
Palpa 3,393 E10
Pampachiri 428 F10
Pampacolca 2,010 F10
Pampas 3,850 E9
Panao 1,363 E7
Pantoja 457 E3
Parinari 375 E5
Paruro 1,727 F9
Pataz 759 D6
Paucarbamba 534 E9
Paucartambo, Cusco 1,620 G9
Paucartambo, Pasco 3,497 E8
Pevas 1,325 G4
Picota 2,288 D6
Pimentel 9,129 B6
Pinquén G9
Pisac 1,566 G9
Pisco 53,414 D9
Piura 186,354 B5
Pizacoma 400 H11
Pomabamba 2,489 D7
Porvenir E5
Pozuzo 326 E8
Puca Barranca E4
Pucallpa 91,953 E7
Pucará 2,268 G10
Pucaurco 628 G4
Pucusana 3,329 D9
Puerto Alianza D5
Puerto América 240 D5
Puerto Arturo F3
Puerto Bermúdez 1,133 E8
Puerto Caballas E10
Puerto Chicama 3,136 C6
Puerto Eten 2,575 B6
Puerto Inca 1,286 E7
Puerto José Pardo D4
Puerto Leguía, Loreto D4
Puerto Leguía, Puno G9
Puerto Maldonado 12,609 H9
Puerto Morín C7
Puerto Ocopa 1,088 E8
Puerto Pardo F7
Puerto Pizarro B4
Puerto Portillo 86 F7
Puerto Prado 328 E8
Puerto Samanco 1,435 C7
Puerto Tahuantinsuyo G9
Puerto Victoria E7
Puno 66,477 G10
Punta de Bombón 4,647 F11
Punta Moreno C6
Puquina 1,026 G11
Puquio 8,099 F10
Putina 5,414 H10
Querecotillo 10,637 B5
Quicacha 255 F10
Quilca 235 F11
Quillabamba 16,837 F9
Quince Mil G9
Ramón Castilla 1,811 G5
Recuay 2,764 D7
Requena 8,270 F5
Reventazón B6
Rioja 9,876 D6
Salaverry 5,539 C7
Saña 40,144 C6
Sandia 1,682 H10
San José 4,070 B6
San José de Sisa 3,782 D6
San Juan E10
San Lorenzo 124 H8
San Martín E3
San Miguel, Ayacucho 1,440 F9
San Miguel, Cajamarca 1,798 C6
San Pedro de Lloc 11,463 C6
San Ramón 7,145 E8
Santa 20,490 C7
Santa Clotilde 1,068 E4
Santa Cruz, Cajamarca 2,739 C6
Santa Cruz, Loreto 449 E5
Santa Elena 368 F5
Santa María de Nanay 294 F4
Santiago 5,092 E10
Santiago de Cao 22,119 C6
Santiago de Chocorvos 525 E9
Santiago de Chuco 5,189 C7
Santo Tomás, Amazonas 1,093 C6
Santo Tomás, Cusco 2,755 G10
Santo Tomás de Andoas 272 D4
San Vicente de Cañete 15,277 D9
Saposoa 4,541 D6
Saquena 2,755 F5
Satipo 9,208 E8
Sauce 2,263 D6
Sayán 5,129 D8
Sechura 11,724 B5
Sicuani 21,176 G10
Sihuas 2,178 D7
Sullana 80,947 B5
Sumbay G10
Sumbilca 1,155 D8
Supe 10,061 D8
Tacna 92,640 G11
Tahuamanu 2,619 H8
Talara 55,122 B5
Tambo de Mora 2,790 D9
Tambo Grande 10,087 B5
Tamshiyacu 2,040 F5
Tarapoto 33,429 D6
Tarata 2,624 H11
Tarma 34,369 E8
Tarqui E3
Tayabamba 1,649 D7
Ticaco 781 H11
Tingo María 25,030 D7
Tiruntán 723 E6
Tocache 5,940 D7
Tonegrama D4
Toparà D9
Toquepala G11
Torata 6,320 G11
Tournavista E7
Trujillo 354,557 C7
Tumbes 48,187 B4
Ubinas 422 G11
Uchiza 2,471 D7
Unini F8
Urcos 4,155 G9
Urubamba 4,686 F9
Vinchos 735 E9
Virú 6,587 C7
Vitor 416 G11
Yambrasbamba 277 D5
Yanahuanca 5,109 D8
Yanaoca 1,152 G10
Yauca 1,805 E10
Yauli 1,020 D8
Yauyos 1,296 E9
Yunguyo 7,253 H11
Yurimaguas 22,858 E5
Zarumilla 9,713 B4
Zorritos 4,497 B4

OTHER FEATURES

Acarí (riv.) E10
Aguaytía (riv.) E7
Aguja (pt.) B5
Amazon (riv.) F4
Andes, Cordillera de los (mts.) F10
Apurímac (riv.) F9
Azángaro (riv.) G10
Azul, Cordillera (mts.) E7
Blanca, Cordillera (mts.) D7
Blanco (cape) B5
Blanco (riv.) F6
Boquerón, El (pass) E7
Cañete (riv.) D9
Casma (riv.) C7
Chimbote (bay) C7
Chincha (isls.) D9
Coles (pt.) G11
Cóndor, Cordillera del (range) C5
Coropuna, Nudo (mt.) F10
Corrientes (riv.) E4
El Boquerón (pass) E7
El Misti (mt.) G11
Ene (riv.) E8
Ferrol (pen.) C7
Grande (riv.) E10
Guañape (isls.) C7
Heath (riv.) H9
Huallaga (riv.) D5
Huasaga (riv.) D4
Huascarán (mt.) D7
Huayabamba (riv.) D6
Ica (riv.) E10
Inambari (riv.) H9
Independencia (bay) D10
Independencia (isl.) D10
Junín (lake) E8
Juruá (riv.) F7
Lachay (pt.) D8
Lobos de Afuera (isls.) B6
Lobos de Tierra (isl.) B6
Locumba (riv.) G11
Madre de Dios (riv.) G9
Majes (riv.) F11
Mantaro (riv.) E8
Manú (riv.) G8
Marañón (riv.) E5
Mayo (riv.) D6
Misti, El (mt.) G11
Montaña, La (reg.) F8
Morona (riv.) D5
Nanay (riv.) E4
Napo (riv.) F4
Negra, Cordillera (mts.) D7
Negra (pt.) B6
Nermete (pt.) B5
Occidental, Cordillera (range) F10
Ocoña (riv.) F11
Oriental, Cordillera (range) H10
Pachitea (riv.) E7
Paita (bay) B5
Pampas (riv.) E9
Paracas (pen.) D9
Parinacochas (lake) F10
Pariñas (pt.) B5
Pastaza (riv.) D5
Pativilca (riv.) D8
Perené (riv.) E8
Pichis (riv.) E8
Piedras, Las (riv.) G8
Pisco (bay) D9
Pisco (riv.) D9
Piura (riv.) B5
Puinagua, Canal de (riv.) E5
Purús (riv.) G8
Putumayo (riv.) G4
Rímac (riv.) D9
Salcantay (mt.) F9
Sama (riv.) G11
San Gallán (isl.) D9
San Lorenzo (isl.) D9
San Nicolás (bay) E10
Santa (riv.) C7
Santiago (riv.) D4
Sechura (bay) B5
Tahuamanu (riv.) H8
Tambo (riv.) G11
Tambopata (riv.) H9
Tapiche (riv.) E6
Tigre (riv.) E4
Titicaca (lake) H10
Tumbes (riv.) B4
Ucayali (riv.) F5

(continued on following page)

Peru and Ecuador ; Guianas

(continued)

* City and suburbs
○Population of district.

Agriculture, Industry and Resources

DOMINANT LAND USE
Diversified Tropical Crops (chiefly plantation agriculture)
Upland Cultivated Areas
Upland Livestock Grazing, Limited Agriculture
Extensive Livestock Ranching
Forests
Nonagricultural Land
MAJOR MINERAL OCCURRENCES
Ag Silver
Au Gold
C Coal
Cu Copper
Fe Iron Ore
Hg Mercury
Mn Manganese
Mo Molybdenum
Na Salt
O Petroleum
P Phosphates
Pb Lead
Sb Antimony
V Vanadium
W Tungsten
Zn Zinc
Water Power
Major Industrial Areas
Guayaquil
Talara
Chimbote
Lima
Crayfish
Tuna
Anchovies
Soles
Bananas
Coffee
Cacao
Cattle
Hogs
Corn
Wheat
Sheep
Rice
Goats
Sugar-cane
Cotton
Cinchona
Rubber
Wild
Potatoes
Llamas and Alpacas

Agriculture, Industry and Resources

DOMINANT LAND USE
Diversified Tropical Crops (chiefly plantation agriculture)
Extensive Livestock Ranching
Forests
MAJOR MINERAL OCCURRENCES
Al Bauxite
Au Gold
D Diamonds
Mn Manganese
Water Power
Crabs
Shrimp
Bananas
Sugar-cane
Rice
Sugarcane
Manioc

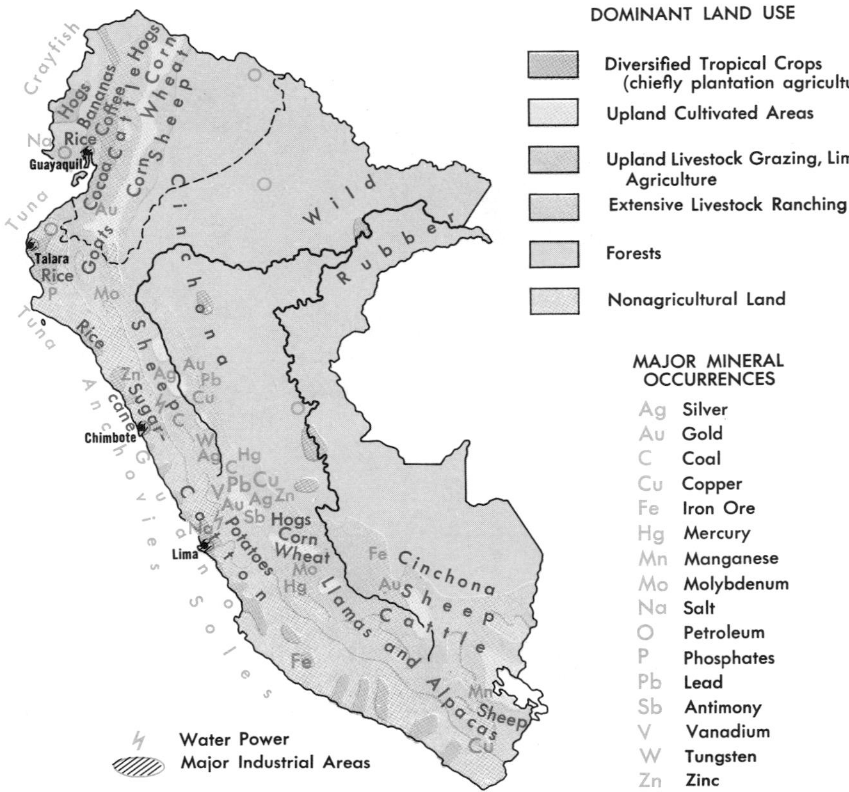

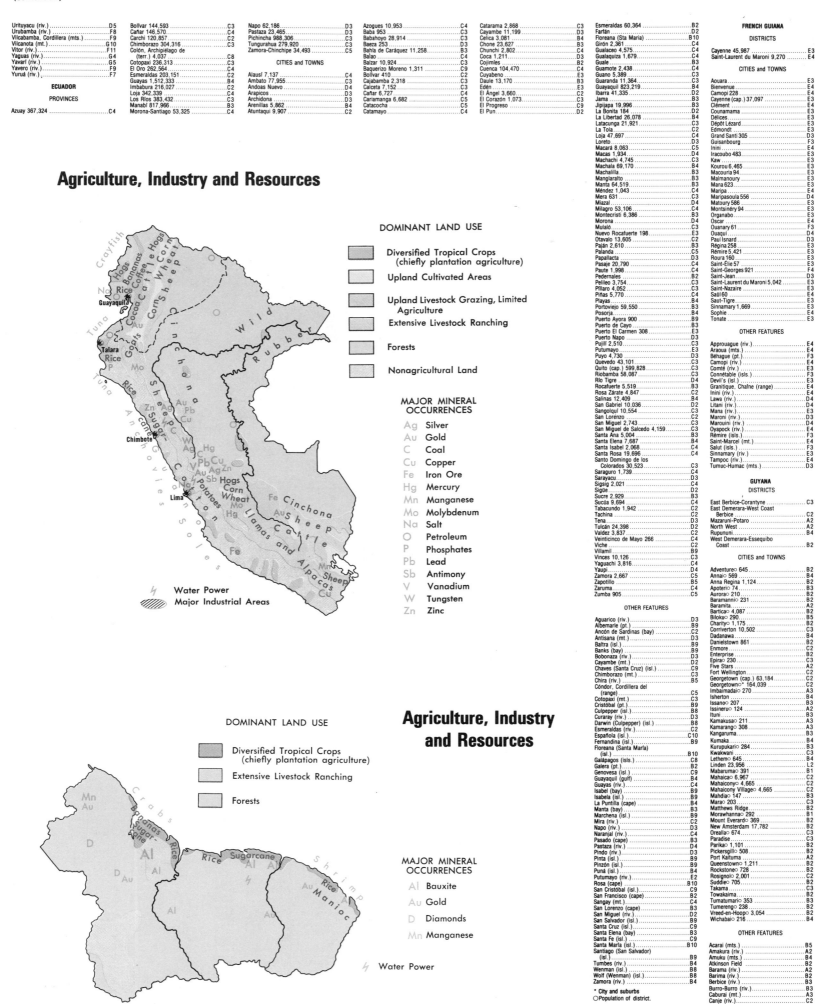

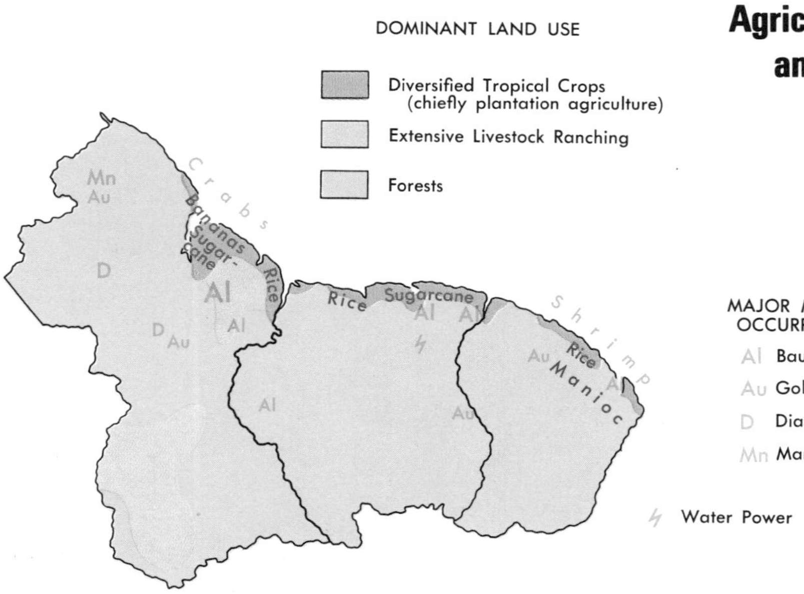

GUYANA

AREA 83,000 sq. mi. (214,970 sq. km.)
POPULATION 793,000
CAPITAL Georgetown
LARGEST CITY Georgetown
HIGHEST POINT Mt. Roraima 9,094 ft. (2,772 m.)
MONETARY UNIT Guyana dollar
MAJOR LANGUAGES English, Hindi
MAJOR RELIGIONS Christianity, Hinduism, Islam

SURINAME

AREA 55,144 sq. mi. (142,823 sq. km.)
POPULATION 354,860
CAPITAL Paramaribo
LARGEST CITY Paramaribo
HIGHEST POINT Julianatop 4,200 ft. (1,280 m.)
MONETARY UNIT Suriname guilder
MAJOR LANGUAGES Dutch, Hindi, Indonesian
MAJOR RELIGIONS Christianity, Islam, Hinduism

FRENCH GUIANA

AREA 35,135 sq. mi. (91,000 sq. km.)
POPULATION 73,022
CAPITAL Cayenne
LARGEST CITY Cayenne
HIGHEST POINT 2,723 ft. (830 m.)
MONETARY UNIT French franc
MAJOR LANGUAGE French
MAJOR RELIGIONS Roman Catholicism, Protestantism

Courantyne (riv.) C3
Cuyuni (riv.) B2
Demerara (riv.) B3
Enwarak (mt.) B3
Essequibo (riv.) B3
Great (fall) B3
Ireng (riv.) B3
Kaieteur (fall) B3
Kamaria (falls) B2
Kuyuwini (riv.) B4
Kwitaro (riv.) B4
Leguan (isl.) B2
Marudi (mts.) B5
Mazaruni (riv.) A2
Moruka (riv.) B2
New (riv.) C4
Pakaraima (mts.) A3
Playa (pt.) B1
Pomeroon (riv.) B2
Potaro (riv.) B3
Puruni (riv.) B2
Roraima (mt.) A3
Rupununi (riv.) B4
Sororieng (mt.) B2
Surwakwima (fall) A2
Takutu (riv.) B4
Venamo (mt.) A3
Waini (riv.) B2
Wenamu (riv.) A2

SURINAME

DISTRICTS

Brokopondo 17,763 .... D4
Commewijne 18,740 .... D3
Coronie 3,251 .... C3
Marowijne 25,911 .... D4
Nickerie 35,178 .... C3
Para 16,635 .... D3
Paramaribo 102,297 .... D2
Saramacca 13,554 .... C3
Suriname 151,585 .... D3

CITIES and TOWNS

Ajoewa C4
Alalapadu C4
Albina 1,000 .... D3
Asidonhoppo D4
Berg en Dal D3
Bitagron C3
Brokopondo D3
Burnside C2
Calcutta 1,100 .... C3
Cottica D4
Domburg 1,200 .... D3
Groningen 600 .... D2
Huwelijkszorg C2
Kwakoegron D3
Lelydorp 300 .... D3
Majoli D4
Mariënburg 3,500 .... D2
Moengo 2,100 .... D3
Nieuw-Amsterdam 1,400 .... D2
Nieuw-Nickerie 7,400 .... C2
Paramaribo (cap.) ⊙ 167,905 .... D2
Paranam D3
Totness 1,300 .... C3
Uitkijk D3
Wageningen 800 .... C3
Zanderij D3

OTHER FEATURES

Bakhuys (mts.) C3
Coeroeni (riv.) C4
Commewijne (riv.) D3
Coppename (riv.) C3
Corantijn (riv.) C3
Cottica (riv.) D3
Eilerts de Haan (mts.) C4
Frederik Willem IV (falls) C4
Julianatop (mt.) C4
Kayser (mts.) C4
Lely (mts.) D3
Litani (riv.) D4
Marowijne (riv.) D3
Nickerie (riv.) C3
Orange (mts.) . j. D4
Saramacca (riv.) D3
Sipwliwini (riv.) C3
Suriname (riv.) D3
Tapanahoni (riv.) D4
Toekomstig (res.) C3
Van Blommestein (lake) D3
Wilhelmina (mts.) C4

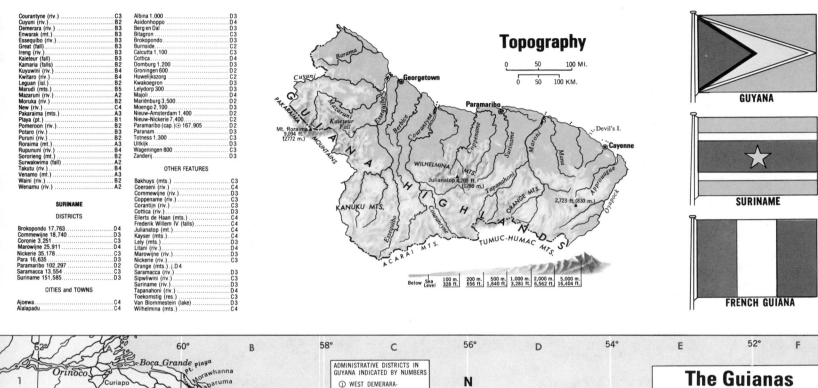

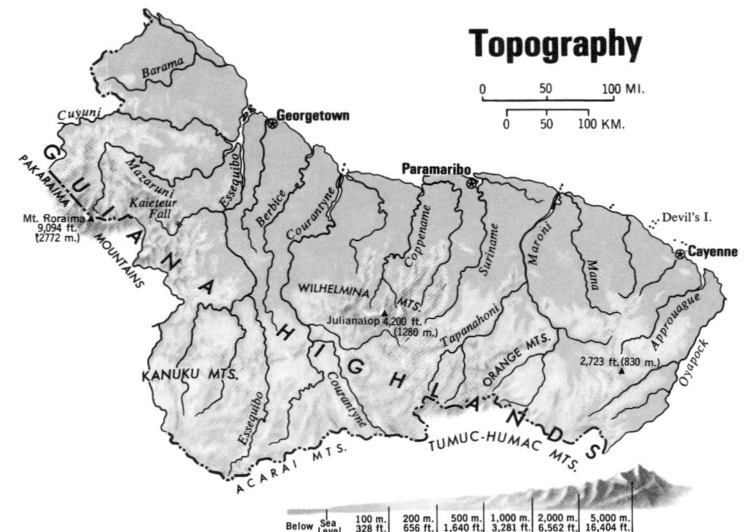

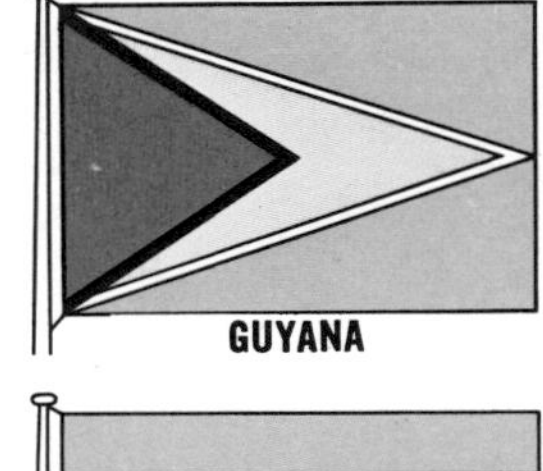

GUYANA

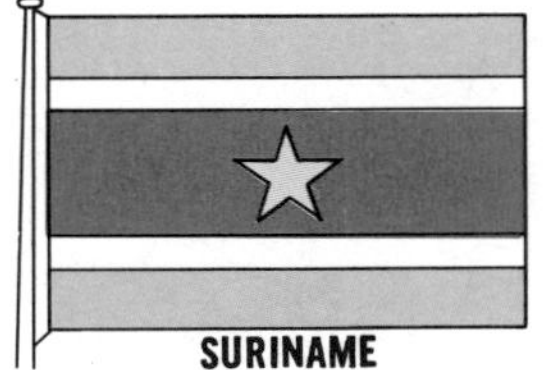

SURINAME

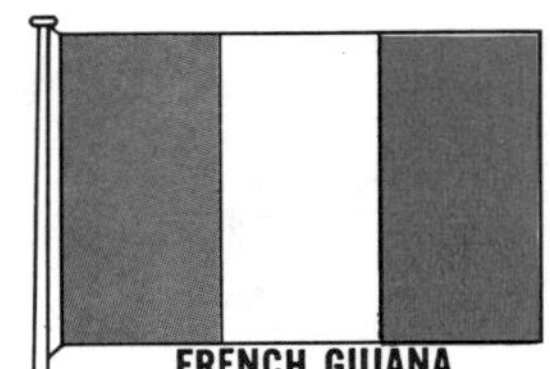

FRENCH GUIANA

The Guianas

LAMBERT CONFORMAL CONIC PROJECTION

SCALE OF MILES: 0 30 60 120
KILOMETERS: 0 30 60 120

Capitals of Countries ☆
Other Capitals ⊙
International Boundaries
Other Boundaries

Scale 1:3,650,000

ADMINISTRATIVE DISTRICTS IN GUYANA INDICATED BY NUMBERS

① WEST DEMERARA-ESSEQUIBO COAST B2
② EAST DEMERARA-WEST COAST BERBICE C2

ADMINISTRATIVE DISTRICTS IN SURINAME INDICATED BY NUMBERS

① SURINAME D2
② PARA D2

Longitude West of Greenwich

Brazil
BIPOLAR OBLIQUE CONIC CONFORMAL PROJECTION
SCALE OF MILES
0 50 100 200 300
KILOMETERS
0 50 100 200 300
Capitals of Countries
State Capitals
International Boundaries
State Boundaries
Scale 1:14,700,000
© Copyright HAMMOND INCORPORATED, Maplewood, N. J.
Longitude 48° West of Greenwich 44°
ATLANTIC OCEAN
SURINAME
FR. GUIANA
GUYANA
AMAPÁ
RORAIMA
AMAZONAS
PARÁ
MARANHÃO
PIAUÍ
CEARÁ
RIO GRANDE DO NORTE
PARAÍBA
PERNAMBUCO
ALAGOAS
SERGIPE
BAHIA
GOIÁS
MATO GROSSO
MATO GROSSO DO SUL
MINAS GERAIS
ESPÍRITO SANTO
RIO DE JANEIRO
SÃO PAULO
PARANÁ
SANTA CATARINA
RIO GRANDE DO SUL
RONDÔNIA
FEDERAL DISTRICT
BOLIVIA
PARAGUAY
ARGENTINA
URUGUAY
Brasília
Manaus
Belém
São Luís
Teresina
Fortaleza (Ceará)
Natal
João Pessoa
Recife (Pernambuco)
Maceió
Aracaju
Salvador (Bahia)
Vitória
Belo Horizonte
Rio de Janeiro
Niterói
São Paulo
Santos
Curitiba
Florianópolis
Porto Alegre
Goiânia
Cuiabá
Campo Grande
Macapá
Asunción
Amazon
Tropic of Capricorn
BRAZIL WESTERN PART
COLOMBIA
VENEZUELA
PERU
ACRE
Pico da Neblina 9,889 ft. (3014 m.)

STATES and TERRITORIES

Acre 301,605 ... G10
Alagoas 1,987,581 ... G5
Amapá (terr.) 175,634 ... D2
Amazonas 1,432,066 ... G9
Bahia 9,474,263 ... F6
Ceará 5,294,876 ... G4
Espírito Santo 2,023,821 ... F7
Federal District 1,177,393 ... E6
Goiás 3,865,482 ... D6
Maranhão 4,002,599 ... E4
Mato Grosso 1,141,661 ... B6
Mato Grosso do Sul 1,370,333 ... C7
Minas Gerais 13,390,805 ... E7
Pará 3,411,868 ... C4
Paraíba 2,772,600 ... G4
Paraná 7,630,466 ... D9
Pernambuco 6,147,102 ... G5
Piauí 2,140,066 ... F4
Rio de Janeiro 11,297,327 ... F8
Rio Grande do Norte 1,899,720 ... G4
Rio Grande do Sul 7,777,212 ... C10
Rondônia (terr.) 492,810 ... H10
Roraima (terr.) 79,153 ... H8
Santa Catarina 3,628,751 ... D9
São Paulo 25,040,698 ... D8
Sergipe 1,141,834 ... G5

CITIES and TOWNS

Abaeté 12,861 ... E7
Abaetetuba 33,031 ... D3
Acaraú 7,144 ... F3
Acopiara 10,747 ... G4
Açu 20,544 ... G4
Agudos 18,790 ... *B3
Alagoa Grande 14,204 ... H4
Alagoinhas 76,377 ... G6
Alcobaça 3,430 ... G7
Alegre 9,441 ... *F2
Alegrete 54,786 ... B10
Além Paraíba 23,028 ... *E2
Alenquer 16,477 ... C3
Alfenas 31,815 ... *D2
Altamira 24,846 ... C3
Altos 13,621 ... F4
Amambaí 12,507 ... C8
Amapá 2,676 ... D2
Amarante 6,848 ... F4
Amargosa 11,118 ... F6
Americana 121,794 ... *C3
Amparo 26,970 ... *C3
Anápolis 160,520 ... D7
Anchieta 5,741 ... F8
Andaraí 2,476 ... F6
Andradina 42,036 ... D8
Andrelândia 8,737 ... *D2
Angra dos Reis 24,894 ... *D3
Antonina 11,950 ... *B4
Aparecida 27,265 ... *D3
Apiaí 7,809 ... *B4
Aquidauana 21,514 ... C8
Aracaju 288,106 ... G5
Aracati 20,282 ... G4
Araçatuba 113,486 ... *A2
Araçuaí 12,292 ... F7
Araguari 73,302 ... D7
Araranguá 22,468 ... D10
Araraquara 77,202 ... *B2
Araras 54,323 ... *C3
Araxá 51,339 ... E7
Arcoverde 40,646 ... G5
Areia Branca 12,979 ... G4
Assis 57,217 ... *A3
Avaré 40,716 ... *B3
Bacabal 43,229 ... E4
Bagé 66,743 ... C10
Bahia (Salvador) 1,496,276 ... G6
Baixo Guandu 13,714 ... F7
Balsas 13,566 ... E4
Bambuí 14,172 ... *C2
Barão de Cocais 11,950 ... *E1
Barbacena 69,675 ... *E2
Barcelos 1,846 ... H9
Bariri 15,372 ... *B3
Barra 10,809 ... F5
Barra do Corda 19,280 ... E4
Barra do Piraí 51,214 ... *E3
Barra Mansa 123,421 ... *D3
Barras 8,904 ... F4
Barreiras 30,355 ... E6
Barreiros 19,419 ... H5
Barretos 65,294 ... *B2
Batatais 30,478 ... *C2
Baturité 12,388 ... G4
Bauru 178,861 ... *B3
Bebedouro 39,070 ... *B2
Bela Vista 11,936 ... C8
Belém 758,117 ... E3
Belém †1,000,349 ... E3
Belo Horizonte 1,442,483 ... *D1
Belo Horizonte †2,541,788 ... *D1
Benjamin Constant 6,563 ... G9
Bento Gonçalves 40,323 ... C10
Betim 71,599 ... *D2
Bicas 8,611 ... *E2
Birigui 45,348 ... *A2
Blumenau 144,819 ... D9
Boa Esperança 17,394 ... *D2
Boa Vista 43,131 ... H8
Bocaiúva 16,616 ... E7
Bom Conselho 13,196 ... G5
Bom Despacho 22,941 ... *D1
Bom Jesus da Lapa 19,978 ... F6
Bom Sucesso 10,331 ... *D2
Borba 5,366 ... H9
Bragança Paulista 61,021 ... *C3
Brasiléia 4,835 ... G10
Brasília (cap.) 411,305 ... E6
Brasília de Minas 10,171 ... F7
Brejo 5,859 ... F3
Breves 31,452 ... D3
Brumado 24,663 ... F6
Brusque 37,898 ... D9

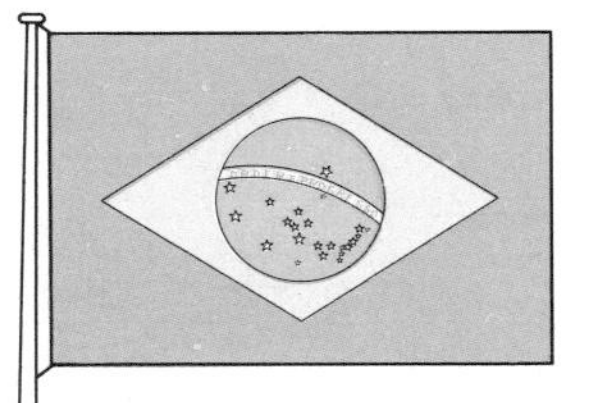

Cabedelo 18,581 ... H4
Cabo Frio 40,668 ... *F3
Caçador 25,287 ... D9
Caçapava 45,258 ... *D3
Caçapava do Sul 15,180 ... C10
Cáceres 33,472 ... B7
Cachoeira 11,520 ... G6
Cachoeira do Sul 59,967 ... C10
Cachoeiro de Itapemirim 84,994 ... G8
Caeté 23,331 ... *E1
Caetité 8,823 ... F6
Caiapônia 9,358 ... C7
Caicó 30,777 ... G4
Cajazeiras 30,834 ... G4
Cajuru 9,670 ... *C2
Camaquã 28,078 ... C10
Cambará 13,218 ... *A3
Cambuí 8,552 ... *C3
Cametá 15,539 ... D3
Camocim 19,921 ... F3
Campina Grande 222,229 ... G4
Campinas 566,517 ... *C3
Campo Belo 30,392 ... *D2
Campo Formoso 10,324 ... F5
Campo Grande 282,844 ... C8
Campo Largo 34,506 ... *B4
Campo Maior 24,009 ... F4
Campos 174,218 ... *F2
Cananéia 5,581 ... *C4
Canavieiras 14,076 ... G6
Canindé 18,573 ... G4
Canoas 214,115 ... D10
Canoinhas 25,880 ... D9
Capanema 28,272 ... E3
Capão Bonito 24,081 ... *B4
Caraguatatuba 22,932 ... *D3
Carangola 15,621 ... *E2
Caratinga 39,621 ... *E1
Caravelas 3,704 ... G7
Carazinho 41,913 ... C10
Carolina 10,136 ... E4
Caruaru 137,636 ... G5
Casa Branca 13,739 ... *C2
Cascavel 16,238 ... G4
Cássia 10,701 ... *C2
Castanhal 51,797 ... E3
Castelo 9,162 ... F8
Castro 21,079 ... *B4
Castro Alves 11,286 ... G6
Cataguases 40,659 ... *E2
Catalão 30,516 ... E7
Catanduva 64,813 ... *B2
Catolé do Rocha 12,165 ... G4
Caxambu 16,221 ... *D2
Caxias 56,755 ... F4
Caxias do Sul 198,824 ... D10
Ceará (Fortaleza) 648,815 ... G3
Ceará-Mirim 17,097 ... H4
Ceres 13,671 ... D6
Chapecó 53,198 ... C9
Coari 14,841 ... H9
Codajás 4,923 ... H9
Codó 11,593 ... E4
Colatina 61,057 ... F7
Conceição do Araguaia 18,143 ... D5
Concórdia 17,973 ... D9
Conselheiro Lafaiete 66,262 ... *E2
Corinto 17,056 ... E7
Cornélio Procópio 31,201 ... D8
Coroatá 16,070 ... F3
Coromandel 11,604 ... E7
Corumbá 66,014 ... B7
Coxim 14,876 ... C7
Crateús 29,905 ... F4
Crato 49,244 ... G4
Criciúma 74,003 ... D10
Cristalina 10,521 ... E7
Cruz Alta 53,315 ... C10
Cruzeiro 55,175 ... *D3
Cruzeiro do Sul 11,189 ... G10
Cubatão 78,327 ... *C3
Cuiabá 167,894 ... C6
Curitiba 843,733 ... *B4
Curitiba †1,441,743 ... *B4
Currais Novos 25,663 ... G4
Cururupu 10,358 ... E3
Curvelo 37,734 ... E7
Diamantina 20,197 ... F7
Divinópolis 108,344 ... *D2
Dois Córregos 11,811 ... *B3
Dom Pedrito 25,773 ... C10
Dores do Indaiá 13,058 ... E7
Dourados 76,838 ... C8
Duque de Caxias 306,057 ... *E3
Erexim 46,927 ... C9
Esperança 12,964 ... G4
Esplanada 9,822 ... G5
Estância 28,250 ... G5
Feira de Santana 225,003 ... G5
Fernandópolis 39,737 ... *A2
Floriano 35,761 ... F4
Florianópolis 153,547 ... E9

AREA 3,284,426 sq. mi. (8,506,663 sq. km.)
POPULATION 119,098,992
CAPITAL Brasília
LARGEST CITY São Paulo (greater)
HIGHEST POINT Pico da Neblina 9,889 ft. (3,014 m.)
MONETARY UNIT cruzeiro
MAJOR LANGUAGE Portuguese
MAJOR RELIGION Roman Catholicism

Topography

0 200 400 MI.
0 200 400 KM.

Fonte Boa 3,278 ... G9
Formiga 36,681 ... *D2
Formosa 29,304 ... E6
Fortaleza 648,815 ... G3
Fortaleza †1,581,588 ... G3
Foz do Iguaçu 93,619 ... C9
Franca 143,630 ... *C2
Frutal 22,955 ... *B2
Garanhuns 64,854 ... G5
Garça 26,527 ... *B3
Goiana 30,108 ... H4
Goiânia 703,263 ... D7
Goiás 15,768 ... D6
Governador Valadares 173,699 ... F7
Grajaú 11,147 ... E4
Guacuí 12,715 ... *F2
Guajará-Mirim 19,992 ... H10
Guarapuava 17,189 ... C9
Guaratinguetá 68,370 ... *D3
Guarujá 67,730 ... *C4
Guarulhos 395,117 ... *C3
Guaxupé 23,637 ... *C2
Guiratinga 8,981 ... C7
Gurupi 27,319 ... D5
Humaitá 10,004 ... H10
Ibaiti 11,352 ... *A3
Ibiá 11,161 ... E7
Ibicaraí 18,202 ... G6
Ibitinga 23,359 ... *B2
Icó 13,007 ... G4
Igarapava 15,342 ... *C2
Igarapé-Miri 12,172 ... D3
Iguape 16,827 ... *C4
Iguatu 39,611 ... G4
Ijuí 51,925 ... C10
Ilhéus 71,240 ... G6
Imbituba 9,998 ... D10
Imperatriz 111,818 ... E4
Inhumas 23,455 ... D7
Ipameri 14,163 ... E7
Ipu 12,787 ... F4
Irati 21,956 ... *A4
Itabaiana, Paraíba 17,843 ... H4

Itabaiana, Sergipe 26,055 ... G5
Itaberaba 27,590 ... F6
Itabira 57,691 ... F7
Itabirito 22,978 ... *E2
Itabuna 129,938 ... G6
Itacoatiara 26,737 ... B3
Itaituba 19,644 ... C4
Itajaí 78,867 ... D9
Itajubá 53,506 ... *D3
Itanhaem 26,181 ... *C4
Itapecerica 10,234 ... *D2
Itapecuru-Mirim 12,216 ... F3
Itapemirim 16,829 ... F8
Itaperuna 34,644 ... *F2
Itapetinga 36,897 ... G6
Itapetininga 61,344 ... *B3
Itapeva 36,551 ... *B3
Itapipoca 19,463 ... G3
Itapira 36,308 ... *C3
Itápolis 13,750 ... *B2
Itaporanga 8,988 ... G4
Itaqui 23,136 ... B10
Itararé 24,368 ... *B4
Itatiba 35,537 ... *C3
Itaúna 49,372 ... *D2
Itu 62,211 ... *C3
Ituaçu 1,749 ... F6
Ituiutaba 65,178 ... D7
Itumbiara 56,602 ... D7
Iturama 12,363 ... *A1
Ituverava 21,323 ... *C2
Jaboatão 67,120 ... H5
Jaboticabal 40,276 ... *B2
Jacareí 103,652 ... *D3
Jacarezinho 23,684 ... *A3
Jacobina 26,723 ... F5
Jacupiranga 7,044 ... *B4
Jaguaquara 11,336 ... F6
Jaguarão 18,165 ... C11
Jaguariaíva 8,566 ... *B4
Januária 20,484 ... E6
Jataí 40,957 ... D7
Jaú 59,522 ... *B3
Jequié 84,792 ... F6

Jequitinhonha 10,900 ... F7
Ji-Paraná 31,724 ... H10
Joaçaba 16,195 ... D9
João Pessoa 290,424 ... H4
João Pinheiro 17,013 ... E7
Joinvile 217,074 ... D9
Juazeiro 60,940 ... G5
Juazeiro do Norte 125,248 ... F4
Juiz de Fora 299,728 ... *E2
Jundiaí 210,015 ... *C3
Lages 108,768 ... D9
Laguna 27,743 ... D10
Lambari 9,722 ... *D2
Lapa 13,314 ... D9
Laranjeiras do Sul 19,329 ... C9
Lavras 35,345 ... *D2
Leme 40,155 ... *C3
Leopoldina 28,554 ... *E2
Limeira 137,812 ... *C3
Limoeiro 36,088 ... H4
Limoeiro do Norte 13,112 ... G4
Linhares 51,575 ... F7
Lins 44,633 ... *B2
Londrina 258,054 ... D8
Lorena 51,276 ... *D3
Luís Correia 3,576 ... F3
Luz 10,068 ... *D1
Luziânia 67,284 ... E7
Macaé 39,644 ... *F3
Macaíba 17,036 ... H4
Macapá 89,081 ... D2
Macau 17,543 ... G4
Maceió 376,479 ... H5
Machado 16,164 ... *C2
Mafra 26,226 ... D9
Magé 37,597 ... *E3
Mamanguape 16,321 ... H4
Manacapuru 17,016 ... H9
Manaus 613,068 ... H9
Manhuaçu 22,678 ... *E2
Manhumirim 11,085 ... *E2
Manicoré 9,532 ... H9
Marabá 41,564 ... D4
Maracaju 9,699 ... C8

Maragogipe 13,512 ... G6
Maranguape 20,098 ... G3
Marechal Deodoro 9,400 ... H5
Mariana 11,785 ... *E2
Marília 103,904 ... *A3
Maringá 158,047 ... D8
Mata de São João 23,741 ... G6
Mato Grosso (Vila Bela da Santissima Trindade) 1,401 ... B6
Maués 10,846 ... B3
Mazagão 1,824 ... D3
Mineiros 16,844 ... C7
Miracema 15,545 ... *E2
Mirassol 25,173 ... *B2
Mococa 33,682 ... *C2
Mogi das Cruzes 122,265 ... *C3
Mogi-Mirim 41,827 ... *C3
Monte Alegre 10,646 ... C3
Monte Aprazível 9,767 ... *A2
Monteiro 11,051 ... G4
Montenegro 27,246 ... D10
Montes Claros 151,881 ... E7
Morrinhos 20,154 ... D7
Mossoró 118,007 ... G4
Muriaé 50,040 ... *E2
Muzambinho 8,803 ... *C2
Nanuque 34,445 ... F7
Natal 376,552 ... H4
Nazaré 18,068 ... G6
Niquelândia 8,828 ... D6
Niterói 386,185 ... *E3
Nova Cruz 12,824 ... H4
Nova Era 11,126 ... *E1
Nova Friburgo 88,943 ... *E3
Nova Iguaçu 491,802 ... *E3
Nova Lima 35,035 ... *E2
Nova Russas 10,021 ... F4
Novo Hamburgo 132,066 ... D10
Novo Horizonte 18,439 ... *B2
Óbidos 17,143 ... C3
Oeiras 12,406 ... F4
Olímpia 24,376 ... *B2
Olinda 266,392 ... H4

Oliveira 22,642 ... *D2
Oriximiná 12,078 ... C3
Orlândia 22,924 ... *C2
Osasco 376,689 ... *C3
Ourinhos 52,698 ... *B3
Ouro Preto 27,821 ... *E2
Palmares 40,624 ... H5
Palmas 15,823 ... C9
Palmeira 11,521 ... *B4
Palmeira das Missões 23,943 ... C9
Pará (Belém) 758,117 ... E3
Paracatu 29,911 ... E7
Pará de Minas 37,127 ... *D1
Paraguaçu Paulista 17,399 ... D8
Paraíba do Sul 13,510 ... *E3
Paranaíba 21,305 ... D7
Paranaguá 68,366 ... *B4
Parati 8,684 ... *D3
Parintins 29,369 ... B3
Parnaíba 78,718 ... F3
Passo Fundo 103,121 ... D10
Passos 56,998 ... *C2
Patos 58,735 ... G4
Patos de Minas 59,896 ... E7
Patrocínio 29,520 ... E7
Pau dos Ferros 12,985 ... G4
Paulo Afonso 62,066 ... G5
Pederneiras 18,864 ... *B3
Pedra Azul 13,615 ... F6
Pedreiras 30,843 ... E4
Pedro Segundo 9,693 ... F4
Pelotas 197,092 ... C10
Penápolis 32,168 ... *A2
Penedo 27,064 ... G5
Pernambuco (Recife) 1,184,215 ... H5
Petrolina 73,436 ... G5
Petrópolis 149,427 ... *E3
Picos 33,098 ... F4
Piedade 13,054 ... *C3
Pilar 14,778 ... H5
Pindamonhangaba 51,174 ... *D3

(continued on following page)

Pinhal (Espírito Santo do
Pinhal) 23,235 . . . . *C3
Pinheiro 19,556 . . . . E3
Piquete 10,316 . . . . *D3
Piracanjuba 11,151 . . . . D7
Piracicaba 179,395 . . . . *C3
Piracuruca 9,419 . . . . F3
Piraí do Sul 13,709 . . . . *B4
Piraju 16,288 . . . . *B3
Pirapora 31,533 . . . . E7
Pirassununga 32,510 . . . . . *C2
Pires do Rio 16,659 . . . . D7
Piripiri 29,497 . . . . F4
Pitangui 12,116 . . . . *D1
Piúí 17,327 . . . . *D2
Poções 16,036 . . . . F6
Poconé 12,960 . . . . B7
Poços de Caldas 81,448 . . . *C2
Pombal 14,831 . . . . G4
Pompéia 11,282 . . . . *A3
Ponta Grossa 171,111 . . . . *B4
Ponta Porã 25,807 . . . . C8
Ponte Nova 34,807 . . . . *E2
Porangatu 21,192 . . . . D6
Porto Alegre 1,108,883 . . . D10
Porto Alegre †2,232,370 . . D10
Porto Feliz 19,680 . . . . *C3
Porto Nacional 19,052 . . . . . E5
Porto Seguro 5,007 . . . . G7
Porto União 19,426 . . . . D9
Porto Velho 101,644 . . . . . H10
Pouso Alegre 50,517 . . . . . *D3
Presidente Dutra 14,506 . . . . E4
Presidente Prudente
127,623 . . . . D8
Presidente Venceslau 26,720 D8
Propriá 19,034 . . . . G5
Promissão 15,333 . . . . *B2
Prudentópolis 8,645 . . . . D9
Quaraí 15,091 . . . . C10
Quixadá 25,149 . . . . G4
Quixeramobim 14,387 . . . . . . F4
Raposos 11,078 . . . . *E2
Raul Soares 10,055 . . . . . . *E2
Recife 1,184,215 . . . . H5
Recife †2,348,362 . . . . H5
Registro 28,702 . . . . *C4
Remanso 13,067 . . . . F5
Resende 36,633 . . . . *D3
Ribamar (São José de
Ribamar) 17,560 . . . . F3
Ribeirão Preto 300,704 . . . . *C2
Rio Bonito 20,561 . . . . *E3
Rio Branco 87,462 . . . . G10
Rio Claro 103,174 . . . . *C3
Rio de Janeiro 5,093,237 . . *E3
Rio de Janeiro †9,018,637 . *E3
Rio do Sul 33,408 . . . . D9
Rio Grande 124,706 . . . . . . D11
Rio Negro 15,851 . . . . D9
Rio Pardo 18,370 . . . . C10
Rio Pomba 9,319 . . . . *E2
Rio Tinto 12,511 . . . . H4
Rio Verde 47,639 . . . . D7
Rio Verde de Mato Grosso
10,001 . . . . C7
Rosário 11,669 . . . . F3
Rosário do Sul 30,753 . . . . C10
Russas 16,259 . . . . G4
Sabará 22,883 . . . . *E1
Sacramento 10,524 . . . . . . *C1
Salgueiro 25,915 . . . . G5
Salinas 12,613 . . . . F7
Salinópolis 10,395 . . . . E3
Salto 42,351 . . . . *C3
Salvador 1,496,276 . . . . G6
Salvador †1,772,018 . . . . . . G6
Santa Cruz 13,172 . . . . G4
Santa Cruz do Rio Pardo
20,507 . . . . *B3
Santa Cruz do Sul 52,050 . . C10
Santa Helena de Goiás
20,067 . . . . D7
Santa Leopoldina 1,217 . . . . G7
Santa Maria 151,202 . . . . . C10
Santa Maria da Vitória
16,294 . . . . F6
Santana do Ipanema 15,311 . G5
Santana do Livramento
58,165 . . . . C10
Santarém 101,534 . . . . C3
Santa Rita do Sapucaí
15,005 . . . . *D3
Santa Vitória do Palmar
14,758 . . . . C11
Santiago 30,406 . . . . C10
Santo Amaro 29,627 . . . . . . G6
Santo Ângelo 50,161 . . . . . C10
Santo André 549,278 . . . . . *C3
Santo Antônio da Platina
21,284 . . . . *A3
Santos 411,023 . . . . *C3
Santos Dumont 31,053 . . . . *E2
São Bento 9,607 . . . . E3
São Bernardo do Campo
381,261 . . . . *C3
São Borja 41,598 . . . . C10
São Carlos 109,231 . . . . . . *C3
São Cristóvão 11,720 . . . . . . G5
São Fidélis 11,713 . . . . *F2
São Francisco 12,011 . . . . . . E6
São Francisco do Sul
13,914 . . . . E9
São Gabriel 40,497 . . . . C10
São Gonçalo 221,278 . . . . . . F8
São João da Boa Vista
45,712 . . . . *C2
São João del Rei 53,401 . . *D2
São João dos Patos 12,848 . F4
São João Nepomuceno
12,752 . . . . *E2
São Joaquim da Barra
26,273 . . . . *C2

São José 37,562 . . . . D9
São José do Rio Pardo
21,914 . . . . *C2
São José do Rio Preto
171,982 . . . . *B2
Cassiporé (cape) D2
Caviana (isl.) D2
Chavantes, Serra dos
(range) D5
Claro (riv.) D7
Comprida (isl.) *C4
Cuiabá (riv.) B7
Culuene (riv.) C6
Curuá (riv.) C4
Doce (riv.) *E2, F7
Dois Irmãos, Serra (range) . . F5
Espigão Mestre (Geral
de Goiás) (range) E6
Espinhaço, Serra do (range) . F7
Estrondo, Serra do (range) . . D4
Feia (lake) *F3
Feio (riv.) *B2
Formosa, Serra (range) C5
Frio (cape) *F3
Furnas (dam) *C2
Geral de Goiás, Serra
(range) E6
Gi-Paraná (riv.) H10
Gradaús, Serra dos (range) . D4
Grajaú (riv.) E4
Grande (isl.) *D3
Grande (riv.) *B2, E8
Guanabara (bay) *E3
Guaporé (riv.) H10
Gurguéia (riv.) E5
Gurupi, Serra do (range) E4
Gurupi (riv.) E3
Ibicuí (riv.) C10
Içá (riv.) G9
Iguaçu (riv.) C9
Iguazú (falls) C9
Ilha Grande (bay) *D3
Iriri (riv.) C4
Itaipu (dam) C9
Itaipu (res.) C9
Itapecuru (riv.) F4
Itapi (riv.) B3
Itapicuru (riv.) G5
Itararé (riv.) *B3
Ivaí (riv.) C8
Jacuípe (riv.) F5
Jaguaribe (riv.) G4

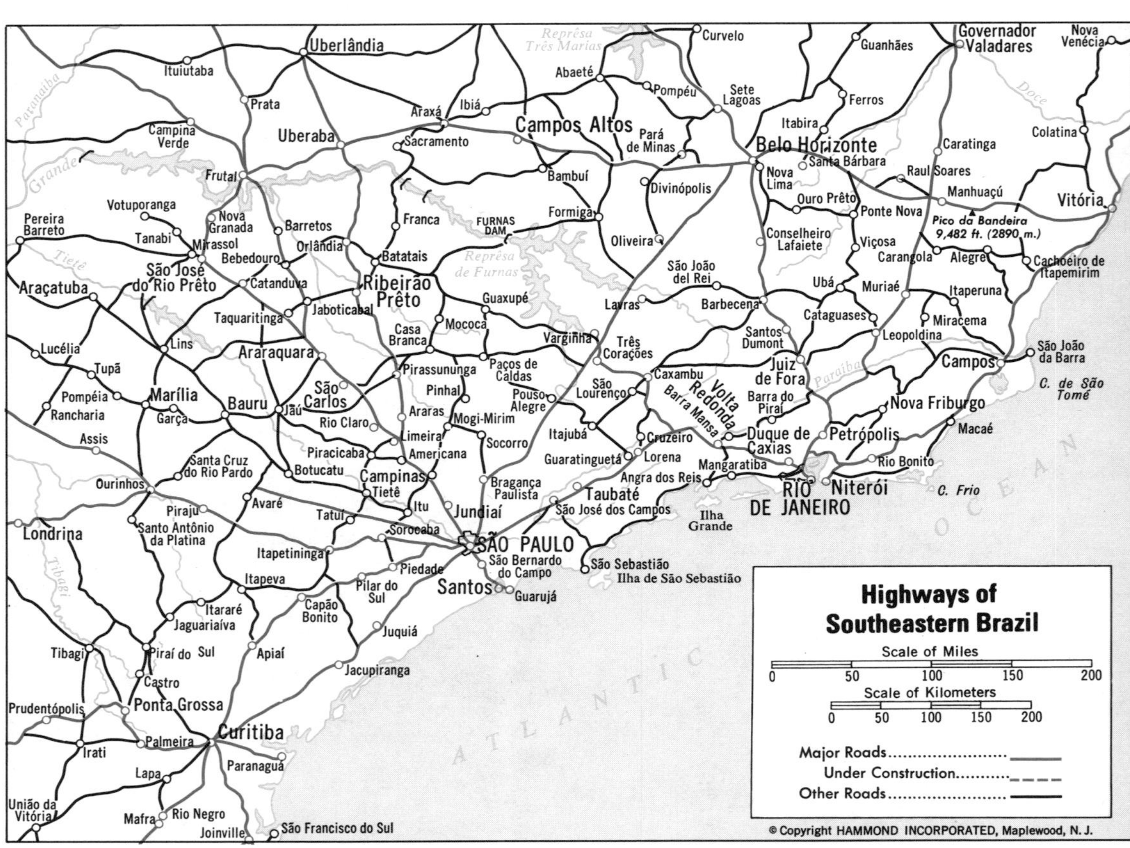

Agriculture, Industry and Resources

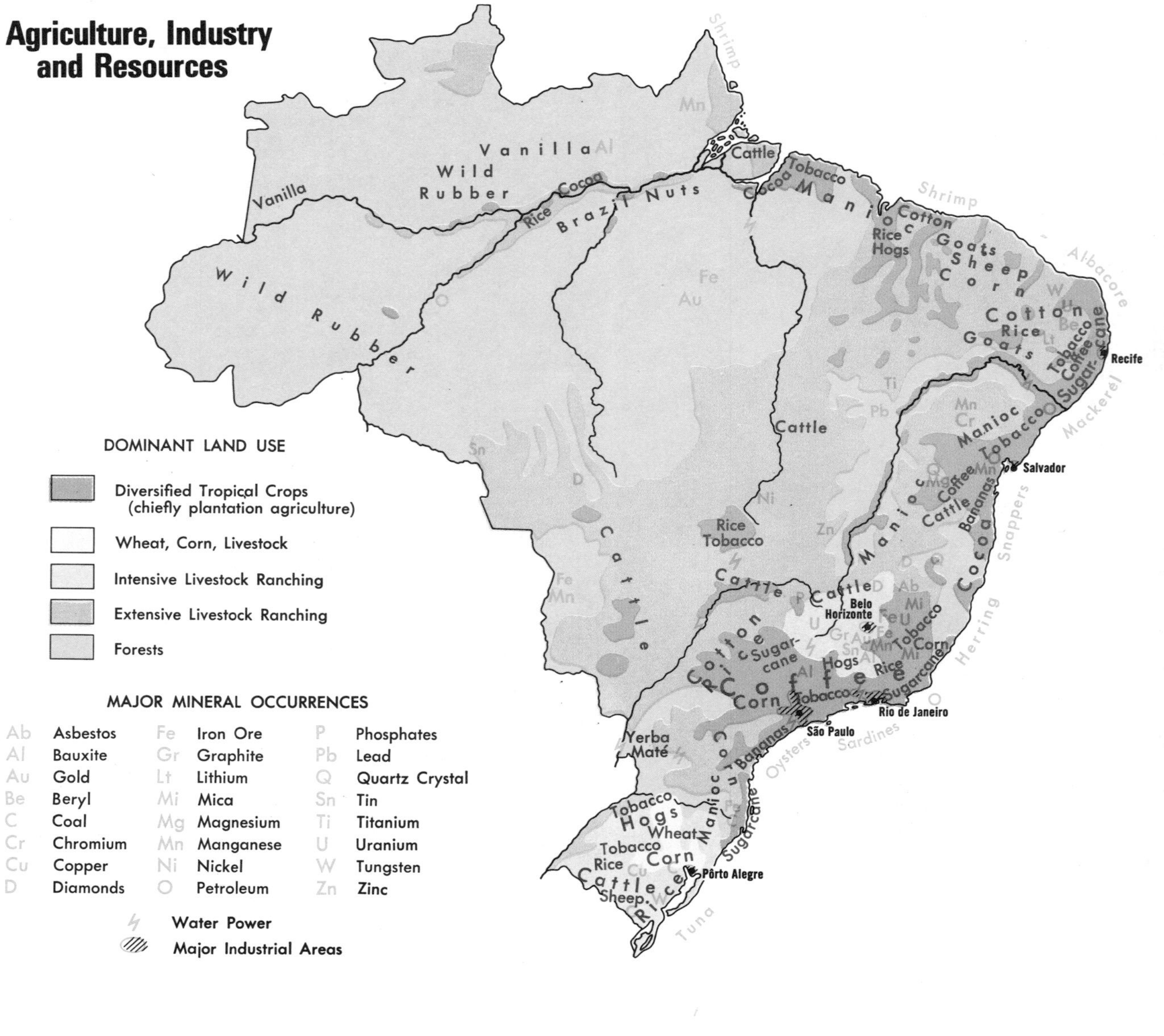

DOMINANT LAND USE

Diversified Tropical Crops (chiefly plantation agriculture)
Wheat, Corn, Livestock
Intensive Livestock Ranching
Extensive Livestock Ranching
Forests

MAJOR MINERAL OCCURRENCES

Ab Asbestos
Al Bauxite
Au Gold
Be Beryl
C Coal
Cr Chromium
Cu Copper
D Diamonds
Fe Iron Ore
Gr Graphite
Lt Lithium
Mi Mica
Mg Magnesium
Mn Manganese
Ni Nickel
O Petroleum
P Phosphates
Pb Lead
Q Quartz Crystal
Sn Tin
Ti Titanium
U Uranium
W Tungsten
Zn Zinc

Water Power
Major Industrial Areas

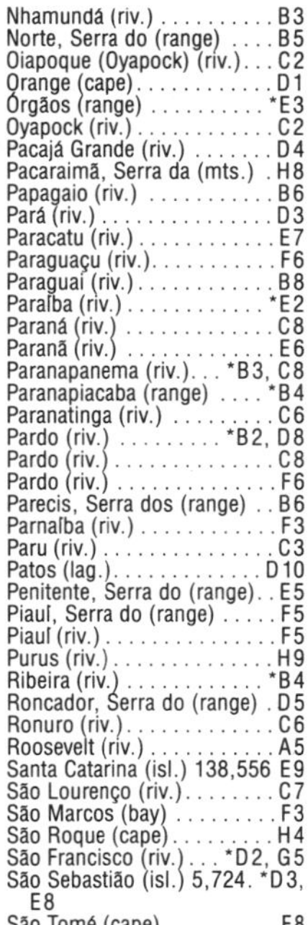

OTHER FEATURES

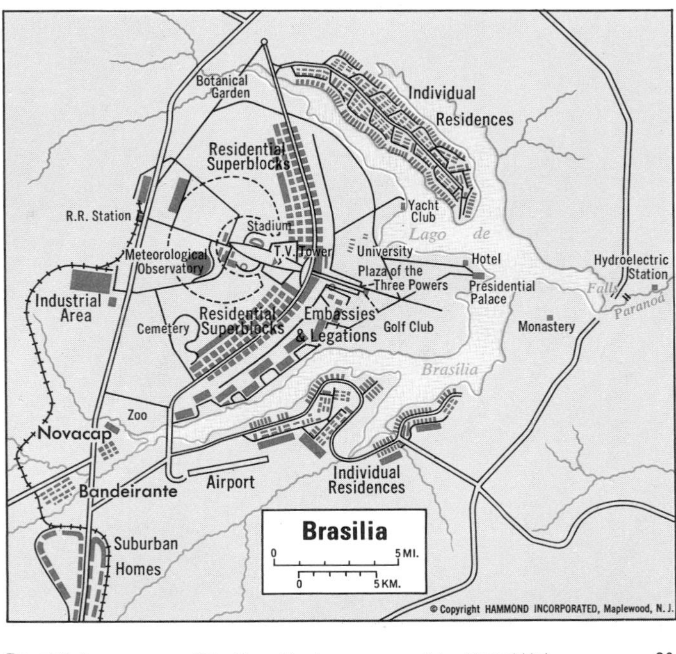

†Population of met. area.
*preceding reference indicates that the name will be found on S.E. Brazil map, page 135.

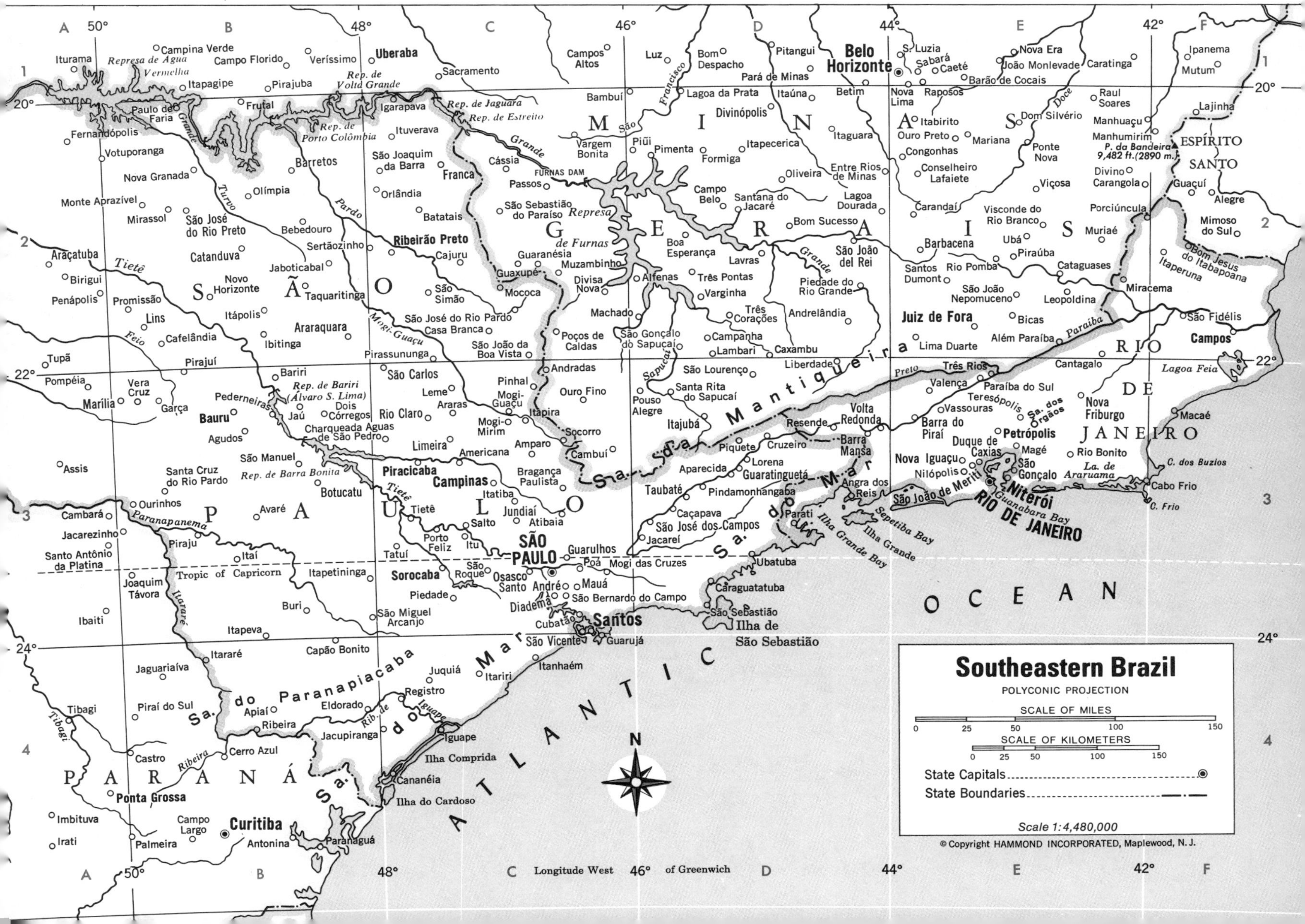

Southeastern Brazil

POLYCONIC PROJECTION

SCALE OF MILES
0 25 50 100 150

SCALE OF KILOMETERS
0 25 50 100 150

State Capitals
State Boundaries

Scale 1:4,480,000

Longitude West 46° of Greenwich

DEPARTMENTS

Beni, El 168,367 .... C3
Chuquisaca 358,516 .... C6
Cochabamba 720,952 .... C5
El Beni 168,367 .... C3
La Paz 1,465,078 .... A4
Oruro 310,409 .... A6
Pando 34,493 .... B2
Potosí 657,743 .... B7
Santa Cruz 710,724 .... E5
Tarija 187,204 .... D7

CITIES and TOWNS

Abapó 466 .... D6
Acchilla 208 .... C7
Achacachi 3,621 .... A5
Aiquile 3,465 .... C6
Alcalá 236 .... C6
Alejandría‡ 198 .... C3
Alto Seco‡ 3,414 .... D6
Amarete 992 .... A4
Ananea 302 .... A4
Ancoraimes 769 .... A4
Andamarca‡ 5,187 .... B6
Añimbo 443 .... C7
Anzaldo 1,056 .... C5
Apolo 1,043 .... A4
Araca‡ 3,537 .... B5
Arampampa 829 .... B5
Arani 2,200 .... C5
Arcopongo‡ 2,223 .... B5
Aroma‡ 873 .... B6
Arque 1,254 .... B5
Arroyo Grande A2
Ascención (Añez) D4
Asunción B2
Asunta 45 .... B5
Atén 199 .... A4
Atocha‡ 3,964 .... B7
Ayacucho 729 .... D5
Ayata 479 .... A4
Azurduy 1,234 .... C6
Barrera B3
Baures 592 .... D3
Bella Flor A2
Bella Vista E3
Berenguela‡ 2,412 .... A5
Betanzos 1,097 .... C6
Bolívar B3
Bolpebra A2
Boyuibe 537 .... D7
Buena Vista, Santa Cruz D5
Cabezas 298 .... D6
Cachuela Esperanza 1,073 .... C2
Caiza 838 .... C7
Cajuata 447 .... B5
Calacoto 415 .... A5
Calamarca 802 .... A5
Callapa 636 .... A5
Camacho‡ 875 .... C7
Camargo 1,609 .... C7
Camatindi‡ 297 .... D7
Camiri 4,969 .... D7
Candelaria‡ 468 .... F5
Canquella 148 .... A7
Capinota 1,734 .... B5
Capirenda D7
Caquiaviri 760 .... A5
Carabuco 626 .... A4
Caracollo 909 .... B5
Caranavi‡ 525 .... B4
Carandaiti 1,403 .... D7
Caraparí 351 .... D7
Carmen‡ 845 .... B2
Cataricahua 3,240 .... B6
Cavari 249 .... B5
Cavinas‡ 1,011 .... B3
Chachacomani 159 .... A6
Chacoma‡ 330 .... A6
Chaguaya 643 .... C7
Challacollo 284 .... B6
Challana‡ 1,206 .... A4
Challapata 2,529 .... B6
Chapacura‡ 152 .... A2
Chaquí 291 .... C6
Charagua 1,185 .... D6
Charaña 794 .... A5
Chayanta 1,272 .... B6
Chiguana 154 .... A7
Chiñijo 27 .... A4
Chive‡ 336 .... A3
Chocaya 444 .... B7
Choquecota‡ 1,976 .... A6
Chulumani 2,362 .... B5
Chuma 931 .... A4
Chuquichambi‡ 1,094 .... B5
Chuquichuqui‡ 1,892 .... C6
Cliza 3,121 .... C5
Cobija 3,650 .... A2
Cocani‡ 658 .... B7
Cocapata‡ 2,855 .... B5

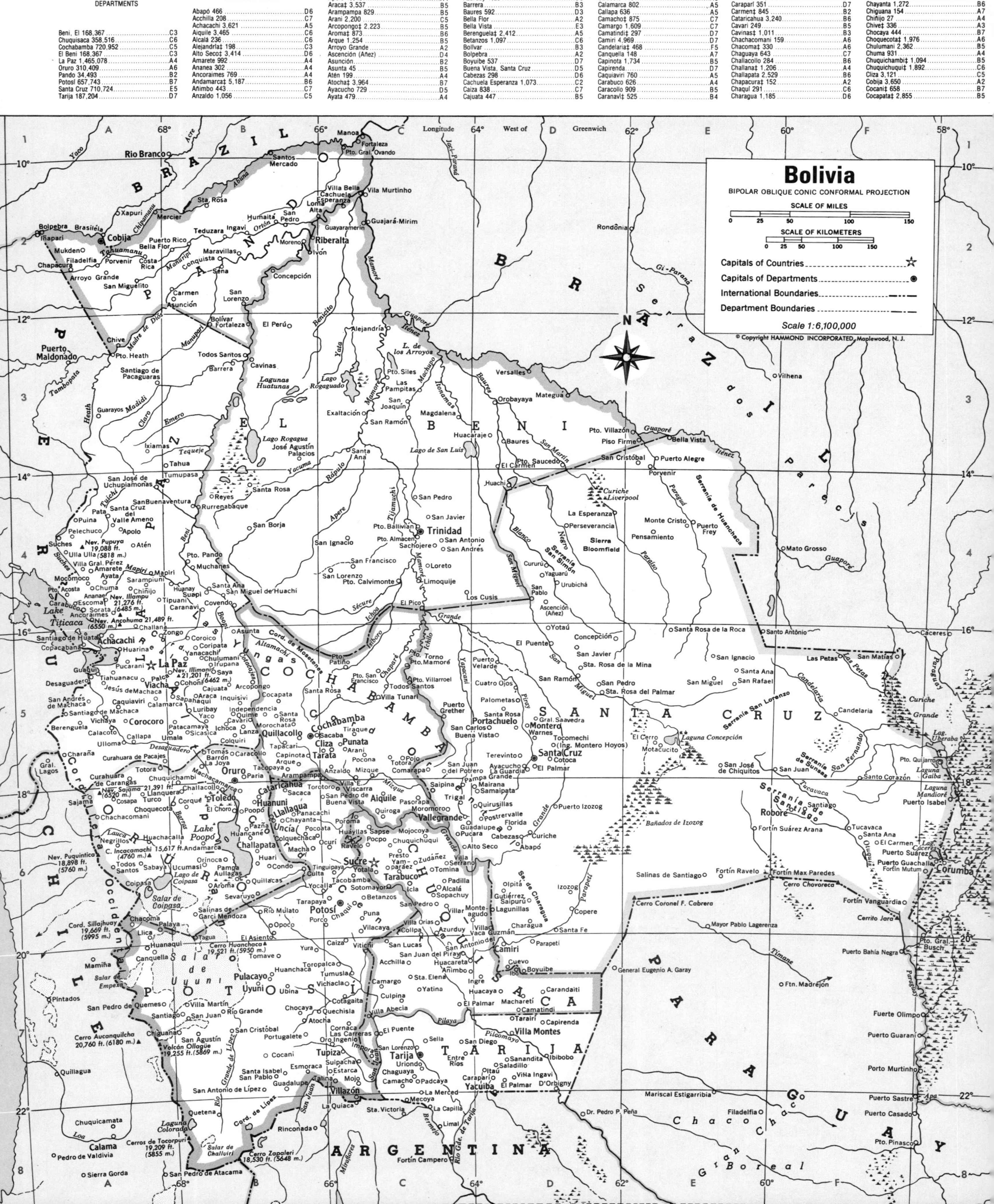

AREA 424,163 sq. mi. (1,098,582 sq. km.)
POPULATION 5,600,000
CAPITALS La Paz, Sucre
LARGEST CITY La Paz
HIGHEST POINT Nevada Ancohuma 21,489 ft. (6,550 m.)
MONETARY UNIT Bolivian peso
MAJOR LANGUAGES Spanish, Quechua, Aymara
MAJOR RELIGION Roman Catholicism

Cochabamba 204,684 C5
Cohoni 890 B5
Coipasa‡ 202 A6
Collpa 481 C6
Colquechaca 1,070 B6
Colquiri 806 B5
Comarapa 1,096 C5
Concepción, El Beni‡ 61 B2
Concepción, Santa Cruz 1,056 D5
Condo‡ 5,525 B6
Conquista‡ 1,162 B2
Copacabana 1,981 A5
Copere D6
Coripata 1,647 B5
Cornaca 264 C7
Corocoro 4,431 A5
Coroico 2,235 B5
Corque 423 B6
Cosapa 297 A6
Costa Rica‡ 43 A2
Cotagaita 1,353 C7
Cotoca 915 D5
Covendo 71 B4
Cuatro Ojos‡ 465 D5
Cuevo 902 D7
Culpina 981 C7
Culta‡ 4,412 B6
Curahuara de Carangas 235 A5
Curahuara de Pacajes 510 A5
Curiche 257 D6
Cururú D4
Desaguadero 201 A5
D'Orbigny‡ 214 D7
El Asiento B6
El Carmen, El Beni 232 D3
El Carmen, Santa Cruz F6
El Cerro 117 E5
El Choro 224 B6
El Palmar, Chuquisaca‡ 772 D7
El Palmar, Santa Cruz 437 D5
El Palmar, Tarija 832 D7
El Perú B3
El Pico C4
El Puente, Santa Cruz‡ 1,185 D5
El Puente, Tarija‡ 1,310 C7
Entre Ríos 1,011 C7
Escoma 220 A4
Esmoraca‡ 1,137 B7
Estarca‡ 2,331 C7
Exaltación, El Beni 405 C3
Filadelfia‡ 942 A2
Florida, Santa Cruz 128 D6
Fortaleza‡ 765 B3
Fortaleza C1
Fortín Campero‡ 87 C8
Fortín Max Paredes F6
Fortín Mutum F6
Fortín Ravelo E6
Fortín Suárez Arana F6
Fortín Vanguardia F6
General Saavedra 1,006 D5
Guadalupe, Potosí 71 B7
Guadalupe, Santa Cruz 2,355 C6
Guaqui 2,266 A5
Guayaramerín 1,470 C2
Huacaraje 673 D3
Huacareta 239 C7
Huacaya 229 D7
Huachacalla 801 A6
Huachi D4
Huanaqui 359 A7
Huanay 574 B4
Huancané 148 B6
Huanchaca B7
Huanuni 5,696 B6
Huari 1,070 B6
Huarina 1,151 A5
Huayllas 206 C6
Humaitá‡ 429 B2
Ibibobo D7
Ibo D7
Ichoca 591 B5
Icla 196 C6
Impora 274 C7
Independencia 1,742 B5
Ingavi‡ 111 B2
Ingeniero Montero Hoyos (Tocomechi) 575 D5
Ingre 162 D7
Inquisivi 530 B5
Irupana 1,937 B5
Itaú 102 D7
Ivón‡ 772 C2
Ixiamas 292 A3
Izozog‡ 2,759 D6
Jesús de Machaca 529 A5
José Agustín Palacios‡ 2,273 B3
La Capilla‡ 1,870 C8
La Esmeralda D8
La Esperanza D4
La Guardia 470 D5
Lagunillas 840 D6
La Joya 401 B5
La Merced‡ 688 C8
Lanza 526 B5
La Paz (cap.) 635,283 B5
Las Carreras 155 C7
Las Pampitas‡ 71 C3
Las Petas‡ 383 F5
Limal‡ 524 C8
Limoquije C4
Llallagua 6,719 B6
Llanquera 613 A6
Llica 560 A6
Loma Alta B2
Loreto 589 C4
Los Cusis D4
Luribay 392 B5
Macha 1,050 B6
Machacamarca 1,746 B5
Machareti‡ 1,164 D7
Magdalena 1,724 C3
Mairana 508 D6
Manoa C1
Mapiri 289 B4
Maravillas B2
Mateguá 38 D3
Mecoya‡ 585 C8
Mercier‡ 272 B2
Mizque 870 C5
Mocomoco 977 A4
Mojo 469 C7
Mojocoya 498 C6
Monteagudo 971 D6
Monte Cristo E4
Montero 2,713 D5
Moreno B2
Morochata 461 B5
Moromoro 556 C6
Motacucito‡ 585 E5
Muchanes B4
Mukden‡ 84 A2
Negrillos 85 A6
Ocurí 1,531 C6
Opoco B6
Orinoca‡ 2,380 B6
Orobayaya‡ 1,132 D3
Oro Ingenio‡ 945 C7
Oruro 124,213 B5
Padcaya 324 C7
Padilla 2,462 C6
Palaya 300 A6
Palca 887 A5
Palometas‡ 3,453 D5
Pampa Aullagas‡ 1,834 B6
Pampa Grande 727 D5
Panacachi 952 B6
Paria 335 B5
Pasorapa 1,016 C6
Pata 122 A4
Patacamaya 1,278 B5
Pazña 671 B6
Pelechuco 873 A4
Pensamiento E4
Perseverancia D4
Piso Firme D3
Pocoata 859 B6
Pocona 518 C5
Pocpo‡ 2,791 C6
Pojo 1,047 C5
Poopó 736 B6
Porco 817 B6
Poroma 171 C6
Portachuelo 2,456 D5
Portugalete‡ 1,590 B7
Porvenir, Pando‡ 846 A2
Porvenir, Santa Cruz E4
Postrervalle 750 D6
Potosí 77,397 C6
Presto 725 C6
Pucara 762 C6
Pucarani 1,041 A5
Puerto Acosta 1,302 A4
Puerto Alegre E3
Puerto Almacen 358 C4
Puerto Ballivián C4
Puerto Calvimonte C4
Puerto Frey E4
Puerto General Ovando 50
Puerto Grether C5
Puerto Guachalla F6
Puerto Heath‡ 570 A3
Puerto Isabel F6
Puerto Izozog D6
Puerto Mamoré C5
Puerto Pando B4
Puerto Patiño C5
Puerto Quijarro G5
Puerto Rico‡ 539 B2
Puerto San Francisco C5
Puerto Saucedo D3
Puerto Siles 357 C3
Puerto Suárez 1,159 F6
Puerto Torno C5
Puerto Velarde D5
Puerto Villarroel C5
Puerto Villazón D3
Puina A4
Pulacayo 7,984 B7
Puna 852 C6
Punata 5,014 C5
Quechisla 171 C7
Queteña 183 B8
Quillacas 1,170 B6
Quillacollo 9,123 B5
Quime 1,256 B5
Quiroga‡ 3,467 C6
Quirusillas 433 D6
Ravelo 907 C6
Reyes 1,404 B4
Riberalta 6,549 C2
Río Grande 281 B7
Río Mulato 381 B6
Roboré 3,715 F6
Rurrenabaque 1,225 B4
Sabaya 649 A6
Sacaba 2,752 C5
Sacaca 1,778 B6
Sachojere 401 C4
Saipina 573 C6
Sajama 231 A6
Saladillo‡ 1,315 D7
Salinas de Garci Mendoza 335 B6
Salinas de Santiago E6
Samaipata 1,656 D6
San Agustín‡ 810 B7
Sanandita 379 D7
San Andrés 399 C4
San Andrés de Machaca 101 A5
San Antonio, El Beni 436 C4
San Antonio de Lípez‡ 177 B7
San Antonio del Parapetí 497 D7
San Borja 708 B4
San Buenaventura 307 A4
San Carlos 570 D5
San Cristóbal, Potosí‡ 1,200 B7
San Cristóbal, Santa Cruz E3
San Diego‡ 773 D7
San Francisco, El Beni 185 C4
San Ignacio, El Beni 1,757 C4
San Ignacio, Santa Cruz 1,819 E5
San Javier, El Beni 233 C4
San Javier, Santa Cruz 564 D5
San Joaquín 1,959 C3
San José de Chiquitos 1,933 E5
San José de Uchupiamonas 277 A4
San Juan, Potosí 131 B7
San Juan, Santa Cruz‡ 1,482 F5
San Juan del Piray 541 C7
San Juan del Potrero 263 C5
San Lorenzo, El Beni 496 C4
San Lorenzo, Pando‡ 317 B2
San Lorenzo, Tarija 785 C7
San Lucas 925 C7
San Matías 887 F5
San Miguel 502 E5
San Miguel de Huachi 25 B4
San Miguelito A2
San Pablo, Potosí 11 B7
San Pablo, Santa Cruz D4
San Pedro, Chuquisaca 182 C6
San Pedro, El Beni 262 C4
San Pedro, Pando‡ 312 B2
San Pedro, Santa Cruz 80 D5
San Pedro de Buena Vista 1,094 C6
San Pedro de Quemes‡ 290 A7
San Rafael‡ 1,282 E5
San Ramón, El Beni 1,161 C3
San Ramón, Santa Cruz 379 D5
Santa Ana, El Beni 2,225 C3
Santa Ana, La Paz 171 B4
Santa Ana, Santa Cruz 275 E5
Santa Ana, Santa Cruz 663 F6
Santa Cruz, Santa Cruz 254,682 D5
Santa Cruz del Valle Ameno 442 A4
Santa Elena‡ 4,474 C7
Santa Fe D6
Santa Isabel‡ 323 B7
Santa Rosa, Cochabamba‡ 942 B5
Santa Rosa, Cochabamba‡ 276 C5
Santa Rosa, El Beni 765 B4
Santa Rosa, Pando‡ 105 B2
Santa Rosa, Santa Cruz 995 D5
Santa Rosa de la Mina 99 D5
Santa Rosa de la Roca 101 E5
Santa Rosa del Palmar 441 E5
Santiago, Potosí 172 A7
Santiago, Santa Cruz 765 F6
Santiago de Huata 948 A5
Santiago de Machaca 218 A5
Santiago de Pacaguaras A3
Santo Corazón‡ 963 F5
Santos Mercado B1
Sapahaqui 55 B5
Sapse‡ 89 C6
Sarampiuni 138 A4
Saya 339 B5
Sella C7
Sena‡ 660 B2
Sevaruyo 475 B6
Sicasica 1,486 B5
Sopachuy 713 C6
Sorata 2,087 A4
Sotomayor 510 C6
Suapi‡ 1,750 B4
Suches‡ 231 A4
Sucre (cap.) 63,625 C6
Suipacha‡ 2,701 C7
Tacobamba‡ 6,933 C6
Tacopaya 795 B5
Tagua B6
Tahua B3
Talina 122 B7
Tapacarí 980 B5
Tarabuco 2,833 C6
Tarairí‡ 394 D7
Tarapaya 357 B6
Tarata 3,016 C5
Tarija 38,916 C7
Teduzara‡ 271 B2
Terevinto‡ 3,790 D5
Tiahuanacu 1,227 A5
Tinguipaya 766 C6
Tipuani‡ 1,216 B4
Tiraque 1,390 C5
Tocomechi 575 D5
Todos Santos, Cochabamba 408 C5
Todos Santos, La Paz B3
Todos Santos, Oruro 68 A6
Toledo 3,273 B6
Tomás Barrón 1,852 B5
Tomave 201 B7
Tomina 708 C6
Toropalca‡ 199 B7
Torotoro 1,233 C6
Totora, Cochabamba C5
Totora, Oruro A5
Trigal 749 C6
Trinidad, El Beni 27,487 C4
Trinidad, Pando‡ 332 B2
Tucavaca F6
Tumupasa 349 B4
Tumusla‡ 526 C7
Tupiza 8,248 C7
Turco 131 A6
Ubina‡ 462 B7
Ucumasi‡ 1,040 B6
Ulla Ulla 52 A4
Ulloma 116 A5
Umala 481 B5
Uncía 4,507 B6
Uriondo 860 C7
Urubichá 1,369 D4
Uyuni 6,968 B7
Vallegrande 5,094 C6
Versalles 83 D3
Viacha 6,607 A5
Vichacla 317 C7
Vichaya 422 A5
Vilacaya 200 C6
Villa Abecia 539 C7
Villa Bella 88 C2
Villa E. Viscarra 658 C6
Villa General Pérez 802 A4
Villa Ingavi 122 D7
Villa Martín 543 B7
Villa Montes 3,105 D7
Villa Orías 404 C6
Villar 322 C6
Villa Serrano 1,570 C6
Villa Tunari 510 C5
Villa Vaca Guzmán 699 D6
Villazón 6,261 C7
Vitichi 1,515 C7
Warnes 1,571 D5
Yaco 835 B5
Yacuiba 5,027 D7
Yaguarú D4
Yamparaéz 725 C6
Yanacachi‡ 1,964 B5
Yatina‡ 1,850 C7
Yocalla‡ 1,814 B6
Yotala 1,554 C6
Yotaú D5
Yura 136 B7
Zongo 141 B5
Zudáñez 1,868 C6

OTHER FEATURES

Abuná (riv.) B2
Altamachi (riv.) B5
Ancohuma, Nevada (mt.) A4
Apere (riv.) C4
Arroyas, Los (lake) C3
Barras (riv.) B6
Baures (riv.) D3
Beni (riv.) B2
Benicito (riv.) C3
Bermejo (riv.) C8
Blanco (riv.) D4
Bloomfield, Sierra (mts.) D4
Boopi (riv.) B4
Cáceres (lag.) G6
Candelaria (riv.) F5
Capitán Ustarés, Cerro (mt.) E6
Central, Cordillera (range) C6
Challviri (salt dep.) B8
Chaparé (riv.) C5
Charagua, Sierra de (mts.) D6
Chipamanu (riv.) A2
Chovoreca, Cerro (mt.) F6
Claro (riv.) A3
Coipasa (lake) B6
Coipasa (salt dep.) A6
Colorada (lag.) A8
Concepción (lag.) E5
Coronel F. Gabrera E6
Cotacajes (riv.) B5
Desaguadero (riv.) B5
Emero (riv.) B3
Empexa (salt dep.) A7
Gaiba (lag.) F5
Grande (marsh) F5
Grande (riv.) C4
Grande (riv.) C6
Grande de Lípez (riv.) B7
Guaporé (riv.) C3
Heath (riv.) A3
Huanchaca, Cerro (mt.) B7
Huanchaca, Serranía de (mts.) E4
Huatunas (lag.) B3
Ichilo (riv.) C5
Ichoa (riv.) C4
Illampu, Nevada (mt.) A4
Illimani, Nevada (mt.) B5
Incacamachi, Cerro (mt.) A6
Isiboro (riv.) C5
Iténez (Guaporé) (riv.) C3
Itonamas (riv.) C3
Izozog (swamp) E6
Jara, Cerrito (mt.) F6
Las Yungas (reg.) B5
Lauca (riv.) A6
Lípez, Cordillera de (range) B8
Liverpool (swamp) D4
Machupo (riv.) C3
Madidi (riv.) A3
Madre de Diós (riv.) A3
Mamoré (riv.) C2
Mandioré (lag.) F6
Manuripi (riv.) B2
Mizque (riv.) C6
Mosetenes, Cordillera de (range) B5
Negro (riv.) D4
Occidental, Cordillera (range) A6
Ollagüe (vol.) B7
Oriental, Cordillera (range) C5
Ortón (riv.) B2
Otuquis (riv.) F6
Paraguá (riv.) E4
Paraguay (riv.) F7
Parapetí (riv.) D6
Petas, Las (riv.) F5
Pilaya (riv.) C7
Pilcomayo (riv.) D7
Piray (riv.) D5
Poopó (lake) B6
Pupuya, Nevada (mt.) A4
Puquintica, Nevado (mt.) A6
Rápulo (riv.) C4
Real, Cordillera (range) A5
Rogagua (lake) B3
Rogaguado (lake) C3
Sajama, Nevada (mt.) A6
San Fernando (riv.) F5
San Juan (riv.) C7
San Lorenzo, Serranía (mts.) E5
San Luis (lake) C3
San Martín (riv.) D3
San Miguel (riv.) D4
San Simón, Serranía (mts.) D4
Santiago, Serranía de (mts.) F6
Sécure (riv.) C4
Sillajhuay, Cordillera (mt.) A6
Suches (riv.) A4
Sunsas, Serranía de (mts.) F5
Tahuamanu (riv.) A2
Tarija, Rio Grande de (riv.) C8
Tequeje (riv.) B3
Tijamuchi (riv.) C4
Titicaca (lake) A4
Tocorpuri, Cerros de (mt.) A8
Tucavaca (riv.) F6
Tuichi (riv.) A4
Uberaba (lag.) G5
Uyuni (salt dep.) B7
Yacuma (riv.) B3
Yapacaní (riv.) C5
Yata (riv.) C3
Yungas, Las (reg.) B5
Zapaleri, Cerro (mt.) B8

‡Population of canton.

Topography

0 100 200 MI.
0 100 200 KM.

Below Sea Level | 100 m. 328 ft. | 200 m. 656 ft. | 500 m. 1,640 ft. | 1,000 m. 3,281 ft. | 2,000 m. 6,562 ft. | 5,000 m. 16,404 ft.

Agriculture, Industry and Resources

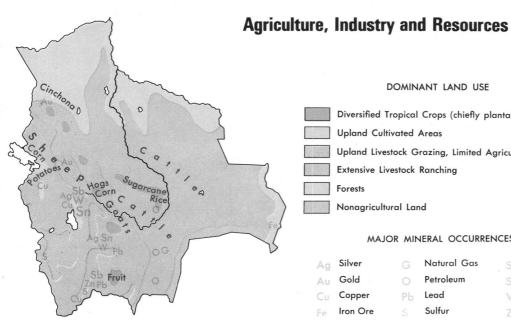

DOMINANT LAND USE

- Diversified Tropical Crops (chiefly plantation agriculture)
- Upland Cultivated Areas
- Upland Livestock Grazing, Limited Agriculture
- Extensive Livestock Ranching
- Forests
- Nonagricultural Land

MAJOR MINERAL OCCURRENCES

- Ag Silver
- Au Gold
- Cu Copper
- Fe Iron Ore
- G Natural Gas
- O Petroleum
- Pb Lead
- S Sulfur
- Sb Antimony
- Sn Tin
- W Tungsten
- Zn Zinc

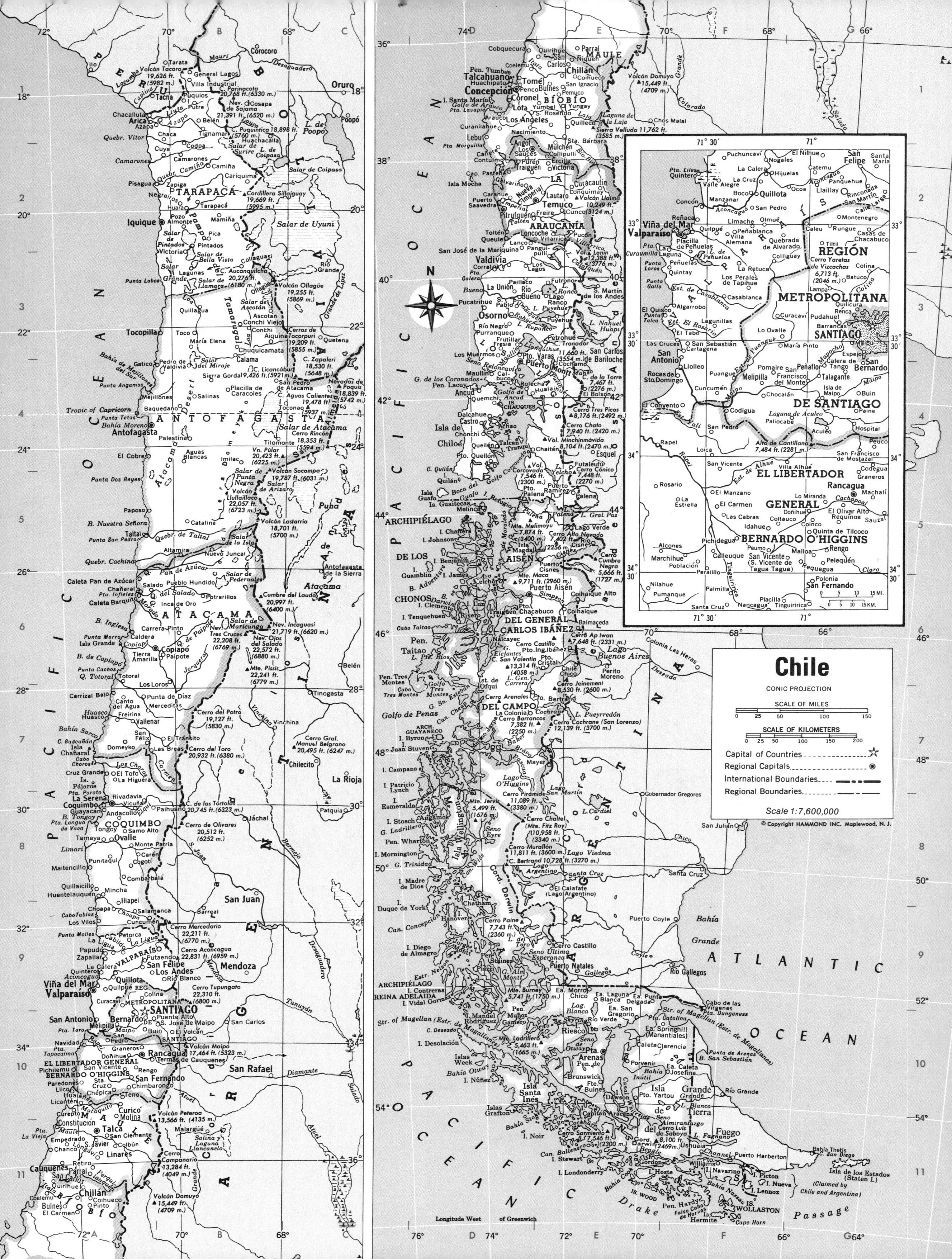
Chile
CONIC PROJECTION
SCALE OF MILES
0 25 50 100 150
SCALE OF KILOMETERS
0 25 50 100 150 200
Capital of Countries
Regional Capitals
International Boundaries
Regional Boundaries
Scale 1:7,600,000
© Copyright HAMMOND INC. Maplewood, N. J.
Longitude West of Greenwich
PACIFIC OCEAN
ATLANTIC OCEAN
ARGENTINA
PERU
BOLIVIA
TARAPACÁ
ANTOFAGASTA
ATACAMA
COQUIMBO
VALPARAÍSO
METROPOLITANA
SANTIAGO
EL LIBERTADOR GENERAL BERNARDO O'HIGGINS
MAULE
BÍOBÍO
LA ARAUCANÍA
LOS LAGOS
AISÉN DEL GENERAL CARLOS IBÁÑEZ DEL CAMPO
MAGALLANES
REGIÓN METROPOLITANA DE SANTIAGO
VALPARAÍSO
EL LIBERTADOR GENERAL BERNARDO O'HIGGINS
Viña del Mar
Valparaíso
San Antonio
Rancagua
San Fernando
Arica
Iquique
Tocopilla
Antofagasta
Copiapó
La Serena
Coquimbo
Talca
Chillán
Concepción
Temuco
Valdivia
Osorno
Puerto Montt
Puerto Aisén
Punta Arenas
Tropic of Capricorn
Drake Passage
Str. of Magellan (Estr. de Magallanes)
Cape Horn
Tierra del Fuego
Isla Grande de Tierra del Fuego
Chiloé
Mendoza
San Juan
San Rafael
Río Gallegos
Salar de Atacama
Salar de Uyuni
Atacama Desert
Volcán Ojos del Salado 22,572 ft. (6880 m.)
Cerro Aconcagua 22,831 ft. (6959 m.)
Isla de los Estados (Staten I.)
(Claimed by Chile and Argentina)

AREA 292,257 sq. mi. (756,946 sq. km.)
POPULATION 11,275,440
CAPITAL Santiago
LARGEST CITY Santiago
HIGHEST POINT Ojos del Salado 22,572 ft. (6,880 m.)
MONETARY UNIT Chilean escudo
MAJOR LANGUAGE Spanish
MAJOR RELIGION Roman Catholicism

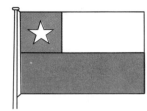

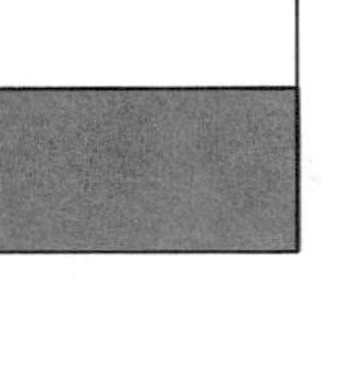

REGIONS

Aisén del General Carlos Ibáñez del Campo 65,478 . . . . . E6
Antofagasta 341,203 . . . . . B4
Atacama 183,071 . . . . . B6
Bíobío 1,516,552 . . . . . E1
Coquimbo 419,178 . . . . . A8
El Libertador General Bernardo O'Higgins 584,989 . . . . . A10
La Araucanía 692,924 . . . . . E2
Los Lagos 843,430 . . . . . D3
Magallanes 132,333 . . . . . E10
Maule 723,224 . . . . . A11
Santiago, Región Metropolitana de (Santiago Metropolitan Region) 4,294,938 . . . . . A9
Tarapacá 273,427 . . . . . B2
Valparaíso 1,204,693 . . . . . A9

CITIES and TOWNS

Achao ○11,501 . . . . . D4
Aguas Blancas ○203 . . . . . B4
Algarrobo ○3,941 . . . . . F3
Ancud 11,900 . . . . . D4
Andacollo 6,000 . . . . . A8
Angol 42,670 . . . . . D1
Antofagasta 125,100 . . . . . A4
Arauco 5,400 . . . . . D1
Arica 87,700 . . . . . A1
Ascotán B3
Barrancas ○184,241 . . . . . G3
Belén ○925 . . . . . B1
Buin 11,800 . . . . . G4
Bulnes 6,900 . . . . . E1
Cabildo 5,800 . . . . . A9
Calama 45,900 . . . . . B3
Calbuco ○21,673 . . . . . D4
Caldera ○3,268 . . . . . A6
Calera de Tango ○6,198 . . . G4
Calle Larga ○7,172 . . . . . G2
Cañete 7,900 . . . . . D2
Carahue ○12,733 . . . . . D2
Cartagena ○7,124 . . . . . F3
Casablanca 5,500 . . . . . F3
Casas de Chacabuco G2
Castro 11,200 . . . . . D4
Catalina ○1,637 . . . . . B5
Catemu ○8,728 . . . . . G2
Cauquenes 20,200 . . . . . A11
Cerro Castillo ○537 . . . . . E9
Cerro Manantiales F10
Chaitén ○4,067 . . . . . E4
Chañaral ○36,949 . . . . . A6
Chanco ○12,433 . . . . . A11
Chépica ○11,199 . . . . . A10
Chillán 128,515 . . . . . A11
Chimbarongo 5,300 . . . . . A10
Chonchi ○8,911 . . . . . D4
Chuquicamata 22,100 . . . . . B3
Cobquecura ○6,298 . . . . . D1
Cochamó ○5,042 . . . . . E3
Codegua ○6,757 . . . . . G4
Codpa ○950 . . . . . B1
Coelemu 5,400 . . . . . D1
Coihaique 32,129 . . . . . E6
Coihueco ○17,276 . . . . . A11
Coinco ○4,942 . . . . . G5
Colbún ○12,924 . . . . . A11
Colina 7,400 . . . . . G3
Collipulli 7,200 . . . . . E2
Coltauco ○11,857 . . . . . F5
Combarbalá ○17,332 . . . . . A8
Concepción 206,226 . . . . . D1
Constitución 11,500 . . . . . A11
Contulmo ○13,987 . . . . . D2
Copiapó 45,200 . . . . . B6
Coquimbo 73,953 . . . . . A8
Coronel 37,300 . . . . . D1
Corral ○5,533 . . . . . D3
Cunco ○18,836 . . . . . E2
Curacautín 9,800 . . . . . E2
Curacaví 5,800 . . . . . G3
Curanilahue 13,200 . . . . . D1
Curepto ○13,020 . . . . . A10
Curicó 41,300 . . . . . A10
Dalcahue ○7,084 . . . . . D4
Domeiko A7
Doñihue ○8,837 . . . . . G5
El Carmen ○13,226 . . . . . A11
El Monte 7,000 . . . . . G4
El Quisco ○2,152 . . . . . E3
El Tabo ○2,180 . . . . . F3
El Tofo A7
Empedrado ○7,887 . . . . . A11
Ercilla ○8,061 . . . . . E2
Estancia Caleta Josefina ○1,042 . . . . . F10
Estancia Morro Chico ○785 . E9
Estancia San Gregorio ○1,156 . . . . . E9
Estancia Springhill (Cerro Manantiales) F10
Freire ○23,313 . . . . . E2
Freirina ○5,523 . . . . . A7
Fresia ○15,359 . . . . . D3
Frutillar ○12,721 . . . . . D3
Futaleufú ○2,366 . . . . . E4
Futrono ○7,109 . . . . . E3
Galvarino ○9,495 . . . . . D2
General Lagos ○810 . . . . . B1
Graneros 8,900 . . . . . G5
Guayacán A8
Hijuelas ○7,128 . . . . . F2
Hualañé ○6,912 . . . . . A10
Huara ○1,934 . . . . . B2
Huasco ○4,971 . . . . . A7
Illapel 12,200 . . . . . A8
Inca de Oro 1,406 . . . . . B6
Iquique 64,500 . . . . . A2
Isla de Maipo ○12,903 . . . . G4
La Calera 24,600 . . . . . F2
La Cruz ○8,907 . . . . . F2
La Estrella ○3,707 . . . . . F5
Lago Ranco ○12,767 . . . . . E3
Lagunas ○5,653 . . . . . B3
La Higuera ○6,991 . . . . . A7
La Ligua 7,500 . . . . . A9
Lampa ○10,220 . . . . . G3
Lanco 5,200 . . . . . D2
Las Cabras ○12,119 . . . . . F5
La Serena 99,908 . . . . . A8
La Unión 15,200 . . . . . D3
Lautaro 11,900 . . . . . E2
Lebu 12,500 . . . . . D1
Licantén ○6,354 . . . . . A10
Limache 15,200 . . . . . F2
Linares 37,900 . . . . . A11
Llay-Llay 9,700 . . . . . G2
Loica F4
Loncoche ○17,539 . . . . . D2
Longaví ○15,909 . . . . . A11
Lonquimay ○9,524 . . . . . E2
Los Andes 23,500 . . . . . B9
Los Ángeles 49,500 . . . . . D1
Los Lagos ○14,934 . . . . . D3
Los Muermos ○9,296 . . . . . D3
Los Sauces ○7,613 . . . . . D2
Los Vilos ○10,453 . . . . . A9
Lota 48,100 . . . . . D1
Machall 5,800 . . . . . G5
Maipú ○117,872 . . . . . G3
Malloa ○9,742 . . . . . G5
Marchigüe ○4,451 . . . . . F5
Marla Elena 5,900 . . . . . B3
Marla Pinto ○5,980 . . . . . G3
Maulln ○14,544 . . . . . D4
Mejillones ○3,333 . . . . . A4
Melipilla 23,900 . . . . . F4
Mincha ○11,329 . . . . . A8
Molina 9,400 . . . . . A10
Monte Patria ○18,927 . . . . . A8
Mulchén 13,700 . . . . . E1
Nacimiento ○17,651 . . . . . D1
Nancagua ○11,076 . . . . . F6
Navidad ○6,618 . . . . . A10
Negreiros ○1,144 . . . . . B2
Ñiquén ○13,640 . . . . . E1
Nogales ○18,529 . . . . . F2
Nueva Imperial 8,000 . . . . . D2
Olivar Alto ○5,414 . . . . . G5
Ollagüe B3
Olmué ○8,804 . . . . . F2
Osorno 68,800 . . . . . D3
Ovalle 31,700 . . . . . A8
Paihuano ○6,048 . . . . . B8
Paillaco 5,200 . . . . . D3
Paine ○21,876 . . . . . G4
Palena ○2,508 . . . . . E5
Palmilla ○7,965 . . . . . F6
Panguipulli 5,700 . . . . . E2
Panquehue ○4,230 . . . . . G2
Papudo ○2,594 . . . . . A9
Paredones ○7,404 . . . . . A10
Parral 17,000 . . . . . A11
Pedro de Valdivia 6,200 . . . . B4
Pemuco ○7,577 . . . . . E1
Peñaflor 15,500 . . . . . G4
Penco ○33,962 . . . . . D1
Peñuelas F3
Petorca ○8,343 . . . . . A9
Petrohué E3
Peumo ○11,308 . . . . . F5
Pica ○1,487 . . . . . B2
Pichidegua ○13,550 . . . . . F5
Pichilemu ○8,042 . . . . . A10
Pinto ○8,687 . . . . . A11
Pisagua ○1,880 . . . . . A2
Pitrufquén 7,800 . . . . . D2
Placilla ○6,441 . . . . . F6
Porvenir ○4,000 . . . . . E10
Potrerillos 5,800 . . . . . B6
Pozo Almonte ○1,798 . . . . . B2
Puchuncaví ○7,542 . . . . . F2
Pucón 18,000 . . . . . E2
Pudahuel G3
Pueblo Hundido 6,200 . . . . . B6
Puente Alto 65,100 . . . . . B10
Puerto Aisén 17,848 . . . . . E6
Puerto Cisnes ○2,800 . . . . . E5

Puerto Ingeniero Ibáñez ○1,900 . . . . . E6
Puerto Montt 119,059 . . . . . E4
Puerto Natales 17,280 . . . . . E9
Puerto Quellón ○7,734 . . . . D4
Puerto Varas 10,900 . . . . . E3
Puerto Williams ○949 . . . . F11
Pumanque ○3,137 . . . . . F6
Punitaqui ○16,167 . . . . . A8
Punta Arenas 2,140 . . . . . E10
Purén ○11,604 . . . . . D2
Purranque 5,900 . . . . . D3
Putaendo ○12,806 . . . . . A9
Putre ○855 . . . . . B1
Puyehue E3
Queilén ○6,055 . . . . . D4
Quemchi ○6,707 . . . . . D4
Quilicura 8,100 . . . . . G3
Quillagua B3
Quilleco ○16,043 . . . . . E1
Quillota 36,500 . . . . . F2
Quilpué 40,600 . . . . . F2
Quinta de Tilcoco ○6,513 . . G5
Quintero 9,900 . . . . . F2
Quirihue ○11,178 . . . . . E1
Rancagua 140,589 . . . . . G5
Renca ○67,168 . . . . . G3
Rengo 12,400 . . . . . G5
Requlnoa ○10,730 . . . . . G5
Retiro ○15,146 . . . . . A11
Rinconada San Martín ○4,118 . . . . . G2
Río Blanco B9
Río Bueno 9,600 . . . . . D3
Río Negro 5,100 . . . . . D3
Río Verde ○554 . . . . . E10
Rocas de Santo Domingo ○4,114 . . . . . F4
Rosario ○3,383 . . . . . F5
Salamanca ○18,741 . . . . . A9
Samo Alto ○5,689 . . . . . A8
San Antonio 46,700 . . . . . F3
San Bernardo ○117,766 . . . G4
San Carlos 17,000 . . . . . E1
San Clemente ○23,273 . . . A11
San Felipe 26,100 . . . . . G2
San Fernando 23,600 . . . . . G6
San Francisco de Mostazal ○11,439 . . . . . G4
San Ignacio ○13,523 . . . . . E1
San Javier 10,800 . . . . . A11
San José de Maipo ○9,601 . . . . . B10
San Pablo ○7,978 . . . . . D3
San Pedro ○8,255 . . . . . F4
San Pedro de Atacama C4
San Rosendo ○14,337 . . . . . E1
Santa Bárbara ○14,345 . . . . E1
Santa Cruz 8,600 . . . . . F6
Santa María ○8,162 . . . . . G2
Santiago (cap.) 3,614,947 . . G3
Santiago *3,672,374 . . . . . G3
San Vicente F4
San Vicente (San Vicente de Tagua Tagua) ○28,333 F5
Sierra Gorda ○8,805 . . . . . B4
Talagante 16,500 . . . . . G4
Talca 133,160 . . . . . A11
Talcahuano 148,300 . . . . . D1
Taltal 6,400 . . . . . A5
Tamaya A8
Tarapacá B2
Temuco 197,232 . . . . . E2
Teno ○17,675 . . . . . A10
Termas de Cauquenes B10
Tierra Amarilla ○7,899 . . . . A6
Tiltil ○9,198 . . . . . G2
Toco ○8,734 . . . . . B3
Toconao C4
Tocopilla 22,000 . . . . . A3
Toltén ○16,265 . . . . . D2
Tomé 29,600 . . . . . D1
Traiguén 11,400 . . . . . D2
Valdivia 115,536 . . . . . D3
Vallenar 26,800 . . . . . A7
Valparaíso 271,580 . . . . . E2
Victoria 16,500 . . . . . D2
Vicuña 5,100 . . . . . A8
Villa Alemana 29,600 . . . . . F2
Villa Alhué ○5,078 . . . . . G4
Villarrica 25,091 . . . . . E2
Viña del Mar 281,361 . . . . . F2
Yumbel ○21,858 . . . . . E1
Yungay ○10,725 . . . . . E1
Zapallar ○2,894 . . . . . A9
Zapiga B2

OTHER FEATURES

Aconcagua (riv.) F2
Aculeo (lag.) G4
Adventure (bay) D5
Aguas Calientes, Cerro (mt.) C4
Almirantazgo (bay) F11
Almirante Montt (gulf) D9
Ancud (gulf) D4
Angamos (isl.) D8
Angamos (pt.) A4
Ap Iwan, Cerro (mt.) E6
Arauco (gulf) D1
Arenales, Cerro (mt.) D7
Atacama (des.) B4
Atacama, Salar de (salt dep.) C4
Aucanquilcha, Cerro (mt.) . . B3
Azapa, Quebrada (riv.) B1
Baker (riv.) D7
Ballenero (chan.) E11
Bascuñán (cape) A7
Beagle (chan.) E11
Bella Vista, Salar de (salt dep.) B3
Benjamín (isl.) D5
Bío-Bío (riv.) E2
Blanca (lag.) E10
Blanco (lake) F10
Bravo (riv.) D7
Brunswick (pen.) E10
Bueno (riv.) D3
Buenos Aires (lake) E6
Byron (isl.) D7
Cachapoal (riv.) G5
Cachina, Quebrada (riv.) A5
Cachos (pt.) A6
Calafquén (lake) E3
Camarones (riv.) A2
Camiña, Quebrada (riv.) B2
Campana (isl.) D7
Campanario, Cerro (mt.) . . A10
Capitán Aracena (isl.) E10
Carmen (riv.) B7
Castillo, Cerro (mt.) E6
Catalina (pt.) F10
Chaffers (isl.) D5
Chaltel, Cerro (mt.) E8
Chañaral (isl.) A7
Chatham (isl.) D9
Chauques (isls.) D4
Cheap (chan.) D7
Chiloé (isl.) 119,286 . . . . . D4
Choapa (riv.) A9
Chonos (arch.) D6
Choros (cape) A7
Cisnes (riv.) E5
Clarence (isl.) E10
Clemente (isl.) D6
Cochrane (lake) E7
Cochrane, Cerro (mt.) E7
Cockburn (chan.) E11
Concepción (chan.) D9
Cónico, Cerro (mt.) E4
Contreras (isl.) D9
Cook (bay) E11
Copiapó (bay) A6
Copiapó (riv.) A6
Corcovado (gulf) D4
Corcovado (vol.) D5
Coronados (gulf) D4
Curaumilla (pt.) E2
Darwin (bay) D6
Darwin, Cordillera (mts.) . . . D8
Darwin, Cordillera (mts.) . . E11

(continued on following page)

(continued)

Dawson (isl.) E10
Deseado (cape) D10
Desolación (isl.) D10
Diego de Almagro (isl.) D9
Domeyko, Cordillera (mts.) . B4
Dos Reyes (pt.) A5
Drake (passg.) E11
Dungeness (pt.) F10
Duque de York (isl.) C9
Elefantes (gulf) D6
Elqui (riv.) A8
Esmeralda (isl.) C8
Eyre (bay) D8
Fagnano (lake) F11
Fitz Roy (Chaltel) (mt.) E8
Galera (pt.) D3
General Paz (lake) E5
Gordon (isl.) E11
Grafton (isls.) D10
Grande (isl.) A6
Grande (riv.) F10
Grande, Salar (salt dep.) . . . B3
Grande de Tierra
del Fuego (isl.) E11
Guafo (gulf) D5
Guafo (isl.) D5
Guaitecas (isls.) D5
Guamblin (isl.) D5
Guayaneco (arch.) D7
Hanover (isl.) D9
Hardy (pen.) F11
Hermite (isls.) F11
Horn (cape) F11
Hornos, Falso (cape) F11
Hoste (isl.) F11
Huasco (riv.) A7
Imperial (riv.) D2
Incaguasi, Nevada (mt.) C6
Infieles (pt.) A6
Inglesa (bay) A6
Inútil (bay) E10
James (isl.) D5
Johnson (isl.) D5
Jorge Montt (isl.) D9
Juan Stuven (isl.) D7
Lacuy (pen.) D4
Ladrillero (gulf) C8
Ladrillero (mt.) E10
Laja (riv.) E1
La Laja (lag.) E1
La Ligua (riv.) A9
Lanín (vol.) E2
Lastarria (vol.) B5
Lauca (riv.) B1
Lavapié (pt.) D1
La Vieja (pt.) A11
Lengua de Vaca (pt.) A8
Lennox (isl.) F11
Liles (pt.) F2
Limarí (riv.) A8
Llaima (vol.) E2
Llamara, Salar de (salt dep.) B3
Llanquihue (lake) E3
Llullaillaco (vol.) B5
Lluta (riv.) B1
Loa (riv.) B3
Lobos (pt.) A3
Londonderry (isl.) E11
Loros (pt.) E3
Luz (isl.) D6
Macá (mt.) D5
Madre de Dios (isl.) D8

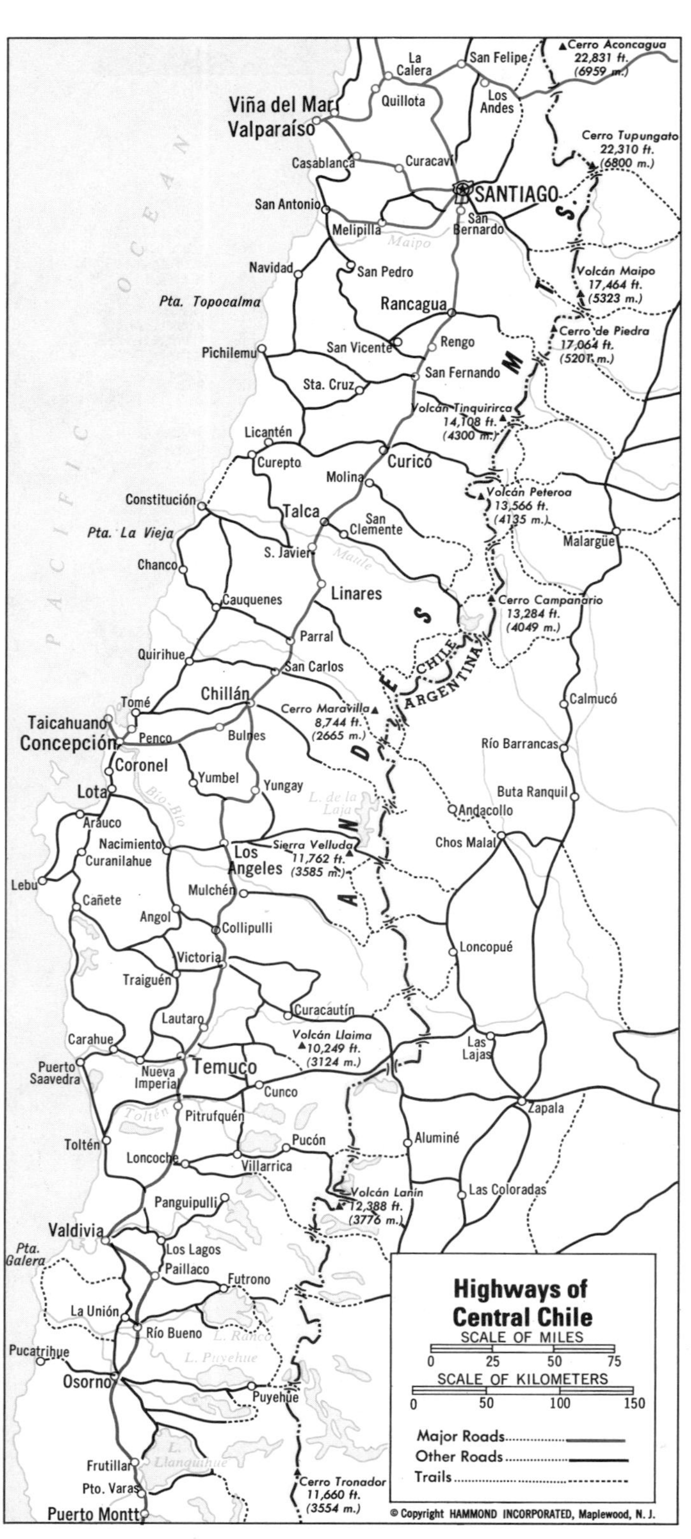

Agriculture, Industry and Resources

DOMINANT LAND USE

- Cereals, Livestock
- Mediterranean Agriculture (cereals, fruit, livestock)
- Pasture Livestock
- Extensive Livestock Ranching
- Limited Seasonal Grazing
- Forests
- Nonagricultural Land

MAJOR MINERAL OCCURRENCES

Ag	Silver	Hg	Mercury
Au	Gold	Id	Iodine
C	Coal	Mn	Manganese
Cu	Copper	Mo	Molybdenum
Fe	Iron Ore	N	Nitrates
G	Natural Gas	Na	Salt
Gp	Gypsum	O	Petroleum
		S	Sulfur

Water Power — Major Industrial Areas

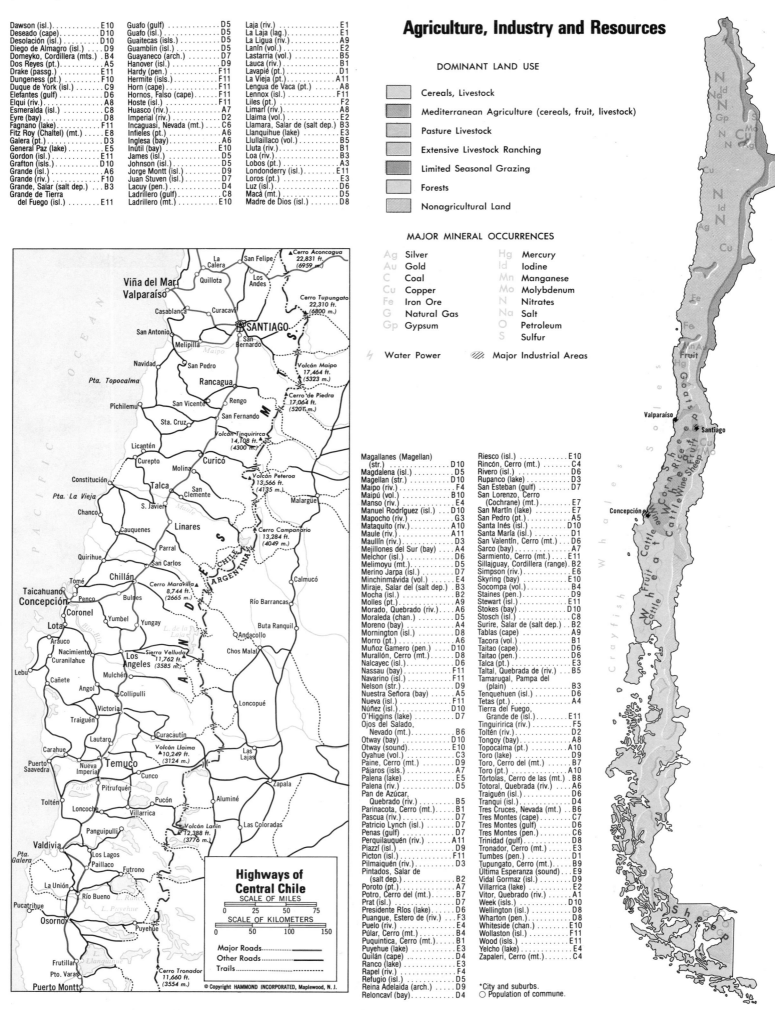

Valparaíso
Santiago
Concepción

Magallanes (Magellan)
(str.) D10
Magdalena (isl.) D5
Magellan (str.) D10
Maipo (riv.) F4
Maipú (vol.) B10
Manso (riv.) E4
Manuel Rodríguez (isl.) . . . D10
Mapocho (riv.) G3
Mataquito (riv.) A10
Maule (riv.) A11
Maullín (riv.) D3
Mejillones del Sur (bay) A4
Melchor (isl.) D6
Melimoyu (mt.) D5
Merino Jarpa (isl.) D7
Minchinmávida (vol.) E4
Miraje, Salar del (salt dep.) . B3
Mocha (isl.) B2
Molles (pt.) A9
Morado, Quebrado (riv.) A6
Moraleda (chan.) D5
Moreno (bay) A4
Mornington (isl.) D8
Morro (pt.) A6
Muñoz Gamero (pen.) D10
Murallón, Cerro (mt.) D8
Nalcayec (isl.) D6
Nassau (bay) F11
Navarino (isl.) F11
Nelson (str.) D9
Nuestra Señora (bay) A5
Nueva (isl.) F11
Núñez (isl.) D10
O'Higgins (lake) D7
Ojos del Salado,
Nevado (mt.) B6
Otway (bay) D10
Otway (sound) E10
Oyahue (vol.) C3
Paine, Cerro (mt.) D9
Pájaros (isls.) A7
Palena (lake) E5
Palena (riv.) D5
Pan de Azúcar,
Quebrado (riv.) B5
Parinacota, Cerro (mt.) B1
Pascua (riv.) D7
Patricio Lynch (isl.) D7
Penas (gulf) D7
Perquilauquén (riv.) A11
Piazzí (isl.) D9
Picton (isl.) F11
Pilmaiquén (riv.) D3
Pintados, Salar de
(salt dep.) B2
Poroto (pt.) A7
Potro, Cerro del (mt.) B7
Prat (isl.) D7
Presidente Ríos (lake) D6
Puangue, Estero de (riv.) . . . F3
Puelo (riv.) E4
Púlar, Cerro (mt.) B4
Puquintica, Cerro (mt.) B1
Puyehue (lake) E3
Quilán (cape) D4
Ranco (lake) E3
Rapel (riv.) F4
Refugio (isl.) D5
Reina Adelaida (arch.) D9
Reloncaví (bay) D4
Riesco (isl.) E10
Rincón, Cerro (mt.) C4
Rivero (isl.) D6
Rupanco (lake) D3
San Esteban (gulf) D7
San Lorenzo, Cerro
(Cochrane) (mt.) E7
San Martín (lake) E7
San Pedro (pt.) A5
Santa Inés (isl.) D10
Santa María (isl.) D1
San Valentín, Cerro (mt.) . . . D6
Sarco (bay) A7
Sarmiento, Cerro (mt.) E11
Sillajguay, Cordillera (range) . B2
Simpson (riv.) E6
Skyring (bay) E10
Socompa (vol.) B4
Staines (pen.) D9
Stewart (isl.) E11
Stokes (bay) D10
Stosch (isl.) C8
Surire, Salar de (salt dep.) . . B2
Tablas (cape) A9
Tacora (vol.) B1
Taitao (cape) D6
Taitao (pen.) D6
Talca (pt.) E3
Taltal, Quebrada de (riv.) . . . B5
Tamarugal, Pampa del
(plain) B3
Tenquehuen (isl.) D6
Tetas (pt.) A4
Tierra del Fuego,
Grande de (isl.) E11
Tinguiririca (riv.) F5
Toltén (riv.) D2
Tongoy (bay) A8
Topocalma (pt.) A10
Toro (lake) D9
Toro, Cerro del (mt.) B7
Toro (pt.) A10
Tórtolas, Cerro de las (mt.) . B8
Totoral, Quebrada (riv.) A6
Traiguén (isl.) D6
Tranqui (isl.) D4
Tres Cruces, Nevada (mt.) . . B6
Tres Montes (cape) C7
Tres Montes (gulf) D6
Tres Montes (pen.) C6
Trinidad (gulf) D8
Tronador, Cerro (mt.) E3
Tumbes (pen.) D1
Tupungato, Cerro (mt.) B9
Última Esperanza (sound) . . . E9
Vidal Gormaz (isl.) D9
Villarrica (lake) E2
Vitor, Quebrado (riv.) A1
Week (isls.) D10
Wellington (isl.) D8
Wharton (pen.) D8
Whiteside (chan.) E10
Wollaston (isl.) F11
Wood (isls.) E11
Yelcho (lake) E4
Zapaleri, Cerro (mt.) C4

*City and suburbs.
○ Population of commune.

PROVINCES

Buenos Aires 10,796,036 . . . D4
Catamarca 206,204 . . . . C2
Chaco 692,410 . . . . D2
Chubut 262,196 . . . . C5
Córdoba 2,407,135 . . . . D3
Corrientes 657,716 . . . . E2
Distrito Federal 2,908,001 . . H7
Entre Ríos 902,241 . . . . E3
Formosa 292,479 . . . . D1
Jujuy 408,514 . . . . C1
La Pampa 207,132 . . . . C4
La Rioja 163,342 . . . . C2
Mendoza 1,187,305 . . . . C4
Misiones 579,579 . . . . F2
Neuquén 241,904 . . . . C4
Río Negro 383,896 . . . . C5
Salta 662,369 . . . . D1
San Juan 469,973 . . . . C3
San Luis 212,837 . . . . C3
Santa Cruz 114,479 . . . . C6
Santa Fe 2,457,188 . . . . D3
Santiago del Estero 652,318 D2
Tierra del Fuego, Antártida, e Islas del Atlántico Sur 29,451 . . . . C7
Tucumán 968,066 . . . . C2

CITIES and TOWNS

Abra Pampa 2,929 . . . . C1
Adolfo Alsina 7,707 . . . . . . D4
Aguaray 4,802 . . . . D1
Aguilares 20,286 . . . . C2
Aimogasta 4,640 . . . . C2
Alberti 6,440 . . . . G7
Alcorta 5,818 . . . . F6
Algarrobo del Águila C4
Allen 14,041 . . . . C4
Alpachiri 1,657 . . . . D4
Alta Gracia 30,628 . . . . D3
Aluminé 1,560 . . . . B4
Alvear 5,419 . . . . E2
Ameghino 2,775 . . . . D3
Añatuya 15,025 . . . . D2
Andalgalá 6,853 . . . . C2
Antofagasta de la Sierra C2
Apóstoles 11,252 . . . . E2
Arrecifes 17,719 . . . . F7
Arroyo Seco 12,886 . . . . . . F6
Ascensión 3,031 . . . . F7
Avellaneda 330,654 . . . . G7
Ayacucho 12,363 . . . . E4
Azul 43,582 . . . . E4
Bahía Blanca 220,765 . . . . . D4
Bahía Bustamante C6
Bahía Thetis C7
Balcarce 28,985 . . . . E4
Balnearia 4,531 . . . . D3
Baradero 20,103 . . . . G6
Barrancas 3,602 . . . . F6
Barranqueras E2
Barreal 2,739 . . . . C3
Basavilbaso 7,657 . . . . G6
Belén 7,411 . . . . C2
Bella Vista, Corrientes 14,229 . . . . E2
Bella Vista, Tucumán 9,177 . D2
Bell Ville 26,559 . . . . D3
Bolívar 16,382 . . . . D4
Bovril 4,735 . . . . G5
Bragado 27,101 . . . . F7
Buenos Aires (cap.) 2,908,001 . . . . H7
Buenos Aires *9,927,404 . . . H7
Cafayate 5,048 . . . . C2
Calafate B7
Calchaquí 5,958 . . . . F5
Caleta Olivia 20,141 . . . . . . C6
Camarones C5
Campana 51,498 . . . . G6
Cañada de Gómez 24,706 . . . F6
Canals 6,627 . . . . D3
Cañuelas 14,831 . . . . G7
Carcarañá 11,121 . . . . F6
Carlos Casares 13,286 . . . . . F7
Carlos Tejedor 4,421 . . . . . . D4
Carmen de Areco 7,882 . . . . F7
Carmen de Patagones 13,981 . . . . D5
Casilda 23,492 . . . . F6
Castelli 4,507 . . . . H7
Catamarca 88,432 . . . . C2
Caucete 14,512 . . . . C3
Ceres 10,743 . . . . D2
Chabás 5,156 . . . . F6
Chacabuco 26,492 . . . . F7
Chajarí 15,242 . . . . G5
Chamical 6,333 . . . . C3
Charadai 1,078 . . . . D2
Charata 13,070 . . . . D2
Chascomús 21,864 . . . . H7
Chepes 4,775 . . . . C3
Chicoana 1,844 . . . . C2
Chilecito 14,010 . . . . C2
Chivilcoy 43,779 . . . . F7
Choele-Choel 6,191 . . . . C4
Chos-Malal 4,823 . . . . C4
Cinco Saltos 15,094 . . . . C4
Cipolletti 40,123 . . . . C4
Clorinda 21,008 . . . . E2
Colón, Buenos Aires 16,070 . F6
Colón, Entre Ríos 11,648 . . . G6
Colonia Las Heras 3,176 . . . . C6
Comandante Fontana 4,468 . D2
Comandante Luis Piedrabuena 2,492 . . . . C6
Comodoro Rivadavia 96,865 . C6
Concepción 29,359 . . . . C2
Concepción de la Sierra 2,778 . . . . E2
Concepción del Uruguay 46,065 . . . . G6
Concordia 93,618 . . . . G5
Constanza 1,313 . . . . G6
Córdoba 982,018 . . . . D3
Coronda 11,554 . . . . F6
Coronel Brandsen 10,484 . . . H7
Coronel Dorrego 10,661 . . . . D4
Coronel Pringles 16,592 . . . . D4
Coronel Suárez 16,359 . . . . . D4

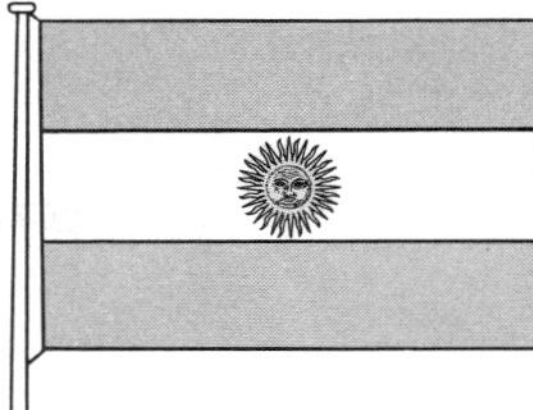

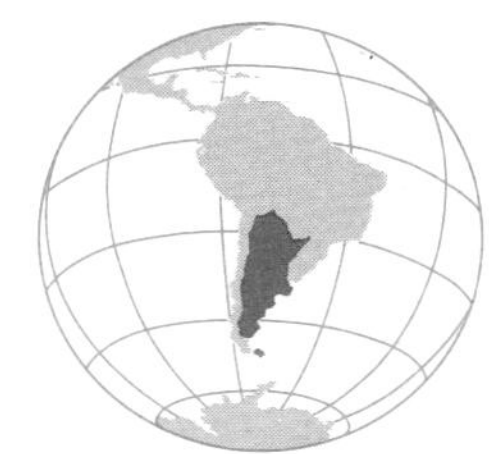

AREA 1,072,070 sq. mi. (2,776,661 sq. km.)
POPULATION 28,438,000
CAPITAL Buenos Aires
LARGEST CITY Buenos Aires
HIGHEST POINT Cerro Aconcagua 22,831 ft. (6,959 m.)
MONETARY UNIT Argentine peso
MAJOR LANGUAGE Spanish
MAJOR RELIGION Roman Catholicism

Agriculture, Industry and Resources

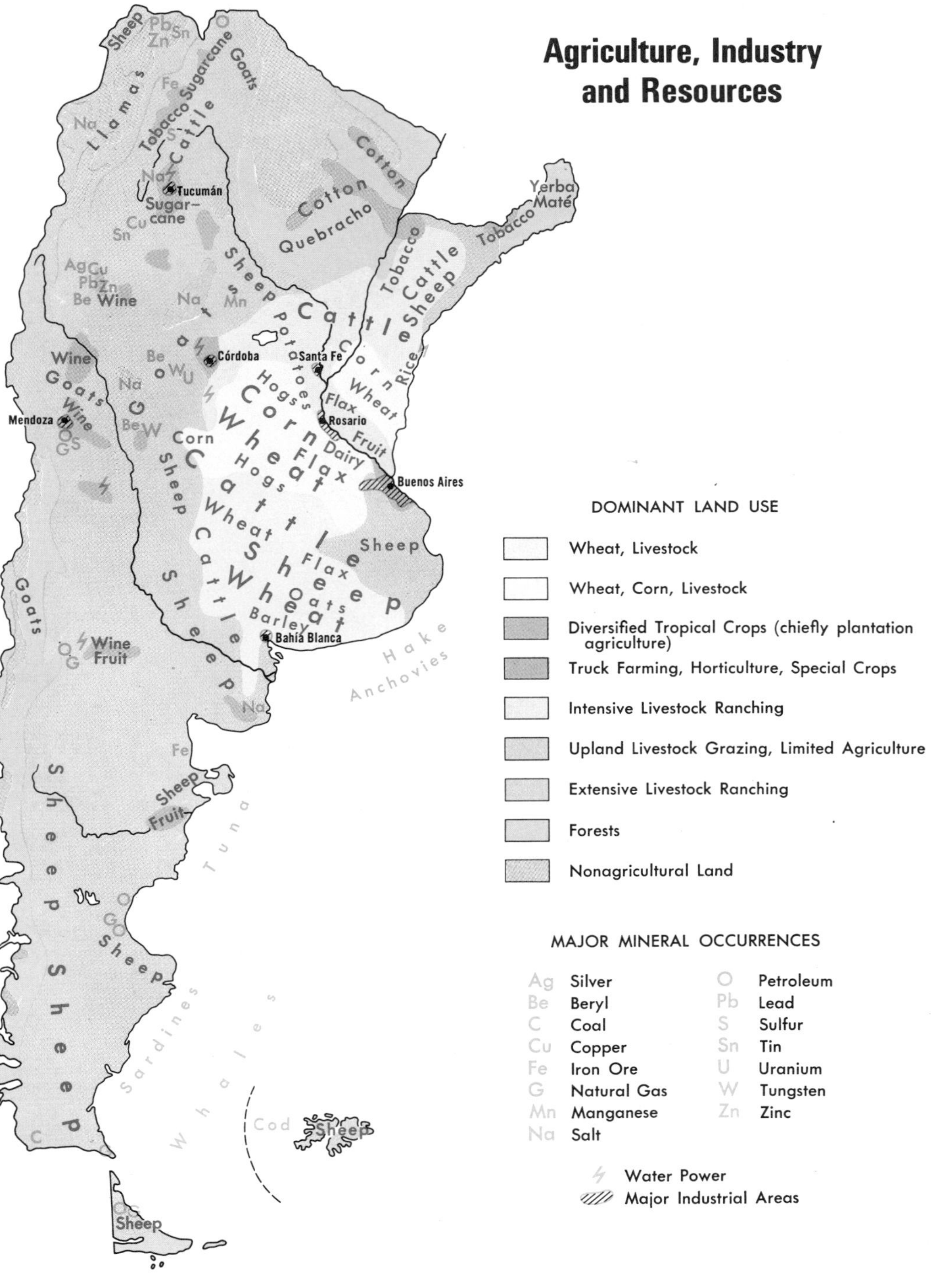

Sheep
Llamas
Tobacco
Sugarcane
Goats
Cattle
Cotton
Tucumán
Sugar-cane
Quebracho
Yerba Maté
Tobacco
Cattle
Sheep
Wine
Córdoba
Santa Fe
Potatoes
Corn
Wheat
Hogs
Flax
Rice
Rosario
Fruit
Dairy
Mendoza
Buenos Aires
Barley
Oats
Bahía Blanca
Hake
Anchovies
Fruit
Tuna
Sardines
Whales
Cod
DOMINANT LAND USE
Wheat, Livestock
Wheat, Corn, Livestock
Diversified Tropical Crops (chiefly plantation agriculture)
Truck Farming, Horticulture, Special Crops
Intensive Livestock Ranching
Upland Livestock Grazing, Limited Agriculture
Extensive Livestock Ranching
Forests
Nonagricultural Land
MAJOR MINERAL OCCURRENCES
Ag Silver
Be Beryl
C Coal
Cu Copper
Fe Iron Ore
G Natural Gas
Mn Manganese
Na Salt
O Petroleum
Pb Lead
S Sulfur
Sn Tin
U Uranium
W Tungsten
Zn Zinc
Water Power
Major Industrial Areas

Coronel Vidal 4,774 . . . . E4
Corral de Bustos 8,613 . . . . . D3
Corrientes 179,590 . . . . E2
Cosquín 13,929 . . . . D3
Crespo 10,668 . . . . F6
Cruz del Eje 23,473 . . . . C3
Curuzú Cuatiá 24,955 . . . . . . G5
Cutral-Có 25,870 . . . . C4
Daireaux 8,150 . . . . D4
Deán Funes 16,306 . . . . D3
Diamante 13,464 . . . . F6
Dolavon 1,778 . . . . C5
Dolores 19,307 . . . . E4
Eduardo Castex 5,397 . . . . . D4
El Bolsón 5,001 . . . . B5
Eldorado 22,821 . . . . F2
El Maitén 2,350 . . . . B5
Elortondo 4,939 . . . . F6
El Quebrachal 2,202 . . . . D2
Embarcación 9,016 . . . . D1
Empedrado 4,732 . . . . E2
Escobar 70,829 . . . . G7
Esperanza 22,838 . . . . F5
Esquel 17,228 . . . . B5
Esquina 10,380 . . . . G5
Famatina 1,237 . . . . C2
Federación 7,259 . . . . G5
Felipe Yofré 1,140 . . . . G4
Fernández 6,062 . . . . D2
Fiambalá 1,201 . . . . C2
Firmat 13,588 . . . . F6
Formosa 95,067 . . . . E2
Fortín Olmos 1,101 . . . . F4
Frías 20,901 . . . . D2
Gaiman 2,651 . . . . C5
Gálvez 14,711 . . . . F6
General Acha 7,647 . . . . C4
General Alvear, Buenos Aires 5,481 . . . . F7
General Alvear, Mendoza 21,250 . . . . C3
General Arenales 3,332 . . . . . F7
General Belgrano 10,909 . . . G7
General Conesa 3,566 . . . . . . C5
General Galarza 3,057 . . . . . . C6
General Güemes 15,534 . . . . D1
General José de San Martín 16,296 . . . . . . E2
General Juan Madariaga 13,409 . . . . E4
General La Madrid 5,154 . . . D4
General Las Heras 6,005 . . . G7
General Paz 5,127 . . . . H7
General Pico 30,180 . . . . D4
General Ramírez 5,393 . . . . . F6
General Roca 38,296 . . . . C4
General San Martín, Buenos Aires 384,306 . . . . G7
General San Martín, La Pampa 2,168 . . . . D4
General Viamonte 10,112 . . . F7
General Villegas 11,307 . . . . D4
Gobernador Crespo 2,972 . . . F5
Godoy Cruz 141,553 . . . . C3
Goya 47,357 . . . . G4
Gualeguay 24,883 . . . . G6
Gualeguaychú 51,057 . . . . . . G6
Guandacol 1,351 . . . . C2
Hasenkamp 2,804 . . . . F5
Helvecia 3,927 . . . . F5
Hernandarias 3,002 . . . . F5
Hernando 8,619 . . . . D3
Huinca Renancó 7,187 . . . . . D3
Humahuaca 3,963 . . . . C1
Humberto (Humberto Primo) 4,163 . . . . F5
Ibarreta 5,262 . . . . D2
Ibicuy 3,082 . . . . G6
Ingeniero Huergo 3,385 . . . . C4
Ingeniero Jacobacci 4,045 . . C5
Ingeniero Luiggi 3,002 . . . . . D4
Intendente Alvear 3,640 . . . . D4
Itatí 3,269 . . . . E2
Ituzaingó 8,687 . . . . E2
Jáchal 8,832 . . . . C3
Jesús María 17,594 . . . . D3
Joaquín V. González 6,054 . . D2
Juárez 11,798 . . . . E4
Jujuy 124,487 . . . . C1
Junín 62,080 . . . . F7
Junín de los Andes 5,638 . . . B4
La Banda 46,994 . . . . D2
Laboulaye 16,883 . . . . D3
La Carlota 8,614 . . . . D3
La Cruz 4,132 . . . . E2
La Cumbre 6,110 . . . . C3
La Falda 12,502 . . . . D3
Laguna Paiva 11,129 . . . . . . F5
Lanús 465,891 . . . . H7
La Paz, Entre Ríos 14,920 . . G5
La Paz, Mendoza 4,604 . . . . C3
La Plata 560,341 . . . . H7
Laprida 6,495 . . . . D4
La Quiaca 8,289 . . . . C1
La Rioja 66,826 . . . . C2
Larroque 3,147 . . . . F5
Las Flores 18,287 . . . . E4
Las Lomitas 4,047 . . . . D1
Las Palmas 5,061 . . . . E2
Las Parejas 7,430 . . . . F6
Las Rosas 9,725 . . . . F6
Las Varillas 10,605 . . . . D3
La Toma 4,325 . . . . C3
Lincoln 19,009 . . . . F7
Lobería 8,898 . . . . E4
Lobos 20,798 . . . . G7
Lomas de Zamora 508,620 . G7
Lucas González 3,015 . . . . . G6
Luján 38,919 . . . . G7
Lules 11,391 . . . . C2
Maciel 4,066 . . . . F6
Magdalena 7,135 . . . . H7
Maipú 7,289 . . . . E4
Malabrigo 3,294 . . . . F4
Malargüe 9,496 . . . . C4
Maquinchao 1,299 . . . . C5
Marcos Juárez 19,827 . . . . . D3
Mar del Plata 407,024 . . . . . E4
Máximo Paz 3,216 . . . . F6
Mburucuyá 3,044 . . . . E2
Médanos 4,511 . . . . D4
Mendoza 596,796 . . . . C3
Mercedes, Buenos Aires 46,581 . . . . G7
Mercedes, Corrientes 20,603 . . . . G4
Mercedes, San Luis 50,856 . C3
Merlo 293,059 . . . . G7
Metán 18,928 . . . . D2
Miramar 15,473 . . . . E4
Monte Caseros 18,247 . . . . . G5
Monte Quemado 4,707 . . . . . D2
Monteros 15,832 . . . . C2
Morón 596,769 . . . . G7
Morteros 11,456 . . . . D3
Navarro 7,176 . . . . G7
Necochea 50,939 . . . . E4
Neuquén 90,037 . . . . C4
Nogoyá 15,862 . . . . F6
Ñorquincó B5
Nueve de Julio 26,608 . . . . . F7
Oberá 27,311 . . . . F2
Olavarría 63,686 . . . . D4
Oliva 9,231 . . . . D3
Palo Santo 3,088 . . . . E2
Paraná 159,581 . . . . F5
Paso de Los Libres 24,112 . . E2
Pedro Luro 3,142 . . . . D4
Pehuajó 25,613 . . . . D4
Pellegrini 3,940 . . . . D4
Pergamino 68,989 . . . . F6
Pico Truncado 9,626 . . . . C6
Pigüé 10,793 . . . . D4
Pilar 3,805 . . . . F5
Pirané 9,039 . . . . E2
Plaza Huincul 7,988 . . . . B4

(continued on following page)

(continued)

Posadas 139,941 ... E2
Presidencia de la Plaza 4,904 ... D2
Presidencia Roque Sáenz Peña 49,261 ... D2
Puán 4,148 ... D4
Puerto Deseado 4,017 ... D6
Puerto Harberton ... C7
Puerto Iguazú 10,250 ... F2
Puerto Madryn 20,709 ... C5
Puerto Rico 8,195 ... D1
Punta Alta 54,375 ... D4
Quequén 11,737 ... E4
Quimili 8,972 ... D2
Quines 3,352 ... C3
Quitilipi 9,937 ... D2
Rafaela 53,132 ... F5
Ramallo 8,248 ... F6
Rauch 8,348 ... E4
Rawson 12,981 ... D5
Reconquista 32,442 ... F4
Recreo 3,502 ... C2
Resistencia 218,438 ... E2
Rinconada ... C1
Río Colorado 7,361 ... D4
Río Cuarto 110,148 ... D3
Río Gallegos 43,479 ... C7
Río Grande 13,271 ... C7
Río Segundo 12,839 ... D3
Río Tercero 34,735 ... D3
Rivadavia 10,953 ... C3
Rojas 14,247 ... F7
Romang 4,017 ... F4
Roque Pérez 5,434 ... G7
Rosario 954,606 ... F6
Rosario de la Frontera 13,531 ... D2
Rosario de Lerma 9,540 ... C1
Rosario del Tala 9,552 ... G6
Rufino 15,306 ... D3
Saladas 7,345 ... E2
Saladillo 14,806 ... G7
Salliqueló 5,479 ... D4
Salta 260,323 ... C1
Salto 18,462 ... F7
San Antonio de Areco 12,932 ... G7
San Antonio de los Cobres 2,357 ... C1
San Antonio Oeste 8,690 ... C5
San Carlos 7,613 ... F6
San Carlos de Bariloche 48,222 ... B5
San Cayetano 5,960 ... E4
San Cristóbal 13,345 ... F5
San Fernando 128,939 ... G7
San Francisco, Córdoba 58,616 ... D3
San Francisco, San Luis 2,448 ... C3
San Genaro 2,977 ... F6
San Ignacio 3,437 ... E2
San Jaime de la Frontera 2,811 ... G5
San Javier 7,557 ... F5
San José de Feliciano 4,986 ... G5
San Juan 290,479 ... C3
San Julián 4,278 ... C6
San Justo 14,135 ... F5
San Luis 70,632 ... C3
San Martín 29,746 ... C3
San Martín de los Andes 9,507 ... C5
San Miguel del Monte 8,414 ... G7
San Miguel de Tucumán 496,914 ... D2
San Nicolás 96,313 ... F6
San Pedro, Buenos Aires 27,058 ... F6
San Pedro, Jujuy 36,907 ... D1
San Rafael 70,477 ... C3
San Ramón de la Nva. Orán 32,955 ... D1
San Salvador 4,342 ... G5
San Sebastián ... C7
Santa Cruz 2,353 ... C7
Santa Elena 14,655 ... F5
Santa Fe 287,240 ... F5
Santa Lucía 4,452 ... E2
Santa María 5,380 ... C2
Santa Rosa, Córdoba 4,306 ... D3
Santa Rosa, La Pampa 51,689 ... C4
Santa Rosa, San Luis 2,878 ... C3
Santa Victoria ... D1
Santiago del Estero 148,357 ... D2
Santo Tomé, Corrientes 14,352 ... E2
Santo Tomé, Santa Fe 35,363 ... F5
Sarmiento 6,313 ... B6
Sauce 4,677 ... G5
Sierra Grande 9,585 ... C5
Suipacha 4,505 ... G7
Sunchales 12,493 ... F5
Suncho Corral 3,837 ... D2
Tafí Viejo 26,625 ... C2
Tandil 78,821 ... E4
Tapalquén 5,356 ... E4
Tartagal 31,367 ... D1
Tigre 199,366 ... G7
Tinogasta 7,829 ... C2
Toay 3,617 ... D4
Tornquist 4,696 ... D4
Tostado 10,492 ... D2
Trelew 52,073 ... C5
Trenque Lauquen 22,504 ... D4
Tres Arroyos 42,118 ... D4
Trevelín 2,935 ... B5
Tunuyán 14,665 ... C3
Urdinarrain 5,472 ... G6
Ushuaia 10,988 ... C7
Valcheta 2,994 ... C5
Vedia 6,273 ... F7
Veinticinco de Mayo 18,936 ... F7
Venado Tuerto 46,775 ... D3
Vera 13,555 ... F5
Verónica 5,657 ... H7
Viale 5,635 ... F5
Vicente López 289,815 ... G7
Victoria 18,883 ... F6
Victorica 3,895 ... C4
Vicuña Mackenna 5,665 ... D3
Viedma 24,338 ... D5
Villa Ángela 25,586 ... D2
Villa Atuel 2,774 ... C3
Villa Cañas 7,303 ... F6
Villa Constitución 36,157 ... F6
Villa del Rosario 10,133 ... D3
Villa Dolores 21,508 ... C3
Villa Elisa 4,106 ... G6
Villa Federal 9,222 ... G5
Villaguay 18,699 ... G5
Villa Guillermina 2,971 ... D2
Villa Huidobro 4,154 ... D3
Villa María 67,490 ... D3
Villa María Grande 4,517 ... F5
Villa Nueva 4,604 ... C3
Villa Ocampo 9,162 ... D2
Villa Regina 14,017 ... C4
Villa San José 6,800 ... G6
Villa San Martín 6,237 ... D2
Vinchina 1,070 ... C2
Zapala 18,293 ... B4
Zárate 65,504 ... G6
Zavalla 3,800 ... F6

OTHER FEATURES

Aconcagua, Cerro (mt.) ... C3
Andes, Cordillera de los (mts.) ... C2
Argentino (lake) ... B7
Arizaro, Salar de (salt dep.) ... C2
Arrecifes (riv.) ... G6
Atacama, Puna de (reg.) ... C2
Atuel (riv.) ... C4
Bermejo (riv.) ... E2
Blanca (bay) ... D4
Brazo Sur, Pilcomayo (riv.) ... E1
Buenos Aires (lake) ... B6
Campanario, Cerro (mt.) ... C4
Chaco Austral (reg.) ... D2
Chaco Central (reg.) ... D1
Chico (riv.) ... C5
Chico (riv.) ... C6
Chubut (riv.) ... C5
Colhué Huapi (lake) ... C6
Colorado (riv.) ... D4
Cónico, Cerro (mt.) ... B5
Corrientes (riv.) ... E2
Coyle (riv.) ... B7
Delgada (pt.) ... D5
Desaguadero (riv.) ... C3
Deseado (riv.) ... C6
Diamante (riv.) ... C3
Domuyo (vol.) ... B4
Dos Bahias (cape)) ... D5
Dulce (riv.) ... D2
Dungeness (pt.) ... C7
El Chocón (res.) ... C4
Estados, Los (isl.) ... D7
Fagnano (lake) ... C7
Famatina, Sierra de (mts.) ... C2
Feliciano (riv.) ... G5
Gallegos (riv.) ... B7
General Manuel Belgrano, Cerro (mt.) ... C2
Gran Chaco (reg.) ... D1
Grande (bay) ... C7
Grande (falls) ... E3
Grande de Tierra del Fuego (isl.) ... C7
Gualeguay (riv.) ... G5
Guayaquilaró (riv.) ... G5
Iguazú (falls) ... F2
Iguazú Nat'l Park ... E2
Lanín (vol.) ... B4
Lanín Nat'l Park ... B4
Lechiguanas (isls.) ... G6
Lennox (isl.) ... C8
Limay (riv.) ... C4
Llancanelo, Salina y Laguna (salt lake) ... C4
Llullaillaco (vol.) ... C1
Magallenes (Magellan) (str.) ... C7
Maipo (vol.) ... C3
Mar Chiquita (lake) ... D3
Mendoza (riv.) ... C3
Mercedario, Cerro (mt.) ... B3
Mogotes (pt.) ... E4
Montemayor (plat.) ... C5
Nahuel Huapi (lake) ... B5
Nahuel Huapi Nat'l Park ... B5
Negro (riv.) ... D4
Neuquén (riv.) ... C4
Ninfas (pt.) ... D5
Norte (pt.) ... D5
Nuevo (gulf) ... D5
Ojos del Salado, Cerro (mt.) ... C2
Pampa de las Tres Hermanas (plain) ... C6
Pampas (plain) ... D4
Paraná (riv.) ... E2
Patagonia (reg.) ... C5
Peteroa (vol.) ... B4
Pilcomayo (riv.) ... E1
Pissis (mt.) ... C2
Plata, Río de la (est.) ... E4
Pueyrredón (lake) ... B6
Puna de Atacama (reg.) ... C2
Quinto (riv.) ... D3
Rincón, Cerro (mt.) ... C1
Saladillo (riv.) ... D2
Salado (riv.) ... C4
Salado (riv.) ... H7
Salado del Norte (riv.) ... D2
Salí (riv.) ... C2
Salto (riv.) ... F7
Samborombón (bay) ... E4
San Antonio (cape) ... E4
San Diego (cape) ... D7
San Jorge (gulf) ... C6
San Juan (riv.) ... C3
San Lorenzo, Cerro (mt.) ... B6
San Martín (lake) ... B6
San Matías (gulf) ... D5
Santa Cruz (riv.) ... B7
Senguerr (riv.) ... B6
Staten (Los Estados) (isl.) ... D7
Tarija (riv.) ... D1
Tercero (riv.) ... D3
Teuco (riv.) ... D1
Tierra del Fuego, Grande de (isl.) ... C7
Toro, Cerro del (mt.) ... B2
Tres Puntas (cape) ... D6
Trinidad (isl.) ... D4
Tronador (mt.) ... B5
Tunuyán (riv.) ... C3
Tupungato, Cerro (mt.) ... B3
Uruguay (riv.) ... E3
Valdés (pen.) ... D5
Viedma (lake) ... B6
Zapaleri, Cerro (mt.) ... C1

FALKLAND ISLANDS

CITIES and TOWNS

Stanley (cap.) 1,050 ... E7

OTHER FEATURES

Adventure (sound) ... E7
Choiseul (sound) ... E7
East Falkland (isl.) 1,491 ... E7
Falkland (isls.) ... D7
Falkland (sound) ... D7
George (isl.) ... E7
Jason (isls.) ... D7
Lively (isl.) ... E7
Malvinas (Falkland) (isls.) ... D7
Pebble (isl.) ... E7
Saunders (isl.) ... E7
Weddel (isl.) ... D7
West Falkland (isl.) 322 ... D7

*City and suburbs.

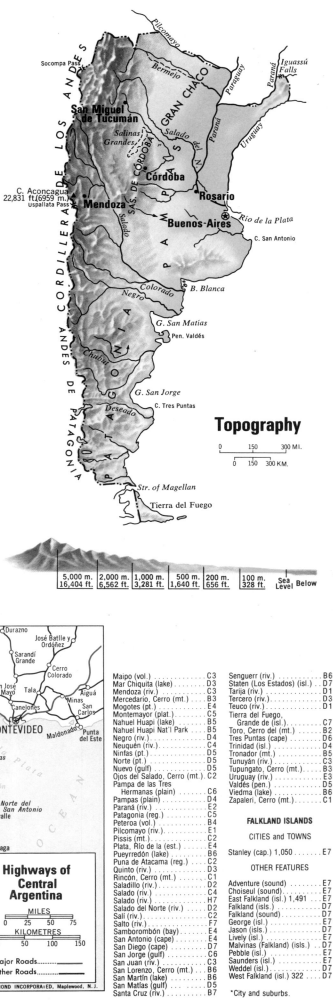

Topography

0 150 300 MI.
0 150 300 KM.

5,000 m. 16,404 ft. | 2,000 m. 6,562 ft. | 1,000 m. 3,281 ft. | 500 m. 1,640 ft. | 200 m. 656 ft. | 100 m. 328 ft. | Sea Level | Below

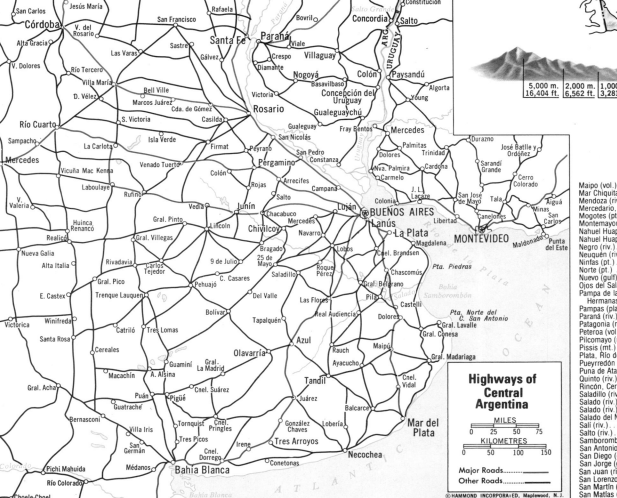

Highways of Central Argentina

MILES 0 25 50 75
KILOMETRES 0 50 100 150
Major Roads
Other Roads

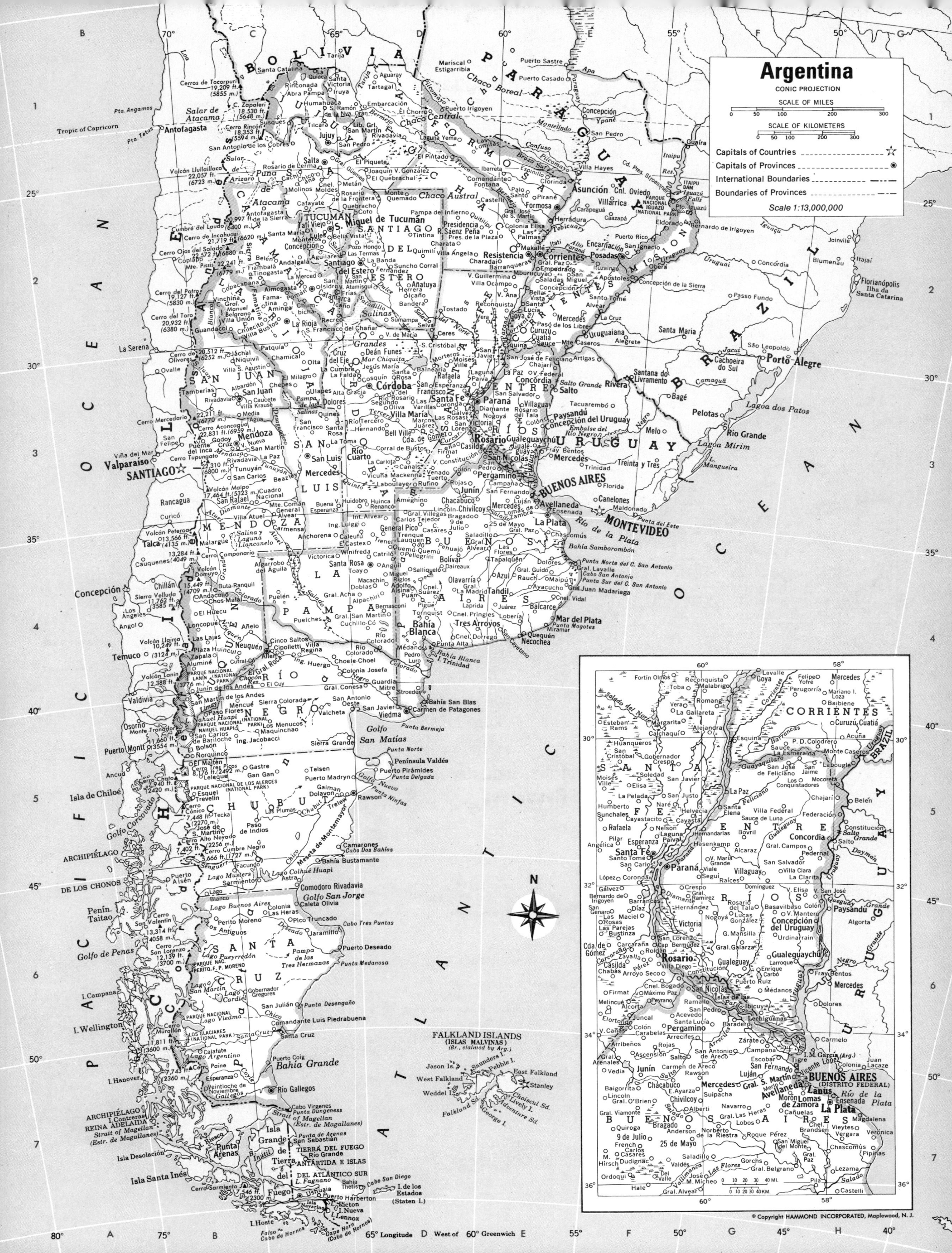

Argentina
CONIC PROJECTION
SCALE OF MILES
0 50 100 200 300
SCALE OF KILOMETERS
0 50 100 200 300
Capitals of Countries
Capitals of Provinces
International Boundaries
Boundaries of Provinces
Scale 1:13,000,000
BOLIVIA
PARAGUAY
BRAZIL
URUGUAY
CHILE
PACIFIC OCEAN
ATLANTIC OCEAN
Tropic of Capricorn
BUENOS AIRES
MONTEVIDEO
SANTIAGO
Asunción
Córdoba
Rosario
Santa Fe
Paraná
Mendoza
Tucumán
S. Miguel de Tucumán
Salta
Jujuy
Corrientes
Resistencia
Posadas
Formosa
La Plata
Mar del Plata
Bahía Blanca
Neuquén
Viedma
Rawson
Santa Rosa
San Luis
San Juan
La Rioja
Catamarca
Santiago del Estero
Río Gallegos
Ushuaia
Punta Arenas
Valparaíso
Antofagasta
Porto Alegre
Florianópolis
Stanley
FALKLAND ISLANDS
(ISLAS MALVINAS)
(Br., claimed by Arg.)
East Falkland
West Falkland
Golfo San Matías
Golfo San Jorge
Bahía Grande
Strait of Magellan
TIERRA DEL FUEGO
Isla Grande de Tierra del Fuego
Cape Horn
Río de la Plata
Lagoa dos Patos
Lagoa Mirim
Salar de Atacama
Cerro Aconcagua 22,831 ft. (6959 m.)
CORRIENTES
ENTRE RÍOS
SANTA FE
BUENOS AIRES (DISTRITO FEDERAL)
65° Longitude D West of 60° Greenwich E
© Copyright HAMMOND INCORPORATED, Maplewood, N. J.

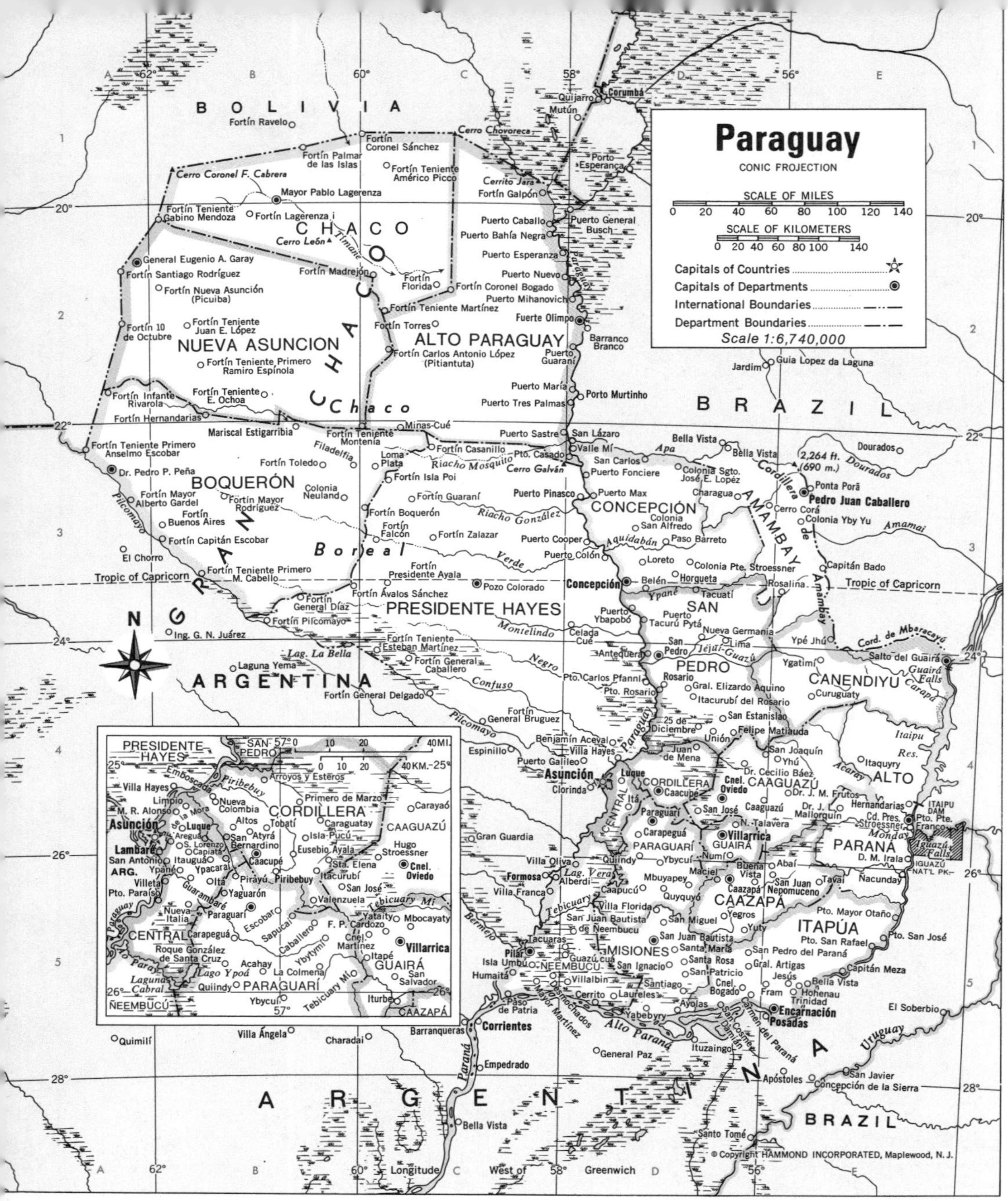

Paraguay

CONIC PROJECTION

SCALE OF MILES: 0 20 40 60 80 100 120 140

SCALE OF KILOMETERS: 0 20 40 60 80 100 140

Capitals of Countries ☆
Capitals of Departments ◉
International Boundaries
Department Boundaries

Scale 1:6,740,000

PARAGUAY

DEPARTMENTS

Alto Paraguay C2
Alto Paraná E4
Amambay D3
Asunción A4
Boquerón B3
Caaguazú D-E4
Caazapá D-E5
Canendiyu E4
Central D4
Chaco B-C2
Concepción D3
Cordillera D4
Guaira D4
Itapúa E5
Misiones D5
Ñeembucú C-D5
Nueva Asunción B2
Paraguarí D4-5
Presidente Hayes C3
San Pedro D4-5

CITIES and TOWNS

Abaí 1,507 .... E4
Acahay 1,937 .... B5
Alberdi 2,346 .... D5
Altos 1,441 .... B4
Antequera 1,281 .... D4
Areguá 3,941 .... B4
Arroyos y Esteros 1,253 .... B4
Asunción (cap.) 387,676 .... A4
Atyrá 1,427 .... B4
Ayolas 309 .... D5
Belén 1,219 .... D3
Bella Vista 3,101 .... D3
Bella Vista 1,421 .... E5
Benjamín Aceval 2,877 .... C4
Buena Vista 1,353 .... D5
Caacupé 7,278 .... B5
Caaguazú 7,950 .... D4
Caapucú 1,400 .... D5
Caazapá 3,132 .... D5
Caballero 1,225 .... B5
Capiatá 2,827 .... B4
Capitán Bado 915 .... E3
Capitán Meza 375 .... E5
Caraguatay 1,439 .... B4
Carapeguá 3,416 .... B5
Carayaó 1,190 .... C4
Carmen del Paraná 1,980 .... D5
Cerrito 958 .... D5
Ciudad Presidente
Stroessner 7,085 .... E4
Concepción 19,392 .... D3
Coronel Bogado 3,973 .... D5
Coronel Martínez 1,598 .... B5
Coronel Oviedo 13,786 .... C5
Curuguaty 1,112 .... E4
Desmochados 551 .... C5
Doctor Cecilio Báez 1,300 .... D4
Doctor Juan L. Mallorquín 1,913 .... E4
Doctor Juan Manuel
Frutos 1,494 .... E4
Doctor M. Irala 468 .... E4
Emboscada 1,222 .... B4
Encarnación 23,343 .... E5
Escobar 548 .... B5
Eusebio Ayala 4,328 .... B4
Fernando de la Mora 36,834 .... B4
Filadelfia 1,438 .... B3
Fram 1,090 .... E5
Fuerte Olimpo 3,063 .... C2
General Artigas 3,542 .... D5
General Elizardo Aquino 1,304 .... D4
General Eugenio A. Garay 740 .... A2
Guarambaré 3,640 .... B5
Hernandarias 3,898 .... E4
Hohenau 1,121 .... E5
Horqueta 4,328 .... D3
Hugo Stroessner 536 .... C4
Humaitá 938 .... C5
Isla Pucú 1,766 .... B4
Isla Umbú 236 .... C5
Itá 7,041 .... B5
Itacurubí 1,997 .... B5
Itacurubí del Rosario 2,467 .... D4
Itapé 1,376 .... C5
Itaquyry E4
Itauguá 3,767 .... B5
Iturbe 3,413 .... C5
Jesús 1,495 .... E5
Juan de Mena 1,027 .... D4
La Colmena 1,804 .... B5
Lambaré 31,656 .... A4
Laureles 435 .... D5
Lima 1,098 .... D3
Limpio 2,219 .... B4
Loreto 1,258 .... D3
Luque 13,921 .... B4
Maciel 376 .... D5
Mariano Roque Alonso 1,492 .... A4
Mariscal Estigarribia 3,150 .... B3
Mayor Martínez 324 .... C5
Mayor Pablo Lagerenza B1
Mbocayaty 925 .... C5
Mbuyapey 1,560 .... D5
Ñacunday 380 .... E5
Natalicio Talavera 1,228 .... D4
Nueva Germania 572 .... D3
Nueva Italia 1,517 .... B5
Ñumí 941 .... D4
Paraguarí 5,036 .... B5
Paso de Patria 698 .... C5
Pedro Juan Caballero 21,033 .... E3
Pilar 12,506 .... C5
Pirayú 2,698 .... B5
Piribebuy 4,497 .... B5
Primero de Marzo 696 .... B4
Puerto Casado 4,078 .... C3
Puerto Guaraní 302 .... C2
Puerto Pinasco 5,477 .... C3
Puerto Presidente Franco 4,152 .... E4
Puerto Sastre 160 .... C3
Quiindy 2,664 .... B5
Quyquyó 928 .... D5
Roque González de Santa
Cruz 1,375 .... B5
Rosario 4,165 .... D4
Salto del Guairá E4
San Antonio 4,906 .... A5
San Bernardino 949 .... B4
San Cosme y Damián 602 .... D5
San Estanislao 4,753 .... D4
San Ignacio 6,116 .... D5
San Joaquin 536 .... E4
San José 3,102 .... B5
San Juan Bautista 6,457 .... D5
San Juan Bautista de
Neembucú 688 .... D5
San Juan Nepomuceno 2,974 .... E5
San Lázaro 1,767 .... D3
San Lorenzo 11,616 .... B4
San Miguel 1,030 .... D5
San Patricio 1,130 .... D5
San Pedro 3,186 .... D3
San Pedro del Paraná 2,723 .... D5
San Salvador 1,393 .... C5
Santa Elena 1,439 .... B5
Santa María 793 .... D5
Santa Rosa 3,736 .... D5
Santiago 1,265 .... D5
Sapucaí 1,864 .... B5
Tacuaras 193 .... C5
Tacuatí 836 .... D3
Tavai 472 .... E5
Tebicuary Mí 183 .... B5
Tobatí 4,983 .... B4
Trinidad 837 .... E5
Unión 1,286 .... D4
Valenzuela 1,108 .... B5
Valle Mí 1,318 .... D3
25 de Diciembre 439 .... D4
Villa Florida 1,261 .... D5
Villa Franca 359 .... C5
Villa Hayes 4,749 .... A4
Villa Oliva 564 .... C5
Villarrica 17,687 .... C5
Villeta 3,156 .... A5
Yabebyry 797 .... D5
Yaguarón 3,368 .... B5
Yataity 1,159 .... C5
Ybycuí 1,736 .... B5
Ybytymí 816 .... B5
Yegros 1,051 .... D5
Ygatimí 396 .... E4
Yhú 964 .... E4
Ypacaraí 5,195 .... B5
Ypané 1,474 .... B5
Ypé Jhú 645 .... E3
Yuty 2,392 .... D5

OTHER FEATURES

Acaray (riv.) E4
Alto Paraná (riv.) D5
Amambay, Cordillera de (mts.) D-E3
Apa (riv.) D3
Aquidabán (riv.) D3
Chaco Boreal (reg.) B2-3
Chovoreca (mt.) C1
Confuso (riv.) C4
Coronel F. Cabrera (mt.) B1
González, Riacho (riv.) C3
Gran Chaco (reg.) B2-3
Iguazú (falls) E4
Itaipu (res.) E4
Jara (hill) C1
Mbaracayú, Cordillera de (mts.) E3
Monday (riv.) E4
Montelindo (riv.) C3
Mosquito, Riacho (riv.) C3
Negro (riv.) C4
Paraguay (riv.) D4
Pilcomayo (riv.) C4
Tebicuary (riv.) C5
Tímane (riv.) B2
Vera (lag.) D5
Verde (riv.) C3

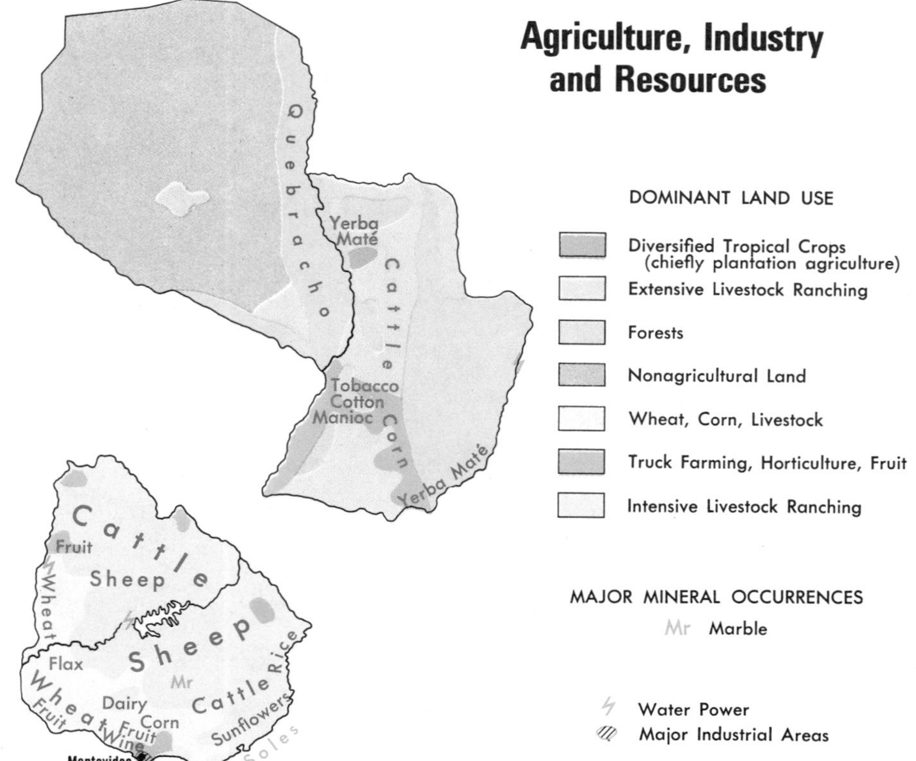

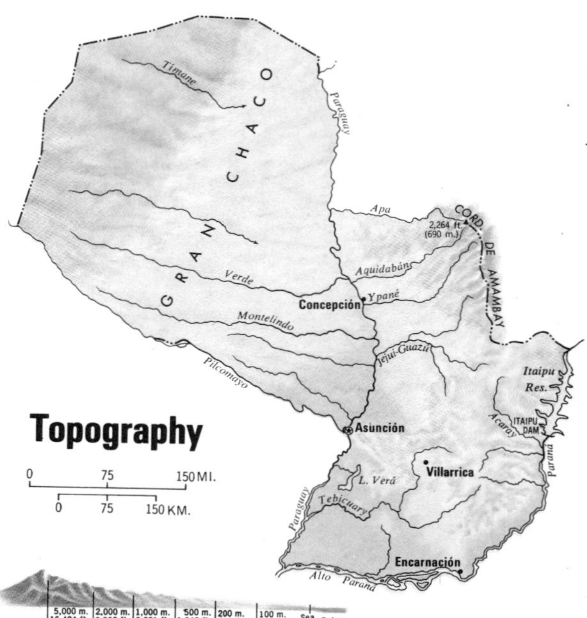

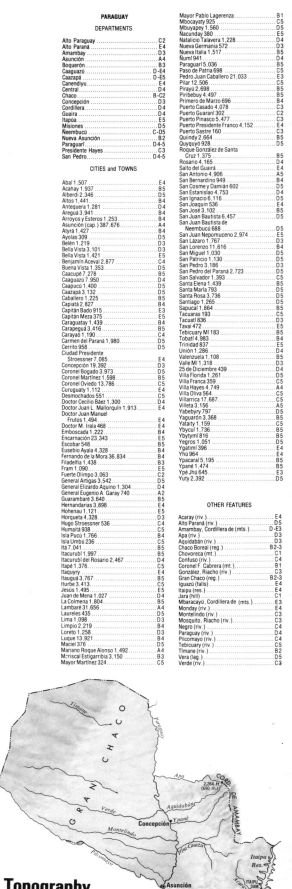

URUGUAY

DEPARTMENTS

Artigas 52,843 .... B1
Canelones 258,195 .... D5
Cerro Largo 71,023 .... E3
Colonia 105,350 .... B5
Durazno 53,635 .... C3
Flores 23,530 .... C4
Florida 63,987 .... D4
Lavalleja 65,823 .... D5
Maldonado 61,259 .... E5
Montevideo 1,202,757 .... B7
Paysandú 88,029 .... B3
Río Negro 46,861 .... B3
Rivera 77,086 .... D2
Rocha 55,097 .... E4
Salto 92,183 .... B2
San José 79,563 .... C5
Soriano 77,906 .... B4
Tacuarembó 76,964 .... D3
Treinta y Tres 43,419 .... E4

CITIES and TOWNS

Aceguá 930 .... E2
Achar 606 .... C3
Agraciada 638 .... A4
Aguas Corrientes 992 .... A6
Aiguá 2,470 .... E5
Algorta 1,372 .... B3
Artigas 29,256 .... C1
Atlántida 2,268 .... B6
Balneario El Tesoro E5
Balneario La Barra E5
Balneario Solís 288 .... D5
Baltasar Brum 1,753 .... B1
Belén 2,129 .... B1
Bella Unión 7,778 .... B1
Bernabé Rivera 540 .... B1
Blanquillo 1,053 .... D3
Cañada Nieto 503 .... B4
Canelones 15,938 .... B6
Cardal 847 .... C5
Cardona 4,126 .... B4
Cardozo 143 .... C3
Carlos Reyles 961 .... C4
Carmelo 13,631 .... A4
Carmen 2,318 .... D4
Carrasco B7
Castillos 6,446 .... F5
Casupá 2,265 .... D5
Cebollatí 1,233 .... F4
Cerrillos 1,690 .... A6
Cerro Chato, Treinta y Tres 1,850 .... D4
Chamizo 486 .... D5
Chuy 4,472 .... F4
Colón, Lavalleja 367 .... E4
Colonia 16,895 .... B5
Colonia Lavalleja C2
Colonia Rossel y Rius 130 .... D4
Colonia Valdense 2,113 .... B5
Conchillas 748 .... B5
Constitución 3,217 .... A2
Costa Azul 453 .... E5
Cufré 430 .... B5
Cuñapirú D2
Curtina 723 .... C3
Diez y Nueve (19) de Abril 308 .... E5
Diez y Ocho (18) de Julio 742 .... F4
Dolores 12,771 .... A4
Durazno 25,811 .... C4
Egaña 667 .... B4
Empalme Olmos 2,084 .... B6
Estación Atlántida 1,845 .... B6
Estación Migues 241 .... C6
Florida 25,030 .... C5
Fortaleza de Santa Teresa F5
Fraile Muerto 2,468 .... E3
Fray Bentos 19,569 .... A4
Fray Marcos 1,573 .... D5
Garzón 258 .... E5
General Enrique Martínez 973 .... F4
Goñi 278 .... C4
Grecco 447 .... B3
Guichón 4,720 .... B3
Ituzaingó 717 .... A6
Javier de Viana 286 .... C1
Joanico 692 .... B6
Joaquín Suárez, Canelones 3,517 .... B6
José Batlle y Ordóñez 2,044 .... D4
José Enrique Rodó 1,334 .... B4
José Pedro Varela 3,541 .... E4
Juan L. Lacaze 11,133 .... B5
Julio María Sanz E4
La Bolsa C1
La Coronilla 571 .... F4
La Cruz 633 .... C4
La Cuchilla F3
La Floresta C7
La Lata E2
La Paloma 1,558 .... F5
La Paz, Canelones 14,402 .... B6
La Paz, Colonia B5
La Pedrera 116 .... F5
Lascano 6,043 .... E4
Las Flores 403 .... D5
La Sierra D5
Las Piedras 53,983 .... B6
Las Toscas 893 .... E3
Libertad 6,071 .... C5
Lorenzo Geyres 474 .... B3
Mal Abrigo 209 .... C5
Maldonado 22,159 .... D6
Mariscala 1,393 .... E5
Mazangano E3
Melo 38,260 .... E3
Mercedes 34,667 .... B4
Merinos 403 .... C3
Miguelete 533 .... B5
Migues 2,183 .... C6
Minas 35,433 .... D5
Minas de Corrales 2,518 .... D2
Montes 2,217 .... D5
Montevideo (cap.) 1,173,254 .... B7
Nico Pérez D4
Nueva Helvecia 8,598 .... B5
Nueva Palmira 6,934 .... A4
Nuevo Berlín 1,970 .... B3
Ombúes de Lavalle 1,689 .... B4
Ombúes de Oribe C4
Palmitas 1,332 .... B4
Pan de Azúcar 4,862 .... D5
Pando 16,184 .... B6
Paso de la Laguna, Salto B2
Paso de la Laguna, Tacuarembó D3
Paso de León B1
Paso del Borracho D2
Paso del Cerro 317 .... C2
Paso de los Toros 13,178 .... C3
Paso Potrero C2
Paysandú 62,412 .... A3
Peralta C3
Piedra Sola 233 .... C3
Piedras Coloradas 487 .... B3
Piñera 261 .... C3
Pintado, Artigas C1
Piraraja 774 .... E4
Piriápolis 5,221 .... D5
Porvenir 705 .... B3
Progreso 8,257 .... B6
Pueblo del Sauce E4
Pueblo Nuevo B2
Punta del Este 6,914 .... E6
Quebracho 1,514 .... B2
Reboledo 373 .... D4
Rio Branco 5,697 .... F3
Rivera 49,013 .... D1
Rocha 21,612 .... E5
Rodríguez 1,575 .... C5
Rosario 8,302 .... B5
Salto 72,94 .... B2
San Antonio, Canelones 1,122 .... B6
San Bautista 1,472 .... B6
San Carlos 16,883 .... E5
San Gregorio, San José C4
San Gregorio, Tacuarembó 2,892 .... D3
San Jacinto 2,292 .... C6
San Javier 1,583 .... A3
San José de Mayo 28,427 .... C5
San Ramón 6,570 .... D5
San Servando F3
Santa Catalina 885 .... B4
Santa Clara de Olimar 2,867 .... D3
Santa Lucía 14,101 .... B6
Santa Rosa 2,736 .... B6
Santiago Vázquez 1,323 .... A7
Sarandí del Yi 6,326 .... D4
Sarandí de Navarro 259 .... C3
Sarandí Grande 5,598 .... C4
Sauce, Canelones 3,942 .... B6
Sauce del Yi D4
Saucedo B2
Sequeira C1
Solís 356 .... D5
Solís de Mataojo 1,763 .... D5
Soriano 1,125 .... A4
Tacuarembó 34,152 .... D2
Tala 3,611 .... D5
Tambores 1,534 .... C2
Toledo 3,127 .... B6
Tomás Gomensoro 2,105 .... B1
Totoral C3
Tranqueras 3,922 .... D2
Treinta y Tres 25,757 .... E4
Tres Bocas B2
Tres Islas E3
Trinidad 17,598 .... B4
Tupambaé 1,039 .... E3
Unión B7
Valentines 153 .... E4
Veinticinco (25) de Agosto 1,891 .... A6
Veinticinco (25) de Mayo 1,744 .... C5
Velázquez 1,042 .... E5
Vergara 2,822 .... E3
Vichadero 1,989 .... E2
Villa Darwin 507 .... B4
Villa del Cerro A7
Young 11,080 .... B3
Zapicán 764 .... E4
Zapucay D2

OTHER FEATURES

Aiguá (riv.) E4
Alférez (riv.) E5
Arapey Chico (riv.) B1
Arapey Grande (riv.) B2
Belén (range) C1
Bonete (dam) C3
Brava (pt.) B7
Cañas (range) C2
Caraguatá (riv.) D3
Castillos (lag.) F5
Cebollatí (riv.) F4
Cordobés (riv.) D3
Cuareim (riv.) B1
Cuñapirú, Arroyo (riv.) D2
Daymán (range) B2
Daymán (riv.) B2
Durazno, Grande del (range) D4
Espinillo (pt.) A7
Este (pt.) D6
Flores (isl.) D5
Garzón (lag.) E5
Grande (range) D4
Grande, Arroyo (riv.) B4
Grande Inferior (range) C4
Haedo (range) C2
India Muerta (riv.) E4
José Ignacio (lag.) E5
Lobos (isl.) E6
Maciel, Arroyo (riv.) C4
Merín (lag.) F4
Mirador Nacional (mt.) D5
Negra (lag.) F5
Negra (range) D2
Negro (riv.) B4
Negro, Arroyo (riv.) B3
Olimar Grande (riv.) E4
Pando (riv.) B6
Parao (riv.) E3
Plata, La (riv.) B5
Polonio (cape) F5
Quequay Chico (riv.) B3
Quequay Grande (riv.) B3
Río Negro (res.) D3
Rocha (lag.) E5
Salto Grande (falls) A2
San José (riv.) C4
San Miguel (swamp) F4
San Salvador (riv.) B4
Santa Ana (range) D2
Santa Lucía (riv.) D5
Santa Lucía Chico (riv.) D4
Santa María (cape) F5
Sauce (lag.) D5
Sopas, Arroyo (riv.) C2
Tacuarembó (riv.) D2
Tacuarí (riv.) E3
Tigre (isl.) A7
Uruguay (riv.) A3
Yaguarón (riv.) F3
Yi (riv.) B4

PARAGUAY

AREA 157,047 sq. mi. (406,752 sq. km.)
POPULATION 2,973,000
CAPITAL Asunción
LARGEST CITY Asunción
HIGHEST POINT Amambay Range 2,264 ft. (690 m.)
MONETARY UNIT guaraní
MAJOR LANGUAGES Spanish, Guaraní
MAJOR RELIGION Roman Catholicism

URUGUAY

AREA 72,172 sq. mi. (186,925 sq. km.)
POPULATION 2,899,000
CAPITAL Montevideo
LARGEST CITY Montevideo
HIGHEST POINT Mirador Nacional 1,644 ft. (501 m.)
MONETARY UNIT Uruguayan peso
MAJOR LANGUAGE Spanish
MAJOR RELIGION Roman Catholicism

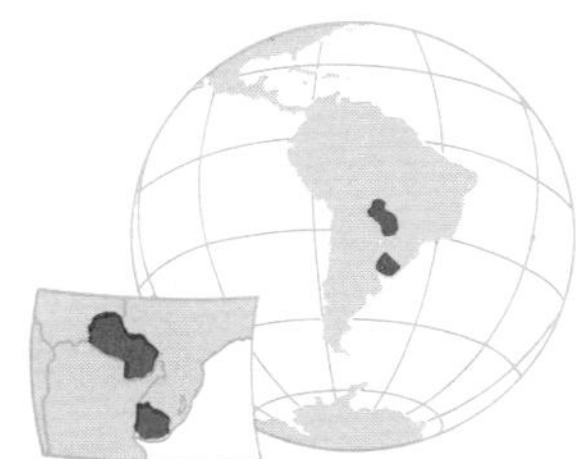

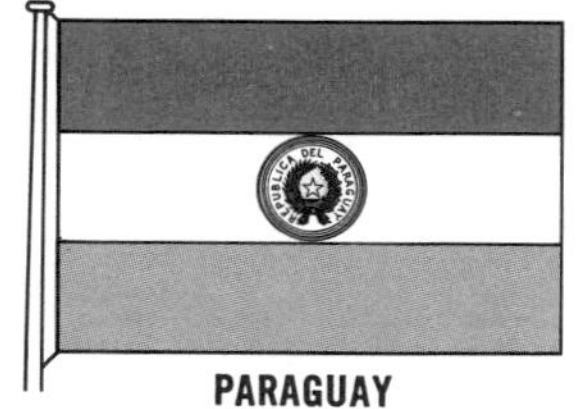

PARAGUAY

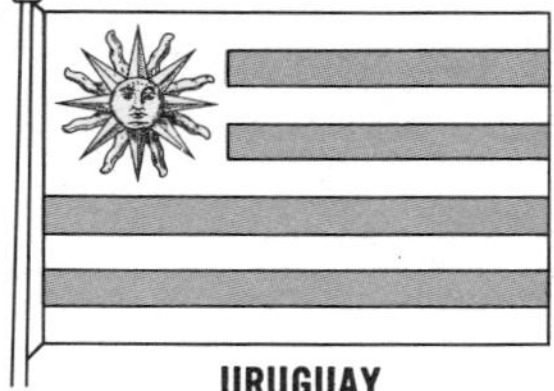

URUGUAY

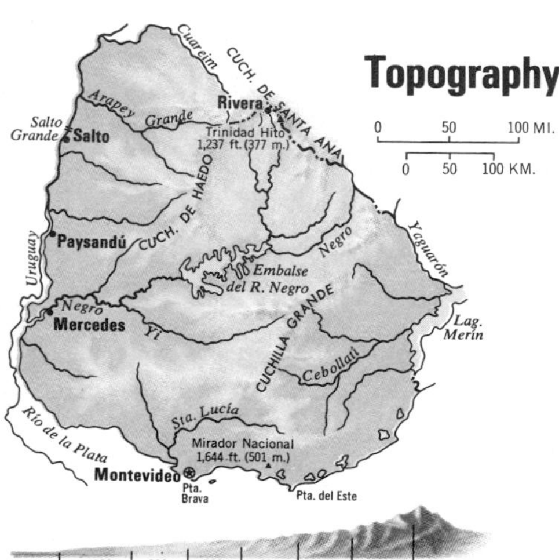

Uruguay

CONIC PROJECTION

SCALE OF MILES 0 20 40 60

SCALE OF KILOMETERS 0 20 40 60

Capitals of Countries
Department Capitals
International Boundaries
Department Boundaries

Scale 1:3,800,000

Longitude 56° West of Greenwich 55°

North America
LAMBERT AZIMUTHAL EQUAL-AREA PROJECTION
MILES
0 100 200 400 600 800
KILOMETERS
0 100 200 400 600 800
Capitals of Countries
Other Capitals
International Boundaries
Other Boundaries
Scale 1:36,600,000
© Copyright HAMMOND INCORPORATED, Maplewood, N.J.
ARCTIC OCEAN
NORTH POLE
EAST SIBERIAN SEA
CHUKCHI SEA
BERING SEA
BEAUFORT SEA
LINCOLN SEA
GREENLAND SEA
NORWEGIAN SEA
ASIA
U.S.S.R.
EUROPE
UNITED KINGDOM
SCOTLAND
NORWAY
DEN.
ICELAND
Reykjavík
GREENLAND (KALÂTDLIT-NUNÂT) (Den.)
Arctic Circle
Denmark Strait
Davis Strait
Baffin Bay
Baffin Island
Hudson Strait
Hudson Bay
LABRADOR SEA
ATLANTIC OCEAN
PACIFIC OCEAN
Gulf of Alaska
ALASKA
UNITED STATES
YUKON TERRITORY
NORTHWEST TERRITORIES
BRITISH COLUMBIA
ALBERTA
SASKATCHEWAN
MANITOBA
ONTARIO
QUEBEC
NEWFOUNDLAND
CANADA
UNITED STATES
WASH.
OREG.
IDAHO
MONT.
WYO.
N. DAK.
S. DAK.
MINN.
WIS.
MICH.
IOWA
NEBR.
NEV.
CALIF.
UTAH
COLO.
KANS.
MO.
ILL.
IND.
OHIO
PA.
N.Y.
ARIZ.
N. MEX.
OKLA.
TEXAS
ARK.
LA.
MISS.
ALA.
GA.
FLA.
TENN.
KY.
N.C.
S.C.
VA.
W.VA.
Washington D.C.
New York
Chicago
Los Angeles
San Francisco
Gulf of Mexico
MEXICO
Mexico City
Tropic of Cancer
BAHAMAS
CUBA
HAITI
DOMINICAN REP.
JAMAICA
PUERTO RICO
WEST INDIES
GREATER ANTILLES
CARIBBEAN SEA
BELIZE
GUATEMALA
HONDURAS
EL SALVADOR
NICARAGUA
COSTA RICA
PANAMA
COLOMBIA
VENEZUELA
ECUADOR
PERU
BRAZIL
BOLIVIA
SOUTH AMERICA
Equator
GALÁPAGOS IS. (Ecuador)
Clipperton (Fr.)
Bermuda (U.K.)
N
Longitude West 90° of Greenwich

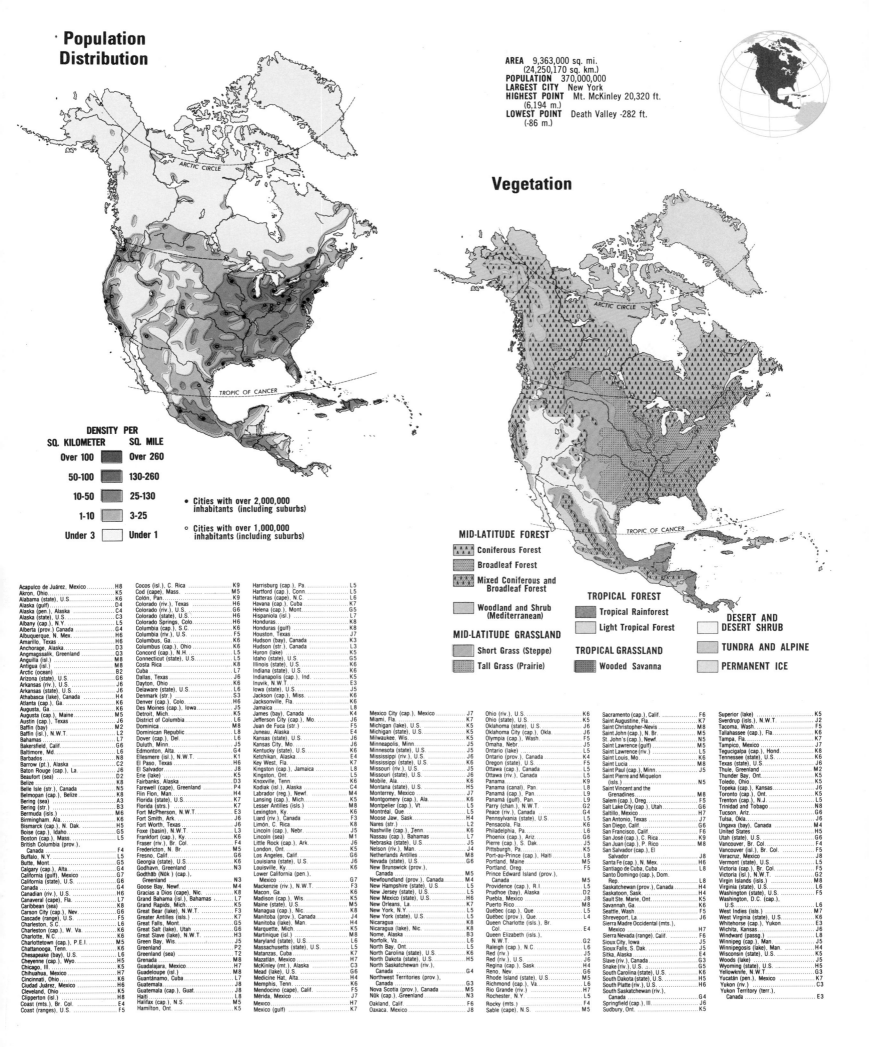

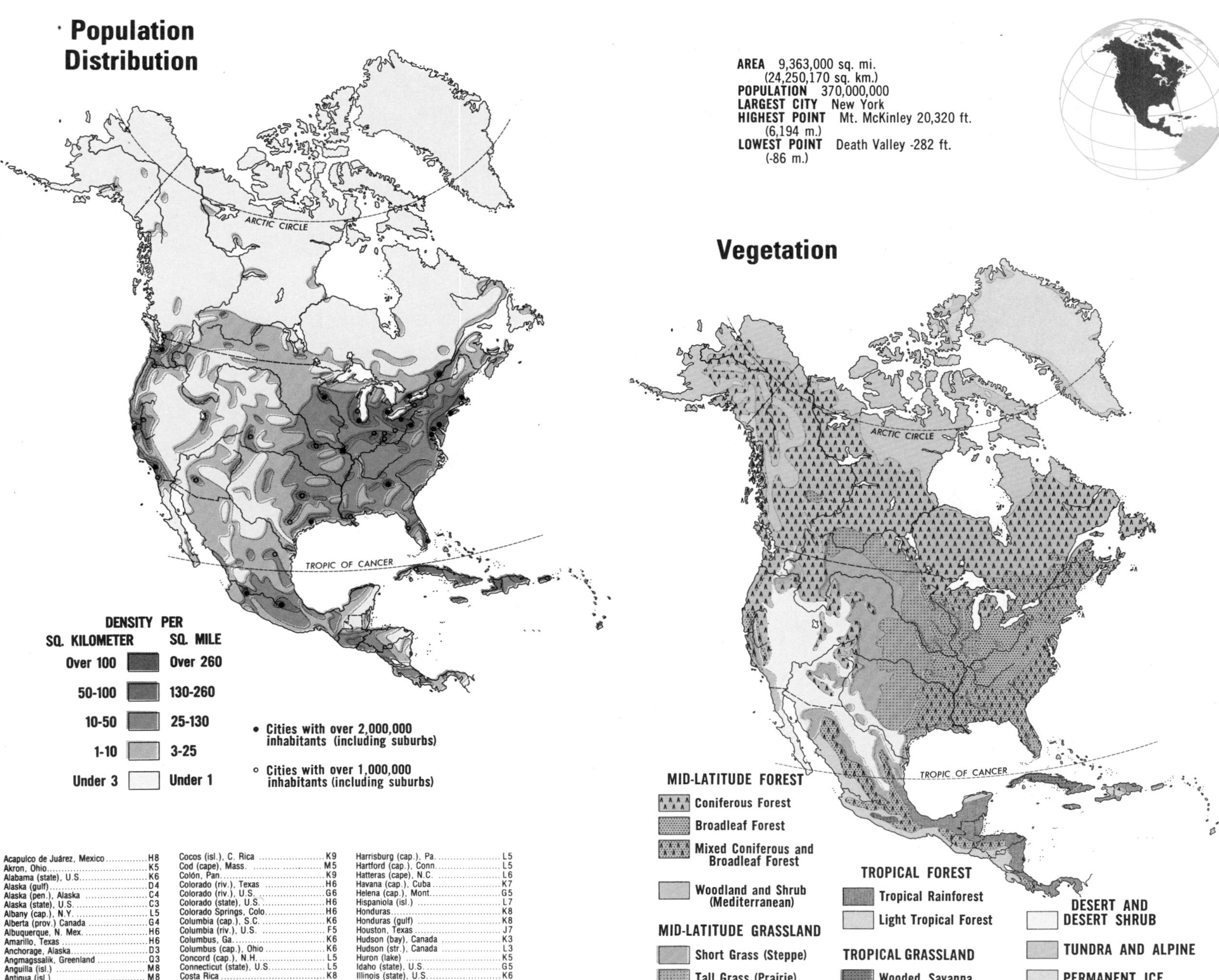
Population Distribution
ARCTIC CIRCLE
TROPIC OF CANCER
DENSITY PER
SQ. KILOMETER
SQ. MILE
Over 100
Over 260
50-100
130-260
10-50
25-130
1-10
3-25
Under 3
Under 1
• Cities with over 2,000,000 inhabitants (including suburbs)
○ Cities with over 1,000,000 inhabitants (including suburbs)
AREA 9,363,000 sq. mi. (24,250,170 sq. km.)
POPULATION 370,000,000
LARGEST CITY New York
HIGHEST POINT Mt. McKinley 20,320 ft. (6,194 m.)
LOWEST POINT Death Valley -282 ft. (-86 m.)
Vegetation
ARCTIC CIRCLE
TROPIC OF CANCER
MID-LATITUDE FOREST
Coniferous Forest
Broadleaf Forest
Mixed Coniferous and Broadleaf Forest
Woodland and Shrub (Mediterranean)
MID-LATITUDE GRASSLAND
Short Grass (Steppe)
Tall Grass (Prairie)
TROPICAL FOREST
Tropical Rainforest
Light Tropical Forest
TROPICAL GRASSLAND
Wooded Savanna
DESERT AND DESERT SHRUB
TUNDRA AND ALPINE
PERMANENT ICE

Average January Temperature

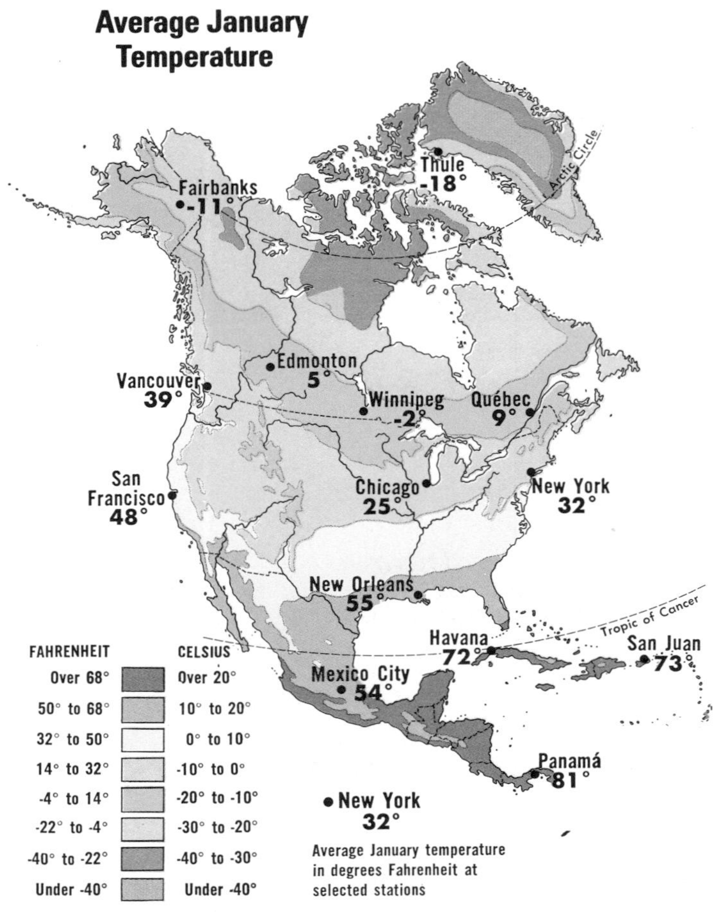
Thule
-18°
Fairbanks
-11°
Arctic Circle
Edmonton
5°
Vancouver
39°
Winnipeg
-2°
Québec
9°
San Francisco
48°
Chicago
25°
New York
32°
New Orleans
55°
Tropic of Cancer
Havana
72°
San Juan
73°
Mexico City
54°
Panamá
81°
FAHRENHEIT
CELSIUS
Over 68° Over 20°
50° to 68° 10° to 20°
32° to 50° 0° to 10°
14° to 32° -10° to 0°
-4° to 14° -20° to -10°
-22° to -4° -30° to -20°
-40° to -22° -40° to -30°
Under -40° Under -40°
New York
32°
Average January temperature in degrees Fahrenheit at selected stations

Average July Temperature

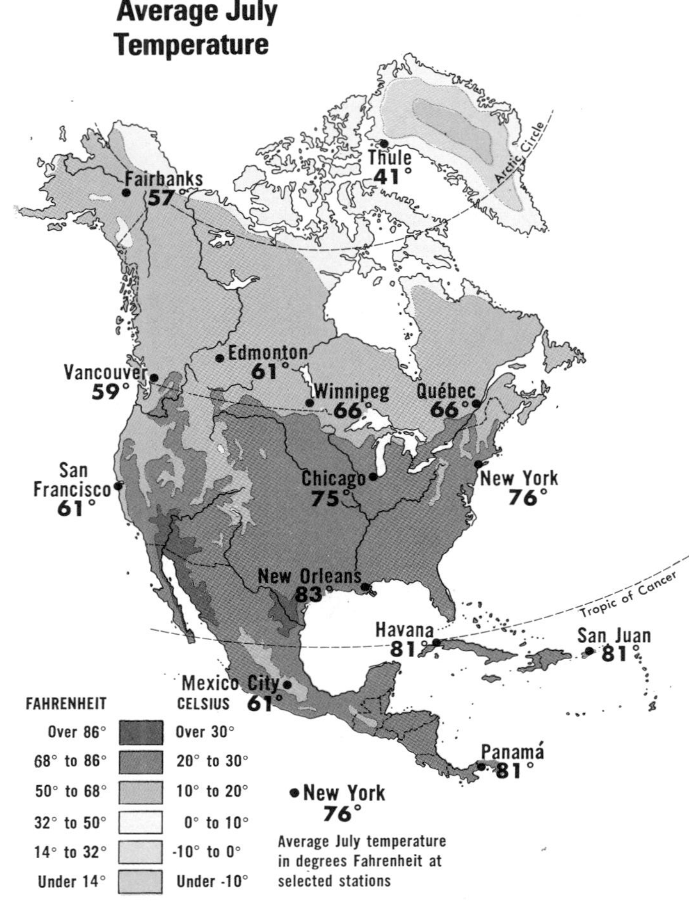
Thule
41°
Fairbanks
57°
Arctic Circle
Edmonton
61°
Vancouver
59°
Winnipeg
66°
Québec
66°
San Francisco
61°
Chicago
75°
New York
76°
New Orleans
83°
Tropic of Cancer
Havana
81°
San Juan
81°
Mexico City
61°
Panamá
81°
FAHRENHEIT
CELSIUS
Over 86° Over 30°
68° to 86° 20° to 30°
50° to 68° 10° to 20°
32° to 50° 0° to 10°
14° to 32° -10° to 0°
Under 14° Under -10°
New York
76°
Average July temperature in degrees Fahrenheit at selected stations

Rainfall

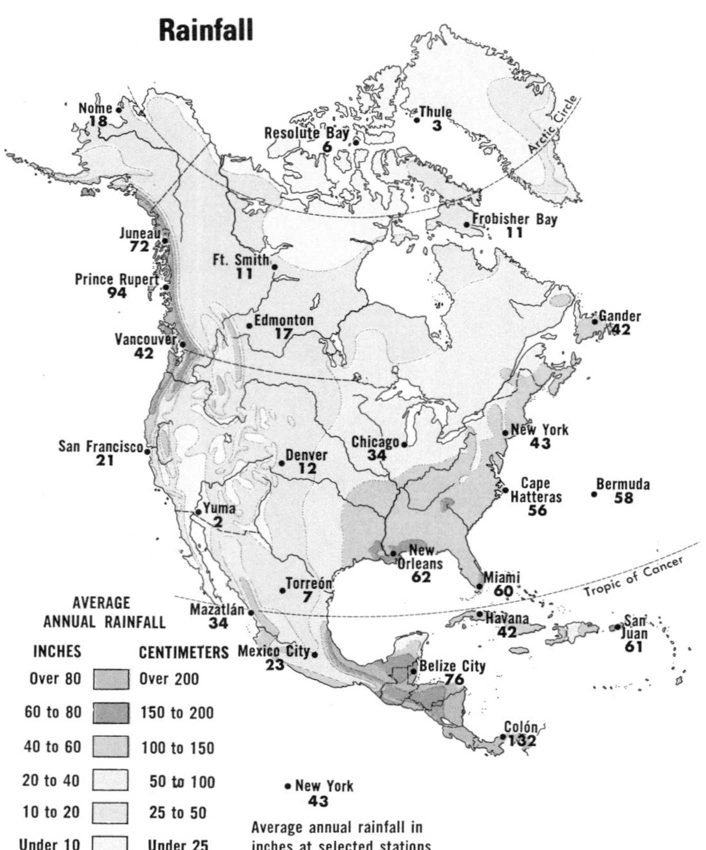
Nome
18
Thule
3
Resolute Bay
6
Arctic Circle
Frobisher Bay
11
Juneau
72
Ft. Smith
11
Prince Rupert
94
Gander
42
Edmonton
17
Vancouver
42
New York
43
San Francisco
21
Chicago
34
Denver
12
Cape Hatteras
56
Bermuda
58
Yuma
2
New Orleans
62
Miami
60
Tropic of Cancer
Torreón
7
Mazatlán
34
Havana
42
San Juan
61
Mexico City
23
Belize City
76
Colón
132
AVERAGE ANNUAL RAINFALL
INCHES
CENTIMETERS
Over 80 Over 200
60 to 80 150 to 200
40 to 60 100 to 150
20 to 40 50 to 100
10 to 20 25 to 50
Under 10 Under 25
New York
43
Average annual rainfall in inches at selected stations

Vegetation/Relief

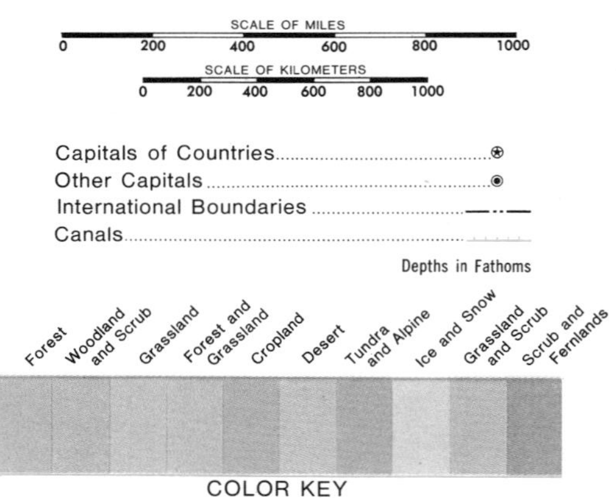
SCALE OF MILES
0 200 400 600 800 1000
SCALE OF KILOMETERS
0 200 400 600 800 1000
Capitals of Countries
Other Capitals
International Boundaries
Canals
Depths in Fathoms
Forest
Woodland and Scrub
Grassland
Forest and Grassland
Cropland
Desert
Tundra and Alpine
Ice and Snow
Grassland and Scrub
Scrub and Fernlands
COLOR KEY

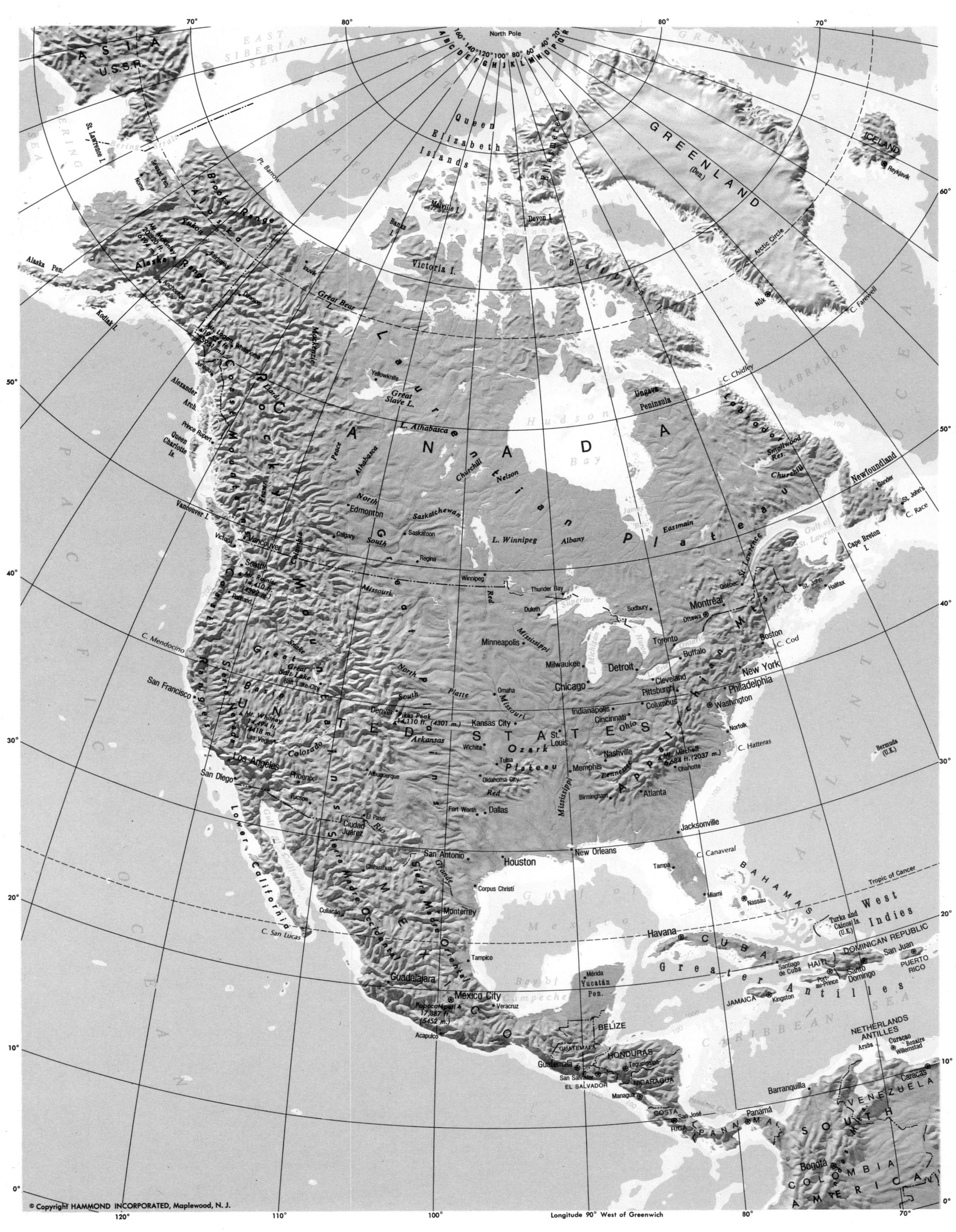

North Pole
ASIA
U.S.S.R.
EAST SIBERIAN SEA
BERING SEA
Bering Strait
St. Lawrence I.
Nome
Pt. Barrow
Brooks Range
Alaska
Yukon
Mt. McKinley 20,320 ft. (6194 m.)
Fairbanks
Alaska Range
Anchorage
Alaska Pen.
Kodiak I.
Gulf of Alaska
Inuvik
Dawson
Whitehorse
Mt. Logan 19,524 ft. (5951 m.)
Juneau
Mackenzie
Great Bear L.
Queen Elizabeth Islands
Ellesmere I.
Melville I.
Banks I.
Devon I.
Victoria I.
Baffin I.
Baffin Bay
GREENLAND (Den.)
GREENLAND SEA
ICELAND
Reykjavík
Nûk
Arctic Circle
C. Farewell
Davis Strait
C. Chidley
LABRADOR SEA
Ungava Peninsula
Labrador
Smallwood Res.
Churchill
Newfoundland
Gander
St. John's
C. Race
Gulf of St. Lawrence
Cape Breton I.
Halifax
St. John
Yellowknife
Great Slave L.
L. Athabasca
Laurentian Plateau
CANADA
Hudson Bay
James Bay
Eastmain
Albany
Nelson
Churchill
Peace
Athabasca
North Saskatchewan
South Saskatchewan
Edmonton
Calgary
Saskatoon
Regina
L. Winnipeg
Winnipeg
Alexander Arch.
Prince Rupert
Queen Charlotte Is.
Coast Mts.
Rocky Mountains
Fraser
Vancouver I.
Victoria
Vancouver
Seattle
Mt. Rainier 14,410 ft. (4392 m.)
Portland
Columbia
Snake
C. Mendocino
Cascade Range
Great Basin
Great Salt Lake
Salt Lake City
San Francisco
Sierra Nevada
Coast Ranges
Mt. Whitney 14,494 ft. (4418 m.)
Las Vegas
Los Angeles
San Diego
Colorado
Phoenix
Tucson
Albuquerque
Great Plains
Missouri
North Platte
South Platte
Denver
Pikes Peak 14,110 ft. (4301 m.)
Arkansas
Wichita
Kansas City
Omaha
Red
Thunder Bay
Duluth
L. Superior
Sudbury
Minneapolis
Mississippi
Milwaukee
L. Michigan
L. Huron
L. Ontario
L. Erie
Detroit
Chicago
Toronto
Buffalo
Cleveland
Pittsburgh
Columbus
Indianapolis
Cincinnati
Ohio
St. Louis
UNITED STATES
Ozark Plateau
Tulsa
Oklahoma City
Fort Worth
Dallas
Nashville
Memphis
Tennessee
Birmingham
Atlanta
Appalachian Mts.
Mt. Mitchell 6,684 ft. (2037 m.)
Charlotte
Ottawa
Montréal
Québec
St. Lawrence
Boston
C. Cod
New York
Philadelphia
Washington
Norfolk
C. Hatteras
Bermuda (U.K.)
Jacksonville
New Orleans
Houston
San Antonio
Corpus Christi
Tampa
C. Canaveral
Miami
BAHAMAS
Nassau
Tropic of Cancer
El Paso
Ciudad Juárez
Rio Grande
Chihuahua
Lower California
Gulf of California
C. San Lucas
Culiacán
Sierra Madre Occidental
Sierra Madre Oriental
Monterrey
Tampico
Gulf of Mexico
MEXICO
Guadalajara
Mexico City
Popocatepetl 17,887 ft. (5452 m.)
Veracruz
Acapulco
Bay of Campeche
Mérida
Yucatán Pen.
BELIZE
GUATEMALA
Guatemala
HONDURAS
Tegucigalpa
San Salvador
EL SALVADOR
NICARAGUA
Managua
COSTA RICA
San José
Panama Canal
PANAMA
Panamá
Havana
CUBA
Santiago de Cuba
Greater Antilles
West Indies
Turks and Caicos Is. (U.K.)
HAITI
Port-au-Prince
DOMINICAN REPUBLIC
Santo Domingo
San Juan
PUERTO RICO
JAMAICA
Kingston
CARIBBEAN SEA
NETHERLANDS ANTILLES
Aruba
Curaçao
Bonaire
Willemstad
Barranquilla
Caracas
VENEZUELA
COLOMBIA
Bogotá
SOUTH AMERICA
PACIFIC OCEAN
ATLANTIC OCEAN
Longitude 90° West of Greenwich

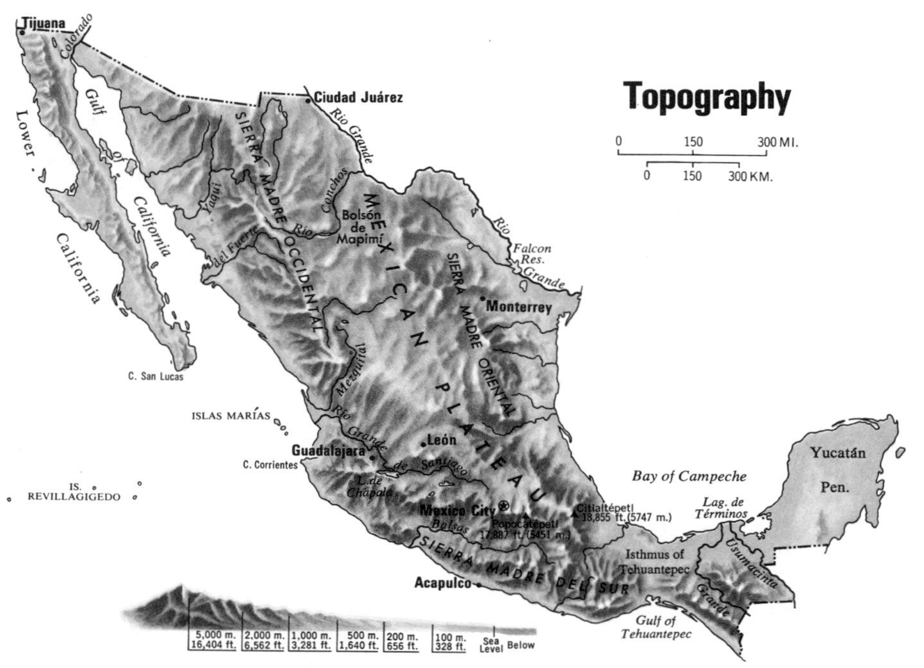

STATES

Aguascalientes 504,300 .... H6
Baja California 1,227,400 .... B1
Baja California Sur 221,000 .... C3
Campeche 371,800 .... O7
Chiapas 2,097,500 .... N8
Chihuahua 1,935,100 .... F2
Coahuila 1,561,000 .... H3
Colima 339,400 .... G7
Distrito Federal 9,377,300 .... L1
Durango 1,160,300 .... G4
Guanajuato 3,045,600 .... J6
Guerrero 2,174,200 .... J8
Hidalgo 1,518,200 .... K6
Jalisco 4,296,500 .... H6
México 7,542,300 .... K7
Michoacán 3,049,400 .... H7
Morelos 931,400 .... K7
Nayarit 729,500 .... G6
Nuevo León 2,463,500 .... K4
Oaxaca 2,517,500 .... L8
Puebla 3,285,300 .... L7
Querétaro 730,900 .... J6
Quintana Roo 209,900 .... P7
San Luis Potosí 1,669,900 .... J5
Sinaloa 1,882,200 .... F4
Sonora 1,498,100 .... D2
Tabasco 1,150,000 .... N7
Tamaulipas 1,924,900 .... K4
Tlaxcala 548,500 .... N1
Veracruz 5,263,800 .... L7
Yucatán 1,034,300 .... P6
Zacatecas 1,144,700 .... H5

CITIES and TOWNS

Acala 11,483 .... N8
Acámbaro 32,257 .... J7
Acaponeta 11,844 .... G5
Acapulco de Juárez 309,254 .... K8
Acatlán de Osorio 7,624 .... K7
Acatzingo de Hidalgo 6,905 .... N2
Acayucan 21,173 .... M8
Aconchi 1,596 .... D2
Actopan, Hidalgo 11,037 .... K6
Actopan, Veracruz 2,265 .... Q1
Agua Dulce 21,060 .... M7
Agualeguas 2,502 .... J3
Agua Prieta 20,754 .... E1
Aguascalientes 181,277 .... H6
Aguililla 5,715 .... H7
Ahome 4,182 .... E4
Ahuacatitlán 6,436 .... L1
Ahuacatlán 5,350 .... G6
Ahumada 6,466 .... F1
Ajalpan 8,238 .... L7
Alamo 9,954 .... L6
Álamos 4,269 .... E3
Aldama, Chihuahua 6,047 .... G2
Aldama, Tamaulipas 3,033 .... L5
Aljojuca 3,204 .... O1
Allende, Coahuila 11,076 .... J2
Allende, Nuevo León 9,914 .... J4
Almoloya del Río 3,714 .... K1
Altamira 6,053 .... L5
Altar 2,519 .... D1
Altepexi 6,661 .... L7
Alto Lucero 3,698 .... P1
Altotonga 6,754 .... P1
Alvarado 15,592 .... M7
Amatlán de los Reyes 3,664 .... P2
Amealco 2,960 .... K6
Ameca 21,018 .... H6
Amecameca de Juárez 16,276 .... L1
Amozoc de Mota 9,203 .... N2
Anáhuac, Chihuahua 10,886 .... F2
Anáhuac, Nuevo León 8,168 .... J3
Angostura 2,663 .... E4
Antiguo Morelos 1,569 .... K5
Apan 13,705 .... M1
Apatzingán de la Constitución 44,849 .... H7
Apizaco 21,189 .... N1
Aquiles Serdán 2,565 .... G2
Aramberri 1,786 .... J5
Arandas 18,934 .... H6
Arcelia 10,024 .... J7
Ario de Rosales 8,774 .... J7
Arizpe 1,736 .... D1
Armería 10,616 .... G7
Arriaga 13,193 .... N8
Arteaga 5,324 .... H7
Ascensión 4,104 .... E1
Asunción Nochixtlán 3,235 .... L8
Atlixco 41,967 .... M2
Atotonilco el Alto 16,271 .... H6
Atoyac de Álvarez 8,874 .... J8
Autlán de Navarro 20,398 .... G7
Axochiapan 8,283 .... M2
Ayutla de los Libres 3,618 .... K8
Azcapotzalco 534,554 .... L1
Azoyú 3,446 .... K8
Bacadéhuachi 1,514 .... E2
Bacalar 2,121 .... P7
Bachíniva 1,809 .... F2
Bácum 2,668 .... D3
Bahía Tortugas 1,457 .... B3
Balancán de Domínguez 3,669 .... O8
Bamoa 5,866 .... E4
Banderilla 3,488 .... P1
Baviácora 2,049 .... E2
Benjamín Hill 5,366 .... D1
Bernardino de Sahagún 12,327 .... M1
Boca del Río 2,354 .... Q2
Bolonchén de Rejón 2,342 .... O7
Buenaventura 3,924 .... F2
Burgos 673 .... K4
Cabo San Lucas 1,534 .... E5
Cacahoatán 5,079 .... N9
Cadereyta Jiménez 13,586 .... K4
Calkiní 6,870 .... O6
Calnali 3,318 .... K6
Calpulálpan 8,659 .... M1
Calvillo 6,453 .... H6
Campeche 69,506 .... O7
Cananea 17,518 .... D1
Canatlán 5,983 .... G4
Cancún 326 .... Q6
Candela 1,689 .... J3
Candelaria 1,982 .... O7
Cañitas de Felipe Pescador 4,885 .... H5
Capulhuac de Mirafuentes 8,289 .... K1
Carbo 2,804 .... D2
Cárdenas, San Luis Potosí 12,020 .... K6
Cárdenas, Tabasco 15,643 .... N8
Carichic 1,520 .... F2
Castaños 8,996 .... J3
Catemaco 11,786 .... M7
Ceballos 2,937 .... H3
Cedral 4,057 .... J5
Celaya 79,977 .... J6
Celestún 1,490 .... O6
Cerritos 10,421 .... J5
Cerro Azul 20,259 .... L6
Chahuites 5,218 .... M8
Chalchihuites 1,894 .... G5
Chalco de Díaz Covarrubias 12,172 .... M1
Champotón 6,606 .... O7
Charcas 10,491 .... J5
Chetumal 23,685 .... Q7
Chiapa de Corzo 8,571 .... N8
Chiautempan 12,327 .... N1
Chietla 4,602 .... M2
Chignahuapan 3,805 .... N1
Chihuahua 327,313 .... F2
Chilapa de Álvarez 9,204 .... K8
Chilpancingo de los Bravos 36,193 .... K8
China, Nuevo León 4,958 .... K4
Chocomán 5,114 .... P2
Choix 2,503 .... E3
Cholula de Rivadavia 15,399 .... M1
Cihuatlán 9,451 .... G7
Cintalapa de Figueroa 12,036 .... N8
Ciudad Acuña (Villa Acuña) 30,276 .... J2
Ciudad Altamirano 8,694 .... J7
Ciudad Camargo, Chihuahua 24,030 .... G3
Ciudad Camargo, Tamaulipas 5,953 .... K3
Ciudad del Carmen 34,656 .... N7
Ciudad Delicias 52,446 .... G2
Ciudad del Maíz 5,241 .... K5
Ciudad de Río Grande 11,651 .... H5
Ciudad Guerrero 3,110 .... F2
Ciudad Guzmán 48,166 .... H7
Ciudad Hidalgo, Chiapas 4,105 .... N9
Ciudad Hidalgo, Michoacán 24,692 .... J7
Ciudad Juárez 424,135 .... F1
Ciudad Lerdo 19,803 .... H4
Ciudad Madero 115,302 .... L5
Ciudad Mante 51,247 .... K5
Ciudad Mendoza 18,696 .... O2
Ciudad Miguel Alemán 11,259 .... K3
Ciudad Obregón 144,795 .... E3
Ciudad Río Bravo 39,018 .... K4
Ciudad Satélite 35,083 .... L1
Ciudad Serdán 9,581 .... O2
Ciudad Valles 47,587 .... K5
Ciudad Victoria 83,897 .... K5
Coalcomán de Matamoros 4,875 .... H7
Coatepec 21,542 .... P1
Coatetelco 5,268 .... L2
Coatzacoalcos 69,753 .... M7
Coatzingo 3,038 .... N2
Cocorit 4,478 .... E3
Colima 58,450 .... H7
Colón 3,346 .... K6
Colotlán 6,135 .... H5
Comala 5,592 .... H7
Comalcalco 14,963 .... N7
Comitán de Domínguez 21,249 .... O8
Compostela 9,801 .... G6
Concepción del Oro 8,144 .... J4
Concordia 3,947 .... G5
Contla 7,517 .... N1
Copala 3,783 .... K8
Coquimatlán 6,212 .... G7
Córdoba 78,495 .... P2
Cosalá 2,279 .... F4
Cosamaloapan de Carpio 19,766 .... M7
Cosautlán de Carvajal 2,039 .... P1
Coscomatepec de Bravo 6,023 .... P2
Coslo 2,680 .... H5
Costa Rica 11,795 .... F4
Cotija de la Paz 9,178 .... H7
Coyoacán 339,446 .... L1
Coyotepec 8,888 .... L1
Coyuca de Benítez 6,328 .... J8
Coyuca de Catalán 2,926 .... J7
Coyutla 3,726 .... L6
Cozumel 5,858 .... Q6
Creel 2,449 .... E3
Cuatrociénagas de Carranza 5,523 .... H3
Cuauhtémoc 26,598 .... F2
Cuautepec de Hinojosa 5,501 .... K6
Cuautitlán de Romero Rubio 11,439 .... L1
Cuautla Morelos 13,946 .... L2
Cuencamé de Ceniceros 3,774 .... H4
Cuernavaca 239,813 .... L2
Cuicatlán 2,733 .... L8
Cuitlahuac 4,813 .... P2
Culiacán 228,001 .... F4
Cumpas 2,395 .... E1
Cunduacán 4,397 .... N7
Dimas 2,194 .... F5
Doctor Arroyo 4,290 .... K5
Dolores Hidalgo de la Independencia Naci 16,849 .... J6
Durango 182,633 .... G1
Dzibalchén 1,917 .... P7
Dzidzantún 7,064 .... P6
Dzitbalché 4,393 .... P6
Ebano 17,489 .... K5
Ecatepec de Morelos 11,899 .... L1
Ejutla de Crespo 5,263 .... L8
Eldorado 8,115 .... E4
El Fuerte 7,179 .... E3
El Porvenir 3,030 .... G1
El Potosí 2,032 .... J4
El Salto 7,818 .... G5
El Zacatón 2,686 .... J5
Empalme 24,927 .... D2
Encarnación de Díaz 10,474 .... H6
Ensenada 77,687 .... A1
Escalón 2,998 .... G3
Escarcega 7,248 .... O7
Escuinapa de Hidalgo 16,442 .... G5
Escuintla 4,111 .... N9
Esperanza, Puebla 4,258 .... O2
Esperanza, Sonora 11,762 .... E3
Espita 5,394 .... Q6
Esqueda 1,458 .... E1
Etchojoa 4,398 .... E3
Ezequiel Montes 3,139 .... K6
Fortín de las Flores 9,358 .... P2
Francisco I. Madero 12,613 .... H4
Fresnillo de González Echererría 44,475 .... H5
Frontera 10,066 .... N7
Galeana, Nuevo León 3,429 .... J4
General Bravo 2,894 .... K4
General Cepeda 3,486 .... J4
General Terán 5,354 .... K4
Gómez Farías 3,030 .... F2
Gómez Palacio 79,650 .... G4
González 6,440 .... K5
Guadalajara 1,478,383 .... H6
Guadalajara* 2,343,034 .... H6
Guadalupe, Nuevo León 51,899 .... K4
Guadalupe, Zacatecas 13,246 .... H5
Guadalupe Bravo 3,333 .... F1
Guadalupe Victoria, Durango 7,931 .... H4
Guadalupe Victoria, Puebla 3,946 .... O1
Guamúchil 17,151 .... E4
Guanajuato 36,809 .... J6
Guasave 26,080 .... E4
Guaymas 57,492 .... D3
Gustavo Díaz Ordaz 10,154 .... K3
Gutiérrez Zamora 9,099 .... L6
Halachó 4,804 .... O6
Hecelchakán 4,279 .... O6
Hermosillo 232,691 .... D2
Heroica Caborca 20,771 .... C1
Heroica Nogales 52,108 .... D1
Hidalgo, Tamaulipas 2,450 .... K4
Hidalgo del Parral (Parral) 57,619 .... G3
Hopelchén 3,699 .... P7
Huajuapan de León 13,822 .... L8
Huamantla 15,565 .... N1
Huaquechula 2,294 .... M2
Huatabampo 18,506 .... D3
Huatusco de Chicuellar 9,501 .... P2
Huauchinango 16,826 .... L6
Huautla de Jiménez 6,132 .... L7
Huehuetlán el Chico 2,667 .... M2
Huejotzingo 8,552 .... M1
Huejutla 6,854 .... K6
Huetamo 9,333 .... J7
Hueyotlipan de Hidalgo 2,353 .... M1
Huimanguillo 7,075 .... N8
Huitzilán 3,573 .... O1
Huitzuco de los Figueroa 9,406 .... K7
Huixcolotla 4,039 .... N2
Huixtepec 5,927 .... L8
Huixtla 15,737 .... N9
Hunucmá 8,020 .... O6
Ignacio de la Llave 3,962 .... Q2
Iguala de la Independencia 45,355 .... K7
Imuris 1,958 .... D1
Irapuato 135,596 .... J6
Isla Mujeres 2,663 .... Q6
Isla, Veracruz 8,075 .... M7
Ixmiquilpan 6,048 .... K6
Ixtapa J8
Ixtapalapa 522,095 .... L1
Ixtenco 5,035 .... N1
Ixtepec 14,025 .... M8
Ixtlán del Río 10,986 .... G6
Izamal 9,749 .... P6
Izúcar de Matamoros 21,164 .... M2
Jala 4,535 .... G6
Jalacingo 3,427 .... P1
Jalapa Enríquez 161,352 .... P1
Jalpa 9,904 .... H6
Jalpa de Méndez 4,785 .... N7
Jalpan 1,878 .... K6
Jáltipan de Morelos 15,170 .... M8
Jantetelco 2,015 .... L2
Jaumave 3,072 .... K5
Jerez de García Salinas 20,325 .... H5
Jico 7,269 .... P1
Jilotepec de Abasolo 4,252 .... K7
Jiménez, Chihuahua 18,095 .... G3
Joachín 3,918 .... Q2
Jojutla de Juárez 14,438 .... L2
Jonacatepec 3,868 .... M2
Jonuta 2,746 .... N7
José Cardel 5,396 .... Q1
Juan Aldama 9,667 .... H4
Juchipila 6,328 .... H6
Juchitán de Zaragoza 30,218 .... M8
Kantunilkin 1,970 .... Q6
La Barca 18,055 .... H6
La Barra de Navidad 1,829 .... G7
La Concordia 3,559 .... N9
La Cruz, Sinaloa 4,218 .... F5
Lagos de Moreno 33,782 .... J6
La Huerta 4,328 .... G7
La Paz, Baja California Sur 46,011 .... D5
La Paz, San Luis Potosí 3,735 .... J5
La Piedad Cavadas 34,963 .... H6
Las Choapas 20,166 .... M7
Las Hadas G7
Las Nieves 2,262 .... G3
Las Rosas 7,658 .... N8
León 468,887 .... J6
Lerdo de Tejada 11,628 .... M8
Lerma 4,158 .... O7
Libres 4,830 .... O1
Linares 24,456 .... K4
Llera de Canales 3,564 .... K5
Loma Bonita 15,804 .... M7
Loreto, Baja California 2,570 .... D4
Loreto, Zacatecas 7,132 .... J5
Los Mochis 67,953 .... E4
Los Reyes de Salgado 19,452 .... H7
Macuspana 12,293 .... N8
Madera 9,759 .... F2
Magdalena de Kino 10,281 .... D1
Maltrata 5,457 .... O2
Manzanillo 20,777 .... G7
Mapastepec 5,907 .... N9
Mapimí 2,737 .... G4
Martínez de la Torre 17,203 .... L6
Mascota 5,674 .... G6
Matamoros, Coahuila 15,125 .... H4
Matamoros, Tamaulipas 165,124 .... L4
Matehuala 28,799 .... J5
Matías Romero 13,200 .... M8
Maxcanú 6,505 .... O6
Mazatlán 147,010 .... F5
Melchor Múzquiz 18,868 .... H3
Melchor Ocampo del Balsas 4,766 .... H8
Meoquí 12,308 .... G2
Mérida 233,912 .... P6
Metepec 4,625 .... M2
Metlatonoc 1,870 .... K8
Mexicali 317,228 .... B1
Mexico City (cap.) 9,377,300 .... L1
Mexico City* 13,993,866 .... L1
Miacatlán 3,980 .... K2
Mier 5,636 .... K3
Miguel Auza 9,303 .... H4
Minatitlán 68,397 .... M8
Mineral del Monte 8,887 .... K6
Miquihuana 1,971 .... J5
Misantla 8,799 .... P1
Miahuatlán de Porfirio Díaz 5,714 .... L8
Mocorito 3,993 .... F4
Moctezuma, San Luis Potosí 1,734 .... J5
Moctezuma, Sonora 2,700 .... E2
Monclova 78,134 .... J3
Montemorelos 18,642 .... K4
Monterrey 1,006,221 .... J4
Monterrey* 1,923,402 .... J4
Morelia 199,099 .... J7
Morelos 4,241 .... J2
Morelos Cañada 2,288 .... O2
Moroleón 25,620 .... J6
Motozintla de Mendoza 4,682 .... N9
Motul de Felipe Carillo Puerto 12,949 .... P6
Muna 5,491 .... P6
Naco 3,580 .... D1
Nacozari 2,976 .... E1
Nadadores 2,461 .... H3
Naica 7,190 .... G2
Namiquipa 4,875 .... F2
Nanacamilpa 6,356 .... M1
Naolinco de Victoria 4,365 .... P1
Naranjos 14,732 .... L6
Naucalpan de Juárez 9,425 .... L1
Nautla 1,935 .... L6
Nava 4,097 .... J2
Navojoa 43,817 .... E3
Navolato 12,799 .... E4
Nazas 2,881 .... G4
Netzahualcóyotl 580,436 .... L1
Nieves 3,966 .... H5
Nochistlán 8,780 .... H6
Nogales 14,254 .... P2
Nombre de Dios 3,188 .... G5
Nopalucan de la Granja 3,002 .... O1
Nueva Casas Grandes 20,023 .... F1
Nueva Ciudad Guerrero 3,300 .... K3
Nueva Italia de Ruiz 14,718 .... J7
Nueva Rosita 34,706 .... J2
Nuevo Ideal 5,252 .... G4
Nuevo Laredo 184,622 .... J3
Oaxaca de Juárez 114,948 .... L8
Ocampo, Coahuila 1,613 .... H3
Ocampo, Tamaulipas 4,801 .... K5
Ocosingo 2,946 .... O8
Ocotlán 35,361 .... H6
Ocotlán de Morelos 5,882 .... L8
Ojinaga 12,757 .... G2
Ojocaliente 7,582 .... H5
Ometepec 7,342 .... K8
Oriental 6,009 .... O1
Orizaba 105,150 .... P2
Otumba de Gómez Farías 3,198 .... M1
Oxkutzcab 8,182 .... P6
Ozuluama 2,851 .... L6
Ozumba de Alzate 6,876 .... M1
Pachuca de Soto 83,892 .... K6
Padilla 4,581 .... K5
Palenque 2,595 .... O8
Palizada 2,332 .... O7
Palomas 2,129 .... F1

Panabá 3,056 ..... P6
Pánuco 14,277 ..... K6
Papanoa 3,033 ..... J8
Papantla de Olarte 26,773 ..... L6
Paralso 7,561 ..... N7
Parral 57,619 ..... G3
Parras de la Fuente 18,207 ..... H4
Paso de Ovejas 4,371 ..... Q2
Pátzcuaro 17,299 ..... J7
Pedro Montoya 4,563 ..... K6
Pénjamo 9,245 ..... J6
Peñón Blanco 2,726 ..... H4
Pericos 4,445 ..... F4
Perote 12,742 ..... O1
Petatlán 9,419 ..... J8
Peto 8,362 ..... P6
Pichucalco 4,615 ..... N8
Piedras Negras, Coahuila 41,033 ..... J2
Piedras Negras, Veracruz 4,099 ..... Q2
Pijijiapan 5,053 ..... N9
Pitiquito 2,268 ..... D1
Potam 2,825 ..... D3
Poza Rica de Hidalgo 152,276 ..... L6
Praxedis G. Guerrero 2,399 ..... G1
Profesor Rafael Ramírez 5,338 ..... O1
Progreso 17,518 ..... P6
Puebla de Zaragoza 465,985 ..... N2
Puente de Ixtla 10,435 ..... K2
Puerto Ángel 1,489 ..... L9
Puerto Escondido 3,845 ..... L9
Puerto Juárez 100 ..... Q6
Puerto Madero 1,908 ..... N9
Puerto Peñasco 8,452 ..... C1
Puerto Vallarta 24,155 ..... G6
Purificación 3,311 ..... G7
Puruándiro 9,956 ..... J7
Putla de Guerrero 3.572 ..... L8
Quecholac 3,374 ..... O2
Querétaro 142,448 ..... J6
Ramos Arizpe 6,205 ..... J4
Rayón, San Luis Potosí 4,451 ..... K6
Rayón, Sonora D2
Reynosa 181,646 ..... K3
Rincón de Romos 8,348 ..... H5
Ríoverde 16,804 ..... J6
Rodeo 2,584 ..... G4
Rosamorada 2,635 ..... G5

(continued on following page)

AREA 761,601 sq. mi. (1,972,546 sq. km.)
POPULATION 67,395,826
CAPITAL Mexico City
LARGEST CITY Mexico City
HIGHEST POINT Citlaltépetl 18,855 ft. (5,747 m.)
MONETARY UNIT Mexican peso
MAJOR LANGUAGE Spanish
MAJOR RELIGION Roman Catholicism

States Indicated by Numbers

1	Tlaxcala	6	Querétaro
2	Morelos	7	Guanajuato
3	Distrito Federal	8	Aguascalientes
4	México	9	Nayarit
5	Hidalgo	10	Colima

Longitude West of Greenwich

(continued)

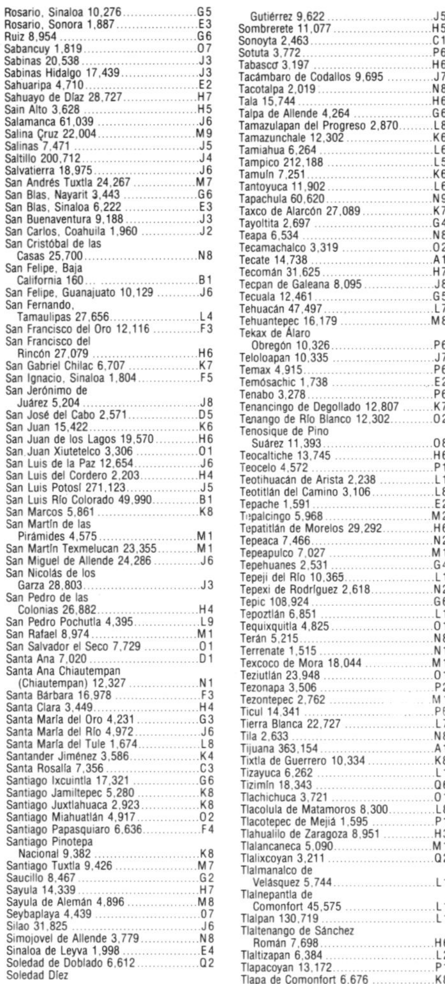

Rosario, Sinaloa 10,276 G5
Rosario, Sonora 1,887 E3
Ruiz 8,954 G6
Sabancuy 1,819 O7
Sabinas 20,538 J3
Sabinas Hidalgo 17,439 J3
Sahuaripa 4,710 E2
Sahuayo de Díaz 28,727 H7
Sain Alto 3,628 H5
Salamanca 61,039 J6
Salina Çruz 22,004 M9
Salinas 7,471 J5
Saltillo 200,712 J4
Salvatierra 18,975 J6
San Andrés Tuxtla 24,267 M7
San Blas, Nayarit 3,443 G6
San Blas, Sinaloa 6,222 E3
San Buenaventura 9,188 J3
San Carlos, Coahuila 1,960 J2
San Cristóbal de las Casas 25,700 N8
San Felipe, Baja California 160 B1
San Felipe, Guanajuato 10,129 J6
San Fernando, Tamaulipas 27,656 L4
San Francisco del Oro 12,116 F3
San Francisco del Rincón 27,079 H6
San Gabriel Chilac 6,707 K7
San Ignacio, Sinaloa 1,804 F5
San Jerónimo de Juárez 5,204 J8
San José del Cabo 2,571 D5
San Juan 15,422 K6
San Juan de los Lagos 19,570 H6
San Juan Xiutetelco 3,306 O1
San Luis de la Paz 12,654 J6
San Luis del Cordero 2,203 H4
San Luis Potosí 271,123 J5
San Luis Río Colorado 49,990 B1
San Marcos 5,861 K8
San Martín de las Pirámides 4,575 M1
San Martín Texmelucan 23,355 M1
San Miguel de Allende 24,286 J6
San Nicolás de los Garza 28,803 J3
San Pedro de las Colonias 26,882 H4
San Pedro Pochutla 4,395 L9
San Rafael 8,974 M1
San Salvador el Seco 7,729 O1
Santa Ana 7,020 D1
Santa Ana Chiautempan (Chiautempan) 12,327 N1
Santa Bárbara 16,978 F3
Santa Clara 3,449 H4
Santa María del Oro 4,231 G3
Santa María del Río 4,972 J6
Santa María del Tule 1,674 L8
Santander Jiménez 3,586 K4
Santa Rosalía 7,356 C3
Santiago Ixcuintla 17,321 G6
Santiago Jamiltepec 5,280 K8
Santiago Juxtlahuaca 2,923 K8
Santiago Miahuatlán 4,917 O2
Santiago Papasquiaro 6,636 F4
Santiago Pinotepa Nacional 9,382 K8
Santiago Tuxtla 9,426 M7
Saucillo 8,467 G2
Sayula 14,339 H7
Sayula de Alemán 4,896 M8
Seybaplaya 4,439 O7
Silao 31,825 J6
Simojovel de Allende 3,779 N8
Sinaloa de Leyva 1,998 E4
Soledad de Doblado 6,612 Q2
Soledad Díez
Gutiérrez 9,622 J5
Sombrerete 11,077 H5
Sonoyta 2,463 C1
Sotuta 3,772 P6
Tabasco 3,197 H6
Tacámbaro de Codallos 9,695 J7
Tacotalpa 2,019 N8
Tala 15,744 H6
Talpa de Allende 4,264 G6
Tamazulapan del Progreso 2,870 L8
Tamazunchale 12,302 K6
Tamiahua 6,264 L6
Tampico 212,188 L5
Tamuín 7,251 K6
Tantoyuca 11,902 L6
Tapachula 60,620 N9
Taxco de Alarcón 27,089 K7
Tayoltita 2,697 G4
Teapa 6,534 N8
Tecamachalco 3,319 O2
Tecate 14,738 A1
Tecomán 31,625 H7
Tecpan de Galeana 8,095 J8
Tecuala 12,461 G5
Tehuacán 47,497 L7
Tehuantepec 16,179 M8
Tekax de Álaro Obregón 10,326 P6
Teloloapan 10,335 J7
Temax 4,915 P6
Temósachic 1,738 E2
Tenabo 3,278 P6
Tenancingo de Degollado 12,807 K7
Tenango de Río Blanco 12,302 O2
Tenosique de Pino Suárez 11,393 O8
Teocaltiche 13,745 H6
Teocelo 4,572 P1
Teotihuacán de Arista 2,238 L1
Teotitlán del Camino 3,106 L8
Tepache 1,591 E2
Tepalcingo 5,968 M2
Tepatitlán de Morelos 29,292 H6
Tepeaca 7,466 N2
Tepeapulco 7,027 M1
Tepehuanes 2,531 G4
Tepeji del Río 10,365 L1
Tepexi de Rodríguez 2,618 N2
Tepic 108,924 G6
Tepoztlán 6,851 L1
Tequixquitla 4,825 O1
Terán 5,215 N8
Terrenate 1,515 N1
Texcoco de Mora 18,044 M1
Teziutlán 23,948 O1
Tezonapa 3,506 P2
Tezontepec 2,762 M1
Ticul 14,341 P6
Tierra Blanca 22,727 L7
Tila 2,633 N8
Tijuana 363,154 A1
Tixtla de Guerrero 10,334 K8
Tizayuca 6,262 L1
Tizimín 18,343 Q6
Tlachichuca 3,721 O1
Tlacolula de Matamoros 8,300 L8
Tlacotepec de Mejiá 1,595 P1
Tlahualilo de Zaragoza 8,951 H3
Tlalancaneca 5,090 M1
Tlalixcoyan 3,211 Q2
Tlalmanalco de Velásquez 5,744 L1
Tlalnepantla de Comonfort 45,575 L1
Tlalpan 130,719 L1
Tlaltenango de Sánchez Román 7,698 H6
Tlaltizapan 6,384 L2
Tlapacoyan 13,172 P1
Tlapa de Comonfort 6,676 K8

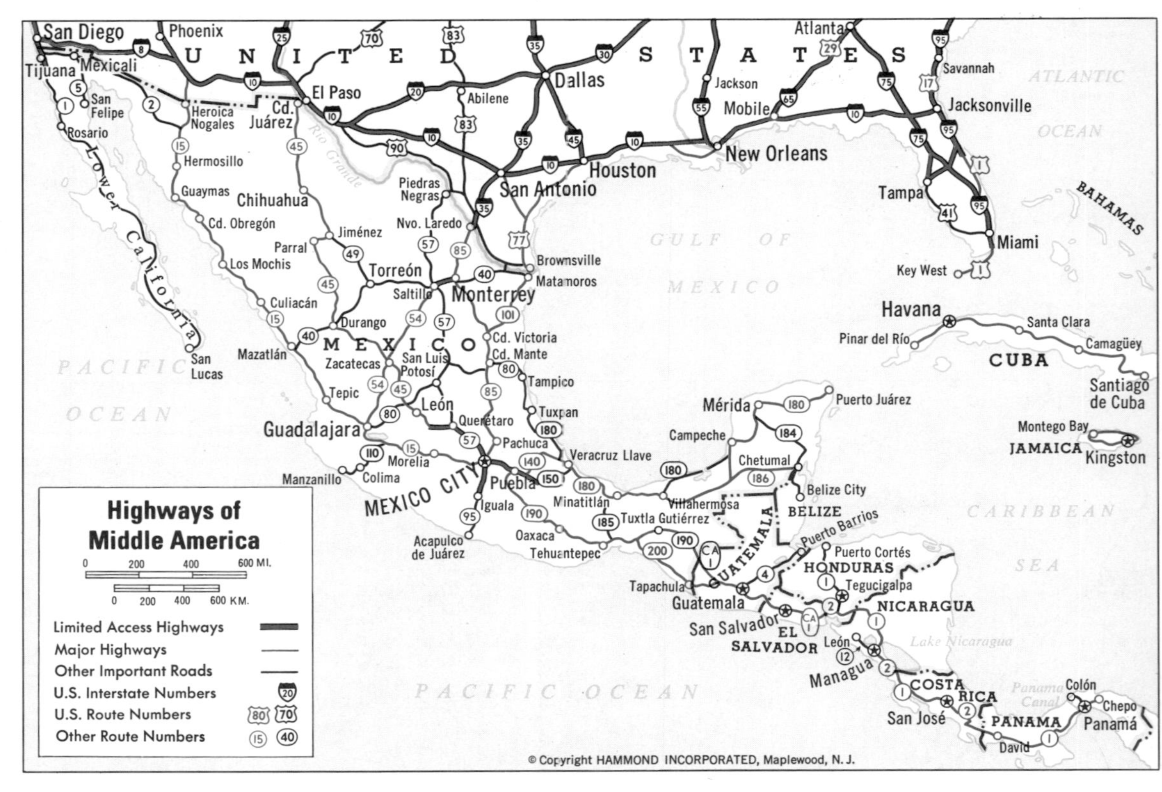

Tlaquepaque 59,760 G6
Tlatlauquitepec 4,272 O1
Tlaquiltenango 8,625 L2
Tlaxcala de Xicotencatl 9,972 M1
Tlaxco 4,969 N1
Tlaxiaco 4,477 L8
Tlayacapan 3,538 L1
Tochimilco 3,190 M2
Todos Santos 2,400 D5
Toluca de Lerdo 136,092 K7
Tomatlán 2,695 G6
Tonalá 15,611 N8
Topolobampo 4,685 E4
Torreón 244,309 H4
Tula, Tamaulipas 5,407 K5
Tula de Allende 10,720 K6
Tulancingo 35,799 K7
Tulcingo del Valle 2,983 M2
Tultepec 8,321 L1
Tuxpan, Jalisco 14,693 H7
Tuxpan, Nayarit 20,322 G6
Tuxpan de Rodríguez Cano 33,901 L6
Tuxtepec 17,701 L7
Tuxtla Gutiérrez 66,851 N8
Tzucabab 4,876 P7
Umán 8,371 P6
Unión de Tula 6,399 G7
Unión Hidalgo 8,658 M8
Ures 3,681 D2
Úrsulo Galván 2,637 Q1
Uruapan del Progreso 108,124 H7
Valladolid 14,663 P6
Valle de Allende 4,973 G3
Valle de Bravo 7,628 J7
Valle Hermoso 19,278 L4
Vanegas 2,042 J5
Venado 2,790 J5
Venustiano Carranza 23,624 N8
Veracruz 255,646 Q1
Vicam 4,104 D3
Vicente Guerrero, Durango 8,451 G5
Victor Rosales 7,629 H5
Viesca 2,923 H4
Villa Acuña 30,276 J2
Villa Cuauhtémoc 6,611 L5
Villa de Cos 1,850 H5
Villa de Guadelupe Hidalgo 88,537 L1
Villa Frontera 25,761 J3
Villa García 2,765 J5
Villahermosa 133,181 N8
Villa Hidalgo 2,126 E1
Villaldama 2,350 J3
Villa Matamoros 1,998 G3
Villanueva 5,895 H5
Villa Unión, Coahuila 4,058 J2
Villa Unión, Durango 4,042 H5
Villa Unión, Sinaloa 6,789 F5
Villa Vicente Guerrero 18,280 N1
Xaltocan 2,524 N1
Xicoténcatl 6,374 K5
Xicotepec de Juárez 12,656 L6
Xochihuehuetlán 3,268 K8
Xochimilco 116,493 L1
Xochitlán 3,312 N2
Yajalón 4,506 N8
Yanga 3,843 P2
Yaqui 8,061 D3
Yautepec 13,952 L2
Yavaros 1,959 E3
Yécora E2
Yecuatla 2,816 P1
Yehualtepec 2,558 O2
Zaachila 7,270 L8
Zacapoaxtla 4,527 O1
Zacapu 31,989 J7
Zacatepec 16,839 L2
Zacatecas 50,251 H5
Zacatelco 14,117 N1
Zacatlán 7,909 N1
Zacoalco de Torres 11,343 H6
Zamora de Hidalgo 5,775 H7
Zaragoza, Coahuila 6,797 J2
Zaragoza, Chihuahua 3,984 F1
Zaragoza, Puebla 4,754 O1
Zempoala 5,064 Q1
Zihuatenejo 4,879 J8
Zimatlán de Álvarez 5,746 L8
Zitácuaro 36,911 J7
Zongolica 2,378 P2
Zumpango de Ocampo 12,923 L1
Zumpango del Río 8,162 J8

OTHER FEATURES

Ágiobampo (bay) E3
Aguanaval (riv.) H4
Amistad (res.) J2
Ángel de la Guarda (isl.) C2
Antigua (riv.) Q1
Arena (pt.) E5
Arenas (cay) O5
Atoyac (riv.) N2
Atoyac (riv.) Q2
Babia (riv.) J2
Bacalar (lake) P7
Ballenas (bay) C3
Balsas (riv.) J7
Banderas (bay) G6
Bavispe, Río de (riv.) E1
Blanco (riv.) Q2
Bravo (Grande) (riv.) G2
Burro (mts.) J2
California (gulf) D3
Campeche (bank) O6
Campeche (bay) N7
Candelaria (riv.) O8
Carmen (isl.) D3
Casas Grandes (riv.) F1
Catoche (cape) Q6
Cedros (isl.) B2
Cerralvo (isl.) E4
Chamela (bay) G7
Chapala (lake) H6
Chetumal (bay) P8
Chichén-Itzá (ruin) P6
Citlaltépetl (mt.) O2
Clarión (isl.) B7
Colorado (riv.) B1
Conchos (riv.) G2
Corrientes (cape) F6
Coyuca (riv.) O1
Creciente (isl.) D5
Cuitzeo (lake) J7
Delgada (pt.) L7
Dzibichaltún (ruin) P6
El Azúcar (res.) K3
Espíritu Santo (isl.) D4
Falcón (res.) K3
Falso (cape) D5
Fuerte (riv.) E3
Giganta, Sierra de la (mts.) D4
Grande (riv.) G2
Grande (riv.) N8
Grande de Santiago (riv.) G6
Grijalva (riv.) N7
Guzmán (lake) F1
Herrero (pt.) Q7
Hondo (riv.) P7
Jesús María (reef) L4
La Boquilla (res.) G3
La Paz (bay) D4
Lobos (cape) C2
Lobos (pt.) D3
Lower California (pen.) C3
Madre (lag.) L4
Madre del Sur, Sierra (mts.) K8
Madre Occidental, Sierra (mts.) F3
Madre Oriental, Sierra (mts.) J4
Magdalena (bay) C4
Maldonado (pt.) K8
Mapimí (depr.) G3
María Cleófas (isl.) F6
María Madre (isl.) F6
María Magdalena (isl.) F6
Mexico (gulf) N4
Mezquital (riv.) G5
Mita (pt.) G6
Mitla (ruin) M8
Moctezuma (riv.) K6
Monserrate (isl.) D4
Montague (isl.) B1
Muerto, Mar (lag.) N9
Nauhcampatépetl (mt.) O1
Nayarit, Sierra (mts.) G5
Nazas (riv.) G4
Nuevo, Bajo (reef) O6
Orizaba (Citlaltépetl) (mt.) O2
Palenque (ruin) O8
Palmito de la Virgen (isl.) F5
Palmito del Verde (isl.) F5
Pánuco (riv.) K5
Paricutín (vol.) H7
Pátzcuaro (lake) J7
Pérez (isl.) P5
Petacalco (bay) H8
Popocatépetl (mt.) M1
Ramos (riv.) G4
Revillagigedo (isls.) C7
Roca Partida (isl.) C7
Sabinas (riv.) J3
San Antonio (reef) L4
San Benedicto (isl.) D7
San Benito (isl.) B2
San Jorge (bay) C1
San José (isl.) D4
San Lázaro (cape) C4
San Lucas (cape) E5
San Marcos (isl.) D3
San Rafael (reef) L4
Santa Ana (reef) N7
Santa Catalina (isl.) D4
Santa Cruz (isl.) D4
Santa Eugenia (pt.) B3
Santa Margarita (isl.) C4
Santa María (lake) F1
Santa María (riv.) F1
Santiaguillo (lake) G4
Sebastián Vizcaíno (bay) B2
Socorro (isl.) D7
Sonora (riv.) D2
Superior (lag.) M9
Teacapán (inlet) F5
Tehuantepec (gulf) M9
Tehuantepec (isth.) M8
Teotihuacán (ruin) M1
Términos (lag.) O7
Tiburón (isl.) C2
Triángulo Este (isl.) N6
Triángulo Oeste (isl.) N6
Tula (riv.) L1
Urique (riv.) F3
Usumacinta (riv.) O8
Uxmal (ruins) P6
Valsequillo (res.) N2
Verde (riv.) F3
Verde (riv.) L8
Yaqui (riv.) E2

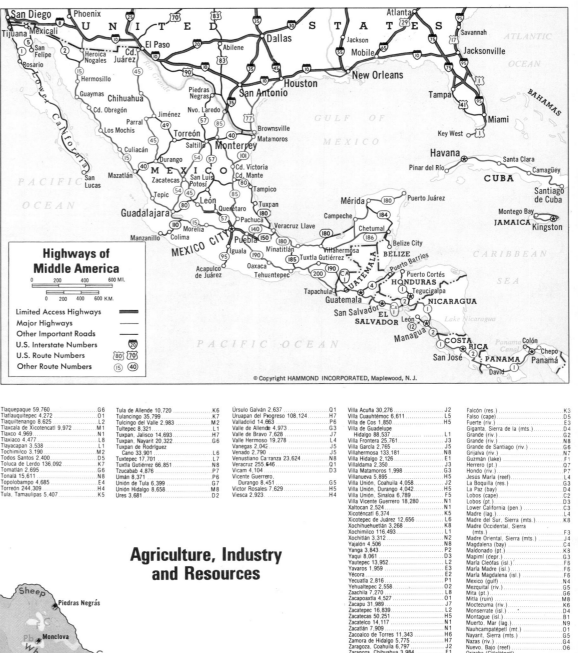

*City and suburbs.

Agriculture, Industry and Resources

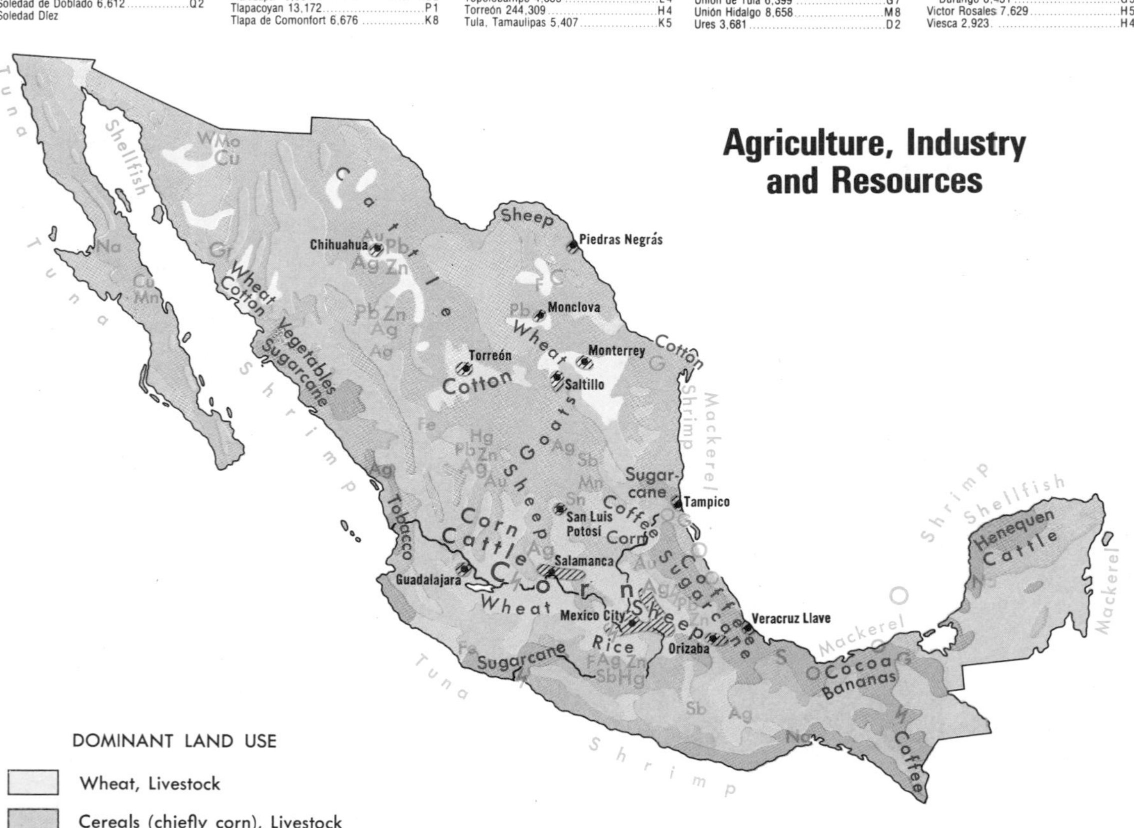

GUATEMALA

AREA 42,042 sq. mi. (108,889 sq. km.)
POPULATION 7,262,419
CAPITAL Guatemala
LARGEST CITY Guatemala
HIGHEST POINT Tajumulco 13,845 ft. (4,220 m.)
MONETARY UNIT quetzal
MAJOR LANGUAGES Spanish, Quiché
MAJOR RELIGION Roman Catholicism

BELIZE

AREA 8,867 sq. mi. (22,966 sq. km.)
POPULATION 144,857
CAPITAL Belmopan
LARGEST CITY Belize City
HIGHEST POINT Victoria Peak 3,681 ft. (1,122 m.)
MONETARY UNIT Belize dollar
MAJOR LANGUAGES English, Spanish, Mayan
MAJOR RELIGIONS Roman Catholicism, Protestantism

EL SALVADOR

AREA 8,260 sq. mi. (21,393 sq. km.)
POPULATION 4,813,000
CAPITAL San Salvador
LARGEST CITY San Salvador
HIGHEST POINT Santa Ana 7,825 ft. (2,385 m.)
MONETARY UNIT colón
MAJOR LANGUAGE Spanish
MAJOR RELIGION Roman Catholicism

HONDURAS

AREA 43,277 sq. mi. (112,087 sq. km.)
POPULATION 3,691,000
CAPITAL Tegucigalpa
LARGEST CITY Tegucigalpa
HIGHEST POINT Las Minas 9,347 ft. (2,849 m.)
MONETARY UNIT lempira
MAJOR LANGUAGE Spanish
MAJOR RELIGION Roman Catholicism

NICARAGUA

AREA 45,698 sq. mi. (118,358 sq. km.)
POPULATION 2,703,000
CAPITAL Managua
LARGEST CITY Managua
HIGHEST POINT Cerro Mocotón 6,913 ft. (2,107 m.)
MONETARY UNIT córdoba
MAJOR LANGUAGE Spanish
MAJOR RELIGION Roman Catholicism

COSTA RICA

AREA 19,575 sq. mi. (50,700 sq. km.)
POPULATION 2,245,000
CAPITAL San José
LARGEST CITY San José
HIGHEST POINT Chirripó Grande 12,530 ft. (3,819 m.)
MONETARY UNIT colón
MAJOR LANGUAGE Spanish
MAJOR RELIGION Roman Catholicism

PANAMA

AREA 29,761 sq. mi. (77,082 sq. km.)
POPULATION 1,830,175
CAPITAL Panamá
LARGEST CITY Panamá
HIGHEST POINT Vol. Baru 11,401 ft. (3,475 m.)
MONETARY UNIT balboa
MAJOR LANGUAGE Spanish
MAJOR RELIGION Roman Catholicism

Agriculture, Industry and Resources

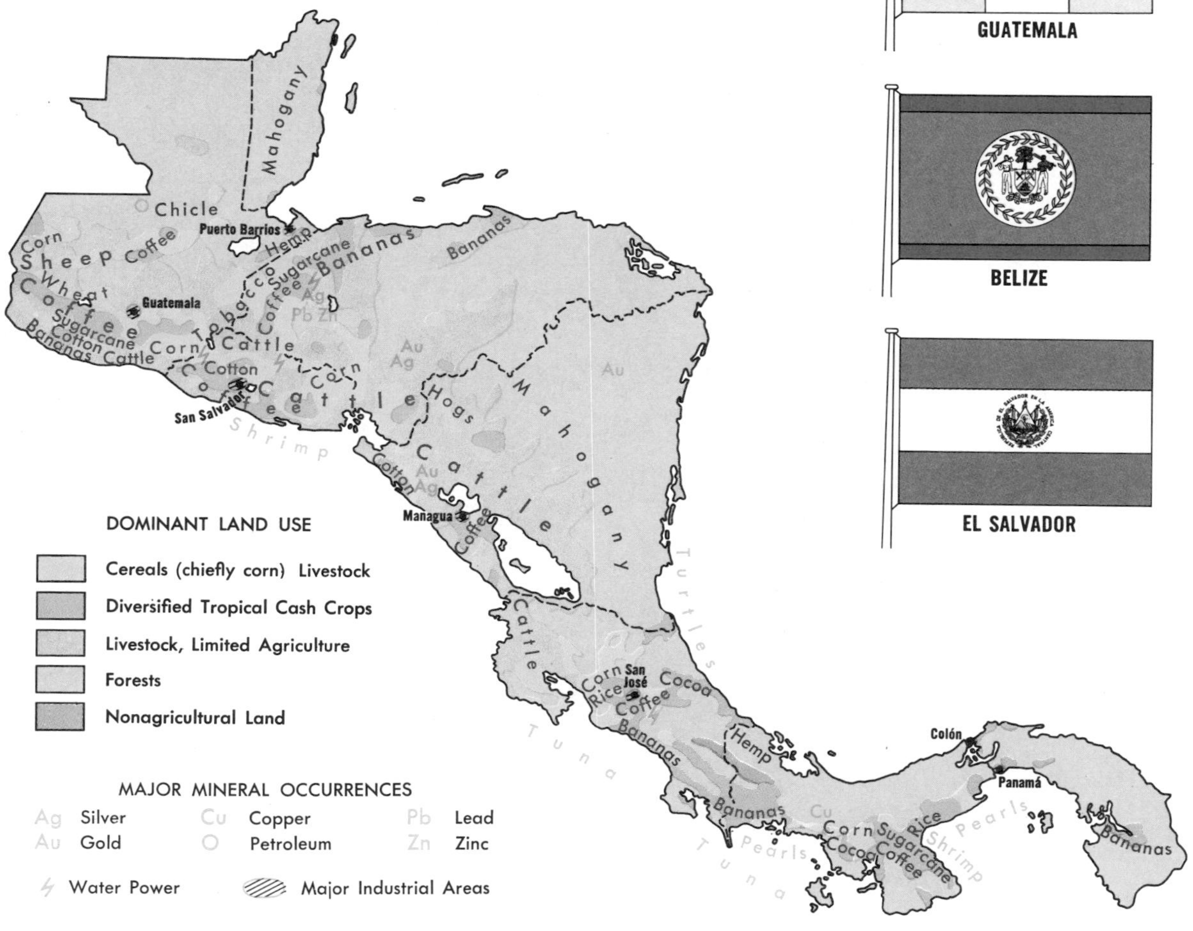

DOMINANT LAND USE

- Cereals (chiefly corn) Livestock
- Diversified Tropical Cash Crops
- Livestock, Limited Agriculture
- Forests
- Nonagricultural Land

MAJOR MINERAL OCCURRENCES

- Ag Silver
- Au Gold
- Cu Copper
- O Petroleum
- Pb Lead
- Zn Zinc

Water Power

Major Industrial Areas

GUATEMALA

HONDURAS

BELIZE

NICARAGUA

EL SALVADOR

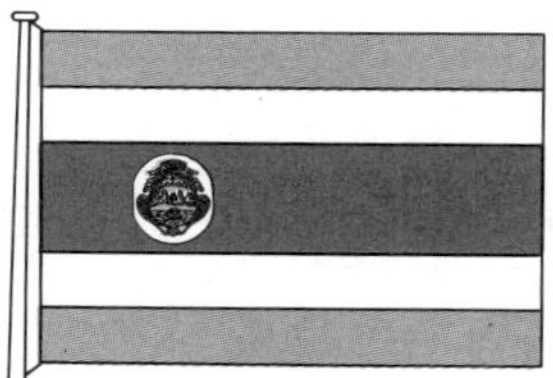

COSTA RICA

PANAMA

BELIZE

CITIES and TOWNS

Belize City 39,887 .... C2
Belize City* 50,925 .... C2
Belmopan (cap.) 2,932 .... C2
Corozal Town 6,862 .... C1
Hattieville 904 .... C2
Libertad 856 .... C1
Orange Walk Town 8,441 .... C1
Punta Gorda 2,219 .... C2
San Ignacio 5,606 .... C2
Stann Creek Town 6,627 .... C2

OTHER FEATURES

Ambergris (cay) D1
Belize (riv.) C2
Bokel (cay) D2
Glover (reef) D2
Half Moon (cay) D2
Hondo (riv.) C1
Honduras (gulf) D2
Mauger (cay) D2
New (riv.) C2
Saint Georges (cay) D2
Sarstún (riv.) C3
Turneffe (isls.) D2

COSTA RICA

CITIES and TOWNS

Alajuela 33,122 .... E6
Atenas 1,728 .... E6
Bagaces 2,129 .... E5
Boruca⊙ 1,892 .... F6
Buenos Aires⊙ 302 .... F6
Cañas 6,053 .... E5
Cartago 21,753 .... F6
Ciudad Quesada 9,754 .... E5
Esparta 4,699 .... E5
Filadelfia 2,958 .... E5
Golfito 6,962 .... F6
Grecia 8,355 .... E5
Guácimo 1,168 .... F5
Guápiles 3,524 .... F5
Heredia 22,700 .... E5
Las Juntas 1,129 .... E5
Liberia 10,802 .... E5
Limón 29,621 .... F6
Miramar 1,673 .... E5
Nicoya 7,474 .... E5
Orotina 3,170 .... E6
Palmares 3,083 .... F6
Paralso 8,446 .... F6
Puerto Cortés 2,070 .... F6
Puntarenas 26,331 .... E6
Quepos 2,155 .... E6
San José (cap.) 215,441 .... F5
San José* 391,107 .... F5
San Marcos 917 .... E6
San Ramón 9,245 .... E5
Santa Cruz 5,777 .... E5
Santo Domingo 5,148 .... F6
Siquirres 4,361 .... F5
Turrialba 12,151 .... F6

(continued on following page)

(continued)

OTHER FEATURES

Blanca (pt.) F5
Blanco (cape) E6
Blanco (peak) F6
Burica (pt.) F6
Cahuita (pt.) F6
Caño (isl.) F6
Carreta (pt.) F6
Chirripó Grande (mt.) F6
Coronada (bay) F6
Cuilapa Miravalles (vol.) E5
Dulce (gulf) F6
Góngora (mt.) E5
Guionos (pt.) E6
Irazú (mt.) F6
Judas (pt.) E6
Llerena (pt.) F6
Matapalo (cape) F6
Nicoya (gulf) E6
Nicoya (pen.) E6
Papagayo (gulf) E5
Salinas (bay) D5
San Juan (riv.) E5
Santa Elena (cape) D5
Talamanca (range) F6
Velas (cape) D5

EL SALVADOR

CITIES and TOWNS

Acajutla 8,598 ..... B4
Ahuachapán 17,242 ..... B4
Atiquizaya 7,035 ..... C3
Chalatenango 7,633 ..... C3
Chinameca 6,303 ..... C4
Cojutepeque 20,615 ..... C4
Estanzuelas 2,548 ..... C4
Ilobasco 6,572 ..... C4
Intipucá 3,469 ..... D4
Jucuarán 1,443 ..... C4
La Libertad C4
La Palma 1,998 ..... C3
La Unión 17,207 ..... D4
Metapán 7,704 ..... C3
Nueva San Salvador 35,106 ..... C4
Puerto de la Concordia C4
San Francisco Gotera 4,725 ..... C4
San Miguel 59,304 ..... D4
San Salvador (cap.) 337,171 ..... C4
Santa Ana 96,306 ..... C4
Santa Rosa de Lima 5,707 ..... D4
San Vicente 18,872 ..... C4
Sensuntepeque 7,226 ..... C4
Sonsonate 33,562 ..... C4
Suchitoto 5,540 ..... C4
Texistepeque 1,722 ..... C3
Usulután 19,616 ..... C4
Zacatecoluca 15,718 ..... C4

OTHER FEATURES

Fonseca (gulf) D4
Güija (lake) C3
Lempa (riv.) C4
Remedios (pt.) B4
Santa Ana (mt.) C4

GUATEMALA

CITIES and TOWNS

Amatitlán 15,251 ..... B3
Antigua 17,994 ..... B3
Asunción Mita 7,477 ..... C3
Cahabón 1,344 ..... C3
Chajul 4,329 ..... B3
Champerico 5,722 ..... A3
Chichicastenango 2,635 ..... B3
Chimaltenango 12,860 ..... B3
Chiquimula 16,126 ..... C3
Coatepeque 15,979 ..... A3
Cobán 11,418 ..... B3
Comalapa 10,980 ..... B3
Cubulco 2,021 ..... B3
Cuilapa 4,287 ..... B3
Cuilco 862 ..... B3
Dolores 973 ..... C2
El Estor 2,324 ..... C3
El Progreso 4,009 ..... B3
Escuintla 33,205 ..... B3
Flores 1,477 ..... C2
Gualán 5,169 ..... C3
Guatemala (cap.) 700,538 ..... B3
Huehuetenango 12,570 ..... B3
Ipala 3,386 ..... C3
Iztapa 1,237 ..... B4
Jacaltenango 4,517 ..... B3
Jalapa 13,788 ..... B3
Jutiapa 8,210 ..... B3
La Gomera 2,394 ..... B3
La Libertad 908 ..... B2
Livingston 2,898 ..... C3
Los Amates 1,383 ..... C3
Masagua 1,178 ..... B3
Mazatenango 23,285 ..... B3
Momostenango 5,210 ..... B3
Morales 2,113 ..... C3
Ocós 741 ..... A3
Panzós 1,643 ..... C3
Puerto Barrios 22,598 ..... C3
Quezaltenango 53,021 ..... B3
Quezaltepeque 2,222 ..... C3
Rabinal 4,625 ..... B3
Retalhuleu 19,060 ..... B3
Río Hondo 1,416 ..... C3
Sacapulas 1,439 ..... B3
Salamá 5,529 ..... B3
San Andrés 1,066 ..... B2
San Felipe 3,210 ..... B3
San José 9,402 ..... B4
San Luis 1,136 ..... C2
San Luis Jilotepeque 6,055 ..... C3
San Marcos 5,700 ..... B3
San Martín Jilotepeque 3,770 ..... B3
San Mateo Ixtatán 1,834 ..... B3
San Pedro Carchá 4,465 ..... B3
Santa Cruz del Quiché 7,651 ..... B3
Santa Rosa de Lima 1,161 ..... B3
Sololá 3,960 ..... B3
Tacaná 1,280 ..... A3
Tejutla 1,205 ..... B3
Tikal C2
Totonicapán 8,568 ..... B3
Zacapa 12,688 ..... C3

OTHER FEATURES

Atitlán (lake) B3
Atitlán (vol.) B3
Azul (riv.) C2
Chixoy (riv.) B2
Güija (lake) C3
Honduras (gulf) D2
Izabal (lake) C3
Minas (mts.) C3
Motagua (riv.) C3
Pasión (riv.) B2
Petén-Itzá (lake) B2
San Pedro (riv.) B2
Sarstún (riv.) C3
Tacaná (vol.) A3
Tajumulco (vol.) B3
Tres Puntas (cape) C3
Usumacinta (riv.) B2

HONDURAS

CITIES and TOWNS

Amapala 2,274 ..... D4
Brus Laguna 933 ..... E3
Catacamas 9,134 ..... E3
Cedros 917 ..... D3
Choloma 961 ..... C3
Choluteca 26,152 ..... D4
Comayagua 15,941 ..... D3
Corquín 2,629 ..... C3
Danlí 10,825 ..... D3
El Dulce Nombre 1,297 ..... E3

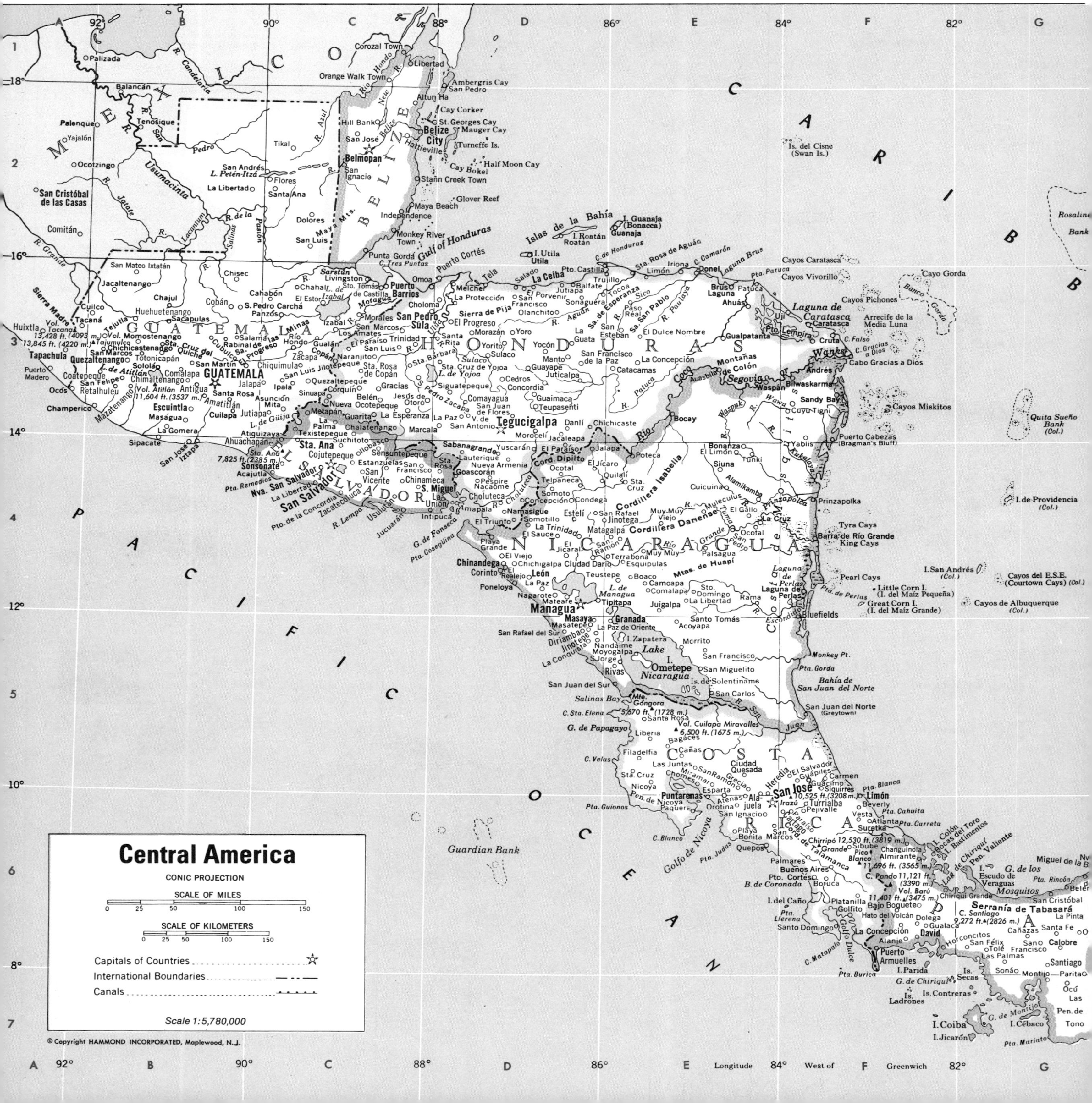

Central America

CONIC PROJECTION

SCALE OF MILES: 0 – 25 – 50 – 100 – 150

SCALE OF KILOMETERS: 0 – 25 – 50 – 100 – 150

Capitals of Countries ☆
International Boundaries
Canals

Scale 1:5,780,000

Longitude 84° West of Greenwich

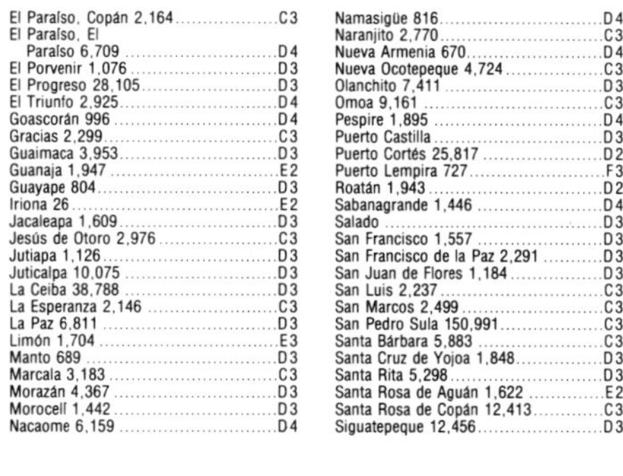

El Paraíso, Copán 2,164 C3
El Paraíso, El Paraíso 6,709 D4
El Porvenir 1,076 D3
El Progreso 28,105 D3
El Triunfo 2,925 D4
Goascorán 996 D4
Gracias 2,299 C3
Guaimaca 3,953 D3
Guanaja 1,947 E2
Guayape 804 D3
Iriona 26 E2
Jacaleapa 1,609 D3
Jesús de Otoro 2,976 C3
Jutiapa 1,126 D3
Juticalpa 10,075 D3
La Ceiba 38,788 D3
La Esperanza 2,146 C3
La Paz 6,811 D3
Limón 1,704 E3
Manto 689 D3
Marcala 3,183 C3
Morazán 4,367 D3
Morocelí 1,442 D3
Nacaome 6,159 D4
Namasigüe 816 D4
Naranjito 2,770 C3
Nueva Armenia 670 D4
Nueva Ocotepeque 4,724 C3
Olanchito 7,411 D3
Omoa 9,161 C3
Pespire 1,895 D4
Puerto Castilla D3
Puerto Cortés 25,817 D2
Puerto Lempira 727 F3
Roatán 1,943 D2
Sabanagrande 1,446 D4
Salado D3
San Francisco 1,557 D3
San Francisco de la Paz 2,291 D3
San Juan de Flores 1,184 D3
San Luis 2,237 C3
San Marcos 2,499 C3
San Pedro Sula 150,991 C3
Santa Bárbara 5,883 C3
Santa Cruz de Yojoa 1,848 D3
Santa Rita 5,298 D3
Santa Rosa de Aguán 1,622 E2
Santa Rosa de Copán 12,413 C3
Siguatepeque 12,456 D3

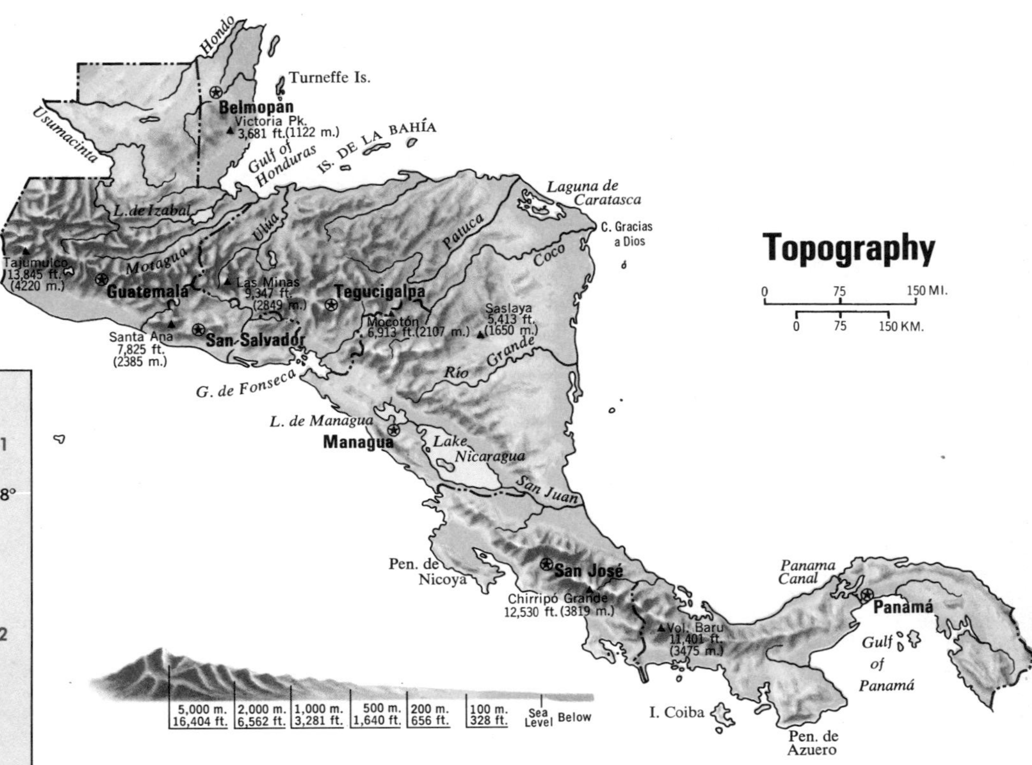

Topography

0 75 150 MI.
0 75 150 KM.

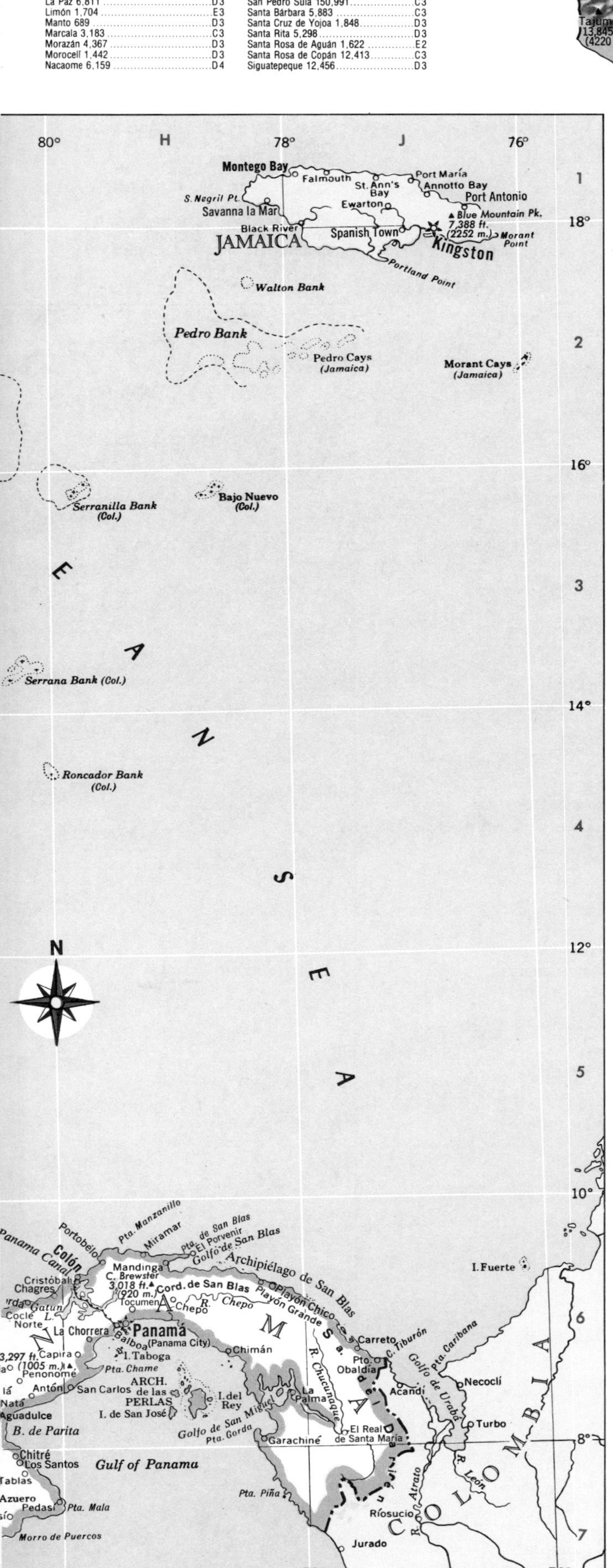

Sinuapa 831 C3
Sonaguera 2,264 D3
Sulaco 1,121 D3
Tegucigalpa (cap.) 273,894 D3
Tegucigalpa* 305,387 D3
Tela 19,055 D3
Teupasenti 2,003 D3
Tocoa 2,803 E3
Trinidad 1,598 C3
Trujillo 3,961 E3
Utila 1,177 D2
Villa de San Antonio 2,359 D3
Yorito 770 D3
Yoro 4,449 D3
Yuscarán 1,835 D4

OTHER FEATURES

Aguán (riv.) D3
Bahía (isls.) D2
Bonacca (Guanaja) (isl.) E2
Brus (lag.) E2
Camarón (cape) E2
Caratasca (cays) F2
Caratasca (lag.) F3
Choluteca (riv.) D4
Cisne (isls.) F2
Coco (riv.) E3
Colón (mts.) E3
Esperanza (mts.) E3
Falso (cape) F3
Fonseca (gulf) D4
Gorda (bank) F3
Guanaja (isl.) E2
Honduras (cape) E2
Honduras (gulf) D2
Patuca (pt.) E3
Patuca (riv.) E3
Paulaya (riv.) E3
Pija, Sierra de (mts.) D3
Roatán (isl.) D2
San Pablo, Sierra (mts.) E3
Segovia (Coco) (riv.) E3
Sico (riv.) E3
Sulaco (riv.) D3
Swan (Cisne) (isls.) F2
Ulúa (riv.) D3
Utila (isl.) D2
Wanks (Coco) (riv.) E3
Yojoa (lake) D3

NICARAGUA

CITIES and TOWNS

Acoyapa 2,588 E5
Barra de Río Grande F4
Bluefields 14,252 F4
Boaco 6,372 E4
Bonanza E4
Bragman's Bluff (Puerto Cabezas) 5,457 F3
Cabo Gracias a Dios○ 3,846 F3
Camoapa 4,385 E4
Chichigalpa 14,498 D4
Chinandega 30,441 D4
Ciudad Darío 5,304 D4
Condega 3,414 D4
Corinto 13,404 D4
Diriamba 10,085 D5
El Jícaro 1,669 E4
El Limón E4
El Realejo 2,229 D4
El Sauce 3,202 D4
El Viejo 8,507 D4
Esquipulas 2,232 E4
Estelí 20,222 D4
Granada 34,976 E5
Greytown (San Juan del Norte) 294 F5
Jalapa 3,633 E4
Jinotega 9,506 E4
Jinotepe 12,473 D5
Juigalpa 8,497 E4
La Cruz 150 E4
La Libertad 1,286 E4
La Paz Central 6,175 D4
La Paz de Oriente 957 E5
La Trinidad 3,548 D4
León 55,625 D4
Managua (cap.) 398,514 D4
Managua* 404,634 D4
Masatepe 6,307 D5
Masaya 30,753 D5
Matagalpa 21,385 E4
Mateare 1,405 D4
Morrito 368 E5
Moyogalpa 1,551 E5
Muy Muy 1,373 E4
Nagarote 7,185 D4
Nandaime 5,631 E5
Ocotal, Segovia 8,215 D4
Poneloya D4
Prinzapolka 8,979 F4
Puerto Cabezas 5,457 F3
Quilalí 1,245 E4
Rama 1,341 E4
Rivas 10,125 E5
San Carlos 2,022 E5
San Jorge 2,874 E5
San Juan del Norte 294 F5
San Juan del Sur 2,393 D5
San Miguelito 1,312 E5
San Rafael del Norte 1,938 E4
San Rafael del Sur 2,914 D5
San Ramón 477 E4
Santo Domingo 1,949 E4
Santo Tomás 2,309 E5
Siuna E4
Somotillo 1,864 D4
Somoto 5,847 D4
Telpaneca 991 D4
Terrabona 904 E4
Teustepe 1,060 E4
Tipitapa 5,758 E4
Waspán 1,246 E3

OTHER FEATURES

Coco (riv.) E3
Cosegüina (pt.) D4
Dariense, Cordillera (range) E4
Dipilto, Cordillera (range) D4
Escondido (riv.) F4
Fonseca (gulf) D4
Gorda (pt.) F5
Gracias a Dios (cape) F3
Grande (riv.) E4
Great Corn (isl.) F4
Huapí (mts.) E4
Isabelia, Cordillera (range) E4
King (cays) F4
Kukalaya (riv.) F4
Little Corn (isl.) F4
Maíz Grande (Great Corn) (isl.) F4
Maíz Pequeña (Little Corn) (isl.) F4
Managua (lake) E4
Miskitos (cays) F3
Monkey (pt.) F5
Mosquitos, Costa de (reg.) E4
Nicaragua (lake) E5
Ometepe (isl.) E5
Pearl (cays) F4
Perlas (pt.) F4
Prinzapolca (riv.) F4
Salinas (bay) D5
San Juan (riv.) E5
San Juan del Norte (bay) F5
Solentiname (isls.) E5
Tuma (riv.) E4
Tyra (cays) F4
Waspuk (riv.) E3
Wawa (riv.) E3
Zapatera (isl.) E5

PANAMA

CITIES and TOWNS

Aguadulce 10,659 G6
Alanje 866 F6
Almirante 4,664 F6
Antón 4,259 G6
Bajo Boquete 2,831 F6
Balboa 1,952 H6
Bocas del Toro 2,515 F6
Cañazas 1,526 G6
Capira 1,749 G6
Changuinola 9,528 F6
Chepo 4,529 H6
Chiriquí Grande F6
Chitré 17,156 G7
Coclé del Norte G6
Colón 59,832 H6
Cristóbal⊙ 7,959 G6
David 50,621 F6
Dolega 1,019 F6
El Real de Santa María 912 J6
Garachiné 1,116 H6
Gualaca 1,510 F6
Horconcitos 1,090 F6
La Chorrera 36,971 H6
La Concepción 10,460 F6
La Palma 1,634 H6
La Pintada 1,100 G6
Las Palmas 738 G6
Las Tablas 5,230 G7
Los Santos 4,644 G7
Mandinga 81 H6
Montijo 1,152 G6
Natá 5,603 G6
Nuevo Chagres 306 G6
Ocú 2,353 G7
Panamá (cap.) 388,638 H6
Panamá* 498,624 H6
Parita 1,616 G6
Pedasí 934 G7
Penonomé 7,389 G6
Playón Chico 1,395 H6
Portobelo 551 H6
Puerto Armuelles 12,488 F6
Puerto Obaldía 491 J6
San Francisco 990 G6
Santa Fe 490 G6
Santiago 21,809 G6
Soná 4,471 G6
Tocumen⊙ 21,745 H6
Tolé 1,052 G6
Tonosí 891 G7

OTHER FEATURES

Azuero (pen.) G7
Bastimentos (isl.) G6
Brewster, Cerro (mt.) H6
Burica, Punta (cape) F6
Cébaco (isl.) G7
Chepo (riv.) H6
Chiriquí (gulf) F7
Chiriquí (lag.) G6
Chucunaque (riv.) J6
Coiba, Isla de (isl.) F7
Colón, Isla de (isl.) G6
Contreras (isls.) F7
Darién (mts.) J6
Escudo de Veraguas (isl.) G6
Gatun (lake) G6
Gorda (pt.) H6
Jicarón (isl.) F7
Ladrones (isls.) F7
Manzanillo (pt.) H6
Montijo (gulf) G7
Mosquitos, Golfo de los (gulf) G6
Panama (gulf) H7
Pando, Cerro (mt.) F6
Parida (isl.) F6
Parita (bay) G6
Perlas (arch.) H6
Puercos, Morro de (head) H7
Rey (isl.) H6
Rincón (pt.) G6
San Blas, Golfo de (bay) H6
San Blas, Pta. de (pt.) H6
San Blas, Cordillera de (mts.) H6
San José (isl.) H6
San Miguel, Golfo de (bay) H6
Santiago, Cerro (mt.) G6
Secas (isls.) G7
Tabasará (mts.) G6
Taboga (isl.) H6
Tiburón (pt.) J6
Valiente (pen.) G6

*City and suburbs.
○Population of sub-district or division.
⊙Population of district.

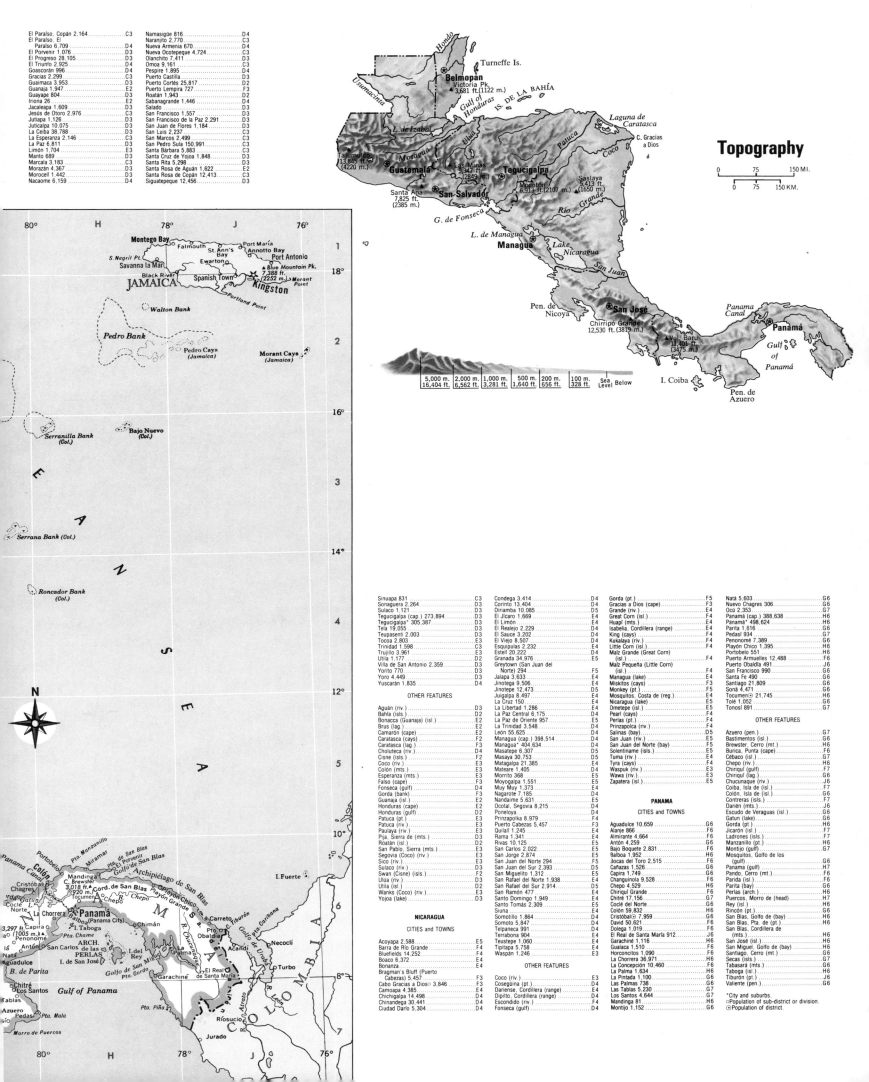

CUBA

HAITI

DOMINICAN REPUBLIC

JAMAICA

TRINIDAD AND TOBAGO

BARBADOS

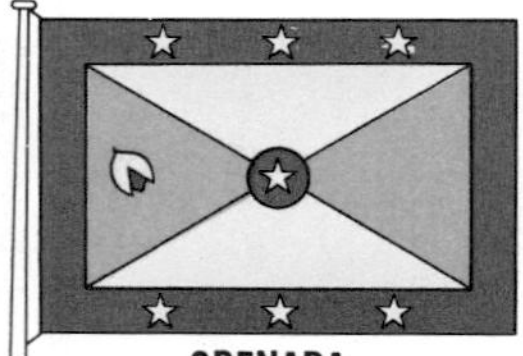

GRENADA

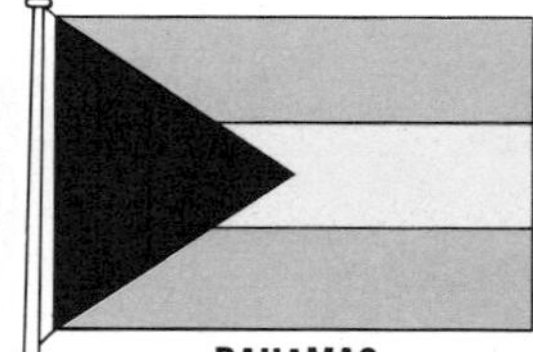

BAHAMAS

DOMINICA

ST. LUCIA

ST. VINC. & GRENS.

ANTIGUA AND BARBUDA

CUBA

AREA 44,206 sq. mi. (114,494 sq. km.)
POPULATION 9,706,369
CAPITAL Havana
LARGEST CITY Havana
HIGHEST POINT Pico Turquino 6,561 ft. (2,000 m.)
MONETARY UNIT Cuban peso
MAJOR LANGUAGE Spanish
MAJOR RELIGION Roman Catholicism

HAITI

AREA 10,694 sq. mi. (27,697 sq. km.)
POPULATION 5,053,792
CAPITAL Port-au-Prince
LARGEST CITY Port-au-Prince
HIGHEST POINT Pic La Selle 8,793 ft. (2,680 m.)
MONETARY UNIT gourde
MAJOR LANGUAGES Creole French, French
MAJOR RELIGION Roman Catholicism

DOMINICAN REPUBLIC

AREA 18,704 sq. mi. (48,443 sq. km.)
POPULATION 5,647,977
CAPITAL Santo Domingo
LARGEST CITY Santo Domingo
HIGHEST POINT Pico Duarte 10,417 ft. (3,175 m.)
MONETARY UNIT Dominican peso
MAJOR LANGUAGE Spanish
MAJOR RELIGION Roman Catholicism

JAMAICA

AREA 4,411 sq. mi. (11,424 sq. km.)
POPULATION 2,184,000
CAPITAL Kingston
LARGEST CITY Kingston
HIGHEST POINT Blue Mountain Peak 7,402 ft. (2,256 m.)
MONETARY UNIT Jamaican dollar
MAJOR LANGUAGE English
MAJOR RELIGIONS Protestantism, Roman Catholicism

PUERTO RICO

AREA 3,515 sq. mi. (9,104 sq. km.)
POPULATION 3,196,520
CAPITAL San Juan
MONETARY UNIT U.S. dollar
MAJOR LANGUAGES Spanish, English
MAJOR RELIGION Roman Catholicism

NETHERLANDS ANTILLES

AREA 390 sq. mi. (1,010 sq. km.)
POPULATION 246,000
CAPITAL Willemstad
MONETARY UNIT Antilles guilder
MAJOR LANGUAGES Dutch, Papiamento, English
MAJOR RELIGIONS Roman Catholicism, Protestantism

BERMUDA

AREA 21 sq. mi. (54 sq. km.)
POPULATION 67,761
CAPITAL Hamilton
MONETARY UNIT Bermuda dollar
MAJOR LANGUAGE English
MAJOR RELIGION Protestantism

ANGUILLA

Anguilla (isl.) 6,519 ... F3

ANTIGUA and BARBUDA

Antigua (isl.) 76,213 ... G3
Barbuda (isl.) 1,071 ... G3
Caribbean (sea) ... B4
Codrington 1,071 ... G3
Falmouth 1,134 ... F3
Redonda (isl.) ... F3
Saint John's (cap.) 21,814 ... G3

BAHAMAS

Acklins (isl.) 616 ... C2
Andros (isl.) 8,397 ... B1
Atwood (Samana) (cay) ... D2
Berry (isls.) 509 ... B1
Biminis, The (isls.) 1,432 ... B1
Caicos (passg.) ... D2
Cat (isl.) 2,143 ... C1
Cay Sal (bank) ... B2
Crooked (isl.) 517 ... D2
Crooked Island (passg.) ... C2
Eleuthera (isl.) 8,326 ... C1
Exuma (cays) ... C1
Exuma (sound) ... C1
Flamingo (cay) ... C2
Freeport 22,301 ... B1
Grand Bahama (isl.) 33,102 ... B1
Great Abaco (isl.) 7,324 ... C1
Great Bahama (bank) ... B1
Great Exuma (isl.) ... C2
Great Inagua (isl.) 939 ... D2
Great Isaac (isl.) ... B1
Gun (cay) ... B1
Harbour (isl.) ... C1
Little Inagua (isl.) ... D2
Long (cay) 33 ... C2
Long (isl.) 3,353 ... C2
Mayaguana (isl.) 476 ... D2
Mayaguana (passg.) ... D2
Mira Por Vos (cays) ... C2
Nassau (cap.) 135,437 ... C1
New Providence (isl.) 135,437 ... C1
North East Providence (chan.) ... C1
North West Providence (chan.) ... B1
Old Bahama (chan.) ... B2
Plana (cays) ... D2
Ragged (isl.) 146 ... C2
Rum (cay) ... C2
Samana (cay) ... D2
San Salvador (isl.) ... D1
Santarén (chan.) ... B1
Tongue of the Ocean (chan.) ... C1
Verde (cay) ... C2
Watling (San Salvador) (isl.) ... C1

BARBADOS

Bridgetown (cap.) 7,552 ... G4
Speightstown ... G4

BERMUDA

Bermuda (isl.) ... H3
Castle (harb.) ... H2
Great (sound) ... G3
Hamilton (cap.) 1,617 ... G3
Harrington (sound) ... G3
Ireland (isl.) ... G3
North (rapid) ... H2
Saint Davids (isl.) ... H2
Saint George 1,647 ... H2
Saint George's (isl.) ... H2
Somerset (isl.) ... G3

CAYMAN ISLANDS

Bartlett Deep ... B3
Cayman Brac (isl.) 1,603 ... B3
George Town (cap.) 7,617 ... B3
Grand Cayman (isl.) 15,000 ... B3
Little Cayman (isl.) 74 ... B3
Misteriosa (bank) ... A3

CUBA

Bayamo 109,201 ... C2
Camagüey 245,235 ... B2
Cienfuegos 107,396 ... B2
Florida (str.) ... B1
Guanabacoa 89,741 ... B2
Guantánamo 178,129 ... C2
Havana (cap.) 1,924,886 ... A2
Holguín 190,155 ... C2
Juventud (Pines) (isl.) 57,879 ... A2
Manzanillo 95,420 ... C2
Marianao ○127,563 ... A2
Matanzas 103,302 ... B2
Pinar del Río 104,598 ... A2
San Felipe (cays) ... A2
Santa Clara 175,113 ... B2
Santiago de Cuba 362,432 ... C3
Windward (passg.) ... C3

DOMINICA

Portsmouth 2,329 ... G4
Roseau (cap.) 9,968 ... G4

DOMINICAN REPUBLIC

La Romana 91,571 ... E3
San Francisco de Macorís 64,906 ... E3
San Pedro de Macorís 78,562 ... E3
Santiago 278,638 ... D3
Santo Domingo (cap.) 1,313,172 ... E3

GRENADA

Carriacou (isl.) 6,052 ... G4
Gouyave 2,498 ... F4
Grenadines (isls.) ... G4
Saint George's (cap.) 6,463 ... F5

GUADELOUPE

Basse-Terre (cap.) 13,397 ... F4
Saint-Barthélemy (isl.) 3,059 ... F3
Saint Martin (isl.) 8,072 ... F3

HAITI

Cap-Haïtien 64,406 ... D3
Gonaïves 34,209 ... D3
Port-au-Prince (cap.) 449,831 ... D3
Gonâve (isl.) ... D3
Jamaica (chan.) ... C3
Tortuga (isl.) ... D2

JAMAICA

Blue Mountain (peak) ... C3
Jamaica (chan.) ... C3
Kingston (cap.) 106,791 ... C3
Montego Bay 43,521 ... B3
Pedro (cays) ... C3
Savanna-la-Mar 11,759 ... B3

MARTINIQUE

Fort-de-France (cap.) 96,649 ... G4
Saint-Pierre 4,923 ... G4
Pelée (vol.) ... G4

MONTSERRAT

Plymouth (cap.) 1,623 ... F3

NETHERLANDS ANTILLES

Aruba (isl.) ... E4
Bonaire (isl.) ... E4
Curaçao (isl.) ... E4
Oranjestad 10,100 ... D4
Saba (isl.) ... F3
Saint Eustatius (isl.) ... F3
Saint Martin (Sint Maarten) (isl.) ... F3
Willemstad (cap.) 95,000 ... E4

PUERTO RICO

Bayamón 185,087 ... G1
Caguas 87,214 ... G1
Culebra (isl.) 1,265 ... G1
Mayagüez 82,968 ... F1
Mona (passg.) ... E3
Ponce 161,739 ... F1
San Juan (cap.) 424,600 ... G1
Vieques (isl.) 7,662 ... G1

SAINT CHRISTOPHER and NEVIS

Basseterre (cap.) 14,725 ... F3
Nevis (isl.) 9,300 ... F3
Saint Christopher (isl.) 35,104 ... F3

SAINT LUCIA

Castries (cap.) •42,770 ... G4
Vieux Fort •10,675 ... G4

SAINT VINCENT and THE GRENADINES

Bequia (isl.) ... G4
Georgetown 1,100 ... G4
Grenadines (isls.) 8,371 ... G4
Kingstown (cap.) 17,117 ... G4

TRINIDAD and TOBAGO

Port-of-Spain (cap.) 67,978 ... G5
Scarborough 6,057 ... G5
Tobago (isl.) 39,695 ... G5
Trinidad (isl.) 1,020,130 ... G5

TURKS and CAICOS ISLANDS

Caicos (isls.) 4,008 ... D2
Cockburn Harbour ... D2
Grand Caicos (isl.) 371 ... D2
Grand Turk (isl.) 3,146 ... D2
Providenciales (isl.) 979 ... D2
Turks (isls.) 3,348 ... D2

VIRGIN ISLANDS (British)

Anegada (isl.) 89 ... H1
Jost Van Dyke (isl.) 135 ... G1
Road Town (cap.) 2,200 ... H1
Tortola (isl.) 9,257 ... H1
Virgin Gorda (isl.) 1,443 ... H1

VIRGIN ISLANDS (U.S.)

Charlotte Amalie (cap.) 11,842 ... H1
Christiansted 2,914 ... H2
Fredriksted 1,046 ... G2
Saint Croix (isl.) 49,725 ... H2
Saint John (isl.) 2,472 ... H1
Saint Thomas (isl.) 44,372 ... G1

WEST INDIES

Antilles, Greater (isls.) ... B2
Antilles, Lesser (isls.) ... E4
Aves (Bird) (isl.) ... F4
Hispaniola (isl.) ... D2
Leeward (isls.) ... F3
Navassa (isl.) ... C3
Windward (isls.) ... G4

• Population of district.
○ Population of municipality.

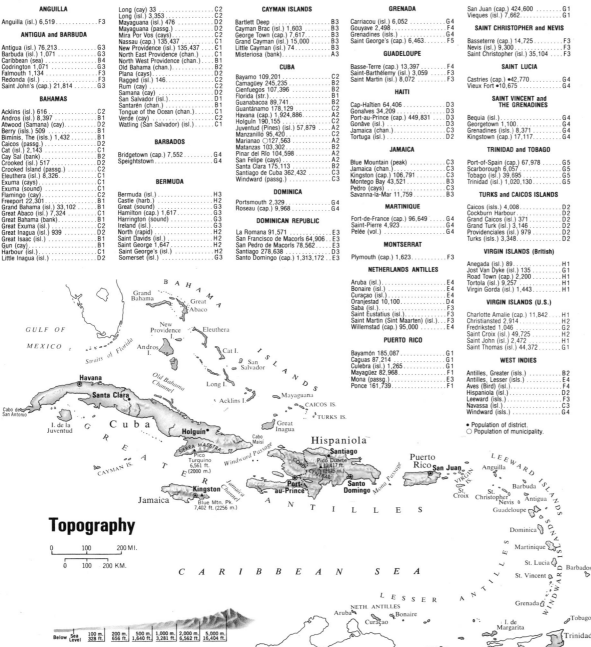

Topography

0 100 200 MI.
0 100 200 KM.

Below Sea Level | 100 m. 328 ft. | 200 m. 656 ft. | 500 m. 1,640 ft. | 1,000 m. 3,281 ft. | 2,000 m. 6,562 ft. | 5,000 m. 16,404 ft.

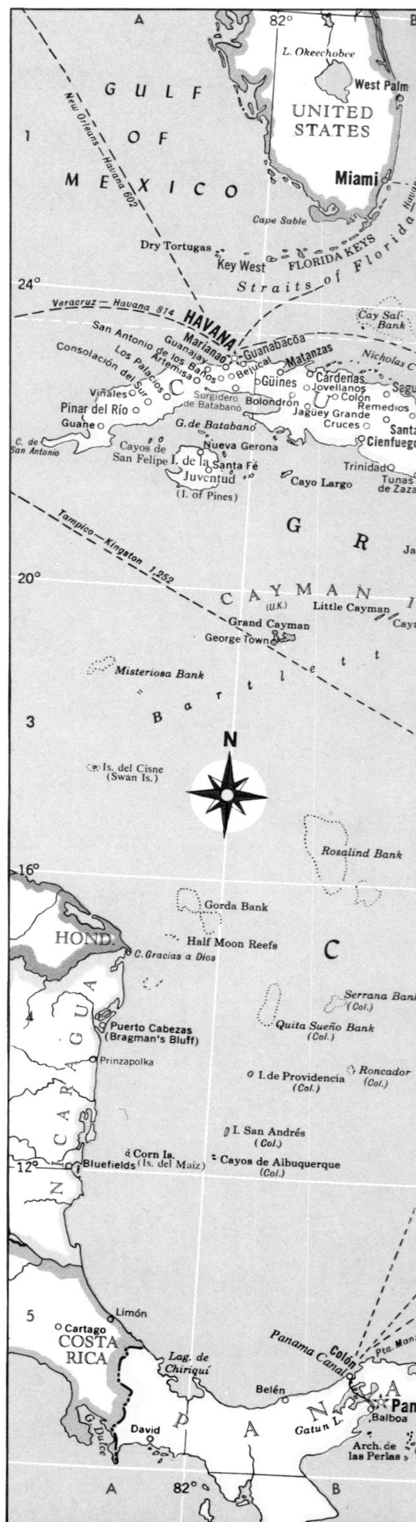

TRINIDAD AND TOBAGO

AREA 1,980 sq. mi. (5,128 sq. km.)
POPULATION 1,067,108
CAPITAL Port of Spain
LARGEST CITY Port of Spain
HIGHEST POINT Mt. Aripo 3,084 ft. (940 m.)
MONETARY UNIT Trinidad and Tobago dollar
MAJOR LANGUAGES English, Hindi
MAJOR RELIGIONS Roman Catholicism, Protestantism, Hinduism, Islam

SAINT CHRISTOPHER-NEVIS

BARBADOS

AREA 166 sq. mi. (430 sq. km.)
POPULATION 248,983
CAPITAL Bridgetown
LARGEST CITY Bridgetown
HIGHEST POINT Mt. Hillaby 1,104 ft. (336 m.)
MONETARY UNIT Barbadian dollar
MAJOR LANGUAGE English
MAJOR RELIGION Protestantism

BAHAMAS

AREA 5,382 sq. mi. (13,939 sq. km.)
POPULATION 209,505
CAPITAL Nassau
LARGEST CITY Nassau
HIGHEST POINT Mt. Alvernia 206 ft. (63 m.)
MONETARY UNIT Bahamian dollar
MAJOR LANGUAGE English
MAJOR RELIGIONS Roman Catholicism, Protestantism

GRENADA

AREA 133 sq. mi. (344 sq. km.)
POPULATION 103,103
CAPITAL St. George's
LARGEST CITY St. George's
HIGHEST POINT Mt. St. Catherine 2,757 ft. (840 m.)
MONETARY UNIT East Caribbean dollar
MAJOR LANGUAGES English, French patois
MAJOR RELIGIONS Roman Catholicism, Protestantism

DOMINICA

AREA 290 sq. mi. (751 sq. km.)
POPULATION 74,089
CAPITAL Roseau
HIGHEST POINT Morne Diablotin 4,747 ft. (1,447 m.)
MONETARY UNIT Dominican dollar
MAJOR LANGUAGES English, French patois
MAJOR RELIGIONS Roman Catholicism, Protestantism

SAINT LUCIA

AREA 238 sq. mi. (616 sq. km.)
POPULATION 115,783
CAPITAL Castries
HIGHEST POINT Mt. Gimie 3,117 ft. (950 m.)
MONETARY UNIT East Caribbean dollar
MAJOR LANGUAGES English, French patois
MAJOR RELIGIONS Roman Catholicism, Protestantism

SAINT VINCENT AND THE GRENADINES

AREA 150 sq. mi. (388 sq. km.)
POPULATION 124,000
CAPITAL Kingstown
HIGHEST POINT Soufrière 4,000 ft. (1,219 m.)
MONETARY UNIT East Caribbean dollar
MAJOR LANGUAGE English
MAJOR RELIGIONS Protestantism, Roman Catholicism

ANTIGUA AND BARBUDA

AREA 171 sq. mi. (443 sq. km.)
POPULATION 75,000
CAPITAL St. John's
HIGHEST POINT Boggy Peak 1,319 ft. (402 m.)
MONETARY UNIT East Caribbean dollar
MAJOR LANGUAGE English
MAJOR RELIGION Protestantism

SAINT CHRISTOPHER-NEVIS

AREA 104 sq. mi. (269 sq. km.)
POPULATION 44,404
CAPITAL Basseterre
HIGHEST POINT Mt. Misery 4,314 ft. (1,315 m.)
MONETARY UNIT East Caribbean dollar
MAJOR LANGUAGE English
MAJOR RELIGIONS Protestantism, Roman Catholicism

The West Indies

CONIC PROJECTION

SCALE OF MILES

SCALE OF KILOMETERS

Capitals ☆

Scale 1:11,200,000

Distances are given in Nautical Miles

Puerto Rico

Bermuda Islands

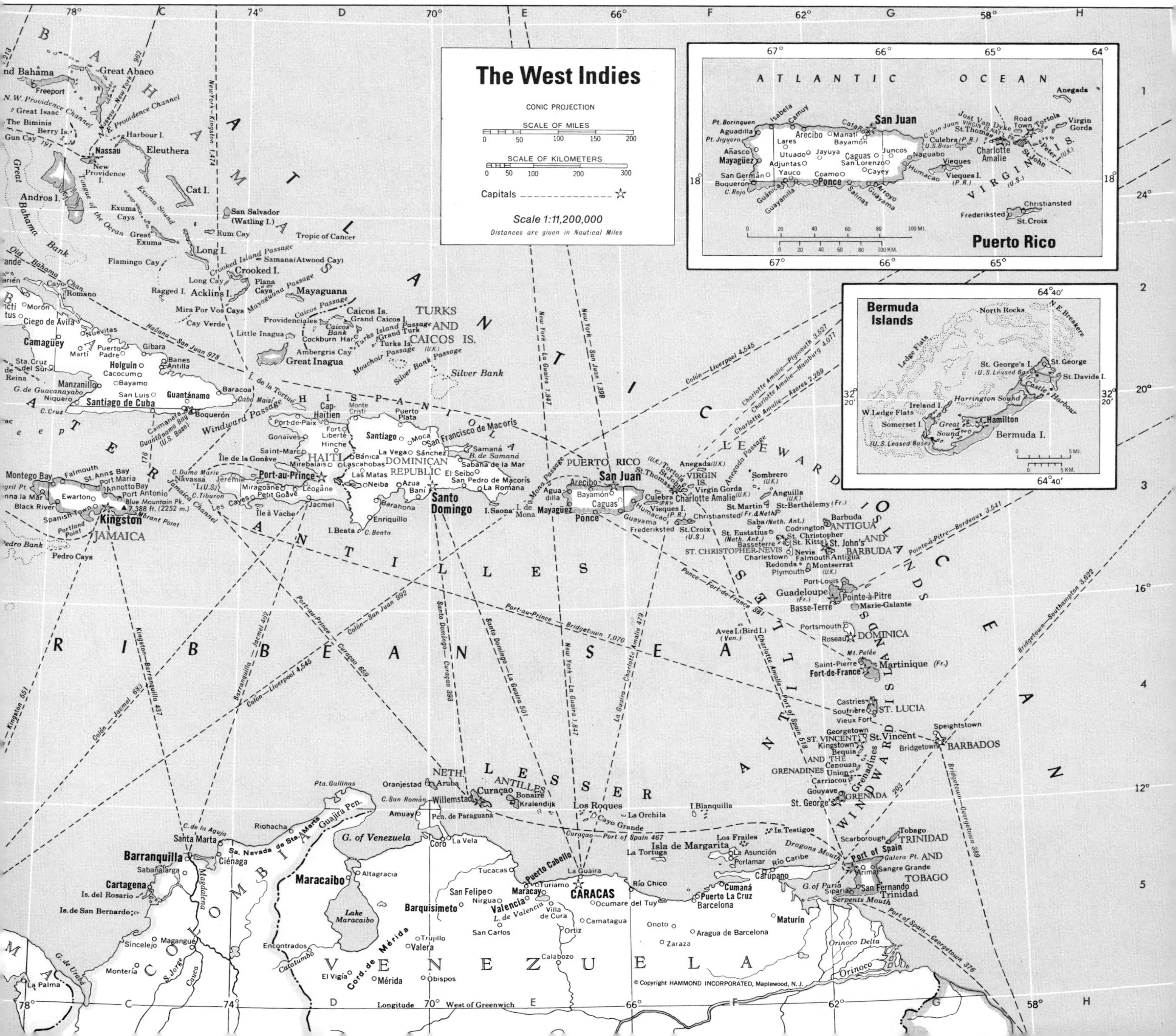

CUBA

PROVINCES

Camagüey 664,566 G2
Ciego de Ávila 320,961 F2
Cienfuegos 326,412 E2
Granma 739,335 H4
Guantánamo 466,609 K4
Habana 1,924,886 C1
Habana, La (Havana) 586,029 C1
Holguín 911,034 J3
Juventud (municipio especial) 57,879 C2
Las Tunas 436,341 H3
Matanzas 557,628 D1
Pinar del Río 640,740 A2
Sancti Spíritus 399,700 F2
Santiago de Cuba 909,506 H4
Villa Clara 764,743 E1

CITIES and TOWNS

Abreus 14,267 D2
Agramonte 4,603 D1
Aguada de Pasajeros 20,219 D2
Alacranes 4,959 D1
Alonso Rojas 1,427 B2
Alquízar 12,691 C1
Altagracia 1,722 G3
Alto Songo-La Maya 25,188 J4
Amarillas 2,767 D2
Amazonas 1,066 F2
Antilla 10,052 J3
Arroyo Blanco 1,431 F2
Artemisa 45,689 B1
Báez 4,178 E2
Báguanos 12,678 J3
Bahía Honda 16,901 B1
Baire 4,879 H4
Banao 803 F2
Banes 38,905 J3
Baracoa 36,702 K4
Baraguá 12,633 F2
Bauta 26,826 C1
Bayamo 109,201 H4
Bejucal 15,649 C1
Bolondrón 5,840 D1
Buenaventura 4,711 H3
Buenavista 1,303 F2
Buey Arriba 8,017 H4
Cabaiguán 36,544 E2
Cabañas 4,897 B1
Cabezas 5,262 D1
Cacocum 14,145 H3
Caibarién 32,094 F2
Caimanera 6,664 J4
Calabazar de Sagua 9,023 E1
Calimete 19,925 D1
Camagüey 245,235 G3
Camajuaní 26,653 E2
Campechuela 20,743 G4
Canasí 1,637 C1
Candelaria 10,810 B1
Cárdenas 65,585 D1
Cartagena 2,166 D2
Cascajal 3,530 E1
Cauto del Embarcadero 949 H4
Cauto el Cristo 1,626 J3
Central Amancio Rodríguez 22,506 G3
Central Bolivia 6,301 G2
Central Brasil 4,904 G2
Central Cándido González 3,414 G3
Central Colombia 16,799 G3
Central Frank País 9,066 K3
Central Guatemala 5,584 J3
Central Haití 3,609 G3
Central Los Reynaldos 3,997 J4
Central Loynaz Echevarría 3,245 J3
Central Manuel Tames 7,864 K4
Céspedes 6,634 G2
Chambas 19,877 F2
Chaparra 8,428 H3
Cidra 3,567 D1
Ciego de Ávila 80,010 F2
Cienfuegos 107,396 D2
Colón 47,010 D1
Condado 33,115 E2
Consolación del Norte 4,681 B1
Consolación del Sur 34,334 B2
Contramaestre 44,991 G3
Corralillo 15,822 D1
Cruces 20,324 E2
Cueto 23,183 J3
Cumanayagua 25,338 E2
Daiquirí J4
Delicias 10,562 H3
Dos Caminos 3,772 J4
Dos Ríos 1,786 J4
El Caney 3,921 J4
El Cobre 3,952 J4
El Santo 2,473 E1
Encrucijada 23,029 E1
Esmeralda 17,205 G1
Esperanza 9,241 E2
Florencia 6,979 F2
Florida 43,881 G3
Fomento 17,310 E2
Gaspar 2,682 F2
Gibara 23,137 J3
Guáimaro 29,712 G3
Guanabacoa 89,741 C1
Guanajay 21,042 B1
Guane 14,126 A2
Guantánamo 178,129 K4
Guaro 3,086 J3
Guasimal 3,057 E2
Guayabal 3,703 G3
Guayos 6,753 F2
Güines 51,691 C1
Güira de Melena 19,851 C1
Guisa 15,182 H4
Havana (cap.) 1,924,886 C1
Herradura 3,762 B1
Holguín 190,155 J3
Ignacio Agramonte 1,487 G3
Imías 4,491 K4
Isabela de Sagua 3,721 E1
Jagüey Grande 30,205 D2
Jamaica 5,128 K4
Jaruco 16,844 C1
Jatibonico 17,047 F2
Jíbaro 1,263 F2
Jiguaní 25,069 H4
Jobabo 14,899 H3
Jovellanos 35,043 D1
La Coloma 3,462 B2
La Maya-Alto Songo 25,188 J4
Las Martinas 4,511 A2
Limonar 9,629 D1
Los Arabos 10,664 E1
Los Palacios 21,884 B1
Lugareño 4,396 G3
Mabay 6,176 H4
Maceo 2,652 H3
Majagua 9,110 F2
Manacas 5,914 E1
Manatí 11,054 H3
Manguito 2,739 D1
Manicaragua 33,900 E2
Mantua 9,165 A2
Mapos (Amazonas) 1,066 F2
Manzanillo 95,420 H4
Marianao ○127,563 C1
Mariel 24,115 B1
Martí 11,474 D1
Matanzas 103,302 C1
Máximo Gómez, Ciego de Ávila 5,116 F2
Máximo Gómez, Matanzas 4,970 D1
Mayajigua 4,425 F2
Mayarí 54,699 J3
Mayarí Arriba 2,302 J4
Media Luna 13,794 G4
Mendoza 2,914 A2
Meneses 4,768 F2
Minas 17,675 G2
Minas de Matahambre 14,976 A1
Moa 28,696 K3
Morón 40,396 F2
Nicaro 9,506 J3
Niquero 15,544 G4
Nueva Gerona 17,175 B2
Nuevitas 35,103 G2
Orozco 4,256 B1
Palma Soriano 66,222 J4
Palmira 19,680 E2
Pedro Betancourt 22,915 D1
Perico 20,633 D1
Pilón 10,194 H4
Pinar del Río 104,598 B2
Placetas 46,038 E2
Primero Enero 14,807 F2
Puerto Esperanza 3,499 A1
Puerto Padre 46,806 H3
Quemado de Güines 11,208 E1
Rancho Veloz 3,966 D1
Ranchuelo 34,255 E2
Regla 38,491 C1
Remedios 27,722 E2
República Dominicana 2,540 F2
Río Cauto 19,550 H4
Rodas 16,350 E2
Sagua de Tánamo 15,327 K3
Sagua la Grande 52,315 E1
San Andrés 2,127 H3
San Antonio de los Baños 28,137 C1
San Cristóbal 30,769 B1
Sancti Spíritus 79,542 E2
San Diego de los Baños 1,430 B1
San Germán 12,362 J3
San José de las Lajas 37,149 C1
San José de los Ramos 1,726 D1
San Juan y Martínez 13,227 B2
San Luis, Pinar del Río 5,677 B2
San Luis, Santiago de Cuba 32,826 J4
San Nicolás 12,368 C1
San Ramón 2,676 H4
Santa Clara 175,113 E2
Santa Cruz del Norte 15,239 C1

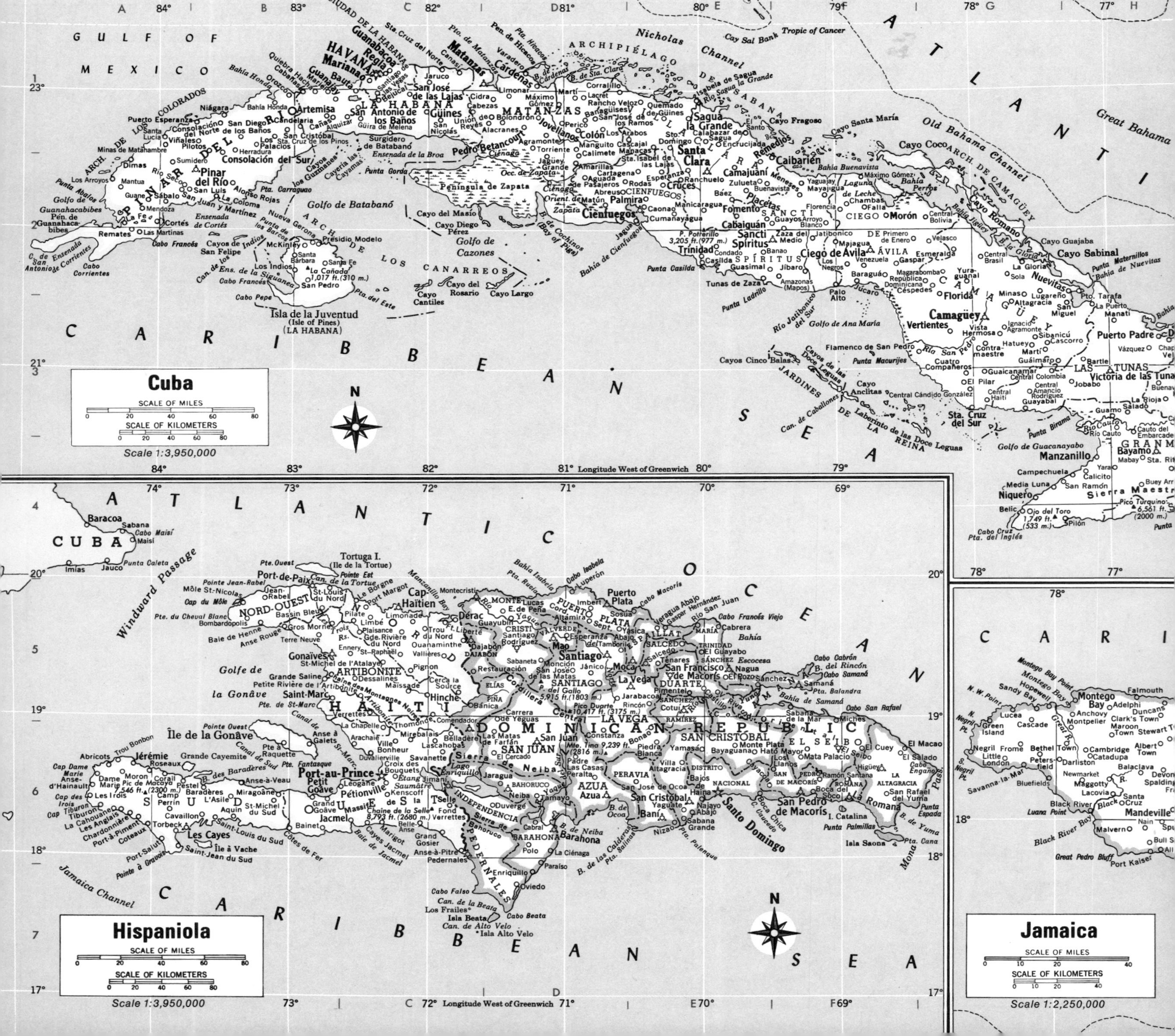

Santa Cruz de los Pinos 3,545 . . . B1
Santa Cruz del Sur 27,142 . . G3
Santa Fe 3,925 . . . B2
Santa Isabel de las Lajas 7,279 . . . E2
Santa Lucía 3,734 . . . J3
Santa Rita 6,358 . . . H4
Santiago de Cuba 362,432 . . J4
Santiago de las Vegas 29,325 . . . C1
Santo Domingo 32,950 . . . E1
Sibanicú 14,252 . . . G3
Sola 2,436 . . . G2
Sumidero 980 . . . A2
Surgidero de Batabanó 11,533 . . . C1
Tacajó 4,469 . . . J3
Torriente 1,759 . . . D11
Trinidad 42,080 . . . E2
Unión de Reyes 28,422 . . . C1
Varadero 14,737 . . . D1
Vázquez 3,851 . . . H3
Velasco 5,618 . . . H3
Venezuela 13,744 . . . F2
Vertientes 25,178 . . . G3
Victoria de las Tunas 87,522 H3
Viñales 2,049 . . . A1
Yaguajay 30,720 . . . F2
Yara 238,879 . . . H4
Zaza del Medio 7,495 . . . F2
Zulueta 5,425 . . . E2

OTHER FEATURES

Abalos (pt.) . . . A2
Ana María (gulf) . . . F3
Anclitas (cay) . . . F3
Batabanó (gulf) . . . C2
Birama (pt.) . . . G4
Broa (inlet) . . . C1
Buenavista (bay) . . . F2
Caballones (chan.) . . . F3
Camagüey (arch.) . . . G2
Cantiles (cay) . . . C3
Cárdenas (bay) . . . D1
Carraguao (pt.) . . . B2
Casilda (pt.) . . . E2
Cauto (riv.) . . . H3
Cayamas (cays) . . . C2
Cazones (gulf) . . . C2
Cienfuegos (bay) . . . D2
Cinco Balas (cays) . . . E3
Cochinos (bay) . . . D2
Coco (cay) . . . G1
Corrientes (cape) . . . A2
Corrientes (inlet) . . . A2
Cortés (inlet) . . . B2
Cristal, Sierra del (mts.) . . . J3
Cruz (cape) . . . G4
Diego Pérez (cay) . . . C2
Doce Leguas (cays) . . . F3
Este (pt.) . . . C3
Fragoso (cay) . . . F1
Francés (cape) . . . A2
Gorda (pt.) . . . C2
Gran Piedra (mt.) . . . J4
Guacanayabo (gulf) . . . G4
Guajaba (cay) . . . G2
Guanahacabibes (gulf) . . . A2
Guanahacabibes (pen.) . . . A2
Guantánamo (bay) . . . J4
Guantánamo Bay U.S. Nav. Reserve . . . K4
Guarico (pt.) . . . K3
Guzmanes (cays) . . . B2
Hicacos (pen.) . . . D1
Hicacos (pt.) . . . D1
Honda (bay) . . . B1
Indios (chan.) . . . B2
Inglés (pt.) . . . G4
Jardines de la Reina (arch.) . F3
Jatibonico del Sur (riv.) . . . F3
Jigüey (bay) . . . G2
Juventud, Isla de la (Pines) (isl.) 57,879 . . . B3
Laberinto de las Doce Leguas (cays) . . . F3
Ladrillo (pt.) . . . E3
Largo (cay) . . . D2
Leche (lag.) . . . F2
Los Barcos (pt.) . . . B2
Los Canarreos (arch.) . . . C2
Los Colorados (arch.) . . . A1
Lucrecia (cape) . . . J3
Macurijes (pt.) . . . F3
Maestra, Sierra (mts.) . . . H4
Maisí (cape) . . . K4
Mangle (pt.) . . . J3
Masío (cay) . . . C2
Matanzas (bay) . . . D1
Nicholas (chan.) . . . E1
Nipe (bay) . . . J3
Nuevitas (bay) . . . H2
Ojo del Toro (mt.) . . . G4
Old Bahama (chan.) . . . G1
Pepe (cape) . . . B3
Perros (bay) . . . G2
Pigs (Cochinos) (bay) . . . D2
Pines (Isla de la Juventud) (isl.) 7,879 . . . B3
Potrerillo (peak) . . . E2
Quemado (pt.) . . . K4
Romano (cay) . . . G2
Rosario (cay) . . . C2
Sabana (arch.) . . . E1
Sabinal (cay) . . . H2
Sagua la Grande (riv.) . . . E1
San Antonio (cape) . . . A2
San Felipe (cays) . . . B2
San Pedro (riv.) . . . G3
Santa Clara (bay) . . . D1
Santa María (cay) . . . F1
Siguanea (bay) . . . B2
Tabacal (pt.) . . . H4
Toa, Cuchillas de (mts.) . . . K4
Tortuguilla (pt.) . . . K4
Turquino (peak) . . . H4
Zapata (pen.) . . . C2
Zapata Occidental (swamp) . . D2
Zapata Oriental (swamp) . . . D2

DOMINICAN REPUBLIC

PROVINCES

Azua 142,770 . . . D6
Bahoruco 78,636 . . . D6
Barahona 137,160 . . . D6
Dajabón 57,709 . . . D5
Distrito Nacional 1,550,739 . E6
Duarte 235,544 . . . E5
Elías Piña 65,384 . . . C5
El Seibo 157,866 . . . F6
Espaillat 164,017 . . . E5
Independencia 38,768 . . . D6
La Altagracia 100,112 . . . F6
La Romana 109,769 . . . F6
La Vega 385,043 . . . D6
María Trinidad Sánchez 112,629 . . . E5
Monte Cristi 83,407 . . . D5
Pedernales 17,006 . . . D7
Peravia 168,123 . . . E6
Puerto Plata 206,757 . . . D5
Salcedo 99,191 . . . E5
Samaná 65,699 . . . E5
Sánchez Ramírez 126,567 . . E5
San Cristóbal 446,132 . . . E6
San Juan 239,957 . . . D6
San Pedro de Macorís 152,890 . . . F6
Santiago 550,372 . . . D5
Santiago Rodríguez 55,411 . D5
Valverde 100,319 . . . D5

CITIES and TOWNS

Altamira 2,759 . . . D5
Azua 31,481 . . . D6
Bajos de Haina 33,135 . . . E6
Baní 36,705 . . . E6
Barahona 49,334 . . . D6
Bonao 44,486 . . . E6
Cabrera 2,542 . . . E5
Comendador 5,962 . . . C6
Constanza 15,141 . . . D6
Cotuí 16,688 . . . E5
Dajabón 8,808 . . . D5
El Seibo 13,511 . . . F6
Hato Mayor 17,859 . . . F6
Higüey 33,501 . . . F6
Imbert 5,315 . . . D5
Jarabacoa 13,416 . . . E5
Jimaní 3,327 . . . C6
La Romana 91,571 . . . F6
La Vega 52,432 . . . E5
Luperón 2,500 . . . D5
Mao 33,527 . . . D5
Moca 31,176 . . . D5
Monción 3,344 . . . D5
Nagua 20,912 . . . E5
Puerto Plata 45,348 . . . D5
Sabana de la Mar 9,983 . . . F5
Sabaneta 9,170 . . . D5
Samaná 5,023 . . . F5
Sánchez 7,919 . . . E5
San Cristóbal 58,520 . . . E6
San Francisco de Macorís 64,906 . . . E5
San Juan 49,764 . . . D6
San Pedro de Macorís 78,562 . . . F6
Santiago 278,638 . . . D5
Santo Domingo (cap.) 1,313,172 . . . E6
Tenares 4,065 . . . E5
Villa Altagracia 20,890 . . . E6

OTHER FEATURES

Alto Velo (chan.) . . . C7
Alto Velo (isl.) . . . D7
Balandra (pt.) . . . F5
Beata (cape) . . . D7
Beata (chan.) . . . C7
Beata (isl.) . . . C7
Cabrón (cape) . . . F5
Calderas (bay) . . . D6
Cana (pt.) . . . F6
Catalina (isl.) . . . F6
Caucedo (capee) . . . E6
Central, Cordillera (range) . . D5
Duarte (peak) . . . D5
Engaño (cape) . . . F6
Enriquillo (lake) . . . C6
Escocesa (bay) . . . E5
Espada (pt.) . . . F6
Falso (cape) . . . C7
Francés Viejo (cape) . . . E5
Gallo (mt.) . . . D5
Isabela (bay) . . . D5
Isabela (cape) . . . D5
Los Frailes (isl.) . . . C7
Macorís (cape) . . . E5
Manzanillo (bay) . . . C5
Mona (passg.) . . . F6
Neiba (bay) . . . D6
Neiba, Sierra de (mts.) . . . D6
Ocoa (bay) . . . D6
Oriental, Cordillera (range) . . F6
Palenque (pt.) . . . E6
Palmillas (pt.) . . . F6
Rincón (bay) . . . F5
Rucia (pt.) . . . D5
Salinas (pt.) . . . E6
Samaná (bay) . . . F5
Samaná (cape) . . . F5
San Rafael (cape) . . . F5
Saona (isl.) . . . F6
Septentrional, Cordillera (range) . . . D5
Tina (mt.) . . . D6
Yaque del Norte (riv.) . . . D5
Yaque del Sur (riv.) . . . D6
Yuma (bay) . . . F6
Yuna (riv.) . . . E5

HAITI

DEPARTMENTS

Artibonite . . . C5
Nord . . . C5
Nord-Ouest . . . B5
Ouest . . . C6
Sud . . . A6

CITIES and TOWNS

Anse-à-Galets 3,623 . . . B6
Anse-d'Hainault 5,220 . . . A6
Aquin 3,820 . . . B6
Cap-Haïtien 64,406 . . . C5
Croix des Bouquets 4,365 . . C6
Dame Marie 4,320 . . . A6
Dérac 1,300 . . . C5
Dessalines 7,984 . . . C5
Fort Liberté 5,012 . . . C5
Gonaïves 34,209 . . . B5
Grande Rivière du Nord 6,007 . . . C5
Gros Morne 4,739 . . . B5
Hinche 10,070 . . . C5
Jacmel 13,730 . . . C6
Jérémie 18,493 . . . A6
Kenscoff 2,605 . . . C6
Lascahobas 3,805 . . . C6
Léogâne 5,782 . . . C6
Les Cayes 34,090 . . . B6
Limbé 10,476 . . . C5
Miragoâne 4,327 . . . B6
Mirebalais 6,069 . . . C6
Ouanaminthe 7,276 . . . C5
Pétionville 35,333 . . . C6
Petite Rivière de l'Artibonite 10,099 . . . B5
Petit Goâve 7,310 . . . B6
Pignon 4,576 . . . C5
Port-au-Prince (cap.) 449,831 . . . C6
Port-de-Paix 15,540 . . . B5
Saint-Louis du Nord 7,203 . . B5
Saint-Marc 24,165 . . . B5
Saint-Michel de l'Atalaye 7,559 . . . C5
Saint-Raaphaël 3,889 . . . C5
Trou du Nord 7,637 . . . C5
Verrettes 3,670 . . . C5

OTHER FEATURES

Artibonite (riv.) . . . C5
Baradères (bay) . . . B6
Cheval Blanc (pt.) . . . B5
Dame Marie (cape) . . . A6
Est (pt.) . . . C4
Fantasque (pt.) . . . B6
Gonâve (gulf) . . . B5
Gonâve (isl.) . . . B6
Grande Cayemite (isl.) . . . B6
Gravois (pt.) . . . A7
Irois (cape) . . . A6
Jean-Rabel (pt.) . . . B5
Macaya (mt.) . . . A6
Manzanillo (bay) . . . C5
Môle (cape) . . . B5
Noires (mts.) . . . C5
Ouest (pt.) . . . B4
Ouest (pt.) . . . B6
Saint-Marc (chan.) . . . B6
Saint-Marc (pt.) . . . B5
Saumâtre (lake) . . . C6
Selle (peak) . . . C6
Sud (chan.) . . . B6
Tortue (chan.) . . . C5
Tortue (Tortuga) (isl.) . . . C4
Tortuga (isl.) . . . C4
Trois-Rivières (riv.) . . . B5
Vache (isl.) . . . B6
Windward (passg.) . . . A5

JAMAICA

CITIES and TOWNS

Alley . . . J7
Alligator Pond . . . H6
Anchovy 2,558 . . . H5
Annotto Bay . . . K6
Bamboo 2,971 . . . J6
Bath . . . K6
Black River 2,701 . . . H6
Bog Walk . . . J6
Bowden . . . K6
Browns Town 5,479 . . . J6
Bull Savanna-Junction 5,110 . . . H6
Cambridge 2,449 . . . H6
Catadupa . . . H6
Christiana . . . H6
Discovery Bay 1,814 . . . J5
Falmouth 3,937 . . . H5
Green Island . . . G6
Hope Bay . . . K6
Kingston (cap.) 106,791 . . . K6
Kingston *516,865 . . . J7
Linstead . . . J6
Lucea 3,635 . . . G5
Mandeville 14,421 . . . H6
Maroon Town 2,717 . . . H6
May Pen 26,074 . . . J6
Montego Bay 43,521 . . . H5
Montpelier . . . H6
Morant Bay 7,465 . . . K7
Negril . . . G6
Ocho Rios 5,851 . . . J6
Oracabessa . . . J5
Port Antonio 10,538 . . . K6
Port Kaiser . . . H7
Port Maria 5,259 . . . J6
Port Morant . . . K6
Saint Ann's Bay 7,101 . . . J5
Saint Margaret's Bay . . . K6
Savanna-la-Mar 11,759 . . . G6
Spanish Town 40,731 . . . J6
Williamsfield . . . H6

OTHER FEATURES

Black (riv.) . . . H6
Black River (bay) . . . G6
Blue (mts.) . . . J6
Blue Mountain (peak) . . . K6
Galina (pt.) . . . J6
Grande (riv.) . . . K6
Great (riv.) . . . H6
Great Pedro Bluff (prom.) . . . H6
Long (bay) . . . H7
Luana (pt.) . . . G6
Minho (riv.) . . . J6
Montego (bay) . . . G5
Montego Bay ((pt.) . . . G5
North East (pt.) . . . K6
North Negril (pt.) . . . G6
North West (pt.) . . . G5
Old Harbour (bay) . . . J6
Portland (pt.) . . . J7
Sir John's (peak) . . . K6
South East (pt.) . . . K6
South Negril (pt.) . . . G6

*City and Suburbs.
○ Population of municipality.

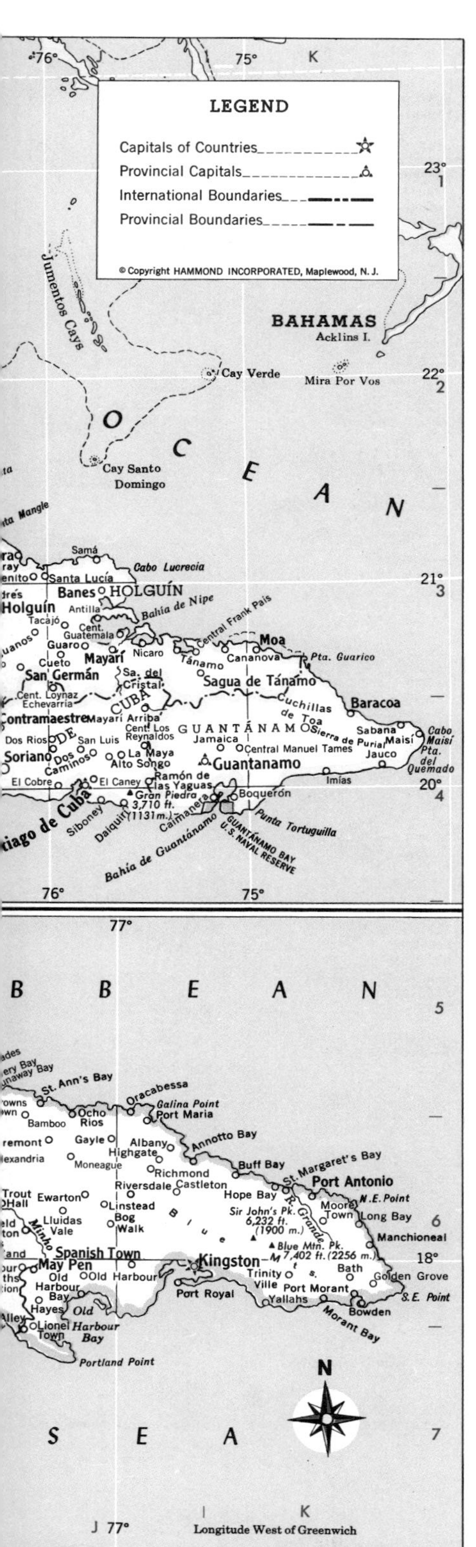

Agriculture, Industry and Resources

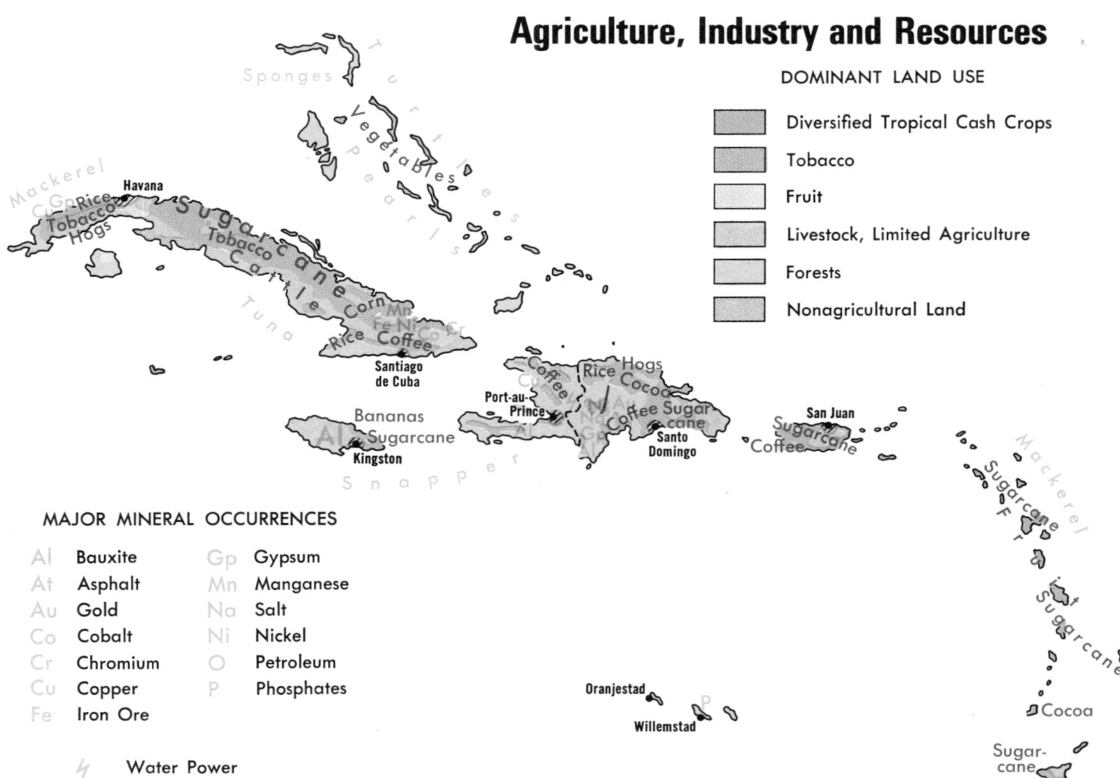

West Indies

(continued)

PUERTO RICO

DISTRICTS

Aguadilla A1
Arecibo C1
Bayamón D1
Guayama D2
Humacao E2
Mayagüez B2
Ponce C2
San Juan D1

CITIES and TOWNS

Adjuntas 5,239 B2
Aguada 5,025 A1
Aguadilla 22,039 A1
Aguas Buenas 3,766 E2
Aibonito 9,331 D2
Añasco 5,646 A1
Ángeles ○2,817 B2
Arecibo 48,779 B1
Arroyo 8,435 E3
Bahomamey A1
Bajadero 3,678 C1
Barceloneta 4,502 C1
Barranquitas 3,618 D2
Bayamón 185,087 D1
Boquerón ○3,675 A3
Cabo Rojo 10,292 A2
Caguas 87,214 E2
Caguas †156,819 E2
Camuy 3,834 B1
Carolina 147,835 E1
Cataño 26,243 D1
Cayey 23,305 D2
Ceiba 4,973 F2
Central Aguirre 1,049 D3
Ciales 3,582 C1
Cidra 6,069 D2
Coamo 12,851 D2
Comerío 5,736 D2
Coquí 3,018 D3
Corozal 5,889 D1
Coto Laurel ○5,192 C2
Culebra (Dewey) 938 G1
Dorado 10,203 D1
Ensenada B3
Esperanza 1,130 G2
Fajardo 26,928 F1
Florida 3,641 C1
Guánica 9,628 B3
Guayama 21,097 E3
Guayanilla 6,163 B3
Guaynabo 65,075 D1
Gurabo 7,645 E2
Hatillo 5,019 B1
Hato Rey E1
Hormigüeros 12,031 A2
Humacao 19,147 E2
Isabela 12,087 A1
Isabel Segunda 2,330 G2
Jayuya 3,588 C2
Jobos 4,194 D3
Juana Díaz 10,469 C2
Juncos 7,851 E2
Lajas 4,275 A2
Lares 5,224 B2
Las Piedras 4,857 E2
Levittown 31,613 D1
Loíza 3,932 E1
Loíza Aldea E1
Luquillo 4,531 F1
Manatí 17,347 C1
Maricao 1,390 B2
Mayagüez 82,968 A2
Mayagüez †98,155 A2
Moca 3,960 A1
Naguabo 4,135 F2
Naranjito 2,849 D1
Palmer 1,566 F1
Palo Seco 1,172 D1
Parguera A3
Patillas 3,172 E2
Peñuelas 4,235 B2
Playa de Fajardo F1
Playa de Humacao ○5,573 F2
Ponce 161,739 C3
Ponce †168,272 C3
Puerto Nuevo D1
Puerto Real 2,390 A2
Puerto Real (Playa de Fajardo) F1
Punta Santiago (Playa de Humacao) ○5,573 F2
Quebradillas 3,770 B1
Río Blanco 1,433 F2
Río Grande 12,047 E1
Río Piedras E1
Rosario A2
Sabana Grande 7,435 B2
Sabana Seca 11,431 D1
Salinas 6,220 D3
San Antonio 2,681 A1
San Germán 13,054 A2
San Juan (cap.) 424,600 E1
San Juan †1,081,193 E1
San Lorenzo 8,880 E2
San Sebastián 10,619 B1
Santa Isabel 6,948 C3
Santurce E1
Tallaboa 1,059 B3
Toa Alta 4,427 D1
Toa Baja 1,992 D1
Trujillo Alto 41,141 E1
Utuado 11,113 B2
Vega Alta 10,582 D1
Vega Baja 18,233 D1
Vieques (Isabel Segunda) 2,330 G2
Villalba 3,469 C2
Yabucoa 6,797 E2
Yauco 14,594 B2

OTHER FEATURES

Aguadilla (bay) A1
Algarrobo (pt.) A2
Añasco (bay) A1
Arenas (pt.) F2
Bauta (riv.) C2
Bayamón (riv.) D1
Boquerón (bay) A3
Borinquen (pt.) A1
Cabullones (pt.) C3
Caja de Muertos (isl.) C3
Camuy (riv.) B1
Canovanas (riv.) E1
Caonillas (lake) C2
Carite (lake) E2
Carraízo (lake) E1
Cayey, Sierra de (mts.) D2
Central, Cordillera (range) C2
Cerro Gordo (pt.) D1
Coamo (res.) D3
Coamo (riv.) D3
Culebra (isl.) 1,265 G1
Culebrinas (riv.) A1
Culebrita (isl.) G2
El Toro (mt.) F2
El Yunque (mt.) F1
Este (pt.) G2
Fajardo (riv.) F1
Figuras (pt.) E3
Fosforescente (bay) A3
Grande de Añasco (riv.) B2
Grande de Arecibo (riv.) C1
Grande de Loíza (riv.) E1
Grande de Manatí (riv.) C1
Guajataca (lake) B1
Guanajibo (pt.) A2
Guanajibo (riv.) A2
Guánica (lake) B3
Guaniquilla (pt.) A2
Guayabal (lake) C2
Guayanés (pt.) F2
Guayanés (riv.) E2
Guayanilla (bay) B3
Guayo (lake) B2
Guilarte (mt.) B2
Honda (bay) F2
Jacaguas (riv.) C2
Jaicoa, Cordillera (mts.) B1
Jiguero (pt.) A1
Jobos (bay) D3
Lima (pt.) F2
Luquillo, Sierra de (mts.) E2
Mangillo (pt.) B3
Mayagüez (bay) A2
Miquillo (pt.) F1
Molinos (pt.) G1
Mona (passg.) A2
Negra (pt.) G2
Nigua (riv.) D2
Ola Grande (pt.) D3
Palmas Altas (pt.) C1
Patillas (lake) E2
Petrona (pt.) D3
Pirata (mt.) F2
Plata (riv.) D2
Puerca (pt.) F2
Puerto Medio Mundo (bay) F2
Punta, Cerro de (mt.) C2
Ramey A.F.B. A1
Rincón (bay) D3
Rojo (cape) A3
Roosevelt Road Naval Res. F2
Salinas (pt.) D1
San José (lag.) E1
San Juan, Cabezas de (prom.) F1
San Juan Nat'l Hist. Site D1
Soldado (pt.) G2
Sucia (bay) A3
Tanamá (riv.) B1
Toro, El (mt.) F2
Torrecilla (lag.) E1
Tortuguero (lag.) D1
Tuna (pt.) E3
Vacía Talega (pt.) E1
Vieques (isl.) 7,662 G2
Vieques (passg.) F2
Vieques (sound) G2
Yagüez (riv.) A2
Yauco (lake) B2
Yeguas ((pt.) F3

ANTIGUA

CITIES and TOWNS

All Saints 1,796 E11
Cedar Grove 1,460 E11
Falmouth 1,134 E11
Freetown 1,250 E11
Jennings 1,370 D11
Liberta 2,394 E11
Old Road 1,244 D11
Parham 1,570 E11
Saint John's (cap.) 21,814 E11
Willikies 1,843 E11

OTHER FEATURES

Antigua (isl.) 76,213 E11
Boggy (peak) D11
Boon (pt.) E11
Green (isl.) E11
Guiana (isl.) E11
Long (isl.) E11
Saint John's (harb.) C11
Standfast (pt.) E11
Willoughby (bay) E11

BARBADOS

CITIES and TOWNS

Bathsheba B8
Belleplaine B8
Bridgetown (cap.) 7,552 B9
Carlton B8
Cave Hill B9
Checker Hall B8
Codrington B8
Crab Hill B8
Crane C9
Drax Hall B8
Ellerton B9
Greenland B8
Holetown B8
Kendal B8
Lodge Hill B8
Marchfield B9
Mount Standfast B8
Oistins B9
Rose Hill B8
Rouen B9
Saint Lawrence B9
Saint Martins C9
Scarboro B9
Seawell B9
Six Mens B8
Speightstown B8
Spring Hall B8
Welchman Hall B8

OTHER FEATURES

Carlisle (bay) B9
Hillaby (mt.) B8
Long (bay) B9
North (pt.) B8
Oistins (bay) B9
Pelican (isl.) B9
Ragged (pt.) C8
Sam Lord's Castle C9
South (pt.) B9

DOMINICA

CITIES and TOWNS

Barroui 1,480 E6
Castle Bruce 1,975 E6
Coulihaut 1,735 E6
Delice F7
Grand Bay 3,152 F7
Hampstead E5
La Plaine F6
Mahout 2,095 E6
Marigot 3,183 E6
Petit Soufrière F6
Portsmouth 2,329 E5
Rosalie F6
Roseau (cap.) 9,968 E7
Roseau *16,035 E7
Saint Joseph 2,643 E6
Salybia F6
Soufrière E7
Vieille Case E5
Wesley 2,002 F5

OTHER FEATURES

Capuchin (cape) E5
Carib Reserve F6
Clyde (riv.) F6
Crumpton (pt.) F5
Diablotin, Morne (mt.) E6
Dominica (passg.) E5
Douglas (bay) E5
Grand (bay) F7
Jaquet (pt.) E5
Layou (riv.) E6
Martinique (passg.) E7
Micotrin (mt.) F6
Pagoua (bay) F6
Prince Rupert (bay) E5
Scotts (head) E7
Soufrière (bay) E7
Trois Pitons, Morne (mt.) E6

GRENADA

CITIES and TOWNS

Gouyave 2,498 C8
Grand Roy C8
Grenville 1,723 D8
Hermitage D8
La Taste D8
Marquis D8
Mount Tivoli D8
Saint George's (cap.) 6,463 C9
Saint George's *34,624 C9
Sauteurs 605 D8
Victoria 1,673 D8
Woodford C8

OTHER FEATURES

Bedford (pt.) D8
David (pt.) D8
Great Bacolet (pt.) D8
Green (isl.) D8
Grenville (bay) D8
Gros (pt.) C8
Halifax (harb.) C8
Irvin's (bay) D8
Les Tantes (isls.) D7
Molinière (pt.) C8
Prickly (pt.) C9
Ronde (isl.) D7
Saint Catherine (mt.) D8
Saline (pt.) C9
Sinai (mt.) D8
Telescope (pt.) D8

GUADELOUPE

Total Population 329,017

CITIES and TOWNS

Anse-Bertrand 1,921 A5
Baie-Mahault 5,874 A6
Baillif 3,844 A7
Bananier A7
Basse-Terre (cap.) 13,397 A7
Bouillante 1,821 A6
Bourg-des-Saintes 907 A7
Capesterre 7,541 A7
Ferry A6
Gosier 13,741 B6
Gourbeyre 5,637 A7
Goyave 1,709 A6
Grand-Bourg 3,249 B7
Lamentin 2,319 A6
Les Abymes 51,837 B6
Morne-à-l'Eau 9,457 A6
Moule 9,800 B6
Petit-Bourg 5,097 A6
Petit-Canal 1,581 A6
Pigeon A6
Pointe-à-Pitre 25,151 B6
Pointe-Noire 2,180 A6
Port-Louis 4,517 B5
Saint-Claude 6,755 A7
Sainte-Anne 11,527 B6
Sainte-Marguerite B6
Sainte-Marie A6
Sainte-Rose 4,805 A6
Saint-François 3,141 B6
Trois-Rivières 7,881 A7
Vieux-Fort 1,073 B7
Vieux-Habitants 4,065 A7

OTHER FEATURES

Allègre (pt.) A6
Antigues (pt.) A5
Basse-Terre (isl.) 138,777 A6
Châteaux (pt.) B6
Constant, Morne (hill) B7
Désirade, La (isl.) 1,602 B6
Fajou (isl.) A6
Grand Cul-de-Sac Marin (bay) A6
Grande-Terre (isl.) B6
Grande Vigie (pt.) B5
Grand-Îlet (isl.) A7
Guadeloupe (isl.) 167,896 B6
Guadeloupe (passg.) A5
Guadeloupe Nat'l Park A6
Kahouanne (isl.) A6
Marie-Galante (isl.) 13,757 B7
Nord (pt.) B7
Nord-Est (bay) B6
Petit Cul-de-Sac Marin (bay) A6
Petite-Terre (isls.) B6
Saintes (chan.) A7
Saintes (isls.) 2,901 A7
Salée (riv.) A6
Sans Toucher (mt.) A6
Soufrière (mt.) A7
Terre-de-Bas (isl.) 1,427 A7
Terre-de-Haut (isl.) 1,453 A7
Vieux-Fort (pt.) A7

MARTINIQUE

Total Population 330,220

CITIES and TOWNS

Ajoupa-Bouillon 1,569 C5
Basse-Pointe 2,163 C5
Bellefontaine 818 C6
Case-Pilote 1,776 C6
Ducos 4,429 D6
Fond-Saint-Denis 962 C6
Fort-de-France (cap.) 96,649 C6
Grand' Rivière 1,053 C5
Gros-Morne 1,976 D6
La Trinité 3,380 D6
Le Carbet 2,321 C6
Le François 2,940 D6
Le Lamentin 6,872 D6
Le Lorrain 2,024 D6
Le Marin 2,651 D7
Le Morne-Rouge 2,650 C5
Le Prêcheur 1,350 C5
Le Robert 3,610 D6
Le Saint-Esprit 3,947 D6
Les Trois-Îlets 1,484 D6
Le Vauclin 3,054 D6
Macouba 1,142 C5
Marigot 1,765 D5
Rivière-Pilote 1,587 D7
Rivière-Salée 1,859 D7
Sainte-Luce 1,502 D7
Sainte-Marie 3,966 D5
Saint-Joseph 2,052 D6
Saint-Pierre 4,923 C6
Schoelcher 16,412 C6

OTHER FEATURES

Cabet, Pitons du (mt.) C6
Cabrits (isl.) D7
Caravelle (pen.) D6
Cul-de-Sac du Marin (bay) D7
Diable (pt.) D5
Ferré (cape) E7
Fort-de-France (bay) C6
Galion (bay) D6
Lézarde (riv.) D6
Long (isl.) D6
Lorrain (riv.) D5
Martinique (passg.) C5
Pelée (vol.) C5
Pilote (riv.) D7
Ramiers (isl.) C6
Ramville (isl.) D6
Robert (harb.) D6
Rose (pt.) D6
Saint-Martin (cape) C5
Saint-Pierre (bay) C6
Salines (pt.) D7
Salomon (pt.) C7
Vauclin (mt.) D6

NETHERLANDS ANTILLES

CITIES and TOWNS

Aresji D9
Ascension F8
Bacuna E8
Balashi E10
Boven Bolivia E8
Bubali D10
Bushiribana E10
Dokterstuin F8
Druif D1
Emmastad F9
Entrejo E8
Fontein E8
Fuik G9
Groot Sint Joris G9
Hato G8
Kralendijk (cap.), Bonaire 2,500 E8
Lago E10
Lagoen F8
Montanja di Reij G9
New Port G9
Noord di Salinja E8
Onima E8
Oranjestad (cap.), Aruba 10,100 D10
Otrabanda F9
Patrick F8
Rincon E8
Rooi E8
Santa Barbara G9
Santa Catharina G9
Savaneta E10
Savonet F8
Sint Anna D1
Sint Jan D8
Sint Kruis F8
Sint Martha F8
Sint Michiel F9
Sint Nicolaas E10
Sint Willebrordus F8
Terra Corra E8
Westpunt, Aruba D10
Westpunt, Curaçao F8
Willemstad (cap.) 95,000 F9
Willemstad *130,000 F9

OTHER FEATURES

Aruba (isl.) 55,148 E9
Basora (pt.) E10
Bonaire (isl.) 8,087 E9
Bullen (bay) F8
Caracas (bay) G9
Curaçao (isl.) 145,430 G7
Goto (lake) D8
Jamanota (mt.) E10
Kanon (pt.) G9
Klein Bonaire (isl.) E8
Kudarebe (pt.) D9
Lac (bay) D9
Lacre (pt.) E9
Malmok (mt.) E8
Noord (pt.) D8
Noord (pt.) F8
Paarden (bay) D10
Palm (beach) D10
Pekelmeer (lake) E9
Piscadera (bay) F9
Schottegat (bay) G9
Sint Anna (bay) F9
Sint Christoffel (mt.) F8
Sint Joris (bay) G9
Slag (bay) D8
Vierkant (pt.) E8

SAINT CHRISTOPHER and NEVIS

CITIES and TOWNS

Basseterre (cap.) 14,725 C10
Cayon C10
Charlestown 1,326 C11
Cotton Ground 471 C11
Dieppe Bay C10
Frigate Bay C10
Gingerland D11
Golden Rock C10
Newcastle D11
Old Road Town C10
Sadlers Village C10
Sandy Point 862 C10
Tabernacle C10
Zion Hill D11

OTHER FEATURES

Brimstone (hill) C10
Dogwood (pt.) D11
Fort (pt.) C11
Great Salt (pond) D10
Heldens (pt.) C10
Horse Shoe (pt.) C11
Misery (mt.) C10
Monkey (hill) C10
Narrows, The (str.) D11
Nevis (isl.) 9,300 D11
Nevis (peak) D11
North Friars (bay) D10
Pinney's (beach) D11
Saint Christopher (Saint Kitts) (isl.) 35,104 D10
South Friars (bay) C10

SAINT LUCIA

CITIES and TOWNS

Anse la Raye •5,007 F6
Canaries •2,075 G6
Castries (cap.) •42,770 G6
Choc G5
Choiseul •6,382 F7
Dauphin G5
Dennery •9,654 G6
Gros Islet •10,329 G5
Laborie •6,944 G7
Marigot G6
Marquis G6
Micoud •12,264 G6
Praslin G6
Soufrière •7,456 F6
Vieux Fort •10,675 G7

OTHER FEATURES

Beaumont (pt.) F6
Canaries, Piton (mt.) G6
Cannelles (pt.) G7
Cannelles (riv.) G6
Cap (pt.) G5
Choc (bay) G5
Fond d'Or (bay) G6
Gimie (mt.) G6
Grand Caille (pt.) F6
Grand Cul de Sac (riv.) G6
Gros Islet (bay) G5
Gros Piton (mt.) G6
La Sorcière (mt.) G6
Maria (isls.) G7
Ministre (pt.) G7
Moule-à-Chique (cape) G7
Petit Piton (mt.) G6
Pigeon (isl.) G5
Port Castries (harb.) G6
Port Praslin (bay) G6
Roseau (riv.) G6
Saint Lucia (chan.) G5
Saint Vincent (chan.) G7
Savannes (bay) G7
Sorcière, La (mt.) G6
Soufrière (bay) F6
Vierge (pt.) G6

SAINT VINCENT and THE GRENADINES

CITIES and TOWNS

Barrouallie 1,298 A9
Calliaqua 627 A9
Camden Park A9
Colonarie A9
Georgetown 1,100 A8
Kingstown (cap.) 17,117 A9
Kingstown *23,330 A9
Layou 1,147 A9
Wallibu A8

OTHER FEATURES

Colonarie (pt.) A9
Cumberland (bay) A8
Dark (head) A8
De Volet (pt.) A8
Espagnol (pt.) A8
Greathead (bay) A9
Kingstown (bay) A9
Owia (bay) A8
Porter (pt.) A8
Richmond (peak) A8
Saint Andrew (mt.) A9
Saint Vincent (passg.) A8
Soufrière (mt.) A8
Yambou (head) A9

TRINIDAD and TOBAGO

CITIES and TOWNS

Arima 11,390 B10
Arouca B10
Basse Terre B11
Biche B10
Blanchisseuse B10
California A11
Carapichaima B10
Caroni B10
Cedros A11
Chaguanas 6,122 B10
Chaguaramas A10
Couva 3,635 B10
Cunapo B10
Ecclesville B11
Flanagin Town B10
Fullarton A11
Fyzabad 1,564 A11
Grande Rivière B10
Guaico B10
Guayaguayare B11
La Brea 1,487 A11
Marabella 18,158 A11
Matelot B10
Matura B10
Mayaro 2,638 B11
Moruga B11
Mucurapo A10
Palo Seco A11
Peñal 3,606 B11
Point Fortin 6,538 A11
Port-of-Spain (cap.) 67,978 A10
Princes Town 8,288 B11
Redhead B10
Rio Claro 2,423 B11
Saint Joseph 4,132 B10
Saint Joseph B11
San Fernando 33,490 A11
San Francique A11
Sangre Grande 8,948 B1
San Juan A10
Sans Souci B10
Siparia 5,773 B11
Tabaquite 2,309 B11
Tacarigua B10
Talparo B10
Toco 1,287 B10
Tunapuna 10,251 B10
Upper Manzanilla B1
Valencia B10
Waterloo A10

OTHER FEATURES

Aripo, El Cerro del (mt.) B10
Boca Grande (passg.) A10
Chacachacare (isl.) A10
Chupara (pt.) B10
Cocos (bay) B10
Dragons Mouth (str.) A10
El Tucuche (mt.) B10
Erin (bay) A11
Galeota (pt.) B11
Galera (pt.) C10
Guapo (bay) A11
Guatuaro (pt.) B11
Icacos (pt.) A11
Maracas (bay) C10
Pitch (lake) A11

VIRGIN ISLANDS (Br.)

CITIES and TOWNS

Road Town (cap.) 2,200 D3
West End C4

OTHER FEATURES

Flanagan (passg.) D4
Frenchman (cay) D4
Great Thatch (isl.) C4
Great Tobago (isl.) B3
Jost Van Dyke (isl.) 135 C3
Little Tobago (isl.) B3
Narrows, The (str.) C4
Norman (isl.) D4
Peter (isl.) D4
Road (bay) D3
Sage (mt.) D4
Sir Francis Drake (chan.) D4
Tortola (isl.) 9,257 D3

VIRGIN ISLANDS (U.S.)

CITIES and TOWNS

Bethlehem E4
Canebay E3
Charlotte Amalie (cap.) 11,842 B4
Christiansted 2,914 F4
Cruz Bay 1,928 C4
Diamond F4
Eastend D4
Emmaus C4
Fredensdal F4
Frederiksted 1,046 E4
Grove Place 3,599 E4
Kingshill F4
Longford F4
Negro Bay E4

OTHER FEATURES

Altona (lag.) F4
Annaly (bay) E3
Baron Bluff (prom.) E3
Bordeaux (mt.) C4
Brass (isls.) A4
Buck (isl.) G3
Buck Island (chan.) F3
Buck Island Reef Nat'l Mon. G3
Butler (bay) E4
Caneel (bay) B4
Capella (isls.) B5
Christiansted Nat'l Hist. Site F4
Coral (bay) C4
Crown (mt.) A4
Dutch Cap (cay) A4
Eagle (mt.) E4
East (pt.) G4
Flanagan (passg.) D4
Flat (cays) A4
Grass (pt.) G4
Great (pond) F4
Great Pond (bay) F4
Green (cay) F4
Hams Bluff (prom.) E3
Hans Lollik (isls.) B4
Hassel (isl.) B4
Jersey (bay) B4
Krause Lagoon (chan.) F4
Leeward (passg.) B4
Long (pt.) B4
Long (pt.) E4
Lovango (cay) C4
Magens (bay) B4
Maho (bay) C4
Narrows, The (str.) C4
Nullberg (mt.) B4
Perseverance (bay) A4
Picara (pt.) B4
Pillsbury (sound) B4
Privateer (pt.) D4
Pull (pt.) F3
Ram (head) C5
Red (pt.) D4
Reef (bay) C4
Saba (isl.) A4
Saint Croix (isl.) 49,725 G4
Saint James (isls.) B4
Saint John (isl.) 2,472 C4
Saint Thomas (harb.) B4
Saint Thomas (isl.) 44,372 A4
Salt (cay) A4
Salt (riv.) F4
Salt River (bay) F3
Sandy (pt.) D4
Savana (isl.) A4
Southwest (cape) E4
Tague (bay) G4
Thatch (cay) B4
Turner Hole (bay) G4
U.S. Nav. Air Sta. A4
Virgin (str.) A4
Virgin Isls. Nat'l Park C4
Water (isl.) A4
Westend Saltpond (lag.) E4

*City and suburbs.
• Population of district.
†Population of met. area.
○ Population of municipality.

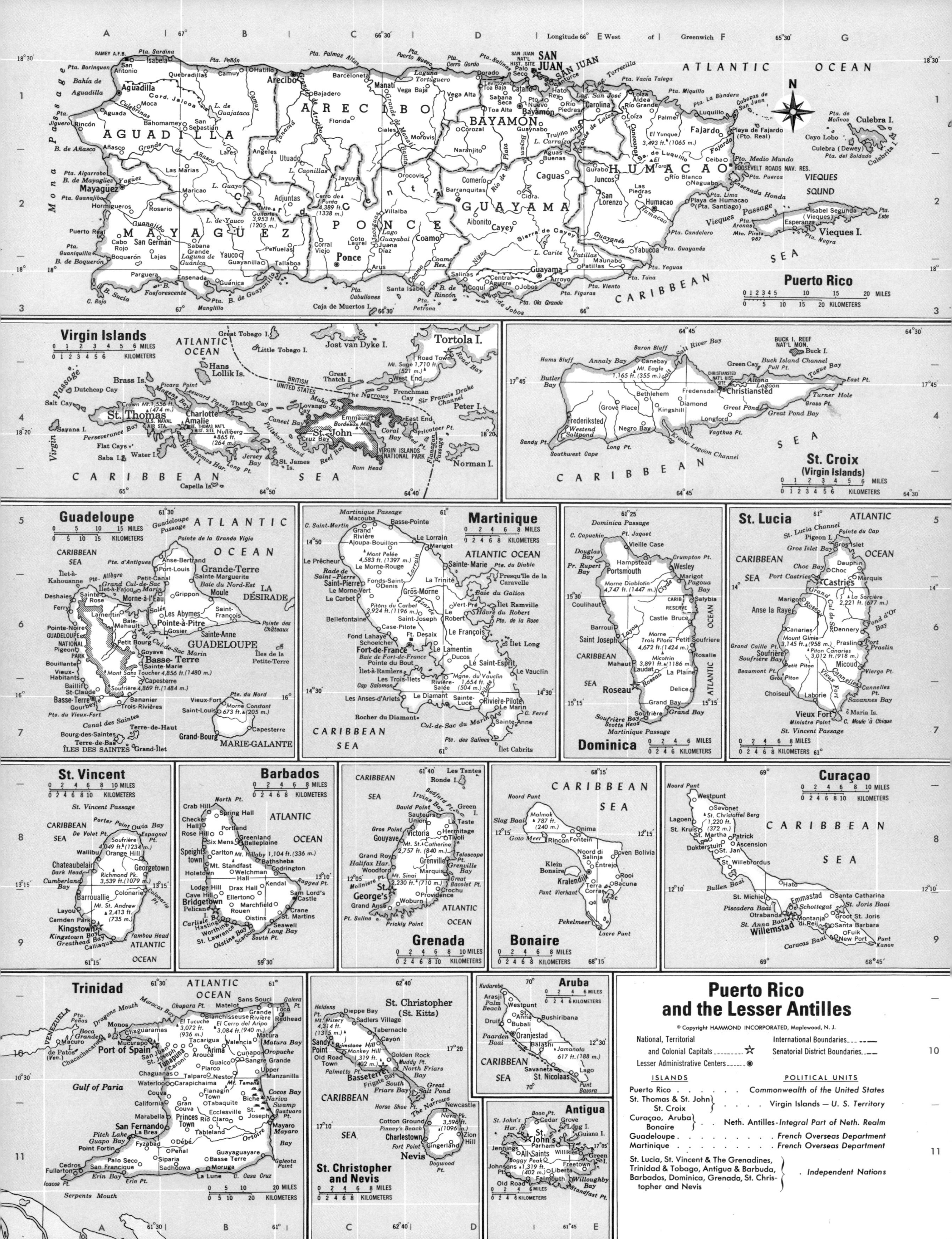

Puerto Rico
and the Lesser Antilles
© Copyright HAMMOND INCORPORATED, Maplewood, N. J.
National, Territorial and Colonial Capitals
Lesser Administrative Centers
International Boundaries
Senatorial District Boundaries
ISLANDS
POLITICAL UNITS
Puerto Rico . . . . . . Commonwealth of the United States
St. Thomas & St. John, St. Croix . . . . Virgin Islands — U. S. Territory
Curaçao, Aruba, Bonaire . . . . Neth. Antilles-Integral Part of Neth. Realm
Guadeloupe . . . . . . French Overseas Department
Martinique . . . . . . French Overseas Department
St. Lucia, St. Vincent & The Grenadines, Trinidad & Tobago, Antigua & Barbuda, Barbados, Dominica, Grenada, St. Christopher and Nevis . Independent Nations
Longitude 66° West of Greenwich
Puerto Rico
ATLANTIC OCEAN
CARIBBEAN SEA
Mona Passage
AGUADILLA
ARECIBO
BAYAMON
HUMACAO
MAYAGÜEZ
PONCE
GUAYAMA
Cordillera Central
SAN JUAN
Aguadilla
Arecibo
Mayagüez
Ponce
Caguas
Humacao
Guayama
Fajardo
Bayamón
Carolina
Cayey
Coamo
Yauco
San Germán
Cerro de Punta 4,389 ft. (1338 m.)
El Yunque 3,493 ft. (1065 m.)
Mte. Guilarte 3,953 ft. (1205 m.)
Culebra I.
Vieques I.
VIEQUES SOUND
Vieques Passage
ROOSEVELT ROADS NAV. RES.
Caja de Muertos I.
0 5 10 15 20 MILES
0 5 10 15 20 KILOMETERS
Virgin Islands
ATLANTIC OCEAN
CARIBBEAN SEA
St. Thomas
Charlotte Amalie
St. John
Tortola I.
Road Town
Jost van Dyke I.
BRITISH
UNITED STATES
VIRGIN ISLANDS NATIONAL PARK
St. Croix (Virgin Islands)
Christiansted
Frederiksted
Salt River Bay
Buck I.
Guadeloupe
Pointe-à-Pitre
Basse-Terre
Grande-Terre
LA DÉSIRADE
MARIE-GALANTE
ÎLES DES SAINTES
Soufrière 4,869 ft. (1484 m.)
Martinique
Fort-de-France
Mont Pelée 4,583 ft. (1397 m.)
ATLANTIC OCEAN
Dominica
Roseau
Portsmouth
Morne Diablotin 4,747 ft. (1447 m.)
St. Lucia
Castries
Vieux Fort
Soufrière
Mount Gimie 3,145 ft. (958 m.)
St. Vincent
Kingstown
Soufrière 4,049 ft. (1234 m.)
Barbados
Bridgetown
Mt. Hillaby 1,104 ft. (336 m.)
Grenada
St. George's
Mt. St. Catherine 2,757 ft. (840 m.)
Bonaire
Kralendijk
Curaçao
Willemstad
St. Christoffel Berg 1,220 ft. (372 m.)
Trinidad
Port of Spain
San Fernando
Gulf of Paria
Serpents Mouth
Dragons Mouth
VENEZUELA
El Cerro del Aripo 3,084 ft. (940 m.)
St. Christopher (St. Kitts)
Basseterre
Charlestown
Nevis
St. Christopher and Nevis
Mt. Misery 4,314 ft. (1315 m.)
Aruba
Oranjestad
Jamanota 617 ft. (188 m.)
Antigua
St. John's
Boggy Peak 1,319 ft. (402 m.)

Abitibi (lake), Ont. H 6
Aklavik, N.W.T. 721 C 2
Albany (riv.), Ont. H 5
Alberta (prov.) 2,237,724 E 5
Amherst, N.S. 9,684 K 6
Amos, Que. 9,421 J 6
Anticosti (isl.), Que. K 6
Athabasca (lake) F 4
Athabasca (riv.), Alta. E 4
Axel Heiburg (isl.), N.W.T. N 3
Baffin (reg.), N.W.T. 8,300 G 1
Baffin (bay), N.W.T. J 1
Baffin (isl.), N.W.T. J 1
Baker Lake, N.W.T. 954 G 3
Banff Nat'l Park, Alta. E 5
Banks (isl.), N.W.T. D 1
Bathurst, N. Br. 15,705 K 6
Belle Isle (str.), Newf. L 5
Bonavista, Newf. 4,460 L 6
Boothia (pen.), N.W.T. G 1
Brandon, Man. 36,242 F 6
British Columbia (prov.) 2,744,467 D 4
Cabot (str.) K 6
Calgary, Alta. 592,743 E 5
Cambridge Bay, N.W.T. 815 F 2
Campbellton, N. Br. 9,818 K 6
Camrose, Alta. 12,570 E 5
Cape Breton (isl.), N.S. K 6
Cartwright, Newf. 658 L 5
Channel-Port aux Basques, Newf. 5,988 L 6
Charlottetown (cap.), P.E.I. 15,282 K 6
Chatham, N. Br. 6,779 K 6
Chesterfield Inlet, N.W.T. 249 G 3
Chibougamau, Que. 10,732 J 6
Chicoutimi, Que. 60,064 J 6
Chidley (cape), Newf. K 3
Chilliwack, Br. Col. ○40,642 D 6
Churchill, Man. 1,186 G 4
Coast (mts.) C 4
Coppermine, N.W.T. 809 E 2
Corner Brook, Newf. 24,339 K 6
Cornwall, Ont. 46,144 J 7
Cranbrook, Br. Col. 15,915 E 6
Cree (lake), Sask. F 4
Dartmouth, N.S. 62,277 K 7
Dauphin, Man. 8,971 F 5
Davis (str.), N.W.T. K 1
Dawson, Yukon 697 C 3
Devon (isl.), N.W.T. M 3
Drumheller, Alta. 6,508 E 5
Edmonton (cap.), Alta. 532,246 E 5
Edmundston, N. Br. 12,044 K 6
Ellesmere (isl.), N.W.T. N 3
Eskimo Point, N.W.T. 1,022 G 3
Estevan, Sask. 9,174 F 6
Finlay (riv.), Br. Col. D 4
Flin Flon, Man.-Sask. 8,261 F 4
Fogo (isl.), Newf. L 6
Fort-Chimo, Que. K 4
Fort Frances, Ont. 8,906 G 6
Fort Franklin, N.W.T. 521 D 3
Fort-George, Que. 2,222 J 5
Fort McMurray, Alta. 31,000 E 4
Fort McPherson, N.W.T. 632 C 2
Fort Nelson, Br. Col. 3,724 D 4
Fort Providence, N.W.T. 605 E 3
Fort Saskatchewan, Alta. 12,169 E 5
Fort Simpson, N.W.T. 980 D 3
Fort Smith (reg.), N.W.T. 22,384 E 3
Fort Smith, N.W.T. 2,298 E 3
Foxe (basin), N.W.T. J 2
Franklin (dist.), N.W.T. H 1
Fraser (riv.), Br. Col. D 5
Fredericton, N. Br. 43,723 K 6
Frobisher Bay, N.W.T. 2,333 K 3
Fundy (bay) K 7
Gander, Newf. 10,404 L 6
Gaspé, Que. 17,261 K 6
Georgian (bay), Ont. H 6
Geraldton, Ont. 2,956 H 6
Glace Bay, N.S. 21,466 L 6
Goose Bay, Newf. 7,103 K 5
Gouin (res.), Que. J 6
Grand Falls, Newf. 8,765 L 6
Grande Prairie, Alta. 24,263 E 4
Great Bear (lake), N.W.T. D 2
Great Slave (lake), N.W.T. E 3
Guelph, Ont. 71,207 H 7
Halifax (cap.), N.S. 114,594 K 7
Hamilton, Ont. 306,434 H 7
Harbour Grace, Newf. 2,988 L 6
Havre-St-Pierre, Que. 3,200 K 5
Hay River, N.W.T. 2,863 E 3
Hearst, Ont. 5,533 H 6
Hecate (str.), Br. Col. C 5
Hull, Que. 56,225 J 6
Inuvik (reg.), N.W.T. 7,485 D 2
Inuvik, N.W.T. 3,147 C 2
Iroquois Falls, Ont. 6,339 H 6
Jasper Nat'l Park, Alta. E 5
Jonquière, Que. 60,354 J 6
Juan de Fuca (str.), Br. Col. D 6
Kamloops, Br. Col. 64,048 D 5
Kane (basin), N.W.T. N 3
Kapuskasing, Ont. 12,014 H 6
Keewatin (reg.), N.W.T. 4,327 G 2
Kelowna, Br. Col. 59,196 E 6
Kenora, Ont. 9,817 G 5
Kingston, Ont. 52,616 J 7
Kirkland Lake, Ont. 12,219 H 6
Kitikmeot (reg.), N.W.T. 3,245 F 1
Kitimat, Br. Col. 12,462 D 5
Kluane (lake), Yukon C 3
Kootenay (lake), Br. Col. E 5
Labrador (reg.), Newf. K 4
Lacombe, Alta. 5,591 E 5
Lake Harbour, N.W.T. 252 J 3
Lake Louise, Alta. 355 E 5
Lancaster (sound), N.W.T. H 1
Leduc, Alta. 12,471 E 5
Lesser Slave (lake), Alta. E 4
Lethbridge, Alta. 54,072 E 6
Liard (riv.) D 3
Lloydminster, Alta.-Sask. 15,031 E 5
Logan (mt.), Yukon B 3
London, Ont. 254,280 H 7
Lunenburg, N.S. 3,014 K 7
Mackenzie (dist.), N.W.T. E 3
Mackenzie (riv.), N.W.T. C 2
Magdalen (isls.), Que. K 6
Manicouagan (riv.), Que. K 5
Manitoba (lake), Man. G 5
Manitoba (prov.) 1,026,241 G 5
Manitoulin (isl.), Ont. H 6
Maple Creek, Sask. 2,470 F 6
Marathon, Ont. 2,271 H 6
Mayo, Yukon 398 C 3
M'Clintock (chan.), N.W.T. F 1
Medicine Hat, Alta. 40,380 E 5
Melville, Sask. 5,092 F 5
Melville (isl.), N.W.T. E 1
Merritt, Br. Col. 6,110 D 5
Minto (lake), Que. J 4
Mistassibi (riv.), Que. J 5
Mistassini (lake), Que. J 5
Moncton, N. Br. 54,743 K 6
Mont-Joli, Que. 6,359 K 6
Mont-Laurier, Que. 8,405 J 6
Montréal, Que. 980,354 J 7
Moose Jaw, Sask. 33,941 F 6
Moosomin, Sask. 2,579 F 5
Moosonee, Ont. 1,433 H 5
Morden, Man. 4,579 G 6
Nain, Newf. 938 K 4
Nanaimo, Br. Col. 47,069 D 6
Nares (str.), N.W.T. N 3
Nelson, Br. Col. 9,143 E 6
Nelson (riv.), Man. G 4
New Brunswick (prov.) 696,423 K
Newfoundland (isl.) L 6
Newfoundland (prov.) 567,681 L 5
New Westminster, Br. Col. 38,550 D 6
Niagara Falls, Ont. 70,960 J 7
Norman Wells, N.W.T. 420 D 2
North Battleford, Sask. 14,030 F 5
North Bay, Ont. 51,268 J 6
North Magnetic Pole F 1
North Saskatchewan (riv.) E 5
N. Vancouver, Br. Col. 33,952 D 6
Northwest Territories 45,741 E 2
Nova Scotia (prov.) 847,422 K 7
Okanagan (lake), Br. Col. D 6
Ontario (prov.) 8,625,107 H 5
Ottawa (cap.), Canada 295,163 J 6
Ottawa (riv.) J 6
Owen Sound, Ont. 19,883 H 7
Pangnirtung, N.W.T. 839 K 2
Parry (chan.), N.W.T. E-H 1
Parry Sound, Ont. 6,124 J 6
Peace (riv.), Alta. E 4
Peace River, Alta. 5,907 E 4
Peel (riv.) C 2
Pelly (riv.), Yukon C 3
Pembroke, Ont. 14,026 J 6
Péribonca (riv.), Que. J 5
Peterborough, Ont. 60,620 J 7
Pond Inlet, N.W.T. 705 J 1
Portage la Prairie, Man. 13,086 G 5
Port Radium, N.W.T. 56 E 2
Poste-de-la-Baleine, Que. 435 J 4
Povungnituk, Que. J 3
Prince Albert, Sask. 31,380 F 5
Prince Albert Nat'l Park, Sask. F 5
Prince Edward Island (prov.) 122,506 K 6
Prince George, Br. Col. 67,559 D 5
Prince Patrick (isl.), N.W.T. M 3
Prince Rupert, Br. Col. 16,197 C 5
Québec (prov.) 6,438,403 J 5
Québec (cap.), Que. 166,474 J 6
Queen Charlotte (isls.), Br. Col. C 5
Queen Elizabeth (isls.), N.W.T. M 3
Quesnel, Br. Col. 8,240 D 5
Race (cape), Newf. L 6
Rainy (lake), Ont. G 6
Rainy River, Ont. 1,061 G 6
Rankin Inlet, N.W.T. 1,109 G 3
Ray (cape), Newf. K 6
Red Deer, Alta. 46,393 E 5
Regina (cap.), Sask. 162,613 F 5
Reindeer (lake) F 4
Revelstoke, Br. Col. 5,544 E 5
Riding Mountain Nat'l Park, Man. F 5
Rimouski, Que. 29,120 K 6
Rivière-du-Loup, Que. 13,459 K 6
Roberval, Que. 11,429 J 6
Robson (mt.), Br. Col. D 5
Rocky (mts.) D 4
Rocky Mountain House, Alta. 4,698 E 5
Rouyn, Que. 17,224 J 6
Sable (cape), N.S. K 7
Sable (isl.), N.S. L 7
Saint Elias (mt.), Yukon B 3
Saint John, N. Br. 80,521 K 6
St. John's (cap.), Newf. 83,770 L 6
Saint Lawrence (riv.) K 6

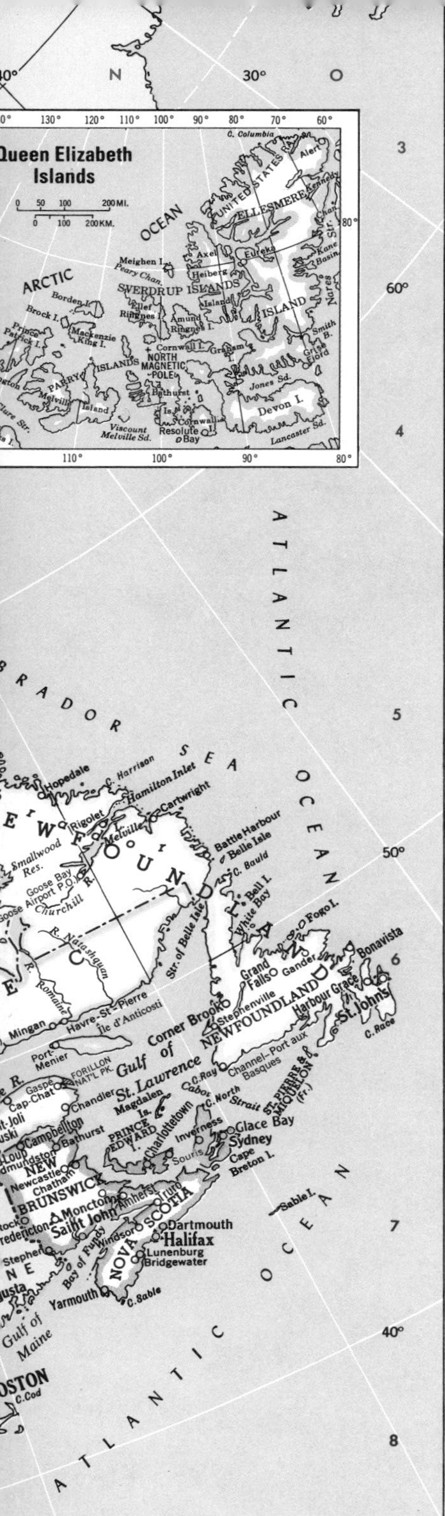

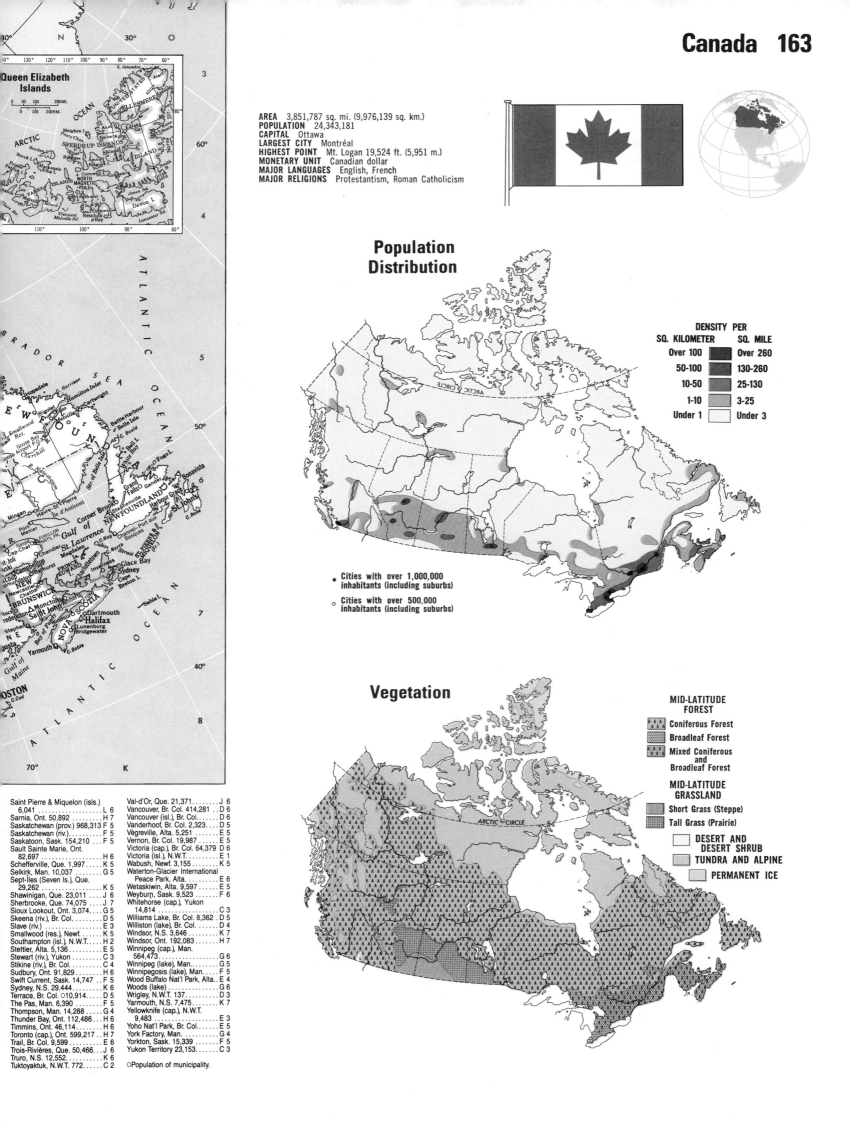

AREA 3,851,787 sq. mi. (9,976,139 sq. km.)
POPULATION 24,343,181
CAPITAL Ottawa
LARGEST CITY Montréal
HIGHEST POINT Mt. Logan 19,524 ft. (5,951 m.)
MONETARY UNIT Canadian dollar
MAJOR LANGUAGES English, French
MAJOR RELIGIONS Protestantism, Roman Catholicism

Population Distribution

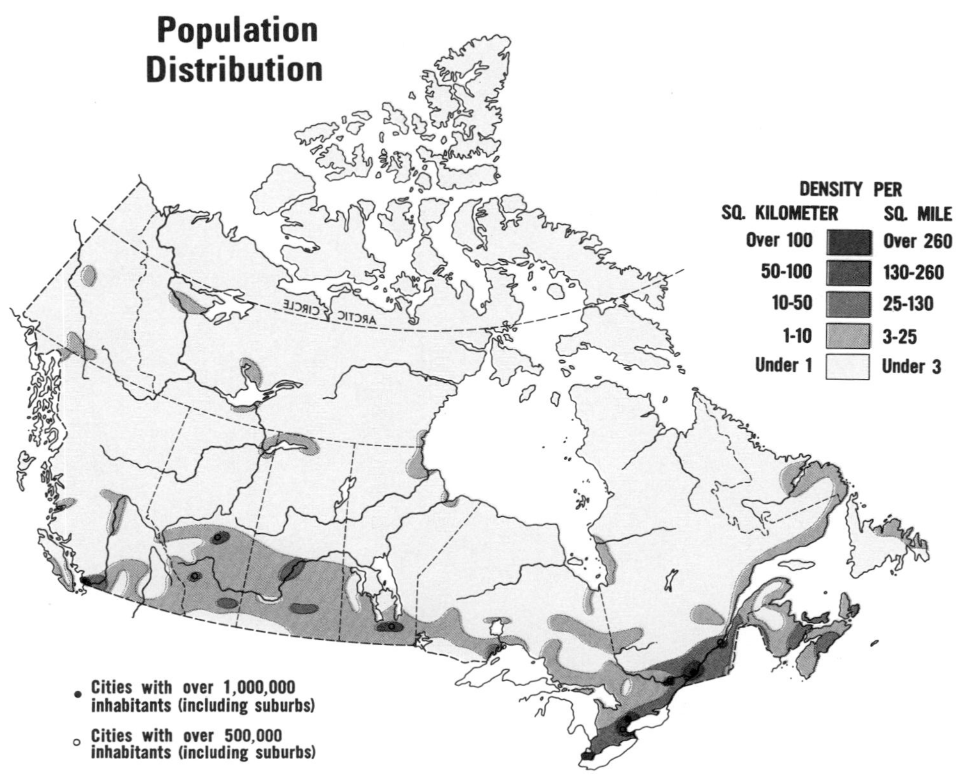

Vegetation

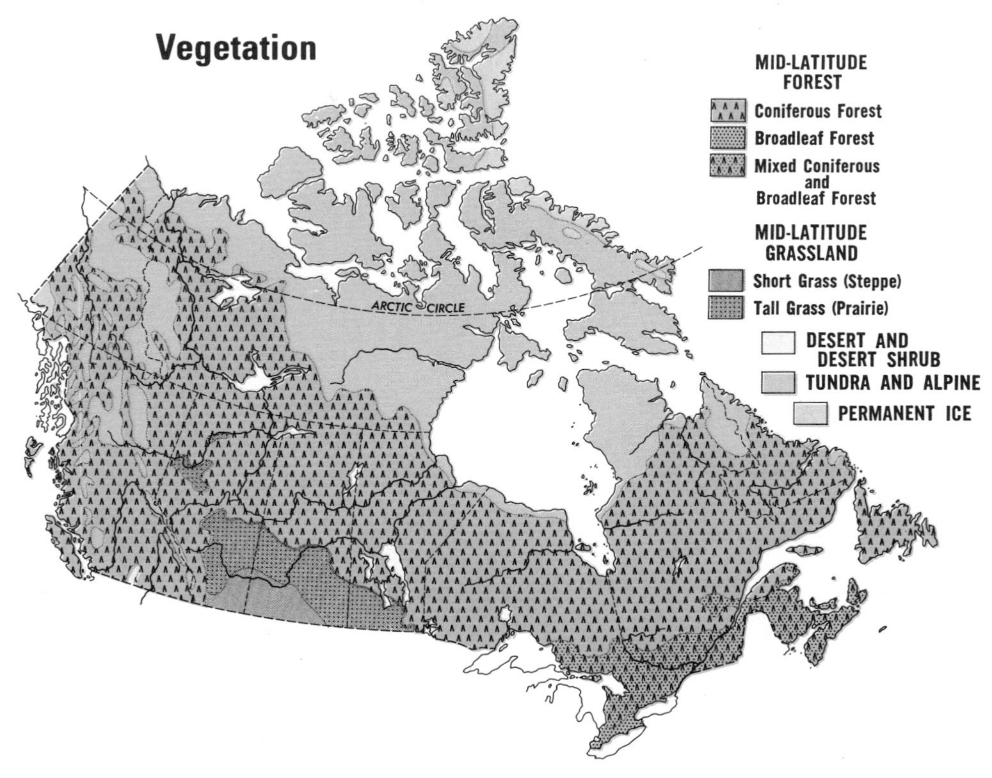

○Population of municipality.

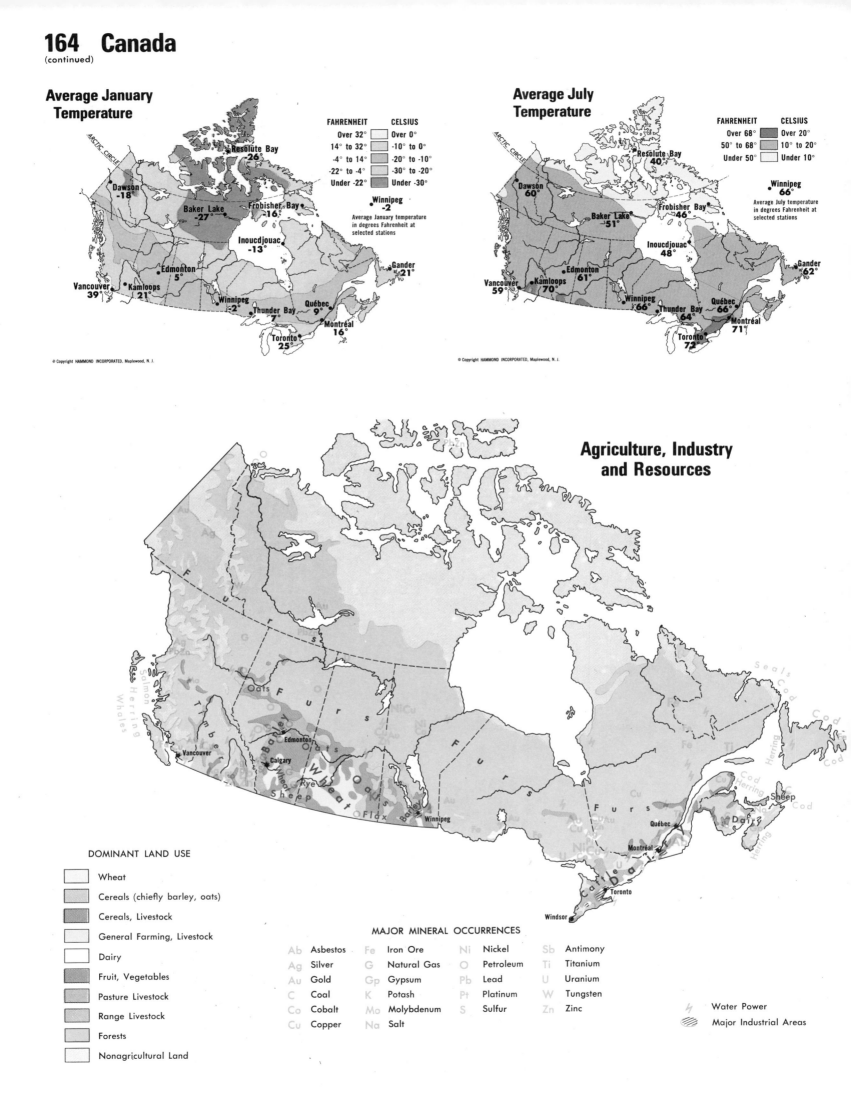

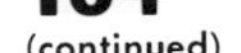

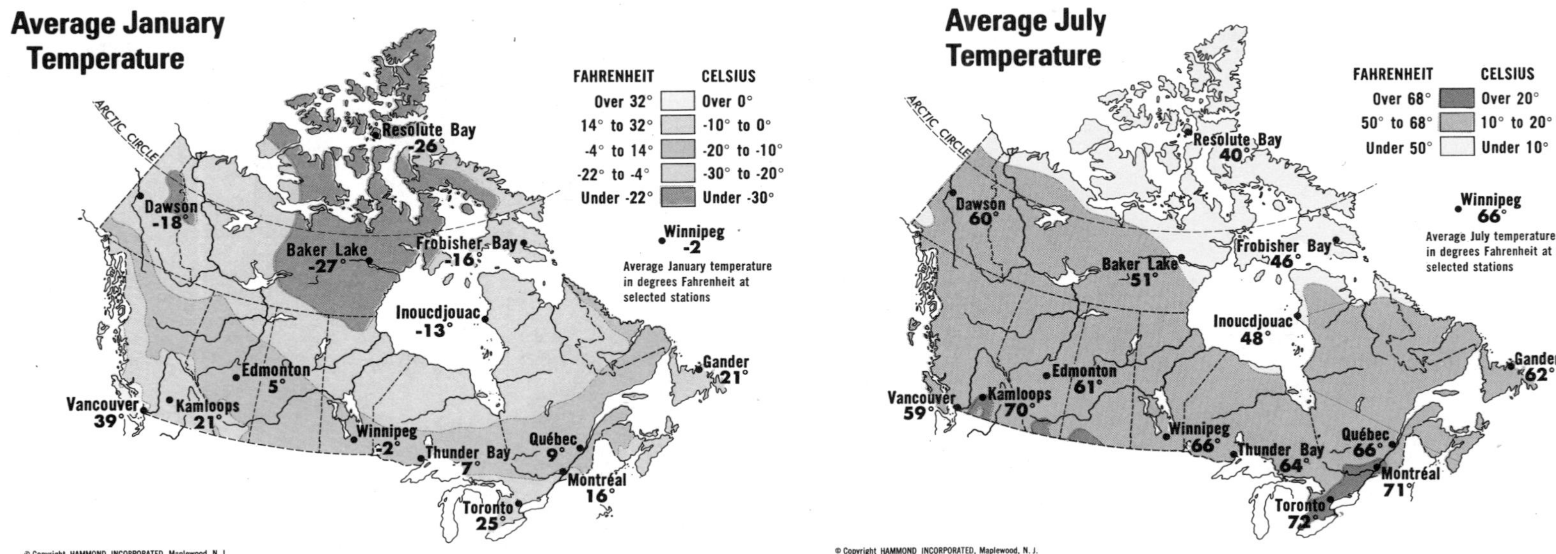

Agriculture, Industry and Resources

DOMINANT LAND USE

- Wheat
- Cereals (chiefly barley, oats)
- Cereals, Livestock
- General Farming, Livestock
- Dairy
- Fruit, Vegetables
- Pasture Livestock
- Range Livestock
- Forests
- Nonagricultural Land

MAJOR MINERAL OCCURRENCES

Ab	Asbestos	Fe	Iron Ore	Ni	Nickel	Sb	Antimony
Ag	Silver	G	Natural Gas	O	Petroleum	Ti	Titanium
Au	Gold	Gp	Gypsum	Pb	Lead	U	Uranium
C	Coal	K	Potash	Pt	Platinum	W	Tungsten
Co	Cobalt	Mo	Molybdenum	S	Sulfur	Zn	Zinc
Cu	Copper	Na	Salt				

Water Power

Major Industrial Areas

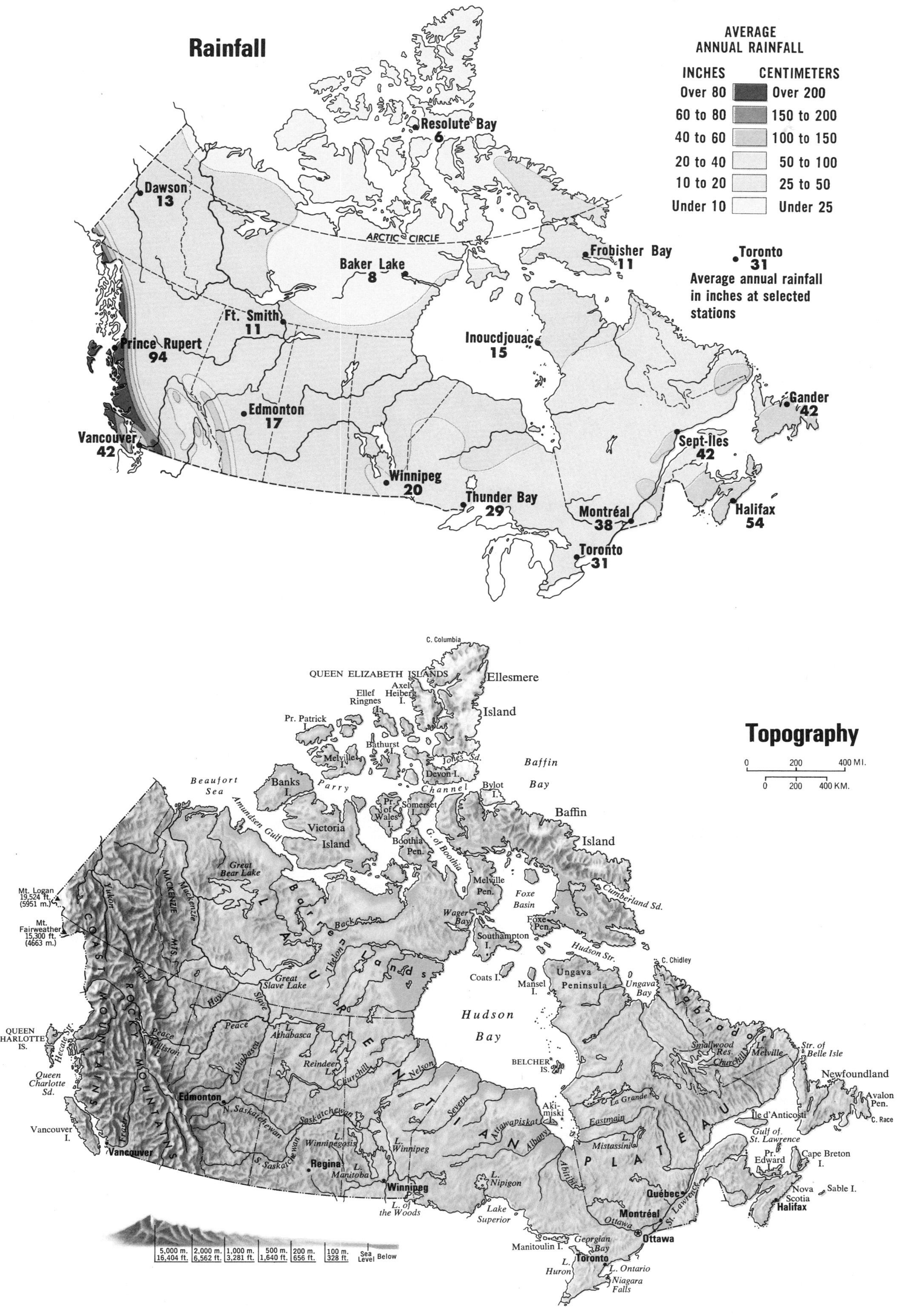
Rainfall
AVERAGE
ANNUAL RAINFALL
INCHES
CENTIMETERS
Over 80
Over 200
60 to 80
150 to 200
40 to 60
100 to 150
20 to 40
50 to 100
10 to 20
25 to 50
Under 10
Under 25
Toronto
31
Average annual rainfall in inches at selected stations
Resolute Bay
6
Dawson
13
ARCTIC CIRCLE
Baker Lake
8
Frobisher Bay
11
Ft. Smith
11
Prince Rupert
94
Inoucdjouac
15
Edmonton
17
Gander
42
Vancouver
42
Sept-Îles
42
Winnipeg
20
Thunder Bay
29
Montréal
38
Halifax
54
Toronto
31
Topography
0
200
400 MI.
0
200
400 KM.
C. Columbia
QUEEN ELIZABETH ISLANDS
Ellesmere
Island
Axel Heiberg I.
Ellef Ringnes I.
Pr. Patrick I.
Bathurst I.
Melville I.
Jones Sd.
Devon I.
Baffin
Bay
Bylot I.
Beaufort Sea
Banks I.
Parry Channel
Amundsen Gulf
Victoria Island
Pr. of Wales I.
Somerset I.
Baffin
Island
Boothia Pen.
G. of Boothia
Great Bear Lake
Melville Pen.
Foxe Basin
Cumberland Sd.
Mt. Logan 19,524 ft. (5951 m.)
Mt. Fairweather 15,300 ft. (4663 m.)
Yukon
MACKENZIE MTS.
Mackenzie
Barren Lands
Back
Wager Bay
Foxe Pen.
Southampton I.
Hudson Str.
C. Chidley
COAST MOUNTAINS
ROCKY MOUNTAINS
Great Slave Lake
Thelon
Coats I.
Mansel I.
Ungava Peninsula
Ungava Bay
Labrador
Hay
Slave
LAURENTIAN PLATEAU
Hudson
Bay
QUEEN CHARLOTTE IS.
Hecate Str.
Peace
Williston
Peace
Athabasca
Athabasca
Reindeer L.
Churchill
Nelson
BELCHER IS.
Smallwood Res.
Churchill
L. Melville
Str. of Belle Isle
Newfoundland
Queen Charlotte Sd.
Edmonton
N. Saskatchewan
Saskatchewan
Severn
Aki-miski
La Grande
Eastmain
Avalon Pen.
C. Race
Île d'Anticosti
Vancouver I.
Fraser
Vancouver
L. Winnipegosis
L. Winnipeg
Attawapiskat
Albany
L. Mistassini
Gulf of St. Lawrence
Pr. Edward I.
Cape Breton I.
S. Saskatchewan
Regina
L. Manitoba
Winnipeg
L. Nipigon
Abitibi
Québec
St. Lawrence
Nova Scotia
Halifax
Sable I.
L. of the Woods
Lake Superior
Montréal
Ottawa
Ottawa
Manitoulin I.
Georgian Bay
Toronto
L. Huron
L. Ontario
Niagara Falls
5,000 m. 16,404 ft.
2,000 m. 6,562 ft.
1,000 m. 3,281 ft.
500 m. 1,640 ft.
200 m. 656 ft.
100 m. 328 ft.
Sea Level
Below

Newfoundland
including Labrador
SCALE
0 25 50 100 150 MI.
0 25 50 100 150 KM.
Capitals of Provinces
Provincial Boundaries
Provincial Boundary according to Imperial Privy Council decision, 1927
Scale 1:5,200,000
Ungava Bay
QUÉBEC
LABRADOR SEA
LABRADOR
ATLANTIC OCEAN
Gulf of St. Lawrence
Cabot Strait
Honguedo Passage
Jacques Cartier (Mingan) Passage
Île d'Anticosti
St. Lawrence River
Chaleur Bay
Gaspé Pen.
NEW BRUNSWICK
PRINCE EDWARD ISLAND
MAGDALEN ISLANDS (Quebec)
ST PIERRE & MIQUELON (Fr.)
Str. of Belle Isle
Newfoundland
Avalon Peninsula
Trinity Bay
Conception Bay
Placentia Bay
Bonavista Bay
Notre Dame Bay
White Bay
Fortune Bay
Schefferville
Labrador City
Wabush
Churchill Falls
Goose Bay
Happy Valley
Smallwood Reservoir
Lake Melville
MEALY MTS.
Hopedale
Nain
Makkovik
Cartwright
Sept-Îles
Port-Cartier
Havre-St-Pierre
Gaspé
Campbellton
Bathurst
Newcastle
Chatham
Corner Brook
Stephenville
Deer Lake
Springdale
Grand Falls
Windsor
Gander
Lewisporte
Botwood
Bonavista
Clarenville
Marystown
Burin
Grand Bank
Fortune
Harbour Breton
Burgeo
Channel-Port aux Basques
Placentia
Carbonear
Harbour Grace
St. John's
Mt. Pearl
GROS MORNE NAT'L PARK
TERRA NOVA NAT'L PARK
LONG RANGE MTS.
Longitude West of Greenwich
© Copyright HAMMOND INCORPORATED, Maplewood, N.J.

NEWFOUNDLAND

CITIES and TOWNS

Admiral's Beach 362 D2
Admiral's Cove 99 D2
Anchor Point 368 C3
Aquaforte 200 D2
Argentia 93 C2
Arnold's Cove 1,124 C2
Avondale 890 D2
Badger 1,090 C4
Badger's Quay-Valleyfield-Pool's Island 1,566 D4
Baie Verte 2,491 C4
Battle Harbour C3
Bauline 423 D2
Bay Bulls 1,081 D2
Bay de Verde 786 D2
Bay L'Argent 483 D4
Bay Roberts 4,512 D2
Bellburns 147 C3
Belleoram 565 C3
Bellevue 286 D2
Bide Arm 339 C3
Big Pond 167 D2
Birchy Bay 707 D4
Bird Cove 400 C3
Bishop's Falls 4,395 C4
Black Tickle 194 C3
Blackhead Road 1,855 D2
Blaketown 617 D2
Bloomfield 715 D2
Bonavista 4,460 D1
Botwood 4,074 C4
Branch 462 D2
Brigus 898 D2
Broad Cove 198 D2
Brooklyn 197 D2
Brownsdale 199 D2
Buchans 1,655 C4
Bunyan's Cove 590 C2
Burgeo 2,504 C4
Burin 2,904 C2
Burnt Islands 991 C4
Burnt Point 260 D2
Calvert 482 D2
Campbellton 703 D4
Cape Broyle 698 D2
Cape Ray 484 C4
Caplin Cove 150 D2
Carbonear 5,335 D2
Carmanville 966 D4
Cartwright 658 C3
Catalina 1,162 D2
Cavendish 343 D2
Champney's West 141 D2
Chance Cove 498 D2
Change Islands 580 D4
Channel-Port aux Basques 5,988 C4
Chapel Arm 689 D2
Charlottetown 330 D2
Charlottetown 250 C3
Churchill Falls 936 B3
Clarenville 2,878 C2
Clarke's Beach 1,009 D2
Codroy 346 C4
Colinet 318 D2
Colliers 819 D2
Come By Chance 337 C2
Conception Harbour 917 D2
Conche 464 C3
Cook's Harbour 388 C3
Corner Brook 24,339 C4
Cow Head 695 C4
Cox's Cove 980 C4
Cupids 706 D2
Daniell's Harbour 614 C3
Dark Cove 1,344 D4
Davis Inlet 240 B2
Deep Bight 243 C2
Deer Lake 4,348 C4
Dildo 877 D2
Dunville 1,817 D2
Durrell 1,145 D4
Eastport 597 D1
Elliston 527 D2
Embree 846 C4
Englee 998 C3
English Harbour 118 D2
English Harbour West 327 C4
Fermeuse 584 D2
Ferryland 795 D2
Flat Bay 322 C4
Flat Rock 808 D2
Fleur de Lys 616 C3
Flowers Cove 459 C3
Fogo 1,105 D4
Forteau 520 C3
Fortune 2,473 C4
Fox Harbour 280 C3
Fox Harbour 538 D2
François 219 C4
Freshwater 1,276 C2
Freshwater 209 D2
Gambo 2,932 D4
Gander 10,404 D4
Garnish 761 C4
Gaskiers-Point la Haye 505 D2
Gaultois 558 C4
Georges Brook 356 D2
Glenwood 1,129 D4
Glovertown 2,165 C1
Goobies 185 D2
Goose Bay-Happy Valley 7,103 B3
Gooseberry Cove 195 C2
Goose Cove 134 C2
Goose Cove 368 C3
Goulds 4,242 D2
Grand Bank 3,901 C4
Grand Falls 8,765 C4
Grates Cove 275 D2
Green Island Cove 222 C3
Green's Harbour 785 D2
Greenspond 423 D4
Grey River 234 C4
Gull Island 362 D2
Hampden 838 C4
Hant's Harbour 542 D2
Happy Adventure 352 D2
Happy Valley-Goose Bay 7,103 B3
Harbour Breton 2,464 C4
Harbour Deep 278 C3
Harbour Grace 2,988 D2
Harbour Main-Chapel Cove-Lakeview 1,303 D2
Hare Bay 1,520 D4
Hawke's Bay 553 C3
Head of Bay d'Espoir 586 C4
Heart's Content 625 D2
Heart's Delight-Islington 899 D2
Heart's Desire 416 D2
Heatherton 328 C4
Hermitage 863 C4
Hickman's Harbour 479 D2
Hillview 295 D2
Hodge's Cove 438 D2
Holyrood 1,789 D2
Hopedale 425 B2
Howley 456 C4
Isle aux Morts 1,238 C4
Jackson's Arm 623 C4
Jeffrey's 276 C4
Jerseyside 641 B3
Job's Cove 201 D2
Joe Batt's Arm-Barr'd Islands 1,155 D4
Keels 129 D1
Kelligrews (Foxtrap-Greeleytown-Peachtown-Kelligrews) 2,292 D2
Kilbride 5,014 D2
King's Cove 253 D1
King's Point 825 C4
Kippens 1,219 C4
Labrador City 11,538 A3
Lamaline 548 C4
L'Anse-au-Clair 267 C3
L'Anse-au-Loup 589 C3
L'Anse au Meadow 66 C3
La Poile 186 C4
Lark Harbour 783 C4
La Scie 1,422 C4
Lawn 999 C4
Lethbridge 686 D2
Lewisporte 3,963 C4
Little Bay Islands 407 C4
Little Catalina 750 D2
Little Heart's Ease 467 D2
Lodge Bay 124 C3
Long Harbour-Mount Arlington Heights 660 D2
Lourdes 932 C4
Lower Island Cove 415 D2
Lumsden 645 D4
Main Brook 514 C3
Makkovik 347 C2
Markland 344 D2
Mary's Harbour 408 C3
Marystown 6,299 D4
McCallum 243 C4
Melrose 416 D2
Middle Arm, Green Bay 575 C4
Millertown 228 C4
Milltown-Head of Bay d'Espoir 1,376 C4
Milton 258 D2
Mobile 171 D2
Mount Carmel-Mitchell's Brook-St. Catherine's 699 D2
Mount Pearl 11,543 D2
Musgrave Harbour 1,554 D4
Musgravetown 635 C2
Nain 938 B2
New Bonaventure 106 D2
New Chelsea 144 D2
New Harbour 777 D2
Newmans Cove 231 D2
New Perlican 350 D2
Newtown 511 D4
Nippers Harbour 259 C4
Norman's Cove-Long Cove 1,152 D2
Norris Arm 1,216 C4
Norris Point 1,033 C4
North Harbour 151 D2
North River 245 D2
North West Brook 279 C2
North West River 515 B3
O'Donnells 280 D2
Old Bonaventure 111 D2
Old Perlican 709 D2
Paradise 2,861 D2
Parkers Cove 424 D4
Parson's Pond 605 C3
Pasadena 2,685 C4
Patrick's Cove 155 C2
Perry's Cove 141 D2
Peterview 1,119 C4
Petites 108 C4
Petley 147 D2
Petty Harbour-Maddox Cove 853 D2
Picadilly 524 C4
Pinware River 201 C3
Placentia 2,204 C2
Plate Cove 474 D2
Point La Haye 195 D2
Point Lance 141 C2
Point Leamington 848 C4
Point Verde 296 C2
Pollards Point 502 C4
Port au Bras 366 D4
Port au Choix 1,311 C3
Port au Port 603 C4
Port Blandford 702 C2
Port Hope Simpson 581 C3
Port Kirwan 164 D2
Port Rexton 489 D2
Port Saunders 769 C3
Portugal Cove 2,361 D2
Portugal Cove South 371 D2
Port Union 671 D2
Postville 223 B3
Pouch Cove 1,522 D2
Princeton 204 D2
Raleigh 373 C3
Ramea 1,386 C4
Red Bay 316 C3
Red Head Cove 225 D2
Rencontre East 230 C4
Renews-Cappahayden 578 D2
Rigolet 271 C3
Riverhead 431 D2
River of Ponds 304 C3
Robert's Arm 1,005 C4
Rocky Harbour 1,273 C4
Roddickton 1,142 C3
Rose Blanche-Harbour le Cou 975 C4
Rushoon 520 D4
Saint Alban's 1,968 C4
Saint Andrew's 262 C4
Saint Anthony 3,107 C3
Saint Brendan's 468 D4
Saint Bride's 599 C2
Saint George's 1,756 C4
St. John's (cap.) 83,770 D2
Saint Joseph's 262 D2
Saint Lawrence 2,012 C4
Saint Lunaire-Griquet 1,010 C3
Saint Mary's 701 D2
Saint Paul's 454 C4
Saint Phillips 1,365 D2
Saint Shotts 239 D2
Saint Vincent's-Saint Stephens-Peter's River 796 D2
Sally's Cove 100 C4
Salmon Cove 786 D2
Seal Cove 751 C3
Seal Cove-White Bay 498 C4
Seldom-Little Seldom 560 D4
Ship Harbour 265 D2
Shoal Cove 223 C3
Shoal Harbour 1,000 C2
South Branch 264 C4
South Brook, Hall's Bay Dist. 786 C4
South Brook, Humber Dist. 477 C4
Southern Harbour 772 C2
South River 645 D2
Spaniard's Bay 2,125 D2
Springdale 3,501 C4
Stephenville 8,876 C4
Stephenville Crossing 2,172 C4
Summerford 1,198 C4
Summerville 346 D2
Sunnyside 703 D2
Sweet Bay 204 D2
Swift Current 329 C2
Terrenceville 796 D4
Tilting 427 D4
Torbay 3,394 D2
Tors Cove 355 D2
Traytown 383 D1
Trepassey 1,473 D2
Trinity 522 D2
Trinity 375 D4
Trout River 759 C4
Twillingate 1,506 C4
Upper Island Cove 2,025 D2
Victoria 1,870 D2
Wabana 4,254 D2
Wabush 3,155 A3
Wesleyville 1,125 D4
Western Bay 463 D2
West Saint Modeste 273 C3
Whitbourne 1,233 D2
Wild Cove 152 C3
Windsor 5,747 C4
Winterton 753 D2
Witless Bay 907 D2

OTHER FEATURES

Alexis (riv.) C3
Anguille (cape) C4
Annieopscotch (mts.) C4
Ashuanipi (lake) A3
Ashuanipi (riv.) A3
Atikonak (lake) B3
Attikamagen (lake) A3
Avalon (pen.) D2
Barachois Pond Prov. Park C4
Bauld (cape) C3
Bell (isl.) C3
Bell (isl.) D2
Belle Isle (isl.) C3
Belle Isle (str.) C3
Blackhead (bay) D2
Bonavista (bay) D1
Bonavista (cape) D1
Bonne (bay) C4
Branch (riv.) C2
Broyle (cape) D2
Bull Arm (inlet) D2
Burin (pen.) C4
Butter Pot Prov. Park D2
Cabot (str.) B4
Canada (bay) C3
Chidley (cape) B1
Churchill (falls) B3
Churchill (riv.) B3
Cirque (mt.) B2
Clode (sound) D2
Conception (bay) D2
Deep (inlet) B2
Double Mer (lake) C3
Dyke (lake) A3
Eagle (riv.) C3
Espoir (bay) C4
Exploits (riv.) C4
Fogo (isl.) D4
Fortune (bay) C4
Freels (cape) D3
Gander (lake) D4
Gander (riv.) D4
Glover (isl.) C4
Goose (riv.) B3
Grand (lake) B3
Grand (lake) C4
Grates (pt.) D2
Great Colinet (isl.) D2
Grey (isls.) C3
Groais (isl.) C3
Gros Morne (mt.) C4
Gros Morne Nat'l Park C4
Groswater (bay) C3
Hamilton (inlet) C3
Hamilton (sound) D4
Hare (bay) C3
Hawke (hills) D2
Hebron (fjord) B2
Hermitage (bay) C4
Holyrood (bay) D2
Horse (isls.) C3
Horse Chops (head) D2
Humber (riv.) C4
Ingornachoix (bay) C3
Ireland's Eye (isl.) D2
Islands (bay) C4
Kaipokok (bay) B3
Kanairiktok (riv.) B3
Kaumajet (mts.) B2
Kingurutik (mesa) B2
Labrador (reg.) B2
Labrador (sea) C2
La Manche Valley Prov. Park D2
La Poile (bay) C4
Little Mecatina (riv.) B3
Long (isl.) C2
Long (lake) A3
Long (pt.) C4
Long Range (mts.) C4
Main Topsail (mt.) C4
Makkovik (cape) C2
McLelan (str.) B1
Mealy (lake) C3
Meelpaeg (lake) C4
Melville (lake) C3
Menihek (lakes) A3
Merasheen (isl.) C2
Mistaken (pt.) D2
Mistastin (lake) B2
Nachvak (fjord) B2
Naskaupi (riv.) B3
Newfoundland (isl.) C4
Newman (sound) D2
New World (isl.) D4
Norman (cape) C3
North Aulatsivik (isl.) B2
Notre Dame (bay) C4
Okak (bay) B2
Ossokmanuan (res.) B3
Petitsikapau (lake) A3
Pine (cape) D2
Pinware (riv.) C3
Pistolet (bay) C3
Placentia (bay) C2
Ponds (isl.) C3
Port au Port (bay) C4
Port au Port (pen.) C4
Port Manvers (harb.) B2
Race (cape) D2
Ramah (bay) B2
Ramea (isls.) C4
Random (isl.) D2
Random (sound) D2
Ray (cape) C4
Red (isl.) C2
Red Indian (lake) C4
Red Wine (riv.) B3
Rocky (riv.) D2
Round (pond) C4
Saglek (bay) B2
Saint Francis (cape) D2
Saint George (cape) C4
Saint George's (bay) C4
Saint John (bay) C3
Saint John (cape) C3
Saint Lawrence (gulf) B4
Saint Lewis (cape) C3
Saint Mary's (bay) C2
Saint Mary's (cape) C2
Saint Michaels (bay) C3
Salmonier (riv.) D2
Sandwich (bay) C3
Shabogamo (lake) A3
Shoal (bay) D2
Smallwood (res.) B3
Smith (sound) D2
South Aulatsivik (isl.) B2
Spear (cape) D2
Squires Mem. Park C4
Swale (isl.) D1
Terra Nova (riv.) C2
Terra Nova Nat'l Park D2
Territok (cape) B2
Thoresby (mt.) B2
Torbay (pt.) D2
Torngat (mts.) B2
Trespassey (bay) D2
Trinity (bay) D2
Tunungayualok (isl.) B2
Ukasiksalik (isl.) B2
Victoria (lake) C4
White (bay) C3
White Bear (lake) C4
White Handkerchief (cape) B2

SAINT PIERRE and MIQUELON

CITIES and TOWNS

Saint-Pierre (cap.) 5,415 C4

OTHER FEATURES

Miquelon (isl.) 626 C4
Saint Pierre (isl.) 5,415 C4

AREA 156,184 sq. mi. (404,517 sq. km.)
POPULATION 567,681
CAPITAL St. John's
LARGEST CITY St. John's
HIGHEST POINT in Torngat Mountains 5,420 ft. (1,652 m.)
SETTLED IN 1610
ADMITTED TO CONFEDERATION 1949
PROVINCIAL FLOWER Pitcher Plant

Agriculture, Industry and Resources

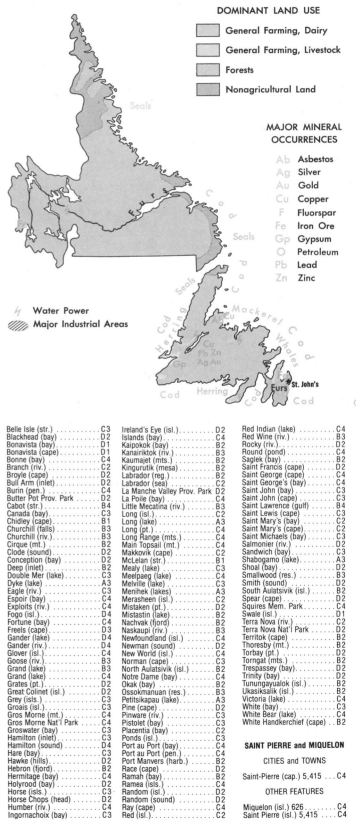

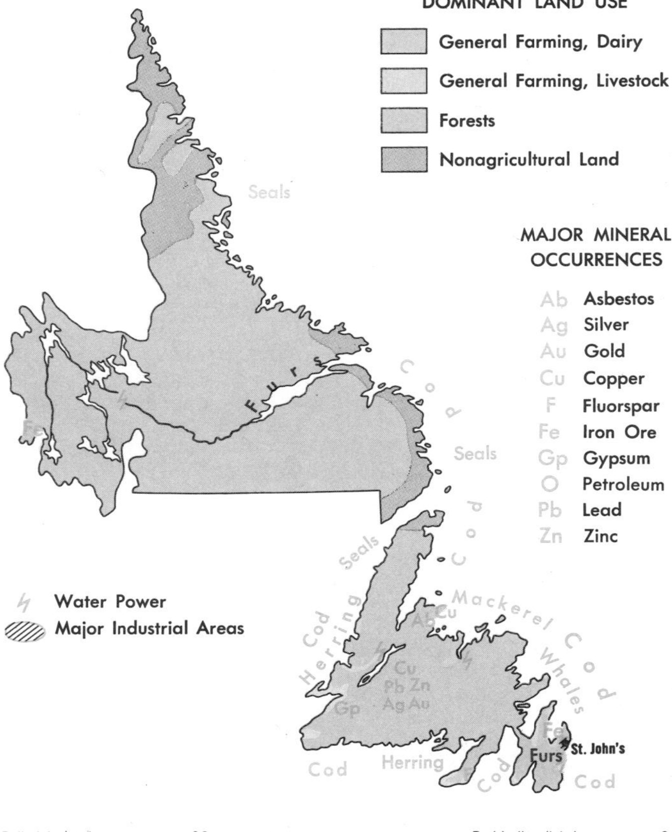

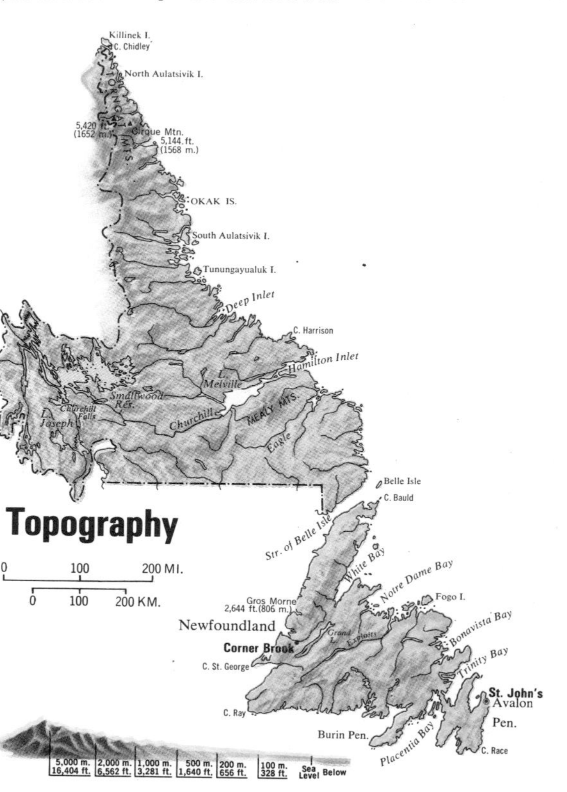

Topography

Nova Scotia and Prince Edward Island

NOVA SCOTIA

COUNTIES

Annapolis 22,522 .... C 4
Antigonish 18,110 .... F 3
Cape Breton 127,035 .... H 3
Colchester 43,224 .... E 3
Cumberland 35,231 .... D 3
Digby 21,689 .... C 4
Guysborough 12,752 .... F 3
Halifax 288,126 .... E 4
Hants 33,121 .... D 4
Inverness 22,337 .... G 2
Kings 49,739 .... D 4
Lunenburg 45,746 .... D 4
Pictou 50,350 .... F 3
Queens 13,126 .... C 4
Richmond 12,284 .... H 3
Shelburne 17,328 .... C 5
Victoria 8,432 .... H 2
Yarmouth 26,290 .... C 5

CITIES and TOWNS

Alder Point 651 .... H 2
Aldershot .... D 3
Amherst⊙ 9,684 .... D 3
Annapolis Royal⊙ 631 .... C 4
Antigonish⊙ 5,205 .... F 3
Arichat 824 .... H 3
Aylesford 744 .... D 3
Baddeck⊙ 972 .... H 2
Barrington Passage 722 .... C 5
Bear River-Sissiboo 854 .... C 4
Beaverbank 1,322 .... E 4
Berwick 1,699 .... D 4
Bridgetown 1,047 .... C 4
Bridgewater 6,669 .... D 4
Brookfield 619 .... E 3
Brooklyn 1,269 .... D 4
Cambridge Station 799 .... D 3
Canning 763 .... D 3
Canso 1,255 .... H 3
Centreville 765 .... D 3
Chéticamp 1,022 .... G 2
Chester 1,131 .... D 4
Chester Basin 639 .... D 4
Church Point 318 .... B 4
Clark's Harbour 1,059 .... C 5
Coldbrook Station 617 .... D 3
Cow Bay 670 .... E 4
Dartmouth 62,277 .... E 4
Debert 618 .... E 3
Digby⊙ 2,558 .... C 4
Dominion 2,856 .... J 2
Donkin 873 .... J 2
Ellershouse-Hartville 662 .... D 4
Elmsdale 1,172 .... E 4
Enfield 1,510 .... E 4
Fall River 1,897 .... E 4
Falmouth 1,110 .... D 3
Glace Bay 21,466 .... J 2
Guysborough⊙ 496 .... G 3
Halifax (cap.)⊙ 114,594 .... E 4
Halifax *277,727 .... E 4
Hantsport 1,395 .... D 3
Herring Cove 1,323 .... E 4
Hilden 1,262 .... E 3
Ingonish 471 .... H 2
Inverness 2,013 .... G 2
Judique 925 .... G 3
Kentville⊙ 4,974 .... D 3
Kingston 1,612 .... D 4
Lakeside 936 .... E 4
Lantz 1,172 .... E 4
Liverpool⊙ 3,304 .... D 4
Lockeport 929 .... C 5
Louisbourg 1,410 .... J 3
Louisdale 979 .... G 3
Lower West Pubnico 790 .... C 5
Lunenburg⊙ 3,014 .... D 4
Mahone Bay 1,228 .... D 4
Meteghan 890 .... B 4
Middleton 1,834 .... C 4
Milford Station 748 .... E 3
Milton 1,678 .... D 4
Mount Uniacke 1,145 .... E 4
Mulgrave 1,099 .... G 3
Musquodoboit Harbour 936 .... E 4
New Glasgow 10,464 .... F 3
New Victoria 1,374 .... H 2
New Waterford 8,808 .... J 2
North Sydney 7,820 .... H 2
Oxford 1,470 .... E 3
Parrsboro 1,799 .... D 3
Pictou⊙ 4,628 .... F 3
Porters Lake 893 .... E 4
Port Hastings 312 .... G 3
Port Hawkesbury 3,850 .... G 3
Port Hood⊙ 701 .... G 2
Port Morien 717 .... J 2
Port Williams 1,227 .... D 3
Prospect 693 .... E 4
Pugwash 648 .... E 3
Reserve Mines 2,472 .... H 2
River Hébert 835 .... D 3
Saint Peters 669 .... H 3
Sandy Point 691 .... C 5
Scotchtown 2,037 .... H 2
Sheet Harbour 819 .... F 4
Shelburne⊙ 2,303 .... C 5
Shubenacadie 984 .... E 3
Springhill 4,896 .... E 3
Stellarton 5,435 .... F 3
Stewiacke 1,174 .... E 3
Sydney⊙ 29,444 .... H 2
Sydney Mines 8,501 .... H 2
Terence Bay 960 .... E 4
Thorburn 1,014 .... F 3
Three Mile Plains 1,355 .... D 4
Timberlea 1,159 .... E 4
Trenton 3,154 .... F 3
Truro⊙ 12,552 .... E 3
Waterville 687 .... D 3
Waverley 1,699 .... E 4
Wedgeport 827 .... C 5
Western Shore 1,712 .... D 4
Westmount 3,097 .... H 2
Westville 4,522 .... F 3
Wileville 746 .... D 4
Windsor⊙ 3,646 .... D 3
Wolfville 3,235 .... D 3
Yarmouth⊙ 7,475 .... B 5

OTHER FEATURES

Advocate (bay) .... D 3
Ainslie (lake) .... G 2
Amet (sound) .... E 3
Andrew (isl.) .... H 3
Annapolis (basin) .... C 4
Annapolis (riv.) .... C 4
Antigonish (harb.) .... G 3
Argos (cape) .... G 3
Aspy (bay) .... H 2
Avon (riv.) .... D 4
Baccaro (pt.) .... C 5
Baddeck (riv.) .... H 2
Barachois (pt.) .... G 4
Barren (isl.) .... G 4
Barrington (bay) .... C 5
Bedford (basin) .... E 4
Berry (head) .... G 3
Boularderie (isl.) .... H 2
Bras d'Or (lake) .... H 3
Breton (cape) .... J 3
Brier (isl.) .... B 4
Canso (cape) .... H 3
Canso (str.) .... G 3
Cap d'Or (cape) .... D 3

Nova Scotia and Prince Edward Island

SCALE

0 10 20 30 40 50 MI.

0 10 20 30 40 50 KM.

Provincial Capitals ⊛
County Seats ⊙
Provincial Boundaries
County Boundaries

Scale 1:1,950,000

Longitude West of Greenwich

Cape Breton (isl.) . . . . J 2
Cape Breton Highlands Nat'l Park . . . . H 2
Cape Negro (isl.) . . . . C 5
Cape Sable (isl.) . . . . C 5
Capstan (cape) . . . . D 3
Caribou (isl.) . . . . F 3
Carleton (riv.) . . . . C 4
Charlotte (lake) . . . . F 4
Chebogue (harb.) . . . . B 5
Chedabucto (bay) . . . . G 3
Chéticamp (isl.) . . . . G 2
Chignecto (bay) . . . . D 3
Chignecto (cape) . . . . C 3
Chignecto (isth.) . . . . D 3
Clam (bay) . . . . F 4
Cliff (cape) . . . . E 3
Clyde (riv.) . . . . C 5
Cobequid (bay) . . . . E 3
Coddle (harb.) . . . . G 3
Coldspring (head) . . . . E 3
Cole (harb.) . . . . E 4
Country (harb.) . . . . G 3
Craignish (hills) . . . . G 3
Cross (isl.) . . . . D 4
Cumberland (basin) . . . . D 3
Dalhousie (mt.) . . . . E 3
Dauphin (cape) . . . . H 2
Digby Gut (chan.) . . . . C 4
Digby Neck (pen.) . . . . B 4
East (bay) . . . . H 3
East (riv.) . . . . F 3
East Bay (hills) . . . . H 3
Egmont (cape) . . . . H 2
Eigg (mt.) . . . . F 3
Fisher (lake) . . . . C 4
Five (isls.) . . . . D 3
Forchu (bay) . . . . H 3
Forchu (cape) . . . . B 5
Framboise Cove (bay) . . . . H 3
Fundy (bay) . . . . C 3
Gabarus (bay) . . . . H 3
Gabarus (cape) . . . . J 3
Gaspereau (lake) . . . . D 4
George (cape) . . . . G 3
George (lake) . . . . B 5

PRINCE EDWARD ISLAND

AREA 2,184 sq. mi. (5,657 sq. km.)
POPULATION 122,506
CAPITAL Charlottetown
LARGEST CITY Charlottetown
HIGHEST POINT 465 ft. (142 m.)
SETTLED IN 1720
ADMITTED TO CONFEDERATION 1873
PROVINCIAL FLOWER Lady's Slipper

NOVA SCOTIA

AREA 21,425 sq. mi. (55,491 sq. km.)
POPULATION 847,442
CAPITAL Halifax
LARGEST CITY Halifax
HIGHEST POINT Cape Breton Highlands 1,747 ft. (532 m.)
SETTLED IN 1605
ADMITTED TO CONFEDERATION 1867
PROVINCIAL FLOWER Trailing Arbutus or Mayflower

Gold (riv.) . . . . D 4
Goose (isl.) . . . . F 4
Goose (isl.) . . . . G 3
Governor (lake) . . . . F 3
Great Bras d'Or (chan.) . . . . . . H 2
Great Pubnico (lake) . . . . C 5
Green (pt.) . . . . C 5
Greville (bay) . . . . D 3
Guysborough (riv.) . . . . G 3
Halifax (harb.) . . . . E 4
Harding (pt.) . . . . D 5
Haute (isl.) . . . . C 3
Hébert (riv.) . . . . D 3
Henry (isl.) . . . . G 3
Indian (harb.) . . . . G 3
Ingonish North (bay) . . . . H 2
Janvrin (isl.) . . . . G 3
Jeddore (harb.) . . . . F 4
John (cape) . . . . E 3
Joli (pt.) . . . . D 5
Jordan (bay) . . . . C 5
Jordan (lake) . . . . C 4
Jordan (riv.) . . . . C 5
Kejimkujik (lake) . . . . C 4
Kejimkujik Nat'l Park . . . . C 4
Kennetcook (riv.) . . . . E 3
La Have (isl.) . . . . D 4
La Have (riv.) . . . . D 4
Linzee (cape) . . . . G 2
Liscomb (isl.) . . . . G 4
Little River (harb.) . . . . B 5
Liverpool (bay) . . . . D 5
Lomond, Loch (lake) . . . . H 3
Long (isl.) . . . . B 4
Louisbourg Nat'l Hist. Park . . . J 3
Lunenburg (bay) . . . . D 4
Mabou (harb.) . . . . G 2
Mabou Highlands (hills) . . . . . . G 2
Madame (isl.) . . . . H 3
Mahone (bay) . . . . D 4
Malagash (pt.) . . . . E 3
Margaree (isl.) . . . . F 4
McNutt (isl.) . . . . C 5
Medway (harb.) . . . . D 4
Medway (riv.) . . . . C 4
Merigomish (harb.) . . . . F 3
Mersey (riv.) . . . . C 4
Michaud (pt.) . . . . H 3
Minas (basin) . . . . D 3
Minas (chan.) . . . . D 3
Mira (bay) . . . . J 2
Mira (riv.) . . . . H 3
Mocodome (cape) . . . . G 3
Molega (lake) . . . . D 4
Morien (cape) . . . . J 2
Mouton (isl.) . . . . D 5
Mud (isl.) . . . . B 5
Mulgrave (lake) . . . . F 3
Musquodoboit (riv.) . . . . E 4
Necum Teuch (harb.) . . . . F 4
Nichol (isl.) . . . . F 4
North (cape) . . . . H 1
North (mt.) . . . . D 3
North Aspy (riv.) . . . . H 2
North Bay Ingonish (bay) . . . . . H 2
North East Margaree (riv.) . . . . H 2
Northumberland (str.) . . . . E 2
Nuttby (mt.) . . . . E 3
Oak (isl.) . . . . E 3
Ocean (lake) . . . . G 3
Ohio (riv.) . . . . D 4
Panuke (lake) . . . . D 4
Paradise (lake) . . . . C 4
Pennant (pt.) . . . . E 4
Percé (cape) . . . . J 2
Peskowesk (lake) . . . . C 4
Petit-de-Grat (isl.) . . . . H 3
Petpeswick (head) . . . . E 4
Philip (riv.) . . . . E 3
Pictou (hârb.) . . . . F 3
Pictou (isl.) . . . . F 3
Pleasant (bay) . . . . H 2
Ponhook (lake) . . . . D 4
Porters (lake) . . . . E 4
Port Hebert (harb.) . . . . D 5
Port Hood (isl.) . . . . G 2
Port Joli (harb.) . . . . D 5
Port Mouton (harb.) . . . . D 5
Poulet Cove (bay) . . . . H 2
Prim (pt.) . . . . C 4
Pubnico (harb.) . . . . C 5
Pugwash (harb.) . . . . E 3
Roseway (riv.) . . . . C 4
Rossignol (lake) . . . . C 4
Sable (cape) . . . . C 5
Sable (isl.) . . . . J 5
Saint Andrews (chan.) . . . . H 2
Saint Anns (bay) . . . . H 2
Saint Georges (bay) . . . . G 3
Saint Lawrence (bay) . . . . H 1
Saint Lawrence (cape) . . . . H 1
Saint Margarets (bay) . . . . E 4
Saint Mary (cape) . . . . B 4
Saint Marys (bay) . . . . B 4
Saint Mary's (riv.) . . . . F 3
Saint Patrick (chan.) . . . . G 3
Saint Paul (isl.) . . . . H 1
Saint Peters (bay) . . . . H 3

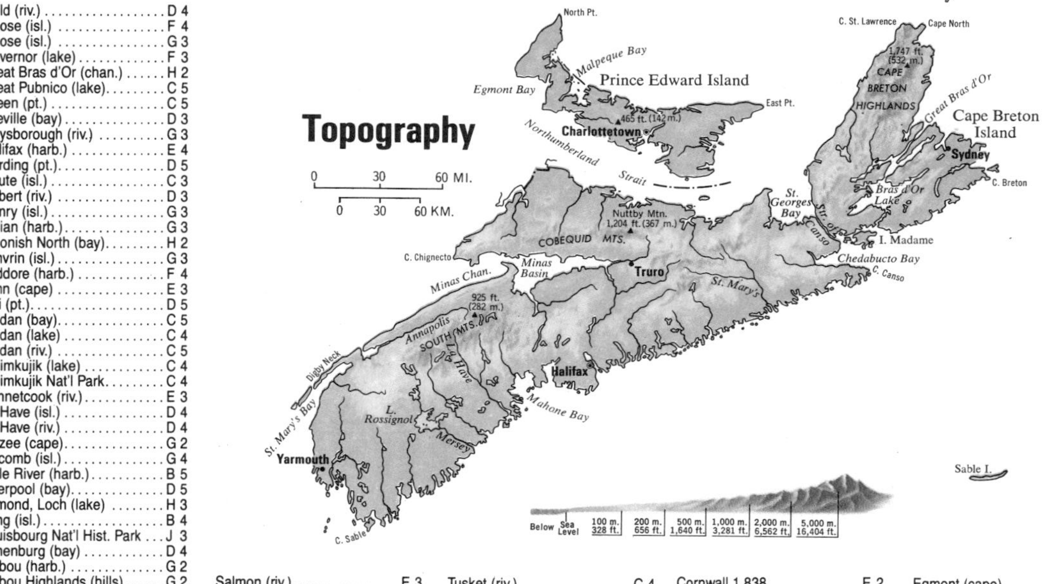

Salmon (riv.) . . . . E 3
Salmon (riv.) . . . . G 3
Scatarie (isl.) . . . . J 2
Scots (bay) . . . . D 3
Seall (isl.) . . . . B 5
Sheet (harb.) . . . . F 4
Sherbrooke (lake) . . . . D 4
Sherbrooke (riv.) . . . . D 4
Shoal (bay) . . . . F 4
Shubenacadie (lake) . . . . E 4
Shubenacadie (riv.) . . . . E 3
Sissiboo (riv.) . . . . C 4
Smoky (cape) . . . . H 2
Sober (isl.) . . . . F 4
South West Margaree (riv.) . . . G 2
Split (cape) . . . . D 3
Spry (harb.) . . . . F 4
Stewiacke (riv.) . . . . E 3
Sydney (harb.) . . . . H 2
Tangier (riv.) . . . . F 4
Taylor (head) . . . . F 4
Tobeatic (lake) . . . . C 4
Tor (bay) . . . . G 3
Tupper (lake) . . . . D 4
Tusket (isl.) . . . . B 5
Tusket (riv.) . . . . C 4
Verte (bay) . . . . D 2
Wallace (harb.) . . . . E 3
West (bay) . . . . G 3
West (pt.) . . . . H 5
West (riv.) . . . . F 3
Western (head) . . . . D 5
West Liscomb (riv.) . . . . F 3
West Saint Mary's (riv.) . . . . . . F 3
Whitehaven (harb.) . . . . G 3
Yarmouth (sound) . . . . B 5

PRINCE EDWARD ISLAND

COUNTIES

Kings 19,215 . . . . F 2
Prince 42,821 . . . . D 2
Queens 60,470 . . . . E 2

CITIES and TOWNS

Alberton 1,020 . . . . E 2
Bunbury 1,024 . . . . F 2
Charlottetown (cap.)⊙ 15,282 . E 2
Cornwall 1,838 . . . . E 2
Georgetown⊙ 737 . . . . F 2
Kensington 1,143 . . . . E 2
Miscouche 752 . . . . D 2
Montague 1,957 . . . . F 2
Murray Harbour 443 . . . . F 2
North Rustico 688 . . . . E 2
O'Leary 736 . . . . D 2
Parkdale 2,018 . . . . E 2
Saint Edward 650 . . . . D 2
Saint Eleanors 2,716 . . . . E 2
Sherwood 5,681 . . . . E 2
Souris 1,413 . . . . F 2
Summerside⊙ 7,828 . . . . E 2
Tignish 982 . . . . D 2
Wilmot 1,563 . . . . E 2

OTHER FEATURES

Bedeque (bay) . . . . E 2
Boughton (isl.) . . . . F 2
Cardigan (bay) . . . . F 2
Cascumpeque (bay) . . . . E 2
East (pt.) . . . . G 2
Egmont (bay) . . . . D 2
Egmont (cape) . . . . D 2
Hillsborough (bay) . . . . E 2
Hog (isl.) . . . . E 2
Kildare (cape) . . . . E 2
Lennox (isl.) . . . . E 2
Malpeque (bay) . . . . E 2
New London (bay) . . . . E 2
North (pt.) . . . . E 1
Northumberland (str.) . . . . D 2
Panmure (isl.) . . . . F 2
Prim (pt.) . . . . E 2
Prince Edward Island Nat'l Park . . . . E 2
Rollo (bay) . . . . F 2
Saint Lawrence (gulf) . . . . F 2
Saint Peters (bay) . . . . F 2
Saint Peters (isl.) . . . . E 2
Savage (harb.) . . . . F 2
Tracadie (bay) . . . . F 2
West (pt.) . . . . D 2
Wood (isls.) . . . . F 3

⊙County seat.
*Population of metropolitan area.

Agriculture, Industry and Resources

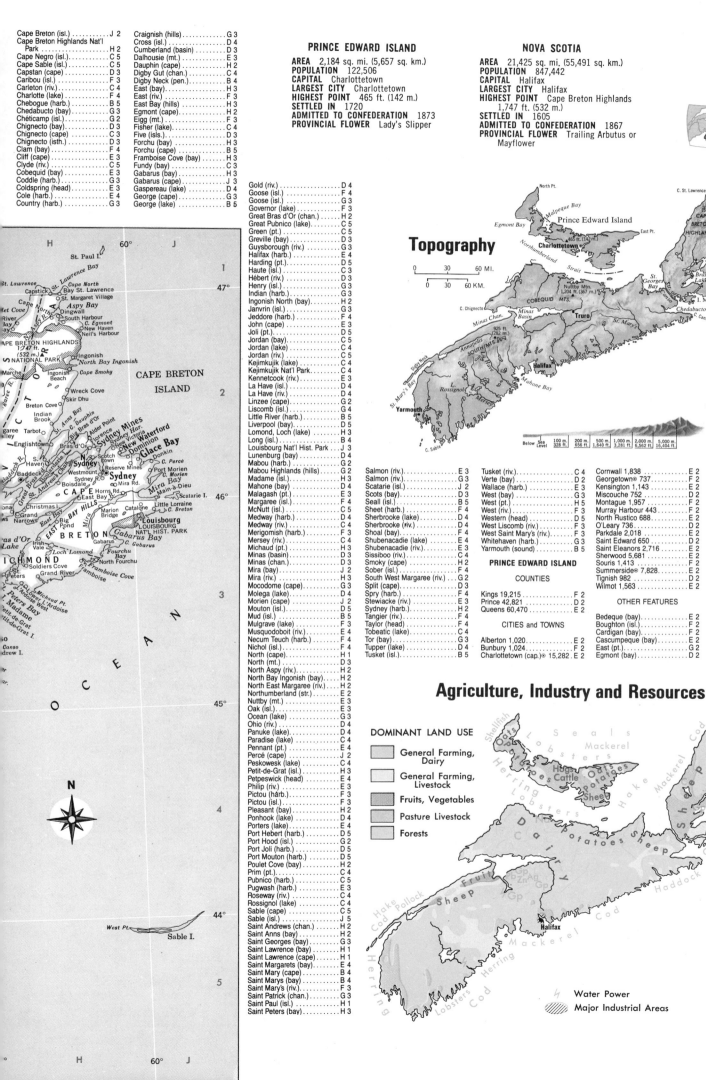

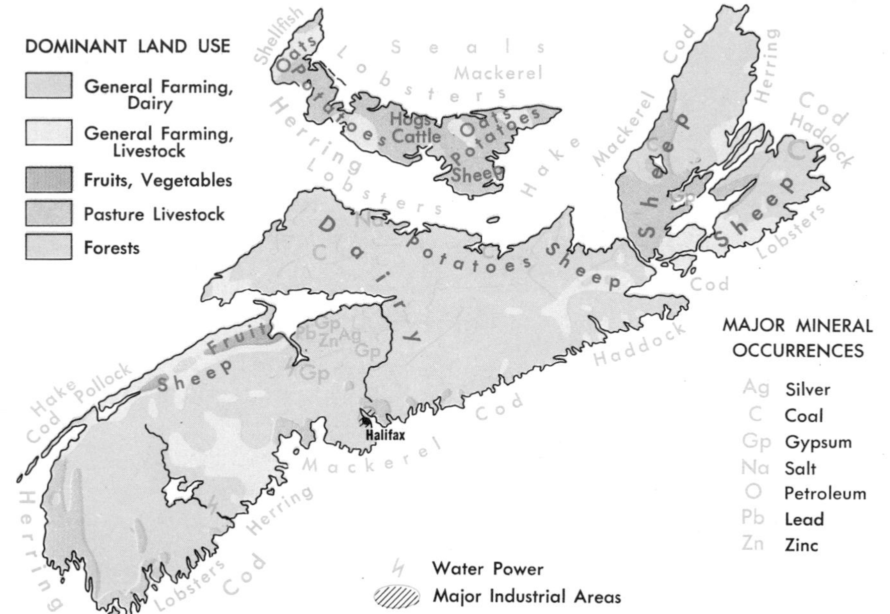

COUNTIES

Albert 23,632 . . . . . F 3
Carleton 24,659 . . . . . C 2
Charlotte 26,571 . . . . . C 3
Gloucester 86,156 . . . . . E 1
Kent 30,799 . . . . . E 2
King's 51,114 . . . . . E 3
Madawaska 34,892 . . . . . B 1
Northumberland 54,134 . . . . . D 2
Queen's 12,485 . . . . . D 3
Restigouche 40,593 . . . . . C 1
Saint John 86,148 . . . . . E 3
Sunbury 21,012 . . . . . D 3
Victoria 20,815 . . . . . C 1
Westmorland 107,640 . . . . . F 2
York 74,213 . . . . . C 3

CITIES and TOWNS

Acadie Siding 64 . . . . . E 2
Acadieville 176 . . . . . E 2
Adamsville 94 . . . . . E 2
Albert Mines 120 . . . . . F 3
Alcida 174 . . . . . E 1
Aldouane 64 . . . . . E 2
Allardville 478 . . . . . E 1
Alma 329 . . . . . F 3
Anagance 114 . . . . . E 3
Anse-Bleue 562 . . . . . E 1
Apohaqui 341 . . . . . E 3
Argyle 63 . . . . . C 2
Armstrong Brook 191 . . . . . E 1
Aroostook 403 . . . . . C 2
Arthurette 178 . . . . . C 2
Astle 201 . . . . . D 2
Atholville 1,694 . . . . . D 1
Aulac 113 . . . . . F 3
Back Bay 455 . . . . . D 3
Baie-Sainte-Anne 709 . . . . . F 1
Baie-Verte 175 . . . . . F 2
Bairdsville 81 . . . . . C 2
Baker Brook 527 . . . . . B 1
Balmoral 1,823 . . . . . D 1
Barachois 686 . . . . . F 2
Barnaby River 38 . . . . . E 2
Barnettville 117 . . . . . E 2
Bartibog Bridge 122 . . . . . E 1
Bas-Caraquet 1,859 . . . . . F 1
Bass River 112 . . . . . E 2
Bath 794 . . . . . C 2
Bathurst⊙ 15,705 . . . . . E 1
Bayfield 81 . . . . . G 2
Bayside . . . . . C 3
Beaubois 211 . . . . . E 1
Beaver Brook Station 95 . . . . . E 1
Beaver Harbour 316 . . . . . D 3
Beechwood 111 . . . . . C 2
Beersville 52 . . . . . E 2
Belledune 690 . . . . . E 1
Bellefleur 83 . . . . . C 1
Bellefond 243 . . . . . E 1
Belleisle Creek 145 . . . . . E 3
Benjamin River 171 . . . . . D 1
Ben Lomond . . . . . E 3
Benton 101 . . . . . C 3
Beresford 3,652 . . . . . E 1
Berry Mills 238 . . . . . E 2
Bertrand 1,268 . . . . . E 1
Berwick 129 . . . . . E 3
Black Point 131 . . . . . D 1
Black River 150 . . . . . E 3
Blacks Harbour 1,356 . . . . . D 3
Blackville 892 . . . . . E 2
Blissfield 119 . . . . . D 2
Bloomfield Ridge 153 . . . . . D 2
Bloomfield Station 62 . . . . . E 3
Bocabec 34 . . . . . C 3
Boiestown 299 . . . . . D 2
Bonny River 153 . . . . . D 3
Bossé 193 . . . . . B 1
Bourgeois 215 . . . . . F 2
Brantville 1,066 . . . . . E 1
Breau-Village 293 . . . . . F 2
Brest 94 . . . . . E 2
Brewers Mills 199 . . . . . C 2
Briggs Corner 89 . . . . . E 2
Bristol 824 . . . . . C 2
Brockway (Lower Brockway-Brockway) 97 . . . . . C 3
Browns Flat 295 . . . . . D 3
Buctouche 2,476 . . . . . F 2
Burnsville 156 . . . . . E 1
Burton⊙ 291 . . . . . D 3
Burtts Corner 484 . . . . . D 2
Cambridge-Narrows 433 . . . . . E 3
Campbellton 9,818 . . . . . D 1
Canaan 115 . . . . . E 2
Canaan Forks 78 . . . . . E 2
Canaan Road 86 . . . . . E 2
Canterbury 474 . . . . . C 3
Cap-Bateau 417 . . . . . F 1
Cape Tormentine 229 . . . . . G 2
Cap Lumière 262 . . . . . F 2
Cap-Pelé 2,199 . . . . . F 2
Caraquet 4,315 . . . . . E 1
Carlingford 229 . . . . . C 2
Carlisle 75 . . . . . C 2
Caron Brook 171 . . . . . B 1
Carrolls Crossing 119 . . . . . D 2
Castalia 145 . . . . . D 4
Central Blissville 155 . . . . . D 3
Centre-Saint-Simon (St. Simon) 991 . . . . . E 1
Centreville 577 . . . . . C 2
Chance Harbour 63 . . . . . D 3
Charlo 1,603 . . . . . D 1
Chatham 6,779 . . . . . E 1
Chatham Head . . . . . E 2
Chipman 1,829 . . . . . E 2
Clair 915 . . . . . B 1
Clarendon 80 . . . . . D 3
Cliffordvale (Limestone-Cliffordvale) 69 . . . . . C 2
Clifton 194 . . . . . E 1
Coal Branch 90 . . . . . E 2
Coal Creek 61 . . . . . E 2
Cocagne Cape 278 . . . . . F 2
Cocagne-Cocagne Sud 600 . . . . . F 2
Codys 125 . . . . . E 3
Coldstream 217 . . . . . C 2
Coles Island 150 . . . . . E 3
College Bridge 536 . . . . . F 3
Collette 198 . . . . . E 2
Connell 58 . . . . . C 2
Connors 96 . . . . . B 1
Cork 54 . . . . . D 3
Cornhill 111 . . . . . E 3
Coughlan 181 . . . . . E 2
Cross Creek 192 . . . . . D 2
Cumberland Bay 231 . . . . . E 2
Dalhousie⊙ 4,958 . . . . . D 1
Dalhousie Junction 105 . . . . . D 1
Darlington 749 . . . . . D 1
Daulnay 398 . . . . . E 1
Dawsonville 278 . . . . . C 1
Debec 200 . . . . . C 2
Dieppe 8,511 . . . . . F 2
Dipper Harbour 166 . . . . . D 3
Doaktown 1,009 . . . . . D 2
Dorchester⊙ 1,101 . . . . . F 3
Dorchester Crossing 605 . . . . . F 2
Douglastown 1,091 . . . . . E 1
Drummond 849 . . . . . C 1
Duguayville 337 . . . . . E 1
Dumfries 150 . . . . . C 3
Dupuis Corner 303 . . . . . F 2
Durham Bridge 255 . . . . . D 2
East Riverside-Kingshurst 989 . . . . . E 3
Edmundston⊙ 12,044 . . . . . B 1
Eel River Bridge 377 . . . . . F 1
Eel River Crossing 1,431 . . . . . D 1
Elgin 301 . . . . . E 3
Enniskillen 63 . . . . . D 3
Escuminac 194 . . . . . F 1
Evandale 58 . . . . . D 3
Evangeline 356 . . . . . F 1
Everett 48 . . . . . C 1
Fairfield 250 . . . . . E 3
Fairhaven 142 . . . . . C 4
Fairisle 415 . . . . . E 1
Fairvale 3,960 . . . . . E 3
Ferry Road 325 . . . . . E 1
Fielding 197 . . . . . C 2
Five Fingers 189 . . . . . C 1
Flatlands 249 . . . . . D 1
Florenceville 709 . . . . . C 2
Forest City 25 . . . . . C 3
Fosterville 58 . . . . . C 3
Four Falls 69 . . . . . C 2
Fredericton (cap.)⊙ 43,723 . . . . . D 3
Fredericton Junction 711 . . . . . D 3
Gagetown⊙ 618 . . . . . D 3
Gardner Creek 56 . . . . . E 3
Geary 654 . . . . . D 3
Germantown 62 . . . . . F 3
Gillespie 96 . . . . . C 2
Glassville 147 . . . . . C 2
Glencoe 147 . . . . . D 1
Glenlivet 284 . . . . . D 1
Gloucester Junction 36 . . . . . E 1
Gondola Point 3,076 . . . . . D 3
Grafton 385 . . . . . C 2
Grand Bay 3,173 . . . . . D 3
Grande-Anse 817 . . . . . E 1
Grand Falls 6,203 . . . . . C 1
Grand Falls Hill 152 . . . . . C 1
Grand Harbour 614 . . . . . D 4
Gray Rapids 266 . . . . . E 2
Hammondvale 72 . . . . . E 3
Hampstead 87 . . . . . D 3
Hampton⊙ 3,141 . . . . . E 3
Harcourt 127 . . . . . E 2
Hardwicke 114 . . . . . E 1
Hardwood Ridge 191 . . . . . D 2
Hartland 846 . . . . . C 2
Harvey, Albert 58 . . . . . F 3
Harvey, York 356 . . . . . D 3
Hatfield Point 176 . . . . . E 3

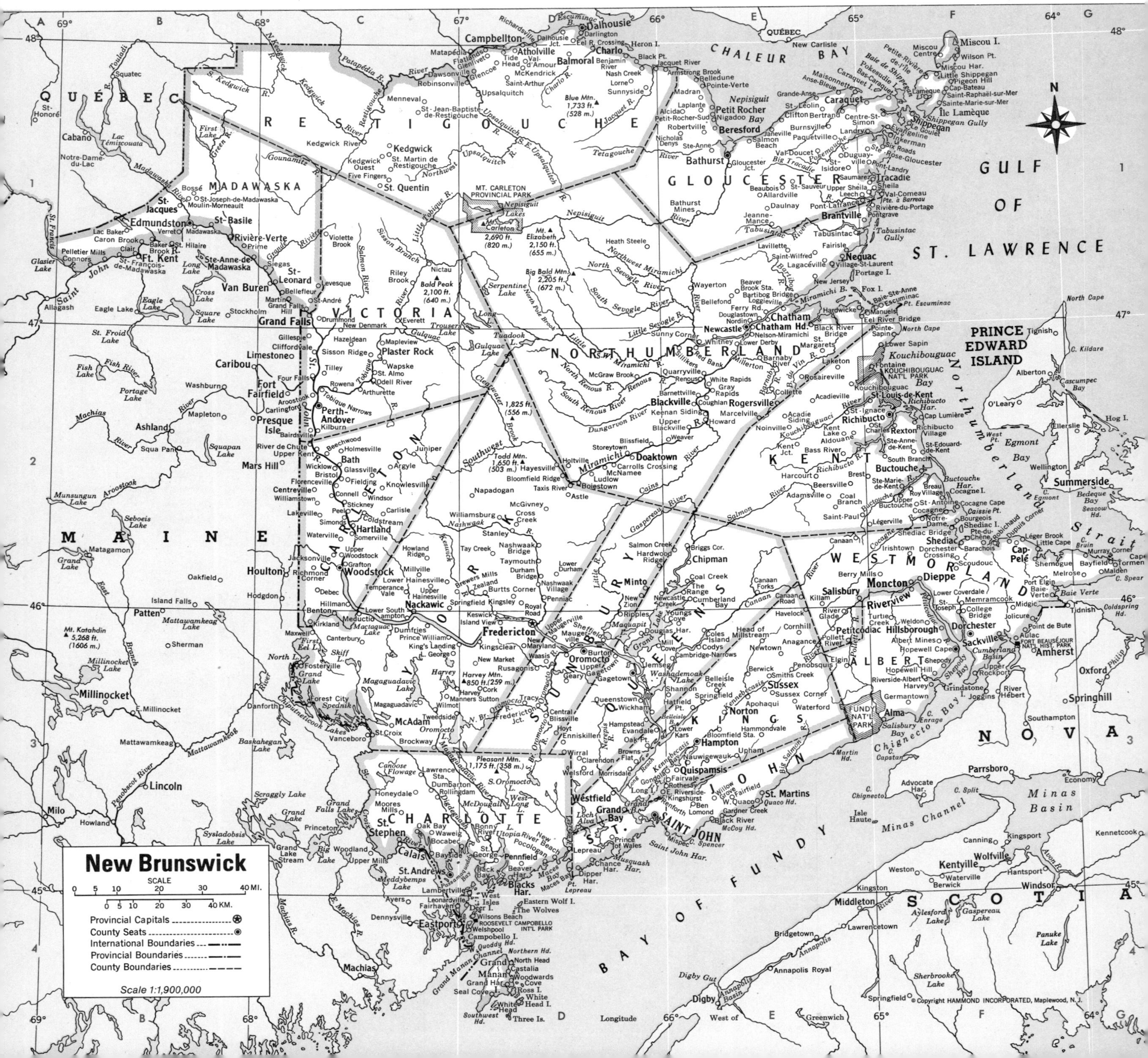

Havelock 439 . . . . . E 3
Hayesville 107 . . . . . D 2
Hazeldean 108 . . . . . C 2
Head of Millstream 61 . . . . . E 3
Hillman 69 . . . . . C 2
Hillsborough 1,239 . . . . . F 3
Holmesville 146 . . . . . C 2
Holtville 222 . . . . . D 2
Honeydale 77 . . . . . C 3
Hopewell Cape⊙ 144 . . . . . F 3
Hopewell Hill 172 . . . . . F 3
Howard 77 . . . . . E 2
Howland Ridge 55 . . . . . C 2
Hoyt 114 . . . . . D 3
Inkerman 396 . . . . . F 1
Irishtown 605 . . . . . F 2
Island View 240 . . . . . D 3
Jacksonville 363 . . . . . C 2
Jacquet River 778 . . . . . E 1
Janeville 204 . . . . . E 1
Jeanne Mance 89 . . . . . E 1
Jemseg 228 . . . . . D 3
Jolicure 96 . . . . . F 3
Juniper 525 . . . . . C 2
Kedgwick 1,222 . . . . . C 1
Keenan Siding 86 . . . . . E 2
Kent Junction 112 . . . . . E 2
Kent Lake 57 . . . . . E 2
Keswick 260 . . . . . D 3
Kilburn 134 . . . . . C 2
Killam 60 . . . . . E 2
Kingsclear 250 . . . . . D 3
Kingsley 145 . . . . . D 2
Kirkland 69 . . . . . C 3
Knowlesville 82 . . . . . C 2
Kouchibouguac 213 . . . . . F 2
Lac Baker 292 . . . . . B 1
Lagacéville 227 . . . . . E 1
Lake George 170 . . . . . C 3
Laketon 81 . . . . . E 2
Lakeville 201 . . . . . C 2
Lambertville 109 . . . . . C 3
Lamèque 1,571 . . . . . F 1
Landry 281 . . . . . E 1
Laplante 197 . . . . . E 1
Lavillette 576 . . . . . E 1
Lawrence Station 229 . . . . . C 3
Leech 584 . . . . . E 1
Léger Brook . . . . . F 2
Légerville 184 . . . . . F 2
Le Goulet 1,173 . . . . . F 1
Leonardville 158 . . . . . C 4
Lepreau 208 . . . . . D 3
Levesque 77 . . . . . C 1
Little Cape 513 . . . . . F 2
Little Shippegan 131 . . . . . F 1
Loggieville 781 . . . . . E 1
Lorne 937 . . . . . D 1
Lower Coverdale 616 . . . . . F 2
Lower Derby 206 . . . . . E 2
Lower Durham 52 . . . . . D 2
Lower Hainesville 66 . . . . . C 2
Lower Kars 30 . . . . . E 3
Lower Millstream 184 . . . . . E 3
Lower Sapin . . . . . F 2
Lower Southampton . . . . . C 3
Ludlow 100 . . . . . D 2
Maces Bay 182 . . . . . D 3
Madran 247 . . . . . E 1
Magaguadavic 126 . . . . . C 3
Maisonnette 757 . . . . . E 1
Malden 93 . . . . . G 2
Manners Sutton 159 . . . . . D 3
Manuels 332 . . . . . F 1
Mapleview 65 . . . . . C 2
Marcelville 61 . . . . . E 2
Martin 104 . . . . . C 1
Maugerville 249 . . . . . D 3
Maxwell 64 . . . . . C 3
McAdam 1,837 . . . . . C 3
McGivney 156 . . . . . D 2
McKendrick 608 . . . . . D 1
McNamee 147 . . . . . D 2
Meductic 234 . . . . . C 3
Melrose 121 . . . . . F 2
Memramcook 276 . . . . . F 2
Menneval 110 . . . . . C 1
Midgic Station 208 . . . . . F 3
Mill Cove 253 . . . . . D 3
Millerton 130 . . . . . E 2
Millville 309 . . . . . C 2
Minto 3,399 . . . . . D 2
Miscou Centre 554 . . . . . F 1
Miscou Harbour 106 . . . . . F 1
Mispec 180 . . . . . E 3
Moncton 54,743 . . . . . F 2
Moores Mills 117 . . . . . C 3
Morrisdale 202 . . . . . D 3
Moulin-Morneault 459 . . . . . B 1
Murray Corner 233 . . . . . G 2
Nackawic 1,357 . . . . . C 2
Napadogan 103 . . . . . D 2
Nash Creek 235 . . . . . D 1
Nashwaak Bridge 142 . . . . . D 2
Nashwaak Village 258 . . . . . D 2
Nauwigewauk 139 . . . . . E 3
Neguac 1,755 . . . . . E 1
Nelson-Miramichi 1,452 . . . . . E 2
Newcastle⊙ 6,284 . . . . . E 2
Newcastle Creek 210 . . . . . D 2
New Denmark 112 . . . . . C 1
New Jersey 65 . . . . . E 1
New Market 143 . . . . . D 3
New Maryland 485 . . . . . D 3
New River Beach 33 . . . . . D 3
Newtown 154 . . . . . E 3
New Zion 171 . . . . . D 2
Nicholas Denys 170 . . . . . D 1
Nictau 30 . . . . . C 1
Nigadoo 1,075 . . . . . E 1
Noinville 50 . . . . . E 2
Nordin 393 . . . . . E 1
North Head 661 . . . . . D 4
Norton 1,372 . . . . . E 3
Notre-Dame 344 . . . . . F 2
Oak Bay 183 . . . . . C 3
Oak Point 83 . . . . . D 3
Oromocto 9,064 . . . . . D 3
Paquetville 626 . . . . . E 1
Peel 117 . . . . . C 2
Pelletier Mills 88 . . . . . B 1
Pennfield . . . . . D 3
Penniac 179 . . . . . D 2
Penobsquis 259 . . . . . E 3
Perth-Andover⊙ 1,872 . . . . . C 2
Petitcodiac 1,401 . . . . . E 3
Petite-Rivière-de-l'Île 549 . . . . . F 1
Petit Rocher 1,860 . . . . . E 1
Petit Rocher Sud . . . . . E 1
Pigeon Hill 595 . . . . . F 1
Plaster Rock 1,222 . . . . . C 2
Pocologan 150 . . . . . D 3
Point de Bute 155 . . . . . F 3
Pointe-du-Chêne 482 . . . . . F 2
Pointe-Sapin 331 . . . . . F 2
Pointe-Verte 1,335 . . . . . E 1
Pollett River 73 . . . . . E 3
Pontgrave 229 . . . . . F 1
Pont-Lafrance 875 . . . . . E 1
Pont-Landry 444 . . . . . F 1
Port Elgin 504 . . . . . F 2
Prime 89 . . . . . B 1
Prince of Wales 138 . . . . . D 3
Prince William 225 . . . . . C 3
Quarryville 205 . . . . . E 2
Queenstown 112 . . . . . D 3
Quispamsis 6,022 . . . . . E 3
Red Bank 141 . . . . . E 2
Renforth 1,490 . . . . . E 3
Renous 192 . . . . . E 2
Rexton 928 . . . . . F 2
Richardsville . . . . . D 1
Richibucto⊙ 1,722 . . . . . E 2
Richibucto Village 442 . . . . . F 2
Richmond Corner 84 . . . . . C 2
Riley Brook 126 . . . . . C 1
Ripples 233 . . . . . D 3
River de Chute 22 . . . . . C 2
River Glade 268 . . . . . E 3
Riverside-Albert 478 . . . . . F 3
Riverview 14,907 . . . . . F 2
Rivière-du-Portage 661 . . . . . F 1
Rivière Verte 1,054 . . . . . B 1
Robertville 733 . . . . . E 1
Robichaud 485 . . . . . F 2
Robinsonville 206 . . . . . C 1
Rogersville 1,237 . . . . . E 2
Rollingdam 65 . . . . . C 3
Rosaireville 86 . . . . . E 2
Rothesay 1,764 . . . . . E 3
Rowena 73 . . . . . C 2
Roy 173 . . . . . F 2
Royal Road 41 . . . . . D 2
Rusagonis 231 . . . . . D 3
Sackville 5,654 . . . . . F 3
Saint Almo 17 . . . . . C 2
Saint-André 385 . . . . . C 1
Saint Andrews⊙ 1,760 . . . . . C 3
Saint-Antoine 1,217 . . . . . F 2
Saint Arthur 369 . . . . . D 1
Saint-Basile 3,214 . . . . . B 1
Saint-Charles 355 . . . . . F 2
Saint Croix 86 . . . . . C 3
Sainte-Anne 329 . . . . . E 1
Sainte-Anne-de-Kent 337 . . . . . F 2
Sainte-Anne-de-Madawaska 1,332 . . . . . B 1
Saint-Édouard-de-Kent 157 . . . . . F 2
Sainte-Marie-de-Kent 283 . . . . . F 2
Sainte-Marie-sur-Mer 539 . . . . . F 1
Sainte-Rose-Gloucester 410 . . . . . F 1
Saint-François-de-Madawaska 753 . . . . . B 1
Saint George 1,163 . . . . . D 3
Saint Hilaire 244 . . . . . B 1
Saint-Ignace 96 . . . . . F 2
Saint-Isidore 794 . . . . . E 1
Saint-Jacques 2,297 . . . . . B 1
Saint-Jean-Baptiste-de-Restigouche 228 . . . . . C 1
Saint John⊙ 80,521 . . . . . E 3
Saint-Joseph 630 . . . . . F 3
Saint-Joseph-de-Madawaska 173 . . . . . B 1
Saint-Léolin 799 . . . . . E 1
Saint Leonard 1,566 . . . . . C 1
Saint-Louis-de-Kent 1,166 . . . . . F 2
Saint Margarets 63 . . . . . E 2
Saint Martin de Restigouche 124 . . . . . C 1
Saint Martins 530 . . . . . E 3
Saint-Paul 365 . . . . . E 2
Saint Quentin 2,334 . . . . . C 1
Saint-Raphaël-sur-Mer 562 . . . . . F 1
Saint Sauveur 252 . . . . . E 1
Saint Stephen 5,120 . . . . . C 3
Saint Wilfred . . . . . E 1
Salisbury 1,672 . . . . . E 2
Salmon Beach 277 . . . . . E 1
Salmon Creek 38 . . . . . E 2
Saumarez 690 . . . . . E 1
Scoudouc 207 . . . . . F 2
Seal Cove 548 . . . . . D 4
Shannon 39 . . . . . E 3
Shediac 4,285 . . . . . F 2
Shediac Bridge 441 . . . . . F 2
Sheffield 112 . . . . . D 3
Sheila 1,172 . . . . . F 1
Shemogue 199 . . . . . F 2
Shepody 86 . . . . . F 3
Shippegan 2,471 . . . . . F 1
Siegas 227 . . . . . C 1
Sillikers 292 . . . . . E 2
Simonds 221 . . . . . C 2
Sisson Ridge 170 . . . . . C 2
Six Roads 239 . . . . . F 1
Smiths Creek 163 . . . . . E 3
Somerville 326 . . . . . C 2
South Branch 86 . . . . . F 2
Springfield, King's 116 . . . . . E 3
Springfield, York 130 . . . . . C 2
Stanley 432 . . . . . D 2
Stickney 232 . . . . . C 2
Storeytown 140 . . . . . D 2
Sunny Corner 405 . . . . . E 2
Sunnyside 87 . . . . . D 1
Sussex 3,972 . . . . . E 3
Sussex Corner 1,023 . . . . . E 3
Tabusintac 231 . . . . . E 1

AREA 28,354 sq. mi. (73,437 sq. km.)
POPULATION 696,403
CAPITAL Fredericton
LARGEST CITY Saint John
HIGHEST POINT Mt. Carleton 2,690 ft. (820 m.)
SETTLED IN 1611
ADMITTED TO CONFEDERATION 1867
PROVINCIAL FLOWER Purple Violet

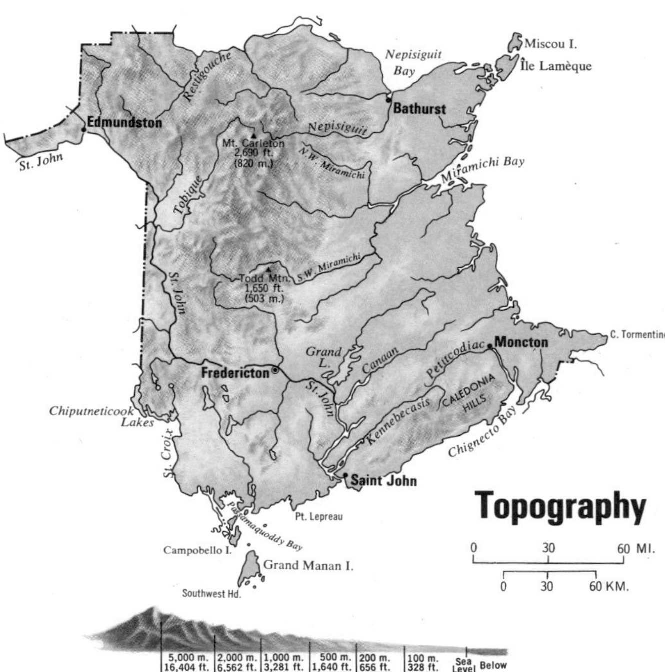

Taxis River 118 . . . . . D 2
Tay Creek 161 . . . . . D 2
Taymouth 301 . . . . . D 2
Temperance Vale 357 . . . . . C 2
The Range 58 . . . . . E 2
Thibault 306 . . . . . C 1
Tide Head 952 . . . . . D 1
Tilley 95 . . . . . C 2
Tobique Narrows 140 . . . . . C 2
Tracadie 2,452 . . . . . F 1
Tracy 636 . . . . . D 3
Turtle Creek 81 . . . . . F 3
Tweedside 87 . . . . . C 3
Upham 107 . . . . . E 3
Upper Blackville 60 . . . . . E 2
Upper Buctouche 158 . . . . . F 2
Upper Gagetown 236 . . . . . D 3
Upper Hainesville 189 . . . . . C 2
Upper Kent 203 . . . . . C 2
Upper Maugerville 543 . . . . . D 3
Upper Mills 153 . . . . . C 3
Upper Rockport 18 . . . . . F 3
Upper Sheila 706 . . . . . E 1
Upper Woodstock 257 . . . . . C 2
Upsalquitch 112 . . . . . D 1
Val-Comeau 534 . . . . . F 1
Val d'Amour 462 . . . . . D 1
Val Doucet 505 . . . . . E 1
Verret 637 . . . . . B 1
Village-Saint-Laurent 187 . . . . . E 1
Waasis 264 . . . . . D 3
Wapske 195 . . . . . C 2
Waterford 120 . . . . . E 3
Waterville 181 . . . . . C 2
Waweig . . . . . C 3
Wayerton 188 . . . . . E 1
Weaver 86 . . . . . E 2
Weldon 227 . . . . . F 3
Welsford 230 . . . . . D 3
Welshpool 260 . . . . . D 4
Westfield 1,100 . . . . . D 3
West Quaco 48 . . . . . E 3
White Head 185 . . . . . D 4
White Rapids 238 . . . . . E 2
Whitney 216 . . . . . E 2
Wickham 72 . . . . . D 3
Wicklow 143 . . . . . C 2
Williamsburg 258 . . . . . D 2
Williamstown 156 . . . . . C 2
Willow Grove 509 . . . . . E 3
Wilmot 57 . . . . . C 3
Wilson Point 45 . . . . . F 1
Wilsons Beach 844 . . . . . D 4
Windsor 43 . . . . . C 2
Wirral 110 . . . . . D 3
Woodstock⊙ 4,649 . . . . . C 2
Woodwards Cove 146 . . . . . D 4
Youngs Cove 65 . . . . . E 3
Zealand 458 . . . . . D 2

OTHER FEATURES

Bald (mt.) . . . . . C 1
Bartibog (riv.) . . . . . E 1
Bay du Vin (riv.) . . . . . E 2
Big Tracadie (riv.) . . . . . E 1
Buctouche (harb.) . . . . . F 2
Buctouche (riv.) . . . . . F 2
Campobello (isl.) . . . . . D 4
Canaan (riv.) . . . . . E 2
Carleton (mt.) . . . . . D 1
Chaleur (bay) . . . . . E 1
Chignecto (bay) . . . . . F 3
Chiputneticook (lakes) . . . . . C 3
Cocagne (isl.) . . . . . F 2
Cumberland (basin) . . . . . F 3
Deer (isl.) . . . . . D 4
Digdeguash (riv.) . . . . . C 3
Escuminac (bay) . . . . . D 1
Escuminac (pt.) . . . . . F 1
Fundy (bay) . . . . . E 3
Fundy Nat'l Park . . . . . E 3
Gaspereau (riv.) . . . . . D 2
Grand (bay) . . . . . D 3
Grand (lake) . . . . . C 3
Grand (lake) . . . . . D 3
Grand Manan (chan.) . . . . . C 4
Grand Manan (isl.) . . . . . D 4
Grande (riv.) . . . . . C 1
Green (riv.) . . . . . B 1
Hammond (riv.) . . . . . E 3
Harvey (lake) . . . . . C 3
Heron (isl.) . . . . . D 1
Kedgwick (riv.) . . . . . C 1
Kennebecasis (riv.) . . . . . E 3
Keswick (riv.) . . . . . C 2
Kouchibouguac (bay) . . . . . F 2
Kouchibouguacis (riv.) . . . . . E 2
Kouchibouguac Nat'l Park . . . . . F 2
Lamèque (isl.) . . . . . F 1
Lepreau (riv.) . . . . . D 3
Little (riv.) . . . . . D 2
Long (isl.) . . . . . D 3
Long Reach (inlet) . . . . . D 3
Maces (bay) . . . . . D 3
Mactaquac (lake) . . . . . C 3
Madawaska (riv.) . . . . . B 1
Magaguadavic (lake) . . . . . C 3
Magaguadavic (riv.) . . . . . C 3
Miramichi (bay) . . . . . E 1
Miscou (isl.) . . . . . F 1
Miscou (pt.) . . . . . F 1
Mount Carleton Prov. Park . . . . . D 1
Musquash (harb.) . . . . . D 3
Nashwaak (riv.) . . . . . D 2
Nepisiguit (bay) . . . . . E 1
Nepisiguit (riv.) . . . . . D 1
Nerepis (riv.) . . . . . D 3
Northern (head) . . . . . D 4
North Sevogle (riv.) . . . . . D 1
Northumberland (str.) . . . . . F 2
Northwest Miramichi (riv.) . . . . . D 1
Oromocto (lake) . . . . . C 3
Oromocto (riv.) . . . . . D 3
Passamaquoddy (bay) . . . . . C 3
Patapédia (riv.) . . . . . C 1
Petitcodiac (riv.) . . . . . F 3
Pokemouche (riv.) . . . . . E 1
Pokesudie (isl.) . . . . . F 1
Pollett (riv.) . . . . . E 3
Quaco (head) . . . . . E 3
Renous (riv.) . . . . . D 2
Restigouche (riv.) . . . . . C 1
Richibucto (harb.) . . . . . F 2
Richibucto (riv.) . . . . . E 2
Roosevelt Campobello Int'l Park . . . . . D 4
Saint Croix (riv.) . . . . . C 3
Saint Francis (riv.) . . . . . A 1
Saint John (harb.) . . . . . E 3
Saint John (riv.) . . . . . C 2
Saint Lawrence (gulf) . . . . . F 1
Salisbury (bay) . . . . . F 3
Salmon (riv.) . . . . . C 1
Salmon (riv.) . . . . . E 2
Shediac (isl.) . . . . . F 2
Shepody (bay) . . . . . F 3
Shippegan (bay) . . . . . E 1
Shippegan Gully (str.) . . . . . F 1
South Sevogle (riv.) . . . . . D 1
Southwest (head) . . . . . D 4
Southwest Miramichi (riv.) . . . . . D 2
Spear (cape) . . . . . G 2
Spednik (lake) . . . . . C 3
Spencer (cape) . . . . . E 3
Tabusintac (riv.) . . . . . E 1
Tabusintac Gully (str.) . . . . . F 1
Tetagouche (riv.) . . . . . D 1
Tobique (riv.) . . . . . C 2
Upsalquitch (riv.) . . . . . D 1
Utopia (lake) . . . . . D 3
Verte (bay) . . . . . G 2
Washademoak (lake) . . . . . E 3
West (isls.) . . . . . D 4
White Head (isl.) . . . . . D 4

⊙County seat.

Agriculture, Industry and Resources

Herring
Cod
Potatoes
Oats
Pb
Zn
Cu
Ag
Sheep
Herring
Lobsters
Potatoes
Oats
Dairy
Sheep
Sb
Saint John
Sardines
Herring

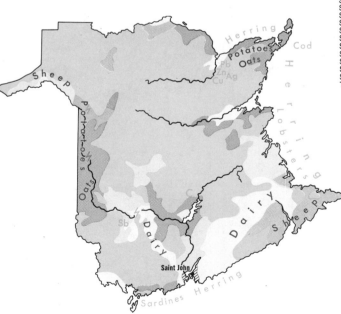

DOMINANT LAND USE

- Cereals, Livestock
- Dairy
- Potatoes
- General Farming, Livestock
- Pasture Livestock
- Forests

MAJOR MINERAL OCCURRENCES

- Ag Silver
- C Coal
- Cu Copper
- Pb Lead
- Sb Antimony
- Zn Zinc
- Water Power
- Major Industrial Areas

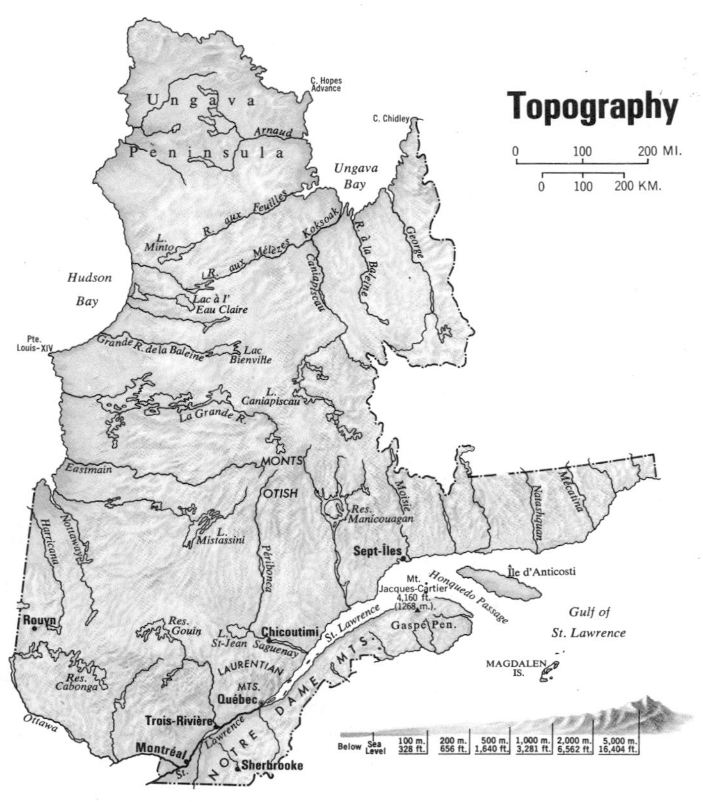

COUNTIES

Argenteuil 32,454 . . . C 4
Arthabaska 59,277 . . . E 4
Bagot 26,840 . . . E 4
Beauce 73,427 . . . G 3
Beauharnois 54,034 . . . C 4
Bellechasse 23,559 . . . G 3
Berthier 31,096 . . . C 3
Bonaventure 40,487 . . . C 2
Brome 17,436 . . . E 4
Chambly 307,090 . . . J 4
Champlain 119,595 . . . E 2
Charlevoix-Est 17,448 . . . G 2
Charlevoix-Ouest 14,172 . . . G 2
Châteauguay 59,968 . . . D 4
Chicoutimi 174,441 . . . G 1
Compton 20,536 . . . F 4
Deux-Montagnes 71,252 . . . C 4
Dorchester 33,949 . . . C 3
Drummond 69,770 . . . E 4
Frontenac 26,814 . . . G 4
Gaspé-Est 41,173 . . . D 1
Gaspé-Ouest 18,943 . . . C 1
Gatineau 54,229 . . . B 3
Hull 131,213 . . . B 4
Huntingdon 16,953 . . . C 4
Iberville 23,180 . . . D 4
Île-de-Montréal 1,760,122 . . . H 4
Île-Jésus 268,335 . . . H 4
Joliette 60,384 . . . C 3
Kamouraska 28,642 . . . H 2
Labelle 34,395 . . . B 3
Lac-Saint-Jean-Est 47,891 . . . F 1
Lac-Saint-Jean-Ouest 62,952 . E 1
Laprairie 105,962 . . . H 4
L'Assomption 109,705 . . . D 4
Lévis 94,104 . . . J 3
L'Islet 22,062 . . . G 2
Lotbinière 29,653 . . . F 3
Maskinongé 20,763 . . . D 3
Matane 29,955 . . . B 1
Matapédia 23,715 . . . B 2
Mégantic 57,892 . . . F 3
Missisquoi 36,161 . . . D 4
Montcalm 27,557 . . . C 3
Montmagny 25,622 . . . G 3
Montmorency No. 1 23,048 . . . F 2
Montmorency No. 2 6,436 . . . G 3
Napierville 13,562 . . . D 4
Nicolet 33,513 . . . E 3
Papineau 37,975 . . . B 4
Pontiac 20,283 . . . A 3
Portneuf 58,843 . . . E 3
Québec 458,980 . . . F 3
Richelieu 53,058 . . . D 4
Richmond 40,871 . . . E 4
Rimouski 69,099 . . . J 1
Rivière-du-Loup 41,250 . . . H 2
Rouville 42,391 . . . D 4
Saguenay 115,881 . . . H 1
Saint-Hyacinthe 55,888 . . . D 4
Saint-Jean 55,576 . . . D 4
Saint-Maurice 107,703 . . . D 3
Shefford 70,733 . . . E 4
Sherbrooke 115,983 . . . E 4
Soulanges 15,429 . . . C 4
Stanstead 38,186 . . . F 4
Témiscouata 52,570 . . . J 2
Terrebonne 193,865 . . . H 4
Vaudreuil 50,043 . . . C 4
Verchères 63,353 . . . J 4
Wolfe 15,635 . . . F 4
Yamaska 14,797 . . . E 3

CITIES and TOWNS

Acton Vale 4,371 . . . E 4
Albanel 992 . . . E 1
Alma⊙ 26,322 . . . F 1
Amqui⊙ 4,048 . . . B 2
Ancienne-Lorette 12,935 . . . H 3
Angers . . . B 4
Anjou 37,346 . . . H 4
Annaville 712 . . . E 3
Armagh 878 . . . G 3
Arthabaska⊙ 6,827 . . . F 3
Arvida . . . F 1
Asbestos 7,967 . . . F 4
Ascot Corner 847 . . . F 4
Audet 760 . . . G 4
Ayer's Cliff⊙ 810 . . . E 4
Aylmer 26,695 . . . B 4
Baie-Comeau 12,866 . . . A 1
Baie-d'Urfé 3,674 . . . G 4
Baie-Saint-Paul⊙ 3,961 . . . G 2
Baie-Trinité 749 . . . B 1
Beaconsfield 19,613 . . . H 4
Beauceville 4,302 . . . G 3
Beauharnois⊙ 7,025 . . . D 4
Beaumont 791 . . . F 3
Beauport 60,447 . . . J 3
Beaupré 2,740 . . . G 2
Bécancour⊙ 10,247 . . . E 3
Bedford⊙ 2,832 . . . E 4
Beebe Plain 1,072 . . . E 4
Bélair (Val-Bélair) 12,695 . . . H 3
Beloeil 17,540 . . . D 4
Bernierville 2,120 . . . F 3
Berthier-en-Bas 562 . . . G 3
Berthierville⊙ 4,049 . . . D 3
Bic 2,994 . . . J 1
Biencourt 824 . . . J 2
Black Lake 5,148 . . . F 3
Blainville 14,682 . . . H 4
Boischatel 3,345 . . . J 3
Bois-des-Filion 4,943 . . . H 4
Bolduc 1,565 . . . G 4
Bonaventure 1,371 . . . C 2
Boucherville 29,704 . . . J 4
Bromont 2,731 . . . E 4
Bromptonville 3,035 . . . F 4
Brossard 52,232 . . . H 4
Brownsburg 2,875 . . . C 4
Buckingham 7,992 . . . B 4
Cabano 3,291 . . . J 2
Cacouna 1,160 . . . H 2
Calumet 729 . . . C 4
Candiac 8,502 . . . J 4
Cap-à-l'Aigle 819 . . . G 2
Cap-Chat 3,464 . . . B 1
Cap-de-la-Madeleine 32,626 . E 3
Caplan-Rivière Caplan 1,139 . C 2
Cap-Saint-Ignace 1,485 . . . G 2
Cap-Santé⊙ 671 . . . F 3
Carignan 4,544 . . . J 4
Carleton 2,710 . . . C 2
Causapscal 2,501 . . . B 2
Chambly 12,190 . . . J 4
Chambord 961 . . . E 1
Chandler 3,946 . . . D 2
Charlemagne 4,827 . . . H 4
Charlesbourg 68,326 . . . J 3
Charny 8,240 . . . J 3
Châteauguay 36,928 . . . H 4
Château-Richer⊙ 3,628 . . . F 3
Chénéville 633 . . . B 4
Chicoutimi⊙ 60,064 . . . G 1
Chicoutimi-Jonquière *135,172 . . . G 1
Chute-aux-Outardes 2,280 . . . A 1
Clermont 3,621 . . . G 2
Coaticook 6,271 . . . F 4
Coleraine 1,660 . . . F 4
Compton 728 . . . F 4
Contrecoeur 5,449 . . . D 4
Cookshire⊙ 1,480 . . . F 4
Coteau-du-Lac 1,247 . . . C 4
Coteau-Landing⊙ 1,386 . . . C 4
Côte-Saint-Luc 27,531 . . . H 4
Courcelles 608 . . . G 4
Courville . . . J 3
Cowansville 12,240 . . . E 4
Crabtree 1,950 . . . D 4
Danville 2,200 . . . E 4
Daveluyville 1,257 . . . E 3
Deauville 942 . . . E 4
Dégelis 3,477 . . . J 2
Delisle 4,011 . . . F 1
Delson 4,935 . . . H 4
Desbiens 1,541 . . . E 1
Deschaillons-sur-Saint-Laurent 950 . . . E 3
Deschambault 977 . . . E 3
Deschênes . . . B 4
Deux-Montagnes 9,944 . . . H 4
Didyme 667 . . . E 1
Disraëli 3,181 . . . F 4
Dolbeau 8,766 . . . E 1
Dollard-des-Ormeaux 39,940 . H 4
Donnacona 5,731 . . . F 3
Dorion 5,749 . . . C 4
Dorval 17,727 . . . H 4
Dosquet 703 . . . F 3
Douville . . . D 4
Drummondville⊙ 27,347 . . . E 4
Drummondville-Sud 9,220 . . . E 4
Dunham 2,887 . . . E 4
Durham-Sud 1,045 . . . E 4
East Angus 4,016 . . . F 4
East Broughton 1,397 . . . F 3
East Broughton Station 1,302 . F 3
Eastman 612 . . . E 4
Entrelacs 1,735 . . . C 3
Farnham 6,498 . . . E 4
Ferme-Neuve 2,266 . . . B 3
Forestville 4,271 . . . H 1
Frampton 684 . . . G 3
Francoeur 1,422 . . . F 3
Gaspé 17,261 . . . D 1
Gatineau 74,988 . . . B 4
Giffard . . . J 3
Girardville 1,128 . . . E 1
Gracefield 869 . . . A 3
Granby 38,069 . . . E 4
Grand'Mère 15,442 . . . E 3
Grande-Rivière 4,420 . . . D 2
Grandes-Bergeronnes 748 . . . H 1
Grande-Vallée 700 . . . D 1
Greenfield Park 18,527 . . . J 4
Grenville 1,417 . . . C 4
Gros-Morne 672 . . . C 1
Hampstead 7,598 . . . H 4
Ham-Sud⊙ 62 . . . F 4
Hauterive 13,995 . . . A 1
Hébertville 2,515 . . . F 1
Hébertville-Station 1,442 . . . F 1
Hemmingford 737 . . . D 4
Henryville 595 . . . D 4
Howick 639 . . . D 4
Hudson 4,414 . . . C 4
Hull⊙ 56,225 . . . B 4
Huntingdon⊙ 3,018 . . . C 4
Île-Perrot 5,945 . . . G 4
Iberville⊙ 8,587 . . . D 4
Inverness⊙ 329 . . . F 3
Joliette⊙ 16,987 . . . D 3
Jonquière 60,354 . . . F 1
Jonquière-Chicoutimi *135,172 . . . F 1
Kingsey Falls 818 . . . E 4
Kirkland 10,476 . . . H 4
Knowlton (Lac-Brome)⊙ 4,316 . . . E 4
La Baie 20,935 . . . G 1
Labelle 1,534 . . . C 3
Lac-à-la-Croix 1,017 . . . F 1
Lac-Alouette-Lac-Brière 1,356 D 4
Lac-au-Saumon 1,332 . . . B 2
Lac-aux-Sables 838 . . . E 3
Lac-Beaufort . . . F 3
Lac-Bouchette 1,703 . . . E 1
Lac-Carré 717 . . . C 3
Lac-des-Écorces 766 . . . B 3
Lac-Drolet 1,120 . . . G 4
Lac-Etchemin 2,729 . . . G 3
Lachenaie 8,631 . . . D 4
Lachine 37,521 . . . H 4
Lachute⊙ 11,729 . . . C 4
Lac-Mégantic⊙ 6,119 . . . G 4
Lacolle 1,319 . . . D 4
Lac-Saint-Charles 5,837 . . . H 3
Lafontaine 4,799 . . . C 4
La Guadeloupe 1,692 . . . F 4
La Malbaie⊙ 4,030 . . . G 2
Lambton 1,559 . . . F 4
L'Annonciation 2,384 . . . C 3
Lanoraie (Lanoraie-d'Autry) 1,613 . . . D 4
La Pêche 4,977 . . . B 4
La Pérade 1,039 . . . E 3
La Pocatière 4,560 . . . H 2
La Prairie⊙ 10,627 . . . J 4
La Providence . . . E 4
Larouche 662 . . . F 1
La Salle 76,299 . . . H 4
L'Ascension 1,287 . . . F 1
L'Assomption⊙ 4,844 . . . D 4
La Station-du-Coteau 892 . . . C 4
Laterrière 788 . . . F 1
La Tuque 11,556 . . . E 2
Laurentides 1,947 . . . D 4
Laurier-Station 1,123 . . . F 3
Laurierville 939 . . . F 3
Lauzon 13,362 . . . J 3
Laval 268,335 . . . H 4
Lavaltrie 2,053 . . . D 4
L'Avenir 1,116 . . . E 4
Lawrenceville 562 . . . E 4
Le Moyne 6,137 . . . J 4
L'Épiphanie 2,971 . . . D 4
Léry 2,239 . . . H 4
Lévis 17,895 . . . J 3
Lennoxville 3,922 . . . F 4
Les Méchins 803 . . . B 1
Linière 1,168 . . . G 3
L'Islet 1,070 . . . G 2
L'Islet-sur-Mer 774 . . . G 2
L'Isle-Verte 1,142 . . . G 1
Longueuil⊙ 124,320 . . . J 4
Loretteville⊙ 15,060 . . . H 3
Lorraine 6,881 . . . H 4
Louiseville⊙ 3,735 . . . E 3
Luceville 1,524 . . . J 1
Lyster 830 . . . F 3
Magog 13,604 . . . E 4
Maniwaki⊙ 5,424 . . . B 3
Manseau 626 . . . E 3
Maple Grove 2,009 . . . H 4
Maria 1,178 . . . C 2
Marieville⊙ 4,877 . . . D 4
Mascouche 20,345 . . . H 4
Maskinongé 1,005 . . . E 3
Masson 4,264 . . . B 4
Massueville 671 . . . E 4
Matane⊙ 13,612 . . . B 1
Matapédia 586 . . . B 2
Melocheville 1,892 . . . C 4
Mercier 6,352 . . . H 4
Metabetchouan 3,406 . . . F 1
Mirabel⊙ 14,080 . . . H 4
Mistassini 6,682 . . . E 1
Montauban 557 . . . E 3
Mont-Carmel 807 . . . H 2
Montcerf 570 . . . A 3
Montebello 1,229 . . . B 4
Mont-Joli 6,359 . . . J 1
Mont-Laurier⊙ 8,405 . . . B 3
Mont-Louis 756 . . . C 1
Montmagny⊙ 12,405 . . . G 3
Montréal⊙ 980,354 . . . H 4
Montréal *2,828,349 . . . H 4
Montréal-Est 3,778 . . . J 4
Montréal-Nord 94,914 . . . H 4
Mont-Rolland 1,517 . . . C 4
Mont-Royal 19,247 . . . H 4
Mont-Saint-Hilaire 10,066 . . . D 4
Morin Heights 592 . . . C 4
Murdochville 3,396 . . . C 1
Nantes 1,167 . . . F 4

Agriculture, Industry and Resources

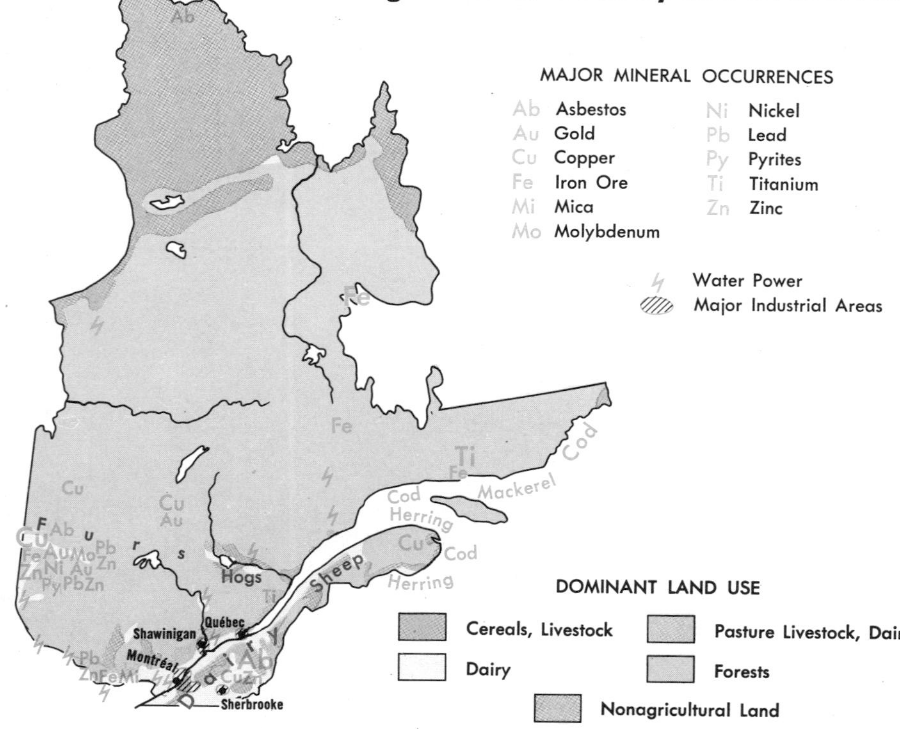

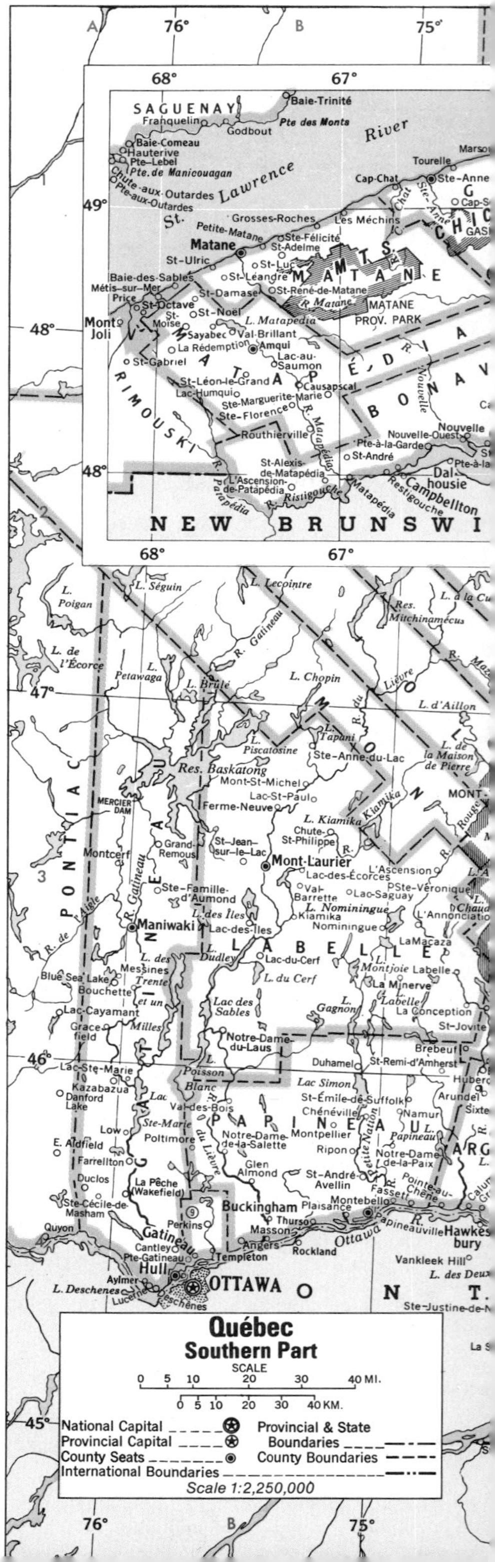

MAJOR MINERAL OCCURRENCES

Ab	Asbestos	Ni	Nickel
Au	Gold	Pb	Lead
Cu	Copper	Py	Pyrites
Fe	Iron Ore	Ti	Titanium
Mi	Mica	Zn	Zinc
Mo	Molybdenum		

Water Power
Major Industrial Areas

DOMINANT LAND USE

Cereals, Livestock
Pasture Livestock, Dairy
Dairy
Forests
Nonagricultural Land

Québec Southern Part

SCALE
0 5 10 20 30 40 MI.
0 5 10 20 30 40 KM.
National Capital
Provincial Capital
County Seats
International Boundaries
Provincial & State Boundaries
County Boundaries
Scale 1:2,250,000

Napierville◎ 2,343 .... D 4
Neuville 996.................. F 3
New Carlisle◎ 1,292.......... D 2
New Richmond 4,257........ C 2
Nicolet 4,880................ E 3
Nominingue 881 .... B 3
Normandin 4,041 .... E 1
North Hatley 689............. F 4
Notre-Dame-de-la-Doré 1,064 E 1
Notre-Dame-des-Laurentides . H 3
Notre-Dame-des-Prairies 6,150 .... D 3
Notre-Dame-du-Bon-Conseil 1,089 .... E 4
Notre-Dame-du-Lac◎ 2,258 .. J 2
Nouvelle 669 .... C 2
Oka 1,538..................... C 4
Omerville 1,398.............. E 4
Ormstown 1,659 .... D 4
Orsainville .... H 3
Otis 673 .... G 1
Otterburn Park 4,268 .... D 4
Outremont 24,338............. H 4
Pabos 1,295................... D 2
Pabos-Mills 1,565 .... D 2
Papineauville◎ 1,481 .... C 4
Paspébiac 1,914 .... D 2
Percé◎ 4,839.................. D 1
Petit-Cap 1,023............... D 1
Petite-Matane 1,065......... B 1
Petit-Saguenay (Saint-François-d'Assise) 804 .... G 1
Pierrefonds 38,390........... H 4
Pierreville 1,212 .... E 3
Pincourt 8,750................ D 4
Pintendre 1,849............... J 3
Plaisance 748 .... B 4
Plessisville 7,249 .... F 3
Pohénégamook 3,702 .... H 2
Pointe-à-la-Croix 1,481 ...... C 2
Pointe-au-Père 796........... J 1
Pointe-au-Pic 1,054 .... G 2
Pointe-aux-Outardes 1,056... A 1
Pointe-aux-Trembles 36,270 .. J 4
Pointe-Calumet 2,935 .... G 4
Pointe-Claire 24,571.......... H 4
Pointe-du-Lac 5,359.......... E 3
Pointe-Gatineau .... B 4
Pointe-Lebel 1,573 .... A 1
Pont-Rouge 3,580............. F 3
Port-Alfred 8,621............. G 1
Portneuf 1,333................ F 3
Portneuf-sur-Mer (Rivière-Portneuf-sur-Mer) 1,255 ... H 1
Price 2,273................... A 1
Princeville 4,023 .... F 3
Proulxville 588 .... E 3
Québec (cap.) 166,474 ...... H 3
Québec *576,075 .... H 3
Quyon 744 .... A 4
Rawdon 2,958 .... D 3
Repentigny 34,419........... J 4
Richelieu 1,832............... D 4
Richmond◎ 3,568.............. E 4
Rigaud 2,268.................. C 4
Rimouski◎ 29,120 .... J 1
Rimouski-Est 2,506 .... J 1
Ripon 620..................... B 4
Rivière-à-Pierre 615......... E 3
Rivière-au-Renard 2,211 ..... D 1
Rivière-Bleue 1,690 .... J 2
Rivière-Bois-Clair 604 .... F 3
Rivière-du-Loup◎ 13,459..... H 2
Rivière-du-Moulin .... G 1
Rivière-Éternité 659.......... G 1
Rivière-Portneuf-Portneuf-sur-Mer 1,255 .... H 1
Robertsonville 1,987 .... F 3
Roberval◎ 11,429.............. E 1
Rock Island 1,179............. E 4
Rosemère 7,778 .... H 4
Rougemont 972................ D 4
Roxboro 6,292................. H 4
Roxton Falls 1,245 .... E 4
Sacré-Coeur-de-Saguenay 1,678 .... H 1
Saint-Adelme 618.............. B 1
Saint-Adelphe 1,159........... E 3
Saint-Adolphe-d'Howard 1,686 .... C 4
Saint-Adrien 597.............. F 4
Saint-Agapitville 2,954....... F 3
Saint-Aimé-des-Lacs 861 .... G 2
Saint-Alban 673............... E 3
Saint-Alexandre-de-Kamouraska 1,048........... H 2
Saint-Alexis-des-Monts 1,984. D 3
Saint-Amable 2,424 .... J 4
Saint-Ambroise 3,606......... F 1
Saint-Anaclet 1,377 .... J 1
Saint-André-Avellin 1,312 .... B 4
Saint-André-Est 1,293 .... C 4
Saint-Anselme 1,808 .... F 3
Saint-Antoine 7,012 .... H 4
Saint-Antonin 941............ H 2
Saint-Aubert 884.............. G 2
Saint-Augustin-de-Québec 2,475 .... E 3
Saint-Basile-Sud 1,719 .... F 3
Saint-Basile-le-Grand 7,658 .. J 4
Saint-Benjamin 1,027......... G 3
Saint-Bernard 585 .... F 3
Saint-Bernard-sur-Mer 711 ... G 2
Saint-Boniface-de-Shawinigan 3,164 .... D 3
Saint-Bruno 2,580............ F 1
Saint-Bruno-de-Montarville 22,880 .... J 4
Saint-Camille-de-Bellechasse 1,744 .... G 3
Saint-Casimir 1,133 .... E 3
Saint-Césaire 2,935 .... D 4
Saint-Charles 1,019 .... G 3
Saint-Charles-de-Mandeville 1,392 .... D 3
Saint-Chrysostome 1,018 .... D 4
Saint-Côme 660 .... D 3
Saint-Constant 9,938 .... H 4
Saint-Cyprien 860............ J 2
Saint-Cyrille 1,041 .... E 4
Saint-Damien-de-Buckland 1,522 .... G 3
Saint-David 5,380............. J 3
Saint-David-de-Falardeau 1,876 .... F 1
Saint-Denis 861 .... D 4

AREA 594,857 sq. mi. (1,540,680 sq. km.)
POPULATION 6,438,403
CAPITAL Québec
LARGEST CITY Montréal
HIGHEST POINT Mont D'Iberville 5,420 ft. (1,652 m.)
SETTLED IN 1608
ADMITTED TO CONFEDERATION 1867
PROVINCIAL FLOWER White Garden Lily

Saint-Dominique 2,068 ...... E 4
Saint-Donat-de-Montcalm 1,521 .... C 3
Sainte-Adèle 4,675........... C 4
Sainte-Agathe 709 .... F 3
Sainte-Agathe-des-Monts 5,641 .... C 3
Sainte-Anne-de-Beaupré 3,292 .... F 2
Sainte-Anne-de-Bellevue 3,981 .... H 4
Sainte-Anne-des-Monts◎ 6,062 .... C 1
Sainte-Anne-des-Plaines 4,258 .... H 4
Sainte-Anne-du-Lac 686 ...... B 3
Sainte-Aurélie 1,045.......... G 3
Sainte-Blandine 849.......... J 1
Sainte-Catherine 1,474 ...... F 3
Sainte-Claire 1,566........... G 3
Sainte-Croix◎ 1,814.......... F 3
Sainte-Félicité 711 .... B 1
Sainte-Foy 68,883 .... H 3
Sainte-Geneviève 2,573 ..... H 4
Sainte-Geneviève-de-Batiscan◎ 356 .... E 3
Sainte-Hélène-de-Bagot 1,328 .... E 4
Sainte-Hénédine◎ 639........ F 3
Sainte-Julie-de-Verchères 14,243 .... J 4
Sainte-Julienne◎ 750......... D 4
Sainte-Justine 1,080 .... G 3
Saint-Élie 639 .... E 3
Saint-Elzéar 743.............. F 3
Sainte-Marie 8,937........... G 3
Sainte-Martine◎ 2,196....... D 4
Saint-Émile 5,216............ H 3
Sainte-Monique 705.......... F 1
Sainte-Pétronille 982 .... J 3
Sainte-Perpétue-de-L'Islet 1,232 .... H 2
Saint-Éphrem-de-Tring 973 ... G 3
Saint-Épiphane 647 .... H 2
Sainte-Pudentienne 866 ..... E 4
Sainte-Rosalie 2,862 .... E 4
Saint-Esprit 1,068............ D 4
Sainte-Thérèse 18,750....... H 4
Sainte-Thérèse-Ouest (Boisbriand) 13,471 .... H 4
Sainte-Thècle 1,703 .... E 3
Saint-Étienne-de-Grès 845 ... E 3
Saint-Étienne-de-Lauzon 1,218 .... J 3

Gaspé Peninsula

COUNTIES indicated by numbers:

No.	County	Key
1	Iberville	D4
2	Napierville	D4
3	Rouville	E4
4	St-Hyacinthe	D4
5	Île-de-Montréal	D4
6	Deux-Montagnes	C4
7	Soulanges	C4
8	Beauharnois	C4
9	Hull	B4
10	Île-Jésus	D4
11	Richelieu	D4
12	Vaudreuil	C4

Internal divisions represent Municipal Counties

Longitude 72° West of Greenwich

(continued)

Saint-Eustache 29,716 H 4
Saint-Fabien 1,361 J 1
Saint-Félicien 9,058 E 1
Saint-Félix-de-Valois 1,462 D 3
Saint-Ferréol-les-Neiges 1,758 G 2
Saint-Flavien 734 F 3
Saint-François-de-Sales 831 E 1
Saint-François-du-Lac⊙ 942 E 3
Saint-Fulgence 950 G 1
Saint-Gabriel 3,161 D 3
Saint-Gabriel-de-Rimouski 779 J 1
Saint-Gédéon, Frontenac 1,569 G 4
Saint-Gédéon, Lac-St-Jean-E. 1,000 F 1
Saint-Georges, Beauce 10,342 G 3
Saint-Georges, Champlain 3,344 E 3
Saint-Georges-Ouest 6,378 G 3
Saint-Germain-de-Grantham 1,373 E 4
Saint-Gervais 973 G 3
Saint-Gilles 912 F 3
Saint-Grégoire (Mont-St-Grégoire) 740 D 4
Saint-Henri 1,970 J 3
Saint-Honoré, Beauce 1,116 G 4
Saint-Honoré, Chicoutimi 1,790 F 1
Saint-Hubert 60,573 J 4
Saint-Hubert-de-Témiscouata 871 J 2
Saint-Hyacinthe⊙ 38,246 D 4
Saint-Isidore 811 F 3
Saint-Isidore-de-Laprairie 769 D 4
Saint-Jacques 2,152 D 4
Saint-Jacques-le-Mineur 1,203 H 4
Saint-Jean-Chrysostome 6,930 J 3
Saint-Jean-de-Dieu 1,377 J 1
Saint-Jean-de-Matha 931 D 3
Saint-Jean-Port-Joli⊙ 1,813 G 2
Saint-Jean-sur-Richelieu⊙ 35,640 D 4
Saint-Jérôme 25,123 H 4
Saint-Joachim 1,139 G 2
Saint-Joseph-de-Beauce 3,216 G 3
Saint-Joseph-de-Sorel 2,545 D 3
Saint-Jovite 3,841 C 3
Saint-Lambert 20,557 J 4
Saint-Laurent 65,900 H 4
Saint-Lazare 731 G 3
Saint-Léonard 79,429 H 4
Saint-Léonard-d'Aston 992 E 3
Saint-Léon-de-Chicoutimi 749 F 1
Saint-Léon-de-Standon 816 G 3
Saint-Léon-le-Grand 722 B 2
Saint-Liboire⊙ 746 E 4
Saint-Louis-de-Gonzague 615 D 4
Saint-Louis-de-Terrebonne 14,172 H 4
Saint-Louis-du-Ha! Ha! 809 H 2
Saint-Luc 8,815 D 4
Saint-Luc-de-Matane 598 B 1
Saint-Marc-des-Carrières 2,822 E 3
Saint-Méthode-de-Frontenac 925 F 3
Saint-Michel-de-Bellechasse 963 G 3
Saint-Michel-des-Saints 1,584 D 3
Saint-Nazaire-de-Chicoutimi 962 F 1
Saint-Nérée 970 G 3
Saint-Nicolas 5,074 H 3
Saint-Noël 666 B 1
Saint-Odilon 580 G 3
Saint-Omer 718 C 2
Saint-Ours 625 D 4
Saint-Pacôme 1,996 G 2
Saint-Pamphile 3,428 H 3
Saint-Pascal⊙ 2,763 H 2
Saint-Paul-de-Montminy 602 G 3
Saint-Paulin 663 D 3
Saint-Paul-l'Ermite (Le Gardeur) 8,312 J 4
Saint-Philippe-de-Néri 715 H 2
Saint-Pie 1,725 E 4
Saint-Pierre 5,305 H 4
Saint-Pierre-d'Orléans 880 G 3
Saint-Polycarpe 602 C 4
Saint-Prime 2,522 E 1
Saint-Prosper-de-Dorchester 2,150 G 3
Saint-Raphaël⊙ 1,346 G 3
Saint-Raymond 3,605 F 3
Saint-Rédempteur 4,463 J 3
Saint-Régis 1,370 C 4
Saint-Rémi 5,146 D 4
Saint-Roch-de-l'Achigan 1,160 D 4
Saint-Roch-de-Richelieu 1,650 D 4
Saint-Romuald-d'Etchemin⊙ 9,849 J 3
Saint-Sauveur-des-Monts 2,348 C 4
Saint-Siméon 1,152 G 2
Saint-Simon 602 H 1
Saint-Stanislas 1,443 E 3
Saint-Sylvère 1,006 E 3
Saint-Timothée 2,113 D 4
Saint-Tite 3,031 E 3
Saint-Tite-des-Caps 626 G 2
Saint-Ubald 1,605 E 3
Saint-Ulric 792 B 1
Saint-Urbain-de-Charlevoix 1,079 G 2
Saint-Victor 1,104 G 3
Saint-Zacharie 1,284 G 3
Saint-Zotique 1,774 C 4
Sault-au-Mouton 828 H 1
Sawyerville 939 F 4
Sayabec 1,721 B 2
Scotstown 762 F 4
Senneville 1,221 G 4
Shannon 3,488 F 3
Shawbridge 942 C 4
Shawinigan 23,011 E 3
Shawinigan-Sud 11,325 E 3
Shawville 1,608 A 4
Sherbrooke⊙ 74,075 E 4
Sherrington 614 D 4
Sillery 12,825 J 3
Sorel⊙ 20,347 D 4
Squatec 1,000 J 2
Stanstead Plain 1,093 F 4
Sutton 1,599 E 4
Tadoussac⊙ 900 H 1
Templeton B 4
Terrebonne 11,769 H 4
Thetford Mines 19,965 F 3
Thurso 2,780 B 4
Tourelle (Tourelle-Grand-Tourelle) 942 C 1
Tourville 659 H 2
Tracy 12,843 D 3
Tring-Jonction 1,315 F 3
Trois-Pistoles 4,445 H 1
Trois-Rivières 50,466 E 3
Trois-Rivières *111,453 E 3
Trois-Rivières-Ouest 13,107 E 3
Upton 926 E 4
Val-Barrette 609 B 3
Val-Brillant 687 B 1
Valcourt 2,601 E 4
Val-David 2,336 C 3
Vallée-Jonction 1,200 G 3
Valleyfield (Salaberry-de-Valleyfield) 29,574 C 4
Vanier 10,725 J 3
Varennes 8,764 J 4
Vaudreuil⊙ 7,608 C 4
Verchères⊙ 4,473 J 4
Verdun 61,287 H 4
Victoriaville 21,838 F 3
Villeneuve J 3
Warwick 2,847 F 4
Waterloo⊙ 4,664 E 4
Waterville 1,397 F 4
Weedon-Centre 1,263 F 4
Westmount 20,480 H 4
Wickham 2,043 E 4
Windsor 5,233 F 4
Wottonville 673 F 4
Yamachiche⊙ 1,258 E 3

OTHER FEATURES

Alma (isl.) F 1
Aylmer (lake) F 4
Baskatong (res.) B 3
Batiscan (riv.) E 2
Bécancour (riv.) F 3
Bonaventure (isl.) D 1
Bonaventure (riv.) C 1
Brome (lake) E 4
Brompton (lake) E 4
Cascapédia (riv.) C 1
Chaleur (bay) C 2
Champlain (lake) D 4
Chaudière (riv.) G 4
Chic-Chocs (mts.) C 1
Chicoutimi (riv.) F 2
Coudres (isl.) G 2
Deschênes (lake) A 4
Deux Montagnes (lake) C 4
Ditton (riv.) F 4
Forillon Nat'l Park D 1
Fort Chambly Nat'l Hist. Park J 4
Gaspé (bay) D 1
Gaspé (cape) D 1
Gaspé (pen.) D 2
Gaspésie Prov. Park C 1
Gatineau (riv.) B 3
Îles (lake) B 3
Jacques-Cartier (mt.) C 1
Jacques-Cartier (riv.) F 2
Kénogami (lake) F 1
Kiamika (lake) B 3
La Maurice Nat'l Park D 3
Laurentides Prov. Park F 2
Lièvre (riv.) B 4
Lièvres (isl.) H 2
Maskinongé (riv.) D 3
Matane (riv.) B 1
Matane Prov. Park B 1
Matapédia (riv.) B 2
Mégantic (lake) G 4
Memphremagog (lake) E 4
Mercier (dam) A 3
Métabetchouane (riv.) F 1
Mille Îles (riv.) H 4
Montmorency (riv.) F 2
Mont-Tremblant Prov. Park C 3
Nicolet (riv.) E 3
Nominingue (lake) B 3
Nord (riv.) C 4
Orléans (isl.) F 3
Ottawa (riv.) B 4
Ouareau (riv.) D 3
Ouelle (riv.) H 2
Patapédia (riv.) B 2
Péribonca (riv.) F 1
Petite Nation (riv.) B 4
Prairies (riv.) H 4
Rimouski (riv.) J 1
Ristigouche (riv.) B 2
Saguenay (riv.) G 1
Sainte-Anne (riv.) F 3
Sainte-Anne (riv.) G 2
Saint-François (lake) F 4
Saint-François (riv.) E 4
Saint-Jean (lake) E 1
Saint Lawrence (gulf) D 2
Saint Lawrence (riv.) H 1
Saint-Louis (lake) H 4
Saint-Maurice (riv.) E 2
Saint-Pierre (lake) E 3
Shawinigan (riv.) E 3
Shipshaw (riv.) F 1
Soeurs (isl.) H 4
Témiscouata (lake) H 2
Tremblant (lake) C 3
Trente et un Milles (lake) B 3
Verte (isl.) H 1
Yamaska (riv.) E 4
York (riv.) D 1

⊙County seat.
*Population of metropolitan area.

QUÉBEC, NORTHERN

INTERNAL DIVISIONS

Abitibi (county) 93,529 B 2
Abitibi (terr.) B 3
Berthier (county) 31,096 B 3
Bonaventure (county) 40,487 D 3
Champlain (county) 119,595 C 3
Charlevoix-Est (co.) 17,448 C 3
Charlevoix-Ouest (county) 14,172 C 3
Chicoutimi (county) 174,441 C 2
Gaspé-Est (county) 41,173 E 3
Gaspé-Ouest (county) 18,943 D 3
Gatineau (county) 54,229 B 3
Joliette (county) 60,384 B 3
Lac-Saint-Jean-Est (county) 47,891 C 3
Lac-Saint-Jean-Ouest (county) 62,952 C 2
Maskinongé (county) 20,763 C 3
Matane (county) 29,955 D 3
Matapédia (county) 23,715 D 3
Mistassini (terr.) B 2
Montcalm (county) 27,557 B 3
Montmorency No. I (county) 23,048 C 3
Nouveau-Québec (terr.) E 1
Pontiac (county) 20,283 B 3
Portneuf (county) 58,843 C 3
Québec (county) 458,980 C 3
Rimouski (county) 69,099 D 3
Saguenay (county) 115,881 D 2
Saint-Maurice (co.) 107,703 C 3
Témiscamingue (co.) 52,570 B 3

CITIES and TOWNS

Alma⊙ 26,322 C 3
Amos⊙ 9,421 B 3
Baie-Comeau 12,866 D 3
Baie-du-Poste 1,690 C 2
Chicoutimi⊙ 60,064 C 3
Gaspé 17,261 E 3
Hauterive 13,995 D 3
Jonquière 60,354 C 3
Lévis 17,895 C 3
La Tuque 11,556 C 3
Manicouagan D 2
Maniwaki⊙ 5,424 B 3
Matane⊙ 13,612 D 3
Mistassini (Baie-du-Poste) 1,690 C 2
Mont-Laurier⊙ 8,405 B 3
Montmagny⊙ 12,405 C 3
New Carlisle⊙ 781 E 3
Nouveau-Comptoir B 2
Percé⊙ 4,839 E 3
Port-Cartier-Ouest D 3
Port-Menier⊙ 275 E 3
Povungnituk 745 E 1
Québec (cap.)⊙ 166,474 C 3
Rimouski⊙ 29,120 D 3
Rivière-au-Tonnerre 480 D 2
Rivière-du-Loup 13,459 D 3
Rouyn 17,224 B 3
Sept-Îles 29,262 D 2
Seven Islands (Sept-Îles) 29,262 D 2
Shawinigan 23,011 C 3
Tadoussac 900 C 3
Val d'Or 21,371 B 3
Ville-Marie 2,651 B 3

OTHER FEATURES

Allard (lake) E 2
Anticosti (isl.) E 3
Baleine, Grand Rivière de la (riv.) B 1
Bell (riv.) B 3
Betsiamites (riv.) C 2
Bienville (lake) C 2
Broadback (riv.) B 2
Cabonga (res.) B 3
Caniapiscau (riv.) D 1
Eastmain (riv.) B 2
Eau Claire (lake) C 1
Feuilles (riv.) C 1
Gaspésie Prov. Park D 3
George (riv.) F 2
Gouin (res.) C 3
Grande Rivière, La (riv.) B 2
Honguedo (passage) E 3
Hudson (bay) A 1
Hudson (str.) F 1
Jacques-Cartier (passage) E 3
James (bay) A 2
Koksoak (riv.) D 1
Laurentides Prov. Park C 3
Louis-XIV (pt.) B 2
Manicouagan (res.) D 2
Minto (lake) E 2
Mistassibi (riv.) C 3
Mistassini (lake) C 2
Moisie (riv.) D 2
Natashquan (riv.) E 2
Nottaway (riv.) B 2
Nouveau-Québec (crater) F 1
Otish (mts.) C 2
Ottawa (riv.) B 3
Péribonca (riv.) C 3
Plétipi (lake) C 2
Saguenay (riv.) C 3
Saint-Jean (lake) C 3
Saint Lawrence (gulf) E 3
Saint Lawrence (riv.) D 3
Ungava (pen.) E 1

⊙County seat.
*Population of metropolitan area.

Northern Québec

SCALE 0 50 100 150 200 MI.
0 50 100 150 200 KM.

Provincial Capital ⊛ · Provincial Boundaries
County Seats ⊙ · County Boundaries
International Boundaries · Territorial Boundaries

Scale 1:8,400,000

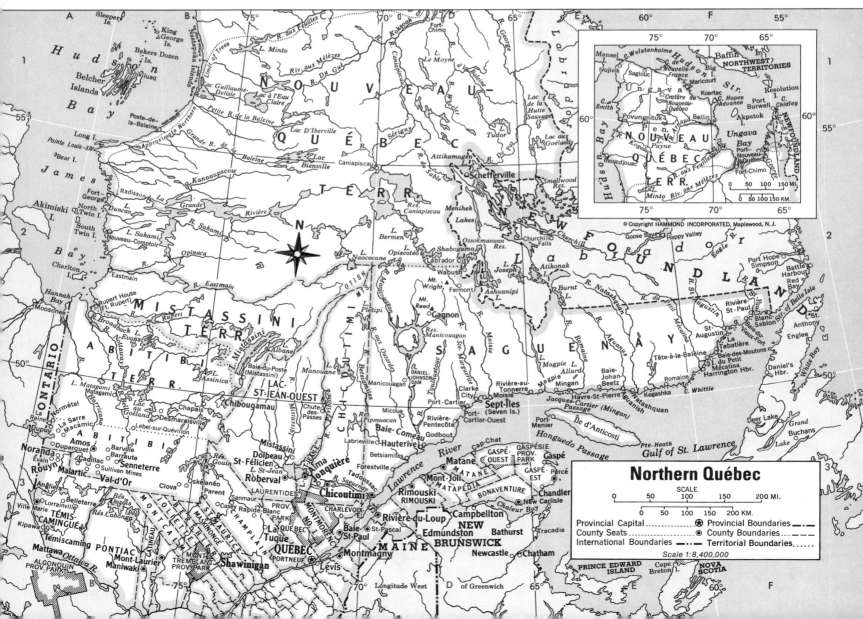

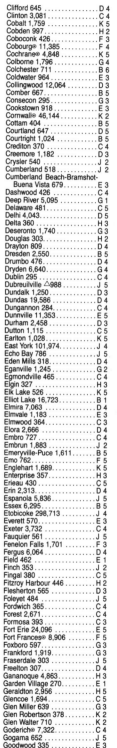

ONTARIO, NORTHERN

INTERNAL DIVISIONS

Algoma (terr. dist.) 133,553 . . . D 3
Cochrane (terr. dist.) 96,875 . . D 2
Kenora (terr. dist.) 59,421 . . . . C 2
Manitoulin (terr. dist.) 11,001 . D 3
Nipissing (terr. dist.) 80,268 . . E 3
Parry Sound (terr. dist.) 33,528 . . . . E 3
Rainy River (terr. dist.) 22,798 B 3
Renfrew (county) 87,484 . . . . . E 3
Sudbury (reg. munic.) 159,779 . . . . D 3
Sudbury (terr. dist.) 27,068 . . . D 3
Thunder Bay (terr. dist.) 153,997 . . . . C 3
Timiskaming (terr. dist.) 41,288 . . . . D 3

CITIES and TOWNS

Chalk River 1,010 . . . . E 3
Elliot Lake 16,723 . . . . D 3
Fort Albany 482 . . . . D 2
Fort Frances⊙ 8,906 . . . . B 3
Kapuskasing 12,014 . . . . D 3
Kenora⊙ 9,817 . . . . B 3
Kirkland Lake 12,219 . . . . D 3
Moose Factory 1,452 . . . . D 2
Moosonee 1,433 . . . . D 2
Nickel Centre 12,318 . . . . D 3
North Bay⊙ 51,268 . . . . E 3
Pembroke⊙ 14,026 . . . . E 3
Sault Sainte Marie⊙ 82,697 . . D 3
Sudbury 91,829 . . . . D 3
Thunder Bay⊙ 112,486 . . . . . . C 3
Timmins 46,114 . . . . D 3
Valley East 20,433 . . . . D 3

OTHER FEATURES

Abitibi (lake) . . . . E 3
Abitibi (riv.) . . . . D 2
Albany (riv.) . . . . C 2
Algonquin Prov. Park . . . . E 3
Asheweig (riv.) . . . . C 2
Attawapiskat (lake) . . . . C 2
Attawapiskat (riv.) . . . . C 2
Basswood (lake) . . . . B 3
Berens (riv.) . . . . A 2
Big Trout (lake) . . . . B 2
Black Duck (riv.) . . . . C 1
Bloodvein (riv.) . . . . A 2
Caribou (isl.) . . . . C 3
Cobham (riv.) . . . . A 2
Eabamet (lake) . . . . C 2
Ekwan (riv.) . . . . C 2
English (riv.) . . . . B 2
Fawn (riv.) . . . . C 2
Finger (lake) . . . . B 2
Georgian (bay) . . . . D 3
Hannah (bay) . . . . D 2
Henrietta Maria (cape) . . . . D 1
Hudson (bay) . . . . D 1
Huron (lake) . . . . D 3
James (bay) . . . . D 2
Kapiskau (riv.) . . . . D 2
Kapuskasing (riv.) . . . . D 3
Kenogami (riv.) . . . . C 2
Kesagami (riv.) . . . . E 2
Lake of the Woods (lake) . . . . . B 3
Lake Superior Prov. Park . . . . . D 3
Little Current (riv.) . . . . C 2
Long (lake) . . . . C 3
Manitoulin (isl.) . . . . D 3
Mattagami (riv.) . . . . D 3
Michipicoten (isl.) . . . . C 3
Mille Lacs (lake) . . . . B 3
Missinaibi (lake) . . . . D 3
Missinaibi (riv.) . . . . D 2
Missisa (lake) . . . . D 2
Nipigon (lake) . . . . C 3
Nipissing (lake) . . . . E 3
North (chan.) . . . . D 3
North Caribou (lake) . . . . B 2
Nungesser (lake) . . . . B 2
Ogidaki (mt.) . . . . D 3
Ogoki (riv.) . . . . C 2
Opazatika (riv.) . . . . D 3
Opinnagau (riv.) . . . . D 2
Otoskwin (riv.) . . . . B 2
Ottawa (riv.) . . . . E 3
Pipestone (riv.) . . . . B 2
Polar Bear Prov. Park . . . . D 2
Pukaskwa Prov. Park . . . . C 3
Quetico Prov. Park . . . . B 3
Rainy (lake) . . . . B 3
Red (lake) . . . . B 2
Sachigo (riv.) . . . . B 2
Saganaga (lake) . . . . B 3
Saint Ignace (isl.) . . . . C 3
Saint Joseph (lake) . . . . B 2
Sandy (lake) . . . . B 2
Savant (lake) . . . . B 2
Seine (riv.) . . . . B 3
Seul (lake) . . . . B 2
Severn (lake) . . . . B 2
Severn (riv.) . . . . B 2
Shamattawa (riv.) . . . . C 2
Shibogama (lake) . . . . C 2
Sibley Prov. Park . . . . C 3
Slate (isls.) . . . . C 3
Stout (lake) . . . . B 2
Superior (lake) . . . . C 3
Sutton (lake) . . . . D 2
Sutton (riv.) . . . . D 2
Timagami (lake) . . . . D 3
Timiskaming (lake) . . . . E 3
Trout (lake) . . . . B 2
Wabuk (pt.) . . . . D 1
Winisk (lake) . . . . C 2
Winisk (riv.) . . . . C 2
Winnipeg (riv.) . . . . A 2
Woods (lake) . . . . B 3

ONTARIO

INTERNAL DIVISIONS

Algoma (terr. dist.) 133,553 . . . J 5
Brant (county) 104,427 . . . . . . D 4
Bruce (county) 60,020 . . . . C 3
Cochrane (terr. dist.) 96,875 . . J 4
Dufferin (county) 31,145 . . . . . D 3
Dundas (county) 18,946 . . . . . J 2
Durham (reg. munic.) 283,639 F 3
Elgin (county) 69,707 . . . . C 5
Essex (county) 312,467 . . . . . . B 5
Frontenac (county) 108,133 . . H 3
Glengarry (county) 20,254 . . . K 2
Grenville (county) 27,176 . . . . J 3
Grey (county) 73,824 . . . . D 3
Haldimand-Norfolk (reg. munic.) 89,456 . . . . E 5
Haliburton (county) 11,361 . . . F 2
Halton (reg. munic.) 253,883 . E 4
Hamilton-Wentworth (reg. munic.) 411,445 . . . . D 4
Hastings (county) 106,883 . . . G 3
Huron (county) 56,127 . . . . C 4
Kenora (terr. dist.) 59,421 . . . . G 5
Kent (county) 107,022 . . . . B 5
Lambton (county) 123,445 . . . B 5
Lanark (county) 45,676 . . . . . . H 3
Leeds (county) 53,765 . . . . H 3
Lennox and Addington (county) 33,040 . . . . G 3
Manitoulin (terr. dist.) 11,001 . B 2
Middlesex (county) 318,184 . . C 4
Muskoka (dist. munic.) 38,370 . . . . E 3
Niagara (reg. munic.) 368,288 E 4
Nipissing (terr. dist.) 80,268 . . F 2
Northumberland (county) 64,966 . . . . G 3
Ottawa-Carleton (reg. munic.) 546,849 . . . . J 2
Oxford (county) 85,920 . . . . . . D 4
Parry Sound (terr. dist.) 33,528 . . . . D 2
Peel (reg. munic.) 490,731 . . . E 4
Perth (county) 66,096 . . . . C 4
Peterborough (county) 102,452 . . . . F 3
Prescott (county) 30,365 . . . . . K 2
Prince Edward (county) 22,336 . . . . G 3
Rainy River (terr. dist.) 22,798 G 5
Renfrew (county) 87,484 . . . . . G 2
Russell (county) 22,412 . . . . . . J 2
Simcoe (county) 225,071 . . . . E 3
Stormont (county) 61,927 . . . . K 2
Sudbury (reg. munic.) 159,779 . . . . K 6
Sudbury (terr. dist.) 27,068 . . . J 5
Thunder Bay (terr. dist.) 153,997 . . . . H 5
Timiskaming (terr. dist.) 41,288 . . . . K 5
Toronto (metro. munic.) 2,137,395 . . . . K 4
Victoria (county) 47,854 . . . . . . F 3
Waterloo (reg. munic.) 305,496 . . . . D 4
Wellington (county) 129,432 . . D 4
York (reg. munic.) 252,053 . . . E 4

CITIES and TOWNS

Ailsa Craig 765 . . . . C 4
Ajax 25,475 . . . . E 4
Alban 342 . . . . D 1
Alexandria 3,271 . . . . K 2
Alfred 1,057 . . . . K 2
Alliston 4,712 . . . . E 3
Almonte 3,855 . . . . H 2
Alvinston 736 . . . . B 5
Amherstburg 5,685 . . . . A 5
Amherst View 6,110 . . . . H 3
Ancaster 14,428 . . . . D 4
Angus 3,085 . . . . E 3
Apsley 264 . . . . F 3
Arkona 473 . . . . C 4
Armstrong 378 . . . . H 4
Arnprior 5,828 . . . . H 2
Aroland 291 . . . . H 4
Arthur 1,700 . . . . D 4
Astorville 340 . . . . E 1
Athens 948 . . . . J 3
Atherley 366 . . . . E 3
Atikokan 4,452 . . . . G 5

AREA 412,580 sq. mi. (1,068,582 sq. km.)
POPULATION 8,625,107
CAPITAL Toronto
LARGEST CITY Toronto
HIGHEST POINT in Timiskaming Dist. 2,275 ft. (693 m.)
SETTLED IN 1749
ADMITTED TO CONFEDERATION 1867
PROVINCIAL FLOWER White Trillium

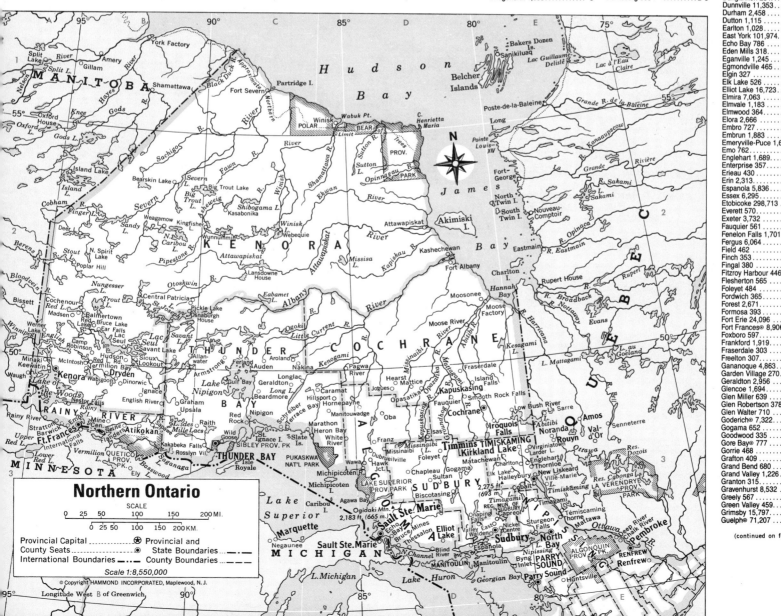

Atwood 723 . . . . D 4
Aurora 16,267 . . . . J 3
Avonmore 273 . . . . K 2
Aylmer 5,254 . . . . C 5
Ayr 1,295 . . . . D 4
Ayton 424 . . . . D 3
Baden 945 . . . . D 4
Bala 577 . . . . E 2
Bancroft 2,329 . . . . G 2
Barrie⊙ 38,423 . . . . E 3
Barry's Bay 1,216 . . . . G 2
Batawa 430 . . . . G 3
Bath 1,071 . . . . H 3
Bayfield 649 . . . . C 4
Beachburg 682 . . . . H 2
Beachville 917 . . . . D 4
Beardmore 583 . . . . H 5
Beaverton 1,952 . . . . E 3
Beeton 1,989 . . . . E 3
Belle River 3,568 . . . . B 5
Belleville⊙ 34,881 . . . . G 3
Belmont 831 . . . . C 5
Bethany 365 . . . . F 3
Bewdley 508 . . . . F 3
Binbrook 306 . . . . E 4
Blackstock 720 . . . . F 3
Blenheim 4,044 . . . . C 5
Blind River 3,444 . . . . J 5
Bloomfield 718 . . . . G 4
Blyth 926 . . . . C 4
Bobcaygeon 1,625 . . . . F 3
Bonfield 540 . . . . E 1
Bothwell 915 . . . . C 5
Bourget 1,057 . . . . J 2
Bracebridge⊙ 9,063 . . . . E 2
Bradford 7,370 . . . . E 3
Braeside 492 . . . . H 2
Brampton⊙ 149,030 . . . . J 4
Brantford⊙ 74,315 . . . . D 4
Bridgenorth 1,633 . . . . F 3
Brigden 635 . . . . B 5
Brighton 3,147 . . . . G 3
Britt 419 . . . . D 2
Brockville⊙ 19,896 . . . . J 3
Bruce Mines 635 . . . . J 5
Brussels 962 . . . . C 4
Burford 1,461 . . . . D 4
Burgessville 302 . . . . D 4
Burk's Falls 922 . . . . E 2
Burlington 114,853 . . . . E 4
Cache Bay 665 . . . . D 1
Caesarea 551 . . . . F 3
Calabogie 256 . . . . H 2
Caledon 26,645 . . . . E 4
Callander 1,158 . . . . E 1
Cambridge 77,183 . . . . D 4
Campbellford 3,409 . . . . G 3
Cannington 1,623 . . . . E 3
Capreol 3,845 . . . . K 5
Caramat 265 . . . . H 5
Cardinal 1,753 . . . . J 3
Carleton Place 5,626 . . . . H 2
Carlisle 781 . . . . D 4
Carlsbad Springs 616 . . . . J 2
Carp 707 . . . . H 2
Cartier 590 . . . . J 5
Casselman 1,675 . . . . J 2
Castleton 346 . . . . F 3
Chalk River 1,010 . . . . G 1
Chapleau 3,243 . . . . J 5
Charing Cross 443 . . . . B 5
Chatham⊙ 40,952 . . . . B 5
Chatsworth 383 . . . . D 3
Cherry Valley 289 . . . . G 4
Chesley 1,840 . . . . C 3
Chesterville 1,430 . . . . J 2
Chute-à-Blondeau 365 . . . . K 2
City View . . . . J 2
Clarence Creek 796 . . . . J 2
Clarksburg 508 . . . . D 3
Clifford 645 . . . . D 4
Clinton 3,081 . . . . C 4
Cobalt 1,759 . . . . K 5
Cobden 997 . . . . H 2
Coboconk 426 . . . . F 3
Cobourg⊙ 11,385 . . . . F 4
Cochrane⊙ 4,848 . . . . K 5
Colborne 1,796 . . . . G 4
Colchester 711 . . . . B 6
Coldwater 964 . . . . E 3
Collingwood 12,064 . . . . D 3
Comber 667 . . . . B 5
Consecon 295 . . . . G 3
Cookstown 918 . . . . E 3
Cornwall⊙ 46,144 . . . . K 2
Cottam 404 . . . . B 5
Courtland 647 . . . . D 5
Courtright 1,024 . . . . B 5
Crediton 370 . . . . C 4
Creemore 1,182 . . . . D 3
Crysler 540 . . . . J 2
Cumberland 518 . . . . J 2
Cumberland Beach-Bramshot-Buena Vista 679 . . . . E 3
Dashwood 426 . . . . C 4
Deep River 5,095 . . . . G 1
Delaware 481 . . . . C 5
Delhi 4,043 . . . . D 5
Delta 360 . . . . H 3
Deseronto 1,740 . . . . G 3
Douglas 303 . . . . H 2
Drayton 809 . . . . D 4
Dresden 2,550 . . . . B 5
Drumbo 476 . . . . D 4
Dryden 6,640 . . . . G 4
Dublin 295 . . . . C 4
Dubreuilville △988 . . . . J 5
Dundalk 1,250 . . . . D 3
Dundas 19,586 . . . . D 4
Dungannon 284 . . . . C 4
Dunnville 11,353 . . . . E 5
Durham 2,458 . . . . D 3
Dutton 1,115 . . . . C 5
Earlton 1,028 . . . . K 5
East York 101,974 . . . . J 4
Echo Bay 786 . . . . J 5
Eden Mills 318 . . . . D 4
Eganville 1,245 . . . . G 2
Egmondville 465 . . . . C 4
Elgin 327 . . . . H 3
Elk Lake 526 . . . . K 5
Elliot Lake 16,723 . . . . B 1
Elmira 7,063 . . . . D 4
Elmvale 1,183 . . . . E 3
Elmwood 364 . . . . C 3
Elora 2,666 . . . . D 4
Embro 727 . . . . C 4
Embrun 1,883 . . . . J 2
Emeryville-Puce 1,611 . . . . B 5
Emo 762 . . . . F 5
Englehart 1,689 . . . . K 5
Enterprise 357 . . . . H 3
Erieau 430 . . . . C 5
Erin 2,313 . . . . D 4
Espanola 5,836 . . . . J 5
Essex 6,295 . . . . B 5
Etobicoke 298,713 . . . . J 4
Everett 570 . . . . E 3
Exeter 3,732 . . . . C 4
Fauquier 561 . . . . J 5
Fenelon Falls 1,701 . . . . F 3
Fergus 6,064 . . . . D 4
Field 462 . . . . E 1
Finch 353 . . . . J 2
Fingal 380 . . . . C 5
Fitzroy Harbour 446 . . . . H 2
Flesherton 565 . . . . D 3
Foleyet 484 . . . . J 5
Fordwich 365 . . . . C 4
Forest 2,671 . . . . C 4
Formosa 393 . . . . C 3
Fort Erie 24,096 . . . . E 5
Fort Frances⊙ 8,906 . . . . F 5
Foxboro 597 . . . . G 3
Frankford 1,919 . . . . G 3
Fraserdale 303 . . . . J 5
Freelton 307 . . . . D 4
Gananoque 4,863 . . . . H 3
Garden Village 270 . . . . E 1
Geraldton 2,956 . . . . H 5
Glencoe 1,694 . . . . C 5
Glen Miller 639 . . . . G 3
Glen Robertson 378 . . . . K 2
Glen Walter 710 . . . . K 2
Goderich⊙ 7,322 . . . . C 4
Gogama 652 . . . . J 5
Goodwood 335 . . . . E 3
Gore Bay⊙ 777 . . . . B 2
Gorrie 468 . . . . C 4
Grafton 409 . . . . G 4
Grand Bend 680 . . . . C 4
Grand Valley 1,226 . . . . D 4
Granton 315 . . . . C 4
Gravenhurst 8,532 . . . . E 3
Greely 567 . . . . J 2
Green Valley 459 . . . . K 2
Grimsby 15,797 . . . . E 4
Guelph⊙ 71,207 . . . . D 4

(continued on following page)

Northern Ontario

SCALE
0 25 50 100 150 200 MI.
0 25 50 100 150 200 KM.

Provincial Capital ⊛ Provincial and State Boundaries
County Seats ⊙ International Boundaries County Boundaries

Scale 1:8,550,000

Longitude West of Greenwich

(continued)

Haileybury◎ 4,925 .... K 5
Haldimand 16,866 .... E 5
Haliburton 1,443 .... F 2
Halton Hills 35,190 .... E 4
Hamilton◎ 306,434 .... E 4
Hamilton *542,095 .... E 4
Hanover 6,316 .... C 3
Harriston 1,954 .... D 4
Harrow 2,274 .... B 5
Harrowsmith 599 .... H 3
Harwood 332 .... F 3
Hastings 975 .... G 3
Havelock 1,385 .... G 3
Hawkesbury 9,877 .... K 2
Hawkestone 275 .... E 3
Hawk Junction 349 .... J 5
Hearst 5,533 .... J 5
Hensall 973 .... C 4
Hepworth 393 .... C 3
Hickson 263 .... D 4
Highgate 435 .... C 5
Hillsburgh 1,065 .... D 4
Hillsdale 370 .... E 3
Holland Landing 2,771 .... E 3
Honey Harbour 505 .... E 3
Hornepayne 1,848 .... J 5
Hudson 515 .... G 4
Huntsville 11,467 .... E 2
Huron Park 1,104 .... C 4
Ignace 2,499 .... G 5
Ilderton 301 .... C 4
Ingersoll 8,494 .... C 4
Ingleside 1,400 .... J 2
Innerkip 715 .... D 4
Inverhuron 438 .... C 3
Iron Bridge 821 .... A 1

Iroquois 1,211 .... J 3
Iroquois Falls 6,339 .... J 5
Johnstown 789 .... J 3
Kakabeka Falls 300 .... G 5
Kanata 19,728 .... J 2
Kapuskasing 12,014 .... J 5
Kars 449 .... J 2
Kearney 538 .... E 2
Keene 353 .... F 3
Keewatin 1,863 .... F 5
Kemptville 2,362 .... J 2
Kenora◎ 9,817 .... F 4
Killaloe Station 634 .... G 2
Killarney 433 .... C 2
Kincardine 5,778 .... C 3
Kingston◎ 52,616 .... H 3
Kingsville 5,134 .... B 6
Kinmount 262 .... F 3
Kirkland Lake 12,219 .... K 5
Kitchener◎ 139,734 .... D 4
Kitchener *287,801 .... D 4
Komoka 1,152 .... C 5
Lakefield 2,374 .... F 3
Lanark 753 .... H 2
Lancaster 637 .... K 2
Langton 348 .... D 5
Lansdowne 540 .... H 3
Larder Lake 1,084 .... K 5
Latchford 397 .... K 5
Leamington 12,528 .... B 5
Limoges 930 .... J 2
Lincoln 14,196 .... E 4
Linden Beach 579 .... B 6
Lindsay◎ 13,596 .... F 3
Linwood 450 .... D 4
Lion's Head 467 .... C 2

Lisle 265 .... E 3
Listowel 5,026 .... D 4
Little Britain 265 .... F 3
Little Current 1,507 .... B 2
London◎ 254,280 .... C 5
London *283,668 .... C 5
Longlac 2,431 .... H 5
Long Sault 1,227 .... K 2
L'Orignal◎ 1,819 .... K 2
Lucan 1,616 .... C 4
Lucknow 1,088 .... C 4
Lyn 518 .... J 3
Lynden 451 .... D 4
Lynhurst 685 .... C 5
MacGregor's Bay 861 .... G 2
MacTier 647 .... E 2
Madawaska 264 .... F 2
Madoc 1,249 .... G 3
Maitland 667 .... J 3
Mallorytown 368 .... J 3
Manitouwadge 3,155 .... H 5
Manitowaning 518 .... C 2
Manotick-Hillside Gardens 2,694 .... J 2
Marathon 2,271 .... H 5
Markdale 1,289 .... D 3
Markham 77,037 .... K 4
Markstay 444 .... D 1
Marmora 1,304 .... G 3
Martintown 388 .... K 2
Massey 1,274 .... C 1
Matachewan 444 .... J 5
Matheson 966 .... K 5
Mattawa 2,652 .... F 1
Mattice 803 .... J 5
Maxville 836 .... K 2

Maynooth 277 .... G 2
McGregor 1,145 .... B 5
McKerrow 260 .... C 1
Meaford 4,367 .... D 3
Melbourne 346 .... C 5
Merlin 745 .... B 5
Merrickville 984 .... J 3
Metcalfe 687 .... J 2
Midhurst 1,457 .... E 3
Midland 12,132 .... D 3
Mildmay 928 .... C 3
Milford Bay 401 .... E 2
Millbank 337 .... D 4
Millbrook 927 .... F 3
Milton◎ 28,067 .... E 4
Milverton 1,463 .... D 4
Minaki 319 .... F 4
Mindemoya 376 .... B 2
Minden◎ 838 .... F 3
Mississauga 315,056 .... J 4
Mitchell 2,777 .... C 4
Monkton 520 .... C 4
Moonbeam 838 .... J 5
Moorefield 308 .... D 4
Mooretown 344 .... B 5
Moose Creek 393 .... K 2
Morewood 264 .... J 2
Morpeth 284 .... C 5
Morrisburg 2,308 .... J 3
Mount Albert 1,165 .... E 3
Mount Brydges 1,557 .... C 5
Mount Forest 3,474 .... D 4
Mount Hope 557 .... E 4
Munster 1,531 .... J 2
Nakina 936 .... H 4
Nanticoke◎ 19,816 .... E 5

Napanee 4,803 .... G 3
Navan 419 .... J 2
Neustadt 511 .... D 3
Newboro 260 .... H 3
Newburgh 617 .... H 3
Newbury 441 .... C 5
Newcastle 32,229 .... F 4
New Hamburg 3,923 .... D 4
New Liskeard 5,551 .... K 5
Newmarket◎ 29,753 .... E 3
Niagara Falls 70,960 .... E 4
Niagara-on-the-Lake 12,186 .... E 4
Nickel Centre 12,318 .... D 1
Nipigon 2,377 .... H 5
Nobel 386 .... D 2
Nobleton 1,861 .... J 3
Noelville 702 .... D 1
North Bay◎ 51,268 .... E 1
North Gower 818 .... J 2
North York 559,521 .... J 4
Norwich 2,117 .... D 5
Norwood 1,278 .... F 3
Nottawa 360 .... D 3
Oakville 75,773 .... E 4
Oakwood 404 .... F 3
Odessa 849 .... H 3
Oil City 266 .... B 5
Oil Springs 627 .... B 5
Omemee 819 .... F 3
Onaping Falls 6,198 .... J 5
Opasatika 413 .... J 5
Orangeville◎ 13,740 .... D 4
Orillia 23,955 .... E 3
Osgoode 1,138 .... J 2
Oshawa 117,519 .... F 4
Oshawa *154,217 .... F 4

Ottawa◎ (cap.), Canada 295,163 .... J 2
Ottawa-Hull *717,978 .... J 2
Otterville 776 .... D 5
Owen Sound◎ 19,883 .... D 3
Paincourt 414 .... B 5
Paisley 1,039 .... C 3
Pakenham 367 .... H 2
Palmerston 1,989 .... D 4
Paris 7,485 .... D 4
Parkhill 1,358 .... C 4
Parry Sound◎ 6,124 .... E 2
Pefferlaw 857 .... E 3
Pelham 11,104 .... E 4
Pembroke◎ 14,026 .... G 2
Penetanguishene 5,315 .... D 3
Perth◎ 5,655 .... H 3
Petawawa 5,520 .... G 2
Peterborough◎ 60,620 .... F 3
Petrolia 4,234 .... B 5
Pickering 37,754 .... K 4
Picton◎ 4,361 .... G 3
Plantagenet 870 .... K 2
Plattsville 495 .... D 4
Point Edward 2,383 .... B 4
Pontypool 759 .... F 3
Port Burwell 655 .... D 5
Port Carling 629 .... E 2
Port Colborne 19,225 .... E 5
Port Elgin 6,131 .... C 3
Port Franks 547 .... C 4
Port Hope 9,992 .... F 4
Port Lambton 921 .... B 5
Portland 271 .... H 3
Port McNicoll 1,883 .... E 3
Port Perry 4,712 .... E 3

Port Rowan 811 .... D 5
Port Stanley 1,891 .... C 5
Pottageville 286 .... J 3
Powassan 1,169 .... E 1
Prescott◎ 4,670 .... J 3
Princeton 462 .... D 4
Puce-Emeryville 1,611 .... B 5
Rainy River 1,061 .... F 5
Ramore 382 .... K 5
Rayside-Balfour 15,017 .... K 5
Red Rock 1,260 .... H 5
Renfrew 8,283 .... H 2
Richards Landing 405 .... J 5
Richmond 2,880 .... J 2
Richmond Hill 37,778 .... J 4
Ridgetown 3,062 .... C 5
Ripley 591 .... C 3
River Valley 275 .... D 1
Rockcliffe Park 1,869 .... J 2
Rockland 3,961 .... J 2
Rockwood 1,068 .... D 4
Rodney 1,007 .... C 5
Rosslyn Village 362 .... G 5
Round Lake Centre 255 .... G 2
Russell 1,099 .... J 2
Ruthven 649 .... B 6
Saint Albert 254 .... J 2
Saint Catharines◎ 124,018 .... E 4
Saint Catharines-Niagara *304,353 .... E 4
Saint Charles 382 .... D 1
Saint Clair Beach 2,845 .... B 5
Saint Clements 890 .... D 4
Saint-Eugène 470 .... K 2
Saint George 865 .... D 4
Saint Isidore de Prescott 746 .... K 2

Saint Jacobs 1,189 . . . . D 4
Saint Mary's 4,883 . . . . C 4
Saint Thomas⊙ 28,165 . . . . . . C 5
Saint Williams 442 . . . . D 5
Salem 825 . . . . D 4
Sarnia⊙ 50,892 . . . . B 5
Sauble Beach 729 . . . . C 3
Sault Sainte Marie⊙ 82,697 . . J 5
Scarborough 443,353 . . . . K 4
Schomberg 923 . . . . J 3
Schreiber 1,968 . . . . H 5
Scotland 600 . . . . D 4
Seaforth 2,114 . . . . C 4
Searchmont 384 . . . . J 5
Sebringville 579 . . . . C 4
Seeleys Bay 503 . . . . H 3
Shakespeare 602 . . . . D 4
Shallow Lake 418 . . . . C 3
Shannonville 314 . . . . G 3
Shanty Bay 358 . . . . E 3
Sharbot Lake 495 . . . . H 3
Shedden 292 . . . . C 5
Shelburne 2,862 . . . . D 3
Simcoe⊙ 14,326 . . . . D 5
Sioux Lookout 3,074 . . . . G 4
Sioux Narrows 394 . . . . F 5
Smithfield 349 . . . . G 3
Smiths Falls 8,831 . . . . H 3
Smithville 1,936 . . . . E 4
Smooth Rock Falls 2,352 . . . . J 5
Sombra 420 . . . . B 5
Southampton 2,830 . . . . C 3
South Mountain 285 . . . . J 3
South River 1,109 . . . . E 2
Spanish 1,063 . . . . J 5
Sparta 283 . . . . C 5
Spencerville 438 . . . . J 3
Springfield 555 . . . . C 5
Springford 309 . . . . D 5
Stayner 2,530 . . . . E 3
Stirling 1,638 . . . . G 3
Stittsville 2,652 . . . . J 2
Stoney Creek 36,762 . . . . E 4
Stoney Point 1,090 . . . . B 5
Straffordville 752 . . . . D 5
Stratford⊙ 26,262 . . . . C 4
Strathroy 8,748 . . . . C 5
Sturgeon Falls 6,045 . . . . E 1
Sudbury⊙ 91,829 . . . . K 5
Sudbury *149,923 . . . . K 5
Sunderland 703 . . . . E 3
Sundridge 734 . . . . E 2
Sydenham 595 . . . . H 3
Tamworth 402 . . . . H 3
Tara 687 . . . . C 3
Tavistock 1,885 . . . . D 4
Tecumseh 6,364 . . . . B 5
Teeswater 1,026 . . . . C 3
Terrace Bay 2,639 . . . . H 5
Thamesford 1,920 . . . . C 4
Thamesville 961 . . . . C 5
Thedford 694 . . . . C 4
Thessalon 1,620 . . . . J 5
Thornbury 1,435 . . . . D 3
Thorndale 581 . . . . C 4
Thornton 414 . . . . E 3
Thorold 15,412 . . . . E 4
Thunder Bay⊙ 112,486 . . . . . . H 5
Thunder Bay *121,379 . . . . . . H 5
Tilbury 4,298 . . . . B 5
Tillsonburg 10,487 . . . . D 5
Timmins 46,114 . . . . J 5

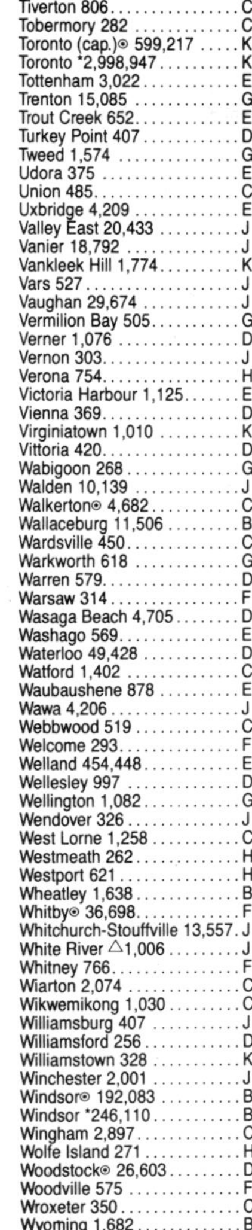

Tiverton 806 . . . . C 3
Tobermory 282 . . . . C 2
Toronto (cap.)⊙ 599,217 . . . . . K 4
Toronto *2,998,947 . . . . K 4
Tottenham 3,022 . . . . E 3
Trenton 15,085 . . . . G 3
Trout Creek 652 . . . . E 2
Turkey Point 407 . . . . D 5
Tweed 1,574 . . . . G 3
Udora 375 . . . . E 3
Union 485 . . . . C 5
Uxbridge 4,209 . . . . E 3
Valley East 20,433 . . . . J 5
Vanier 18,792 . . . . J 2
Vankleek Hill 1,774 . . . . K 2
Vars 527 . . . . J 2
Vaughan 29,674 . . . . J 4
Vermilion Bay 505 . . . . G 4
Verner 1,076 . . . . D 1
Vernon 303 . . . . J 2
Verona 754 . . . . H 3
Victoria Harbour 1,125 . . . . . . E 3
Vienna 369 . . . . D 5
Virginiatown 1,010 . . . . K 5
Vittoria 420 . . . . D 5
Wabigoon 268 . . . . G 5
Walden 10,139 . . . . J 5
Walkerton⊙ 4,682 . . . . C 3
Wallaceburg 11,506 . . . . B 5
Wardsville 450 . . . . C 5
Warkworth 618 . . . . G 3
Warren 579 . . . . D 1
Warsaw 314 . . . . F 3
Wasaga Beach 4,705 . . . . D 3
Washago 569 . . . . E 3
Waterloo 49,428 . . . . D 4
Watford 1,402 . . . . C 5
Waubaushene 878 . . . . E 3
Wawa 4,206 . . . . J 5
Webbwood 519 . . . . C 1
Welcome 293 . . . . F 4
Welland 454,448 . . . . E 5
Wellesley 997 . . . . D 4
Wellington 1,082 . . . . G 4
Wendover 326 . . . . J 2
West Lorne 1,258 . . . . C 5
Westmeath 262 . . . . H 2
Westport 621 . . . . H 3
Wheatley 1,638 . . . . B 5
Whitby⊙ 36,698 . . . . F 4
Whitchurch-Stouffville 13,557 . J 3
White River △1,006 . . . . J 5
Whitney 766 . . . . F 2
Wiarton 2,074 . . . . C 3
Wikwemikong 1,030 . . . . C 2
Williamsburg 407 . . . . J 3
Williamsford 256 . . . . D 3
Williamstown 328 . . . . K 2
Winchester 2,001 . . . . J 2
Windsor⊙ 192,083 . . . . B 5
Windsor *246,110 . . . . B 5
Wingham 2,897 . . . . C 4
Wolfe Island 271 . . . . H 3
Woodstock⊙ 26,603 . . . . D 4
Woodville 575 . . . . F 3
Wroxeter 350 . . . . C 4
Wyoming 1,682 . . . . B 5
Yarker 319 . . . . H 3
York 134,617 . . . . J 4
Zephyr 330 . . . . E 3
Zurich 795 . . . . C 4

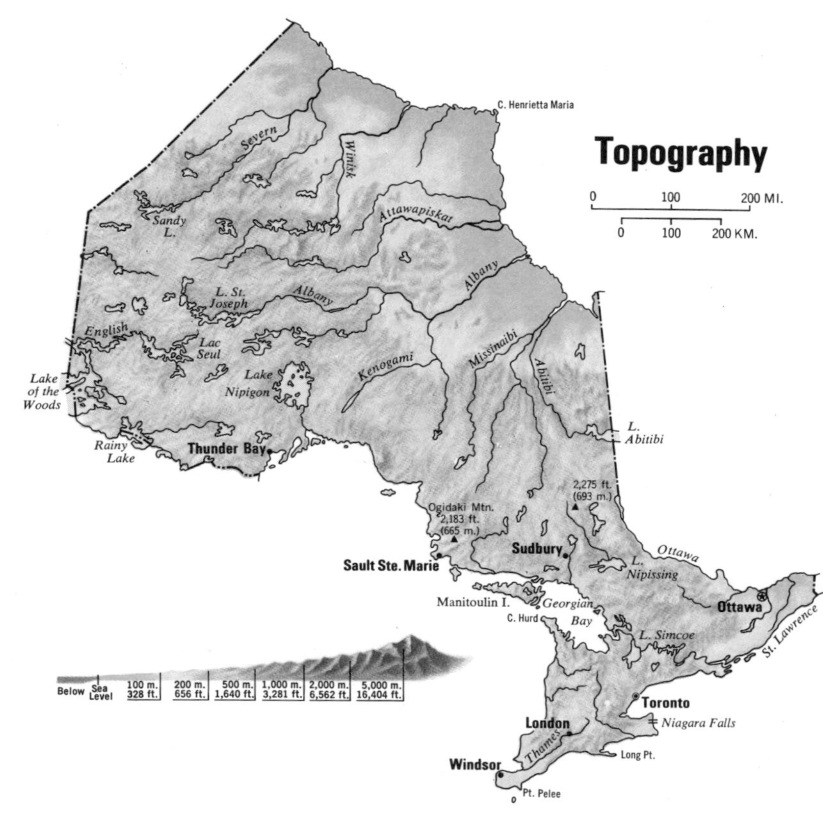

OTHER FEATURES

Abitibi (riv.) . . . . J 5
Algonquin Prov. Park . . . . F 2
Amherst (isl.) . . . . H 3
Balsam (lake) . . . . F 3
Barrie (isl.) . . . . B 1
Bays (lake) . . . . F 2
Big Rideau (lake) . . . . H 3
Black (riv.) . . . . E 3
Bruce (pen.) . . . . C 2
Buckhorn (lake) . . . . F 3
Cabot (head) . . . . C 2
Charleston (lake) . . . . J 3
Christian (isl.) . . . . D 3
Clear (lake) . . . . F 3
Cockburn (isl.) . . . . A 2
Couchiching (lake) . . . . E 3
Croker (cape) . . . . D 3
Don (riv.) . . . . J 4
Doré (lake) . . . . G 2
Douglas (pt.) . . . . C 3
Erie (lake) . . . . E 5
Flowerpot (isl.) . . . . C 2
French (riv.) . . . . D 1
Georgian (bay) . . . . D 2
Georgian Bay Is. Nat'l Park . . . . C 2, D 3
Georgina (isl.) . . . . E 3
Grand (riv.) . . . . D 4
Humber (riv.) . . . . J 3
Hurd (cape) . . . . C 2
Huron (lake) . . . . B 3
Ipperwash Prov. Park . . . . C 4
Joseph (lake) . . . . E 2
Killarney Prov. Park . . . . C 1
Killbear Point Prov. Park . . . . . D 2
Lake of the Woods (lake) . . . . . F 5
Lake Superior Prov. Park . . . . . J 5
Lonely (isl.) . . . . C 2
Long (pt.) . . . . D 5
Long Point (bay) . . . . D 5
Madawaska (riv.) . . . . G 2
Magnetawan (riv.) . . . . D 2
Main (chan.) . . . . C 2
Manitou (lake) . . . . C 2
Manitoulin (isl.) . . . . B 2
Mattagami (riv.) . . . . J 5
Michipicoten (isl.) . . . . H 5
Missinaibi (riv.) . . . . J 5
Mississagi (riv.) . . . . A 1
Mississippi (lake) . . . . H 2
Muskoka (lake) . . . . E 2
Niagara (riv.) . . . . E 4
Nipigon (lake) . . . . H 5
Nipissing (lake) . . . . E 1
North (chan.) . . . . A 1
Nottawasaga (bay) . . . . D 3
Ogidaki (mt.) . . . . J 5
Ontario (lake) . . . . G 4
Opeongo (lake) . . . . F 2
Ottawa (riv.) . . . . H 2
Owen (sound) . . . . D 3
Panache (lake) . . . . C 1
Parry (isl.) . . . . D 2
Parry (sound) . . . . D 2
Pelee (pt.) . . . . B 6
Petre (pt.) . . . . G 4
Point Pelee Nat'l Park . . . . B 5
Presqu'île Prov. Park . . . . G 4
Pukaskwa Prov. Park . . . . H 5
Quetico Prov. Park . . . . G 5
Rainy (lake) . . . . G 5
Rice (lake) . . . . F 3
Rideau (lake) . . . . H 3
Rondeau Prov. Park . . . . C 5
Rosseau (lake) . . . . E 2
Saint Clair (lake) . . . . B 5
Saint Clair (riv.) . . . . B 5
Saint Lawrence (lake) . . . . K 3
Saint Lawrence (riv.) . . . . J 3
Saint Lawrence Is. Nat'l Park . J 3
Saugeen (riv.) . . . . C 3
Scugog (lake) . . . . F 3
Seul (lake) . . . . G 4
Severn (riv.) . . . . E 3
Sibley Prov. Park . . . . H 5
Simcoe (lake) . . . . E 3
South (bay) . . . . C 2
Spanish (riv.) . . . . C 1
Stony (lake) . . . . G 3
Superior (lake) . . . . H 5
Sydenham (riv.) . . . . B 5
Thames (riv.) . . . . B 5
Theano (pt.) . . . . J 5
Thousand (isls.) . . . . H 3
Timagami (lake) . . . . K 5
Trout (lake) . . . . E 1
Vernon (lake) . . . . E 2
Walpole (isl.) . . . . B 5
Welland (canal) . . . . E 5
Woods (lake) . . . . F 5

⊙County seat.
*Population of metropolitan area.
△Population of town or township.

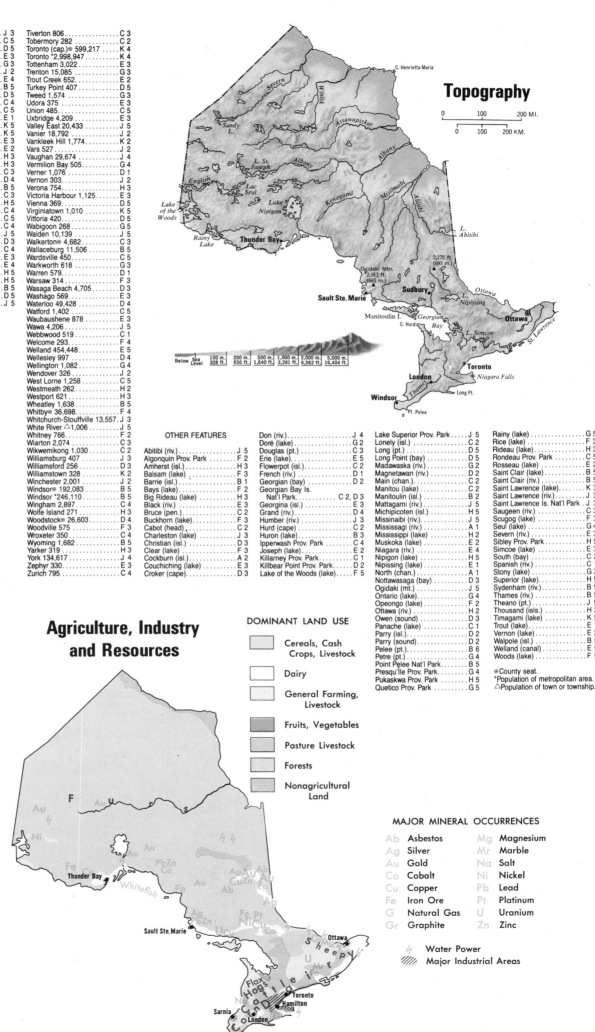

Agriculture, Industry and Resources

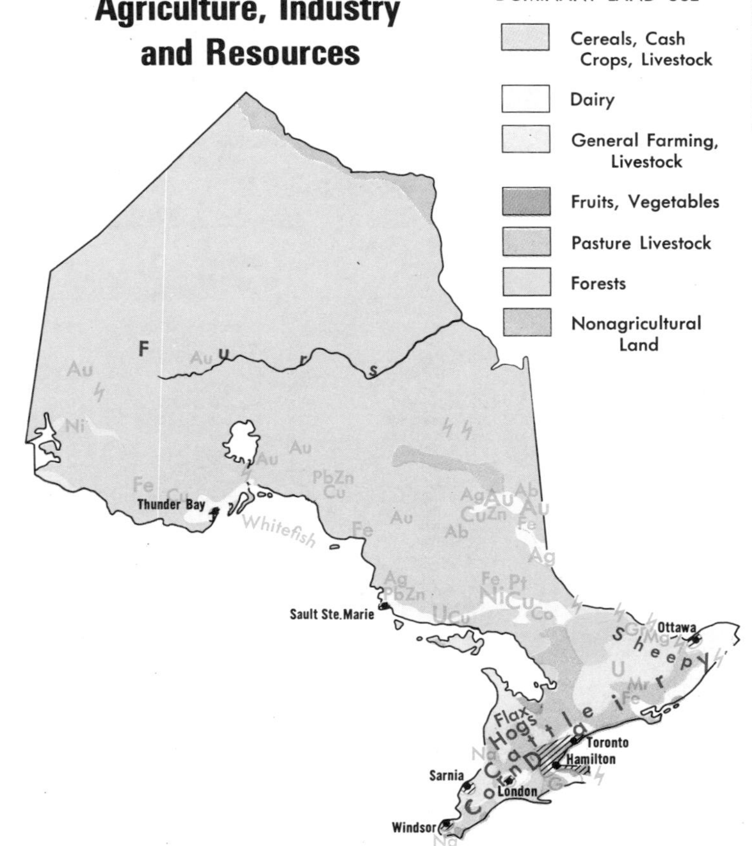

MAJOR MINERAL OCCURRENCES

Ab	Asbestos	Mg	Magnesium
Ag	Silver	Mr	Marble
Au	Gold	Na	Salt
Co	Cobalt	Ni	Nickel
Cu	Copper	Pb	Lead
Fe	Iron Ore	Pt	Platinum
G	Natural Gas	U	Uranium
Gr	Graphite	Zn	Zinc

Water Power
Major Industrial Areas

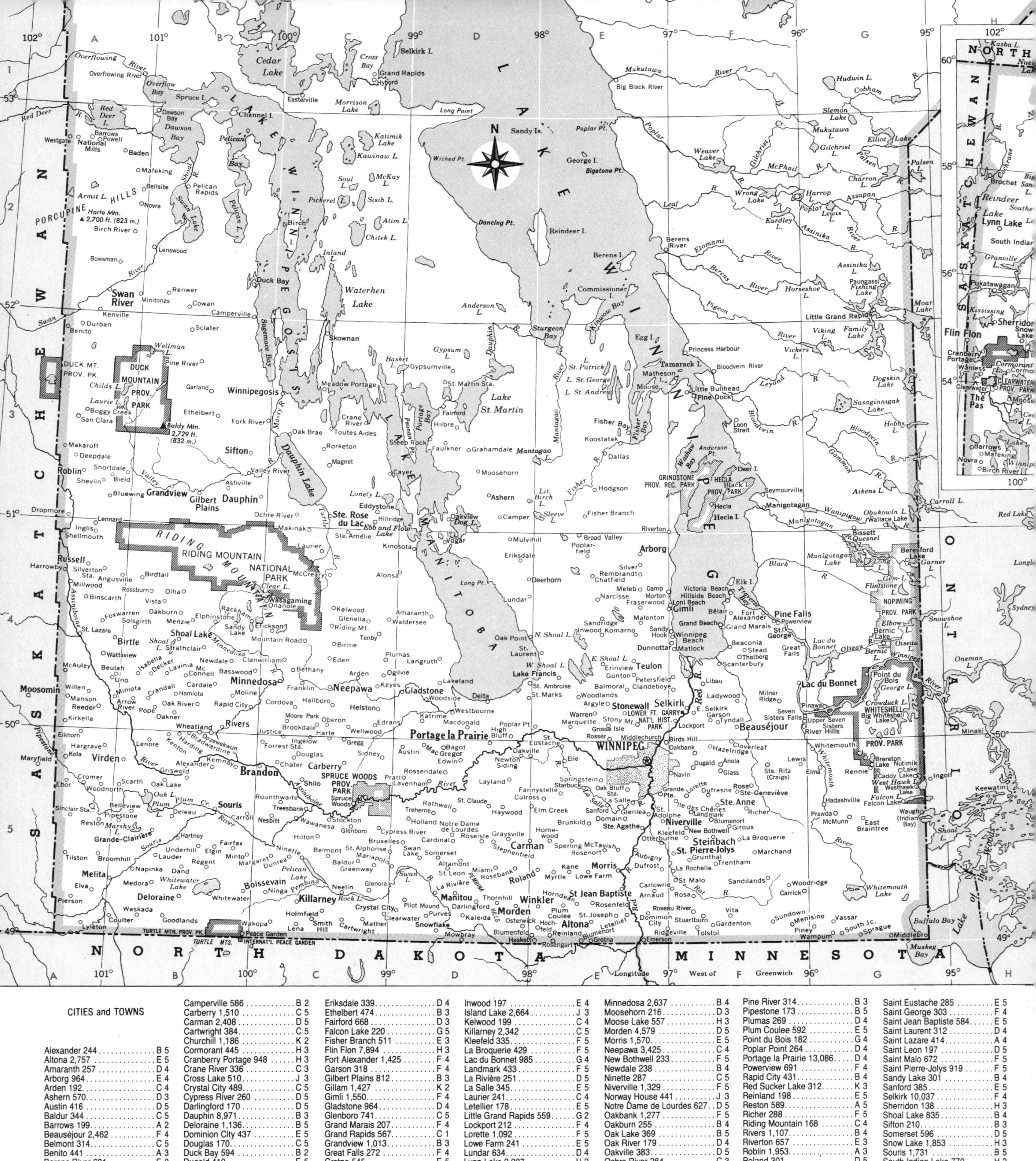

CITIES and TOWNS

Alexander 244 . . . . B 5
Altona 2,757 . . . . E 5
Amaranth 257 . . . . D 4
Arborg 964 . . . . E 4
Arden 192 . . . . C 4
Ashern 570 . . . . D 3
Austin 416 . . . . D 5
Baldur 344 . . . . C 5
Barrows 199 . . . . A 2
Beauséjour 2,462 . . . . F 4
Belmont 314 . . . . C 5
Benito 441 . . . . A 3
Berens River 681 . . . . F 2
Binscarth 472 . . . . A 4
Birch River 597 . . . . A 2
Birds Hill 711 . . . . F 4
Birtle 887 . . . . B 4
Bloodvein River 413 . . . . F 3
Blumenort 533 . . . . F 5
Boissevain 1,660 . . . . C 5
Bowsman 454 . . . . A 2
Brandon 36,242 . . . . C 5
Brochet 215 . . . . H 2
Camperville 586 . . . . B 2
Carberry 1,510 . . . . C 5
Carman 2,408 . . . . D 5
Cartwright 384 . . . . C 5
Churchill 1,186 . . . . K 2
Cormorant 445 . . . . H 3
Cranberry Portage 948 . . . . H 3
Crane River 336 . . . . C 3
Cross Lake 510 . . . . J 3
Crystal City 489 . . . . C 5
Cypress River 260 . . . . D 5
Darlingford 170 . . . . D 5
Dauphin 8,971 . . . . B 3
Deloraine 1,136 . . . . B 5
Dominion City 437 . . . . E 5
Douglas 170 . . . . C 5
Duck Bay 594 . . . . B 2
Dugald 410 . . . . F 5
Dunnottar 287 . . . . E 4
Easterville 589 . . . . C 1
East Selkirk 985 . . . . F 4
Elgin 172 . . . . B 5
Elie 450 . . . . E 5
Elkhorn 509 . . . . A 5
Elm Creek 293 . . . . E 5
Elphinstone 201 . . . . B 4
Emerson 762 . . . . E 5
Erickson 540 . . . . C 4
Eriksdale 339 . . . . D 4
Ethelbert 474 . . . . B 3
Fairford 668 . . . . D 3
Falcon Lake 220 . . . . G 5
Fisher Branch 511 . . . . E 3
Flin Flon 7,894 . . . . H 3
Fort Alexander 1,425 . . . . F 4
Garson 318 . . . . F 4
Gilbert Plains 812 . . . . B 3
Gillam 1,427 . . . . K 2
Gimli 1,550 . . . . F 4
Gladstone 964 . . . . D 4
Glenboro 741 . . . . C 5
Grand Marais 207 . . . . F 4
Grand Rapids 567 . . . . C 1
Grandview 1,013 . . . . B 3
Great Falls 272 . . . . F 4
Gretna 545 . . . . E 5
Grosse Isle 171 . . . . E 4
Grunthal 572 . . . . F 5
Hamiota 728 . . . . B 4
Hartney 490 . . . . B 5
Haywood 240 . . . . D 5
Hillridge 201 . . . . C 3
Hochfeld 187 . . . . E 5
Holland 418 . . . . D 5
Île des Chênes 814 . . . . F 5
Inglis 209 . . . . A 4
Inwood 197 . . . . E 4
Island Lake 2,664 . . . . J 3
Kelwood 199 . . . . C 4
Killarney 2,342 . . . . C 5
Kleefeld 335 . . . . F 5
La Broquerie 429 . . . . F 5
Lac du Bonnet 985 . . . . G 4
Landmark 433 . . . . F 5
La Rivière 251 . . . . D 5
La Salle 345 . . . . E 5
Laurier 241 . . . . C 4
Letellier 178 . . . . E 5
Little Grand Rapids 559 . . . . G 2
Lockport 212 . . . . F 4
Lorette 1,092 . . . . F 5
Lowe Farm 241 . . . . E 5
Lundar 634 . . . . D 4
Lynn Lake 2,087 . . . . H 2
MacGregor 795 . . . . D 5
Mafeking 266 . . . . B 2
Manigotagan 216 . . . . F 3
Manitou 861 . . . . D 5
McCreary 618 . . . . C 4
Melita 1,156 . . . . A 5
Miami 401 . . . . D 5
Middlechurch 342 . . . . E 4
Miniota 247 . . . . B 4
Minitonas 628 . . . . B 2
Minnedosa 2,637 . . . . B 4
Moosehorn 216 . . . . D 3
Moose Lake 557 . . . . H 3
Morden 4,579 . . . . D 5
Morris 1,570 . . . . E 5
Neepawa 3,425 . . . . C 4
New Bothwell 233 . . . . F 5
Newdale 238 . . . . B 4
Ninette 287 . . . . C 5
Niverville 1,329 . . . . F 5
Norway House 441 . . . . J 3
Notre Dame de Lourdes 627 . . D 5
Oakbank 1,277 . . . . F 5
Oakburn 255 . . . . B 4
Oak Lake 369 . . . . B 5
Oak River 179 . . . . D 4
Oakville 383 . . . . D 5
Ochre River 284 . . . . C 3
Onanole 386 . . . . C 4
Oozewekwun 453 . . . . B 5
Paungassi 296 . . . . G 2
Pelican Rapids 178 . . . . B 2
Petersfield 170 . . . . E 4
Pierson 238 . . . . A 5
Pikwitonei 175 . . . . J 3
Pilot Mound 838 . . . . D 5
Pinawa 2,006 . . . . G 4
Pine Falls 885 . . . . F 4
Pine River 314 . . . . B 3
Pipestone 173 . . . . B 5
Plumas 269 . . . . D 4
Plum Coulee 592 . . . . E 5
Point du Bois 182 . . . . G 4
Poplar Point 264 . . . . D 4
Portage la Prairie 13,086 . . . . D 4
Powerview 691 . . . . F 4
Rapid City 431 . . . . B 4
Red Sucker Lake 312 . . . . K 3
Reinland 198 . . . . E 5
Reston 589 . . . . A 5
Richer 288 . . . . F 5
Riding Mountain 168 . . . . C 4
Rivers 1,107 . . . . B 4
Riverton 657 . . . . E 3
Roblin 1,953 . . . . A 3
Roland 301 . . . . D 5
Rorketon 229 . . . . C 3
Rosenfeld 263 . . . . E 5
Rossburn 696 . . . . B 4
Russell 1,660 . . . . A 4
Saint Adolphe 928 . . . . E 5
Saint Ambroise 263 . . . . E 4
Saint Claude 592 . . . . D 5
Sainte Agathe 326 . . . . E 5
Sainte Anne 1,338 . . . . F 5
Sainte Rose du Lac 1,090 . . . . C 3
Saint Eustache 285 . . . . E 5
Saint George 303 . . . . F 4
Saint Jean Baptiste 584 . . . . E 5
Saint Laurent 312 . . . . D 4
Saint Lazare 414 . . . . A 4
Saint Leon 197 . . . . D 5
Saint Malo 672 . . . . F 5
Saint Pierre-Jolys 919 . . . . F 5
Sandy Lake 301 . . . . B 4
Sanford 385 . . . . E 5
Selkirk 10,037 . . . . F 4
Sherridon 138 . . . . H 3
Shoal Lake 835 . . . . B 4
Sifton 210 . . . . B 3
Somerset 596 . . . . D 5
Snow Lake 1,853 . . . . H 3
Souris 1,731 . . . . B 5
South Indian Lake 770 . . . . H 2
Split Lake 985 . . . . J 2
Sprague 199 . . . . G 5
Starbuck 224 . . . . E 5
Steinbach 6,676 . . . . F 5
Stonewall 2,210 . . . . E 4
Stony Mountain 1,313 . . . . E 4
Strathclair 390 . . . . B 4
Swan Lake 367 . . . . D 5
Swan River 3,782 . . . . A 2
Teulon 925 . . . . E 4

The Pas 6,390 H 3
Thicket Portage 195 J 3
Thompson 14,288 J 2
Treherne 743 D 5
Tyndall 421 F 4
Virden 2,940 A 5
Vita 364 F 5
Wabowden 655 J 3
Wallace Lake •2,044 G 3
Wanless 193 H 3
Warren 459 E 4
Waskada 239 B 5
Wawanesa 492 C 5
Whitemouth 320 G 5
Whitewater •856 B 5
Winkler 5,046 E 5
Winnipeg (cap.) 564,473 E 5
Winnipeg *584,842 E 5
Winnipeg Beach 565 F 4
Winnipegosis 855 B 3
Woodlands 185 E 4
Wooodridge 170 G 5
York Landing 229 J 2

AREA 250,999 sq. mi. (650,087 sq. km.)
POPULATION 1,026,241
CAPITAL Winnipeg
LARGEST CITY Winnipeg
HIGHEST POINT Baldy Mtn. 2,729 ft. (832 m.)
SETTLED IN 1812
ADMITTED TO CONFEDERATION 1870
PROVINCIAL FLOWER Prairie Crocus

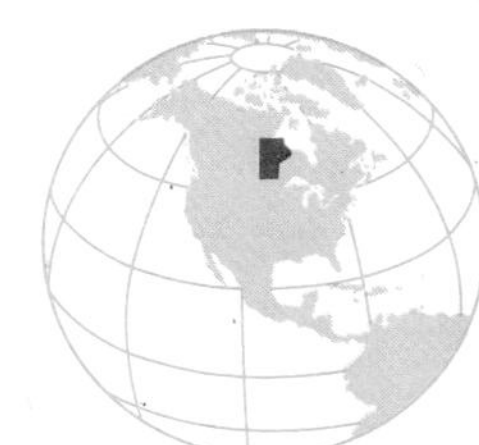

OTHER FEATURES

Aikens (lake) G 3
Anderson (lake) D 2
Anderson (pt.) F 3
Armit (lake) A 2
Assapan (riv.) G 2
Assiniboine (riv.) C 5
Assinika (lake) G 2
Assinika (riv.) G 2
Atim (lake) C 2
Baldy (mt.) B 3
Basket (lake) C 3
Beaverhill (lake) J 3
Berens (isl.) E 2
Berens (riv.) F 2
Bernic (lake) G 4
Big Sand (lake) H 2
Bigstone (lake) J 3
Bigstone (pt.) E 2
Bigstone (riv.) J 3
Birch (isl.) C 2
Black (isl.) F 3
Black (riv.) F 4
Bloodvein (riv.) F 3
Bonnet (lake) G 4
Buffalo (bay) G 5
Burntwood (riv.) J 2
Caribou (riv.) J 1
Carroll (lake) G 3
Cedar (lake) B 1
Channel (isl.) B 2
Charron (lake) G 2
Childs (lake) A 3
Chitek (lake) C 2
Churchill (cape) K 2
Churchill (riv.) J 2
Clear (lake) C 4
Clearwater Lake Prov. Park H 3
Cobham (riv.) G 1
Cochrane (riv.) H 2
Commissioner (isl.) E 2
Cormorant (lake) H 3
Cross (bay) C 1
Cross (lake) J 3
Crowduck (lake) G 4
Dancing (pt.) D 2
Dauphin (lake) C 3
Dauphin (riv.) D 3
Dawson (bay) B 2
Dog (lake) D 3
Dogskin (lake) G 3
Duck Mountain Prov. Park B 3
Eardley (lake) F 2
East Shoal (lake) E 4
Ebb and Flow (lake) C 3
Egg (isl.) E 3
Elbow (lake) G 4
Elk (isl.) F 4
Elliot (lake) G 2
Etawney (lake) J 2
Etomami (riv.) F 2
Falcon (lake) G 5
Family (lake) G 3
Fisher (bay) E 3
Fisher (riv.) E 3
Fishing (lake) G 2
Flintstone (lake) G 4
Fox (riv.) K 2
Gammon (riv.) G 3
Garner (lake) G 4
Gem (lake) G 4
George (isl.) E 2
George (lake) G 4
Gilchrist (creek) F 2
Gilchrist (lake) G 2
Gods (lake) K 3
Gods (riv.) K 3
Granville (lake) H 2
Grass (riv.) J 3
Grass River Prov. Park H 3
Grindstone Prov. Rec. Park F 3
Gunisao (lake) J 3
Gypsum (lake) D 3
Harrop (lake) G 2
Harte (mt.) A 2
Hayes (riv.) K 3
Hecla (isl.) F 3
Hecla Prov. Park F 3
Hobbs (lake) G 3
Horseshoe (lake) G 2
Hubbart (pt.) K 2
Hudson (bay) K 2
Hudwin (lake) G 1
Inland (lake) C 2
International Peace Garden B 5
Island (lake) K 3
Katimik (lake) C 2
Kawinaw (lake) C 2
Kinwow (bay) E 2
Kississing (lake) H 2
Knee (lake) J 3
Lake of the Woods (lake) H 5
La Salle (riv.) E 5
Laurie (lake) A 3
Leaf (riv.) F 2
Lewis (lake) G 2
Leyond (riv.) F 3
Little Birch (lake) E 3
Lonely (lake) C 3
Long (lake) G 4
Long (pt.) D 1
Long (pt.) D 4
Manigotagan (lake) G 4
Manigotagan (riv.) G 3
Manitoba (lake) D 4
Mantagao (riv.) E 3
Marshy (lake) B 5
McKay (lake) C 2
McPhail (riv.) F 2
Minnedosa (riv.) B 4
Moar (lake) G 2
Molson (lake) J 3
Moose (isl.) E 3
Morrison (lake) C 1
Mossy (riv.) C 3
Mukutawa (lake) G 2
Mukutawa (riv.) E 1
Muskeg (bay) G 6
Nejanilini (lake) J 1
Nelson (riv.) J 2
Nopiming Prov. Park G 4
Northern Indian (lake) J 2
North Knife (lake) J 2
North Seal (riv.) H 2
North Shoal (lake) E 4
Nueltin (lake) H 1
Oak (lake) B 5
Obukowin (lake) G 3
Oiseau (lake) G 4
Oiseau (riv.) G 4
Overflow (bay) A 1
Overflowing (riv.) A 1
Owl (riv.) K 2
Oxford (lake) J 3
Paint (lake) J 2
Palsen (riv.) G 2
Pelican (bay) B 2
Pelican (lake) B 2
Pelican (lake) C 5
Pembina (hills) D 5
Pembina (riv.) C 5
Peonan (pt.) D 3
Pickerel (lake) C 2
Pigeon (riv.) F 2
Pipestone (creek) A 5
Plum (creek) B 5
Plum (lake) B 5
Poplar (riv.) E 2
Porcupine (hills) A 2
Portage (bay) D 3
Punk (isl.) F 3
Quesnel (lake) G 4
Rat (riv.) F 5
Red (riv.) F 4
Red Deer (lake) A 2
Red Deer (riv.) A 2
Reindeer (isl.) E 2
Reindeer (lake) H 2
Riding (mt.) B 4
Riding Mountain Nat'l Park B 4
Rock (lake) C 5
Ross (isl.) J 3
Sagemace (bay) B 3
Saint Andrew (lake) E 3
Saint George (lake) E 3
Saint Martin (lake) D 3
Saint Patrick (lake) E 3
Sale (riv.) E 5
Sandy (isls.) D 2
Sasaginnigak (lake) G 3
Seal (riv.) J 2
Selkirk (isl.) C 1
Setting (lake) H 3
Shoal (lake) G 5
Shoal (riv.) B 2
Sipiwesk (lake) J 3
Sisib (lake) C 2
Sleeve (lake) E 3
Slemon (lake) G 1
Snowshoe (lake) G 4
Soul (lake) C 2
Souris (riv.) B 5
Southern Indian (lake) H 2
South Knife (riv.) J 2
South Seal (riv.) J 2
Split (lake) J 2
Spruce (isl.) B 1
Spruce Woods Prov. Park C 5
Stevenson (lake) J 3
Sturgeon (bay) E 3
Swan (lake) B 2
Swan (lake) D 5
Swan (riv.) A 3
Tadoule (lake) J 2
Tamarack (isl.) F 3
Tatnam (cape) K 2
Traverse (bay) F 4
Turtle (mts.) B 5
Turtle (riv.) C 3
Turtle Mountain Prov. Park B 5
Valley (riv.) B 3
Vickers (lake) F 3
Viking (lake) G 3
Wanipigow (riv.) G 3
Washow (bay) F 3
Waterhen (lake) C 2
Weaver (lake) F 2
Wellman (lake) B 3
West Hawk (lake) G 5
West Shoal (lake) E 4
Whitemouth (lake) G 5
Whitemouth (riv.) G 5
Whiteshell Prov. Park G 4
Whitewater (lake) B 5
Wicked (pt.) D 2
Winnipeg (lake) E 2
Winnipeg (riv.) G 4
Winnipegosis (lake) C 2
Woods (lake) H 5
Wrong (lake) F 2

*Population of metropolitan area.
•Population of rural municipality.

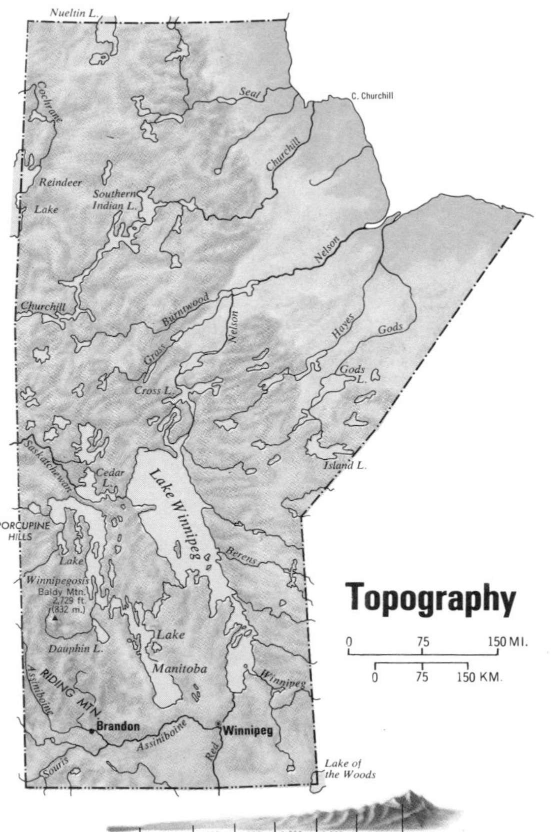

Agriculture, Industry and Resources

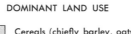

DOMINANT LAND USE

- Cereals (chiefly barley, oats)
- Cereals, Livestock
- Dairy
- Livestock
- Forests
- Nonagricultural Land

MAJOR MINERAL OCCURRENCES

Au	Gold	Ni	Nickel
Co	Cobalt	O	Petroleum
Cu	Copper	Pb	Lead
Na	Salt	Pt	Platinum
		Zn	Zinc

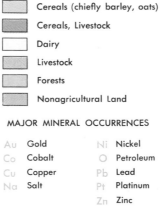

Water Power

Major Industrial Areas

Topography

0 60 120 MI.
0 60 120 KM.

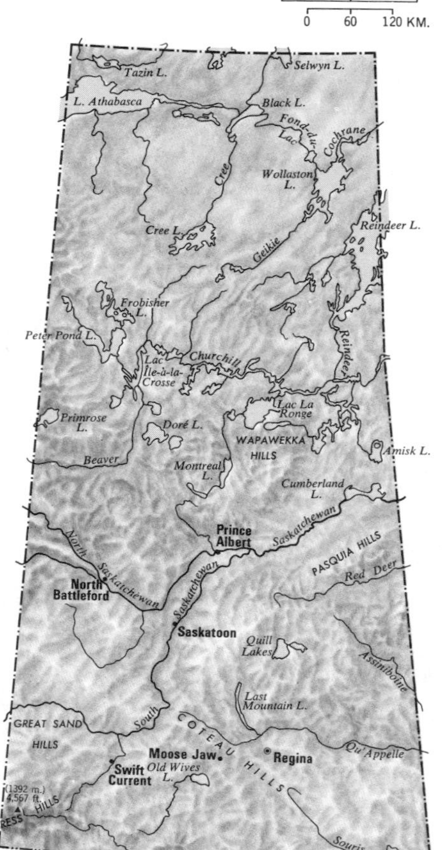

5,000 m. 16,404 ft. | 2,000 m. 6,562 ft. | 1,000 m. 3,281 ft. | 500 m. 1,640 ft. | 200 m. 656 ft. | 100 m. 328 ft. | Sea Level | Below

CITIES and TOWNS

Name	Key
Abbey 218	C 5
Aberdeen 496	E 3
Abernethy 300	H 5
Air Ronge 557	M 3
Alameda 318	J 6
Alida 169	K 6
Allan 871	E 4
Alsask 652	B 4
Annaheim 209	G 3
Antelope •231	C 5
Arborfield 439	H 2
Archerwill 286	H 3
Arcola 493	J 6
Arlington Beach •432	F 4
Asquith 507	D 3
Assiniboia 2,924	E 6
Avonlea 442	G 5
Baildon •799	F 5
Balcarres 739	H 5
Balgonie 777	G 5
Batoche	E 3
Battleford 3,565	C 3
Beauval 606	L 3
Beechy 279	D 5
Bengough 536	F 6
Bethune 369	F 5
Bienfait 835	J 6
Biggar 2,561	C 3
Big River 819	D 2
Birch Hills 957	F 3
Bjorkdale 269	H 3
Blaine Lake 653	D 3
Borden 197	D 3
Brabant Lake 245	M 3
Bradwell 168	E 4
Bredenbury 467	K 5
Briercrest 151	F 5
Broadview 840	J 5
Brock 184	C 4
Browning •687	J 6
Bruno 772	F 3
Buchanan 392	J 4
Buffalo Gap •598	F 6
Buffalo Narrows 1,088	L 3
Burstall 550	B 5
Cabri 632	C 5
Cadillac 173	D 6
Calder 164	K 4
Cana •1,238	J 5
Candle Lake 219	F 2
Cando 163	C 3
Canoe Lake 182	L 3
Canora 2,667	J 4
Canwood 340	E 2
Carievale 246	K 6
Carlyle 1,074	J 6
Carnduff 1,043	K 6
Carrot River 1,169	H 2
Central Butte 548	E 5
Ceylon 184	G 6
Chaplin 389	E 5
Chitek Lake 170	D 2
Choiceland 543	G 2
Christopher Lake 227	F 2
Churchbridge 972	J 5
Clavet 234	E 4
Climax 293	C 6
Cochin 221	C 2
Codette 236	H 2
Coleville 383	B 4
Colonsay 594	F 4
Connaught Heights •982	G 3
Conquest 256	D 4
Consul 153	B 6
Coronach 1,032	F 6
Craik 565	F 4
Craven 206	G 5
Creelman 184	H 6
Creighton 1,636	N 4
Cudworth 947	F 3
Cumberland House 831	J 2
Cupar 669	G 5
Cut Knife 624	B 3
Dalmeny 1,064	E 3
Davidson 1,166	E 4
Debden 403	E 2
Delisle 980	D 4
Denare Beach 592	M 4
Denzil 199	B 3
Deschambault Lake 386	M 3
Dinsmore 398	D 4
Dodsland 272	C 4
Domremy 209	F 3
Drake 211	G 4
Duck Lake 699	E 3
Dundurn 531	E 4
Dysart 275	H 5
Earl Grey 303	G 5
Eastend 723	C 6
Eatonia 528	B 4
Ebenezer 164	J 4
Edam 384	C 2
Edenwold 143	G 5
Elbow 313	E 4
Eldorado 229	L 2
Elfros 199	H 4
Elrose 624	D 4
Elstow 143	E 4
Endeavour 199	J 3
Englefeld 271	G 3
Erwood 149	J 3
Esterhazy 3,065	K 5
Estevan 9,174	J 6
Eston 1,413	C 4
Eyebrow 168	E 5
Fillmore 396	H 6
Fleming 141	K 5
Flin Flon 367	N 4
Foam Lake 1,452	H 4
Fond du Lac 494	L 2
Fort Qu'Appelle 1,827	H 5
Fox Valley 380	B 5
Francis 182	H 5
Frobisher 166	J 6
Frontier 619	C 6
Gainsborough 308	K 6
Gerald 197	K 5
Glaslyn 430	C 2
Glenavon 284	J 5
Glen Ewen 168	K 6
Goodsoil 263	L 4
Govan 394	G 4
Grand Coulee 208	G 5
Gravelbourg 1,338	E 6
Grayson 264	J 5
Green Acres 139	F 2
Green Lake 634	L 4
Grenfell 1,307	J 5
Guernsey 198	F 4
Gull Lake 1,095	C 5
Hafford 557	D 3
Hague 625	E 3
Hanley 484	E 4
Harris 259	D 4
Hawarden 137	E 4
Hearts Hill •552	B 3
Hepburn 411	E 3
Herbert 1,019	D 5
Hodgeville 329	E 5
Holdfast 297	F 5
Hudson Bay 2,361	J 3
Humboldt 4,705	F 3
Hyas 165	J 4
Île-à-la-Crosse 1,035	L 3
Imperial 501	F 4
Indian Head 1,889	H 5
Invermay 353	J 4
Ituna 870	H 4
Jansen 223	G 4
Jasmin •14	H 4
Kamsack 2,688	K 4
Kelliher 397	H 4
Kelvington 1,054	H 3
Kenaston 345	E 4
Kennedy 275	J 5
Kerrobert 1,141	C 4
Kincaid 256	D 6
Kindersley 3,969	B 4
Kinistino 783	F 3
Kipling 1,016	J 5
Kisbey 228	J 6
Kronau 154	G 5
Kyle 516	C 5
Lac Pelletier •586	C 6
Lafleche 583	E 6
Laird 233	E 3
Lake Lenore 361	G 3
La Loche 1,632	L 3
Lampman 651	J 6
Lancer 156	C 5
Landis 277	C 3
Lang 219	G 6
Langenburg 1,324	K 5
Langham 1,151	E 3
Lanigan 1,732	F 4
La Ronge 2,579	L 3
Lashburn 813	B 2
Leader 1,108	B 5
Leask 478	E 2
Lebret 274	H 5
Lemberg 414	H 5
Leoville 393	D 2
Leroy 504	G 4
Lestock 402	G 4
Limerick 164	E 6
Lintlaw 234	H 3
Lipton 364	H 5
Lloydminster 6,034	A 2
Loon Lake 369	B 1
Loreburn 201	E 4
Lucky Lake 333	D 5
Lumsden 1,303	G 5
Luseland 704	B 3
Macdowall 171	E 2
Macklin 976	A 3
Macoun 190	H 6
Maidstone 1,001	B 2
Mankota 375	D 6
Manor 368	K 6
Maple Creek 2,470	B 6
Marcelin 238	E 3
Margo 153	H 4
Marriott •627	D 4
Marsden 229	B 3
Marshall 453	B 2
Martensville 1,966	E 3
Maryfield 431	K 6
Maymont 212	D 3
McLean 189	G 5
Meacham 178	F 3
Meadow Lake 3,857	C 1
Meath Park 262	F 2
Medstead 163	C 2
Melfort 6,010	G 3
Melville 5,092	J 5
Meota 235	C 2
Mervin 155	C 2
Midale 564	H 6
Middle Lake 275	F 3
Milden 251	D 4
Milestone 602	G 5
Montmartre 544	H 5
Montreal Lake 448	F 1
Moose Jaw 33,941	F 5
Moose Range •679	H 2
Moosomin 2,579	K 5
Morse 416	D 5
Mortlach 293	E 5
Mossbank 464	E 6
Muenster 385	F 3
Naicam 886	G 3
Neilburg 354	B 3
Neuanlage 144	E 3
Neudorf 425	J 5
Neuhorst 146	E 3
Nipawin 4,376	H 2
Nokomis 524	F 4
Norquay 552	J 4
North Battleford 14,030	C 3
North Portal 164	J 6
Odessa 232	H 5
Ogema 441	G 6
Osler 527	E 3
Outlook 1,976	E 4
Oxbow 1,191	J 6
Paddockwood 211	F 2
Pangman 227	G 6
Paradise Hill 421	B 2
Patuanak 173	L 3
Paynton 210	B 2
Pelican Narrows 331	N 3
Pelly 391	K 4
Pennant 202	C 5
Pense 472	G 5
Perdue 407	D 3
Pierceland 425	K 4
Pilger 150	F 3
Pilot Butte 1,255	G 5
Pine House 612	M 3
Plenty 175	C 4
Plunkett 150	F 4
Ponteix 769	D 6
Porcupine Plain 937	H 3
Preeceville 1,243	J 4
Prelate 317	B 5
Prince Albert 31,380	F 2
Prud'homme 222	F 3
Punnichy 394	G 4
Qu'Appelle 653	H 5
Quill Lake 514	G 3
Quinton 169	G 4
Rabbit Lake 159	D 2
Radisson 439	D 3
Radville 1,012	G 6
Rama 133	H 4
Raymore 635	G 4
Redvers 859	K 6
Regina (cap.) 162,613	G 5
Regina *164,313	G 5
Regina Beach 603	F 5
Rhein 271	J 4
Richmound 188	B 5
Riverhurst 193	E 5
Rocanville 934	K 5
Roche Percé 142	J 6
Rockglen 511	F 6
Rosetown 2,664	D 4
Rose Valley 538	H 3
Rosthern 1,609	E 3
Rouleau 443	G 5
Saint Benedict 157	F 3
Saint Brieux 401	G 3
Saint Louis 448	F 3
Saint Philips •538	K 4
Saint Walburg 802	B 2
Saltcoats 549	J 4
Sandy Bay 756	N 3
Saskatoon 154,210	E 3
Saskatoon *154,210	E 3
Sceptre 169	B 5
Scott 203	C 3
Sedley 373	H 5
Semans 344	G 4
Shaunavon 2,112	C 6
Sheho 285	H 4
Shell Lake 220	D 2
Shellbrook 1,228	E 2
Simpson 231	F 4
Sintaluta 215	H 5
Smeaton 246	G 2
Southey 697	G 5
Spalding 337	G 3
Spiritwood 926	D 2
Springside 533	J 4
Spy Hill 354	K 5
Star City 527	G 3
Stenen 143	J 4
Stockholm 391	J 5
Stonehenge •701	F 6
Storthoaks 142	K 6
Stoughton 716	J 6
Strasbourg 842	G 4
Sturgis 789	J 4
Swift Current 14,747	D 5
Tantallon 196	K 5
Theodore 473	J 4
Timber Bay 152	F 1
Tisdale 3,107	H 3
Togo 181	K 4
Tompkins 275	C 5
Torch River •2,440	G 2
Torquay 311	H 6
Tramping Lake 178	B 3
Tugaske 175	E 5
Turnor Lake 166	L 3
Turtleford 505	B 2
Unity 2,408	B 3
Uranium City 2,507	L 2
Val Marie 236	D 6
Vanguard 292	D 6
Vanscoy 298	D 4
Vibank 369	H 5
Viscount 386	F 4
Vonda 313	F 3
Wadena 1,495	H 4
Wakaw 1,030	F 3
Waldeck 292	D 5
Waldheim 758	E 3
Walpole •711	K 6
Wapella 487	K 5
Warman 2,076	E 3
Waseca 169	B 2
Waskesiu Lake 176	E 2
Watrous 1,830	F 4
Watson 901	G 3
Wawota 622	J 6
Weldon 279	F 2
Welwyn 170	K 5
Weyburn 9,523	H 6
White City 602	G 5
White Fox 394	H 2
Whitewood 1,003	J 5
Wilcox 202	G 5
Wilkie 1,501	C 3
Willow Bunch 494	F 6
Willow Creek •1,218	B 6
Windthorst 254	J 5
Wiseton 195	D 4
Wishart 212	H 4
Wollaston Lake 248	N 2
Wolseley 904	H 5
Wymark 162	D 5
Wynyard 2,147	G 4
Yarbo 158	K 5
Yellow Grass 477	H 6
Yorkton 15,339	J 4
Young 456	F 4
Zenon Park 273	H 2

OTHER FEATURES

Name	Key
Allan (hills)	E 4
Amisk (lake)	M 4
Antelope (lake)	C 5
Antler (riv.)	K 6
Arm (riv.)	F 5
Assiniboine (riv.)	J 3
Athabasca (lake)	L 2
Bad (lake)	C 4
Bad (hills)	C 4
Basin (lake)	F 3
Batoche Nat'l Hist. Site	E 3
Battle (creek)	B 6
Battle (riv.)	B 3
Bear (hills)	C 4
Beaver (hills)	H 4
Beaver (riv.)	L 4
Beaverlodge (lake)	L 2
Big Muddy (lake)	G 6
Bigstick (lake)	B 5
Birch (lake)	C 2
Bitter (lake)	B 5
Black (lake)	M 2
Boundary (plat.)	B 6
Brightsand (lake)	B 2
Bronson (lake)	B 2

Agriculture, Industry and Resources

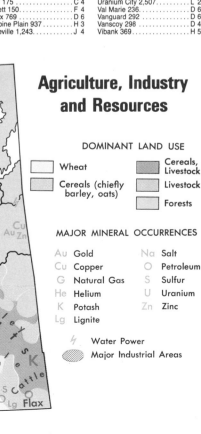

DOMINANT LAND USE

- Wheat
- Cereals (chiefly barley, oats)
- Cereals, Livestock
- Livestock
- Forests

MAJOR MINERAL OCCURRENCES

- Au Gold
- Cu Copper
- G Natural Gas
- He Helium
- K Potash
- Lg Lignite
- Na Salt
- O Petroleum
- S Sulfur
- U Uranium
- Zn Zinc

- Water Power
- Major Industrial Areas

AREA 251,699 sq. mi. (651,900 sq. km.)
POPULATION 968,313
CAPITAL Regina
LARGEST CITY Regina
HIGHEST POINT Cypress Hills 4,567 ft. (1,392 m.)
SETTLED IN 1774
ADMITTED TO CONFEDERATION 1905
PROVINCIAL FLOWER Prairie Lily

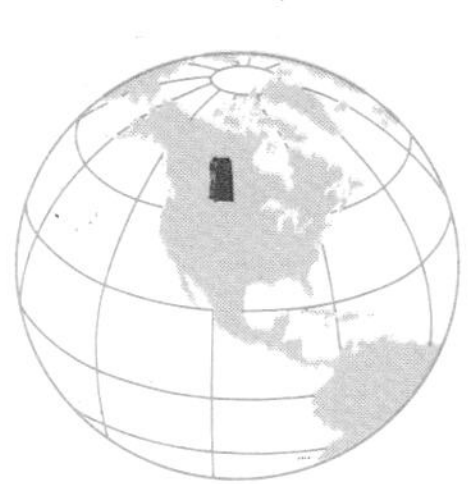

*Population of metropolitan area.
•Population of rural municipality.

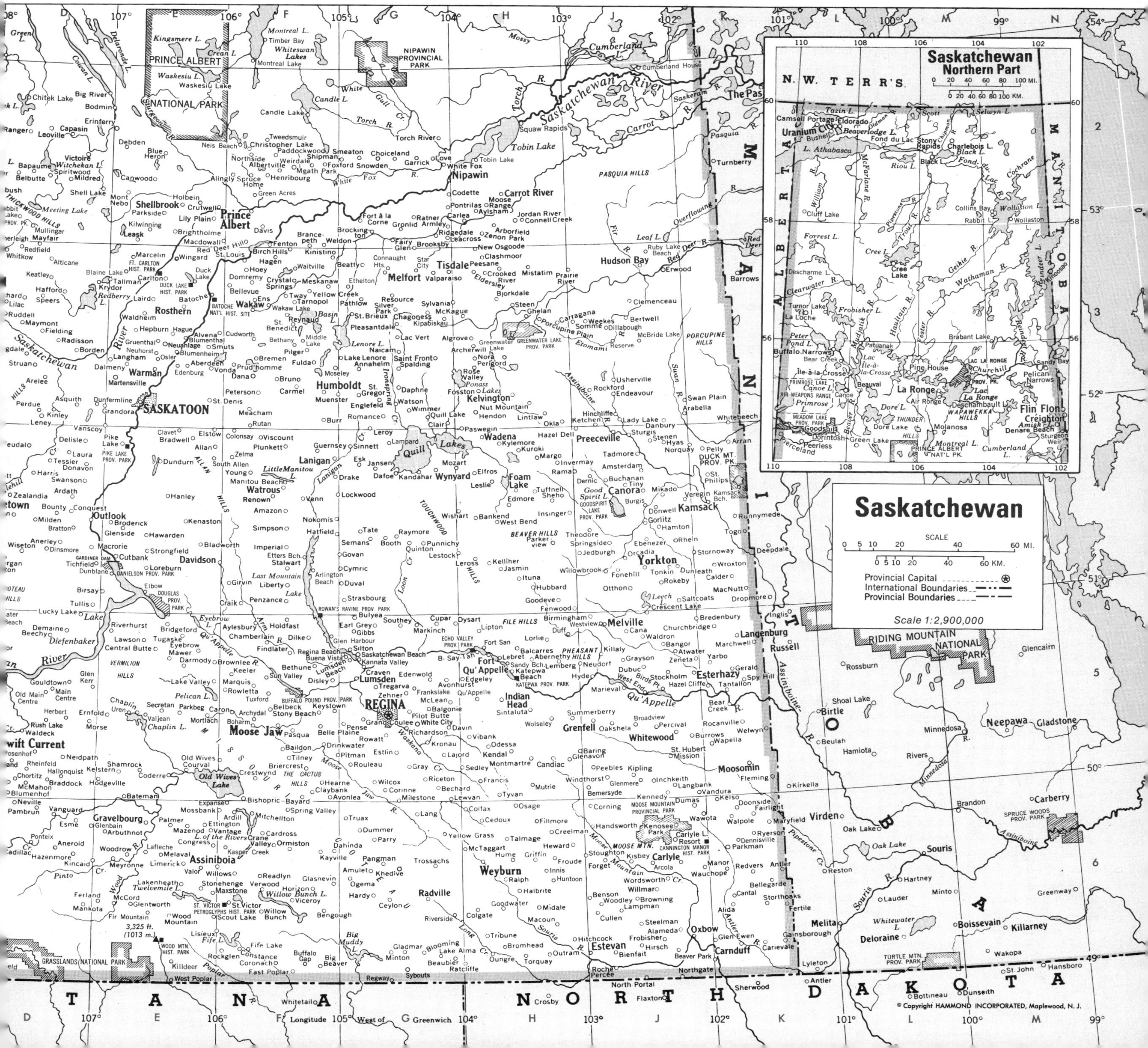

Saskatchewan

Scale 1:2,900,000

Provincial Capital
International Boundaries
Provincial Boundaries

Saskatchewan Northern Part

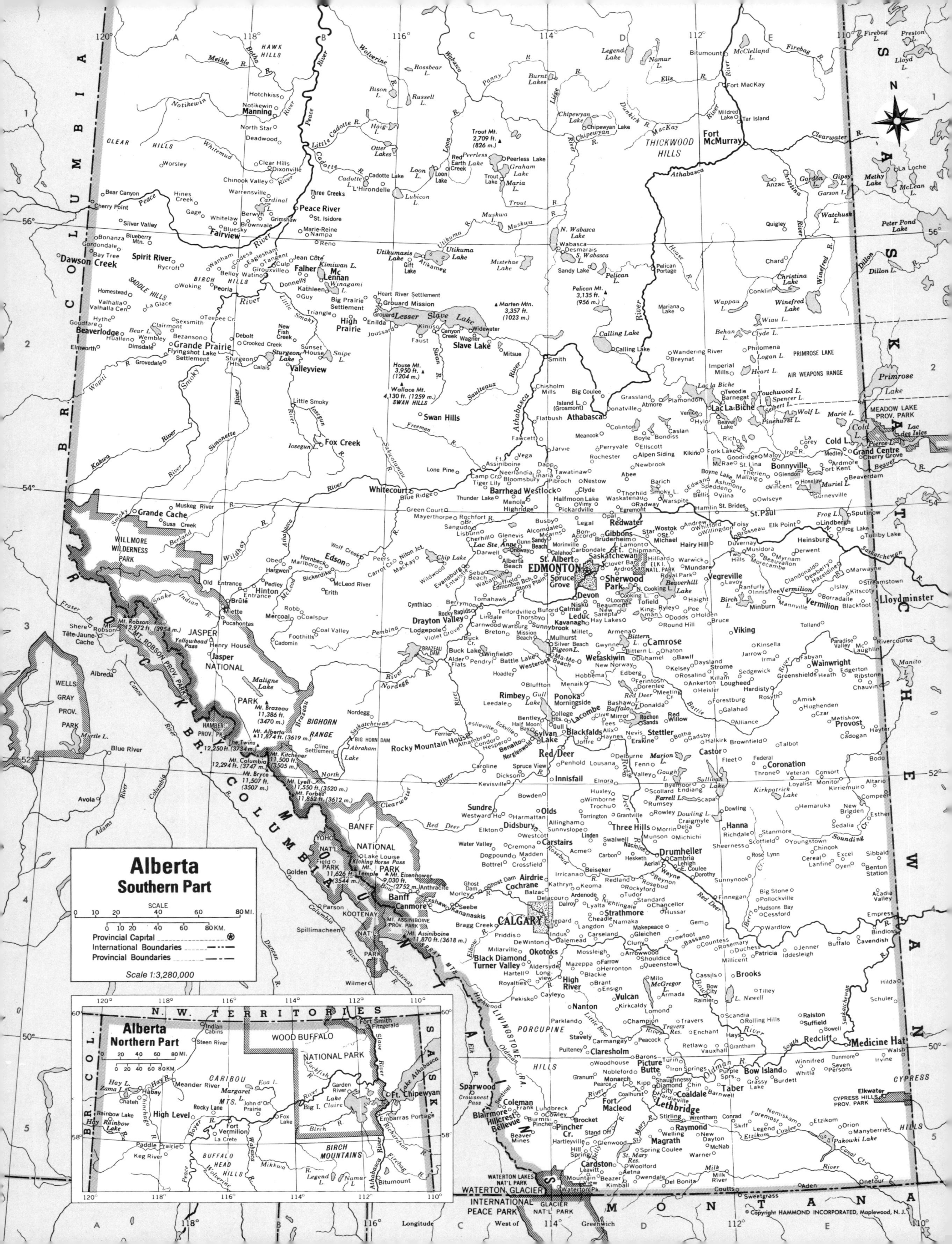

Alberta
Southern Part
SCALE
0 10 20 40 60 80 MI.
0 10 20 40 60 80 KM.
Provincial Capital
International Boundaries
Provincial Boundaries
Scale 1:3,280,000
Alberta
Northern Part
N. W. TERRITORIES
WOOD BUFFALO
NATIONAL PARK
CARIBOU MTS.
BIRCH MOUNTAINS
BUFFALO HEAD HILLS
High Level
Fort Chipewyan
Fort Smith
Fitzgerald
Fort Vermilion
Lake Claire
Lake Athabasca
Bitumount
BRITISH COLUMBIA
SASKATCHEWAN
MONTANA
EDMONTON
CALGARY
Red Deer
Lethbridge
Medicine Hat
Grande Prairie
Peace River
Fort McMurray
Athabasca
Lac La Biche
Lloydminster
Jasper
Banff
Canmore
Drumheller
Camrose
Wetaskiwin
Lacombe
Ponoka
St. Albert
Sherwood Park
Spruce Grove
Whitecourt
Slave Lake
Lesser Slave Lake
Swan Hills
Hinton
Edson
Grande Cache
Fox Creek
Valleyview
High Prairie
Manning
Fairview
Spirit River
Dawson Creek
Beaverlodge
Vermilion
Wainwright
Vegreville
St. Paul
Bonnyville
Cold Lake
Hanna
Brooks
Taber
Cardston
Pincher Cr.
Fort Macleod
Claresholm
High River
Okotoks
Airdrie
Cochrane
Olds
Innisfail
Stettler
Coronation
Provost
Rocky Mountain House
Drayton Valley
Stony Plain
Devon
Leduc
Westlock
Barrhead
Redwater
JASPER NATIONAL PARK
BANFF NATIONAL PARK
WILLMORE WILDERNESS PARK
ELK I. NAT'L PARK
WATERTON LAKES NAT'L PARK
WATERTON GLACIER INTERNATIONAL PEACE PARK
GLACIER NAT'L PARK
CYPRESS HILLS PROV. PARK
MEADOW LAKE PROV. PARK
WELLS GRAY PROV. PARK
Mt. Robson 12,972 ft. (3954 m.)
Mt. Columbia 12,294 ft. (3747 m.)
Mt. Alberta 11,874 ft. (3619 m.)
Mt. Assiniboine 11,870 ft. (3618 m.)
Mt. Forbes 11,852 ft. (3612 m.)
Mt. Brazeau 11,386 ft. (3470 m.)
Mt. Kitchener 11,500 ft. (3505 m.)
Mt. Bryce 11,507 ft. (3507 m.)
Mt. Lyell 11,550 ft. (3520 m.)
Trout Mt. 2,709 ft. (826 m.)
Marten Mtn. 3,357 ft. (1023 m.)
Pelican Mt. 3,135 ft. (956 m.)
House Mt. 3,950 ft. (1204 m.)
Wallace Mt. 4,130 ft. (1259 m.)
Peace River
Athabasca River
North Saskatchewan River
Red Deer River
Bow River
Oldman River
South Saskatchewan River
Milk River
Smoky River
Hay River
Clearwater R.
Beaver R.
Battle R.
PORCUPINE HILLS
THICKWOOD HILLS
CLEAR HILLS
BIRCH HILLS
SADDLE HILLS
HAWK HILLS
SWAN HILLS
PRIMROSE LAKE AIR WEAPONS RANGE
Longitude West of Greenwich
© Copyright HAMMOND INCORPORATED, Maplewood, N. J.

AREA 255,285 sq. mi. (661,185 sq. km.)
POPULATION 2,237,724
CAPITAL Edmonton
LARGEST CITY Edmonton
HIGHEST POINT Mt. Columbia 12,294 ft. (3,747 m.)
SETTLED IN 1861
ADMITTED TO CONFEDERATION 1905
PROVINCIAL FLOWER Wild Rose

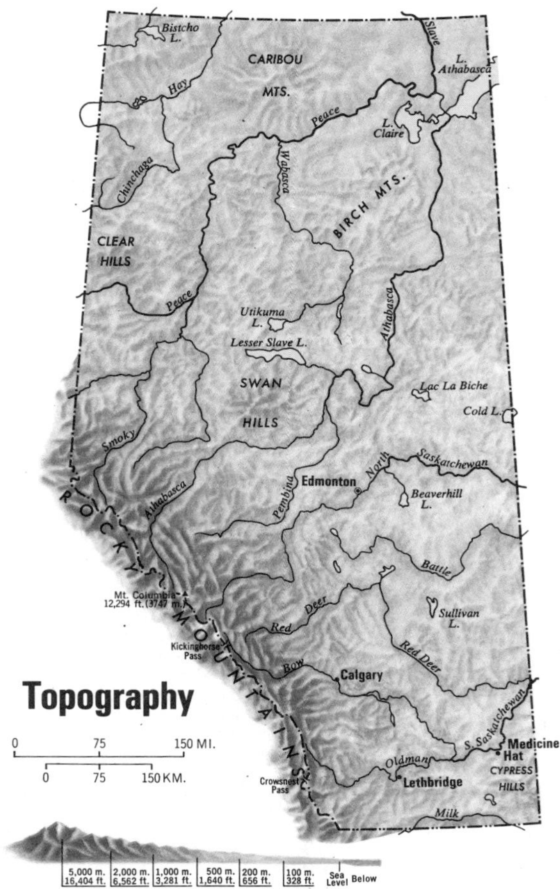

Topography

CITIES and TOWNS

Acme 457 . . . . . D 4
Airdrie 8,414 . . . . . C 4
Alberta Beach 485 . . . . . C 3
Alix 837 . . . . . D 3
Andrew 548 . . . . . D 3
Antler Lake 334 . . . . . D 3
Ardmore 224 . . . . . E 2
Arrowwood 156 . . . . . D 4
Athabasca 1,731 . . . . . D 2
Banff 4,208 . . . . . C 4
Barnwell 359 . . . . . D 5
Barons 315 . . . . . D 4
Barrhead 3,736 . . . . . C 2
Bashaw 875 . . . . . D 3
Bassano 1,200 . . . . . D 4
Bawlf 350 . . . . . D 3
Beaumont 2,638 . . . . . D 3
Beaverlodge 1,937 . . . . . A 2
Beiseker 580 . . . . . D 4
Bentley 823 . . . . . C 3
Berwyn 557 . . . . . B 1
Big Valley 360 . . . . . D 3
Black Diamond 1,444 . . . . . C 4
Blackfalds 1,488 . . . . . D 3
Blackfoot 220 . . . . . E 3
Blackie 298 . . . . . D 4
Bon Accord 1,376 . . . . . D 3
Bonnyville 4,454 . . . . . E 2
Bowden 989 . . . . . C 4
Bow Island 1,491 . . . . . E 5
Boyle 638 . . . . . D 2
Bragg Creek 505 . . . . . C 4
Breton 552 . . . . . C 3
Brooks 9,421 . . . . . E 4
Bruce 88 . . . . . E 3
Bruderheim 1,136 . . . . . D 3
Burdett 220 . . . . . E 5
Calgary 592,743 . . . . . C 4
Calgary *592,743 . . . . . C 4
Calmar 1,003 . . . . . D 3
Camrose 12,570 . . . . . D 3
Canmore 3,484 . . . . . C 4
Carbon 434 . . . . . D 4
Cardston 3,267 . . . . . D 5
Carmangay 266 . . . . . D 4
Caroline 436 . . . . . C 3
Carseland 484 . . . . . D 4
Carstairs 1,587 . . . . . D 4
Castor 1,123 . . . . . D 3
Cereal 249 . . . . . E 4
Champion 339 . . . . . D 4
Chauvin 298 . . . . . E 3
Chipman 266 . . . . . D 3
Clairmont 469 . . . . . A 2
Claresholm 3,493 . . . . . D 4
Clive 364 . . . . . D 3
Clyde 364 . . . . . D 2
Coaldale 4,579 . . . . . D 5
Coalhurst 882 . . . . . D 5
Cochrane 3,544 . . . . . C 4
Cold Lake 2,110 . . . . . E 2
College Heights 267 . . . . . D 3
Consort 632 . . . . . E 3
Cooking Lake 218 . . . . . D 3
Coronation 1,309 . . . . . E 3
Coutts 400 . . . . . D 5
Cowley 304 . . . . . D 5
Cremona 382 . . . . . C 4
Crossfield 1,217 . . . . . C 4
Daysland 679 . . . . . D 3
Delburne 574 . . . . . D 3
Desmarais 260 . . . . . D 2
Devon 3,885 . . . . . D 3
Didsbury 3,095 . . . . . C 4
Donalda 280 . . . . . D 3
Donnelly 336 . . . . . B 2
Drayton Valley 5,042 . . . . . C 3
Drumheller 6,508 . . . . . D 4
Duchess 429 . . . . . E 4
East Coulee 218 . . . . . D 4
Eckville 870 . . . . . C 3
Edgerton 387 . . . . . E 3
Edmonton (cap.) 532,246 . . . . . D 3
Edmonton *657,057 . . . . . D 3
Edmonton Beach 280 . . . . . C 3
Edson 5,835 . . . . . B 3
Elk Point 1,022 . . . . . E 3
Elnora 249 . . . . . D 3
Entwistle 462 . . . . . C 3
Erskine 259 . . . . . D 3
Evansburg 779 . . . . . C 3
Exshaw 353 . . . . . C 4
Fairview 2,869 . . . . . A 1
Falher 1,102 . . . . . B 2
Faust 399 . . . . . C 2
Foremost 568 . . . . . E 5
Forestburg 924 . . . . . D 3
Fort Assiniboine 207 . . . . . C 2
Fort Chipewyan 944 . . . . . C 5
Fort Macleod 3,139 . . . . . D 5
Fort McKay 267 . . . . . E 1
Fort McMurray 31,000 . . . . . E 1
Fort Saskatchewan 12,169 . . . . . D 3
Fort Vermilion 752 . . . . . B 5
Fox Creek 1,978 . . . . . B 2
Fox Lake 634 . . . . . B 5
Gibbons 2,276 . . . . . D 3
Gift Lake 428 . . . . . C 2
Girouxville 325 . . . . . B 2
Gleichen 381 . . . . . D 4
Glendon 430 . . . . . E 2
Glenwood 259 . . . . . D 5
Grand Centre 3,146 . . . . . E 2
Grande Cache 4,523 . . . . . A 3
Grande Prairie 24,263 . . . . . A 2
Granum 399 . . . . . D 5
Grimshaw 2,316 . . . . . B 1
Grouard Mission 221 . . . . . C 2
Hanna 2,806 . . . . . E 4
Hardisty 641 . . . . . E 3
Hay Lakes 302 . . . . . D 3
Heisler 212 . . . . . D 3
High Level 2,194 . . . . . A 5
High Prairie 2,506 . . . . . B 2
High River 4,792 . . . . . D 4
Hines Creek 575 . . . . . A 1
Hinton 8,342 . . . . . B 3
Holden 430 . . . . . D 3
Hughenden 267 . . . . . E 3
Hythe 639 . . . . . A 2
Innisfail 5,247 . . . . . D 3
Innisfree 255 . . . . . E 3
Irma 474 . . . . . E 3
Irricana 558 . . . . . D 4
Irvine 360 . . . . . E 5
Jasper 3,269 . . . . . B 3
John d'Or Prairie 437 . . . . . B 5
Joussard 330 . . . . . B 2
Killam 1,005 . . . . . E 3
Kinuso 285 . . . . . C 2
Kitscoty 497 . . . . . E 3
Lac La Biche 2,007 . . . . . E 2
Lacombe 5,591 . . . . . D 3
La Crete 479 . . . . . B 5
Lake Louise 355 . . . . . B 4
Lamont 1,563 . . . . . D 3
Leduc 12,471 . . . . . D 3
Legal 1,022 . . . . . D 3
Lethbridge 54,072 . . . . . D 5
Linden 407 . . . . . D 4
Little Buffalo Lake 253 . . . . . B 1
Lloydminster 8,997 . . . . . E 3
Longview 301 . . . . . C 4
Lougheed 226 . . . . . E 3
Lundbreck 244 . . . . . C 5
Magrath 1,576 . . . . . D 5
Manning 1,173 . . . . . B 1
Mannville 788 . . . . . E 3
Marlboro 211 . . . . . B 3
Marwayne 500 . . . . . E 3
Mayerthorpe 1,475 . . . . . C 3
McLennan 1,125 . . . . . B 2
Medicine Hat 40,380 . . . . . E 4
Milk River 894 . . . . . D 5
Millet 1,120 . . . . . D 3
Mirror 507 . . . . . D 3
Monarch 212 . . . . . D 5
Morinville 4,657 . . . . . D 3
Morrin 244 . . . . . D 4
Mundare 604 . . . . . D 3
Myrnam 397 . . . . . E 3
Nacmine 369 . . . . . D 4
Nampa 334 . . . . . B 1
Nanton 1,641 . . . . . D 4
New Norway 291 . . . . . D 3
New Sarepta 417 . . . . . D 3
Nobleford 534 . . . . . D 5
North Calling Lake 234 . . . . . D 2
Okotoks 3,847 . . . . . C 4
Olds 4,813 . . . . . D 4
Onoway 621 . . . . . C 3
Oyen 975 . . . . . E 4
Peace River 5,907 . . . . . B 1
Penhold 1,531 . . . . . D 3
Picture Butte 1,404 . . . . . D 5
Pincher Creek 3,757 . . . . . D 5
Plamondon 259 . . . . . D 2
Pollockville 19 . . . . . E 4
Ponoka 5,221 . . . . . D 3
Provost 1,645 . . . . . E 3
Rainbow Lake 504 . . . . . A 5
Ralston 357 . . . . . E 4
Raymond 2,837 . . . . . D 5
Redcliff 3,876 . . . . . E 4
Red Deer 46,393 . . . . . D 3
Redwater 1,932 . . . . . D 3
Rimbey 1,685 . . . . . C 3
Robb 230 . . . . . B 3
Rockyford 329 . . . . . D 4
Rocky Mountain House 4,698 . C 3
Rosemary 328 . . . . . E 4
Rycroft 649 . . . . . A 2
Ryley 483 . . . . . D 3
Saint Albert 31,996 . . . . . D 3
Saint Paul 4,884 . . . . . E 3
Sangudo 398 . . . . . C 3
Sedgewick 879 . . . . . E 3
Sexsmith 1,180 . . . . . A 2
Shaughnessy 270 . . . . . D 5
Sherwood Park 29,285 . . . . . D 3
Slave Lake 4,506 . . . . . C 2
Smith 216 . . . . . D 2
Smoky Lake 1,074 . . . . . D 2
Spirit River 1,104 . . . . . A 2
Spruce Grove 10,326 . . . . . D 3
Standard 379 . . . . . D 4
Stavely 504 . . . . . D 4
Stettler 5,136 . . . . . D 3
Stirling 688 . . . . . D 5
Stony Plain 4,839 . . . . . C 3
Strathmore 2,986 . . . . . D 4
Strome 281 . . . . . E 3
Sundre 1,742 . . . . . C 4
Swan Hills 2,497 . . . . . C 2
Sylvan Lake 3,779 . . . . . C 3
Taber 5,988 . . . . . E 5
Thorhild 576 . . . . . D 2
Thorsby 737 . . . . . C 3
Three Hills 1,787 . . . . . D 4
Tilley 345 . . . . . E 4
Tofield 1,504 . . . . . D 3
Trochu 880 . . . . . D 4
Turner Valley 1,311 . . . . . C 4
Two Hills 1,193 . . . . . E 3
Valleyview 2,061 . . . . . B 2
Vauxhall 1,049 . . . . . D 4
Vegreville 5,251 . . . . . E 3
Vermilion 3,766 . . . . . E 3
Veteran 314 . . . . . E 3
Viking 1,232 . . . . . E 3
Vilna 345 . . . . . E 2
Vulcan 1,489 . . . . . D 4
Wabamun 662 . . . . . C 3
Wabasca 701 . . . . . D 2
Wainwright 4,266 . . . . . E 3
Warburg 501 . . . . . C 3
Warner 477 . . . . . D 5
Waskatenau 290 . . . . . D 2
Wembley 1,169 . . . . . A 2
Westlock 4,424 . . . . . C 2
Wetaskiwin 9,597 . . . . . D 3
Whitecourt 5,585 . . . . . C 2
Wildwood 441 . . . . . C 3
Willingdon 366 . . . . . E 3
Youngstown 297 . . . . . E 4

OTHER FEATURES

Abraham (lake) . . . . . B 3
Alberta (mt.) . . . . . B 3
Assiniboine (mt.) . . . . . C 4
Athabasca (lake) . . . . . C 5
Athabasca (riv.) . . . . . D 1
Banff Nat'l Park . . . . . B 4
Battle (riv.) . . . . . D 3
Bear (lake) . . . . . A 2
Beaver (riv.) . . . . . E 2
Beaverhill (lake) . . . . . D 3
Behan (lake) . . . . . E 2
Belly (riv.) . . . . . D 5
Berland (riv.) . . . . . A 3
Berry (creek) . . . . . E 4
Biche (lake) . . . . . E 2
Big (isl.) . . . . . B 5
Big Horn (dam) . . . . . B 3
Bighorn (range) . . . . . B 3
Birch (hills) . . . . . A 2
Birch (lake) . . . . . E 3
Birch (mts.) . . . . . B 5
Birch (riv.) . . . . . B 5
Bison (lake) . . . . . B 1
Bittern (lake) . . . . . D 3
Botha (riv.) . . . . . B 1
Bow (riv.) . . . . . D 4
Boyer (riv.) . . . . . A 5
Brazeau (mt.) . . . . . B 3
Brazeau (riv.) . . . . . B 3
Buffalo (lake) . . . . . D 3
Buffalo Head (hills) . . . . . B 5
Burnt (lakes) . . . . . C 1
Cadotte (lake) . . . . . B 1
Cadotte (riv.) . . . . . B 1
Calling (lake) . . . . . D 2
Canal (creek) . . . . . E 5
Cardinal (lake) . . . . . B 1
Caribou (mts.) . . . . . B 5
Chinchaga (riv.) . . . . . A 5
Chip (lake) . . . . . C 3
Chipewyan (lake) . . . . . D 1
Chipewyan (riv.) . . . . . D 1
Christina (lake) . . . . . E 2
Christina (riv.) . . . . . E 1
Claire (lake) . . . . . B 5
Clear (hills) . . . . . A 1
Clearwater (riv.) . . . . . C 4
Clearwater (riv.) . . . . . E 1
Clyde (lake) . . . . . E 2
Cold (lake) . . . . . E 2
Columbia (mt.) . . . . . B 3
Crowsnest (pass) . . . . . C 5
Cypress (hills) . . . . . E 5
Cypress Hills Prov. Park . . . . . E 5
Dillon (riv.) . . . . . E 2
Dowling (lake) . . . . . D 4
Dunkirk (riv.) . . . . . D 1
Eisenhower (mt.) . . . . . C 4
Elbow (riv.) . . . . . C 4
Elk Island Nat'l Park . . . . . D 3
Ells (riv.) . . . . . D 1
Etzikom Coulee (riv.) . . . . . E 5
Eva (lake) . . . . . B 5
Farrell (lake) . . . . . D 4
Firebag (riv.) . . . . . E 1
Forbes (mt.) . . . . . B 4
Freeman (riv.) . . . . . C 2
Frog (lake) . . . . . E 3
Garson (lake) . . . . . E 1
Gipsy (lake) . . . . . E 1
Gordon (lake) . . . . . E 1
Gough (lake) . . . . . D 3
Graham (lake) . . . . . C 1
Gull (lake) . . . . . C 3
Haig (lake) . . . . . B 1
Hawk (hills) . . . . . B 1
Hay (lake) . . . . . A 5
Hay (riv.) . . . . . A 5
Heart (lake) . . . . . E 2
Highwood (riv.) . . . . . C 4
House (mt.) . . . . . C 2
House (riv.) . . . . . D 2
Iosegun (lake) . . . . . B 2
Iosegun (riv.) . . . . . B 2
Jackfish (riv.) . . . . . B 5
Jasper Nat'l Park . . . . . A 3
Kakwa (riv.) . . . . . A 2
Kickinghorse (pass) . . . . . B 4
Kimiwan (lake) . . . . . B 2
Kirkpatrick (lake) . . . . . E 4
Kitchener (mt.) . . . . . B 3
Legend (lake) . . . . . D 1
Lesser Slave (lake) . . . . . C 2
Liége (riv.) . . . . . D 1
Little Bow (riv.) . . . . . D 4
Little Cadotte (riv.) . . . . . B 1
Little Smoky (riv.) . . . . . B 2
Livingstone (range) . . . . . C 4
Logan (lake) . . . . . E 2
Loon (lake) . . . . . C 1
Loon (riv.) . . . . . C 1
Lubicon (lake) . . . . . C 1
Lyell (mt.) . . . . . B 4
MacKay (riv.) . . . . . D 1
Maligne (lake) . . . . . B 3
Margaret (lake) . . . . . B 5
Marie (lake) . . . . . E 2
Marion (lake) . . . . . D 3
Marten (mt.) . . . . . C 2
McClelland (lake) . . . . . E 1
McGregor (lake) . . . . . D 4
McLeod (riv.) . . . . . B 3
Meikle (riv.) . . . . . A 1
Mikkwa (riv.) . . . . . B 5
Milk (riv.) . . . . . D 5
Mistehae (lake) . . . . . C 2
Muriel (lake) . . . . . E 2
Muskwa (lake) . . . . . C 1
Muskwa (riv.) . . . . . C 1
Namur (lake) . . . . . D 1
Newell (lake) . . . . . E 4
Nordegg (riv.) . . . . . C 3
North Saskatchewan (riv.) . . . . . E 3
North Wabasca (lake) . . . . . D 1
Notikewin (riv.) . . . . . A 1
Oldman (riv.) . . . . . D 5
Otter (lakes) . . . . . B 1
Pakowki (lake) . . . . . E 5
Panny (riv.) . . . . . C 1
Peace (riv.) . . . . . B 1
Peerless (lake) . . . . . C 1
Pelican (lake) . . . . . D 2
Pelican (mts.) . . . . . D 2
Pembina (riv.) . . . . . C 3
Pigeon (lake) . . . . . D 3
Pinehurst (lake) . . . . . E 2
Porcupine (hills) . . . . . C 4
Primrose (lake) . . . . . E 2
Rainbow (lake) . . . . . A 5
Red Deer (lake) . . . . . D 3
Red Deer (riv.) . . . . . D 4
Richardson (riv.) . . . . . C 5
Rocky (mts.) . . . . . B-C 4
Rosebud (riv.) . . . . . D 4
Russell (lake) . . . . . C 1
Saddle (hills) . . . . . A 2
Sainte Anne (lake) . . . . . C 3
Saint Mary (res.) . . . . . D 5
Saint Mary (riv.) . . . . . D 5
Saulteaux (riv.) . . . . . C 2
Seibert (lake) . . . . . E 2
Simonette (riv.) . . . . . A 2
Slave (riv.) . . . . . C 5
Smoky (riv.) . . . . . A 2
Snake Indian (riv.) . . . . . A 3
Snipe (lake) . . . . . B 2
Sounding (creek) . . . . . E 4
South Saskatchewan (riv.) . . . . . E 4
South Wabasca (lake) . . . . . D 2
Spencer (lake) . . . . . E 2
Spray (mts.) . . . . . C 4
Sturgeon (lake) . . . . . B 2
Sullivan (lake) . . . . . D 3
Swan (hills) . . . . . C 2
Swan (riv.) . . . . . C 2
Temple (mt.) . . . . . B 4
The Twins (mt.) . . . . . B 3
Thickwood (hills) . . . . . D 1
Touchwood (lake) . . . . . E 2
Travers (res.) . . . . . D 4
Trout (mt.) . . . . . C 1
Trout (riv.) . . . . . C 1
Utikuma (lake) . . . . . C 2
Utikuma (riv.) . . . . . C 1
Utikumasis (lake) . . . . . C 2
Vermilion (riv.) . . . . . E 3
Wabasca (riv.) . . . . . C 1
Wallace (mt.) . . . . . C 2
Wapiti (riv.) . . . . . A 2
Wappau (lake) . . . . . E 2
Watchusk (lake) . . . . . E 1
Waterton-Glacier Int'l Peace Park . . . . . C 5
Waterton Lakes Nat'l Park . . . . . C 5
Whitemud (riv.) . . . . . A 1
Wildhay (riv.) . . . . . B 3
Willmore Wilderness Prov. Park . . . . . A 3
Winagami (lake) . . . . . B 2
Winefred (lake) . . . . . E 2
Winefred (riv.) . . . . . E 2
Wolf (lake) . . . . . E 2
Wolverine (riv.) . . . . . B 1
Wood Buffalo Nat'l Park . . . . . B 5
Yellowhead (pass) . . . . . A 3
Zama (lake) . . . . . A 5

*Population of metropolitan area.

Agriculture, Industry and Resources

DOMINANT LAND USE

- Wheat
- Cereals (chiefly barley, oats)
- Cereals, Livestock
- Dairy
- Pasture Livestock
- Range Livestock
- Forests
- Nonagricultural Land

MAJOR MINERAL OCCURRENCES

- C Coal
- G Natural Gas
- Na Salt
- O Petroleum
- S Sulfur
- Water Power
- Major Industrial Areas

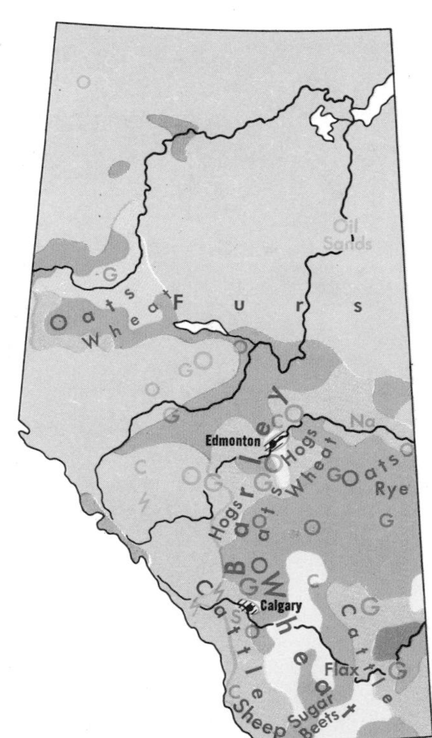

CITIES and TOWNS

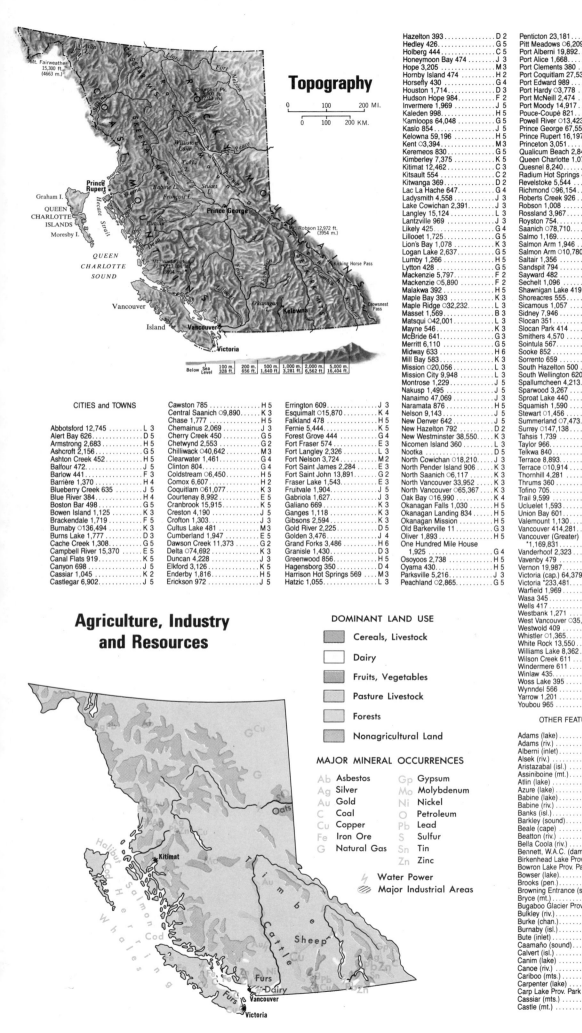

Abbotsford 12,745 L 3
Alert Bay 626 D 5
Armstrong 2,683 H 5
Ashcroft 2,156 G 5
Ashton Creek 452 H 5
Balfour 472 J 5
Barlow 441 F 3
Barrière 1,370 H 4
Blueberry Creek 635 J 5
Blue River 384 H 4
Boston Bar 498 G 5
Bowen Island 1,125 K 3
Brackendale 1,719 F 5
Burnaby ○136,494 K 3
Burns Lake 1,777 D 3
Cache Creek 1,308 G 5
Campbell River 15,370 E 5
Canal Flats 919 K 5
Canyon 698 J 5
Cassiar 1,045 K 2
Castlegar 6,902 J 5
Cawston 785 H 5
Central Saanich ○9,890 K 3
Chase 1,777 H 5
Chemainus 2,069 J 3
Cherry Creek 450 G 5
Chetwynd 2,553 G 2
Chilliwack ○40,642 M 3
Clearwater 1,461 G 4
Clinton 804 G 4
Coldstream ○6,450 H 5
Comox 6,607 H 2
Coquitlam ○61,077 K 3
Courtenay 8,992 E 5
Cranbrook 15,915 K 5
Creston 4,190 J 5
Crofton 1,303 J 3
Cultus Lake 481 M 3
Cumberland 1,947 E 5
Dawson Creek 11,373 G 2
Delta ○74,692 K 3
Duncan 4,228 J 3
Elkford 3,126 K 5
Enderby 1,816 H 5
Erickson 972 J 5
Errington 609 J 3
Esquimalt ○15,870 K 4
Falkland 478 H 5
Fernie 5,444 K 5
Forest Grove 444 G 4
Fort Fraser 574 E 3
Fort Langley 2,326 L 3
Fort Nelson 3,724 M 2
Fort Saint James 2,284 E 3
Fort Saint John 13,891 G 2
Fraser Lake 1,543 E 3
Fruitvale 1,904 J 5
Gabriola 1,627 J 3
Galiano 669 K 3
Ganges 1,118 K 3
Gibsons 2,594 K 3
Gold River 2,225 D 5
Golden 3,476 J 4
Grand Forks 3,486 H 6
Granisle 1,430 D 3
Greenwood 856 H 5
Hagensborg 350 D 4
Harrison Hot Springs 569 M 3
Hatzic 1,055 L 3
Hazelton 393 D 2
Hedley 426 G 5
Holberg 444 C 5
Honeymoon Bay 474 J 3
Hope 3,205 M 3
Hornby Island 474 H 2
Horsefly 430 G 4
Houston 1,714 D 3
Hudson Hope 984 F 2
Invermere 1,969 J 5
Kaleden 998 H 5
Kamloops 64,048 G 5
Kaslo 854 J 5
Kelowna 59,196 H 5
Kent ○3,394 M 3
Keremeos 830 G 5
Kimberley 7,375 K 5
Kitimat 12,462 C 3
Kitsault 554 C 2
Kitwanga 369 D 2
Lac La Hache 647 G 4
Ladysmith 4,558 J 3
Lake Cowichan 2,391 J 3
Langley 15,124 L 3
Lantzville 969 J 3
Likely 425 G 4
Lillooet 1,725 G 5
Lion's Bay 1,078 K 3
Logan Lake 2,637 G 5
Lumby 1,266 H 5
Lytton 428 G 5
Mackenzie 5,797 F 2
Mackenzie ○5,890 F 2
Malakwa 392 H 5
Maple Bay 393 K 3
Maple Ridge ○32,232 L 3
Masset 1,569 B 3
Matsqui ○42,001 L 3
Mayne 546 K 3
McBride 641 G 3
Merritt 6,110 G 5
Midway 633 H 6
Mill Bay 583 K 3
Mission ○20,056 L 3
Mission City 9,948 L 3
Montrose 1,229 J 5
Nakusp 1,495 J 5
Nanaimo 47,069 J 3
Naramata 876 H 5
Nelson 9,143 J 5
New Denver 642 J 5
New Hazelton 792 D 2
New Westminster 38,550 K 3
Nicomen Island 360 L 3
Nootka D 5
North Cowichan ○18,210 J 3
North Pender Island 906 K 3
North Saanich ○6,117 K 3
North Vancouver 33,952 K 3
North Vancouver ○65,367 K 3
Oak Bay ○16,990 K 4
Okanagan Falls 1,030 H 5
Okanagan Landing 834 H 5
Okanagan Mission H 5
Old Barkerville 11 G 3
Oliver 1,893 H 5
One Hundred Mile House 1,925 G 4
Osoyoos 2,738 H 5
Oyama 430 H 5
Parksville 5,216 J 3
Peachland ○2,865 G 5
Penticton 23,181 H 5
Pitt Meadows ○6,209 L 3
Port Alberni 19,892 H 3
Port Alice 1,668 D 5
Port Clements 380 B 3
Port Coquitlam 27,535 L 3
Port Edward 989 B 3
Port Hardy ○3,778 D 5
Port McNeill 2,474 D 5
Port Moody 14,917 L 3
Pouce-Coupé 821 G 2
Powell River ○13,423 E 5
Prince George 67,559 F 3
Prince Rupert 16,197 B 3
Princeton 3,051 G 5
Qualicum Beach 2,844 J 3
Queen Charlotte 1,070 A 3
Quesnel 8,240 F 4
Radium Hot Springs 419 J 5
Revelstoke 5,544 J 5
Richmond ○96,154 K 3
Roberts Creek 926 J 3
Robson 1,008 J 5
Rossland 3,967 H 6
Royston 754 H 2
Saanich ○78,710 K 3
Salmo 1,169 J 5
Salmon Arm 1,946 H 5
Salmon Arm ○10,780 H 5
Saltair 1,356 J 3
Sandspit 794 B 3
Sayward 482 D 5
Sechelt 1,096 J 2
Shawnigan Lake 419 J 3
Shoreacres 555 J 5
Sicamous 1,057 H 5
Sidney 7,946 K 3
Slocan 351 J 5
Slocan Park 414 J 5
Smithers 4,570 D 3
Sointula 567 D 5
Sooke 852 J 4
Sorrento 659 H 5
South Hazelton 500 D 2
South Wellington 620 J 3
Spallumcheen 4,213 H 5
Sparwood 3,267 K 5
Sproat Lake 440 H 3
Squamish 1,590 F 5
Stewart ○1,456 C 2
Summerland ○7,473 G 5
Surrey ○147,138 K 3
Tahsis 1,739 D 5
Taylor 966 G 2
Telkwa 840 D 3
Terrace 8,893 C 3
Terrace ○10,914 C 3
Thornhill 4,281 C 3
Thrums 360 J 5
Tofino 705 E 5
Trail 9,599 J 6
Ucluelet 1,593 E 6
Union Bay 601 H 2
Valemount 1,130 H 4
Vancouver 414,281 K 3
Vancouver (Greater) *1,169,831 K 3
Vanderhoof 2,323 E 3
Vavenby 479 H 4
Vernon 19,987 H 5
Victoria (cap.) 64,379 K 4
Victoria *233,481 K 4
Warfield 1,969 J 5
Wasa 345 K 5
Wells 417 G 3
Westbank 1,271 H 5
West Vancouver ○35,728 K 3
Westwold 409 G 5
Whistler ○1,365 F 5
White Rock 13,550 K 3
Williams Lake 8,362 F 4
Wilson Creek 611 J 2
Windermere 611 K 5
Winlaw 435 J 5
Woss Lake 395 D 5
Wynndel 566 J 5
Yarrow 1,201 M 3
Youbou 965 J 3

OTHER FEATURES

Adams (lake) H 4
Adams (riv.) H 4
Alberni (inlet) H 3
Alsek (riv.) H 1
Aristazabal (isl.) C 4
Assiniboine (mt.) K 5
Atlin (lake) J 1
Azure (lake) G 4
Babine (lake) E 3
Babine (riv.) D 2
Banks (isl.) B 3
Barkley (sound) E 6
Beale (cape) E 6
Beatton (riv.) G 1
Bella Coola (riv.) D 4
Bennett, W.A.C. (dam) F 2
Birkenhead Lake Prov. Park F 5
Bowron Lake Prov. Park G 3
Bowser (lake) C 2
Brooks (pen.) D 5
Browning Entrance (str.) B 3
Bryce (mt.) J 4
Bugaboo Glacier Prov. Park J 5
Bulkley (riv.) D 2
Burke (chan.) D 4
Burnaby (isl.) B 4
Bute (inlet) E 5
Caamaño (sound) C 4
Calvert (isl.) C 4
Canim (lake) G 4
Canoe (riv.) H 4
Cariboo (mts.) G 3
Carpenter (lake) F 5
Carp Lake Prov. Park F 3
Cassiar (mts.) K 2
Castle (mt.) A 2
Charlotte (lake) E 4
Chatham (sound) B 3
Chehalis (lake) L 3
Chilcotin (riv.) E 4
Chilko (lake) F 4
Chilko (riv.) E 4
Chilkoot (pass) J 1
Chuchi (lake) E 2
Churchill (peak) L 2
Clayoquot (sound) D 5
Clearwater (lake) G 4
Clearwater (riv.) G 4
Coast (mts.) D 3
Columbia (lake) K 5
Columbia (mt.) J 4
Columbia (riv.) H 4
Cook (cape) C 5
Cowichan (lake) J 3
Crowsnest (pass) K 5
Cypress Prov. Park K 3
Dean (chan.) D 4
Dean (riv.) D 4
Dease (lake) K 2
Dease (riv.) K 2
Devils Thumb (mt.) A 1
Dixon Entrance (chan.) A 3
Douglas (chan.) C 3
Duncan (riv.) J 5
Dundas (isl.) B 3
Elk (riv.) K 5
Elk Lakes Prov. Park K 5
Eutsuk (lake) D 3
Fairweather (mt.) H 1
Cathedral Prov. Park H 5
Finlay (riv.) E 1
Fitzhugh (sound) D 4
Flathead (riv.) K 6
Flores (isl.) D 5
Fontas (riv.) M 2
Forbes (mt.) J 4
Fort Nelson (riv.) M 2
François (lake) D 3
Fraser (lake) E 3
Fraser (riv.) F 4
Fraser Reach (chan.) C 3
Galiano (isl.) K 3
Gardner (canal) C 3
Garibaldi Prov. Park F 5
Georgia (str.) J 3
Germansen (lake) E 2
Gil (isl.) C 3
Glacier Nat'l Park J 4
Golden Ears Prov. Park L 2
Gordon (riv.) H 3
Graham (isl.) A 3
Graham Reach (chan.) C 3
Grenville (chan.) C 3
Halfway (riv.) F 2
Hamber Prov. Park H 4
Harrison (lake) M 2
Hawkesbury (isl.) C 3
Hazelton (mts.) C 2
Hecate (str.) B 3
Hobson (lake) H 4
Homathko (riv.) E 4
Horsefly (lake) G 4

Agriculture, Industry and Resources

DOMINANT LAND USE

Cereals, Livestock
Dairy
Fruits, Vegetables
Pasture Livestock
Forests
Nonagricultural Land

MAJOR MINERAL OCCURRENCES

Ab Asbestos
Ag Silver
Au Gold
C Coal
Cu Copper
Fe Iron Ore
G Natural Gas
Gp Gypsum
Mo Molybdenum
Ni Nickel
O Petroleum
Pb Lead
S Sulfur
Sn Tin
Zn Zinc

Water Power
Major Industrial Areas

Kitimat
Oats
Timber
Cattle
Sheep
Furs
Dairy
Vancouver
Victoria
Halibut
Cod
Salmon
Herring
Whales

Howe (sound) K 2
Hunter (isl.) C 4
Inklin (riv.) J 2
Inzana (lake) E 3
Isaac (lake) G 3
Iskut (riv.) B 2
Jervis (inlet) E 5
John Jay (mt.) B 2
Johnstone (str.) D 5
Juan de Fuca (str.) J 4
Kates Needle (mt.) A 1
Kechika (riv.) L 2
Kenney (dam) E 3
Kettle (riv.) H 5
Kicking Horse (pass) J 4
King (isl.) D 4
Klinaklini (riv.) E 4
Kloch (lake) E 2
Knight (inlet) E 5
Knox (cape) A 3
Kokanee Glacier Prov. Park J 5
Koocanusa (lake) K 6
Kootenay (lake) J 5
Kootenay (riv.) K 5
Kootenay Nat'l Park J 4
Kotcho (lake) M 2
Kotcho (riv.) M 2
Kunghit (isl.) B 4
Kyuquot (sound) D 5
Langara (isl.) A 3
Laredo (sound) C 4
Liard (riv.) L 2
Lillooet (riv.) F 5
Louise (isl.) B 4
Lower Arrow (lake) H 5
Lyell (isl.) B 4
Lyell (mt.) J 4
Mabel (lake) H 5
Mahood (lake) G 4
Malaspina (str.) J 2
Manning Prov. Park G 5
Masset (inlet) A 3
McCauley (isl.) B 3
McGregor (riv.) G 3
Meziadin (lake) C 2
Milbanke (sound) C 4
Moberly (lake) F 2
Monashee (mts.) H 4
Moresby (isl.) B 4
Morice (lake) D 3
Morice (riv.) D 3
Mount Assiniboine Prov. Park K 5
Mount Edziza Prov. Park and Rec. Area B 1
Mount Revelstoke Nat'l Park H 4
Mount Robson Prov. Park H 3
Muncho Lake Prov. Park L 2
Murray (riv.) G 3
Murtle (lake) H 4
Muskwa (riv.) M 2
Nanika (dam) D 3
Nass (riv.) C 2
Nation (riv.) F 2
Nechako (riv.) E 3
Nitinat (lake) H 3
Nootka (isl.) D 5
Nootka (sound) D 5
North Thompson (riv.) G 4
Observatory (inlet) C 2
Okanagan (lake) H 5
Okanagan Mtn. Prov. Park G 5
Okanogan (riv.) H 6
Omineca (mts.) E 2
Omineca (riv.) E 2
Ootsa (lake) D 3
Owikeno (lake) D 4
Pacific Rim Nat'l Park E 6
Parsnip (riv.) F 3
Peace (riv.) G 2
Pend Oreille (riv.) J 6
Petitot (riv.) M 2
Pinchi (lake) E 3
Pine (riv.) G 2
Pitt (isl.) C 3
Pitt (lake) L 2
Porcher (isl.) B 3
Portland (canal) B 2
Portland (inlet) C 3
Price (isl.) C 4
Princess Royal (isl.) C 3
Principe (chan.) C 3
Prophet (riv.) M 2
Purcell (mts.) J 5
Quatsino (sound) C 5
Queen Charlotte (isls.) B 3
Queen Charlotte (sound) C 4
Queen Charlotte (str.) D 5
Queens (sound) C 4
Quesnel (lake) G 4
Quesnel (riv.) F 4
Rivers (inlet) D 4
Robson (mt.) H 3
Rocky (mts.) F 2
Roderick (isl.) C 4
Rose (pt.) B 3
Saint James (cape) B 4
Salmon (riv.) F 3
Salmon Arm (inlet) J 2
San Juan (riv.) J 3
Schoen Lake Prov. Park E 5
Scott (cape) C 5
Scott (isls.) C 5
Seechelt (inlet) J 2
Seechelt (pen.) J 2
Selkirk (mts.) J 4
Seymour (inlet) D 4
Sheslay (riv.) J 2
Shuswap (lake) H 4
Sikanni Chief (riv.) F 1
Silver Star Prov. Park H 5
Sir Sandford (mt.) H 4
Skagit (riv.) G 6
Skeena (mts.) C 2
Skeena (riv.) C 3
Skidegate (inlet) B 3
Slocan (lake) J 5
Smith (sound) C 4
South Bentinck Arm (inlet) D 4
Stave (lake) L 3
Stephens (isl.) B 3
Stikine (riv.) B 1
Stone Mountain Prov. Park L 2

AREA 366,253 sq. mi. (948,596 sq. km.)
POPULATION 2,744,467
CAPITAL Victoria
LARGEST CITY Vancouver
HIGHEST POINT Mt. Fairweather 15,300 ft. (4,663 m.)
SETTLED IN 1806
ADMITTED TO CONFEDERATION 1871
PROVINCIAL FLOWER Dogwood

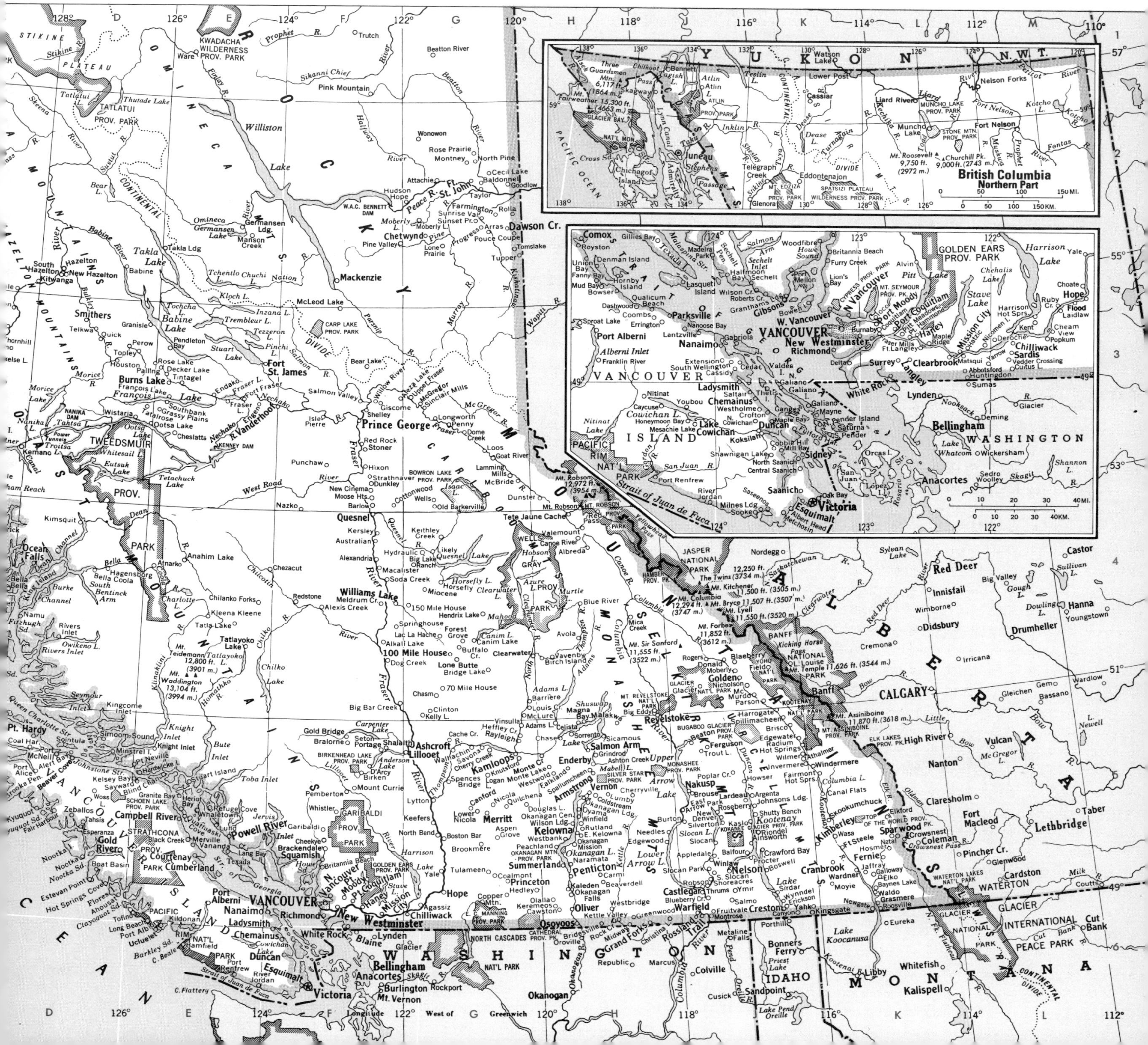

Strathcona Prov. Park E 5
Stuart (lake) E 3
Sustut (riv.) D 2
Tagish (lake) J 1
Tahtsa (lake) D 3
Takla (lake) D 2
Taku (riv.) J 2
Tatlatui (lake) D 2
Tatlayoko (lake) E 4
Tchentlo (lake) E 2
Teslin (lake) K 1
Tetachuck (lake) E 3
Texada (isl.) J 2
Tezzeron (lake) E 3
Thompson (riv.) G 5
Three Guardsmen (mt.) H 1
Thutade (lake) D 2
Tiedemann (mt.) E 4
Toad (riv.) L 2
Toba (inlet) E 5
Tochcha (lake) E 3
Top Of The World Prov. Park K 5
Trembleur (lake) E 3
Troitsa (lake) D 3
Tumeka (lake) C 1
Turnagain (riv.) K 2
Tuya (riv.) K 2
Tweedsmuir Prov. Park D 3
Upper Arrow (lake) H 5
Valdes (isl.) K 3
Vancouver (isl.) D 5
Virago (sound) A 3
Waddington (mt.) E 4
Wapiti (riv.) H 3
Wells Gray Prov. Park H 4
West Road (riv.) E 3
Whitesail (lake) D 3
Williston (lake) F 2
Work (chan.) C 3
Yellowhead (pass) H 4
Yoho Nat'l Park J 4

*Population of metropolitan area.
○Population of municipality.

NORTHWEST TERRITORIES

DISTRICTS

Baffin 8,300 . . . . . J2
Fort Smith 22,384 . . . . . G3
Inuvik 7,485 . . . . . F3
Keewatin 4,327 . . . . . J3
Kitikmeot 3,245 . . . . . G2

CITIES and TOWNS

Aklavik 721 . . . . . E3
Alert M1
Amadjuak L3
Arctic Bay 375 . . . . . K2
Arctic Red River 120 . . . . . E3
Baker Lake 954 . . . . . J3
Bathurst Inlet 20 . . . . . H3
Bay Chimo 60 . . . . . H3
Bell Rock G3
Broughton Island 378 . . . . . M3
Buffalo River Junction G3
Cambridge Bay 815 . . . . . H3
Cape Dorset 784 . . . . . L3
Cape Dyer M3
Cape Smith L3
Chesterfield Inlet 249 . . . . . K3
Clyde (Clyde River) 443 . . . . . M2
Colville Lake 57 . . . . . F3
Coppermine 809 . . . . . G3
Coral Harbour 429 . . . . . K3
Detah 143 . . . . . G3
Dory Point G3
Enterprise 46 . . . . . G3
Eskimo Point 1,022 . . . . . J3
Eureka K2
Fort Franklin 521 . . . . . F3
Fort Good Hope 463 . . . . . F3
Fort Liard 405 . . . . . F3
Fort McPherson 632 . . . . . E3
Fort Norman 286 . . . . . F3
Fort Providence 605 . . . . . G3
Fort Resolution 480 . . . . . G3
Fort Simpson 980 . . . . . F3
Fort Smith 2,298 . . . . . G4
Frobisher Bay 2,333 . . . . . M3
Gjoa Haven 523 . . . . . J3
Grise Fiord 106 . . . . . K2
Hall Beach 349 . . . . . K3
Hay River 2,863 . . . . . G3
Holman Island 300 . . . . . G2
Igloolik 746 . . . . . K3
Inuvik 3,147 . . . . . E3
Isachsen H2
Jean-Marie River 69 . . . . . F3
Kakisa 36 . . . . . G3
Kipisa 43 . . . . . M3
Lac la Martre 268 . . . . . G3
Lake Harbour 252 . . . . . L3
Mould Bay F2
Nahanni Butte 85 . . . . . F3
Nanisivik 261 . . . . . K2
Norman Wells 420 . . . . . F3
Pangnirtung 839 . . . . . M3
Paulatuk 174 . . . . . F3
Pelly Bay 257 . . . . . K3
Pine Point 1,861 . . . . . G3
Pond Inlet 705 . . . . . L2
Port Burwell M3
Port Radium 56 . . . . . G3
Rae-Edzo 1,378 . . . . . G3
Rae Lakes 200 . . . . . G3
Rankin Inlet 1,109 . . . . . G3
Reliance 15 . . . . . H3
Repulse Bay 352 . . . . . K3
Resolute Bay 168 . . . . . J2
Resolution Island M3
Rocher River G3
Sachs Harbour 161 . . . . . F2
Salt River G3
Sawmill Bay G3
Snare Lake 69 . . . . . G3
Snowdrift 253 . . . . . G3
Spence Bay 431 . . . . . J3
Trout Lake 59 . . . . . F3
Tuktoyaktuk 772 . . . . . E3
Tungsten 320 . . . . . F3
Whale Cove 188 . . . . . J3
Wrigley 137 . . . . . F3
Yellowknife (cap.) 9,483 . . . . . G3

OTHER FEATURES

Adelaide (pen.) J3
Admiralty (inlet) K2
Air Force (isl.) L3
Akpatok (isl.) M3
Amadjuak (lake) L3
Amund Ringnes (isl.) J2
Amundsen (gulf) F2
Anderson (riv.) F3
Arctic Red (riv.) E3
Artillery (lake) H3
Auyuittug Nat'l Park M3
Axel Heiberg (isl.) J2
Aylmer (lake) H3
Back (riv.) J3
Baffin (bay) M2
Baffin (isl.) L2
Baker (lake) J3
Banks (isl.) F2
Barbeau (peak) L1
Barrow (str.) J2
Bathurst (cape) F2
Bathurst (inlet) H3
Bathurst (isl.) H2
Beaufort (sea) D2
Bellot (str.) J2
Boothia (gulf) K3
Boothia (pen.) J2
Borden (isl.) G2
Borden (pen.) K2
Brodeur (pen.) K2
Bruce (mts.) L2
Buchan (gulf) L2
Burnside (riv.) G3
Byam Martin (chan.) H2
Byam Martin (isl.) H2
Bylot (isl.) L2
Camsell (riv.) G3
Challenger (mts.) L1
Chantrey (inlet) J3
Chesterfield (inlet) J3
Chidley (cape) M3
Clinton-Colden (lake) H3
Clyde (inlet) M2
Coats (isl.) K3
Coburg (isl.) L2
Columbia (cape) M1
Colville (lake) F3
Committee (bay) K3
Contwoyto (lake) H3
Coppermine (riv.) G3
Cornwall (isl.) J2
Cornwallis (isl.) J2
Coronation (gulf) G3
Croker (bay) K2
Crown Prince Frederik (isl.) K3
Cumberland (pen.) M3
Cumberland (sound) M3
Dalhousie (cape) E2
Davis (str.) M3
Dease (str.) H3
Denmark (bay) H2
Devon (isl.) K2
Dolphin and Union (str.) G3
Dubawnt (lake) H3
Dubawnt (riv.) H3
Dundas (pen.) G2
Dyer (cape) M3
Eclipse (sound) L2
Eglinton (isl.) F2
Ellef Ringnes (isl.) H2
Ellesmere (isl.) K2
Ennadai (lake) H3
Eskimo (lakes) E3
Eureka (sound) K2
Evans (str.) K3
Exeter (sound) M3
Fisher (str.) K3
Fosheim (pen.) K1
Foxe (basin) L3
Foxe (chan.) K3
Foxe (pen.) L3
Franklin (bay) F2
Franklin (mts.) F3
Franklin (str.) J2
Frobisher (bay) M3
Frozen (str.) K3
Fury and Hecla (str.) K3
Gabriel (str.) M3
Garry (lake) H3
Gods Mercy (bay) K3
Great Bear (lake) F3
Great Bear (riv.) F3
Great Slave (lake) G3
Greely (fjord) K1
Grinnell (pen.) J2
Hadley (bay) H2
Hall (basin) M1
Hall (pen.) M3
Hayes (riv.) J3
Hazen (lake) L1
Hazen (str.) G2
Henik (lakes) J3
Henry Kater (cape) M3
Home (bay) M3
Hood (riv.) G3
Horn (mts.) G3
Hornaday (riv.) F3
Horton (riv.) F3
Hottah (lake) G3
Hudson (bay) K3
Hudson (str.) L3
Isachsen (cape) H2
James Ross (str.) J3
Jenny Lind (isl.) H3
Jens Munk (isl.) K3
Jones (sound) K2
Kaminuriak (lake) J3
Kane (basin) L2
Kasba (lake) H3
Kazan (riv.) H3
Keele (riv.) F3
Keith Arm (inlet) F3
Kellett (cape) F2
Kellett (str.) G2
Kennedy (chan.) M1
Kent (pen.) H3
King Christian (isl.) H2
King William (isl.) J3
Lady Ann (str.) K2
La Martre (lake) G3
Lancaster (sound) K2
Lands End (cape) F2
Larsen (sound) J2
Liard (riv.) F4
Lincoln (sea) M1
Liverpool (bay) E2
Lockhart (riv.) H3
Lougheed (isl.) H2
Lyon (inlet) K3
MacKay (lake) G3
Mackenzie (bay) E3
Mackenzie (mts.) E3
Mackenzie (riv.) F3
Mackenzie King (isl.) G2
Macmillan (pass) F3
Maguse (lake) J3
Makinson (inlet) L2
Mansel (isl.) K3
Marian (lake) G3
Markham (inlet) L1
McLeod (bay) G3
M'Clintock (chan.) H2
M'Clure (str.) G2
McTavish Arm (inlet) G3
Meighen (isl.) H1
Melville (isl.) G2
Melville (pen.) K3
Mercy (cape) M3
Mills (lake) G3
Minto (inlet) G2
Mistake (bay) J3
Nahanni Nat'l Park F3
Nansen (sound) J1
Nares (str.) L2
Navy Board (inlet) K2
Nelson Head (prom.) F2
Nettilling (lake) L3
Nonacho (lake) H3
North Arm (inlet) G3
North Magnetic Pole H2
Norwegian (bay) J2
Nottingham (isl.) L3
Nueltin (lake) H3
Ommanney (bay) H2
Padloping (isl.) M3
Parry (bay) K3
Parry (chan.) G2
Parry (isls.) G2
Parry (pen.) F2
Peary (chan.) H2
Peel (sound) J2
Pelly (bay) J3
Penny (str.) J2
Point (lake) G3
Pond (inlet) L2
Prince Albert (pen.) G2
Prince Albert (sound) G2
Prince Charles (isl.) L3
Prince Gustav Adolf (sea) H2
Prince of Wales (isl.) J2
Prince of Wales (str.) G2
Prince Patrick (isl.) F2
Prince Regent (inlet) J2
Queen Elizabeth (isls.) H1
Queen Maud (gulf) H3
Queens (chan.) J2
Raanes (pen.) K2

Topography

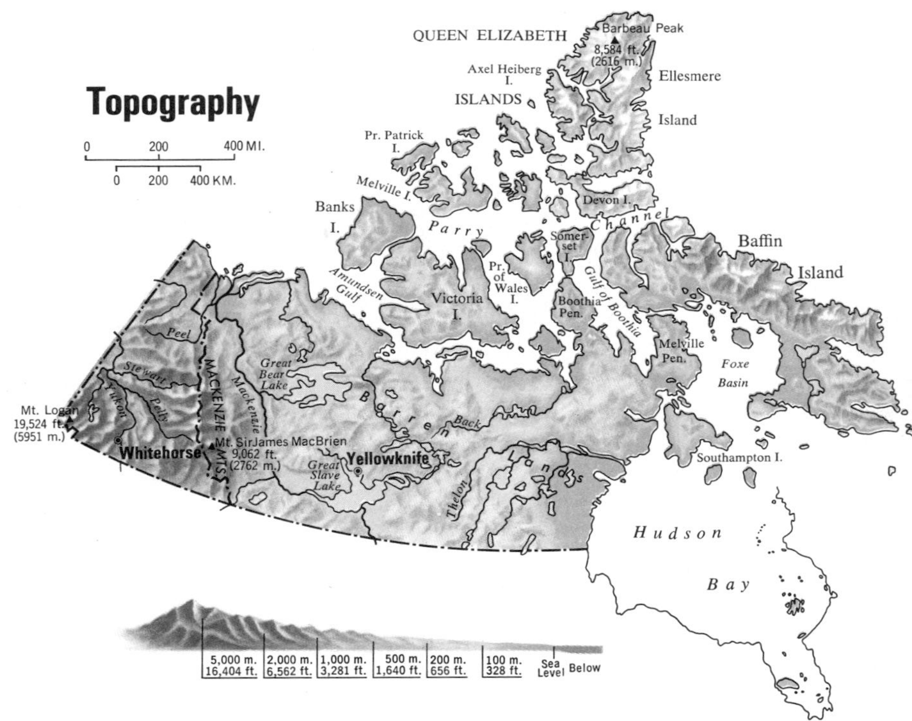

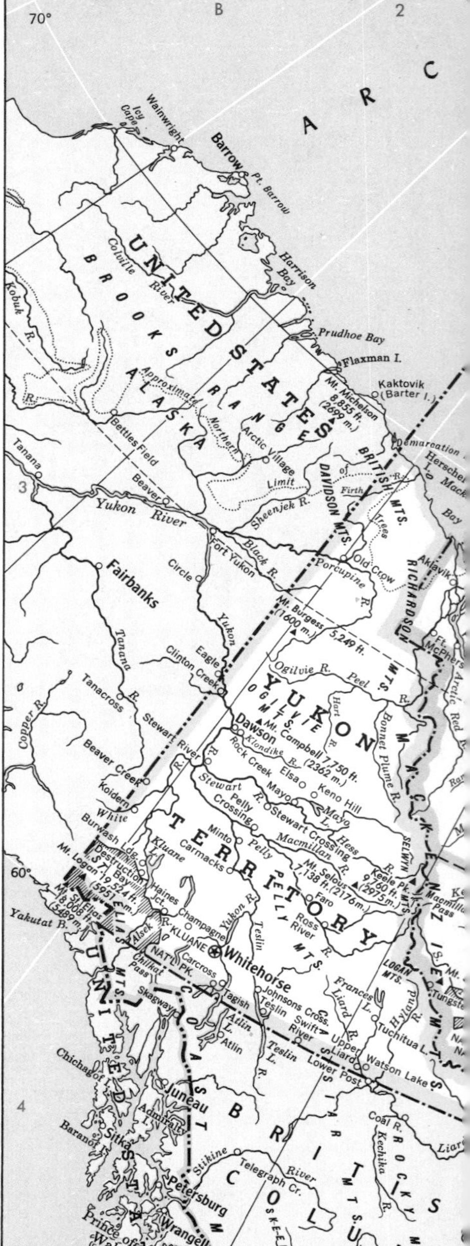

Agriculture, Industry and Resources

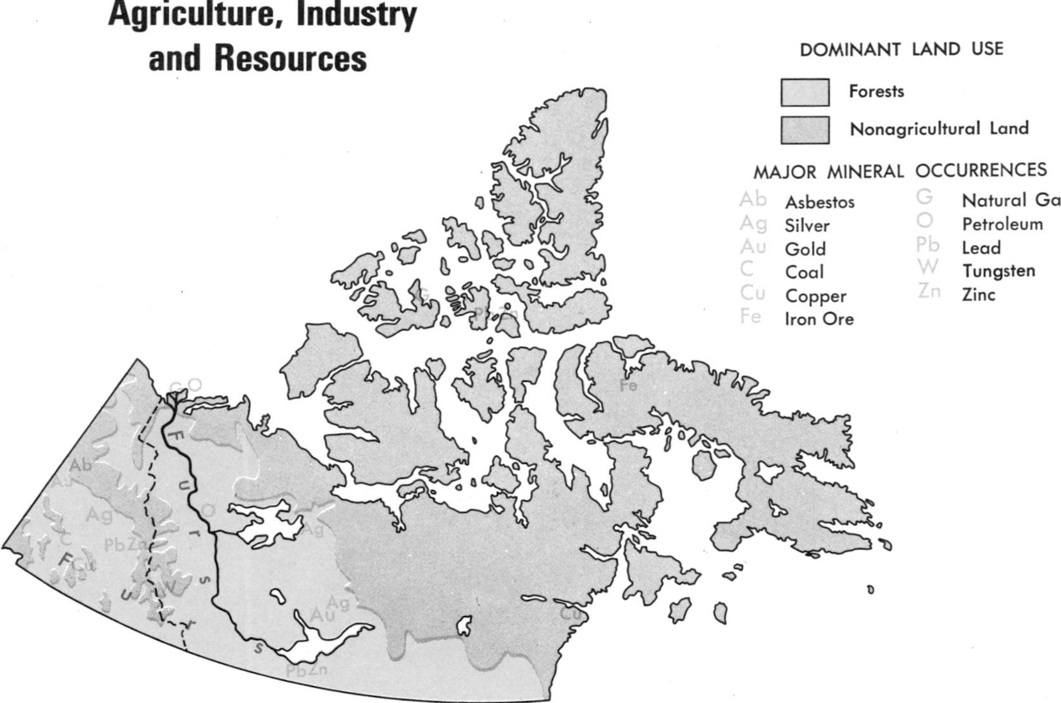

Rae (isth.) K3
Rae (riv.) G3
Rae (str.) J3
Ramparts (riv.) E3
Resolution (isl.) M3
Richard Collinson (inlet) G2
Richards (isl.) E3
Richardson (mts.) E3
Robeson (chan.) M1
Roes Welcome (sound) K3
Rowley (isl.) K3
Royal Geographical Society (isls.) J3
Russell (isl.) J2
Sabine (pen.) H2
Salisbury (isl.) L3
Seahorse (pt.) L3
Selwyn (lake) H4
Sherman (inlet) J3
Simpson (pen.) K3
Sir James MacBrien (mt.) F3
Slave (riv.) G3
Smith (bay) L2
Smith (cape) L3
Smith (sound) L2
Snare (riv.) G3
Snowbird (lake) H3
Somerset (isl.) J2
South (bay) K3
Southampton (isl.) K3
South Nahanni (riv.) F3
Stallworthy (cape) J1
Steensby (inlet) L2
Stefansson (isl.) H2
Sverdrup (chan.) J1
Sverdrup (isls.) J2
Talbot (inlet) L2
Taltson (riv.) G3
Tathlina (lake) G3
Tha-anne (riv.) J3
Thelon (riv.) H3
Thlewiaza (riv.) J3
Trout (lake) F3
Ungava (bay) M4
Vansittart (isl.) K3
Victoria (isl.) G2
Victoria (str.) H3
Viscount Melville (sound) G2
Wager (bay) K3
Wales (isl.) K3
Walsingham (cape) M3
Wellington (chan.) J2
Wholdaia (lake) H3
Winter (harb.) H2
Wollaston (pen.) G3
Wood Buffalo Nat'l Park G3
Wynniatt (bay) G2
Yathkyed (lake) J3
Yellowknife (riv.) G3

YUKON TERRITORY

AREA 207,075 sq. mi. (536,324 sq. km.)
POPULATION 23,153
CAPITAL Whitehorse
LARGEST CITY Whitehorse
HIGHEST POINT Mt. Logan 19,524 ft. (5,951 m.)
SETTLED IN 1897
ADMITTED TO CONFEDERATION 1898
PROVINCIAL FLOWER Fireweed

NORTHWEST TERRITORIES

AREA 1,304,896 sq. mi. (3,379,683 sq. km.)
POPULATION 45,741
CAPITAL Yellowknife
LARGEST CITY Yellowknife
HIGHEST POINT Mt. Sir James MacBrien 9,062 ft. (2,762 m.)
SETTLED IN 1800
ADMITTED TO CONFEDERATION 1870
PROVINCIAL FLOWER Mountain Avens

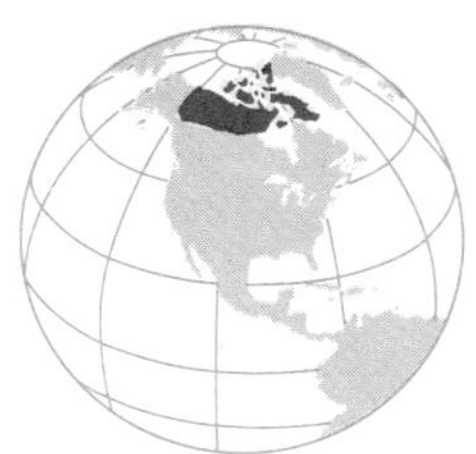

YUKON TERRITORY

CITIES and TOWNS

Beaver Creek 90 D3
Burwash Landing 73 D3
Carcross 216 E3
Carmacks •256 E3
Champagne E3
Clinton Creek D3
Cowley E3
Dawson 697 E3
Destruction Bay 45 E3
Elsa 336 E3
Faro 1,652 E3
Haines Junction •366 E3
Johnson's Crossing 13 E3
Keno Hill 88 E3
Koidern D3
Mayo 398 E3
Minto E3
Old Crow 243 E3
Pelly Crossing 182 E3
Rock Creek 59 E3
Ross River 294 E3
Stewart Crossing 20 E3
Stewart River D3
Swift River 24 E3
Tagish 89 E3
Teslin •310 E3
Tuchitua Lake E3
Upper Liard 130 F3
Watson Lake •748 F3
Whitehorse (cap.) 14,814 E3

OTHER FEATURES

Alsek (riv.) E3
Bonnet Plume (riv.) E3
British (mts.) D3
Campbell (mt.) E3
Cassiar (mts.) E3
Frances (lake) E3
Herschel (isl.) E3
Hess (riv.) E3
Hyland (riv.) F3
Keele (peak) E3
Klondike (riv.) E3
Kluane (lake) E3
Kluane Nat'l Park E3
Liard (riv.) E3
Logan (mt.) D3
Logan (mts.) F3
Mackenzie (bay) E3
Mackenzie (mts.) E3
Macmillan (riv.) E3
Mayo (lake) E3
Ogilvie (mts.) E3
Ogilvie (riv.) E3
Peel (riv.) E3
Pelly (mts.) E3
Pelly (riv.) E3
Porcupine (riv.) E3
Richardson (mts.) E3
Rocky (mts.) F4
Saint Elias (mt.) D3
Saint Elias (mts.) E3
Selous (mt.) E3
Selwyn (mts.) E3
Stewart (riv.) E3
Teslin (lake) E4
Teslin (riv.) E3
White (riv.) D3
Yukon (riv.) E3

• Population of district.

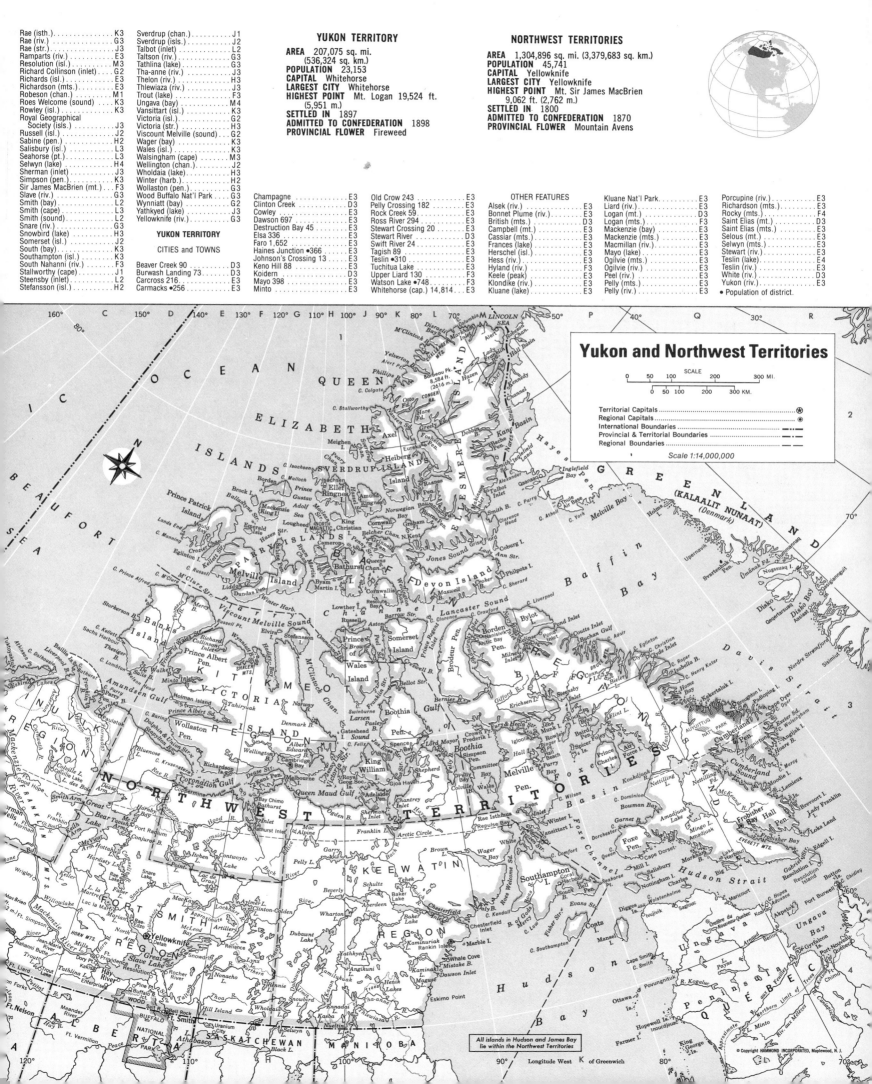

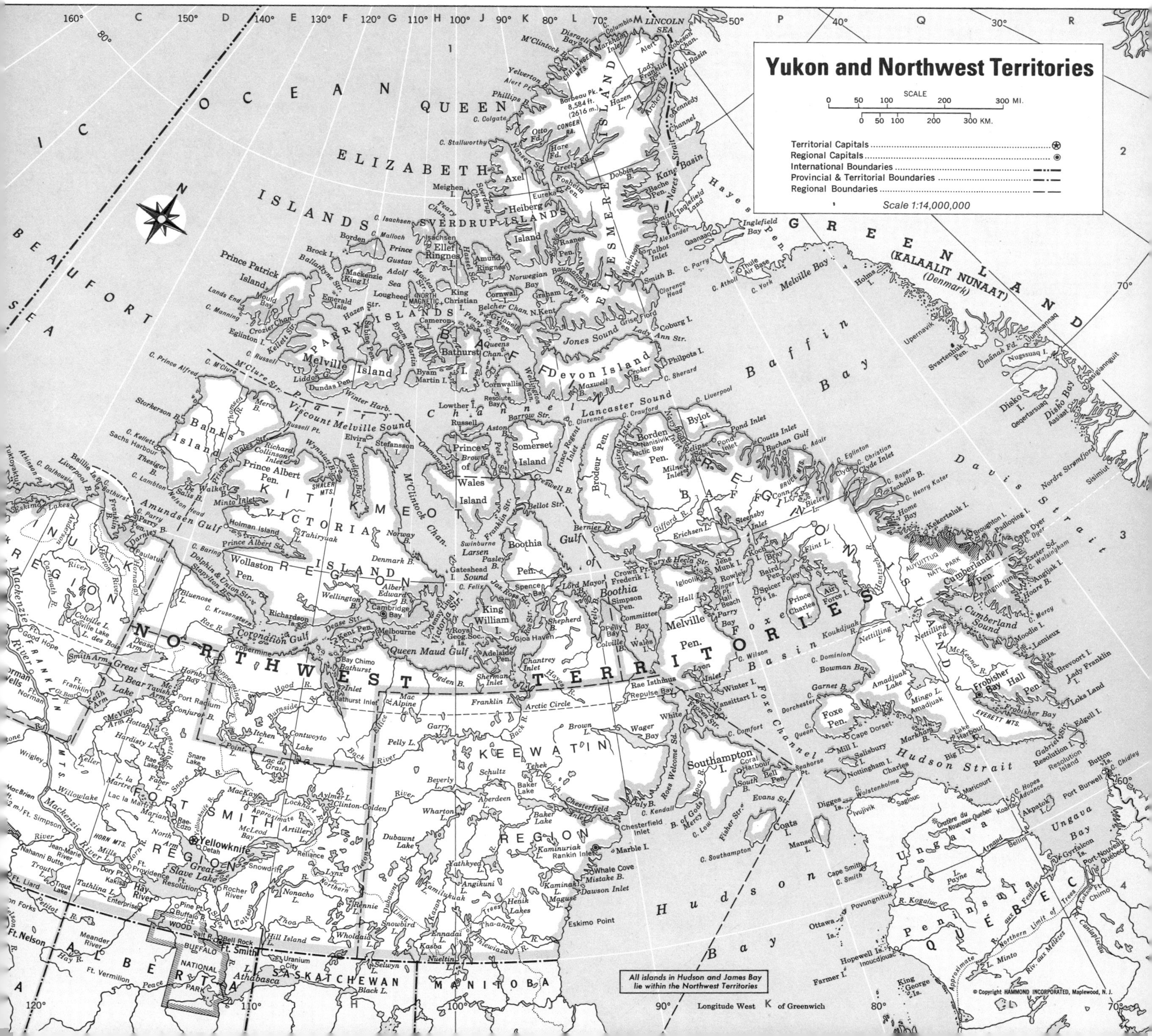

Yukon and Northwest Territories
SCALE
0 50 100 200 300 MI.
0 50 100 200 300 KM.
Territorial Capitals
Regional Capitals
International Boundaries
Provincial & Territorial Boundaries
Regional Boundaries
Scale 1:14,000,000
All islands in Hudson and James Bay lie within the Northwest Territories
Longitude West of Greenwich
© Copyright HAMMOND INCORPORATED, Maplewood, N.J.

Akron, Ohio‡ 660,328 .... K2
Alabama (state) 3,890,061 .... J4
Alaska (state) 400,481 .... C5
Alaska (gulf), Alaska D6
Alaska (range), Alaska C6
Albany (cap.), N.Y.‡ 795,019 .... M2
Albuquerque, N. Mex.‡ 454,499 .... E3
Aleutian (isls.), Alaska D6
Allentown, Pa.‡ 636,714 .... L2
Anchorage, Alaska‡ 173,017 .... D6
Annapolis (cap.), Md. 31,740 .... L3
Ann Arbor, Mich.‡ 264,748 .... K2
Appalachian (mts.) K3
Appleton, Wis.‡ 291,325 .... J2
Arizona (state) 2,717,866 .... D4
Arkansas (state) 2,285,513 .... H3
Arkansas (riv.) H3
Atlanta (cap.), Ga.‡ 2,029,618 .... K4
Atlantic City, N.J.‡ 194,119 .... M3
Attu (isl.), Alaska D6
Augusta, Ga.‡ 327,372 .... K4
Augusta (cap.), Maine 21,819 .... N2
Austin (cap.), Texas‡ 536,450 .... G4
Bakersfield, Calif.‡ 403,089 .... C3
Baltimore, Md.‡ 2,174,023 .... L3
Baton Rouge (cap.), La.‡ 493,973 .... H4
Beaumont, Texas‡ 375,497 .... H4
Bering (sea), Alaska C6
Bering (str.), Alaska C5
Bighorn (riv.) E2
Binghamton, N.Y.‡ 301,336 .... L2
Birmingham, Ala.‡ 847,360 .... J4
Bismarck (cap.), N. Dak.‡ 79,988 .... G1
Bitterroot (range) D1
Black Hills (mts.) F2
Boise (cap.), Idaho‡ 173,076 .... C2
Borah (peak), Idaho D2
Boston (cap.), Mass.‡ 2,763,357 .... M2
Bridgeport, Conn.‡ 395,455 .... M2
Brazos (riv.), Texas G4
Brooks (range), Alaska C5
Buffalo, N.Y.‡ 1,242,573 .... L2
California (state) 23,668,562 .... B3
Canadian (riv.) F3
Canaveral (Kennedy) (cape), Fla. L5
Canton, Ohio‡ 404,421 .... K2
Cape Fear (riv.), N.C. L4
Carson City (cap.), Nev. 32,022 .... C3
Cascade (range) B1
Cedar Rapids, Iowa‡ 169,775 .... H2
Champlain (lake) M2
Charleston, S.C.‡ 430,301 .... L4
Charleston (cap.), W. Va.‡ 269,595 .... K3
Charlotte, N.C.‡ 637,218 .... L3
Chattahoochee (riv.) K4
Chattanooga, Tenn.‡ 426,540 .... J3
Chesapeake (bay) L3
Cheyenne (cap.), Wyo. 47,283 .... E2
Cheyenne (riv.) F2
Chicago, Ill.‡ 7,102,328 .... J2
Cimarron (riv.) G3
Cincinnati, Ohio‡ 1,401,403 .... K3
Cleveland, Ohio‡ 1,898,720 .... K2
Coast (ranges) B2
Cod (cape), Mass. N2
Colorado (state) 2,888,834 .... E3
Colorado (riv.) D4
Colorado (riv.), Texas G4
Colorado Springs, Colo.‡ 317,458 .... F3
Columbia (cap.), S.C.‡ 408,176 .... K4
Columbia (riv.) B1
Columbus, Ga.‡ 239,196 .... K4
Columbus (cap.), Ohio‡ 1,093,293 .... K3
Concord (cap.), N.H. 30,400 .... M2
Connecticut (state) 3,107,576 .... M2
Connecticut (riv.) M2
Corpus Christi, Texas‡ 326,228 .... G5
Cumberland (riv.) J3
Dallas, Texas‡ 2,974,878 .... G4
Davenport, Iowa‡ 383,958 .... H2
Dayton, Ohio‡ 830,070 .... K3
Death Valley (depr.), Calif. C3
Delaware (state) 595,225 .... L3
Delaware (bay) M3
Denver (cap.), Colo.‡ 1,619,921 .... F3
Des Moines (cap.), Iowa‡ 338,048 .... H2
Detroit, Mich.‡ 4,352,762 .... K2
District of Columbia 637,651 .... L3
Dover (cap.), Del. 23,512 .... L3
Duluth, Minn.‡ 266,650 .... H1
Durham, N.C.‡ 530,673 .... L3
Elbert (mt.), Colo. E3
El Paso, Texas‡ 479,899 .... E4
Erie, Pa.‡ 279,780 .... K2
Erie (lake) K2
Eugene, Oreg.‡ 275,226 .... B2
Evansville, Ind.‡ 309,408 .... J3
Everglades, The (swamp), Fla. K5
Fayetteville, N.C.‡ 247,160 .... L3
Flint, Mich.‡ 521,589 .... K2
Florida (state) 9,739,992 .... K5
Florida (keys), Fla. K6
Fort Smith, Ark.‡ 203,269 .... H3
Fort Wayne, Ind.‡ 382,961 .... J2
Fort Worth, Texas 385,141 .... G4
Frankfort (cap.), Ky. 25,973 .... K3
Fresno, Calif.‡ 515,013 .... C3
Galveston, Texas‡ 195,940 .... H5
Gary, Ind.‡ 642,781 .... J2
Georgia (state) 5,464,265 .... K4
Gila (riv.) D4
Glacier Nat'l Park, Mont. D1
Golden Gate (chan.), Calif. B3
Grand Canyon Nat'l Park, Ariz. D3
Grand Rapids, Mich.‡ 601,680 .... K2
Great Salt (lake), Utah D2
Greensboro, N.C.‡ 827,385 .... K3
Greenville, S.C.‡ 568,758 .... K4
Hamilton, Ohio‡ 258,787 .... K3
Harrisburg (cap.), Pa.‡ 446,072 .... L2
Hartford (cap.), Conn.‡ 726,114 .... M2
Hatteras (cape), N.C. M3
Havasu (lake) D4
Hawaii (state) 965,000 .... F5
Hawaii (isl.), Hawaii F6
Helena (cap.), Mont. 23,938 .... D1
Honolulu (cap.), Hawaii‡ 762,874 .... F5
Houston, Texas‡ 2,905,350 .... G5
Huntington, W. Va.‡ 311,350 .... K3
Huntsville, Ala.‡ 308,593 .... J4
Huron (lake), Mich. K2
Idaho (state) 943,935 .... D2
Illinois (state) 11,418,461 .... J3
Indiana (state) 5,490,179 .... J3
Aleutian (isls.), Alaska D6
Iowa (state) 2,913,387 .... H2
Jackson (cap.), Miss.‡ 320,425 .... J4
Jacksonville, Fla.‡ 737,519 .... K4
Jefferson City (cap.), Mo. 33,619 .... H3
Jersey City, N.J.‡ 556,972 .... M2
Johnstown, Pa.‡ 664,506 .... L2
Juneau (cap.), Alaska 19,528 .... E6
Kalamazoo, Mich.‡ 279,192 .... J2
Kansas (state) 2,363,208 .... G3
Kansas City, Kans.-Mo.‡ 1,327,020 .... G3
Kauai (isl.), Hawaii E5
Kentucky (state) 3,661,433 .... J3
Kentucky (lake) J3
Knoxville, Tenn.‡ 476,517 .... K3
Lancaster, Pa.‡ 362,346 .... L2
Lansing (cap.), Mich.‡ 476,517 .... K2
Las Vegas, Nev.‡ 461,816 .... C3
Lawrence, Mass.‡ 281,981 .... M2
Lexington, Ky.‡ 318,136 .... K3
Lima, Ohio‡ 218,244 .... K2
Lincoln (cap.), Nebr.‡ 192,884 .... G2
Little Rock (cap.), Ark.‡ 393,494 .... H4
Long (isl.), N.Y. M2
Long Beach, Calif. 361,334 .... C4
Los Angeles, Calif.‡ 7,477,657 .... C4
Louisiana (state) 4,203,972 .... H4
Louisvillle, Ky.‡ 906,240 .... J3
Lowell, Mass.‡ 233,410 .... M2
Lubbock, Texas‡ 211,651 .... F4
Macon, Ga.‡ 254,623 .... K4
Madison (cap.), Wis.‡ 323,545 .... H2
Maine (state) 1,124,660 .... N1
Maryland (state) 4,216,446 .... L3
Massachusetts (state) 5,737,037 .... M2
Maui (isl.), Hawaii F5
Mauna Kea (mt.), Hawaii G6
Mauna Loa (mt.), Hawaii G6
May (cape), N.J. M3
McKinley (mt.), Alaska D5
Memphis, Tenn.‡ 912,887 .... J3
Mendocino (cape), Calif. A2
Mexico (gulf) J5
Miami, Fla.‡ 1,625,979 .... K5
Michigan (state) 9,258,344 .... J1
Michigan (lake) J2
Milwaukee, Wis.‡ 1,397,143 .... J2
Minneapolis, Minn.‡ 2,114,256 .... H1
Minnesota (state) 4,077,148 .... H1
Mississippi (state) 2,520,638 .... J4
Mississippi (riv.) H4
Missouri (state) 4,917,444 .... H3
Missouri (riv.) H3
Mitchell (mt.), N.C. K3
Mobile, Ala.‡ 442,819 .... J4
Montana (state) 786,690 .... E1
Montgomery (cap.), Ala.‡ 272,687 .... J4
Nantucket (isl.), Mass. N2
Nashville (cap.), Tenn.‡ 850,505 .... J3
Nebraska (state) 1,570,006 .... F2
Nevada (state) 799,184 .... C3
Newark, N.J.‡ 1,965,304 .... L2
New Hampshire (state) 920,610 .... M2
New Haven, Conn.‡ 417,592 .... M2
New Jersey (state) 7,364,158 .... M3
New Mexico (state) 1,299,968 .... E4
New Orleans, La.‡ 1,186,725 .... H5
Newport News, Va.‡ 364,449 .... L3
New York (state) 17,557,288 .... L2
New York, N.Y.‡ 9,119,737 .... M2
Norfolk, Va.‡ 806,691 .... L3
North Carolina (state) 5,874,429 .... L3
North Dakota (state) 652,695 .... F1
Oahu (isl.), Hawaii F5
Oakland, Calif.‡ 3,252,721 .... B3
Ohio (state) 10,797,419 .... K2
Ohio (riv.) J3
Oklahoma (state) 3,025,266 .... G3
Oklahoma City (cap.), Okla.‡ 834,088 .... G3
Olympia (cap.), Wash.‡ 124,264 .... B1
Olympic Nat'l Park, Wash. A1
Omaha, Nebr.‡ 570,399 .... G2
Ontario (lake), N.Y. L2
Oregon (state) 2,632,663 .... B2
Orlando, Fla.‡ 700,699 .... K5
Ozark (mts.) H3
Paterson, N.J.‡ 447,585 .... M2
Pennsylvania (state) L2
Pensacola, Fla.‡ 289,782 .... J4
Peoria, Ill.‡ 365,864 .... J2
Philadelphia, Pa.‡ 4,716,818 .... M2
Phoenix (cap.), Ariz.‡ 1,508,030 .... D4
Pierre (cap.), S. Dak. 11,793 .... F2
Pikes (peak), Colo. E3
Pittsburgh, Pa.‡ 2,263,894 .... L2
Platte (riv.), Nebr. G2
Pontchartrain (lake), La. J5
Portland, Maine‡ 183,625 .... N2
Portland, Oreg.‡ 1,242,187 .... B1
Potomac (riv.) L3
Providence (cap.), R.I.‡ 919,216 .... M2
Racine, Wis.‡ 173,132 .... J2
Raleigh (cap.), N.C.‡ 530,673 .... L3
Rainier (mt.), Wash. B1
Reading, Pa.‡ 312,509 .... L2
Red (riv.) H4
Red River of the North (riv.) G1
Rhode Island (state) 947,154 .... M2
Richmond (cap.), Va.‡ 632,015 .... L3
Rio Grande (riv.) F5
Roanoke, Va.‡ 218,244 .... K3
Rochester, N.Y.‡ 971,079 .... L2
Rockford, Ill.‡ 279,514 .... J2
Rocky (mts.) E3
Sacramento (cap.), Calif.‡ 1,014,002 .... B3
Saginaw, Mich.‡ 224,548 .... K2
Saint Clair (lake), Mich. K2
Saint Lawrence (riv.), N.Y. N1
Saint Louis, Mo.‡ 2,355,276 .... H3

AREA 3,623,420 sq. mi. (9,384,658 sq. km.)
POPULATION 226,504,825
CAPITAL Washington
LARGEST CITY New York
HIGHEST POINT Mt. McKinley 20,320 ft. (6,194 m.)
MONETARY UNIT U.S. dollar
MAJOR LANGUAGE English
MAJOR RELIGIONS Protestantism, Roman Catholicism, Judaism

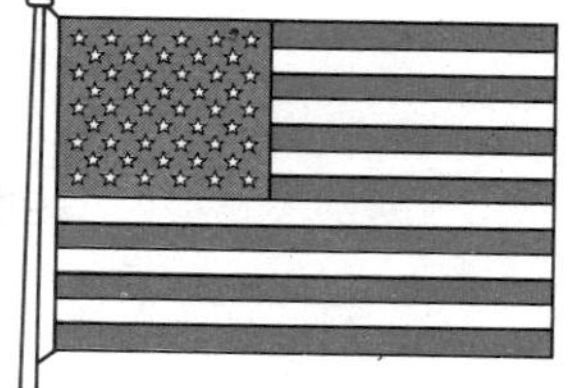

Population Distribution

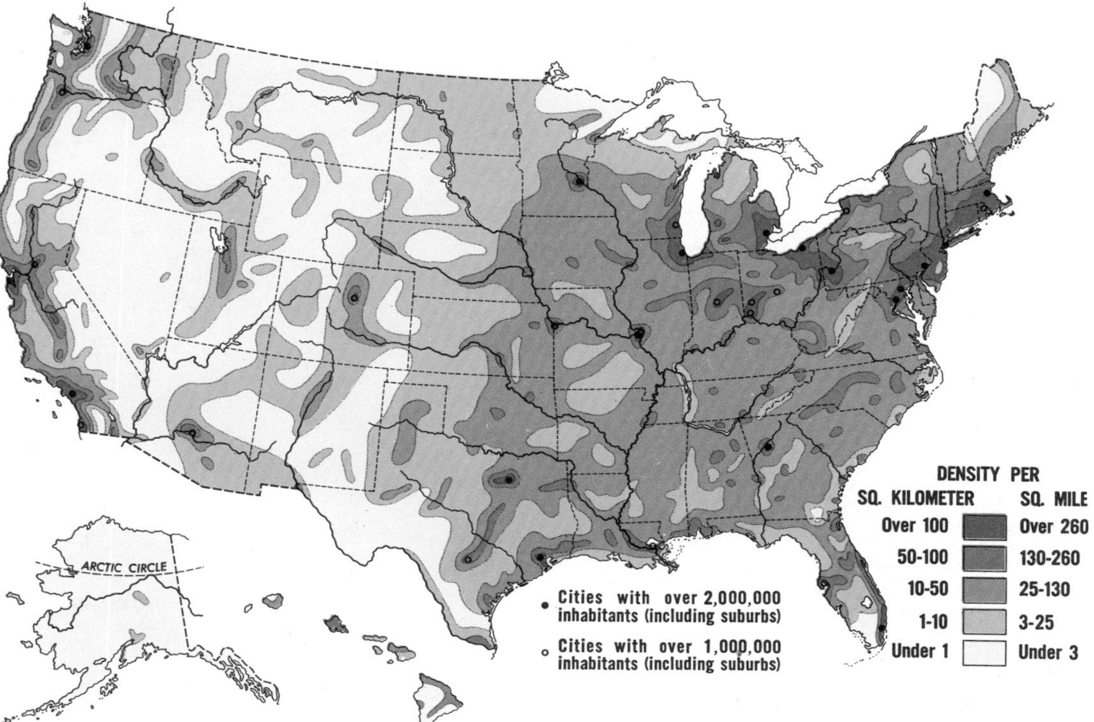

Vegetation

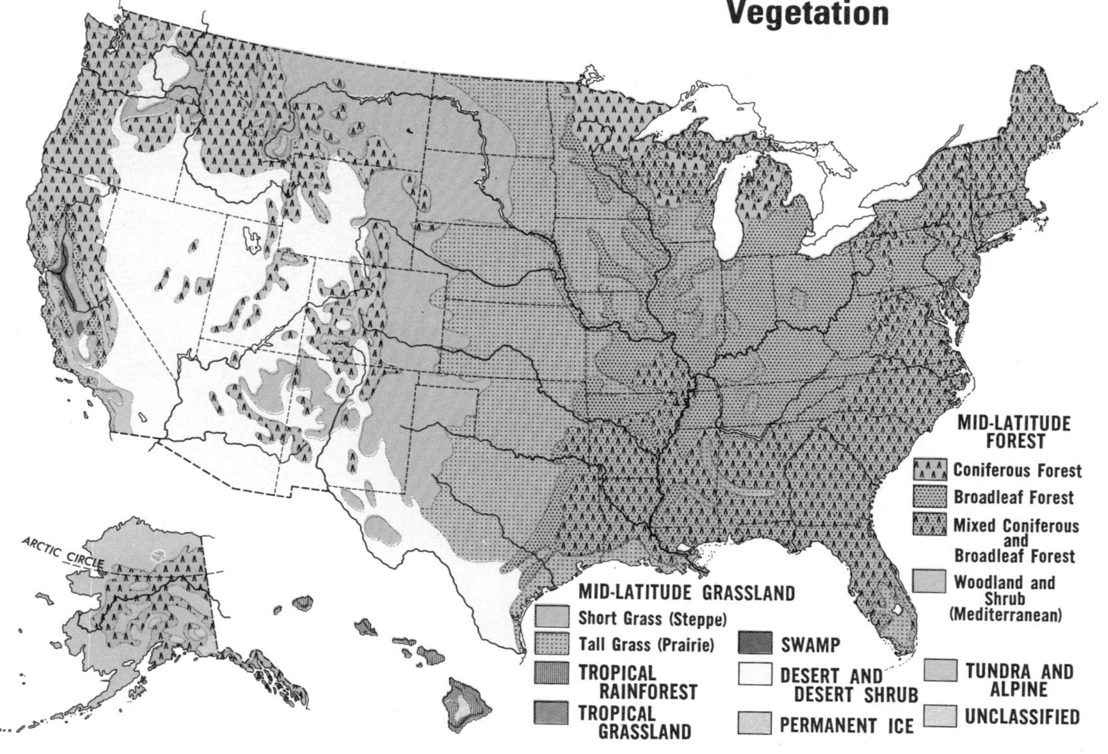

Saint Paul (cap.), Minn. 270,230 .... H1
Sakakawea (lake), N. Dak. F1
Salem (cap.), Oreg.‡ 249,895 .... B1
Salinas, Calif.‡ 290,444 .... B3
Salt Lake City (cap.), Utah‡ 936,255 .... D2
Salton Sea (lake), Calif. C4
San Antonio, Texas‡ 1,071,954 .... G5
San Bernardino, Calif.‡ 1,557,080 .... C4
San Diego, Calif.‡ 1,861,846 .... C4
San Francisco, Calif.‡ 325,721 .... B3
San Joaquin (riv.), Calif. C3
San Jose, Calif.‡ 1,295,071 .... B3
Santa Ana, Calif.‡ 1,931,570 .... C4
Santa Barbara, Calif.‡ 298,660 .... C4
Santa Fe (cap.), N. Mex. 48,899 .... E3
Savannah, Ga.‡ 228,178 .... K4
Scranton, Pa. 88,117 .... L2
Seattle, Wash.‡ 1,606,765 .... B1
Shasta (mt.), Calif. B2
Shreveport, La.‡ 376,646 .... H4
Sierra Nevada (mts.) B3
Snake (riv.) C1
South Bend, Ind.‡ 280,772 .... J2
Spokane, Wash.‡ 341,835 .... C1
South Carolina (state) 3,119,208 .... K4
South Dakota (state) 690,178 .... F2
Springfield (cap.), Ill.‡ 187,338 .... H3
Springfield, Mass.‡ 530,668 .... M2
Springfield, Mo.‡ 207,704 .... H3
Springfield, Ohio‡ 183,885 .... K2
Stockton, Calif.‡ 347,342 .... B3
Superior (lake) J1
Syracuse, N.Y.‡ 642,375 .... L2
Tacoma, Wash.‡ 485,643 .... B1
Tahoe (lake) C3
Tallahassee (cap.), Fla.‡ 159,542 .... K4
Tampa, Fla.‡ 1,569,492 .... K5
Tennessee (state) 4,590,750 .... J3
Terre Haute, Ind.‡ 176,583 .... J3
Texas (state) 14,228,383 .... G4
Toledo, Ohio‡ 791,599 .... K2
Topeka (cap.), Kans.‡ 185,442 .... G3
Trenton (cap.), N.J.‡ 307,863 .... M2
Tucson, Ariz.‡ 531,263 .... D4
Tulsa, Okla.‡ 689,628 .... G3
Utah (state) 1,461,037 .... D3
Utica, N.Y.‡ 320,180 .... M2
Vermont (state) 511,456 .... M2
Virginia (state) 5,346,279 .... L3
Wabash (riv.) J3
Washington (state) 4,130,163 .... B1
Washington, D.C. (cap.), U.S.‡ 3,060,240 .... L3
Waterbury, Conn.‡ 228,059 .... M2
Waterloo, Iowa 75,985 .... H2
West Palm Beach, Fla.‡ 573,125 .... K5
West Virginia (state) 1,949,644 .... K3
Wheeling, W. Va.‡ 185,566 .... K2
Whitney (mt.), Calif. C3
Wichita, Kans.‡ 411,313 .... G3
Wilkes-Barre, Pa. 51,551 .... L2
Wilmington, Del.‡ 524,108 .... M3
Wisconsin (state) 4,705,335 .... J2
Woods (lake), Minn. G1
Worcester, Mass.‡ 372,940 .... M2
Wyoming (state) 470,816 .... E2
Yellowstone Nat'l Park, Wyo. E2
York, Pa.‡ 381,255 .... L3
Yosemite Nat'l Park, Calif. C3
Youngstown, Ohio‡ 531,350 .... K2
Yukon (riv.), Alaska C5

‡ Population of metropolitan area.

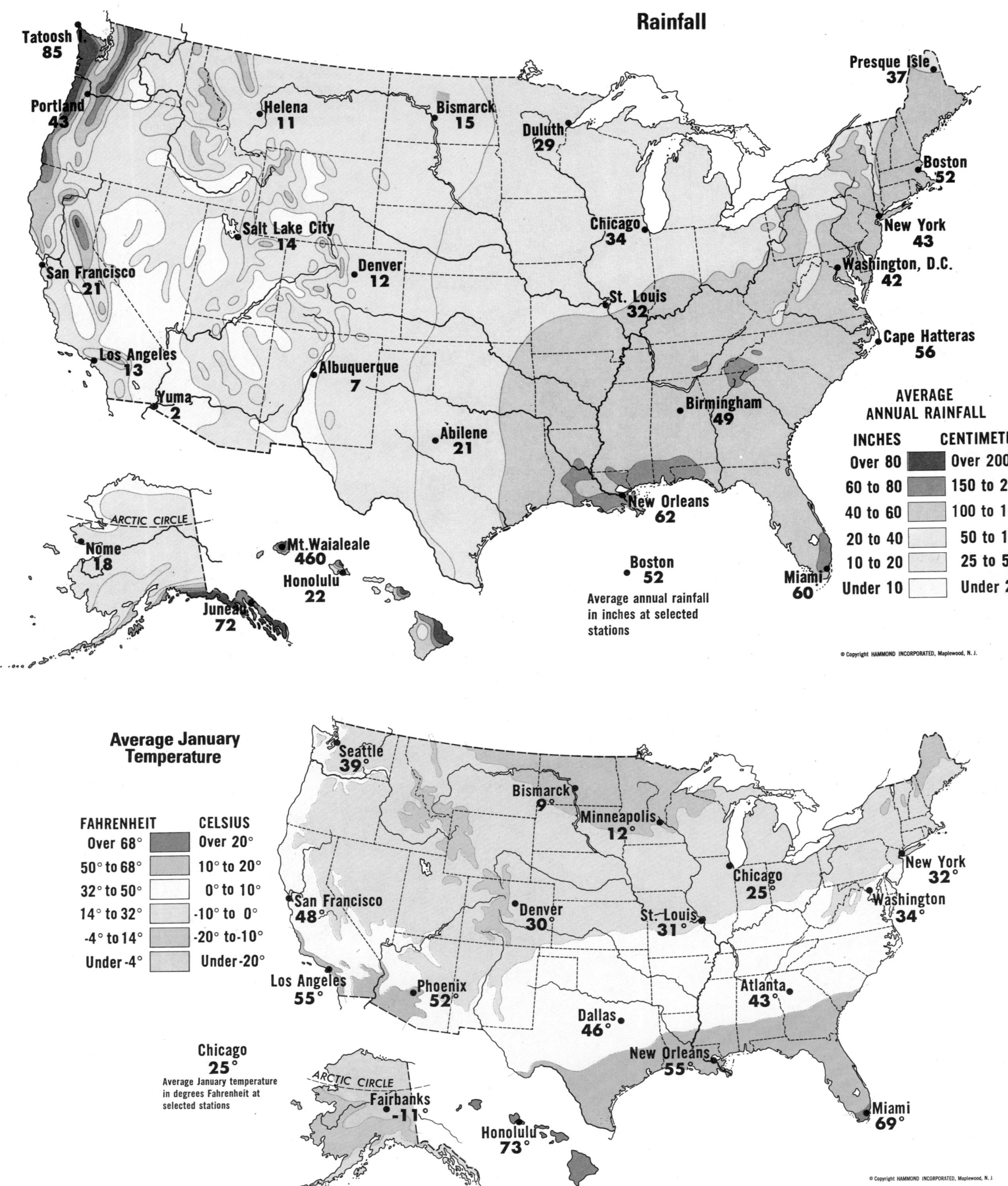
Rainfall
Tatoosh I.
85
Portland
43
Helena
11
Bismarck
15
Duluth
29
Presque Isle
37
Boston
52
Chicago
34
New York
43
Salt Lake City
14
San Francisco
21
Denver
12
Washington, D.C.
42
St. Louis
32
Cape Hatteras
56
Los Angeles
13
Albuquerque
7
Yuma
2
Birmingham
49
Abilene
21
New Orleans
62
ARCTIC CIRCLE
Nome
18
Mt. Waialeale
460
Honolulu
22
Juneau
72
Miami
60
Boston
52
Average annual rainfall in inches at selected stations
AVERAGE ANNUAL RAINFALL
INCHES
CENTIMETE
Over 80
Over 200
60 to 80
150 to 20
40 to 60
100 to 15
20 to 40
50 to 10
10 to 20
25 to 5
Under 10
Under 2
© Copyright HAMMOND INCORPORATED, Maplewood, N. J.
Average January Temperature
FAHRENHEIT
CELSIUS
Over 68°
Over 20°
50° to 68°
10° to 20°
32° to 50°
0° to 10°
14° to 32°
-10° to 0°
-4° to 14°
-20° to -10°
Under -4°
Under -20°
Seattle
39°
Bismarck
9°
Minneapolis
12°
New York
32°
Chicago
25°
San Francisco
48°
Denver
30°
St. Louis
31°
Washington
34°
Los Angeles
55°
Phoenix
52°
Atlanta
43°
Dallas
46°
New Orleans
55°
Chicago
25°
Average January temperature in degrees Fahrenheit at selected stations
ARCTIC CIRCLE
Fairbanks
-11°
Honolulu
73°
Miami
69°
© Copyright HAMMOND INCORPORATED, Maplewood, N. J.

Topography

0 200 400 MI.
0 200 400 KM.
C. Flattery
Seattle
Mt. Rainier 14,410 ft. (4392 m.)
Mt. St. Helens 8,364 ft. (2549 m.)
CASCADE RANGE
COLUMBIA PLATEAU
Columbia
Snake
BITTERROOT RANGE
ROCKY MOUNTAINS
Missouri
Fort Peck Lake
Yellowstone
Lake Sakakawea
Lake Oahe
GREAT PLAINS
James
Red
Rainy
Lake Superior
Keweenaw Pen.
Minneapolis
Mississippi
Wisconsin
Lake Michigan
Lake Huron
Milwaukee
Chicago
Detroit
Lake Erie
Cleveland
Lake Ontario
St. Lawrence
Niagara Falls
Champlain
Gulf of Maine
Boston
C. Cod
Long Island
New York
Philadelphia
Washington
ATLANTIC OCEAN
Chesapeake Bay
C. Hatteras
C. Fear
PACIFIC OCEAN
COAST RANGES
SIERRA NEVADA
Central Valley
Sacramento
San Francisco
Great Basin
Great Salt Lake
Mt. Whitney 14,494 ft. (4418 m.)
Pt. Conception
SANTA BARBARA IS.
Mojave Desert
Los Angeles
San Diego
Lake Mead
Grand Canyon
Colorado
COLORADO PLATEAU
Lake Powell
Phoenix
Gila
Denver
Mt. Elbert 14,431 ft. (4399 m.)
Arkansas
N. Platte
Platte
Des Moines
Illinois
Kansas City
St. Louis
Indianapolis
Wabash
Ohio
OZARK PLATEAU
Tennessee
Memphis
Wheeler L.
ALLEGHENY MTS.
APPALACHIAN MOUNTAINS
PIEDMONT
Mt. Mitchell 6,684 ft. (2037 m.)
ATLANTIC COASTAL PLAIN
Savannah
Atlanta
Chattahoochee
Canadian
Red
LLANO ESTACADO
Rio Grande
Pecos
EDWARDS PLATEAU
Brazos
Colorado
Dallas
Houston
GULF COASTAL PLAIN
New Orleans
Mississippi Delta
Jacksonville
C. Canaveral
L. Okeechobee
The Everglades
Miami
FLORIDA KEYS
Gulf of Mexico
ARCTIC OCEAN
0 200 400 MI.
0 200 400 KM.
BROOKS RA.
Bering Str.
Yukon
Tanana
St. Lawrence I.
Mt. McKinley 20,320 ft. (6194 m.)
Alaska Ra.
Anchorage
BERING SEA
Gulf of Alaska
Kodiak I.
Alaska Pen.
Aleutian Islands
ALEXANDER ARCHIPELAGO
Kauai
Oahu
Honolulu
Molokai
Maui
HAWAIIAN ISLANDS
PACIFIC OCEAN
Mauna Kea 13,796 ft. (4205 m.)
Hawaii
0 50 100 MI.
0 50 100 KM.
5,000 m. 16,404 ft.
2,000 m. 6,562 ft.
1,000 m. 3,281 ft.
500 m. 1,640 ft.
200 m. 656 ft.
100 m. 328 ft.
Sea Level
Below

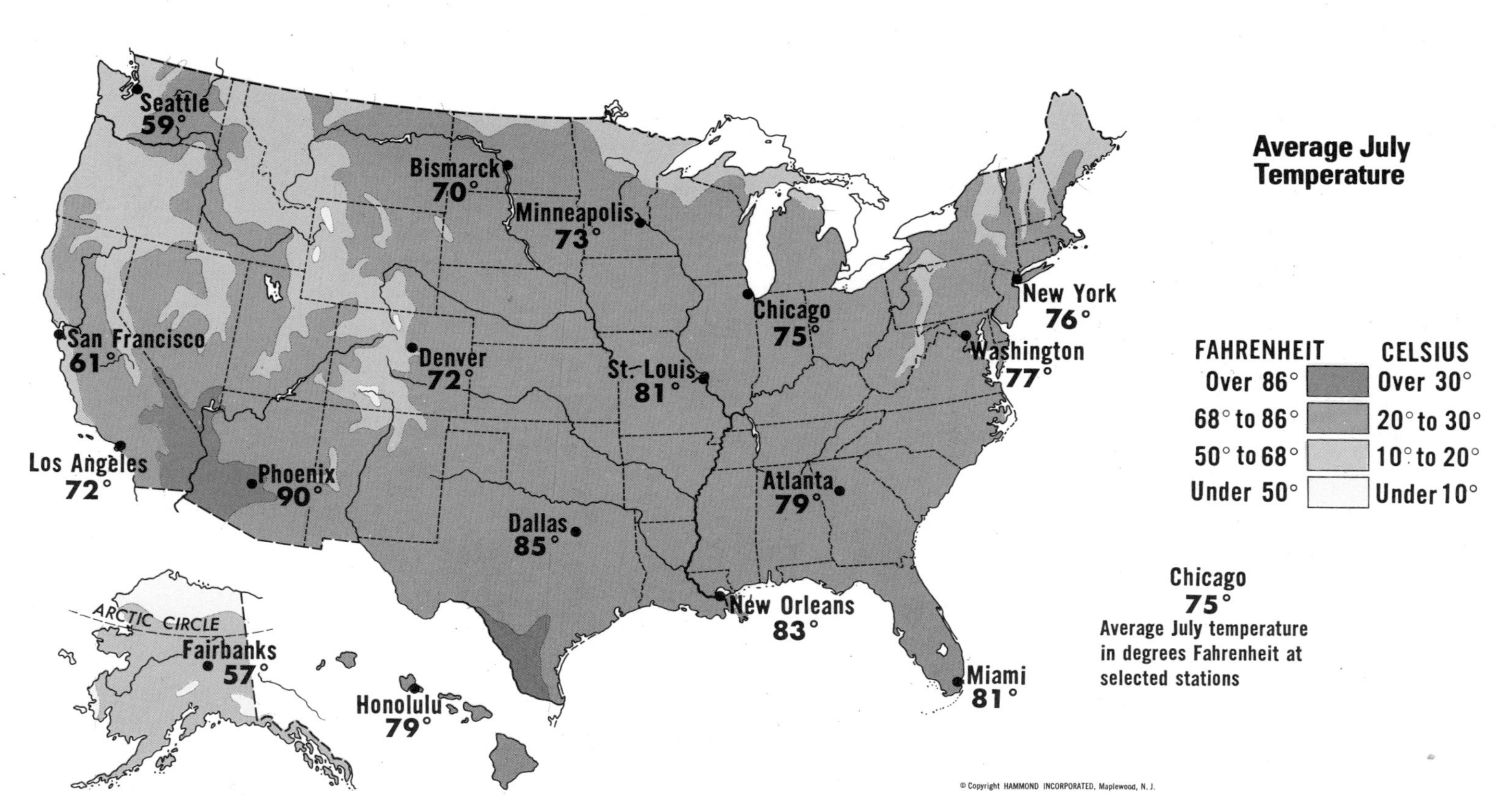

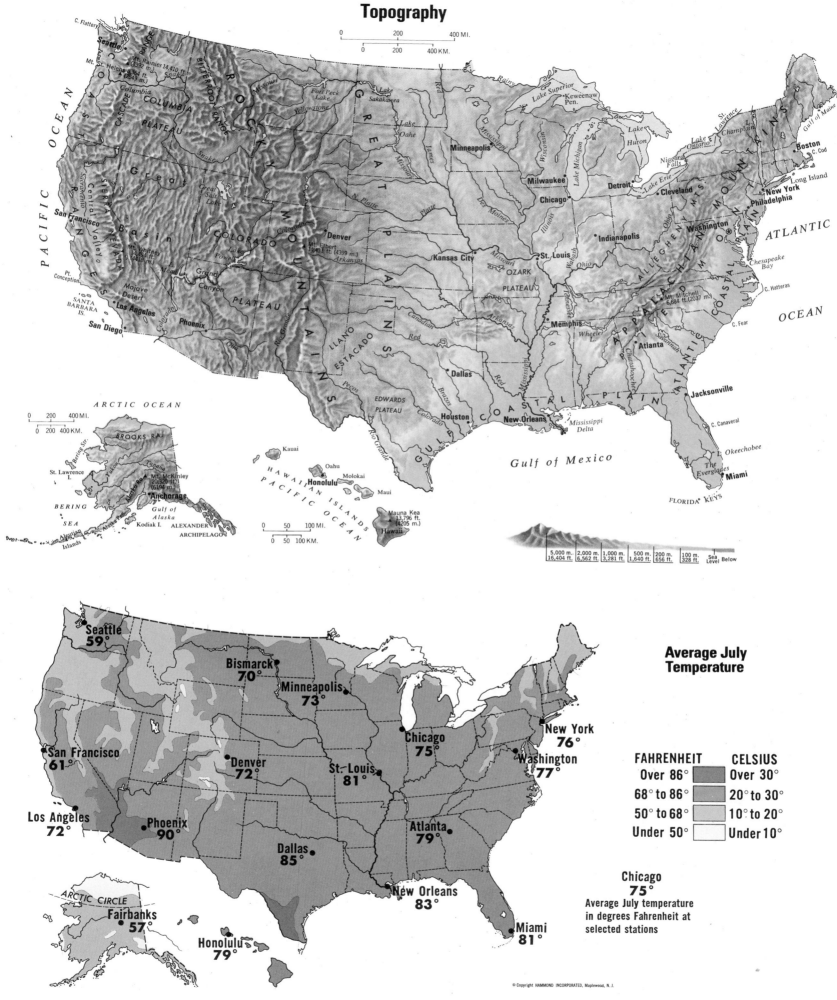

Average July Temperature
Seattle 59°
Bismarck 70°
Minneapolis 73°
San Francisco 61°
Denver 72°
St. Louis 81°
Chicago 75°
New York 76°
Washington 77°
Los Angeles 72°
Phoenix 90°
Dallas 85°
Atlanta 79°
New Orleans 83°
Miami 81°
ARCTIC CIRCLE
Fairbanks 57°
Honolulu 79°
FAHRENHEIT CELSIUS
Over 86° Over 30°
68° to 86° 20° to 30°
50° to 68° 10° to 20°
Under 50° Under 10°
Chicago 75°
Average July temperature in degrees Fahrenheit at selected stations

United States Standard Time Zones

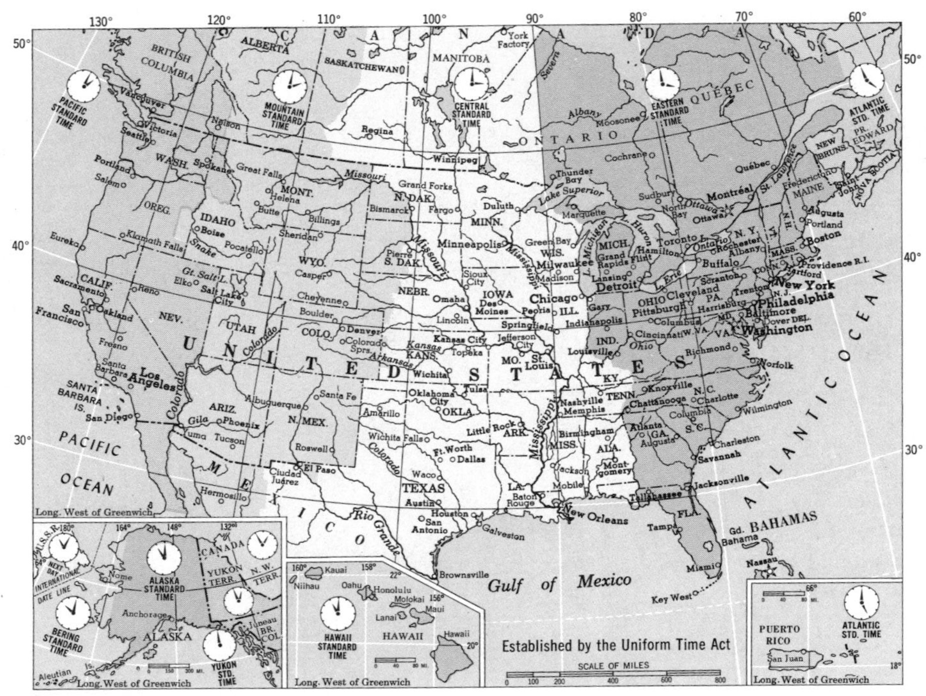

Agriculture, Industry and Resources

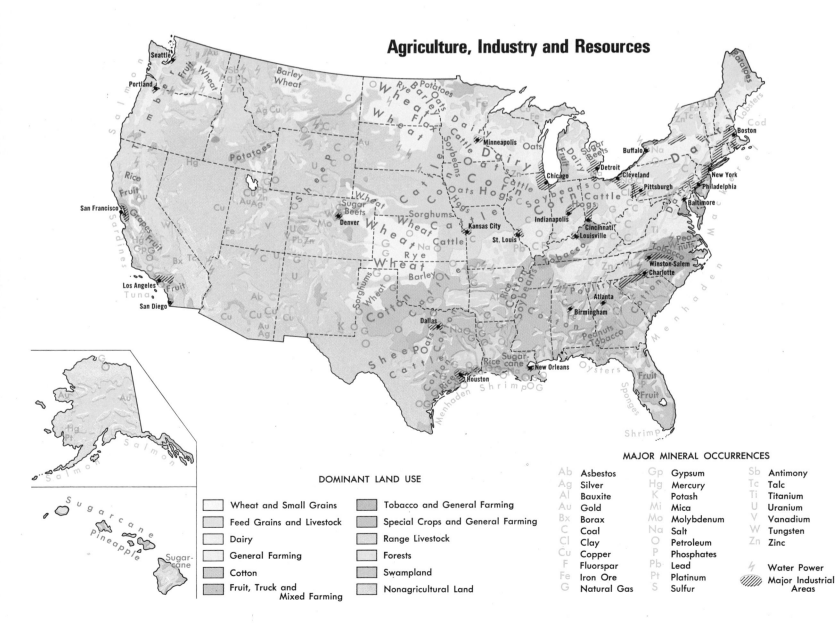

DOMINANT LAND USE

- Wheat and Small Grains
- Feed Grains and Livestock
- Dairy
- General Farming
- Cotton
- Fruit, Truck and Mixed Farming
- Tobacco and General Farming
- Special Crops and General Farming
- Range Livestock
- Forests
- Swampland
- Nonagricultural Land

MAJOR MINERAL OCCURRENCES

Ab	Asbestos	Gp	Gypsum	Sb	Antimony
Ag	Silver	Hg	Mercury	Tc	Talc
Al	Bauxite	K	Potash	Ti	Titanium
Au	Gold	Mi	Mica	U	Uranium
Bx	Borax	Mo	Molybdenum	V	Vanadium
C	Coal	Na	Salt	W	Tungsten
Cl	Clay	O	Petroleum	Zn	Zinc
Cu	Copper	P	Phosphates		
F	Fluorspar	Pb	Lead		Water Power
Fe	Iron Ore	Pt	Platinum		Major Industrial Areas
G	Natural Gas	S	Sulfur		